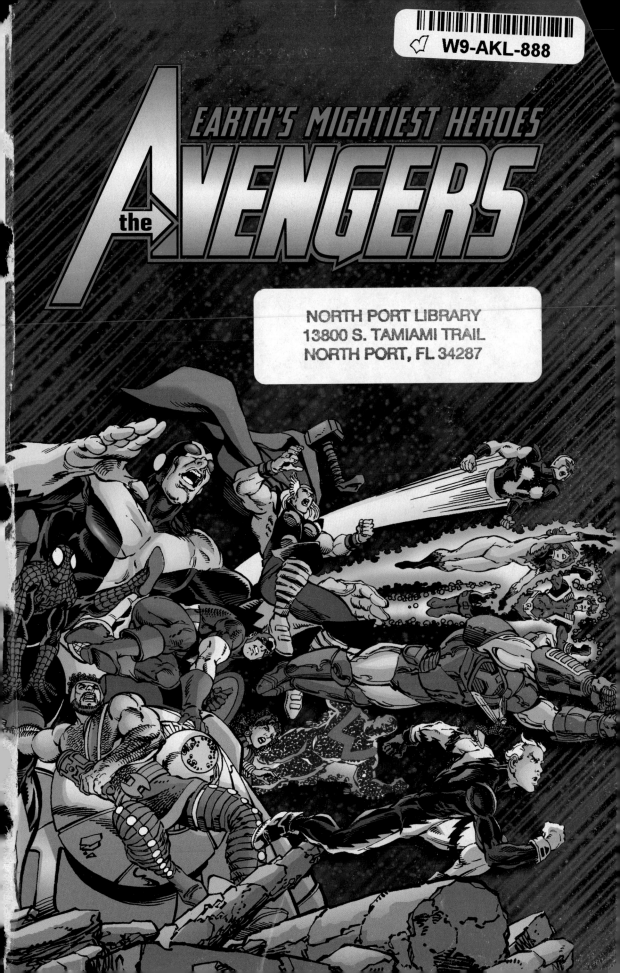

EARTH'S MIGHTIEST HEROES

the AVENGERS

EARTH'S MIGHTIEST HEROES
the AVENGERS

WRITERS
KURT BUSIEK
& Fabian Nicieza

PENCILERS
GEORGE PÉREZ,
Stuart Immonen, Norm Breyfogle, Mark Bagley
& Paul Ryan with Richard Howell

INKERS
Dick Giordano, Al Vey, Wade von Grawbadger, Norm Breyfogle,
Al Milgrom & Greg Adams with Scott Hanna & Richard Howell

COLORISTS
Tom Smith & Joe Rosas

LETTERERS
Richard Starkings & Comicraft's
Albert Deschesne, Wes Abbott & Oscar Gongora

EDITOR
Tom Brevoort

COVERS ARTISTS
George Pérez & Tom Smith

Collection Editor: **Mark D. Beazley**
Assistant Editors: **Nelson Ribeiro & Alex Starbuck** • Editor, Special Projects: **Jennifer Grünwald**
Senior Editor, Special Projects: **Jeff Youngquist**
Research & Layout: **Jeph York** • Senior Vice President of Sales: **David Gabriel**
SVP of Brand Planning & Communications: **Michael Pasciullo**

Editor in Chief: **Axel Alonso** • Chief Creative Officer: **Joe Quesada**
Publisher: **Dan Buckley** • Executive Producer: **Alan Fine**

AVENGERS ASSEMBLE VOL. 3. Contains material originally published in magazine form as AVENGERS #24-34 and ANNUAL 2000, and THUNDERBOLTS #42-44. First printing 2012. ISBN# 978-0-7851-6196-7.
Published by MARVEL WORLDWIDE, INC., a subsidiary of MARVEL ENTERTAINMENT, LLC. OFFICE OF PUBLICATION: 135 West 50th Street, New York, NY 10020. Copyright © 2000 and 2012 Marvel Characters, Inc.
All rights reserved. $34.99 per copy in the U.S. and $38.99 in Canada (GST #R127032852); Canadian Agreement #40668537. All characters featured in this issue and the distinctive names and likenesses thereof,
and all related indicia are trademarks of Marvel Characters, Inc. No similarity between any of the names, characters, persons, and/or institutions in this magazine with those of any living or dead person or institution
is intended, and any such similarity which may exist is purely coincidental. **Printed in the U.S.A.** ALAN FINE, EVP - Office of the President, Marvel Worldwide, Inc. and EVP & CMO Marvel Characters B.V.; DAN
BUCKLEY, Publisher & President - Print, Animation & Digital Divisions; JOE QUESADA, Chief Creative Officer; TOM BREVOORT, SVP of Publishing; DAVID BOGART, SVP of Operations & Procurement, Publishing; RUWAN
JAYATILLEKE, SVP & Associate Publisher, Publishing; C.B. CEBULSKI, SVP of Creator & Content Development; DAVID GABRIEL, SVP of Publishing Sales & Circulation; MICHAEL PASCIULLO, SVP of Brand Planning &
Communications; JIM O'KEEFE, VP of Operations & Logistics; DAN CARR, Executive Director of Publishing Technology; SUSAN CRESPI, Editorial Operations Manager; ALEX MORALES, Publishing Operations Manager;
STAN LEE, Chairman Emeritus. For information regarding advertising in Marvel Comics or on Marvel.com, please contact John Dokes, SVP Integrated Sales and Marketing, at jdokes@marvel.com. For Marvel
subscription inquiries, please call 800-217-9158. **Manufactured between 3/29/2012 and 4/17/2012 by QUAD/GRAPHICS, DUBUQUE, IA, USA.**

10 9 8 7 6 5 4 3 2 1

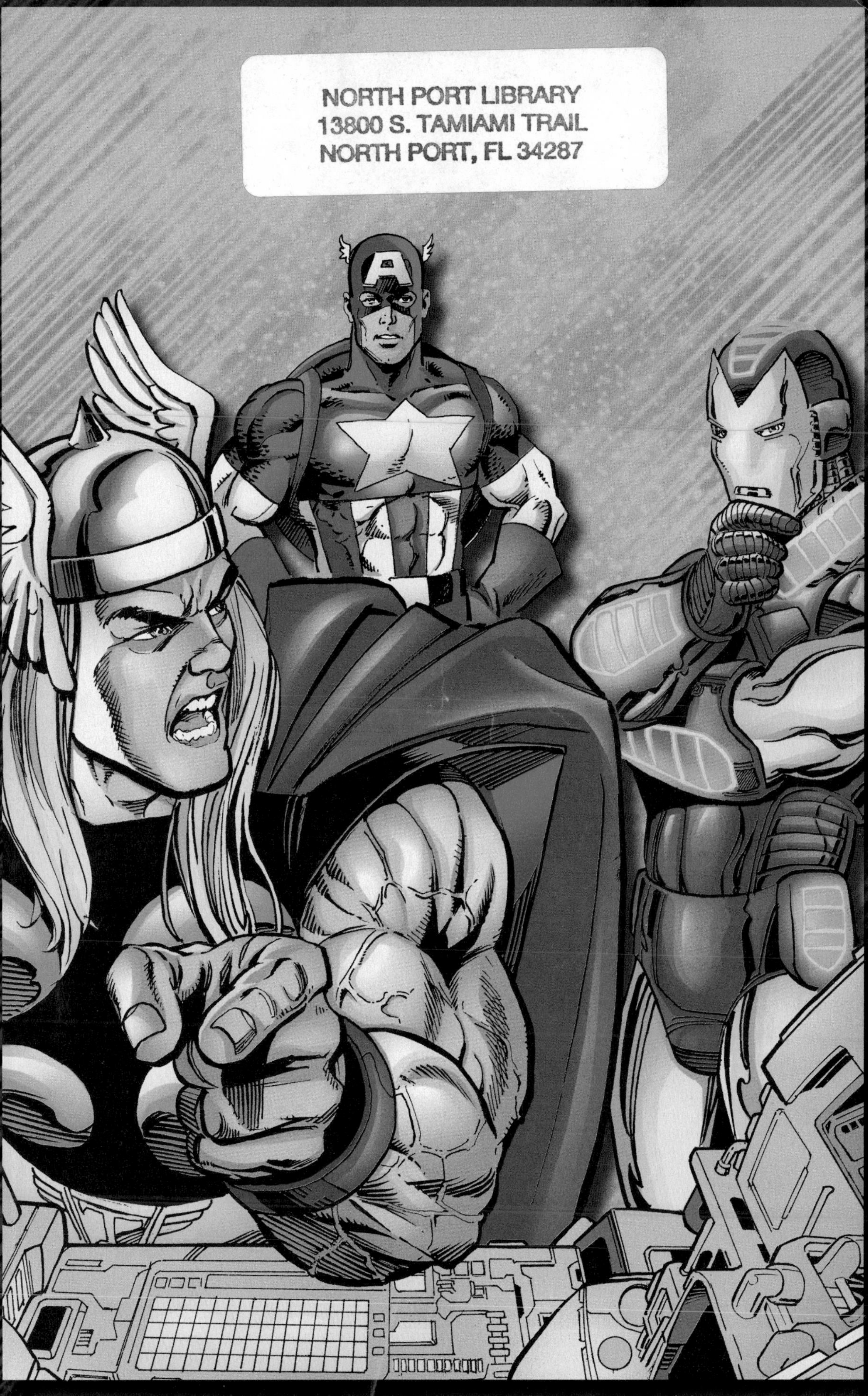

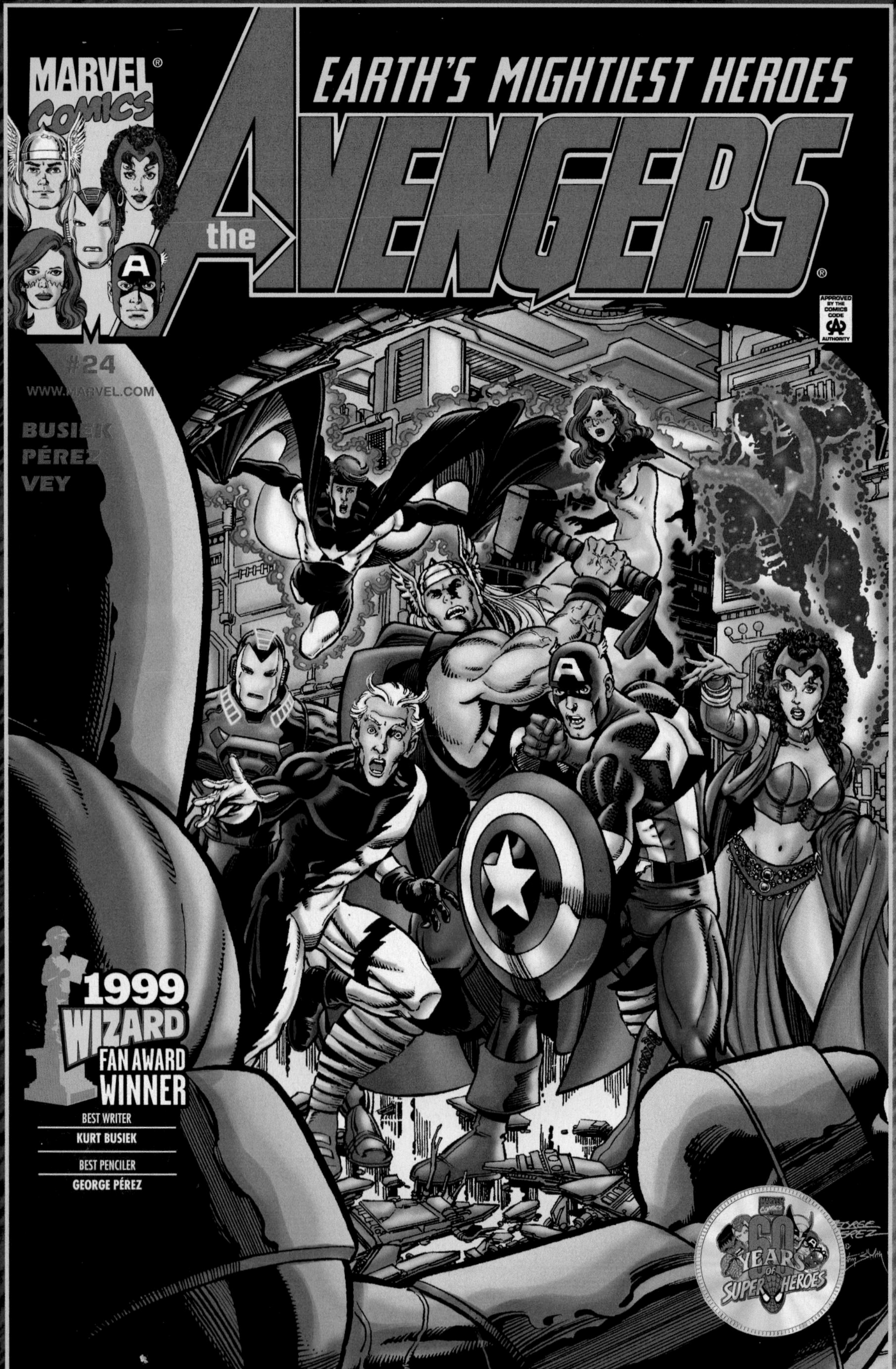
MARVEL®
COMICS
EARTH'S MIGHTIEST HEROES
the AVENGERS®
APPROVED BY THE COMICS CODE AUTHORITY
#24
WWW.MARVEL.COM
BUSIEK
PÉREZ
VEY
1999
WIZARD
FAN AWARD
WINNER
BEST WRITER
KURT BUSIEK
BEST PENCILER
GEORGE PÉREZ
MARVEL COMICS
60 YEARS OF SUPER HEROES

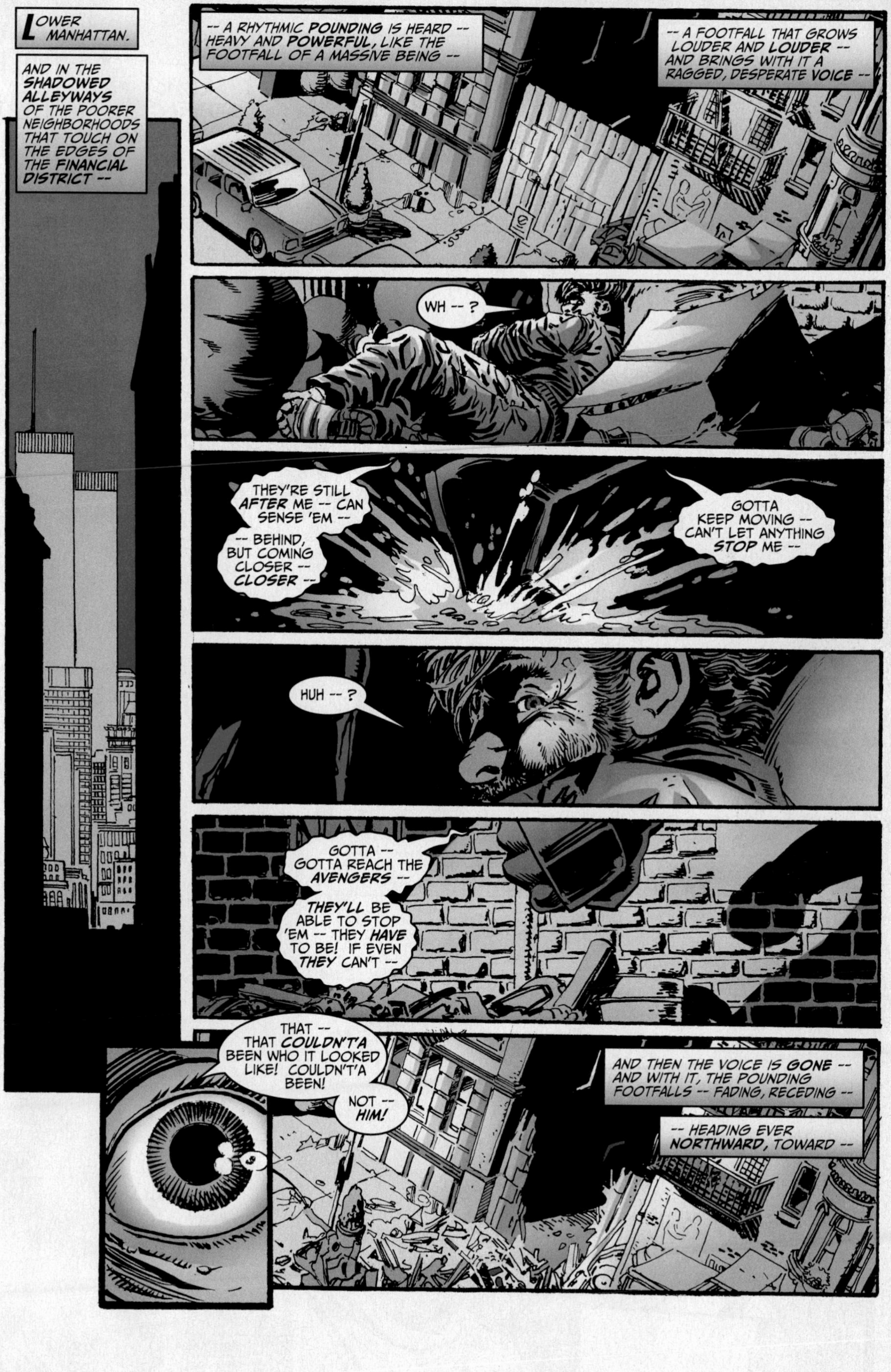
LOWER MANHATTAN.
AND IN THE SHADOWED ALLEYWAYS OF THE POORER NEIGHBORHOODS THAT TOUCH ON THE EDGES OF THE FINANCIAL DISTRICT --
-- A RHYTHMIC POUNDING IS HEARD -- HEAVY AND POWERFUL, LIKE THE FOOTFALL OF A MASSIVE BEING --
-- A FOOTFALL THAT GROWS LOUDER AND LOUDER -- AND BRINGS WITH IT A RAGGED, DESPERATE VOICE --
WH -- ?
THEY'RE STILL AFTER ME -- CAN SENSE 'EM --
-- BEHIND, BUT COMING CLOSER -- CLOSER --
GOTTA KEEP MOVING -- CAN'T LET ANYTHING STOP ME --
HUH -- ?
GOTTA -- GOTTA REACH THE AVENGERS --
THEY'LL BE ABLE TO STOP 'EM -- THEY HAVE TO BE! IF EVEN THEY CAN'T --
THAT -- THAT COULDN'T'A BEEN WHO IT LOOKED LIKE! COULDN'T'A BEEN!
NOT -- HIM!
AND THEN THE VOICE IS GONE -- AND WITH IT, THE POUNDING FOOTFALLS -- FADING, RECEDING --
-- HEADING EVER NORTHWARD, TOWARD --

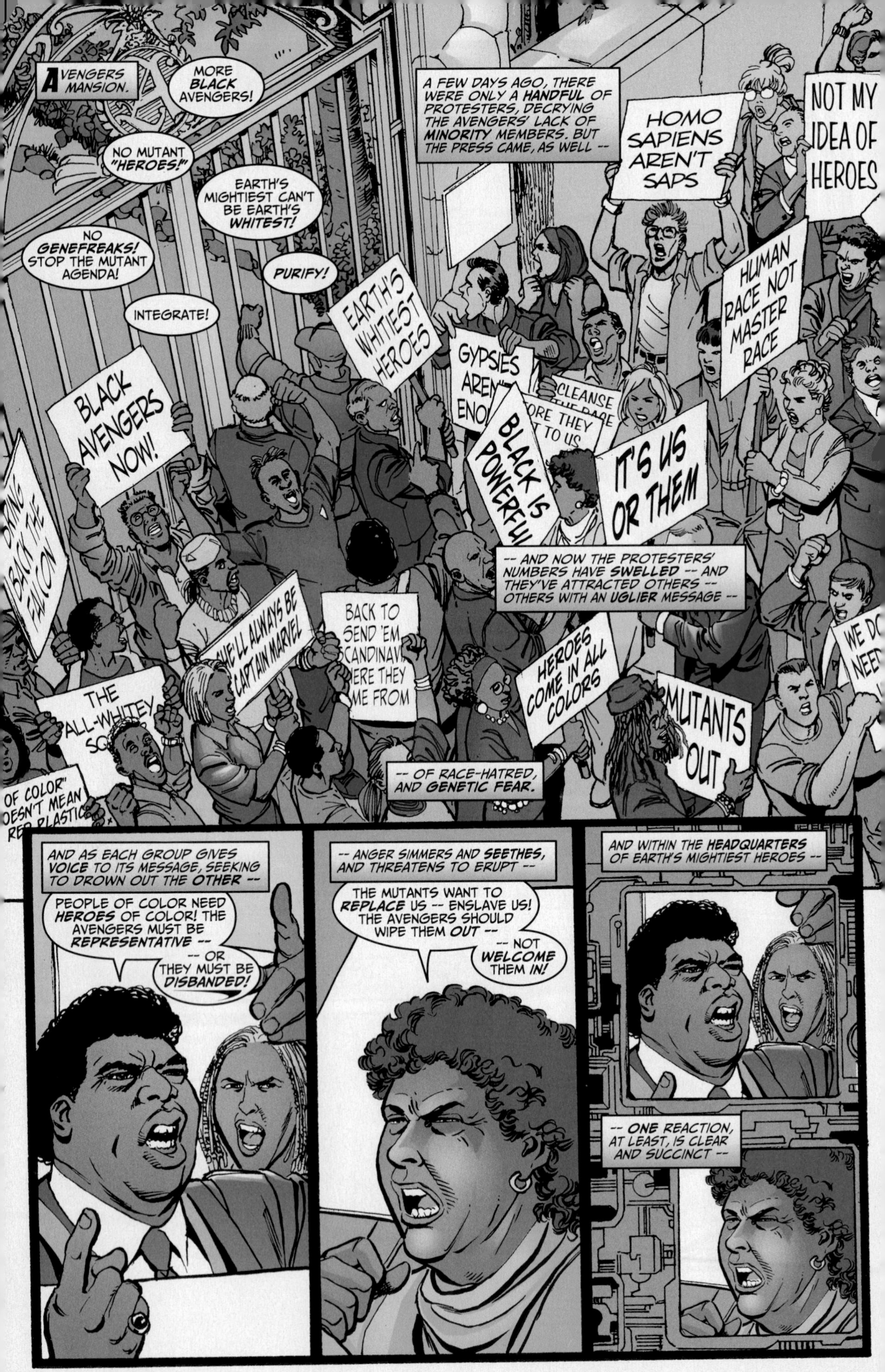
AVENGERS MANSION.
MORE BLACK AVENGERS!
NO MUTANT "HEROES!"
EARTH'S MIGHTIEST CAN'T BE EARTH'S WHITEST!
NO GENEFREAKS! STOP THE MUTANT AGENDA!
PURIFY!
INTEGRATE!
A FEW DAYS AGO, THERE WERE ONLY A HANDFUL OF PROTESTERS, DECRYING THE AVENGERS' LACK OF MINORITY MEMBERS. BUT THE PRESS CAME, AS WELL --
HOMO SAPIENS AREN'T SAPS
NOT MY IDEA OF HEROES
HUMAN RACE NOT MASTER RACE
EARTH'S WHITEST HEROES
BLACK AVENGERS NOW!
BLACK IS POWERFUL
IT'S US OR THEM
-- AND NOW THE PROTESTERS' NUMBERS HAVE SWELLED -- AND THEY'VE ATTRACTED OTHERS -- OTHERS WITH AN UGLIER MESSAGE --
HEROES COME IN ALL COLORS
MUTANTS OUT
-- OF RACE-HATRED, AND GENETIC FEAR.
AND AS EACH GROUP GIVES VOICE TO ITS MESSAGE, SEEKING TO DROWN OUT THE OTHER --
PEOPLE OF COLOR NEED HEROES OF COLOR! THE AVENGERS MUST BE REPRESENTATIVE --
-- OR THEY MUST BE DISBANDED!
-- ANGER SIMMERS AND SEETHES, AND THREATENS TO ERUPT --
THE MUTANTS WANT TO REPLACE US -- ENSLAVE US! THE AVENGERS SHOULD WIPE THEM OUT --
-- NOT WELCOME THEM IN!
AND WITHIN THE HEADQUARTERS OF EARTH'S MIGHTIEST HEROES --
-- ONE REACTION, AT LEAST, IS CLEAR AND SUCCINCT --

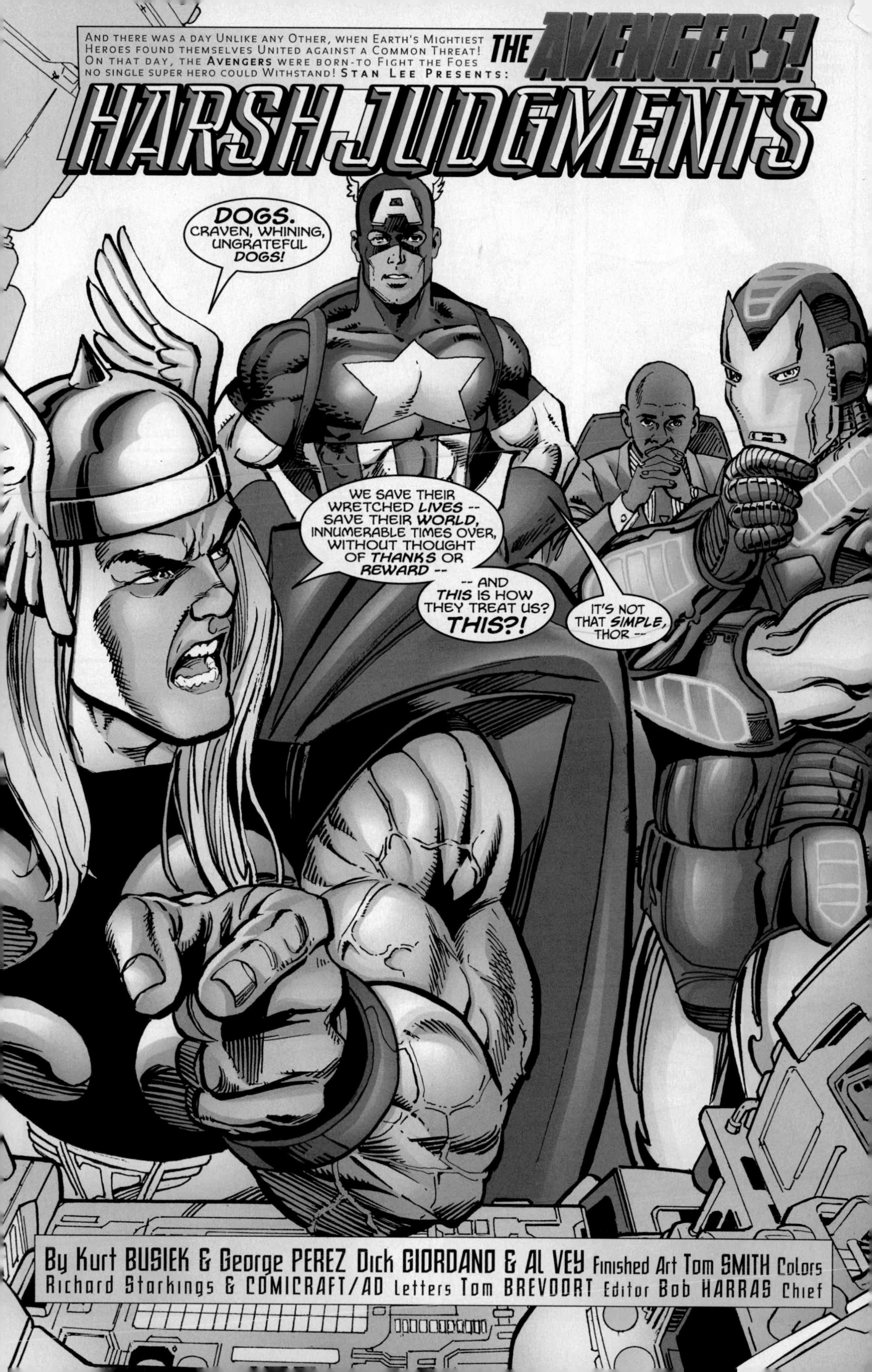

And there was a day Unlike any Other, when Earth's Mightiest Heroes found themselves United against a Common Threat! On that day, the Avengers were born-to Fight the Foes no single super hero could Withstand! Stan Lee Presents:
THE AVENGERS!
HARSH JUDGMENTS
DOGS. CRAVEN, WHINING, UNGRATEFUL DOGS!
WE SAVE THEIR WRETCHED LIVES -- SAVE THEIR WORLD, INNUMERABLE TIMES OVER, WITHOUT THOUGHT OF THANKS OR REWARD --
-- AND THIS IS HOW THEY TREAT US? THIS?!
IT'S NOT THAT SIMPLE, THOR --
By Kurt BUSIEK & George PEREZ Dick GIORDANO & AL VEY Finished Art Tom SMITH Colors
Richard Starkings & COMICRAFT/AD Letters Tom BREVOORT Editor Bob HARRAS Chief

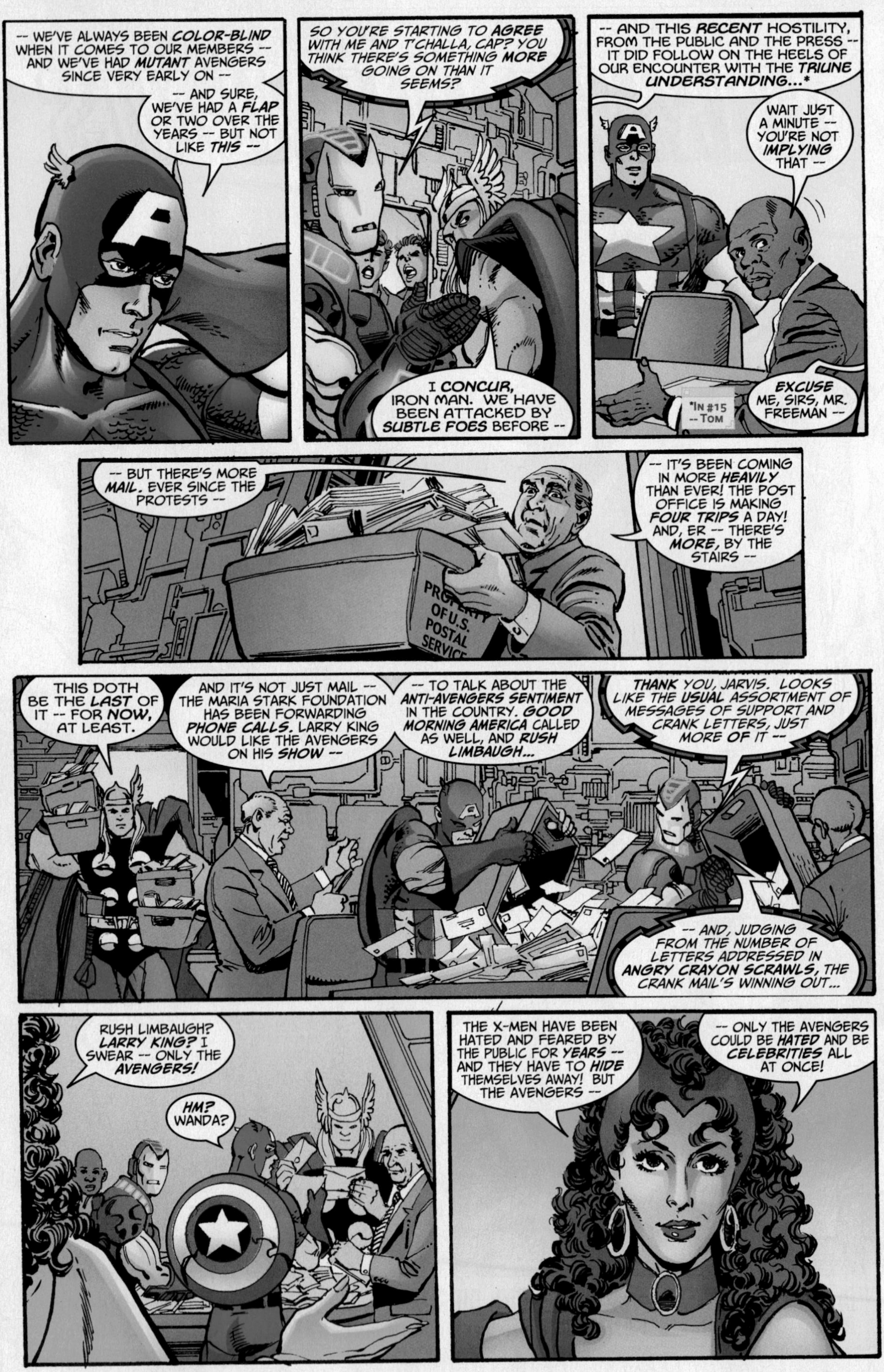
-- WE'VE ALWAYS BEEN COLOR-BLIND WHEN IT COMES TO OUR MEMBERS -- AND WE'VE HAD MUTANT AVENGERS SINCE VERY EARLY ON --
-- AND SURE, WE'VE HAD A FLAP OR TWO OVER THE YEARS -- BUT NOT LIKE THIS --
SO YOU'RE STARTING TO AGREE WITH ME AND T'CHALLA, CAP? YOU THINK THERE'S SOMETHING MORE GOING ON THAN IT SEEMS?
I CONCUR, IRON MAN. WE HAVE BEEN ATTACKED BY SUBTLE FOES BEFORE --
-- AND THIS RECENT HOSTILITY, FROM THE PUBLIC AND THE PRESS -- IT DID FOLLOW ON THE HEELS OF OUR ENCOUNTER WITH THE TRIUNE UNDERSTANDING...*
WAIT JUST A MINUTE -- YOU'RE NOT IMPLYING THAT --
*IN #15 -- TOM
EXCUSE ME, SIRS, MR. FREEMAN --
-- BUT THERE'S MORE MAIL. EVER SINCE THE PROTESTS --
-- IT'S BEEN COMING IN MORE HEAVILY THAN EVER! THE POST OFFICE IS MAKING FOUR TRIPS A DAY! AND, ER -- THERE'S MORE, BY THE STAIRS --
PROPERTY OF U.S. POSTAL SERVICE
THIS DOTH BE THE LAST OF IT -- FOR NOW, AT LEAST.
AND IT'S NOT JUST MAIL -- THE MARIA STARK FOUNDATION HAS BEEN FORWARDING PHONE CALLS. LARRY KING WOULD LIKE THE AVENGERS ON HIS SHOW --
-- TO TALK ABOUT THE ANTI-AVENGERS SENTIMENT IN THE COUNTRY. GOOD MORNING AMERICA CALLED AS WELL, AND RUSH LIMBAUGH...
THANK YOU, JARVIS. LOOKS LIKE THE USUAL ASSORTMENT OF MESSAGES OF SUPPORT AND CRANK LETTERS, JUST MORE OF IT --
-- AND, JUDGING FROM THE NUMBER OF LETTERS ADDRESSED IN ANGRY CRAYON SCRAWLS, THE CRANK MAIL'S WINNING OUT...
RUSH LIMBAUGH? LARRY KING? I SWEAR -- ONLY THE AVENGERS!
HM? WANDA?
THE X-MEN HAVE BEEN HATED AND FEARED BY THE PUBLIC FOR YEARS -- AND THEY HAVE TO HIDE THEMSELVES AWAY! BUT THE AVENGERS --
-- ONLY THE AVENGERS COULD BE HATED AND BE CELEBRITIES ALL AT ONCE!

BUT MY *APOLOGIES*, GENTLEMEN. I DIDN'T STOP BY TO *LAUGH* AT OUR COMPARATIVE MISFORTUNES --

-- BUT TO SEE IF ANYONE KNEW WHERE *SIMON* IS?

HE WAS IN THE *COMM-ROOM*, LAST I SAW.

THANKS, CAP.

AND AS THE YOUNG MUTANT KNOWN AS THE *SCARLET WITCH* STRIDES LITHELY AND PURPOSEFULLY AWAY --

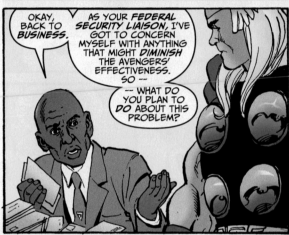

OKAY, BACK TO *BUSINESS*.

AS YOUR *FEDERAL SECURITY LIAISON*, I'VE GOT TO CONCERN MYSELF WITH ANYTHING THAT MIGHT *DIMINISH* THE AVENGERS' EFFECTIVENESS. SO --

-- WHAT DO YOU PLAN TO *DO* ABOUT THIS PROBLEM?

I STILL SAY WE DO *NOTHING*, DUANE. WE'VE DONE NOTHING *WRONG* -- SO WE JUST KEEP *ON*, AS ALWAYS --

I *DISAGREE*, CAP. FAILING TO RESPOND JUST LETS PEOPLE *BELIEVE* THE ACCUSATIONS -- AND I'VE SEEN ENOUGH AT STARK ENTERPRISES TO --

YOU'RE PROBABLY *RIGHT*, OLD FRIEND. I'LL -- GIVE IT SOME *THOUGHT*. IN THE MEANTIME, IF ANYONE WANTS ME --

-- I'LL BE IN THE *COMBAT SIMULATION ROOM*.

WELL, *THAT* WAS BRUSQUE -- !

YES -- AND I MUST CONFESS, IT *WORRIES* ME. CAPTAIN AMERICA SPENDS MORE AND MORE TIME *ALONE* -- TRAINING --

AND AS THE AVENGERS' BUTLER VOICES HIS *WORRIES* --

THOOM THOOM

-- AND A HEAVY TREAD COMES NEARER, EVER NEARER --

BBBBBMMMM

OH, *MAAAN* --

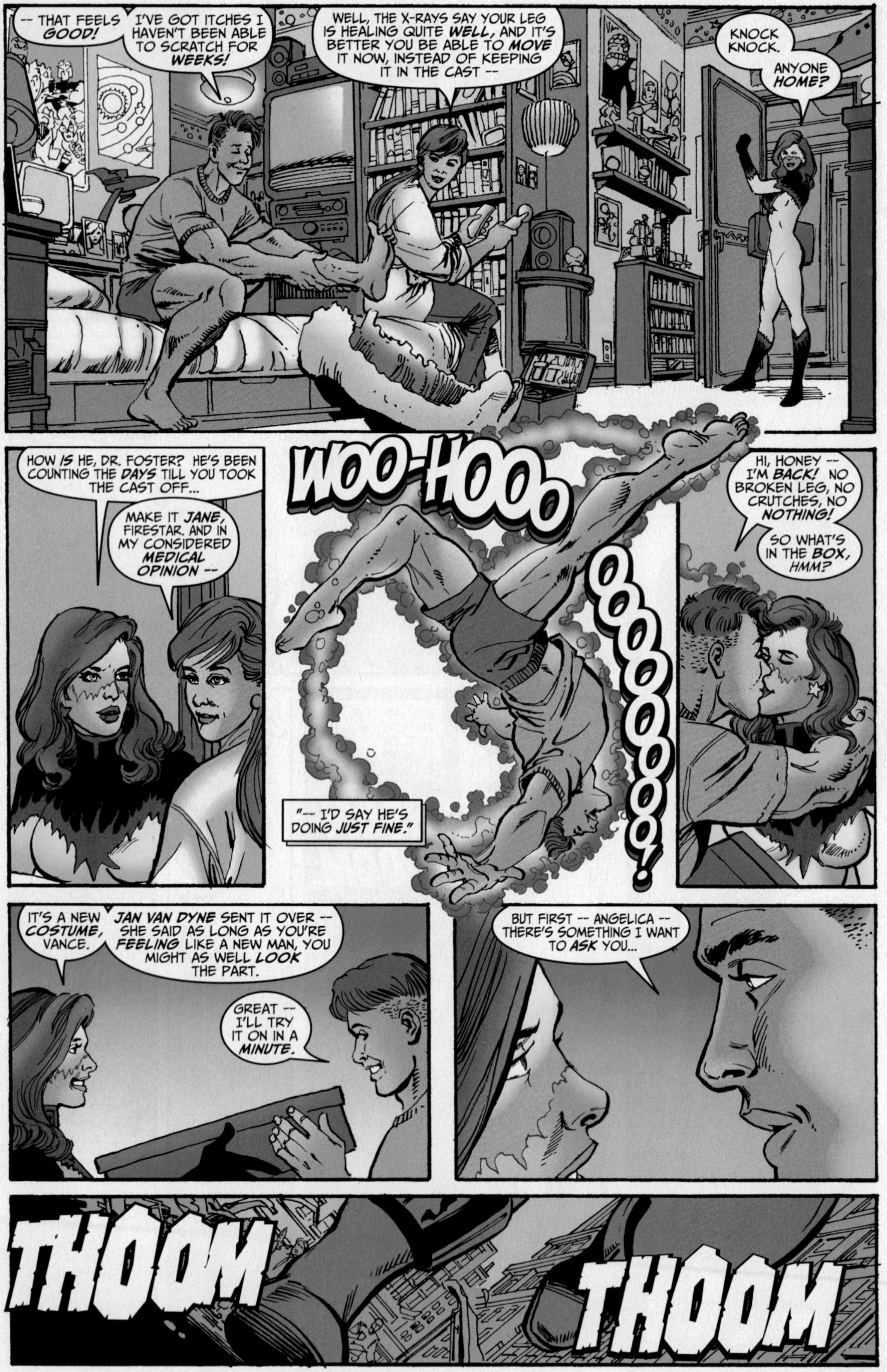

-- THAT FEELS GOOD!
I'VE GOT ITCHES I HAVEN'T BEEN ABLE TO SCRATCH FOR WEEKS!
WELL, THE X-RAYS SAY YOUR LEG IS HEALING QUITE WELL, AND IT'S BETTER YOU BE ABLE TO MOVE IT NOW, INSTEAD OF KEEPING IT IN THE CAST --
KNOCK KNOCK.
ANYONE HOME?
HOW IS HE, DR. FOSTER? HE'S BEEN COUNTING THE DAYS TILL YOU TOOK THE CAST OFF...
MAKE IT JANE, FIRESTAR. AND IN MY CONSIDERED MEDICAL OPINION --
WOO-HOOoOOOOOOOOOO!
"-- I'D SAY HE'S DOING JUST FINE."
HI, HONEY -- I'M BACK! NO BROKEN LEG, NO CRUTCHES, NO NOTHING!
SO WHAT'S IN THE BOX, HMM?
IT'S A NEW COSTUME, VANCE.
JAN VAN DYNE SENT IT OVER -- SHE SAID AS LONG AS YOU'RE FEELING LIKE A NEW MAN, YOU MIGHT AS WELL LOOK THE PART.
GREAT -- I'LL TRY IT ON IN A MINUTE.
BUT FIRST -- ANGELICA -- THERE'S SOMETHING I WANT TO ASK YOU...
THOOM
THOOM

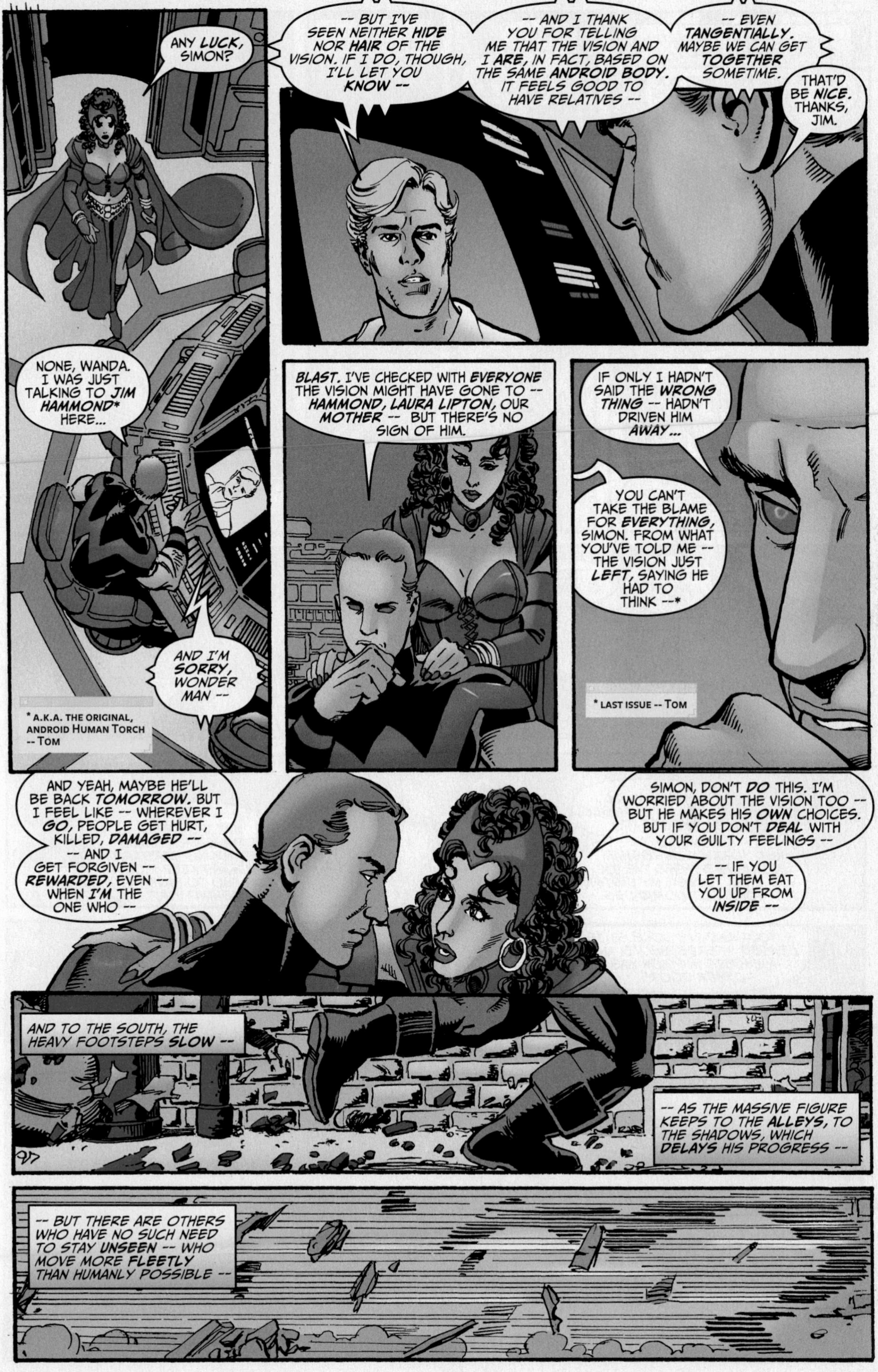
ANY LUCK, SIMON?
-- BUT I'VE SEEN NEITHER HIDE NOR HAIR OF THE VISION. IF I DO, THOUGH, I'LL LET YOU KNOW --
-- AND I THANK YOU FOR TELLING ME THAT THE VISION AND I ARE, IN FACT, BASED ON THE SAME ANDROID BODY. IT FEELS GOOD TO HAVE RELATIVES --
-- EVEN TANGENTIALLY. MAYBE WE CAN GET TOGETHER SOMETIME.
THAT'D BE NICE. THANKS, JIM.
NONE, WANDA. I WAS JUST TALKING TO JIM HAMMOND* HERE...
AND I'M SORRY, WONDER MAN --
* A.K.A. THE ORIGINAL, ANDROID HUMAN TORCH -- TOM
BLAST. I'VE CHECKED WITH EVERYONE THE VISION MIGHT HAVE GONE TO -- HAMMOND, LAURA LIPTON, OUR MOTHER -- BUT THERE'S NO SIGN OF HIM.
IF ONLY I HADN'T SAID THE WRONG THING -- HADN'T DRIVEN HIM AWAY...
YOU CAN'T TAKE THE BLAME FOR EVERYTHING, SIMON. FROM WHAT YOU'VE TOLD ME -- THE VISION JUST LEFT, SAYING HE HAD TO THINK --*
* LAST ISSUE -- TOM
AND YEAH, MAYBE HE'LL BE BACK TOMORROW. BUT I FEEL LIKE -- WHEREVER I GO, PEOPLE GET HURT, KILLED, DAMAGED --
-- AND I GET FORGIVEN -- REWARDED, EVEN -- WHEN I'M THE ONE WHO --
SIMON, DON'T DO THIS. I'M WORRIED ABOUT THE VISION TOO -- BUT HE MAKES HIS OWN CHOICES. BUT IF YOU DON'T DEAL WITH YOUR GUILTY FEELINGS --
-- IF YOU LET THEM EAT YOU UP FROM INSIDE --
AND TO THE SOUTH, THE HEAVY FOOTSTEPS SLOW --
-- AS THE MASSIVE FIGURE KEEPS TO THE ALLEYS, TO THE SHADOWS, WHICH DELAYS HIS PROGRESS --
-- BUT THERE ARE OTHERS WHO HAVE NO SUCH NEED TO STAY UNSEEN -- WHO MOVE MORE FLEETLY THAN HUMANLY POSSIBLE --

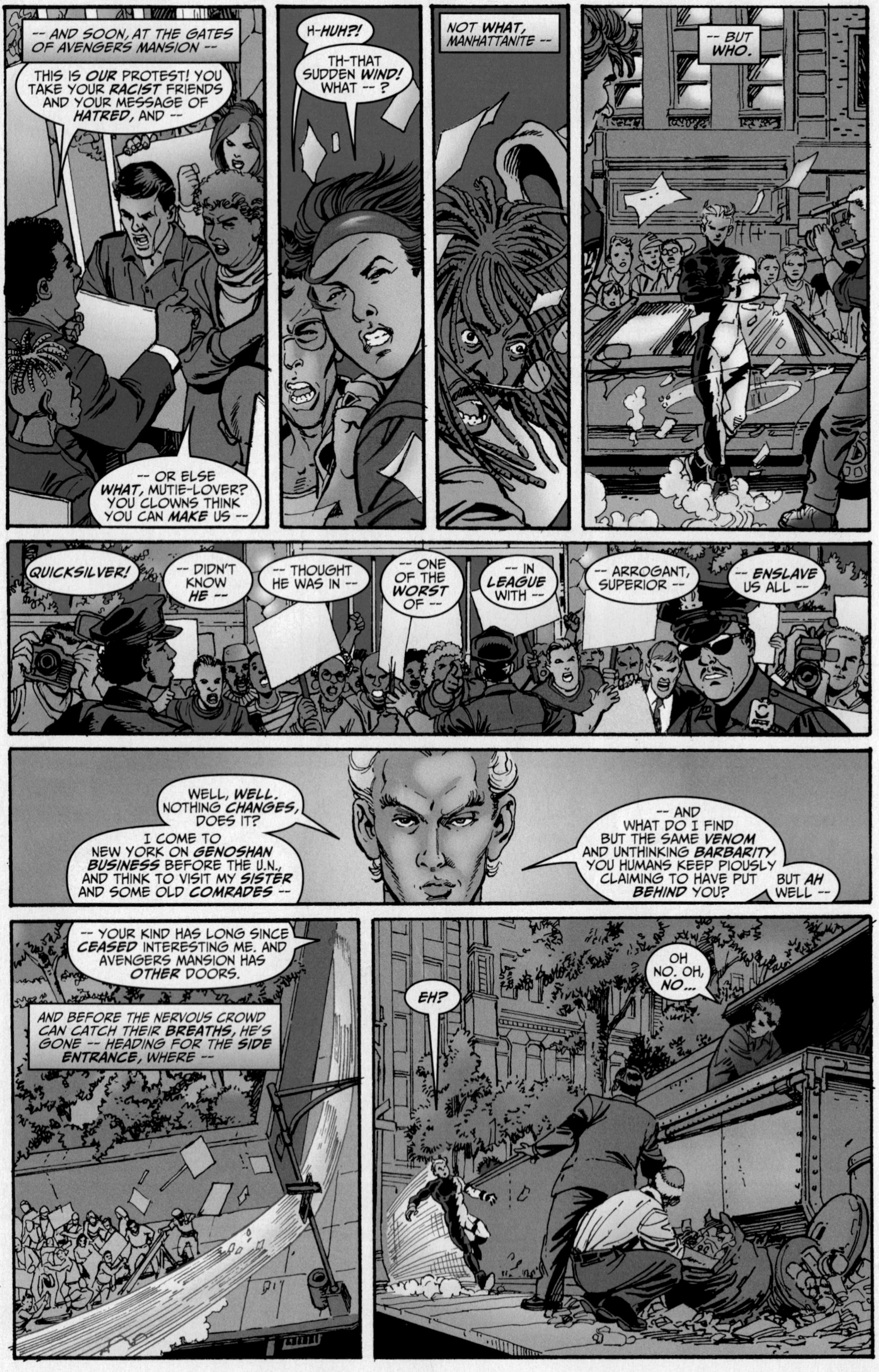
-- AND SOON, AT THE GATES OF AVENGERS MANSION --
THIS IS OUR PROTEST! YOU TAKE YOUR RACIST FRIENDS AND YOUR MESSAGE OF HATRED, AND --
-- OR ELSE WHAT, MUTIE-LOVER? YOU CLOWNS THINK YOU CAN MAKE US --
H-HUH?!
TH-THAT SUDDEN WIND! WHAT -- ?
NOT WHAT, MANHATTANITE --
-- BUT WHO.
QUICKSILVER!
-- DIDN'T KNOW HE --
-- THOUGHT HE WAS IN --
-- ONE OF THE WORST OF --
-- IN LEAGUE WITH --
-- ARROGANT, SUPERIOR --
-- ENSLAVE US ALL --
WELL, WELL. NOTHING CHANGES, DOES IT?
I COME TO NEW YORK ON GENOSHAN BUSINESS BEFORE THE U.N., AND THINK TO VISIT MY SISTER AND SOME OLD COMRADES --
-- AND WHAT DO I FIND BUT THE SAME VENOM AND UNTHINKING BARBARITY YOU HUMANS KEEP PIOUSLY CLAIMING TO HAVE PUT BEHIND YOU?
BUT AH WELL --
-- YOUR KIND HAS LONG SINCE CEASED INTERESTING ME. AND AVENGERS MANSION HAS OTHER DOORS.
AND BEFORE THE NERVOUS CROWD CAN CATCH THEIR BREATHS, HE'S GONE -- HEADING FOR THE SIDE ENTRANCE, WHERE --
EH?
OH NO. OH, NO...

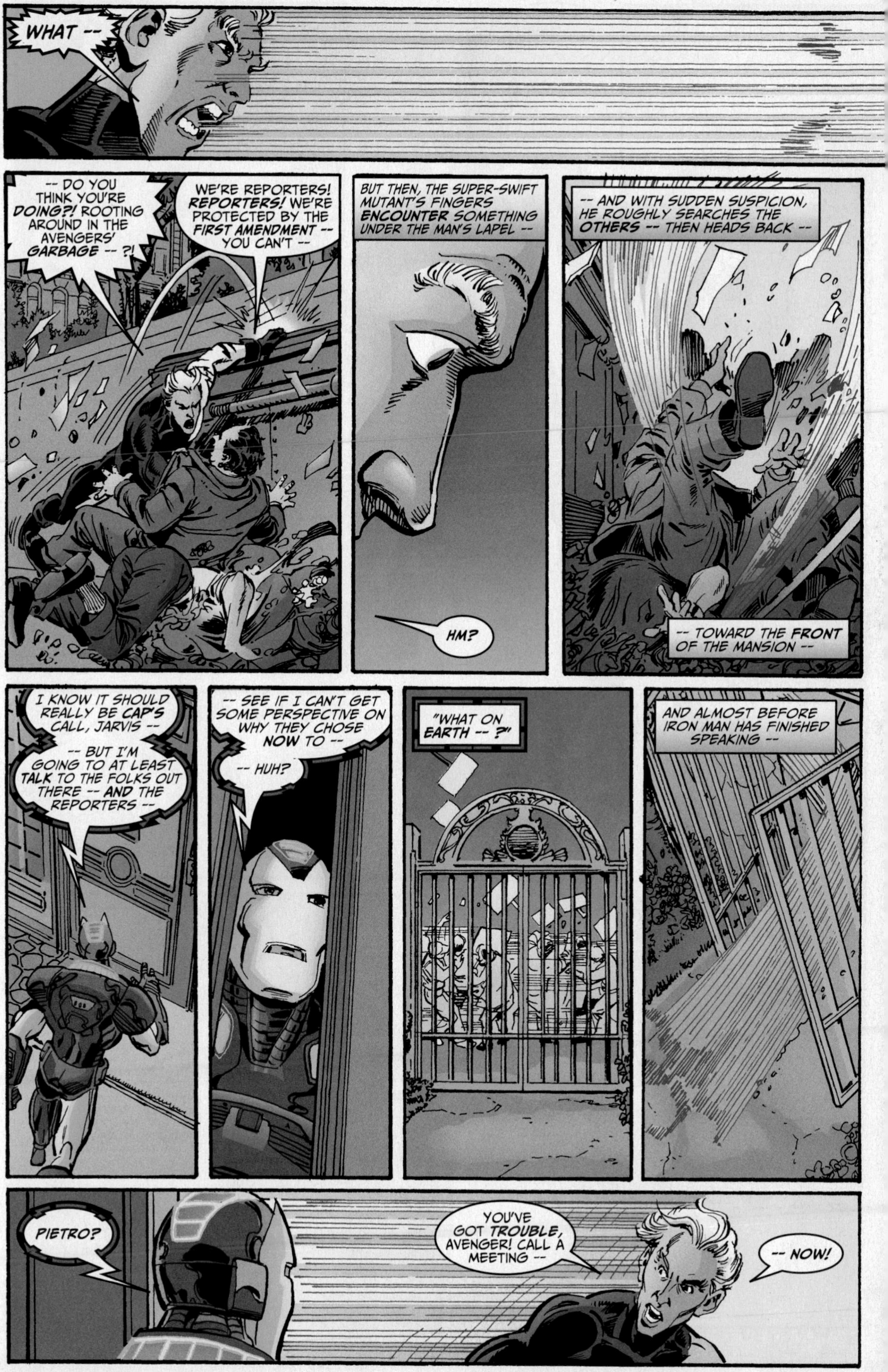
WHAT --
-- DO YOU THINK YOU'RE DOING?! ROOTING AROUND IN THE AVENGERS' GARBAGE -- ?!
WE'RE REPORTERS! REPORTERS! WE'RE PROTECTED BY THE FIRST AMENDMENT -- YOU CAN'T --
BUT THEN, THE SUPER-SWIFT MUTANT'S FINGERS ENCOUNTER SOMETHING UNDER THE MAN'S LAPEL --
HM?
-- AND WITH SUDDEN SUSPICION, HE ROUGHLY SEARCHES THE OTHERS -- THEN HEADS BACK --
-- TOWARD THE FRONT OF THE MANSION --
I KNOW IT SHOULD REALLY BE CAP'S CALL, JARVIS --
-- BUT I'M GOING TO AT LEAST TALK TO THE FOLKS OUT THERE -- AND THE REPORTERS --
-- SEE IF I CAN'T GET SOME PERSPECTIVE ON WHY THEY CHOSE NOW TO --
-- HUH?
"WHAT ON EARTH -- ?"
AND ALMOST BEFORE IRON MAN HAS FINISHED SPEAKING --
PIETRO?
YOU'VE GOT TROUBLE, AVENGER! CALL A MEETING --
-- NOW!

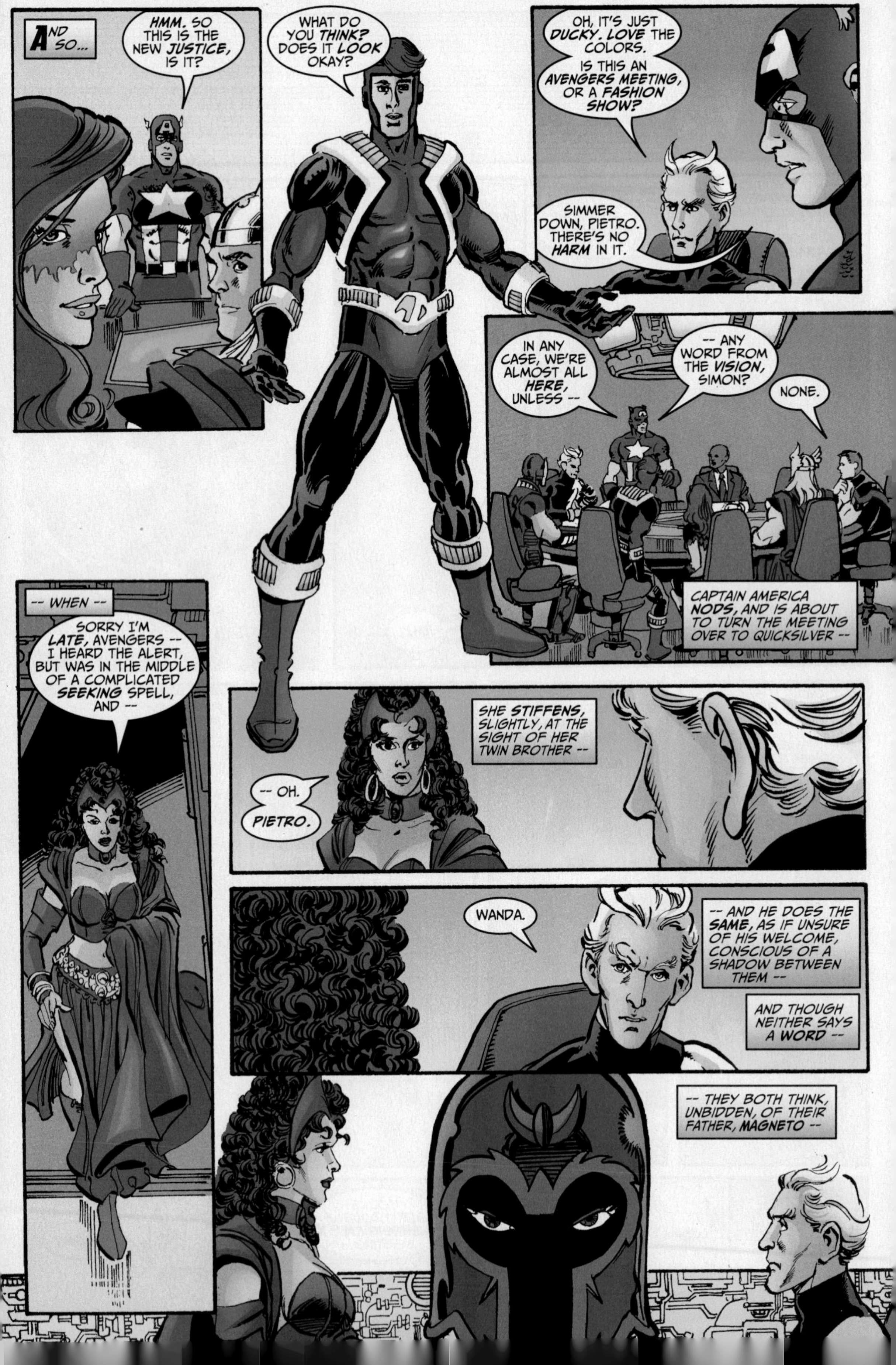
AND SO...
HMM. SO THIS IS THE NEW JUSTICE, IS IT?
WHAT DO YOU THINK? DOES IT LOOK OKAY?
OH, IT'S JUST DUCKY. LOVE THE COLORS.
IS THIS AN AVENGERS MEETING, OR A FASHION SHOW?
SIMMER DOWN, PIETRO. THERE'S NO HARM IN IT.
IN ANY CASE, WE'RE ALMOST ALL HERE, UNLESS --
-- ANY WORD FROM THE VISION, SIMON?
NONE.
CAPTAIN AMERICA NODS, AND IS ABOUT TO TURN THE MEETING OVER TO QUICKSILVER --
-- WHEN --
SORRY I'M LATE, AVENGERS -- I HEARD THE ALERT, BUT WAS IN THE MIDDLE OF A COMPLICATED SEEKING SPELL, AND --
SHE STIFFENS, SLIGHTLY, AT THE SIGHT OF HER TWIN BROTHER --
-- OH. PIETRO.
WANDA.
-- AND HE DOES THE SAME, AS IF UNSURE OF HIS WELCOME, CONSCIOUS OF A SHADOW BETWEEN THEM --
AND THOUGH NEITHER SAYS A WORD --
-- THEY BOTH THINK, UNBIDDEN, OF THEIR FATHER, MAGNETO --

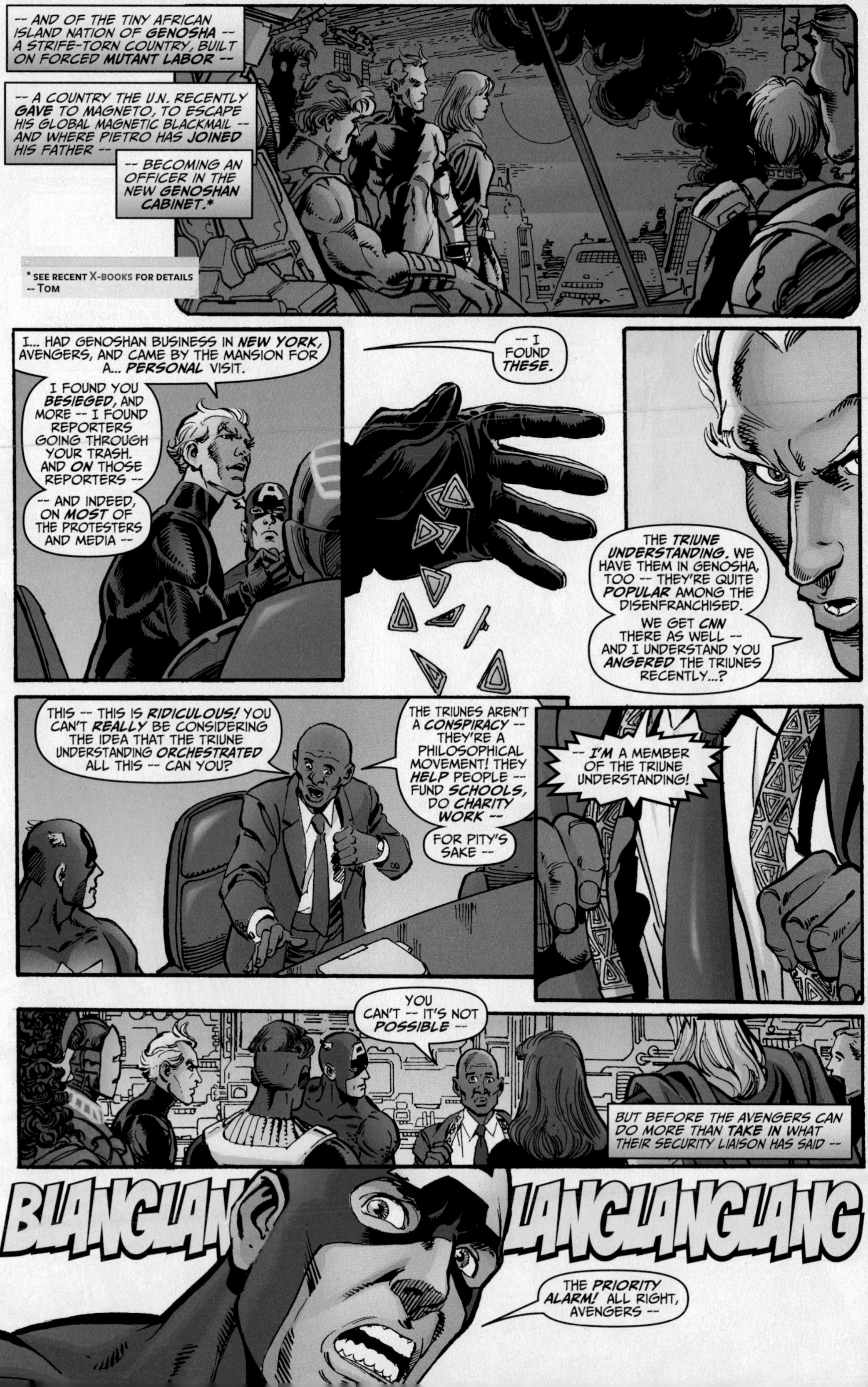

-- AND OF THE TINY AFRICAN ISLAND NATION OF GENOSHA -- A STRIFE-TORN COUNTRY, BUILT ON FORCED MUTANT LABOR --
-- A COUNTRY THE U.N. RECENTLY GAVE TO MAGNETO, TO ESCAPE HIS GLOBAL MAGNETIC BLACKMAIL -- AND WHERE PIETRO HAS JOINED HIS FATHER --
-- BECOMING AN OFFICER IN THE NEW GENOSHAN CABINET.*
* SEE RECENT X-BOOKS FOR DETAILS -- TOM
I... HAD GENOSHAN BUSINESS IN NEW YORK, AVENGERS, AND CAME BY THE MANSION FOR A... PERSONAL VISIT.
I FOUND YOU BESIEGED, AND MORE -- I FOUND REPORTERS GOING THROUGH YOUR TRASH. AND ON THOSE REPORTERS --
-- AND INDEED, ON MOST OF THE PROTESTERS AND MEDIA --
-- I FOUND THESE.
THE TRIUNE UNDERSTANDING. WE HAVE THEM IN GENOSHA, TOO -- THEY'RE QUITE POPULAR AMONG THE DISENFRANCHISED.
WE GET CNN THERE AS WELL -- AND I UNDERSTAND YOU ANGERED THE TRIUNES RECENTLY...?
THIS -- THIS IS RIDICULOUS! YOU CAN'T REALLY BE CONSIDERING THE IDEA THAT THE TRIUNE UNDERSTANDING ORCHESTRATED ALL THIS -- CAN YOU?
THE TRIUNES AREN'T A CONSPIRACY -- THEY'RE A PHILOSOPHICAL MOVEMENT! THEY HELP PEOPLE -- FUND SCHOOLS, DO CHARITY WORK --
FOR PITY'S SAKE --
-- I'M A MEMBER OF THE TRIUNE UNDERSTANDING!
YOU CAN'T -- IT'S NOT POSSIBLE --
BUT BEFORE THE AVENGERS CAN DO MORE THAN TAKE IN WHAT THEIR SECURITY LIAISON HAS SAID --
BLANGLANGLANGLANGLANGLANG
THE PRIORITY ALARM! ALL RIGHT, AVENGERS --

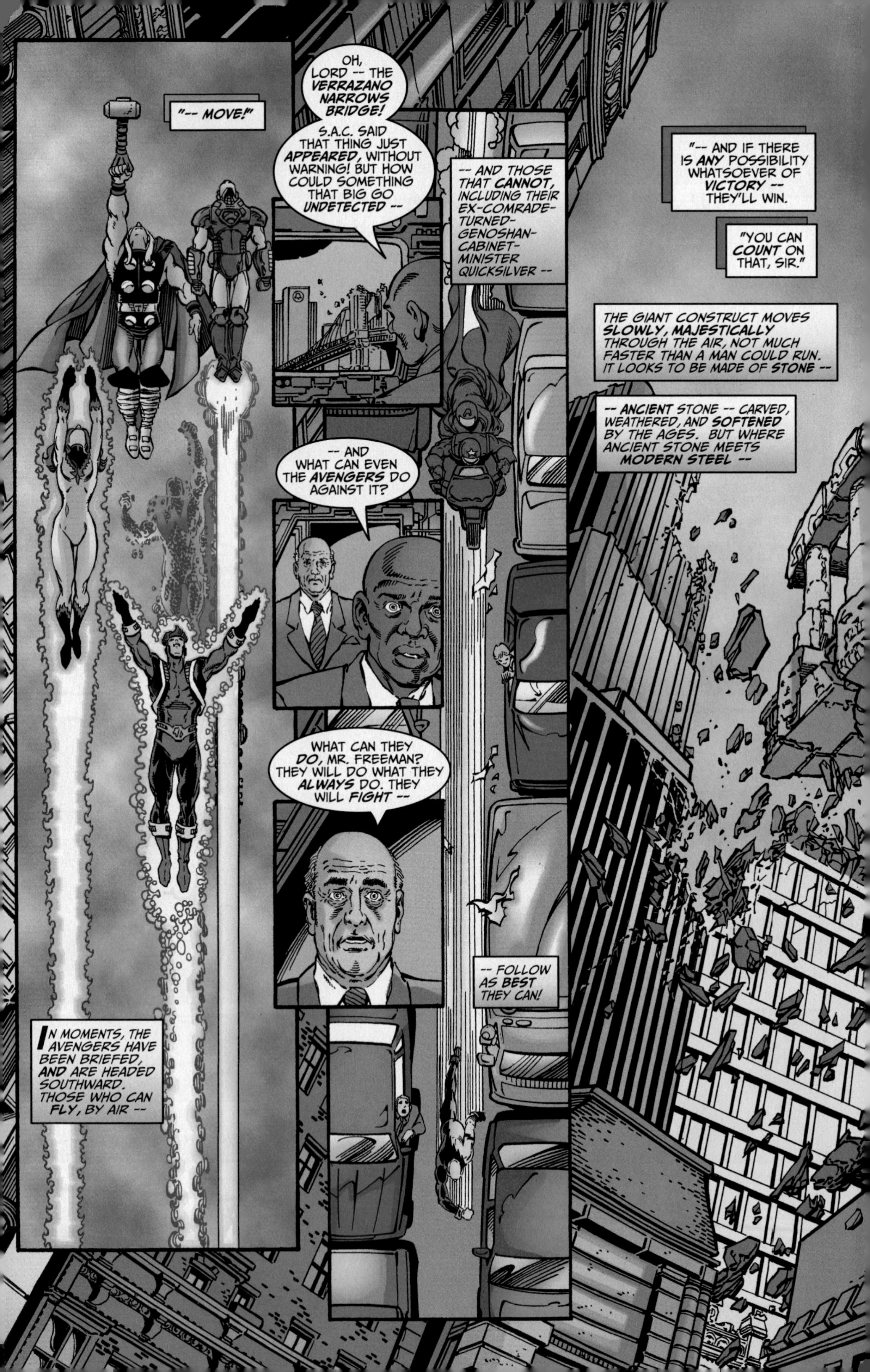
"-- MOVE!"
OH, LORD -- THE VERRAZANO NARROWS BRIDGE!
S.A.C. SAID THAT THING JUST APPEARED, WITHOUT WARNING! BUT HOW COULD SOMETHING THAT BIG GO UNDETECTED --
-- AND WHAT CAN EVEN THE AVENGERS DO AGAINST IT?
WHAT CAN THEY DO, MR. FREEMAN? THEY WILL DO WHAT THEY ALWAYS DO. THEY WILL FIGHT --
IN MOMENTS, THE AVENGERS HAVE BEEN BRIEFED, AND ARE HEADED SOUTHWARD. THOSE WHO CAN FLY, BY AIR --
-- AND THOSE THAT CANNOT, INCLUDING THEIR EX-COMRADE-TURNED-GENOSHAN-CABINET-MINISTER QUICKSILVER --
-- FOLLOW AS BEST THEY CAN!
"-- AND IF THERE IS ANY POSSIBILITY WHATSOEVER OF VICTORY -- THEY'LL WIN.
"YOU CAN COUNT ON THAT, SIR."
THE GIANT CONSTRUCT MOVES SLOWLY, MAJESTICALLY THROUGH THE AIR, NOT MUCH FASTER THAN A MAN COULD RUN. IT LOOKS TO BE MADE OF STONE --
-- ANCIENT STONE -- CARVED, WEATHERED, AND SOFTENED BY THE AGES. BUT WHERE ANCIENT STONE MEETS MODERN STEEL --

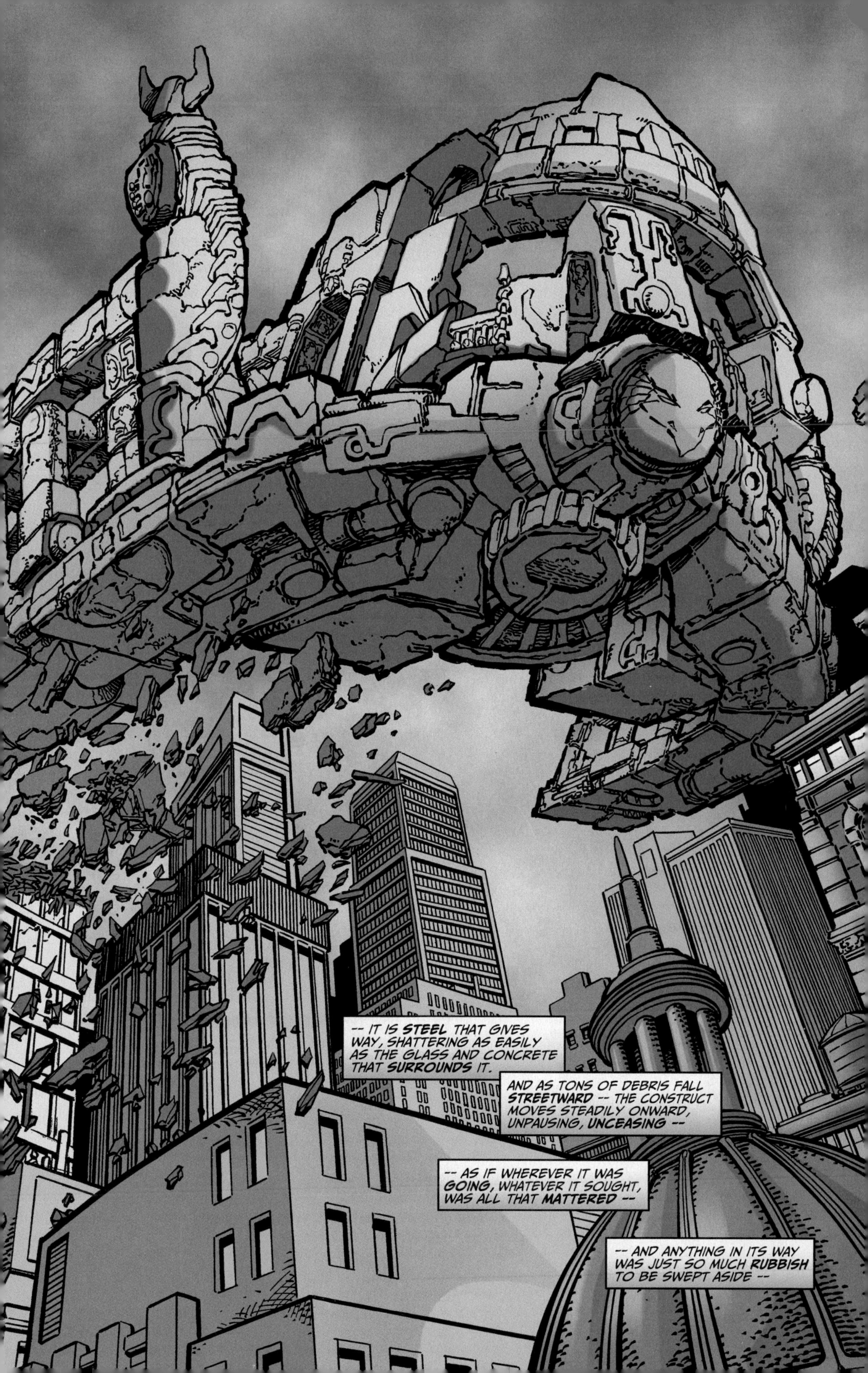
-- IT IS STEEL THAT GIVES WAY, SHATTERING AS EASILY AS THE GLASS AND CONCRETE THAT SURROUNDS IT.
AND AS TONS OF DEBRIS FALL STREETWARD -- THE CONSTRUCT MOVES STEADILY ONWARD, UNPAUSING, UNCEASING --
-- AS IF WHEREVER IT WAS GOING, WHATEVER IT SOUGHT, WAS ALL THAT MATTERED --
-- AND ANYTHING IN ITS WAY WAS JUST SO MUCH RUBBISH TO BE SWEPT ASIDE --

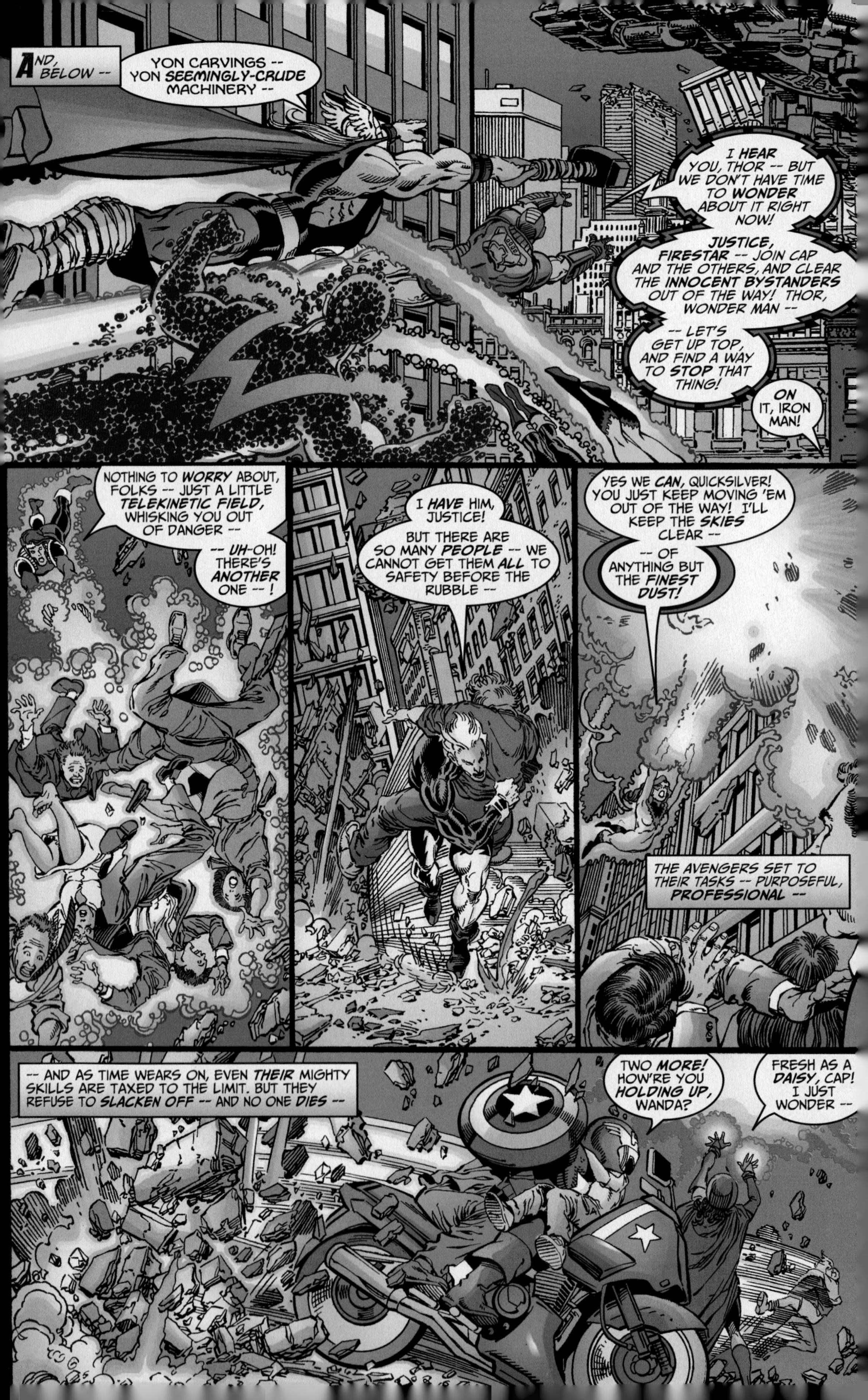
AND, BELOW --
YON CARVINGS -- YON SEEMINGLY-CRUDE MACHINERY --
I HEAR YOU, THOR -- BUT WE DON'T HAVE TIME TO WONDER ABOUT IT RIGHT NOW!
JUSTICE, FIRESTAR -- JOIN CAP AND THE OTHERS, AND CLEAR THE INNOCENT BYSTANDERS OUT OF THE WAY! THOR, WONDER MAN --
-- LET'S GET UP TOP, AND FIND A WAY TO STOP THAT THING!
ON IT, IRON MAN!
NOTHING TO WORRY ABOUT, FOLKS -- JUST A LITTLE TELEKINETIC FIELD, WHISKING YOU OUT OF DANGER --
-- UH-OH! THERE'S ANOTHER ONE -- !
I HAVE HIM, JUSTICE!
BUT THERE ARE SO MANY PEOPLE -- WE CANNOT GET THEM ALL TO SAFETY BEFORE THE RUBBLE --
YES WE CAN, QUICKSILVER! YOU JUST KEEP MOVING 'EM OUT OF THE WAY! I'LL KEEP THE SKIES CLEAR --
-- OF ANYTHING BUT THE FINEST DUST!
THE AVENGERS SET TO THEIR TASKS -- PURPOSEFUL, PROFESSIONAL --
-- AND AS TIME WEARS ON, EVEN THEIR MIGHTY SKILLS ARE TAXED TO THE LIMIT. BUT THEY REFUSE TO SLACKEN OFF -- AND NO ONE DIES --
TWO MORE! HOW'RE YOU HOLDING UP, WANDA?
FRESH AS A DAISY, CAP! I JUST WONDER --

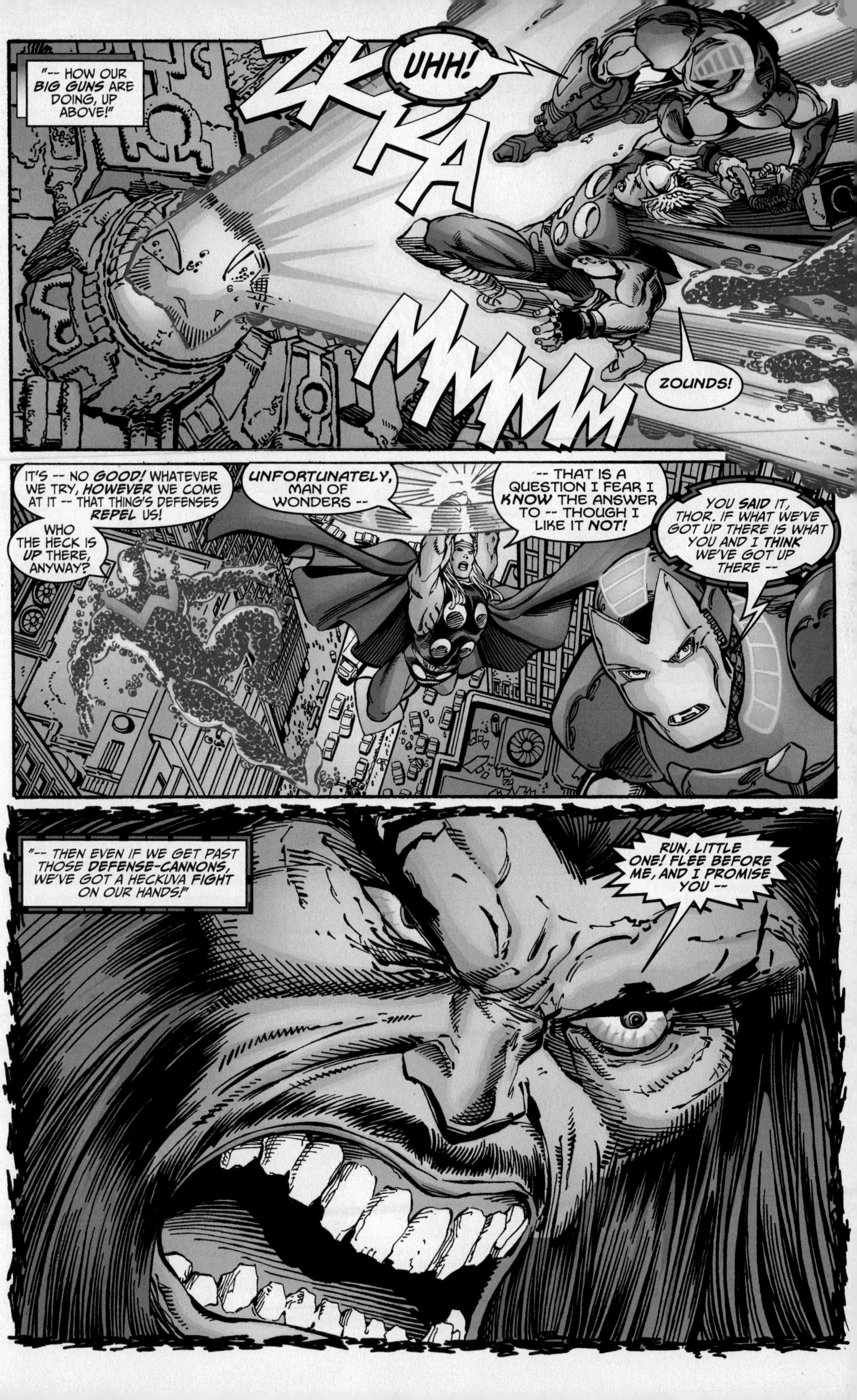
"-- HOW OUR BIG GUNS ARE DOING, UP ABOVE!"
ZZKKA
UHH!
MMMMM
ZOUNDS!
IT'S -- NO GOOD! WHATEVER WE TRY, HOWEVER WE COME AT IT -- THAT THING'S DEFENSES REPEL US!
WHO THE HECK IS UP THERE, ANYWAY?
UNFORTUNATELY, MAN OF WONDERS --
-- THAT IS A QUESTION I FEAR I KNOW THE ANSWER TO -- THOUGH I LIKE IT NOT!
YOU SAID IT, THOR. IF WHAT WE'VE GOT UP THERE IS WHAT YOU AND I THINK WE'VE GOT UP THERE --
"-- THEN EVEN IF WE GET PAST THOSE DEFENSE-CANNONS, WE'VE GOT A HECKUVA FIGHT ON OUR HANDS!"
RUN, LITTLE ONE! FLEE BEFORE ME, AND I PROMISE YOU --

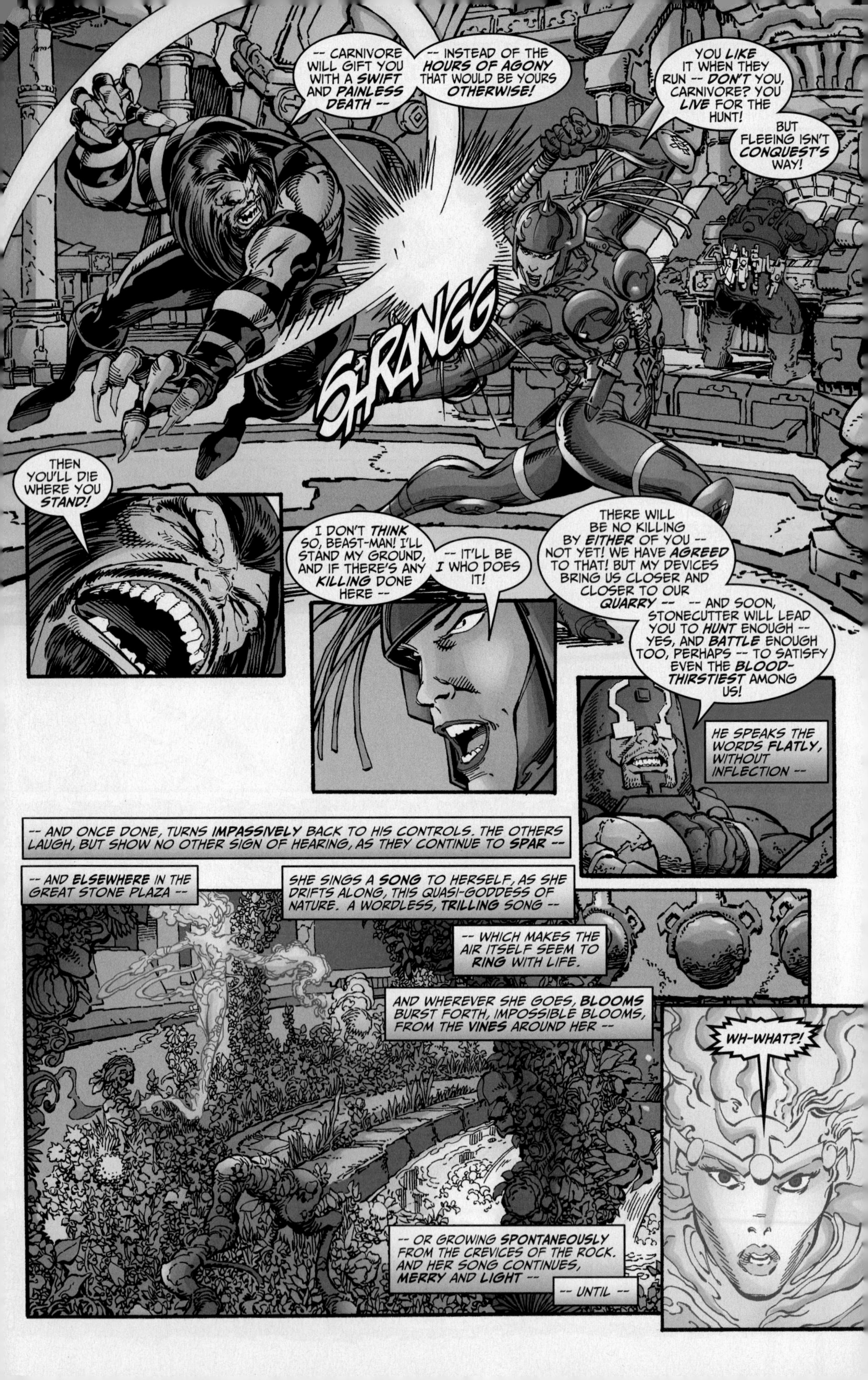
-- CARNIVORE WILL GIFT YOU WITH A SWIFT AND PAINLESS DEATH --
-- INSTEAD OF THE HOURS OF AGONY THAT WOULD BE YOURS OTHERWISE!
YOU LIKE IT WHEN THEY RUN -- DON'T YOU, CARNIVORE? YOU LIVE FOR THE HUNT!
BUT FLEEING ISN'T CONQUEST'S WAY!
SHRANGG
THEN YOU'LL DIE WHERE YOU STAND!
I DON'T THINK SO, BEAST-MAN! I'LL STAND MY GROUND, AND IF THERE'S ANY KILLING DONE HERE --
-- IT'LL BE I WHO DOES IT!
THERE WILL BE NO KILLING BY EITHER OF YOU -- NOT YET! WE HAVE AGREED TO THAT! BUT MY DEVICES BRING US CLOSER AND CLOSER TO OUR QUARRY --
-- AND SOON, STONECUTTER WILL LEAD YOU TO HUNT ENOUGH -- YES, AND BATTLE ENOUGH TOO, PERHAPS -- TO SATISFY EVEN THE BLOOD-THIRSTIEST AMONG US!
HE SPEAKS THE WORDS FLATLY, WITHOUT INFLECTION --
-- AND ONCE DONE, TURNS IMPASSIVELY BACK TO HIS CONTROLS. THE OTHERS LAUGH, BUT SHOW NO OTHER SIGN OF HEARING, AS THEY CONTINUE TO SPAR --
-- AND ELSEWHERE IN THE GREAT STONE PLAZA --
SHE SINGS A SONG TO HERSELF, AS SHE DRIFTS ALONG, THIS QUASI-GODDESS OF NATURE. A WORDLESS, TRILLING SONG --
-- WHICH MAKES THE AIR ITSELF SEEM TO RING WITH LIFE.
AND WHEREVER SHE GOES, BLOOMS BURST FORTH, IMPOSSIBLE BLOOMS, FROM THE VINES AROUND HER --
-- OR GROWING SPONTANEOUSLY FROM THE CREVICES OF THE ROCK. AND HER SONG CONTINUES, MERRY AND LIGHT --
-- UNTIL --
WH-WHAT?!

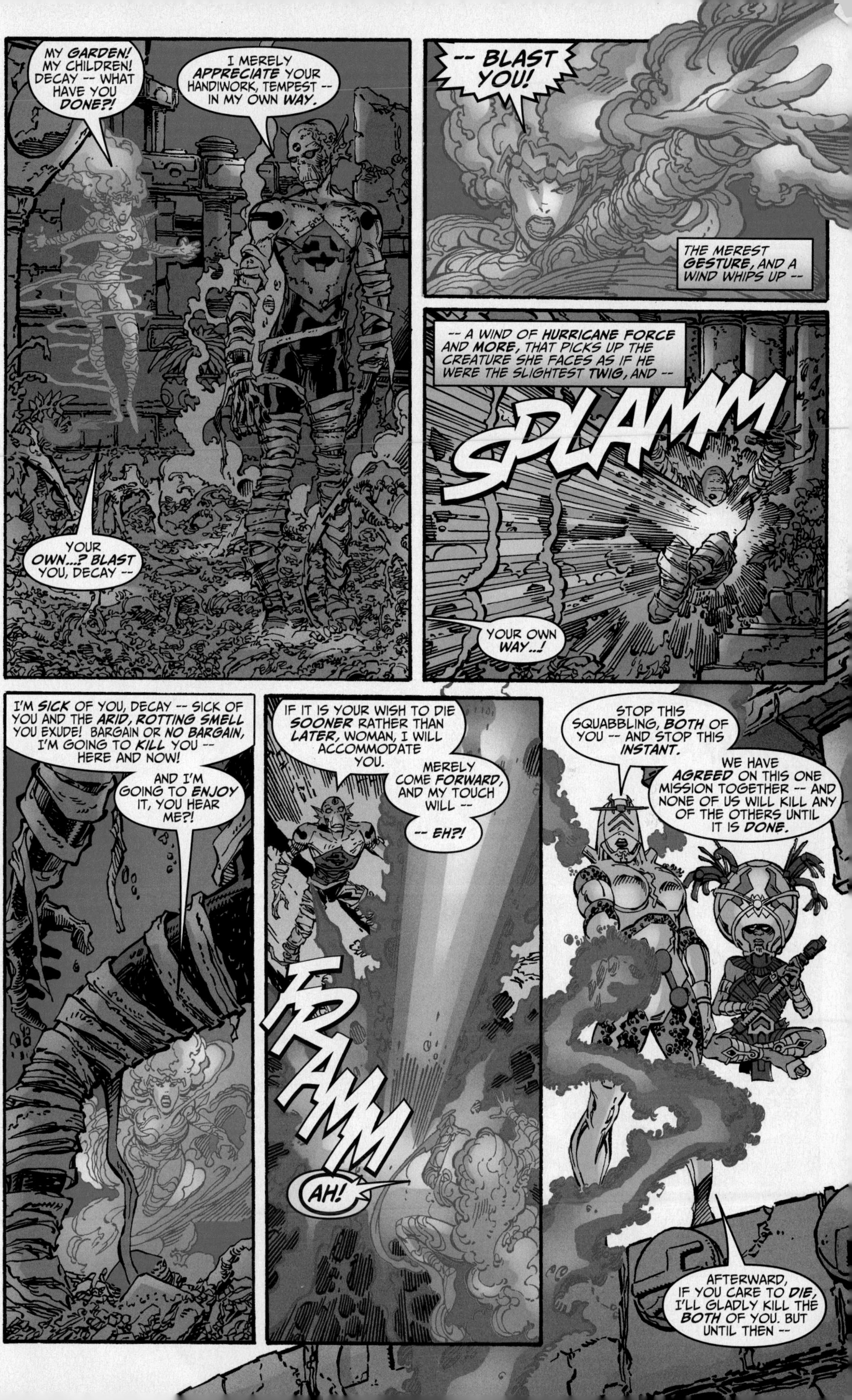
MY GARDEN! MY CHILDREN! DECAY -- WHAT HAVE YOU DONE?!
I MERELY APPRECIATE YOUR HANDIWORK, TEMPEST -- IN MY OWN WAY.
YOUR OWN...? BLAST YOU, DECAY --
-- BLAST YOU!
THE MEREST GESTURE, AND A WIND WHIPS UP --
-- A WIND OF HURRICANE FORCE AND MORE, THAT PICKS UP THE CREATURE SHE FACES AS IF HE WERE THE SLIGHTEST TWIG, AND --
SPLAMM
YOUR OWN WAY...!
I'M SICK OF YOU, DECAY -- SICK OF YOU AND THE ARID, ROTTING SMELL YOU EXUDE! BARGAIN OR NO BARGAIN, I'M GOING TO KILL YOU -- HERE AND NOW!
AND I'M GOING TO ENJOY IT, YOU HEAR ME?!
IF IT IS YOUR WISH TO DIE SOONER RATHER THAN LATER, WOMAN, I WILL ACCOMMODATE YOU.
MERELY COME FORWARD, AND MY TOUCH WILL --
-- EH?!
FRAMM
AH!
STOP THIS SQUABBLING, BOTH OF YOU -- AND STOP THIS INSTANT.
WE HAVE AGREED ON THIS ONE MISSION TOGETHER -- AND NONE OF US WILL KILL ANY OF THE OTHERS UNTIL IT IS DONE.
AFTERWARD, IF YOU CARE TO DIE, I'LL GLADLY KILL THE BOTH OF YOU. BUT UNTIL THEN --

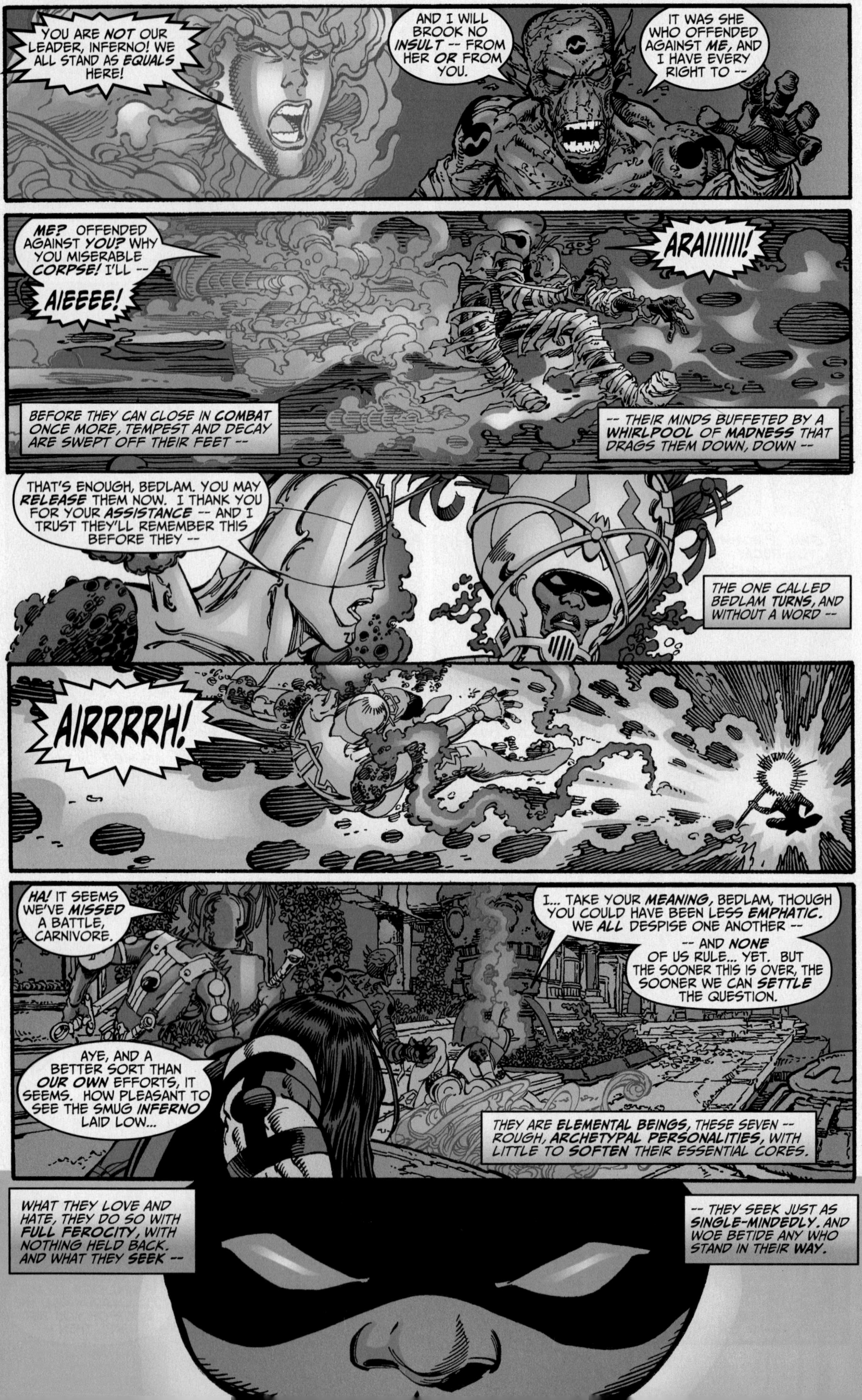

YOU ARE NOT OUR LEADER, INFERNO! WE ALL STAND AS EQUALS HERE!
AND I WILL BROOK NO INSULT -- FROM HER OR FROM YOU.
IT WAS SHE WHO OFFENDED AGAINST ME, AND I HAVE EVERY RIGHT TO --
ME? OFFENDED AGAINST YOU? WHY YOU MISERABLE CORPSE! I'LL --
AIEEEE!
ARAIIIIIII!
BEFORE THEY CAN CLOSE IN COMBAT ONCE MORE, TEMPEST AND DECAY ARE SWEPT OFF THEIR FEET --
-- THEIR MINDS BUFFETED BY A WHIRLPOOL OF MADNESS THAT DRAGS THEM DOWN, DOWN --
THAT'S ENOUGH, BEDLAM. YOU MAY RELEASE THEM NOW. I THANK YOU FOR YOUR ASSISTANCE -- AND I TRUST THEY'LL REMEMBER THIS BEFORE THEY --
THE ONE CALLED BEDLAM TURNS, AND WITHOUT A WORD --
AIRRRRH!
HA! IT SEEMS WE'VE MISSED A BATTLE, CARNIVORE.
I... TAKE YOUR MEANING, BEDLAM, THOUGH YOU COULD HAVE BEEN LESS EMPHATIC. WE ALL DESPISE ONE ANOTHER --
-- AND NONE OF US RULE... YET. BUT THE SOONER THIS IS OVER, THE SOONER WE CAN SETTLE THE QUESTION.
AYE, AND A BETTER SORT THAN OUR OWN EFFORTS, IT SEEMS. HOW PLEASANT TO SEE THE SMUG INFERNO LAID LOW...
THEY ARE ELEMENTAL BEINGS, THESE SEVEN -- ROUGH, ARCHETYPAL PERSONALITIES, WITH LITTLE TO SOFTEN THEIR ESSENTIAL CORES.
WHAT THEY LOVE AND HATE, THEY DO SO WITH FULL FEROCITY, WITH NOTHING HELD BACK. AND WHAT THEY SEEK --
-- THEY SEEK JUST AS SINGLE-MINDEDLY. AND WOE BETIDE ANY WHO STAND IN THEIR WAY.

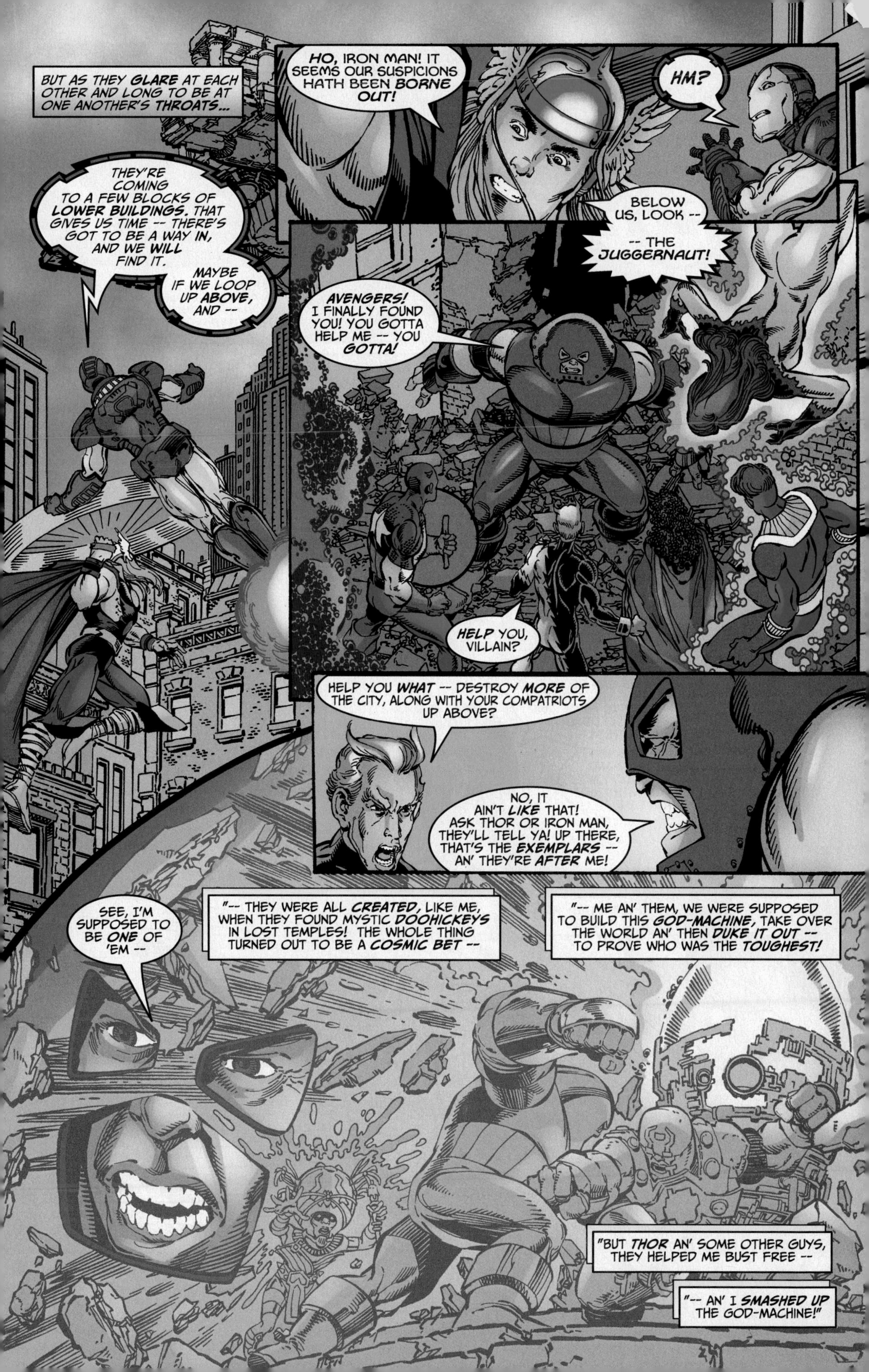
BUT AS THEY GLARE AT EACH OTHER AND LONG TO BE AT ONE ANOTHER'S THROATS...
HO, IRON MAN! IT SEEMS OUR SUSPICIONS HATH BEEN BORNE OUT!
HM?
THEY'RE COMING TO A FEW BLOCKS OF LOWER BUILDINGS. THAT GIVES US TIME -- THERE'S GOT TO BE A WAY IN, AND WE WILL FIND IT.
MAYBE IF WE LOOP UP ABOVE, AND --
BELOW US, LOOK --
-- THE JUGGERNAUT!
AVENGERS! I FINALLY FOUND YOU! YOU GOTTA HELP ME -- YOU GOTTA!
HELP YOU, VILLAIN?
HELP YOU WHAT -- DESTROY MORE OF THE CITY, ALONG WITH YOUR COMPATRIOTS UP ABOVE?
NO, IT AIN'T LIKE THAT! ASK THOR OR IRON MAN, THEY'LL TELL YA! UP THERE, THAT'S THE EXEMPLARS -- AN' THEY'RE AFTER ME!
SEE, I'M SUPPOSED TO BE ONE OF 'EM --
"-- THEY WERE ALL CREATED, LIKE ME, WHEN THEY FOUND MYSTIC DOOHICKEYS IN LOST TEMPLES! THE WHOLE THING TURNED OUT TO BE A COSMIC BET --
"-- ME AN' THEM, WE WERE SUPPOSED TO BUILD THIS GOD-MACHINE, TAKE OVER THE WORLD AN' THEN DUKE IT OUT -- TO PROVE WHO WAS THE TOUGHEST!
"BUT THOR AN' SOME OTHER GUYS, THEY HELPED ME BUST FREE --
"-- AN' I SMASHED UP THE GOD-MACHINE!"

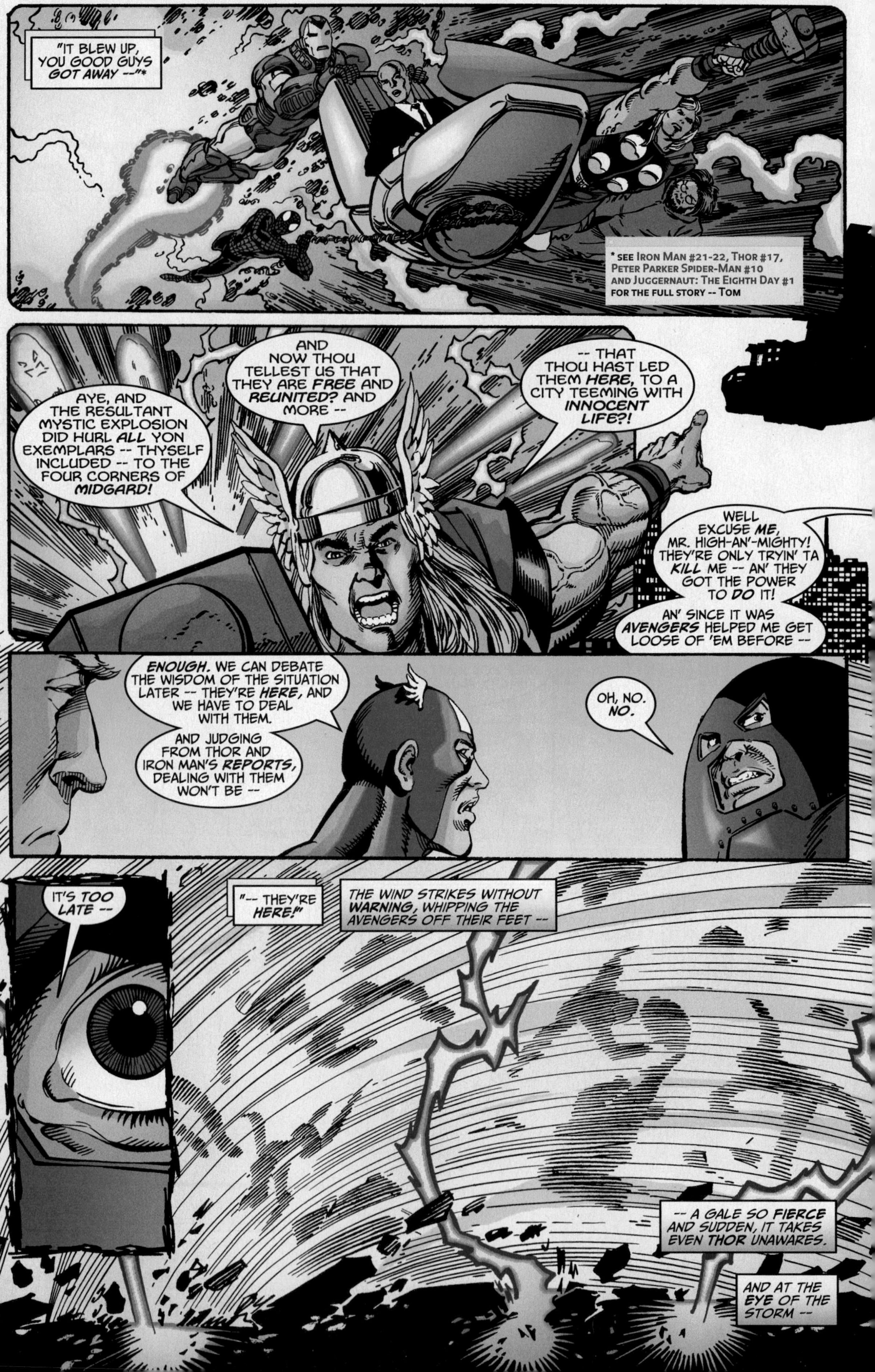
"IT BLEW UP, YOU GOOD GUYS GOT AWAY --"*
* SEE IRON MAN #21-22, THOR #17, PETER PARKER SPIDER-MAN #10 AND JUGGERNAUT: THE EIGHTH DAY #1 FOR THE FULL STORY -- TOM
AYE, AND THE RESULTANT MYSTIC EXPLOSION DID HURL ALL YON EXEMPLARS -- THYSELF INCLUDED -- TO THE FOUR CORNERS OF MIDGARD!
AND NOW THOU TELLEST US THAT THEY ARE FREE AND REUNITED? AND MORE --
-- THAT THOU HAST LED THEM HERE, TO A CITY TEEMING WITH INNOCENT LIFE?!
WELL EXCUSE ME, MR. HIGH-AN'-MIGHTY! THEY'RE ONLY TRYIN' TA KILL ME -- AN' THEY GOT THE POWER TO DO IT!
AN' SINCE IT WAS AVENGERS HELPED ME GET LOOSE OF 'EM BEFORE --
ENOUGH. WE CAN DEBATE THE WISDOM OF THE SITUATION LATER -- THEY'RE HERE, AND WE HAVE TO DEAL WITH THEM.
AND JUDGING FROM THOR AND IRON MAN'S REPORTS, DEALING WITH THEM WON'T BE --
OH, NO. NO.
IT'S TOO LATE --
"-- THEY'RE HERE!"
THE WIND STRIKES WITHOUT WARNING, WHIPPING THE AVENGERS OFF THEIR FEET --
-- A GALE SO FIERCE AND SUDDEN, IT TAKES EVEN THOR UNAWARES.
AND AT THE EYE OF THE STORM --

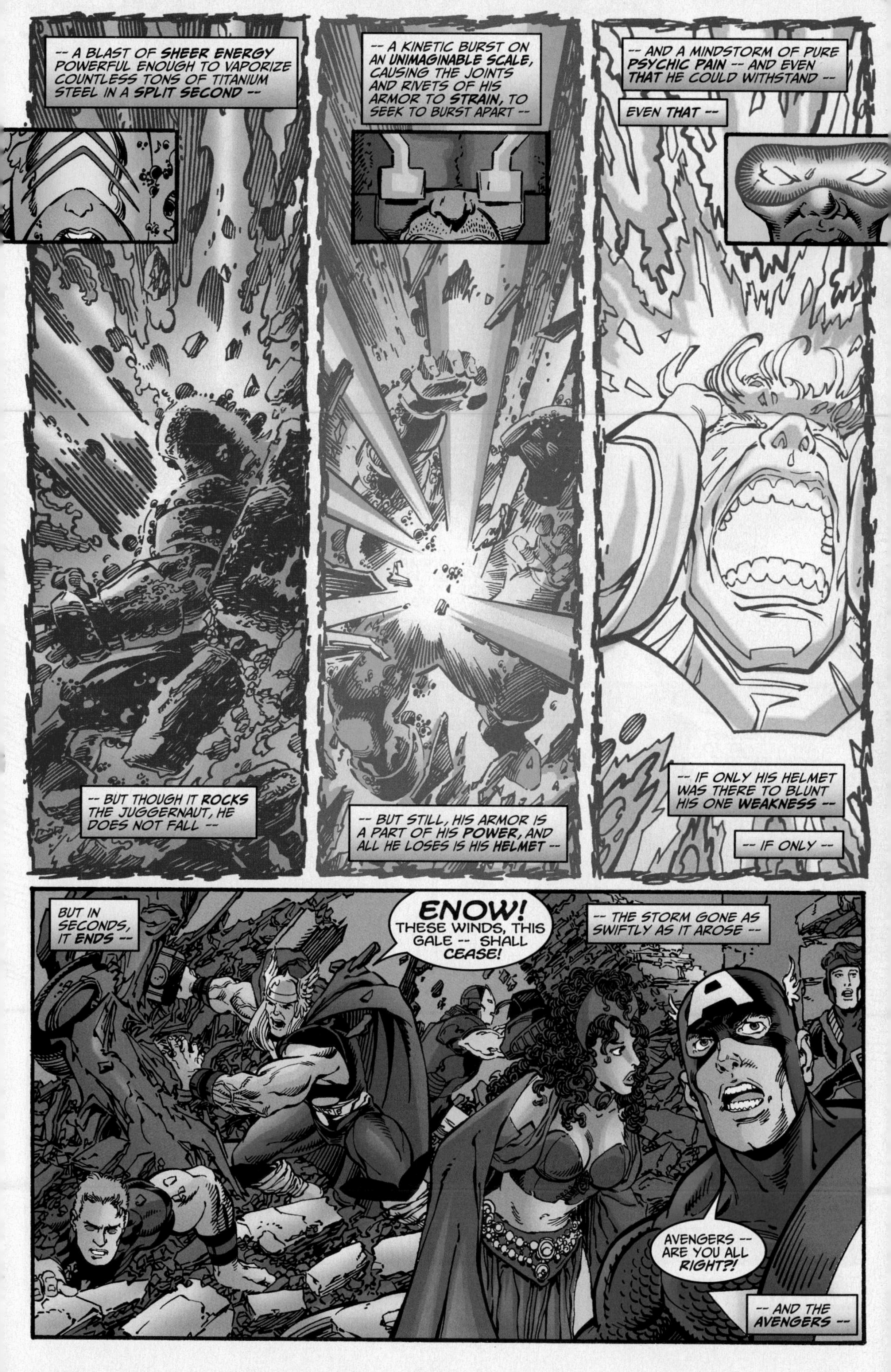

-- A BLAST OF SHEER ENERGY POWERFUL ENOUGH TO VAPORIZE COUNTLESS TONS OF TITANIUM STEEL IN A SPLIT SECOND --
-- BUT THOUGH IT ROCKS THE JUGGERNAUT, HE DOES NOT FALL --
-- A KINETIC BURST ON AN UNIMAGINABLE SCALE, CAUSING THE JOINTS AND RIVETS OF HIS ARMOR TO STRAIN, TO SEEK TO BURST APART --
-- BUT STILL, HIS ARMOR IS A PART OF HIS POWER, AND ALL HE LOSES IS HIS HELMET --
-- AND A MINDSTORM OF PURE PSYCHIC PAIN -- AND EVEN THAT HE COULD WITHSTAND --
EVEN THAT --
-- IF ONLY HIS HELMET WAS THERE TO BLUNT HIS ONE WEAKNESS --
-- IF ONLY --
BUT IN SECONDS, IT ENDS --
ENOW! THESE WINDS, THIS GALE -- SHALL CEASE!
-- THE STORM GONE AS SWIFTLY AS IT AROSE --
AVENGERS -- ARE YOU ALL RIGHT?!
-- AND THE AVENGERS --

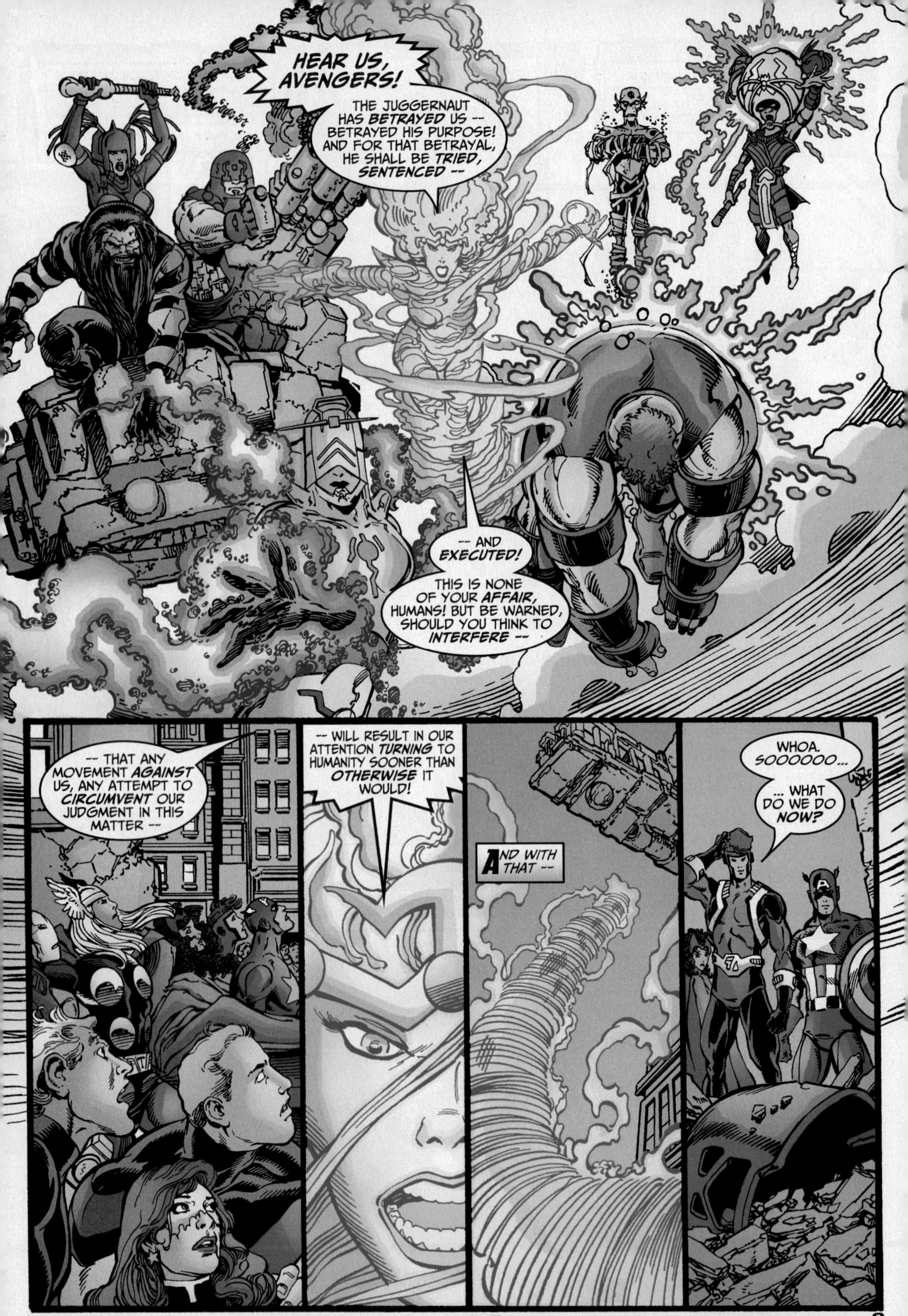
HEAR US, AVENGERS!
THE JUGGERNAUT HAS BETRAYED US -- BETRAYED HIS PURPOSE! AND FOR THAT BETRAYAL, HE SHALL BE TRIED, SENTENCED --
-- AND EXECUTED!
THIS IS NONE OF YOUR AFFAIR, HUMANS! BUT BE WARNED, SHOULD YOU THINK TO INTERFERE --
-- THAT ANY MOVEMENT AGAINST US, ANY ATTEMPT TO CIRCUMVENT OUR JUDGMENT IN THIS MATTER --
-- WILL RESULT IN OUR ATTENTION TURNING TO HUMANITY SOONER THAN OTHERWISE IT WOULD!
AND WITH THAT --
WHOA. SOOOOOO...
... WHAT DO WE DO NOW?

NEXT: TRIAL BY THE GODS! OUR DOUBLE-SIZED TWENTY-FIFTH ISSUE! AND IN THOSE PAGES -- AN AVENGER QUITS! DON'T MISS IT!

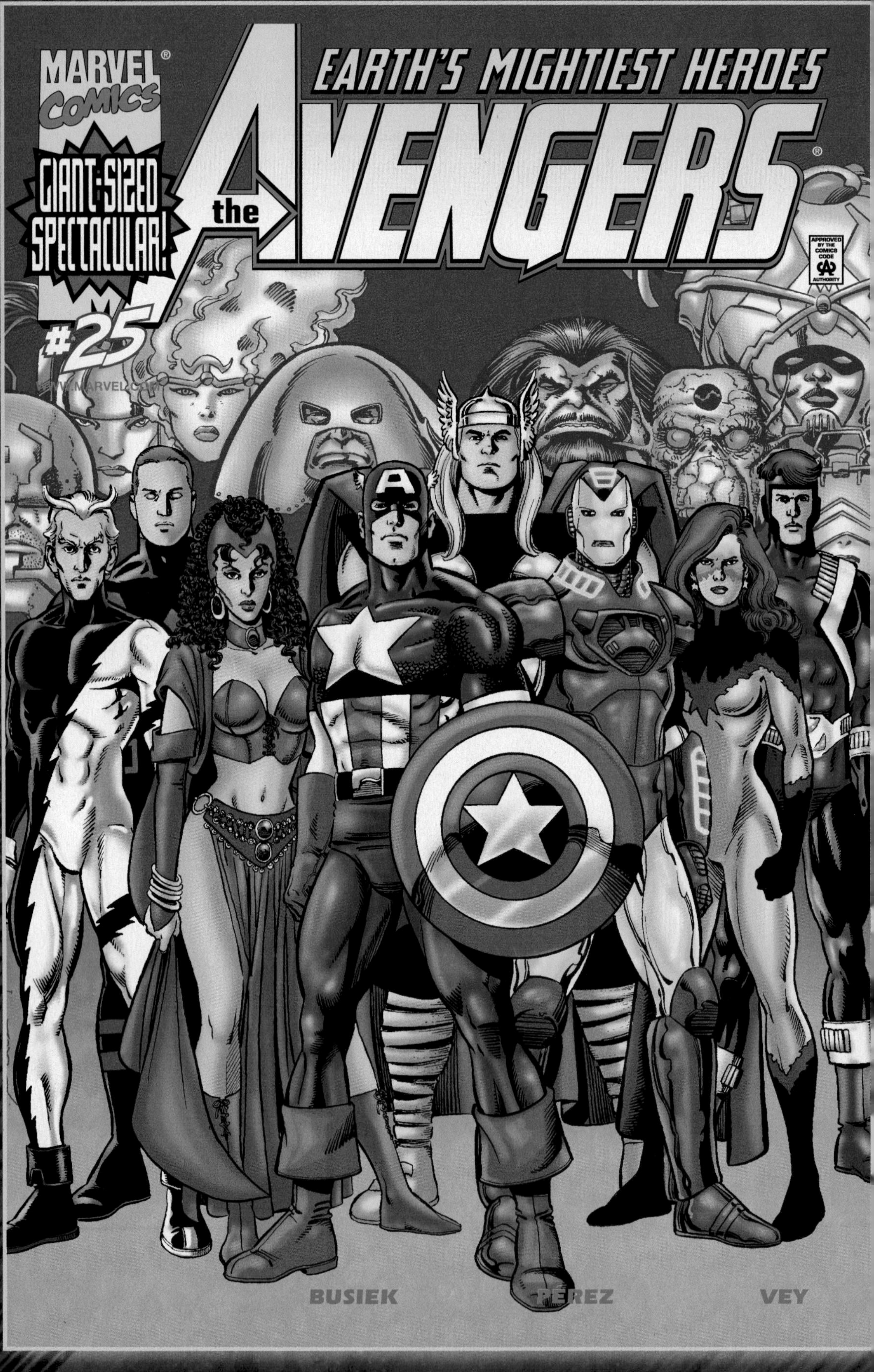
MARVEL COMICS
EARTH'S MIGHTIEST HEROES
the AVENGERS
GIANT-SIZED SPECTACULAR!
#25
APPROVED BY THE COMICS CODE AUTHORITY
BUSIEK
PÉREZ
VEY

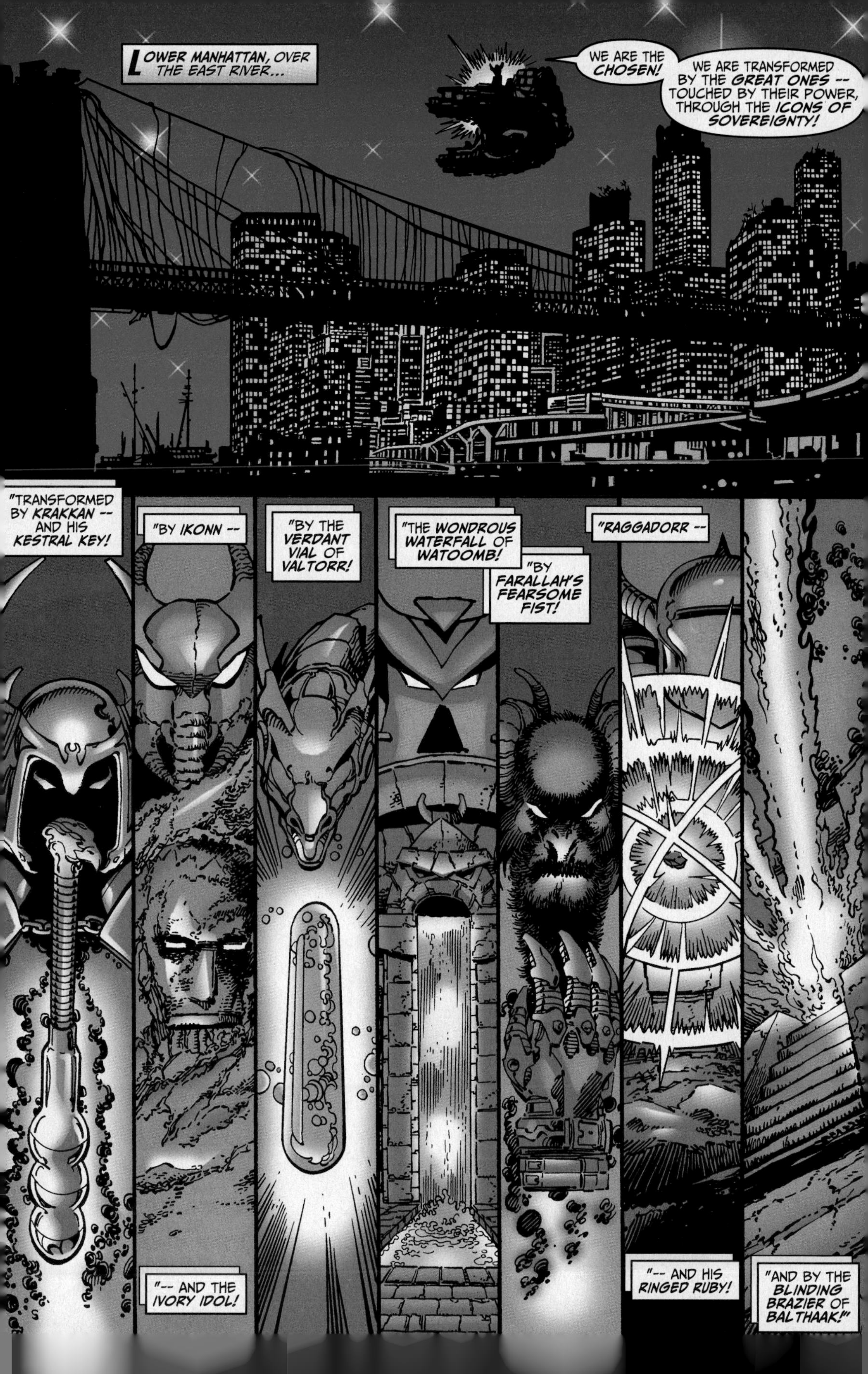
LOWER MANHATTAN, OVER THE EAST RIVER...
WE ARE THE CHOSEN!
WE ARE TRANSFORMED BY THE GREAT ONES -- TOUCHED BY THEIR POWER, THROUGH THE ICONS OF SOVEREIGNTY!
"TRANSFORMED BY KRAKKAN -- AND HIS KESTRAL KEY!
"BY IKONN --
"-- AND THE IVORY IDOL!
"BY THE VERDANT VIAL OF VALTORR!
"THE WONDROUS WATERFALL OF WATOOMB!
"BY FARALLAH'S FEARSOME FIST!
"RAGGADORR --
"-- AND HIS RINGED RUBY!
"AND BY THE BLINDING BRAZIER OF BALTHAAK!"

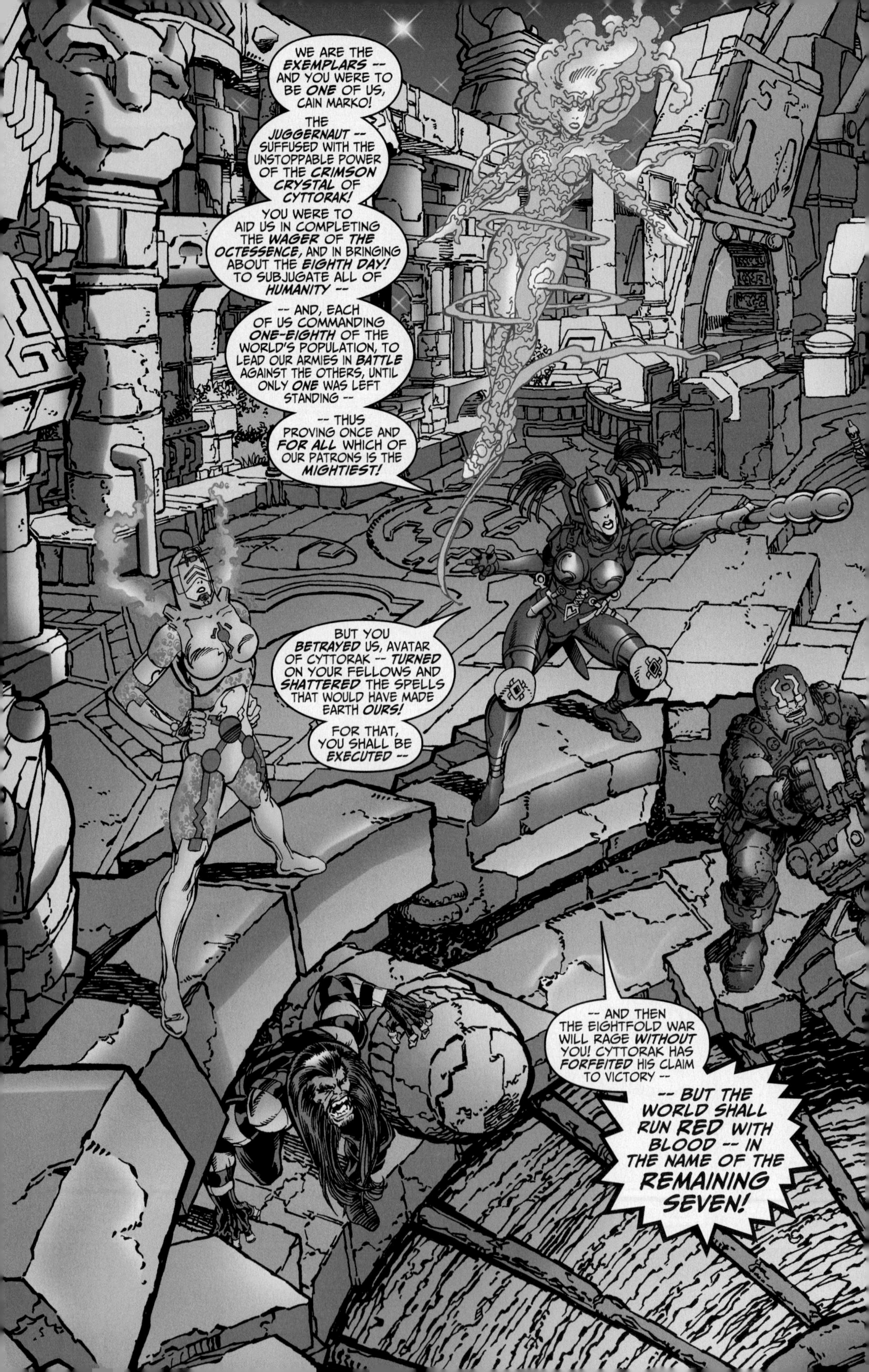
WE ARE THE EXEMPLARS -- AND YOU WERE TO BE ONE OF US, CAIN MARKO!
THE JUGGERNAUT -- SUFFUSED WITH THE UNSTOPPABLE POWER OF THE CRIMSON CRYSTAL OF CYTTORAK!
YOU WERE TO AID US IN COMPLETING THE WAGER OF THE OCTESSENCE, AND IN BRINGING ABOUT THE EIGHTH DAY! TO SUBJUGATE ALL OF HUMANITY --
-- AND, EACH OF US COMMANDING ONE-EIGHTH OF THE WORLD'S POPULATION, TO LEAD OUR ARMIES IN BATTLE AGAINST THE OTHERS, UNTIL ONLY ONE WAS LEFT STANDING --
-- THUS PROVING ONCE AND FOR ALL WHICH OF OUR PATRONS IS THE MIGHTIEST!
BUT YOU BETRAYED US, AVATAR OF CYTTORAK -- TURNED ON YOUR FELLOWS AND SHATTERED THE SPELLS THAT WOULD HAVE MADE EARTH OURS!
FOR THAT, YOU SHALL BE EXECUTED --
-- AND THEN THE EIGHTFOLD WAR WILL RAGE WITHOUT YOU! CYTTORAK HAS FORFEITED HIS CLAIM TO VICTORY --
-- BUT THE WORLD SHALL RUN RED WITH BLOOD -- IN THE NAME OF THE REMAINING SEVEN!

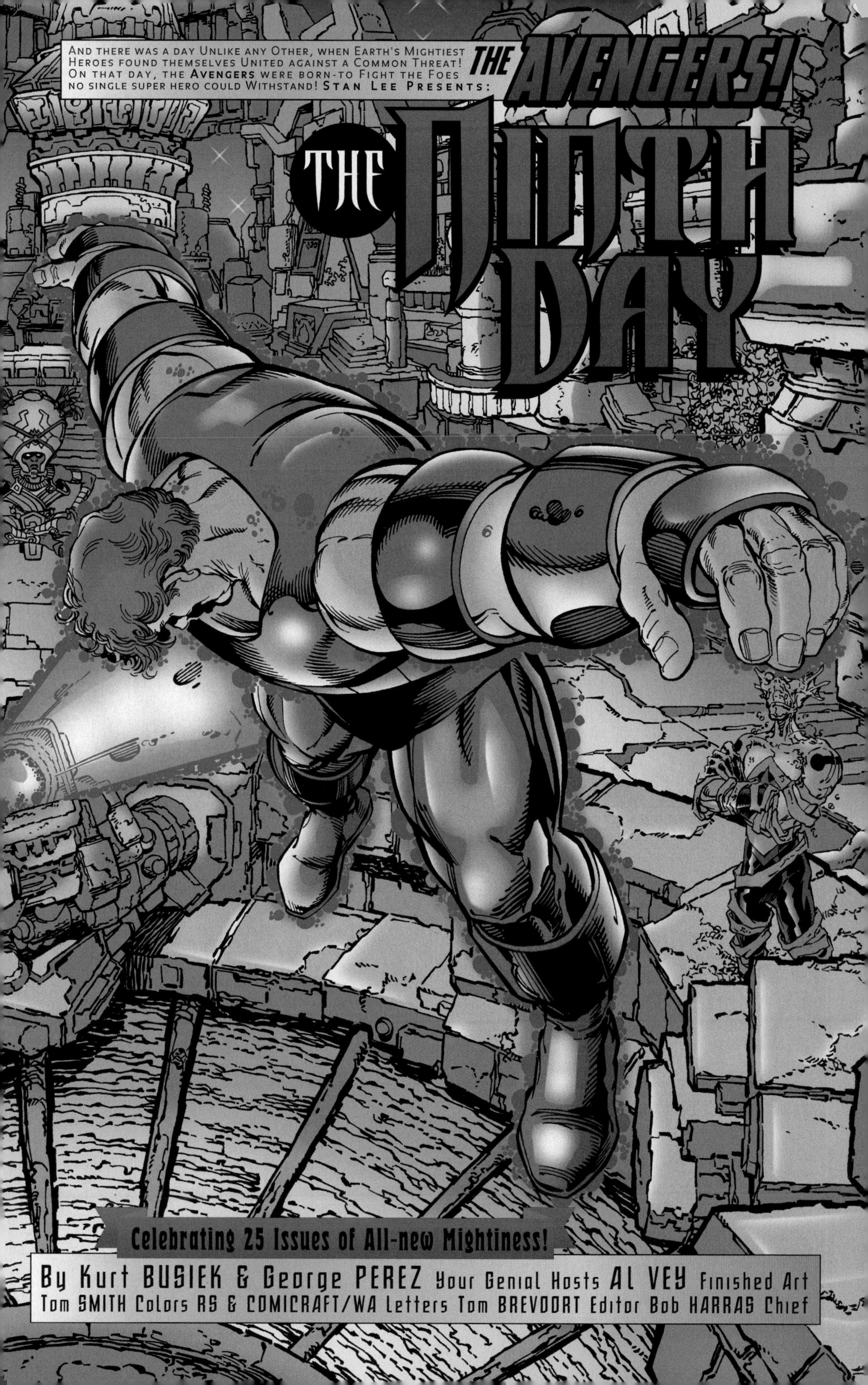
And there was a day Unlike any Other, when Earth's Mightiest Heroes found themselves United against a Common Threat! On that day, the Avengers were born-to Fight the Foes no single super hero could Withstand! Stan Lee Presents:
The Avengers!
The Ninth Day
Celebrating 25 Issues of All-new Mightiness!
By Kurt BUSIEK & George PEREZ Your Genial Hosts AL VEY Finished Art Tom SMITH Colors RS & COMICRAFT/WA Letters Tom BREVOORT Editor Bob HARRAS Chief

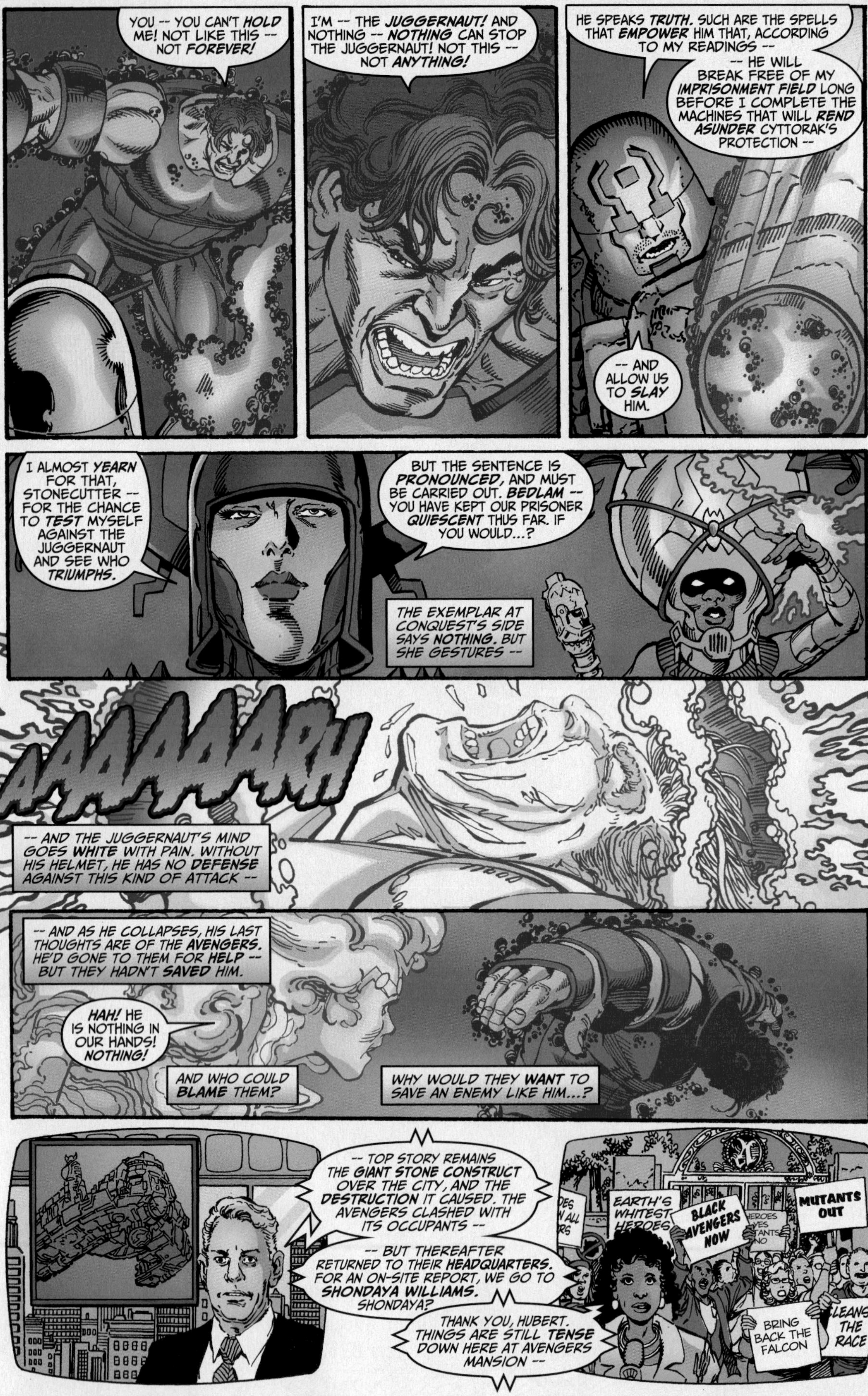
YOU -- YOU CAN'T HOLD ME! NOT LIKE THIS -- NOT FOREVER!
I'M -- THE JUGGERNAUT! AND NOTHING -- NOTHING CAN STOP THE JUGGERNAUT! NOT THIS -- NOT ANYTHING!
HE SPEAKS TRUTH. SUCH ARE THE SPELLS THAT EMPOWER HIM THAT, ACCORDING TO MY READINGS --
-- HE WILL BREAK FREE OF MY IMPRISONMENT FIELD LONG BEFORE I COMPLETE THE MACHINES THAT WILL REND ASUNDER CYTTORAK'S PROTECTION --
-- AND ALLOW US TO SLAY HIM.
I ALMOST YEARN FOR THAT, STONECUTTER -- FOR THE CHANCE TO TEST MYSELF AGAINST THE JUGGERNAUT AND SEE WHO TRIUMPHS.
BUT THE SENTENCE IS PRONOUNCED, AND MUST BE CARRIED OUT. BEDLAM -- YOU HAVE KEPT OUR PRISONER QUIESCENT THUS FAR. IF YOU WOULD...?
THE EXEMPLAR AT CONQUEST'S SIDE SAYS NOTHING. BUT SHE GESTURES --
AAAAAARH
-- AND THE JUGGERNAUT'S MIND GOES WHITE WITH PAIN. WITHOUT HIS HELMET, HE HAS NO DEFENSE AGAINST THIS KIND OF ATTACK --
-- AND AS HE COLLAPSES, HIS LAST THOUGHTS ARE OF THE AVENGERS. HE'D GONE TO THEM FOR HELP -- BUT THEY HADN'T SAVED HIM.
HAH! HE IS NOTHING IN OUR HANDS! NOTHING!
AND WHO COULD BLAME THEM?
WHY WOULD THEY WANT TO SAVE AN ENEMY LIKE HIM...?
-- TOP STORY REMAINS THE GIANT STONE CONSTRUCT OVER THE CITY, AND THE DESTRUCTION IT CAUSED. THE AVENGERS CLASHED WITH ITS OCCUPANTS --
-- BUT THEREAFTER RETURNED TO THEIR HEADQUARTERS. FOR AN ON-SITE REPORT, WE GO TO SHONDAYA WILLIAMS. SHONDAYA?
THANK YOU, HUBERT. THINGS ARE STILL TENSE DOWN HERE AT AVENGERS MANSION --
EARTH'S WHITEST HEROES
BLACK AVENGERS NOW
MUTANTS OUT
BRING BACK THE FALCON
CLEANSE THE RACE

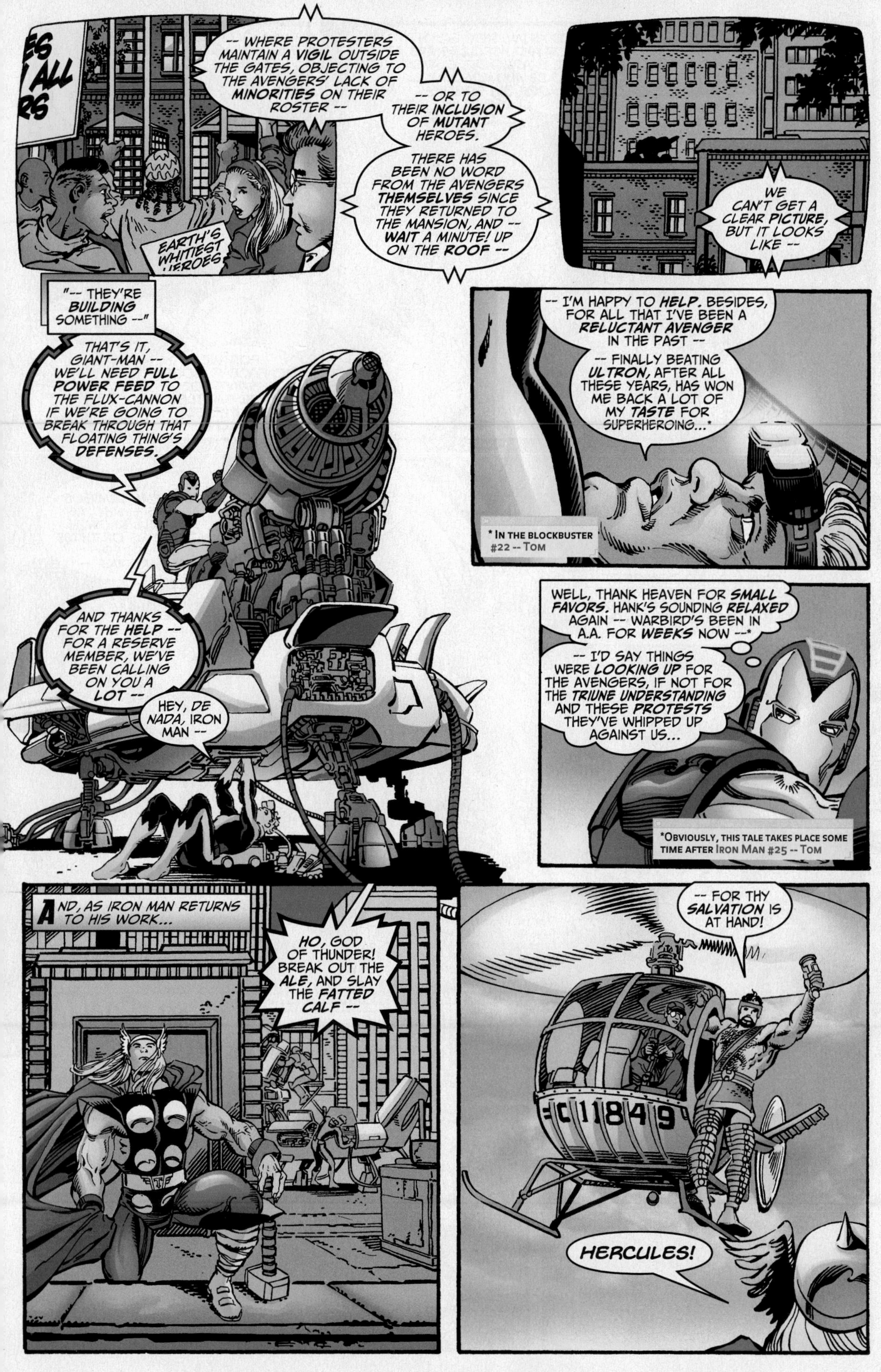
-- WHERE PROTESTERS MAINTAIN A VIGIL OUTSIDE THE GATES, OBJECTING TO THE AVENGERS' LACK OF MINORITIES ON THEIR ROSTER --
-- OR TO THEIR INCLUSION OF MUTANT HEROES.
THERE HAS BEEN NO WORD FROM THE AVENGERS THEMSELVES SINCE THEY RETURNED TO THE MANSION, AND -- WAIT A MINUTE! UP ON THE ROOF --
EARTH'S WHITIEST HEROES
WE CAN'T GET A CLEAR PICTURE, BUT IT LOOKS LIKE --
"-- THEY'RE BUILDING SOMETHING --"
THAT'S IT, GIANT-MAN -- WE'LL NEED FULL POWER FEED TO THE FLUX-CANNON IF WE'RE GOING TO BREAK THROUGH THAT FLOATING THING'S DEFENSES.
AND THANKS FOR THE HELP -- FOR A RESERVE MEMBER, WE'VE BEEN CALLING ON YOU A LOT --
HEY, DE NADA, IRON MAN --
-- I'M HAPPY TO HELP. BESIDES, FOR ALL THAT I'VE BEEN A RELUCTANT AVENGER IN THE PAST --
-- FINALLY BEATING ULTRON, AFTER ALL THESE YEARS, HAS WON ME BACK A LOT OF MY TASTE FOR SUPERHEROING...*
* IN THE BLOCKBUSTER #22 -- TOM
WELL, THANK HEAVEN FOR SMALL FAVORS. HANK'S SOUNDING RELAXED AGAIN -- WARBIRD'S BEEN IN A.A. FOR WEEKS NOW --*
-- I'D SAY THINGS WERE LOOKING UP FOR THE AVENGERS, IF NOT FOR THE TRIUNE UNDERSTANDING AND THESE PROTESTS THEY'VE WHIPPED UP AGAINST US...
*OBVIOUSLY, THIS TALE TAKES PLACE SOME TIME AFTER IRON MAN #25 -- TOM
AND, AS IRON MAN RETURNS TO HIS WORK...
HO, GOD OF THUNDER! BREAK OUT THE ALE, AND SLAY THE FATTED CALF --
-- FOR THY SALVATION IS AT HAND!
C11849
HERCULES!

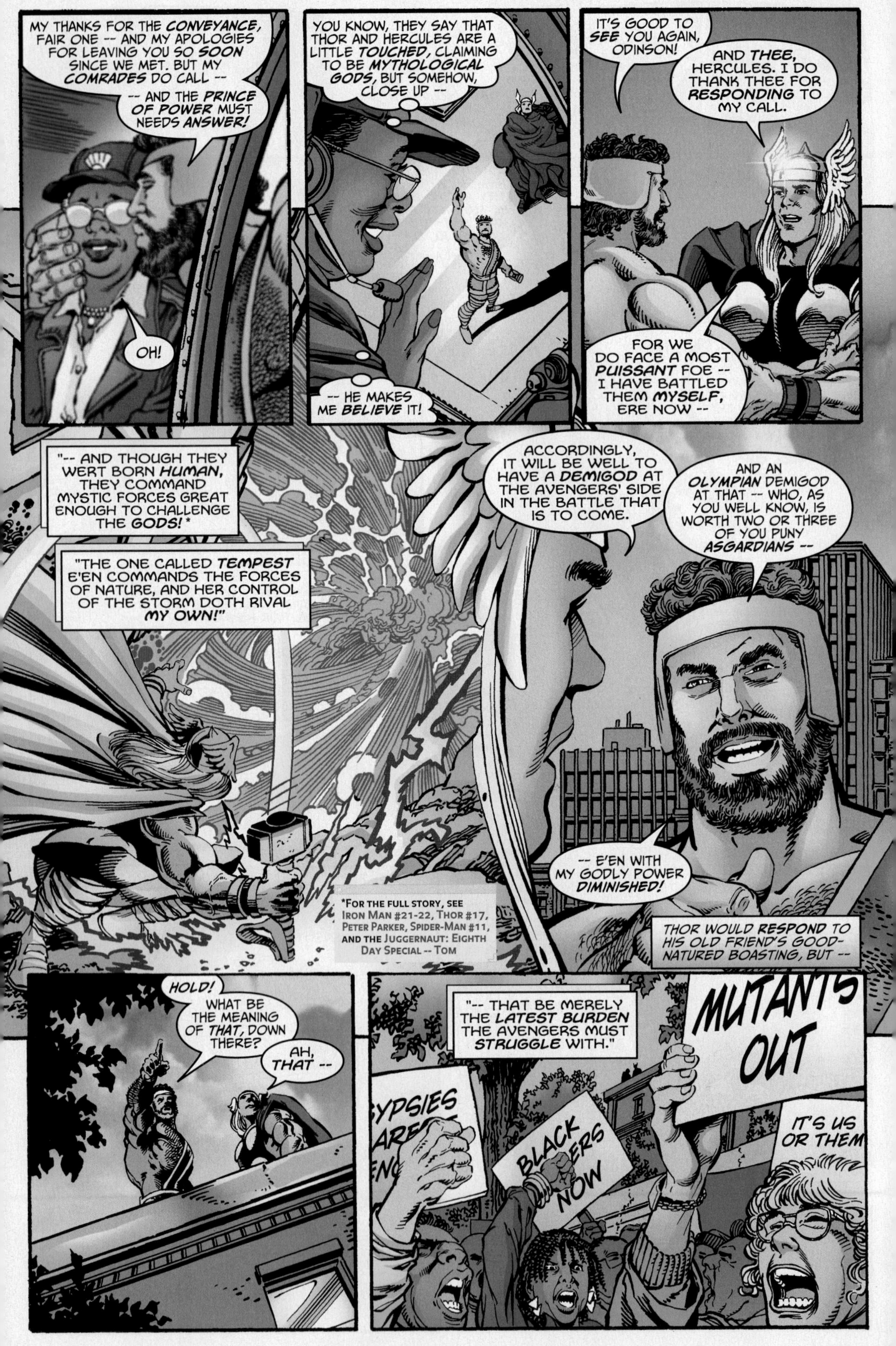
MY THANKS FOR THE CONVEYANCE, FAIR ONE -- AND MY APOLOGIES FOR LEAVING YOU SO SOON SINCE WE MET. BUT MY COMRADES DO CALL --
-- AND THE PRINCE OF POWER MUST NEEDS ANSWER!
OH!
YOU KNOW, THEY SAY THAT THOR AND HERCULES ARE A LITTLE TOUCHED, CLAIMING TO BE MYTHOLOGICAL GODS, BUT SOMEHOW, CLOSE UP --
-- HE MAKES ME BELIEVE IT!
IT'S GOOD TO SEE YOU AGAIN, ODINSON!
AND THEE, HERCULES. I DO THANK THEE FOR RESPONDING TO MY CALL.
FOR WE DO FACE A MOST PUISSANT FOE -- I HAVE BATTLED THEM MYSELF, ERE NOW --
"-- AND THOUGH THEY WERT BORN HUMAN, THEY COMMAND MYSTIC FORCES GREAT ENOUGH TO CHALLENGE THE GODS! *
"THE ONE CALLED TEMPEST E'EN COMMANDS THE FORCES OF NATURE, AND HER CONTROL OF THE STORM DOTH RIVAL MY OWN!"
ACCORDINGLY, IT WILL BE WELL TO HAVE A DEMIGOD AT THE AVENGERS' SIDE IN THE BATTLE THAT IS TO COME.
AND AN OLYMPIAN DEMIGOD AT THAT -- WHO, AS YOU WELL KNOW, IS WORTH TWO OR THREE OF YOU PUNY ASGARDIANS --
-- E'EN WITH MY GODLY POWER DIMINISHED!
*FOR THE FULL STORY, SEE IRON MAN #21-22, THOR #17, PETER PARKER, SPIDER-MAN #11, AND THE JUGGERNAUT: EIGHTH DAY SPECIAL -- TOM
THOR WOULD RESPOND TO HIS OLD FRIEND'S GOOD-NATURED BOASTING, BUT --
HOLD! WHAT BE THE MEANING OF THAT, DOWN THERE?
AH, THAT --
"-- THAT BE MERELY THE LATEST BURDEN THE AVENGERS MUST STRUGGLE WITH."
MUTANTS OUT
IT'S US OR THEM
NOW

THEY DO **OBJECT** TO HOW WE SAFEGUARD THEIR LIVES AND THEIR FUTURES. HALF OF THEM DEMAND THAT WE CHOOSE AVENGERS FOR THEIR **SKIN COLOR** --

-- AND THE OTHER HALF THAT WE **EXCLUDE** AVENGERS FOR AN ACCIDENT OF **BIRTH**.

BOTH SAY WE MUST FOLLOW THEIR WISHES OR BE **UNWORTHY** OF RESPECT.

PFAUGH!

THEY ARE **JACKALS**, THOR. BITING THE HAND THAT KEEPS THEM **SAFE** TO SNAP AND GROWL. THEY ARE **UNDESERVING** OF YOUR PROTECTION.

IT IS AS AGAINST THOR'S NATURE TO **AGREE** WITH HERCULES'S BITTER CONCLUSION AS IT IS FOR HERCULES TO **VOICE** IT UNTHINKINGLY --

-- BUT THOUGH HE STAYS **SILENT** -- HE CAN MARSHAL FEW ARGUMENTS **AGAINST** IT...

FIVE FLOORS DOWN, IN THE SUB-BASEMENT **COMMUNICATIONS** ROOM...

CAPTAIN AMERICA?

AH, **DUANE**, THERE YOU ARE.

DID YOU GET THE **DATA**?

EVERYTHING THE GOVERNMENT KNOWS ABOUT THE EXEMPLARS, RIGHT HERE. AS I'VE SAID... WE'RE EAGER TO **HELP** THE AVENGERS IN THEIR MISSION.

AND BELIEVE ME, DUANE --

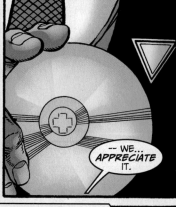

-- WE... **APPRECIATE** IT.

IS THERE A **PROBLEM**, CAP? I MAY BE A **MEMBER** OF THE TRIUNE UNDERSTANDING --

-- BUT I'M STILL THE SAME MAN I'VE **ALWAYS** BEEN. AND THE TRIUNES HAVE BEEN NOTHING BUT **GOOD** FOR ME. DO YOU **REALLY** HOLD IT AGAINST ME?

NO, NO -- OF **COURSE** NOT. LET'S JUST GET TO **WORK**, AND SEE --

 "-- WHAT WE'VE **GOT** HERE."

 **M**EANWHILE, IN THE AVENGERS' UPSTAIRS TROPHY HALL...

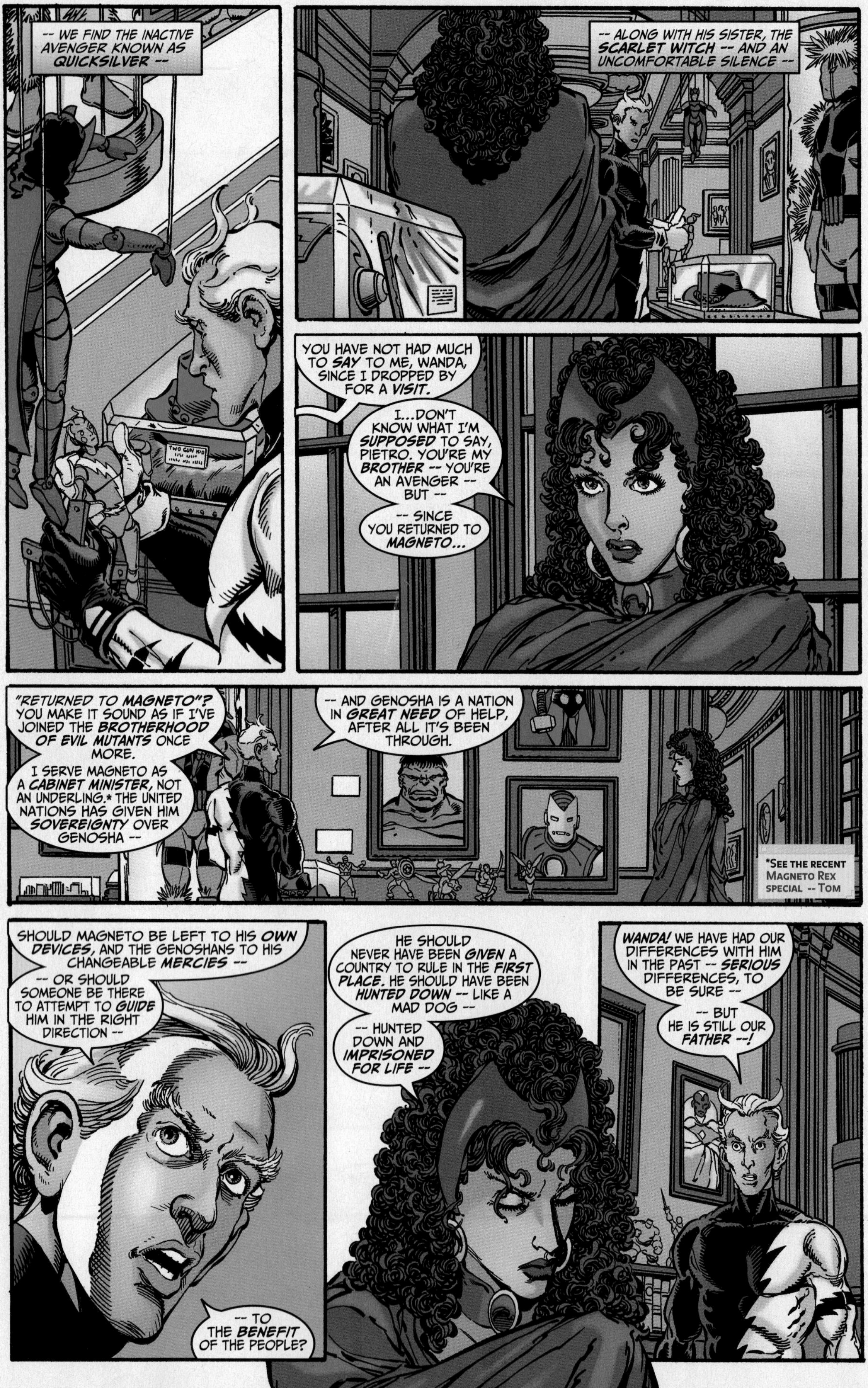
-- WE FIND THE INACTIVE AVENGER KNOWN AS QUICKSILVER --
TWO GUN KID
-- ALONG WITH HIS SISTER, THE SCARLET WITCH -- AND AN UNCOMFORTABLE SILENCE --
YOU HAVE NOT HAD MUCH TO SAY TO ME, WANDA, SINCE I DROPPED BY FOR A VISIT.
I...DON'T KNOW WHAT I'M SUPPOSED TO SAY, PIETRO. YOU'RE MY BROTHER -- YOU'RE AN AVENGER -- BUT --
-- SINCE YOU RETURNED TO MAGNETO...
"RETURNED TO MAGNETO"? YOU MAKE IT SOUND AS IF I'VE JOINED THE BROTHERHOOD OF EVIL MUTANTS ONCE MORE.
I SERVE MAGNETO AS A CABINET MINISTER, NOT AN UNDERLING.* THE UNITED NATIONS HAS GIVEN HIM SOVEREIGNTY OVER GENOSHA --
-- AND GENOSHA IS A NATION IN GREAT NEED OF HELP, AFTER ALL IT'S BEEN THROUGH.
*SEE THE RECENT MAGNETO REX SPECIAL -- TOM
SHOULD MAGNETO BE LEFT TO HIS OWN DEVICES, AND THE GENOSHANS TO HIS CHANGEABLE MERCIES --
-- OR SHOULD SOMEONE BE THERE TO ATTEMPT TO GUIDE HIM IN THE RIGHT DIRECTION --
-- TO THE BENEFIT OF THE PEOPLE?
HE SHOULD NEVER HAVE BEEN GIVEN A COUNTRY TO RULE IN THE FIRST PLACE. HE SHOULD HAVE BEEN HUNTED DOWN -- LIKE A MAD DOG --
-- HUNTED DOWN AND IMPRISONED FOR LIFE --
WANDA! WE HAVE HAD OUR DIFFERENCES WITH HIM IN THE PAST -- SERIOUS DIFFERENCES, TO BE SURE --
-- BUT HE IS STILL OUR FATHER --!

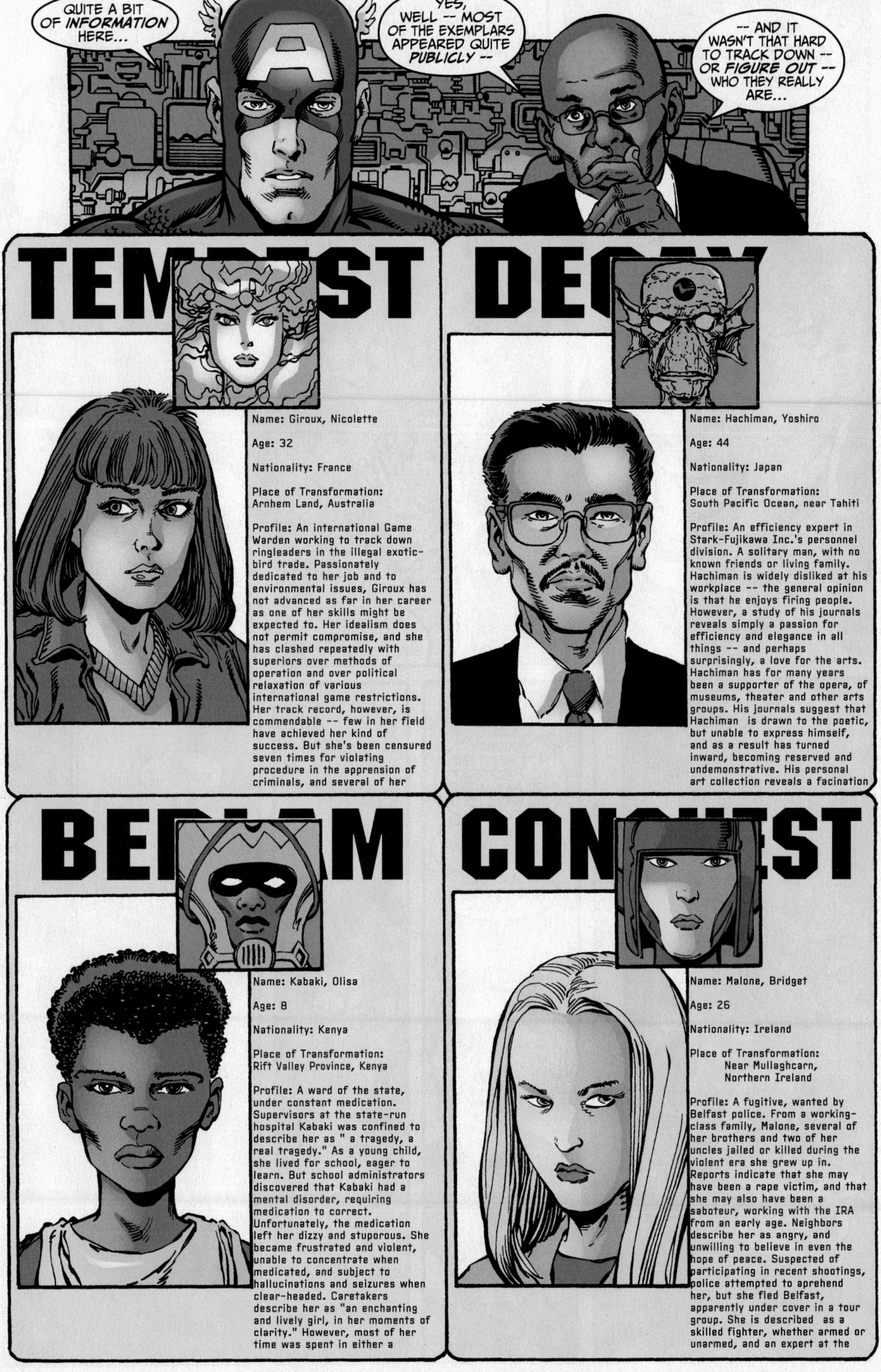
QUITE A BIT OF *INFORMATION* HERE...
YES, WELL -- MOST OF THE EXEMPLARS APPEARED QUITE *PUBLICLY* --
-- AND IT WASN'T THAT HARD TO TRACK DOWN -- OR *FIGURE OUT* -- WHO THEY REALLY ARE...
Name: Giroux, Nicolette
Age: 32
Nationality: France
Place of Transformation: Arnhem Land, Australia
Profile: An international Game Warden working to track down ringleaders in the illegal exotic-bird trade. Passionately dedicated to her job and to environmental issues, Giroux has not advanced as far in her career as one of her skills might be expected to. Her idealism does not permit compromise, and she has clashed repeatedly with superiors over methods of operation and over political relaxation of various international game restrictions. Her track record, however, is commendable -- few in her field have achieved her kind of success. But she's been censured seven times for violating procedure in the apprension of criminals, and several of her
Name: Hachiman, Yoshiro
Age: 44
Nationality: Japan
Place of Transformation: South Pacific Ocean, near Tahiti
Profile: An efficiency expert in Stark-Fujikawa Inc.'s personnel division. A solitary man, with no known friends or living family. Hachiman is widely disliked at his workplace -- the general opinion is that he enjoys firing people. However, a study of his journals reveals simply a passion for efficiency and elegance in all things -- and perhaps surprisingly, a love for the arts. Hachiman has for many years been a supporter of the opera, of museums, theater and other arts groups. His journals suggest that Hachiman is drawn to the poetic, but unable to express himself, and as a result has turned inward, becoming reserved and undemonstrative. His personal art collection reveals a facination
Name: Kabaki, Olisa
Age: 8
Nationality: Kenya
Place of Transformation: Rift Valley Province, Kenya
Profile: A ward of the state, under constant medication. Supervisors at the state-run hospital Kabaki was confined to describe her as " a tragedy, a real tragedy." As a young child, she lived for school, eager to learn. But school administrators discovered that Kabaki had a mental disorder, requiring medication to correct. Unfortunately, the medication left her dizzy and stuporous. She became frustrated and violent, unable to concentrate when medicated, and subject to hallucinations and seizures when clear-headed. Caretakers describe her as "an enchanting and lively girl, in her moments of clarity." However, most of her time was spent in either a
Name: Malone, Bridget
Age: 26
Nationality: Ireland
Place of Transformation: Near Mullaghcarn, Northern Ireland
Profile: A fugitive, wanted by Belfast police. From a working-class family, Malone, several of her brothers and two of her uncles jailed or killed during the violent era she grew up in. Reports indicate that she may have been a rape victim, and that she may also have been a saboteur, working with the IRA from an early age. Neighbors describe her as angry, and unwilling to believe in even the hope of peace. Suspected of participating in recent shootings, police attempted to aprehend her, but she fled Belfast, apparently under cover in a tour group. She is described as a skilled fighter, whether armed or unarmed, and an expert at the

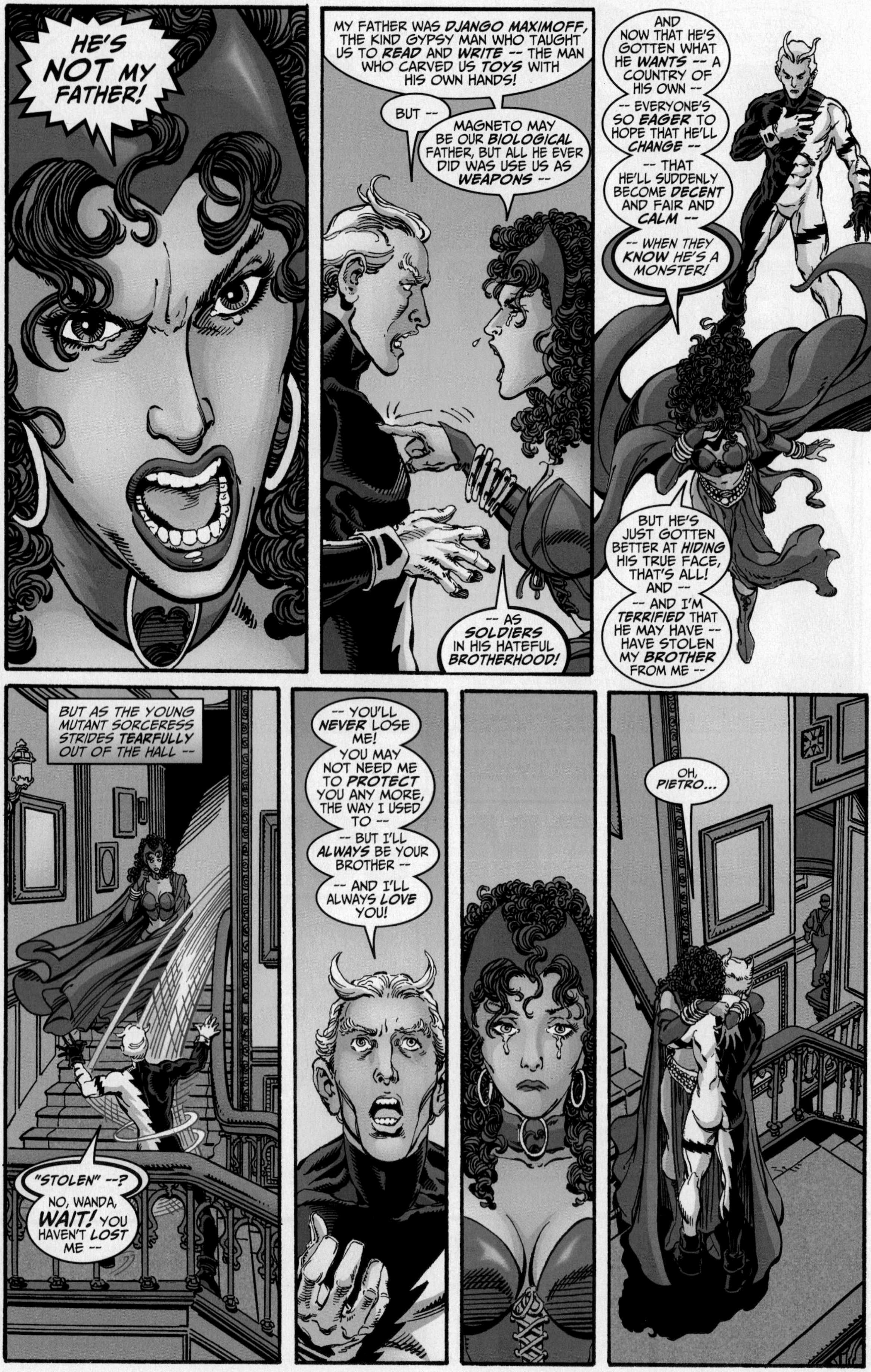
HE'S NOT MY FATHER!
MY FATHER WAS DJANGO MAXIMOFF, THE KIND GYPSY MAN WHO TAUGHT US TO READ AND WRITE -- THE MAN WHO CARVED US TOYS WITH HIS OWN HANDS!
BUT --
MAGNETO MAY BE OUR BIOLOGICAL FATHER, BUT ALL HE EVER DID WAS USE US AS WEAPONS --
-- AS SOLDIERS IN HIS HATEFUL BROTHERHOOD!
AND NOW THAT HE'S GOTTEN WHAT HE WANTS -- A COUNTRY OF HIS OWN --
-- EVERYONE'S SO EAGER TO HOPE THAT HE'LL CHANGE --
-- THAT HE'LL SUDDENLY BECOME DECENT AND FAIR AND CALM --
-- WHEN THEY KNOW HE'S A MONSTER!
BUT HE'S JUST GOTTEN BETTER AT HIDING HIS TRUE FACE, THAT'S ALL! AND --
-- AND I'M TERRIFIED THAT HE MAY HAVE -- HAVE STOLEN MY BROTHER FROM ME --
BUT AS THE YOUNG MUTANT SORCERESS STRIDES TEARFULLY OUT OF THE HALL --
"STOLEN" --?
NO, WANDA, WAIT! YOU HAVEN'T LOST ME --
-- YOU'LL NEVER LOSE ME!
YOU MAY NOT NEED ME TO PROTECT YOU ANY MORE, THE WAY I USED TO --
-- BUT I'LL ALWAYS BE YOUR BROTHER --
-- AND I'LL ALWAYS LOVE YOU!
OH, PIETRO...

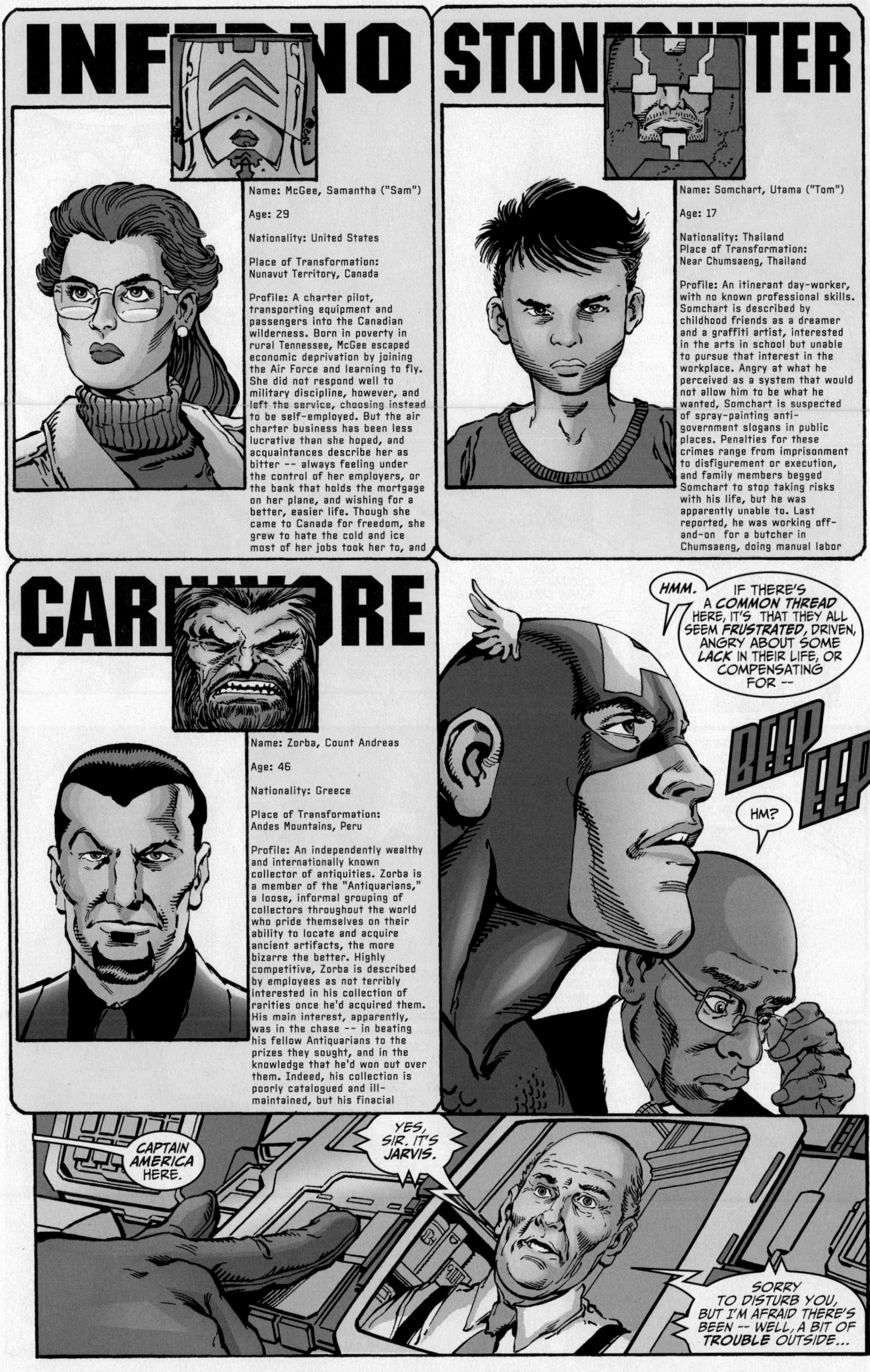
INF NO
Name: McGee, Samantha ("Sam")
Age: 29
Nationality: United States
Place of Transformation: Nunavut Territory, Canada
Profile: A charter pilot, transporting equipment and passengers into the Canadian wilderness. Born in poverty in rural Tennessee, McGee escaped economic deprivation by joining the Air Force and learning to fly. She did not respond well to military discipline, however, and left the service, choosing instead to be self-employed. But the air charter business has been less lucrative than she hoped, and acquaintances describe her as bitter -- always feeling under the control of her employers, or the bank that holds the mortgage on her plane, and wishing for a better, easier life. Though she came to Canada for freedom, she grew to hate the cold and ice most of her jobs took her to, and
STON TER
Name: Somchart, Utama ("Tom")
Age: 17
Nationality: Thailand
Place of Transformation: Near Chumsaeng, Thailand
Profile: An itinerant day-worker, with no known professional skills. Somchart is described by childhood friends as a dreamer and a graffiti artist, interested in the arts in school but unable to pursue that interest in the workplace. Angry at what he perceived as a system that would not allow him to be what he wanted, Somchart is suspected of spray-painting anti-government slogans in public places. Penalties for these crimes range from imprisonment to disfigurement or execution, and family members begged Somchart to stop taking risks with his life, but he was apparently unable to. Last reported, he was working off-and-on for a butcher in Chumsaeng, doing manual labor
CAR ORE
Name: Zorba, Count Andreas
Age: 46
Nationality: Greece
Place of Transformation: Andes Mountains, Peru
Profile: An independently wealthy and internationally known collector of antiquities. Zorba is a member of the "Antiquarians," a loose, informal grouping of collectors throughout the world who pride themselves on their ability to locate and acquire ancient artifacts, the more bizarre the better. Highly competitive, Zorba is described by employees as not terribly interested in his collection of rarities once he'd acquired them. His main interest, apparently, was in the chase -- in beating his fellow Antiquarians to the prizes they sought, and in the knowledge that he'd won out over them. Indeed, his collection is poorly catalogued and ill-maintained, but his finacial
HMM.
IF THERE'S A COMMON THREAD HERE, IT'S THAT THEY ALL SEEM FRUSTRATED, DRIVEN, ANGRY ABOUT SOME LACK IN THEIR LIFE, OR COMPENSATING FOR --
BEEP BEEP
HM?
CAPTAIN AMERICA HERE.
YES, SIR. IT'S JARVIS.
SORRY TO DISTURB YOU, BUT I'M AFRAID THERE'S BEEN -- WELL, A BIT OF TROUBLE OUTSIDE...

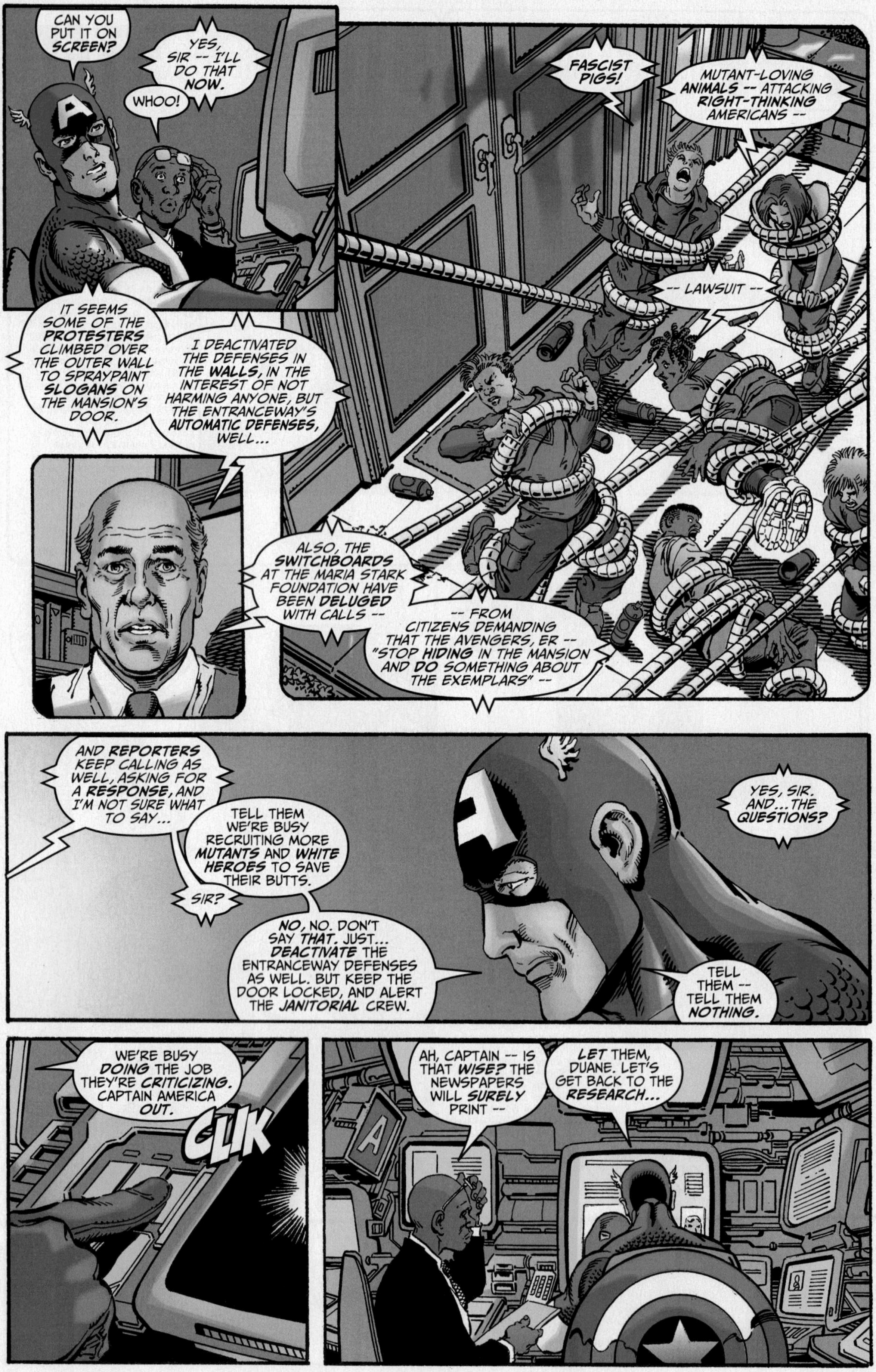
CAN YOU PUT IT ON SCREEN?
YES, SIR -- I'LL DO THAT NOW.
WHOO!
FASCIST PIGS!
MUTANT-LOVING ANIMALS -- ATTACKING RIGHT-THINKING AMERICANS --
-- LAWSUIT --
IT SEEMS SOME OF THE PROTESTERS CLIMBED OVER THE OUTER WALL TO SPRAYPAINT SLOGANS ON THE MANSION'S DOOR.
I DEACTIVATED THE DEFENSES IN THE WALLS, IN THE INTEREST OF NOT HARMING ANYONE, BUT THE ENTRANCEWAY'S AUTOMATIC DEFENSES, WELL...
ALSO, THE SWITCHBOARDS AT THE MARIA STARK FOUNDATION HAVE BEEN DELUGED WITH CALLS --
-- FROM CITIZENS DEMANDING THAT THE AVENGERS, ER -- "STOP HIDING IN THE MANSION AND DO SOMETHING ABOUT THE EXEMPLARS" --
AND REPORTERS KEEP CALLING AS WELL, ASKING FOR A RESPONSE, AND I'M NOT SURE WHAT TO SAY...
TELL THEM WE'RE BUSY RECRUITING MORE MUTANTS AND WHITE HEROES TO SAVE THEIR BUTTS.
SIR?
NO, NO. DON'T SAY THAT. JUST... DEACTIVATE THE ENTRANCEWAY DEFENSES AS WELL. BUT KEEP THE DOOR LOCKED, AND ALERT THE JANITORIAL CREW.
YES, SIR. AND... THE QUESTIONS?
TELL THEM -- TELL THEM NOTHING.
WE'RE BUSY DOING THE JOB THEY'RE CRITICIZING. CAPTAIN AMERICA OUT.
CLIK
AH, CAPTAIN -- IS THAT WISE? THE NEWSPAPERS WILL SURELY PRINT --
LET THEM, DUANE. LET'S GET BACK TO THE RESEARCH...

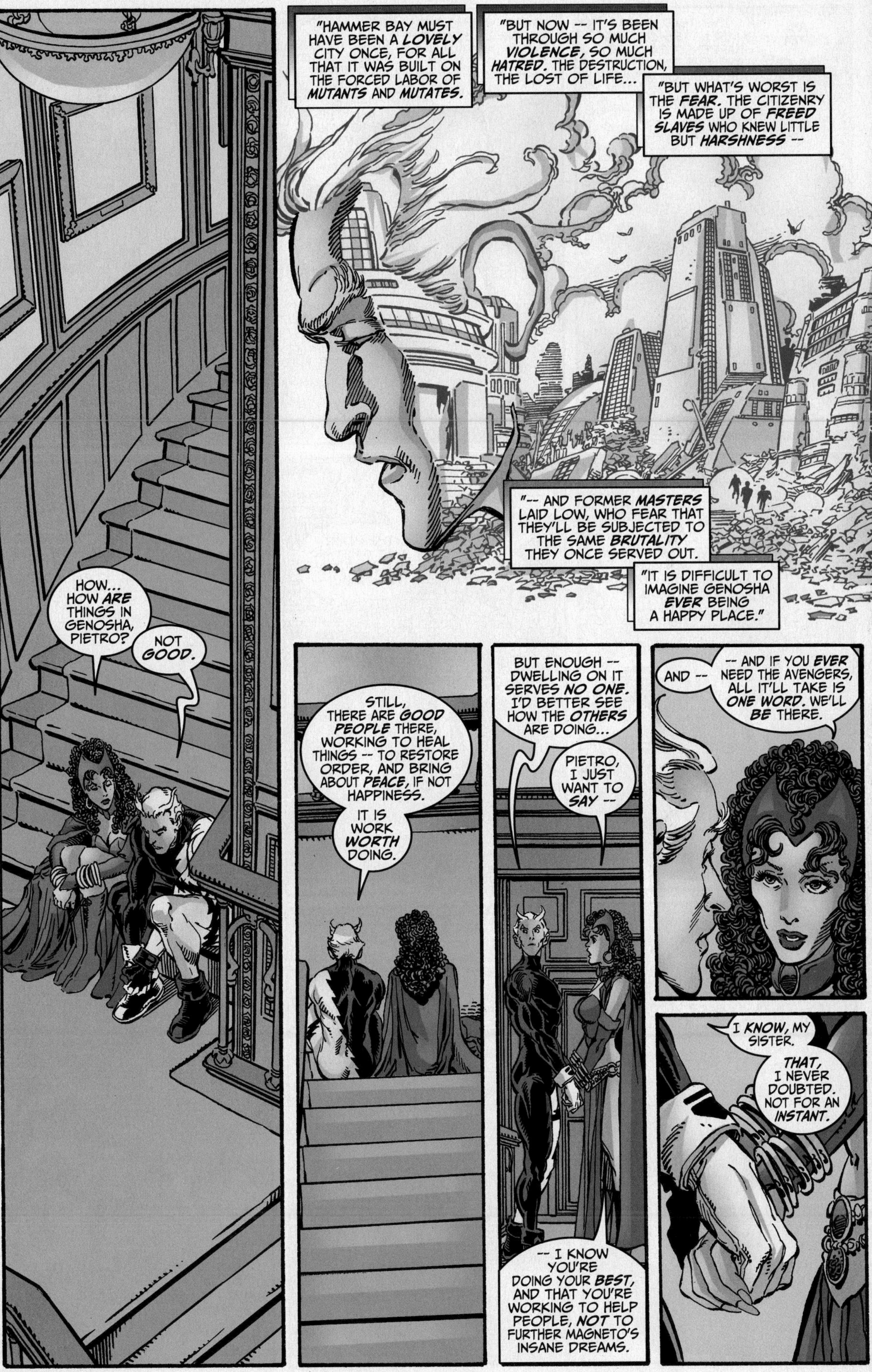

"HAMMER BAY MUST HAVE BEEN A LOVELY CITY ONCE, FOR ALL THAT IT WAS BUILT ON THE FORCED LABOR OF MUTANTS AND MUTATES.
"BUT NOW -- IT'S BEEN THROUGH SO MUCH VIOLENCE, SO MUCH HATRED. THE DESTRUCTION, THE LOST OF LIFE...
"BUT WHAT'S WORST IS THE FEAR. THE CITIZENRY IS MADE UP OF FREED SLAVES WHO KNEW LITTLE BUT HARSHNESS --
"-- AND FORMER MASTERS LAID LOW, WHO FEAR THAT THEY'LL BE SUBJECTED TO THE SAME BRUTALITY THEY ONCE SERVED OUT.
"IT IS DIFFICULT TO IMAGINE GENOSHA EVER BEING A HAPPY PLACE."
HOW... HOW ARE THINGS IN GENOSHA, PIETRO?
NOT GOOD.
STILL, THERE ARE GOOD PEOPLE THERE, WORKING TO HEAL THINGS -- TO RESTORE ORDER, AND BRING ABOUT PEACE, IF NOT HAPPINESS.
IT IS WORK WORTH DOING.
BUT ENOUGH -- DWELLING ON IT SERVES NO ONE. I'D BETTER SEE HOW THE OTHERS ARE DOING...
PIETRO, I JUST WANT TO SAY --
-- I KNOW YOU'RE DOING YOUR BEST, AND THAT YOU'RE WORKING TO HELP PEOPLE, NOT TO FURTHER MAGNETO'S INSANE DREAMS.
AND --
-- AND IF YOU EVER NEED THE AVENGERS, ALL IT'LL TAKE IS ONE WORD. WE'LL BE THERE.
I KNOW, MY SISTER.
THAT, I NEVER DOUBTED. NOT FOR AN INSTANT.

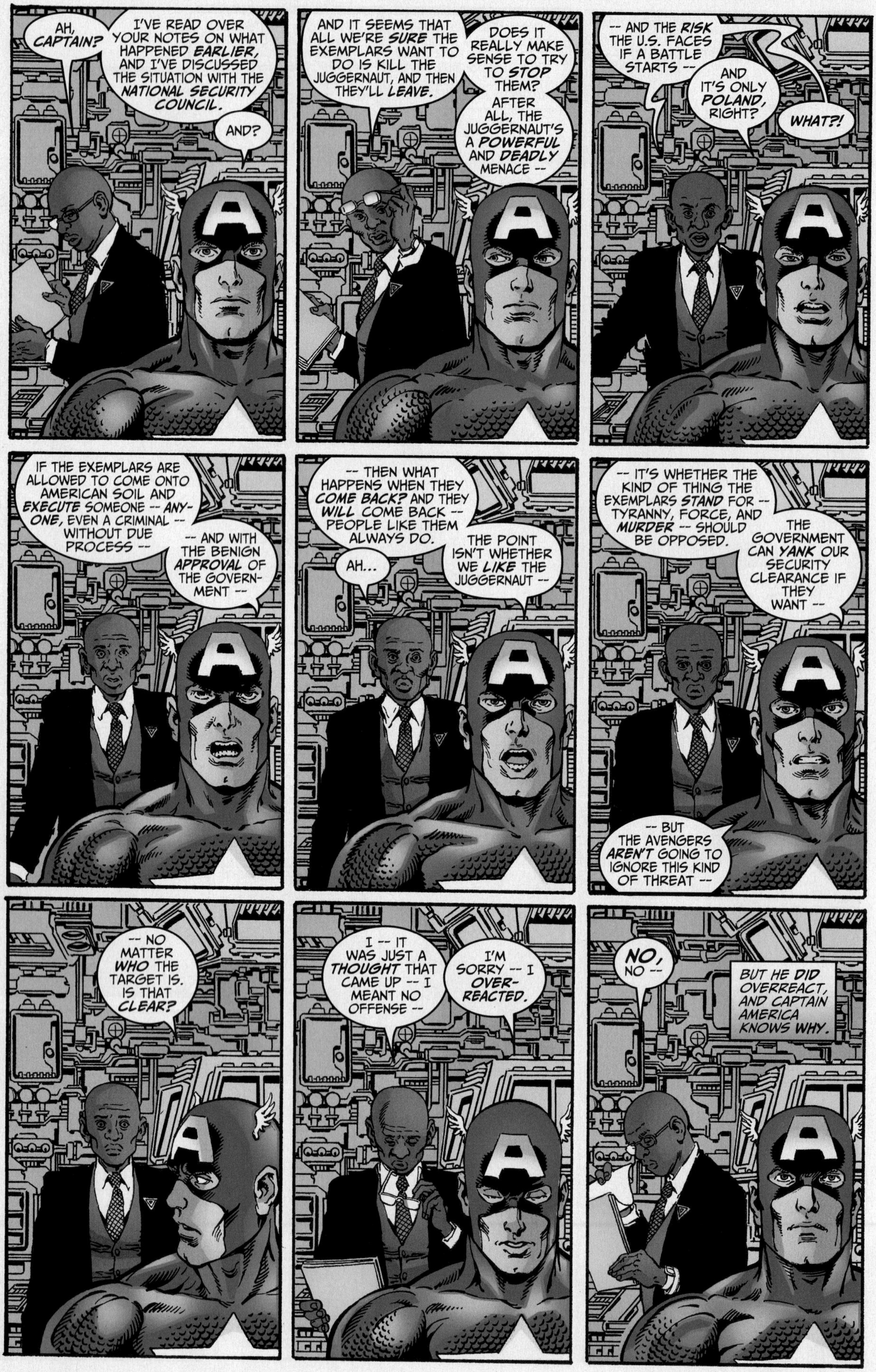
AH, CAPTAIN?
I'VE READ OVER YOUR NOTES ON WHAT HAPPENED EARLIER, AND I'VE DISCUSSED THE SITUATION WITH THE NATIONAL SECURITY COUNCIL.
AND?
AND IT SEEMS THAT ALL WE'RE SURE THE EXEMPLARS WANT TO DO IS KILL THE JUGGERNAUT, AND THEN THEY'LL LEAVE.
DOES IT REALLY MAKE SENSE TO TRY TO STOP THEM?
AFTER ALL, THE JUGGERNAUT'S A POWERFUL AND DEADLY MENACE --
-- AND THE RISK THE U.S. FACES IF A BATTLE STARTS --
AND IT'S ONLY POLAND, RIGHT?
WHAT?!
IF THE EXEMPLARS ARE ALLOWED TO COME ONTO AMERICAN SOIL AND EXECUTE SOMEONE -- ANY-ONE, EVEN A CRIMINAL -- WITHOUT DUE PROCESS --
-- AND WITH THE BENIGN APPROVAL OF THE GOVERN-MENT --
-- THEN WHAT HAPPENS WHEN THEY COME BACK? AND THEY WILL COME BACK -- PEOPLE LIKE THEM ALWAYS DO.
AH...
THE POINT ISN'T WHETHER WE LIKE THE JUGGERNAUT --
-- IT'S WHETHER THE KIND OF THING THE EXEMPLARS STAND FOR -- TYRANNY, FORCE, AND MURDER -- SHOULD BE OPPOSED.
THE GOVERNMENT CAN YANK OUR SECURITY CLEARANCE IF THEY WANT --
-- BUT THE AVENGERS AREN'T GOING TO IGNORE THIS KIND OF THREAT --
-- NO MATTER WHO THE TARGET IS. IS THAT CLEAR?
I -- IT WAS JUST A THOUGHT THAT CAME UP -- I MEANT NO OFFENSE --
I'M SORRY -- I OVER-REACTED.
NO, NO --
BUT HE DID OVERREACT, AND CAPTAIN AMERICA KNOWS WHY.

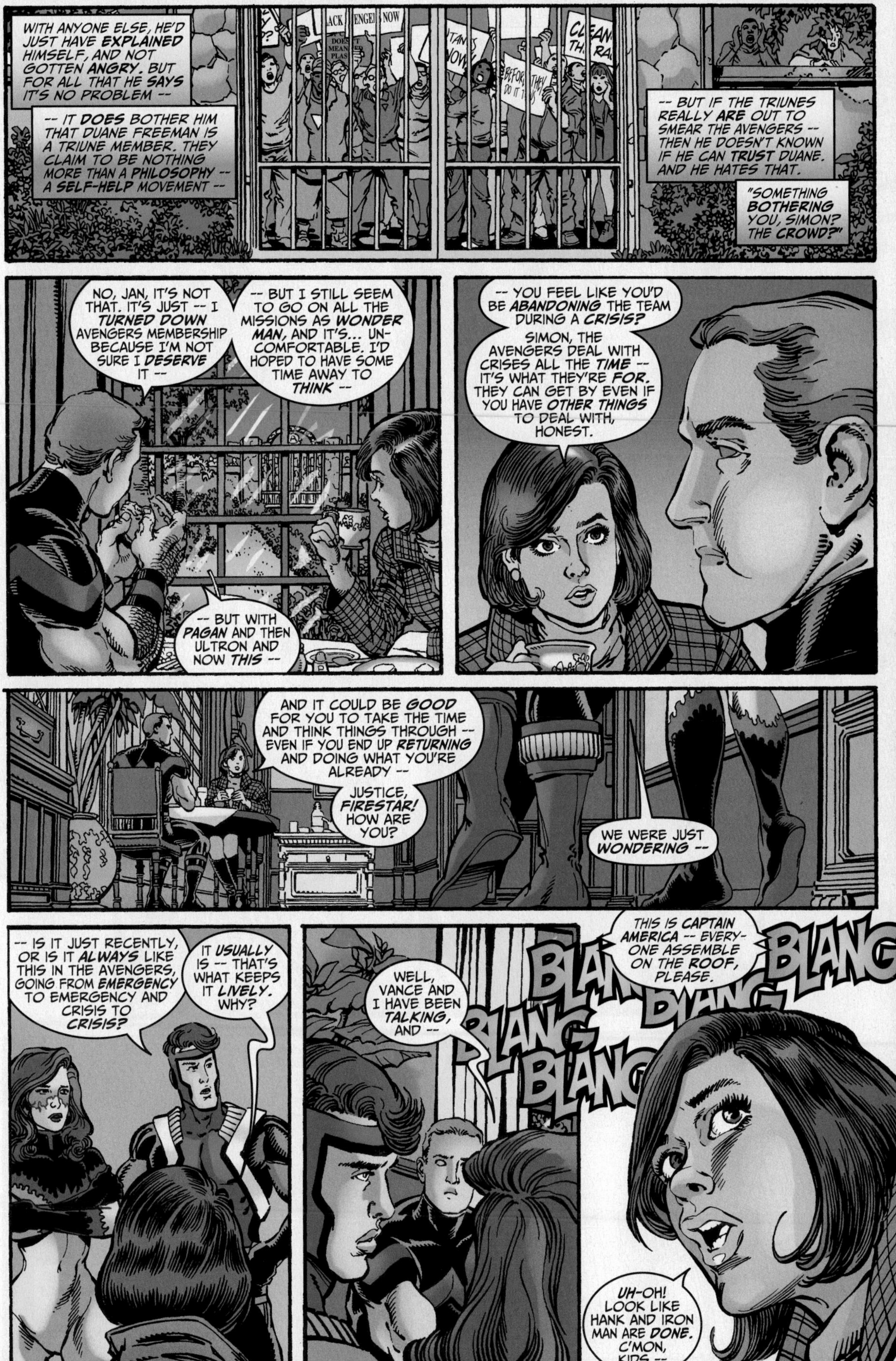

WITH ANYONE ELSE, HE'D JUST HAVE EXPLAINED HIMSELF, AND NOT GOTTEN ANGRY. BUT FOR ALL THAT HE SAYS IT'S NO PROBLEM --
-- IT DOES BOTHER HIM THAT DUANE FREEMAN IS A TRIUNE MEMBER. THEY CLAIM TO BE NOTHING MORE THAN A PHILOSOPHY -- A SELF-HELP MOVEMENT --
-- BUT IF THE TRIUNES REALLY ARE OUT TO SMEAR THE AVENGERS -- THEN HE DOESN'T KNOWN IF HE CAN TRUST DUANE. AND HE HATES THAT.
"SOMETHING BOTHERING YOU, SIMON? THE CROWD?"
NO, JAN, IT'S NOT THAT. IT'S JUST -- I TURNED DOWN AVENGERS MEMBERSHIP BECAUSE I'M NOT SURE I DESERVE IT --
-- BUT WITH PAGAN AND THEN ULTRON AND NOW THIS --
-- BUT I STILL SEEM TO GO ON ALL THE MISSIONS AS WONDER MAN, AND IT'S... UN-COMFORTABLE. I'D HOPED TO HAVE SOME TIME AWAY TO THINK --
-- YOU FEEL LIKE YOU'D BE ABANDONING THE TEAM DURING A CRISIS?
SIMON, THE AVENGERS DEAL WITH CRISES ALL THE TIME -- IT'S WHAT THEY'RE FOR. THEY CAN GET BY EVEN IF YOU HAVE OTHER THINGS TO DEAL WITH, HONEST.
AND IT COULD BE GOOD FOR YOU TO TAKE THE TIME AND THINK THINGS THROUGH -- EVEN IF YOU END UP RETURNING AND DOING WHAT YOU'RE ALREADY --
JUSTICE, FIRESTAR! HOW ARE YOU?
WE WERE JUST WONDERING --
-- IS IT JUST RECENTLY, OR IS IT ALWAYS LIKE THIS IN THE AVENGERS, GOING FROM EMERGENCY TO EMERGENCY AND CRISIS TO CRISIS?
IT USUALLY IS -- THAT'S WHAT KEEPS IT LIVELY. WHY?
WELL, VANCE AND I HAVE BEEN TALKING, AND --
BLANG BLANG BLANG BLANG BLANG
THIS IS CAPTAIN AMERICA -- EVERY-ONE ASSEMBLE ON THE ROOF, PLEASE.
UH-OH! LOOK LIKE HANK AND IRON MAN ARE DONE. C'MON, KIDS --

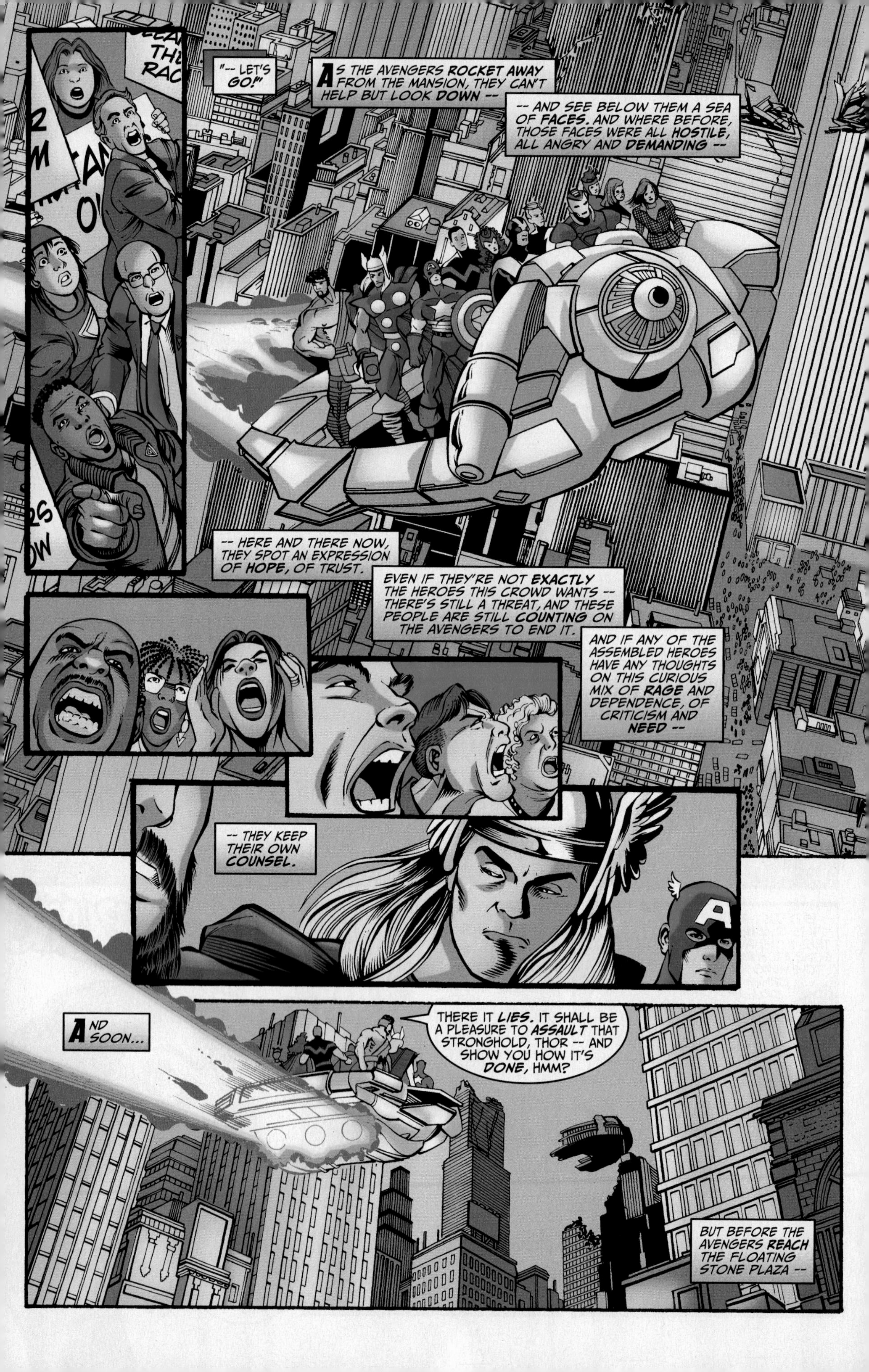

"-- LET'S GO!"
AS THE AVENGERS ROCKET AWAY FROM THE MANSION, THEY CAN'T HELP BUT LOOK DOWN --
-- AND SEE BELOW THEM A SEA OF FACES. AND WHERE BEFORE, THOSE FACES WERE ALL HOSTILE, ALL ANGRY AND DEMANDING --
-- HERE AND THERE NOW, THEY SPOT AN EXPRESSION OF HOPE, OF TRUST.
EVEN IF THEY'RE NOT EXACTLY THE HEROES THIS CROWD WANTS -- THERE'S STILL A THREAT, AND THESE PEOPLE ARE STILL COUNTING ON THE AVENGERS TO END IT.
AND IF ANY OF THE ASSEMBLED HEROES HAVE ANY THOUGHTS ON THIS CURIOUS MIX OF RAGE AND DEPENDENCE, OF CRITICISM AND NEED --
-- THEY KEEP THEIR OWN COUNSEL.
AND SOON...
THERE IT LIES. IT SHALL BE A PLEASURE TO ASSAULT THAT STRONGHOLD, THOR -- AND SHOW YOU HOW IT'S DONE, HMM?
BUT BEFORE THE AVENGERS REACH THE FLOATING STONE PLAZA --

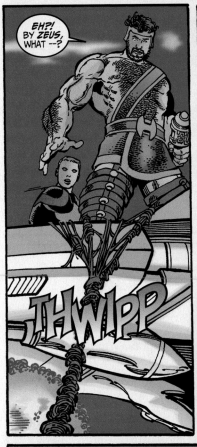

EH?! BY *ZEUS*, WHAT --?

THWIPP

HIYA, FOLKS!

MIND IF I SIT *IN?* THOSE JERKS BUSTED UP SOME OF MY FAVORITE WEB-SLINGING *ROOF-TOPS!*

GLAD TO HAVE YOU, SPIDER-MAN. WE'LL TAKE ALL THE HELP WE CAN GET.

GREAT -- HOPE THAT GOES FOR *ME*, TOO! THE OTHER NEW WARRIORS -- PLUS *DAREDEVIL* AND GUYS LIKE THAT -- ARE DEALING WITH LOOTERS DOWN *BELOW* --

-- BUT I SURE WOULDN'T MIND PLAYING AN INNING IN THE *BIG* LEAGUES!

NOVA! BUCKET-HEAD!

AND SO...

THIS IS GOING TO BE *TRICKY.* THEIR DEFENSIVE SYSTEMS *MODIFY* THEMSELVES -- COMPENSATING FOR ANY ATTACK.

SO WE'VE GOT TO KEEP *SHIFTING* OUR ATTACK FREQUENCIES -- BREAK THROUGH BEFORE THEY CAN *CATCH UP.* READY, HANK?

RARIN' TO GO, SHELL-HEAD.

"THEN -- LET'S DO IT!"

ZAAKKK

FCHROOM

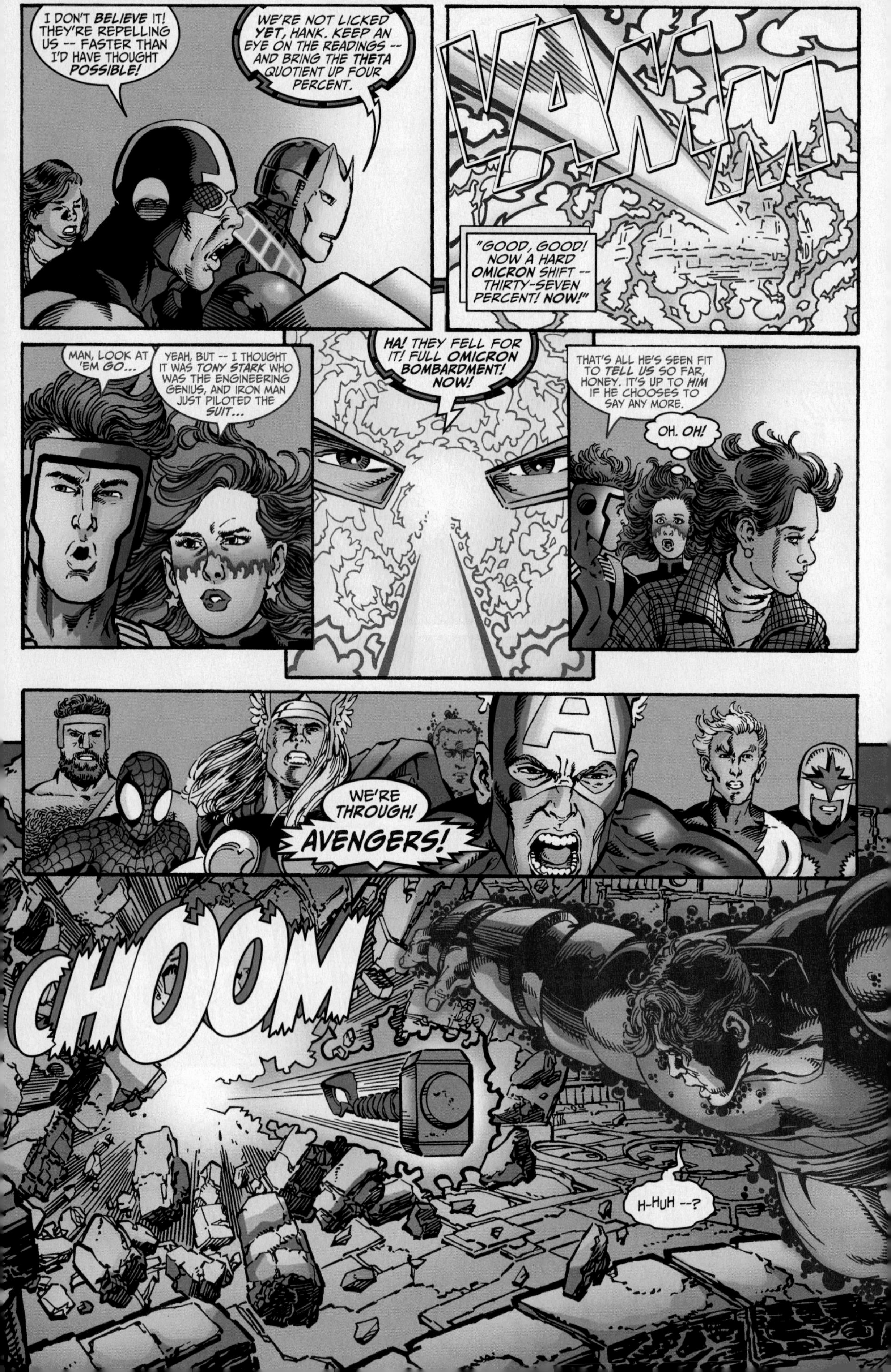
I DON'T BELIEVE IT! THEY'RE REPELLING US -- FASTER THAN I'D HAVE THOUGHT POSSIBLE!
WE'RE NOT LICKED YET, HANK. KEEP AN EYE ON THE READINGS -- AND BRING THE THETA QUOTIENT UP FOUR PERCENT.
VAMM
"GOOD, GOOD! NOW A HARD OMICRON SHIFT -- THIRTY-SEVEN PERCENT! NOW!"
MAN, LOOK AT 'EM GO...
YEAH, BUT -- I THOUGHT IT WAS TONY STARK WHO WAS THE ENGINEERING GENIUS, AND IRON MAN JUST PILOTED THE SUIT...
HA! THEY FELL FOR IT! FULL OMICRON BOMBARDMENT! NOW!
THAT'S ALL HE'S SEEN FIT TO TELL US SO FAR, HONEY. IT'S UP TO HIM IF HE CHOOSES TO SAY ANY MORE.
OH. OH!
WE'RE THROUGH!
AVENGERS!
CHOOM
H-HUH --?

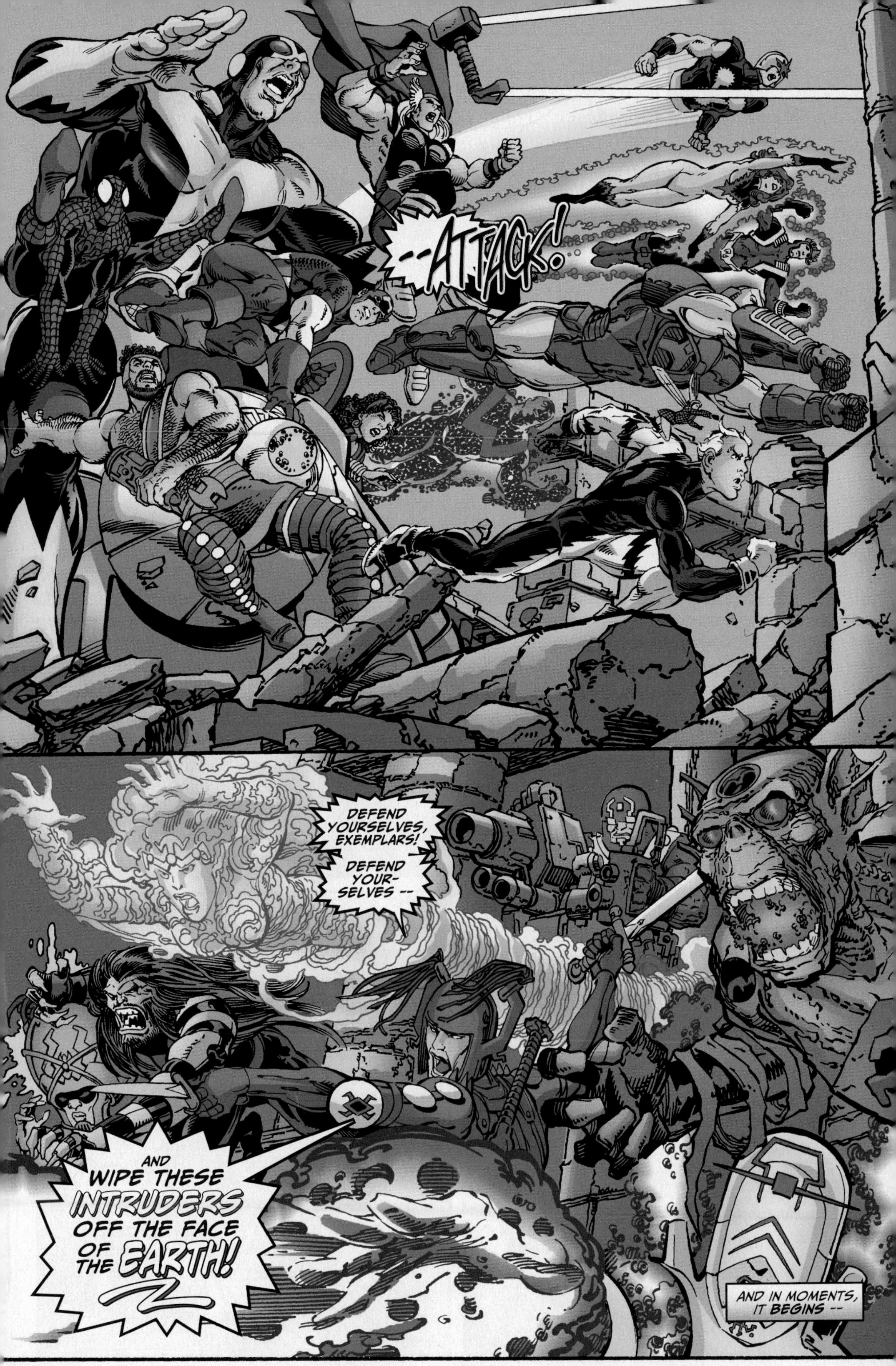
--ATTACK!
DEFEND YOURSELVES, EXEMPLARS!
DEFEND YOUR-SELVES --
AND WIPE THESE INTRUDERS OFF THE FACE OF THE EARTH!
AND IN MOMENTS, IT BEGINS --

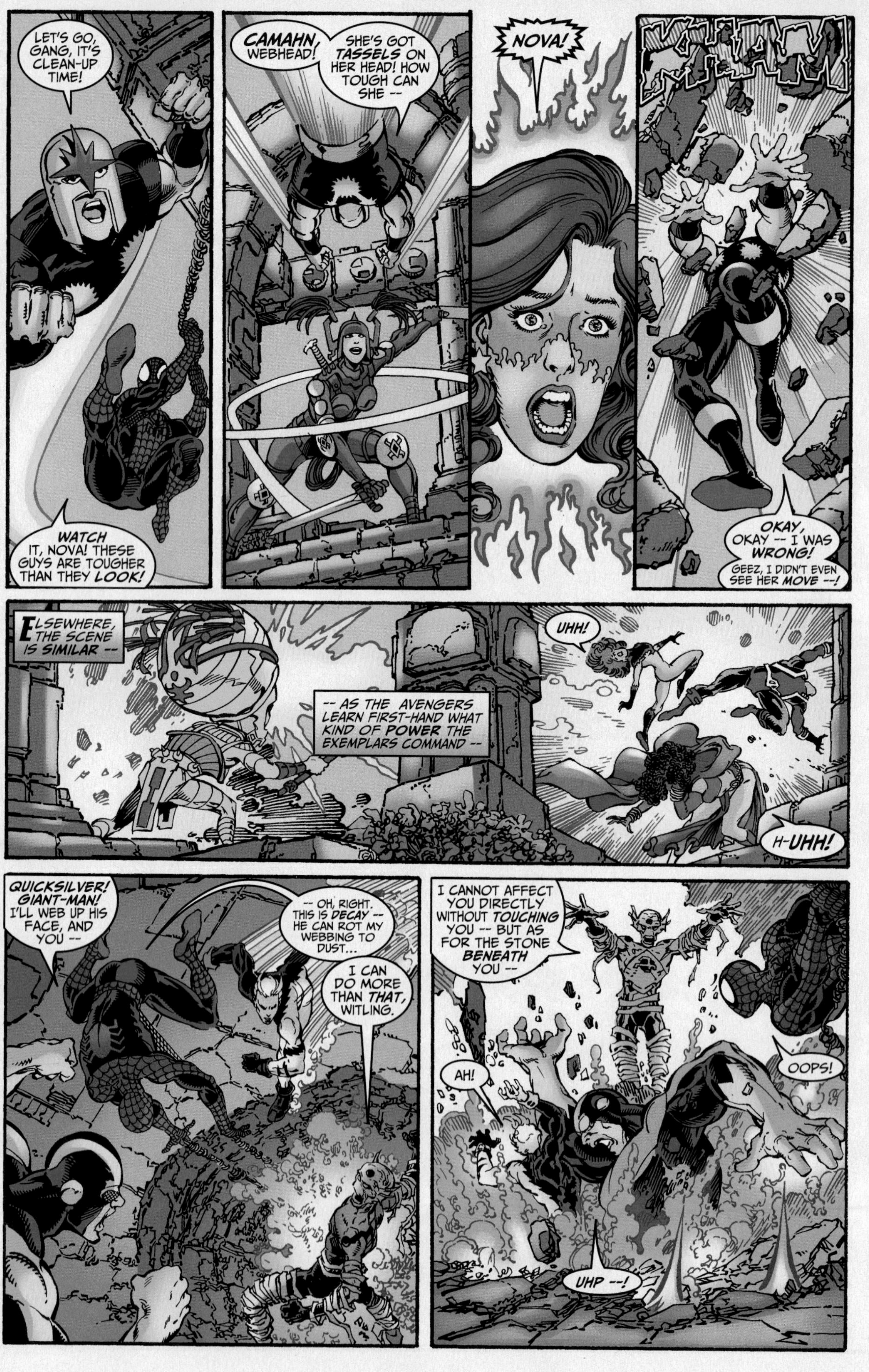
LET'S GO, GANG, IT'S CLEAN-UP TIME!
WATCH IT, NOVA! THESE GUYS ARE TOUGHER THAN THEY LOOK!
CAMAHN, WEBHEAD!
SHE'S GOT TASSELS ON HER HEAD! HOW TOUGH CAN SHE --
NOVA!
OKAY, OKAY -- I WAS WRONG! GEEZ, I DIDN'T EVEN SEE HER MOVE --!
ELSEWHERE, THE SCENE IS SIMILAR --
-- AS THE AVENGERS LEARN FIRST-HAND WHAT KIND OF POWER THE EXEMPLARS COMMAND --
UHH!
H-UHH!
QUICKSILVER! GIANT-MAN! I'LL WEB UP HIS FACE, AND YOU --
-- OH, RIGHT. THIS IS DECAY -- HE CAN ROT MY WEBBING TO DUST...
I CAN DO MORE THAN THAT, WITLING.
I CANNOT AFFECT YOU DIRECTLY WITHOUT TOUCHING YOU -- BUT AS FOR THE STONE BENEATH YOU --
AH!
OOPS!
UHP --!

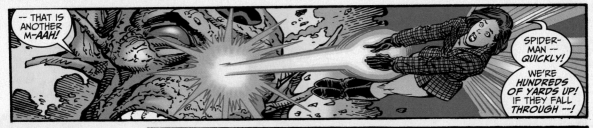

-- THAT IS ANOTHER M--AAH!

SPIDER-MAN -- QUICKLY! WE'RE HUNDREDS OF YARDS UP! IF THEY FALL THROUGH --!

DON'T WORRY, WASP --

TWHIP

-- I'M ON IT!

WHEW!

BUT EVEN AS TWO HEROES ARE RESCUED --

-- ANOTHER PAIR IS IMPERILED --

IRON MAN! USE THY BOOT JETS -- WREST US FREE FROM THIS WHIRL-WIND!

I'M TRYING, HERC! BUT TEMPEST'S WINDS ARE TOO POWERFUL --

-- I CAN'T GET MY GYROS TO STABILIZE --!

-- AND FOR A THIRD --

BACK OFF, CARNIVORE! THIS ONE IS MINE!

FEAUGH! LEAVE THE CHOICE OF TARGETS TO YOUR BETTERS, GIRL! YOU'LL LIVE LONGER!

EITHER OR BOTH OF THEE, CAITIFFS! THE GOD OF THUNDER WILL STILL PREVAIL!

I'LL SHOW YOU, ANIMAL --!

THIS IS INSANE! THEY'VE GOT THE POWER TO BEAT HIM IF THEY WORKED TOGETHER -- BUT THEY'RE TOO ANGRY, TOO COMPETITIVE!

ARRH! CURSE YOUR HIDE, INFERNO!

AND THEY'RE NOTHING LIKE THEIR FILES LED ME TO BELIEVE. THIS IS A BUSH PILOT AND A GRECIAN COUNT?!

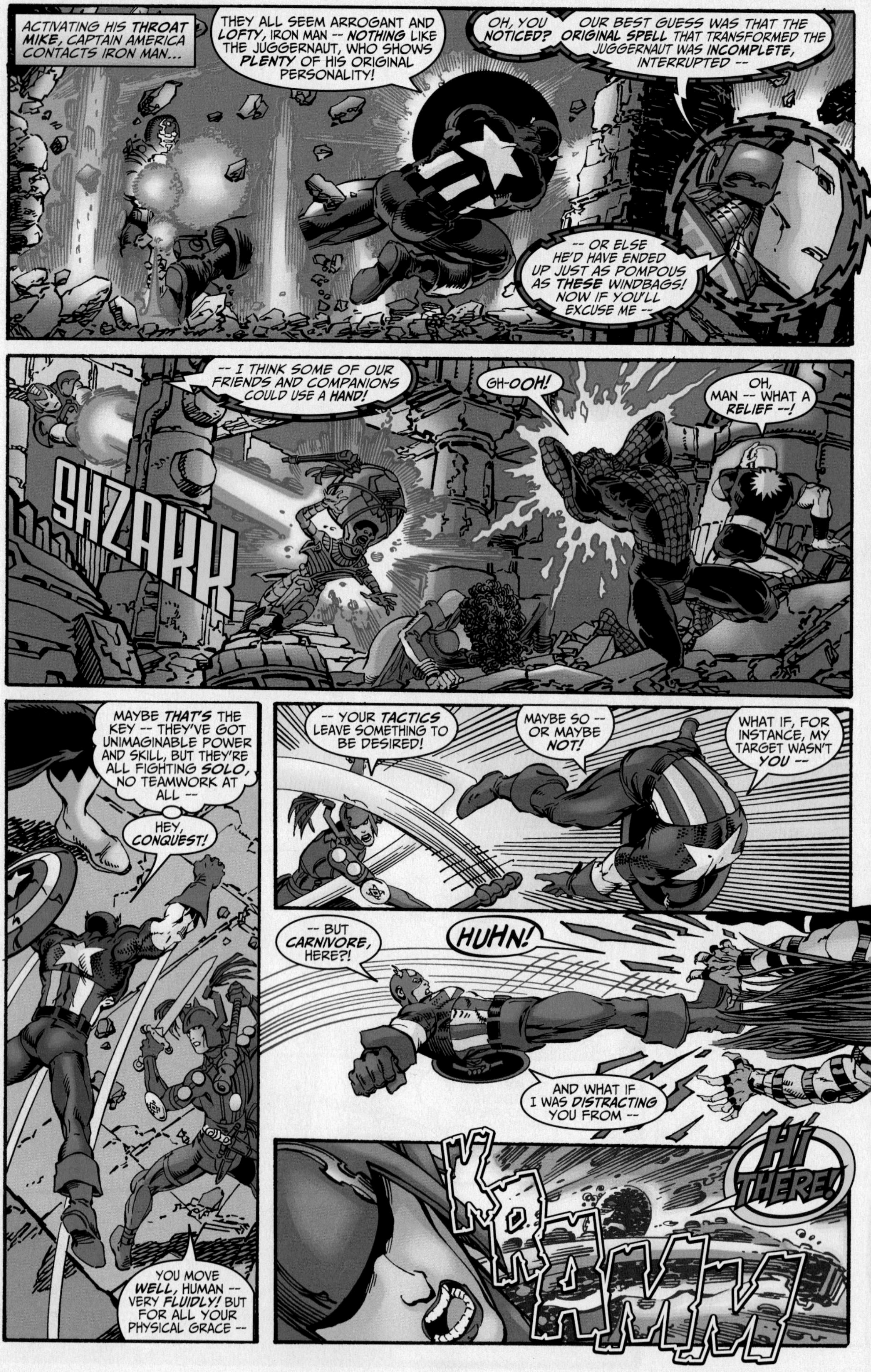
ACTIVATING HIS THROAT MIKE, CAPTAIN AMERICA CONTACTS IRON MAN...
THEY ALL SEEM ARROGANT AND LOFTY, IRON MAN -- NOTHING LIKE THE JUGGERNAUT, WHO SHOWS PLENTY OF HIS ORIGINAL PERSONALITY!
OH, YOU NOTICED?
OUR BEST GUESS WAS THAT THE ORIGINAL SPELL THAT TRANSFORMED THE JUGGERNAUT WAS INCOMPLETE, INTERRUPTED --
-- OR ELSE HE'D HAVE ENDED UP JUST AS POMPOUS AS THESE WINDBAGS! NOW IF YOU'LL EXCUSE ME --
-- I THINK SOME OF OUR FRIENDS AND COMPANIONS COULD USE A HAND!
SHZAKK
GH-OOH!
OH, MAN -- WHAT A RELIEF --!
MAYBE THAT'S THE KEY -- THEY'VE GOT UNIMAGINABLE POWER AND SKILL, BUT THEY'RE ALL FIGHTING SOLO, NO TEAMWORK AT ALL --
HEY, CONQUEST!
YOU MOVE WELL, HUMAN -- VERY FLUIDLY! BUT FOR ALL YOUR PHYSICAL GRACE --
-- YOUR TACTICS LEAVE SOMETHING TO BE DESIRED!
MAYBE SO -- OR MAYBE NOT!
WHAT IF, FOR INSTANCE, MY TARGET WASN'T YOU --
-- BUT CARNIVORE, HERE?!
HUHN!
AND WHAT IF I WAS DISTRACTING YOU FROM --
KRAMM
HI THERE!

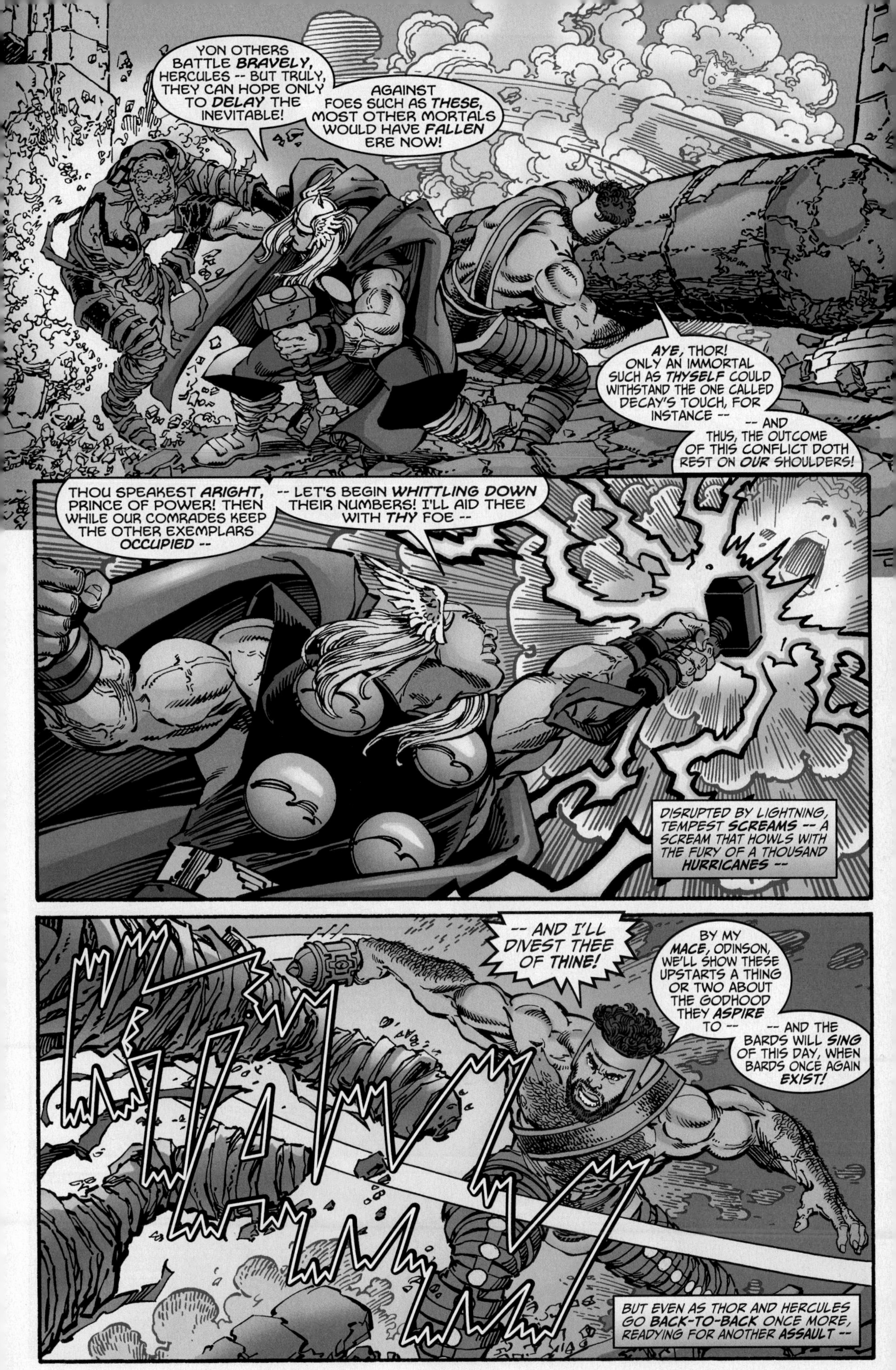
YON OTHERS BATTLE BRAVELY, HERCULES -- BUT TRULY, THEY CAN HOPE ONLY TO DELAY THE INEVITABLE!
AGAINST FOES SUCH AS THESE, MOST OTHER MORTALS WOULD HAVE FALLEN ERE NOW!
AYE, THOR! ONLY AN IMMORTAL SUCH AS THYSELF COULD WITHSTAND THE ONE CALLED DECAY'S TOUCH, FOR INSTANCE --
-- AND THUS, THE OUTCOME OF THIS CONFLICT DOTH REST ON OUR SHOULDERS!
THOU SPEAKEST ARIGHT, PRINCE OF POWER! THEN WHILE OUR COMRADES KEEP THE OTHER EXEMPLARS OCCUPIED --
-- LET'S BEGIN WHITTLING DOWN THEIR NUMBERS! I'LL AID THEE WITH THY FOE --
DISRUPTED BY LIGHTNING, TEMPEST SCREAMS -- A SCREAM THAT HOWLS WITH THE FURY OF A THOUSAND HURRICANES --
-- AND I'LL DIVEST THEE OF THINE!
BY MY MACE, ODINSON, WE'LL SHOW THESE UPSTARTS A THING OR TWO ABOUT THE GODHOOD THEY ASPIRE TO --
-- AND THE BARDS WILL SING OF THIS DAY, WHEN BARDS ONCE AGAIN EXIST!
BUT EVEN AS THOR AND HERCULES GO BACK-TO-BACK ONCE MORE, READYING FOR ANOTHER ASSAULT --

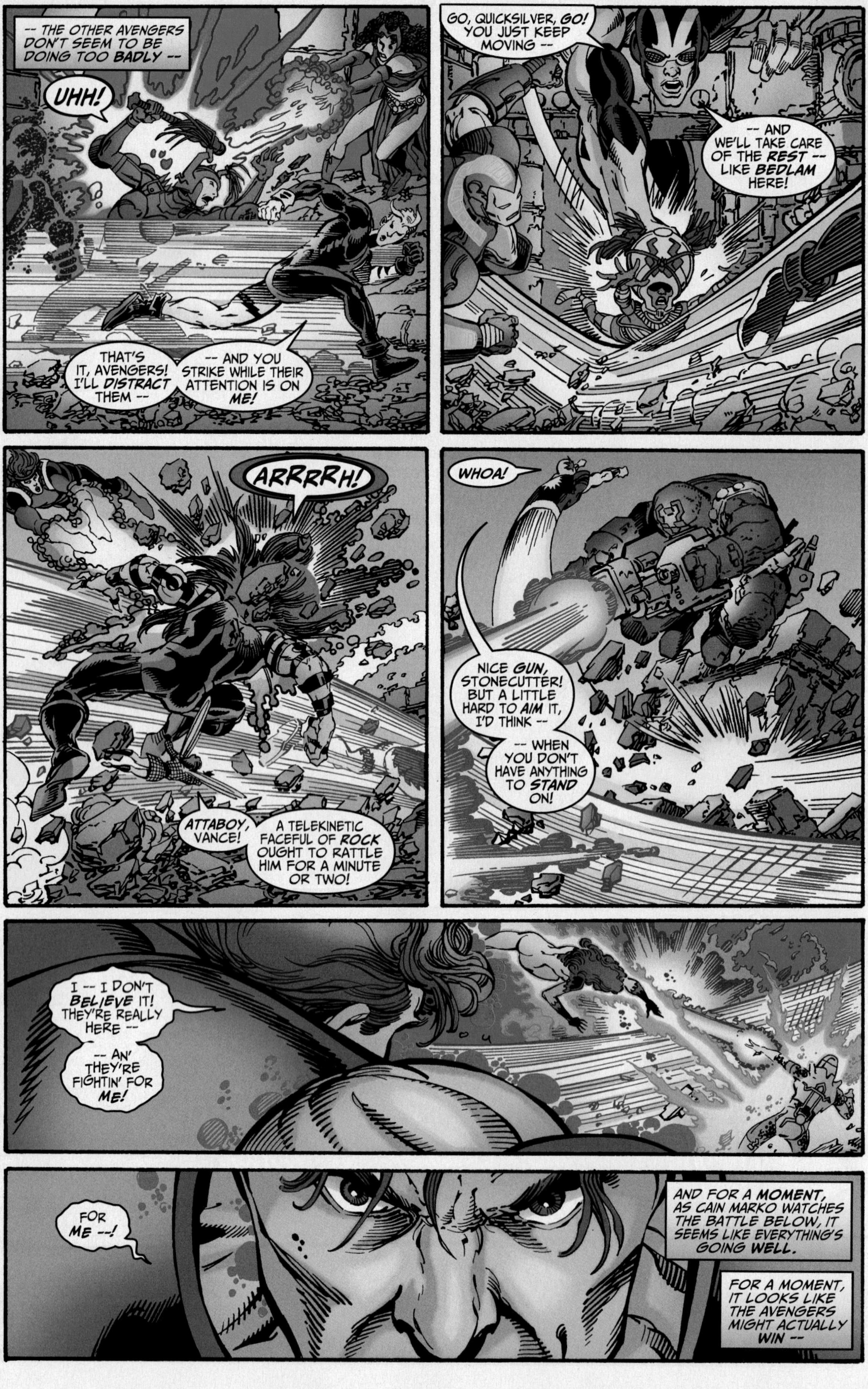
-- THE OTHER AVENGERS DON'T SEEM TO BE DOING TOO BADLY --
UHH!
THAT'S IT, AVENGERS! I'LL DISTRACT THEM --
-- AND YOU STRIKE WHILE THEIR ATTENTION IS ON ME!
GO, QUICKSILVER, GO! YOU JUST KEEP MOVING --
-- AND WE'LL TAKE CARE OF THE REST -- LIKE BEDLAM HERE!
ARRRRH!
ATTABOY, VANCE!
A TELEKINETIC FACEFUL OF ROCK OUGHT TO RATTLE HIM FOR A MINUTE OR TWO!
WHOA!
NICE GUN, STONECUTTER! BUT A LITTLE HARD TO AIM IT, I'D THINK --
-- WHEN YOU DON'T HAVE ANYTHING TO STAND ON!
I -- I DON'T BELIEVE IT! THEY'RE REALLY HERE --
-- AN' THEY'RE FIGHTIN' FOR ME!
FOR ME --!
AND FOR A MOMENT, AS CAIN MARKO WATCHES THE BATTLE BELOW, IT SEEMS LIKE EVERYTHING'S GOING WELL.
FOR A MOMENT, IT LOOKS LIKE THE AVENGERS MIGHT ACTUALLY WIN --

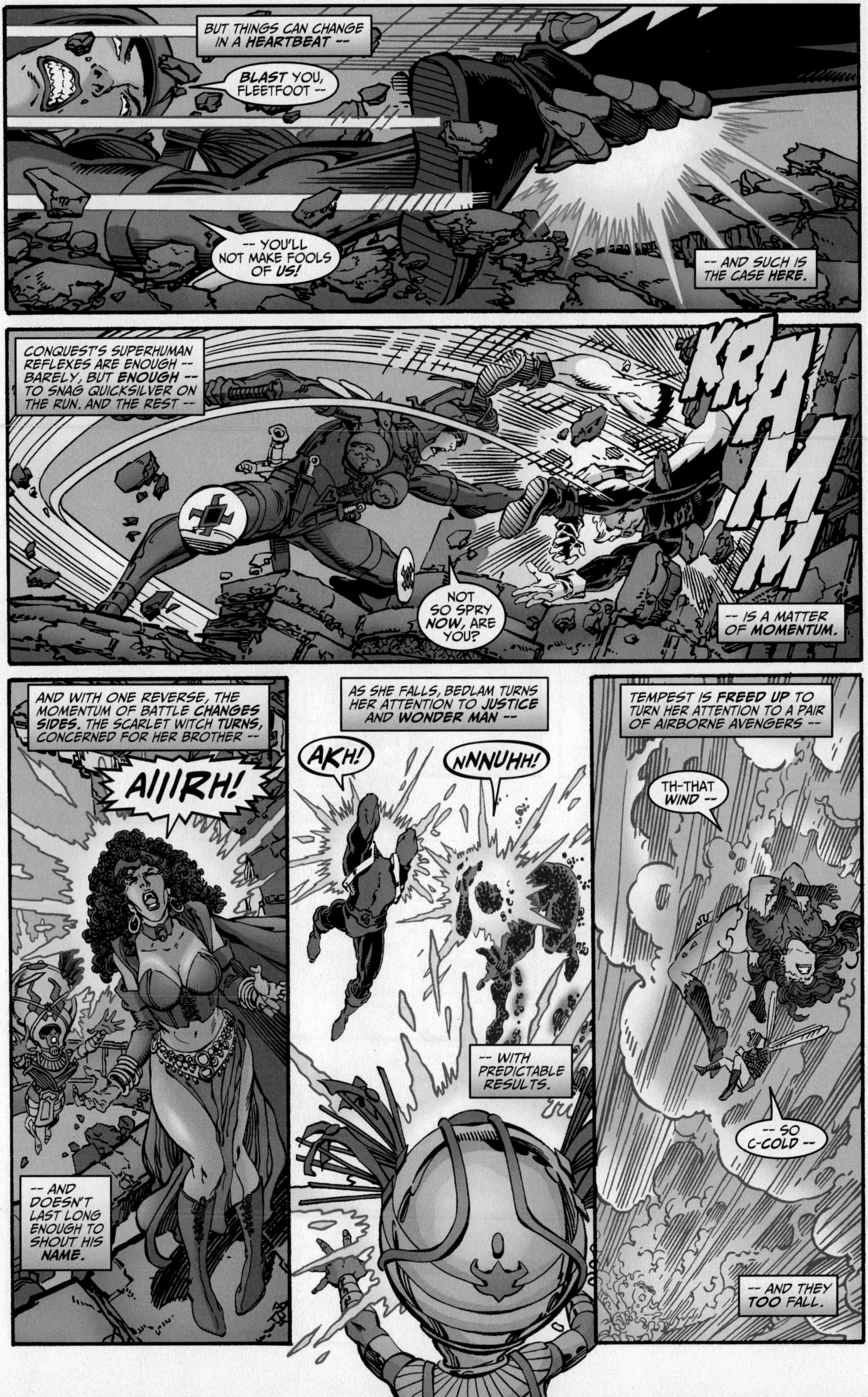

BUT THINGS CAN CHANGE IN A HEARTBEAT --
BLAST YOU, FLEETFOOT --
-- YOU'LL NOT MAKE FOOLS OF US!
-- AND SUCH IS THE CASE HERE.
CONQUEST'S SUPERHUMAN REFLEXES ARE ENOUGH -- BARELY, BUT ENOUGH -- TO SNAG QUICKSILVER ON THE RUN. AND THE REST --
KRAMMM
NOT SO SPRY NOW, ARE YOU?
-- IS A MATTER OF MOMENTUM.
AND WITH ONE REVERSE, THE MOMENTUM OF BATTLE CHANGES SIDES. THE SCARLET WITCH TURNS, CONCERNED FOR HER BROTHER --
AIIIRH!
-- AND DOESN'T LAST LONG ENOUGH TO SHOUT HIS NAME.
AS SHE FALLS, BEDLAM TURNS HER ATTENTION TO JUSTICE AND WONDER MAN --
AKH!
NNNUHH!
-- WITH PREDICTABLE RESULTS.
TEMPEST IS FREED UP TO TURN HER ATTENTION TO A PAIR OF AIRBORNE AVENGERS --
TH-THAT WIND --
-- SO C-COLD --
-- AND THEY TOO FALL.

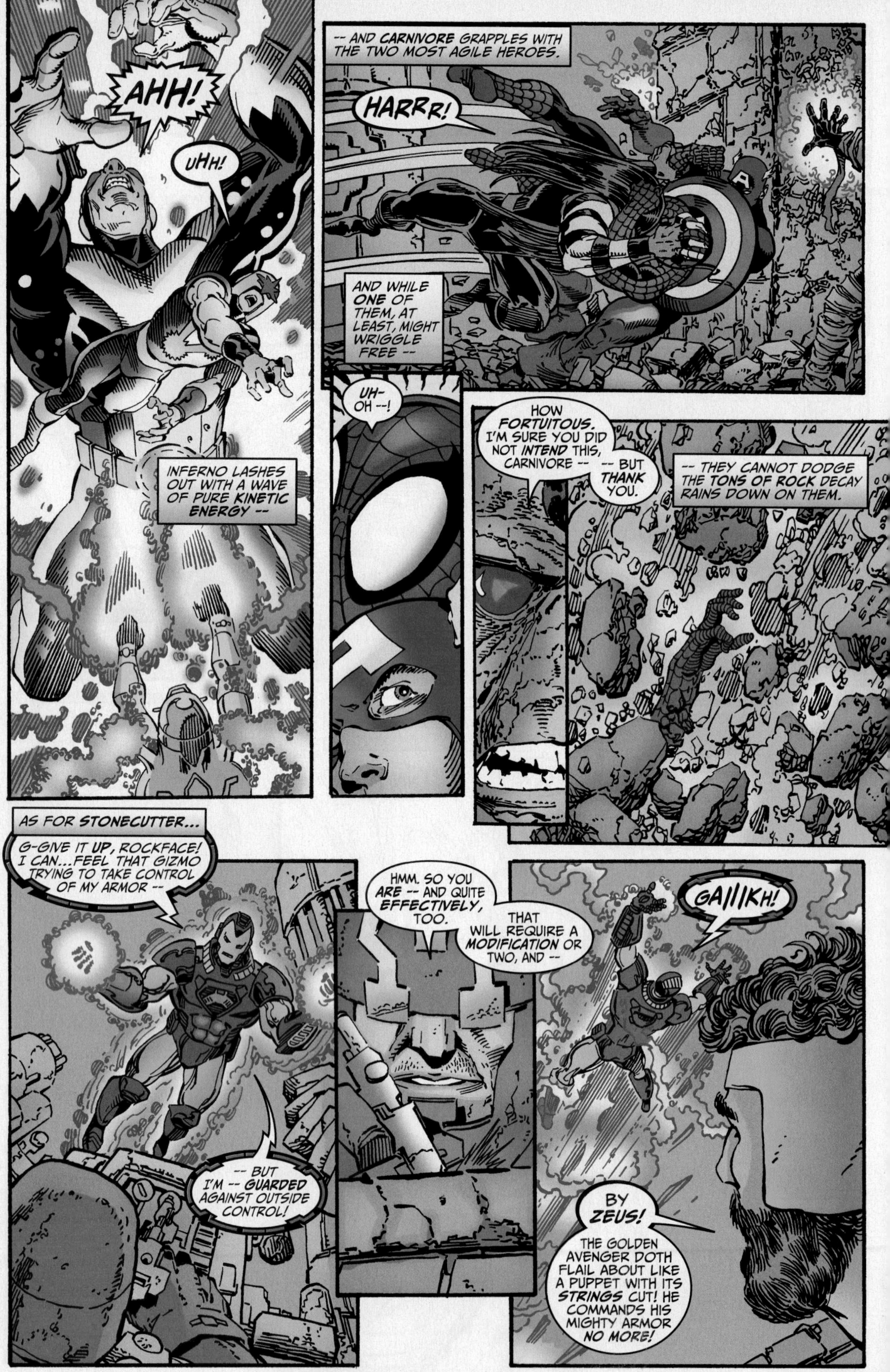
AHH!
UHH!
INFERNO LASHES OUT WITH A WAVE OF PURE KINETIC ENERGY --
-- AND CARNIVORE GRAPPLES WITH THE TWO MOST AGILE HEROES.
HARRR!
AND WHILE ONE OF THEM, AT LEAST, MIGHT WRIGGLE FREE --
UH-OH --!
HOW FORTUITOUS. I'M SURE YOU DID NOT INTEND THIS, CARNIVORE --
-- BUT THANK YOU.
-- THEY CANNOT DODGE THE TONS OF ROCK DECAY RAINS DOWN ON THEM.
AS FOR STONECUTTER...
G-GIVE IT UP, ROCKFACE! I CAN...FEEL THAT GIZMO TRYING TO TAKE CONTROL OF MY ARMOR --
-- BUT I'M -- GUARDED AGAINST OUTSIDE CONTROL!
HMM. SO YOU ARE -- AND QUITE EFFECTIVELY, TOO.
THAT WILL REQUIRE A MODIFICATION OR TWO, AND --
GAIIIKH!
BY ZEUS!
THE GOLDEN AVENGER DOTH FLAIL ABOUT LIKE A PUPPET WITH ITS STRINGS CUT! HE COMMANDS HIS MIGHTY ARMOR NO MORE!

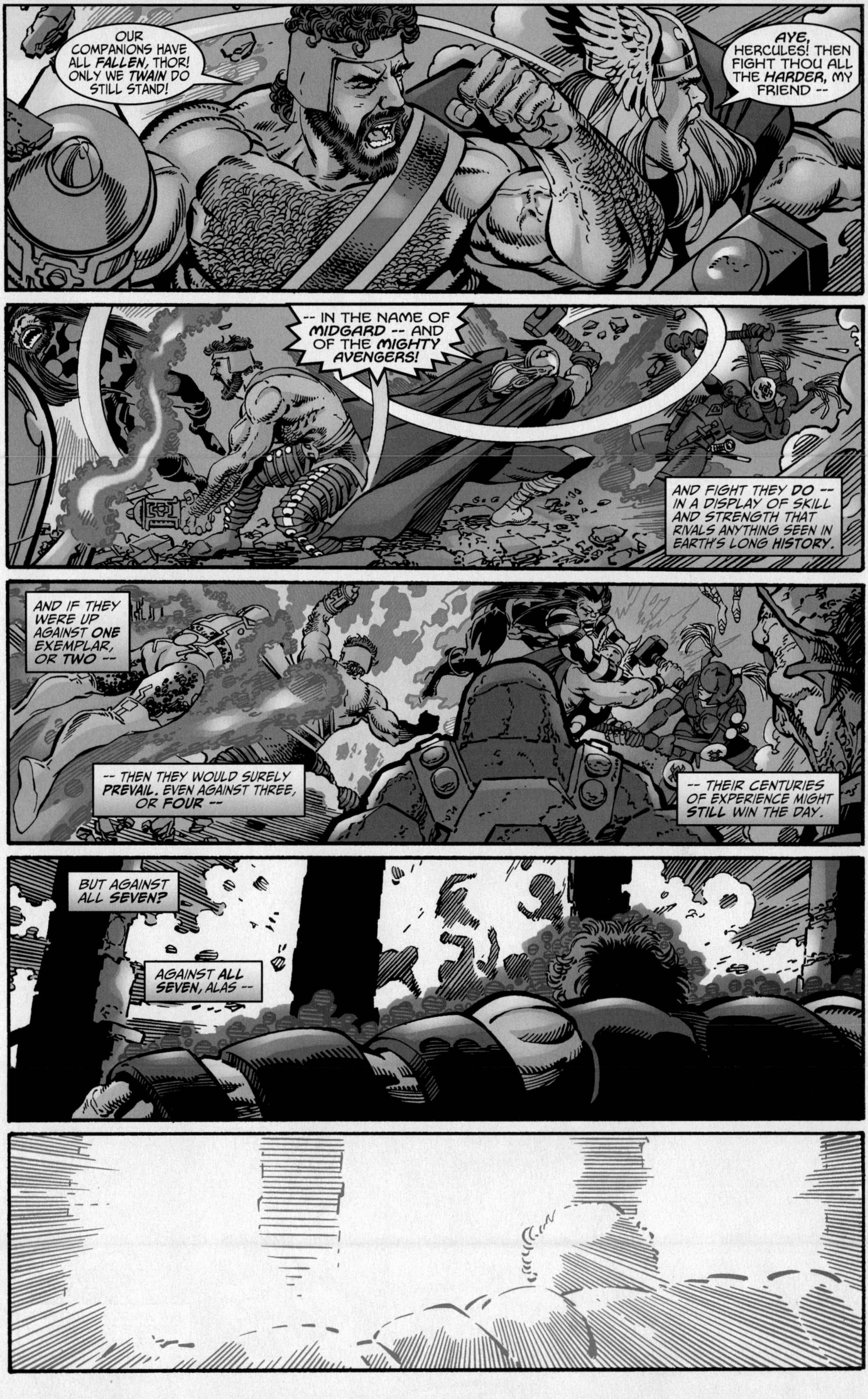
OUR COMPANIONS HAVE ALL FALLEN, THOR! ONLY WE TWAIN DO STILL STAND!
AYE, HERCULES! THEN FIGHT THOU ALL THE HARDER, MY FRIEND --
-- IN THE NAME OF MIDGARD -- AND OF THE MIGHTY AVENGERS!
AND FIGHT THEY DO -- IN A DISPLAY OF SKILL AND STRENGTH THAT RIVALS ANYTHING SEEN IN EARTH'S LONG HISTORY.
AND IF THEY WERE UP AGAINST ONE EXEMPLAR, OR TWO --
-- THEN THEY WOULD SURELY PREVAIL. EVEN AGAINST THREE, OR FOUR --
-- THEIR CENTURIES OF EXPERIENCE MIGHT STILL WIN THE DAY.
BUT AGAINST ALL SEVEN?
AGAINST ALL SEVEN, ALAS --

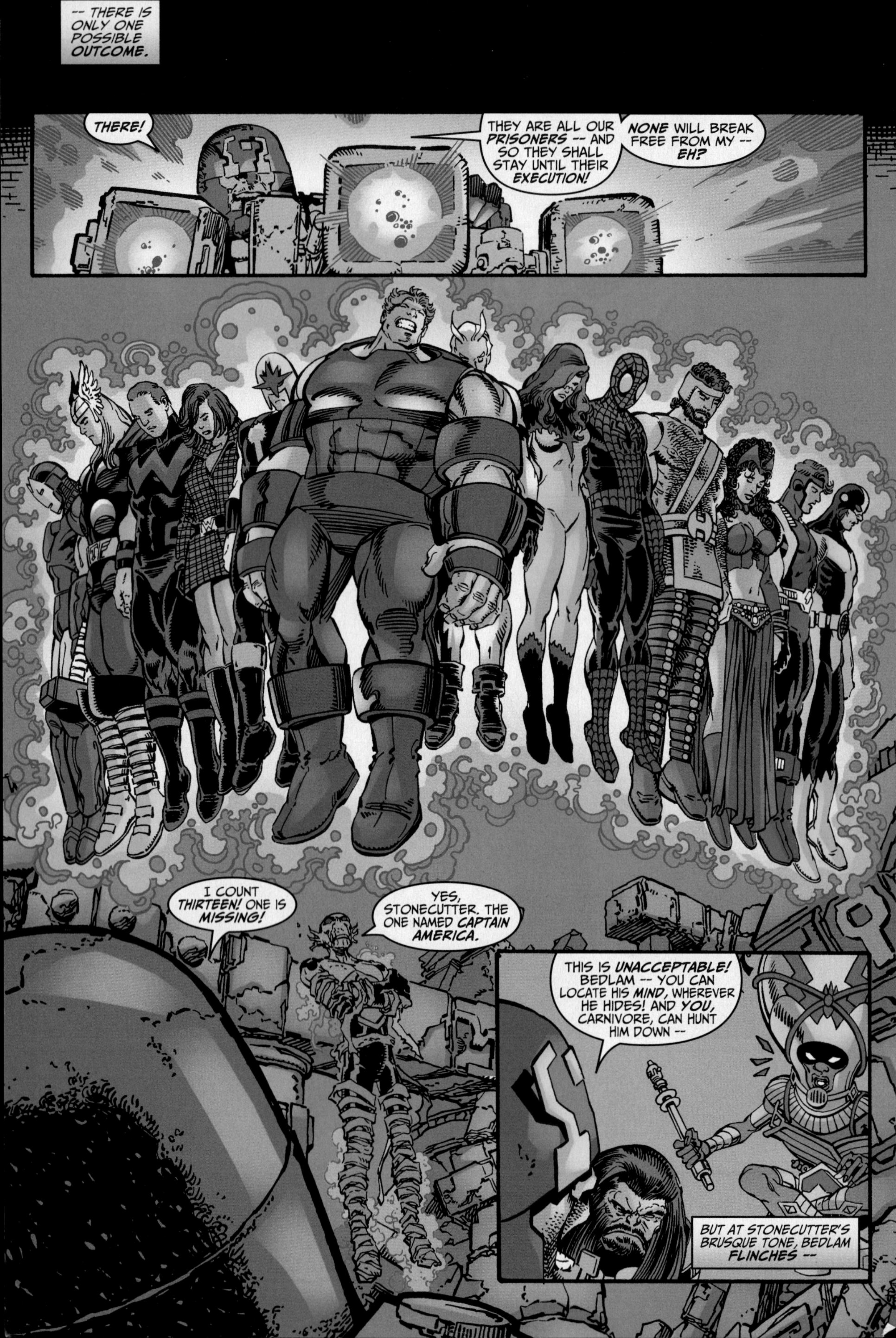
-- THERE IS ONLY ONE POSSIBLE OUTCOME.
THERE!
THEY ARE ALL OUR PRISONERS -- AND SO THEY SHALL STAY UNTIL THEIR EXECUTION!
NONE WILL BREAK FREE FROM MY -- EH?
I COUNT THIRTEEN! ONE IS MISSING!
YES, STONECUTTER. THE ONE NAMED CAPTAIN AMERICA.
THIS IS UNACCEPTABLE! BEDLAM -- YOU CAN LOCATE HIS MIND, WHEREVER HE HIDES! AND YOU, CARNIVORE, CAN HUNT HIM DOWN --
BUT AT STONECUTTER'S BRUSQUE TONE, BEDLAM FLINCHES --

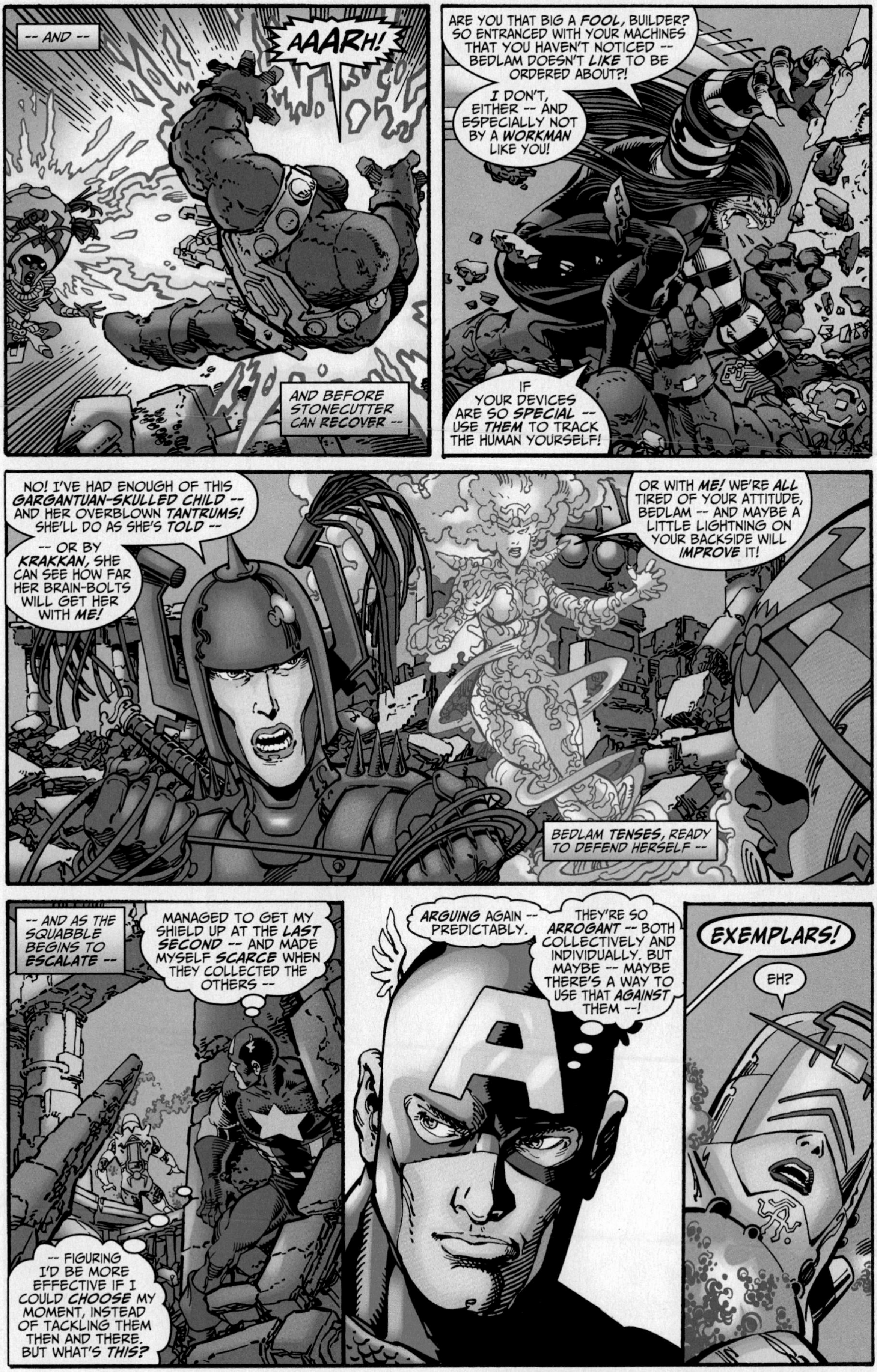
-- AND --
AAARH!
AND BEFORE STONECUTTER CAN RECOVER --
ARE YOU THAT BIG A FOOL, BUILDER? SO ENTRANCED WITH YOUR MACHINES THAT YOU HAVEN'T NOTICED -- BEDLAM DOESN'T LIKE TO BE ORDERED ABOUT?!
I DON'T, EITHER -- AND ESPECIALLY NOT BY A WORKMAN LIKE YOU!
IF YOUR DEVICES ARE SO SPECIAL -- USE THEM TO TRACK THE HUMAN YOURSELF!
NO! I'VE HAD ENOUGH OF THIS GARGANTUAN-SKULLED CHILD -- AND HER OVERBLOWN TANTRUMS! SHE'LL DO AS SHE'S TOLD --
-- OR BY KRAKKAN, SHE CAN SEE HOW FAR HER BRAIN-BOLTS WILL GET HER WITH ME!
OR WITH ME! WE'RE ALL TIRED OF YOUR ATTITUDE, BEDLAM -- AND MAYBE A LITTLE LIGHTNING ON YOUR BACKSIDE WILL IMPROVE IT!
BEDLAM TENSES, READY TO DEFEND HERSELF --
-- AND AS THE SQUABBLE BEGINS TO ESCALATE --
MANAGED TO GET MY SHIELD UP AT THE LAST SECOND -- AND MADE MYSELF SCARCE WHEN THEY COLLECTED THE OTHERS --
-- FIGURING I'D BE MORE EFFECTIVE IF I COULD CHOOSE MY MOMENT, INSTEAD OF TACKLING THEM THEN AND THERE. BUT WHAT'S THIS?
ARGUING AGAIN -- PREDICTABLY.
THEY'RE SO ARROGANT -- BOTH COLLECTIVELY AND INDIVIDUALLY. BUT MAYBE -- MAYBE THERE'S A WAY TO USE THAT AGAINST THEM --!
EXEMPLARS!
EH?

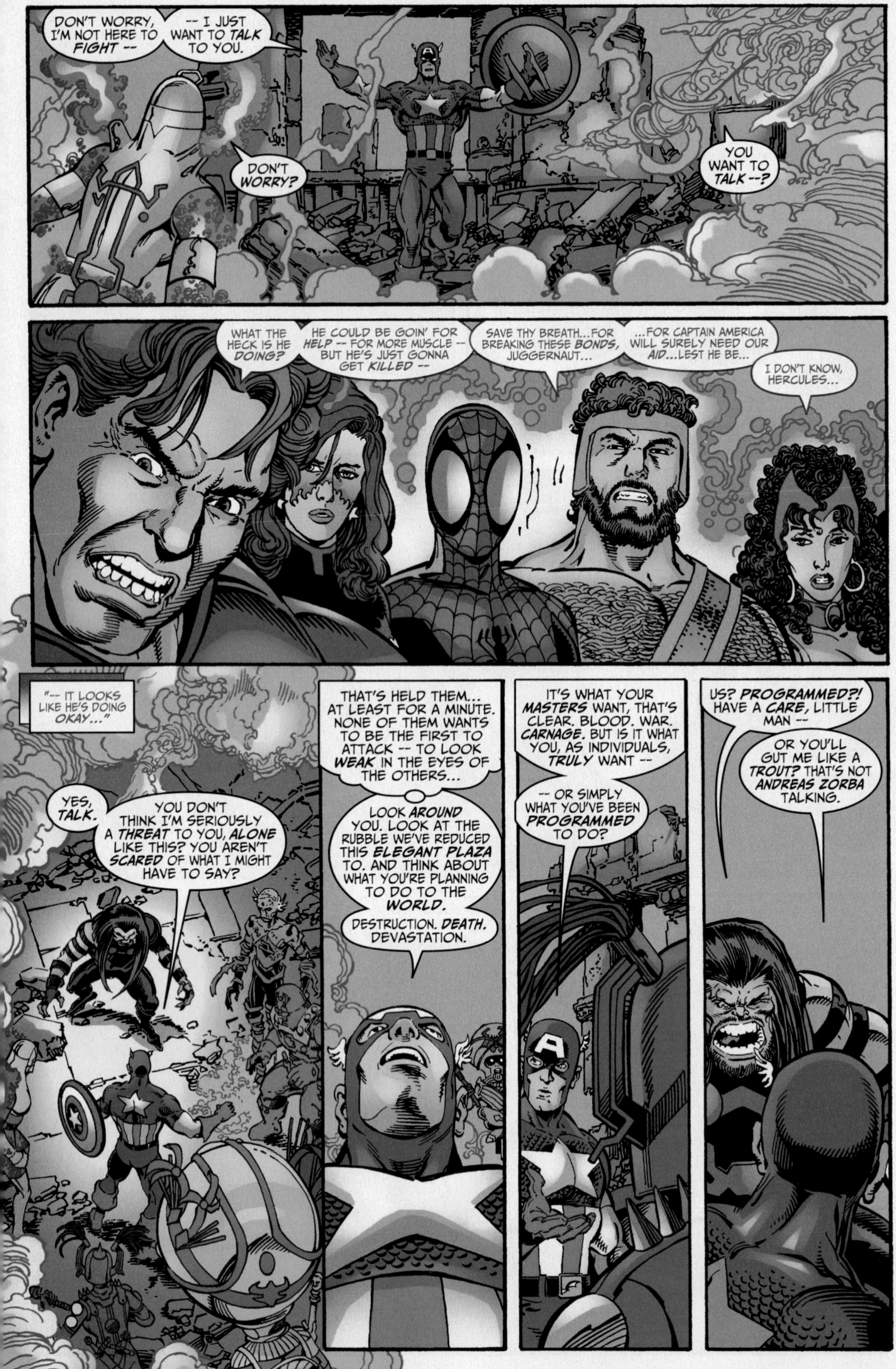
DON'T WORRY, I'M NOT HERE TO FIGHT --
-- I JUST WANT TO TALK TO YOU.
DON'T WORRY?
YOU WANT TO TALK --?
WHAT THE HECK IS HE DOING?
HE COULD BE GOIN' FOR HELP -- FOR MORE MUSCLE -- BUT HE'S JUST GONNA GET KILLED --
SAVE THY BREATH...FOR BREAKING THESE BONDS, JUGGERNAUT...
...FOR CAPTAIN AMERICA WILL SURELY NEED OUR AID...LEST HE BE...
I DON'T KNOW, HERCULES...
"-- IT LOOKS LIKE HE'S DOING OKAY..."
YES, TALK.
YOU DON'T THINK I'M SERIOUSLY A THREAT TO YOU, ALONE LIKE THIS? YOU AREN'T SCARED OF WHAT I MIGHT HAVE TO SAY?
THAT'S HELD THEM... AT LEAST FOR A MINUTE. NONE OF THEM WANTS TO BE THE FIRST TO ATTACK -- TO LOOK WEAK IN THE EYES OF THE OTHERS...
LOOK AROUND YOU. LOOK AT THE RUBBLE WE'VE REDUCED THIS ELEGANT PLAZA TO. AND THINK ABOUT WHAT YOU'RE PLANNING TO DO TO THE WORLD.
DESTRUCTION. DEATH. DEVASTATION.
IT'S WHAT YOUR MASTERS WANT, THAT'S CLEAR. BLOOD. WAR. CARNAGE. BUT IS IT WHAT YOU, AS INDIVIDUALS, TRULY WANT --
-- OR SIMPLY WHAT YOU'VE BEEN PROGRAMMED TO DO?
US? PROGRAMMED?! HAVE A CARE, LITTLE MAN --
OR YOU'LL GUT ME LIKE A TROUT? THAT'S NOT ANDREAS ZORBA TALKING.

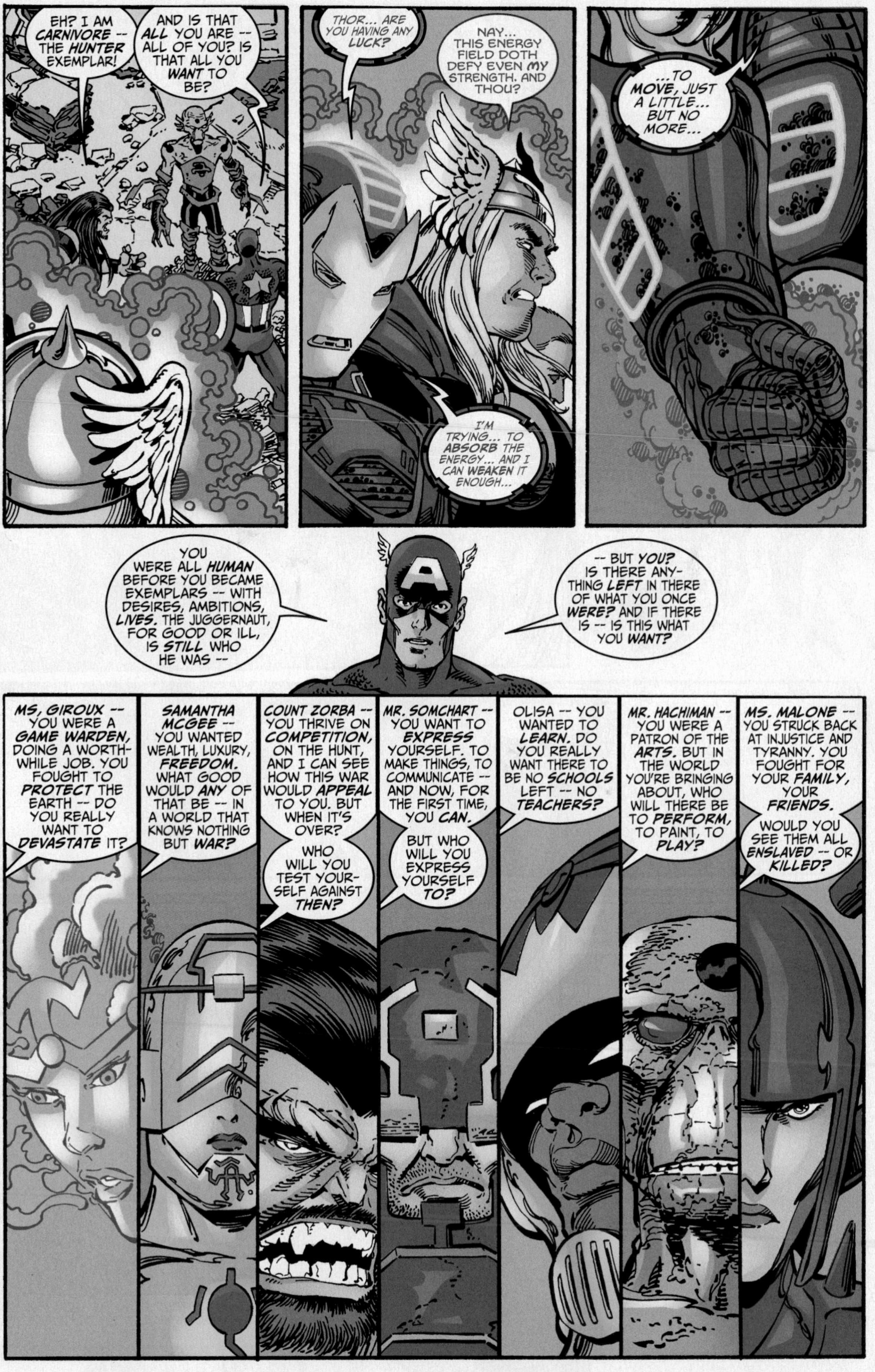
EH? I AM CARNIVORE -- THE HUNTER EXEMPLAR!
AND IS THAT ALL YOU ARE -- ALL OF YOU? IS THAT ALL YOU WANT TO BE?
THOR... ARE YOU HAVING ANY LUCK?
NAY... THIS ENERGY FIELD DOTH DEFY EVEN MY STRENGTH. AND THOU?
I'M TRYING... TO ABSORB THE ENERGY... AND I CAN WEAKEN IT ENOUGH...
...TO MOVE, JUST A LITTLE... BUT NO MORE...
YOU WERE ALL HUMAN BEFORE YOU BECAME EXEMPLARS -- WITH DESIRES, AMBITIONS, LIVES. THE JUGGERNAUT, FOR GOOD OR ILL, IS STILL WHO HE WAS --
-- BUT YOU? IS THERE ANY-THING LEFT IN THERE OF WHAT YOU ONCE WERE? AND IF THERE IS -- IS THIS WHAT YOU WANT?
MS. GIROUX -- YOU WERE A GAME WARDEN, DOING A WORTH-WHILE JOB. YOU FOUGHT TO PROTECT THE EARTH -- DO YOU REALLY WANT TO DEVASTATE IT?
SAMANTHA MCGEE -- YOU WANTED WEALTH, LUXURY, FREEDOM. WHAT GOOD WOULD ANY OF THAT BE -- IN A WORLD THAT KNOWS NOTHING BUT WAR?
COUNT ZORBA -- YOU THRIVE ON COMPETITION, ON THE HUNT, AND I CAN SEE HOW THIS WAR WOULD APPEAL TO YOU. BUT WHEN IT'S OVER?
WHO WILL YOU TEST YOUR-SELF AGAINST THEN?
MR. SOMCHART -- YOU WANT TO EXPRESS YOURSELF. TO MAKE THINGS, TO COMMUNICATE -- AND NOW, FOR THE FIRST TIME, YOU CAN.
BUT WHO WILL YOU EXPRESS YOURSELF TO?
OLISA -- YOU WANTED TO LEARN. DO YOU REALLY WANT THERE TO BE NO SCHOOLS LEFT -- NO TEACHERS?
MR. HACHIMAN -- YOU WERE A PATRON OF THE ARTS. BUT IN THE WORLD YOU'RE BRINGING ABOUT, WHO WILL THERE BE TO PERFORM, TO PAINT, TO PLAY?
MS. MALONE -- YOU STRUCK BACK AT INJUSTICE AND TYRANNY. YOU FOUGHT FOR YOUR FAMILY, YOUR FRIENDS.
WOULD YOU SEE THEM ALL ENSLAVED -- OR KILLED?

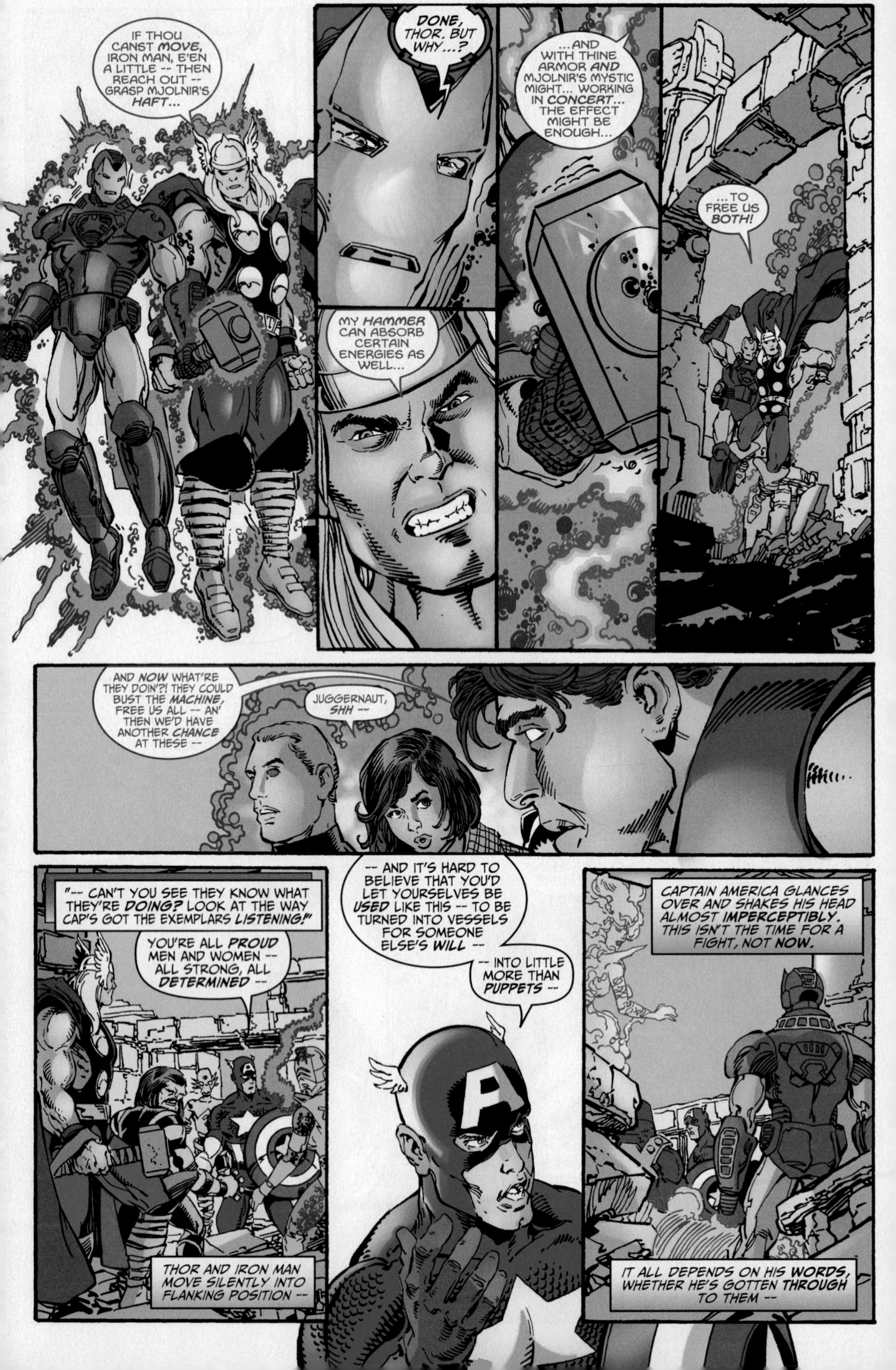
IF THOU CANST MOVE, IRON MAN, E'EN A LITTLE -- THEN REACH OUT -- GRASP MJOLNIR'S HAFT...
DONE, THOR. BUT WHY...?
MY HAMMER CAN ABSORB CERTAIN ENERGIES AS WELL...
...AND WITH THINE ARMOR AND MJOLNIR'S MYSTIC MIGHT... WORKING IN CONCERT... THE EFFECT MIGHT BE ENOUGH...
...TO FREE US BOTH!
AND NOW WHAT'RE THEY DOIN'?! THEY COULD BUST THE MACHINE, FREE US ALL -- AN' THEN WE'D HAVE ANOTHER CHANCE AT THESE --
JUGGERNAUT, SHH --
"-- CAN'T YOU SEE THEY KNOW WHAT THEY'RE DOING? LOOK AT THE WAY CAP'S GOT THE EXEMPLARS LISTENING!"
YOU'RE ALL PROUD MEN AND WOMEN -- ALL STRONG, ALL DETERMINED --
THOR AND IRON MAN MOVE SILENTLY INTO FLANKING POSITION --
-- AND IT'S HARD TO BELIEVE THAT YOU'D LET YOURSELVES BE USED LIKE THIS -- TO BE TURNED INTO VESSELS FOR SOMEONE ELSE'S WILL --
-- INTO LITTLE MORE THAN PUPPETS --
CAPTAIN AMERICA GLANCES OVER AND SHAKES HIS HEAD ALMOST IMPERCEPTIBLY. THIS ISN'T THE TIME FOR A FIGHT, NOT NOW.
IT ALL DEPENDS ON HIS WORDS, WHETHER HE'S GOTTEN THROUGH TO THEM --

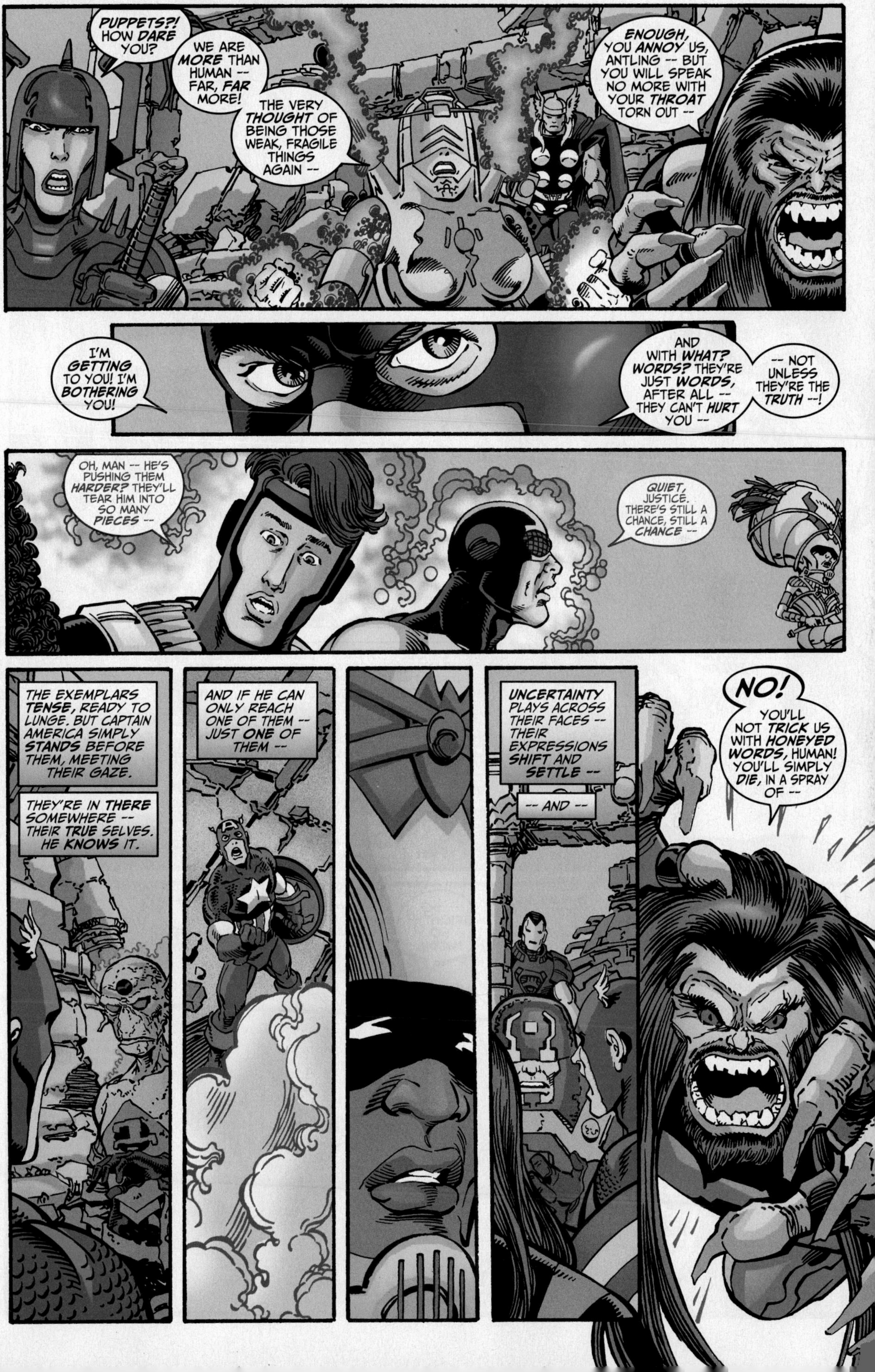
PUPPETS?! HOW DARE YOU?
WE ARE MORE THAN HUMAN -- FAR, FAR MORE!
THE VERY THOUGHT OF BEING THOSE WEAK, FRAGILE THINGS AGAIN --
ENOUGH, YOU ANNOY US, ANTLING -- BUT YOU WILL SPEAK NO MORE WITH YOUR THROAT TORN OUT --
I'M GETTING TO YOU! I'M BOTHERING YOU!
AND WITH WHAT? WORDS? THEY'RE JUST WORDS, AFTER ALL -- THEY CAN'T HURT YOU --
-- NOT UNLESS THEY'RE THE TRUTH --!
OH, MAN -- HE'S PUSHING THEM HARDER? THEY'LL TEAR HIM INTO SO MANY PIECES --
QUIET, JUSTICE. THERE'S STILL A CHANCE, STILL A CHANCE --
THE EXEMPLARS TENSE, READY TO LUNGE. BUT CAPTAIN AMERICA SIMPLY STANDS BEFORE THEM, MEETING THEIR GAZE.
THEY'RE IN THERE SOMEWHERE -- THEIR TRUE SELVES. HE KNOWS IT.
AND IF HE CAN ONLY REACH ONE OF THEM -- JUST ONE OF THEM --
UNCERTAINTY PLAYS ACROSS THEIR FACES -- THEIR EXPRESSIONS SHIFT AND SETTLE --
-- AND --
NO! YOU'LL NOT TRICK US WITH HONEYED WORDS, HUMAN! YOU'LL SIMPLY DIE, IN A SPRAY OF --

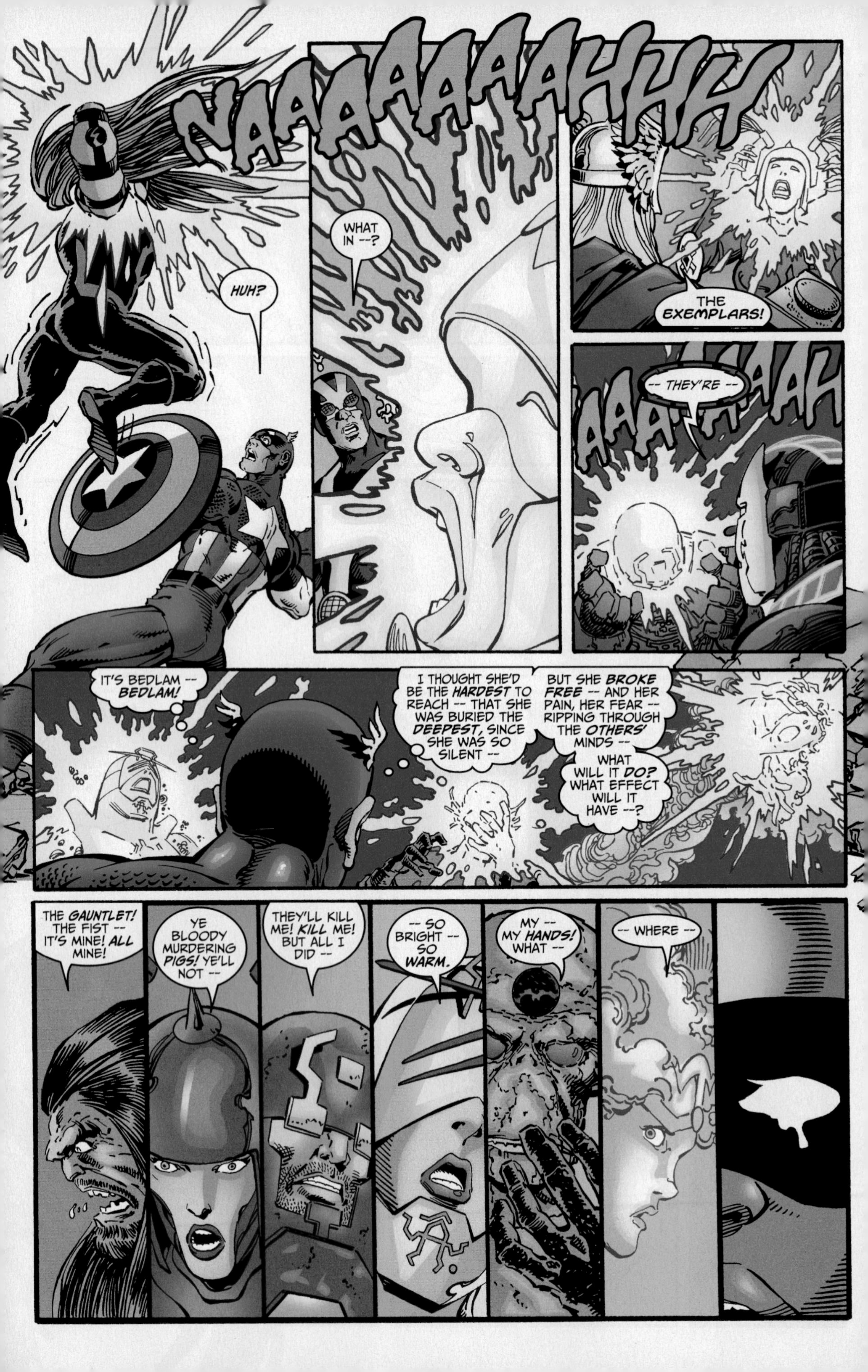
NAAAAAAAHHH
HUH?
WHAT IN --?
THE EXEMPLARS!
-- THEY'RE --
IT'S BEDLAM -- BEDLAM!
I THOUGHT SHE'D BE THE HARDEST TO REACH -- THAT SHE WAS BURIED THE DEEPEST, SINCE SHE WAS SO SILENT --
BUT SHE BROKE FREE -- AND HER PAIN, HER FEAR -- RIPPING THROUGH THE OTHERS' MINDS --
WHAT WILL IT DO? WHAT EFFECT WILL IT HAVE --?
THE GAUNTLET! THE FIST -- IT'S MINE! ALL MINE!
YE BLOODY MURDERING PIGS! YE'LL NOT --
THEY'LL KILL ME! KILL ME! BUT ALL I DID --
-- SO BRIGHT -- SO WARM.
MY -- MY HANDS! WHAT --
-- WHERE --

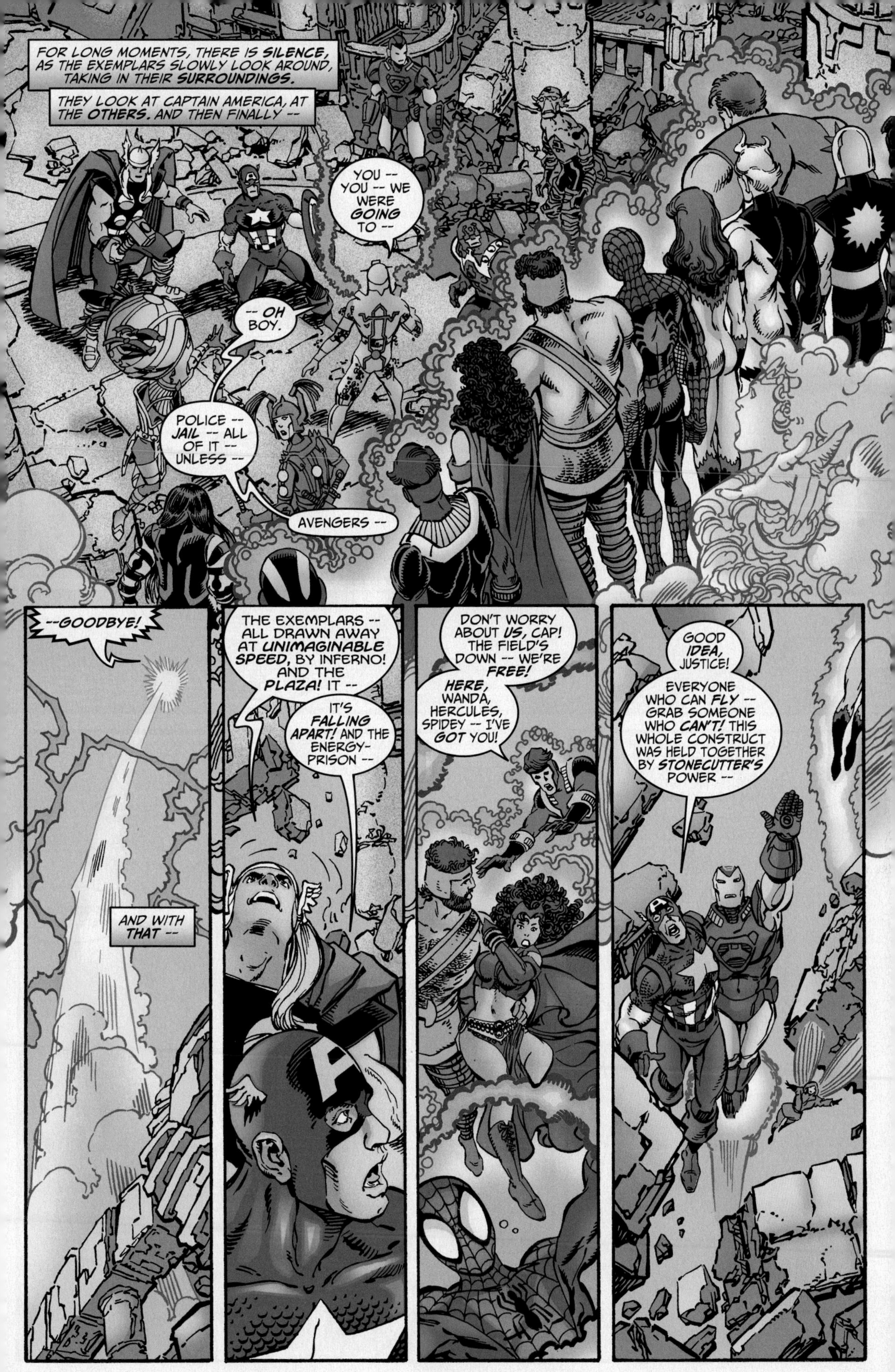
FOR LONG MOMENTS, THERE IS SILENCE, AS THE EXEMPLARS SLOWLY LOOK AROUND, TAKING IN THEIR SURROUNDINGS.
THEY LOOK AT CAPTAIN AMERICA, AT THE OTHERS. AND THEN FINALLY --
YOU -- YOU -- WE WERE GOING TO --
-- OH BOY.
POLICE -- JAIL -- ALL OF IT -- UNLESS --
AVENGERS --
--GOODBYE!
AND WITH THAT --
THE EXEMPLARS -- ALL DRAWN AWAY AT UNIMAGINABLE SPEED, BY INFERNO! AND THE PLAZA! IT --
IT'S FALLING APART! AND THE ENERGY-PRISON --
DON'T WORRY ABOUT US, CAP! THE FIELD'S DOWN -- WE'RE FREE!
HERE, WANDA, HERCULES, SPIDEY -- I'VE GOT YOU!
GOOD IDEA, JUSTICE!
EVERYONE WHO CAN FLY -- GRAB SOMEONE WHO CAN'T! THIS WHOLE CONSTRUCT WAS HELD TOGETHER BY STONECUTTER'S POWER --

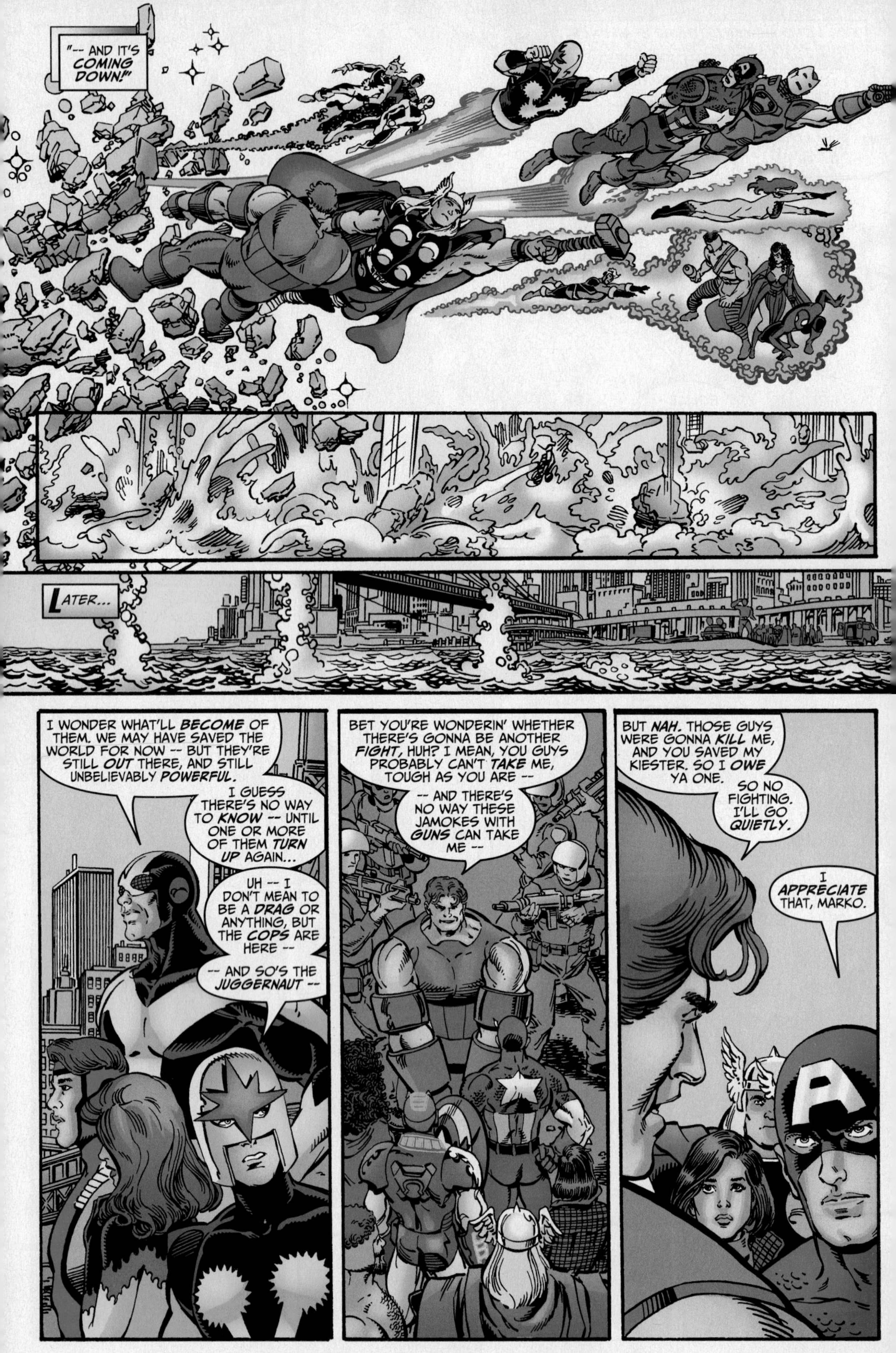
"-- AND IT'S COMING DOWN!"
LATER...
I WONDER WHAT'LL BECOME OF THEM. WE MAY HAVE SAVED THE WORLD FOR NOW -- BUT THEY'RE STILL OUT THERE, AND STILL UNBELIEVABLY POWERFUL.
I GUESS THERE'S NO WAY TO KNOW -- UNTIL ONE OR MORE OF THEM TURN UP AGAIN...
UH -- I DON'T MEAN TO BE A DRAG OR ANYTHING, BUT THE COPS ARE HERE --
-- AND SO'S THE JUGGERNAUT --
BET YOU'RE WONDERIN' WHETHER THERE'S GONNA BE ANOTHER FIGHT, HUH? I MEAN, YOU GUYS PROBABLY CAN'T TAKE ME, TOUGH AS YOU ARE --
-- AND THERE'S NO WAY THESE JAMOKES WITH GUNS CAN TAKE ME --
BUT NAH. THOSE GUYS WERE GONNA KILL ME, AND YOU SAVED MY KIESTER. SO I OWE YA ONE.
SO NO FIGHTING. I'LL GO QUIETLY.
I APPRECIATE THAT, MARKO.

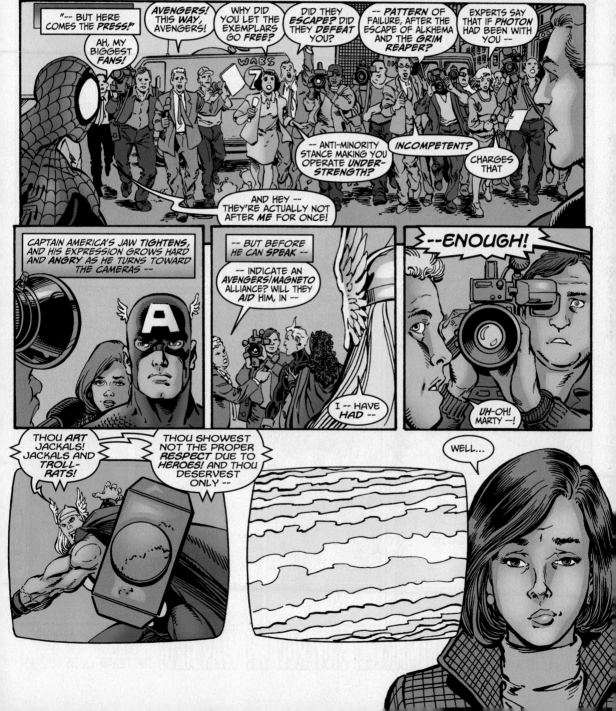

"BESIDES," MUTTERS CAIN MARKO TO HIMSELF AS HE'S TAKEN AWAY, "I DON'T NEED THE *HASSLE.* EASIER TO BUST FREE AND TAKE OFF --

"-- WHEN THE COPS HAVE ME WELL *AWAY* FROM HERE..."

WELL, THAT'S *THAT.* WE'D BETTER GET BACK TO THE *MANSION,* FILE A REPORT ON --

AH, CAP? IT'S NOT AS OVER AS YOU *THINK.* DON'T LOOK NOW --

"-- BUT HERE COMES THE *PRESS!*"

AH, MY BIGGEST FANS!

AVENGERS! THIS *WAY,* AVENGERS!

WHY DID YOU LET THE EXEMPLARS GO FREE?

DID THEY *ESCAPE?* DID THEY *DEFEAT* YOU?

-- *PATTERN* OF FAILURE, AFTER THE ESCAPE OF ALKHEMA AND THE *GRIM REAPER?*

EXPERTS SAY THAT IF *PHOTON* HAD BEEN WITH YOU --

-- ANTI-MINORITY STANCE MAKING YOU OPERATE *UNDER-STRENGTH?*

INCOMPETENT?

CHARGES THAT

AND HEY -- THEY'RE ACTUALLY NOT AFTER *ME* FOR ONCE!

CAPTAIN AMERICA'S JAW TIGHTENS, AND HIS EXPRESSION GROWS HARD AND *ANGRY* AS HE TURNS TOWARD THE CAMERAS --

-- BUT BEFORE HE CAN *SPEAK* --

-- INDICATE AN *AVENGERS/MAGNETO* ALLIANCE? WILL THEY *AID* HIM, IN --

I -- HAVE HAD --

--ENOUGH!

UH-OH! MARTY --!

THOU *ART* JACKALS! JACKALS AND TROLL-RATS!

THOU SHOWEST NOT THE PROPER *RESPECT* DUE TO *HEROES!* AND THOU DESERVEST ONLY --

WELL...

...THAT DIDN'T GO OVER SO WELL, NOW DID IT? I THINK IT'S ON *EVERY* CHANNEL...

-- SCENE AT THE *EAST RIVER* TODAY, AS THE AVENGERS *ASSAULTED* NEWS REPORTERS AFTER --

TREAD *LIGHTLY*, WOMAN. THE THUNDER GOD WILL *NOT* BE --

SORRY, THOR -- DIDN'T MEAN TO *SNIP*. BUT --

BUT WE'RE USED TO HAVING *GOOD RELATIONS* WITH THE PUBLIC AND THE PRESS. AND NOW WE *DON'T*. AND THAT LEADS TO WHAT I'VE GOT TO *SAY*.

WE'VE HAD MUTANTS ON THE TEAM *BEFORE*. WE'VE HAD ALL-WHITE ROSTERS. AND IT'S *NEVER* BEEN LIKE THIS. IT SEEMS OBVIOUS TO ME --

-- THAT SOMEONE IS *TARGETING* US, USING WHATEVER DISCONTENT THEY CAN FIND -- WHATEVER THEY CAN DISTORT OR EXAGGERATE -- *AGAINST* US.

MAYBE IT *IS* THE TRIUNES. MAYBE NOT. BUT EITHER WAY, I'M AT A *LOSS*.

ALL I KNOW HOW TO *DO*, TO CONCENTRATE ON, IS LEADING THIS TEAM TO *VICTORY*.

BUT WE FACE A FOE THAT CAN'T BE FOUGHT *DIRECTLY* -- A FOE THAT IS TURNING OUR EVERY ACT INTO A *BLACK MARK*, AN APPEARANCE OF *WRONGDOING*.

THEY KNOW MY APPROACH, AND THEY'RE USING IT *AGAINST* US, PREDICTING MY SILENCE AND SURE THEIR CHARGES WILL GO *UNANSWERED*.

THE AVENGERS NEED *BETTER* THAN THAT. THEY NEED A LEADER WHO CAN *COMBAT* THIS KIND OF THREAT, WHO *KNOWS* THIS WORLD, LIKE IRON MAN DOES.

ACCORDINGLY --

-- I'M *LEAVING* THE AVENGERS, EFFECTIVE *IMMEDIATELY*. LET *ME* TAKE THE BLAME FOR OUR SO-CALLED FAILURES -- WHILE YOU *REORGANIZE* AROUND SOMEONE WHO CAN DO A *BETTER JOB* IN THE KIND OF BATTLE THE AVENGERS FIND THEMSELVES IN *NOW*.

AND BY THE TIME THEY CAN DO MORE THAN *GASP* --

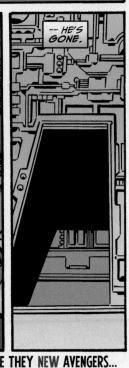

-- HE'S GONE.

NEXT **ANT-MAN! CAPTAIN MARVEL! SILVERCLAW! WARBIRD!** ARE THEY NEW AVENGERS... OR SOMETHING ELSE? THE TRIUNE CRISIS DEEPENS!

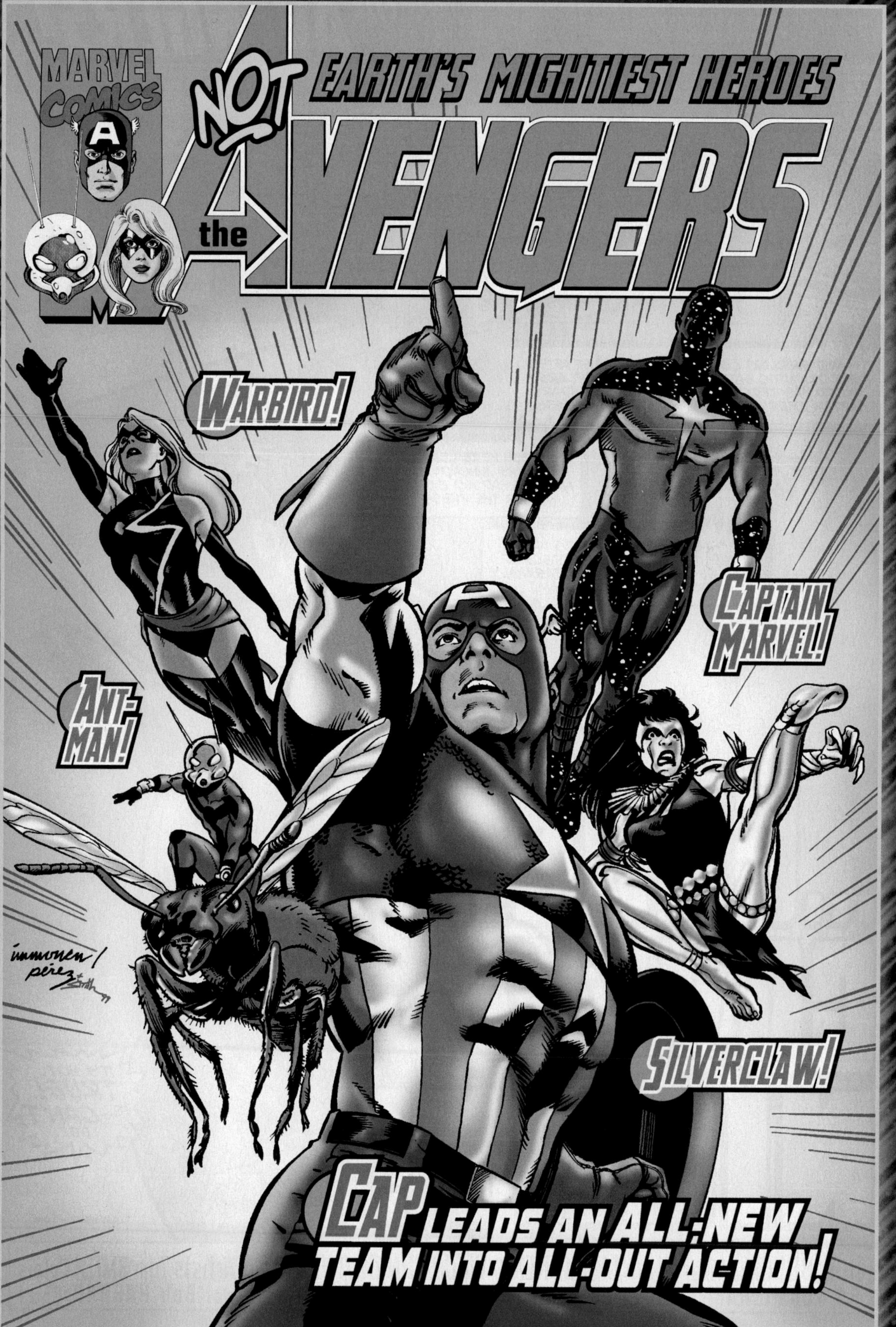
MARVEL COMICS
NOT EARTH'S MIGHTIEST HEROES
the AVENGERS
WARBIRD!
CAPTAIN MARVEL!
ANT-MAN!
SILVERCLAW!
CAP LEADS AN ALL-NEW TEAM INTO ALL-OUT ACTION!

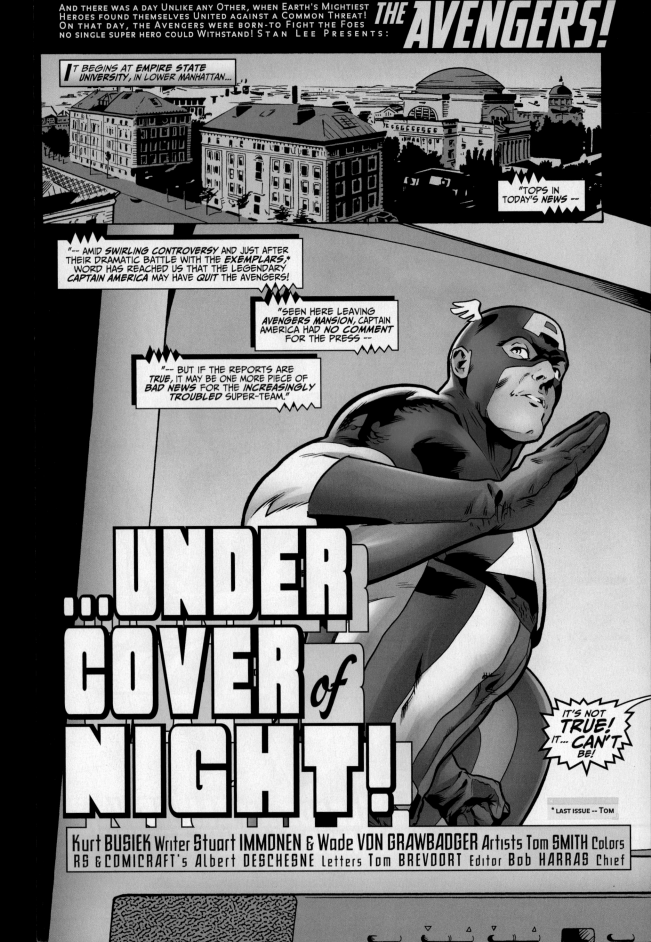

AND THERE WAS A DAY UNLIKE ANY OTHER, WHEN EARTH'S MIGHTIEST HEROES FOUND THEMSELVES UNITED AGAINST A COMMON THREAT! ON THAT DAY, THE AVENGERS WERE BORN-TO FIGHT THE FOES NO SINGLE SUPER HERO COULD WITHSTAND! STAN LEE PRESENTS:

THE AVENGERS!

IT BEGINS AT EMPIRE STATE UNIVERSITY, IN LOWER MANHATTAN...

"TOPS IN TODAY'S NEWS --

"-- AMID *SWIRLING CONTROVERSY* AND JUST AFTER THEIR DRAMATIC BATTLE WITH THE *EXEMPLARS,** WORD HAS REACHED US THAT THE LEGENDARY *CAPTAIN AMERICA* MAY HAVE *QUIT* THE AVENGERS!

"SEEN HERE LEAVING *AVENGERS MANSION,* CAPTAIN AMERICA HAD *NO COMMENT* FOR THE PRESS --

"-- BUT IF THE REPORTS ARE *TRUE,* IT MAY BE ONE MORE PIECE OF *BAD NEWS* FOR THE *INCREASINGLY TROUBLED* SUPER-TEAM."

...UNDER COVER of NIGHT!

IT'S NOT *TRUE!* IT... *CAN'T* BE!

* LAST ISSUE -- TOM

Kurt BUSIEK Writer   Stuart IMMONEN & Wade VON GRAWBADGER Artists   Tom SMITH Colors
RS & COMICRAFT's Albert DESCHESNE Letters   Tom BREVOORT Editor   Bob HARRAS Chief

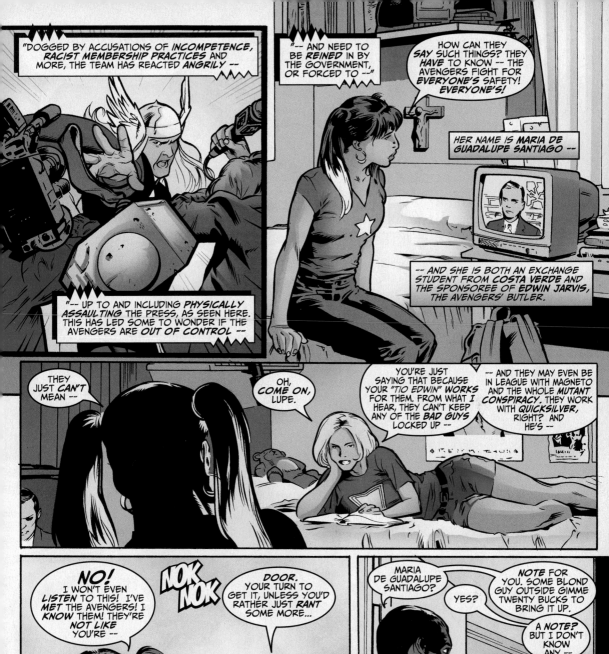

"DOGGED BY ACCUSATIONS OF *INCOMPETENCE,* *RACIST* MEMBERSHIP PRACTICES AND MORE, THE TEAM HAS REACTED *ANGRILY* --"

"-- AND NEED TO BE *REINED* IN BY THE GOVERNMENT, OR FORCED TO --"

HOW CAN THEY *SAY* SUCH THINGS? THEY *HAVE* TO KNOW -- THE AVENGERS FIGHT FOR *EVERYONE'S* SAFETY! *EVERYONE'S!*

HER NAME IS *MARIA DE GUADALUPE SANTIAGO* --

"-- UP TO AND INCLUDING *PHYSICALLY* *ASSAULTING* THE PRESS, AS SEEN HERE. THIS HAS LED SOME TO WONDER IF THE AVENGERS ARE *OUT OF CONTROL* --"

-- AND SHE IS BOTH AN EXCHANGE STUDENT FROM *COSTA VERDE* AND THE *SPONSOREE* OF *EDWIN JARVIS,* THE AVENGERS' BUTLER.

THEY JUST *CAN'T* MEAN --

OH, COME ON, LUPE.

YOU'RE JUST SAYING THAT BECAUSE YOUR *"TIO EDWIN"* WORKS FOR THEM. FROM WHAT I HEAR, THEY CAN'T KEEP ANY OF THE *BAD GUYS* LOCKED UP --

-- AND THEY MAY EVEN BE IN LEAGUE WITH *MAGNETO* AND THE WHOLE *MUTANT CONSPIRACY.* THEY WORK WITH *QUICKSILVER,* RIGHT? AND HE'S --

NO! I WON'T EVEN *LISTEN* TO THIS! I'VE *MET* THE AVENGERS! I *KNOW* THEM! THEY'RE *NOT LIKE* YOU'RE --

NOK NOK

DOOR. YOUR TURN TO GET IT, UNLESS YOU'D RATHER JUST *RANT* SOME MORE...

MARIA DE GUADALUPE SANTIAGO?

YES?

NOTE FOR YOU. SOME BLOND GUY OUTSIDE GIMME *TWENTY BUCKS* TO BRING IT UP.

A *NOTE?* BUT I DON'T *KNOW* ANY --

HER NAME IS *MARIA DE GUADALUPE SANTIAGO* --

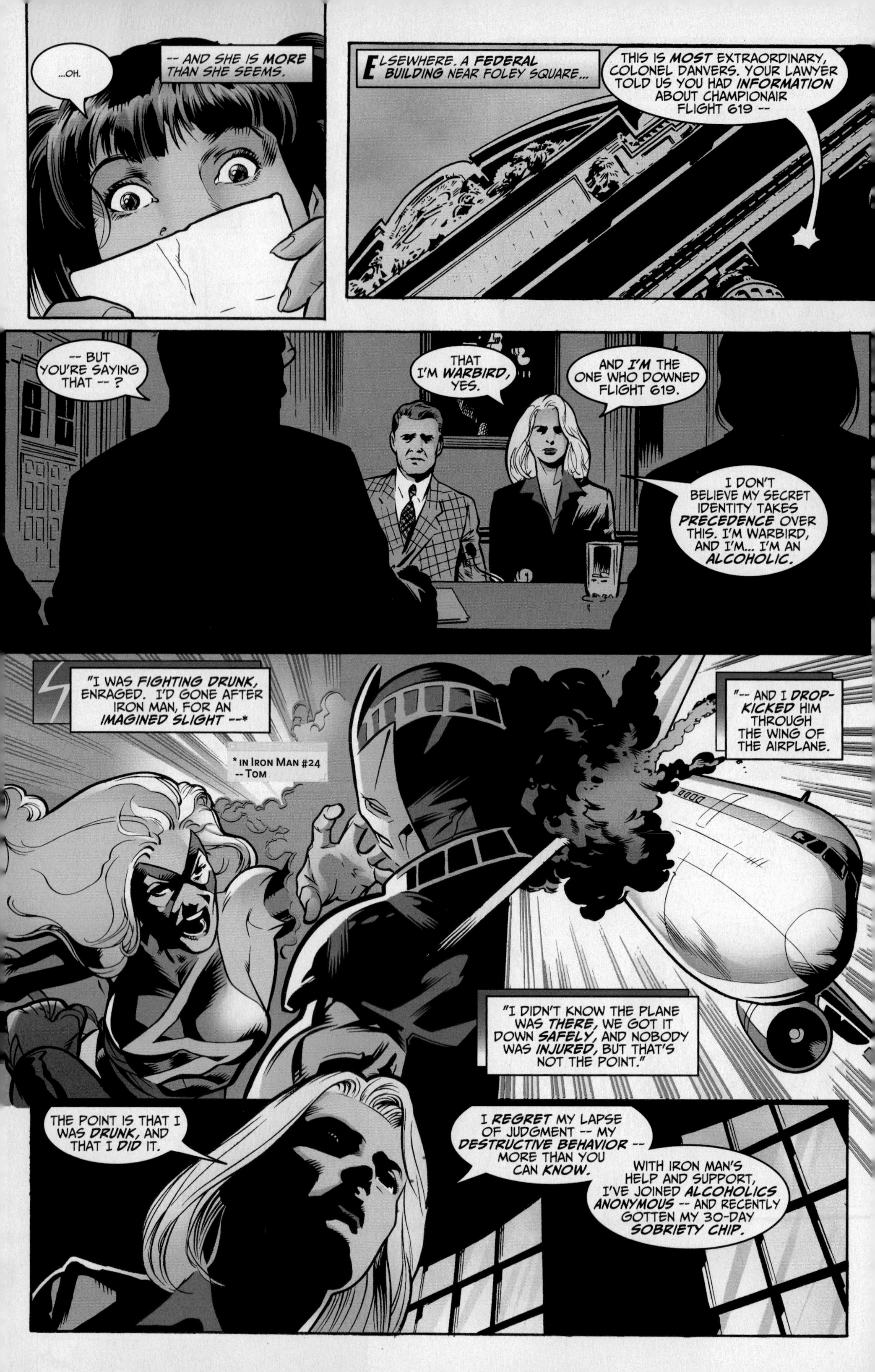
...OH.
-- AND SHE IS MORE THAN SHE SEEMS.
ELSEWHERE. A FEDERAL BUILDING NEAR FOLEY SQUARE...
THIS IS MOST EXTRAORDINARY, COLONEL DANVERS. YOUR LAWYER TOLD US YOU HAD INFORMATION ABOUT CHAMPIONAIR FLIGHT 619 --
-- BUT YOU'RE SAYING THAT -- ?
THAT I'M WARBIRD, YES.
AND I'M THE ONE WHO DOWNED FLIGHT 619.
I DON'T BELIEVE MY SECRET IDENTITY TAKES PRECEDENCE OVER THIS. I'M WARBIRD, AND I'M... I'M AN ALCOHOLIC.
"I WAS FIGHTING DRUNK, ENRAGED. I'D GONE AFTER IRON MAN, FOR AN IMAGINED SLIGHT --*
* IN IRON MAN #24 -- TOM
"-- AND I DROP-KICKED HIM THROUGH THE WING OF THE AIRPLANE.
"I DIDN'T KNOW THE PLANE WAS THERE, WE GOT IT DOWN SAFELY, AND NOBODY WAS INJURED, BUT THAT'S NOT THE POINT."
THE POINT IS THAT I WAS DRUNK, AND THAT I DID IT.
I REGRET MY LAPSE OF JUDGMENT -- MY DESTRUCTIVE BEHAVIOR -- MORE THAN YOU CAN KNOW.
WITH IRON MAN'S HELP AND SUPPORT, I'VE JOINED ALCOHOLICS ANONYMOUS -- AND RECENTLY GOTTEN MY 30-DAY SOBRIETY CHIP.

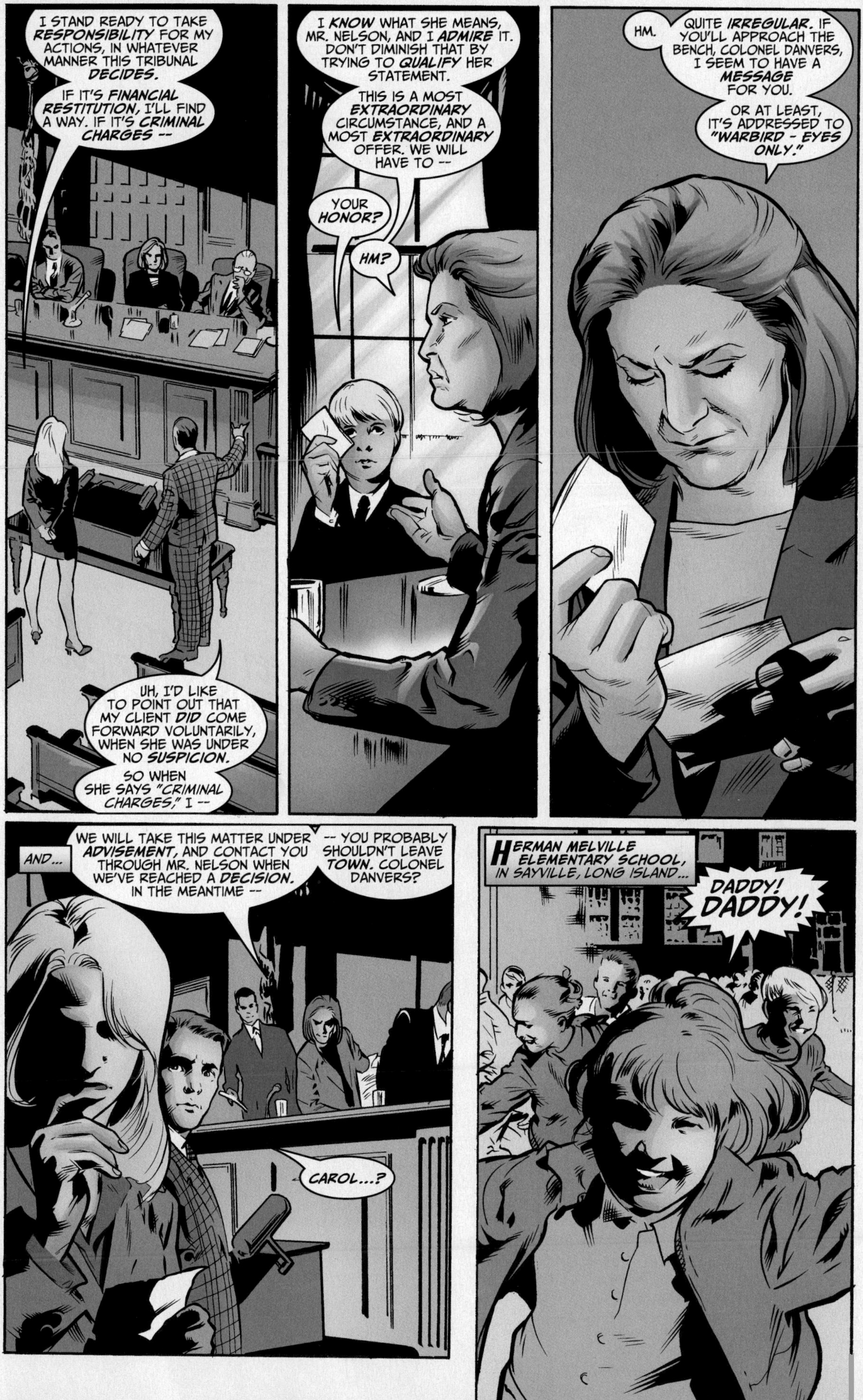
I STAND READY TO TAKE RESPONSIBILITY FOR MY ACTIONS, IN WHATEVER MANNER THIS TRIBUNAL DECIDES.
IF IT'S FINANCIAL RESTITUTION, I'LL FIND A WAY. IF IT'S CRIMINAL CHARGES --
UH, I'D LIKE TO POINT OUT THAT MY CLIENT DID COME FORWARD VOLUNTARILY, WHEN SHE WAS UNDER NO SUSPICION.
SO WHEN SHE SAYS "CRIMINAL CHARGES," I --
I KNOW WHAT SHE MEANS, MR. NELSON, AND I ADMIRE IT. DON'T DIMINISH THAT BY TRYING TO QUALIFY HER STATEMENT.
THIS IS A MOST EXTRAORDINARY CIRCUMSTANCE, AND A MOST EXTRAORDINARY OFFER. WE WILL HAVE TO --
YOUR HONOR?
HM?
HM.
QUITE IRREGULAR. IF YOU'LL APPROACH THE BENCH, COLONEL DANVERS, I SEEM TO HAVE A MESSAGE FOR YOU.
OR AT LEAST, IT'S ADDRESSED TO "WARBIRD - EYES ONLY."
AND...
WE WILL TAKE THIS MATTER UNDER ADVISEMENT, AND CONTACT YOU THROUGH MR. NELSON WHEN WE'VE REACHED A DECISION. IN THE MEANTIME --
-- YOU PROBABLY SHOULDN'T LEAVE TOWN. COLONEL DANVERS?
CAROL...?
HERMAN MELVILLE ELEMENTARY SCHOOL, IN SAYVILLE, LONG ISLAND...
DADDY! DADDY!

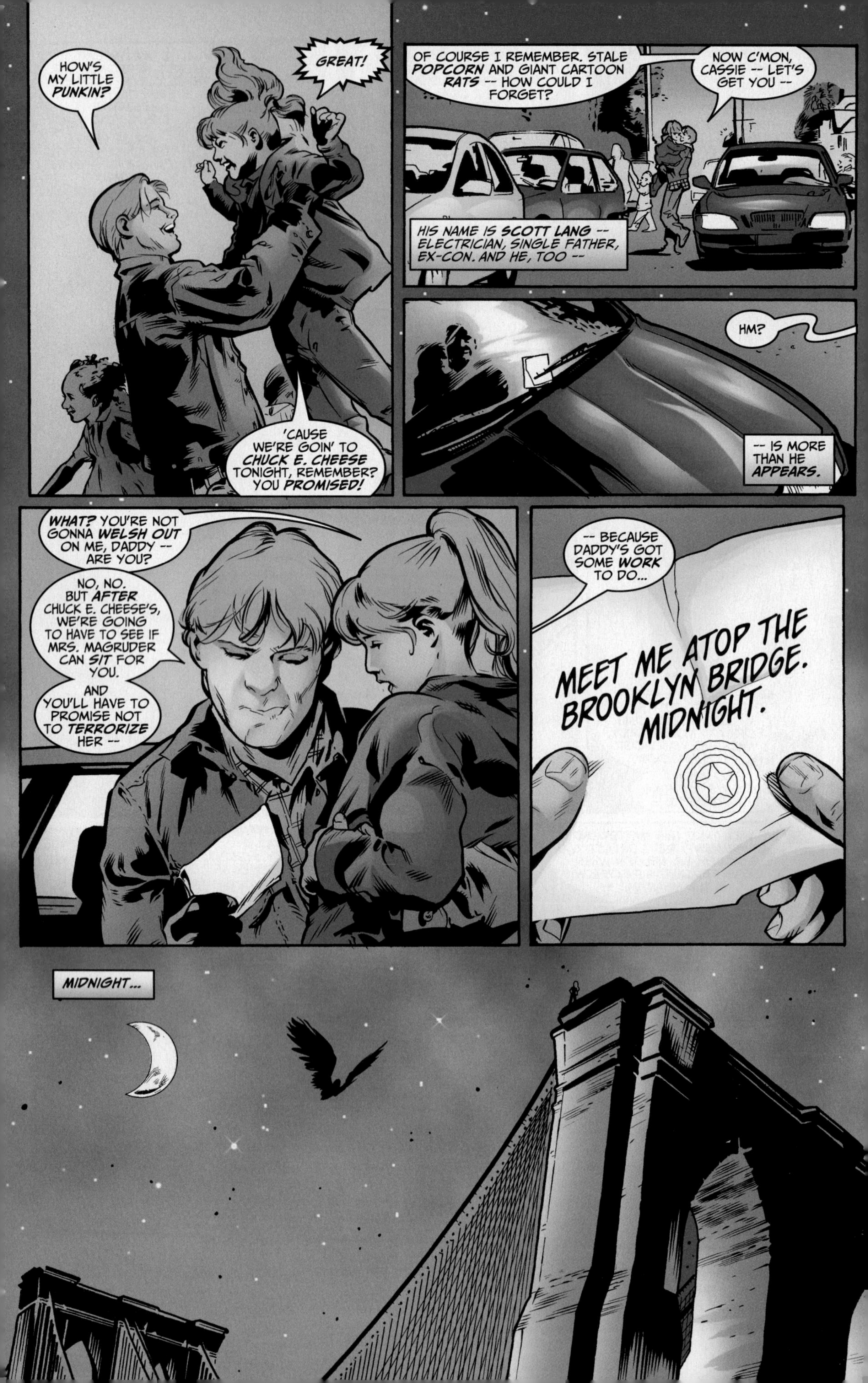
HOW'S MY LITTLE PUNKIN?
GREAT!
'CAUSE WE'RE GOIN' TO CHUCK E. CHEESE TONIGHT, REMEMBER? YOU PROMISED!
OF COURSE I REMEMBER. STALE POPCORN AND GIANT CARTOON RATS -- HOW COULD I FORGET?
NOW C'MON, CASSIE -- LET'S GET YOU --
HIS NAME IS SCOTT LANG -- ELECTRICIAN, SINGLE FATHER, EX-CON. AND HE, TOO --
HM?
-- IS MORE THAN HE APPEARS.
WHAT? YOU'RE NOT GONNA WELSH OUT ON ME, DADDY -- ARE YOU?
NO, NO. BUT AFTER CHUCK E. CHEESE'S, WE'RE GOING TO HAVE TO SEE IF MRS. MAGRUDER CAN SIT FOR YOU.
AND YOU'LL HAVE TO PROMISE NOT TO TERRORIZE HER --
-- BECAUSE DADDY'S GOT SOME WORK TO DO...
MEET ME ATOP THE BROOKLYN BRIDGE. MIDNIGHT.
MIDNIGHT...

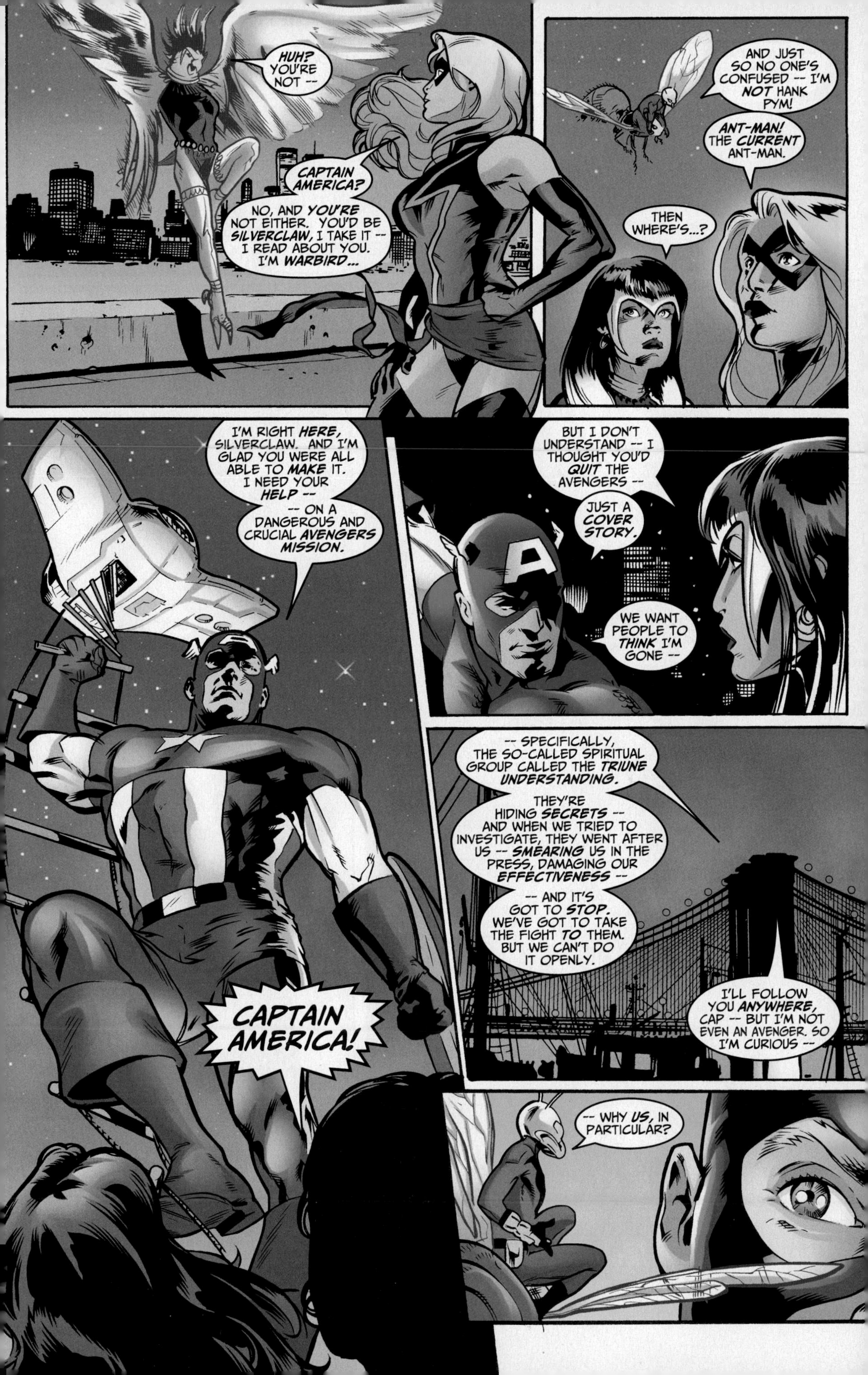
HUH? YOU'RE NOT --
CAPTAIN AMERICA?
NO, AND YOU'RE NOT EITHER. YOU'D BE SILVERCLAW, I TAKE IT -- I READ ABOUT YOU. I'M WARBIRD...
AND JUST SO NO ONE'S CONFUSED -- I'M NOT HANK PYM!
ANT-MAN! THE CURRENT ANT-MAN.
THEN WHERE'S...?
I'M RIGHT HERE, SILVERCLAW. AND I'M GLAD YOU WERE ALL ABLE TO MAKE IT. I NEED YOUR HELP --
-- ON A DANGEROUS AND CRUCIAL AVENGERS MISSION.
CAPTAIN AMERICA!
BUT I DON'T UNDERSTAND -- I THOUGHT YOU'D QUIT THE AVENGERS --
JUST A COVER STORY.
WE WANT PEOPLE TO THINK I'M GONE --
-- SPECIFICALLY, THE SO-CALLED SPIRITUAL GROUP CALLED THE TRIUNE UNDERSTANDING.
THEY'RE HIDING SECRETS -- AND WHEN WE TRIED TO INVESTIGATE, THEY WENT AFTER US -- SMEARING US IN THE PRESS, DAMAGING OUR EFFECTIVENESS --
-- AND IT'S GOT TO STOP. WE'VE GOT TO TAKE THE FIGHT TO THEM. BUT WE CAN'T DO IT OPENLY.
I'LL FOLLOW YOU ANYWHERE, CAP -- BUT I'M NOT EVEN AN AVENGER. SO I'M CURIOUS --
-- WHY US, IN PARTICULAR?

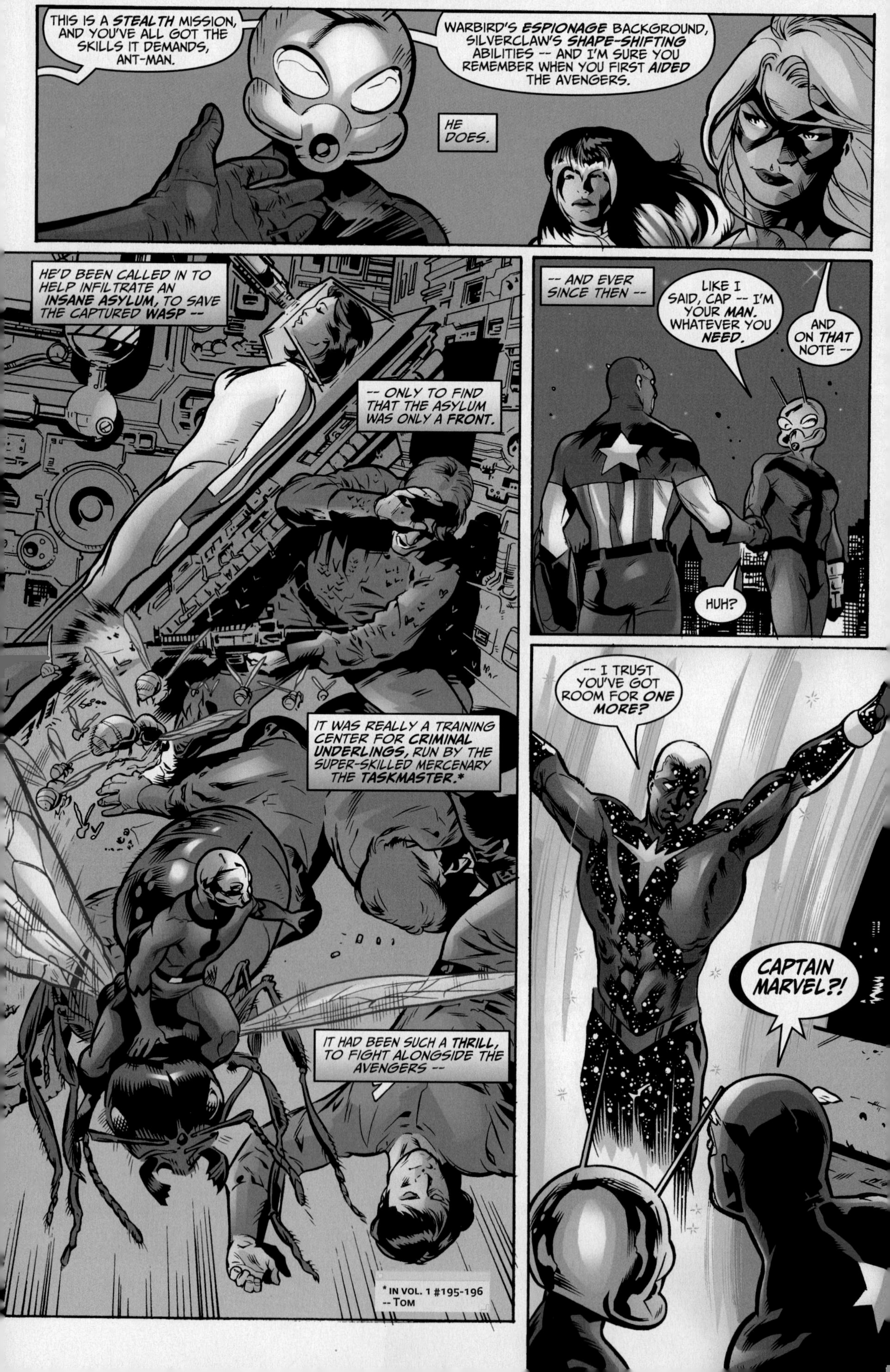
THIS IS A STEALTH MISSION, AND YOU'VE ALL GOT THE SKILLS IT DEMANDS, ANT-MAN.
WARBIRD'S ESPIONAGE BACKGROUND, SILVERCLAW'S SHAPE-SHIFTING ABILITIES -- AND I'M SURE YOU REMEMBER WHEN YOU FIRST AIDED THE AVENGERS.
HE DOES.
HE'D BEEN CALLED IN TO HELP INFILTRATE AN INSANE ASYLUM, TO SAVE THE CAPTURED WASP --
-- ONLY TO FIND THAT THE ASYLUM WAS ONLY A FRONT.
IT WAS REALLY A TRAINING CENTER FOR CRIMINAL UNDERLINGS, RUN BY THE SUPER-SKILLED MERCENARY THE TASKMASTER.*
IT HAD BEEN SUCH A THRILL, TO FIGHT ALONGSIDE THE AVENGERS --
* IN VOL. 1 #195-196 -- TOM
-- AND EVER SINCE THEN --
LIKE I SAID, CAP -- I'M YOUR MAN. WHATEVER YOU NEED.
AND ON THAT NOTE --
HUH?
-- I TRUST YOU'VE GOT ROOM FOR ONE MORE?
CAPTAIN MARVEL?!

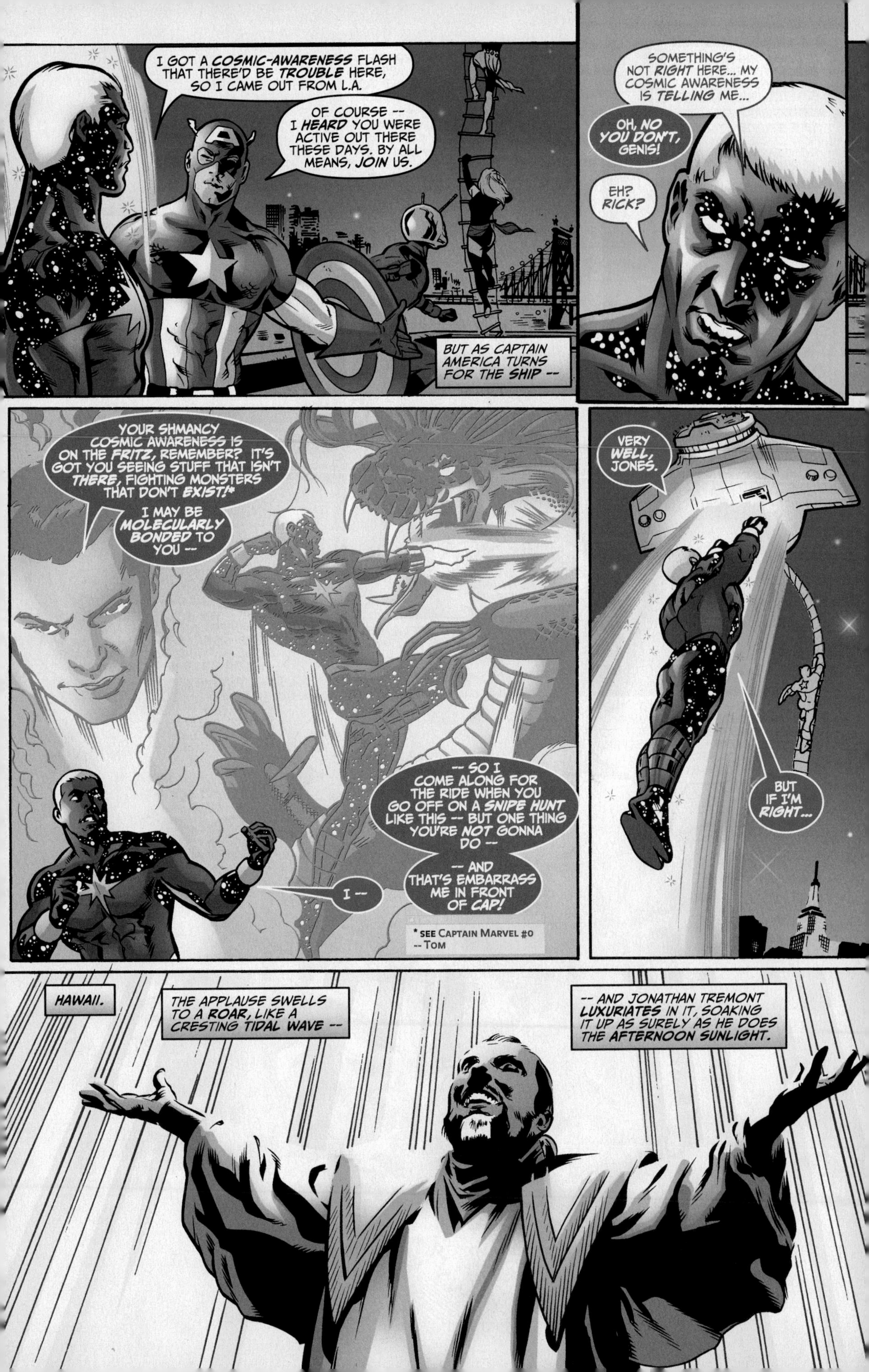
I GOT A COSMIC-AWARENESS FLASH THAT THERE'D BE TROUBLE HERE, SO I CAME OUT FROM L.A.
OF COURSE -- I HEARD YOU WERE ACTIVE OUT THERE THESE DAYS. BY ALL MEANS, JOIN US.
BUT AS CAPTAIN AMERICA TURNS FOR THE SHIP --
SOMETHING'S NOT RIGHT HERE... MY COSMIC AWARENESS IS TELLING ME...
OH, NO YOU DON'T, GENIS!
EH? RICK?
YOUR SHMANCY COSMIC AWARENESS IS ON THE FRITZ, REMEMBER? IT'S GOT YOU SEEING STUFF THAT ISN'T THERE, FIGHTING MONSTERS THAT DON'T EXIST!*
I MAY BE MOLECULARLY BONDED TO YOU --
-- SO I COME ALONG FOR THE RIDE WHEN YOU GO OFF ON A SNIPE HUNT LIKE THIS -- BUT ONE THING YOU'RE NOT GONNA DO --
I --
-- AND THAT'S EMBARRASS ME IN FRONT OF CAP!
* SEE CAPTAIN MARVEL #0 -- TOM
VERY WELL, JONES.
BUT IF I'M RIGHT...
HAWAII.
THE APPLAUSE SWELLS TO A ROAR, LIKE A CRESTING TIDAL WAVE --
-- AND JONATHAN TREMONT LUXURIATES IN IT, SOAKING IT UP AS SURELY AS HE DOES THE AFTERNOON SUNLIGHT.

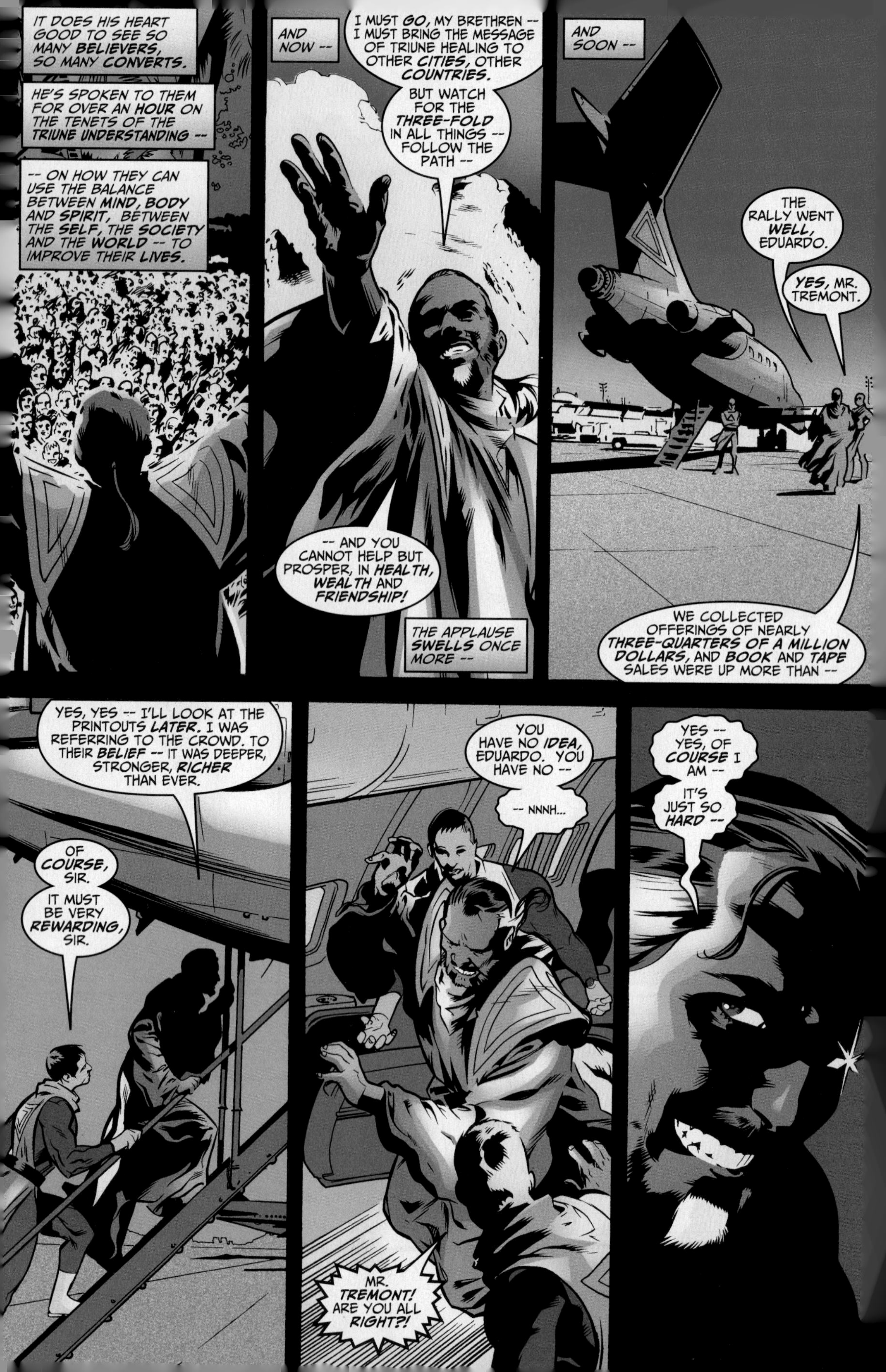
IT DOES HIS HEART GOOD TO SEE SO MANY BELIEVERS, SO MANY CONVERTS.
HE'S SPOKEN TO THEM FOR OVER AN HOUR ON THE TENETS OF THE TRIUNE UNDERSTANDING --
-- ON HOW THEY CAN USE THE BALANCE BETWEEN MIND, BODY AND SPIRIT, BETWEEN THE SELF, THE SOCIETY AND THE WORLD -- TO IMPROVE THEIR LIVES.
AND NOW --
I MUST GO, MY BRETHREN -- I MUST BRING THE MESSAGE OF TRIUNE HEALING TO OTHER CITIES, OTHER COUNTRIES.
BUT WATCH FOR THE THREE-FOLD IN ALL THINGS -- FOLLOW THE PATH --
-- AND YOU CANNOT HELP BUT PROSPER, IN HEALTH, WEALTH AND FRIENDSHIP!
THE APPLAUSE SWELLS ONCE MORE --
AND SOON --
THE RALLY WENT WELL, EDUARDO.
YES, MR. TREMONT.
WE COLLECTED OFFERINGS OF NEARLY THREE-QUARTERS OF A MILLION DOLLARS, AND BOOK AND TAPE SALES WERE UP MORE THAN --
YES, YES -- I'LL LOOK AT THE PRINTOUTS LATER. I WAS REFERRING TO THE CROWD. TO THEIR BELIEF -- IT WAS DEEPER, STRONGER, RICHER THAN EVER.
OF COURSE, SIR.
IT MUST BE VERY REWARDING, SIR.
YOU HAVE NO IDEA, EDUARDO. YOU HAVE NO --
-- NNNH...
MR. TREMONT! ARE YOU ALL RIGHT?!
YES -- YES, OF COURSE I AM --
IT'S JUST SO HARD --

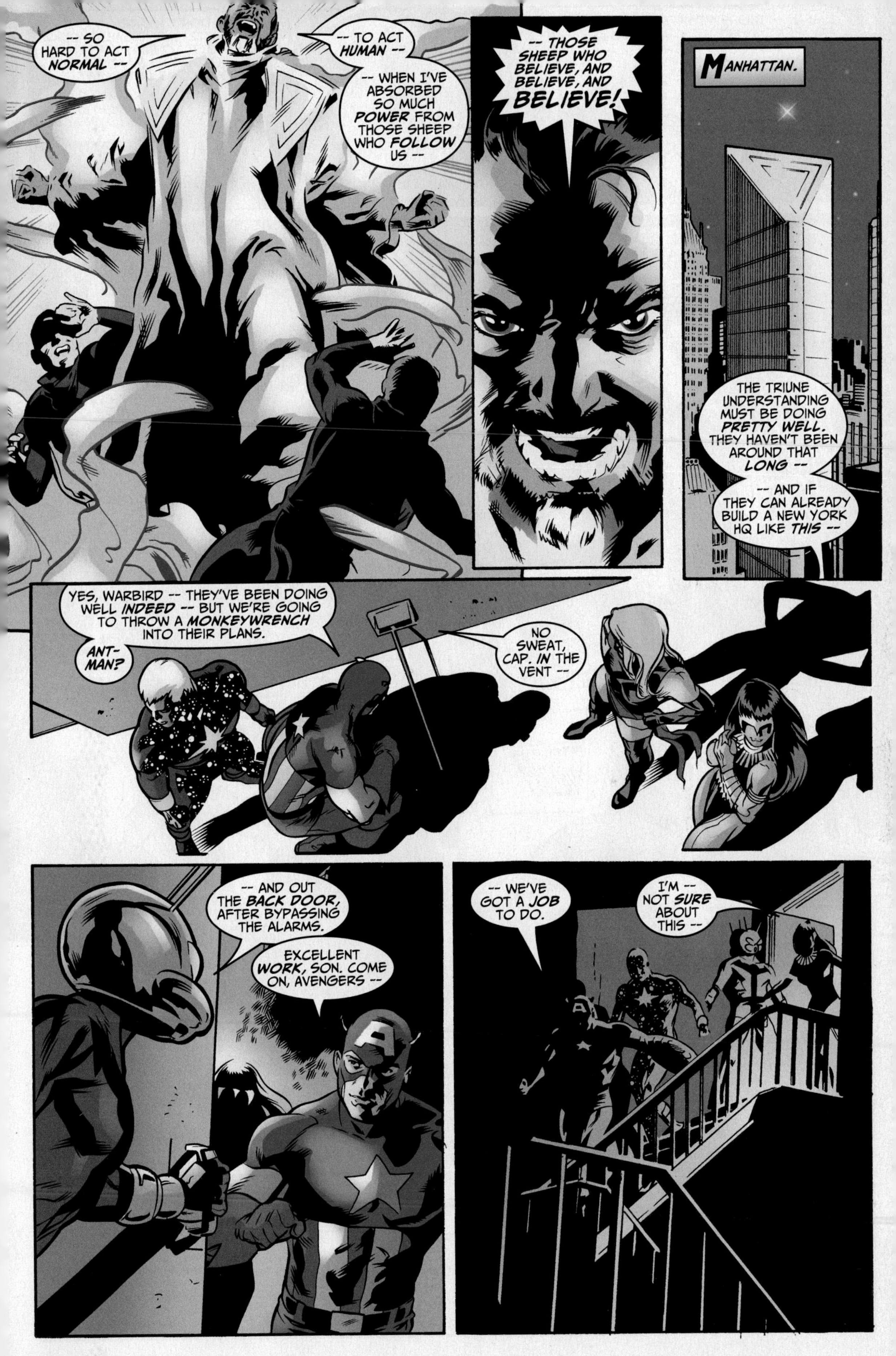
-- SO HARD TO ACT NORMAL --
-- TO ACT HUMAN --
-- WHEN I'VE ABSORBED SO MUCH POWER FROM THOSE SHEEP WHO FOLLOW US --
-- THOSE SHEEP WHO BELIEVE, AND BELIEVE, AND BELIEVE!
MANHATTAN.
THE TRIUNE UNDERSTANDING MUST BE DOING PRETTY WELL. THEY HAVEN'T BEEN AROUND THAT LONG --
-- AND IF THEY CAN ALREADY BUILD A NEW YORK HQ LIKE THIS --
YES, WARBIRD -- THEY'VE BEEN DOING WELL INDEED -- BUT WE'RE GOING TO THROW A MONKEYWRENCH INTO THEIR PLANS.
ANT-MAN?
NO SWEAT, CAP. IN THE VENT --
-- AND OUT THE BACK DOOR, AFTER BYPASSING THE ALARMS.
EXCELLENT WORK, SON. COME ON, AVENGERS --
-- WE'VE GOT A JOB TO DO.
I'M -- NOT SURE ABOUT THIS --

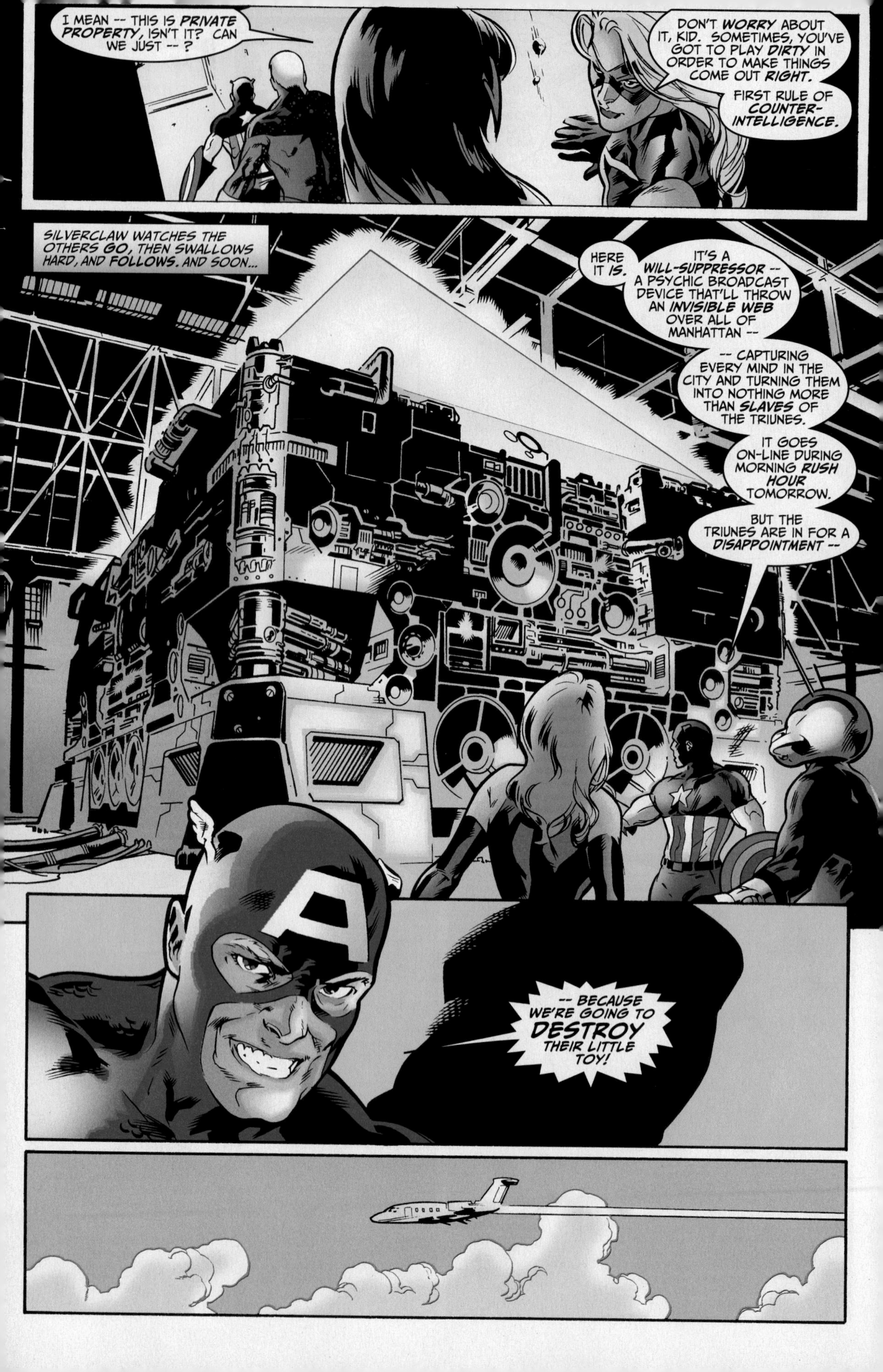
I MEAN -- THIS IS PRIVATE PROPERTY, ISN'T IT? CAN WE JUST -- ?
DON'T WORRY ABOUT IT, KID. SOMETIMES, YOU'VE GOT TO PLAY DIRTY IN ORDER TO MAKE THINGS COME OUT RIGHT.
FIRST RULE OF COUNTER-INTELLIGENCE.
SILVERCLAW WATCHES THE OTHERS GO, THEN SWALLOWS HARD, AND FOLLOWS. AND SOON...
HERE IT IS.
IT'S A WILL-SUPPRESSOR -- A PSYCHIC BROADCAST DEVICE THAT'LL THROW AN INVISIBLE WEB OVER ALL OF MANHATTAN --
-- CAPTURING EVERY MIND IN THE CITY AND TURNING THEM INTO NOTHING MORE THAN SLAVES OF THE TRIUNES.
IT GOES ON-LINE DURING MORNING RUSH HOUR TOMORROW.
BUT THE TRIUNES ARE IN FOR A DISAPPOINTMENT --
-- BECAUSE WE'RE GOING TO DESTROY THEIR LITTLE TOY!

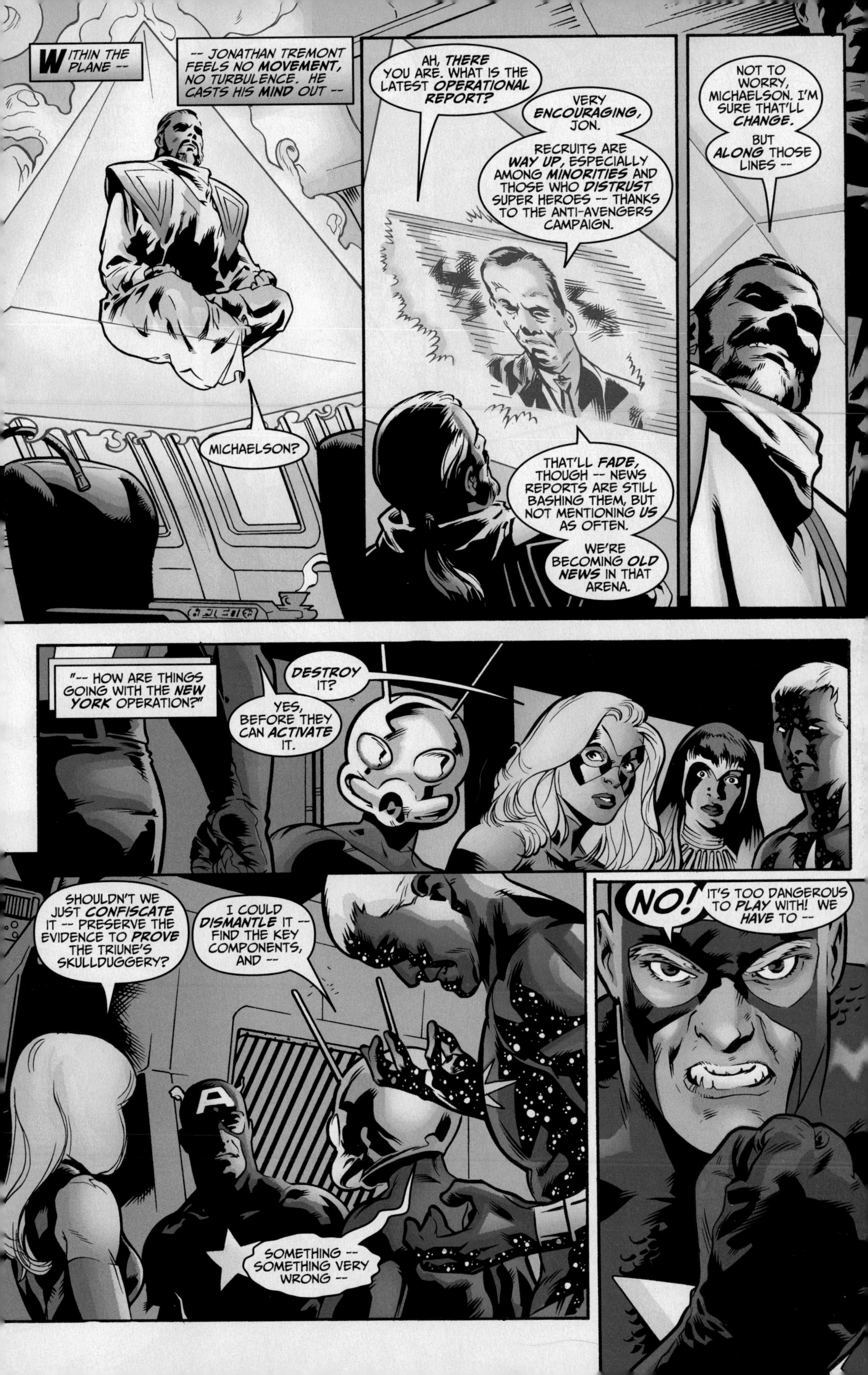
WITHIN THE PLANE --
-- JONATHAN TREMONT FEELS NO MOVEMENT, NO TURBULENCE. HE CASTS HIS MIND OUT --
MICHAELSON?
AH, THERE YOU ARE. WHAT IS THE LATEST OPERATIONAL REPORT?
VERY ENCOURAGING, JON.
RECRUITS ARE WAY UP, ESPECIALLY AMONG MINORITIES AND THOSE WHO DISTRUST SUPER HEROES -- THANKS TO THE ANTI-AVENGERS CAMPAIGN.
THAT'LL FADE, THOUGH -- NEWS REPORTS ARE STILL BASHING THEM, BUT NOT MENTIONING US AS OFTEN.
WE'RE BECOMING OLD NEWS IN THAT ARENA.
NOT TO WORRY, MICHAELSON. I'M SURE THAT'LL CHANGE.
BUT ALONG THOSE LINES --
"-- HOW ARE THINGS GOING WITH THE NEW YORK OPERATION?"
DESTROY IT?
YES, BEFORE THEY CAN ACTIVATE IT.
SHOULDN'T WE JUST CONFISCATE IT -- PRESERVE THE EVIDENCE TO PROVE THE TRIUNE'S SKULLDUGGERY?
I COULD DISMANTLE IT -- FIND THE KEY COMPONENTS, AND --
SOMETHING -- SOMETHING VERY WRONG --
NO!
IT'S TOO DANGEROUS TO PLAY WITH! WE HAVE TO --

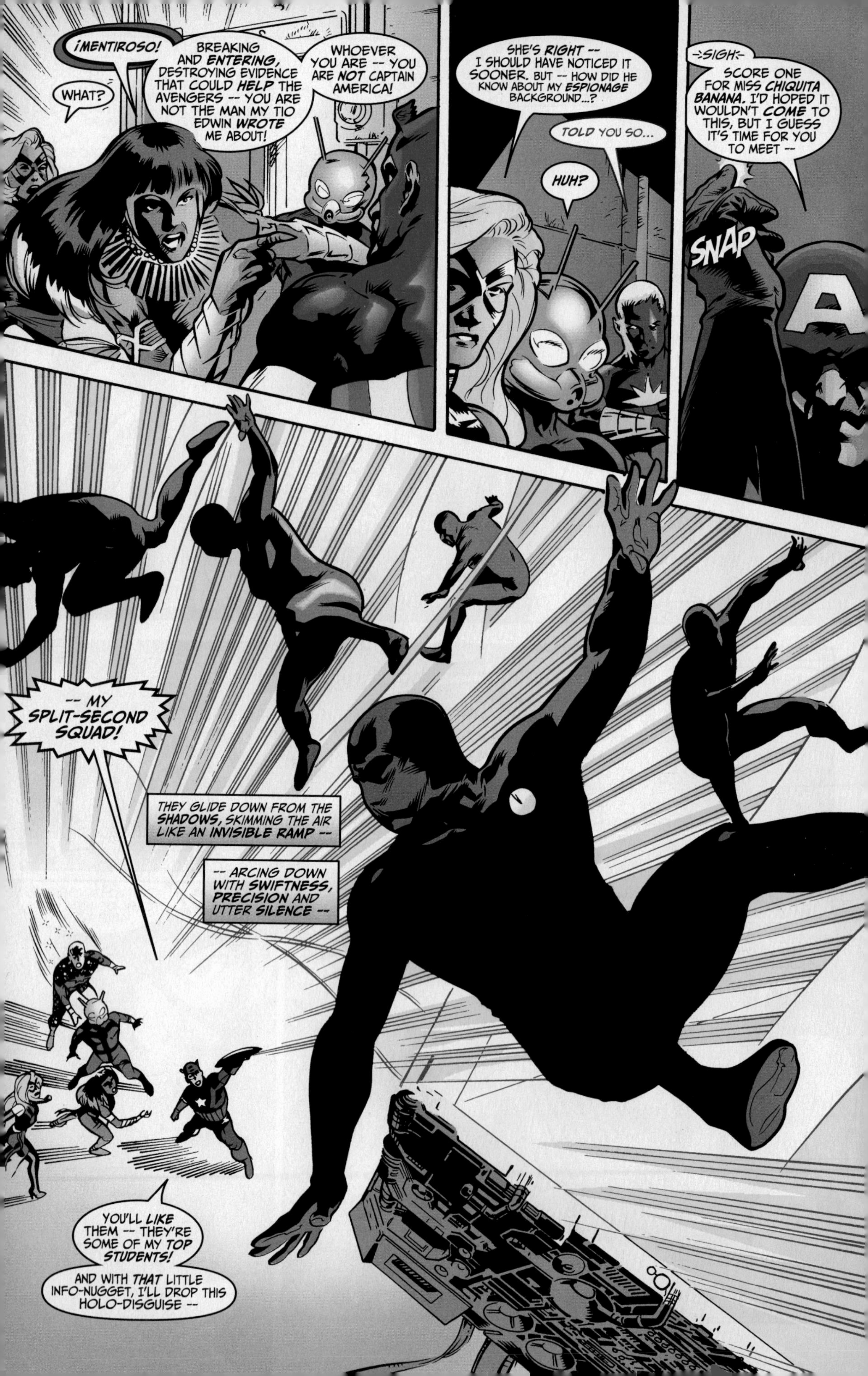
¡MENTIROSO!
WHAT?
BREAKING AND ENTERING, DESTROYING EVIDENCE THAT COULD HELP THE AVENGERS -- YOU ARE NOT THE MAN MY TIO EDWIN WROTE ME ABOUT!
WHOEVER YOU ARE -- YOU ARE NOT CAPTAIN AMERICA!
SHE'S RIGHT -- I SHOULD HAVE NOTICED IT SOONER. BUT -- HOW DID HE KNOW ABOUT MY ESPIONAGE BACKGROUND...?
TOLD YOU SO...
HUH?
-SIGH-
SCORE ONE FOR MISS CHIQUITA BANANA. I'D HOPED IT WOULDN'T COME TO THIS, BUT I GUESS IT'S TIME FOR YOU TO MEET --
SNAP
-- MY SPLIT-SECOND SQUAD!
THEY GLIDE DOWN FROM THE SHADOWS, SKIMMING THE AIR LIKE AN INVISIBLE RAMP --
-- ARCING DOWN WITH SWIFTNESS, PRECISION AND UTTER SILENCE --
YOU'LL LIKE THEM -- THEY'RE SOME OF MY TOP STUDENTS!
AND WITH THAT LITTLE INFO-NUGGET, I'LL DROP THIS HOLO-DISGUISE --

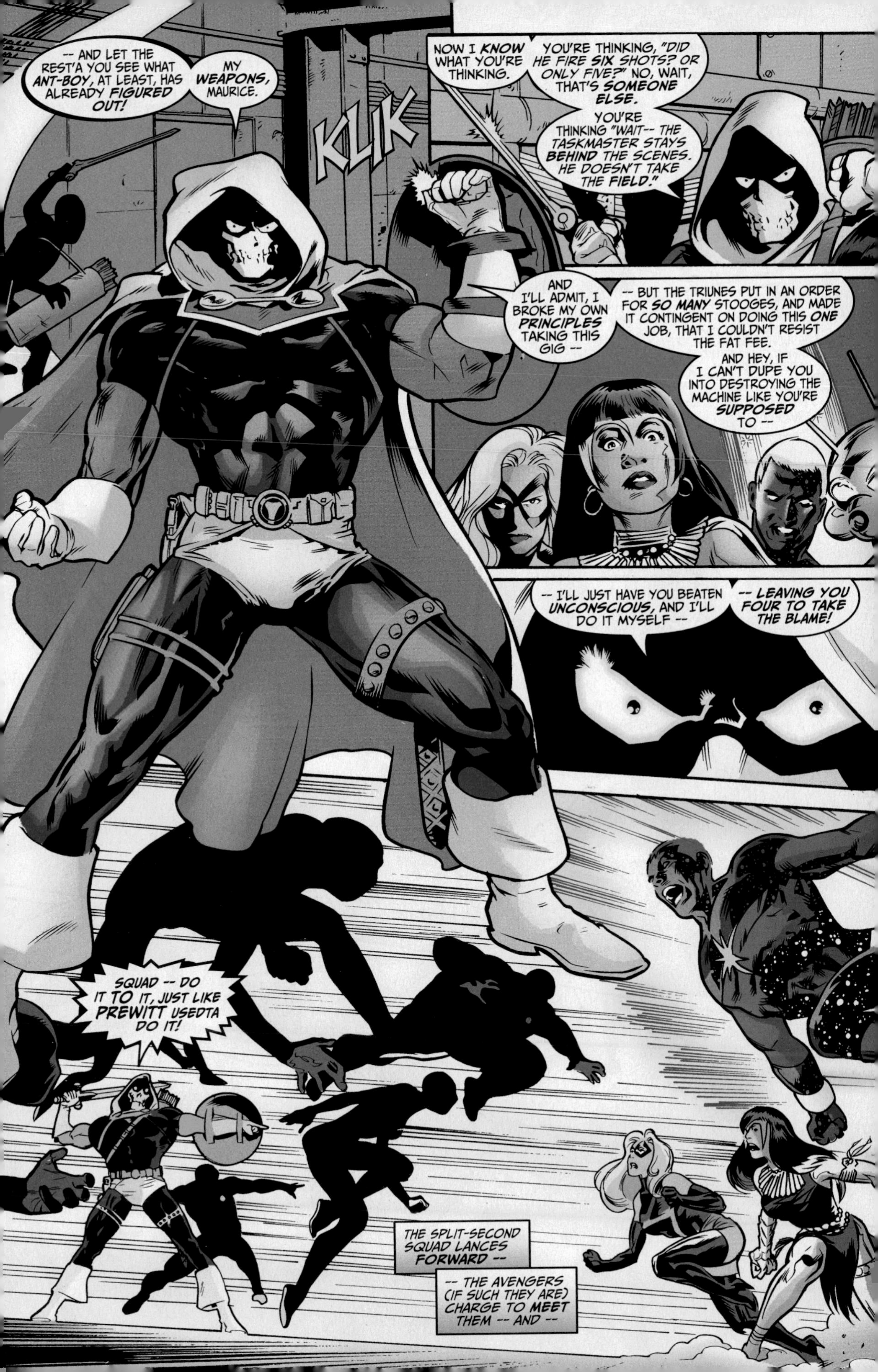
-- AND LET THE REST'A YOU SEE WHAT ANT-BOY, AT LEAST, HAS ALREADY FIGURED OUT!
MY WEAPONS, MAURICE.
KLIK
NOW I KNOW WHAT YOU'RE THINKING.
YOU'RE THINKING, "DID HE FIRE SIX SHOTS? OR ONLY FIVE?" NO, WAIT, THAT'S SOMEONE ELSE.
YOU'RE THINKING "WAIT-- THE TASKMASTER STAYS BEHIND THE SCENES. HE DOESN'T TAKE THE FIELD."
AND I'LL ADMIT, I BROKE MY OWN PRINCIPLES TAKING THIS GIG --
-- BUT THE TRIUNES PUT IN AN ORDER FOR SO MANY STOOGES, AND MADE IT CONTINGENT ON DOING THIS ONE JOB, THAT I COULDN'T RESIST THE FAT FEE.
AND HEY, IF I CAN'T DUPE YOU INTO DESTROYING THE MACHINE LIKE YOU'RE SUPPOSED TO --
-- I'LL JUST HAVE YOU BEATEN UNCONSCIOUS, AND I'LL DO IT MYSELF --
-- LEAVING YOU FOUR TO TAKE THE BLAME!
SQUAD -- DO IT TO IT, JUST LIKE PREWITT USEDTA DO IT!
THE SPLIT-SECOND SQUAD LANCES FORWARD --
-- THE AVENGERS (IF SUCH THEY ARE) CHARGE TO MEET THEM -- AND --

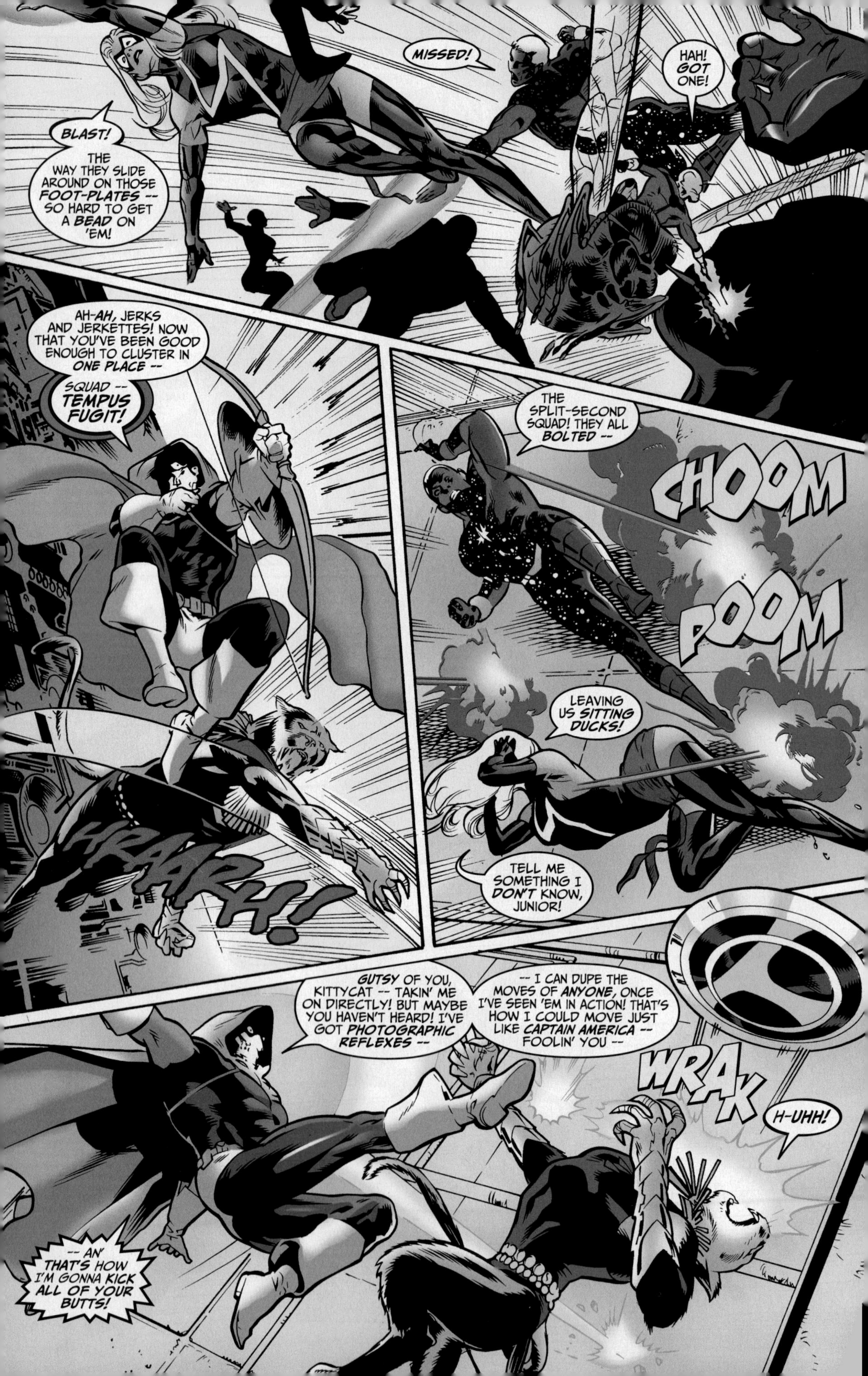
MISSED!
HAH! GOT ONE!
BLAST!
THE WAY THEY SLIDE AROUND ON THOSE FOOT-PLATES -- SO HARD TO GET A BEAD ON 'EM!
AH-AH, JERKS AND JERKETTES! NOW THAT YOU'VE BEEN GOOD ENOUGH TO CLUSTER IN ONE PLACE --
SQUAD -- TEMPUS FUGIT!
THE SPLIT-SECOND SQUAD! THEY ALL BOLTED --
CHOOM
POOM
LEAVING US SITTING DUCKS!
TELL ME SOMETHING I DON'T KNOW, JUNIOR!
HRAARH!!
GUTSY OF YOU, KITTYCAT -- TAKIN' ME ON DIRECTLY! BUT MAYBE YOU HAVEN'T HEARD! I'VE GOT PHOTOGRAPHIC REFLEXES --
-- I CAN DUPE THE MOVES OF ANYONE, ONCE I'VE SEEN 'EM IN ACTION! THAT'S HOW I COULD MOVE JUST LIKE CAPTAIN AMERICA -- FOOLIN' YOU --
WRAK
H-UHH!
-- AN' THAT'S HOW I'M GONNA KICK ALL OF YOUR BUTTS!

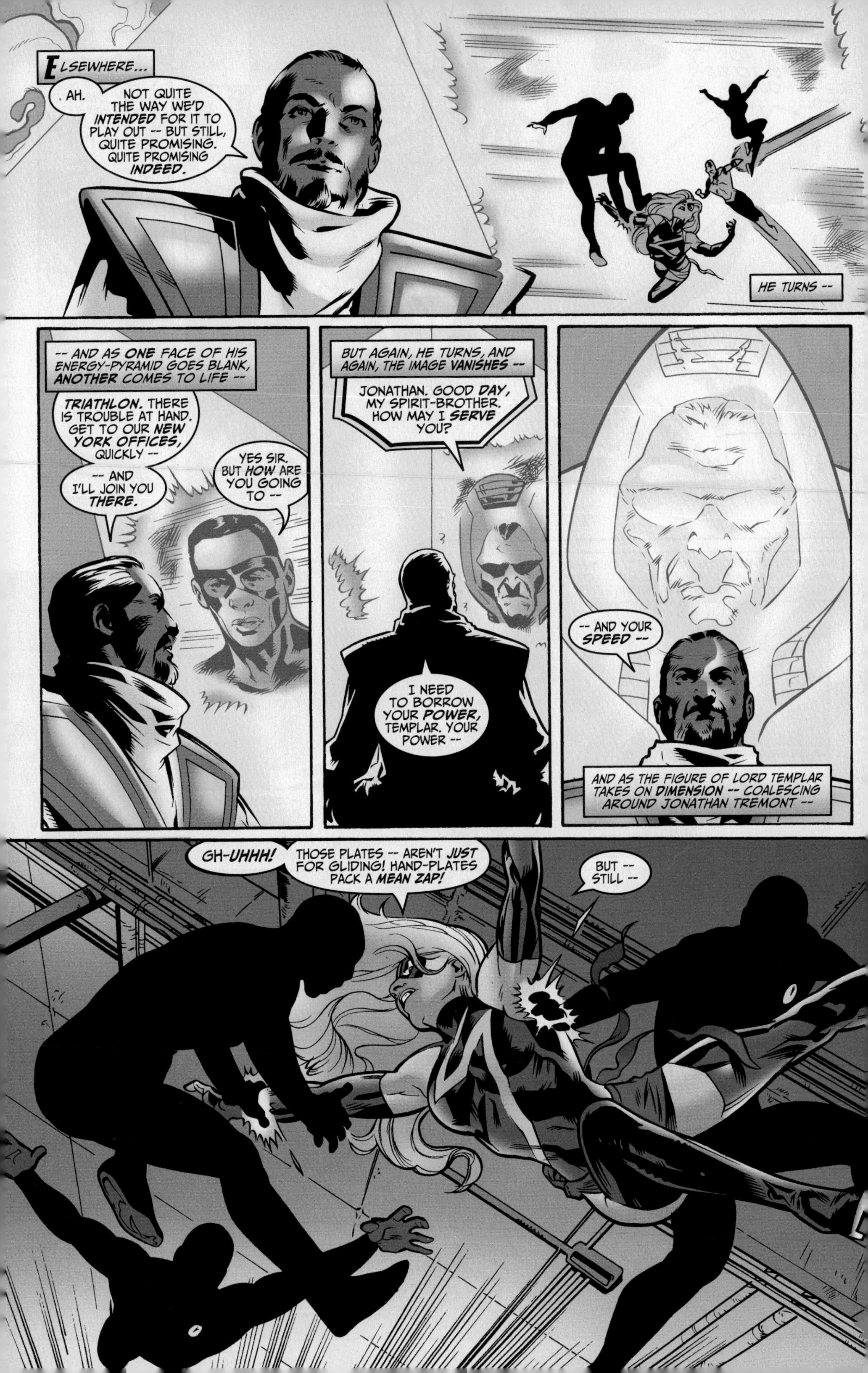
ELSEWHERE...
. AH.
NOT QUITE THE WAY WE'D INTENDED FOR IT TO PLAY OUT -- BUT STILL, QUITE PROMISING. QUITE PROMISING INDEED.
HE TURNS --
-- AND AS ONE FACE OF HIS ENERGY-PYRAMID GOES BLANK, ANOTHER COMES TO LIFE --
TRIATHLON. THERE IS TROUBLE AT HAND. GET TO OUR NEW YORK OFFICES, QUICKLY --
-- AND I'LL JOIN YOU THERE.
YES SIR. BUT HOW ARE YOU GOING TO --
BUT AGAIN, HE TURNS, AND AGAIN, THE IMAGE VANISHES --
JONATHAN. GOOD DAY, MY SPIRIT-BROTHER. HOW MAY I SERVE YOU?
I NEED TO BORROW YOUR POWER, TEMPLAR. YOUR POWER --
-- AND YOUR SPEED --
AND AS THE FIGURE OF LORD TEMPLAR TAKES ON DIMENSION -- COALESCING AROUND JONATHAN TREMONT --
GH-UHHH!
THOSE PLATES -- AREN'T JUST FOR GLIDING! HAND-PLATES PACK A MEAN ZAP!
BUT -- STILL --

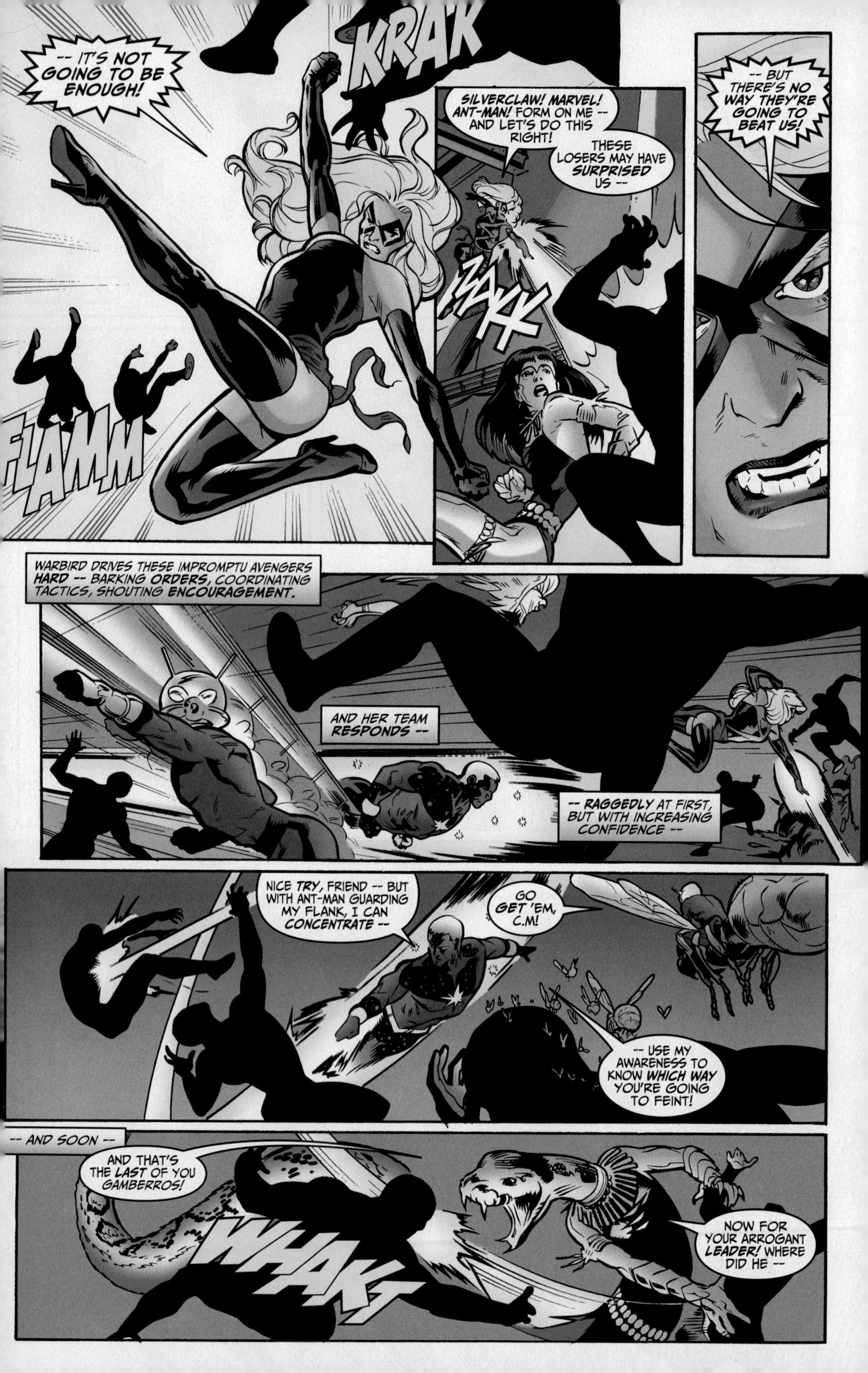
-- IT'S NOT GOING TO BE ENOUGH!
KRAK
SILVERCLAW! MARVEL! ANT-MAN! FORM ON ME -- AND LET'S DO THIS RIGHT!
THESE LOSERS MAY HAVE SURPRISED US --
WAKK
FLAMM
-- BUT THERE'S NO WAY THEY'RE GOING TO BEAT US!
WARBIRD DRIVES THESE IMPROMPTU AVENGERS HARD -- BARKING ORDERS, COORDINATING TACTICS, SHOUTING ENCOURAGEMENT.
AND HER TEAM RESPONDS --
-- RAGGEDLY AT FIRST, BUT WITH INCREASING CONFIDENCE --
NICE TRY, FRIEND -- BUT WITH ANT-MAN GUARDING MY FLANK, I CAN CONCENTRATE --
GO GET 'EM, C.M!
-- USE MY AWARENESS TO KNOW WHICH WAY YOU'RE GOING TO FEINT!
-- AND SOON --
AND THAT'S THE LAST OF YOU GAMBERROS!
WHAKT
NOW FOR YOUR ARROGANT LEADER! WHERE DID HE --

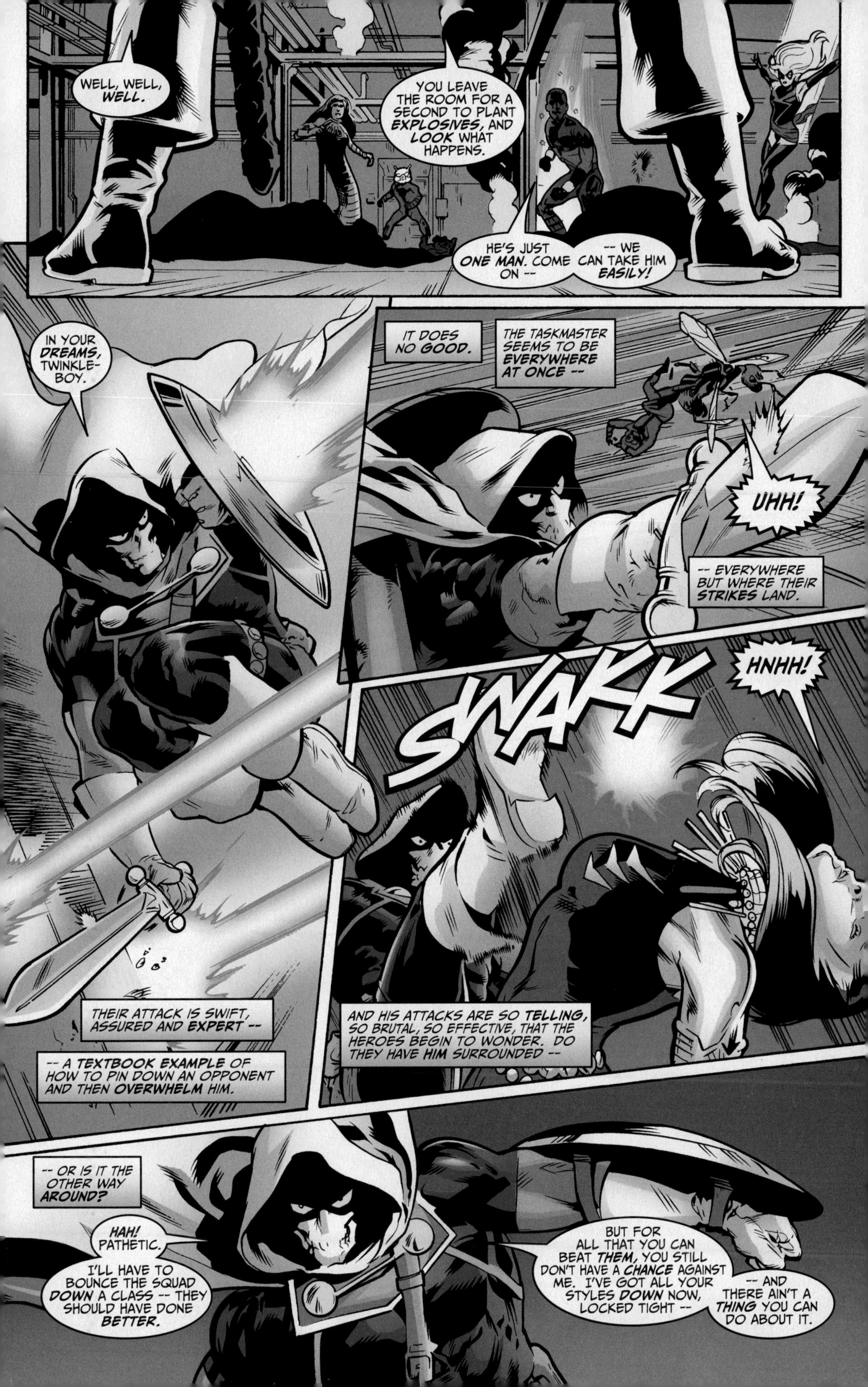

WELL, WELL, WELL.
YOU LEAVE THE ROOM FOR A SECOND TO PLANT EXPLOSIVES, AND LOOK WHAT HAPPENS.
HE'S JUST ONE MAN. COME ON --
-- WE CAN TAKE HIM EASILY!
IN YOUR DREAMS, TWINKLE-BOY.
IT DOES NO GOOD.
THE TASKMASTER SEEMS TO BE EVERYWHERE AT ONCE --
UHH!
-- EVERYWHERE BUT WHERE THEIR STRIKES LAND.
SWAKK
HNHH!
THEIR ATTACK IS SWIFT, ASSURED AND EXPERT --
-- A TEXTBOOK EXAMPLE OF HOW TO PIN DOWN AN OPPONENT AND THEN OVERWHELM HIM.
AND HIS ATTACKS ARE SO TELLING, SO BRUTAL, SO EFFECTIVE, THAT THE HEROES BEGIN TO WONDER. DO THEY HAVE HIM SURROUNDED --
-- OR IS IT THE OTHER WAY AROUND?
HAH! PATHETIC.
I'LL HAVE TO BOUNCE THE SQUAD DOWN A CLASS -- THEY SHOULD HAVE DONE BETTER.
BUT FOR ALL THAT YOU CAN BEAT THEM, YOU STILL DON'T HAVE A CHANCE AGAINST ME. I'VE GOT ALL YOUR STYLES DOWN NOW, LOCKED TIGHT --
-- AND THERE AIN'T A THING YOU CAN DO ABOUT IT.

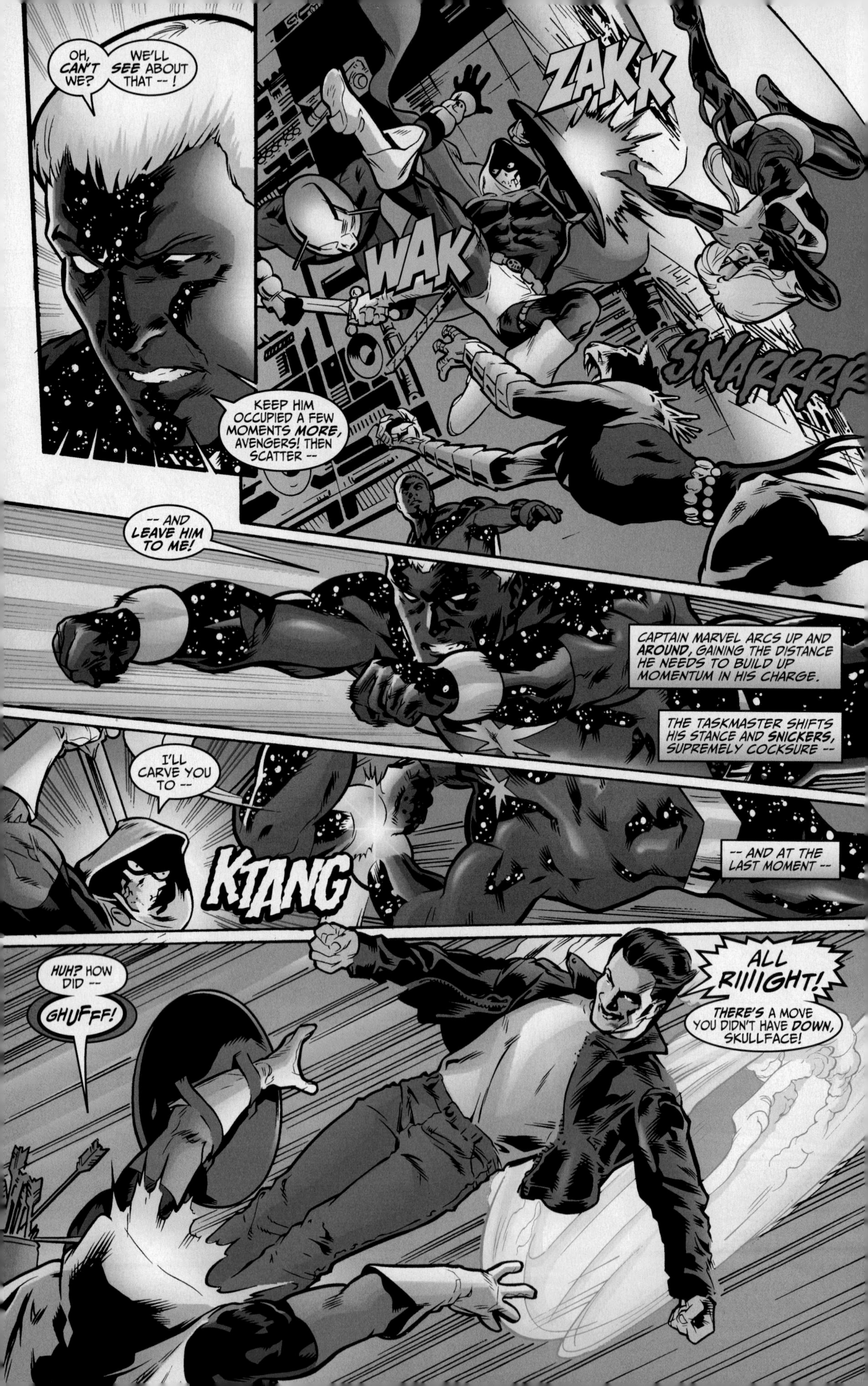

OH, CAN'T WE?
WE'LL SEE ABOUT THAT -- !
ZAKK
WAK
SNARRRR
KEEP HIM OCCUPIED A FEW MOMENTS MORE, AVENGERS! THEN SCATTER --
-- AND LEAVE HIM TO ME!
CAPTAIN MARVEL ARCS UP AND AROUND, GAINING THE DISTANCE HE NEEDS TO BUILD UP MOMENTUM IN HIS CHARGE.
THE TASKMASTER SHIFTS HIS STANCE AND SNICKERS, SUPREMELY COCKSURE --
I'LL CARVE YOU TO --
KTANG
-- AND AT THE LAST MOMENT --
HUH? HOW DID --
GHUFFF!
ALL RIIIIGHT!
THERE'S A MOVE YOU DIDN'T HAVE DOWN, SKULLFACE!

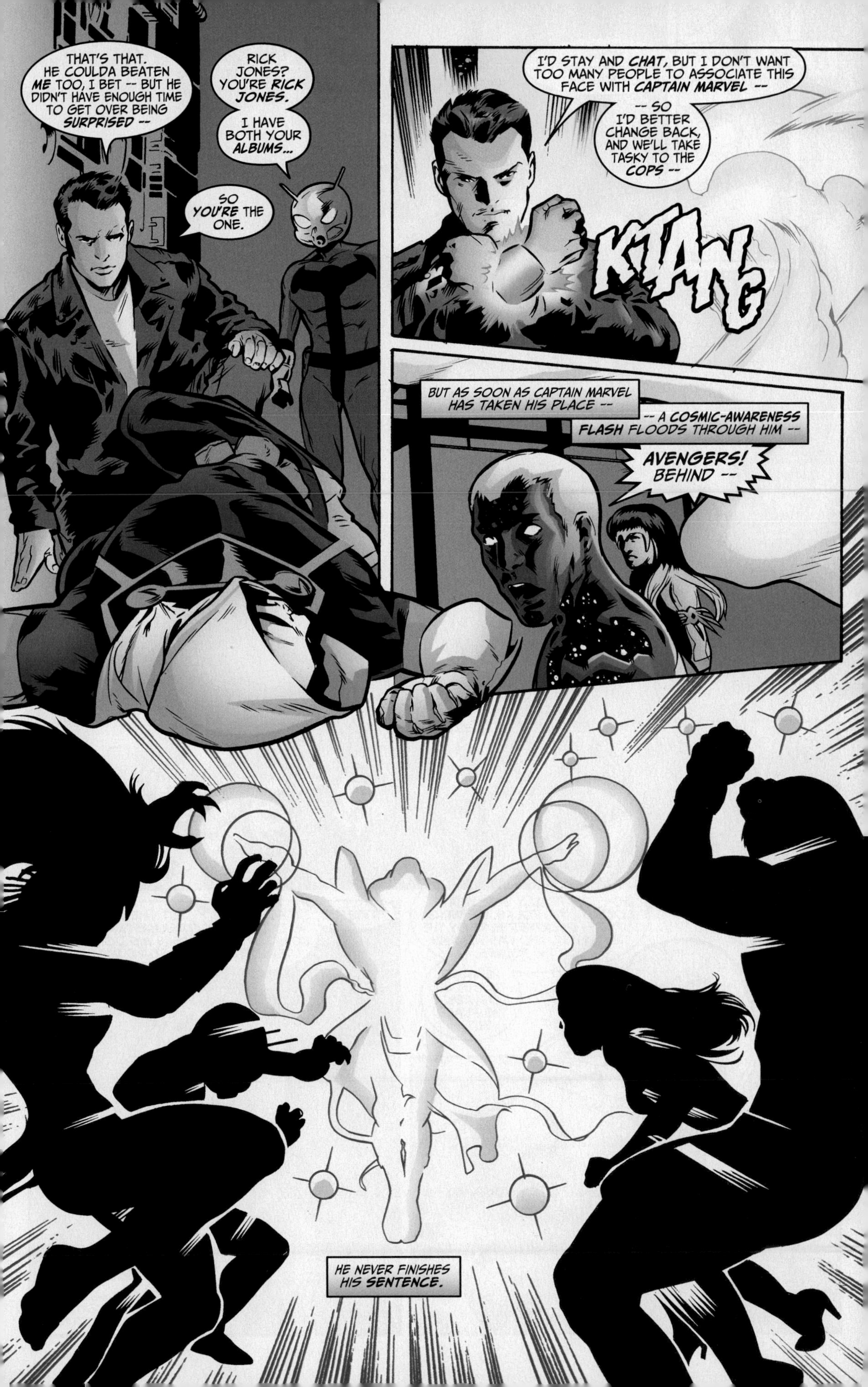

THAT'S THAT. HE COULDA BEATEN ME TOO, I BET -- BUT HE DIDN'T HAVE ENOUGH TIME TO GET OVER BEING SURPRISED --
RICK JONES? YOU'RE RICK JONES.
I HAVE BOTH YOUR ALBUMS...
SO YOU'RE THE ONE.
I'D STAY AND CHAT, BUT I DON'T WANT TOO MANY PEOPLE TO ASSOCIATE THIS FACE WITH CAPTAIN MARVEL --
-- SO I'D BETTER CHANGE BACK, AND WE'LL TAKE TASKY TO THE COPS --
KTANG
BUT AS SOON AS CAPTAIN MARVEL HAS TAKEN HIS PLACE --
-- A COSMIC-AWARENESS FLASH FLOODS THROUGH HIM --
AVENGERS! BEHIND --
HE NEVER FINISHES HIS SENTENCE.

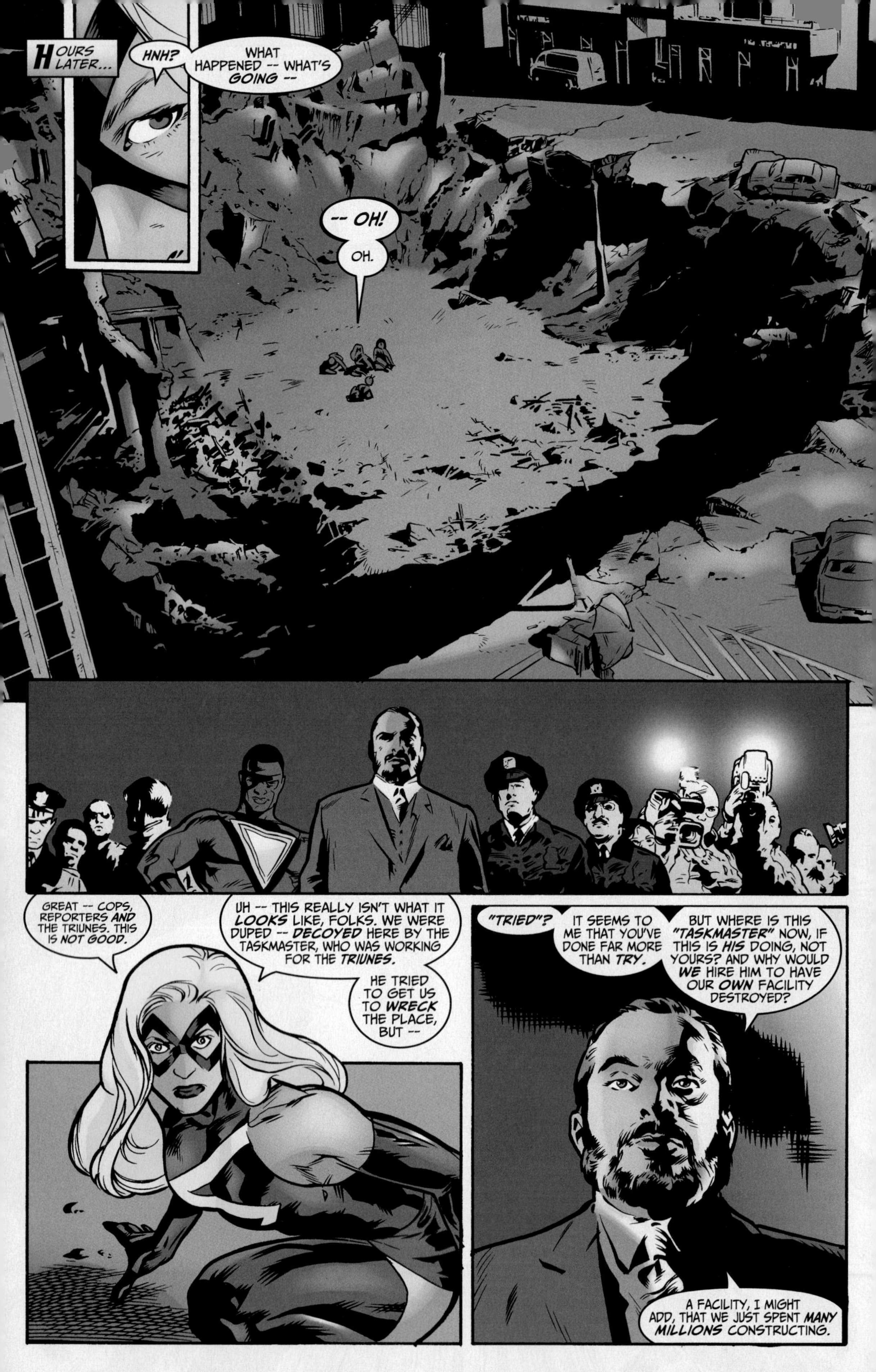
HOURS LATER...
HNH?
WHAT HAPPENED -- WHAT'S GOING --
-- OH!
OH.
GREAT -- COPS, REPORTERS AND THE TRIUNES. THIS IS NOT GOOD.
UH -- THIS REALLY ISN'T WHAT IT LOOKS LIKE, FOLKS. WE WERE DUPED -- DECOYED HERE BY THE TASKMASTER, WHO WAS WORKING FOR THE TRIUNES.
HE TRIED TO GET US TO WRECK THE PLACE, BUT --
"TRIED"?
IT SEEMS TO ME THAT YOU'VE DONE FAR MORE THAN TRY.
BUT WHERE IS THIS "TASKMASTER" NOW, IF THIS IS HIS DOING, NOT YOURS? AND WHY WOULD WE HIRE HIM TO HAVE OUR OWN FACILITY DESTROYED?
A FACILITY, I MIGHT ADD, THAT WE JUST SPENT MANY MILLIONS CONSTRUCTING.

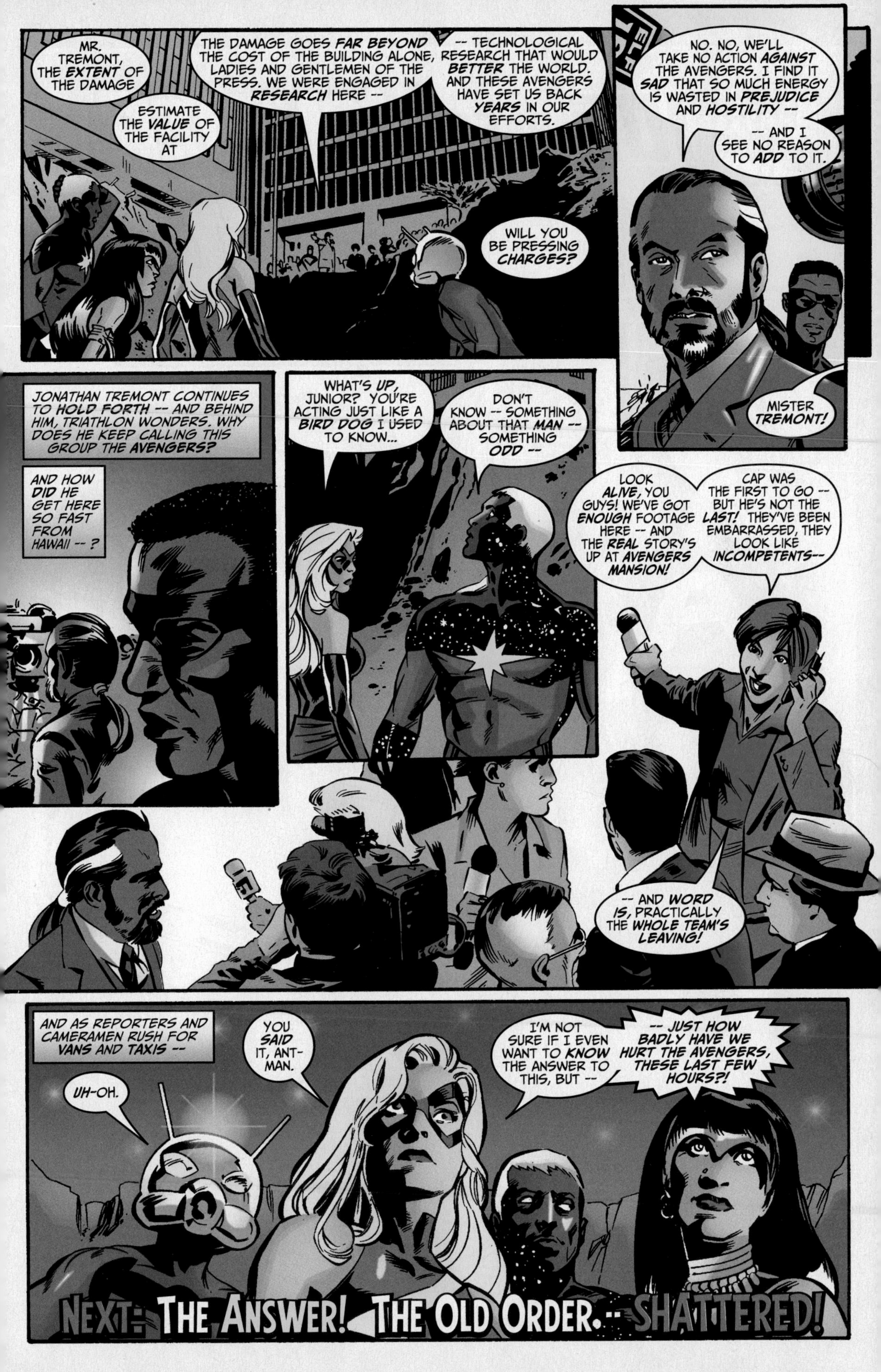
MR. TREMONT, THE EXTENT OF THE DAMAGE
ESTIMATE THE VALUE OF THE FACILITY AT
THE DAMAGE GOES FAR BEYOND THE COST OF THE BUILDING ALONE, LADIES AND GENTLEMEN OF THE PRESS. WE WERE ENGAGED IN RESEARCH HERE --
-- TECHNOLOGICAL RESEARCH THAT WOULD BETTER THE WORLD. AND THESE AVENGERS HAVE SET US BACK YEARS IN OUR EFFORTS.
WILL YOU BE PRESSING CHARGES?
NO. NO, WE'LL TAKE NO ACTION AGAINST THE AVENGERS. I FIND IT SAD THAT SO MUCH ENERGY IS WASTED IN PREJUDICE AND HOSTILITY --
-- AND I SEE NO REASON TO ADD TO IT.
MISTER TREMONT!
JONATHAN TREMONT CONTINUES TO HOLD FORTH -- AND BEHIND HIM, TRIATHLON WONDERS. WHY DOES HE KEEP CALLING THIS GROUP THE AVENGERS?
AND HOW DID HE GET HERE SO FAST FROM HAWAII -- ?
WHAT'S UP, JUNIOR? YOU'RE ACTING JUST LIKE A BIRD DOG I USED TO KNOW...
DON'T KNOW -- SOMETHING ABOUT THAT MAN -- SOMETHING ODD --
LOOK ALIVE, YOU GUYS! WE'VE GOT ENOUGH FOOTAGE HERE -- AND THE REAL STORY'S UP AT AVENGERS MANSION!
CAP WAS THE FIRST TO GO -- BUT HE'S NOT THE LAST! THEY'VE BEEN EMBARRASSED, THEY LOOK LIKE INCOMPETENTS--
-- AND WORD IS, PRACTICALLY THE WHOLE TEAM'S LEAVING!
AND AS REPORTERS AND CAMERAMEN RUSH FOR VANS AND TAXIS --
UH-OH.
YOU SAID IT, ANT-MAN.
I'M NOT SURE IF I EVEN WANT TO KNOW THE ANSWER TO THIS, BUT --
-- JUST HOW BADLY HAVE WE HURT THE AVENGERS, THESE LAST FEW HOURS?!
NEXT: THE ANSWER! THE OLD ORDER.-- SHATTERED!

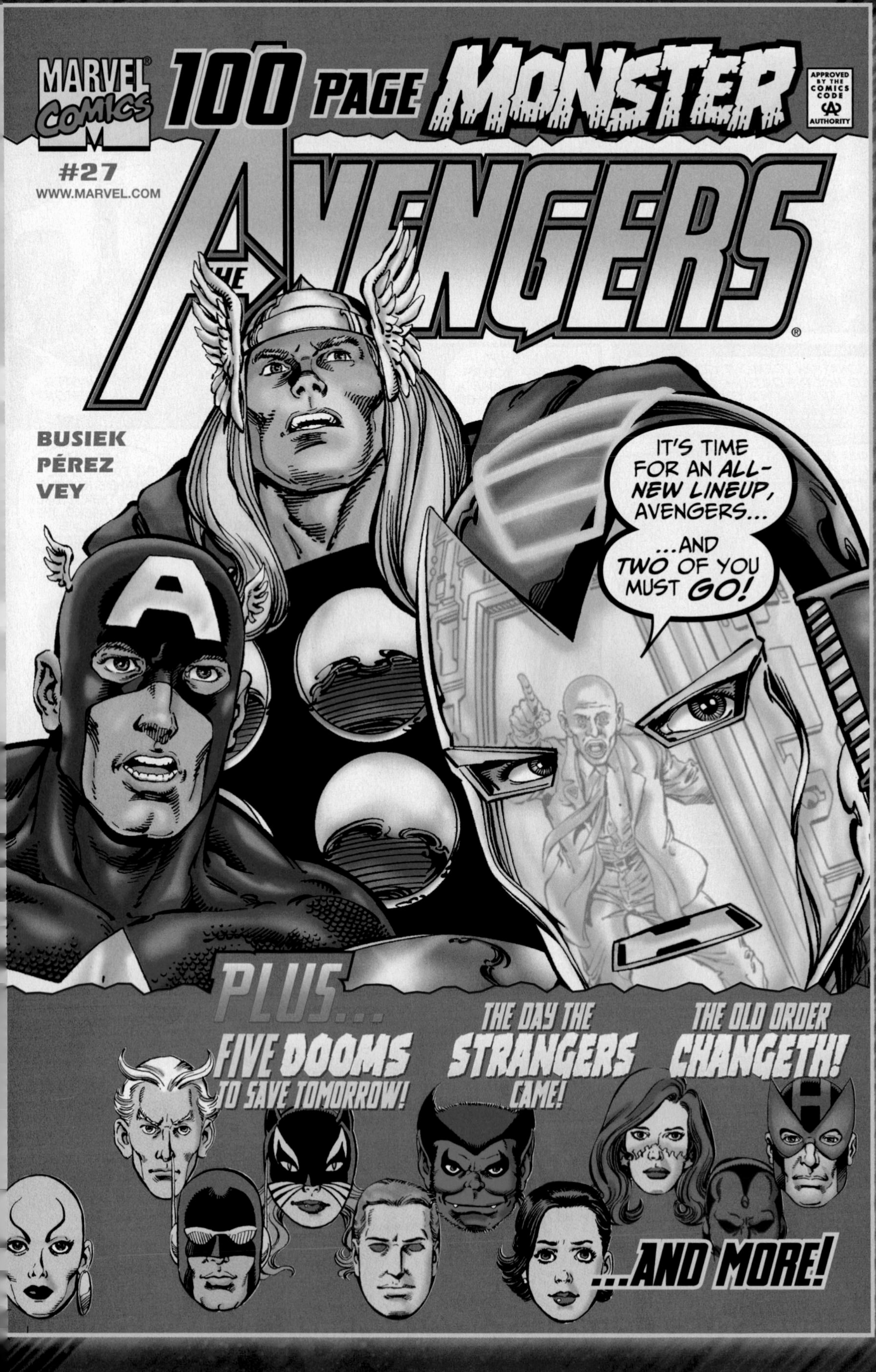

MARVEL® COMICS
100 PAGE MONSTER
APPROVED BY THE COMICS CODE AUTHORITY
#27
WWW.MARVEL.COM
THE AVENGERS®
BUSIEK
PÉREZ
VEY
IT'S TIME FOR AN ALL-NEW LINEUP, AVENGERS...
...AND TWO OF YOU MUST GO!
PLUS...
FIVE DOOMS TO SAVE TOMORROW!
THE DAY THE STRANGERS CAME!
THE OLD ORDER CHANGETH!
...AND MORE!

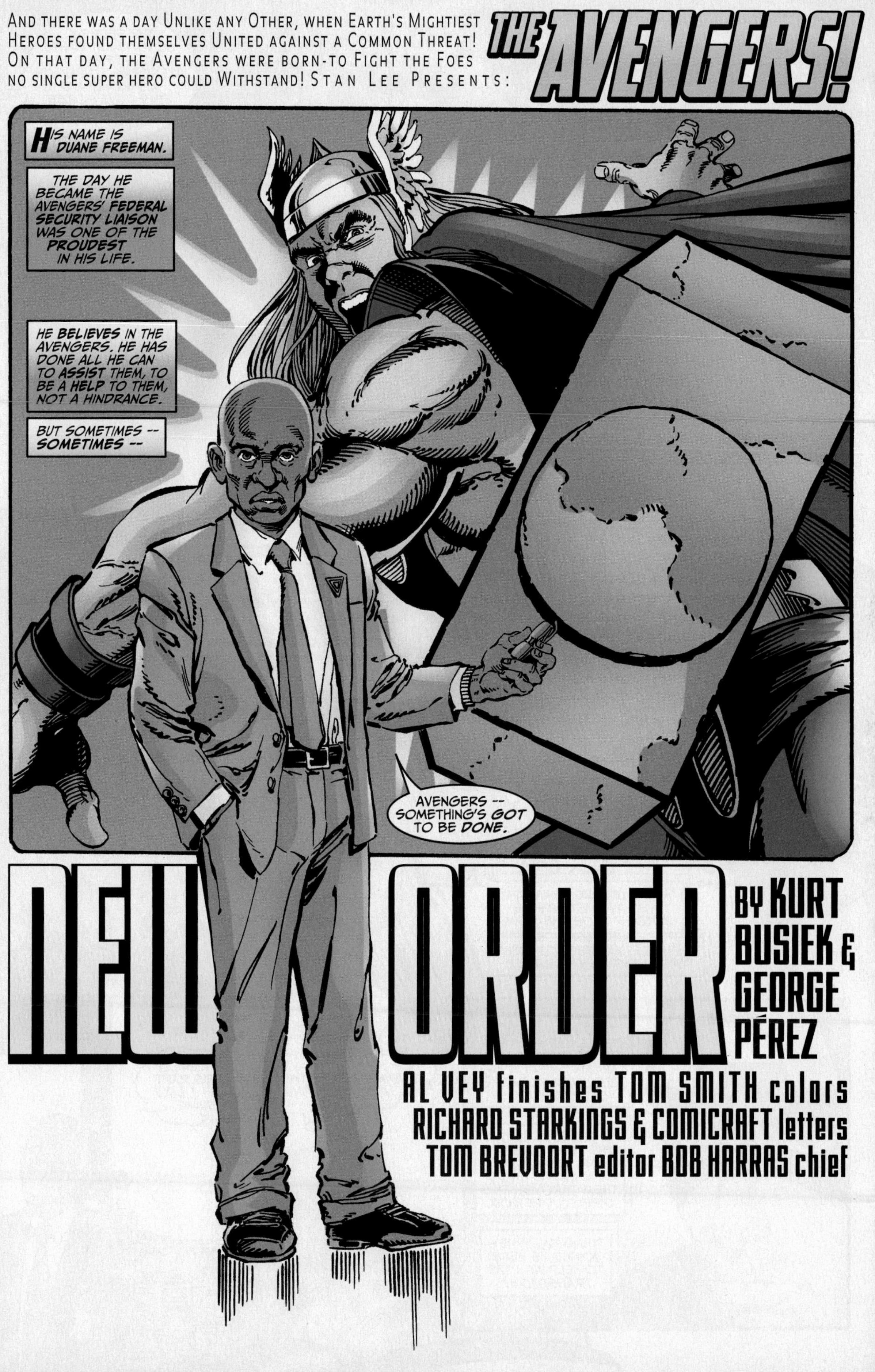

AND THERE WAS A DAY UNLIKE ANY OTHER, WHEN EARTH'S MIGHTIEST HEROES FOUND THEMSELVES UNITED AGAINST A COMMON THREAT! ON THAT DAY, THE AVENGERS WERE BORN-TO FIGHT THE FOES NO SINGLE SUPER HERO COULD WITHSTAND! STAN LEE PRESENTS:
THE AVENGERS!
HIS NAME IS DUANE FREEMAN.
THE DAY HE BECAME THE AVENGERS' FEDERAL SECURITY LIAISON WAS ONE OF THE PROUDEST IN HIS LIFE.
HE BELIEVES IN THE AVENGERS. HE HAS DONE ALL HE CAN TO ASSIST THEM, TO BE A HELP TO THEM, NOT A HINDRANCE.
BUT SOMETIMES -- SOMETIMES --
AVENGERS -- SOMETHING'S GOT TO BE DONE.
NEW ORDER
BY KURT BUSIEK & GEORGE PÉREZ
AL VEY finishes TOM SMITH colors
RICHARD STARKINGS & COMICRAFT letters
TOM BREVOORT editor BOB HARRAS chief

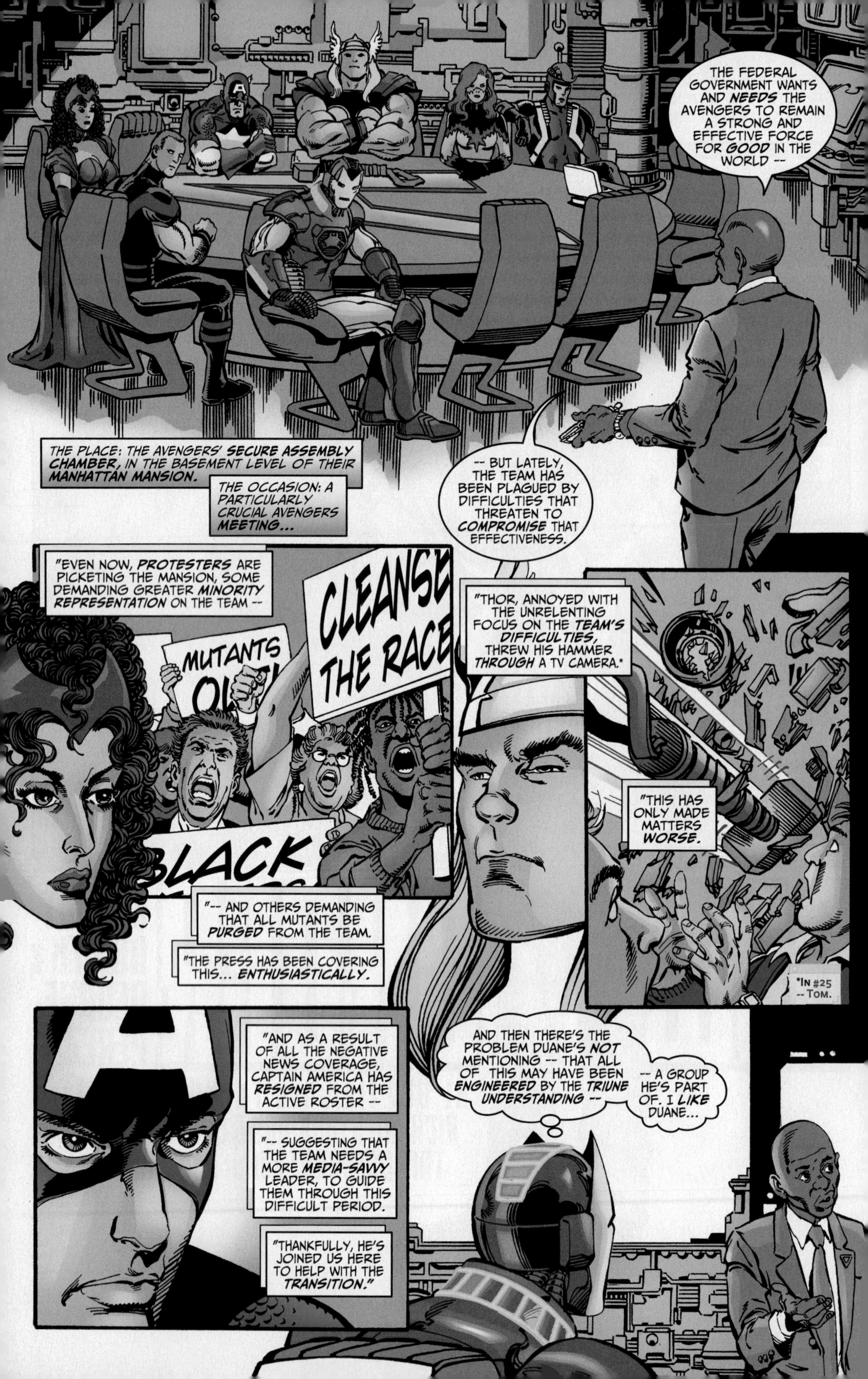
THE FEDERAL GOVERNMENT WANTS AND NEEDS THE AVENGERS TO REMAIN A STRONG AND EFFECTIVE FORCE FOR GOOD IN THE WORLD --
THE PLACE: THE AVENGERS' SECURE ASSEMBLY CHAMBER, IN THE BASEMENT LEVEL OF THEIR MANHATTAN MANSION.
THE OCCASION: A PARTICULARLY CRUCIAL AVENGERS MEETING...
-- BUT LATELY, THE TEAM HAS BEEN PLAGUED BY DIFFICULTIES THAT THREATEN TO COMPROMISE THAT EFFECTIVENESS.
"EVEN NOW, PROTESTERS ARE PICKETING THE MANSION, SOME DEMANDING GREATER MINORITY REPRESENTATION ON THE TEAM --
CLEANSE THE RACE
MUTANTS
BLACK
"-- AND OTHERS DEMANDING THAT ALL MUTANTS BE PURGED FROM THE TEAM.
"THE PRESS HAS BEEN COVERING THIS... ENTHUSIASTICALLY.
"THOR, ANNOYED WITH THE UNRELENTING FOCUS ON THE TEAM'S DIFFICULTIES, THREW HIS HAMMER THROUGH A TV CAMERA.*
"THIS HAS ONLY MADE MATTERS WORSE.
*IN #25 -- TOM.
"AND AS A RESULT OF ALL THE NEGATIVE NEWS COVERAGE, CAPTAIN AMERICA HAS RESIGNED FROM THE ACTIVE ROSTER --
"-- SUGGESTING THAT THE TEAM NEEDS A MORE MEDIA-SAVVY LEADER, TO GUIDE THEM THROUGH THIS DIFFICULT PERIOD.
"THANKFULLY, HE'S JOINED US HERE TO HELP WITH THE TRANSITION."
AND THEN THERE'S THE PROBLEM DUANE'S NOT MENTIONING -- THAT ALL OF THIS MAY HAVE BEEN ENGINEERED BY THE TRIUNE UNDERSTANDING --
-- A GROUP HE'S PART OF. I LIKE DUANE...

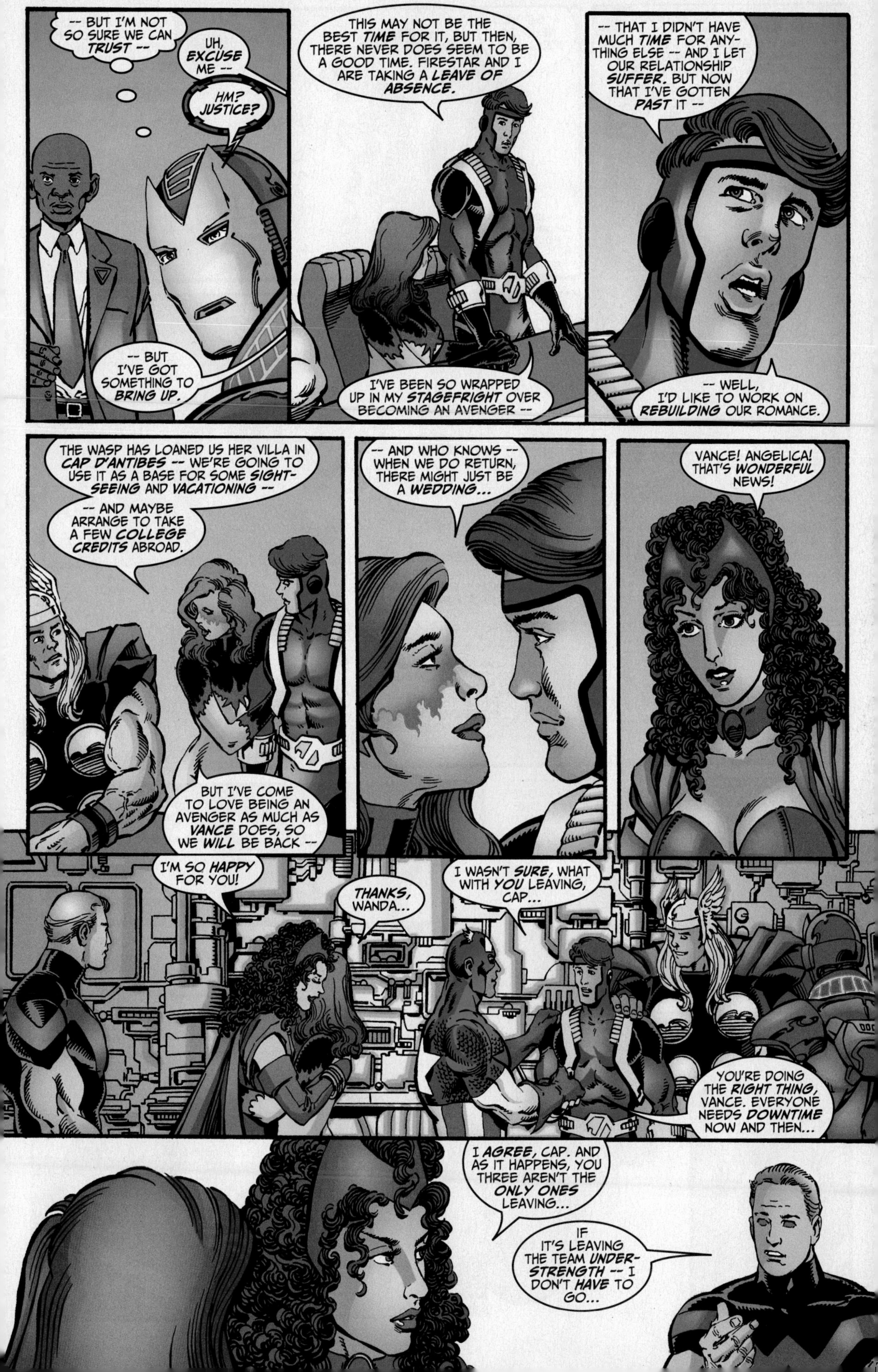
-- BUT I'M NOT SO SURE WE CAN TRUST --
UH, EXCUSE ME --
HM? JUSTICE?
-- BUT I'VE GOT SOMETHING TO BRING UP.
THIS MAY NOT BE THE BEST TIME FOR IT, BUT THEN, THERE NEVER DOES SEEM TO BE A GOOD TIME. FIRESTAR AND I ARE TAKING A LEAVE OF ABSENCE.
I'VE BEEN SO WRAPPED UP IN MY STAGEFRIGHT OVER BECOMING AN AVENGER --
-- THAT I DIDN'T HAVE MUCH TIME FOR ANYTHING ELSE -- AND I LET OUR RELATIONSHIP SUFFER. BUT NOW THAT I'VE GOTTEN PAST IT --
-- WELL, I'D LIKE TO WORK ON REBUILDING OUR ROMANCE.
THE WASP HAS LOANED US HER VILLA IN CAP D'ANTIBES -- WE'RE GOING TO USE IT AS A BASE FOR SOME SIGHT-SEEING AND VACATIONING --
-- AND MAYBE ARRANGE TO TAKE A FEW COLLEGE CREDITS ABROAD.
BUT I'VE COME TO LOVE BEING AN AVENGER AS MUCH AS VANCE DOES, SO WE WILL BE BACK --
-- AND WHO KNOWS -- WHEN WE DO RETURN, THERE MIGHT JUST BE A WEDDING...
VANCE! ANGELICA! THAT'S WONDERFUL NEWS!
I'M SO HAPPY FOR YOU!
THANKS, WANDA...
I WASN'T SURE, WHAT WITH YOU LEAVING, CAP...
YOU'RE DOING THE RIGHT THING, VANCE. EVERYONE NEEDS DOWNTIME NOW AND THEN...
I AGREE, CAP. AND AS IT HAPPENS, YOU THREE AREN'T THE ONLY ONES LEAVING...
IF IT'S LEAVING THE TEAM UNDER-STRENGTH -- I DON'T HAVE TO GO...

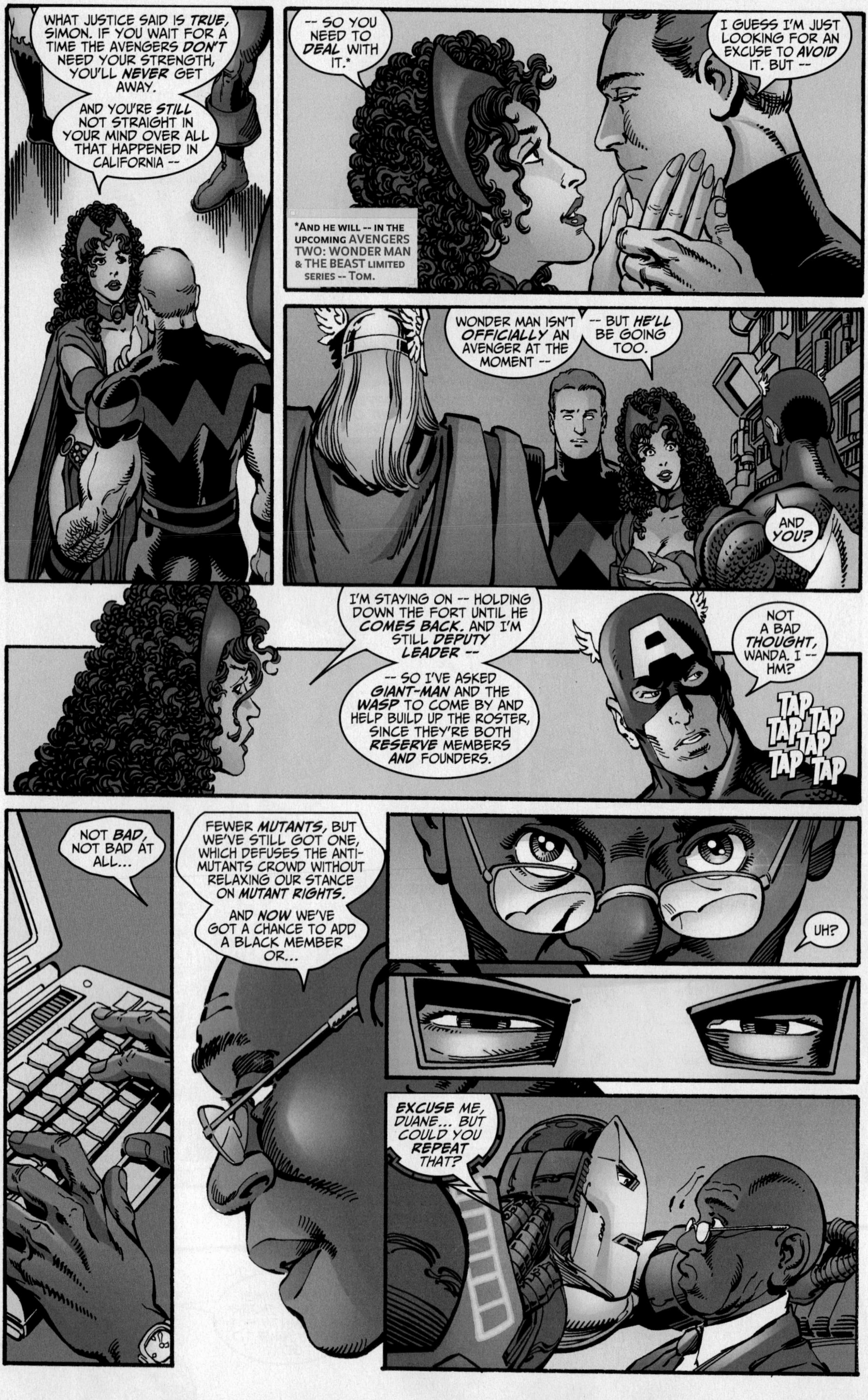
WHAT JUSTICE SAID IS TRUE, SIMON. IF YOU WAIT FOR A TIME THE AVENGERS DON'T NEED YOUR STRENGTH, YOU'LL NEVER GET AWAY.
AND YOU'RE STILL NOT STRAIGHT IN YOUR MIND OVER ALL THAT HAPPENED IN CALIFORNIA --
-- SO YOU NEED TO DEAL WITH IT.*
*AND HE WILL -- IN THE UPCOMING AVENGERS TWO: WONDER MAN & THE BEAST LIMITED SERIES -- TOM.
I GUESS I'M JUST LOOKING FOR AN EXCUSE TO AVOID IT. BUT --
WONDER MAN ISN'T OFFICIALLY AN AVENGER AT THE MOMENT --
-- BUT HE'LL BE GOING TOO.
AND YOU?
I'M STAYING ON -- HOLDING DOWN THE FORT UNTIL HE COMES BACK. AND I'M STILL DEPUTY LEADER --
-- SO I'VE ASKED GIANT-MAN AND THE WASP TO COME BY AND HELP BUILD UP THE ROSTER, SINCE THEY'RE BOTH RESERVE MEMBERS AND FOUNDERS.
NOT A BAD THOUGHT, WANDA. I -- HM?
TAP TAP TAP TAP TAP TAP
NOT BAD, NOT BAD AT ALL...
FEWER MUTANTS, BUT WE'VE STILL GOT ONE, WHICH DEFUSES THE ANTI-MUTANTS CROWD WITHOUT RELAXING OUR STANCE ON MUTANT RIGHTS.
AND NOW WE'VE GOT A CHANCE TO ADD A BLACK MEMBER OR...
UH?
EXCUSE ME, DUANE... BUT COULD YOU REPEAT THAT?

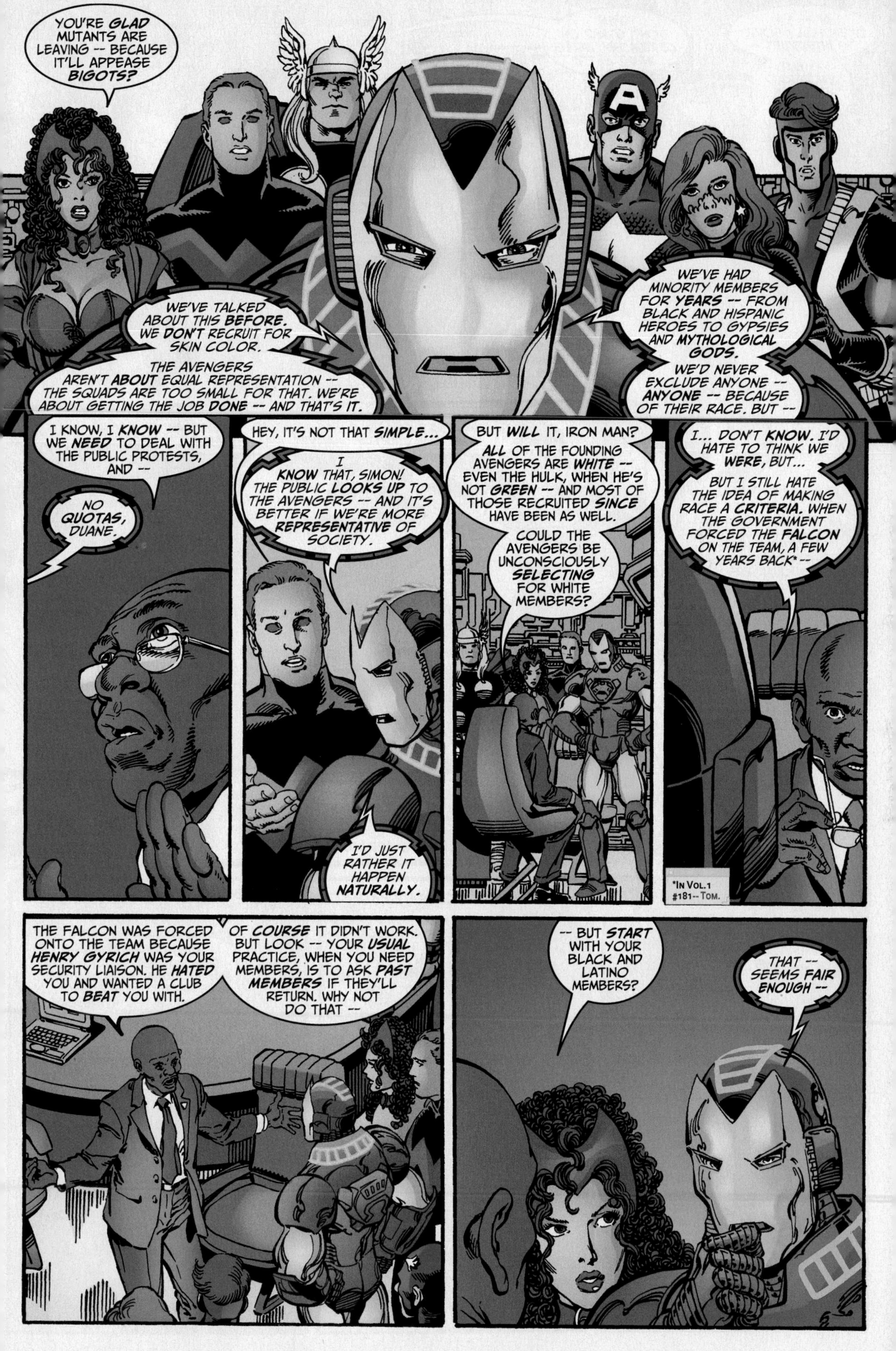

YOU'RE GLAD MUTANTS ARE LEAVING -- BECAUSE IT'LL APPEASE BIGOTS?
WE'VE TALKED ABOUT THIS BEFORE. WE DON'T RECRUIT FOR SKIN COLOR.
THE AVENGERS AREN'T ABOUT EQUAL REPRESENTATION -- THE SQUADS ARE TOO SMALL FOR THAT. WE'RE ABOUT GETTING THE JOB DONE -- AND THAT'S IT.
WE'VE HAD MINORITY MEMBERS FOR YEARS -- FROM BLACK AND HISPANIC HEROES TO GYPSIES AND MYTHOLOGICAL GODS.
WE'D NEVER EXCLUDE ANYONE -- ANYONE -- BECAUSE OF THEIR RACE. BUT --
I KNOW, I KNOW -- BUT WE NEED TO DEAL WITH THE PUBLIC PROTESTS, AND --
NO QUOTAS, DUANE.
HEY, IT'S NOT THAT SIMPLE...
I KNOW THAT, SIMON! THE PUBLIC LOOKS UP TO THE AVENGERS -- AND IT'S BETTER IF WE'RE MORE REPRESENTATIVE OF SOCIETY.
I'D JUST RATHER IT HAPPEN NATURALLY.
BUT WILL IT, IRON MAN?
ALL OF THE FOUNDING AVENGERS ARE WHITE -- EVEN THE HULK, WHEN HE'S NOT GREEN -- AND MOST OF THOSE RECRUITED SINCE HAVE BEEN AS WELL.
COULD THE AVENGERS BE UNCONSCIOUSLY SELECTING FOR WHITE MEMBERS?
I... DON'T KNOW. I'D HATE TO THINK WE WERE, BUT...
BUT I STILL HATE THE IDEA OF MAKING RACE A CRITERIA. WHEN THE GOVERNMENT FORCED THE FALCON ON THE TEAM, A FEW YEARS BACK* --
*IN VOL.1 #181-- TOM.
THE FALCON WAS FORCED ONTO THE TEAM BECAUSE HENRY GYRICH WAS YOUR SECURITY LIAISON. HE HATED YOU AND WANTED A CLUB TO BEAT YOU WITH.
OF COURSE IT DIDN'T WORK. BUT LOOK -- YOUR USUAL PRACTICE, WHEN YOU NEED MEMBERS, IS TO ASK PAST MEMBERS IF THEY'LL RETURN. WHY NOT DO THAT --
-- BUT START WITH YOUR BLACK AND LATINO MEMBERS?
THAT -- SEEMS FAIR ENOUGH --

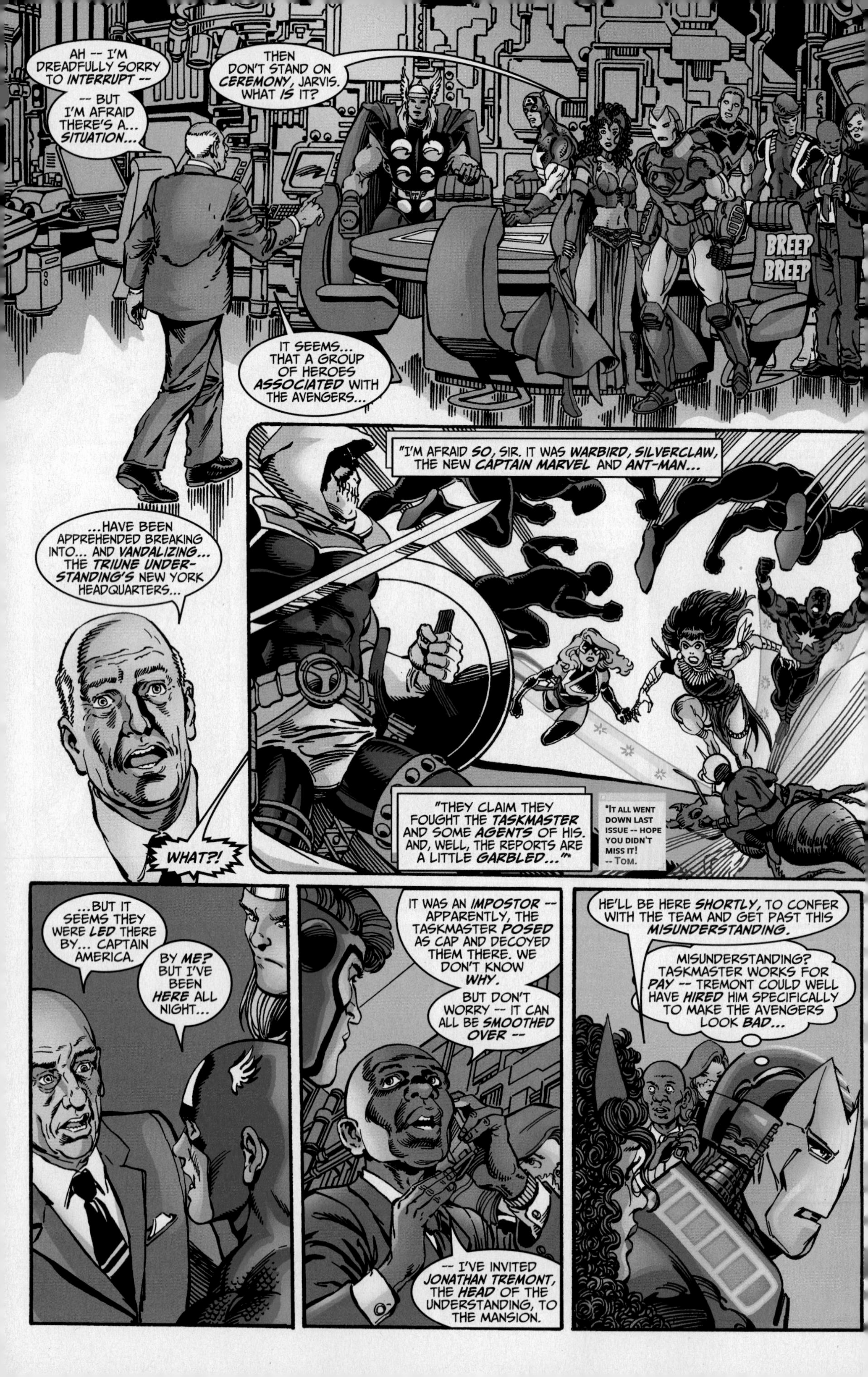
AH -- I'M DREADFULLY SORRY TO INTERRUPT --
-- BUT I'M AFRAID THERE'S A... SITUATION...
THEN DON'T STAND ON CEREMONY, JARVIS. WHAT IS IT?
BREEP BREEP
IT SEEMS... THAT A GROUP OF HEROES ASSOCIATED WITH THE AVENGERS...
"I'M AFRAID SO, SIR. IT WAS WARBIRD, SILVERCLAW, THE NEW CAPTAIN MARVEL AND ANT-MAN...
...HAVE BEEN APPREHENDED BREAKING INTO... AND VANDALIZING... THE TRIUNE UNDER-STANDING'S NEW YORK HEADQUARTERS...
WHAT?!
"THEY CLAIM THEY FOUGHT THE TASKMASTER AND SOME AGENTS OF HIS. AND, WELL, THE REPORTS ARE A LITTLE GARBLED..."*
*IT ALL WENT DOWN LAST ISSUE -- HOPE YOU DIDN'T MISS IT! -- TOM.
...BUT IT SEEMS THEY WERE LED THERE BY... CAPTAIN AMERICA.
BY ME? BUT I'VE BEEN HERE ALL NIGHT...
IT WAS AN IMPOSTOR -- APPARENTLY, THE TASKMASTER POSED AS CAP AND DECOYED THEM THERE. WE DON'T KNOW WHY.
BUT DON'T WORRY -- IT CAN ALL BE SMOOTHED OVER --
-- I'VE INVITED JONATHAN TREMONT, THE HEAD OF THE UNDERSTANDING, TO THE MANSION.
HE'LL BE HERE SHORTLY, TO CONFER WITH THE TEAM AND GET PAST THIS MISUNDERSTANDING.
MISUNDERSTANDING? TASKMASTER WORKS FOR PAY -- TREMONT COULD WELL HAVE HIRED HIM SPECIFICALLY TO MAKE THE AVENGERS LOOK BAD...

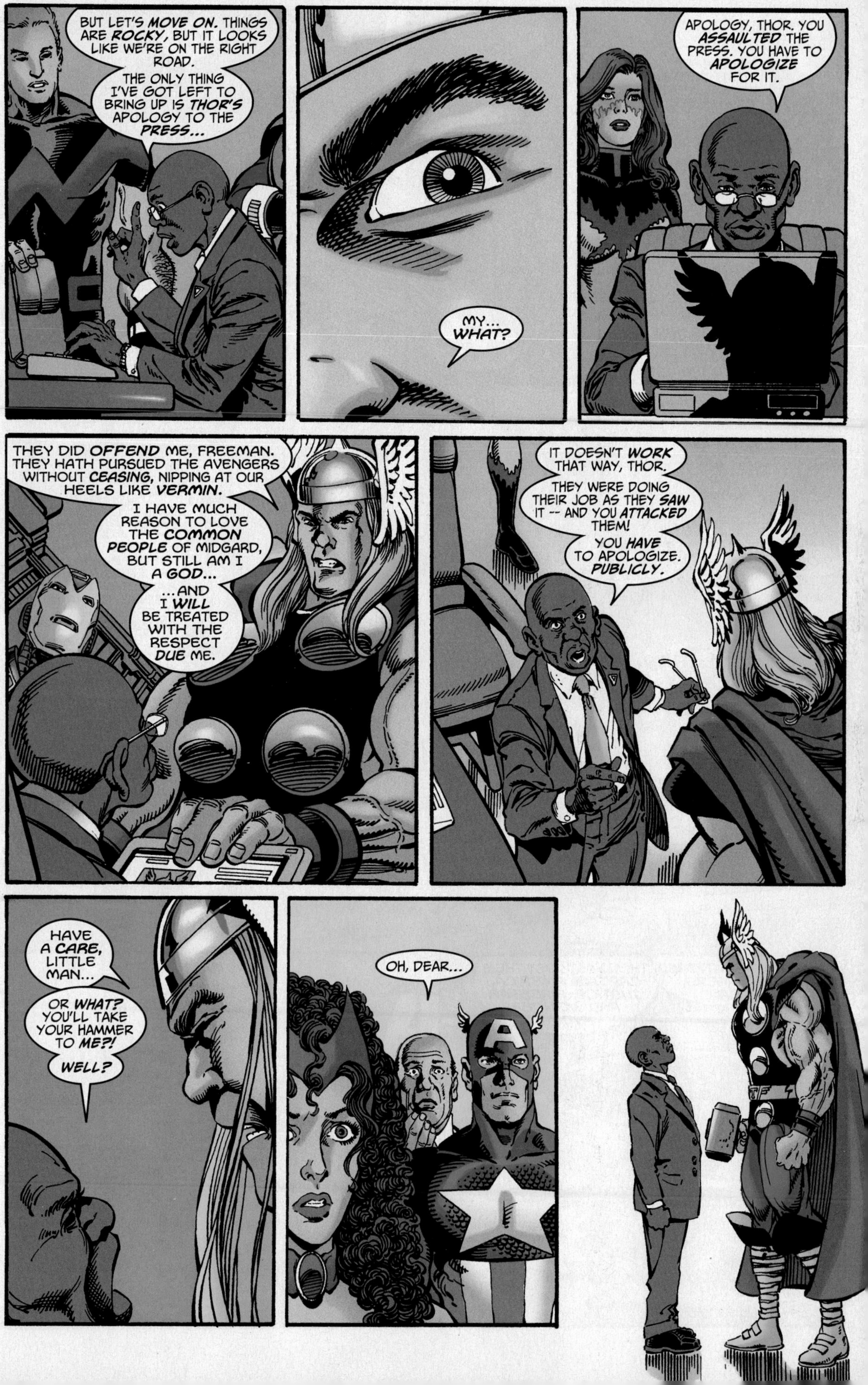
BUT LET'S MOVE ON. THINGS ARE ROCKY, BUT IT LOOKS LIKE WE'RE ON THE RIGHT ROAD.
THE ONLY THING I'VE GOT LEFT TO BRING UP IS THOR'S APOLOGY TO THE PRESS...
MY... WHAT?
APOLOGY, THOR. YOU ASSAULTED THE PRESS. YOU HAVE TO APOLOGIZE FOR IT.
THEY DID OFFEND ME, FREEMAN. THEY HATH PURSUED THE AVENGERS WITHOUT CEASING, NIPPING AT OUR HEELS LIKE VERMIN.
I HAVE MUCH REASON TO LOVE THE COMMON PEOPLE OF MIDGARD, BUT STILL AM I A GOD...
...AND I WILL BE TREATED WITH THE RESPECT DUE ME.
IT DOESN'T WORK THAT WAY, THOR.
THEY WERE DOING THEIR JOB AS THEY SAW IT -- AND YOU ATTACKED THEM!
YOU HAVE TO APOLOGIZE. PUBLICLY.
HAVE A CARE, LITTLE MAN...
OR WHAT? YOU'LL TAKE YOUR HAMMER TO ME?!
WELL?
OH, DEAR...

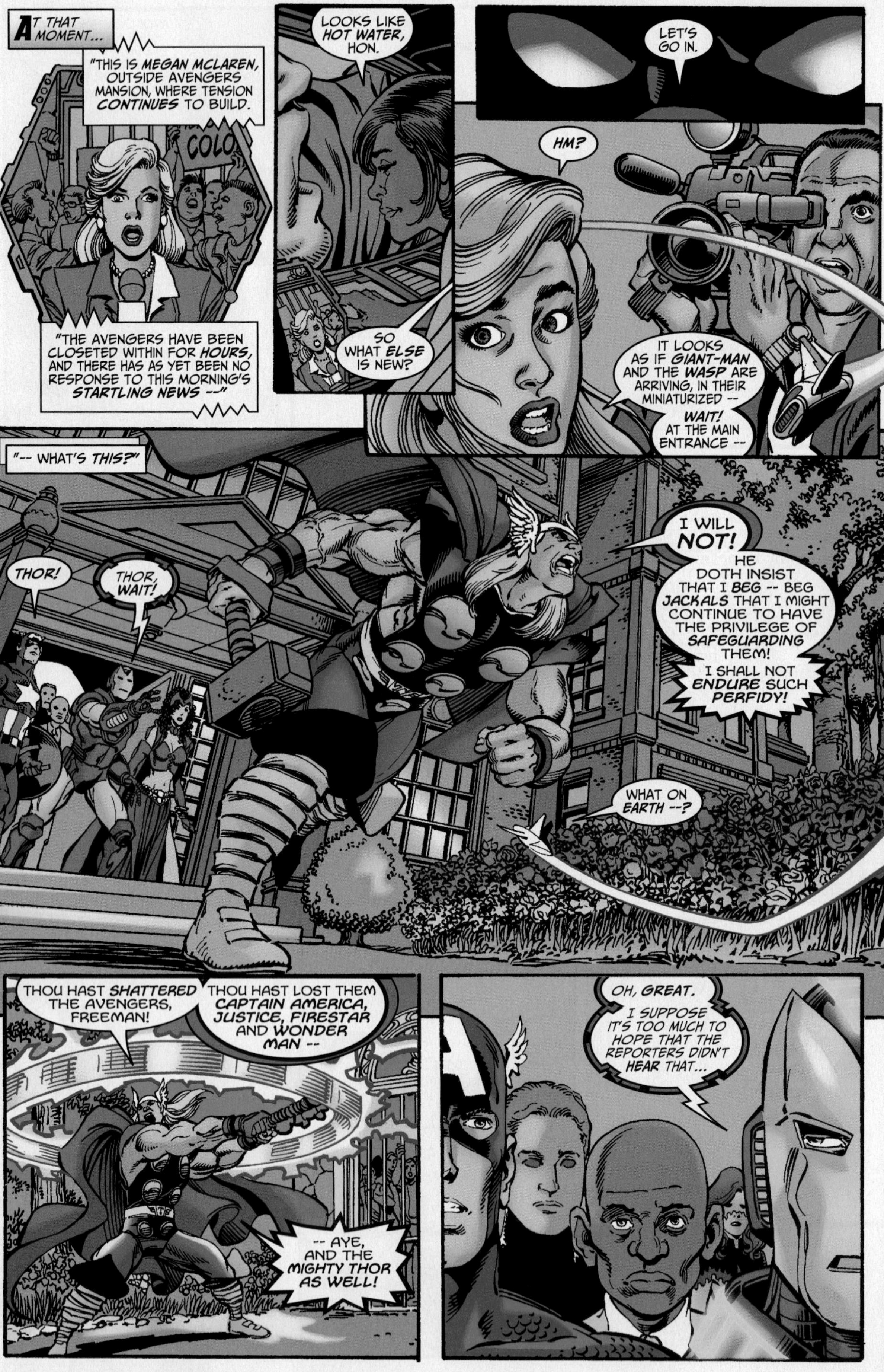
AT THAT MOMENT...
"THIS IS MEGAN MCLAREN, OUTSIDE AVENGERS MANSION, WHERE TENSION CONTINUES TO BUILD.
"THE AVENGERS HAVE BEEN CLOSETED WITHIN FOR HOURS, AND THERE HAS AS YET BEEN NO RESPONSE TO THIS MORNING'S STARTLING NEWS --"
LOOKS LIKE HOT WATER, HON.
SO WHAT ELSE IS NEW?
LET'S GO IN.
HM?
IT LOOKS AS IF GIANT-MAN AND THE WASP ARE ARRIVING, IN THEIR MINIATURIZED --
WAIT! AT THE MAIN ENTRANCE --
"-- WHAT'S THIS?"
THOR!
THOR, WAIT!
I WILL NOT!
HE DOTH INSIST THAT I BEG -- BEG JACKALS THAT I MIGHT CONTINUE TO HAVE THE PRIVILEGE OF SAFEGUARDING THEM!
I SHALL NOT ENDURE SUCH PERFIDY!
WHAT ON EARTH --?
THOU HAST SHATTERED THE AVENGERS, FREEMAN!
THOU HAST LOST THEM CAPTAIN AMERICA, JUSTICE, FIRESTAR AND WONDER MAN --
-- AYE, AND THE MIGHTY THOR AS WELL!
OH, GREAT.
I SUPPOSE IT'S TOO MUCH TO HOPE THAT THE REPORTERS DIDN'T HEAR THAT...

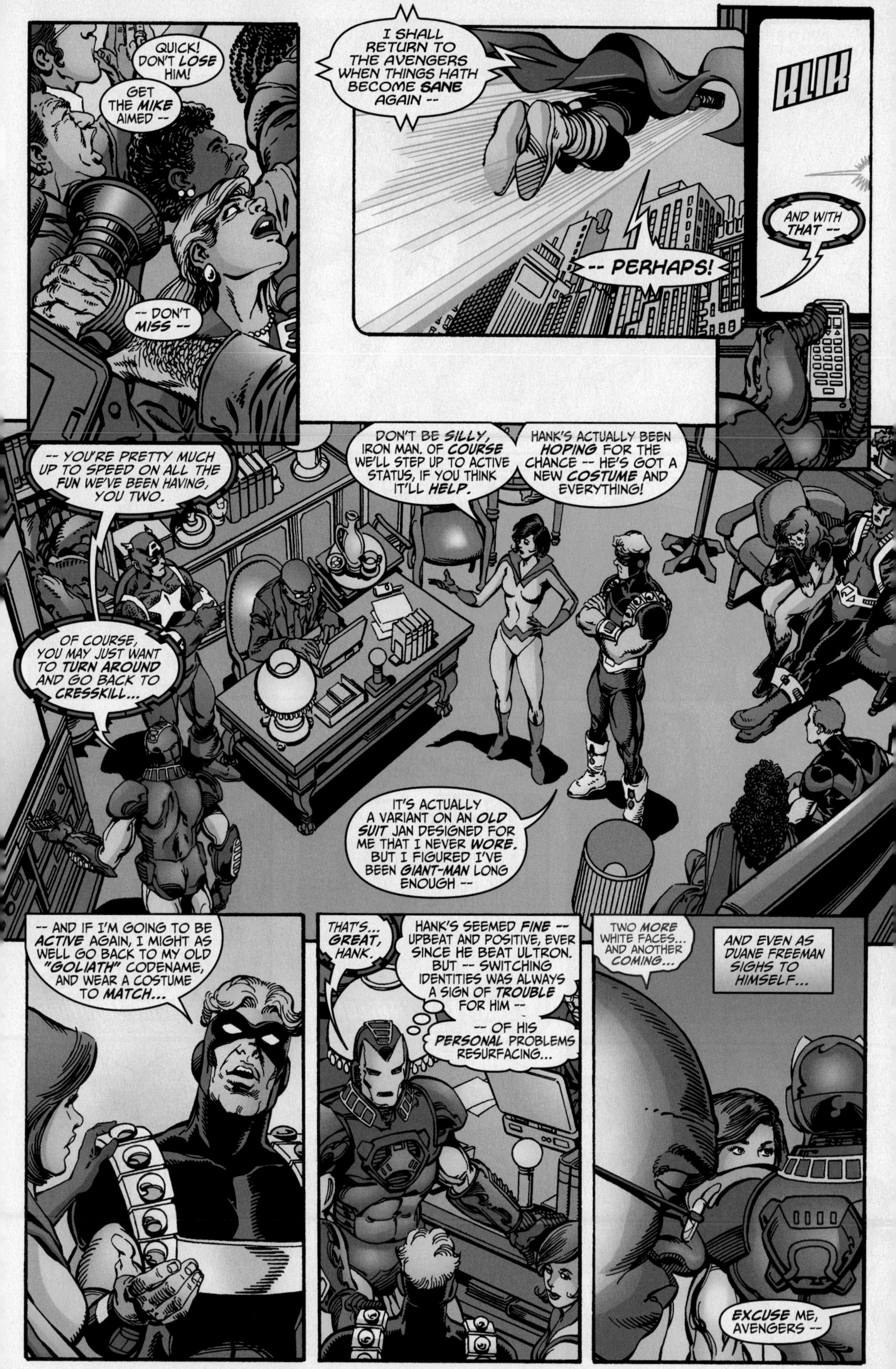
QUICK! DON'T LOSE HIM!
GET THE MIKE AIMED --
-- DON'T MISS --
I SHALL RETURN TO THE AVENGERS WHEN THINGS HATH BECOME SANE AGAIN --
-- PERHAPS!
KLIK
AND WITH THAT --
-- YOU'RE PRETTY MUCH UP TO SPEED ON ALL THE FUN WE'VE BEEN HAVING, YOU TWO.
OF COURSE, YOU MAY JUST WANT TO TURN AROUND AND GO BACK TO CRESSKILL...
DON'T BE SILLY, IRON MAN. OF COURSE WE'LL STEP UP TO ACTIVE STATUS, IF YOU THINK IT'LL HELP.
HANK'S ACTUALLY BEEN HOPING FOR THE CHANCE -- HE'S GOT A NEW COSTUME AND EVERYTHING!
IT'S ACTUALLY A VARIANT ON AN OLD SUIT JAN DESIGNED FOR ME THAT I NEVER WORE. BUT I FIGURED I'VE BEEN GIANT-MAN LONG ENOUGH --
-- AND IF I'M GOING TO BE ACTIVE AGAIN, I MIGHT AS WELL GO BACK TO MY OLD "GOLIATH" CODENAME, AND WEAR A COSTUME TO MATCH...
THAT'S... GREAT, HANK.
HANK'S SEEMED FINE -- UPBEAT AND POSITIVE, EVER SINCE HE BEAT ULTRON. BUT -- SWITCHING IDENTITIES WAS ALWAYS A SIGN OF TROUBLE FOR HIM --
-- OF HIS PERSONAL PROBLEMS RESURFACING...
TWO MORE WHITE FACES... AND ANOTHER COMING...
AND EVEN AS DUANE FREEMAN SIGHS TO HIMSELF...
EXCUSE ME, AVENGERS --

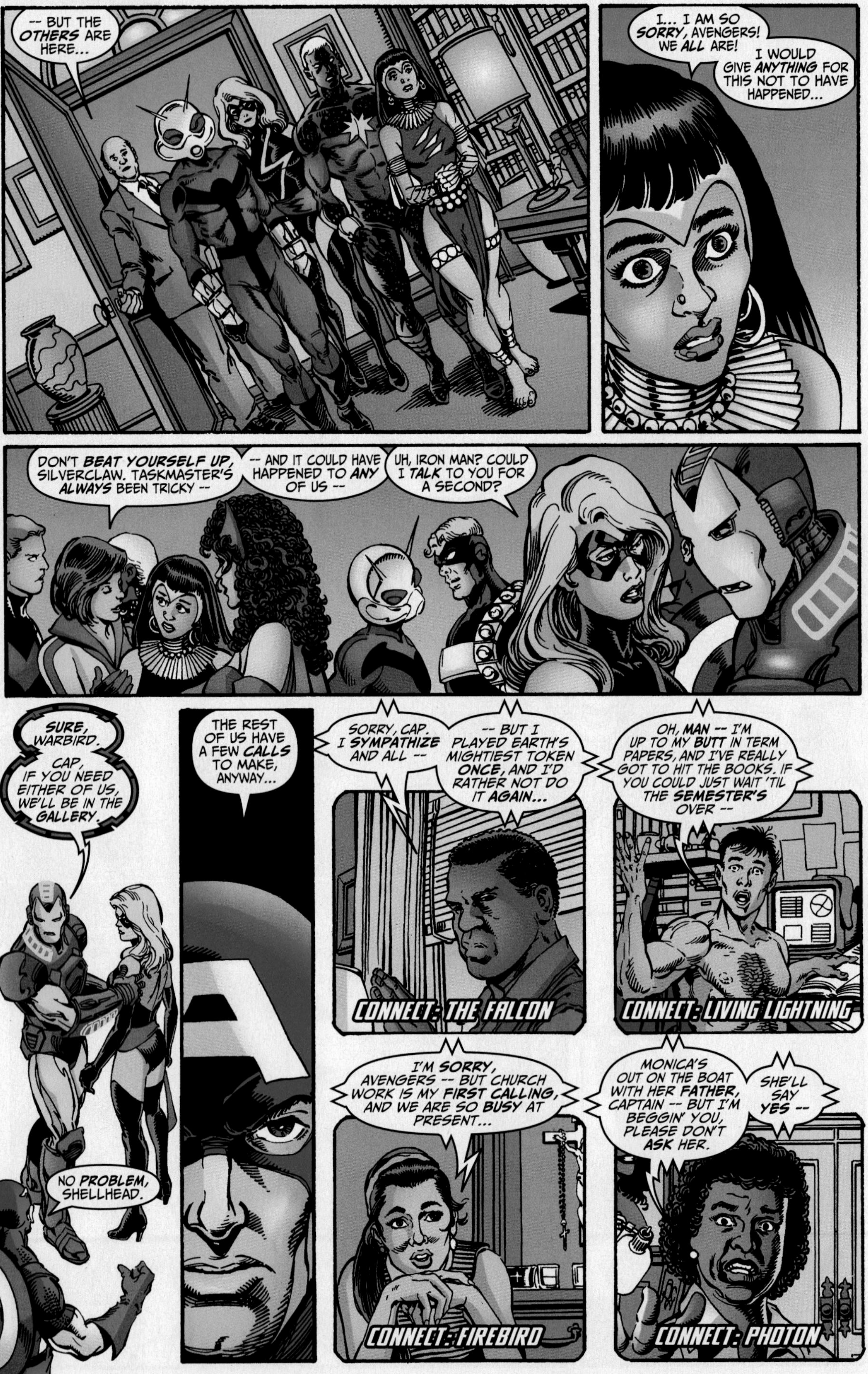

-- BUT THE OTHERS ARE HERE...
I... I AM SO SORRY, AVENGERS! WE ALL ARE!
I WOULD GIVE ANYTHING FOR THIS NOT TO HAVE HAPPENED...
DON'T BEAT YOURSELF UP, SILVERCLAW. TASKMASTER'S ALWAYS BEEN TRICKY --
-- AND IT COULD HAVE HAPPENED TO ANY OF US --
UH, IRON MAN? COULD I TALK TO YOU FOR A SECOND?
SURE, WARBIRD.
CAP, IF YOU NEED EITHER OF US, WE'LL BE IN THE GALLERY.
NO PROBLEM, SHELLHEAD.
THE REST OF US HAVE A FEW CALLS TO MAKE, ANYWAY...
SORRY, CAP. I SYMPATHIZE AND ALL --
-- BUT I PLAYED EARTH'S MIGHTIEST TOKEN ONCE, AND I'D RATHER NOT DO IT AGAIN...
CONNECT: THE FALCON
OH, MAN -- I'M UP TO MY BUTT IN TERM PAPERS, AND I'VE REALLY GOT TO HIT THE BOOKS. IF YOU COULD JUST WAIT 'TIL THE SEMESTER'S OVER --
CONNECT: LIVING LIGHTNING
I'M SORRY, AVENGERS -- BUT CHURCH WORK IS MY FIRST CALLING, AND WE ARE SO BUSY AT PRESENT...
CONNECT: FIREBIRD
MONICA'S OUT ON THE BOAT WITH HER FATHER, CAPTAIN -- BUT I'M BEGGIN' YOU, PLEASE DON'T ASK HER.
SHE'LL SAY YES --
CONNECT: PHOTON

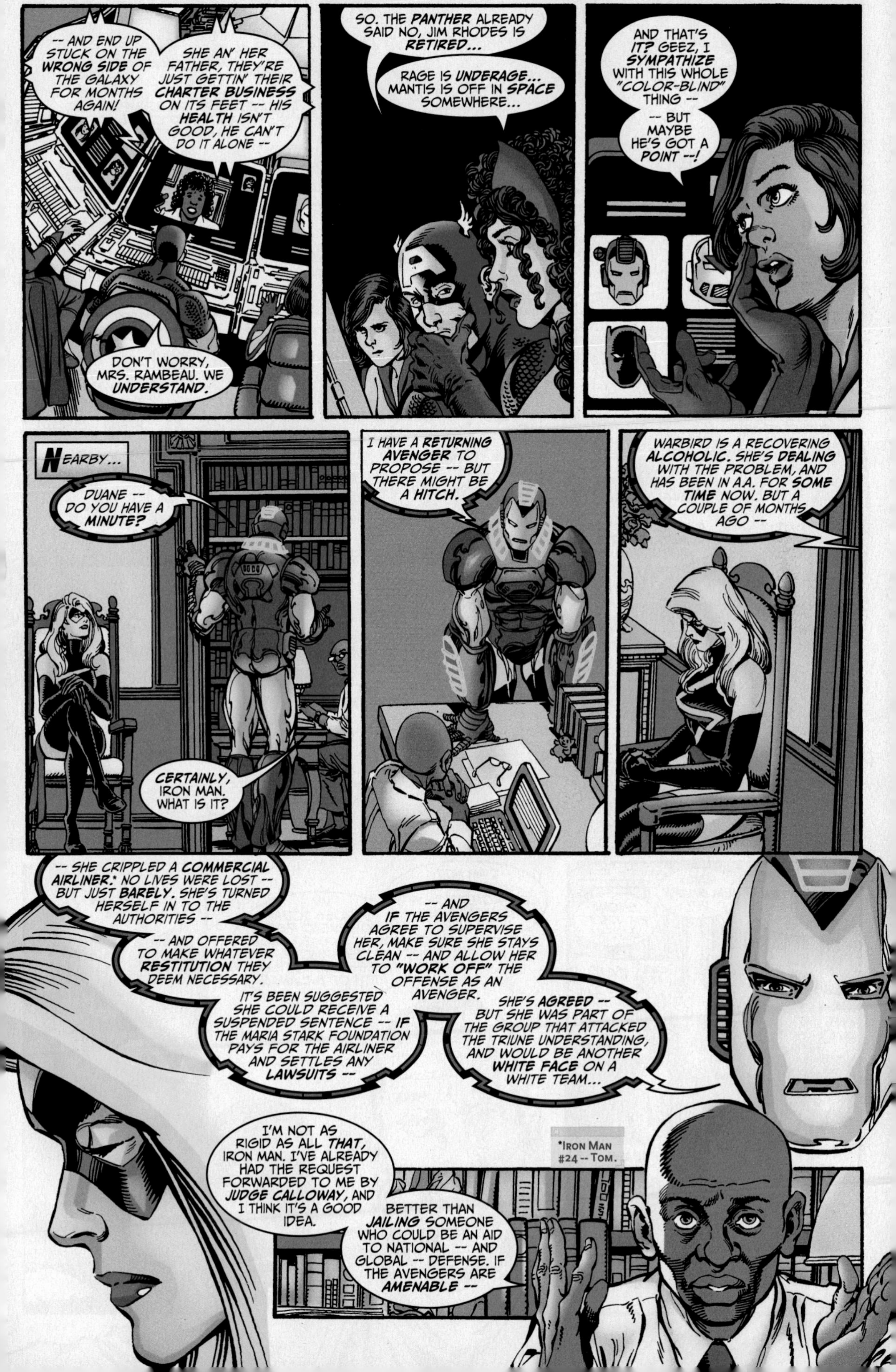
-- AND END UP STUCK ON THE WRONG SIDE OF THE GALAXY FOR MONTHS AGAIN!
SHE AN' HER FATHER, THEY'RE JUST GETTIN' THEIR CHARTER BUSINESS ON ITS FEET -- HIS HEALTH ISN'T GOOD, HE CAN'T DO IT ALONE --
DON'T WORRY, MRS. RAMBEAU. WE UNDERSTAND.
SO. THE PANTHER ALREADY SAID NO, JIM RHODES IS RETIRED...
RAGE IS UNDERAGE... MANTIS IS OFF IN SPACE SOMEWHERE...
AND THAT'S IT? GEEZ, I SYMPATHIZE WITH THIS WHOLE "COLOR-BLIND" THING --
-- BUT MAYBE HE'S GOT A POINT --!
NEARBY...
DUANE -- DO YOU HAVE A MINUTE?
CERTAINLY, IRON MAN. WHAT IS IT?
I HAVE A RETURNING AVENGER TO PROPOSE -- BUT THERE MIGHT BE A HITCH.
WARBIRD IS A RECOVERING ALCOHOLIC. SHE'S DEALING WITH THE PROBLEM, AND HAS BEEN IN A.A. FOR SOME TIME NOW. BUT A COUPLE OF MONTHS AGO --
-- SHE CRIPPLED A COMMERCIAL AIRLINER.* NO LIVES WERE LOST -- BUT JUST BARELY. SHE'S TURNED HERSELF IN TO THE AUTHORITIES --
-- AND OFFERED TO MAKE WHATEVER RESTITUTION THEY DEEM NECESSARY.
IT'S BEEN SUGGESTED SHE COULD RECEIVE A SUSPENDED SENTENCE -- IF THE MARIA STARK FOUNDATION PAYS FOR THE AIRLINER AND SETTLES ANY LAWSUITS --
-- AND IF THE AVENGERS AGREE TO SUPERVISE HER, MAKE SURE SHE STAYS CLEAN -- AND ALLOW HER TO "WORK OFF" THE OFFENSE AS AN AVENGER.
SHE'S AGREED -- BUT SHE WAS PART OF THE GROUP THAT ATTACKED THE TRIUNE UNDERSTANDING, AND WOULD BE ANOTHER WHITE FACE ON A WHITE TEAM...
*IRON MAN #24 -- TOM.
I'M NOT AS RIGID AS ALL THAT, IRON MAN. I'VE ALREADY HAD THE REQUEST FORWARDED TO ME BY JUDGE CALLOWAY, AND I THINK IT'S A GOOD IDEA.
BETTER THAN JAILING SOMEONE WHO COULD BE AN AID TO NATIONAL -- AND GLOBAL -- DEFENSE. IF THE AVENGERS ARE AMENABLE --

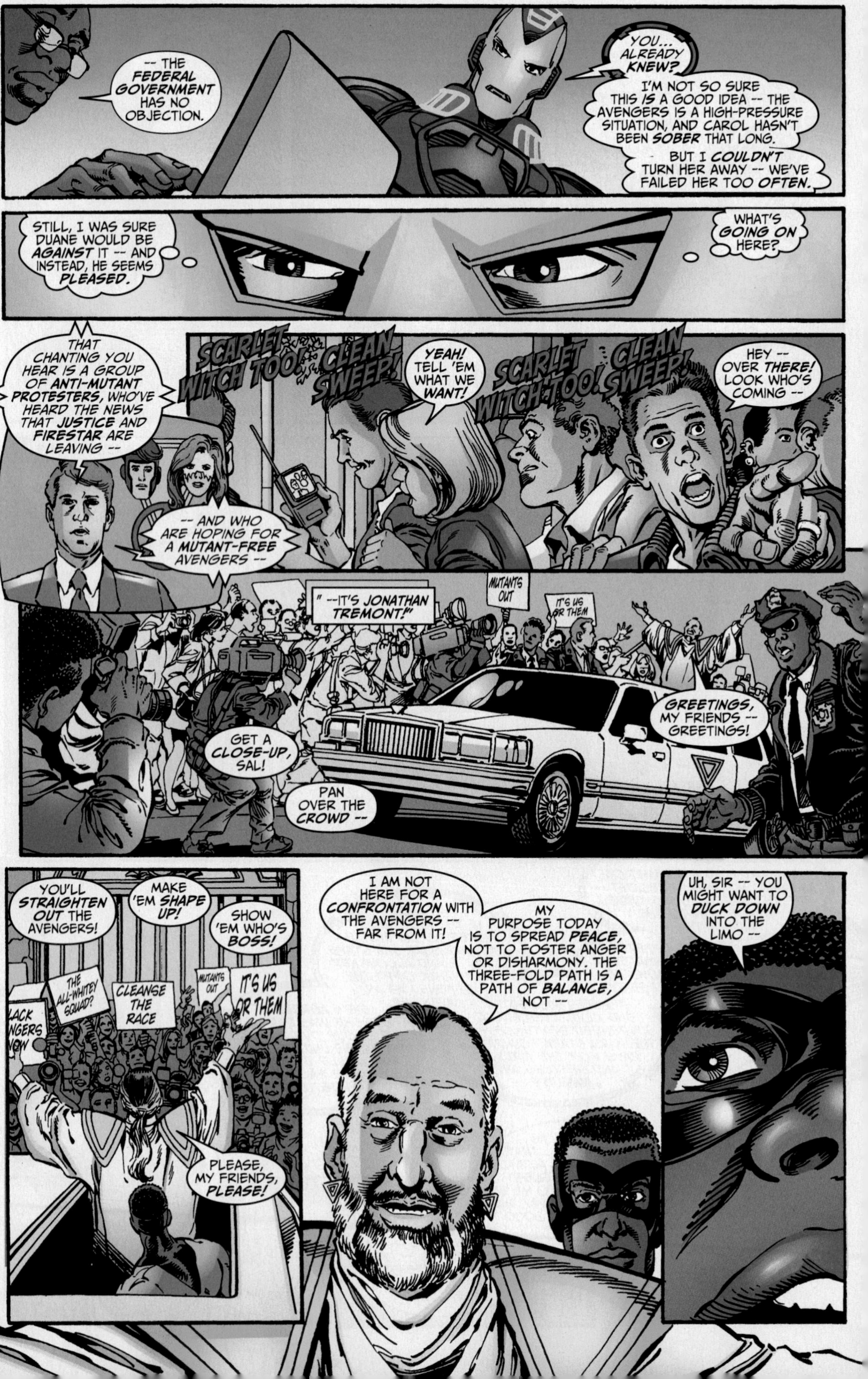
-- THE FEDERAL GOVERNMENT HAS NO OBJECTION.
YOU... ALREADY KNEW?
I'M NOT SO SURE THIS IS A GOOD IDEA -- THE AVENGERS IS A HIGH-PRESSURE SITUATION, AND CAROL HASN'T BEEN SOBER THAT LONG.
BUT I COULDN'T TURN HER AWAY -- WE'VE FAILED HER TOO OFTEN.
STILL, I WAS SURE DUANE WOULD BE AGAINST IT -- AND INSTEAD, HE SEEMS PLEASED.
WHAT'S GOING ON HERE?
THAT CHANTING YOU HEAR IS A GROUP OF ANTI-MUTANT PROTESTERS, WHO'VE HEARD THE NEWS THAT JUSTICE AND FIRESTAR ARE LEAVING --
SCARLET WITCH TOO! CLEAN SWEEP!
YEAH! TELL 'EM WHAT WE WANT!
SCARLET WITCH TOO! CLEAN SWEEP!
HEY -- OVER THERE! LOOK WHO'S COMING --
-- AND WHO ARE HOPING FOR A MUTANT-FREE AVENGERS --
" --IT'S JONATHAN TREMONT!"
MUTANTS OUT
IT'S US OR THEM
GET A CLOSE-UP, SAL!
PAN OVER THE CROWD --
GREETINGS, MY FRIENDS -- GREETINGS!
YOU'LL STRAIGHTEN OUT THE AVENGERS!
MAKE 'EM SHAPE UP!
SHOW 'EM WHO'S BOSS!
THE ALL-WHITEY SQUAD?
CLEANSE THE RACE
MUTANTS OUT
IT'S US OR THEM
PLEASE, MY FRIENDS, PLEASE!
I AM NOT HERE FOR A CONFRONTATION WITH THE AVENGERS -- FAR FROM IT!
MY PURPOSE TODAY IS TO SPREAD PEACE, NOT TO FOSTER ANGER OR DISHARMONY. THE THREE-FOLD PATH IS A PATH OF BALANCE, NOT --
UH, SIR -- YOU MIGHT WANT TO DUCK DOWN INTO THE LIMO --

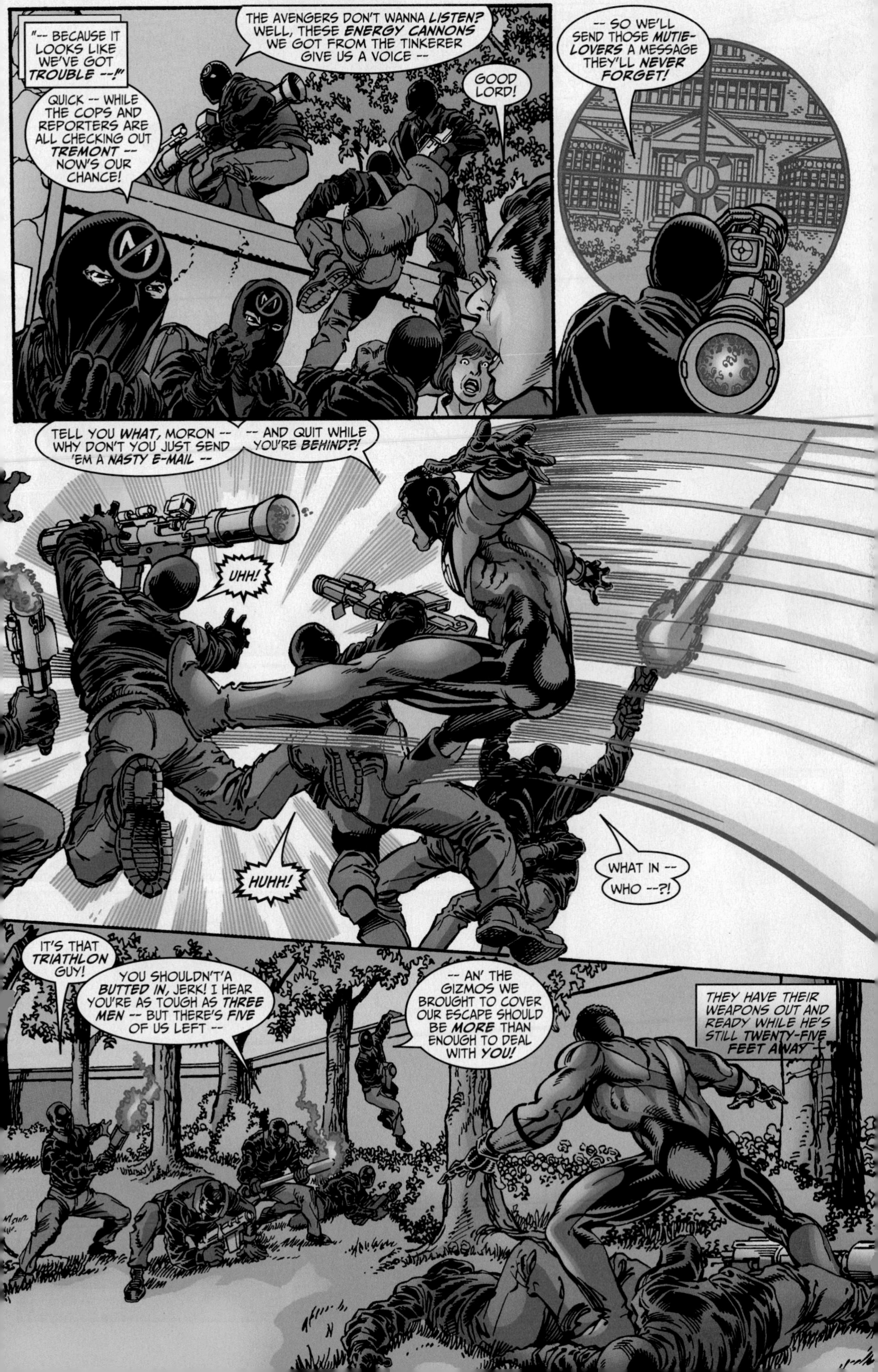
"-- BECAUSE IT LOOKS LIKE WE'VE GOT TROUBLE --!"
QUICK -- WHILE THE COPS AND REPORTERS ARE ALL CHECKING OUT TREMONT -- NOW'S OUR CHANCE!
THE AVENGERS DON'T WANNA LISTEN? WELL, THESE ENERGY CANNONS WE GOT FROM THE TINKERER GIVE US A VOICE --
GOOD LORD!
-- SO WE'LL SEND THOSE MUTIE-LOVERS A MESSAGE THEY'LL NEVER FORGET!
TELL YOU WHAT, MORON -- WHY DON'T YOU JUST SEND 'EM A NASTY E-MAIL --
-- AND QUIT WHILE YOU'RE BEHIND?!
UHH!
HUHH!
WHAT IN -- WHO --?!
IT'S THAT TRIATHLON GUY!
YOU SHOULDN'T'A BUTTED IN, JERK! I HEAR YOU'RE AS TOUGH AS THREE MEN -- BUT THERE'S FIVE OF US LEFT --
-- AN' THE GIZMOS WE BROUGHT TO COVER OUR ESCAPE SHOULD BE MORE THAN ENOUGH TO DEAL WITH YOU!
THEY HAVE THEIR WEAPONS OUT AND READY WHILE HE'S STILL TWENTY-FIVE FEET AWAY --

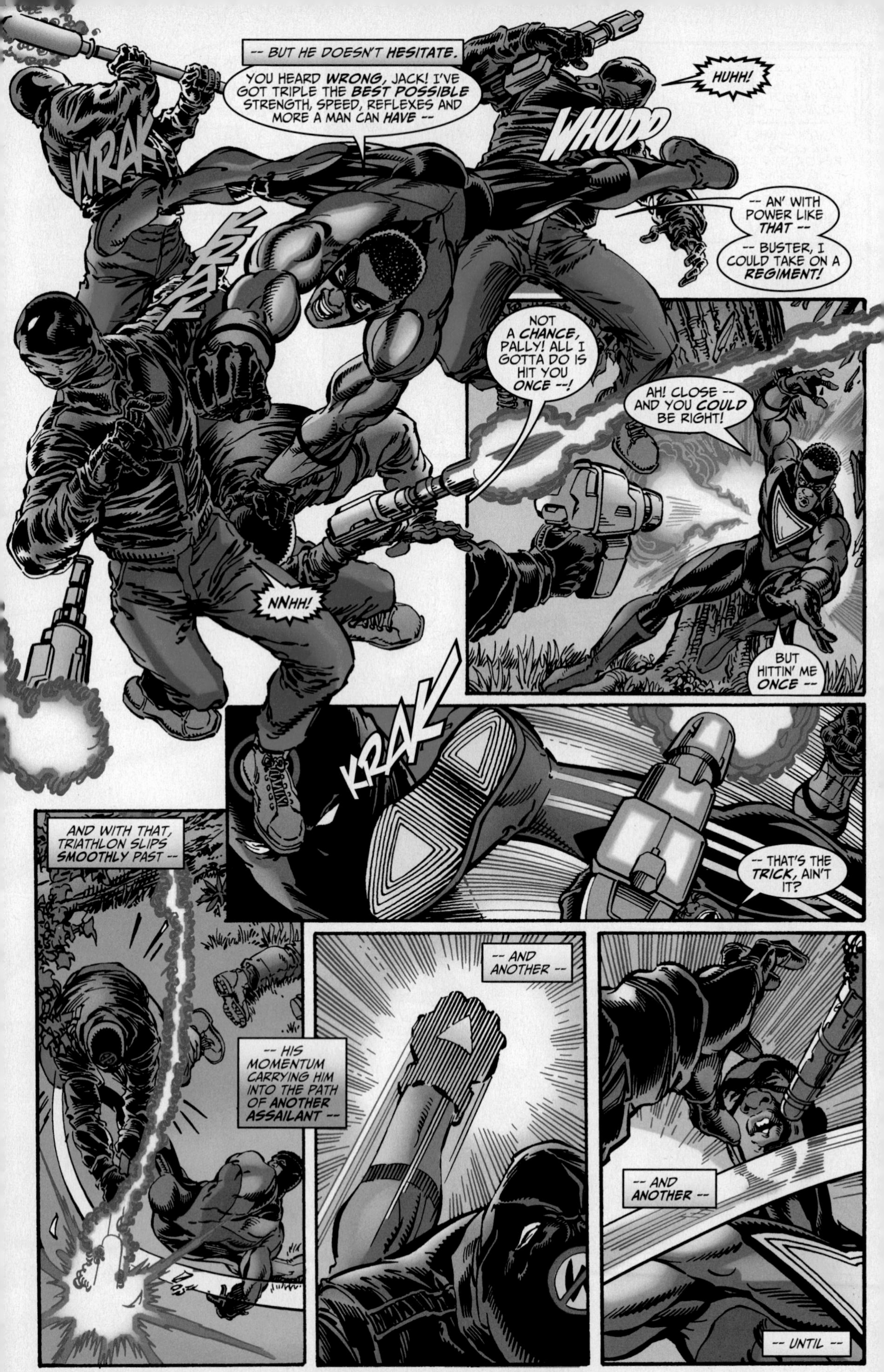
-- BUT HE DOESN'T HESITATE.
YOU HEARD WRONG, JACK! I'VE GOT TRIPLE THE BEST POSSIBLE STRENGTH, SPEED, REFLEXES AND MORE A MAN CAN HAVE --
WRAK
KRAK
WHUDD
HUHH!
-- AN' WITH POWER LIKE THAT --
-- BUSTER, I COULD TAKE ON A REGIMENT!
NOT A CHANCE, PALLY! ALL I GOTTA DO IS HIT YOU ONCE --!
AH! CLOSE -- AND YOU COULD BE RIGHT!
NNHH!
BUT HITTIN' ME ONCE --
KRAK
-- THAT'S THE TRICK, AIN'T IT?
AND WITH THAT, TRIATHLON SLIPS SMOOTHLY PAST --
-- HIS MOMENTUM CARRYING HIM INTO THE PATH OF ANOTHER ASSAILANT --
-- AND ANOTHER --
-- AND ANOTHER --
-- UNTIL --

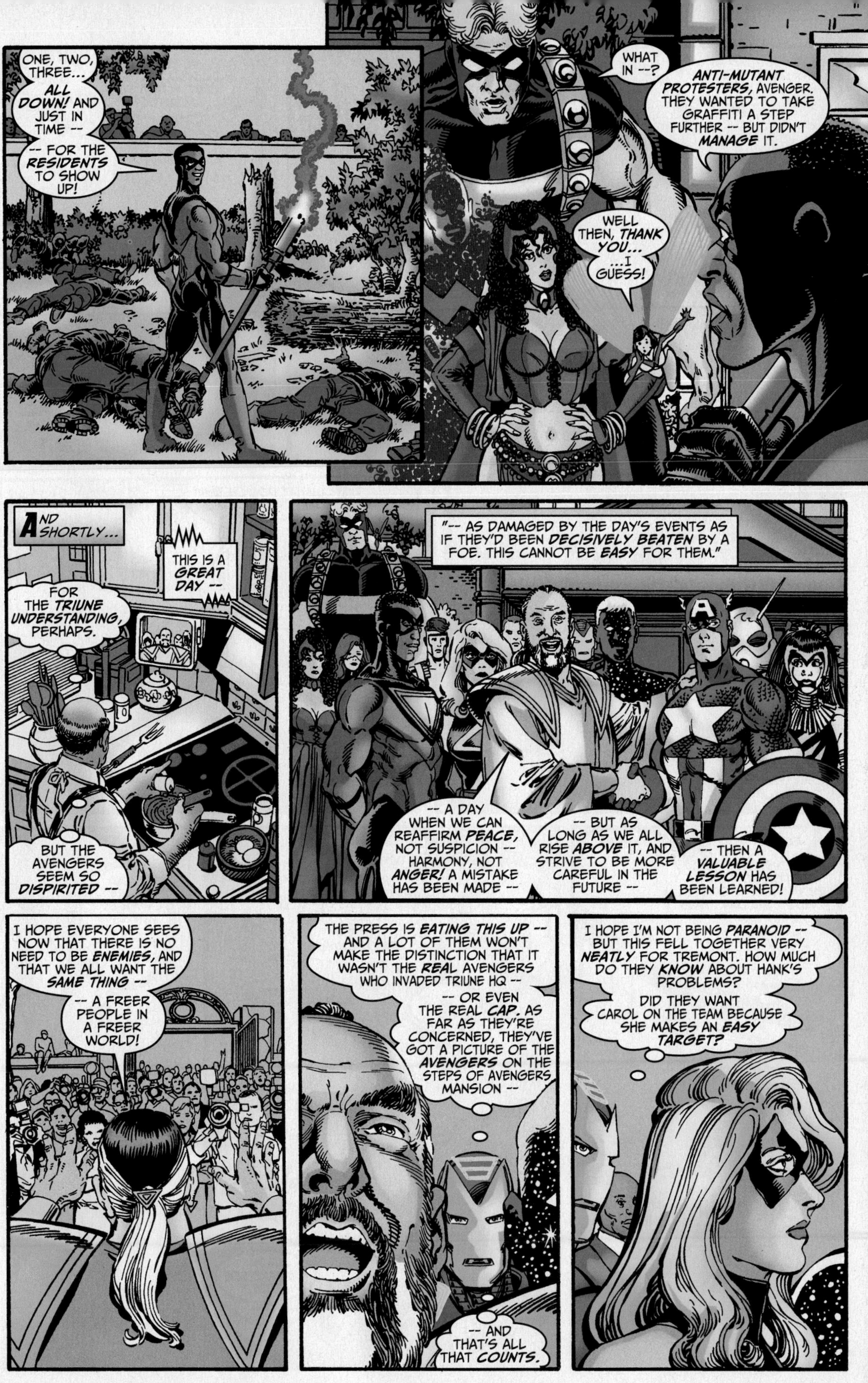
ONE, TWO, THREE... ALL DOWN! AND JUST IN TIME --
-- FOR THE RESIDENTS TO SHOW UP!
WHAT IN --?
ANTI-MUTANT PROTESTERS, AVENGER. THEY WANTED TO TAKE GRAFFITI A STEP FURTHER -- BUT DIDN'T MANAGE IT.
WELL THEN, THANK YOU... ...I GUESS!
AND SHORTLY...
THIS IS A GREAT DAY --
FOR THE TRIUNE UNDERSTANDING, PERHAPS.
BUT THE AVENGERS SEEM SO DISPIRITED --
"-- AS DAMAGED BY THE DAY'S EVENTS AS IF THEY'D BEEN DECISIVELY BEATEN BY A FOE. THIS CANNOT BE EASY FOR THEM."
-- A DAY WHEN WE CAN REAFFIRM PEACE, NOT SUSPICION -- HARMONY, NOT ANGER! A MISTAKE HAS BEEN MADE --
-- BUT AS LONG AS WE ALL RISE ABOVE IT, AND STRIVE TO BE MORE CAREFUL IN THE FUTURE --
-- THEN A VALUABLE LESSON HAS BEEN LEARNED!
I HOPE EVERYONE SEES NOW THAT THERE IS NO NEED TO BE ENEMIES, AND THAT WE ALL WANT THE SAME THING --
-- A FREER PEOPLE IN A FREER WORLD!
THE PRESS IS EATING THIS UP -- AND A LOT OF THEM WON'T MAKE THE DISTINCTION THAT IT WASN'T THE REAL AVENGERS WHO INVADED TRIUNE HQ --
-- OR EVEN THE REAL CAP. AS FAR AS THEY'RE CONCERNED, THEY'VE GOT A PICTURE OF THE AVENGERS ON THE STEPS OF AVENGERS MANSION --
-- AND THAT'S ALL THAT COUNTS.
I HOPE I'M NOT BEING PARANOID -- BUT THIS FELL TOGETHER VERY NEATLY FOR TREMONT. HOW MUCH DO THEY KNOW ABOUT HANK'S PROBLEMS?
DID THEY WANT CAROL ON THE TEAM BECAUSE SHE MAKES AN EASY TARGET?

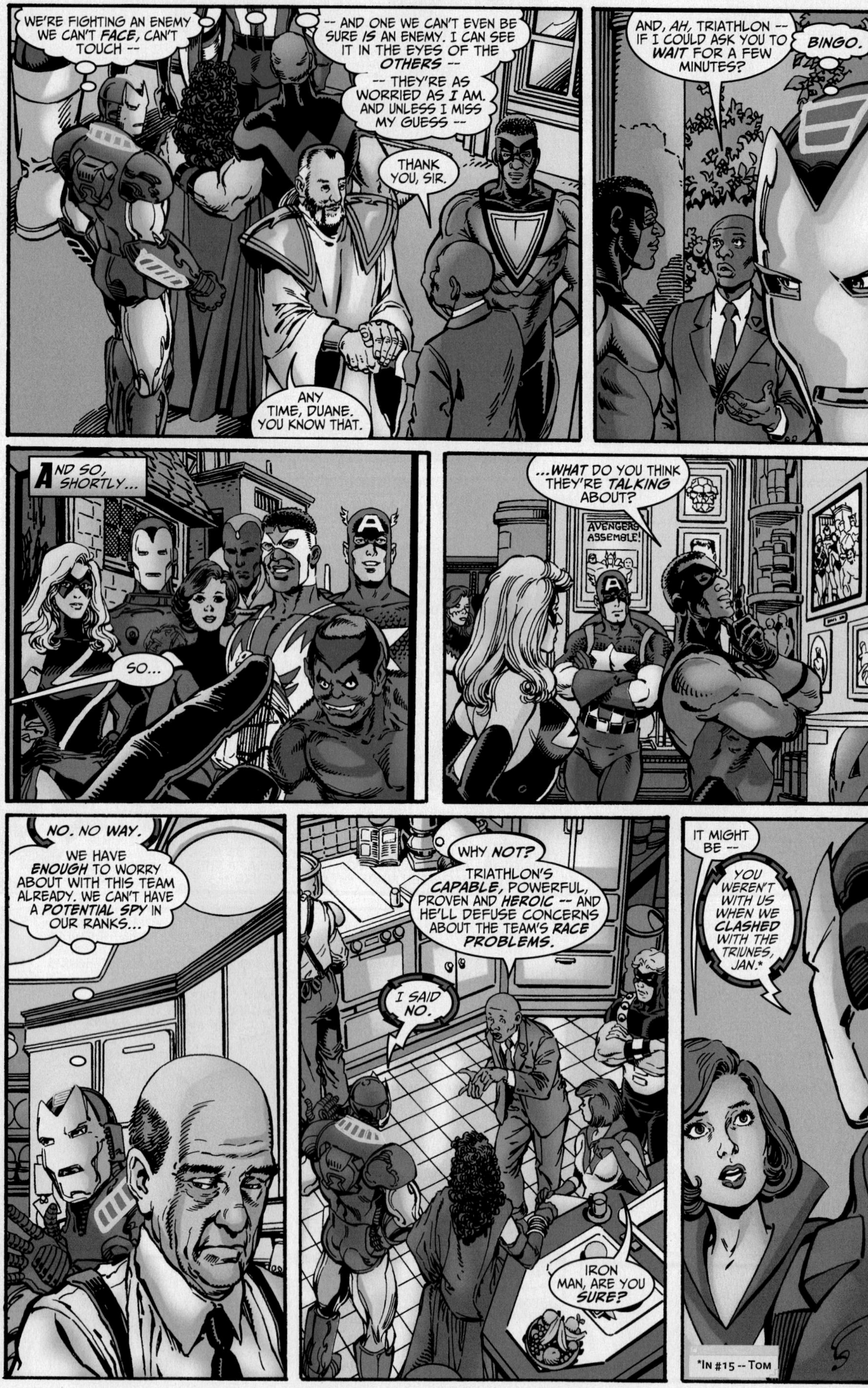
WE'RE FIGHTING AN ENEMY WE CAN'T FACE, CAN'T TOUCH --
-- AND ONE WE CAN'T EVEN BE SURE IS AN ENEMY. I CAN SEE IT IN THE EYES OF THE OTHERS --
-- THEY'RE AS WORRIED AS I AM. AND UNLESS I MISS MY GUESS --
THANK YOU, SIR.
ANY TIME, DUANE. YOU KNOW THAT.
AND, AH, TRIATHLON -- IF I COULD ASK YOU TO WAIT FOR A FEW MINUTES?
BINGO.
AND SO, SHORTLY...
SO...
...WHAT DO YOU THINK THEY'RE TALKING ABOUT?
AVENGERS ASSEMBLE!
NO. NO WAY.
WE HAVE ENOUGH TO WORRY ABOUT WITH THIS TEAM ALREADY. WE CAN'T HAVE A POTENTIAL SPY IN OUR RANKS...
WHY NOT?
TRIATHLON'S CAPABLE, POWERFUL, PROVEN AND HEROIC -- AND HE'LL DEFUSE CONCERNS ABOUT THE TEAM'S RACE PROBLEMS.
I SAID NO.
IRON MAN, ARE YOU SURE?
IT MIGHT BE --
YOU WEREN'T WITH US WHEN WE CLASHED WITH THE TRIUNES, JAN.*
*IN #15 -- TOM

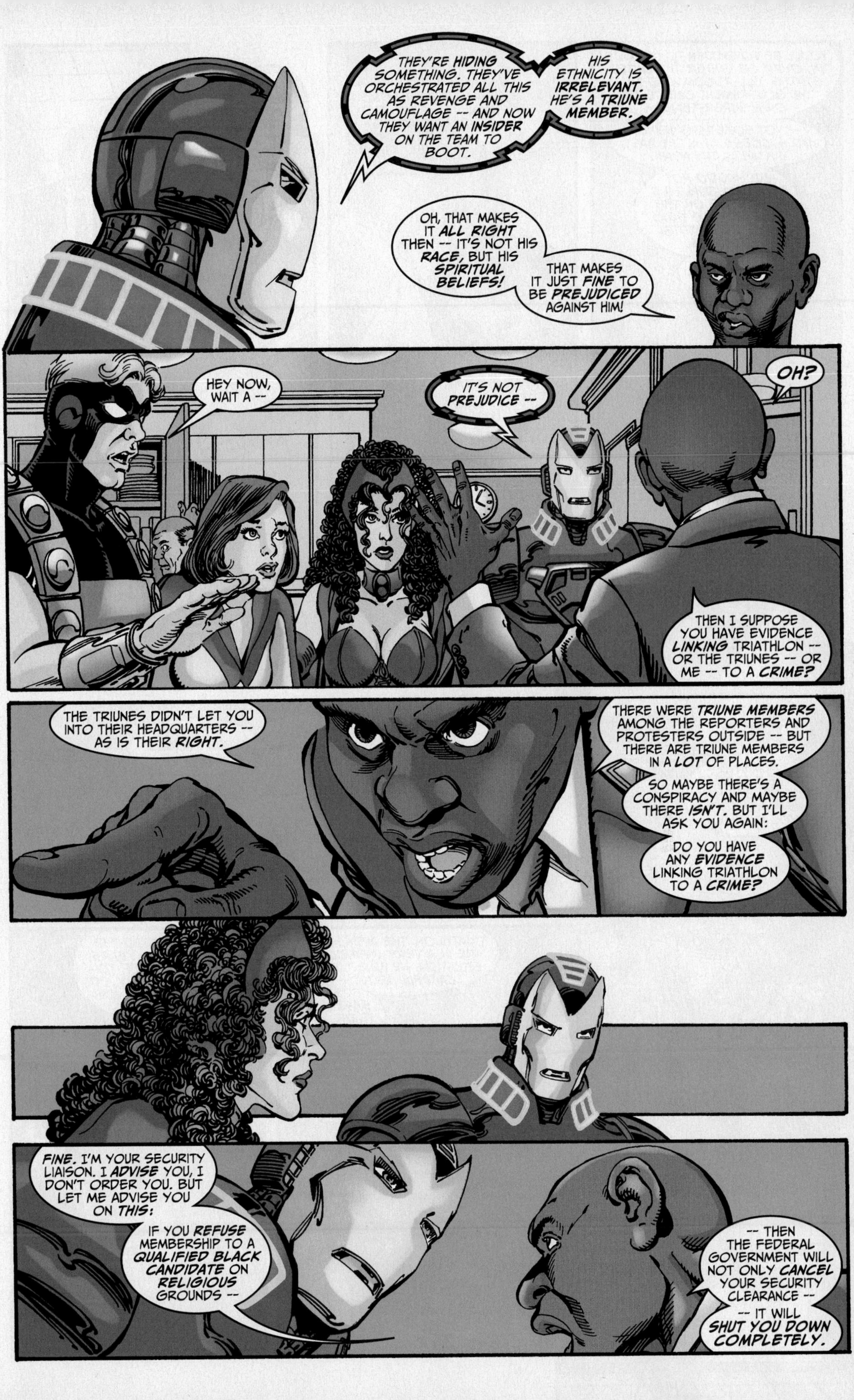
THEY'RE HIDING SOMETHING. THEY'VE ORCHESTRATED ALL THIS AS REVENGE AND CAMOUFLAGE -- AND NOW THEY WANT AN INSIDER ON THE TEAM TO BOOT.
HIS ETHNICITY IS IRRELEVANT. HE'S A TRIUNE MEMBER.
OH, THAT MAKES IT ALL RIGHT THEN -- IT'S NOT HIS RACE, BUT HIS SPIRITUAL BELIEFS!
THAT MAKES IT JUST FINE TO BE PREJUDICED AGAINST HIM!
HEY NOW, WAIT A --
IT'S NOT PREJUDICE --
OH?
THEN I SUPPOSE YOU HAVE EVIDENCE LINKING TRIATHLON -- OR THE TRIUNES -- OR ME -- TO A CRIME?
THE TRIUNES DIDN'T LET YOU INTO THEIR HEADQUARTERS -- AS IS THEIR RIGHT.
THERE WERE TRIUNE MEMBERS AMONG THE REPORTERS AND PROTESTERS OUTSIDE -- BUT THERE ARE TRIUNE MEMBERS IN A LOT OF PLACES.
SO MAYBE THERE'S A CONSPIRACY AND MAYBE THERE ISN'T. BUT I'LL ASK YOU AGAIN:
DO YOU HAVE ANY EVIDENCE LINKING TRIATHLON TO A CRIME?
FINE. I'M YOUR SECURITY LIAISON. I ADVISE YOU, I DON'T ORDER YOU. BUT LET ME ADVISE YOU ON THIS:
IF YOU REFUSE MEMBERSHIP TO A QUALIFIED BLACK CANDIDATE ON RELIGIOUS GROUNDS --
-- THEN THE FEDERAL GOVERNMENT WILL NOT ONLY CANCEL YOUR SECURITY CLEARANCE --
-- IT WILL SHUT YOU DOWN COMPLETELY.

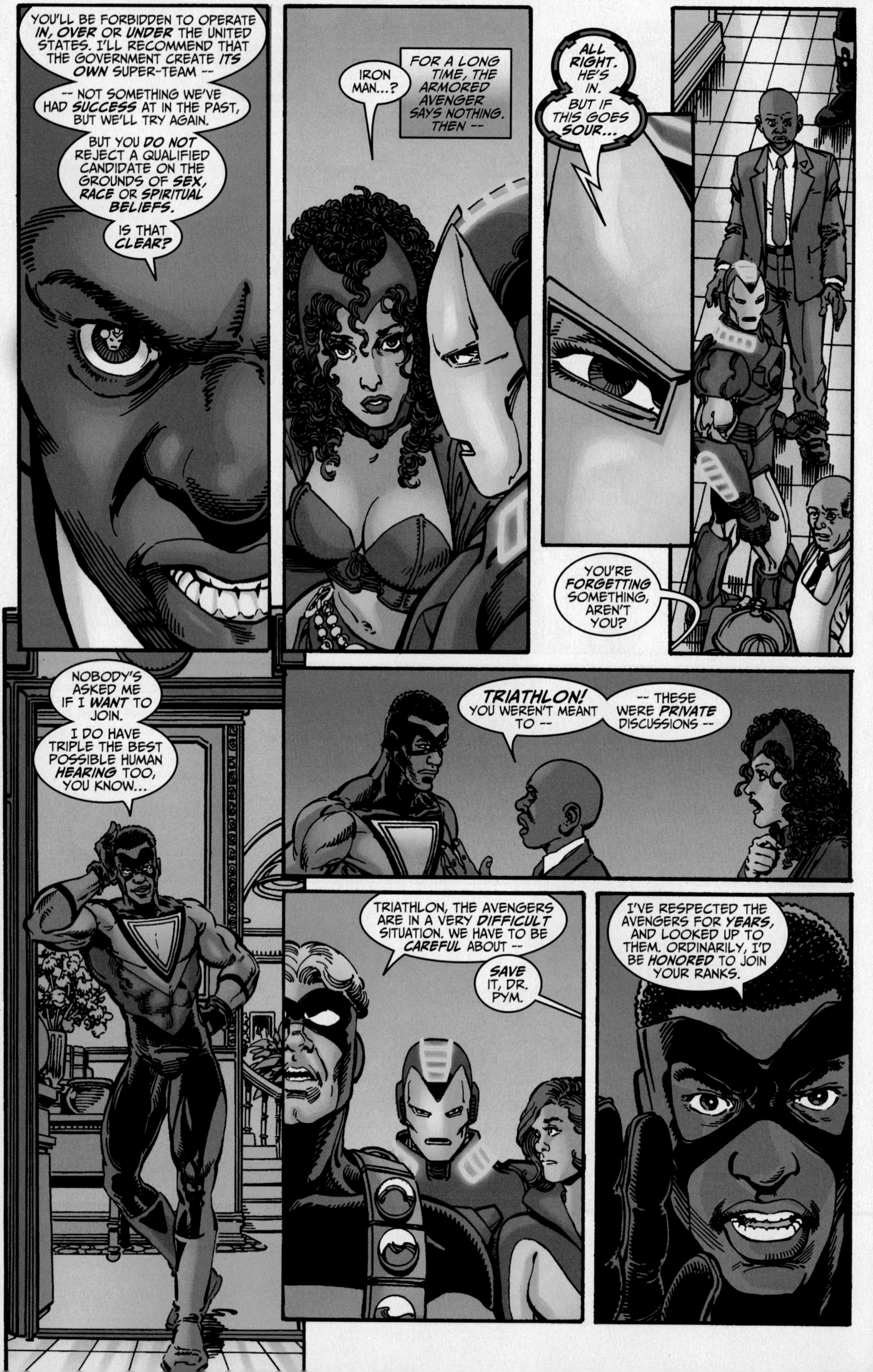
YOU'LL BE FORBIDDEN TO OPERATE IN, OVER OR UNDER THE UNITED STATES. I'LL RECOMMEND THAT THE GOVERNMENT CREATE ITS OWN SUPER-TEAM --
-- NOT SOMETHING WE'VE HAD SUCCESS AT IN THE PAST, BUT WE'LL TRY AGAIN.
BUT YOU DO NOT REJECT A QUALIFIED CANDIDATE ON THE GROUNDS OF SEX, RACE OR SPIRITUAL BELIEFS.
IS THAT CLEAR?
IRON MAN...?
FOR A LONG TIME, THE ARMORED AVENGER SAYS NOTHING. THEN --
ALL RIGHT. HE'S IN.
BUT IF THIS GOES SOUR...
YOU'RE FORGETTING SOMETHING, AREN'T YOU?
NOBODY'S ASKED ME IF I WANT TO JOIN.
I DO HAVE TRIPLE THE BEST POSSIBLE HUMAN HEARING TOO, YOU KNOW...
TRIATHLON! YOU WEREN'T MEANT TO --
-- THESE WERE PRIVATE DISCUSSIONS --
TRIATHLON, THE AVENGERS ARE IN A VERY DIFFICULT SITUATION. WE HAVE TO BE CAREFUL ABOUT --
SAVE IT, DR. PYM.
I'VE RESPECTED THE AVENGERS FOR YEARS, AND LOOKED UP TO THEM. ORDINARILY, I'D BE HONORED TO JOIN YOUR RANKS.

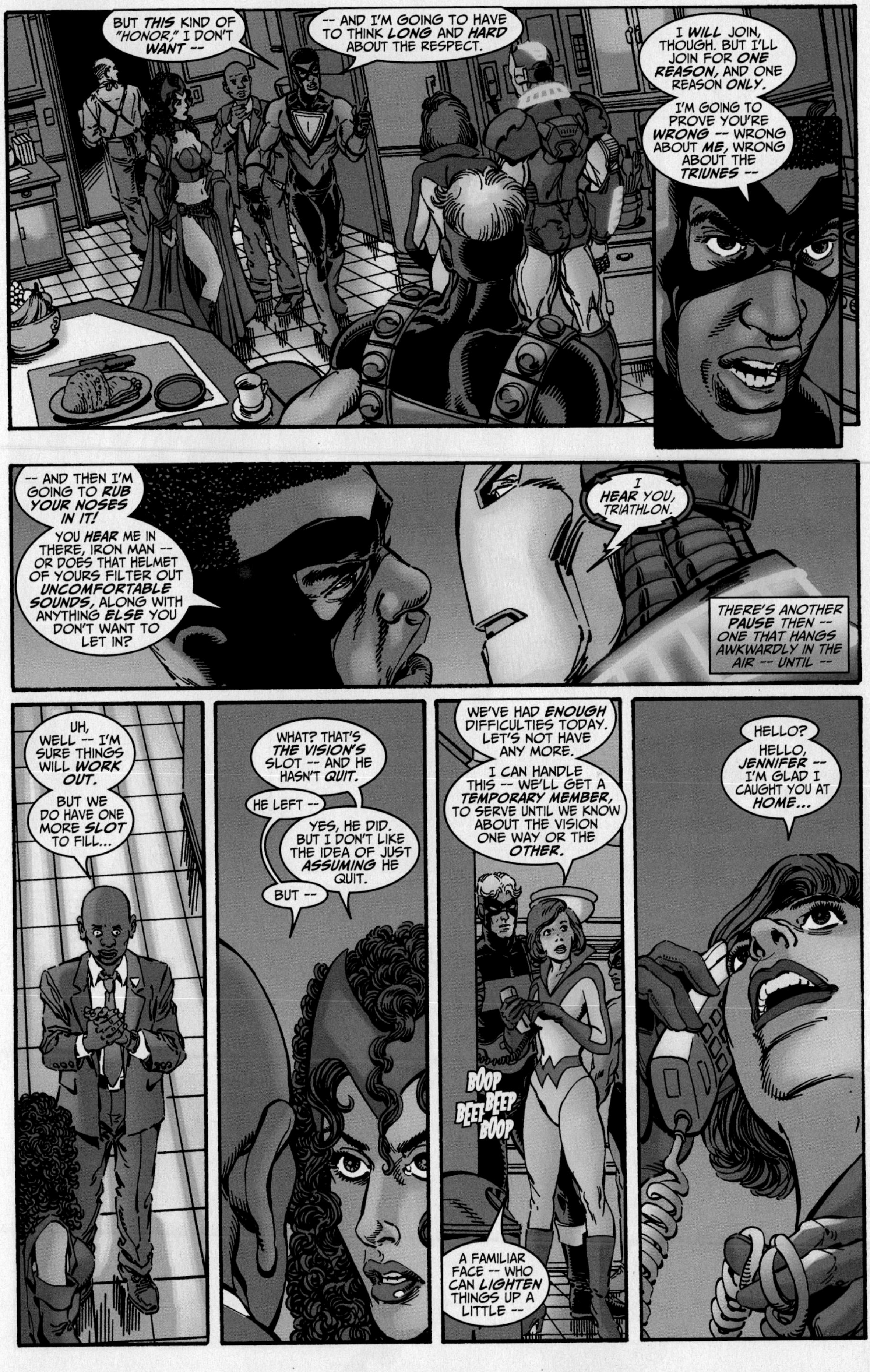
BUT THIS KIND OF "HONOR," I DON'T WANT --
-- AND I'M GOING TO HAVE TO THINK LONG AND HARD ABOUT THE RESPECT.
I WILL JOIN, THOUGH. BUT I'LL JOIN FOR ONE REASON, AND ONE REASON ONLY.
I'M GOING TO PROVE YOU'RE WRONG -- WRONG ABOUT ME, WRONG ABOUT THE TRIUNES --
-- AND THEN I'M GOING TO RUB YOUR NOSES IN IT!
YOU HEAR ME IN THERE, IRON MAN -- OR DOES THAT HELMET OF YOURS FILTER OUT UNCOMFORTABLE SOUNDS, ALONG WITH ANYTHING ELSE YOU DON'T WANT TO LET IN?
I HEAR YOU, TRIATHLON.
THERE'S ANOTHER PAUSE THEN -- ONE THAT HANGS AWKWARDLY IN THE AIR -- UNTIL --
UH, WELL -- I'M SURE THINGS WILL WORK OUT.
BUT WE DO HAVE ONE MORE SLOT TO FILL...
WHAT? THAT'S THE VISION'S SLOT -- AND HE HASN'T QUIT.
HE LEFT --
YES, HE DID. BUT I DON'T LIKE THE IDEA OF JUST ASSUMING HE QUIT.
BUT --
WE'VE HAD ENOUGH DIFFICULTIES TODAY. LET'S NOT HAVE ANY MORE.
I CAN HANDLE THIS -- WE'LL GET A TEMPORARY MEMBER, TO SERVE UNTIL WE KNOW ABOUT THE VISION ONE WAY OR THE OTHER.
BOOP BEEP BEEP BOOP
A FAMILIAR FACE -- WHO CAN LIGHTEN THINGS UP A LITTLE --
HELLO?
HELLO, JENNIFER -- I'M GLAD I CAUGHT YOU AT HOME...

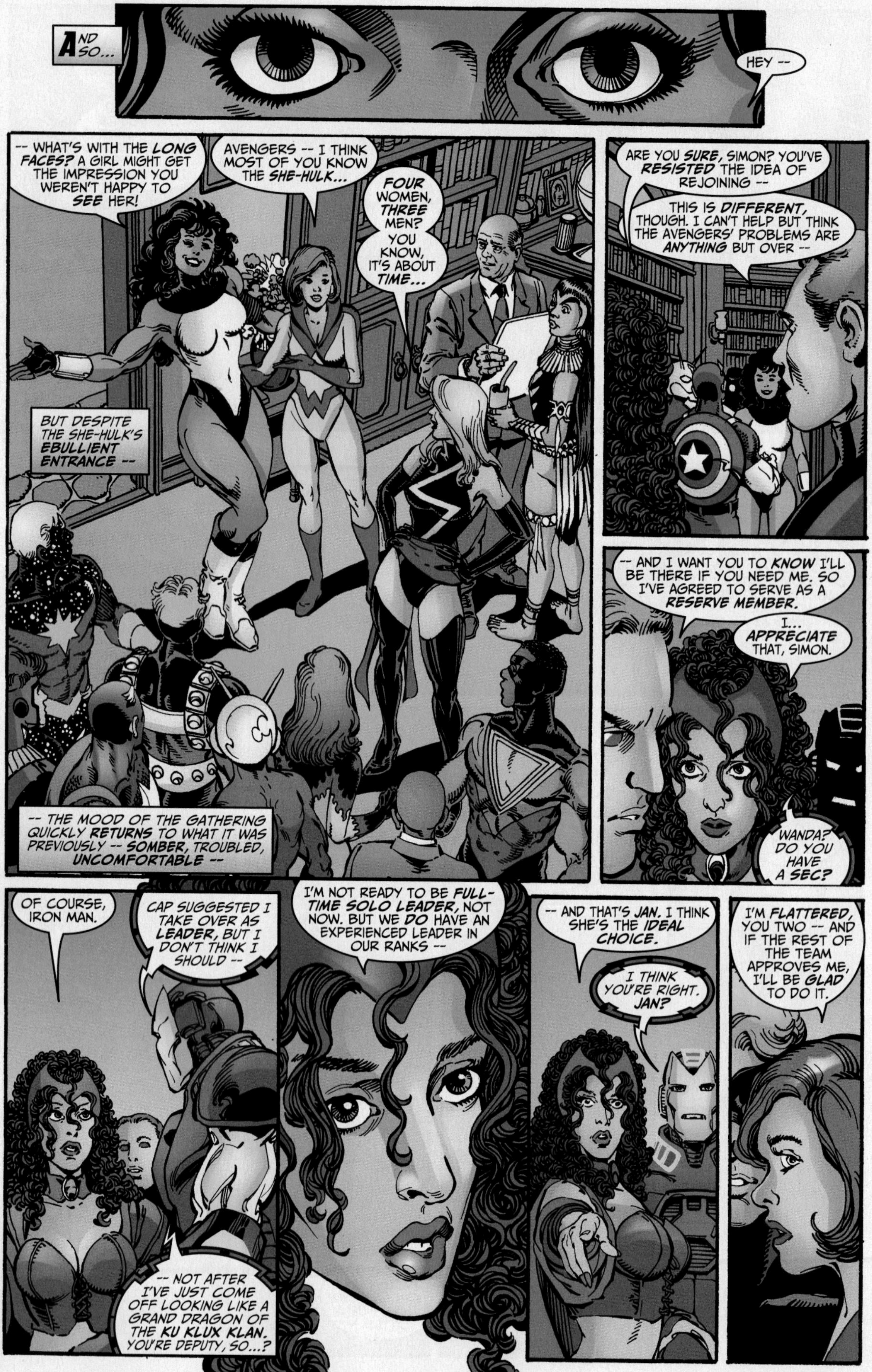
AND SO...
HEY --
-- WHAT'S WITH THE LONG FACES? A GIRL MIGHT GET THE IMPRESSION YOU WEREN'T HAPPY TO SEE HER!
AVENGERS -- I THINK MOST OF YOU KNOW THE SHE-HULK...
FOUR WOMEN, THREE MEN? YOU KNOW, IT'S ABOUT TIME...
BUT DESPITE THE SHE-HULK'S EBULLIENT ENTRANCE --
-- THE MOOD OF THE GATHERING QUICKLY RETURNS TO WHAT IT WAS PREVIOUSLY -- SOMBER, TROUBLED, UNCOMFORTABLE --
ARE YOU SURE, SIMON? YOU'VE RESISTED THE IDEA OF REJOINING --
THIS IS DIFFERENT, THOUGH. I CAN'T HELP BUT THINK THE AVENGERS' PROBLEMS ARE ANYTHING BUT OVER --
-- AND I WANT YOU TO KNOW I'LL BE THERE IF YOU NEED ME. SO I'VE AGREED TO SERVE AS A RESERVE MEMBER.
I... APPRECIATE THAT, SIMON.
WANDA? DO YOU HAVE A SEC?
OF COURSE, IRON MAN.
CAP SUGGESTED I TAKE OVER AS LEADER, BUT I DON'T THINK I SHOULD --
-- NOT AFTER I'VE JUST COME OFF LOOKING LIKE A GRAND DRAGON OF THE KU KLUX KLAN. YOU'RE DEPUTY, SO...?
I'M NOT READY TO BE FULL-TIME SOLO LEADER, NOT NOW. BUT WE DO HAVE AN EXPERIENCED LEADER IN OUR RANKS --
-- AND THAT'S JAN. I THINK SHE'S THE IDEAL CHOICE.
I THINK YOU'RE RIGHT. JAN?
I'M FLATTERED, YOU TWO -- AND IF THE REST OF THE TEAM APPROVES ME, I'LL BE GLAD TO DO IT.

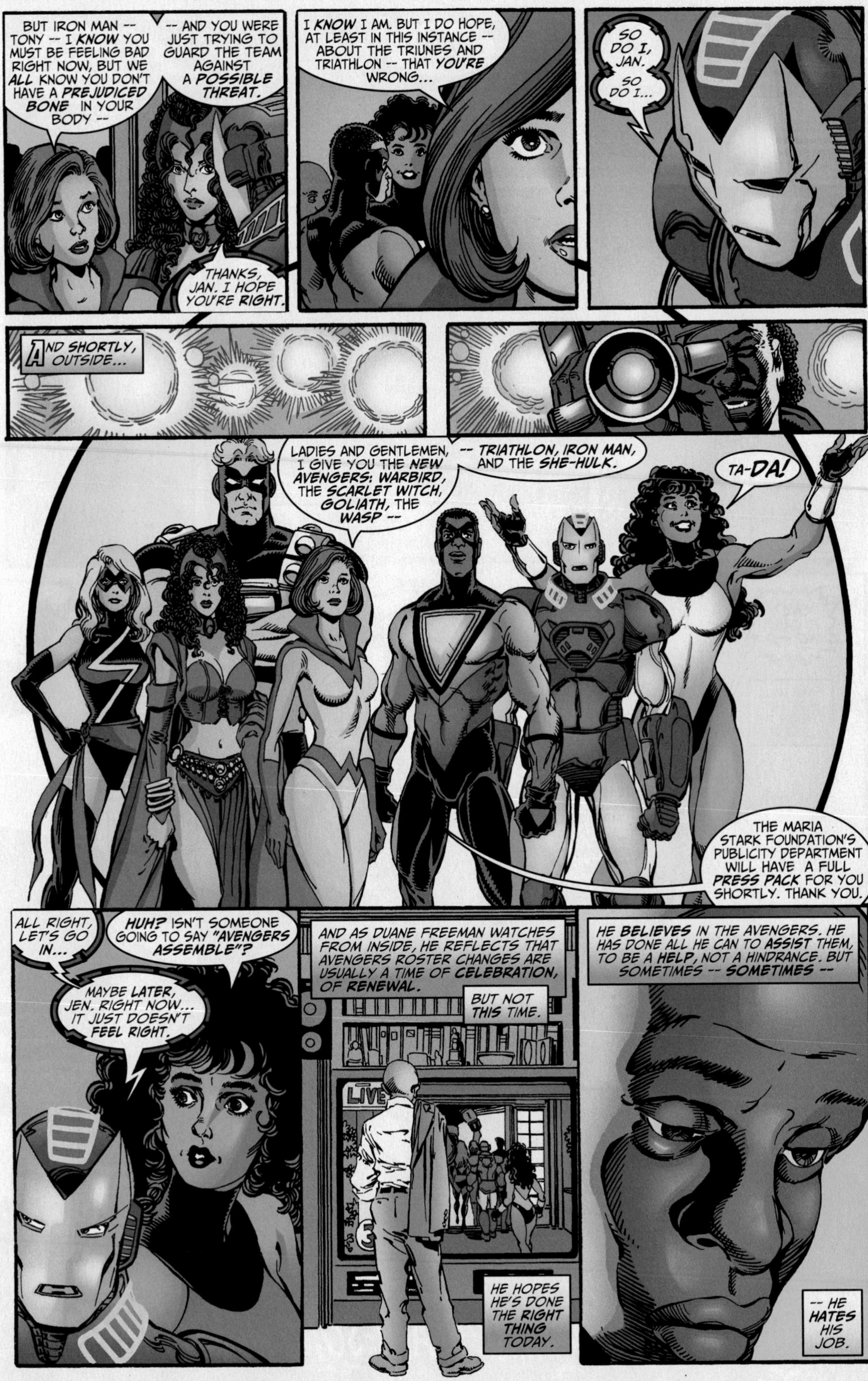
BUT IRON MAN -- TONY -- I KNOW YOU MUST BE FEELING BAD RIGHT NOW, BUT WE ALL KNOW YOU DON'T HAVE A PREJUDICED BONE IN YOUR BODY --
-- AND YOU WERE JUST TRYING TO GUARD THE TEAM AGAINST A POSSIBLE THREAT.
THANKS, JAN. I HOPE YOU'RE RIGHT.
I KNOW I AM. BUT I DO HOPE, AT LEAST IN THIS INSTANCE -- ABOUT THE TRIUNES AND TRIATHLON -- THAT YOU'RE WRONG...
SO DO I, JAN.
SO DO I...
AND SHORTLY, OUTSIDE...
LADIES AND GENTLEMEN, I GIVE YOU THE NEW AVENGERS: WARBIRD, THE SCARLET WITCH, GOLIATH, THE WASP --
-- TRIATHLON, IRON MAN, AND THE SHE-HULK.
TA-DA!
THE MARIA STARK FOUNDATION'S PUBLICITY DEPARTMENT WILL HAVE A FULL PRESS PACK FOR YOU SHORTLY. THANK YOU.
ALL RIGHT, LET'S GO IN...
HUH? ISN'T SOMEONE GOING TO SAY "AVENGERS ASSEMBLE"?
MAYBE LATER, JEN. RIGHT NOW... IT JUST DOESN'T FEEL RIGHT.
AND AS DUANE FREEMAN WATCHES FROM INSIDE, HE REFLECTS THAT AVENGERS ROSTER CHANGES ARE USUALLY A TIME OF CELEBRATION, OF RENEWAL.
BUT NOT THIS TIME.
LIVE
HE HOPES HE'S DONE THE RIGHT THING TODAY.
HE BELIEVES IN THE AVENGERS. HE HAS DONE ALL HE CAN TO ASSIST THEM, TO BE A HELP, NOT A HINDRANCE. BUT SOMETIMES -- SOMETIMES --
-- HE HATES HIS JOB.

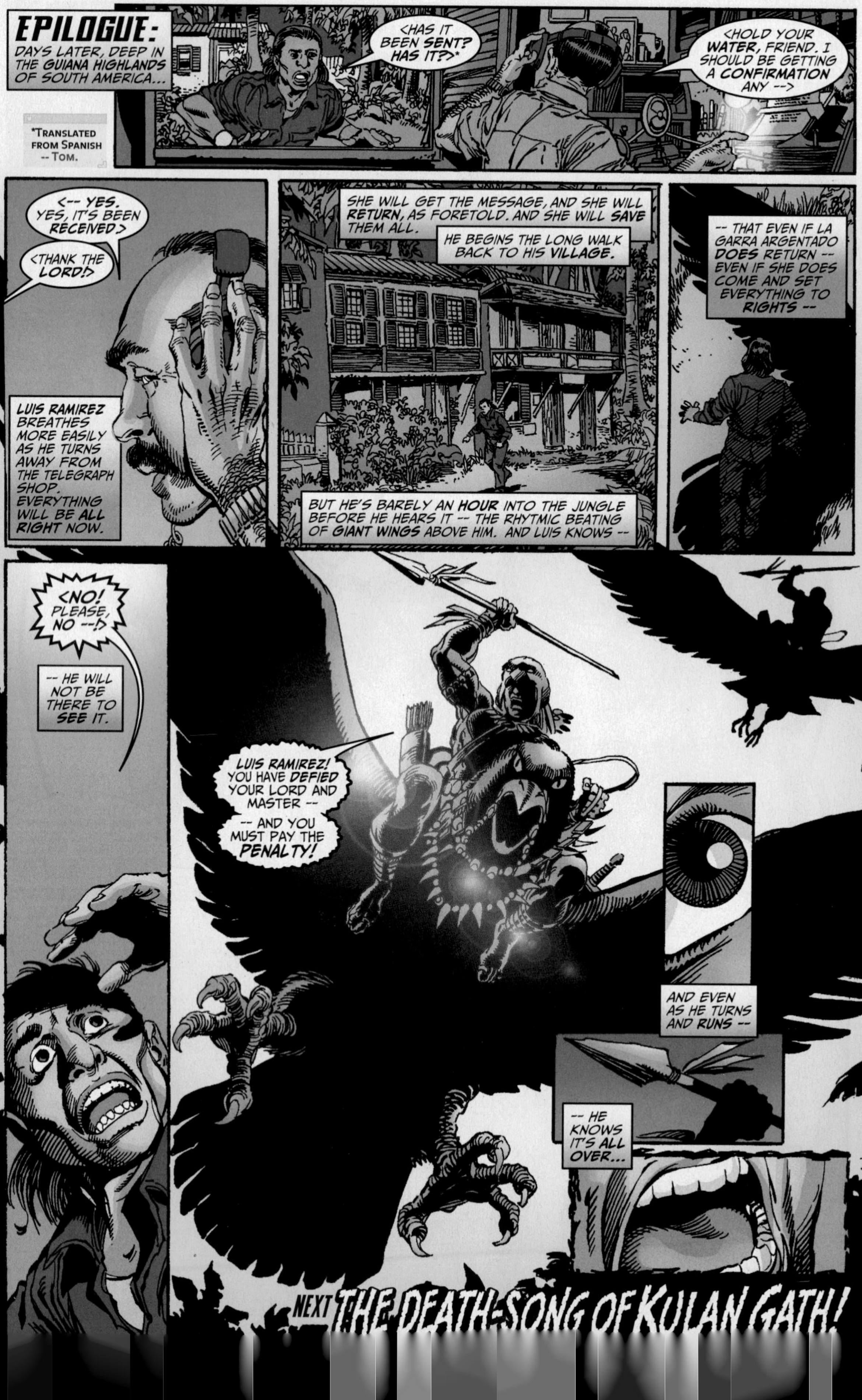
EPILOGUE:
DAYS LATER, DEEP IN THE GUIANA HIGHLANDS OF SOUTH AMERICA...
<HAS IT BEEN SENT? HAS IT?>*
<HOLD YOUR WATER, FRIEND. I SHOULD BE GETTING A CONFIRMATION ANY -->
*TRANSLATED FROM SPANISH -- TOM.
<-- YES. YES, IT'S BEEN RECEIVED.>
<THANK THE LORD!>
LUIS RAMIREZ BREATHES MORE EASILY AS HE TURNS AWAY FROM THE TELEGRAPH SHOP. EVERYTHING WILL BE ALL RIGHT NOW.
SHE WILL GET THE MESSAGE, AND SHE WILL RETURN, AS FORETOLD. AND SHE WILL SAVE THEM ALL.
HE BEGINS THE LONG WALK BACK TO HIS VILLAGE.
BUT HE'S BARELY AN HOUR INTO THE JUNGLE BEFORE HE HEARS IT -- THE RHYTMIC BEATING OF GIANT WINGS ABOVE HIM. AND LUIS KNOWS --
-- THAT EVEN IF LA GARRA ARGENTADO DOES RETURN -- EVEN IF SHE DOES COME AND SET EVERYTHING TO RIGHTS --
<NO! PLEASE, NO --!>
-- HE WILL NOT BE THERE TO SEE IT.
LUIS RAMIREZ! YOU HAVE DEFIED YOUR LORD AND MASTER --
-- AND YOU MUST PAY THE PENALTY!
AND EVEN AS HE TURNS AND RUNS --
-- HE KNOWS IT'S ALL OVER...
NEXT THE DEATH-SONG OF KULAN GATH!

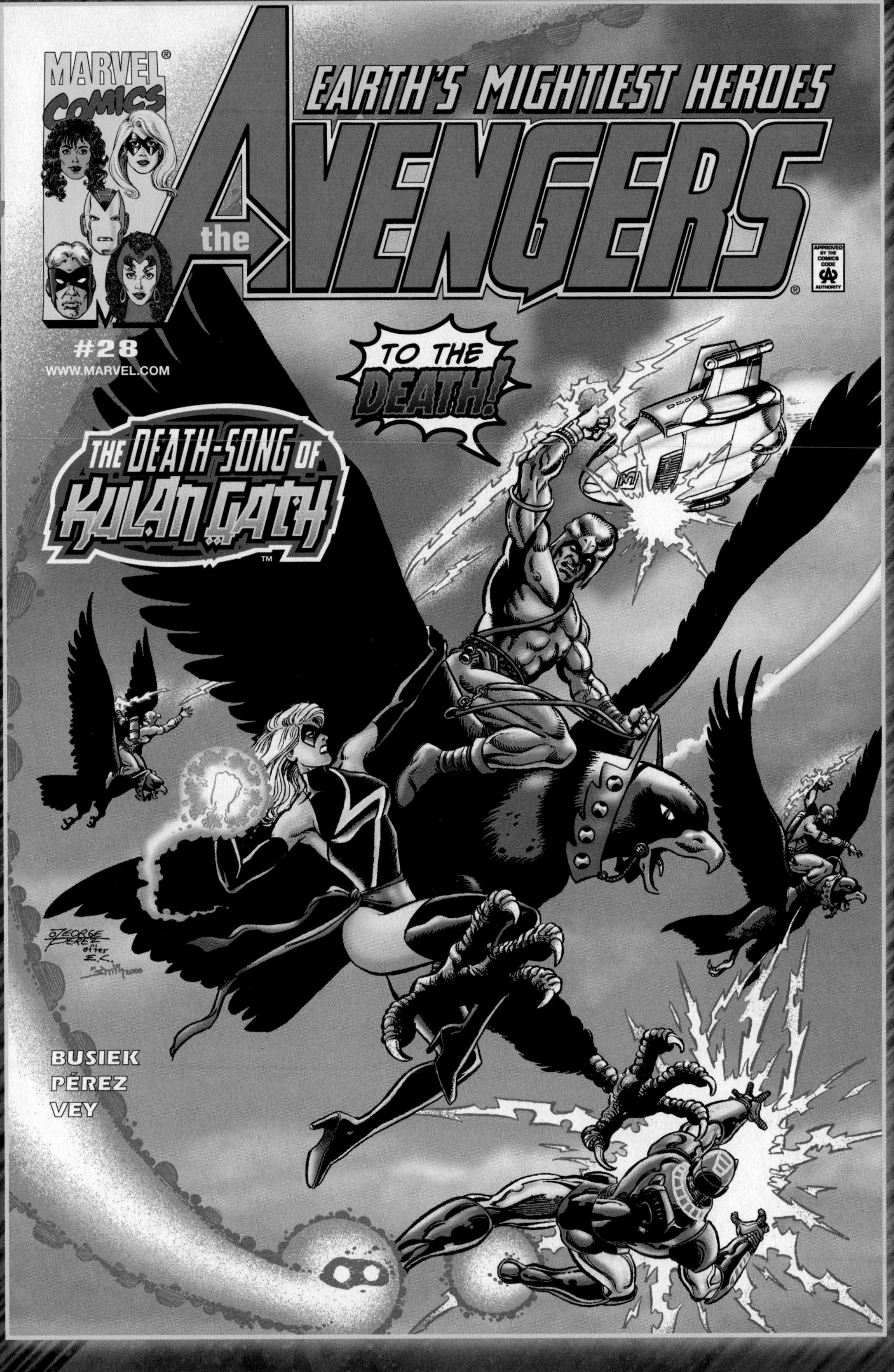
MARVEL COMICS
EARTH'S MIGHTIEST HEROES
the AVENGERS
#28
WWW.MARVEL.COM
TO THE DEATH!
THE DEATH-SONG OF KULAN GATH
BUSIEK
PÉREZ
VEY

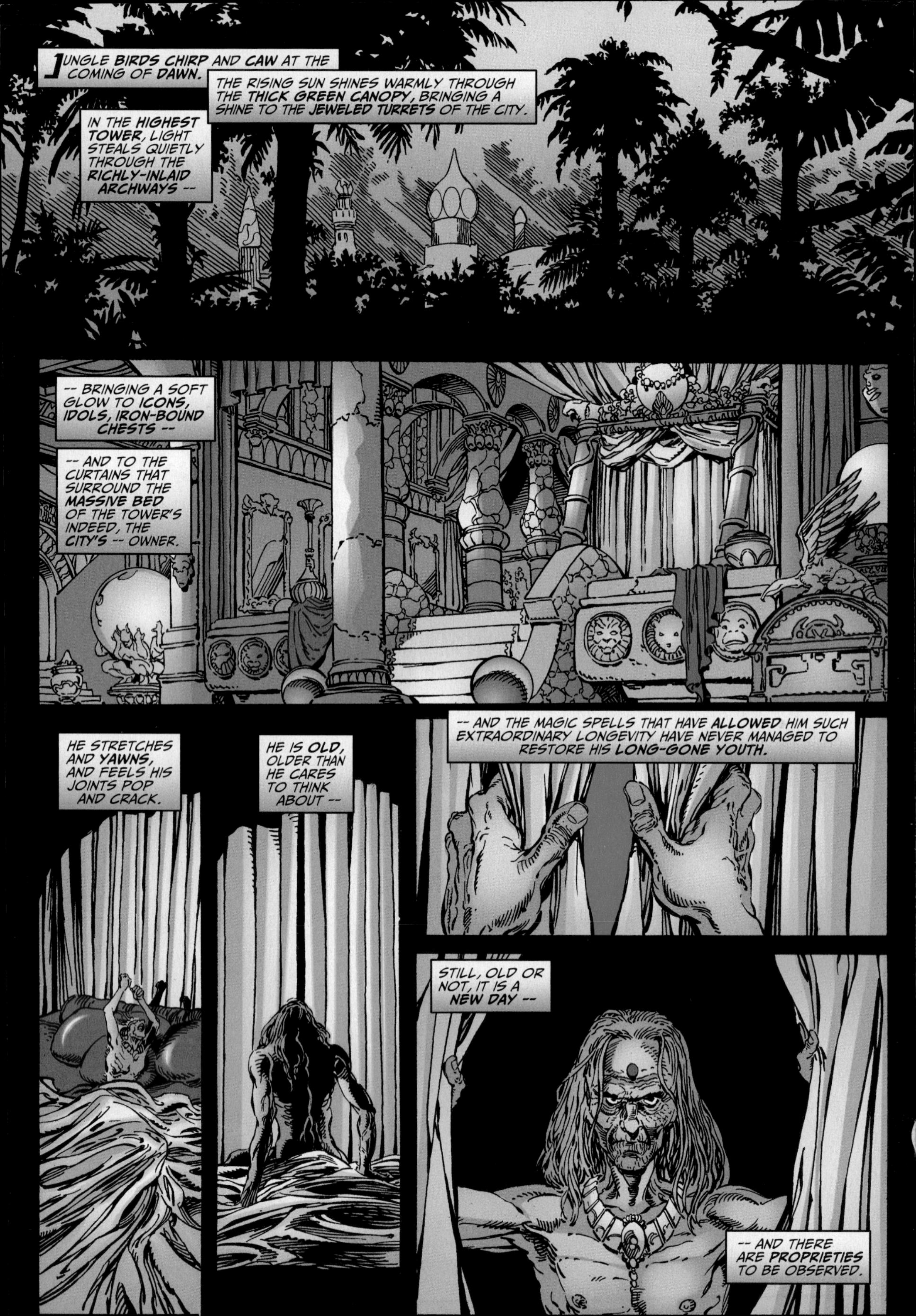
JUNGLE BIRDS CHIRP AND CAW AT THE COMING OF DAWN.
THE RISING SUN SHINES WARMLY THROUGH THE THICK GREEN CANOPY, BRINGING A SHINE TO THE JEWELED TURRETS OF THE CITY.
IN THE HIGHEST TOWER, LIGHT STEALS QUIETLY THROUGH THE RICHLY-INLAID ARCHWAYS --
-- BRINGING A SOFT GLOW TO ICONS, IDOLS, IRON-BOUND CHESTS --
-- AND TO THE CURTAINS THAT SURROUND THE MASSIVE BED OF THE TOWER'S INDEED, THE CITY'S -- OWNER.
HE STRETCHES AND YAWNS, AND FEELS HIS JOINTS POP AND CRACK.
HE IS OLD, OLDER THAN HE CARES TO THINK ABOUT --
-- AND THE MAGIC SPELLS THAT HAVE ALLOWED HIM SUCH EXTRAORDINARY LONGEVITY HAVE NEVER MANAGED TO RESTORE HIS LONG-GONE YOUTH.
STILL, OLD OR NOT, IT IS A NEW DAY --
-- AND THERE ARE PROPRIETIES TO BE OBSERVED.

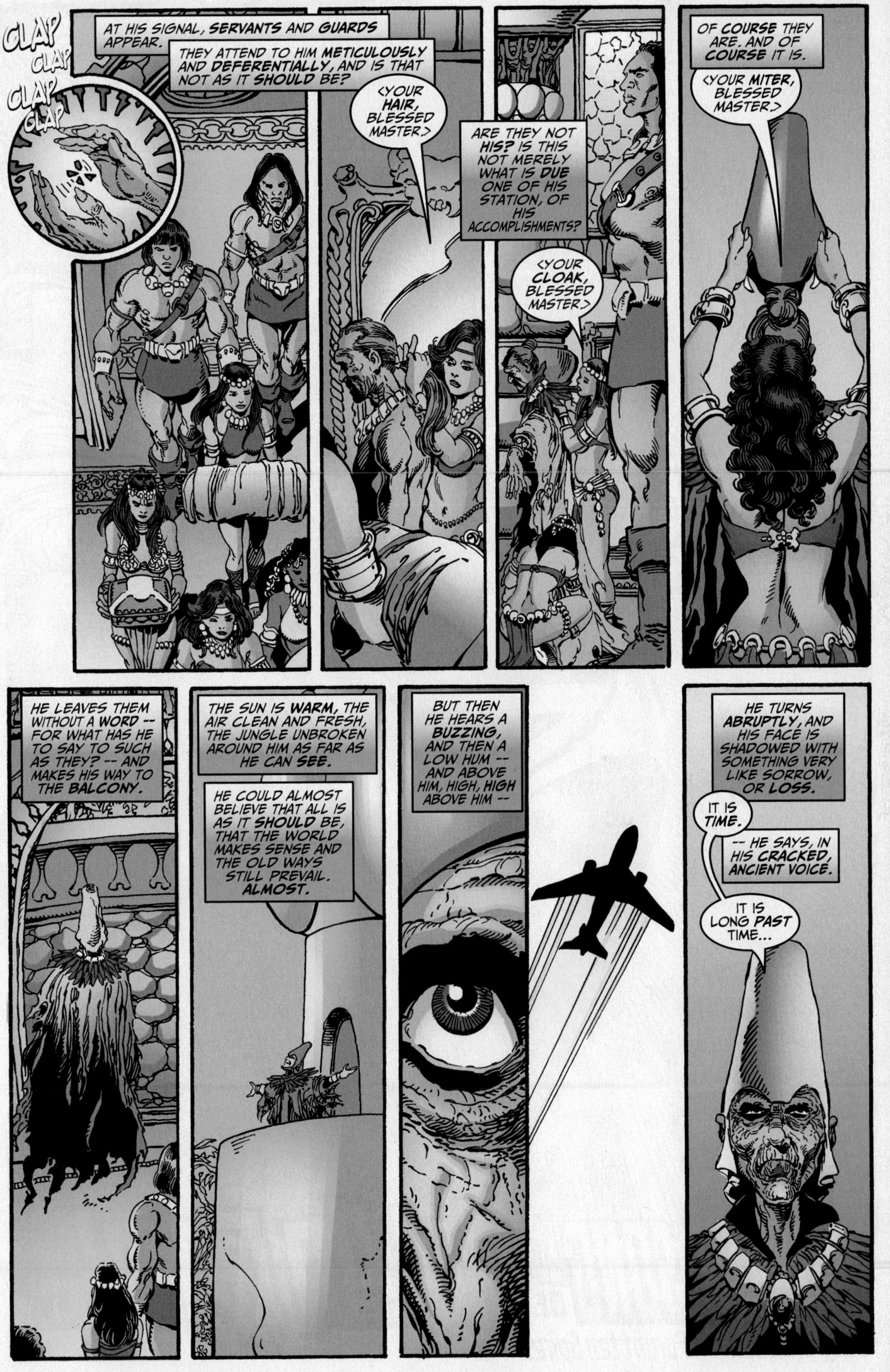
CLAP CLAP CLAP CLAP
AT HIS SIGNAL, SERVANTS AND GUARDS APPEAR.
THEY ATTEND TO HIM METICULOUSLY AND DEFERENTIALLY, AND IS THAT NOT AS IT SHOULD BE?
<YOUR HAIR, BLESSED MASTER.>
ARE THEY NOT HIS? IS THIS NOT MERELY WHAT IS DUE ONE OF HIS STATION, OF HIS ACCOMPLISHMENTS?
<YOUR CLOAK, BLESSED MASTER.>
OF COURSE THEY ARE. AND OF COURSE IT IS.
<YOUR MITER, BLESSED MASTER.>
HE LEAVES THEM WITHOUT A WORD -- FOR WHAT HAS HE TO SAY TO SUCH AS THEY? -- AND MAKES HIS WAY TO THE BALCONY.
THE SUN IS WARM, THE AIR CLEAN AND FRESH, THE JUNGLE UNBROKEN AROUND HIM AS FAR AS HE CAN SEE.
HE COULD ALMOST BELIEVE THAT ALL IS AS IT SHOULD BE, THAT THE WORLD MAKES SENSE AND THE OLD WAYS STILL PREVAIL. ALMOST.
BUT THEN HE HEARS A BUZZING, AND THEN A LOW HUM -- AND ABOVE HIM, HIGH, HIGH ABOVE HIM --
HE TURNS ABRUPTLY, AND HIS FACE IS SHADOWED WITH SOMETHING VERY LIKE SORROW, OR LOSS.
IT IS TIME.
-- HE SAYS, IN HIS CRACKED, ANCIENT VOICE.
IT IS LONG PAST TIME...

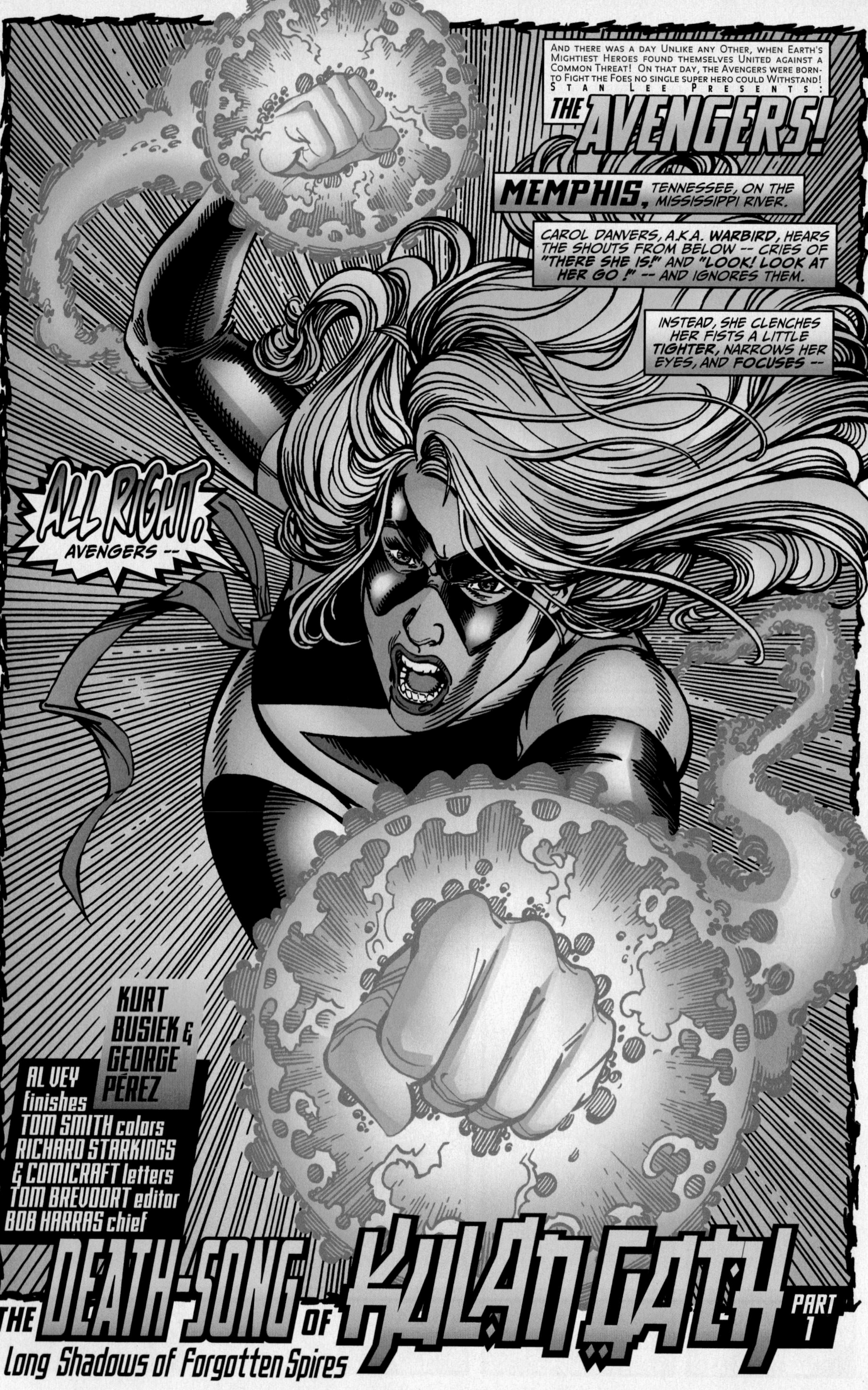

And there was a day Unlike any Other, when Earth's Mightiest Heroes found themselves United against a Common Threat! On that day, the Avengers were born-to Fight the Foes no single super hero could Withstand!
Stan Lee Presents:
THE AVENGERS!
MEMPHIS, TENNESSEE, ON THE MISSISSIPPI RIVER.
CAROL DANVERS, A.K.A. WARBIRD, HEARS THE SHOUTS FROM BELOW -- CRIES OF "THERE SHE IS!" AND "LOOK! LOOK AT HER GO!" -- AND IGNORES THEM.
INSTEAD, SHE CLENCHES HER FISTS A LITTLE TIGHTER, NARROWS HER EYES, AND FOCUSES --
ALL RIGHT. AVENGERS --
KURT BUSIEK & GEORGE PÉREZ
AL VEY finishes
TOM SMITH colors
RICHARD STARKINGS & COMICRAFT letters
TOM BREVOORT editor
BOB HARRAS chief
THE DEATH-SONG OF KULAN GATH PART 1
Long Shadows of Forgotten Spires

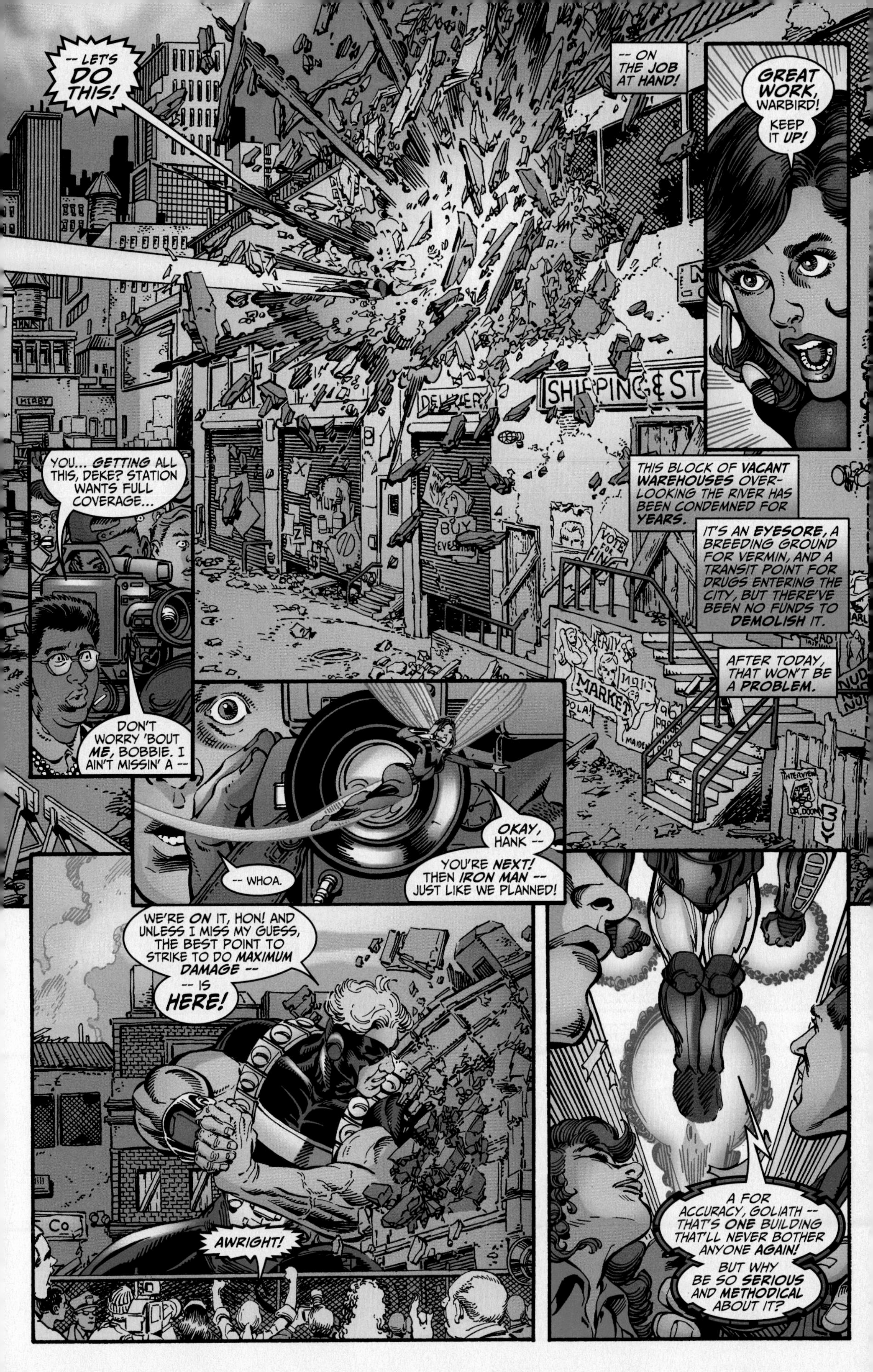
-- LET'S DO THIS!
-- ON THE JOB AT HAND!
GREAT WORK, WARBIRD!
KEEP IT UP!
THIS BLOCK OF VACANT WAREHOUSES OVER-LOOKING THE RIVER HAS BEEN CONDEMNED FOR YEARS.
IT'S AN EYESORE, A BREEDING GROUND FOR VERMIN, AND A TRANSIT POINT FOR DRUGS ENTERING THE CITY, BUT THERE'VE BEEN NO FUNDS TO DEMOLISH IT.
AFTER TODAY, THAT WON'T BE A PROBLEM.
SHIPPING & ST
DELIVERY
BUY
VOTE FOR
MARKET
YOU... GETTING ALL THIS, DEKE? STATION WANTS FULL COVERAGE...
DON'T WORRY 'BOUT ME, BOBBIE. I AIN'T MISSIN' A --
-- WHOA.
OKAY, HANK --
YOU'RE NEXT! THEN IRON MAN -- JUST LIKE WE PLANNED!
WE'RE ON IT, HON! AND UNLESS I MISS MY GUESS, THE BEST POINT TO STRIKE TO DO MAXIMUM DAMAGE --
-- IS HERE!
AWRIGHT!
A FOR ACCURACY, GOLIATH -- THAT'S ONE BUILDING THAT'LL NEVER BOTHER ANYONE AGAIN!
BUT WHY BE SO SERIOUS AND METHODICAL ABOUT IT?

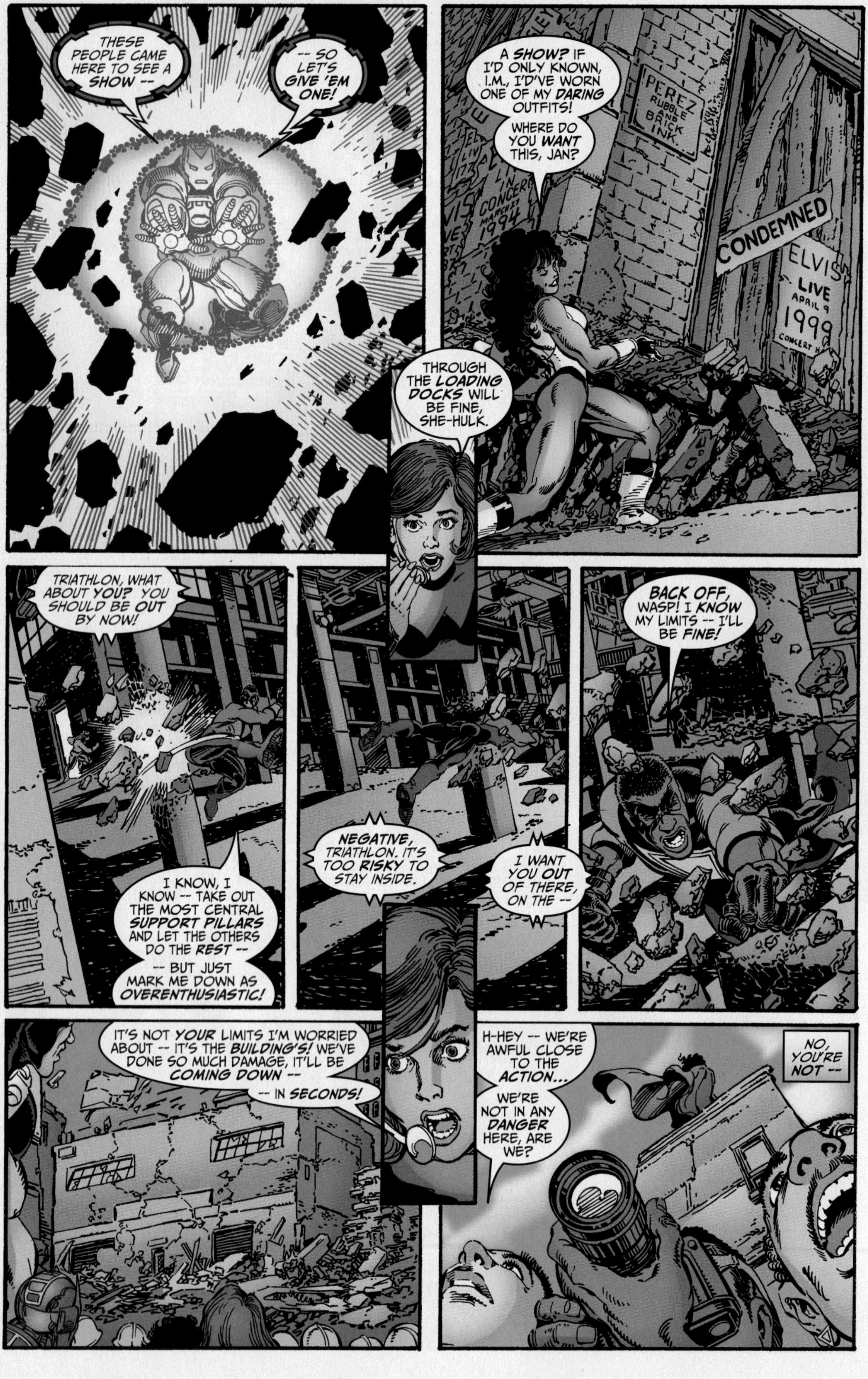
THESE PEOPLE CAME HERE TO SEE A SHOW --
-- SO LET'S GIVE 'EM ONE!
A SHOW? IF I'D ONLY KNOWN, I.M., I'D'VE WORN ONE OF MY DARING OUTFITS!
WHERE DO YOU WANT THIS, JAN?
PEREZ RUBBLE AND BRICK INK.
CONDEMNED
ELVIS LIVE APRIL 9 1999 CONCERT H
THROUGH THE LOADING DOCKS WILL BE FINE, SHE-HULK.
TRIATHLON, WHAT ABOUT YOU? YOU SHOULD BE OUT BY NOW!
I KNOW, I KNOW -- TAKE OUT THE MOST CENTRAL SUPPORT PILLARS AND LET THE OTHERS DO THE REST --
-- BUT JUST MARK ME DOWN AS OVERENTHUSIASTIC!
NEGATIVE, TRIATHLON. IT'S TOO RISKY TO STAY INSIDE.
BACK OFF, WASP! I KNOW MY LIMITS -- I'LL BE FINE!
I WANT YOU OUT OF THERE, ON THE --
IT'S NOT YOUR LIMITS I'M WORRIED ABOUT -- IT'S THE BUILDING'S! WE'VE DONE SO MUCH DAMAGE, IT'LL BE COMING DOWN --
-- IN SECONDS!
H-HEY -- WE'RE AWFUL CLOSE TO THE ACTION...
WE'RE NOT IN ANY DANGER HERE, ARE WE?
NO, YOU'RE NOT --

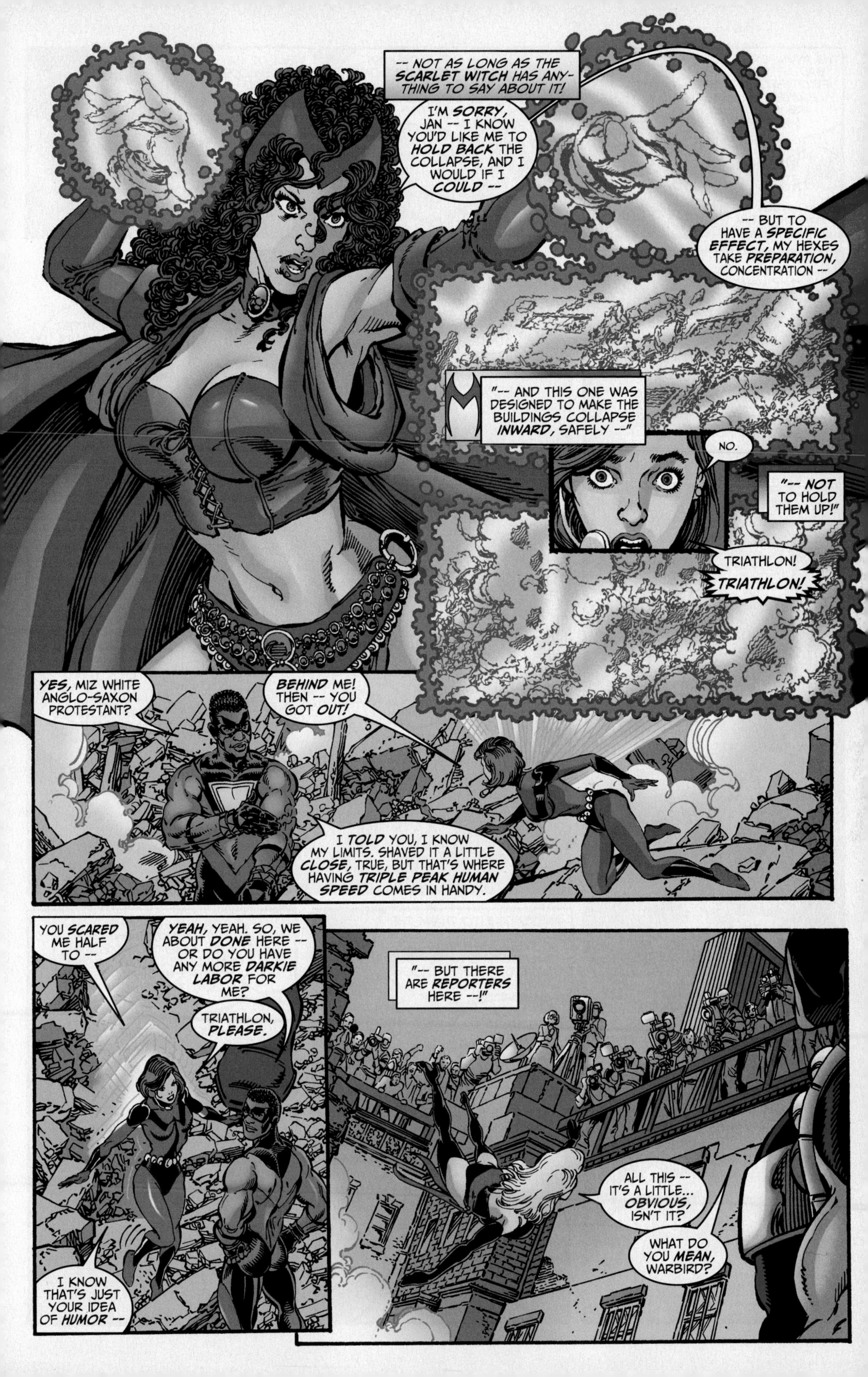
-- NOT AS LONG AS THE SCARLET WITCH HAS ANY-THING TO SAY ABOUT IT!
I'M SORRY, JAN -- I KNOW YOU'D LIKE ME TO HOLD BACK THE COLLAPSE, AND I WOULD IF I COULD --
-- BUT TO HAVE A SPECIFIC EFFECT, MY HEXES TAKE PREPARATION, CONCENTRATION --
"-- AND THIS ONE WAS DESIGNED TO MAKE THE BUILDINGS COLLAPSE INWARD, SAFELY --"
NO.
"-- NOT TO HOLD THEM UP!"
TRIATHLON!
TRIATHLON!
YES, MIZ WHITE ANGLO-SAXON PROTESTANT?
BEHIND ME! THEN -- YOU GOT OUT!
I TOLD YOU, I KNOW MY LIMITS. SHAVED IT A LITTLE CLOSE, TRUE, BUT THAT'S WHERE HAVING TRIPLE PEAK HUMAN SPEED COMES IN HANDY.
YOU SCARED ME HALF TO --
YEAH, YEAH. SO, WE ABOUT DONE HERE -- OR DO YOU HAVE ANY MORE DARKIE LABOR FOR ME?
TRIATHLON, PLEASE.
I KNOW THAT'S JUST YOUR IDEA OF HUMOR --
"-- BUT THERE ARE REPORTERS HERE --!"
ALL THIS -- IT'S A LITTLE... OBVIOUS, ISN'T IT?
WHAT DO YOU MEAN, WARBIRD?

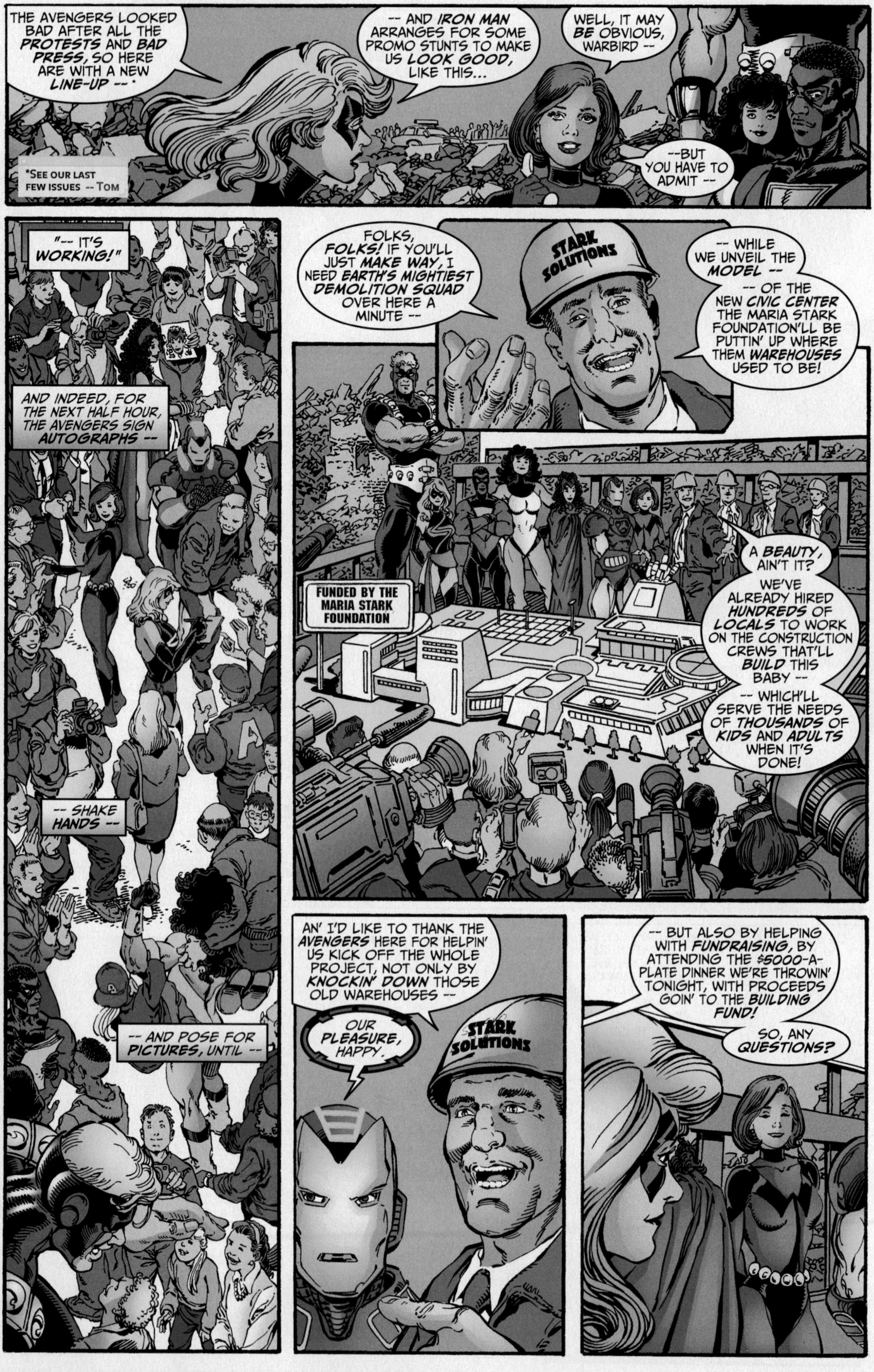
THE AVENGERS LOOKED BAD AFTER ALL THE PROTESTS AND BAD PRESS, SO HERE ARE WITH A NEW LINE-UP -- *
*SEE OUR LAST FEW ISSUES -- TOM
-- AND IRON MAN ARRANGES FOR SOME PROMO STUNTS TO MAKE US LOOK GOOD, LIKE THIS...
WELL, IT MAY BE OBVIOUS, WARBIRD --
--BUT YOU HAVE TO ADMIT --
"-- IT'S WORKING!"
AND INDEED, FOR THE NEXT HALF HOUR, THE AVENGERS SIGN AUTOGRAPHS --
-- SHAKE HANDS --
-- AND POSE FOR PICTURES, UNTIL --
FOLKS, FOLKS! IF YOU'LL JUST MAKE WAY, I NEED EARTH'S MIGHTIEST DEMOLITION SQUAD OVER HERE A MINUTE --
STARK SOLUTIONS
-- WHILE WE UNVEIL THE MODEL --
-- OF THE NEW CIVIC CENTER THE MARIA STARK FOUNDATION'LL BE PUTTIN' UP WHERE THEM WAREHOUSES USED TO BE!
FUNDED BY THE MARIA STARK FOUNDATION
A BEAUTY, AIN'T IT?
WE'VE ALREADY HIRED HUNDREDS OF LOCALS TO WORK ON THE CONSTRUCTION CREWS THAT'LL BUILD THIS BABY --
-- WHICH'LL SERVE THE NEEDS OF THOUSANDS OF KIDS AND ADULTS WHEN IT'S DONE!
AN' I'D LIKE TO THANK THE AVENGERS HERE FOR HELPIN' US KICK OFF THE WHOLE PROJECT, NOT ONLY BY KNOCKIN' DOWN THOSE OLD WAREHOUSES --
OUR PLEASURE, HAPPY.
STARK SOLUTIONS
-- BUT ALSO BY HELPING WITH FUNDRAISING, BY ATTENDING THE $5000-A-PLATE DINNER WE'RE THROWIN' TONIGHT, WITH PROCEEDS GOIN' TO THE BUILDING FUND!
SO, ANY QUESTIONS?

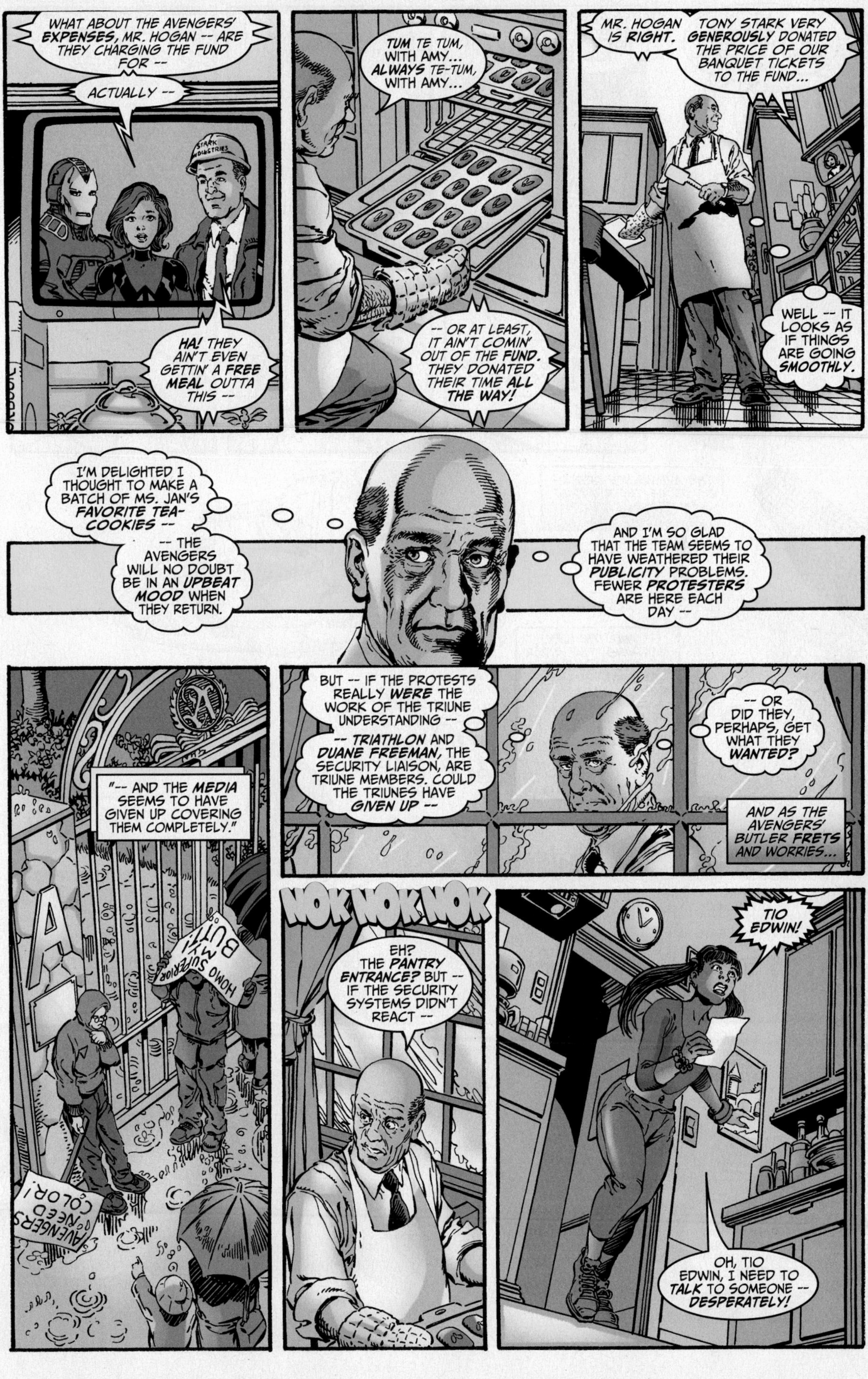

WHAT ABOUT THE AVENGERS' EXPENSES, MR. HOGAN -- ARE THEY CHARGING THE FUND FOR --
ACTUALLY --
STARK INDUSTRIES
HA! THEY AIN'T EVEN GETTIN' A FREE MEAL OUTTA THIS --
TUM TE TUM, WITH AMY... ALWAYS TE-TUM, WITH AMY...
-- OR AT LEAST, IT AIN'T COMIN' OUT OF THE FUND. THEY DONATED THEIR TIME ALL THE WAY!
MR. HOGAN IS RIGHT.
TONY STARK VERY GENEROUSLY DONATED THE PRICE OF OUR BANQUET TICKETS TO THE FUND...
WELL -- IT LOOKS AS IF THINGS ARE GOING SMOOTHLY.
I'M DELIGHTED I THOUGHT TO MAKE A BATCH OF MS. JAN'S FAVORITE TEA-COOKIES --
-- THE AVENGERS WILL NO DOUBT BE IN AN UPBEAT MOOD WHEN THEY RETURN.
AND I'M SO GLAD THAT THE TEAM SEEMS TO HAVE WEATHERED THEIR PUBLICITY PROBLEMS. FEWER PROTESTERS ARE HERE EACH DAY --
"-- AND THE MEDIA SEEMS TO HAVE GIVEN UP COVERING THEM COMPLETELY."
HOMO SUPERIOR MY BUTT!
AVENGERS NEED COLOR!
BUT -- IF THE PROTESTS REALLY WERE THE WORK OF THE TRIUNE UNDERSTANDING --
-- TRIATHLON AND DUANE FREEMAN, THE SECURITY LIAISON, ARE TRIUNE MEMBERS. COULD THE TRIUNES HAVE GIVEN UP --
-- OR DID THEY, PERHAPS, GET WHAT THEY WANTED?
AND AS THE AVENGERS' BUTLER FRETS AND WORRIES...
NOK NOK NOK
EH? THE PANTRY ENTRANCE? BUT -- IF THE SECURITY SYSTEMS DIDN'T REACT --
TIO EDWIN!
OH, TIO EDWIN, I NEED TO TALK TO SOMEONE -- DESPERATELY!

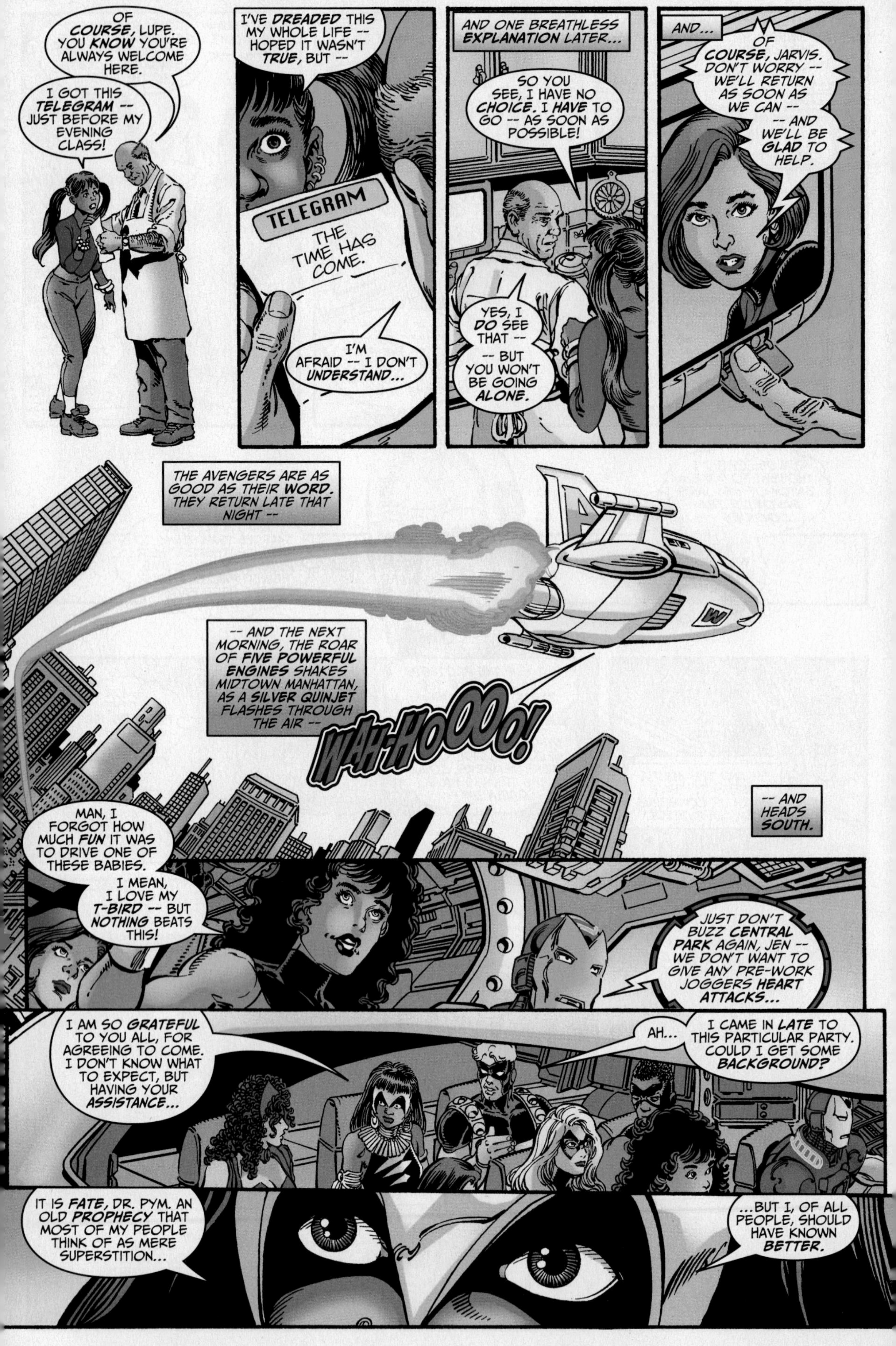
OF COURSE, LUPE. YOU KNOW YOU'RE ALWAYS WELCOME HERE.
I GOT THIS TELEGRAM -- JUST BEFORE MY EVENING CLASS!
I'VE DREADED THIS MY WHOLE LIFE -- HOPED IT WASN'T TRUE, BUT --
TELEGRAM
THE TIME HAS COME.
I'M AFRAID -- I DON'T UNDERSTAND...
AND ONE BREATHLESS EXPLANATION LATER...
SO YOU SEE, I HAVE NO CHOICE. I HAVE TO GO -- AS SOON AS POSSIBLE!
YES, I DO SEE THAT --
-- BUT YOU WON'T BE GOING ALONE.
AND...
OF COURSE, JARVIS. DON'T WORRY -- WE'LL RETURN AS SOON AS WE CAN --
-- AND WE'LL BE GLAD TO HELP.
THE AVENGERS ARE AS GOOD AS THEIR WORD. THEY RETURN LATE THAT NIGHT --
-- AND THE NEXT MORNING, THE ROAR OF FIVE POWERFUL ENGINES SHAKES MIDTOWN MANHATTAN, AS A SILVER QUINJET FLASHES THROUGH THE AIR --
WAH-HOOOOo!
-- AND HEADS SOUTH.
MAN, I FORGOT HOW MUCH FUN IT WAS TO DRIVE ONE OF THESE BABIES.
I MEAN, I LOVE MY T-BIRD -- BUT NOTHING BEATS THIS!
JUST DON'T BUZZ CENTRAL PARK AGAIN, JEN -- WE DON'T WANT TO GIVE ANY PRE-WORK JOGGERS HEART ATTACKS...
I AM SO GRATEFUL TO YOU ALL, FOR AGREEING TO COME. I DON'T KNOW WHAT TO EXPECT, BUT HAVING YOUR ASSISTANCE...
AH...
I CAME IN LATE TO THIS PARTICULAR PARTY. COULD I GET SOME BACKGROUND?
IT IS FATE, DR. PYM. AN OLD PROPHECY THAT MOST OF MY PEOPLE THINK OF AS MERE SUPERSTITION...
...BUT I, OF ALL PEOPLE, SHOULD HAVE KNOWN BETTER.

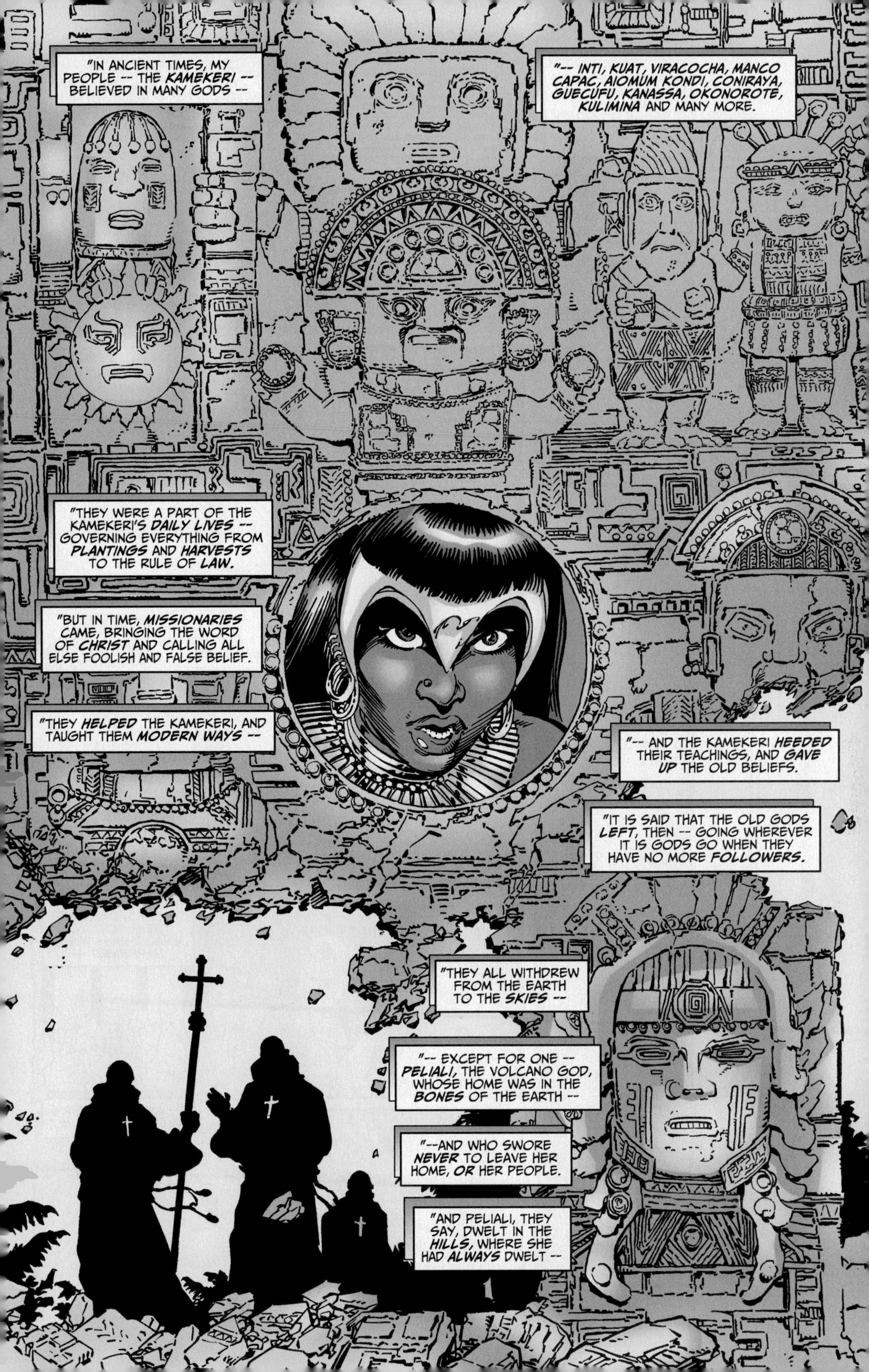
"IN ANCIENT TIMES, MY PEOPLE -- THE KAMEKERI -- BELIEVED IN MANY GODS --
"-- INTI, KUAT, VIRACOCHA, MANCO CAPAC, AIOMÚM KONDI, CONIRAYA, GUECUFU, KANASSA, OKONOROTE, KULIMINA AND MANY MORE.
"THEY WERE A PART OF THE KAMEKERI'S DAILY LIVES -- GOVERNING EVERYTHING FROM PLANTINGS AND HARVESTS TO THE RULE OF LAW.
"BUT IN TIME, MISSIONARIES CAME, BRINGING THE WORD OF CHRIST AND CALLING ALL ELSE FOOLISH AND FALSE BELIEF.
"THEY HELPED THE KAMEKERI, AND TAUGHT THEM MODERN WAYS --
"-- AND THE KAMEKERI HEEDED THEIR TEACHINGS, AND GAVE UP THE OLD BELIEFS.
"IT IS SAID THAT THE OLD GODS LEFT, THEN -- GOING WHEREVER IT IS GODS GO WHEN THEY HAVE NO MORE FOLLOWERS.
"THEY ALL WITHDREW FROM THE EARTH TO THE SKIES --
"-- EXCEPT FOR ONE -- PELIALI, THE VOLCANO GOD, WHOSE HOME WAS IN THE BONES OF THE EARTH --
"--AND WHO SWORE NEVER TO LEAVE HER HOME, OR HER PEOPLE.
"AND PELIALI, THEY SAY, DWELT IN THE HILLS, WHERE SHE HAD ALWAYS DWELT --

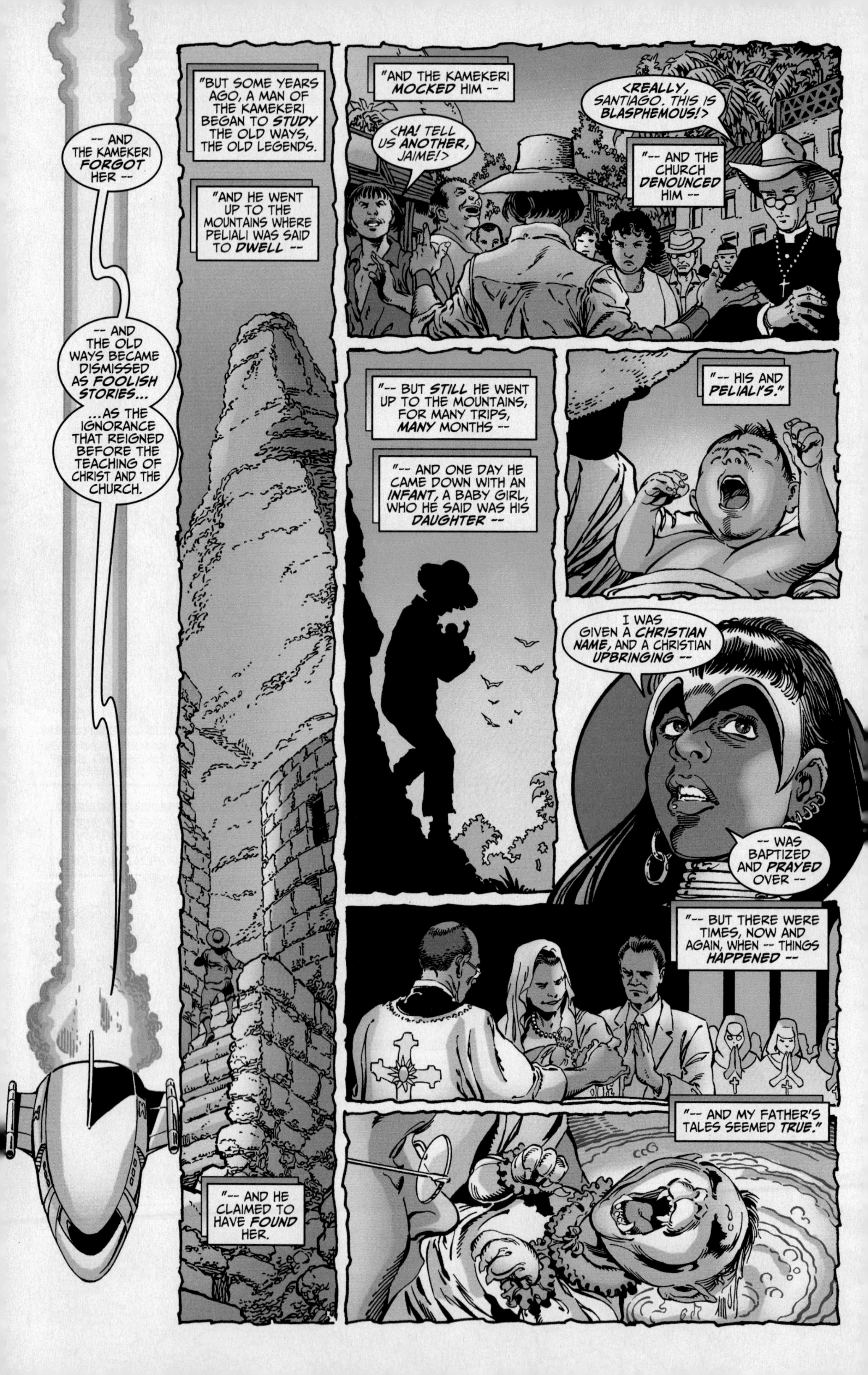
-- AND THE KAMEKERI FORGOT HER --
-- AND THE OLD WAYS BECAME DISMISSED AS FOOLISH STORIES...
...AS THE IGNORANCE THAT REIGNED BEFORE THE TEACHING OF CHRIST AND THE CHURCH.
"BUT SOME YEARS AGO, A MAN OF THE KAMEKERI BEGAN TO STUDY THE OLD WAYS, THE OLD LEGENDS.
"AND HE WENT UP TO THE MOUNTAINS WHERE PELIALI WAS SAID TO DWELL --
"-- AND HE CLAIMED TO HAVE FOUND HER.
"AND THE KAMEKERI MOCKED HIM --
<HA! TELL US ANOTHER, JAIME!>
<REALLY, SANTIAGO. THIS IS BLASPHEMOUS!>
"-- AND THE CHURCH DENOUNCED HIM --
"-- BUT STILL HE WENT UP TO THE MOUNTAINS, FOR MANY TRIPS, MANY MONTHS --
"-- AND ONE DAY HE CAME DOWN WITH AN INFANT, A BABY GIRL, WHO HE SAID WAS HIS DAUGHTER --
"-- HIS AND PELIALI'S."
I WAS GIVEN A CHRISTIAN NAME, AND A CHRISTIAN UPBRINGING --
-- WAS BAPTIZED AND PRAYED OVER --
"-- BUT THERE WERE TIMES, NOW AND AGAIN, WHEN -- THINGS HAPPENED --
"-- AND MY FATHER'S TALES SEEMED TRUE."

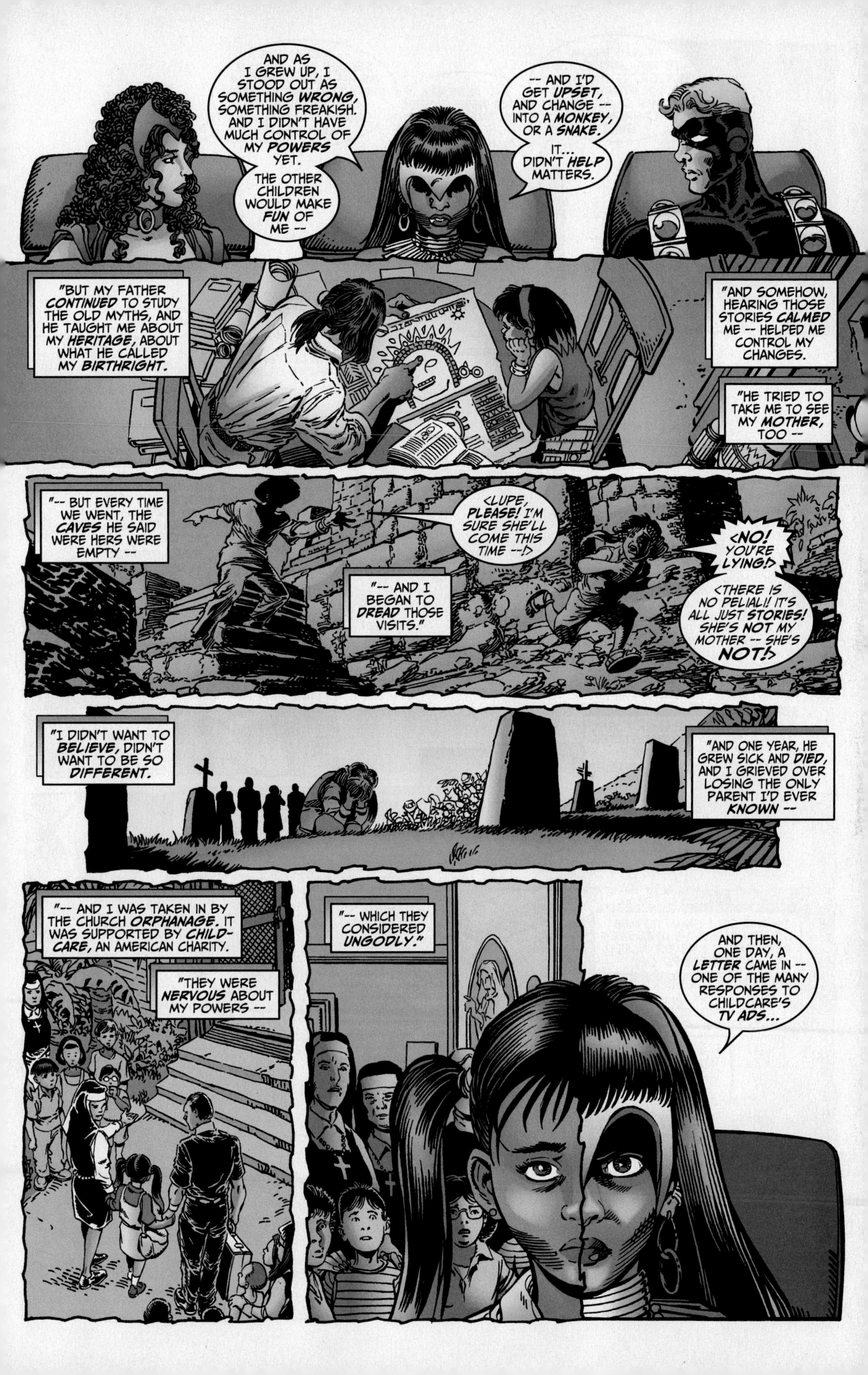
AND AS I GREW UP, I STOOD OUT AS SOMETHING WRONG, SOMETHING FREAKISH. AND I DIDN'T HAVE MUCH CONTROL OF MY POWERS YET.
THE OTHER CHILDREN WOULD MAKE FUN OF ME --
-- AND I'D GET UPSET, AND CHANGE -- INTO A MONKEY, OR A SNAKE.
IT... DIDN'T HELP MATTERS.
"BUT MY FATHER CONTINUED TO STUDY THE OLD MYTHS, AND HE TAUGHT ME ABOUT MY HERITAGE, ABOUT WHAT HE CALLED MY BIRTHRIGHT.
"AND SOMEHOW, HEARING THOSE STORIES CALMED ME -- HELPED ME CONTROL MY CHANGES.
"HE TRIED TO TAKE ME TO SEE MY MOTHER, TOO --
"-- BUT EVERY TIME WE WENT, THE CAVES HE SAID WERE HERS WERE EMPTY --
<LUPE, PLEASE! I'M SURE SHE'LL COME THIS TIME --!>
"-- AND I BEGAN TO DREAD THOSE VISITS."
<NO! YOU'RE LYING!>
<THERE IS NO PELIALI! IT'S ALL JUST STORIES! SHE'S NOT MY MOTHER -- SHE'S NOT!>
"I DIDN'T WANT TO BELIEVE, DIDN'T WANT TO BE SO DIFFERENT.
"AND ONE YEAR, HE GREW SICK AND DIED, AND I GRIEVED OVER LOSING THE ONLY PARENT I'D EVER KNOWN --
"-- AND I WAS TAKEN IN BY THE CHURCH ORPHANAGE. IT WAS SUPPORTED BY CHILD-CARE, AN AMERICAN CHARITY.
"THEY WERE NERVOUS ABOUT MY POWERS --
"-- WHICH THEY CONSIDERED UNGODLY."
AND THEN, ONE DAY, A LETTER CAME IN -- ONE OF THE MANY RESPONSES TO CHILDCARE'S TV ADS...

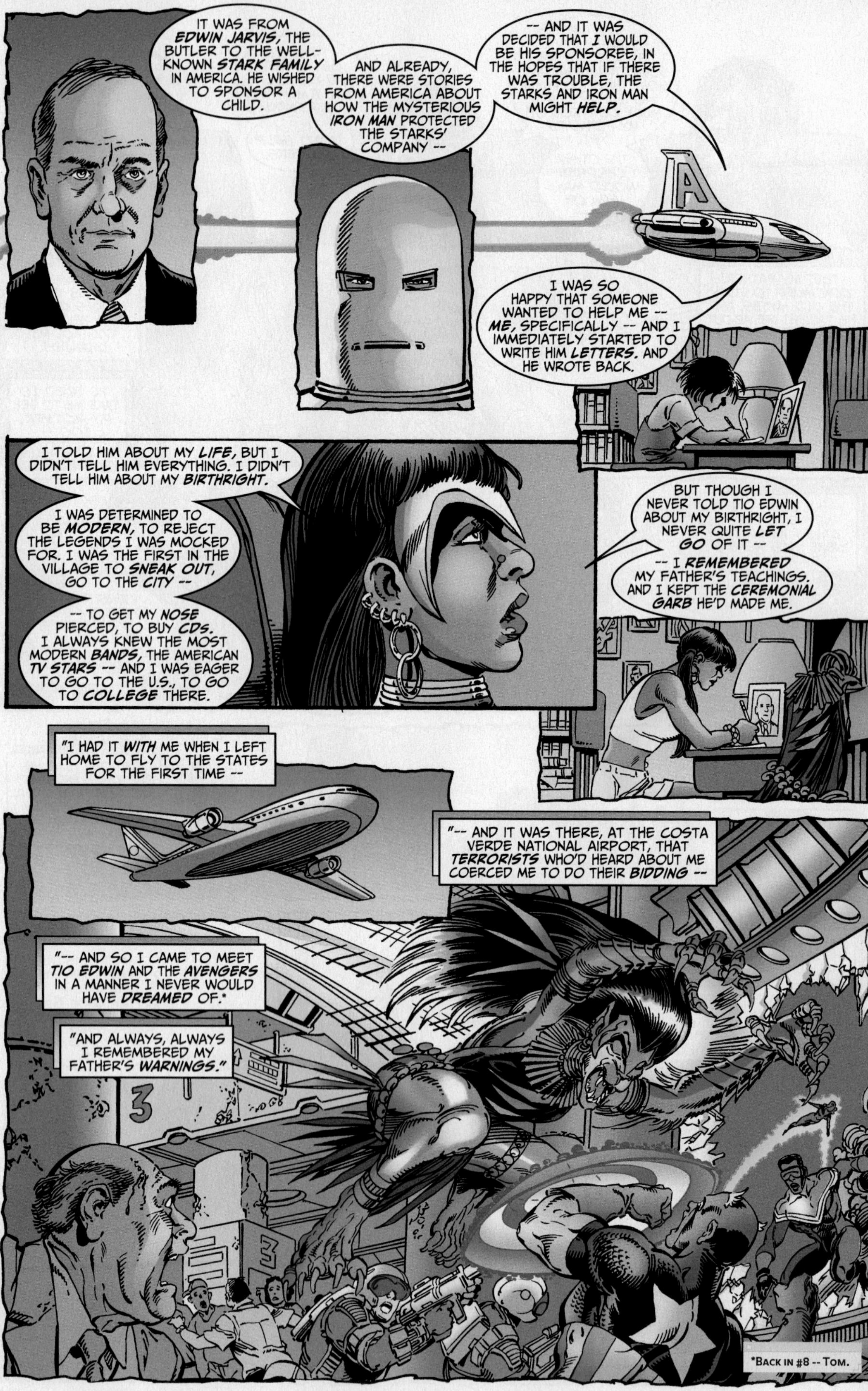

IT WAS FROM EDWIN JARVIS, THE BUTLER TO THE WELL-KNOWN STARK FAMILY IN AMERICA. HE WISHED TO SPONSOR A CHILD.
AND ALREADY, THERE WERE STORIES FROM AMERICA ABOUT HOW THE MYSTERIOUS IRON MAN PROTECTED THE STARKS' COMPANY --
-- AND IT WAS DECIDED THAT I WOULD BE HIS SPONSOREE, IN THE HOPES THAT IF THERE WAS TROUBLE, THE STARKS AND IRON MAN MIGHT HELP.
I WAS SO HAPPY THAT SOMEONE WANTED TO HELP ME -- ME, SPECIFICALLY -- AND I IMMEDIATELY STARTED TO WRITE HIM LETTERS. AND HE WROTE BACK.
I TOLD HIM ABOUT MY LIFE, BUT I DIDN'T TELL HIM EVERYTHING. I DIDN'T TELL HIM ABOUT MY BIRTHRIGHT.
I WAS DETERMINED TO BE MODERN, TO REJECT THE LEGENDS I WAS MOCKED FOR. I WAS THE FIRST IN THE VILLAGE TO SNEAK OUT, GO TO THE CITY --
-- TO GET MY NOSE PIERCED, TO BUY CDS. I ALWAYS KNEW THE MOST MODERN BANDS, THE AMERICAN TV STARS -- AND I WAS EAGER TO GO TO THE U.S., TO GO TO COLLEGE THERE.
BUT THOUGH I NEVER TOLD TIO EDWIN ABOUT MY BIRTHRIGHT, I NEVER QUITE LET GO OF IT --
-- I REMEMBERED MY FATHER'S TEACHINGS. AND I KEPT THE CEREMONIAL GARB HE'D MADE ME.
"I HAD IT WITH ME WHEN I LEFT HOME TO FLY TO THE STATES FOR THE FIRST TIME --
"-- AND IT WAS THERE, AT THE COSTA VERDE NATIONAL AIRPORT, THAT TERRORISTS WHO'D HEARD ABOUT ME COERCED ME TO DO THEIR BIDDING --
"-- AND SO I CAME TO MEET TIO EDWIN AND THE AVENGERS IN A MANNER I NEVER WOULD HAVE DREAMED OF.*
"AND ALWAYS, ALWAYS I REMEMBERED MY FATHER'S WARNINGS."
*BACK IN #8 -- TOM.

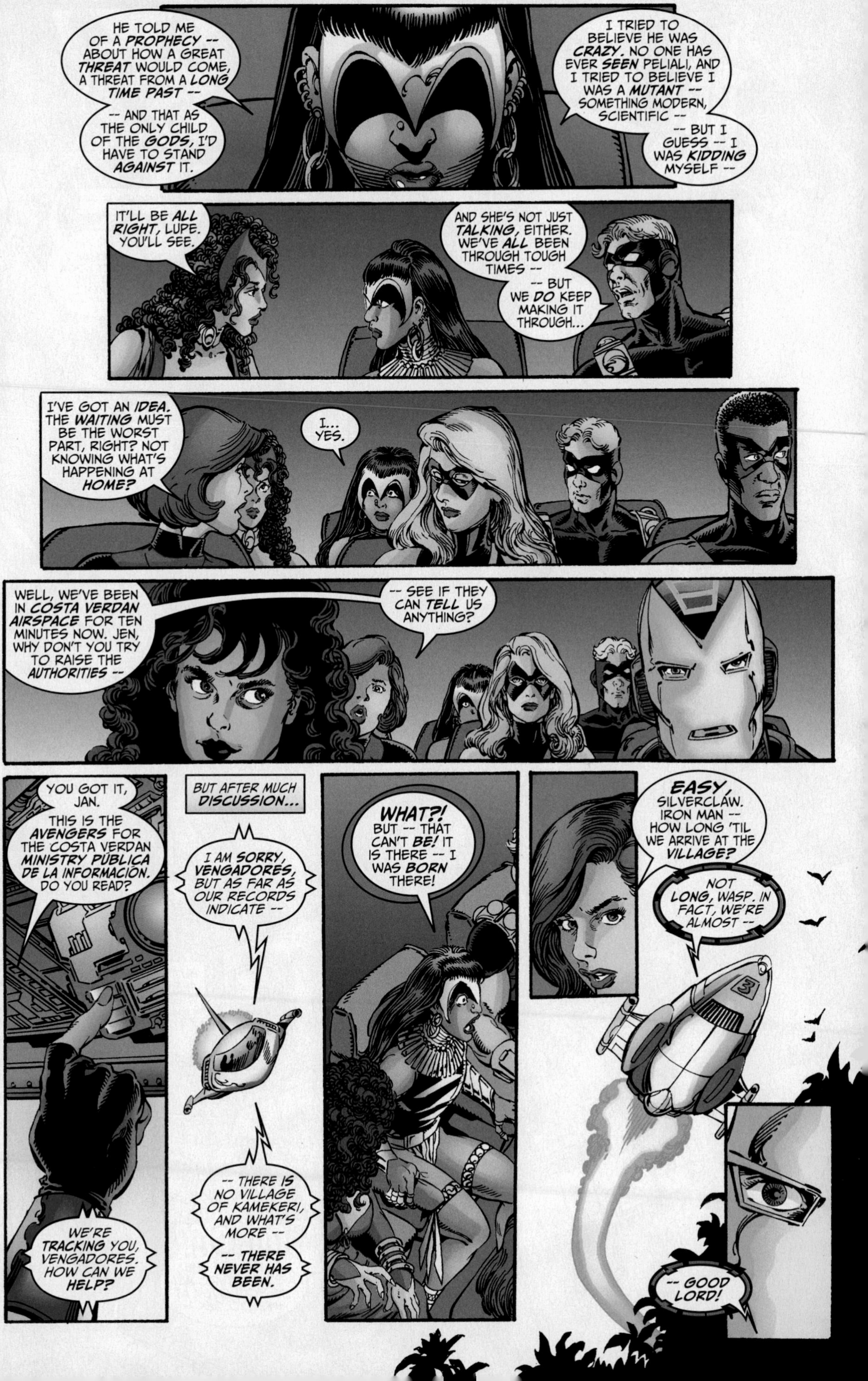
HE TOLD ME OF A PROPHECY -- ABOUT HOW A GREAT THREAT WOULD COME, A THREAT FROM A LONG TIME PAST --
-- AND THAT AS THE ONLY CHILD OF THE GODS, I'D HAVE TO STAND AGAINST IT.
I TRIED TO BELIEVE HE WAS CRAZY. NO ONE HAS EVER SEEN PELIALI, AND I TRIED TO BELIEVE I WAS A MUTANT -- SOMETHING MODERN, SCIENTIFIC --
-- BUT I GUESS -- I WAS KIDDING MYSELF --
IT'LL BE ALL RIGHT, LUPE. YOU'LL SEE.
AND SHE'S NOT JUST TALKING, EITHER. WE'VE ALL BEEN THROUGH TOUGH TIMES --
-- BUT WE DO KEEP MAKING IT THROUGH...
I'VE GOT AN IDEA. THE WAITING MUST BE THE WORST PART, RIGHT? NOT KNOWING WHAT'S HAPPENING AT HOME?
I... YES.
WELL, WE'VE BEEN IN COSTA VERDAN AIRSPACE FOR TEN MINUTES NOW. JEN, WHY DON'T YOU TRY TO RAISE THE AUTHORITIES --
-- SEE IF THEY CAN TELL US ANYTHING?
YOU GOT IT, JAN.
THIS IS THE AVENGERS FOR THE COSTA VERDAN MINISTRY PÚBLICA DE LA INFORMACIÓN. DO YOU READ?
WE'RE TRACKING YOU, VENGADORES. HOW CAN WE HELP?
BUT AFTER MUCH DISCUSSION...
I AM SORRY, VENGADORES, BUT AS FAR AS OUR RECORDS INDICATE --
-- THERE IS NO VILLAGE OF KAMEKERI, AND WHAT'S MORE --
-- THERE NEVER HAS BEEN.
WHAT?! BUT -- THAT CAN'T BE! IT IS THERE -- I WAS BORN THERE!
EASY, SILVERCLAW. IRON MAN -- HOW LONG 'TIL WE ARRIVE AT THE VILLAGE?
NOT LONG, WASP. IN FACT, WE'RE ALMOST --
-- GOOD LORD!

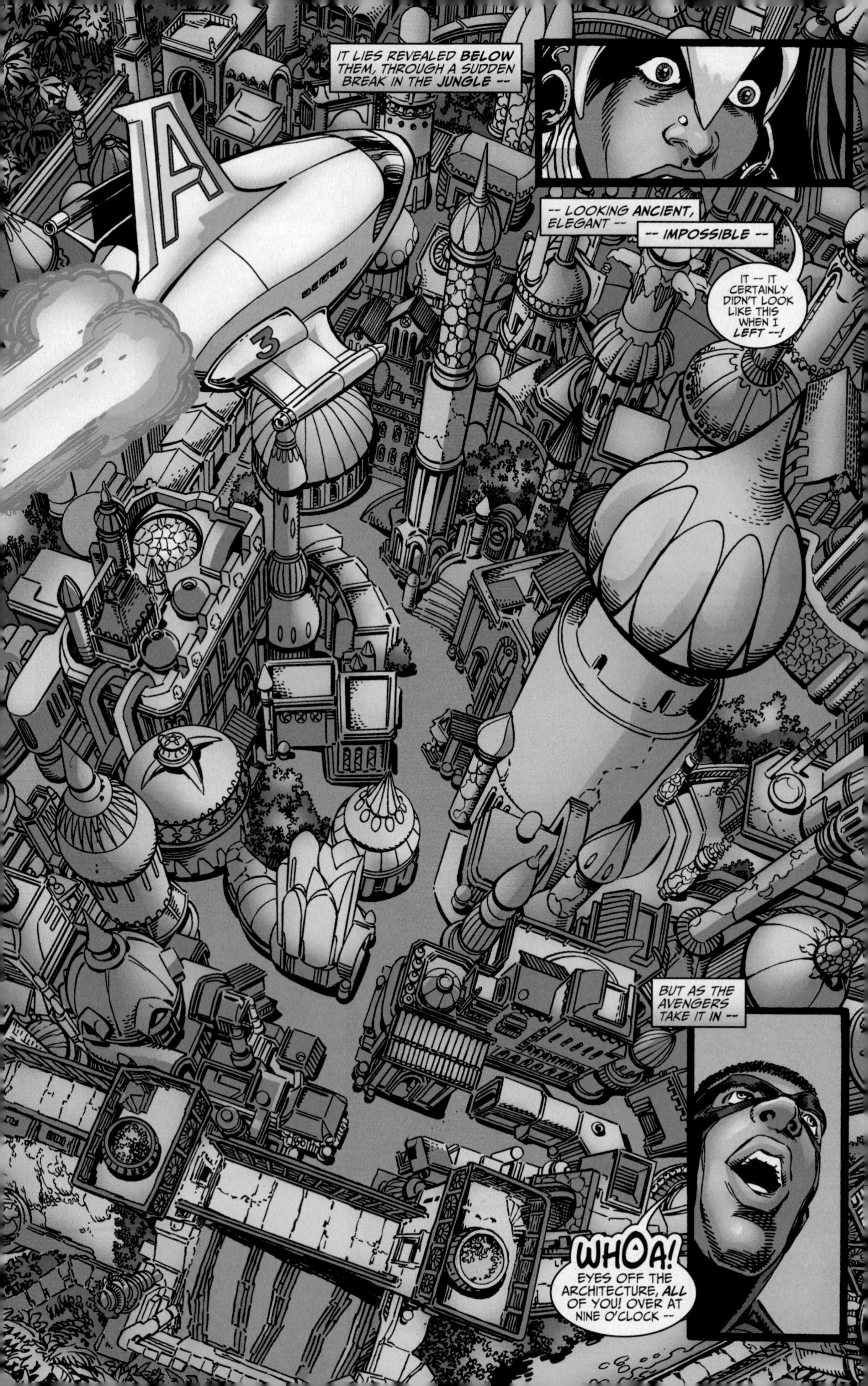
IT LIES REVEALED BELOW THEM, THROUGH A SUDDEN BREAK IN THE JUNGLE --
-- LOOKING ANCIENT, ELEGANT --
-- IMPOSSIBLE --
IT -- IT CERTAINLY DIDN'T LOOK LIKE THIS WHEN I LEFT --!
A
3
BUT AS THE AVENGERS TAKE IT IN --
WHOA! EYES OFF THE ARCHITECTURE, ALL OF YOU! OVER AT NINE O'CLOCK --

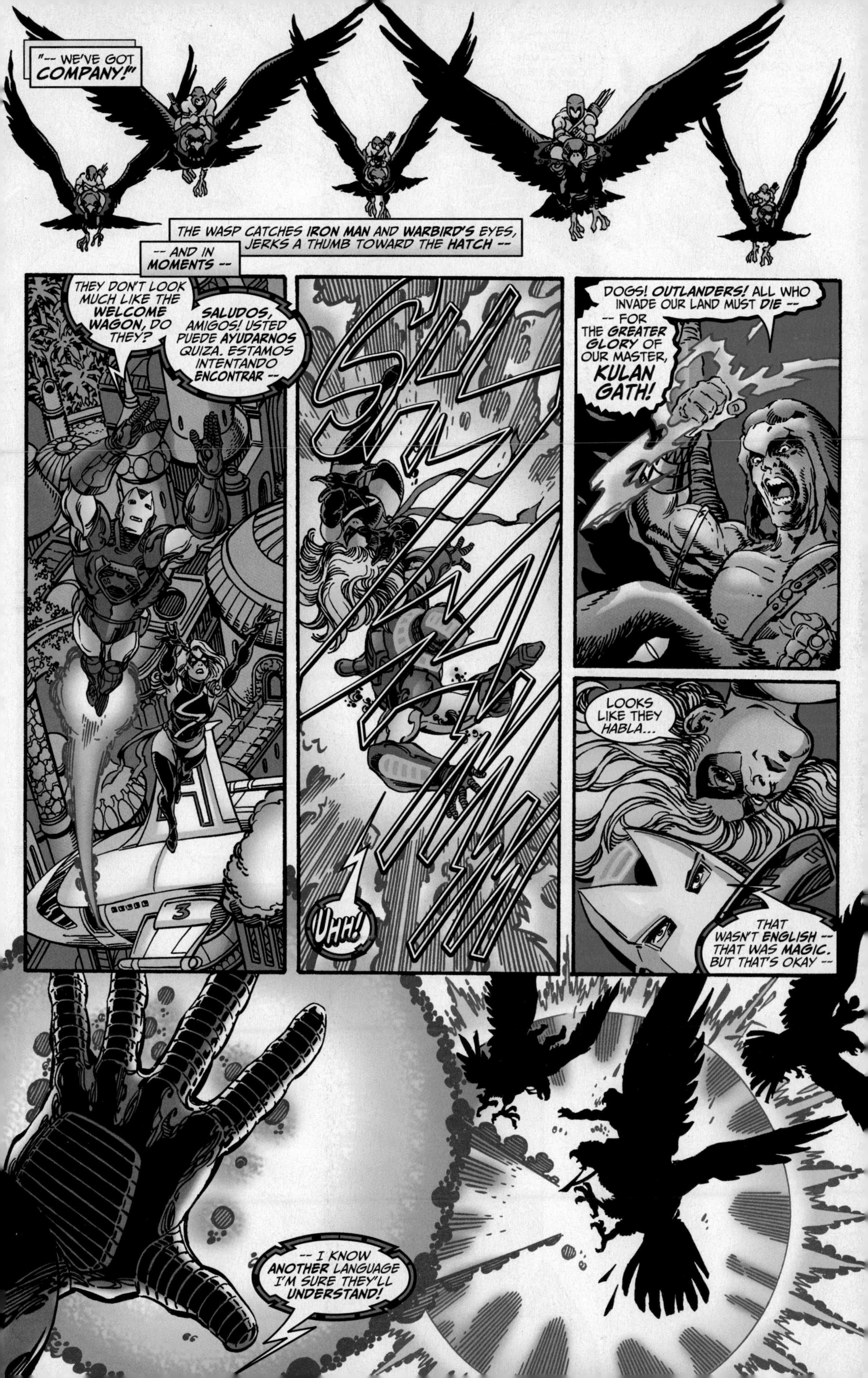
"-- WE'VE GOT COMPANY!"
THE WASP CATCHES IRON MAN AND WARBIRD'S EYES, JERKS A THUMB TOWARD THE HATCH --
-- AND IN MOMENTS --
THEY DON'T LOOK MUCH LIKE THE WELCOME WAGON, DO THEY?
SALUDOS, AMIGOS! USTED PUEDE AYUDARNOS QUIZA. ESTAMOS INTENTANDO ENCONTRAR --
3
SHHHHHHH
UHH!
DOGS! OUTLANDERS! ALL WHO INVADE OUR LAND MUST DIE --
-- FOR THE GREATER GLORY OF OUR MASTER, KULAN GATH!
LOOKS LIKE THEY HABLA...
THAT WASN'T ENGLISH -- THAT WAS MAGIC. BUT THAT'S OKAY --
-- I KNOW ANOTHER LANGUAGE I'M SURE THEY'LL UNDERSTAND!

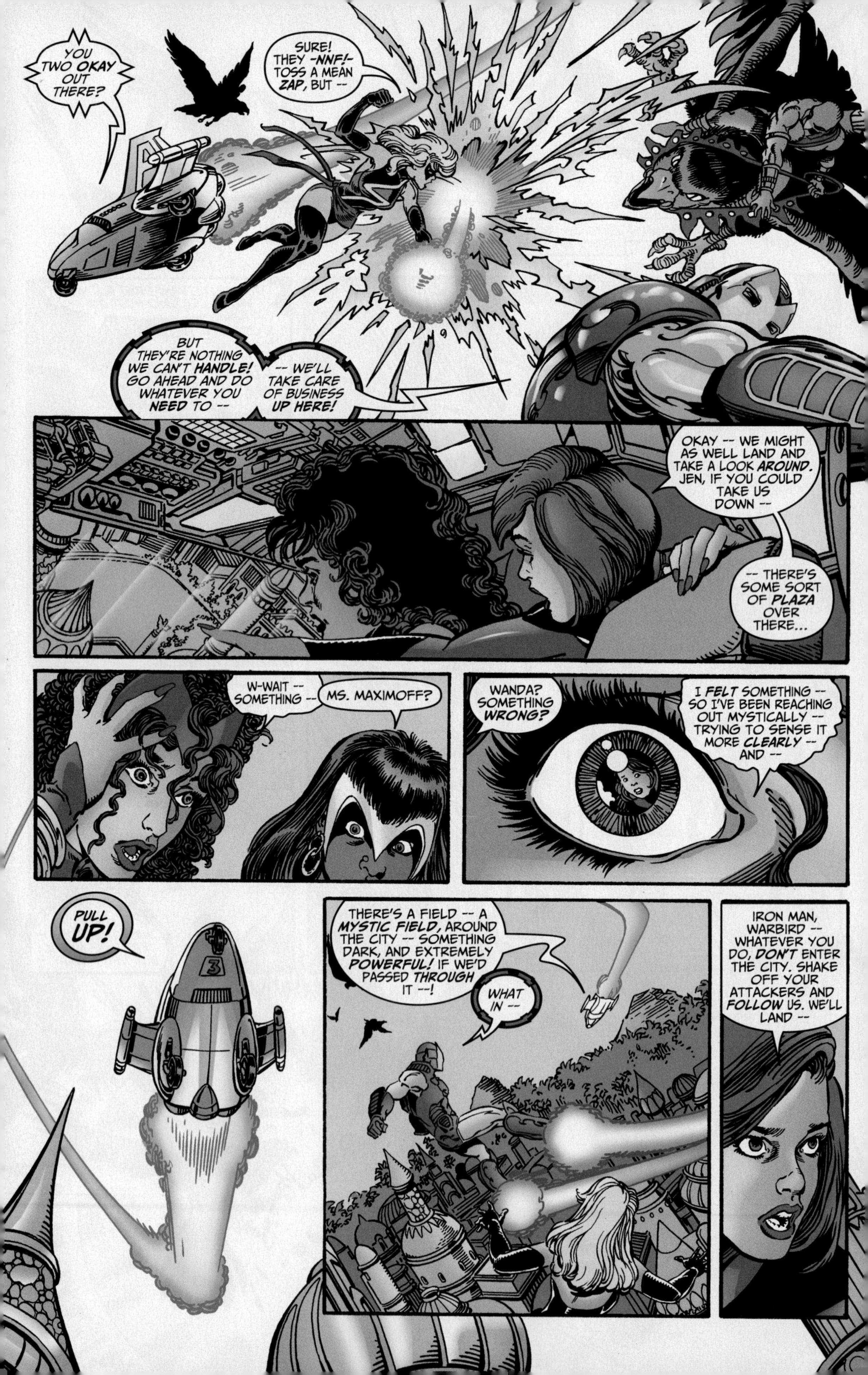
YOU TWO OKAY OUT THERE?
SURE! THEY -NNF!- TOSS A MEAN ZAP, BUT --
BUT THEY'RE NOTHING WE CAN'T HANDLE! GO AHEAD AND DO WHATEVER YOU NEED TO --
-- WE'LL TAKE CARE OF BUSINESS UP HERE!
OKAY -- WE MIGHT AS WELL LAND AND TAKE A LOOK AROUND. JEN, IF YOU COULD TAKE US DOWN --
-- THERE'S SOME SORT OF PLAZA OVER THERE...
W-WAIT -- SOMETHING --
MS. MAXIMOFF?
WANDA? SOMETHING WRONG?
I FELT SOMETHING -- SO I'VE BEEN REACHING OUT MYSTICALLY -- TRYING TO SENSE IT MORE CLEARLY -- AND --
PULL UP!
THERE'S A FIELD -- A MYSTIC FIELD, AROUND THE CITY -- SOMETHING DARK, AND EXTREMELY POWERFUL! IF WE'D PASSED THROUGH IT --!
WHAT IN --
IRON MAN, WARBIRD -- WHATEVER YOU DO, DON'T ENTER THE CITY. SHAKE OFF YOUR ATTACKERS AND FOLLOW US. WE'LL LAND --

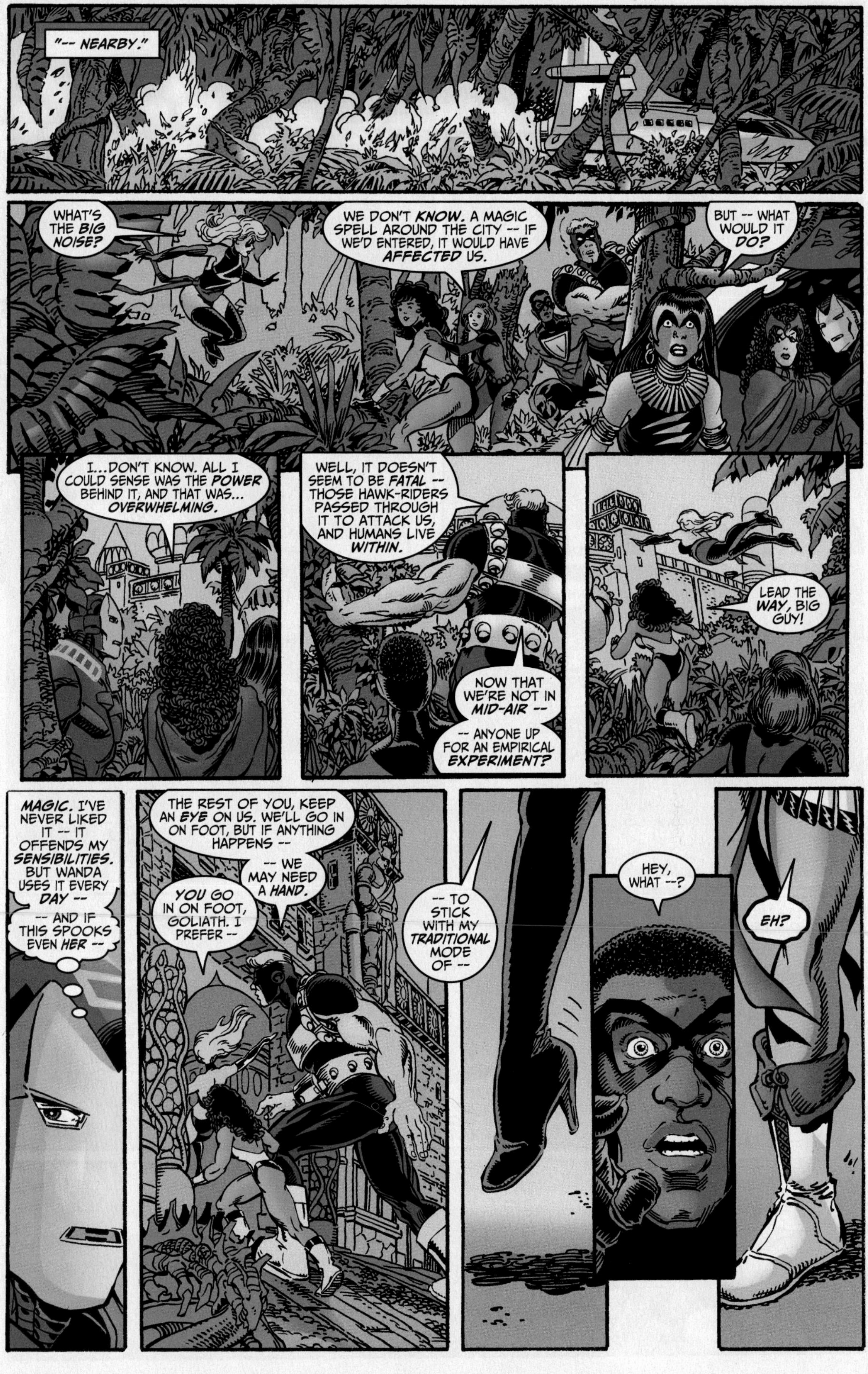
"-- NEARBY."
WHAT'S THE BIG NOISE?
WE DON'T KNOW. A MAGIC SPELL AROUND THE CITY -- IF WE'D ENTERED, IT WOULD HAVE AFFECTED US.
BUT -- WHAT WOULD IT DO?
I...DON'T KNOW. ALL I COULD SENSE WAS THE POWER BEHIND IT, AND THAT WAS... OVERWHELMING.
WELL, IT DOESN'T SEEM TO BE FATAL -- THOSE HAWK-RIDERS PASSED THROUGH IT TO ATTACK US, AND HUMANS LIVE WITHIN.
NOW THAT WE'RE NOT IN MID-AIR --
-- ANYONE UP FOR AN EMPIRICAL EXPERIMENT?
LEAD THE WAY, BIG GUY!
MAGIC. I'VE NEVER LIKED IT -- IT OFFENDS MY SENSIBILITIES. BUT WANDA USES IT EVERY DAY --
-- AND IF THIS SPOOKS EVEN HER --
THE REST OF YOU, KEEP AN EYE ON US. WE'LL GO IN ON FOOT, BUT IF ANYTHING HAPPENS --
-- WE MAY NEED A HAND.
YOU GO IN ON FOOT, GOLIATH. I PREFER --
-- TO STICK WITH MY TRADITIONAL MODE OF --
HEY, WHAT --?
EH?

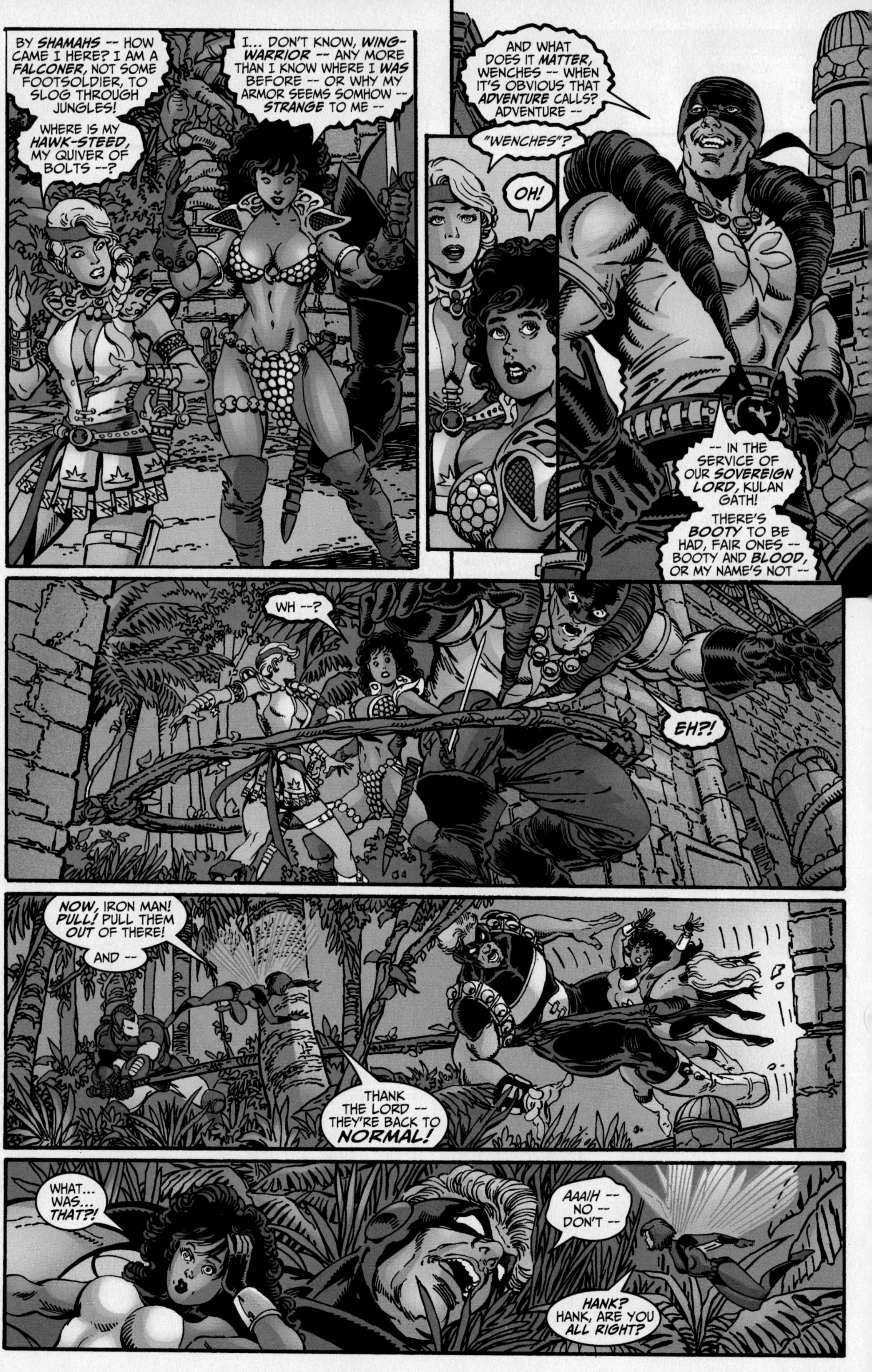
BY *SHAMAHS* -- HOW CAME I HERE? I AM A *FALCONER*, NOT SOME FOOTSOLDIER, TO SLOG THROUGH JUNGLES!
WHERE IS MY *HAWK-STEED*, MY QUIVER OF BOLTS --?
I... DON'T KNOW, *WING-WARRIOR* -- ANY MORE THAN I KNOW WHERE I *WAS* BEFORE -- OR WHY MY ARMOR SEEMS SOMHOW -- *STRANGE* TO ME --
AND WHAT DOES IT *MATTER*, WENCHES -- WHEN IT'S OBVIOUS THAT *ADVENTURE* CALLS? ADVENTURE --
"WENCHES"?
OH!
-- IN THE SERVICE OF OUR *SOVEREIGN LORD*, KULAN GATH!
THERE'S *BOOTY* TO BE HAD, FAIR ONES -- BOOTY AND *BLOOD*, OR MY NAME'S NOT --
WH --?
EH?!
NOW, IRON MAN! *PULL!* PULL THEM *OUT* OF THERE!
AND --
THANK THE LORD -- THEY'RE BACK TO *NORMAL!*
WHAT... WAS... *THAT?!*
AAAIH -- NO -- DON'T --
HANK? HANK, ARE YOU *ALL RIGHT?*

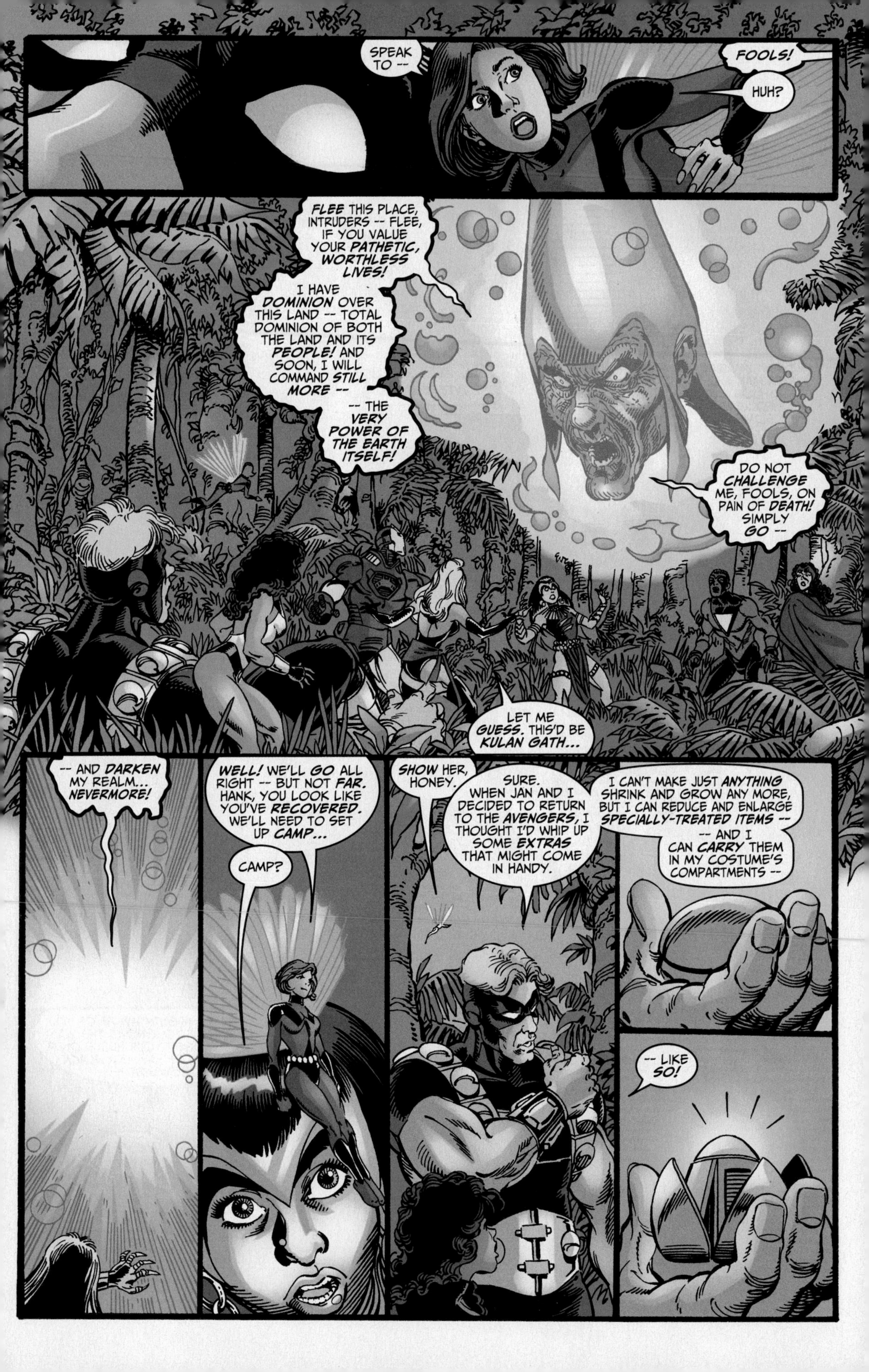
SPEAK TO --
FOOLS!
HUH?
FLEE THIS PLACE, INTRUDERS -- FLEE, IF YOU VALUE YOUR PATHETIC, WORTHLESS LIVES!
I HAVE DOMINION OVER THIS LAND -- TOTAL DOMINION OF BOTH THE LAND AND ITS PEOPLE! AND SOON, I WILL COMMAND STILL MORE --
-- THE VERY POWER OF THE EARTH ITSELF!
DO NOT CHALLENGE ME, FOOLS, ON PAIN OF DEATH! SIMPLY GO --
LET ME GUESS. THIS'D BE KULAN GATH...
-- AND DARKEN MY REALM... NEVERMORE!
WELL! WE'LL GO ALL RIGHT -- BUT NOT FAR. HANK, YOU LOOK LIKE YOU'VE RECOVERED. WE'LL NEED TO SET UP CAMP...
CAMP?
SHOW HER, HONEY.
SURE. WHEN JAN AND I DECIDED TO RETURN TO THE AVENGERS, I THOUGHT I'D WHIP UP SOME EXTRAS THAT MIGHT COME IN HANDY.
I CAN'T MAKE JUST ANYTHING SHRINK AND GROW ANY MORE, BUT I CAN REDUCE AND ENLARGE SPECIALLY-TREATED ITEMS --
-- AND I CAN CARRY THEM IN MY COSTUME'S COMPARTMENTS --
-- LIKE SO!

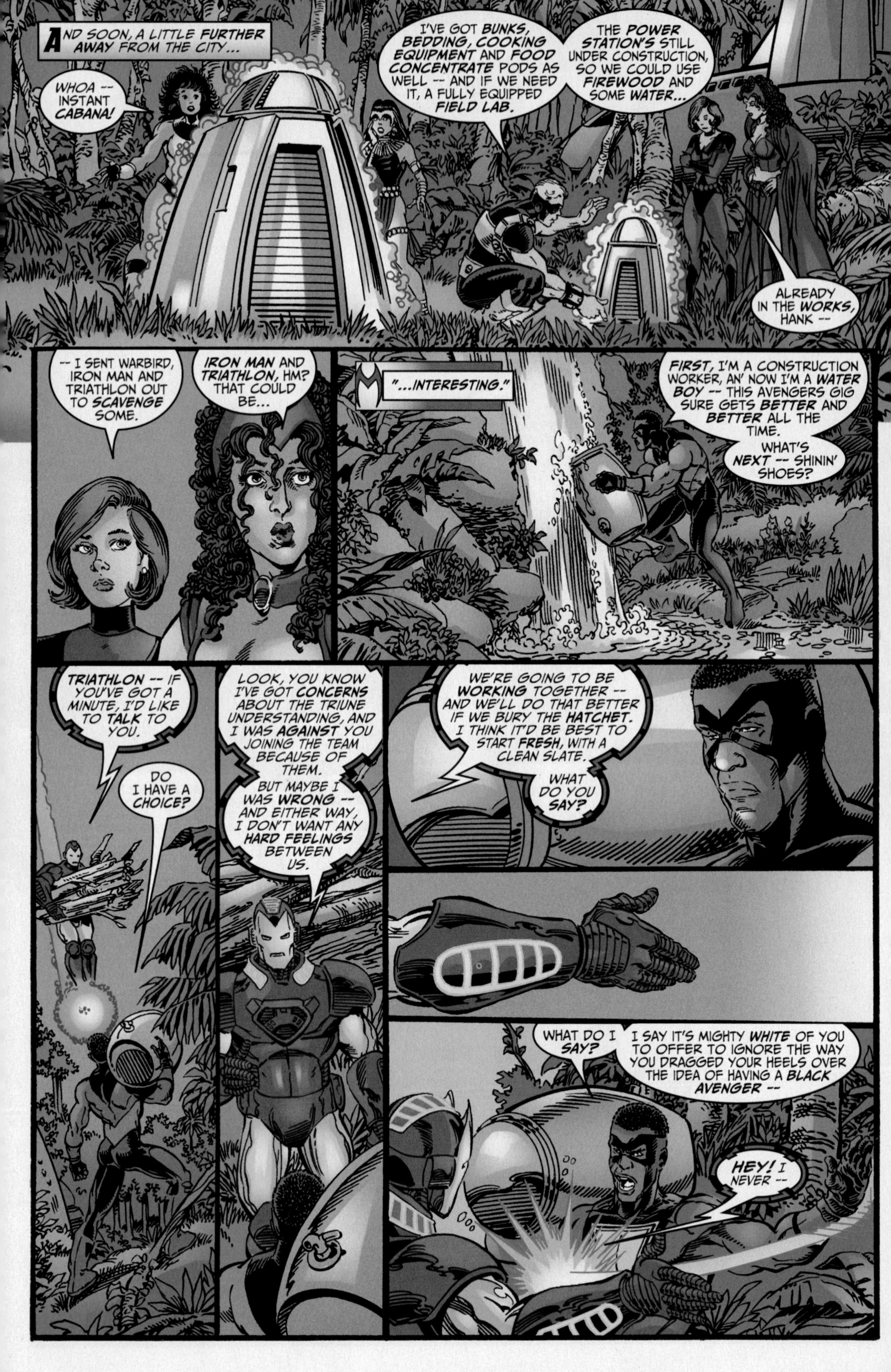
AND SOON, A LITTLE FURTHER AWAY FROM THE CITY...
WHOA -- INSTANT CABANA!
I'VE GOT BUNKS, BEDDING, COOKING EQUIPMENT AND FOOD CONCENTRATE PODS AS WELL -- AND IF WE NEED IT, A FULLY EQUIPPED FIELD LAB.
THE POWER STATION'S STILL UNDER CONSTRUCTION, SO WE COULD USE FIREWOOD AND SOME WATER...
ALREADY IN THE WORKS, HANK --
-- I SENT WARBIRD, IRON MAN AND TRIATHLON OUT TO SCAVENGE SOME.
IRON MAN AND TRIATHLON, HM? THAT COULD BE...
"...INTERESTING."
FIRST, I'M A CONSTRUCTION WORKER, AN' NOW I'M A WATER BOY -- THIS AVENGERS GIG SURE GETS BETTER AND BETTER ALL THE TIME.
WHAT'S NEXT -- SHININ' SHOES?
TRIATHLON -- IF YOU'VE GOT A MINUTE, I'D LIKE TO TALK TO YOU.
DO I HAVE A CHOICE?
LOOK, YOU KNOW I'VE GOT CONCERNS ABOUT THE TRIUNE UNDERSTANDING, AND I WAS AGAINST YOU JOINING THE TEAM BECAUSE OF THEM.
BUT MAYBE I WAS WRONG -- AND EITHER WAY, I DON'T WANT ANY HARD FEELINGS BETWEEN US.
WE'RE GOING TO BE WORKING TOGETHER -- AND WE'LL DO THAT BETTER IF WE BURY THE HATCHET. I THINK IT'D BE BEST TO START FRESH, WITH A CLEAN SLATE.
WHAT DO YOU SAY?
WHAT DO I SAY?
I SAY IT'S MIGHTY WHITE OF YOU TO OFFER TO IGNORE THE WAY YOU DRAGGED YOUR HEELS OVER THE IDEA OF HAVING A BLACK AVENGER --
HEY! I NEVER --

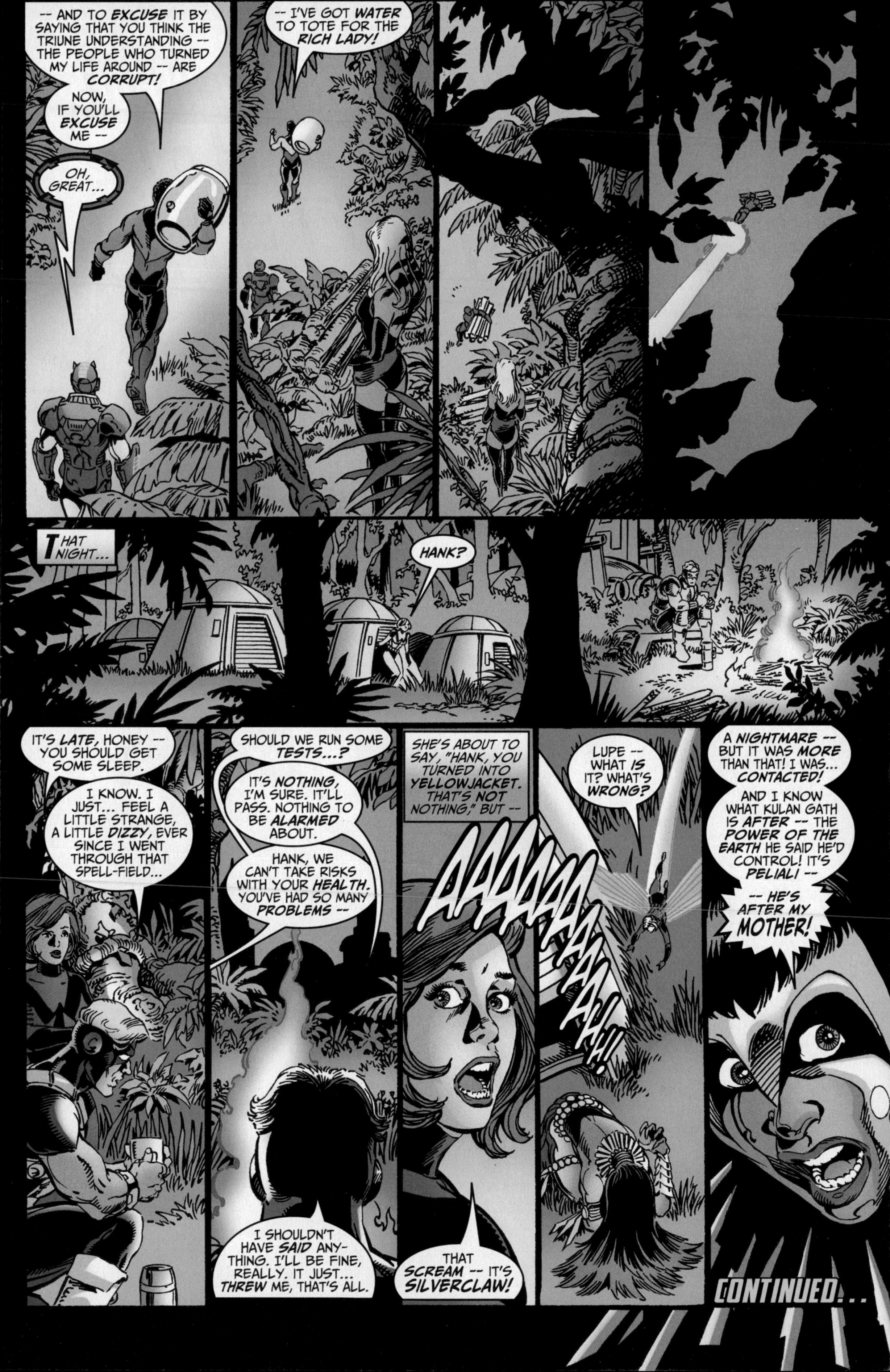
-- AND TO EXCUSE IT BY SAYING THAT YOU THINK THE TRIUNE UNDERSTANDING -- THE PEOPLE WHO TURNED MY LIFE AROUND -- ARE CORRUPT!
NOW, IF YOU'LL EXCUSE ME --
OH, GREAT...
-- I'VE GOT WATER TO TOTE FOR THE RICH LADY!
THAT NIGHT...
HANK?
IT'S LATE, HONEY -- YOU SHOULD GET SOME SLEEP.
I KNOW. I JUST... FEEL A LITTLE STRANGE, A LITTLE DIZZY, EVER SINCE I WENT THROUGH THAT SPELL-FIELD...
SHOULD WE RUN SOME TESTS...?
IT'S NOTHING, I'M SURE. IT'LL PASS. NOTHING TO BE ALARMED ABOUT.
HANK, WE CAN'T TAKE RISKS WITH YOUR HEALTH. YOU'VE HAD SO MANY PROBLEMS --
I SHOULDN'T HAVE SAID ANY-THING. I'LL BE FINE, REALLY. IT JUST... THREW ME, THAT'S ALL.
SHE'S ABOUT TO SAY, "HANK, YOU TURNED INTO YELLOWJACKET. THAT'S NOT NOTHING," BUT --
AAAAAAAAAAAHH!!
THAT SCREAM -- IT'S SILVERCLAW!
LUPE -- WHAT IS IT? WHAT'S WRONG?
A NIGHTMARE -- BUT IT WAS MORE THAN THAT! I WAS... CONTACTED!
AND I KNOW WHAT KULAN GATH IS AFTER -- THE POWER OF THE EARTH HE SAID HE'D CONTROL! IT'S PELIALI --
-- HE'S AFTER MY MOTHER!
CONTINUED...

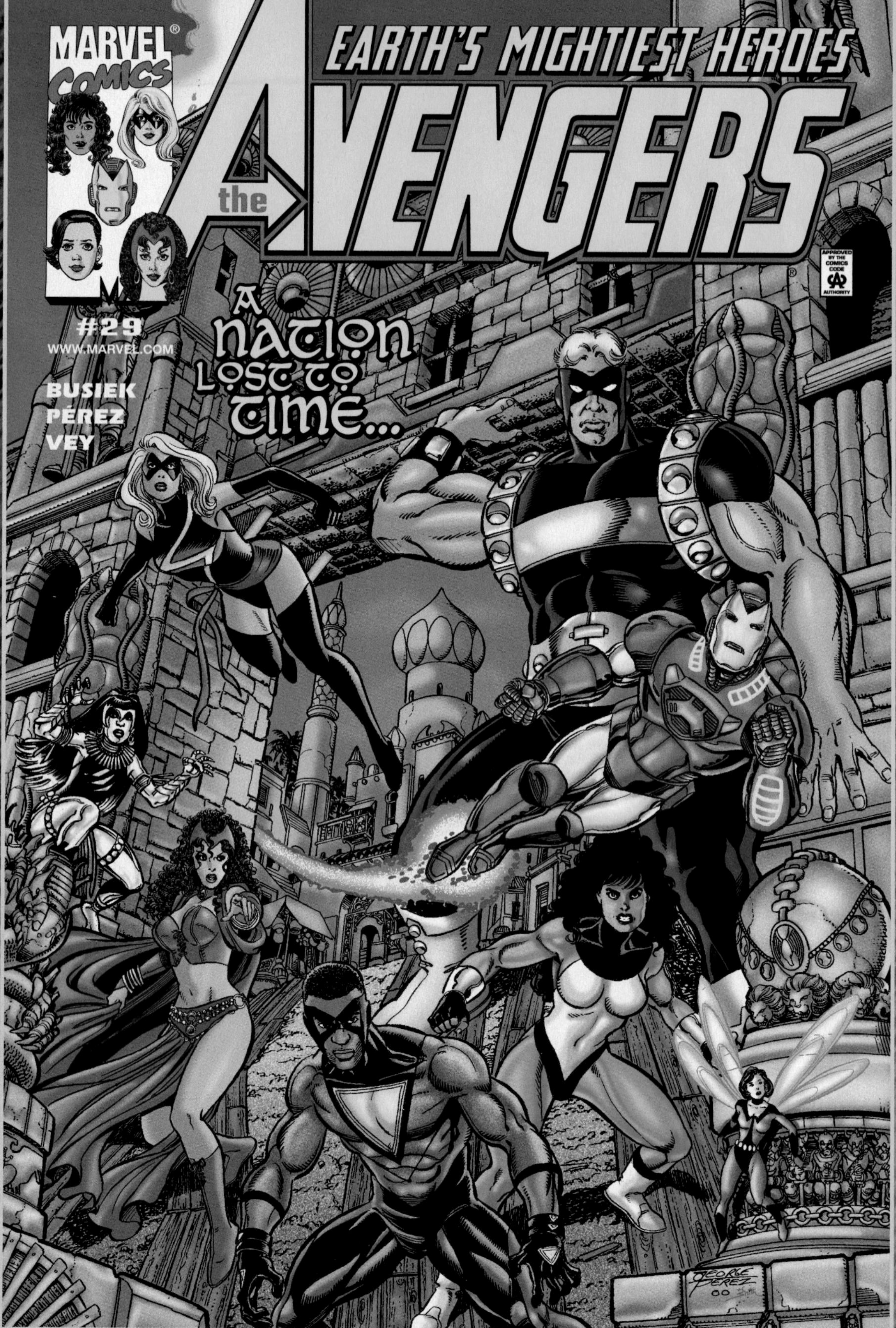
MARVEL COMICS
EARTH'S MIGHTIEST HEROES
the AVENGERS
APPROVED BY THE COMICS CODE AUTHORITY
#29
WWW.MARVEL.COM
A NATION LOST TO TIME...
BUSIEK
PÉREZ
VEY
GEORGE PEREZ

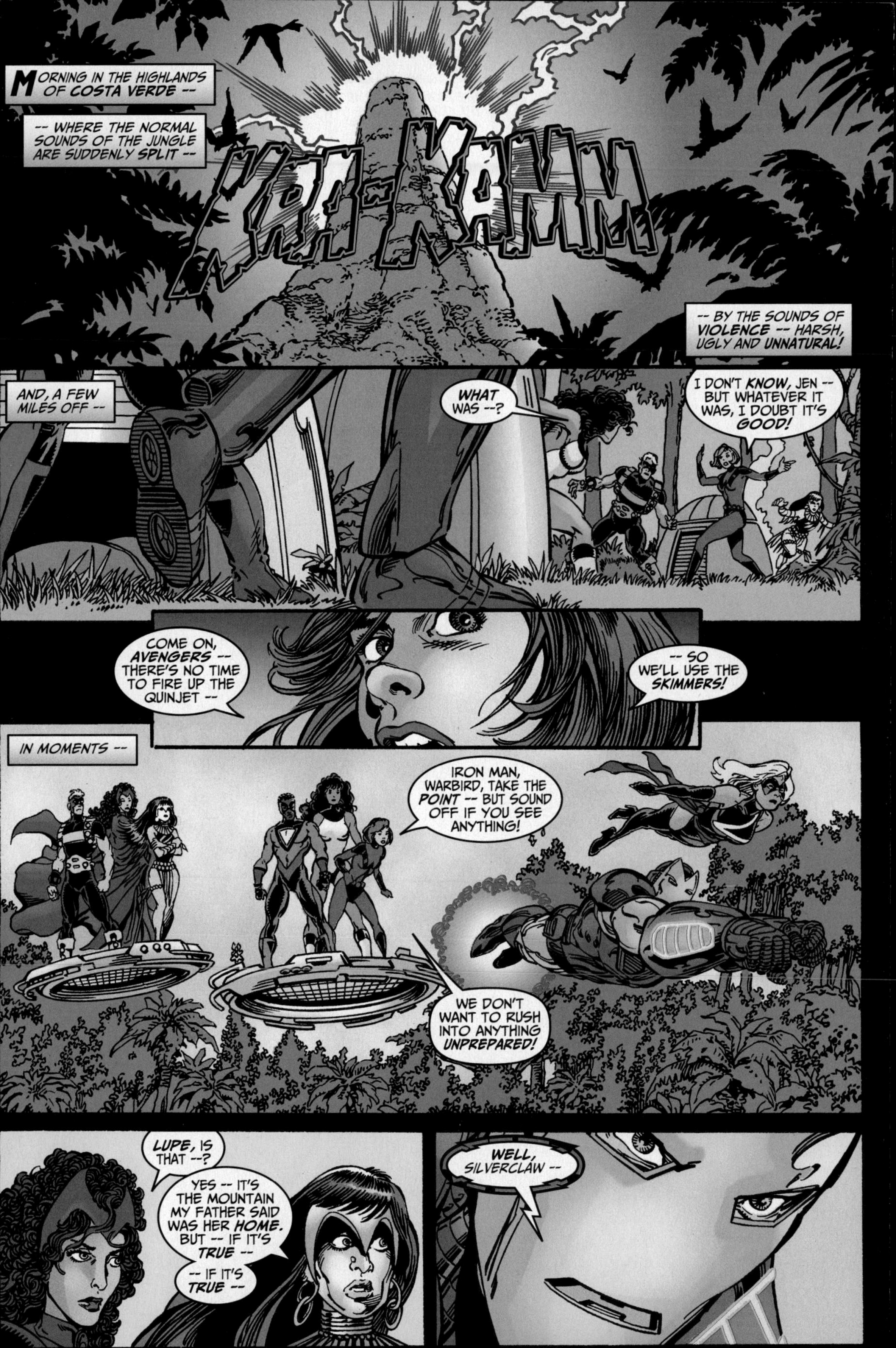
MORNING IN THE HIGHLANDS OF COSTA VERDE --
-- WHERE THE NORMAL SOUNDS OF THE JUNGLE ARE SUDDENLY SPLIT --
KA-KAMM
-- BY THE SOUNDS OF VIOLENCE -- HARSH, UGLY AND UNNATURAL!
AND, A FEW MILES OFF --
WHAT WAS --?
I DON'T KNOW, JEN -- BUT WHATEVER IT WAS, I DOUBT IT'S GOOD!
COME ON, AVENGERS -- THERE'S NO TIME TO FIRE UP THE QUINJET --
-- SO WE'LL USE THE SKIMMERS!
IN MOMENTS --
IRON MAN, WARBIRD, TAKE THE POINT -- BUT SOUND OFF IF YOU SEE ANYTHING!
WE DON'T WANT TO RUSH INTO ANYTHING UNPREPARED!
LUPE, IS THAT --?
YES -- IT'S THE MOUNTAIN MY FATHER SAID WAS HER HOME. BUT -- IF IT'S TRUE --
-- IF IT'S TRUE --
WELL, SILVERCLAW --

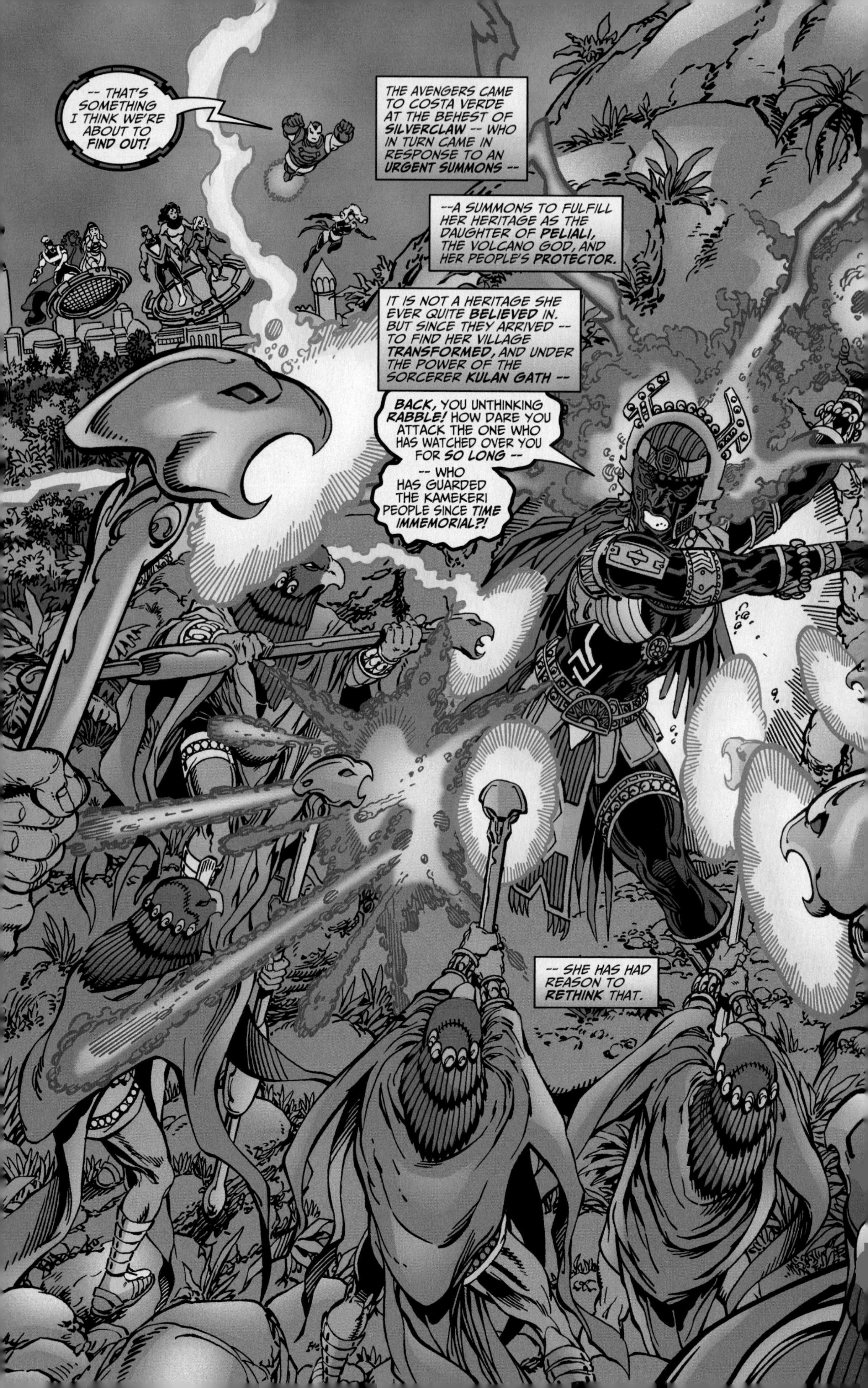
-- THAT'S SOMETHING I THINK WE'RE ABOUT TO FIND OUT!
THE AVENGERS CAME TO COSTA VERDE AT THE BEHEST OF SILVERCLAW -- WHO IN TURN CAME IN RESPONSE TO AN URGENT SUMMONS --
--A SUMMONS TO FULFILL HER HERITAGE AS THE DAUGHTER OF PELIALI, THE VOLCANO GOD, AND HER PEOPLE'S PROTECTOR.
IT IS NOT A HERITAGE SHE EVER QUITE BELIEVED IN. BUT SINCE THEY ARRIVED -- TO FIND HER VILLAGE TRANSFORMED, AND UNDER THE POWER OF THE SORCERER KULAN GATH --
BACK, YOU UNTHINKING RABBLE! HOW DARE YOU ATTACK THE ONE WHO HAS WATCHED OVER YOU FOR SO LONG --
-- WHO HAS GUARDED THE KAMEKERI PEOPLE SINCE TIME IMMEMORIAL?!
-- SHE HAS HAD REASON TO RETHINK THAT.

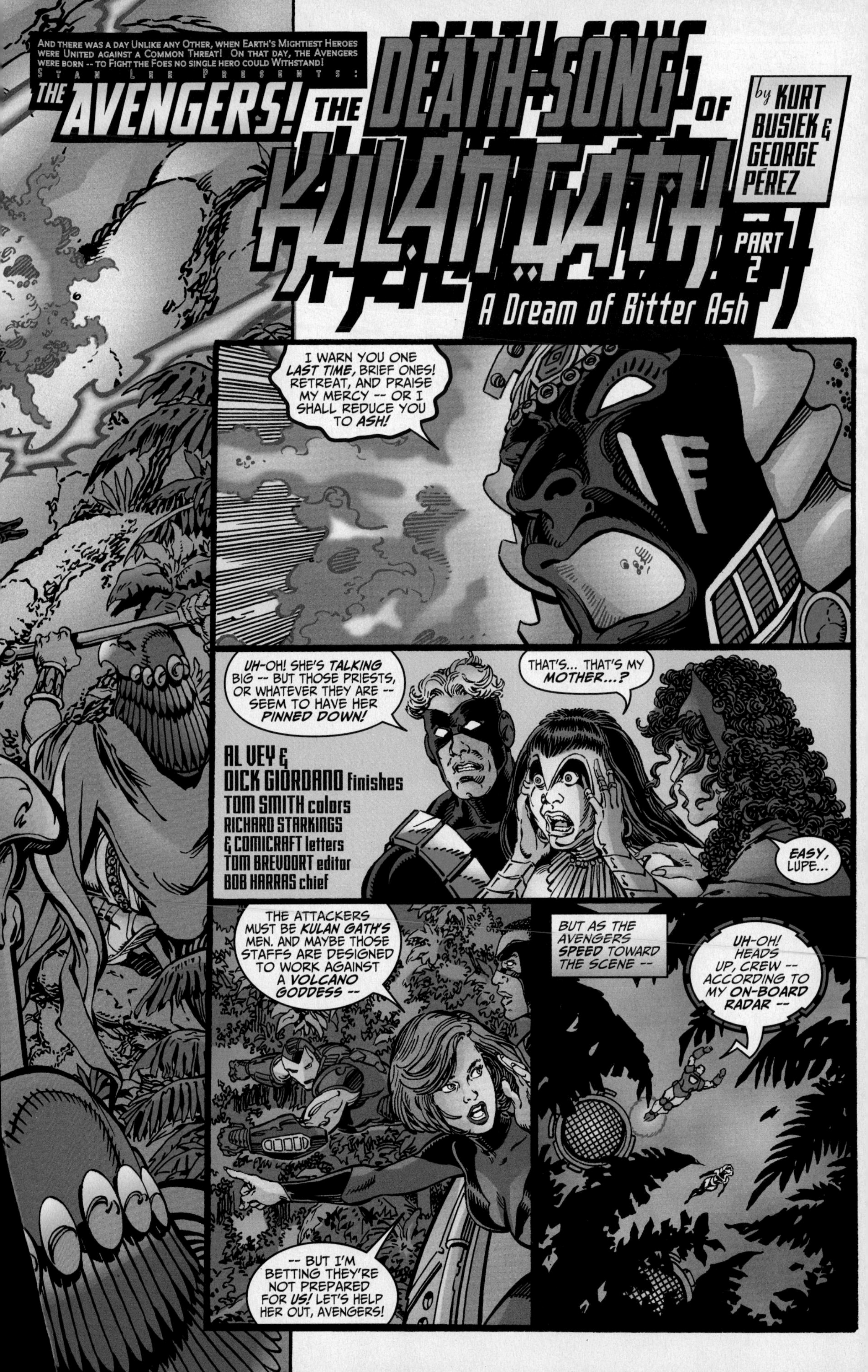

And there was a day Unlike any Other, when Earth's Mightiest Heroes were United against a Common Threat! On that day, the Avengers were born -- to Fight the Foes no single hero could Withstand!
Stan Lee Presents:
THE AVENGERS!
THE DEATH-SONG OF KULAN GATH! PART 2
A Dream of Bitter Ash
by KURT BUSIEK & GEORGE PÉREZ
I WARN YOU ONE LAST TIME, BRIEF ONES! RETREAT, AND PRAISE MY MERCY -- OR I SHALL REDUCE YOU TO ASH!
UH-OH! SHE'S TALKING BIG -- BUT THOSE PRIESTS, OR WHATEVER THEY ARE -- SEEM TO HAVE HER PINNED DOWN!
THAT'S... THAT'S MY MOTHER...?
AL VEY & DICK GIORDANO finishes
TOM SMITH colors
RICHARD STARKINGS & COMICRAFT letters
TOM BREVOORT editor
BOB HARRAS chief
EASY, LUPE...
THE ATTACKERS MUST BE KULAN GATH'S MEN. AND MAYBE THOSE STAFFS ARE DESIGNED TO WORK AGAINST A VOLCANO GODDESS --
-- BUT I'M BETTING THEY'RE NOT PREPARED FOR US! LET'S HELP HER OUT, AVENGERS!
BUT AS THE AVENGERS SPEED TOWARD THE SCENE --
UH-OH! HEADS UP, CREW -- ACCORDING TO MY ON-BOARD RADAR --

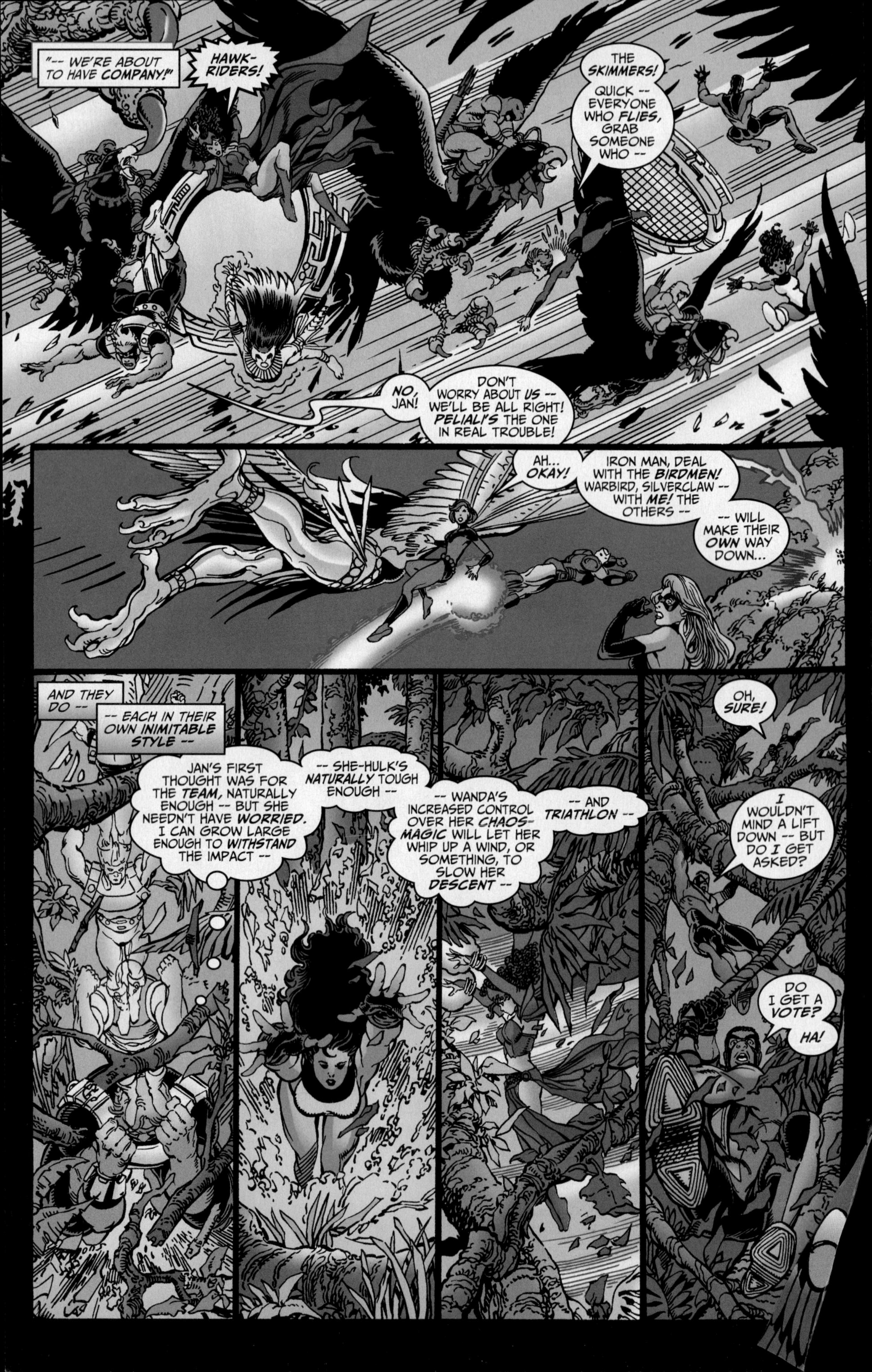
"-- WE'RE ABOUT TO HAVE COMPANY!"
HAWK-RIDERS!
THE SKIMMERS! QUICK -- EVERYONE WHO FLIES, GRAB SOMEONE WHO --
NO, JAN!
DON'T WORRY ABOUT US -- WE'LL BE ALL RIGHT! PELIALI'S THE ONE IN REAL TROUBLE!
AH... OKAY!
IRON MAN, DEAL WITH THE BIRDMEN! WARBIRD, SILVERCLAW -- WITH ME! THE OTHERS --
-- WILL MAKE THEIR OWN WAY DOWN...
AND THEY DO --
-- EACH IN THEIR OWN INIMITABLE STYLE --
JAN'S FIRST THOUGHT WAS FOR THE TEAM, NATURALLY ENOUGH -- BUT SHE NEEDN'T HAVE WORRIED. I CAN GROW LARGE ENOUGH TO WITHSTAND THE IMPACT --
-- SHE-HULK'S NATURALLY TOUGH ENOUGH --
-- WANDA'S INCREASED CONTROL OVER HER CHAOS-MAGIC WILL LET HER WHIP UP A WIND, OR SOMETHING, TO SLOW HER DESCENT --
-- AND TRIATHLON --
OH, SURE!
I WOULDN'T MIND A LIFT DOWN -- BUT DO I GET ASKED?
DO I GET A VOTE?
HA!

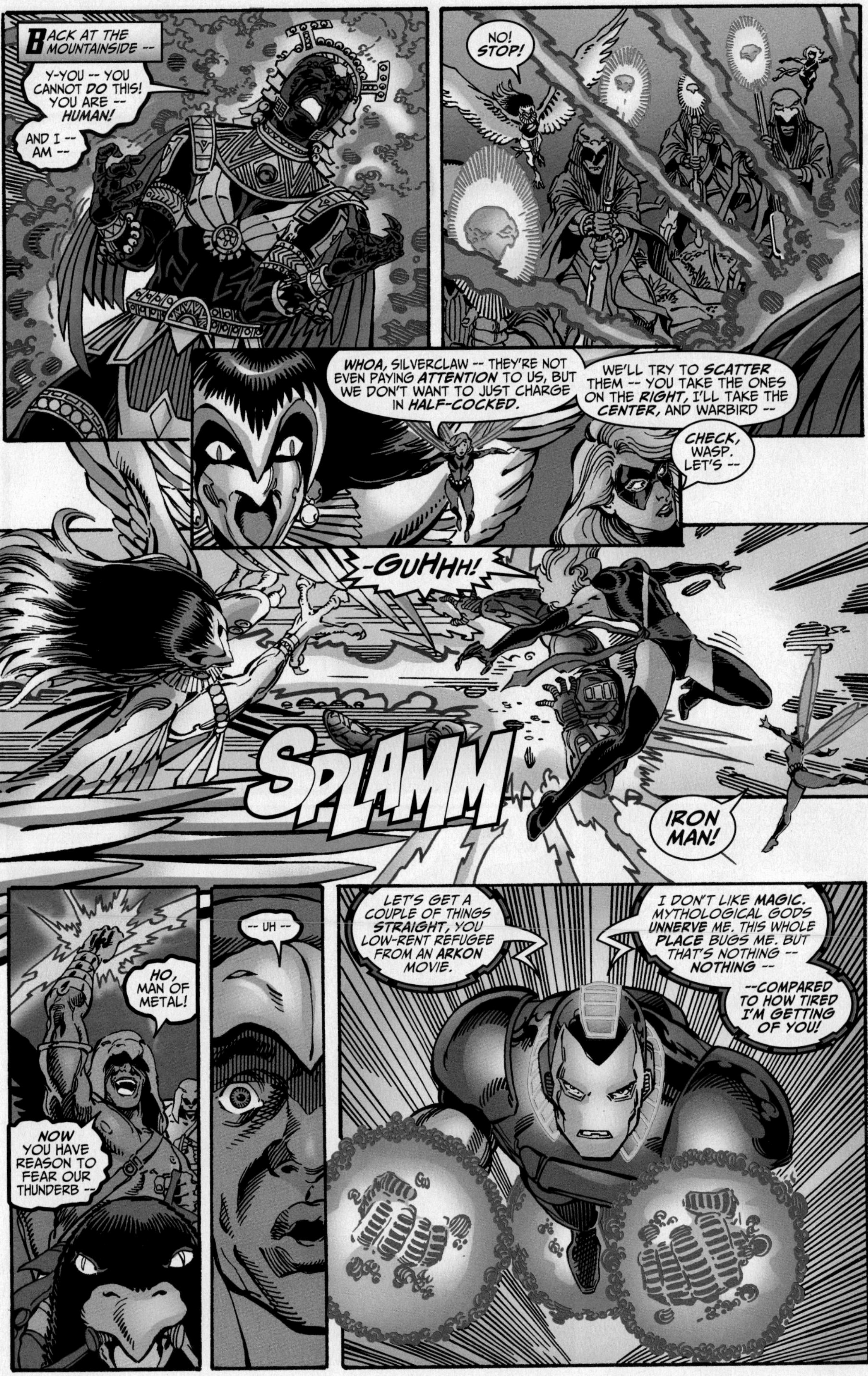
BACK AT THE MOUNTAINSIDE --
Y-YOU -- YOU CANNOT DO THIS! YOU ARE -- HUMAN!
AND I -- AM --
NO! STOP!
WHOA, SILVERCLAW -- THEY'RE NOT EVEN PAYING ATTENTION TO US, BUT WE DON'T WANT TO JUST CHARGE IN HALF-COCKED.
WE'LL TRY TO SCATTER THEM -- YOU TAKE THE ONES ON THE RIGHT, I'LL TAKE THE CENTER, AND WARBIRD --
CHECK, WASP. LET'S --
-GUHHH!
SPLAMM
IRON MAN!
HO, MAN OF METAL!
NOW YOU HAVE REASON TO FEAR OUR THUNDERB --
-- UH --
LET'S GET A COUPLE OF THINGS STRAIGHT, YOU LOW-RENT REFUGEE FROM AN ARKON MOVIE.
I DON'T LIKE MAGIC. MYTHOLOGICAL GODS UNNERVE ME. THIS WHOLE PLACE BUGS ME. BUT THAT'S NOTHING -- NOTHING --
--COMPARED TO HOW TIRED I'M GETTING OF YOU!

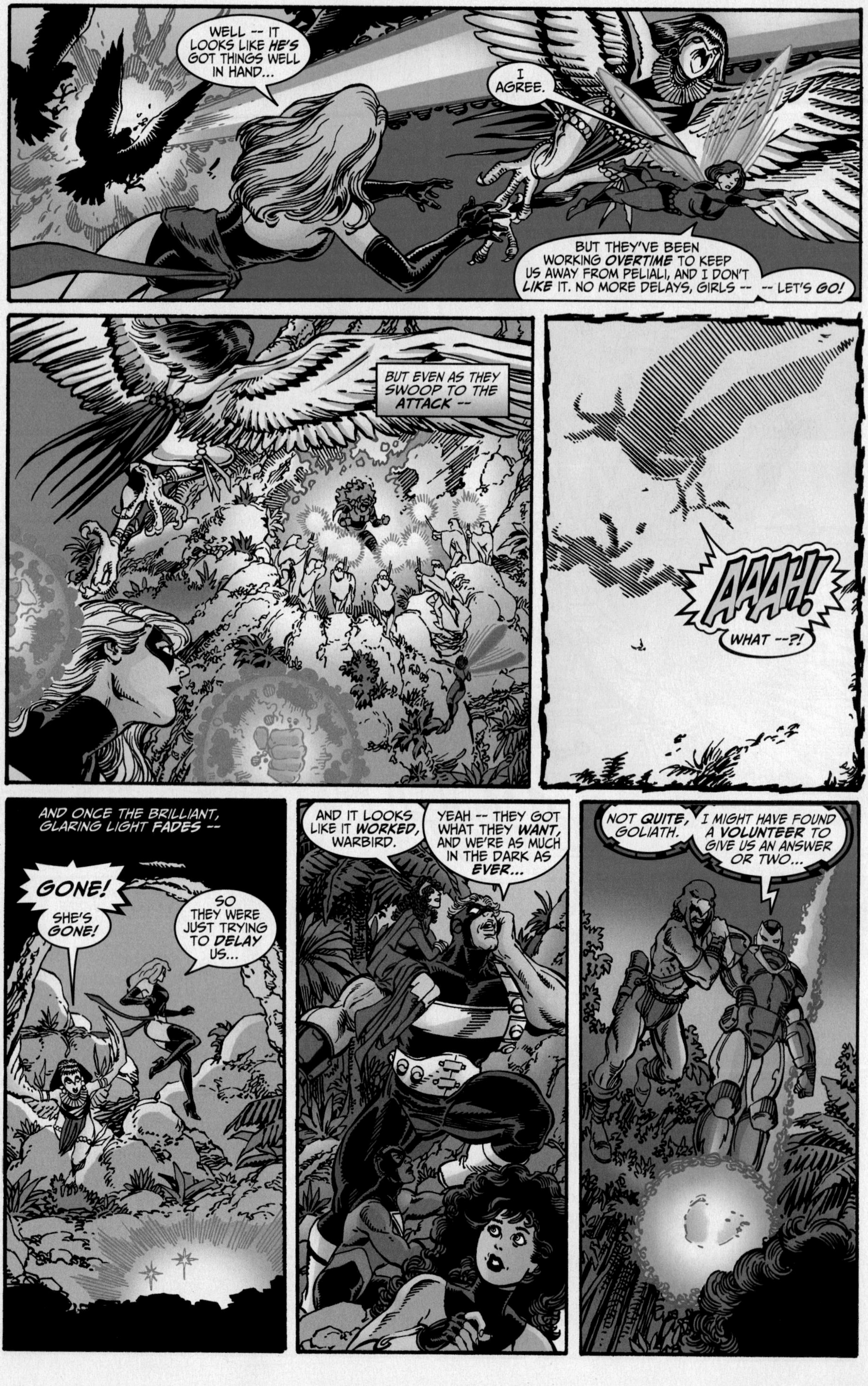
WELL -- IT LOOKS LIKE HE'S GOT THINGS WELL IN HAND...
I AGREE.
BUT THEY'VE BEEN WORKING OVERTIME TO KEEP US AWAY FROM PELIALI, AND I DON'T LIKE IT. NO MORE DELAYS, GIRLS --
-- LET'S GO!
BUT EVEN AS THEY SWOOP TO THE ATTACK --
AAAH!
WHAT --?!
AND ONCE THE BRILLIANT, GLARING LIGHT FADES --
GONE!
SHE'S GONE!
SO THEY WERE JUST TRYING TO DELAY US...
AND IT LOOKS LIKE IT WORKED, WARBIRD.
YEAH -- THEY GOT WHAT THEY WANT, AND WE'RE AS MUCH IN THE DARK AS EVER...
NOT QUITE, GOLIATH.
I MIGHT HAVE FOUND A VOLUNTEER TO GIVE US AN ANSWER OR TWO...

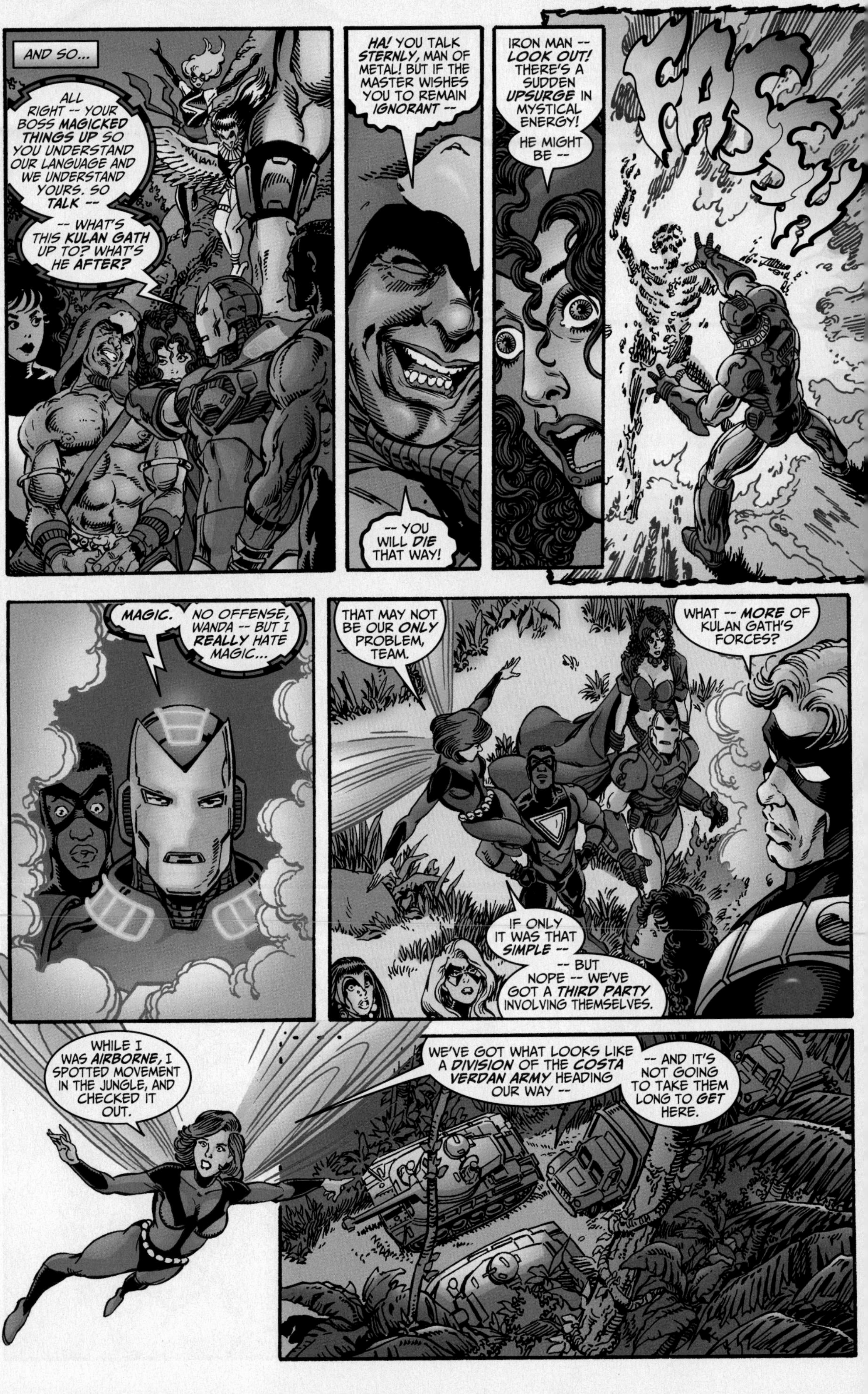
AND SO...
ALL RIGHT -- YOUR BOSS MAGICKED THINGS UP SO YOU UNDERSTAND OUR LANGUAGE AND WE UNDERSTAND YOURS. SO TALK --
-- WHAT'S THIS KULAN GATH UP TO? WHAT'S HE AFTER?
HA! YOU TALK STERNLY, MAN OF METAL! BUT IF THE MASTER WISHES YOU TO REMAIN IGNORANT --
-- YOU WILL DIE THAT WAY!
IRON MAN -- LOOK OUT! THERE'S A SUDDEN UPSURGE IN MYSTICAL ENERGY!
HE MIGHT BE --
FAS
MAGIC.
NO OFFENSE, WANDA -- BUT I REALLY HATE MAGIC...
THAT MAY NOT BE OUR ONLY PROBLEM, TEAM.
WHAT -- MORE OF KULAN GATH'S FORCES?
IF ONLY IT WAS THAT SIMPLE --
-- BUT NOPE -- WE'VE GOT A THIRD PARTY INVOLVING THEMSELVES.
WHILE I WAS AIRBORNE, I SPOTTED MOVEMENT IN THE JUNGLE, AND CHECKED IT OUT.
WE'VE GOT WHAT LOOKS LIKE A DIVISION OF THE COSTA VERDAN ARMY HEADING OUR WAY --
-- AND IT'S NOT GOING TO TAKE THEM LONG TO GET HERE.

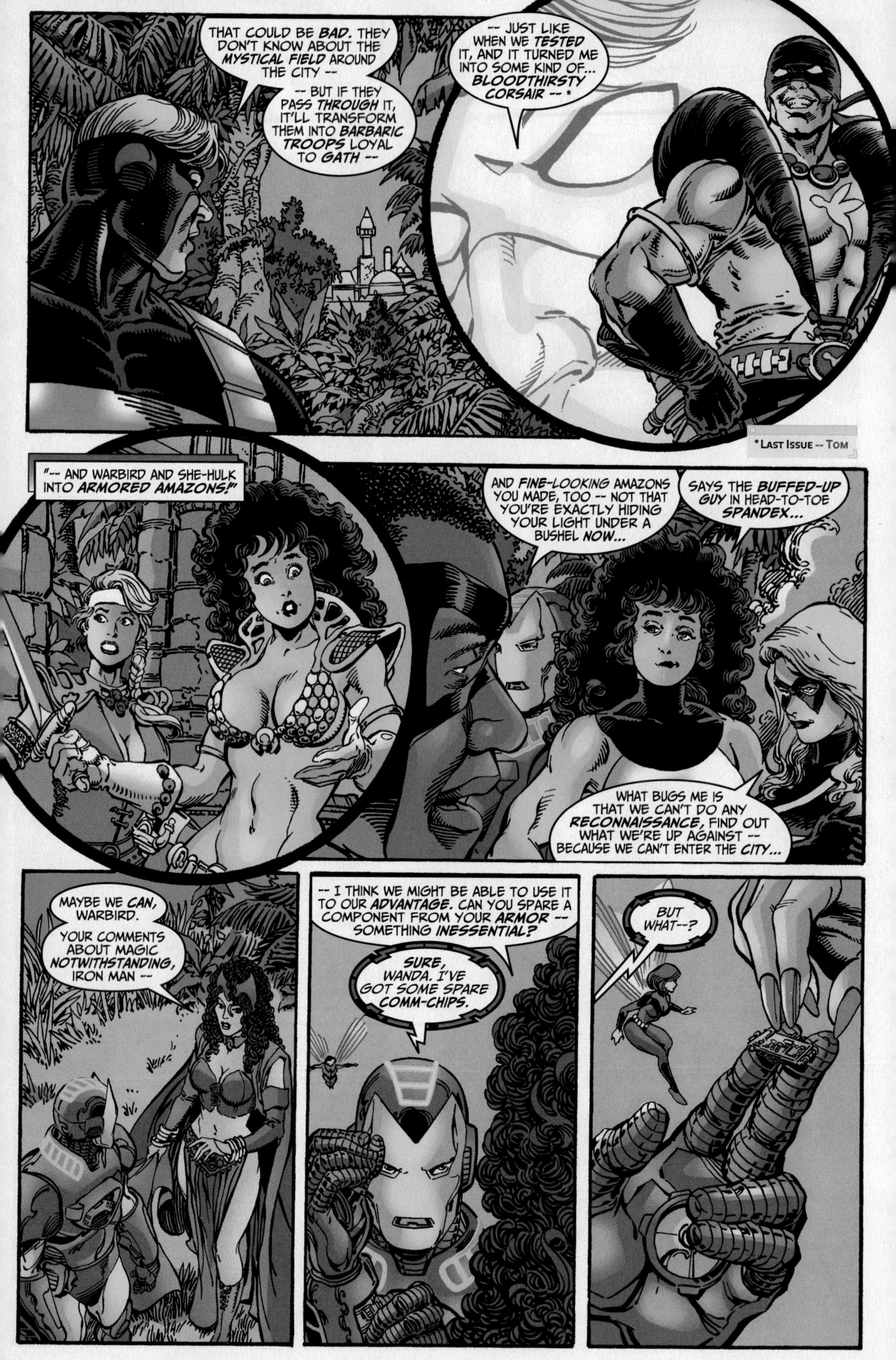
THAT COULD BE BAD. THEY DON'T KNOW ABOUT THE MYSTICAL FIELD AROUND THE CITY --
-- BUT IF THEY PASS THROUGH IT, IT'LL TRANSFORM THEM INTO BARBARIC TROOPS LOYAL TO GATH --
-- JUST LIKE WHEN WE TESTED IT, AND IT TURNED ME INTO SOME KIND OF... BLOODTHIRSTY CORSAIR -- *
*LAST ISSUE -- TOM
"-- AND WARBIRD AND SHE-HULK INTO ARMORED AMAZONS!"
AND FINE-LOOKING AMAZONS YOU MADE, TOO -- NOT THAT YOU'RE EXACTLY HIDING YOUR LIGHT UNDER A BUSHEL NOW...
SAYS THE BUFFED-UP GUY IN HEAD-TO-TOE SPANDEX...
WHAT BUGS ME IS THAT WE CAN'T DO ANY RECONNAISSANCE, FIND OUT WHAT WE'RE UP AGAINST -- BECAUSE WE CAN'T ENTER THE CITY...
MAYBE WE CAN, WARBIRD.
YOUR COMMENTS ABOUT MAGIC NOTWITHSTANDING, IRON MAN --
-- I THINK WE MIGHT BE ABLE TO USE IT TO OUR ADVANTAGE. CAN YOU SPARE A COMPONENT FROM YOUR ARMOR -- SOMETHING INESSENTIAL?
SURE, WANDA. I'VE GOT SOME SPARE COMM-CHIPS.
BUT WHAT--?

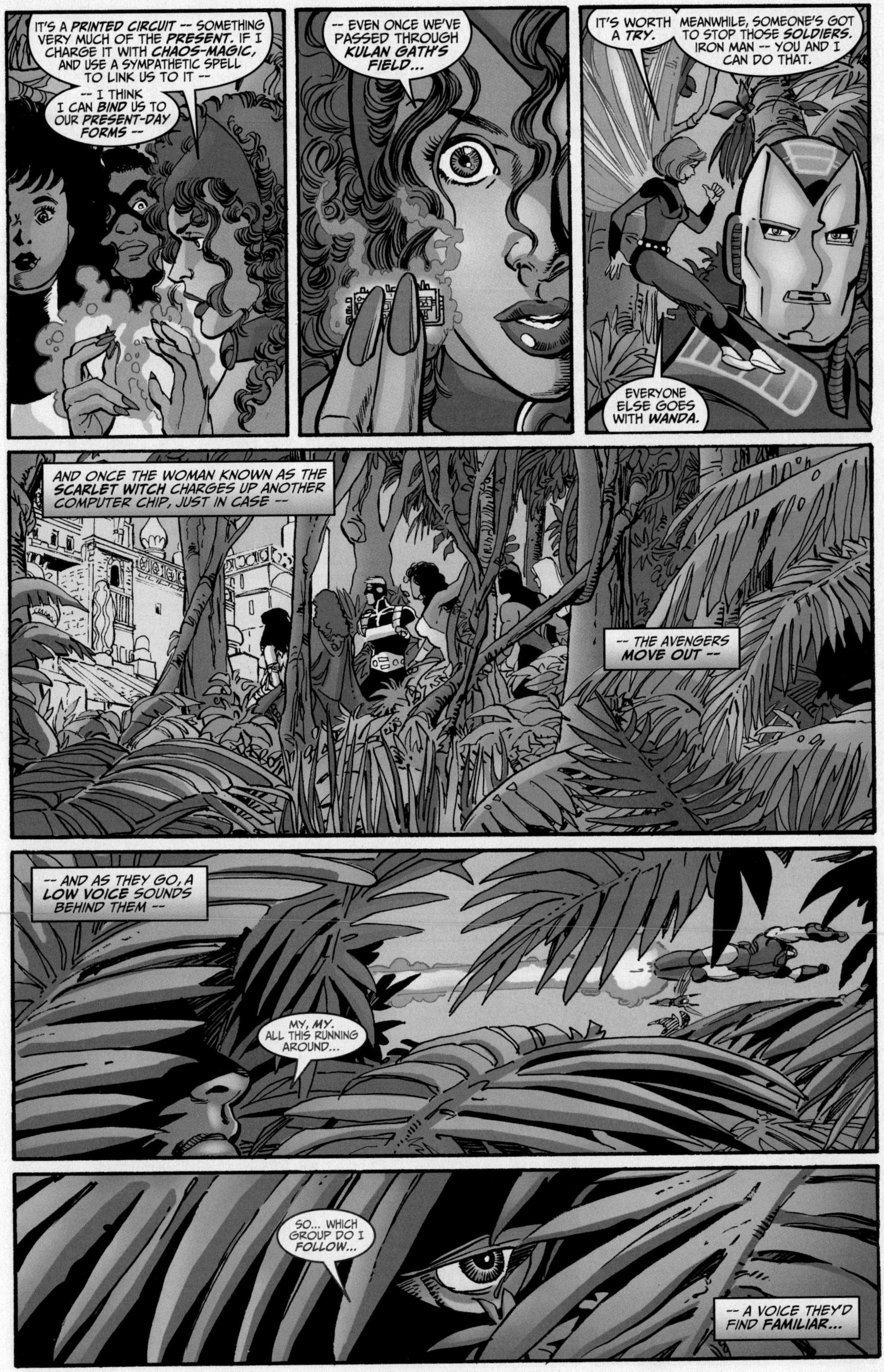
IT'S A PRINTED CIRCUIT -- SOMETHING VERY MUCH OF THE PRESENT. IF I CHARGE IT WITH CHAOS-MAGIC, AND USE A SYMPATHETIC SPELL TO LINK US TO IT --
-- I THINK I CAN BIND US TO OUR PRESENT-DAY FORMS --
-- EVEN ONCE WE'VE PASSED THROUGH KULAN GATH'S FIELD...
IT'S WORTH A TRY.
MEANWHILE, SOMEONE'S GOT TO STOP THOSE SOLDIERS. IRON MAN -- YOU AND I CAN DO THAT.
EVERYONE ELSE GOES WITH WANDA.
AND ONCE THE WOMAN KNOWN AS THE SCARLET WITCH CHARGES UP ANOTHER COMPUTER CHIP, JUST IN CASE --
-- THE AVENGERS MOVE OUT --
-- AND AS THEY GO, A LOW VOICE SOUNDS BEHIND THEM --
MY, MY. ALL THIS RUNNING AROUND...
SO... WHICH GROUP DO I FOLLOW...
-- A VOICE THEY'D FIND FAMILIAR...

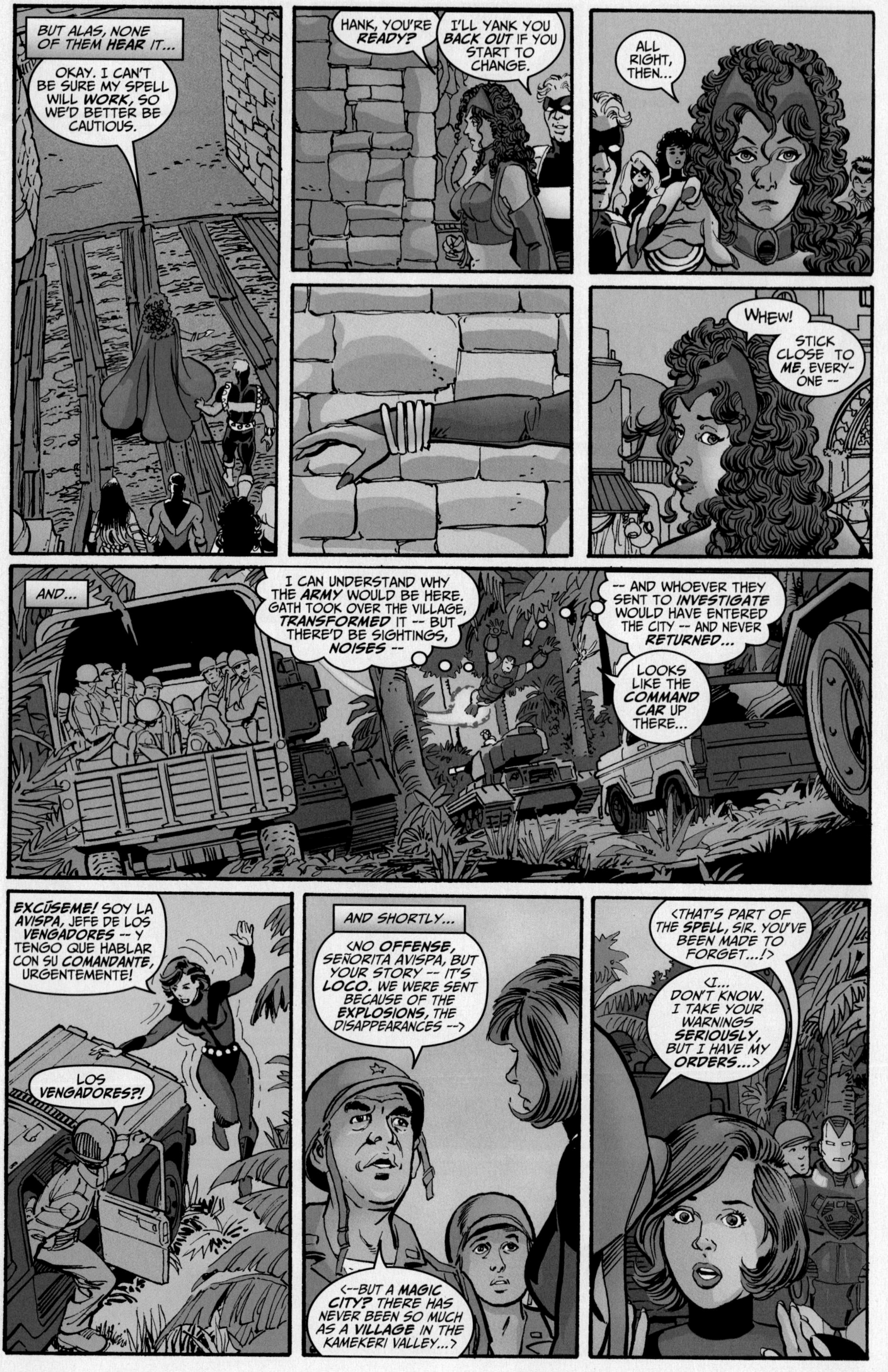
BUT ALAS, NONE OF THEM HEAR IT...
OKAY. I CAN'T BE SURE MY SPELL WILL WORK, SO WE'D BETTER BE CAUTIOUS.
HANK, YOU'RE READY?
I'LL YANK YOU BACK OUT IF YOU START TO CHANGE.
ALL RIGHT, THEN...
WHEW!
STICK CLOSE TO ME, EVERY-ONE --
AND...
I CAN UNDERSTAND WHY THE ARMY WOULD BE HERE. GATH TOOK OVER THE VILLAGE, TRANSFORMED IT -- BUT THERE'D BE SIGHTINGS, NOISES --
-- AND WHOEVER THEY SENT TO INVESTIGATE WOULD HAVE ENTERED THE CITY -- AND NEVER RETURNED...
LOOKS LIKE THE COMMAND CAR UP THERE...
EXCÚSEME! SOY LA AVISPA, JEFE DE LOS VENGADORES -- Y TENGO QUE HABLAR CON SU COMANDANTE, URGENTEMENTE!
LOS VENGADORES?!
AND SHORTLY...
<NO OFFENSE, SEÑORITA AVISPA, BUT YOUR STORY -- IT'S LOCO. WE WERE SENT BECAUSE OF THE EXPLOSIONS, THE DISAPPEARANCES -->
<--BUT A MAGIC CITY? THERE HAS NEVER BEEN SO MUCH AS A VILLAGE IN THE KAMEKERI VALLEY...>
<THAT'S PART OF THE SPELL, SIR. YOU'VE BEEN MADE TO FORGET...!>
<I... DON'T KNOW. I TAKE YOUR WARNINGS SERIOUSLY, BUT I HAVE MY ORDERS...>

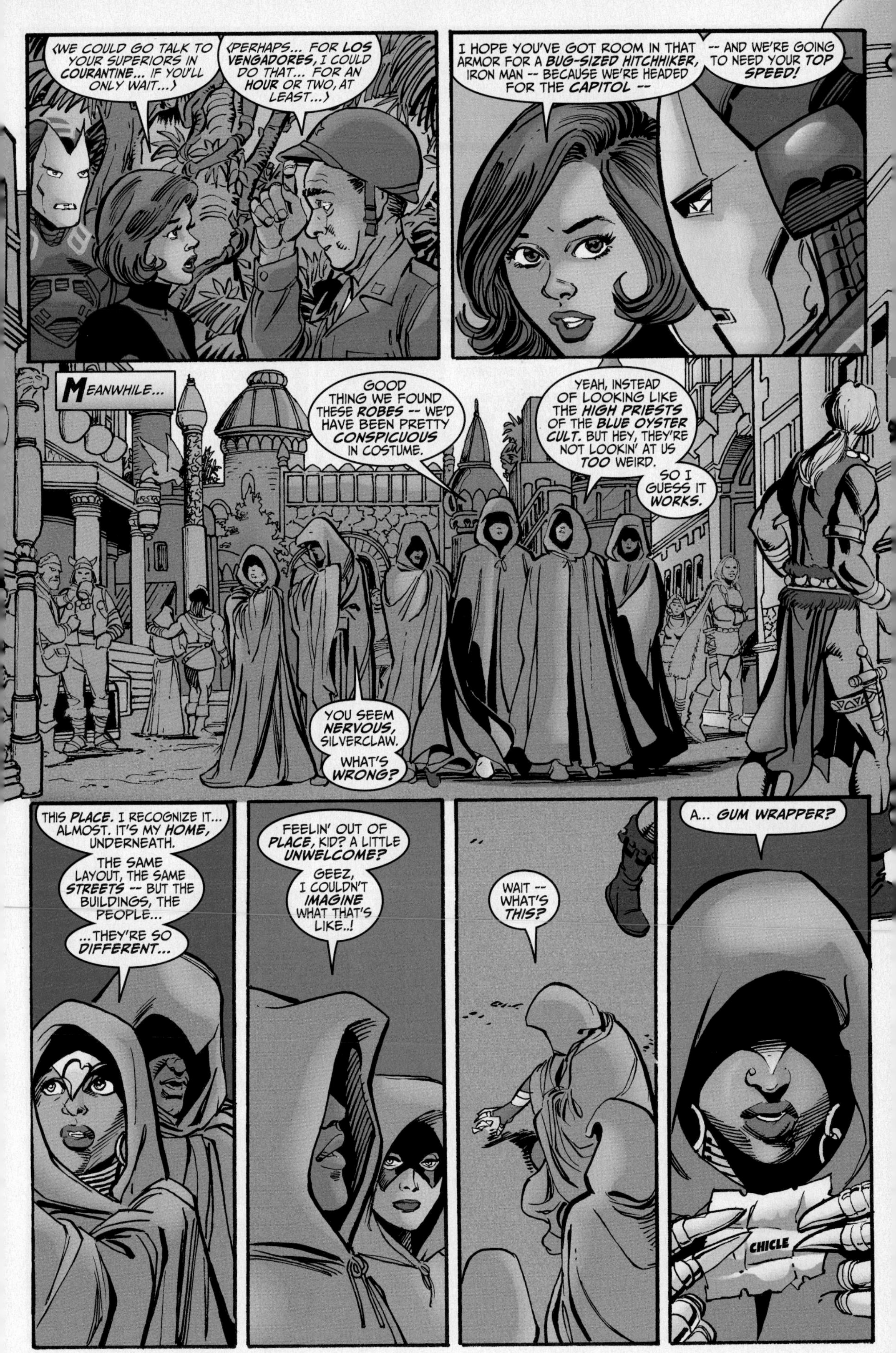

⟨WE COULD GO TALK TO YOUR SUPERIORS IN COURANTINE... IF YOU'LL ONLY WAIT...⟩
⟨PERHAPS... FOR LOS VENGADORES, I COULD DO THAT... FOR AN HOUR OR TWO, AT LEAST...⟩
I HOPE YOU'VE GOT ROOM IN THAT ARMOR FOR A BUG-SIZED HITCHHIKER, IRON MAN -- BECAUSE WE'RE HEADED FOR THE CAPITOL --
-- AND WE'RE GOING TO NEED YOUR TOP SPEED!
MEANWHILE...
GOOD THING WE FOUND THESE ROBES -- WE'D HAVE BEEN PRETTY CONSPICUOUS IN COSTUME.
YEAH, INSTEAD OF LOOKING LIKE THE HIGH PRIESTS OF THE BLUE OYSTER CULT. BUT HEY, THEY'RE NOT LOOKIN' AT US TOO WEIRD.
SO I GUESS IT WORKS.
YOU SEEM NERVOUS, SILVERCLAW.
WHAT'S WRONG?
THIS PLACE. I RECOGNIZE IT... ALMOST. IT'S MY HOME, UNDERNEATH.
THE SAME LAYOUT, THE SAME STREETS -- BUT THE BUILDINGS, THE PEOPLE...
...THEY'RE SO DIFFERENT...
FEELIN' OUT OF PLACE, KID? A LITTLE UNWELCOME?
GEEZ, I COULDN'T IMAGINE WHAT THAT'S LIKE..!
WAIT -- WHAT'S THIS?
A... GUM WRAPPER?
CHICLE

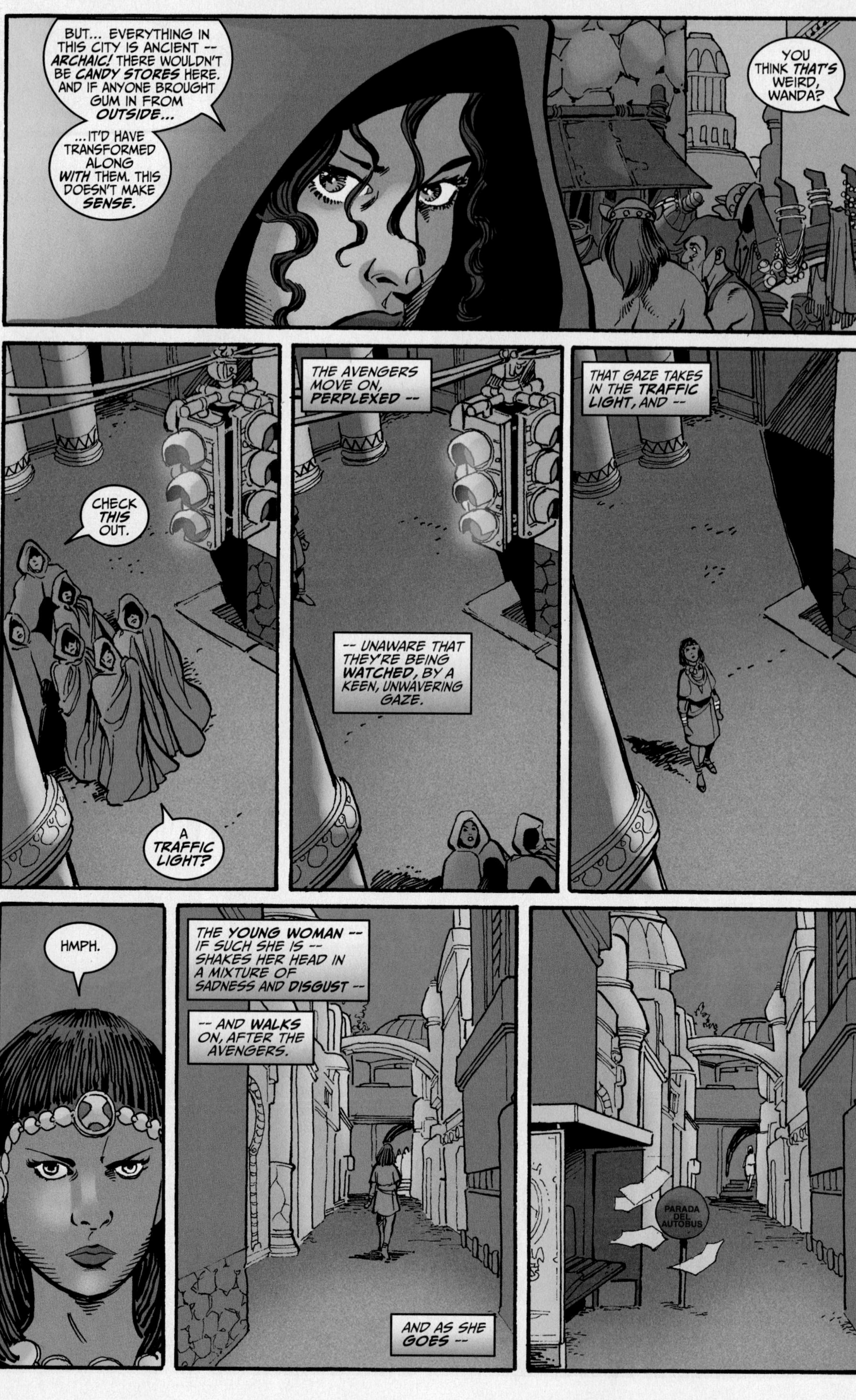
BUT... EVERYTHING IN THIS CITY IS ANCIENT -- ARCHAIC! THERE WOULDN'T BE CANDY STORES HERE. AND IF ANYONE BROUGHT GUM IN FROM OUTSIDE...
...IT'D HAVE TRANSFORMED ALONG WITH THEM. THIS DOESN'T MAKE SENSE.
YOU THINK THAT'S WEIRD, WANDA?
CHECK THIS OUT.
A TRAFFIC LIGHT?
THE AVENGERS MOVE ON, PERPLEXED --
-- UNAWARE THAT THEY'RE BEING WATCHED, BY A KEEN, UNWAVERING GAZE.
THAT GAZE TAKES IN THE TRAFFIC LIGHT, AND --
HMPH.
THE YOUNG WOMAN -- IF SUCH SHE IS -- SHAKES HER HEAD IN A MIXTURE OF SADNESS AND DISGUST --
-- AND WALKS ON, AFTER THE AVENGERS.
AND AS SHE GOES --
PARADA DEL AUTOBUS

AND IN THE SQUARE AHEAD --
NNNH!
GOLIATH!
HANK, ARE YOU ALL RIGHT?!
JUST A... STOMACH THING, I EXPECT. I'LL BE FINE.
HANK, IF YOU'RE HAVING HEALTH PROBLEMS...
I'LL... RUN A WHOLE BATTERY OF TESTS ONCE WE'RE HOME. BUT IT'S NOTHING, I'M SURE OF IT. IT'S ALREADY PASSING.
RIGHT NOW, WHAT WE NEED IS INFORMATION...
...AND WHAT BETTER PLACE TO FIND IT THAN THE NEIGHBORHOOD TAVERN?
I... ALL RIGHT, HANK. BUT ONCE WE'RE HOME...
THEY FILE IN, BUT ONCE AGAIN --
-- THEY DON'T DO SO UNOBSERVED.
SHE WATCHES SILENTLY FOR SOME MOMENTS. THEN SHE MAKES SEVERAL ABRUPT, COMPLEX GESTURES --
-- AND MOVES ON.
AHHH -- SMELL THAT AROMA! SWEAT, UNDERCOOKED MEAT, AND STALE BEER! REMINDS ME OF MY UNDERGRADUATE DAYS!
FOR LAW SCHOOL, OF COURSE, YOU'D HAVE TO ADD AN UNDERTASTE OF PANIC...
IT'S A BAR.

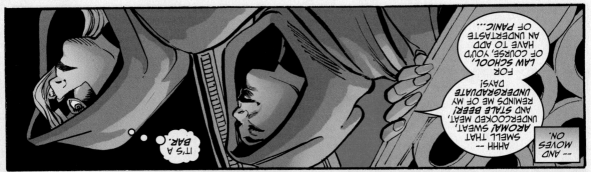

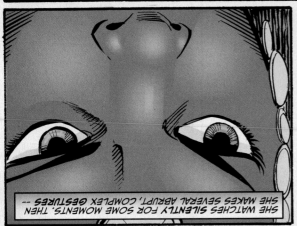

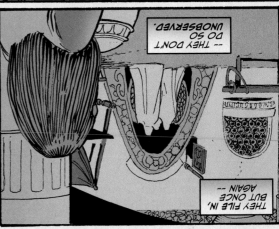

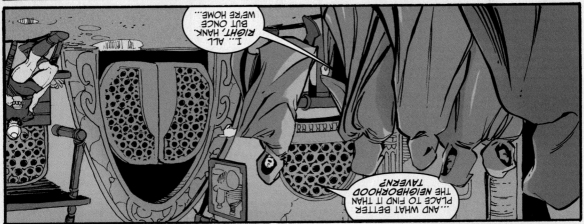

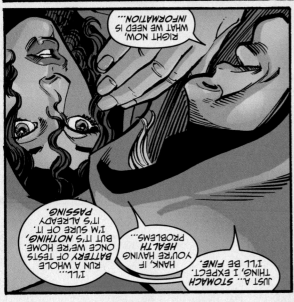

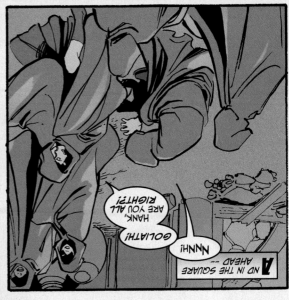

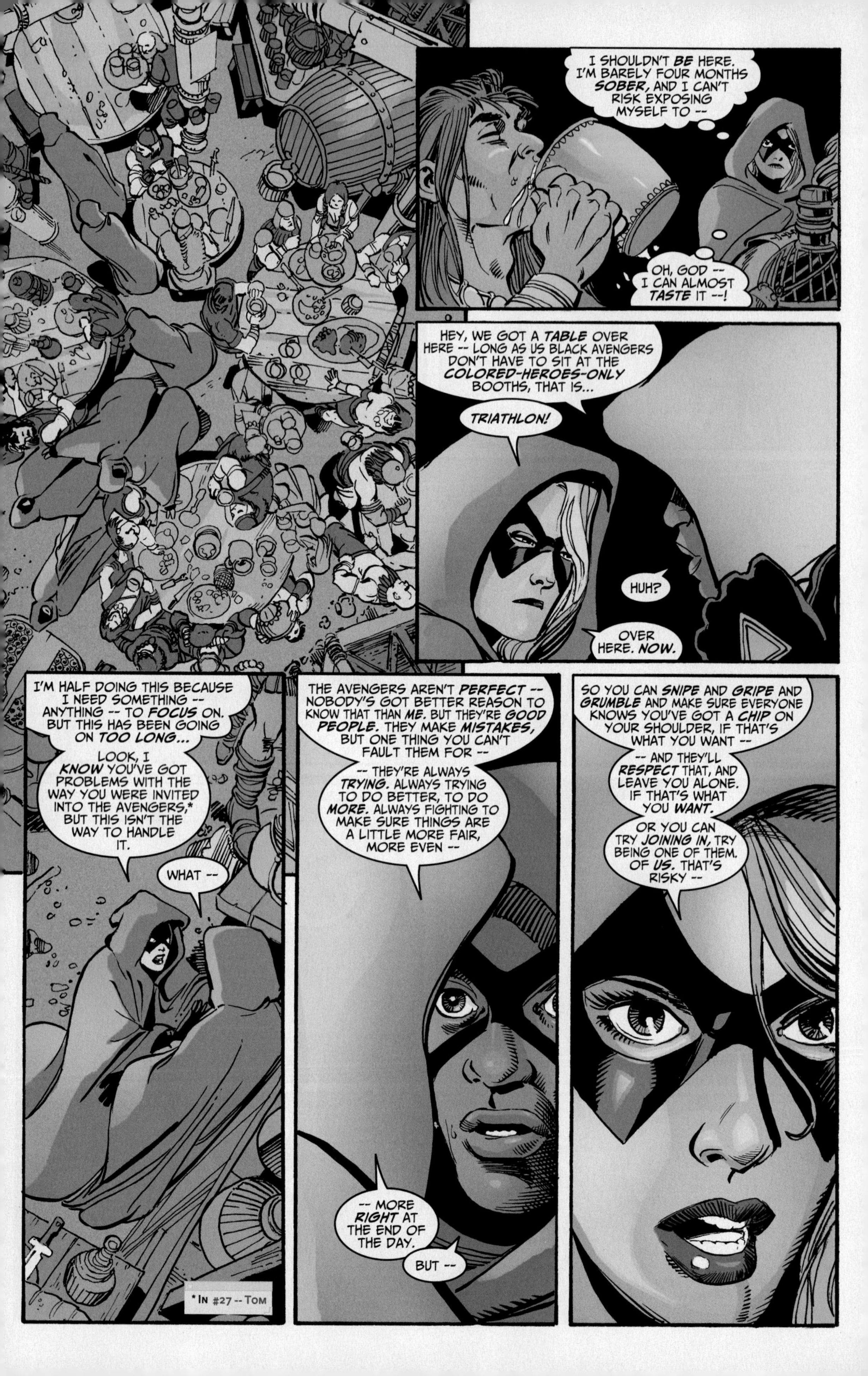
I SHOULDN'T BE HERE. I'M BARELY FOUR MONTHS SOBER, AND I CAN'T RISK EXPOSING MYSELF TO --
OH, GOD -- I CAN ALMOST TASTE IT --!
HEY, WE GOT A TABLE OVER HERE -- LONG AS US BLACK AVENGERS DON'T HAVE TO SIT AT THE COLORED-HEROES-ONLY BOOTHS, THAT IS...
TRIATHLON!
HUH?
OVER HERE. NOW.
I'M HALF DOING THIS BECAUSE I NEED SOMETHING -- ANYTHING -- TO FOCUS ON. BUT THIS HAS BEEN GOING ON TOO LONG...
LOOK, I KNOW YOU'VE GOT PROBLEMS WITH THE WAY YOU WERE INVITED INTO THE AVENGERS,* BUT THIS ISN'T THE WAY TO HANDLE IT.
WHAT --
*IN #27 -- TOM
THE AVENGERS AREN'T PERFECT -- NOBODY'S GOT BETTER REASON TO KNOW THAT THAN ME. BUT THEY'RE GOOD PEOPLE. THEY MAKE MISTAKES, BUT ONE THING YOU CAN'T FAULT THEM FOR --
-- THEY'RE ALWAYS TRYING. ALWAYS TRYING TO DO BETTER, TO DO MORE. ALWAYS FIGHTING TO MAKE SURE THINGS ARE A LITTLE MORE FAIR, MORE EVEN --
-- MORE RIGHT AT THE END OF THE DAY.
BUT --
SO YOU CAN SNIPE AND GRIPE AND GRUMBLE AND MAKE SURE EVERYONE KNOWS YOU'VE GOT A CHIP ON YOUR SHOULDER, IF THAT'S WHAT YOU WANT --
-- AND THEY'LL RESPECT THAT, AND LEAVE YOU ALONE. IF THAT'S WHAT YOU WANT.
OR YOU CAN TRY JOINING IN, TRY BEING ONE OF THEM. OF US. THAT'S RISKY --

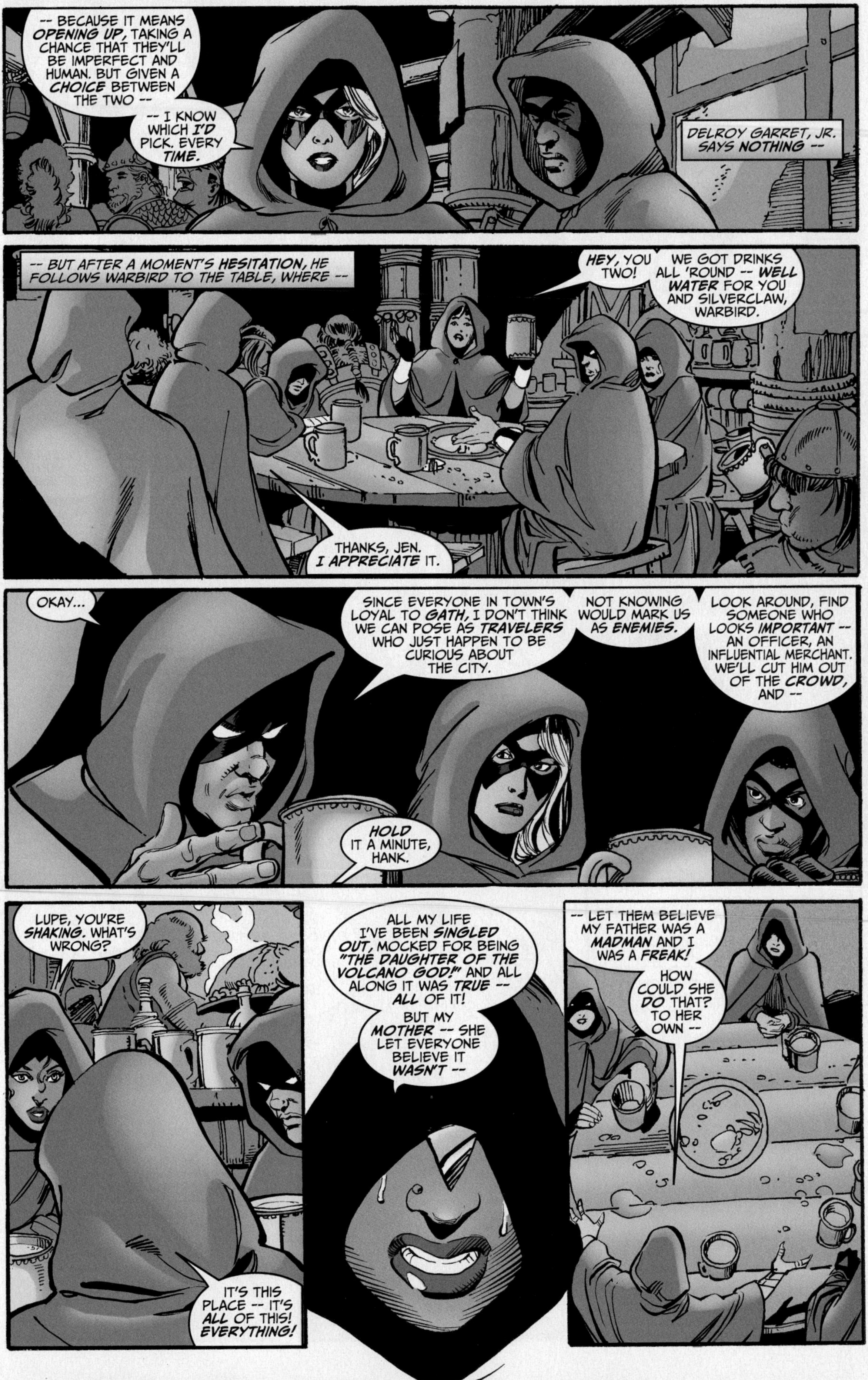
-- BECAUSE IT MEANS OPENING UP, TAKING A CHANCE THAT THEY'LL BE IMPERFECT AND HUMAN. BUT GIVEN A CHOICE BETWEEN THE TWO --
-- I KNOW WHICH I'D PICK. EVERY TIME.
DELROY GARRET, JR. SAYS NOTHING --
-- BUT AFTER A MOMENT'S HESITATION, HE FOLLOWS WARBIRD TO THE TABLE, WHERE --
HEY, YOU TWO!
WE GOT DRINKS ALL 'ROUND -- WELL WATER FOR YOU AND SILVERCLAW, WARBIRD.
THANKS, JEN. I APPRECIATE IT.
OKAY...
SINCE EVERYONE IN TOWN'S LOYAL TO GATH, I DON'T THINK WE CAN POSE AS TRAVELERS WHO JUST HAPPEN TO BE CURIOUS ABOUT THE CITY.
NOT KNOWING WOULD MARK US AS ENEMIES.
LOOK AROUND, FIND SOMEONE WHO LOOKS IMPORTANT -- AN OFFICER, AN INFLUENTIAL MERCHANT. WE'LL CUT HIM OUT OF THE CROWD, AND --
HOLD IT A MINUTE, HANK.
LUPE, YOU'RE SHAKING. WHAT'S WRONG?
IT'S THIS PLACE -- IT'S ALL OF THIS! EVERYTHING!
ALL MY LIFE I'VE BEEN SINGLED OUT, MOCKED FOR BEING "THE DAUGHTER OF THE VOLCANO GOD!" AND ALL ALONG IT WAS TRUE -- ALL OF IT!
BUT MY MOTHER -- SHE LET EVERYONE BELIEVE IT WASN'T --
-- LET THEM BELIEVE MY FATHER WAS A MADMAN AND I WAS A FREAK!
HOW COULD SHE DO THAT? TO HER OWN --

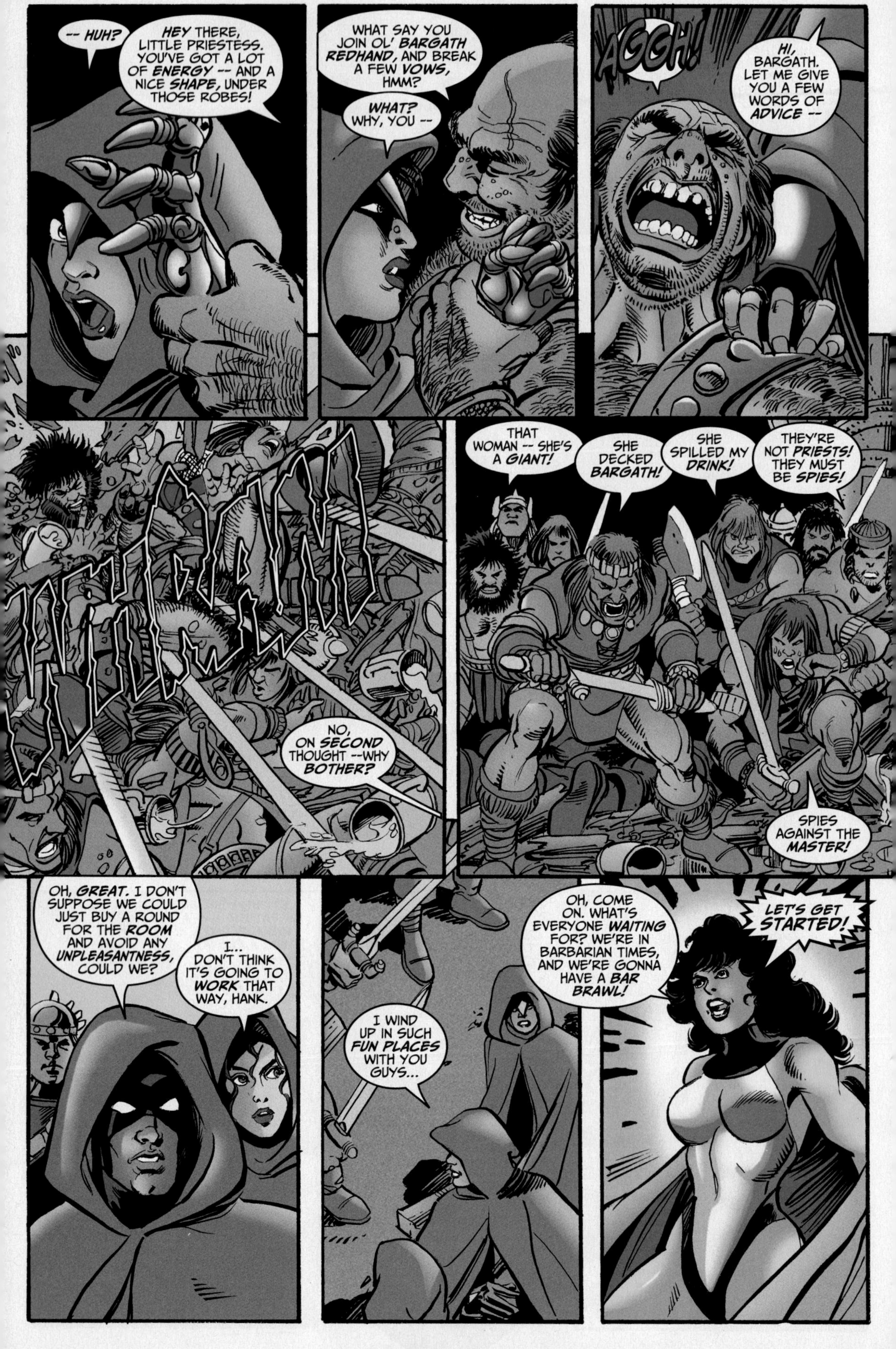
-- HUH?
HEY THERE, LITTLE PRIESTESS. YOU'VE GOT A LOT OF ENERGY -- AND A NICE SHAPE, UNDER THOSE ROBES!
WHAT SAY YOU JOIN OL' BARGATH REDHAND, AND BREAK A FEW VOWS, HMM?
WHAT? WHY, YOU --
AGGH!
HI, BARGATH. LET ME GIVE YOU A FEW WORDS OF ADVICE --
NO, ON SECOND THOUGHT --WHY BOTHER?
THAT WOMAN -- SHE'S A GIANT!
SHE DECKED BARGATH!
SHE SPILLED MY DRINK!
THEY'RE NOT PRIESTS! THEY MUST BE SPIES!
SPIES AGAINST THE MASTER!
OH, GREAT. I DON'T SUPPOSE WE COULD JUST BUY A ROUND FOR THE ROOM AND AVOID ANY UNPLEASANTNESS, COULD WE?
I... DON'T THINK IT'S GOING TO WORK THAT WAY, HANK.
I WIND UP IN SUCH FUN PLACES WITH YOU GUYS...
OH, COME ON. WHAT'S EVERYONE WAITING FOR? WE'RE IN BARBARIAN TIMES, AND WE'RE GONNA HAVE A BAR BRAWL!
LET'S GET STARTED!

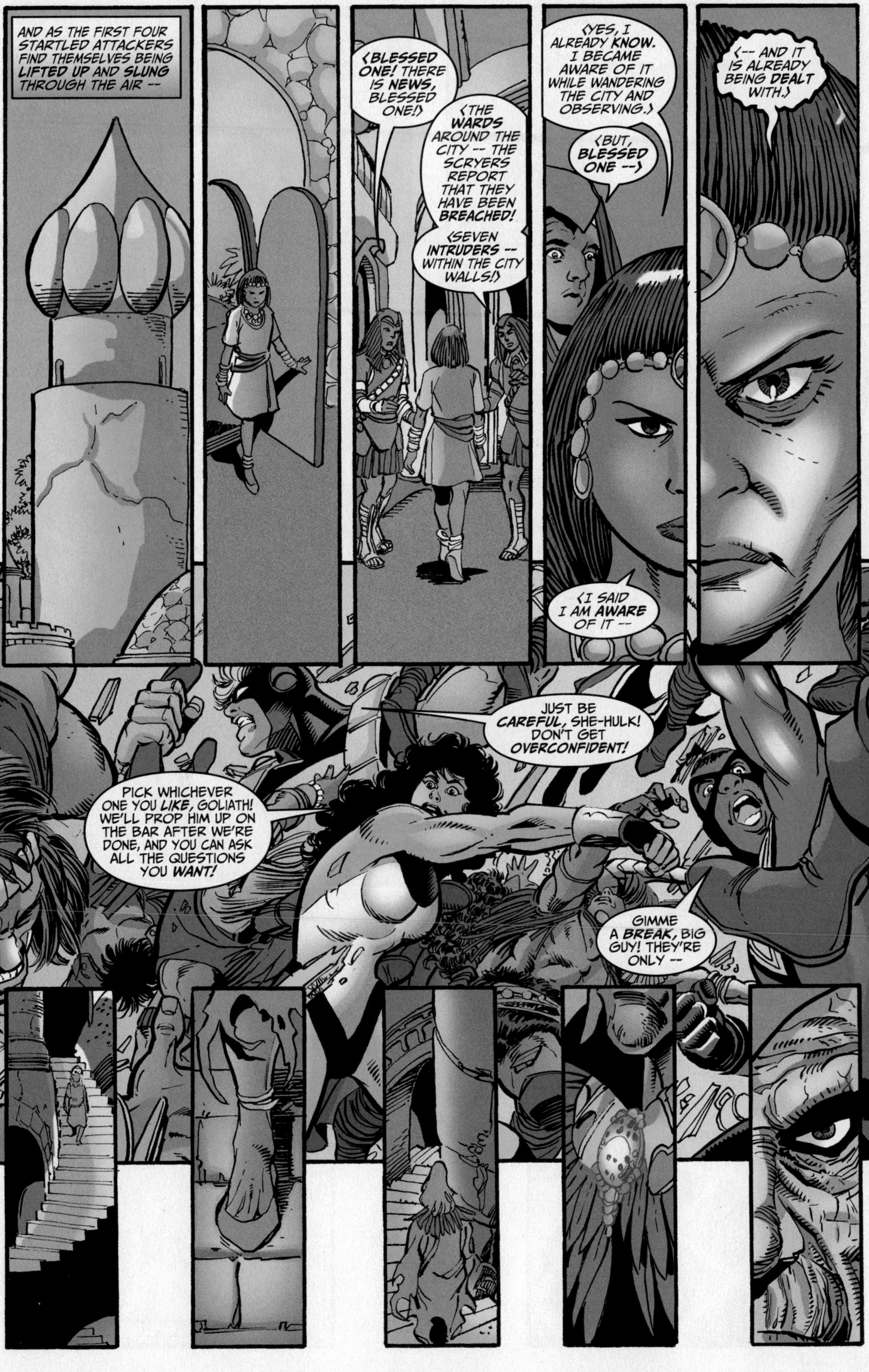
AND AS THE FIRST FOUR STARTLED ATTACKERS FIND THEMSELVES BEING LIFTED UP AND SLUNG THROUGH THE AIR --
‹BLESSED ONE! THERE IS NEWS, BLESSED ONE!›
‹THE WARDS AROUND THE CITY -- THE SCRYERS REPORT THAT THEY HAVE BEEN BREACHED!
‹SEVEN INTRUDERS -- WITHIN THE CITY WALLS!›
‹YES, I ALREADY KNOW. I BECAME AWARE OF IT WHILE WANDERING THE CITY AND OBSERVING.›
‹BUT, BLESSED ONE --›
‹I SAID I AM AWARE OF IT --
‹-- AND IT IS ALREADY BEING DEALT WITH.›
JUST BE CAREFUL, SHE-HULK! DON'T GET OVERCONFIDENT!
PICK WHICHEVER ONE YOU LIKE, GOLIATH! WE'LL PROP HIM UP ON THE BAR AFTER WE'RE DONE, AND YOU CAN ASK ALL THE QUESTIONS YOU WANT!
GIMME A BREAK, BIG GUY! THEY'RE ONLY --

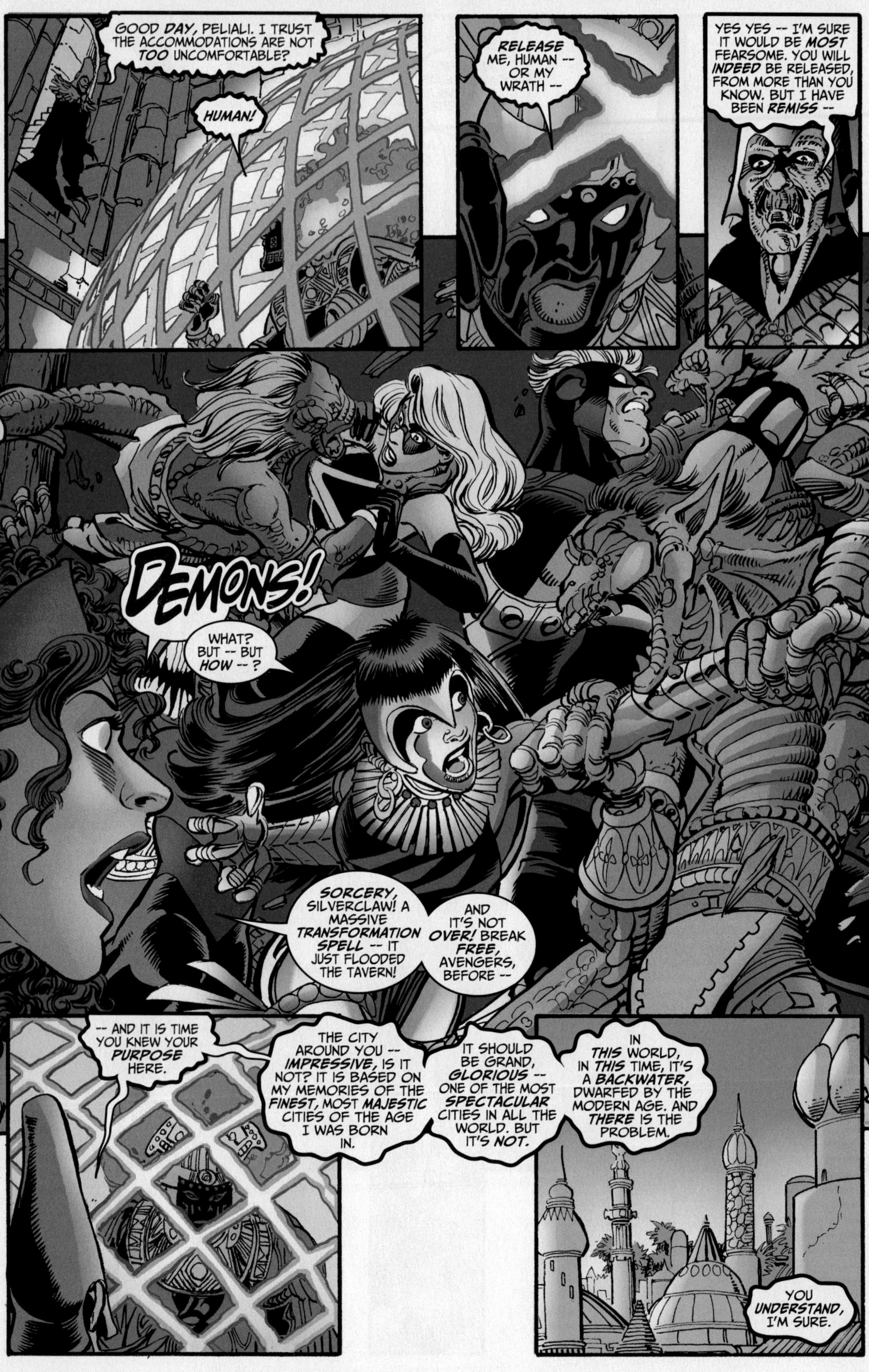
GOOD DAY, PELIALI. I TRUST THE ACCOMMODATIONS ARE NOT TOO UNCOMFORTABLE?
HUMAN!
RELEASE ME, HUMAN -- OR MY WRATH --
YES YES -- I'M SURE IT WOULD BE MOST FEARSOME. YOU WILL INDEED BE RELEASED, FROM MORE THAN YOU KNOW. BUT I HAVE BEEN REMISS --
DEMONS!
WHAT? BUT -- BUT HOW -- ?
SORCERY, SILVERCLAW! A MASSIVE TRANSFORMATION SPELL -- IT JUST FLOODED THE TAVERN!
AND IT'S NOT OVER! BREAK FREE, AVENGERS, BEFORE --
-- AND IT IS TIME YOU KNEW YOUR PURPOSE HERE.
THE CITY AROUND YOU -- IMPRESSIVE, IS IT NOT? IT IS BASED ON MY MEMORIES OF THE FINEST, MOST MAJESTIC CITIES OF THE AGE I WAS BORN IN.
IT SHOULD BE GRAND, GLORIOUS -- ONE OF THE MOST SPECTACULAR CITIES IN ALL THE WORLD. BUT IT'S NOT.
IN THIS WORLD, IN THIS TIME, IT'S A BACKWATER, DWARFED BY THE MODERN AGE. AND THERE IS THE PROBLEM.
YOU UNDERSTAND, I'M SURE.

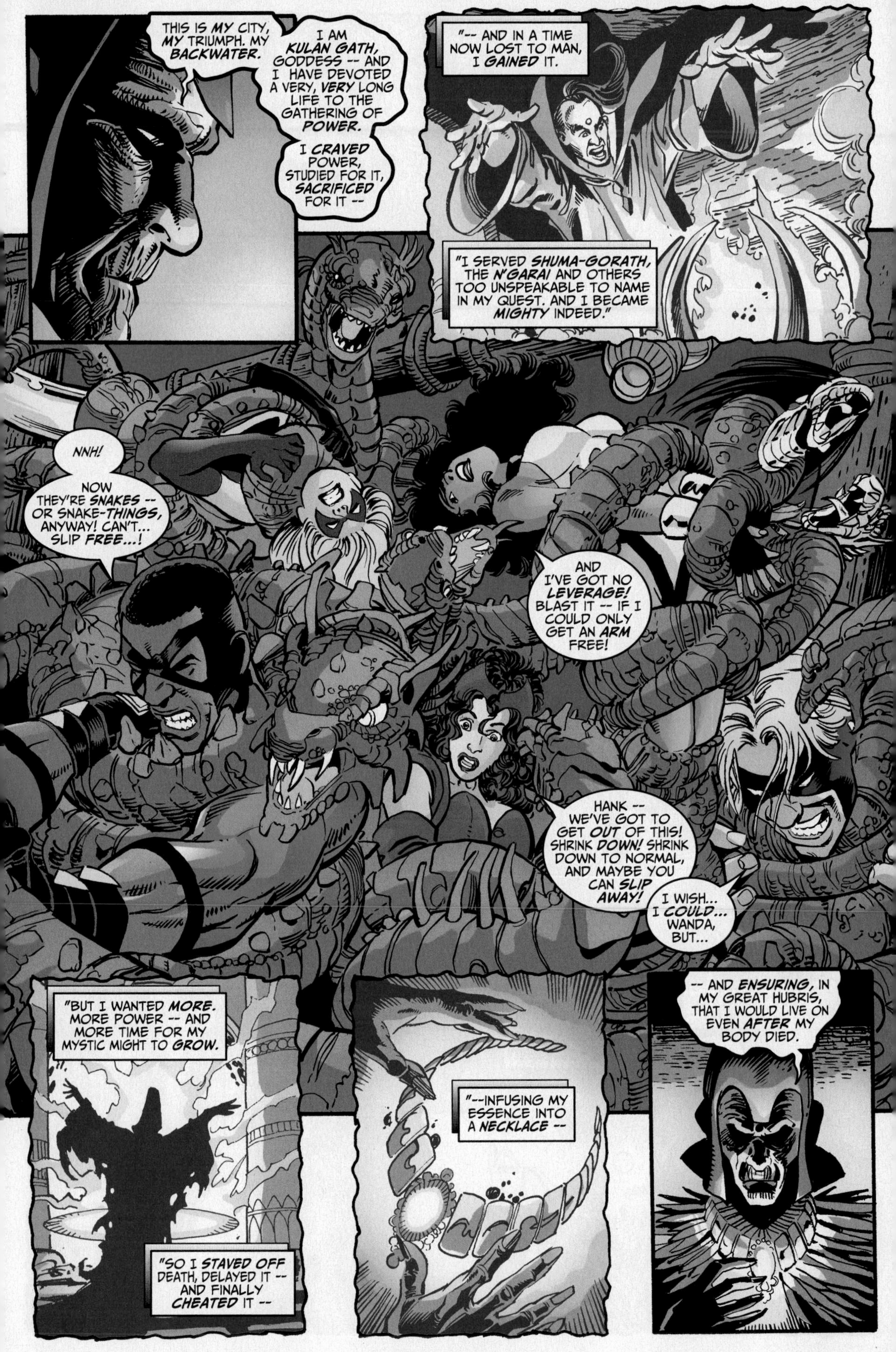
THIS IS MY CITY, MY TRIUMPH. MY BACKWATER.
I AM KULAN GATH, GODDESS -- AND I HAVE DEVOTED A VERY, VERY LONG LIFE TO THE GATHERING OF POWER.
I CRAVED POWER, STUDIED FOR IT, SACRIFICED FOR IT --
"-- AND IN A TIME NOW LOST TO MAN, I GAINED IT.
"I SERVED SHUMA-GORATH, THE N'GARAI AND OTHERS TOO UNSPEAKABLE TO NAME IN MY QUEST. AND I BECAME MIGHTY INDEED."
NNH!
NOW THEY'RE SNAKES -- OR SNAKE-THINGS, ANYWAY! CAN'T... SLIP FREE...!
AND I'VE GOT NO LEVERAGE! BLAST IT -- IF I COULD ONLY GET AN ARM FREE!
HANK -- WE'VE GOT TO GET OUT OF THIS! SHRINK DOWN! SHRINK DOWN TO NORMAL, AND MAYBE YOU CAN SLIP AWAY!
I WISH... I COULD... WANDA, BUT...
"BUT I WANTED MORE. MORE POWER -- AND MORE TIME FOR MY MYSTIC MIGHT TO GROW.
"SO I STAVED OFF DEATH, DELAYED IT -- AND FINALLY CHEATED IT --
"--INFUSING MY ESSENCE INTO A NECKLACE --
-- AND ENSURING, IN MY GREAT HUBRIS, THAT I WOULD LIVE ON EVEN AFTER MY BODY DIED.

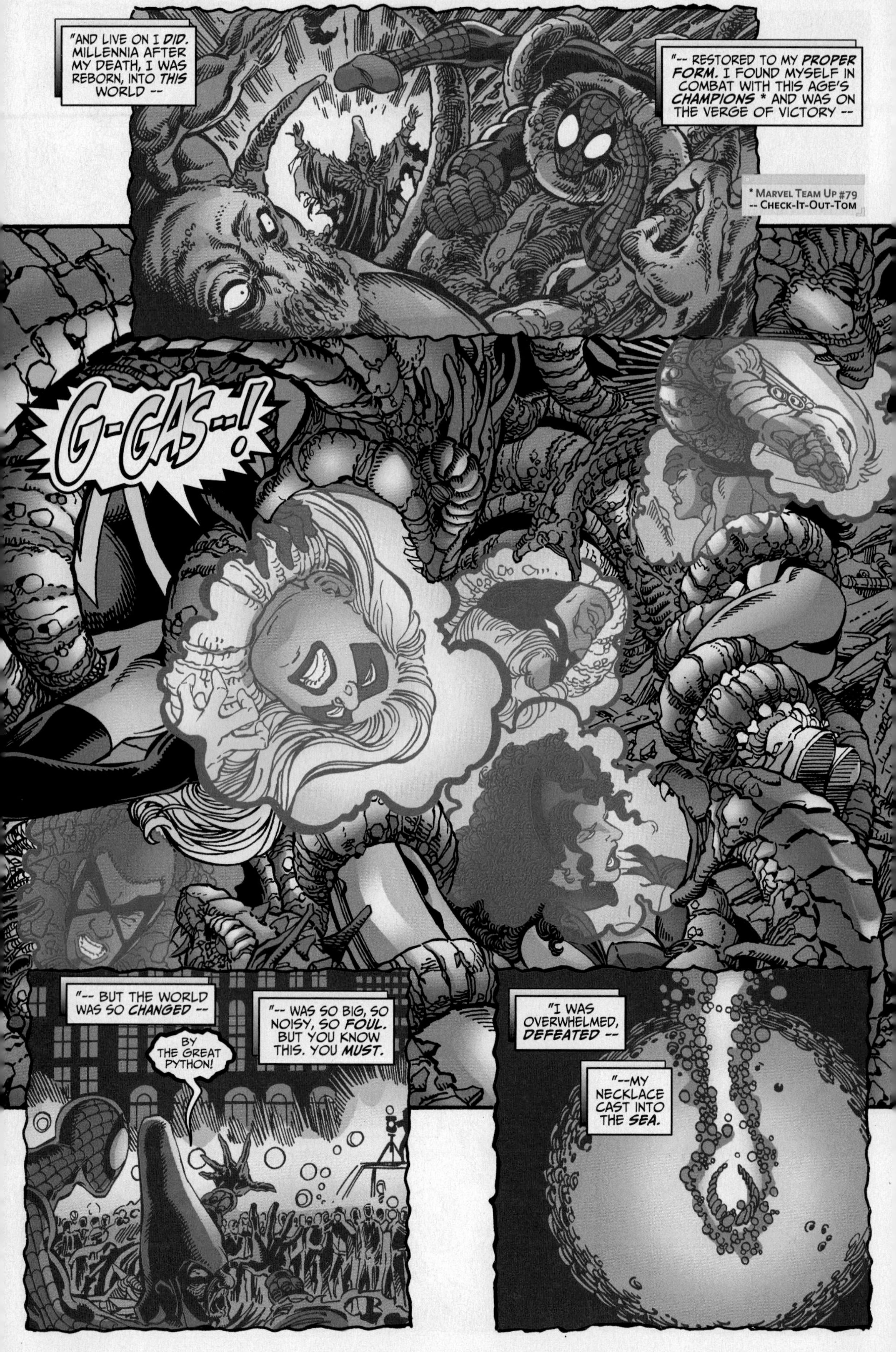
"AND LIVE ON I *DID*. MILLENNIA AFTER MY DEATH, I WAS REBORN, INTO *THIS* WORLD --
"-- RESTORED TO MY *PROPER FORM*. I FOUND MYSELF IN COMBAT WITH THIS AGE'S *CHAMPIONS* * AND WAS ON THE VERGE OF VICTORY --
* MARVEL TEAM UP #79 -- CHECK-IT-OUT-TOM
G-GAS--!
"-- BUT THE WORLD WAS SO *CHANGED* --
"-- WAS SO BIG, SO NOISY, SO *FOUL*. BUT YOU KNOW THIS. YOU *MUST*.
BY THE GREAT PYTHON!
"I WAS OVERWHELMED, *DEFEATED* --
"--MY NECKLACE CAST INTO THE *SEA*.

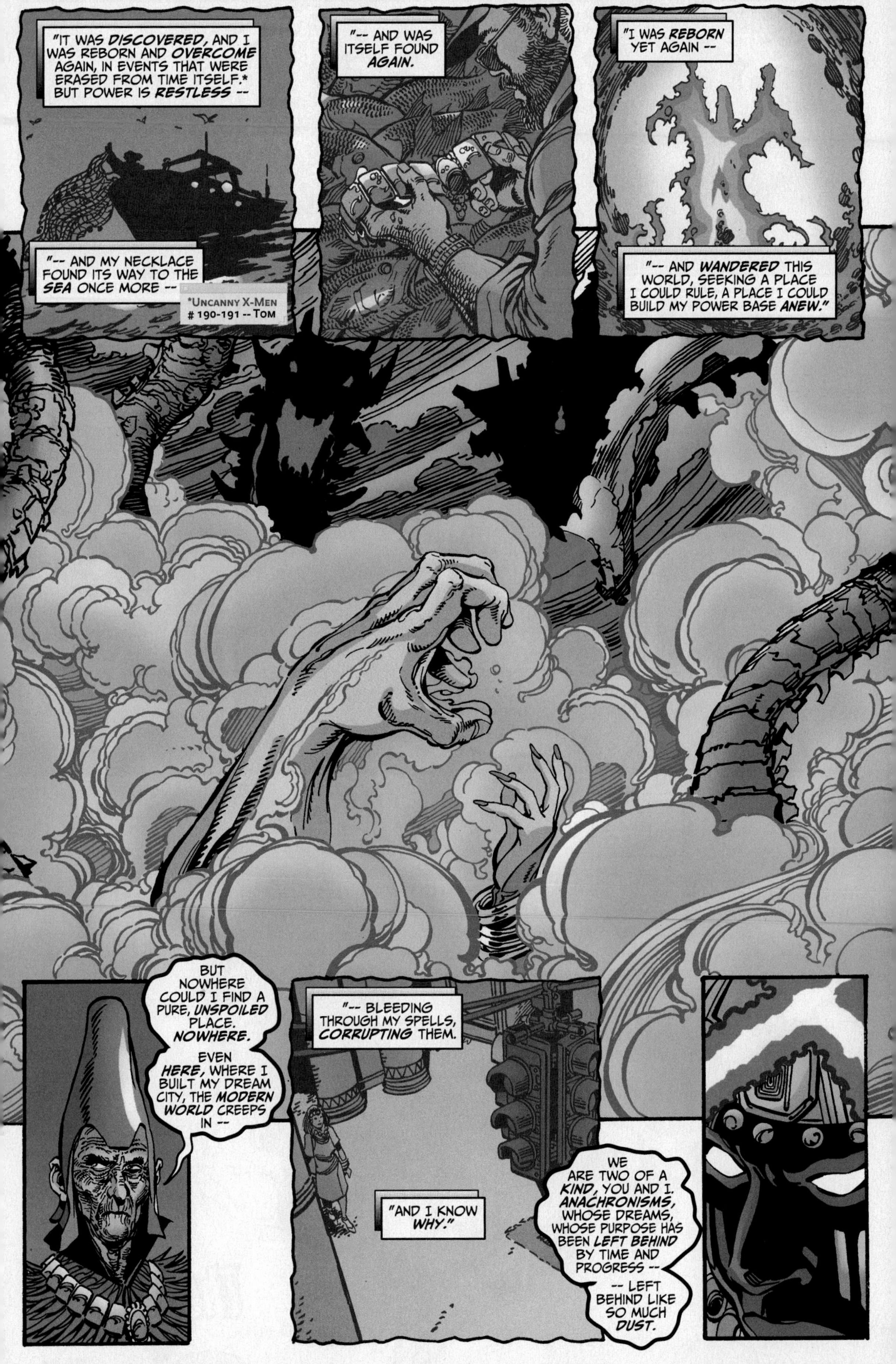
"IT WAS DISCOVERED, AND I WAS REBORN AND OVERCOME AGAIN, IN EVENTS THAT WERE ERASED FROM TIME ITSELF.* BUT POWER IS RESTLESS --
"-- AND MY NECKLACE FOUND ITS WAY TO THE SEA ONCE MORE --
*UNCANNY X-MEN # 190-191 -- TOM
"-- AND WAS ITSELF FOUND AGAIN.
"I WAS REBORN YET AGAIN --
"-- AND WANDERED THIS WORLD, SEEKING A PLACE I COULD RULE, A PLACE I COULD BUILD MY POWER BASE ANEW."
BUT NOWHERE COULD I FIND A PURE, UNSPOILED PLACE. NOWHERE.
EVEN HERE, WHERE I BUILT MY DREAM CITY, THE MODERN WORLD CREEPS IN --
"-- BLEEDING THROUGH MY SPELLS, CORRUPTING THEM.
"AND I KNOW WHY."
WE ARE TWO OF A KIND, YOU AND I. ANACHRONISMS, WHOSE DREAMS, WHOSE PURPOSE HAS BEEN LEFT BEHIND BY TIME AND PROGRESS --
-- LEFT BEHIND LIKE SO MUCH DUST.

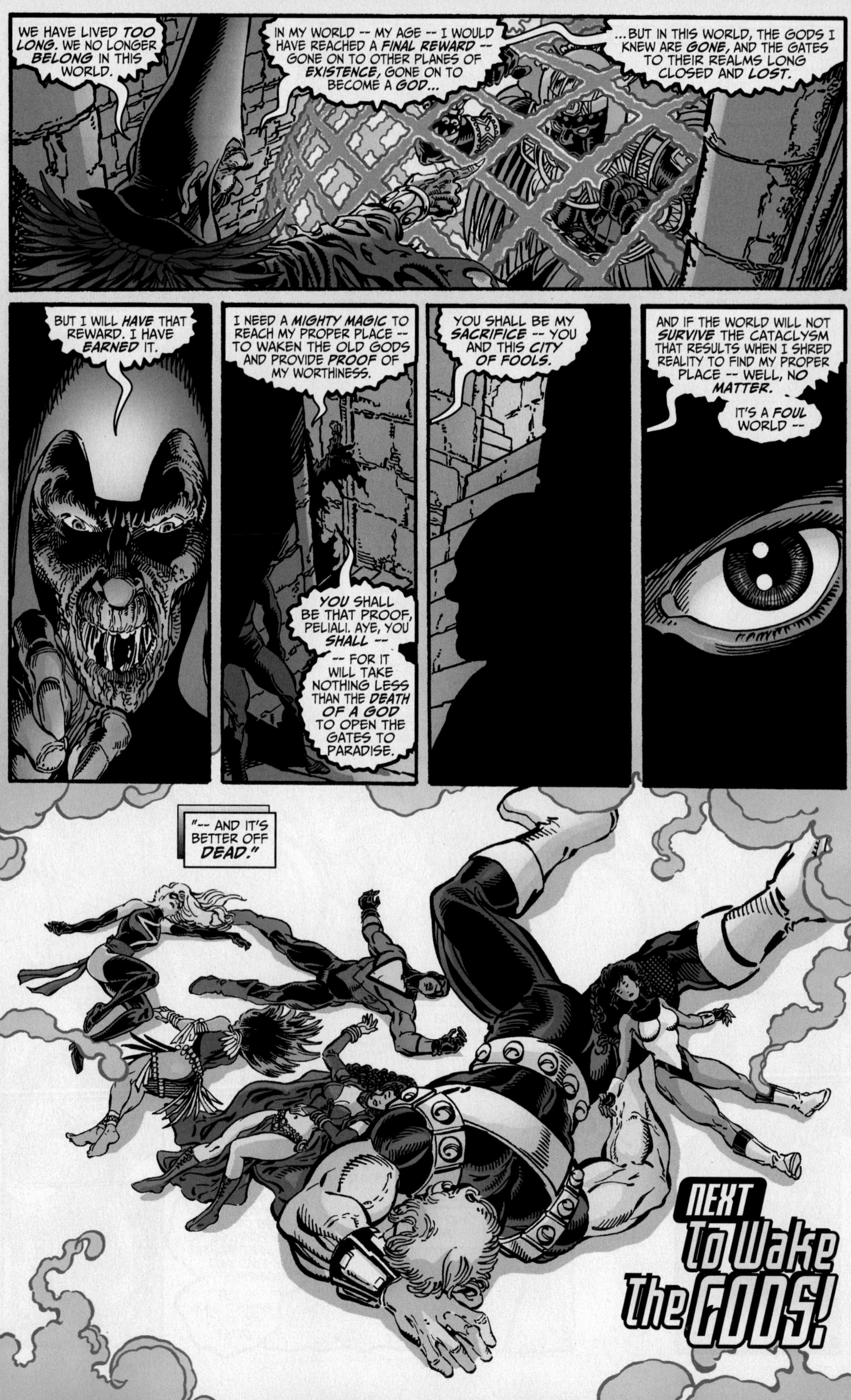
WE HAVE LIVED TOO LONG. WE NO LONGER BELONG IN THIS WORLD.
IN MY WORLD -- MY AGE -- I WOULD HAVE REACHED A FINAL REWARD -- GONE ON TO OTHER PLANES OF EXISTENCE, GONE ON TO BECOME A GOD...
...BUT IN THIS WORLD, THE GODS I KNEW ARE GONE, AND THE GATES TO THEIR REALMS LONG CLOSED AND LOST.
BUT I WILL HAVE THAT REWARD. I HAVE EARNED IT.
I NEED A MIGHTY MAGIC TO REACH MY PROPER PLACE -- TO WAKEN THE OLD GODS AND PROVIDE PROOF OF MY WORTHINESS.
YOU SHALL BE THAT PROOF, PELIALI. AYE, YOU SHALL --
-- FOR IT WILL TAKE NOTHING LESS THAN THE DEATH OF A GOD TO OPEN THE GATES TO PARADISE.
YOU SHALL BE MY SACRIFICE -- YOU AND THIS CITY OF FOOLS.
AND IF THE WORLD WILL NOT SURVIVE THE CATACLYSM THAT RESULTS WHEN I SHRED REALITY TO FIND MY PROPER PLACE -- WELL, NO MATTER.
IT'S A FOUL WORLD --
"-- AND IT'S BETTER OFF DEAD."
NEXT
To Wake The GODS!

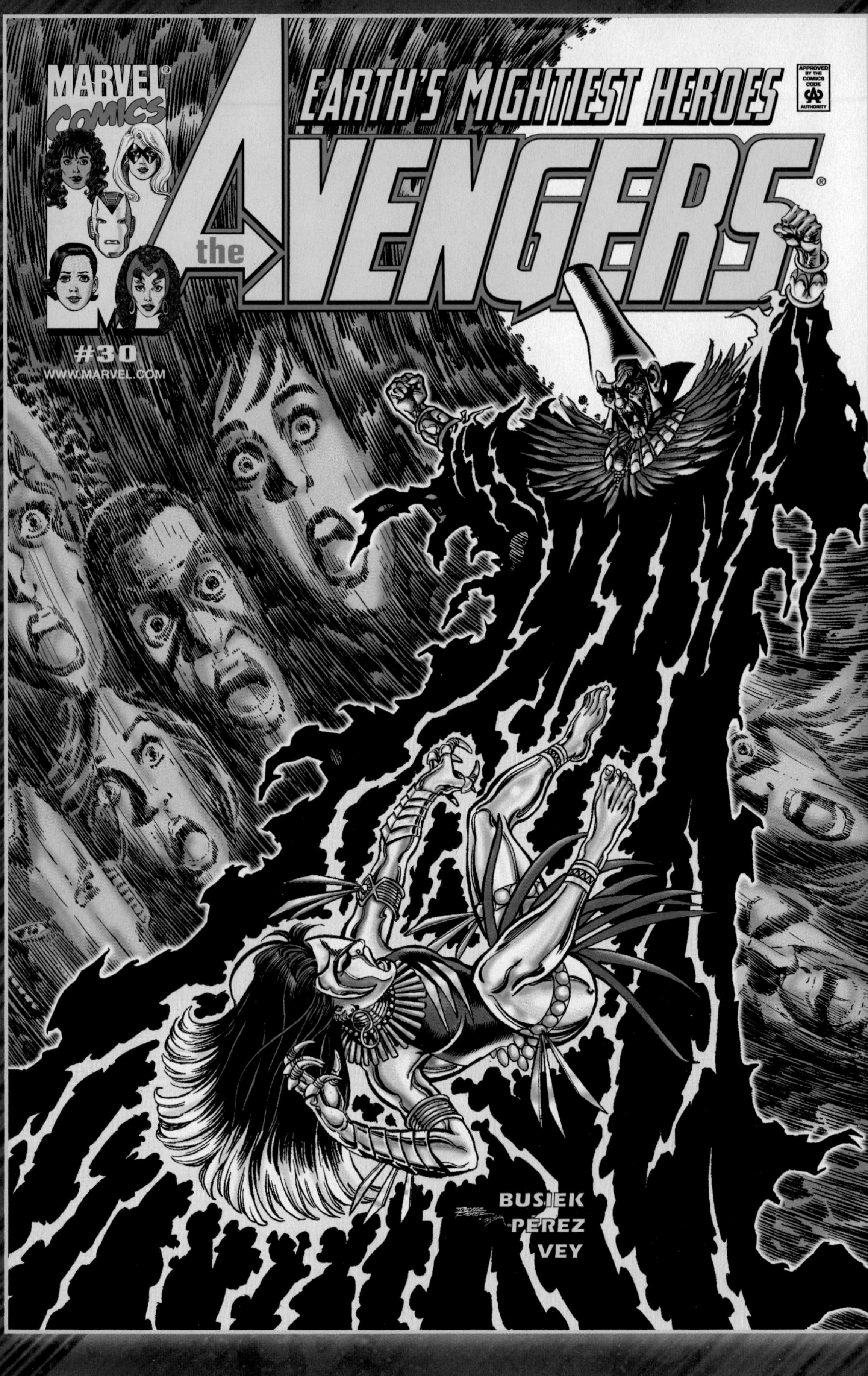
MARVEL COMICS
EARTH'S MIGHTIEST HEROES
the AVENGERS
#30
WWW.MARVEL.COM
APPROVED BY THE COMICS CODE AUTHORITY
BUSIEK
PÉREZ
VEY

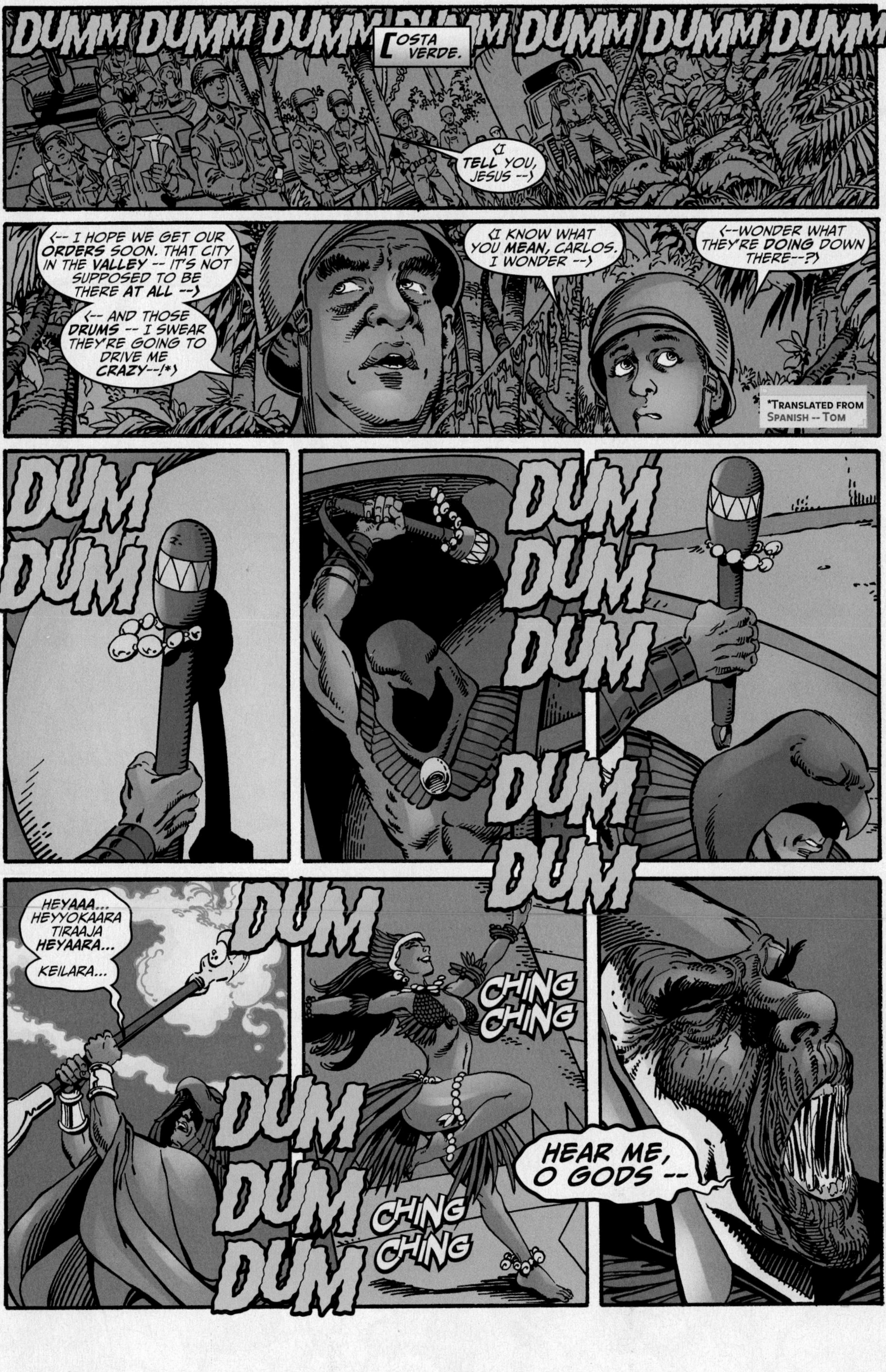
DUMM DUMM DUMM DUMM DUMM DUMM DUMM
COSTA VERDE.
⟨I TELL YOU, JESUS --⟩
⟨-- I HOPE WE GET OUR ORDERS SOON. THAT CITY IN THE VALLEY -- IT'S NOT SUPPOSED TO BE THERE AT ALL --⟩
⟨-- AND THOSE DRUMS -- I SWEAR THEY'RE GOING TO DRIVE ME CRAZY--!*⟩
⟨I KNOW WHAT YOU MEAN, CARLOS. I WONDER --⟩
⟨--WONDER WHAT THEY'RE DOING DOWN THERE--?⟩
*TRANSLATED FROM SPANISH -- TOM
DUM DUM
DUM DUM DUM
DUM DUM
HEYAAA... HEYYOKAARA TIRAAJA HEYAARA...
KEILARA...
DUM
CHING CHING
DUM DUM DUM
CHING CHING
HEAR ME, O GODS --

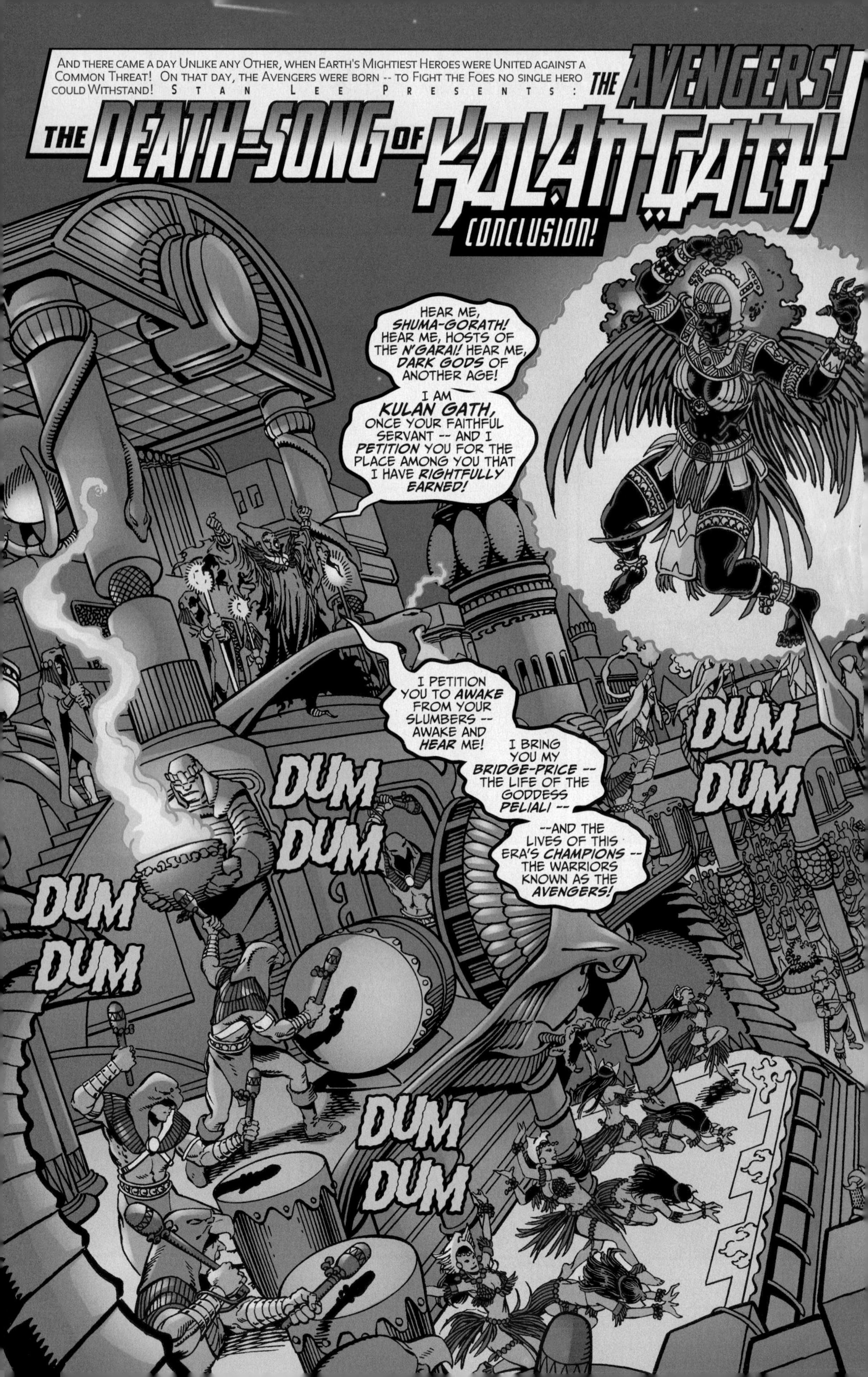
AND THERE CAME A DAY UNLIKE ANY OTHER, WHEN EARTH'S MIGHTIEST HEROES WERE UNITED AGAINST A COMMON THREAT! ON THAT DAY, THE AVENGERS WERE BORN -- TO FIGHT THE FOES NO SINGLE HERO COULD WITHSTAND! STAN LEE PRESENTS: THE AVENGERS!
THE DEATH-SONG OF KULAN GATH
CONCLUSION!
HEAR ME, SHUMA-GORATH! HEAR ME, HOSTS OF THE N'GARAI! HEAR ME, DARK GODS OF ANOTHER AGE!
I AM KULAN GATH, ONCE YOUR FAITHFUL SERVANT -- AND I PETITION YOU FOR THE PLACE AMONG YOU THAT I HAVE RIGHTFULLY EARNED!
I PETITION YOU TO AWAKE FROM YOUR SLUMBERS -- AWAKE AND HEAR ME!
I BRING YOU MY BRIDGE-PRICE -- THE LIFE OF THE GODDESS PELIALI --
--AND THE LIVES OF THIS ERA'S CHAMPIONS -- THE WARRIORS KNOWN AS THE AVENGERS!
DUM DUM
DUM DUM
DUM DUM
DUM DUM

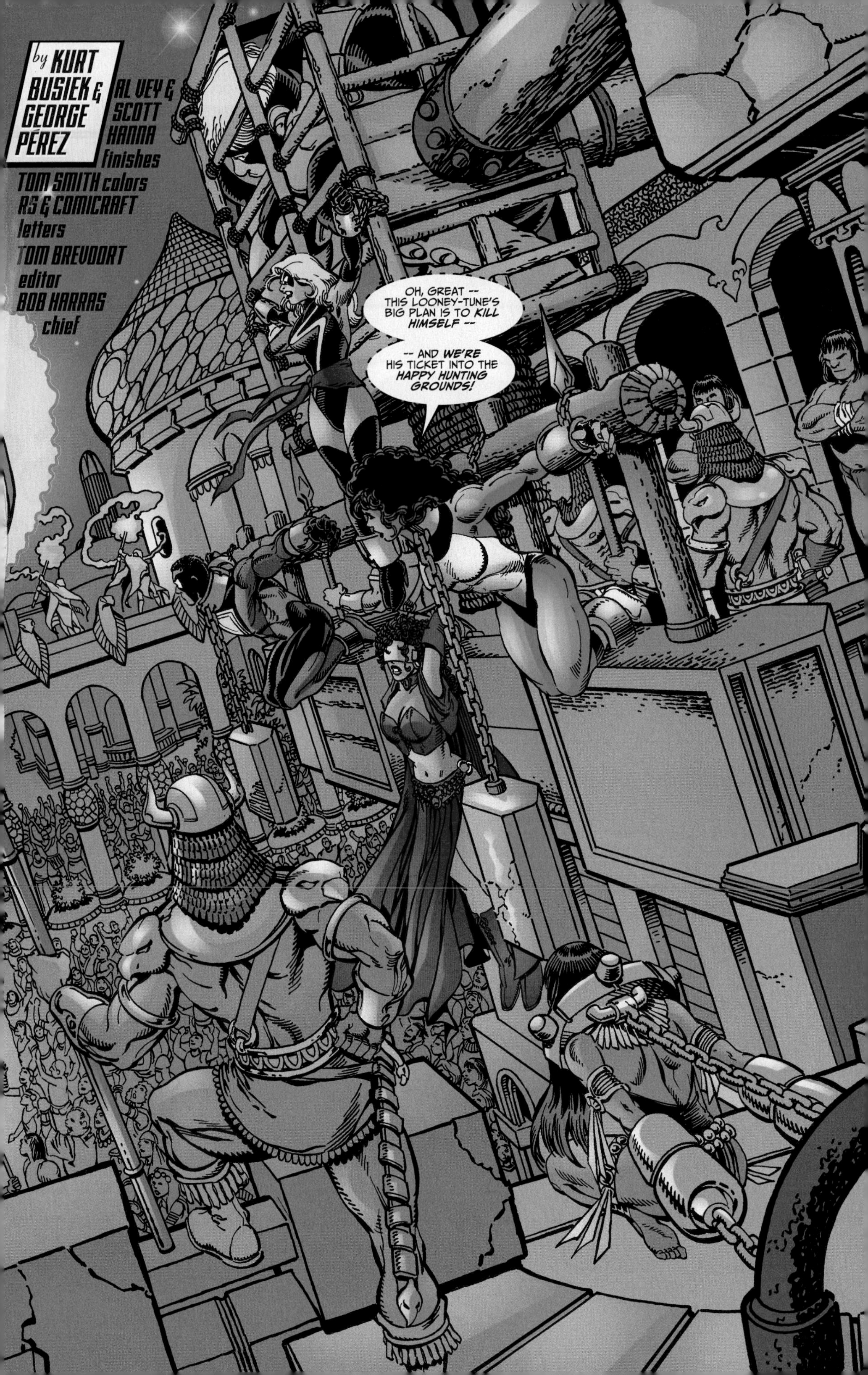
by KURT BUSIEK & GEORGE PÉREZ
AL VEY & SCOTT HANNA finishes
TOM SMITH colors
RS & COMICRAFT letters
TOM BREVOORT editor
BOB HARRAS chief
OH, GREAT -- THIS LOONEY-TUNE'S BIG PLAN IS TO KILL HIMSELF --
-- AND WE'RE HIS TICKET INTO THE HAPPY HUNTING GROUNDS!

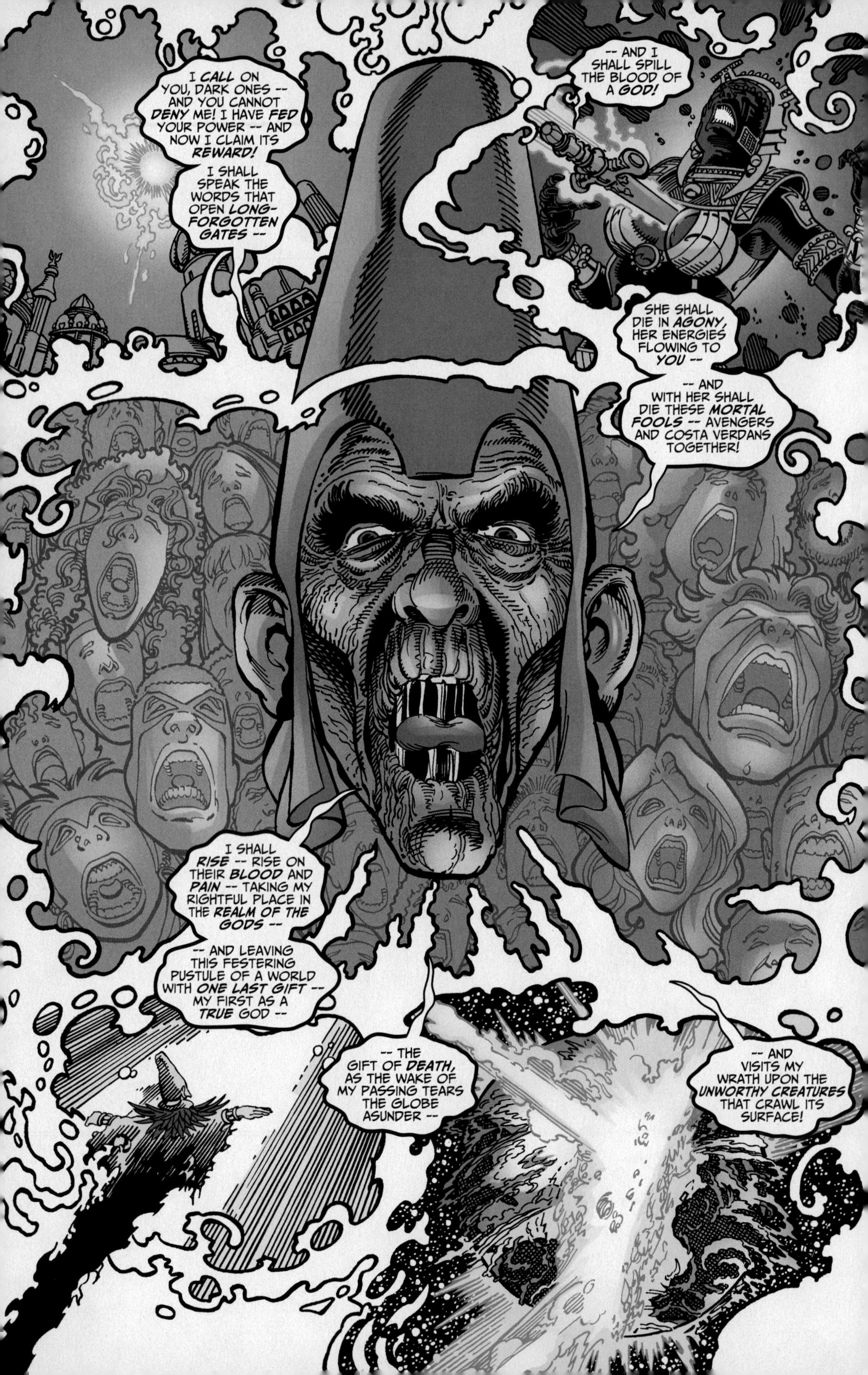
I CALL ON YOU, DARK ONES -- AND YOU CANNOT DENY ME! I HAVE FED YOUR POWER -- AND NOW I CLAIM ITS REWARD!
I SHALL SPEAK THE WORDS THAT OPEN LONG-FORGOTTEN GATES --
-- AND I SHALL SPILL THE BLOOD OF A GOD!
SHE SHALL DIE IN AGONY, HER ENERGIES FLOWING TO YOU --
-- AND WITH HER SHALL DIE THESE MORTAL FOOLS -- AVENGERS AND COSTA VERDANS TOGETHER!
I SHALL RISE -- RISE ON THEIR BLOOD AND PAIN -- TAKING MY RIGHTFUL PLACE IN THE REALM OF THE GODS --
-- AND LEAVING THIS FESTERING PUSTULE OF A WORLD WITH ONE LAST GIFT -- MY FIRST AS A TRUE GOD --
-- THE GIFT OF DEATH, AS THE WAKE OF MY PASSING TEARS THE GLOBE ASUNDER --
-- AND VISITS MY WRATH UPON THE UNWORTHY CREATURES THAT CRAWL ITS SURFACE!

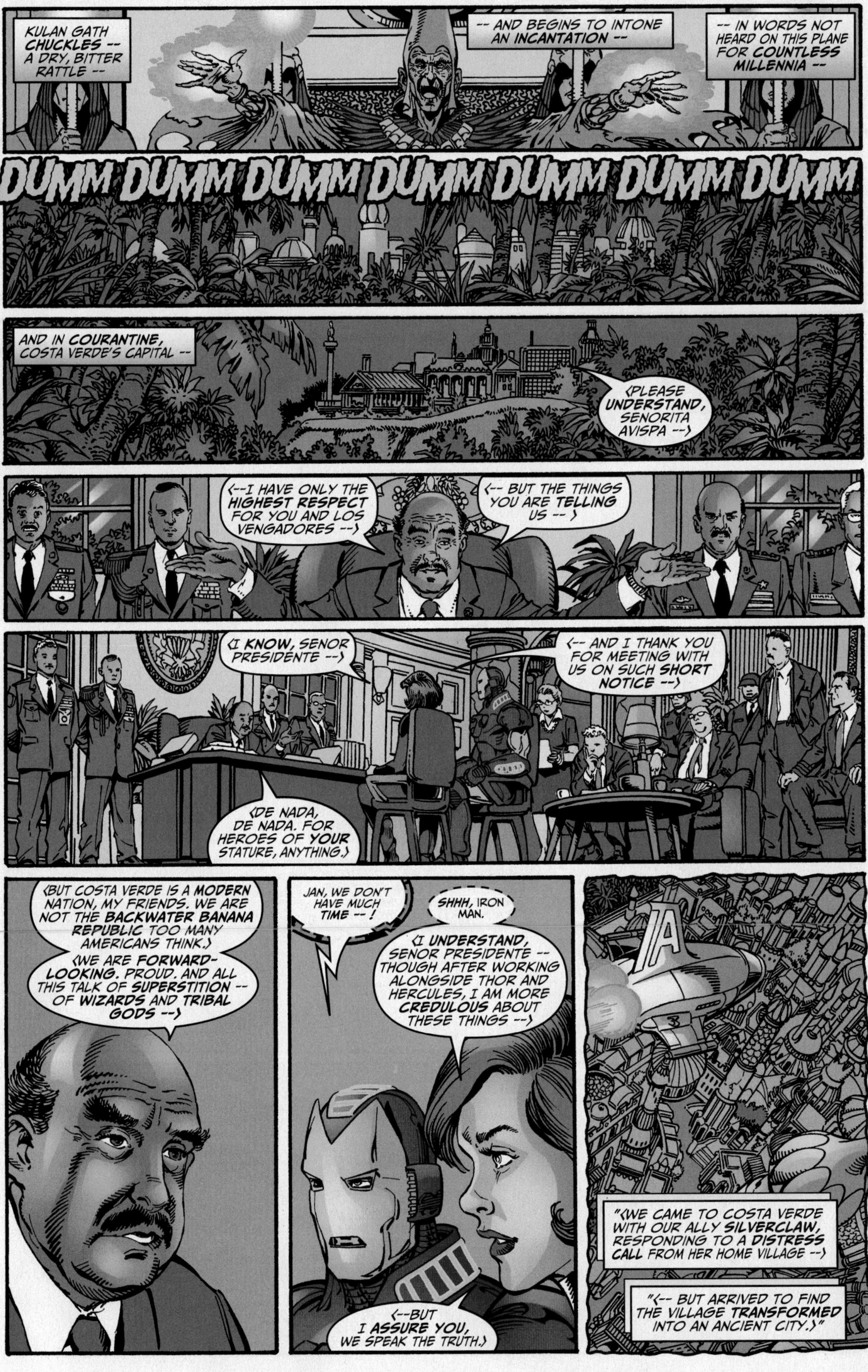

KULAN GATH CHUCKLES -- A DRY, BITTER RATTLE --
-- AND BEGINS TO INTONE AN INCANTATION --
-- IN WORDS NOT HEARD ON THIS PLANE FOR COUNTLESS MILLENNIA --
DUMM DUMM DUMM DUMM DUMM DUMM DUMM
AND IN COURANTINE, COSTA VERDE'S CAPITAL --
‹PLEASE UNDERSTAND, SENORITA AVISPA --›
‹--I HAVE ONLY THE HIGHEST RESPECT FOR YOU AND LOS VENGADORES --›
‹-- BUT THE THINGS YOU ARE TELLING US -- ›
‹I KNOW, SENOR PRESIDENTE --›
‹-- AND I THANK YOU FOR MEETING WITH US ON SUCH SHORT NOTICE --›
‹DE NADA, DE NADA. FOR HEROES OF YOUR STATURE, ANYTHING.›
‹BUT COSTA VERDE IS A MODERN NATION, MY FRIENDS. WE ARE NOT THE BACKWATER BANANA REPUBLIC TOO MANY AMERICANS THINK.›
‹WE ARE FORWARD-LOOKING. PROUD. AND ALL THIS TALK OF SUPERSTITION -- OF WIZARDS AND TRIBAL GODS --›
JAN, WE DON'T HAVE MUCH TIME -- !
SHHH, IRON MAN.
‹I UNDERSTAND, SENOR PRESIDENTE -- THOUGH AFTER WORKING ALONGSIDE THOR AND HERCULES, I AM MORE CREDULOUS ABOUT THESE THINGS --›
‹--BUT I ASSURE YOU, WE SPEAK THE TRUTH.›
"‹WE CAME TO COSTA VERDE WITH OUR ALLY SILVERCLAW, RESPONDING TO A DISTRESS CALL FROM HER HOME VILLAGE --›
"‹-- BUT ARRIVED TO FIND THE VILLAGE TRANSFORMED INTO AN ANCIENT CITY.›"

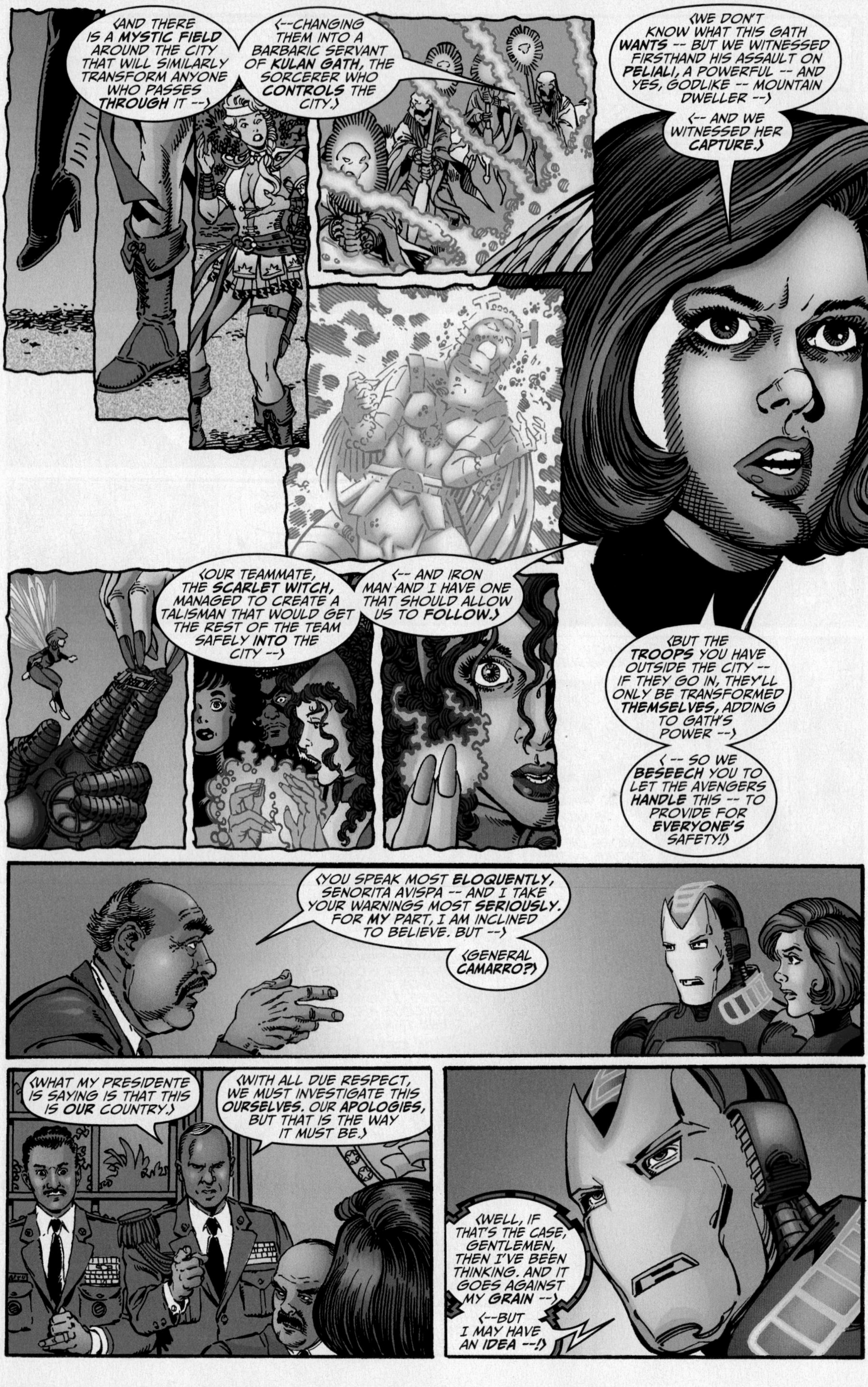
‹AND THERE IS A MYSTIC FIELD AROUND THE CITY THAT WILL SIMILARLY TRANSFORM ANYONE WHO PASSES THROUGH IT --›
‹--CHANGING THEM INTO A BARBARIC SERVANT OF KULAN GATH, THE SORCERER WHO CONTROLS THE CITY.›
‹WE DON'T KNOW WHAT THIS GATH WANTS -- BUT WE WITNESSED FIRSTHAND HIS ASSAULT ON PELIALI, A POWERFUL -- AND YES, GODLIKE -- MOUNTAIN DWELLER --›
‹-- AND WE WITNESSED HER CAPTURE.›
‹OUR TEAMMATE, THE SCARLET WITCH, MANAGED TO CREATE A TALISMAN THAT WOULD GET THE REST OF THE TEAM SAFELY INTO THE CITY --›
‹-- AND IRON MAN AND I HAVE ONE THAT SHOULD ALLOW US TO FOLLOW.›
‹BUT THE TROOPS YOU HAVE OUTSIDE THE CITY -- IF THEY GO IN, THEY'LL ONLY BE TRANSFORMED THEMSELVES, ADDING TO GATH'S POWER --›
‹ -- SO WE BESEECH YOU TO LET THE AVENGERS HANDLE THIS -- TO PROVIDE FOR EVERYONE'S SAFETY!›
‹YOU SPEAK MOST ELOQUENTLY, SENORITA AVISPA -- AND I TAKE YOUR WARNINGS MOST SERIOUSLY. FOR MY PART, I AM INCLINED TO BELIEVE. BUT --›
‹GENERAL CAMARRO?›
‹WHAT MY PRESIDENTE IS SAYING IS THAT THIS IS OUR COUNTRY.›
‹WITH ALL DUE RESPECT, WE MUST INVESTIGATE THIS OURSELVES. OUR APOLOGIES, BUT THAT IS THE WAY IT MUST BE.›
‹WELL, IF THAT'S THE CASE, GENTLEMEN, THEN I'VE BEEN THINKING. AND IT GOES AGAINST MY GRAIN --›
‹--BUT I MAY HAVE AN IDEA --!›

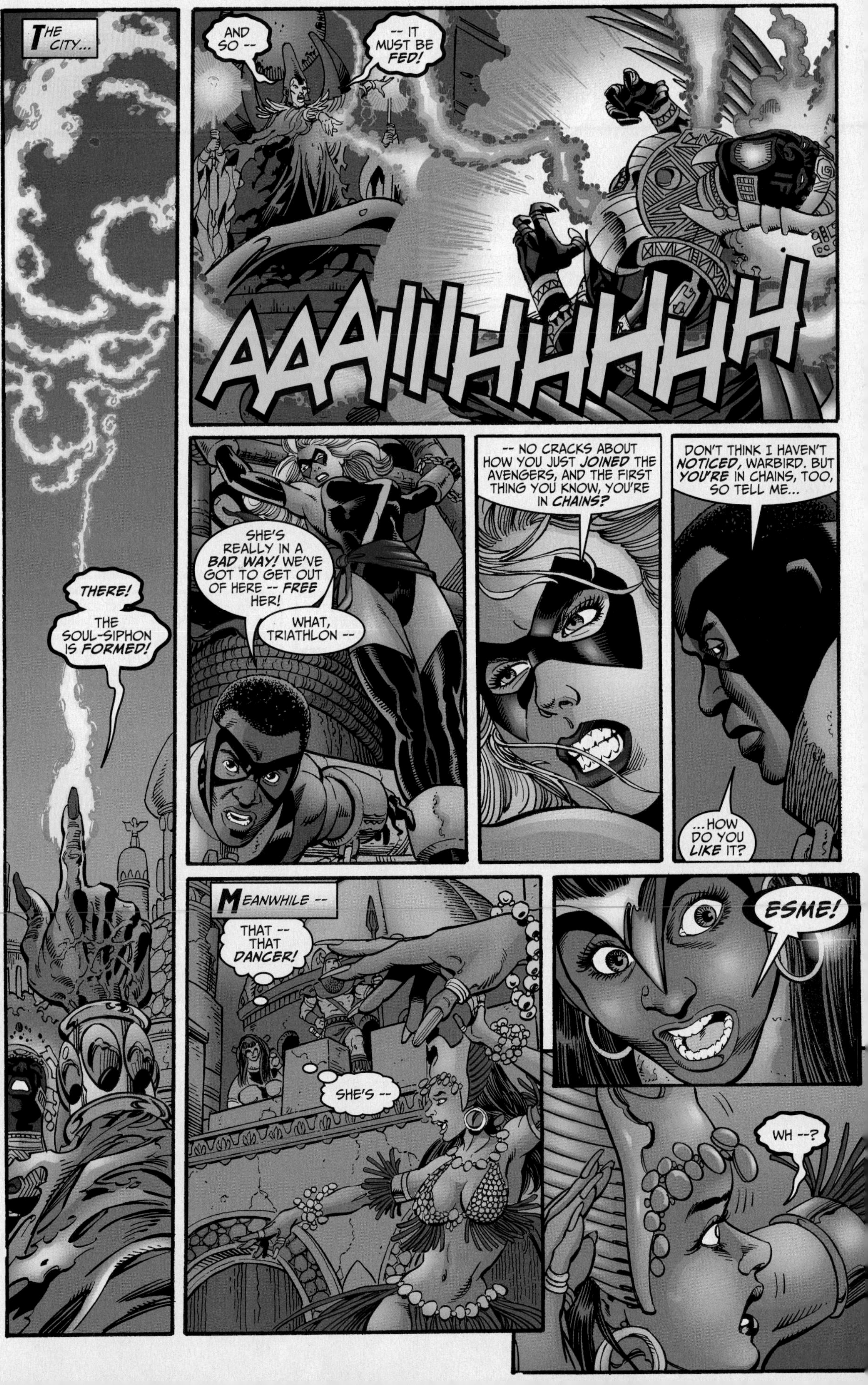
THE CITY...
THERE!
THE SOUL-SIPHON IS FORMED!
AND SO --
-- IT MUST BE FED!
AAAIIIHHHHHH
SHE'S REALLY IN A BAD WAY! WE'VE GOT TO GET OUT OF HERE -- FREE HER!
WHAT, TRIATHLON --
-- NO CRACKS ABOUT HOW YOU JUST JOINED THE AVENGERS, AND THE FIRST THING YOU KNOW, YOU'RE IN CHAINS?
DON'T THINK I HAVEN'T NOTICED, WARBIRD. BUT YOU'RE IN CHAINS, TOO, SO TELL ME...
...HOW DO YOU LIKE IT?
MEANWHILE --
THAT -- THAT DANCER!
SHE'S --
ESME!
WH --?

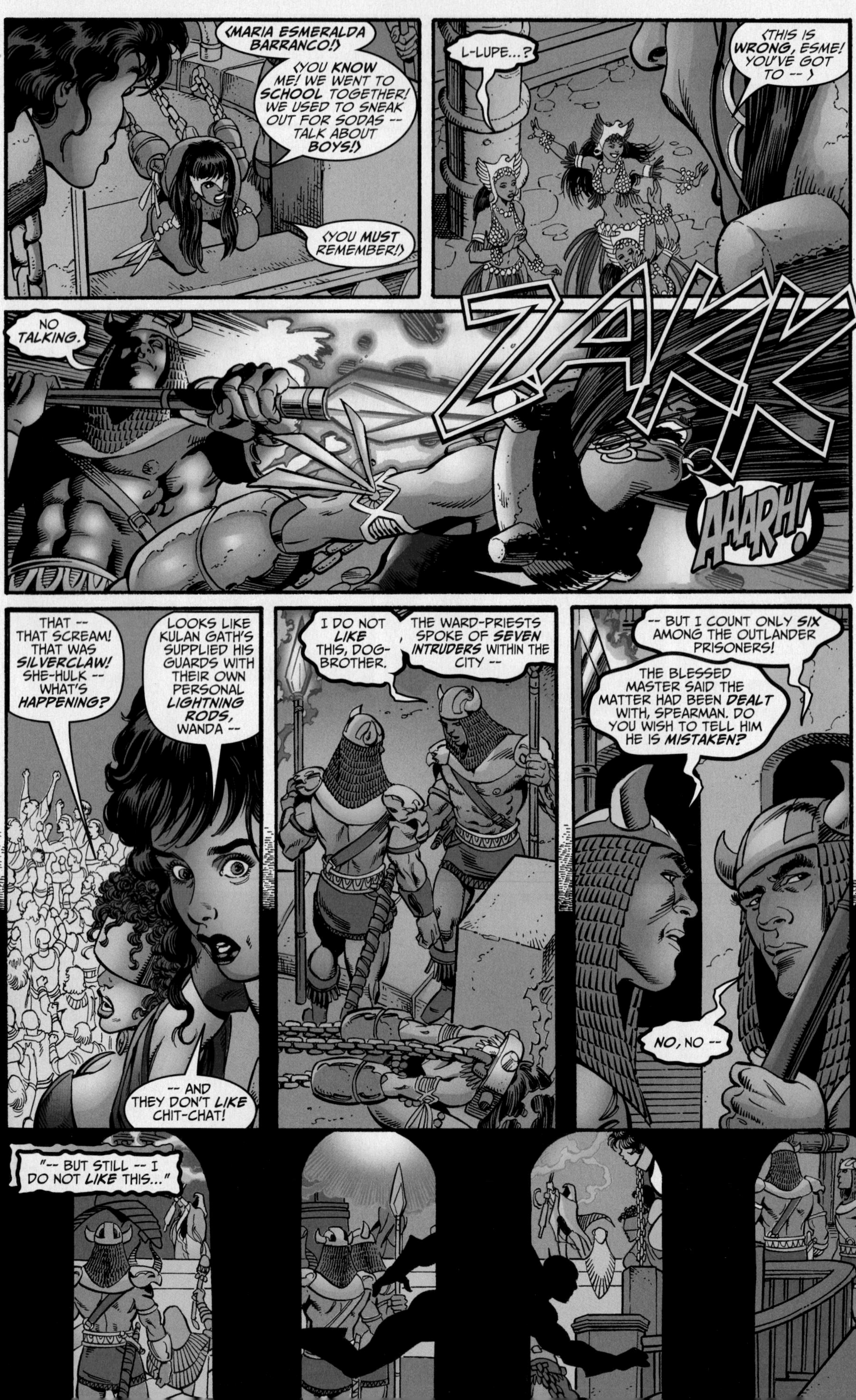
<MARIA ESMERALDA BARRANCO!>
<YOU KNOW ME! WE WENT TO SCHOOL TOGETHER! WE USED TO SNEAK OUT FOR SODAS -- TALK ABOUT BOYS!>
<YOU MUST REMEMBER!>
L-LUPE...?
<THIS IS WRONG, ESME! YOU'VE GOT TO -- >
NO TALKING.
ZAKK
AAARH!
THAT -- THAT SCREAM! THAT WAS SILVERCLAW! SHE-HULK -- WHAT'S HAPPENING?
LOOKS LIKE KULAN GATH'S SUPPLIED HIS GUARDS WITH THEIR OWN PERSONAL LIGHTNING RODS, WANDA --
-- AND THEY DON'T LIKE CHIT-CHAT!
I DO NOT LIKE THIS, DOG-BROTHER.
THE WARD-PRIESTS SPOKE OF SEVEN INTRUDERS WITHIN THE CITY --
-- BUT I COUNT ONLY SIX AMONG THE OUTLANDER PRISONERS!
THE BLESSED MASTER SAID THE MATTER HAD BEEN DEALT WITH, SPEARMAN. DO YOU WISH TO TELL HIM HE IS MISTAKEN?
NO, NO --
"-- BUT STILL -- I DO NOT LIKE THIS..."

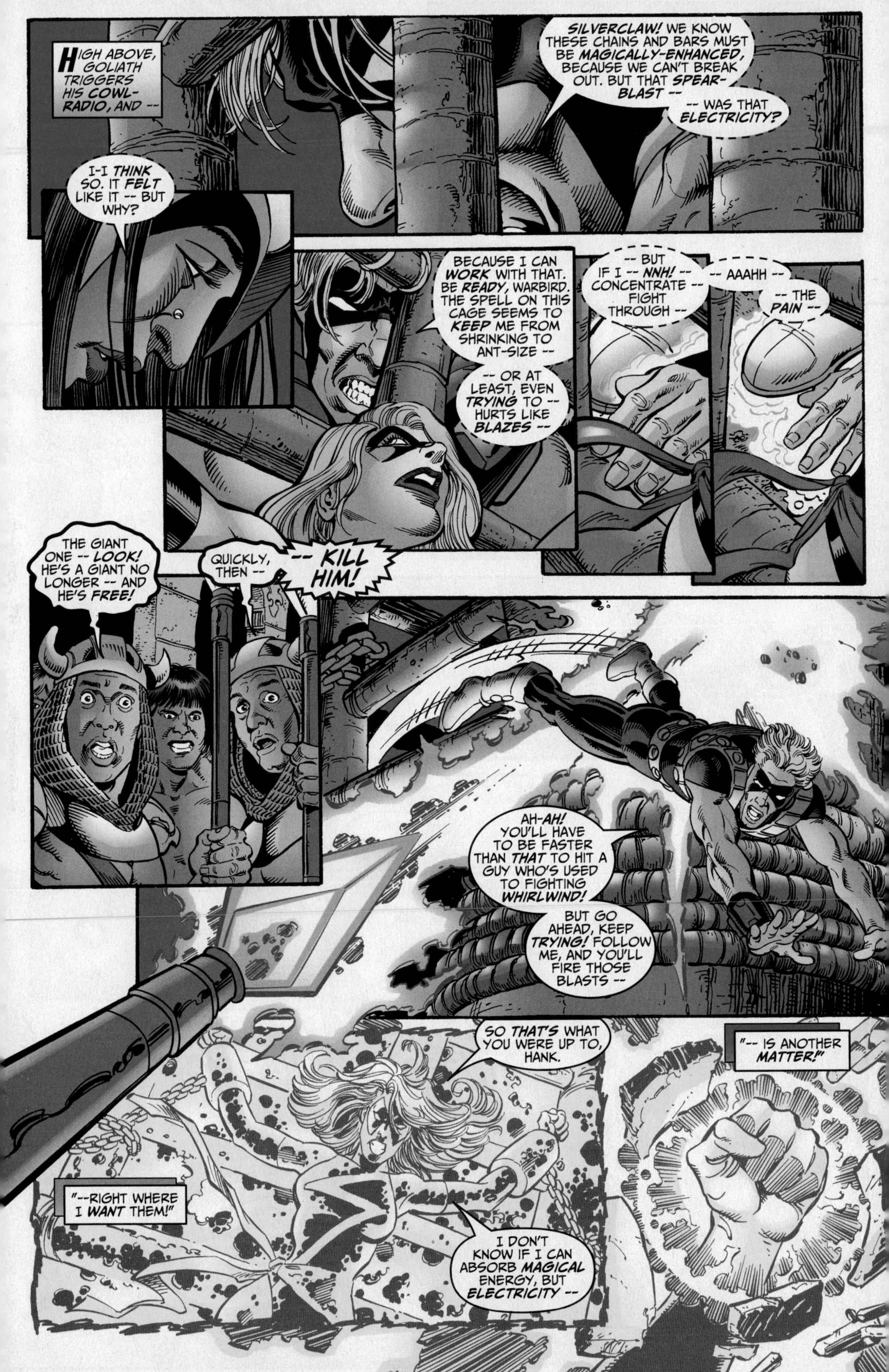
HIGH ABOVE, GOLIATH TRIGGERS HIS COWL-RADIO, AND --
SILVERCLAW! WE KNOW THESE CHAINS AND BARS MUST BE MAGICALLY-ENHANCED, BECAUSE WE CAN'T BREAK OUT. BUT THAT SPEAR-BLAST --
-- WAS THAT ELECTRICITY?
I-I THINK SO. IT FELT LIKE IT -- BUT WHY?
BECAUSE I CAN WORK WITH THAT. BE READY, WARBIRD. THE SPELL ON THIS CAGE SEEMS TO KEEP ME FROM SHRINKING TO ANT-SIZE --
-- OR AT LEAST, EVEN TRYING TO -- HURTS LIKE BLAZES --
-- BUT IF I -- NNH! -- CONCENTRATE -- FIGHT THROUGH --
-- AAAHH --
-- THE PAIN --
THE GIANT ONE -- LOOK! HE'S A GIANT NO LONGER -- AND HE'S FREE!
QUICKLY, THEN --
-- KILL HIM!
AH-AH! YOU'LL HAVE TO BE FASTER THAN THAT TO HIT A GUY WHO'S USED TO FIGHTING WHIRLWIND!
BUT GO AHEAD, KEEP TRYING! FOLLOW ME, AND YOU'LL FIRE THOSE BLASTS --
"--RIGHT WHERE I WANT THEM!"
I DON'T KNOW IF I CAN ABSORB MAGICAL ENERGY, BUT ELECTRICITY --
SO THAT'S WHAT YOU WERE UP TO, HANK.
"-- IS ANOTHER MATTER!"

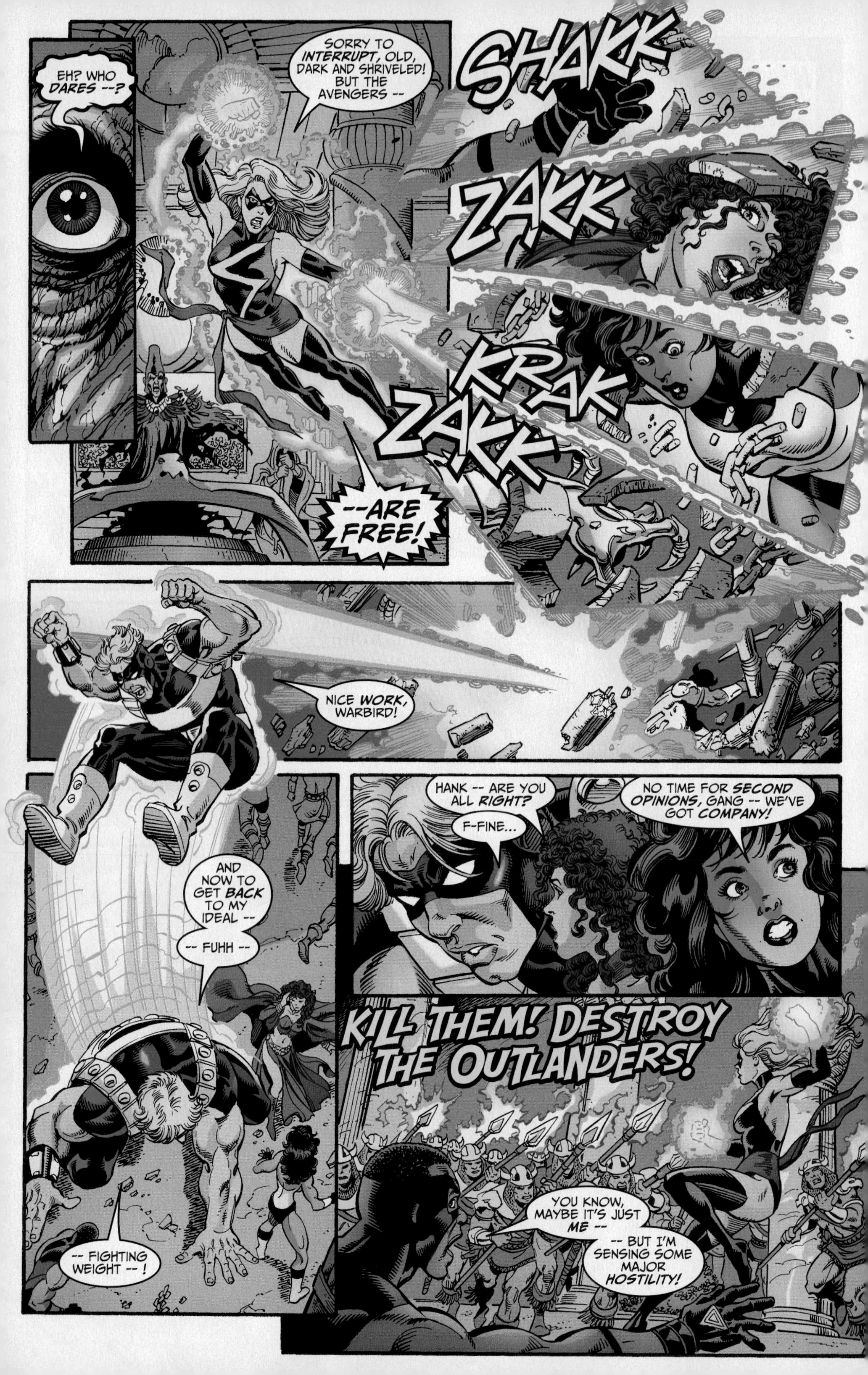
EH? WHO DARES --?
SORRY TO INTERRUPT, OLD, DARK AND SHRIVELED! BUT THE AVENGERS --
SHAKK
ZAKK
KRAK
ZAKK
--ARE FREE!
NICE WORK, WARBIRD!
AND NOW TO GET BACK TO MY IDEAL --
-- FUHH --
-- FIGHTING WEIGHT -- !
HANK -- ARE YOU ALL RIGHT?
F-FINE...
NO TIME FOR SECOND OPINIONS, GANG -- WE'VE GOT COMPANY!
KILL THEM! DESTROY THE OUTLANDERS!
YOU KNOW, MAYBE IT'S JUST ME --
-- BUT I'M SENSING SOME MAJOR HOSTILITY!

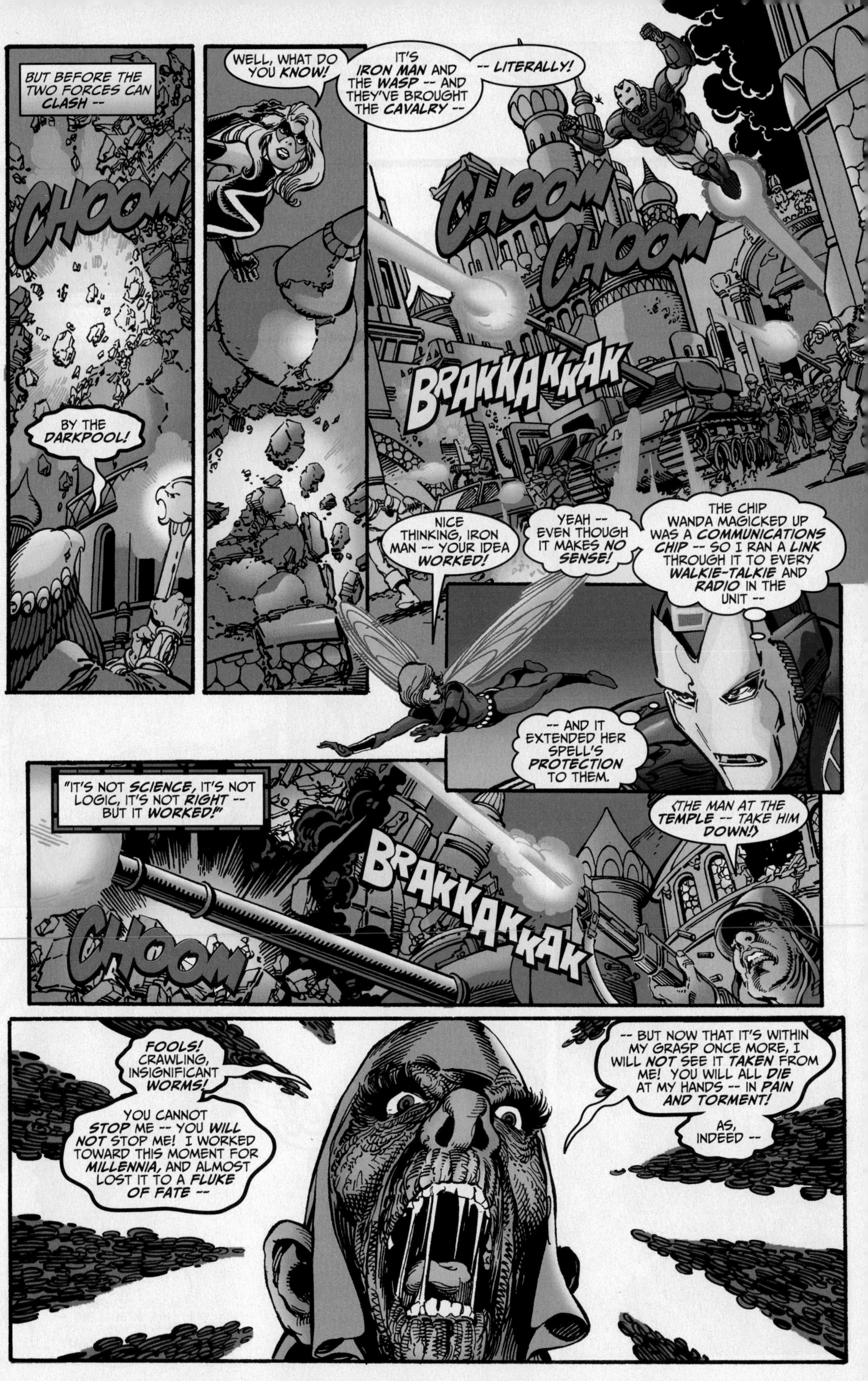
BUT BEFORE THE TWO FORCES CAN CLASH --
CHOOM
BY THE DARKPOOL!
WELL, WHAT DO YOU KNOW!
IT'S IRON MAN AND THE WASP -- AND THEY'VE BROUGHT THE CAVALRY --
-- LITERALLY!
CHOOM
CHOOM
BRAKKAKKAK
NICE THINKING, IRON MAN -- YOUR IDEA WORKED!
YEAH -- EVEN THOUGH IT MAKES NO SENSE!
THE CHIP WANDA MAGICKED UP WAS A COMMUNICATIONS CHIP -- SO I RAN A LINK THROUGH IT TO EVERY WALKIE-TALKIE AND RADIO IN THE UNIT --
-- AND IT EXTENDED HER SPELL'S PROTECTION TO THEM.
"IT'S NOT SCIENCE, IT'S NOT LOGIC, IT'S NOT RIGHT -- BUT IT WORKED!"
‹THE MAN AT THE TEMPLE -- TAKE HIM DOWN!›
BRAKKAKKAK
CHOOM
FOOLS! CRAWLING, INSIGNIFICANT WORMS!
YOU CANNOT STOP ME -- YOU WILL NOT STOP ME! I WORKED TOWARD THIS MOMENT FOR MILLENNIA, AND ALMOST LOST IT TO A FLUKE OF FATE --
-- BUT NOW THAT IT'S WITHIN MY GRASP ONCE MORE, I WILL NOT SEE IT TAKEN FROM ME! YOU WILL ALL DIE AT MY HANDS -- IN PAIN AND TORMENT!
AS, INDEED --

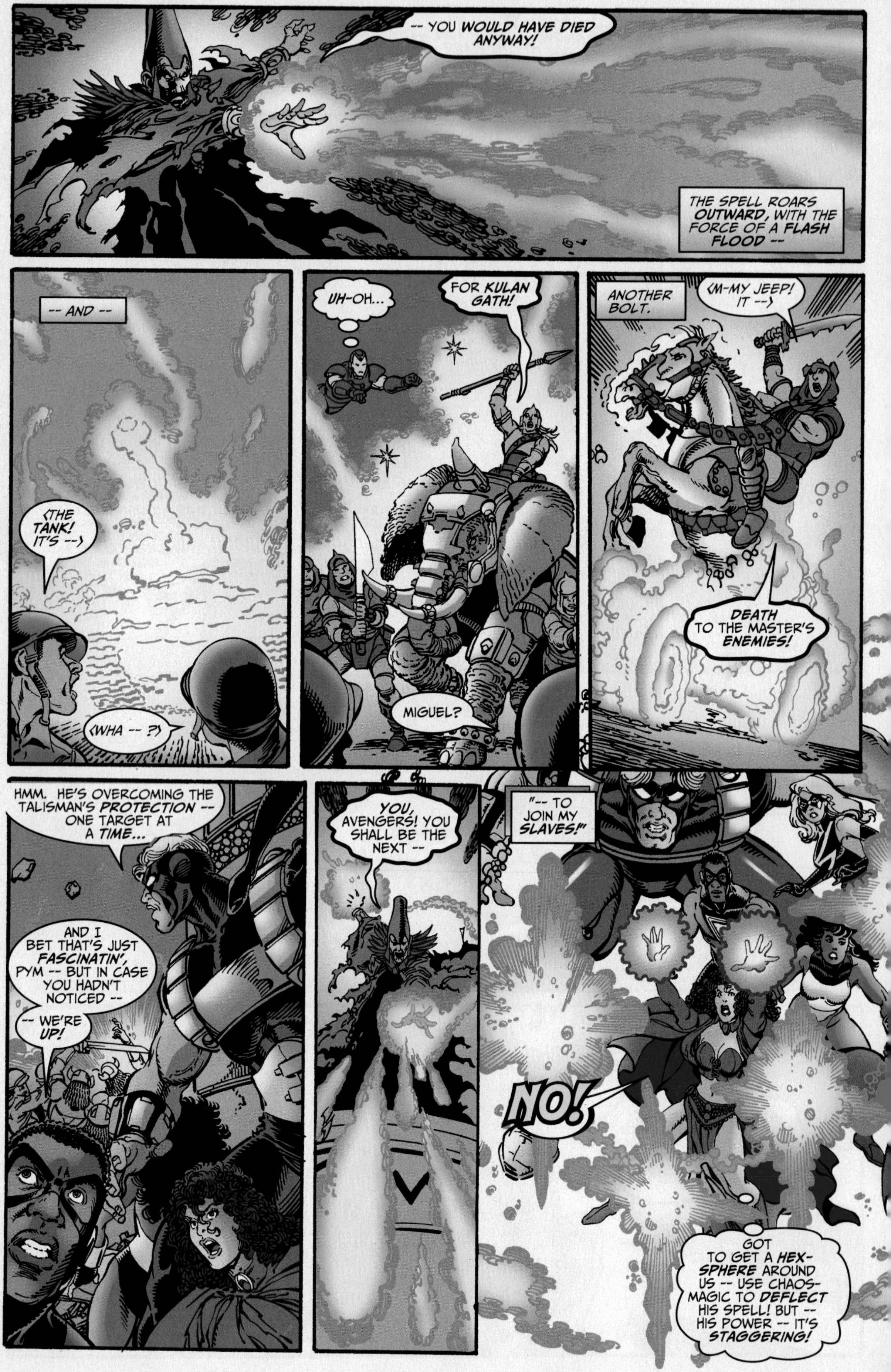
-- YOU WOULD HAVE DIED ANYWAY!
THE SPELL ROARS OUTWARD, WITH THE FORCE OF A FLASH FLOOD --
-- AND --
<THE TANK! IT'S -->
<WHA -- ?>
UH-OH...
FOR KULAN GATH!
MIGUEL?
ANOTHER BOLT.
<M-MY JEEP! IT -->
DEATH TO THE MASTER'S ENEMIES!
HMM. HE'S OVERCOMING THE TALISMAN'S PROTECTION -- ONE TARGET AT A TIME...
AND I BET THAT'S JUST FASCINATIN', PYM -- BUT IN CASE YOU HADN'T NOTICED --
-- WE'RE UP!
YOU, AVENGERS! YOU SHALL BE THE NEXT --
"-- TO JOIN MY SLAVES!"
NO!
GOT TO GET A HEX-SPHERE AROUND US -- USE CHAOS-MAGIC TO DEFLECT HIS SPELL! BUT -- HIS POWER -- IT'S STAGGERING!

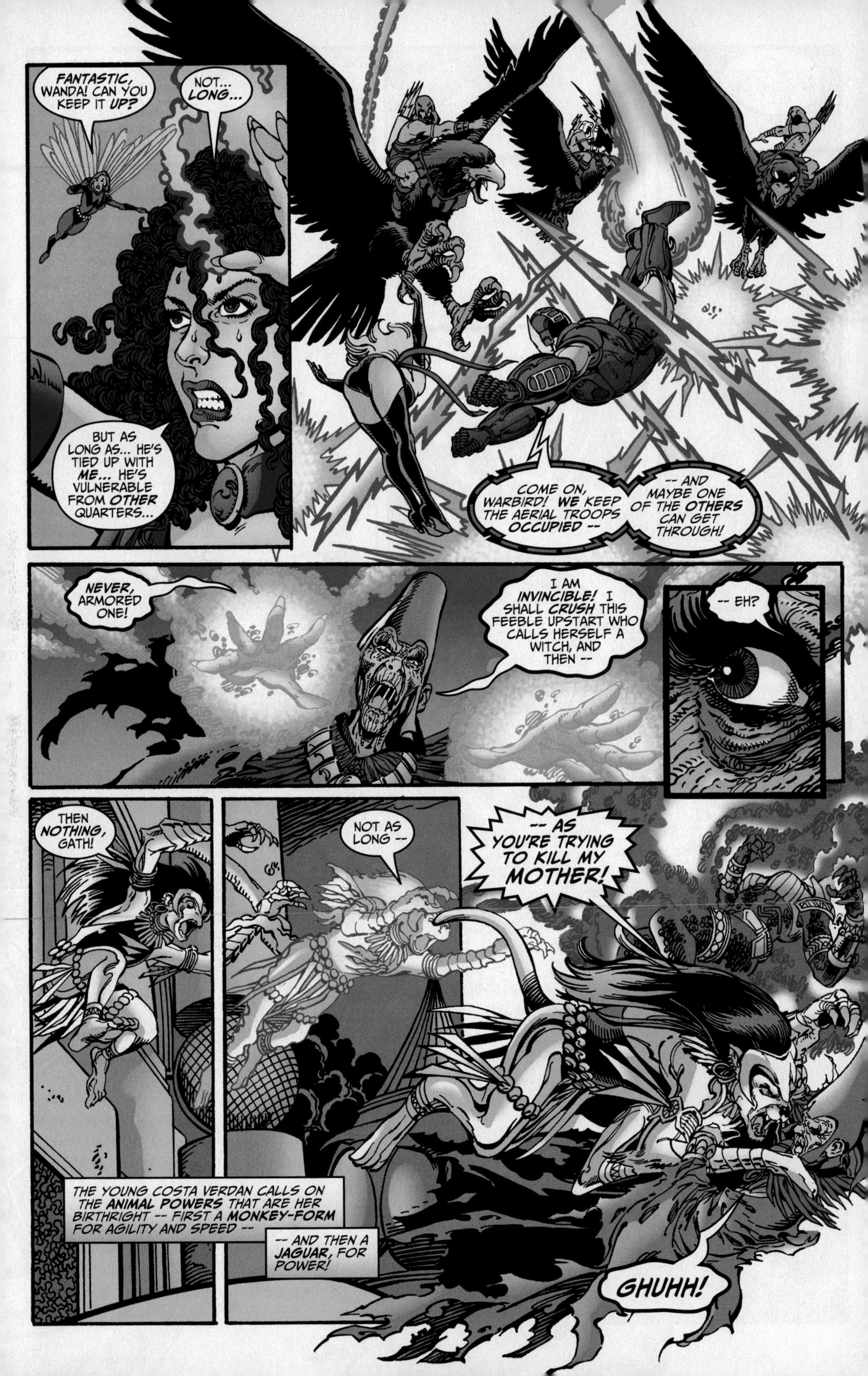
FANTASTIC, WANDA! CAN YOU KEEP IT UP?
NOT... LONG...
BUT AS LONG AS... HE'S TIED UP WITH ME... HE'S VULNERABLE FROM OTHER QUARTERS...
COME ON, WARBIRD! WE KEEP THE AERIAL TROOPS OCCUPIED --
-- AND MAYBE ONE OF THE OTHERS CAN GET THROUGH!
NEVER, ARMORED ONE!
I AM INVINCIBLE! I SHALL CRUSH THIS FEEBLE UPSTART WHO CALLS HERSELF A WITCH, AND THEN --
-- EH?
THEN NOTHING, GATH!
NOT AS LONG --
-- AS YOU'RE TRYING TO KILL MY MOTHER!
THE YOUNG COSTA VERDAN CALLS ON THE ANIMAL POWERS THAT ARE HER BIRTHRIGHT -- FIRST A MONKEY-FORM FOR AGILITY AND SPEED --
-- AND THEN A JAGUAR, FOR POWER!
GHUHH!

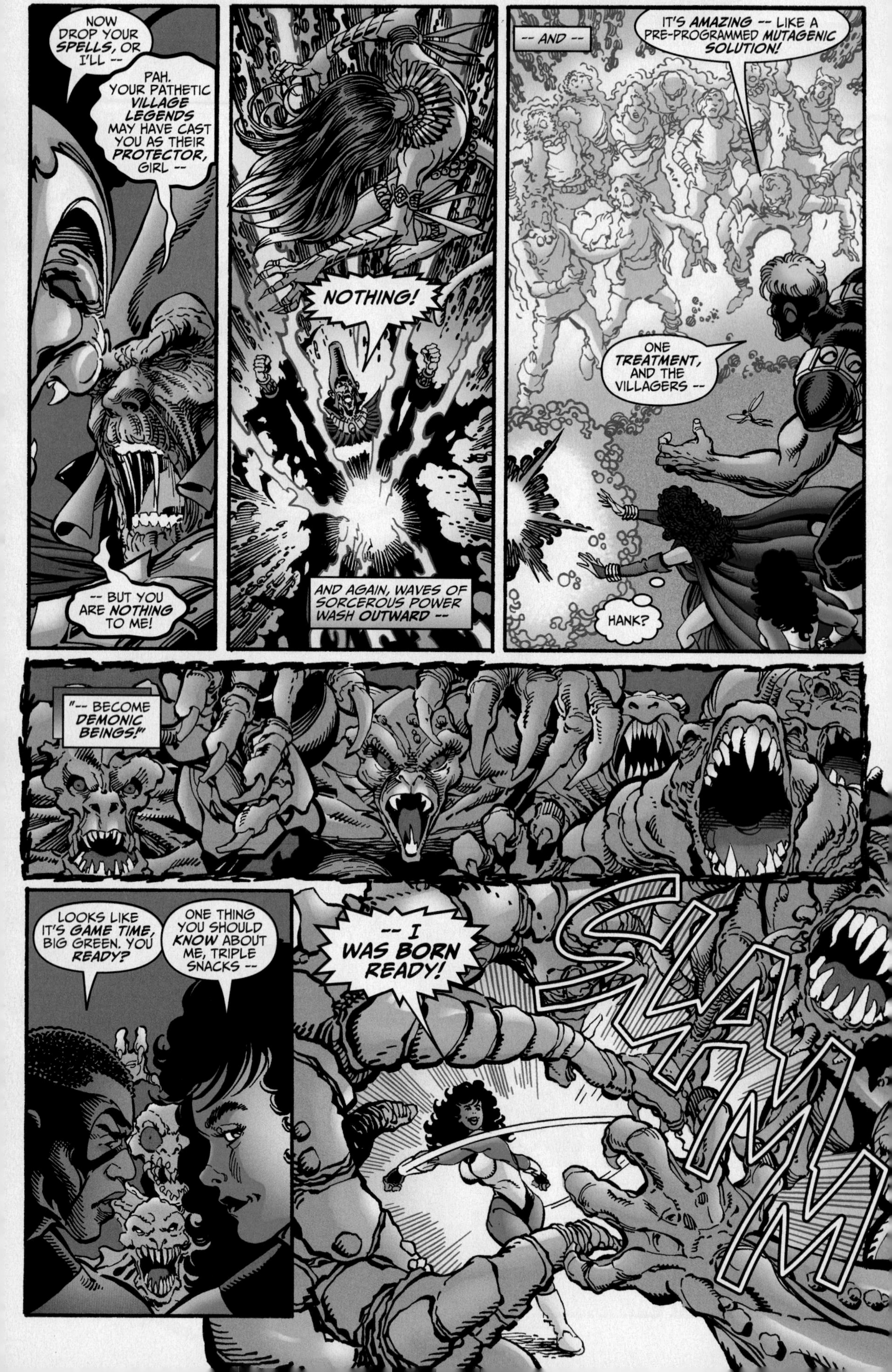
NOW DROP YOUR SPELLS, OR I'LL --
PAH. YOUR PATHETIC VILLAGE LEGENDS MAY HAVE CAST YOU AS THEIR PROTECTOR, GIRL --
-- BUT YOU ARE NOTHING TO ME!
NOTHING!
AND AGAIN, WAVES OF SORCEROUS POWER WASH OUTWARD --
-- AND --
IT'S AMAZING -- LIKE A PRE-PROGRAMMED MUTAGENIC SOLUTION!
ONE TREATMENT, AND THE VILLAGERS --
HANK?
"-- BECOME DEMONIC BEINGS!"
LOOKS LIKE IT'S GAME TIME, BIG GREEN. YOU READY?
ONE THING YOU SHOULD KNOW ABOUT ME, TRIPLE SNACKS --
-- I WAS BORN READY!
SLAMM

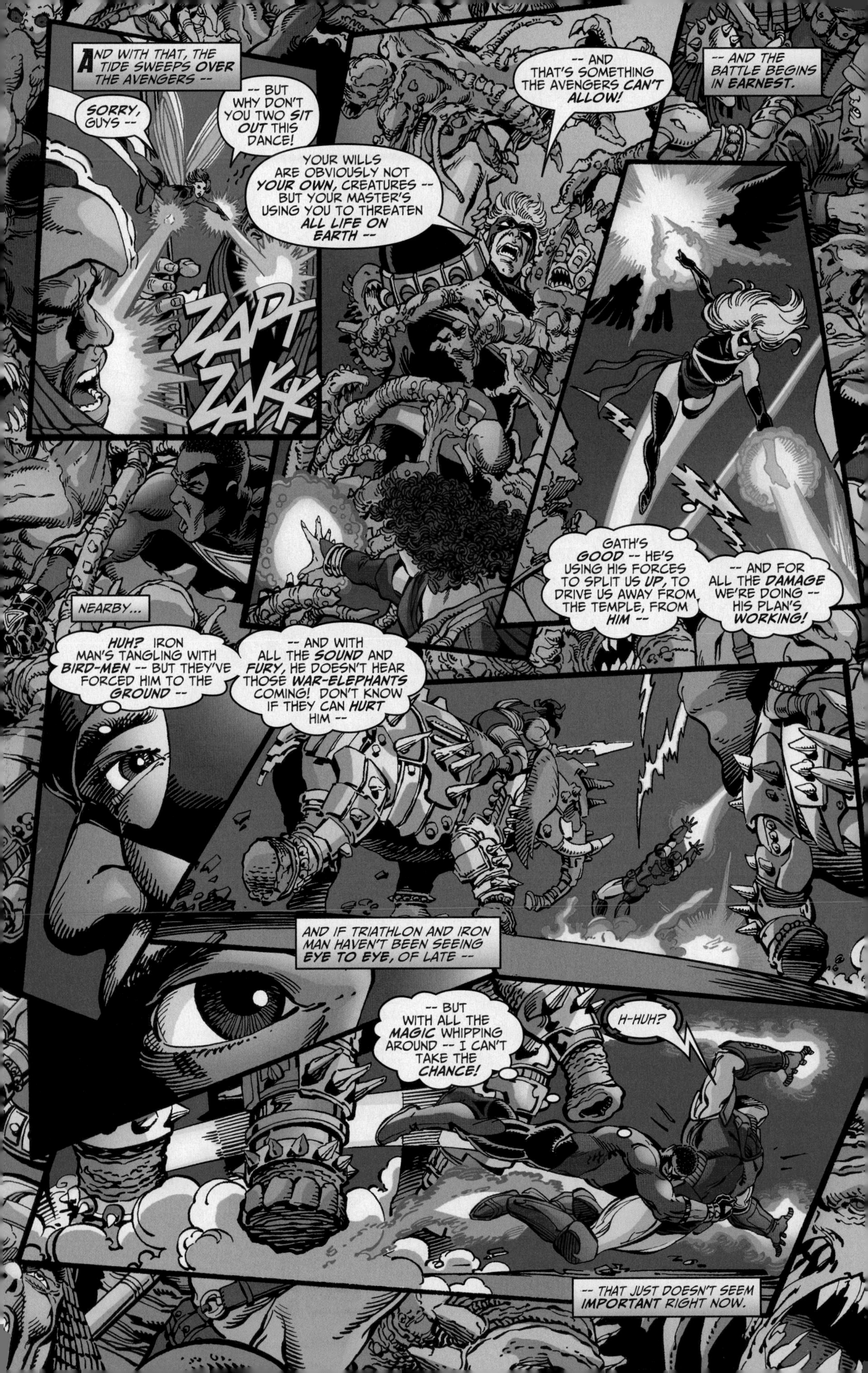
AND WITH THAT, THE TIDE SWEEPS OVER THE AVENGERS --
SORRY, GUYS --
-- BUT WHY DON'T YOU TWO SIT OUT THIS DANCE!
ZAP! ZAKK
YOUR WILLS ARE OBVIOUSLY NOT YOUR OWN, CREATURES -- BUT YOUR MASTER'S USING YOU TO THREATEN ALL LIFE ON EARTH --
-- AND THAT'S SOMETHING THE AVENGERS CAN'T ALLOW!
-- AND THE BATTLE BEGINS IN EARNEST.
GATH'S GOOD -- HE'S USING HIS FORCES TO SPLIT US UP, TO DRIVE US AWAY FROM THE TEMPLE, FROM HIM --
-- AND FOR ALL THE DAMAGE WE'RE DOING -- HIS PLAN'S WORKING!
NEARBY...
HUH? IRON MAN'S TANGLING WITH BIRD-MEN -- BUT THEY'VE FORCED HIM TO THE GROUND --
-- AND WITH ALL THE SOUND AND FURY, HE DOESN'T HEAR THOSE WAR-ELEPHANTS COMING! DON'T KNOW IF THEY CAN HURT HIM --
AND IF TRIATHLON AND IRON MAN HAVEN'T BEEN SEEING EYE TO EYE, OF LATE --
-- BUT WITH ALL THE MAGIC WHIPPING AROUND -- I CAN'T TAKE THE CHANCE!
H-HUH?
-- THAT JUST DOESN'T SEEM IMPORTANT RIGHT NOW.

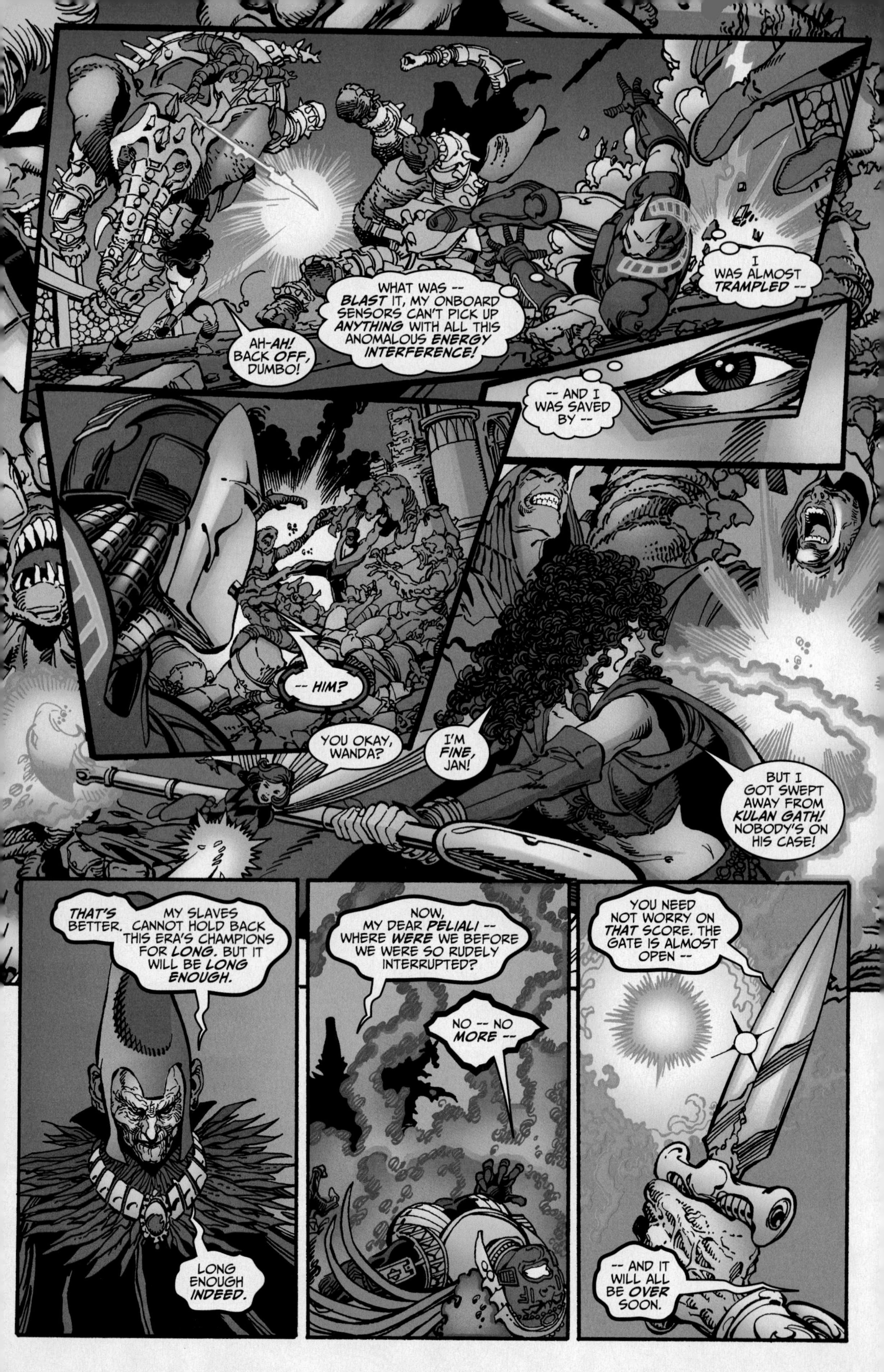

AH-AH! BACK OFF, DUMBO!
WHAT WAS -- BLAST IT, MY ONBOARD SENSORS CAN'T PICK UP ANYTHING WITH ALL THIS ANOMALOUS ENERGY INTERFERENCE!
I WAS ALMOST TRAMPLED --
-- AND I WAS SAVED BY --
-- HIM?
YOU OKAY, WANDA?
I'M FINE, JAN!
BUT I GOT SWEPT AWAY FROM KULAN GATH! NOBODY'S ON HIS CASE!
THAT'S BETTER.
MY SLAVES CANNOT HOLD BACK THIS ERA'S CHAMPIONS FOR LONG. BUT IT WILL BE LONG ENOUGH.
LONG ENOUGH INDEED.
NOW, MY DEAR PELIALI -- WHERE WERE WE BEFORE WE WERE SO RUDELY INTERRUPTED?
NO -- NO MORE --
YOU NEED NOT WORRY ON THAT SCORE. THE GATE IS ALMOST OPEN --
-- AND IT WILL ALL BE OVER SOON.

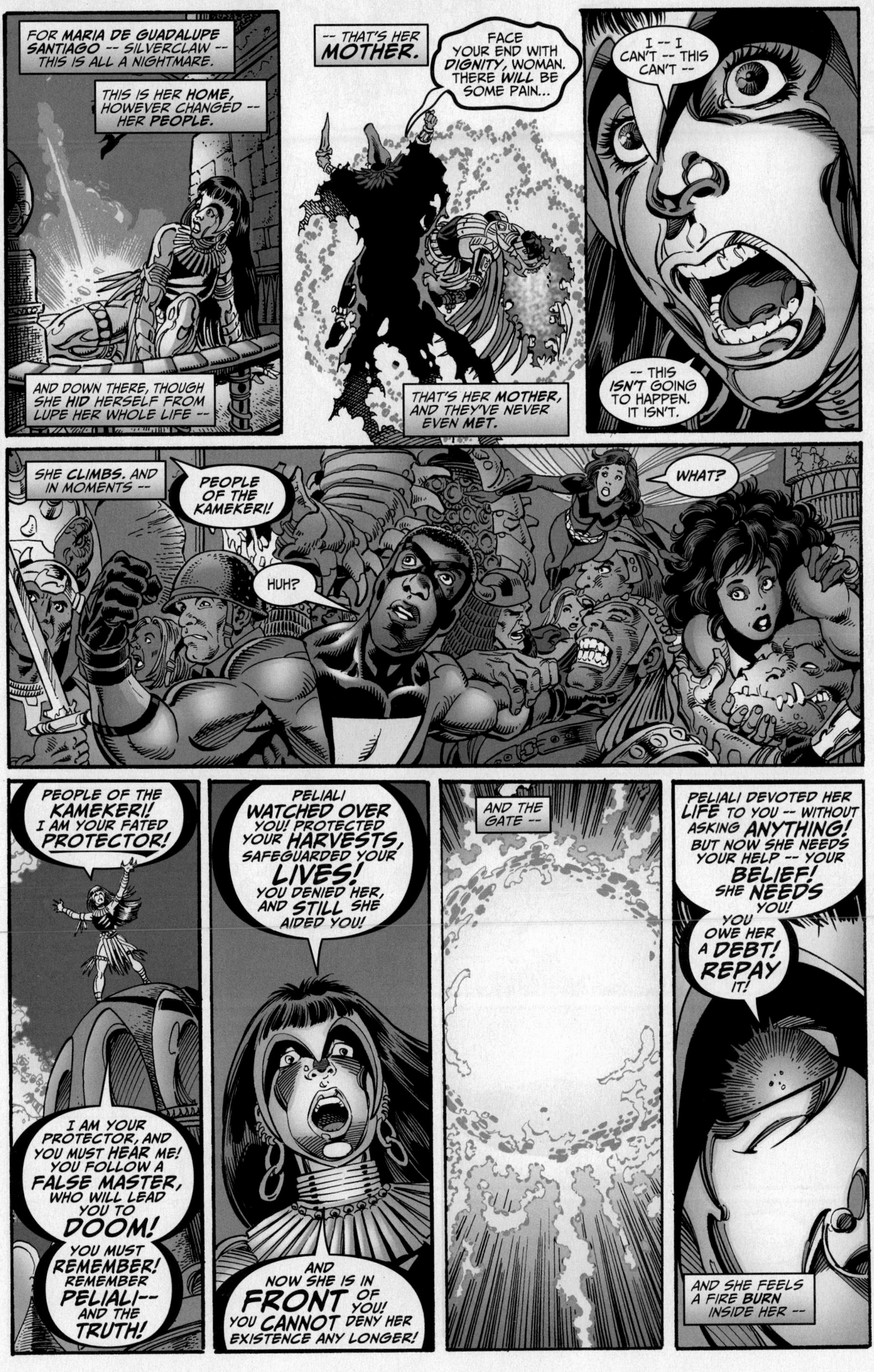
FOR MARIA DE GUADALUPE SANTIAGO -- SILVERCLAW -- THIS IS ALL A NIGHTMARE.
THIS IS HER HOME, HOWEVER CHANGED -- HER PEOPLE.
AND DOWN THERE, THOUGH SHE HID HERSELF FROM LUPE HER WHOLE LIFE --
-- THAT'S HER MOTHER.
FACE YOUR END WITH DIGNITY, WOMAN. THERE WILL BE SOME PAIN...
THAT'S HER MOTHER, AND THEY'VE NEVER EVEN MET.
I -- I CAN'T -- THIS CAN'T --
-- THIS ISN'T GOING TO HAPPEN. IT ISN'T.
SHE CLIMBS. AND IN MOMENTS --
PEOPLE OF THE KAMEKERI!
HUH?
WHAT?
PEOPLE OF THE KAMEKERI! I AM YOUR FATED PROTECTOR!
I AM YOUR PROTECTOR, AND YOU MUST HEAR ME! YOU FOLLOW A FALSE MASTER, WHO WILL LEAD YOU TO DOOM!
YOU MUST REMEMBER! REMEMBER PELIALI-- AND THE TRUTH!
PELIALI WATCHED OVER YOU! PROTECTED YOUR HARVESTS, SAFEGUARDED YOUR LIVES! YOU DENIED HER, AND STILL SHE AIDED YOU!
AND NOW SHE IS IN FRONT OF YOU! YOU CANNOT DENY HER EXISTENCE ANY LONGER!
AND THE GATE --
PELIALI DEVOTED HER LIFE TO YOU -- WITHOUT ASKING ANYTHING! BUT NOW SHE NEEDS YOUR HELP -- YOUR BELIEF! SHE NEEDS YOU!
YOU OWE HER A DEBT! REPAY IT!
AND SHE FEELS A FIRE BURN INSIDE HER --

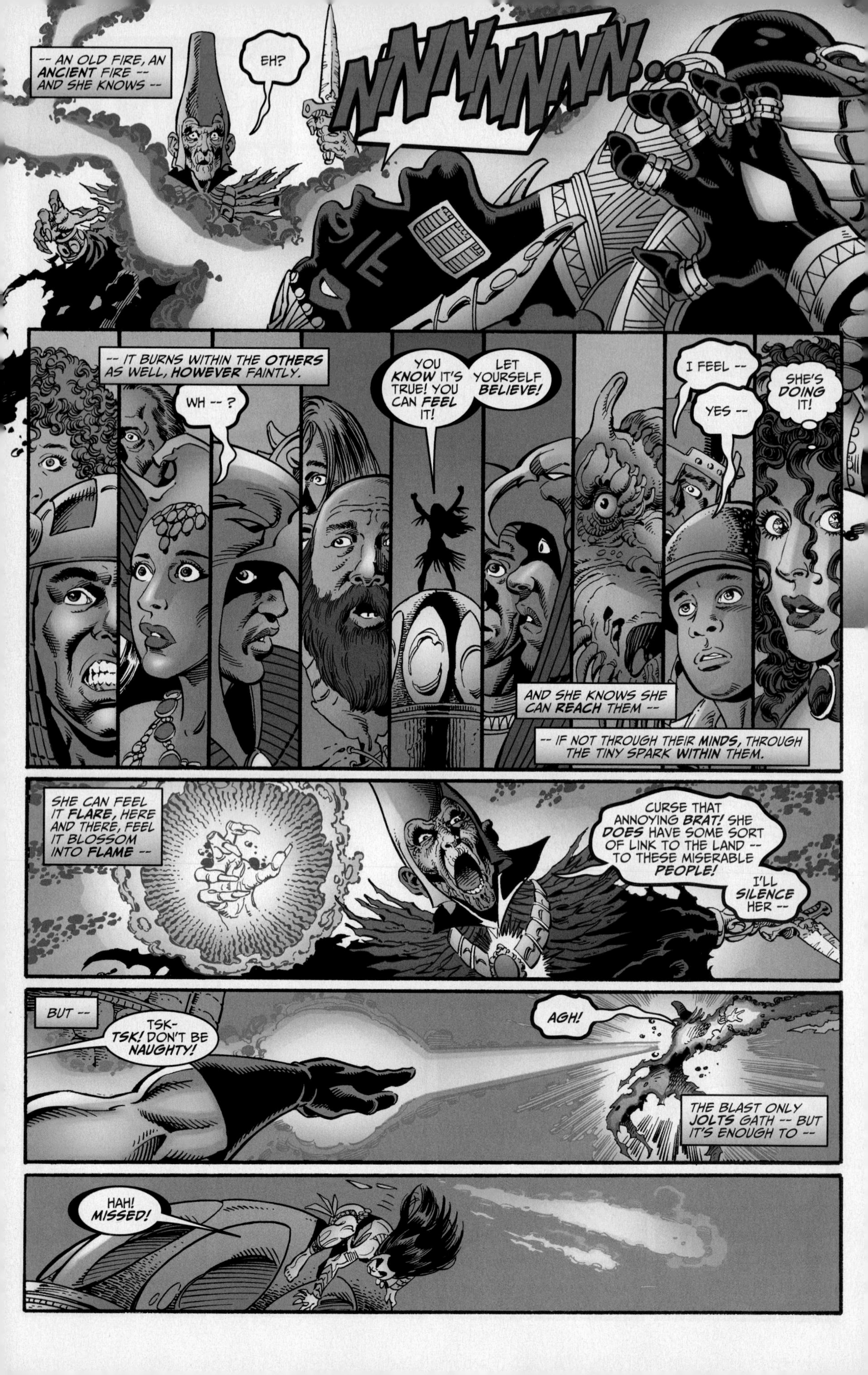
-- AN OLD FIRE, AN ANCIENT FIRE -- AND SHE KNOWS --
EH?
NNNNNNNN...
-- IT BURNS WITHIN THE OTHERS AS WELL, HOWEVER FAINTLY.
WH -- ?
YOU KNOW IT'S TRUE! YOU CAN FEEL IT!
LET YOURSELF BELIEVE!
I FEEL --
YES --
SHE'S DOING IT!
AND SHE KNOWS SHE CAN REACH THEM --
-- IF NOT THROUGH THEIR MINDS, THROUGH THE TINY SPARK WITHIN THEM.
SHE CAN FEEL IT FLARE, HERE AND THERE, FEEL IT BLOSSOM INTO FLAME --
CURSE THAT ANNOYING BRAT! SHE DOES HAVE SOME SORT OF LINK TO THE LAND -- TO THESE MISERABLE PEOPLE!
I'LL SILENCE HER --
BUT --
TSK-TSK! DON'T BE NAUGHTY!
AGH!
THE BLAST ONLY JOLTS GATH -- BUT IT'S ENOUGH TO --
HAH! MISSED!

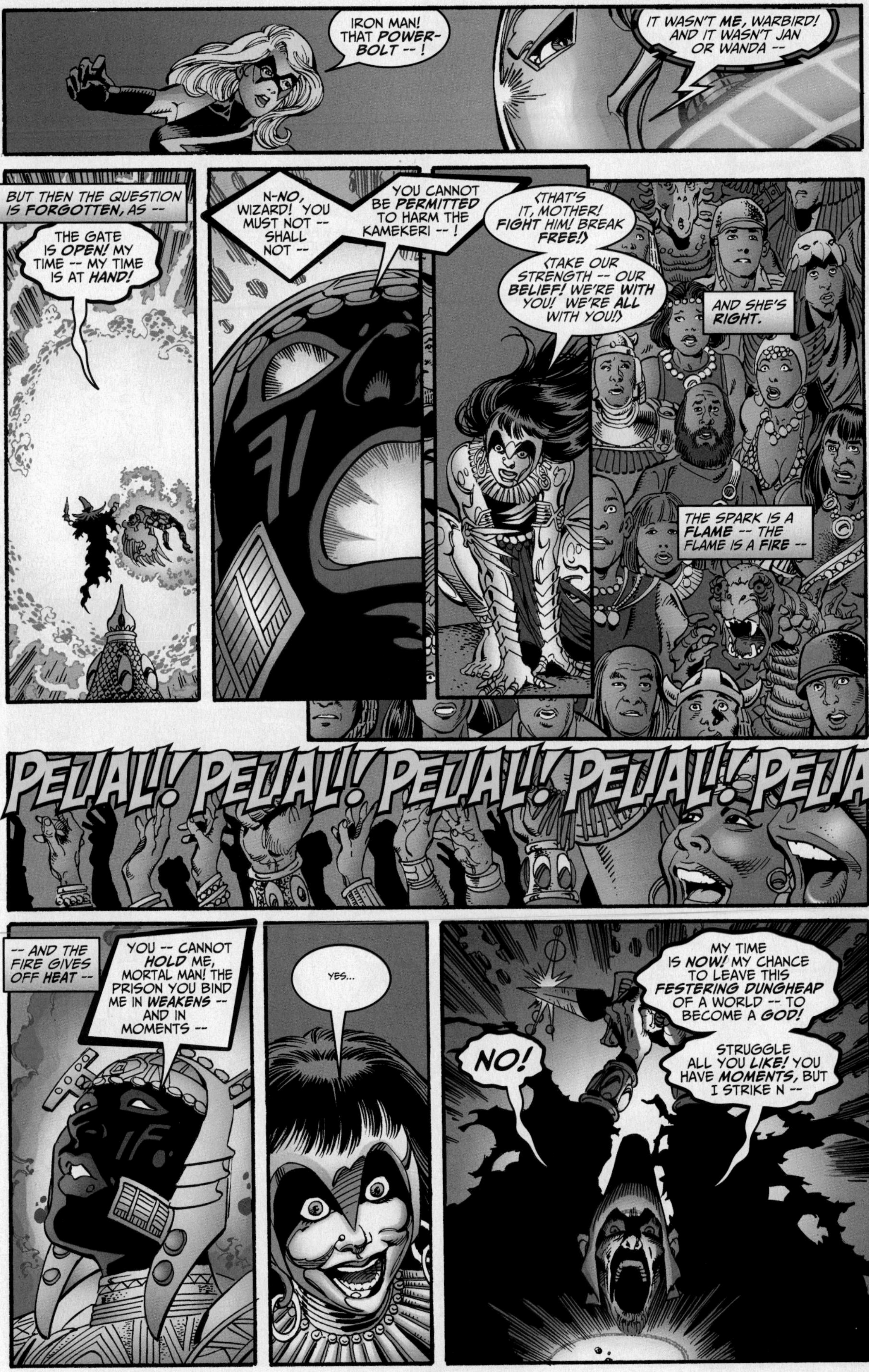
IRON MAN! THAT POWER-BOLT -- !
IT WASN'T ME, WARBIRD! AND IT WASN'T JAN OR WANDA --
BUT THEN THE QUESTION IS FORGOTTEN, AS --
THE GATE IS OPEN! MY TIME -- MY TIME IS AT HAND!
N-NO, WIZARD! YOU MUST NOT -- SHALL NOT --
YOU CANNOT BE PERMITTED TO HARM THE KAMEKERI -- !
<THAT'S IT, MOTHER! FIGHT HIM! BREAK FREE!>
<TAKE OUR STRENGTH -- OUR BELIEF! WE'RE WITH YOU! WE'RE ALL WITH YOU!>
AND SHE'S RIGHT.
THE SPARK IS A FLAME -- THE FLAME IS A FIRE --
PEJAL! PEJAL! PEJAL! PEJAL! PEJAL
-- AND THE FIRE GIVES OFF HEAT --
YOU -- CANNOT HOLD ME, MORTAL MAN! THE PRISON YOU BIND ME IN WEAKENS -- AND IN MOMENTS --
YES...
MY TIME IS NOW! MY CHANCE TO LEAVE THIS FESTERING DUNGHEAP OF A WORLD -- TO BECOME A GOD!
NO!
STRUGGLE ALL YOU LIKE! YOU HAVE MOMENTS, BUT I STRIKE N --

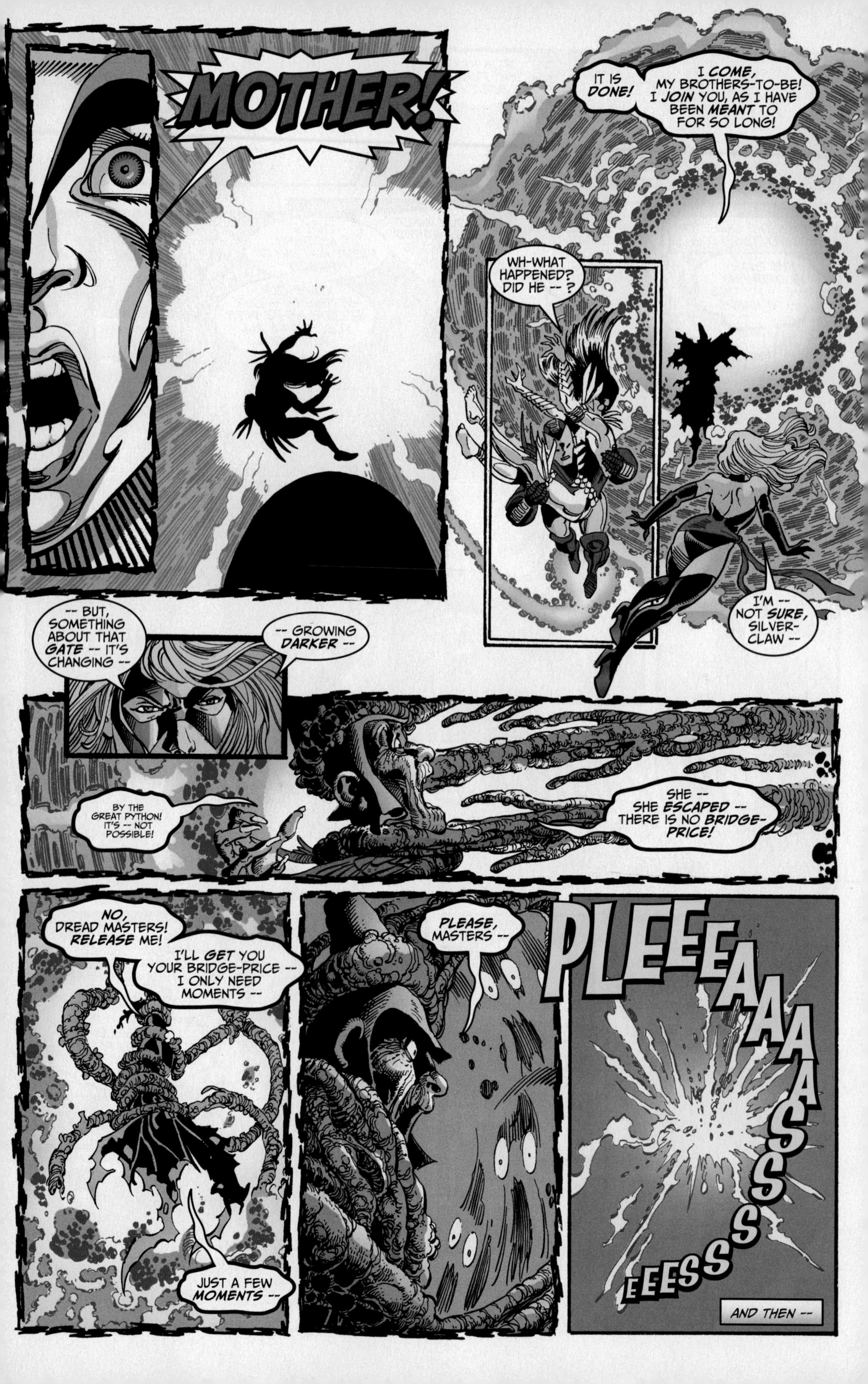
MOTHER!
IT IS DONE!
I COME, MY BROTHERS-TO-BE! I JOIN YOU, AS I HAVE BEEN MEANT TO FOR SO LONG!
WH-WHAT HAPPENED? DID HE -- ?
I'M -- NOT SURE, SILVER-CLAW --
-- BUT, SOMETHING ABOUT THAT GATE -- IT'S CHANGING --
-- GROWING DARKER --
BY THE GREAT PYTHON! IT'S -- NOT POSSIBLE!
SHE -- SHE ESCAPED -- THERE IS NO BRIDGE-PRICE!
NO, DREAD MASTERS! RELEASE ME!
I'LL GET YOU YOUR BRIDGE-PRICE -- I ONLY NEED MOMENTS --
JUST A FEW MOMENTS --
PLEASE, MASTERS --
PLEEEAAAAASSSSEEES
AND THEN --

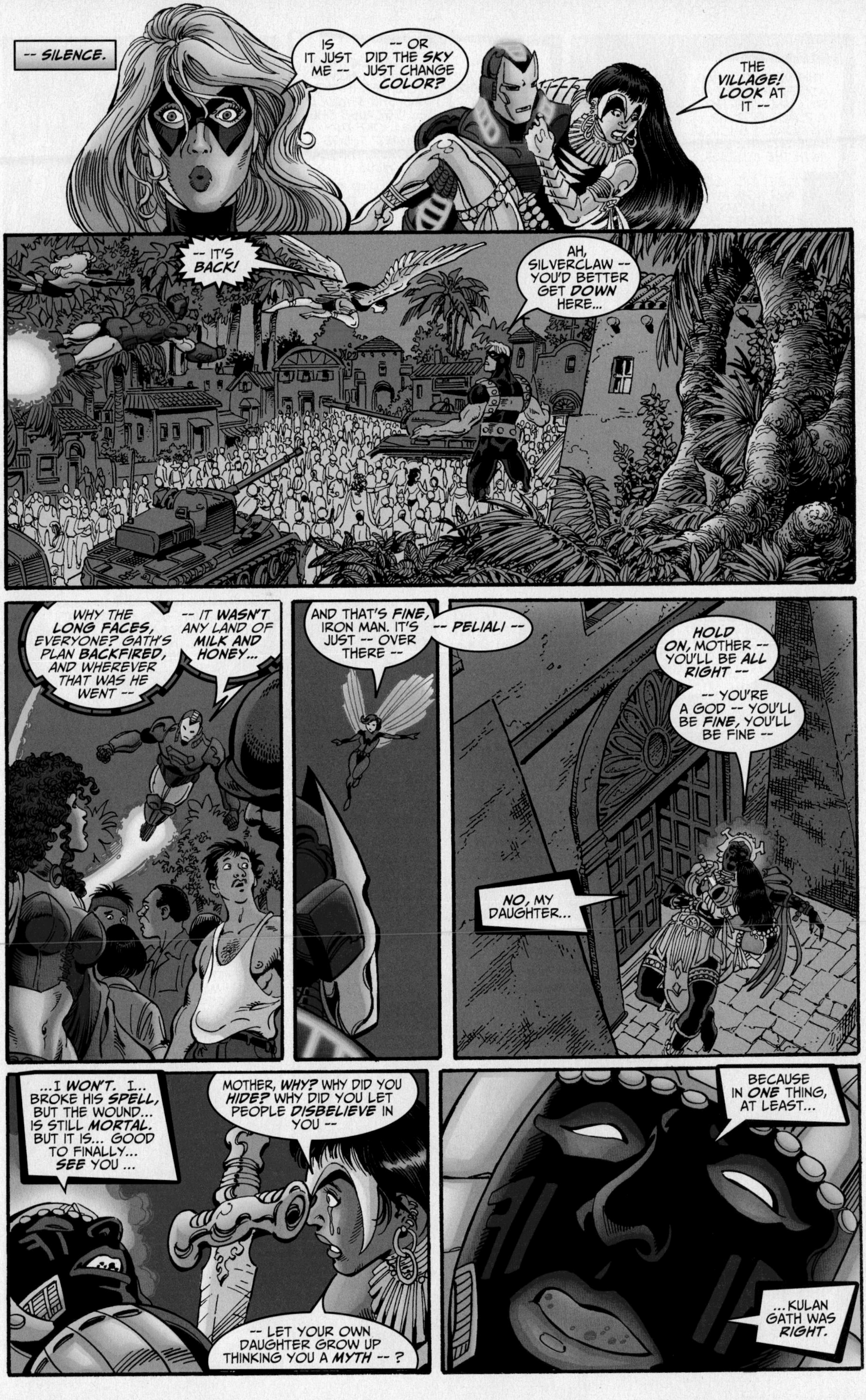
-- SILENCE.
IS IT JUST ME --
-- OR DID THE SKY JUST CHANGE COLOR?
THE VILLAGE! LOOK AT IT --
-- IT'S BACK!
AH, SILVERCLAW -- YOU'D BETTER GET DOWN HERE...
WHY THE LONG FACES, EVERYONE? GATH'S PLAN BACKFIRED, AND WHEREVER THAT WAS HE WENT --
-- IT WASN'T ANY LAND OF MILK AND HONEY...
AND THAT'S FINE, IRON MAN. IT'S JUST -- OVER THERE --
-- PELIALI --
HOLD ON, MOTHER -- YOU'LL BE ALL RIGHT --
-- YOU'RE A GOD -- YOU'LL BE FINE, YOU'LL BE FINE --
NO, MY DAUGHTER...
...I WON'T. I... BROKE HIS SPELL, BUT THE WOUND... IS STILL MORTAL. BUT IT IS... GOOD TO FINALLY... SEE YOU ...
MOTHER, WHY? WHY DID YOU HIDE? WHY DID YOU LET PEOPLE DISBELIEVE IN YOU --
-- LET YOUR OWN DAUGHTER GROW UP THINKING YOU A MYTH -- ?
BECAUSE IN ONE THING, AT LEAST...
...KULAN GATH WAS RIGHT.

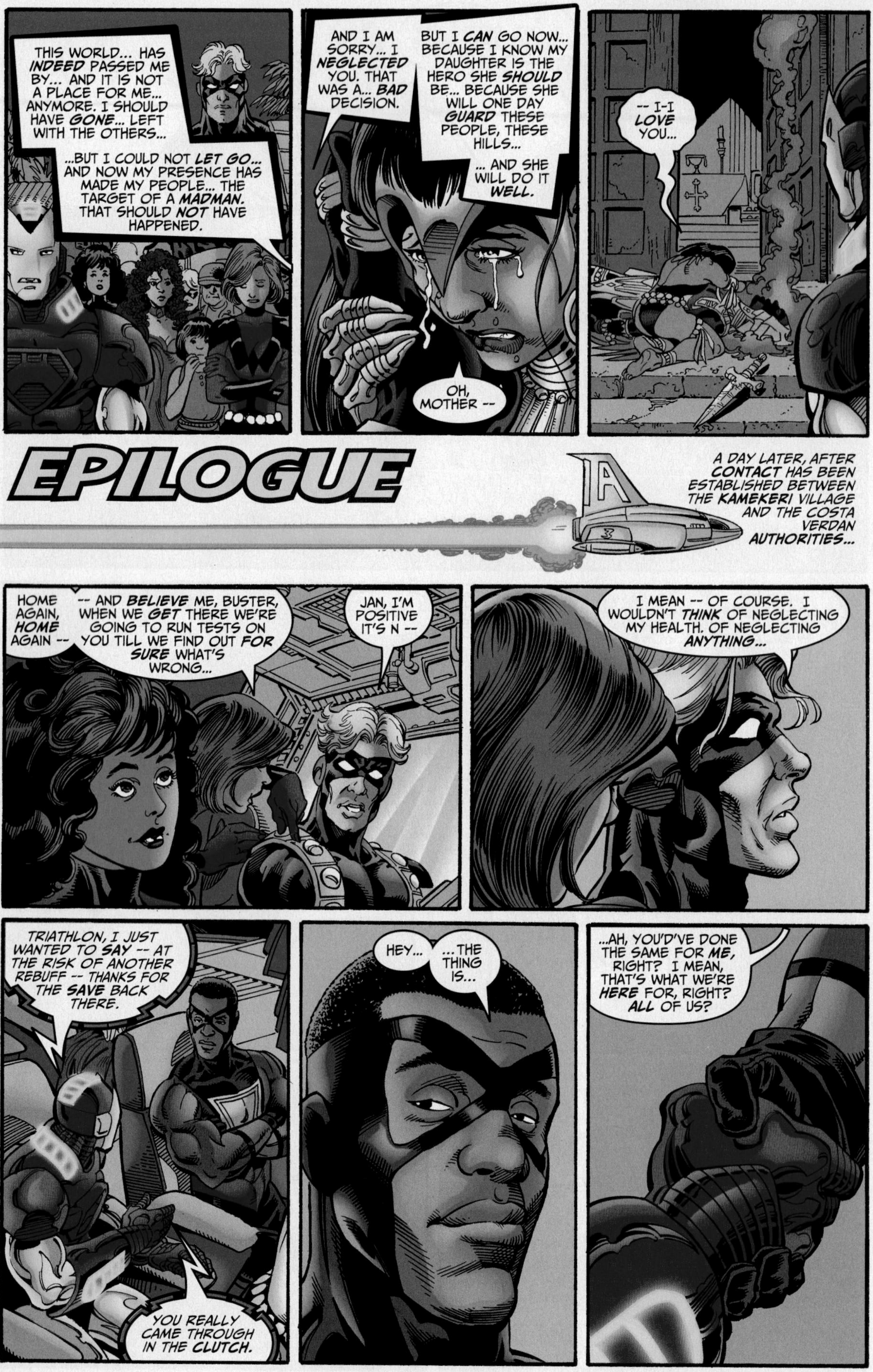
THIS WORLD... HAS INDEED PASSED ME BY... AND IT IS NOT A PLACE FOR ME... ANYMORE. I SHOULD HAVE GONE... LEFT WITH THE OTHERS...
...BUT I COULD NOT LET GO... AND NOW MY PRESENCE HAS MADE MY PEOPLE... THE TARGET OF A MADMAN. THAT SHOULD NOT HAVE HAPPENED.
AND I AM SORRY... I NEGLECTED YOU. THAT WAS A... BAD DECISION.
BUT I CAN GO NOW... BECAUSE I KNOW MY DAUGHTER IS THE HERO SHE SHOULD BE... BECAUSE SHE WILL ONE DAY GUARD THESE PEOPLE, THESE HILLS...
... AND SHE WILL DO IT WELL.
OH, MOTHER --
-- I-I LOVE YOU...
EPILOGUE
A DAY LATER, AFTER CONTACT HAS BEEN ESTABLISHED BETWEEN THE KAMEKERI VILLAGE AND THE COSTA VERDAN AUTHORITIES...
HOME AGAIN, HOME AGAIN --
-- AND BELIEVE ME, BUSTER, WHEN WE GET THERE WE'RE GOING TO RUN TESTS ON YOU TILL WE FIND OUT FOR SURE WHAT'S WRONG...
JAN, I'M POSITIVE IT'S N --
I MEAN -- OF COURSE. I WOULDN'T THINK OF NEGLECTING MY HEALTH. OF NEGLECTING ANYTHING...
TRIATHLON, I JUST WANTED TO SAY -- AT THE RISK OF ANOTHER REBUFF -- THANKS FOR THE SAVE BACK THERE.
YOU REALLY CAME THROUGH IN THE CLUTCH.
HEY...
...THE THING IS...
...AH, YOU'D'VE DONE THE SAME FOR ME, RIGHT? I MEAN, THAT'S WHAT WE'RE HERE FOR, RIGHT? ALL OF US?

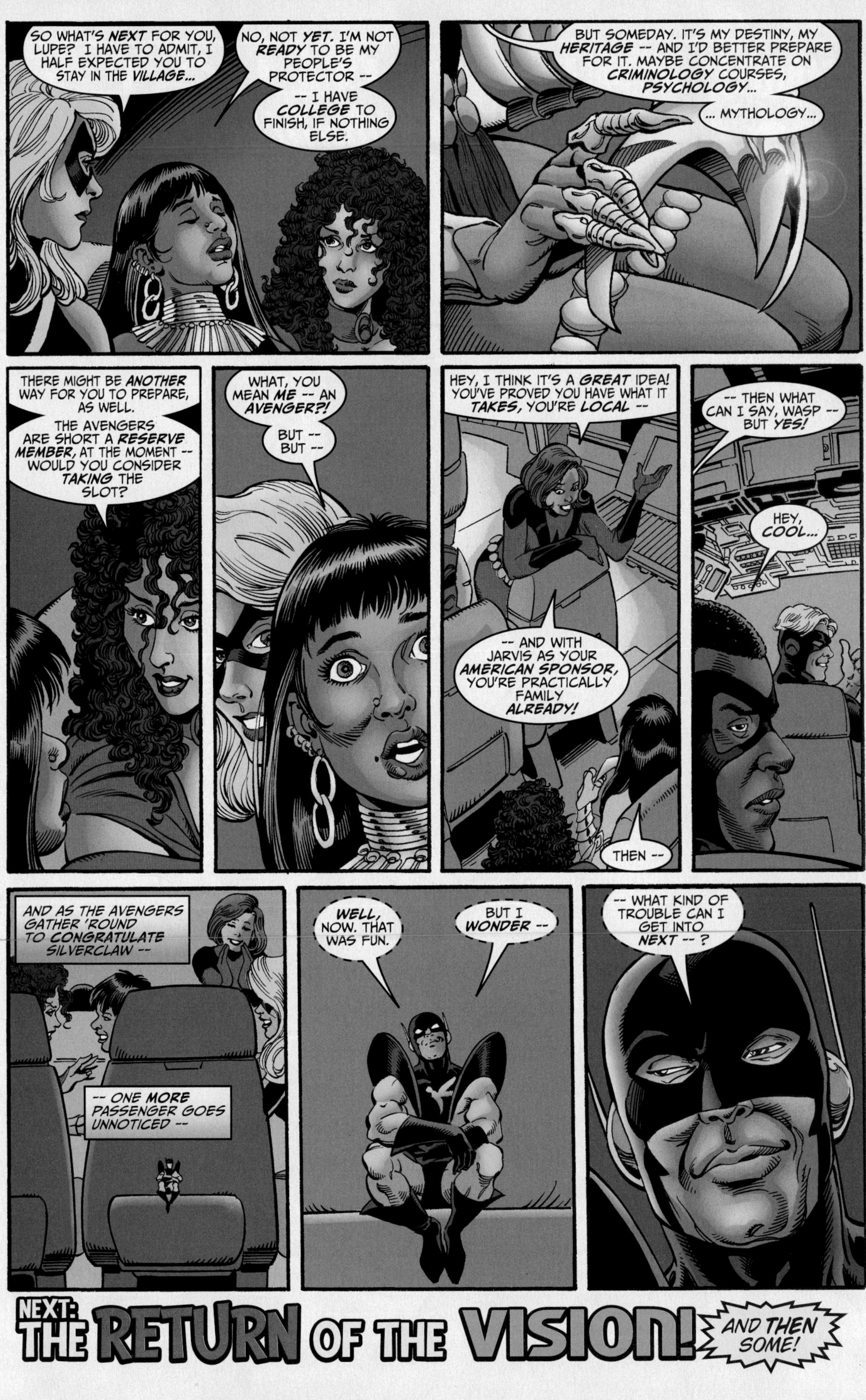
SO WHAT'S NEXT FOR YOU, LUPE? I HAVE TO ADMIT, I HALF EXPECTED YOU TO STAY IN THE VILLAGE...
NO, NOT YET. I'M NOT READY TO BE MY PEOPLE'S PROTECTOR --
-- I HAVE COLLEGE TO FINISH, IF NOTHING ELSE.
BUT SOMEDAY. IT'S MY DESTINY, MY HERITAGE -- AND I'D BETTER PREPARE FOR IT. MAYBE CONCENTRATE ON CRIMINOLOGY COURSES, PSYCHOLOGY...
... MYTHOLOGY...
THERE MIGHT BE ANOTHER WAY FOR YOU TO PREPARE, AS WELL.
THE AVENGERS ARE SHORT A RESERVE MEMBER, AT THE MOMENT -- WOULD YOU CONSIDER TAKING THE SLOT?
WHAT, YOU MEAN ME -- AN AVENGER?!
BUT -- BUT --
HEY, I THINK IT'S A GREAT IDEA! YOU'VE PROVED YOU HAVE WHAT IT TAKES, YOU'RE LOCAL --
-- AND WITH JARVIS AS YOUR AMERICAN SPONSOR, YOU'RE PRACTICALLY FAMILY ALREADY!
THEN --
-- THEN WHAT CAN I SAY, WASP -- BUT YES!
HEY, COOL...
AND AS THE AVENGERS GATHER 'ROUND TO CONGRATULATE SILVERCLAW --
-- ONE MORE PASSENGER GOES UNNOTICED --
WELL, NOW. THAT WAS FUN.
BUT I WONDER --
-- WHAT KIND OF TROUBLE CAN I GET INTO NEXT -- ?
NEXT: THE RETURN OF THE VISION!
AND THEN SOME!

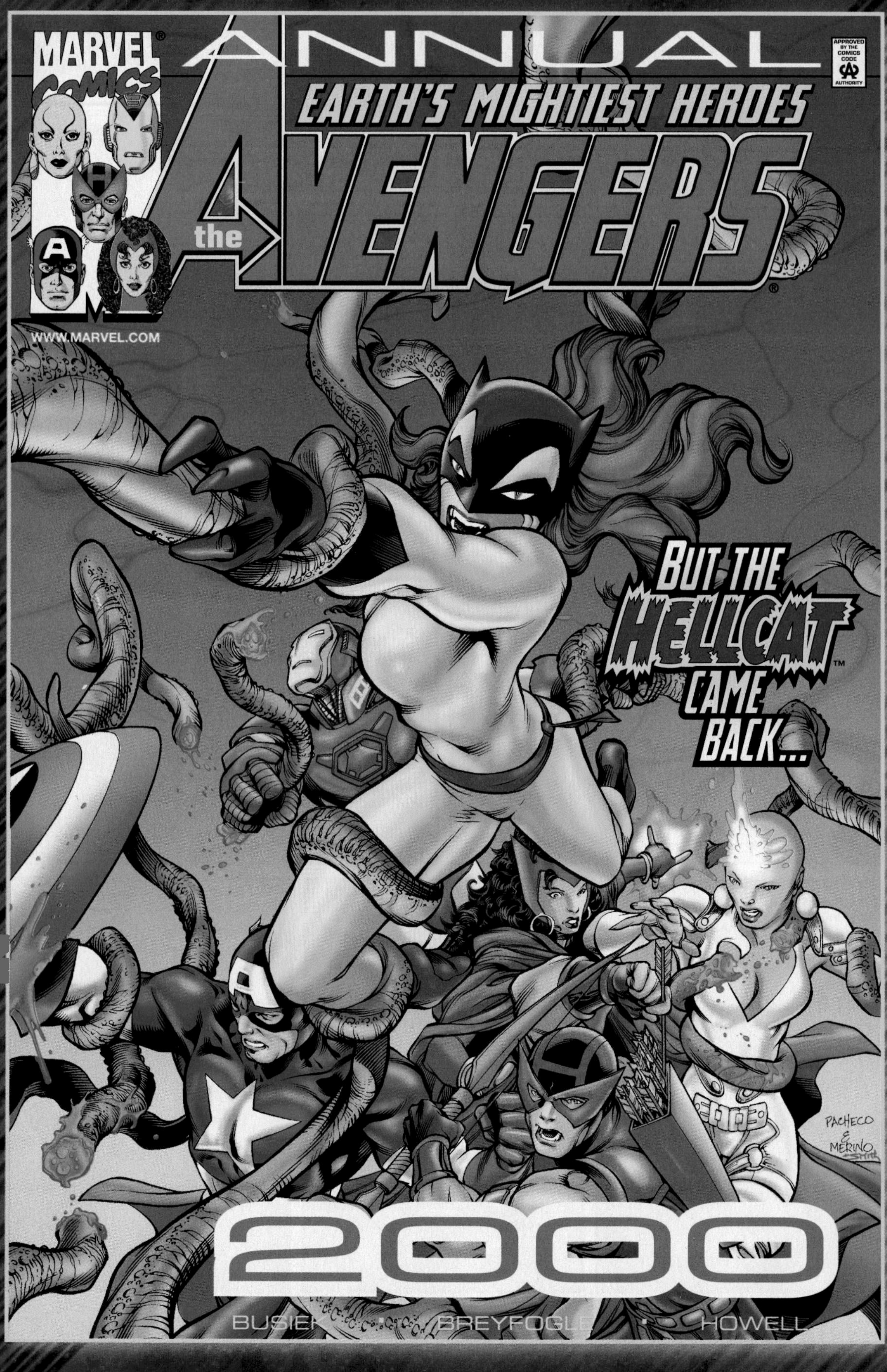
MARVEL COMICS
ANNUAL
APPROVED BY THE COMICS CODE AUTHORITY
EARTH'S MIGHTIEST HEROES
the AVENGERS
WWW.MARVEL.COM
BUT THE HELLCAT™ CAME BACK...
PACHECO & MERINO SMITH
2000
BUSIEK • BREYFOGLE • HOWELL

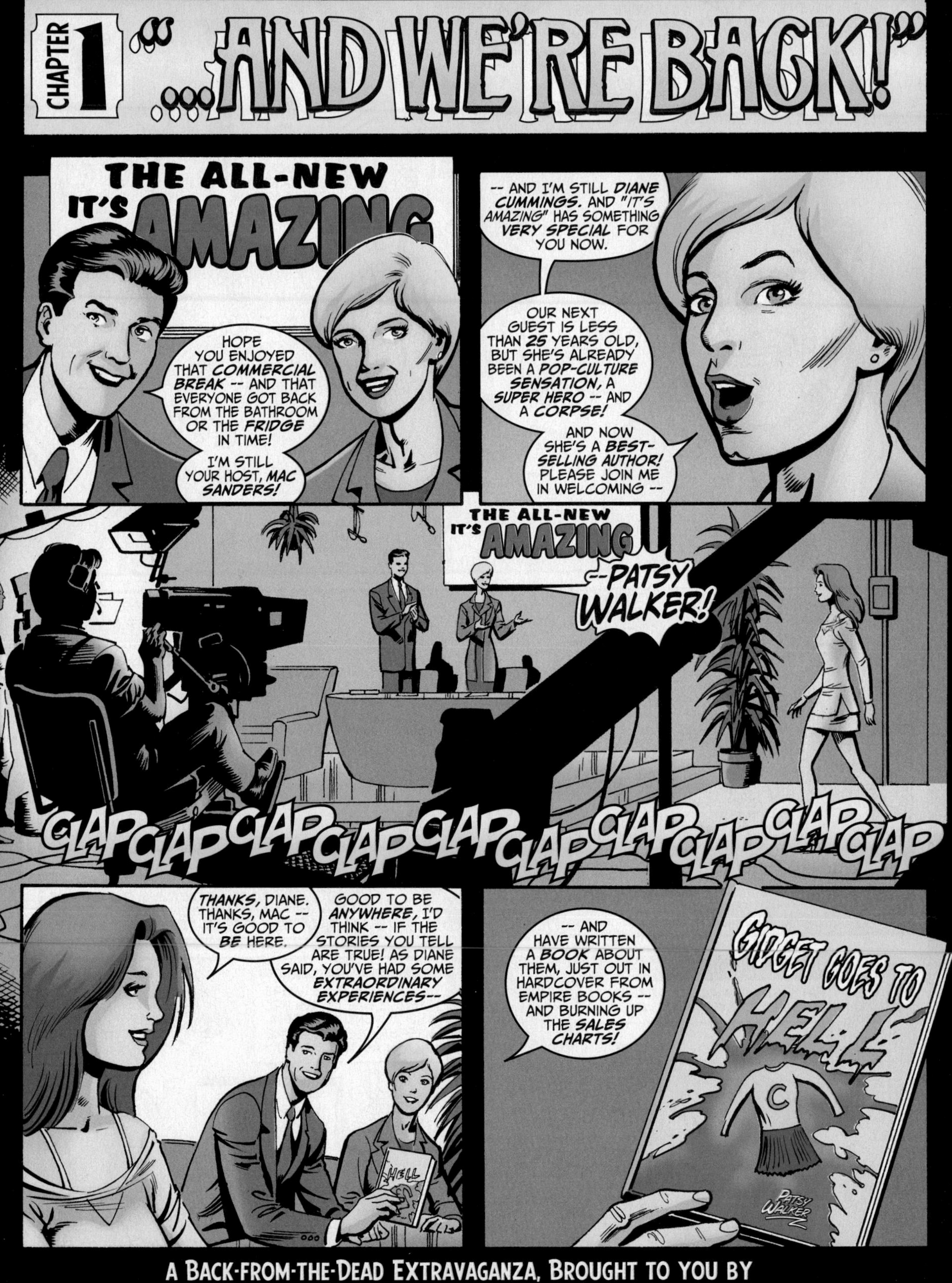

CHAPTER 1 "...AND WE'RE BACK!"
THE ALL-NEW IT'S AMAZING
HOPE YOU ENJOYED THAT COMMERCIAL BREAK -- AND THAT EVERYONE GOT BACK FROM THE BATHROOM OR THE FRIDGE IN TIME!
I'M STILL YOUR HOST, MAC SANDERS!
-- AND I'M STILL DIANE CUMMINGS. AND "IT'S AMAZING" HAS SOMETHING VERY SPECIAL FOR YOU NOW.
OUR NEXT GUEST IS LESS THAN 25 YEARS OLD, BUT SHE'S ALREADY BEEN A POP-CULTURE SENSATION, A SUPER HERO -- AND A CORPSE!
AND NOW SHE'S A BEST-SELLING AUTHOR! PLEASE JOIN ME IN WELCOMING --
THE ALL-NEW IT'S AMAZING
--PATSY WALKER!
CLAP CLAP CLAP CLAP CLAP CLAP CLAP CLAP CLAP CLAP
THANKS, DIANE. THANKS, MAC -- IT'S GOOD TO BE HERE.
GOOD TO BE ANYWHERE, I'D THINK -- IF THE STORIES YOU TELL ARE TRUE! AS DIANE SAID, YOU'VE HAD SOME EXTRAORDINARY EXPERIENCES--
HELL
-- AND HAVE WRITTEN A BOOK ABOUT THEM, JUST OUT IN HARDCOVER FROM EMPIRE BOOKS -- AND BURNING UP THE SALES CHARTS!
GIDGET GOES TO HELL
C
PATSY WALKER

A BACK-FROM-THE-DEAD EXTRAVAGANZA, BROUGHT TO YOU BY
KURT BUSIEK, WRITER... NORM BREYFOGLE, ARTIST... TOM SMITH, COLORIST...
RICHARD STARKINGS & COMICRAFT, LETTERS... TOM BREVOORT, EDITOR... BOB HARRAS, GUARDIAN OF THE GATES!

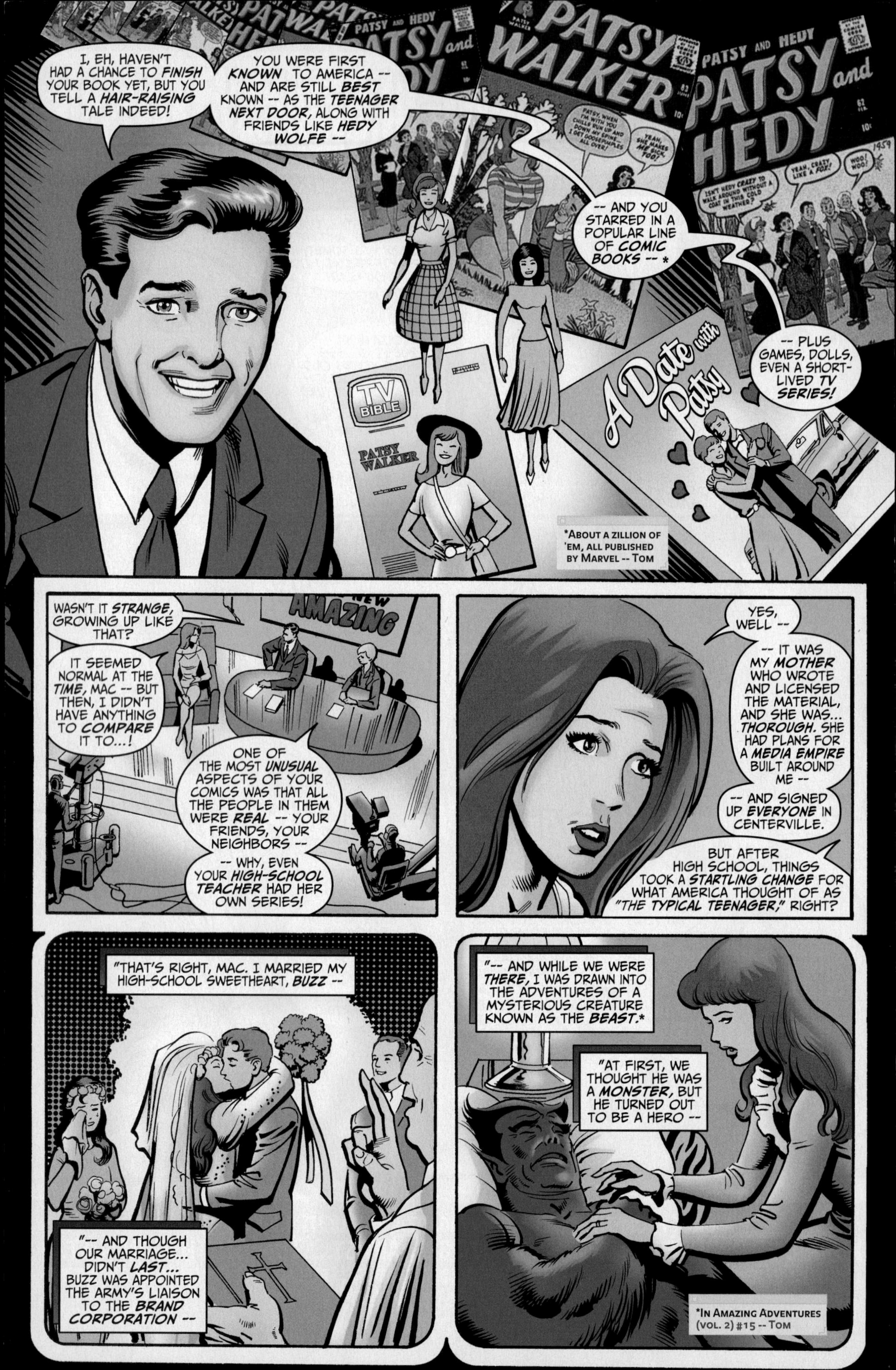
I, EH, HAVEN'T HAD A CHANCE TO *FINISH* YOUR BOOK YET, BUT YOU TELL A *HAIR-RAISING* TALE INDEED!
YOU WERE FIRST *KNOWN* TO AMERICA -- AND ARE STILL *BEST* KNOWN -- AS THE *TEENAGER NEXT DOOR,* ALONG WITH FRIENDS LIKE *HEDY WOLFE* --
PATSY AND HEDY
PATSY WALKER
PATSY and HEDY
-- AND YOU STARRED IN A POPULAR LINE OF *COMIC BOOKS* -- *
-- PLUS GAMES, DOLLS, EVEN A SHORT-LIVED *TV SERIES!*
TV BIBLE
PATSY WALKER
A Date with Patsy
*About a zillion of 'em, all published by Marvel -- Tom
WASN'T IT *STRANGE,* GROWING UP LIKE THAT?
IT SEEMED NORMAL AT THE *TIME,* MAC -- BUT THEN, I DIDN'T HAVE ANYTHING TO *COMPARE* IT TO...!
ONE OF THE MOST *UNUSUAL* ASPECTS OF YOUR COMICS WAS THAT ALL THE PEOPLE IN THEM WERE *REAL* -- YOUR FRIENDS, YOUR NEIGHBORS --
-- WHY, EVEN YOUR *HIGH-SCHOOL TEACHER* HAD HER OWN SERIES!
YES, WELL --
-- IT WAS MY *MOTHER* WHO WROTE AND LICENSED THE MATERIAL, AND SHE WAS... *THOROUGH.* SHE HAD PLANS FOR A *MEDIA EMPIRE* BUILT AROUND ME --
-- AND SIGNED UP *EVERYONE* IN CENTERVILLE.
BUT AFTER HIGH SCHOOL, THINGS TOOK A *STARTLING CHANGE* FOR WHAT AMERICA THOUGHT OF AS "*THE TYPICAL TEENAGER,*" RIGHT?
"THAT'S RIGHT, MAC. I MARRIED MY HIGH-SCHOOL SWEETHEART, *BUZZ* --
"-- AND THOUGH OUR MARRIAGE... DIDN'T *LAST*... BUZZ WAS APPOINTED THE ARMY'S LIAISON TO THE *BRAND CORPORATION* --
"-- AND WHILE WE WERE *THERE,* I WAS DRAWN INTO THE ADVENTURES OF A MYSTERIOUS CREATURE KNOWN AS THE *BEAST.**
"AT FIRST, WE THOUGHT HE WAS A *MONSTER,* BUT HE TURNED OUT TO BE A HERO --
*In Amazing Adventures (vol. 2) #15 -- Tom

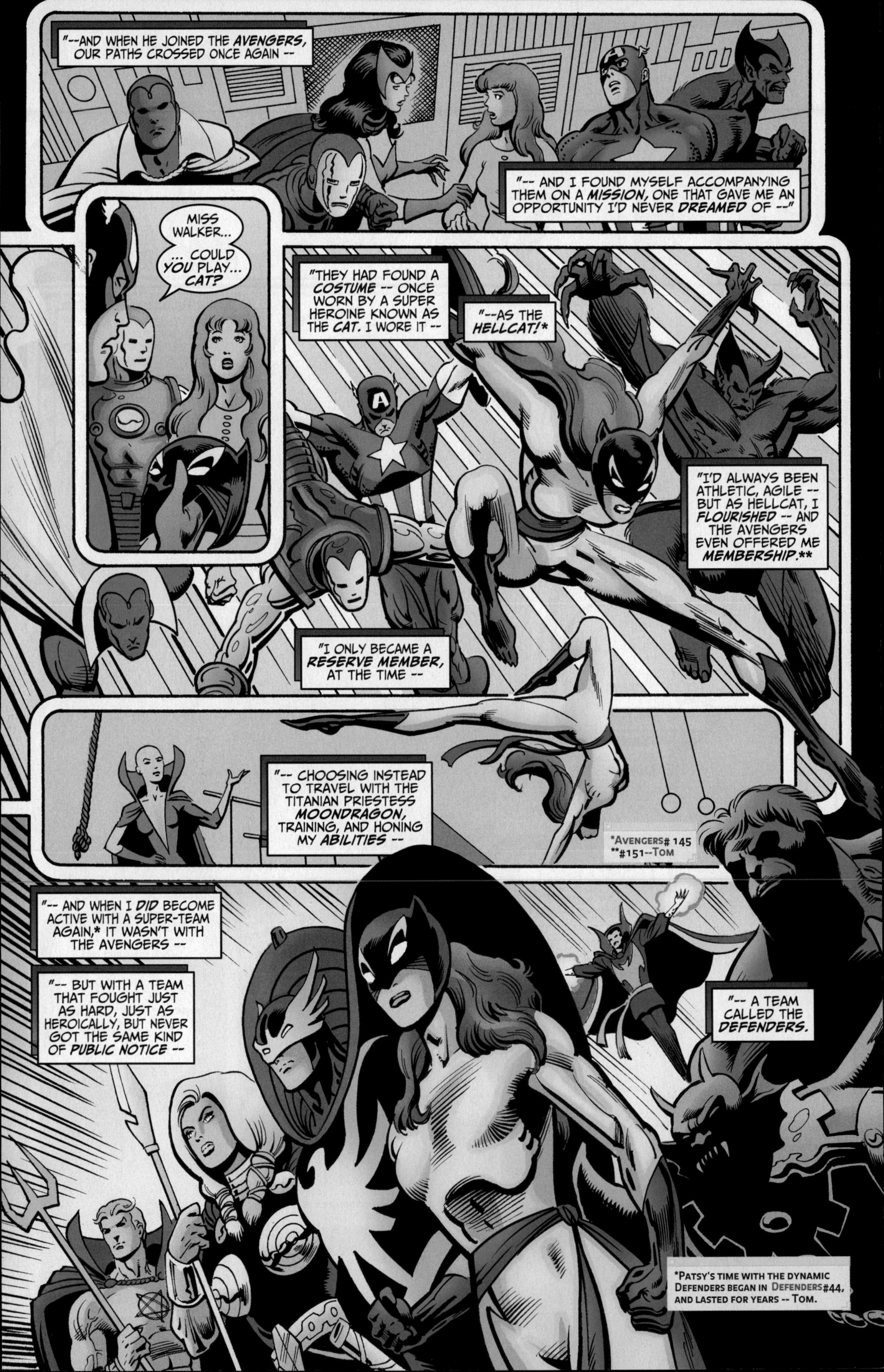
"--AND WHEN HE JOINED THE AVENGERS, OUR PATHS CROSSED ONCE AGAIN --
"-- AND I FOUND MYSELF ACCOMPANYING THEM ON A MISSION, ONE THAT GAVE ME AN OPPORTUNITY I'D NEVER DREAMED OF --"
MISS WALKER...
... COULD YOU PLAY... CAT?
"THEY HAD FOUND A COSTUME -- ONCE WORN BY A SUPER HEROINE KNOWN AS THE CAT. I WORE IT --
"--AS THE HELLCAT!*
"I'D ALWAYS BEEN ATHLETIC, AGILE -- BUT AS HELLCAT, I FLOURISHED -- AND THE AVENGERS EVEN OFFERED ME MEMBERSHIP.**
"I ONLY BECAME A RESERVE MEMBER, AT THE TIME --
"-- CHOOSING INSTEAD TO TRAVEL WITH THE TITANIAN PRIESTESS MOONDRAGON, TRAINING, AND HONING MY ABILITIES --
*AVENGERS# 145
**#151--TOM
"-- AND WHEN I DID BECOME ACTIVE WITH A SUPER-TEAM AGAIN,* IT WASN'T WITH THE AVENGERS --
"-- BUT WITH A TEAM THAT FOUGHT JUST AS HARD, JUST AS HEROICALLY, BUT NEVER GOT THE SAME KIND OF PUBLIC NOTICE --
"-- A TEAM CALLED THE DEFENDERS.
*PATSY'S TIME WITH THE DYNAMIC DEFENDERS BEGAN IN DEFENDERS#44, AND LASTED FOR YEARS -- TOM.

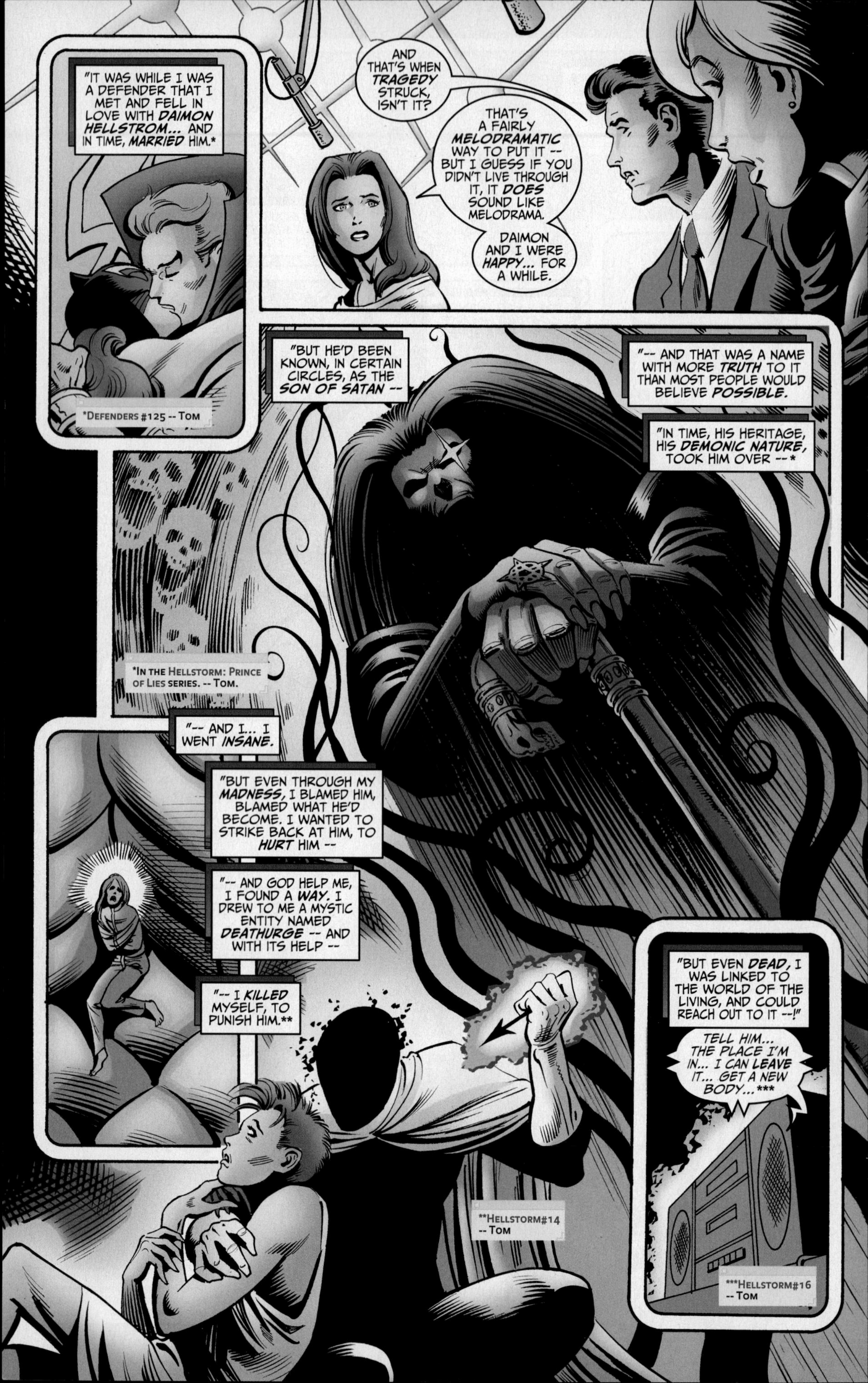
"IT WAS WHILE I WAS A DEFENDER THAT I MET AND FELL IN LOVE WITH DAIMON HELLSTROM... AND IN TIME, MARRIED HIM.*
*DEFENDERS #125 -- TOM
AND THAT'S WHEN TRAGEDY STRUCK, ISN'T IT?
THAT'S A FAIRLY MELODRAMATIC WAY TO PUT IT -- BUT I GUESS IF YOU DIDN'T LIVE THROUGH IT, IT DOES SOUND LIKE MELODRAMA.
DAIMON AND I WERE HAPPY... FOR A WHILE.
"BUT HE'D BEEN KNOWN, IN CERTAIN CIRCLES, AS THE SON OF SATAN --
"-- AND THAT WAS A NAME WITH MORE TRUTH TO IT THAN MOST PEOPLE WOULD BELIEVE POSSIBLE.
"IN TIME, HIS HERITAGE, HIS DEMONIC NATURE, TOOK HIM OVER --*
*IN THE HELLSTORM: PRINCE OF LIES SERIES. -- TOM.
"-- AND I... I WENT INSANE.
"BUT EVEN THROUGH MY MADNESS, I BLAMED HIM, BLAMED WHAT HE'D BECOME. I WANTED TO STRIKE BACK AT HIM, TO HURT HIM --
"-- AND GOD HELP ME, I FOUND A WAY. I DREW TO ME A MYSTIC ENTITY NAMED DEATHURGE -- AND WITH ITS HELP --
"-- I KILLED MYSELF, TO PUNISH HIM.**
**HELLSTORM#14 -- TOM
"BUT EVEN DEAD, I WAS LINKED TO THE WORLD OF THE LIVING, AND COULD REACH OUT TO IT --!"
TELL HIM... THE PLACE I'M IN... I CAN LEAVE IT... GET A NEW BODY...***
***HELLSTORM#16 -- TOM

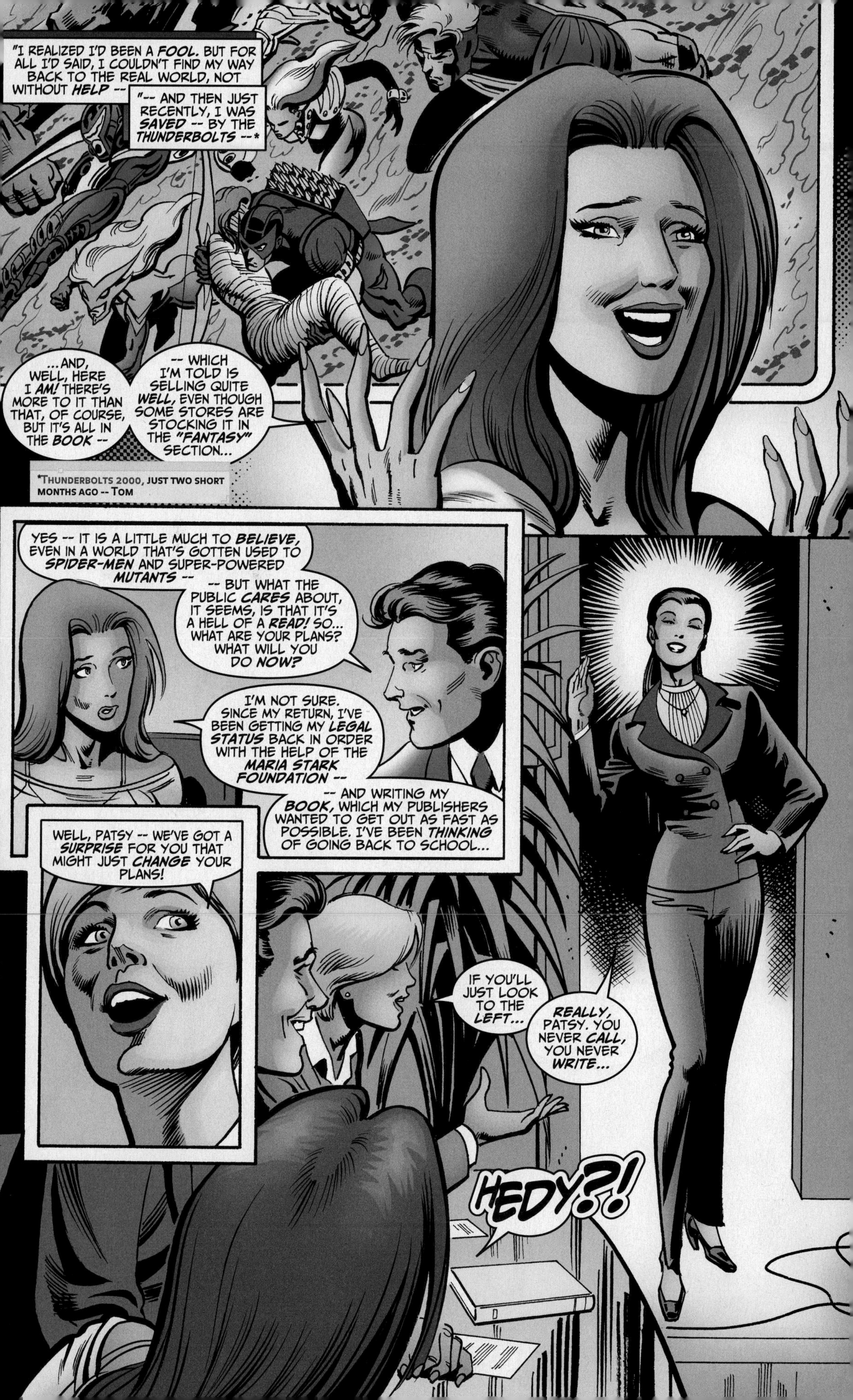
"I REALIZED I'D BEEN A FOOL. BUT FOR ALL I'D SAID, I COULDN'T FIND MY WAY BACK TO THE REAL WORLD, NOT WITHOUT HELP --
"-- AND THEN JUST RECENTLY, I WAS SAVED -- BY THE THUNDERBOLTS --*
...AND, WELL, HERE I AM! THERE'S MORE TO IT THAN THAT, OF COURSE, BUT IT'S ALL IN THE BOOK --
-- WHICH I'M TOLD IS SELLING QUITE WELL, EVEN THOUGH SOME STORES ARE STOCKING IT IN THE "FANTASY" SECTION...
*THUNDERBOLTS 2000, JUST TWO SHORT MONTHS AGO -- TOM
YES -- IT IS A LITTLE MUCH TO BELIEVE, EVEN IN A WORLD THAT'S GOTTEN USED TO SPIDER-MEN AND SUPER-POWERED MUTANTS --
-- BUT WHAT THE PUBLIC CARES ABOUT, IT SEEMS, IS THAT IT'S A HELL OF A READ! SO... WHAT ARE YOUR PLANS? WHAT WILL YOU DO NOW?
I'M NOT SURE. SINCE MY RETURN, I'VE BEEN GETTING MY LEGAL STATUS BACK IN ORDER WITH THE HELP OF THE MARIA STARK FOUNDATION --
-- AND WRITING MY BOOK, WHICH MY PUBLISHERS WANTED TO GET OUT AS FAST AS POSSIBLE. I'VE BEEN THINKING OF GOING BACK TO SCHOOL...
WELL, PATSY -- WE'VE GOT A SURPRISE FOR YOU THAT MIGHT JUST CHANGE YOUR PLANS!
IF YOU'LL JUST LOOK TO THE LEFT...
REALLY, PATSY. YOU NEVER CALL, YOU NEVER WRITE...
HEDY?!

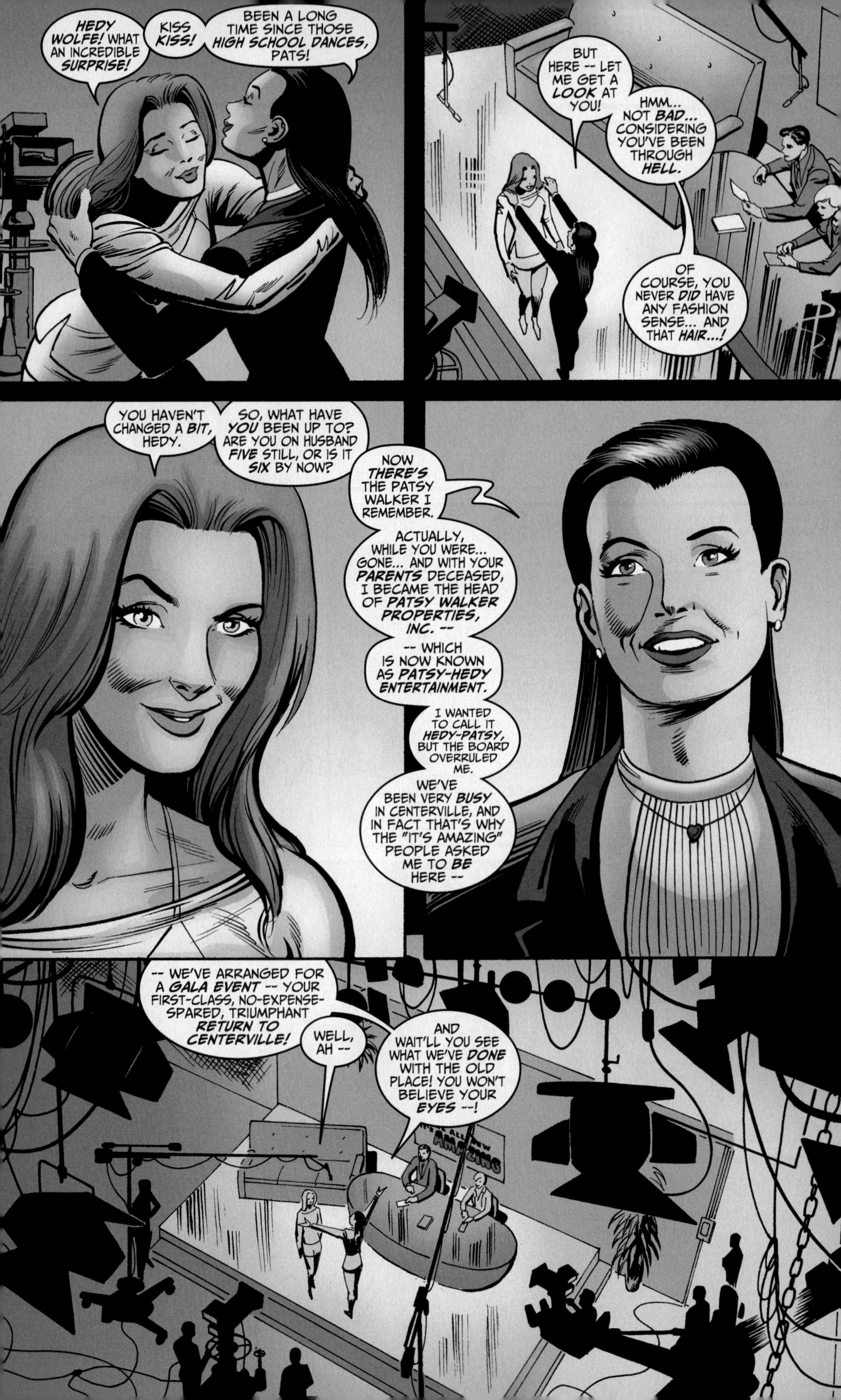
HEDY WOLFE! WHAT AN INCREDIBLE SURPRISE!
KISS KISS!
BEEN A LONG TIME SINCE THOSE HIGH SCHOOL DANCES, PATS!
BUT HERE -- LET ME GET A LOOK AT YOU!
HMM... NOT BAD... CONSIDERING YOU'VE BEEN THROUGH HELL.
OF COURSE, YOU NEVER DID HAVE ANY FASHION SENSE... AND THAT HAIR...!
YOU HAVEN'T CHANGED A BIT, HEDY.
SO, WHAT HAVE YOU BEEN UP TO? ARE YOU ON HUSBAND FIVE STILL, OR IS IT SIX BY NOW?
NOW THERE'S THE PATSY WALKER I REMEMBER.
ACTUALLY, WHILE YOU WERE... GONE... AND WITH YOUR PARENTS DECEASED, I BECAME THE HEAD OF PATSY WALKER PROPERTIES, INC. --
-- WHICH IS NOW KNOWN AS PATSY-HEDY ENTERTAINMENT.
I WANTED TO CALL IT HEDY-PATSY, BUT THE BOARD OVERRULED ME.
WE'VE BEEN VERY BUSY IN CENTERVILLE, AND IN FACT THAT'S WHY THE "IT'S AMAZING" PEOPLE ASKED ME TO BE HERE --
-- WE'VE ARRANGED FOR A GALA EVENT -- YOUR FIRST-CLASS, NO-EXPENSE-SPARED, TRIUMPHANT RETURN TO CENTERVILLE!
WELL, AH --
AND WAIT'LL YOU SEE WHAT WE'VE DONE WITH THE OLD PLACE! YOU WON'T BELIEVE YOUR EYES --!
AMAZING

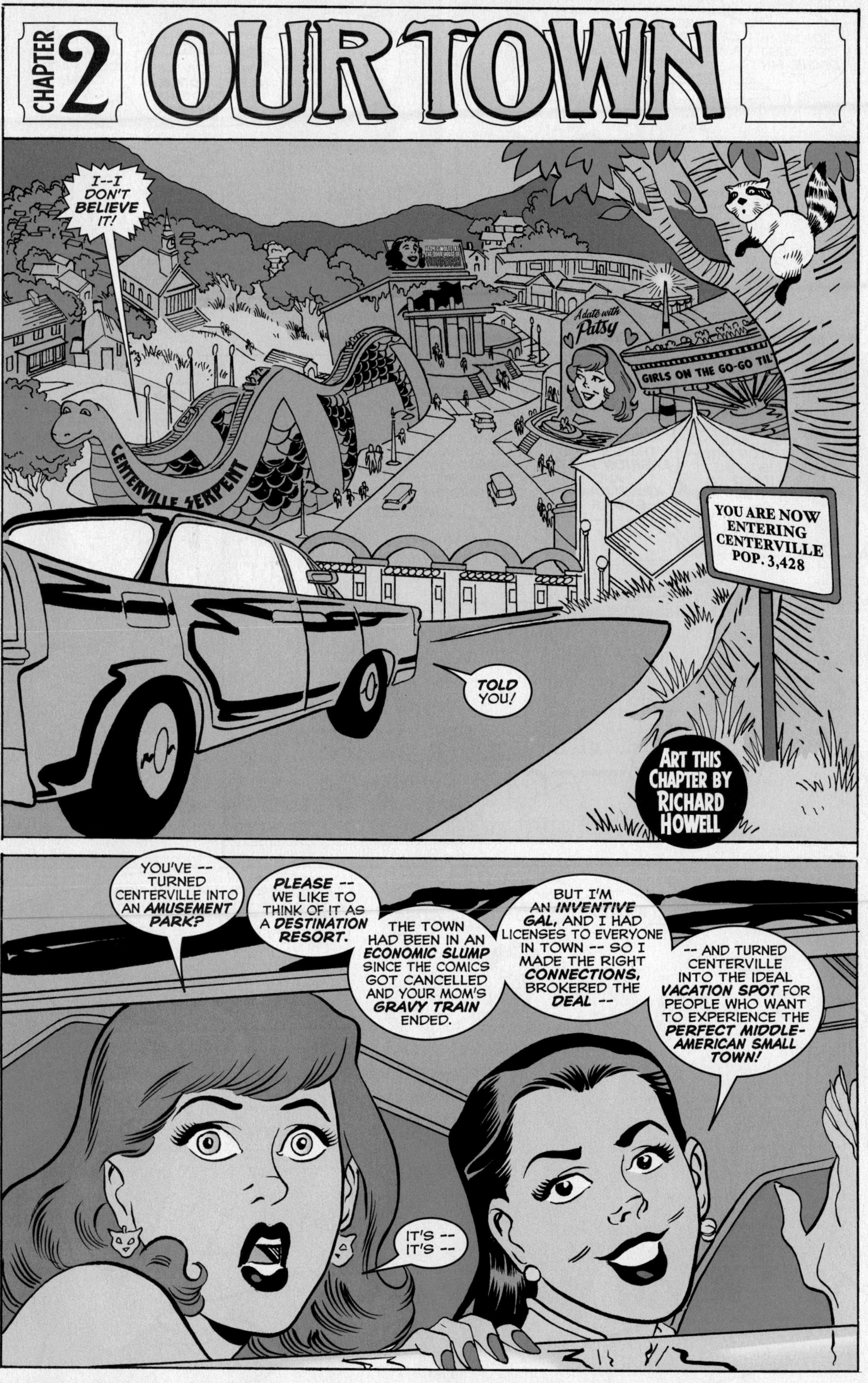
CHAPTER 2 OUR TOWN
I--I DON'T BELIEVE IT!
A date with Patsy
GIRLS ON THE GO-GO TIL
YOU ARE NOW ENTERING CENTERVILLE POP. 3,428
CENTERVILLE SERPENT
TOLD YOU!
ART THIS CHAPTER BY RICHARD HOWELL
YOU'VE -- TURNED CENTERVILLE INTO AN AMUSEMENT PARK?
PLEASE -- WE LIKE TO THINK OF IT AS A DESTINATION RESORT.
THE TOWN HAD BEEN IN AN ECONOMIC SLUMP SINCE THE COMICS GOT CANCELLED AND YOUR MOM'S GRAVY TRAIN ENDED.
BUT I'M AN INVENTIVE GAL, AND I HAD LICENSES TO EVERYONE IN TOWN -- SO I MADE THE RIGHT CONNECTIONS, BROKERED THE DEAL --
-- AND TURNED CENTERVILLE INTO THE IDEAL VACATION SPOT FOR PEOPLE WHO WANT TO EXPERIENCE THE PERFECT MIDDLE-AMERICAN SMALL TOWN!
IT'S -- IT'S --

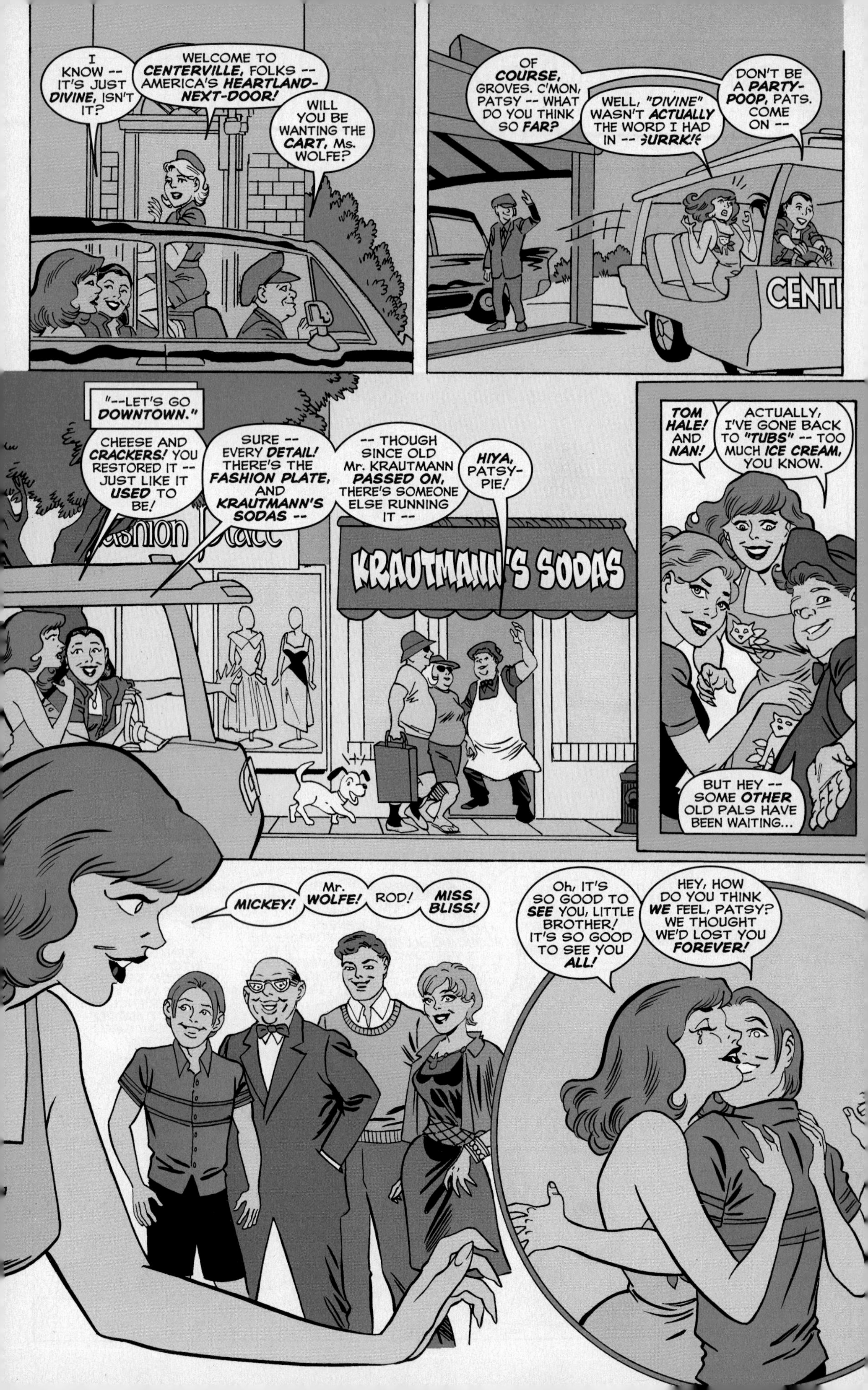
I KNOW -- IT'S JUST DIVINE, ISN'T IT?
WELCOME TO CENTERVILLE, FOLKS -- AMERICA'S HEARTLAND-NEXT-DOOR!
WILL YOU BE WANTING THE CART, Ms. WOLFE?
OF COURSE, GROVES. C'MON, PATSY -- WHAT DO YOU THINK SO FAR?
WELL, "DIVINE" WASN'T ACTUALLY THE WORD I HAD IN -- ЭURRK!Є
DON'T BE A PARTY-POOP, PATS. COME ON --
CENT
"--LET'S GO DOWNTOWN."
CHEESE AND CRACKERS! YOU RESTORED IT -- JUST LIKE IT USED TO BE!
SURE -- EVERY DETAIL! THERE'S THE FASHION PLATE, AND KRAUTMANN'S SODAS --
-- THOUGH SINCE OLD Mr. KRAUTMANN PASSED ON, THERE'S SOMEONE ELSE RUNNING IT --
HIYA, PATSY-PIE!
KRAUTMANN'S SODAS
TOM HALE! AND NAN!
ACTUALLY, I'VE GONE BACK TO "TUBS" -- TOO MUCH ICE CREAM, YOU KNOW.
BUT HEY -- SOME OTHER OLD PALS HAVE BEEN WAITING...
MICKEY!
Mr. WOLFE!
ROD!
MISS BLISS!
Oh, IT'S SO GOOD TO SEE YOU, LITTLE BROTHER! IT'S SO GOOD TO SEE YOU ALL!
HEY, HOW DO YOU THINK WE FEEL, PATSY? WE THOUGHT WE'D LOST YOU FOREVER!

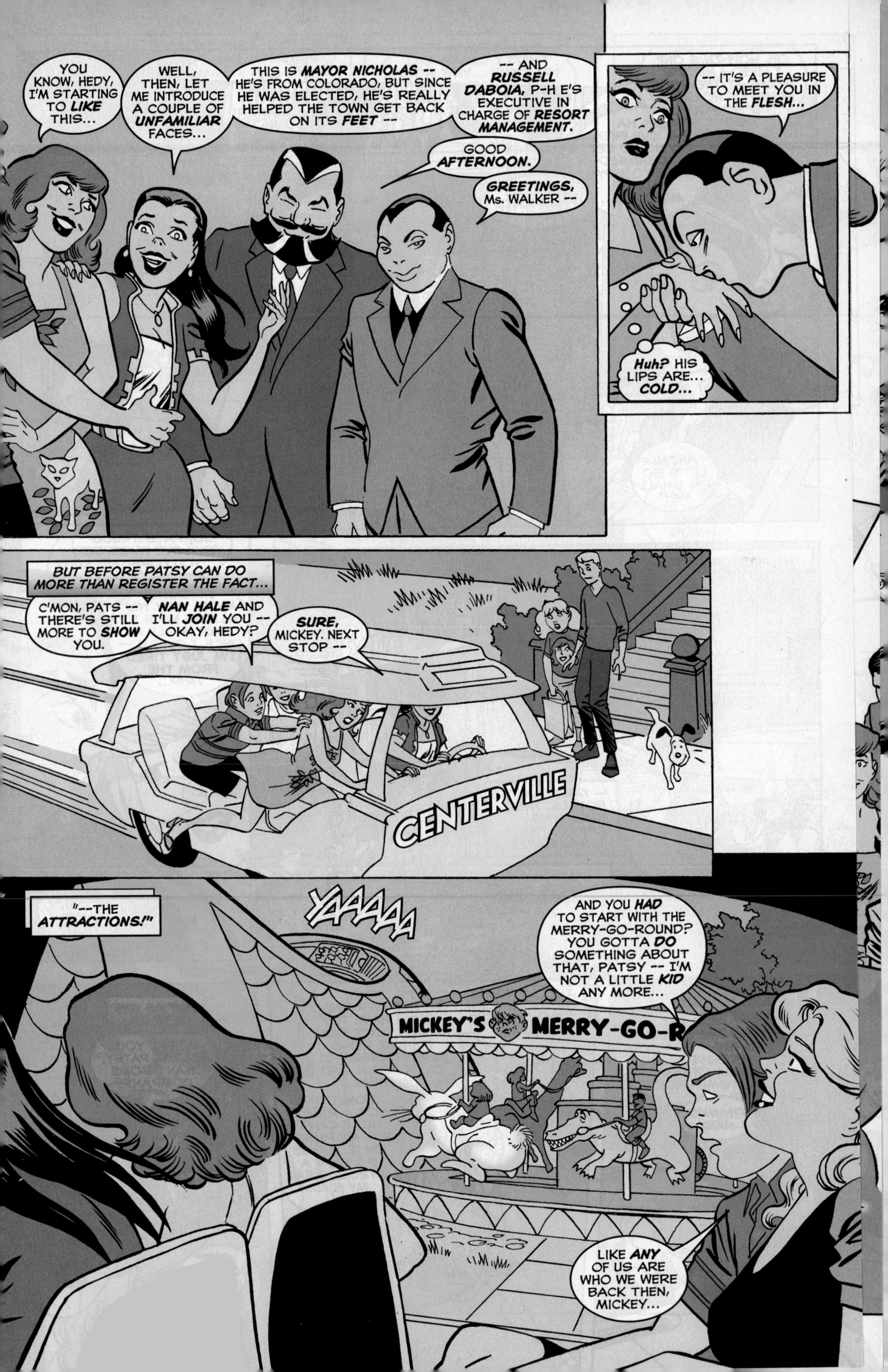

YOU KNOW, HEDY, I'M STARTING TO **LIKE** THIS...
WELL, THEN, LET ME INTRODUCE A COUPLE OF **UNFAMILIAR** FACES...
THIS IS **MAYOR NICHOLAS** -- HE'S FROM COLORADO, BUT SINCE HE WAS ELECTED, HE'S REALLY HELPED THE TOWN GET BACK ON ITS **FEET** --
-- AND **RUSSELL DABOIA,** P-H E'S EXECUTIVE IN CHARGE OF **RESORT MANAGEMENT.**
GOOD **AFTERNOON.**
GREETINGS, Ms. WALKER --
-- IT'S A PLEASURE TO MEET YOU IN THE **FLESH...**
Huh? HIS LIPS ARE... **COLD...**
BUT BEFORE PATSY CAN DO MORE THAN REGISTER THE FACT...
C'MON, PATS -- THERE'S STILL MORE TO **SHOW** YOU.
NAN HALE AND I'LL **JOIN** YOU -- OKAY, HEDY?
SURE, MICKEY. NEXT STOP --
CENTERVILLE
"--THE **ATTRACTIONS!"**
YAAAAA
AND YOU **HAD** TO START WITH THE MERRY-GO-ROUND? YOU GOTTA **DO** SOMETHING ABOUT THAT, PATSY -- I'M NOT A LITTLE **KID** ANY MORE...
MICKEY'S MERRY-GO-R
LIKE **ANY** OF US ARE WHO WE WERE BACK THEN, MICKEY...

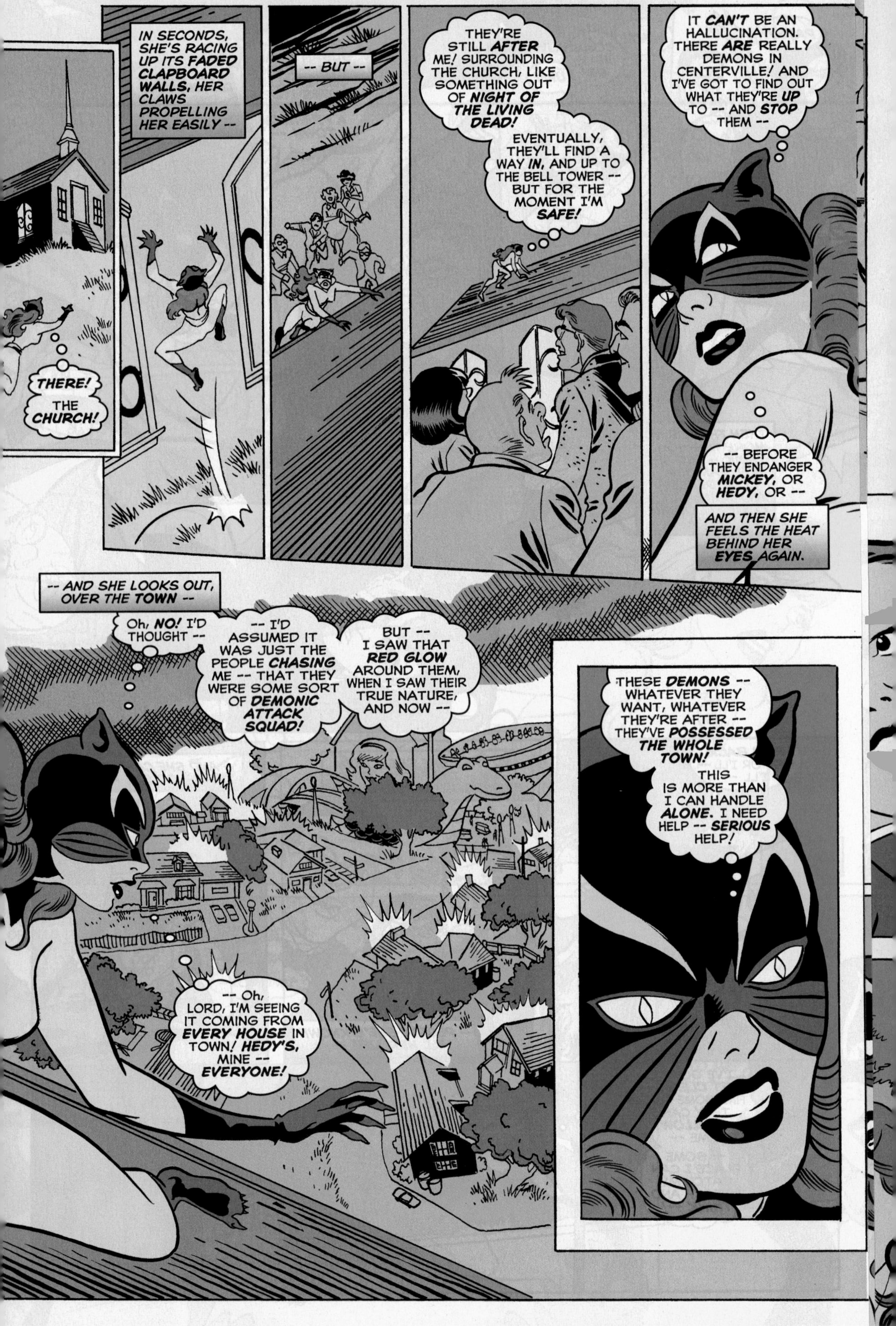
THERE! THE CHURCH!
IN SECONDS, SHE'S RACING UP ITS FADED CLAPBOARD WALLS, HER CLAWS PROPELLING HER EASILY --
-- BUT --
THEY'RE STILL AFTER ME! SURROUNDING THE CHURCH, LIKE SOMETHING OUT OF NIGHT OF THE LIVING DEAD!
EVENTUALLY, THEY'LL FIND A WAY IN, AND UP TO THE BELL TOWER -- BUT FOR THE MOMENT I'M SAFE!
IT CAN'T BE AN HALLUCINATION. THERE ARE REALLY DEMONS IN CENTERVILLE! AND I'VE GOT TO FIND OUT WHAT THEY'RE UP TO -- AND STOP THEM --
-- BEFORE THEY ENDANGER MICKEY, OR HEDY, OR --
AND THEN SHE FEELS THE HEAT BEHIND HER EYES AGAIN.
-- AND SHE LOOKS OUT, OVER THE TOWN --
Oh, NO! I'D THOUGHT --
-- I'D ASSUMED IT WAS JUST THE PEOPLE CHASING ME -- THAT THEY WERE SOME SORT OF DEMONIC ATTACK SQUAD!
BUT -- I SAW THAT RED GLOW AROUND THEM, WHEN I SAW THEIR TRUE NATURE, AND NOW --
-- Oh, LORD, I'M SEEING IT COMING FROM EVERY HOUSE IN TOWN! HEDY'S, MINE -- EVERYONE!
THESE DEMONS -- WHATEVER THEY WANT, WHATEVER THEY'RE AFTER -- THEY'VE POSSESSED THE WHOLE TOWN!
THIS IS MORE THAN I CAN HANDLE ALONE. I NEED HELP -- SERIOUS HELP!

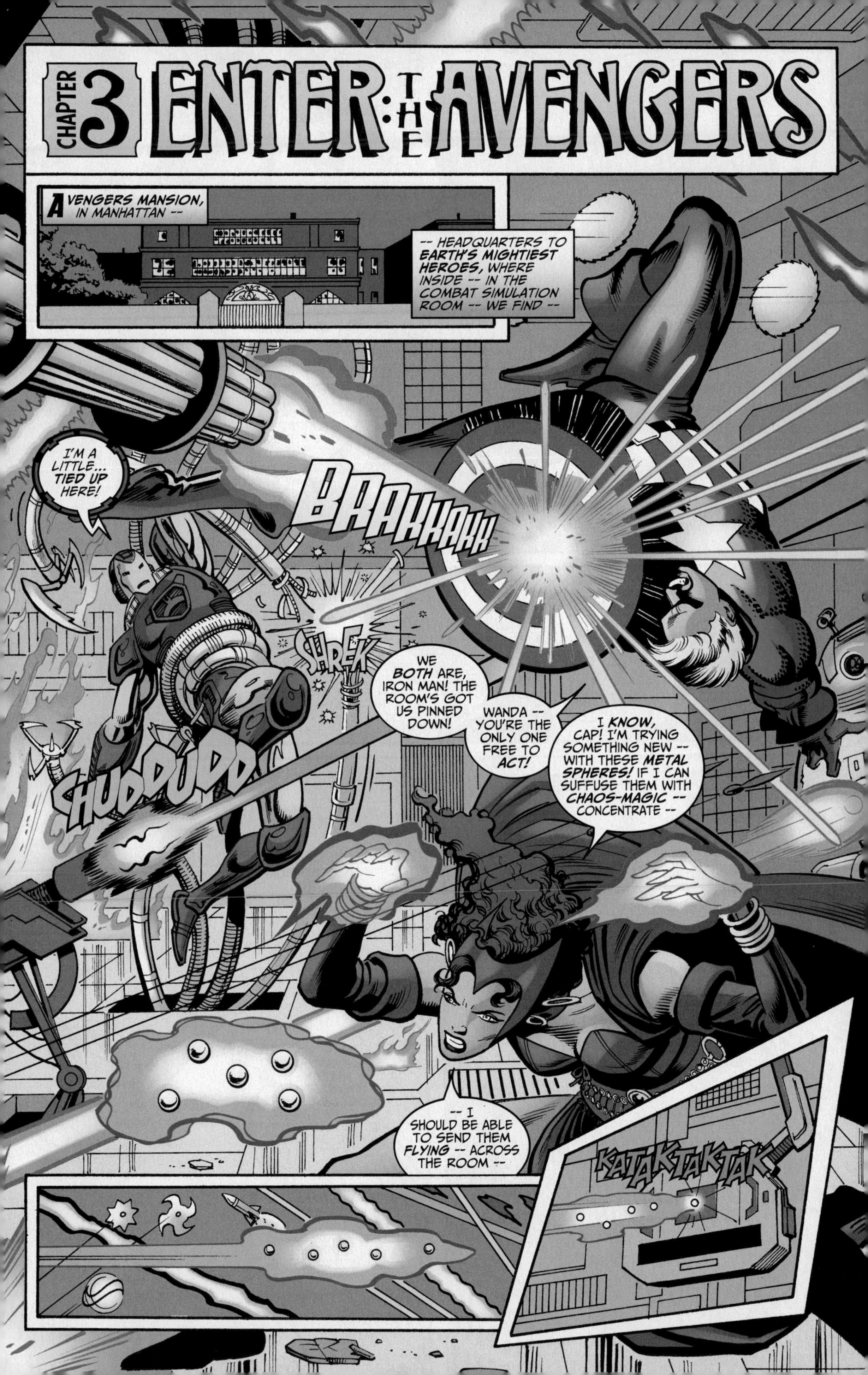
CHAPTER 3 ENTER: THE AVENGERS
AVENGERS MANSION, IN MANHATTAN --
-- HEADQUARTERS TO EARTH'S MIGHTIEST HEROES, WHERE INSIDE -- IN THE COMBAT SIMULATION ROOM -- WE FIND --
I'M A LITTLE... TIED UP HERE!
BRAKKAKK
SHREK
WE BOTH ARE, IRON MAN! THE ROOM'S GOT US PINNED DOWN!
WANDA -- YOU'RE THE ONLY ONE FREE TO ACT!
I KNOW, CAP! I'M TRYING SOMETHING NEW -- WITH THESE METAL SPHERES! IF I CAN SUFFUSE THEM WITH CHAOS-MAGIC -- CONCENTRATE --
CHUDDUDD
-- I SHOULD BE ABLE TO SEND THEM FLYING -- ACROSS THE ROOM --
KATAKTAKTAK

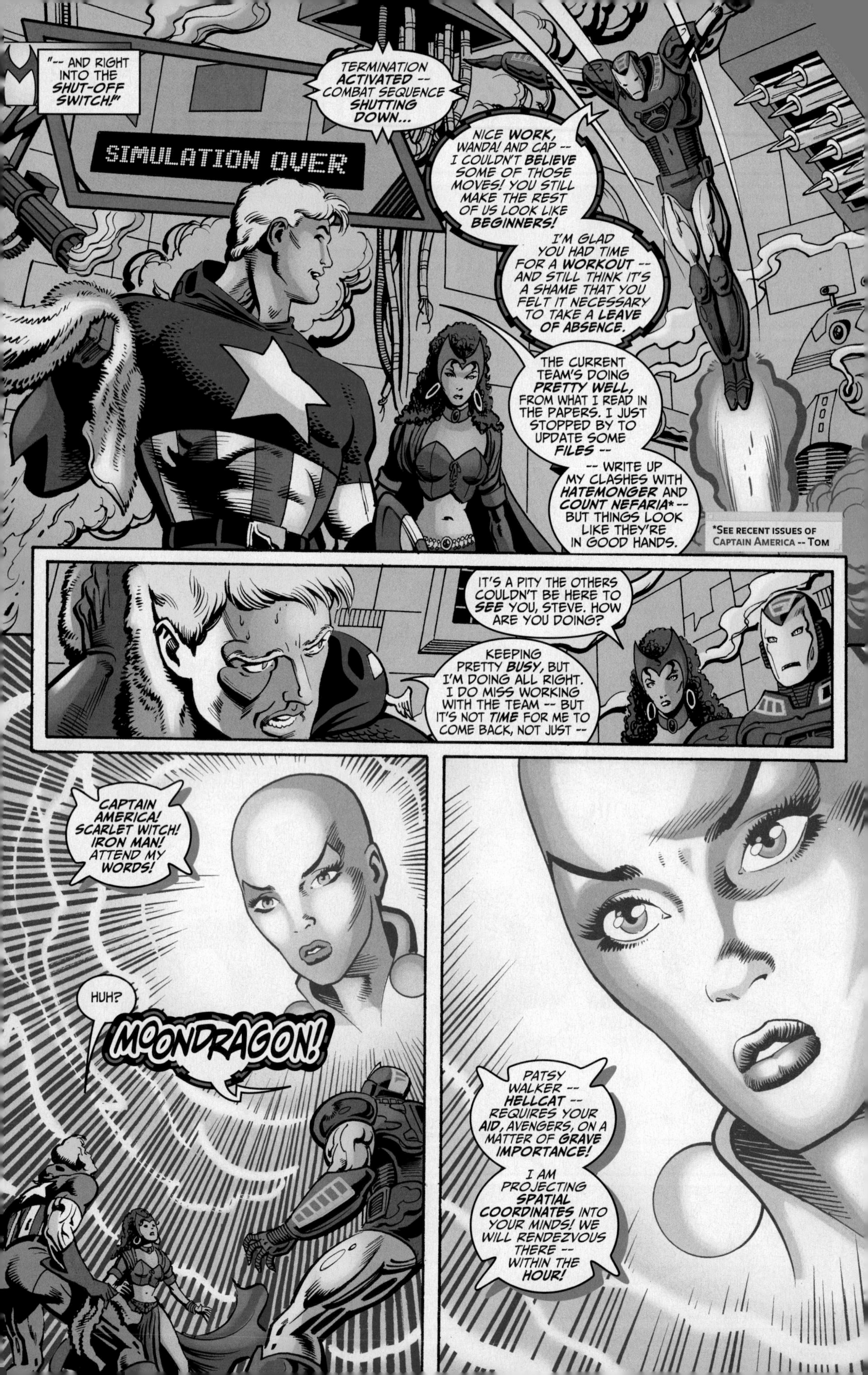
"-- AND RIGHT INTO THE SHUT-OFF SWITCH!"
TERMINATION ACTIVATED -- COMBAT SEQUENCE SHUTTING DOWN...
SIMULATION OVER
NICE WORK, WANDA! AND CAP -- I COULDN'T BELIEVE SOME OF THOSE MOVES! YOU STILL MAKE THE REST OF US LOOK LIKE BEGINNERS!
I'M GLAD YOU HAD TIME FOR A WORKOUT -- AND STILL THINK IT'S A SHAME THAT YOU FELT IT NECESSARY TO TAKE A LEAVE OF ABSENCE.
THE CURRENT TEAM'S DOING PRETTY WELL, FROM WHAT I READ IN THE PAPERS. I JUST STOPPED BY TO UPDATE SOME FILES --
-- WRITE UP MY CLASHES WITH HATEMONGER AND COUNT NEFARIA* -- BUT THINGS LOOK LIKE THEY'RE IN GOOD HANDS.
*SEE RECENT ISSUES OF CAPTAIN AMERICA -- TOM
IT'S A PITY THE OTHERS COULDN'T BE HERE TO SEE YOU, STEVE. HOW ARE YOU DOING?
KEEPING PRETTY BUSY, BUT I'M DOING ALL RIGHT. I DO MISS WORKING WITH THE TEAM -- BUT IT'S NOT TIME FOR ME TO COME BACK, NOT JUST --
CAPTAIN AMERICA! SCARLET WITCH! IRON MAN! ATTEND MY WORDS!
HUH?
MOONDRAGON!
PATSY WALKER -- HELLCAT -- REQUIRES YOUR AID, AVENGERS, ON A MATTER OF GRAVE IMPORTANCE!
I AM PROJECTING SPATIAL COORDINATES INTO YOUR MINDS! WE WILL RENDEZVOUS THERE -- WITHIN THE HOUR!

DO NOT FAIL ME! MOONDRAGON OUT!
WH --?
SOON...
I WILL NEVER GET USED TO THAT WOMAN'S ARROGANCE. SHE DIDN'T EVEN TELL US WHAT KIND OF DANGER HELLCAT'S IN!
JUST, "GET MOVING, AVENGERS -- HERE'S THE ADDRESS!" OF ALL THE --
IN A MINUTE, IRON MAN, YOU'LL BE ABLE TO GRIPE AT HER YOURSELF --
-- BECAUSE ACCORDING TO THE ONBOARD SENSORS --
"-- SHE'S HERE."
VERY GOOD, AVENGERS. NOW HEAD WEST -- WE MUST REACH CENTERVILLE WITH ALL DUE SPEED.
NOW WAIT A --
PATSY ATTEMPTED TO CONTACT YOU VIA HER AVENGERS COMMUNICARD, BUT THE OUTGOING SIGNAL WAS JAMMED.
HOWEVER, I MAINTAIN A LOW-LEVEL AWARENESS OF MY FORMER CHARGE, AND SENSED HER DISTRESS --
-- SO I CONTACTED HER TELEPATHICALLY.
MOONDRAGON, YOU CAN'T JUST --
I AM AN AVENGER, AM I NOT?
INACTIVE, BUT WITH FULL PRIVILEGES, INCLUDING THE RIGHT TO CALL ON THE TEAM IN AN EMERGENCY? VERY WELL.
I COULD SENSE IN YOUR MINDS THAT THERE WERE ONLY THE THREE OF YOU AT THE MANSION, SO I CALLED IN ASSISTANCE. THEY SHOULD BE ARRIVING --
-- NOW.
HAWKEYE! AND SONGBIRD!
HI, GANG --

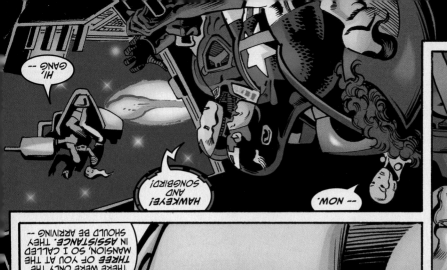

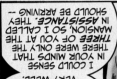

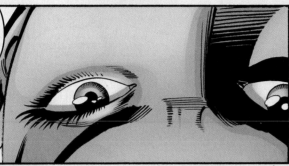

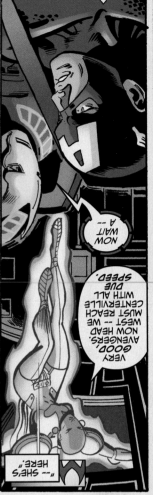

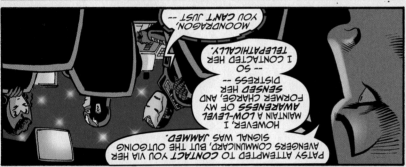

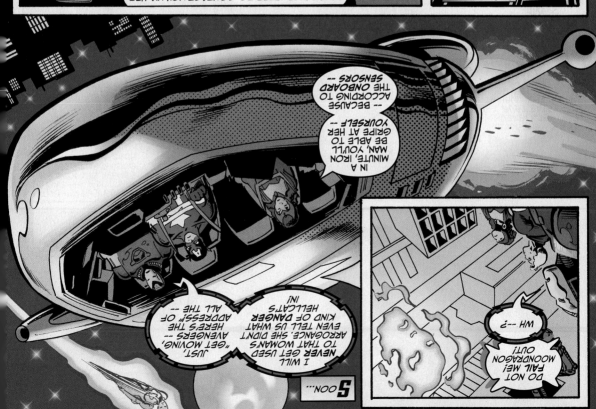

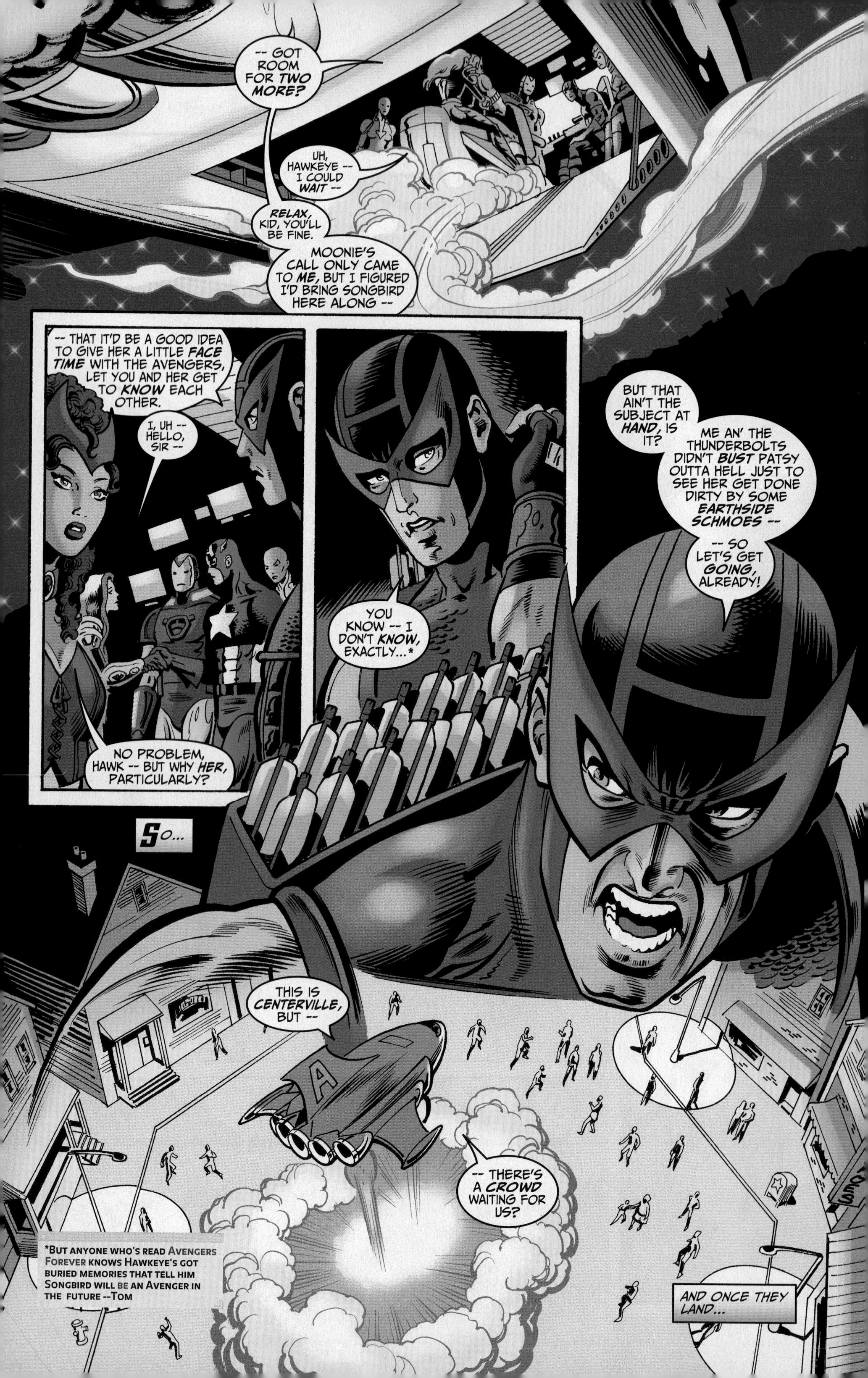
-- GOT ROOM FOR TWO MORE?
UH, HAWKEYE -- I COULD WAIT --
RELAX, KID, YOU'LL BE FINE.
MOONIE'S CALL ONLY CAME TO ME, BUT I FIGURED I'D BRING SONGBIRD HERE ALONG --
-- THAT IT'D BE A GOOD IDEA TO GIVE HER A LITTLE FACE TIME WITH THE AVENGERS, LET YOU AND HER GET TO KNOW EACH OTHER.
I, UH -- HELLO, SIR --
NO PROBLEM, HAWK -- BUT WHY HER, PARTICULARLY?
YOU KNOW -- I DON'T KNOW, EXACTLY...*
BUT THAT AIN'T THE SUBJECT AT HAND, IS IT?
ME AN' THE THUNDERBOLTS DIDN'T BUST PATSY OUTTA HELL JUST TO SEE HER GET DONE DIRTY BY SOME EARTHSIDE SCHMOES --
-- SO LET'S GET GOING, ALREADY!
SO...
THIS IS CENTERVILLE, BUT --
-- THERE'S A CROWD WAITING FOR US?
AND ONCE THEY LAND...
*BUT ANYONE WHO'S READ AVENGERS FOREVER KNOWS HAWKEYE'S GOT BURIED MEMORIES THAT TELL HIM SONGBIRD WILL BE AN AVENGER IN THE FUTURE --TOM

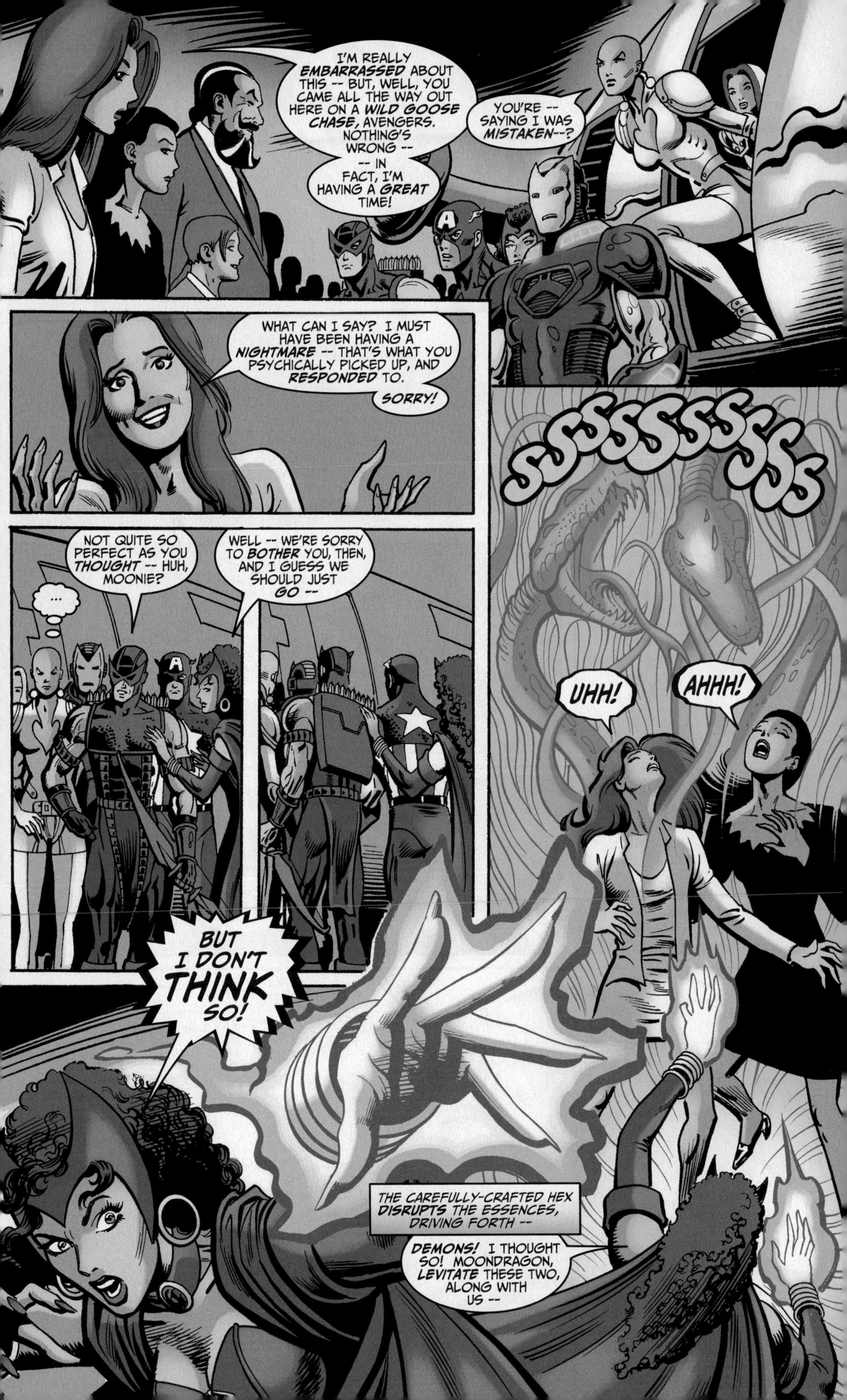
I'M REALLY EMBARRASSED ABOUT THIS -- BUT, WELL, YOU CAME ALL THE WAY OUT HERE ON A WILD GOOSE CHASE, AVENGERS. NOTHING'S WRONG --
-- IN FACT, I'M HAVING A GREAT TIME!
YOU'RE -- SAYING I WAS MISTAKEN--?
WHAT CAN I SAY? I MUST HAVE BEEN HAVING A NIGHTMARE -- THAT'S WHAT YOU PSYCHICALLY PICKED UP, AND RESPONDED TO.
SORRY!
NOT QUITE SO PERFECT AS YOU THOUGHT -- HUH, MOONIE?
...
WELL -- WE'RE SORRY TO BOTHER YOU, THEN, AND I GUESS WE SHOULD JUST GO --
SSSSSSSSSS
UHH!
AHHH!
BUT I DON'T THINK SO!
THE CAREFULLY-CRAFTED HEX DISRUPTS THE ESSENCES, DRIVING FORTH --
DEMONS! I THOUGHT SO! MOONDRAGON, LEVITATE THESE TWO, ALONG WITH US --

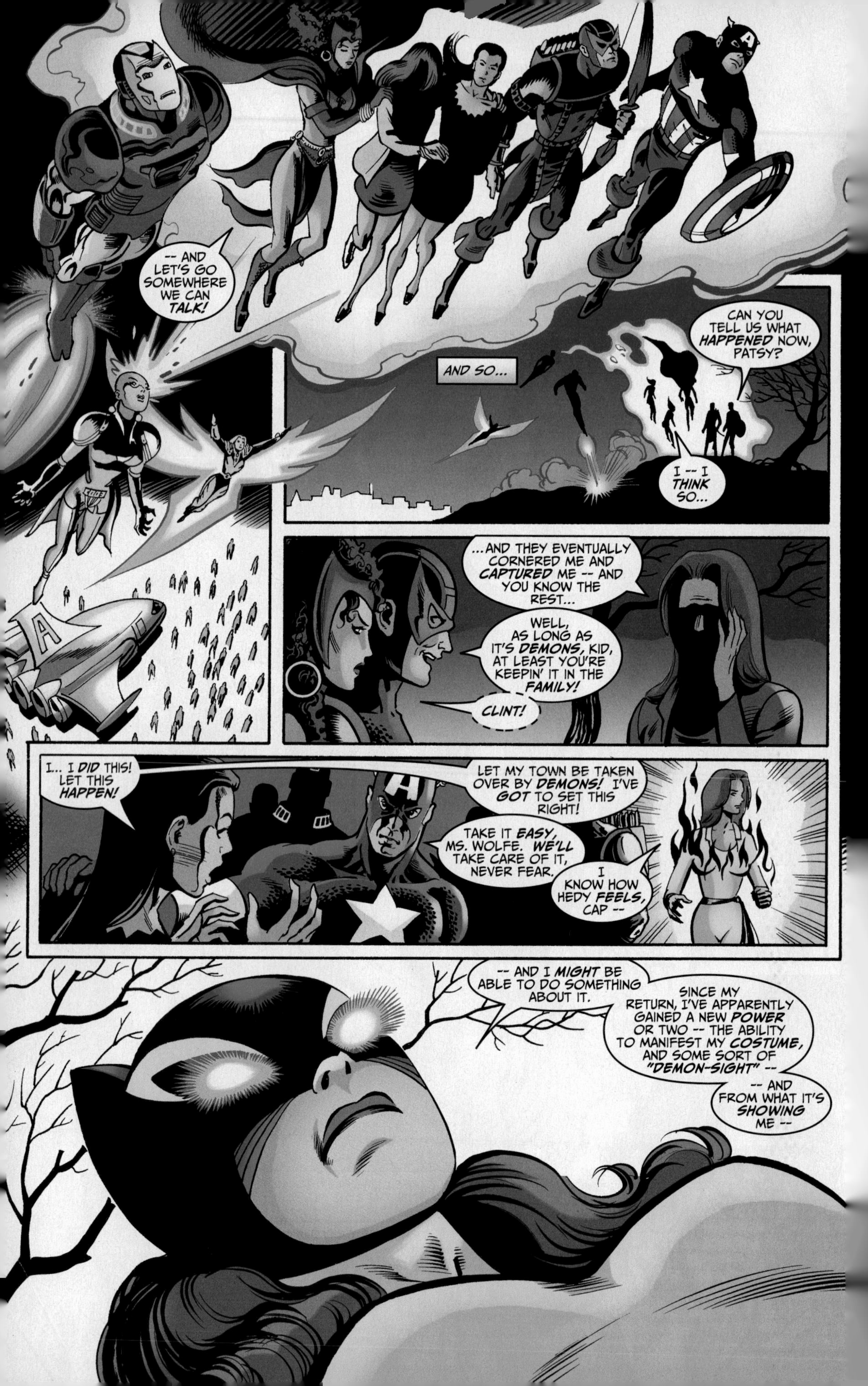
-- AND LET'S GO SOMEWHERE WE CAN *TALK!*
AND SO...
CAN YOU TELL US WHAT *HAPPENED* NOW, PATSY?
I -- I *THINK* SO...
...AND THEY EVENTUALLY CORNERED ME AND *CAPTURED* ME -- AND YOU KNOW THE REST...
WELL, AS LONG AS IT'S *DEMONS,* KID, AT LEAST YOU'RE KEEPIN' IT IN THE *FAMILY!*
CLINT!
I... I *DID* THIS! LET THIS *HAPPEN!*
LET MY TOWN BE TAKEN OVER BY *DEMONS!* I'VE *GOT* TO SET THIS RIGHT!
TAKE IT *EASY,* MS. WOLFE. *WE'LL* TAKE CARE OF IT, NEVER FEAR.
I KNOW HOW HEDY *FEELS,* CAP --
-- AND I *MIGHT* BE ABLE TO DO SOMETHING ABOUT IT.
SINCE MY RETURN, I'VE APPARENTLY GAINED A NEW *POWER* OR TWO -- THE ABILITY TO MANIFEST MY *COSTUME,* AND SOME SORT OF *"DEMON-SIGHT"* --
-- AND FROM WHAT IT'S *SHOWING* ME --

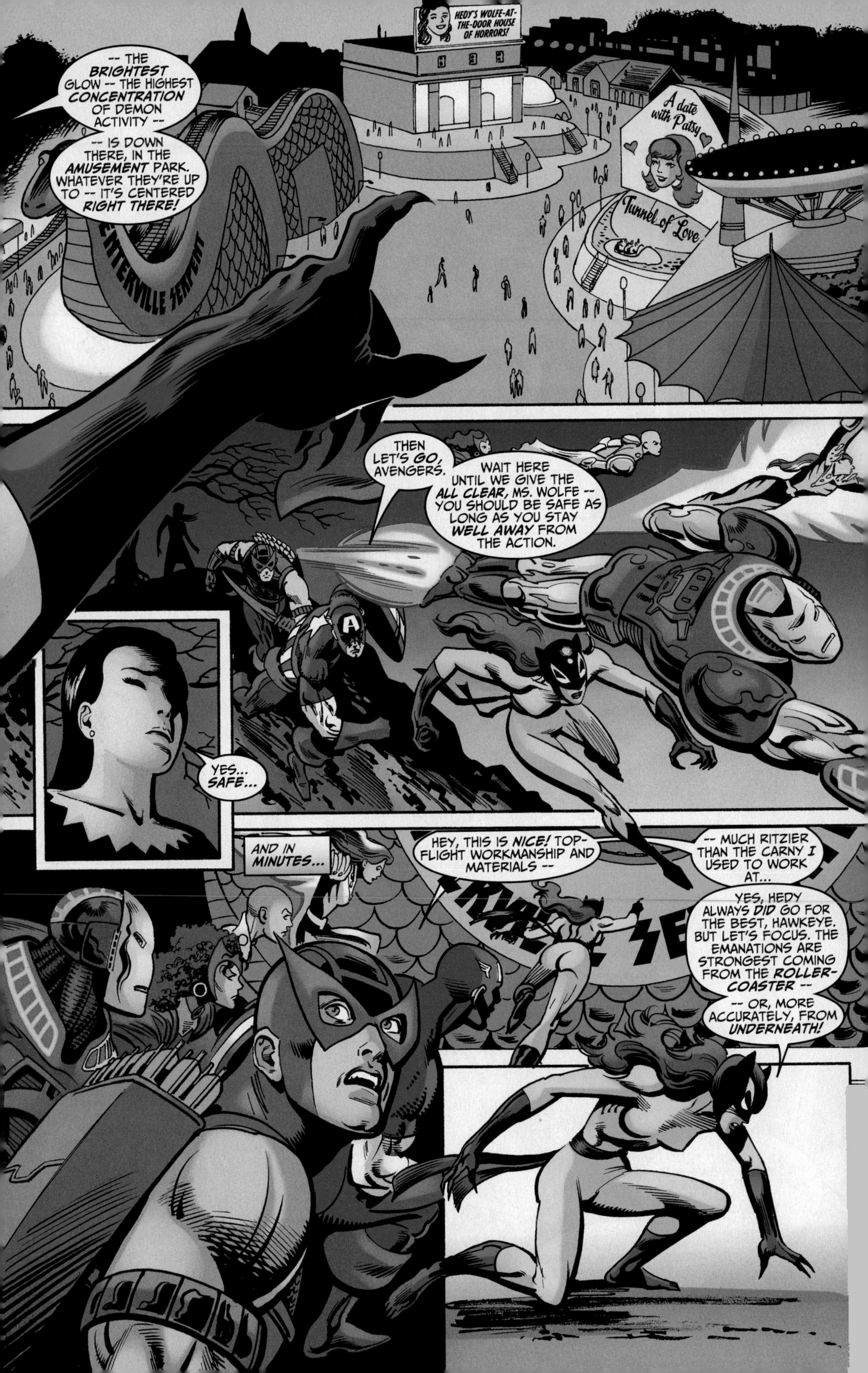
HEDY'S WOLFE-AT-THE-DOOR HOUSE OF HORRORS!
-- THE BRIGHTEST GLOW -- THE HIGHEST CONCENTRATION OF DEMON ACTIVITY --
-- IS DOWN THERE, IN THE AMUSEMENT PARK. WHATEVER THEY'RE UP TO -- IT'S CENTERED RIGHT THERE!
A date with Patsy
Tunnel of Love
THEN LET'S GO, AVENGERS.
WAIT HERE UNTIL WE GIVE THE ALL CLEAR, MS. WOLFE -- YOU SHOULD BE SAFE AS LONG AS YOU STAY WELL AWAY FROM THE ACTION.
YES... SAFE...
AND IN MINUTES...
HEY, THIS IS NICE! TOP-FLIGHT WORKMANSHIP AND MATERIALS --
-- MUCH RITZIER THAN THE CARNY I USED TO WORK AT...
YES, HEDY ALWAYS DID GO FOR THE BEST, HAWKEYE. BUT LET'S FOCUS. THE EMANATIONS ARE STRONGEST COMING FROM THE ROLLER-COASTER --
-- OR, MORE ACCURATELY, FROM UNDERNEATH!

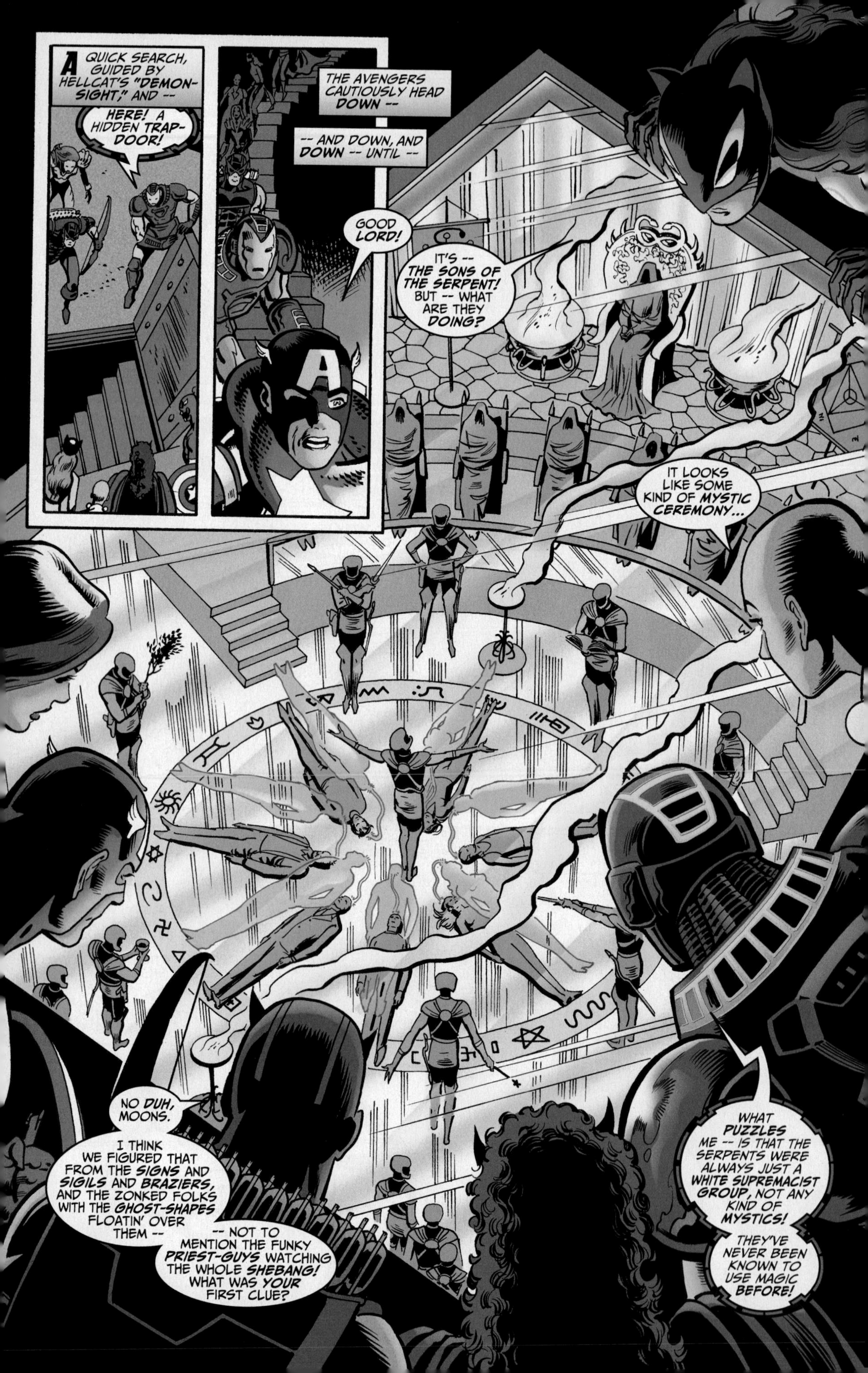
A QUICK SEARCH, GUIDED BY HELLCAT'S "DEMON-SIGHT," AND --
HERE! A HIDDEN TRAP-DOOR!
THE AVENGERS CAUTIOUSLY HEAD DOWN --
-- AND DOWN, AND DOWN -- UNTIL --
GOOD LORD!
IT'S -- THE SONS OF THE SERPENT! BUT -- WHAT ARE THEY DOING?
IT LOOKS LIKE SOME KIND OF MYSTIC CEREMONY...
NO DUH, MOONS.
I THINK WE FIGURED THAT FROM THE SIGNS AND SIGILS AND BRAZIERS, AND THE ZONKED FOLKS WITH THE GHOST-SHAPES FLOATIN' OVER THEM --
-- NOT TO MENTION THE FUNKY PRIEST-GUYS WATCHING THE WHOLE SHEBANG! WHAT WAS YOUR FIRST CLUE?
WHAT PUZZLES ME -- IS THAT THE SERPENTS WERE ALWAYS JUST A WHITE SUPREMACIST GROUP, NOT ANY KIND OF MYSTICS!
THEY'VE NEVER BEEN KNOWN TO USE MAGIC BEFORE!

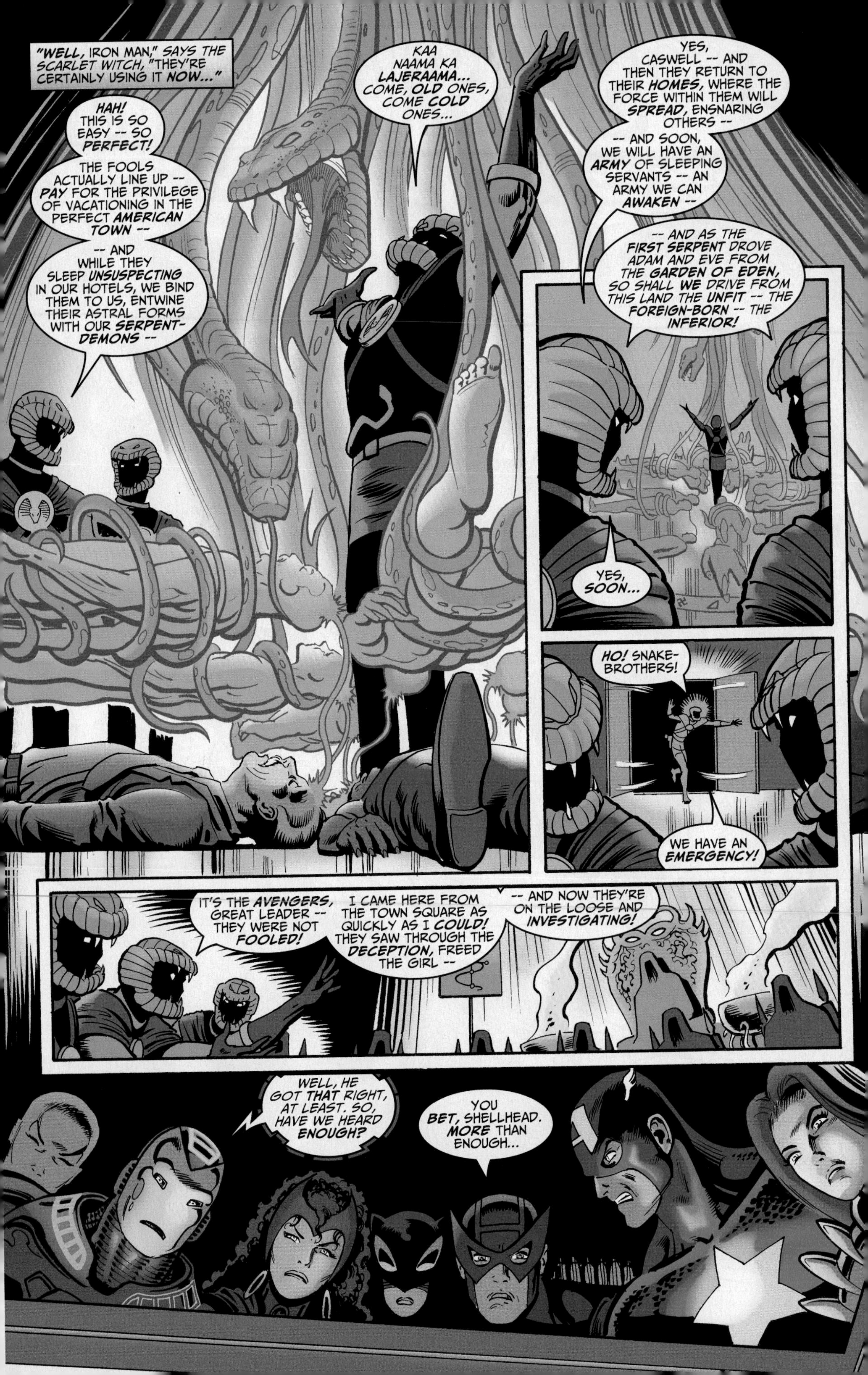
"WELL, IRON MAN," SAYS THE SCARLET WITCH, "THEY'RE CERTAINLY USING IT NOW..."
HAH! THIS IS SO EASY -- SO PERFECT!
THE FOOLS ACTUALLY LINE UP -- PAY FOR THE PRIVILEGE OF VACATIONING IN THE PERFECT AMERICAN TOWN --
-- AND WHILE THEY SLEEP UNSUSPECTING IN OUR HOTELS, WE BIND THEM TO US, ENTWINE THEIR ASTRAL FORMS WITH OUR SERPENT-DEMONS --
KAA NAAMA KA LAJERAAMA... COME, OLD ONES, COME COLD ONES...
YES, CASWELL -- AND THEN THEY RETURN TO THEIR HOMES, WHERE THE FORCE WITHIN THEM WILL SPREAD, ENSNARING OTHERS --
-- AND SOON, WE WILL HAVE AN ARMY OF SLEEPING SERVANTS -- AN ARMY WE CAN AWAKEN --
-- AND AS THE FIRST SERPENT DROVE ADAM AND EVE FROM THE GARDEN OF EDEN, SO SHALL WE DRIVE FROM THIS LAND THE UNFIT -- THE FOREIGN-BORN -- THE INFERIOR!
YES, SOON...
HO! SNAKE-BROTHERS!
WE HAVE AN EMERGENCY!
IT'S THE AVENGERS, GREAT LEADER -- THEY WERE NOT FOOLED!
I CAME HERE FROM THE TOWN SQUARE AS QUICKLY AS I COULD! THEY SAW THROUGH THE DECEPTION, FREED THE GIRL --
-- AND NOW THEY'RE ON THE LOOSE AND INVESTIGATING!
WELL, HE GOT THAT RIGHT, AT LEAST. SO, HAVE WE HEARD ENOUGH?
YOU BET, SHELLHEAD. MORE THAN ENOUGH...

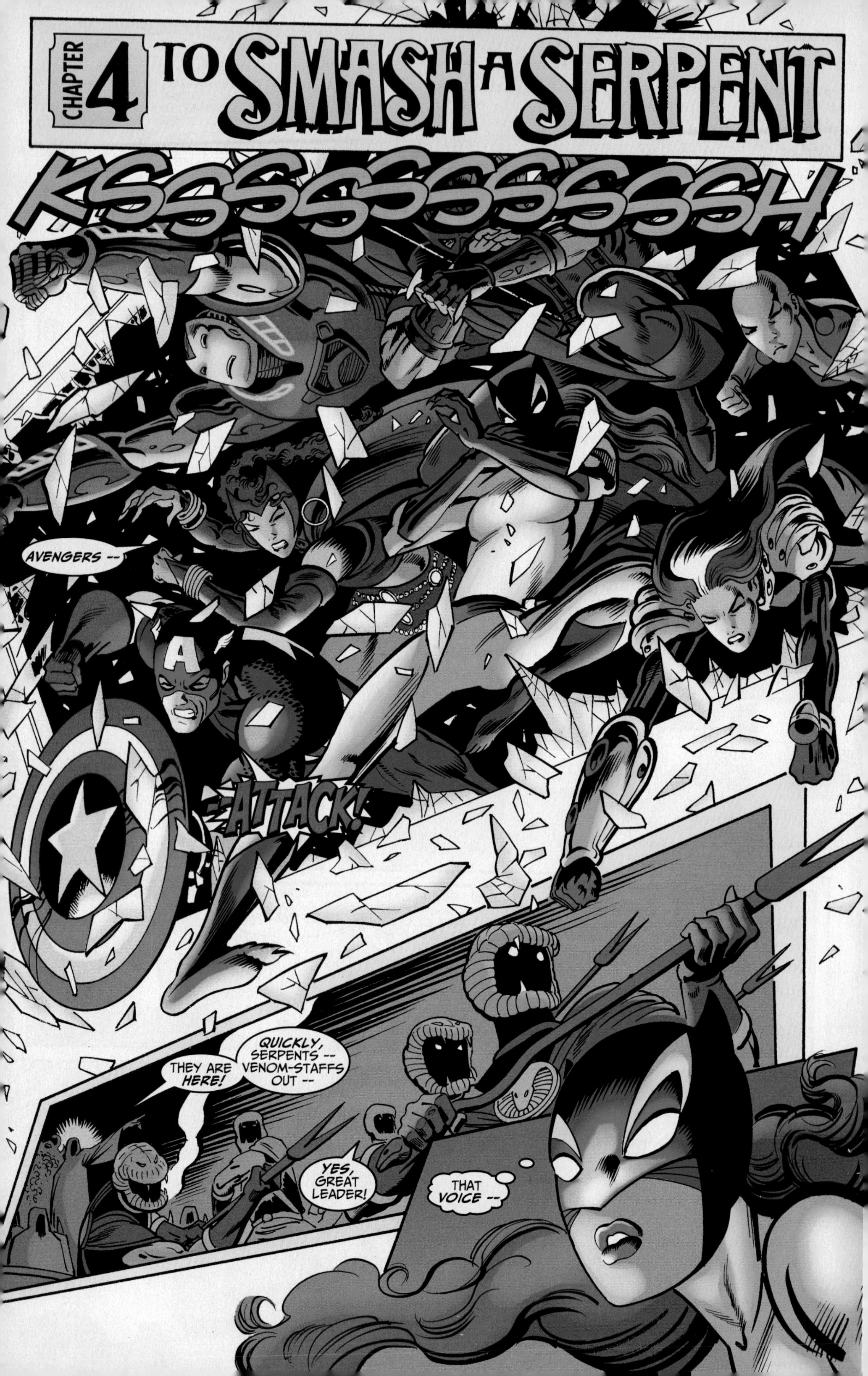
CHAPTER 4 TO SMASH A SERPENT
KSSSSSSSSSSSH
AVENGERS --
-- ATTACK!
THEY ARE HERE!
QUICKLY, SERPENTS -- VENOM-STAFFS OUT --
YES, GREAT LEADER!
THAT VOICE --

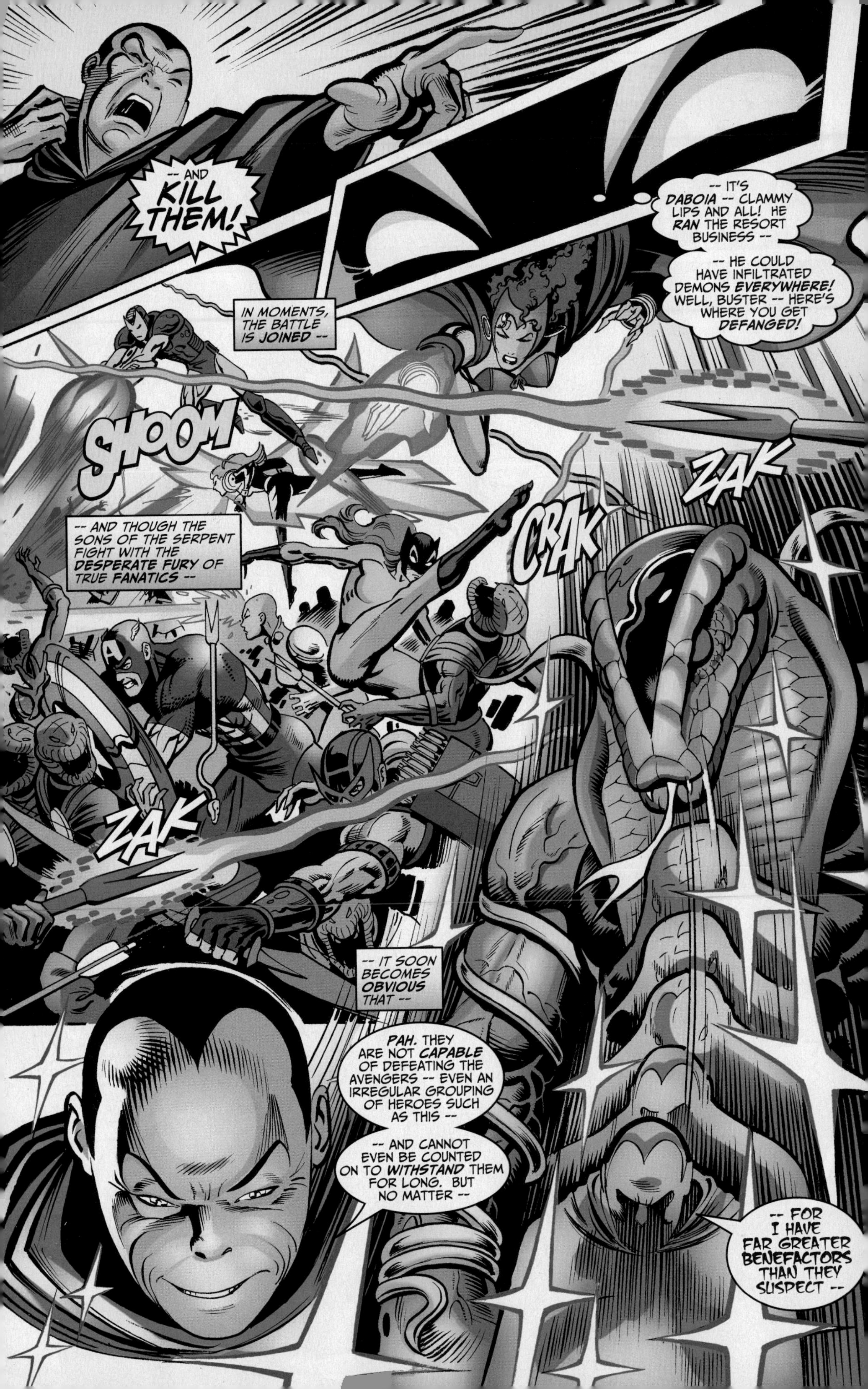
-- AND KILL THEM!
-- IT'S DABOIA -- CLAMMY LIPS AND ALL! HE RAN THE RESORT BUSINESS --
-- HE COULD HAVE INFILTRATED DEMONS EVERYWHERE! WELL, BUSTER -- HERE'S WHERE YOU GET DEFANGED!
IN MOMENTS, THE BATTLE IS JOINED --
SHOOM
ZAK
CRAK
-- AND THOUGH THE SONS OF THE SERPENT FIGHT WITH THE DESPERATE FURY OF TRUE FANATICS --
ZAK
-- IT SOON BECOMES OBVIOUS THAT --
PAH. THEY ARE NOT CAPABLE OF DEFEATING THE AVENGERS -- EVEN AN IRREGULAR GROUPING OF HEROES SUCH AS THIS --
-- AND CANNOT EVEN BE COUNTED ON TO WITHSTAND THEM FOR LONG. BUT NO MATTER --
-- FOR I HAVE FAR GREATER BENEFACTORS THAN THEY SUSPECT --

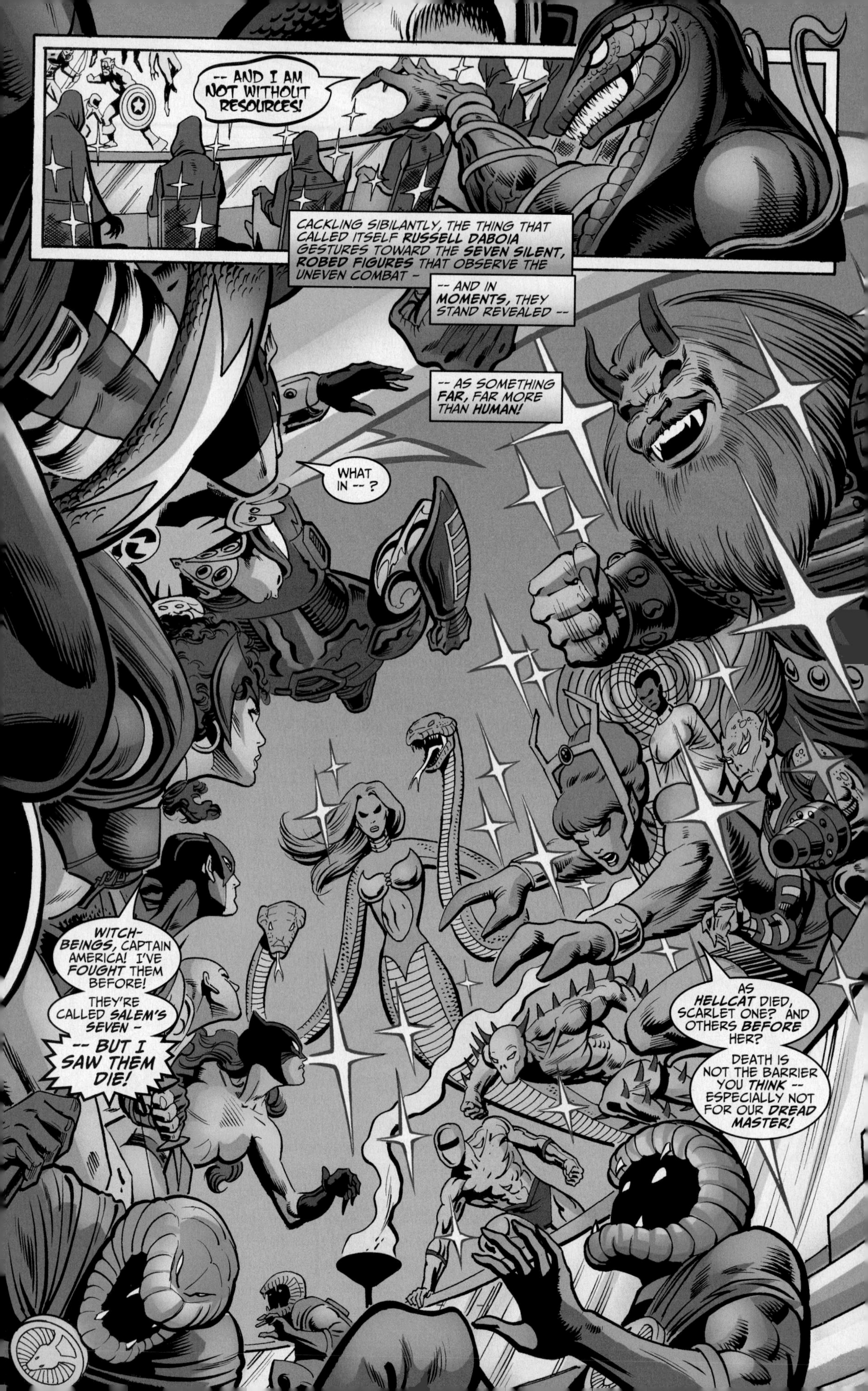
-- AND I AM NOT WITHOUT RESOURCES!
CACKLING SIBILANTLY, THE THING THAT CALLED ITSELF **RUSSELL DABOIA** GESTURES TOWARD THE **SEVEN SILENT, ROBED FIGURES** THAT OBSERVE THE UNEVEN COMBAT -
-- AND IN **MOMENTS,** THEY STAND REVEALED --
-- AS SOMETHING **FAR,** FAR MORE THAN **HUMAN!**
WHAT IN -- ?
WITCH-BEINGS, CAPTAIN AMERICA! I'VE **FOUGHT** THEM BEFORE!
THEY'RE CALLED **SALEM'S SEVEN** -
-- BUT I SAW THEM DIE!
AS **HELLCAT** DIED, SCARLET ONE? AND OTHERS **BEFORE** HER?
DEATH IS NOT THE BARRIER YOU **THINK** -- ESPECIALLY NOT FOR OUR **DREAD MASTER!**

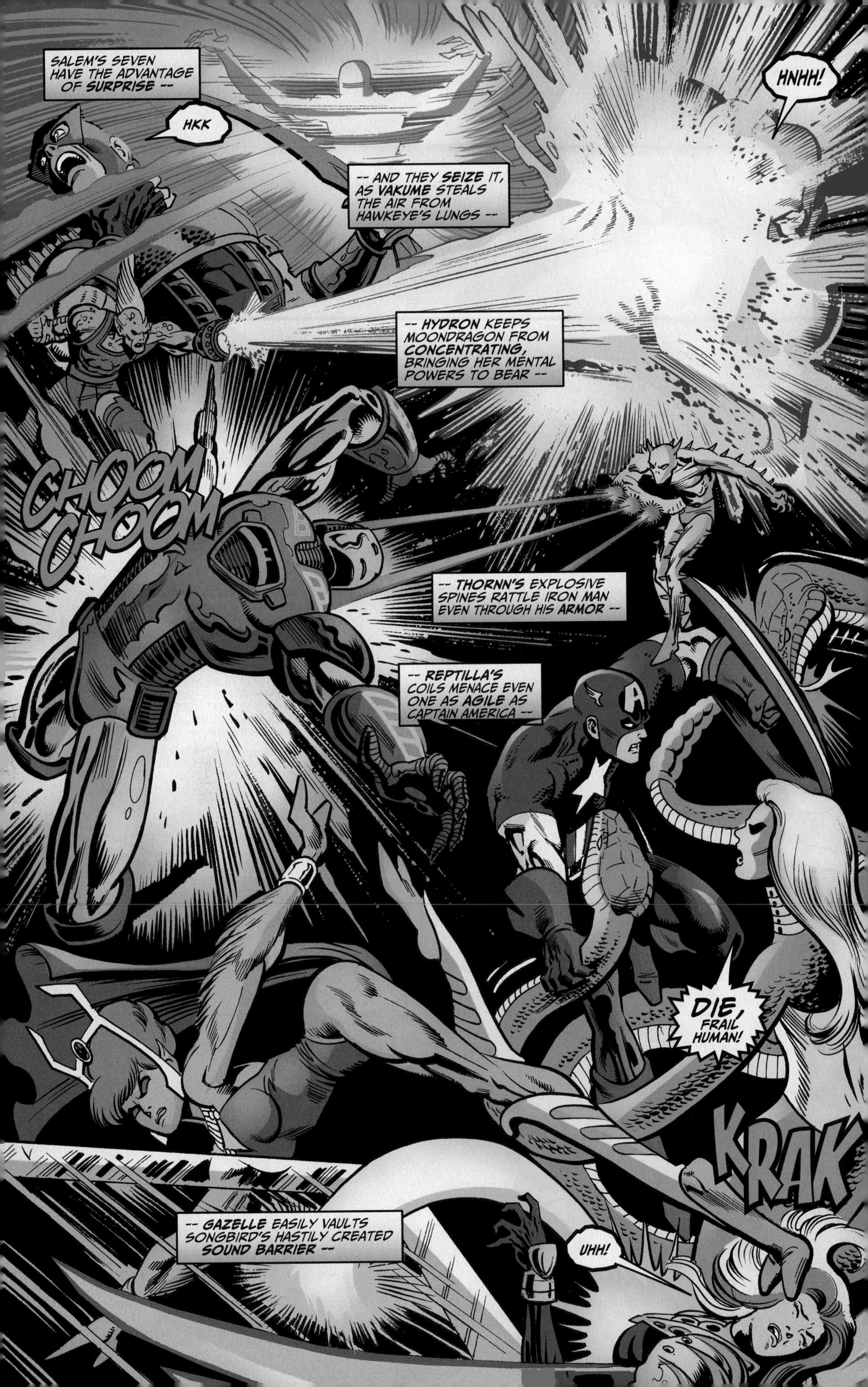
SALEM'S SEVEN HAVE THE ADVANTAGE OF **SURPRISE** --
HKK
HNHH!
-- AND THEY **SEIZE** IT, AS **VAKUME** STEALS THE AIR FROM HAWKEYE'S LUNGS --
-- **HYDRON** KEEPS MOONDRAGON FROM **CONCENTRATING**, BRINGING HER MENTAL POWERS TO BEAR --
CHOOM CHOOM
-- **THORNN'S** EXPLOSIVE SPINES RATTLE IRON MAN EVEN THROUGH HIS **ARMOR** --
-- **REPTILLA'S** COILS MENACE EVEN ONE AS **AGILE** AS CAPTAIN AMERICA --
DIE, FRAIL HUMAN!
KRAK
-- **GAZELLE** EASILY VAULTS SONGBIRD'S HASTILY CREATED **SOUND BARRIER** --
UHH!

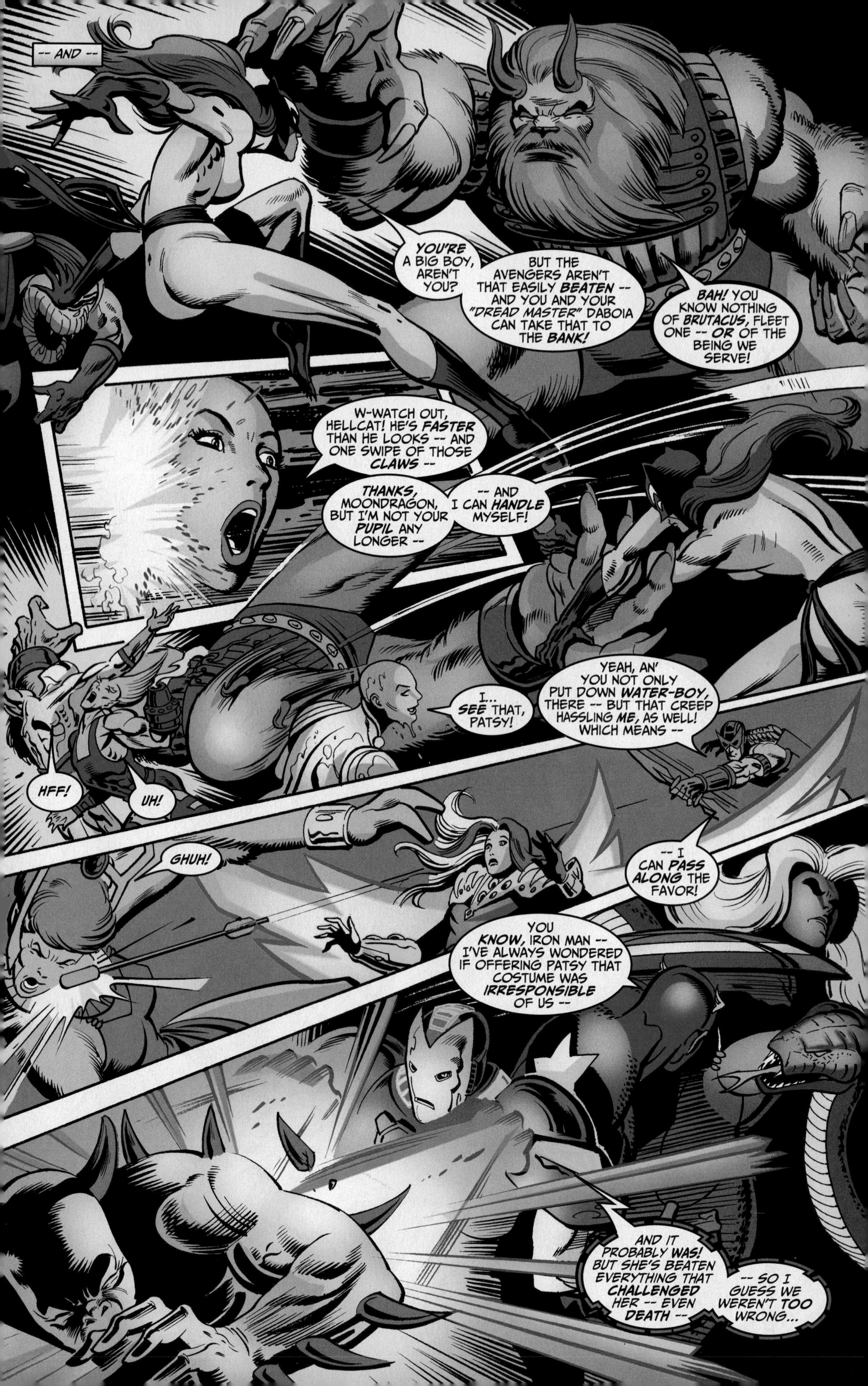
-- AND --
YOU'RE A BIG BOY, AREN'T YOU?
BUT THE AVENGERS AREN'T THAT EASILY BEATEN -- AND YOU AND YOUR "DREAD MASTER" DABOIA CAN TAKE THAT TO THE BANK!
BAH! YOU KNOW NOTHING OF BRUTACUS, FLEET ONE -- OR OF THE BEING WE SERVE!
W-WATCH OUT, HELLCAT! HE'S FASTER THAN HE LOOKS -- AND ONE SWIPE OF THOSE CLAWS --
THANKS, MOONDRAGON, BUT I'M NOT YOUR PUPIL ANY LONGER --
-- AND I CAN HANDLE MYSELF!
I... SEE THAT, PATSY!
YEAH, AN' YOU NOT ONLY PUT DOWN WATER-BOY, THERE -- BUT THAT CREEP HASSLING ME, AS WELL! WHICH MEANS --
HFF!
UH!
GHUH!
-- I CAN PASS ALONG THE FAVOR!
YOU KNOW, IRON MAN -- I'VE ALWAYS WONDERED IF OFFERING PATSY THAT COSTUME WAS IRRESPONSIBLE OF US --
AND IT PROBABLY WAS! BUT SHE'S BEATEN EVERYTHING THAT CHALLENGED HER -- EVEN DEATH --
-- SO I GUESS WE WEREN'T TOO WRONG...

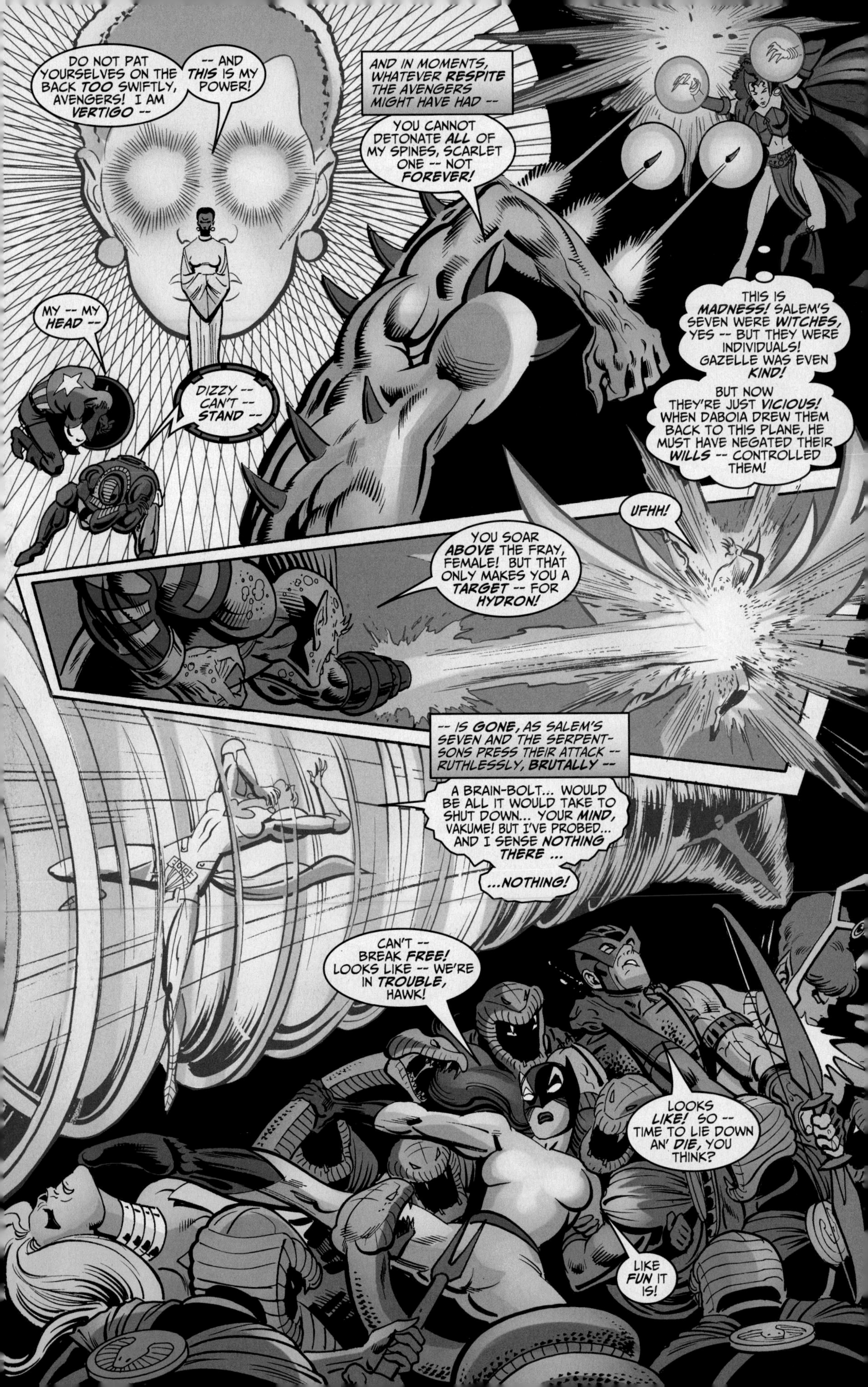
DO NOT PAT YOURSELVES ON THE BACK TOO SWIFTLY, AVENGERS! I AM VERTIGO --
-- AND THIS IS MY POWER!
MY -- MY HEAD --
DIZZY -- CAN'T -- STAND --
AND IN MOMENTS, WHATEVER RESPITE THE AVENGERS MIGHT HAVE HAD --
YOU CANNOT DETONATE ALL OF MY SPINES, SCARLET ONE -- NOT FOREVER!
THIS IS MADNESS! SALEM'S SEVEN WERE WITCHES, YES -- BUT THEY WERE INDIVIDUALS! GAZELLE WAS EVEN KIND!
BUT NOW THEY'RE JUST VICIOUS! WHEN DABOIA DREW THEM BACK TO THIS PLANE, HE MUST HAVE NEGATED THEIR WILLS -- CONTROLLED THEM!
UFHH!
YOU SOAR ABOVE THE FRAY, FEMALE! BUT THAT ONLY MAKES YOU A TARGET -- FOR HYDRON!
-- IS GONE, AS SALEM'S SEVEN AND THE SERPENT-SONS PRESS THEIR ATTACK -- RUTHLESSLY, BRUTALLY --
A BRAIN-BOLT... WOULD BE ALL IT WOULD TAKE TO SHUT DOWN... YOUR MIND, VAKUME! BUT I'VE PROBED... AND I SENSE NOTHING THERE ...
...NOTHING!
CAN'T -- BREAK FREE! LOOKS LIKE -- WE'RE IN TROUBLE, HAWK!
LOOKS LIKE! SO -- TIME TO LIE DOWN AN' DIE, YOU THINK?
LIKE FUN IT IS!

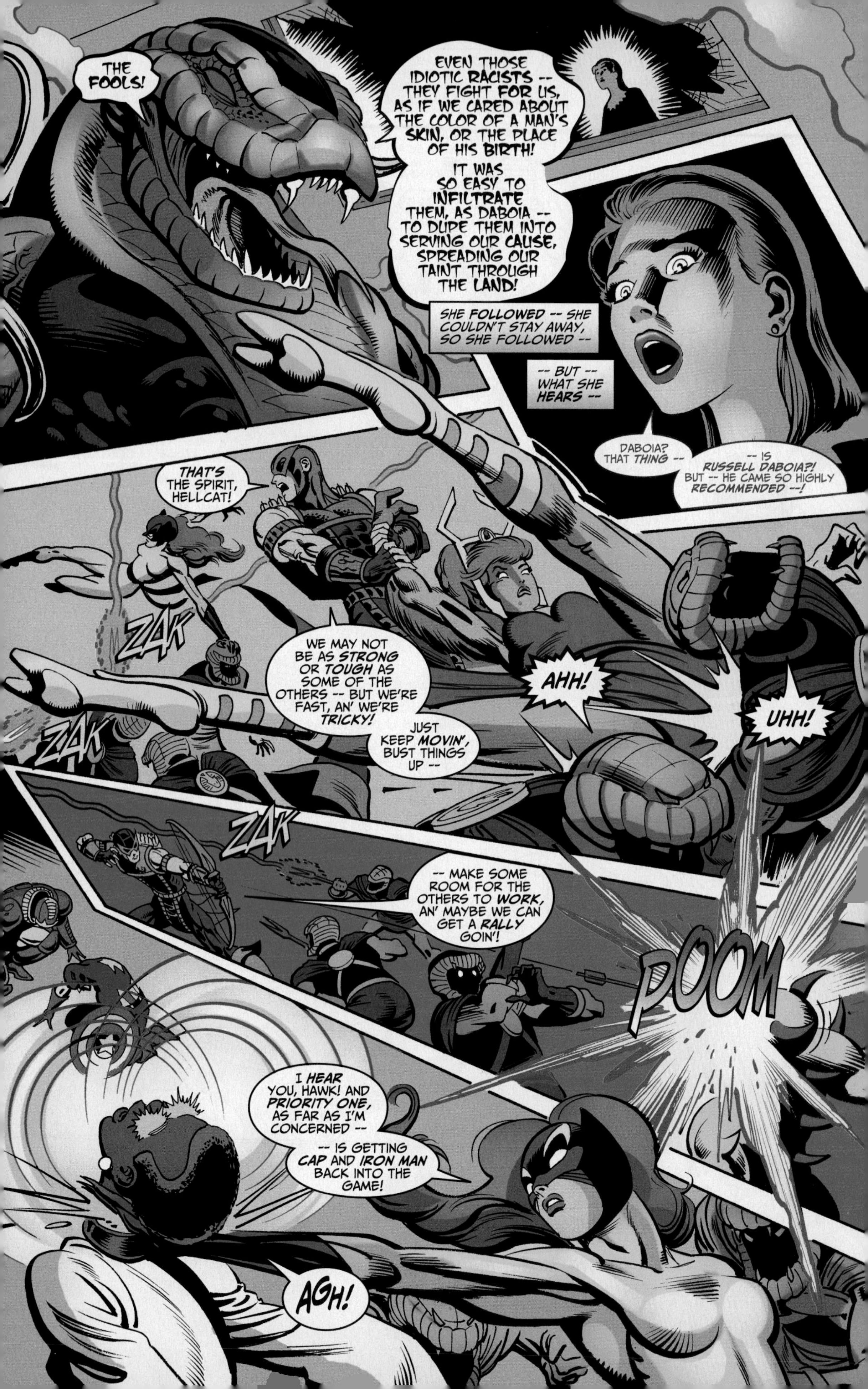
THE FOOLS!
EVEN THOSE IDIOTIC RACISTS -- THEY FIGHT FOR US, AS IF WE CARED ABOUT THE COLOR OF A MAN'S SKIN, OR THE PLACE OF HIS BIRTH!
IT WAS SO EASY TO INFILTRATE THEM, AS DABOIA -- TO DUPE THEM INTO SERVING OUR CAUSE, SPREADING OUR TAINT THROUGH THE LAND!
SHE FOLLOWED -- SHE COULDN'T STAY AWAY, SO SHE FOLLOWED --
-- BUT -- WHAT SHE HEARS --
DABOIA? THAT THING --
-- IS RUSSELL DABOIA?! BUT -- HE CAME SO HIGHLY RECOMMENDED --!
THAT'S THE SPIRIT, HELLCAT!
ZAK
WE MAY NOT BE AS STRONG OR TOUGH AS SOME OF THE OTHERS -- BUT WE'RE FAST, AN' WE'RE TRICKY!
AHH!
UHH!
ZAK
JUST KEEP MOVIN', BUST THINGS UP --
ZAK
-- MAKE SOME ROOM FOR THE OTHERS TO WORK, AN' MAYBE WE CAN GET A RALLY GOIN'!
POOM
I HEAR YOU, HAWK! AND PRIORITY ONE, AS FAR AS I'M CONCERNED --
-- IS GETTING CAP AND IRON MAN BACK INTO THE GAME!
AGH!

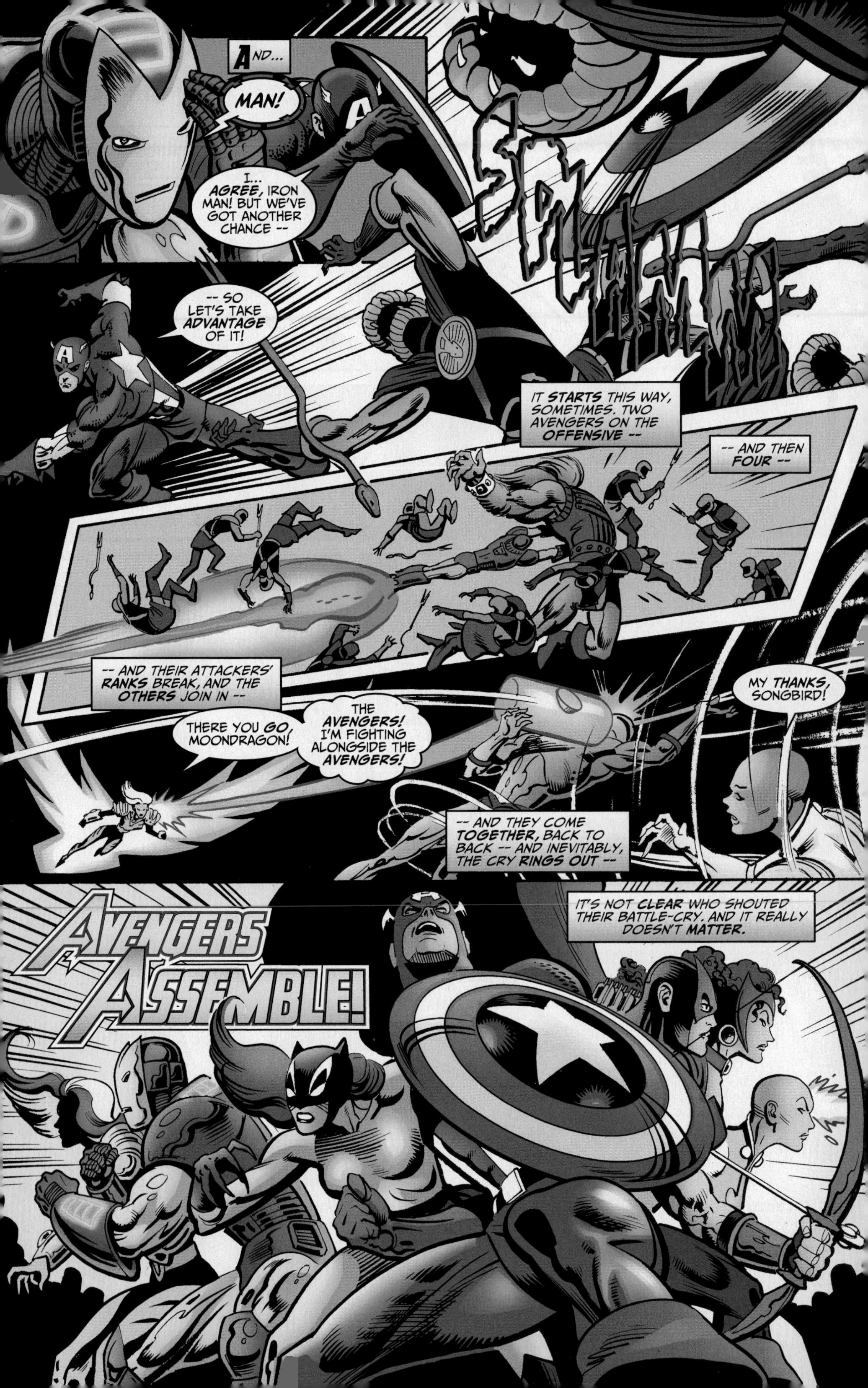
AND...
MAN!
I... AGREE, IRON MAN! BUT WE'VE GOT ANOTHER CHANCE --
-- SO LET'S TAKE ADVANTAGE OF IT!
IT STARTS THIS WAY, SOMETIMES. TWO AVENGERS ON THE OFFENSIVE --
-- AND THEN FOUR --
-- AND THEIR ATTACKERS' RANKS BREAK, AND THE OTHERS JOIN IN --
THERE YOU GO, MOONDRAGON!
THE AVENGERS! I'M FIGHTING ALONGSIDE THE AVENGERS!
MY THANKS, SONGBIRD!
-- AND THEY COME TOGETHER, BACK TO BACK -- AND INEVITABLY, THE CRY RINGS OUT --
AVENGERS ASSEMBLE!
IT'S NOT CLEAR WHO SHOUTED THEIR BATTLE-CRY. AND IT REALLY DOESN'T MATTER.

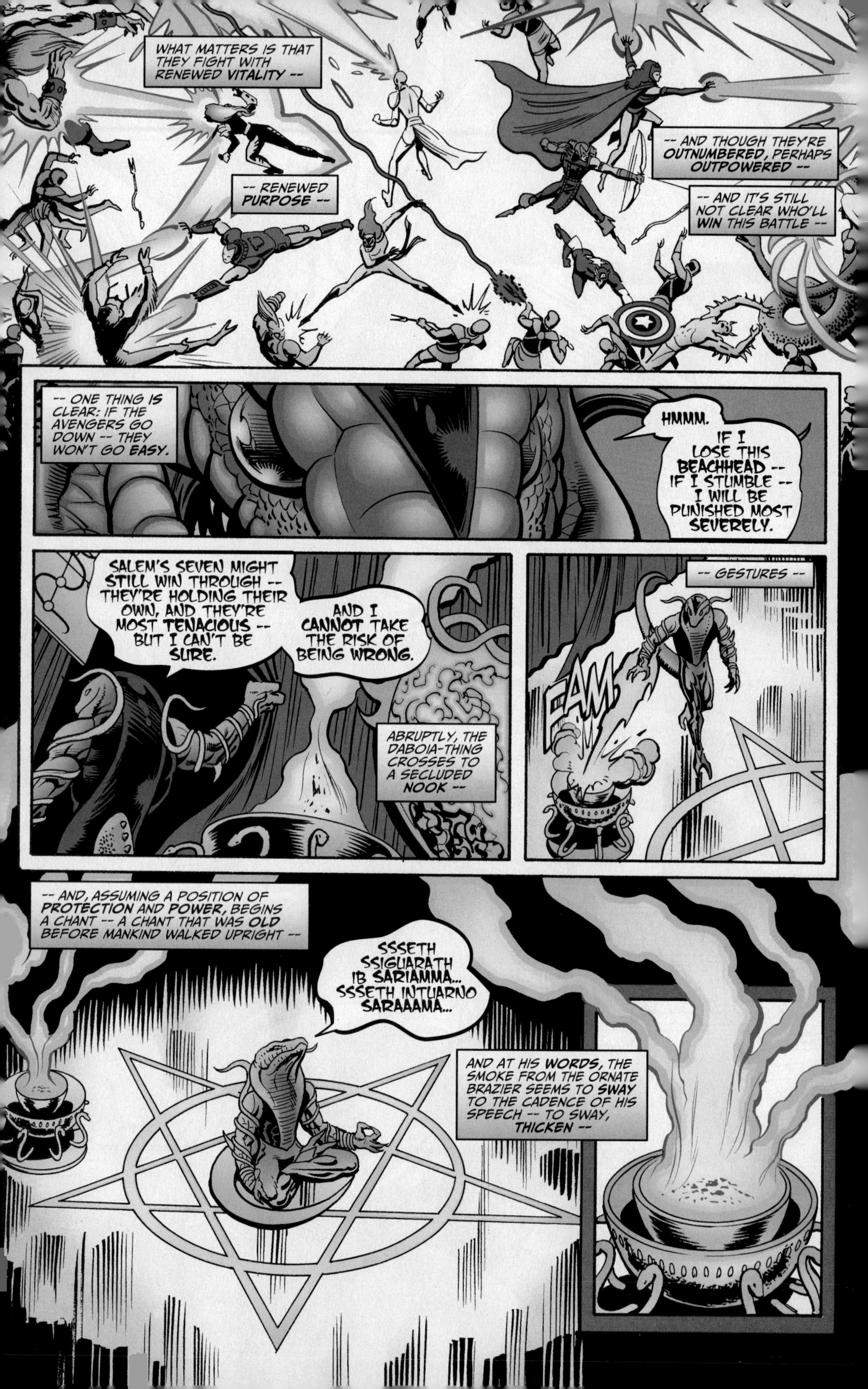
WHAT MATTERS IS THAT THEY FIGHT WITH RENEWED VITALITY --
-- RENEWED PURPOSE --
-- AND THOUGH THEY'RE OUTNUMBERED, PERHAPS OUTPOWERED --
-- AND IT'S STILL NOT CLEAR WHO'LL WIN THIS BATTLE --
-- ONE THING IS CLEAR: IF THE AVENGERS GO DOWN -- THEY WON'T GO EASY.
HMMM.
IF I LOSE THIS BEACHHEAD -- IF I STUMBLE -- I WILL BE PUNISHED MOST SEVERELY.
SALEM'S SEVEN MIGHT STILL WIN THROUGH -- THEY'RE HOLDING THEIR OWN, AND THEY'RE MOST TENACIOUS -- BUT I CAN'T BE SURE.
AND I CANNOT TAKE THE RISK OF BEING WRONG.
ABRUPTLY, THE DABOIA-THING CROSSES TO A SECLUDED NOOK --
-- GESTURES --
FAM
-- AND, ASSUMING A POSITION OF PROTECTION AND POWER, BEGINS A CHANT -- A CHANT THAT WAS OLD BEFORE MANKIND WALKED UPRIGHT --
SSSETH SSIGUARATH IB SARIAMMA... SSSETH INTUARNO SARAAAMA...
AND AT HIS WORDS, THE SMOKE FROM THE ORNATE BRAZIER SEEMS TO SWAY TO THE CADENCE OF HIS SPEECH -- TO SWAY, THICKEN --

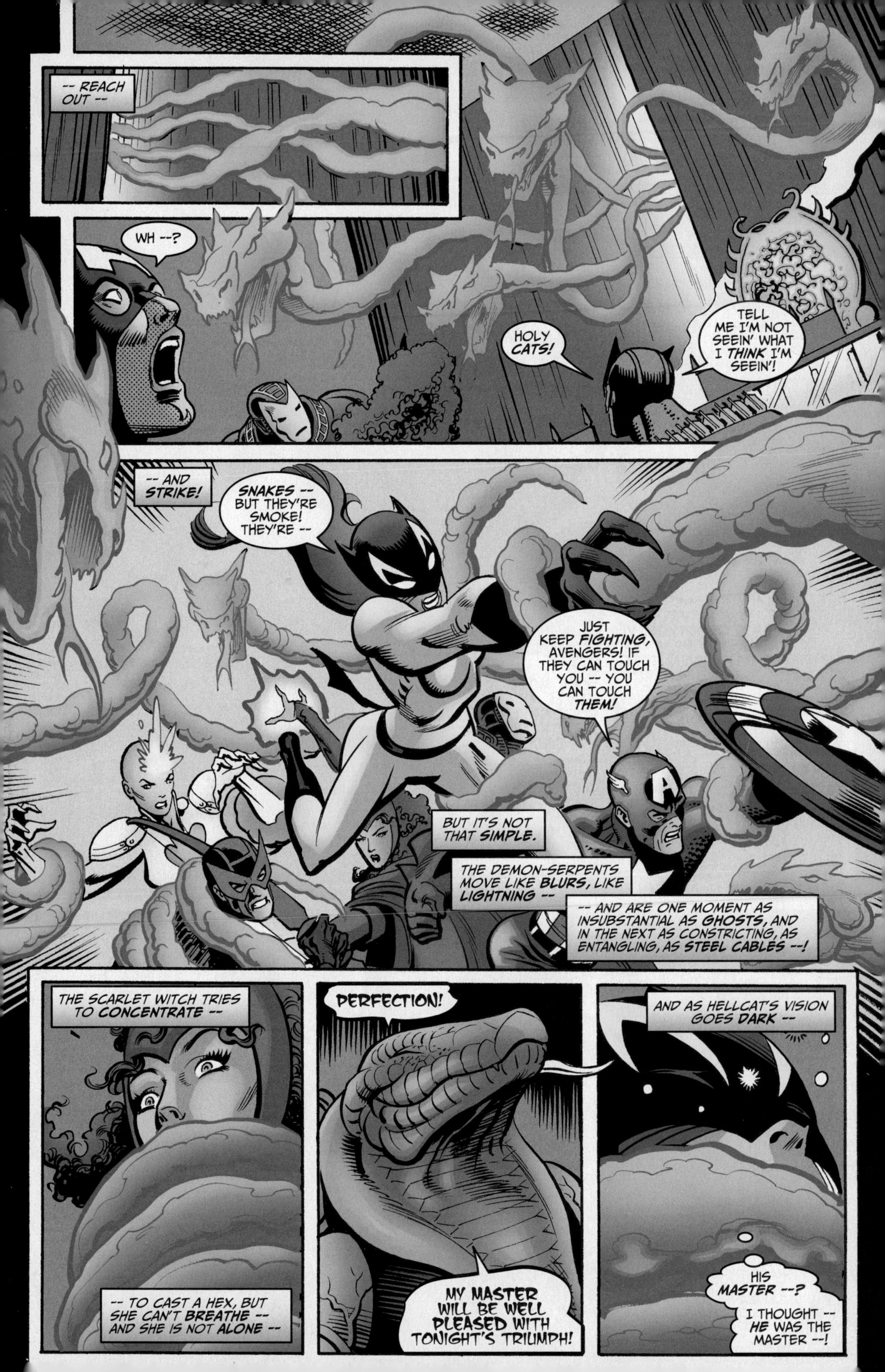
-- REACH OUT --
WH --?
HOLY CATS!
TELL ME I'M NOT SEEIN' WHAT I THINK I'M SEEIN'!
-- AND STRIKE!
SNAKES -- BUT THEY'RE SMOKE! THEY'RE --
JUST KEEP FIGHTING, AVENGERS! IF THEY CAN TOUCH YOU -- YOU CAN TOUCH THEM!
BUT IT'S NOT THAT SIMPLE.
THE DEMON-SERPENTS MOVE LIKE BLURS, LIKE LIGHTNING --
-- AND ARE ONE MOMENT AS INSUBSTANTIAL AS GHOSTS, AND IN THE NEXT AS CONSTRICTING, AS ENTANGLING, AS STEEL CABLES --!
THE SCARLET WITCH TRIES TO CONCENTRATE --
-- TO CAST A HEX, BUT SHE CAN'T BREATHE -- AND SHE IS NOT ALONE --
PERFECTION!
MY MASTER WILL BE WELL PLEASED WITH TONIGHT'S TRIUMPH!
AND AS HELLCAT'S VISION GOES DARK --
HIS MASTER --?
I THOUGHT -- HE WAS THE MASTER --!

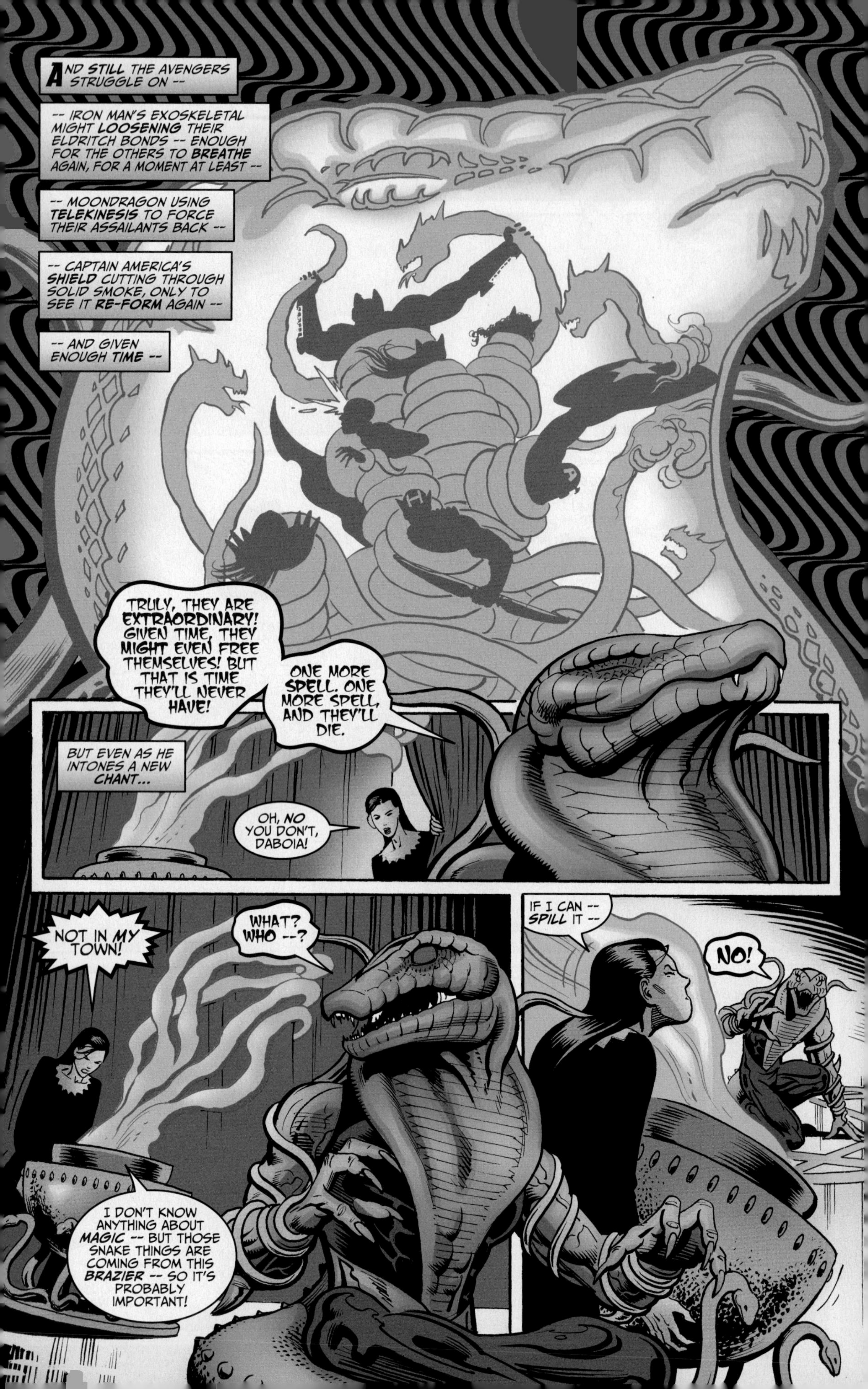
AND STILL THE AVENGERS STRUGGLE ON --
-- IRON MAN'S EXOSKELETAL MIGHT LOOSENING THEIR ELDRITCH BONDS -- ENOUGH FOR THE OTHERS TO BREATHE AGAIN, FOR A MOMENT AT LEAST --
-- MOONDRAGON USING TELEKINESIS TO FORCE THEIR ASSAILANTS BACK --
-- CAPTAIN AMERICA'S SHIELD CUTTING THROUGH SOLID SMOKE, ONLY TO SEE IT RE-FORM AGAIN --
-- AND GIVEN ENOUGH TIME --
TRULY, THEY ARE EXTRAORDINARY! GIVEN TIME, THEY MIGHT EVEN FREE THEMSELVES! BUT THAT IS TIME THEY'LL NEVER HAVE!
ONE MORE SPELL. ONE MORE SPELL, AND THEY'LL DIE.
BUT EVEN AS HE INTONES A NEW CHANT...
OH, NO YOU DON'T, DABOIA!
NOT IN MY TOWN!
WHAT? WHO --?
I DON'T KNOW ANYTHING ABOUT MAGIC -- BUT THOSE SNAKE THINGS ARE COMING FROM THIS BRAZIER -- SO IT'S PROBABLY IMPORTANT!
IF I CAN -- SPILL IT --
NO!

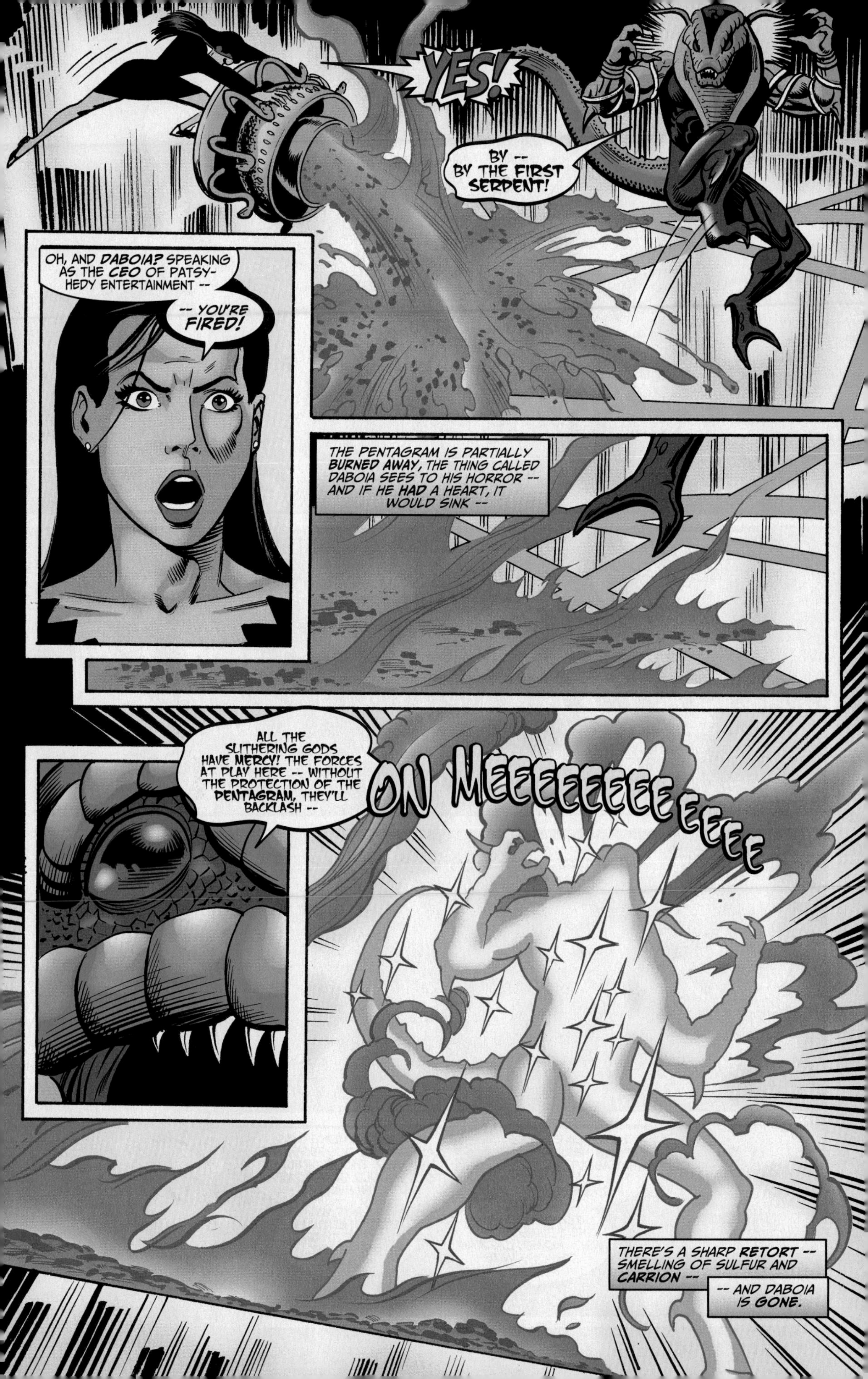
YES!
BY -- BY THE FIRST SERPENT!
OH, AND DABOIA? SPEAKING AS THE CEO OF PATSY-HEDY ENTERTAINMENT --
-- YOU'RE FIRED!
THE PENTAGRAM IS PARTIALLY BURNED AWAY, THE THING CALLED DABOIA SEES TO HIS HORROR -- AND IF HE HAD A HEART, IT WOULD SINK --
ALL THE SLITHERING GODS HAVE MERCY! THE FORCES AT PLAY HERE -- WITHOUT THE PROTECTION OF THE PENTAGRAM, THEY'LL BACKLASH --
ON MEEEEEEEEEEEEE
THERE'S A SHARP RETORT -- SMELLING OF SULFUR AND CARRION --
-- AND DABOIA IS GONE.

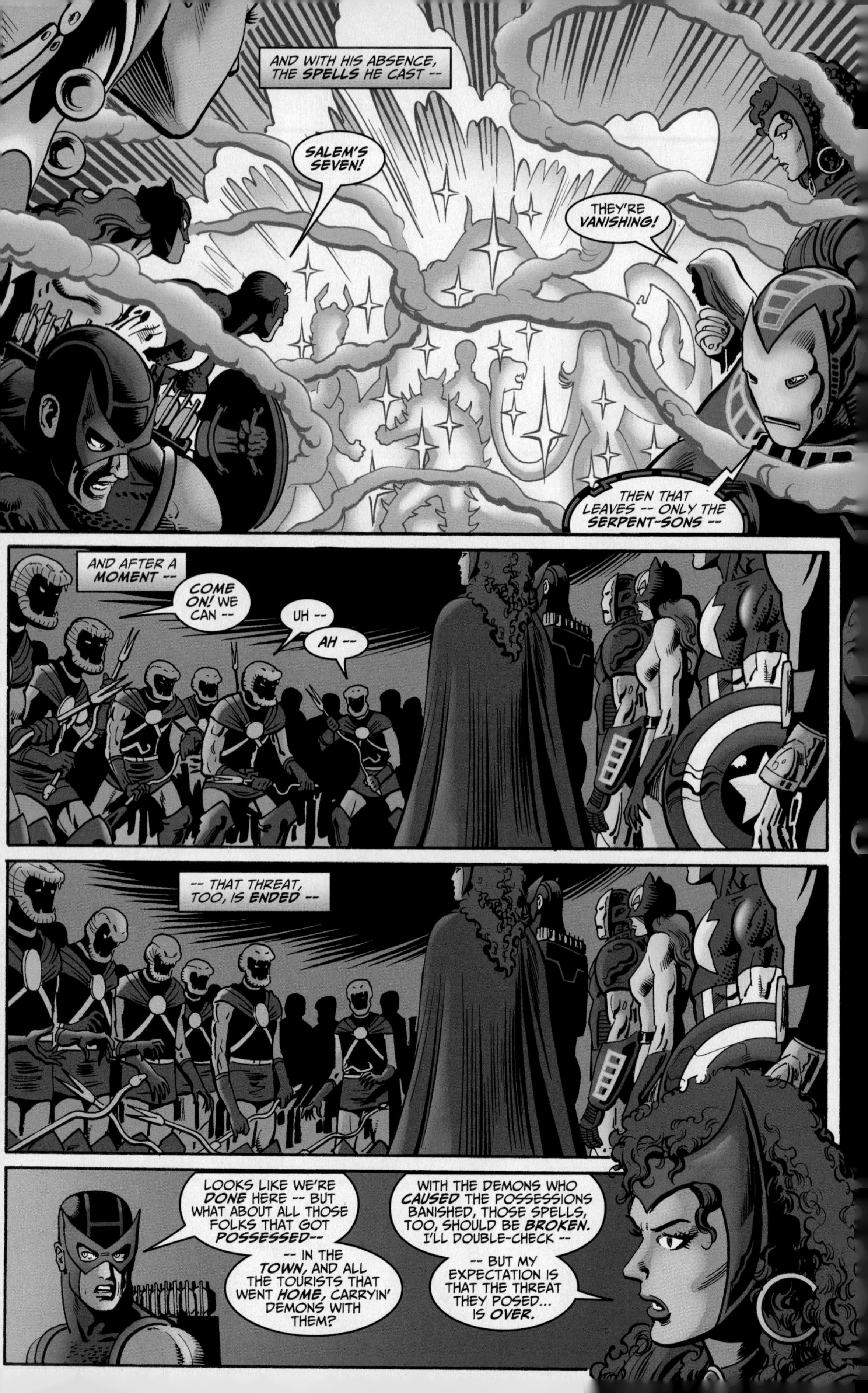
AND WITH HIS ABSENCE, THE SPELLS HE CAST --
SALEM'S SEVEN!
THEY'RE VANISHING!
THEN THAT LEAVES -- ONLY THE SERPENT-SONS --
AND AFTER A MOMENT --
COME ON! WE CAN --
UH --
AH --
-- THAT THREAT, TOO, IS ENDED --
LOOKS LIKE WE'RE DONE HERE -- BUT WHAT ABOUT ALL THOSE FOLKS THAT GOT POSSESSED--
-- IN THE TOWN, AND ALL THE TOURISTS THAT WENT HOME, CARRYIN' DEMONS WITH THEM?
WITH THE DEMONS WHO CAUSED THE POSSESSIONS BANISHED, THOSE SPELLS, TOO, SHOULD BE BROKEN. I'LL DOUBLE-CHECK --
-- BUT MY EXPECTATION IS THAT THE THREAT THEY POSED... IS OVER.

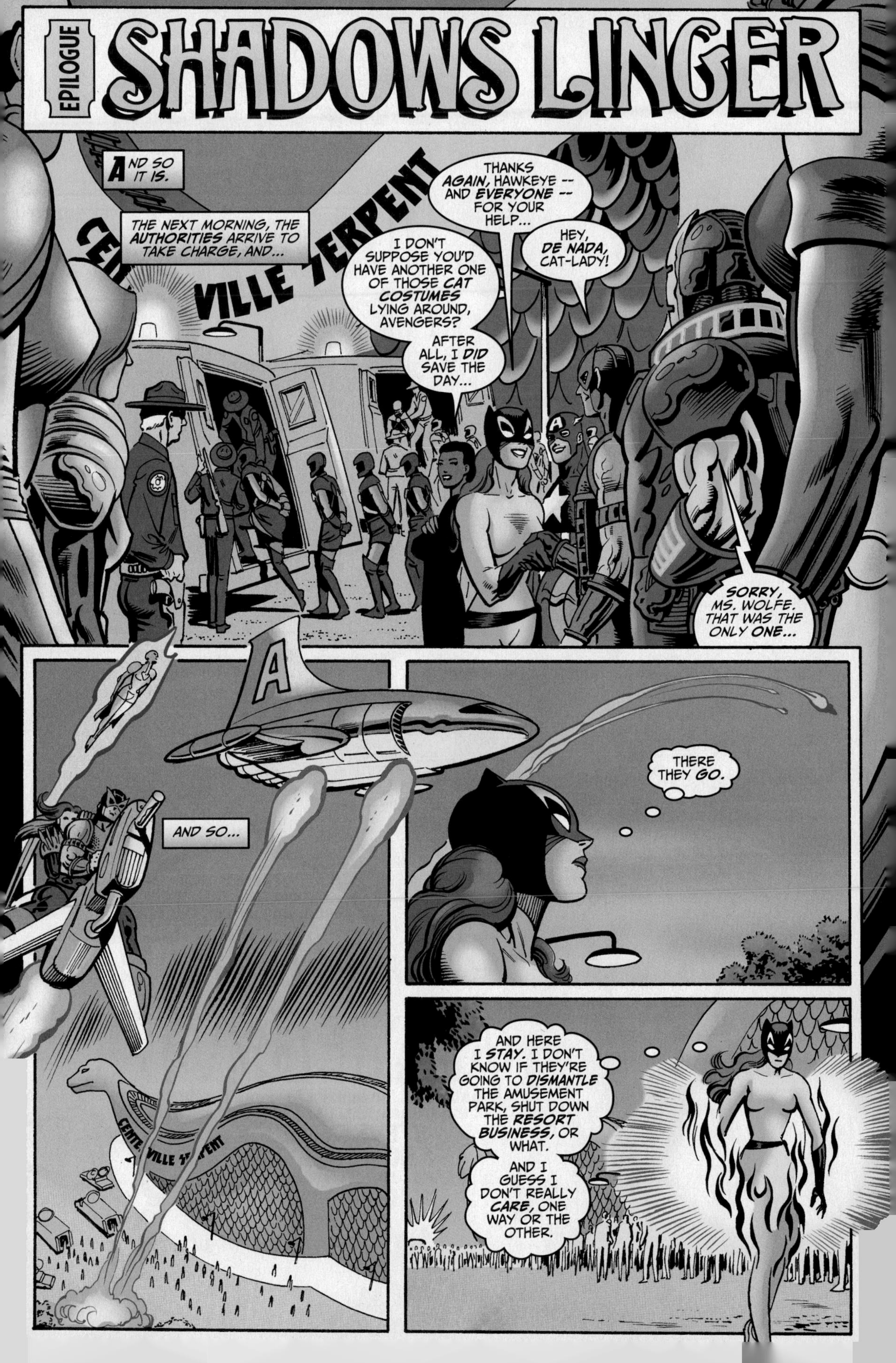
EPILOGUE
SHADOWS LINGER
AND SO IT IS.
THE NEXT MORNING, THE AUTHORITIES ARRIVE TO TAKE CHARGE, AND...
CENTERVILLE SERPENT
THANKS AGAIN, HAWKEYE -- AND EVERYONE -- FOR YOUR HELP...
HEY, DE NADA, CAT-LADY!
I DON'T SUPPOSE YOU'D HAVE ANOTHER ONE OF THOSE CAT COSTUMES LYING AROUND, AVENGERS?
AFTER ALL, I DID SAVE THE DAY...
SORRY, MS. WOLFE. THAT WAS THE ONLY ONE...
AND SO...
THERE THEY GO.
AND HERE I STAY. I DON'T KNOW IF THEY'RE GOING TO DISMANTLE THE AMUSEMENT PARK, SHUT DOWN THE RESORT BUSINESS, OR WHAT.
AND I GUESS I DON'T REALLY CARE, ONE WAY OR THE OTHER.

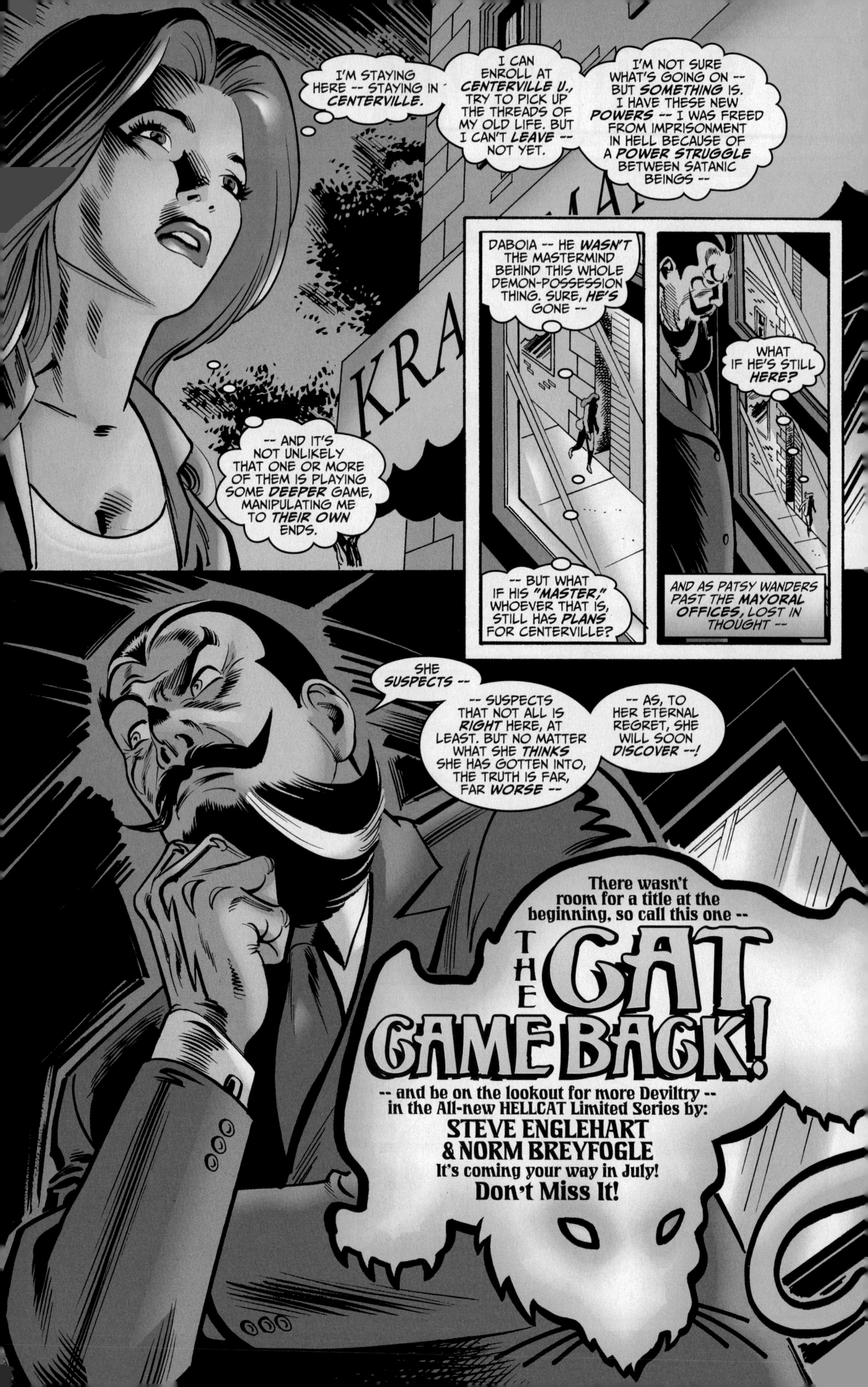
I'M STAYING HERE -- STAYING IN CENTERVILLE.
I CAN ENROLL AT CENTERVILLE U., TRY TO PICK UP THE THREADS OF MY OLD LIFE. BUT I CAN'T LEAVE -- NOT YET.
I'M NOT SURE WHAT'S GOING ON -- BUT SOMETHING IS. I HAVE THESE NEW POWERS -- I WAS FREED FROM IMPRISONMENT IN HELL BECAUSE OF A POWER STRUGGLE BETWEEN SATANIC BEINGS --
-- AND IT'S NOT UNLIKELY THAT ONE OR MORE OF THEM IS PLAYING SOME DEEPER GAME, MANIPULATING ME TO THEIR OWN ENDS.
KRA
DABOIA -- HE WASN'T THE MASTERMIND BEHIND THIS WHOLE DEMON-POSSESSION THING. SURE, HE'S GONE --
-- BUT WHAT IF HIS "MASTER," WHOEVER THAT IS, STILL HAS PLANS FOR CENTERVILLE?
WHAT IF HE'S STILL HERE?
AND AS PATSY WANDERS PAST THE MAYORAL OFFICES, LOST IN THOUGHT --
SHE SUSPECTS --
-- SUSPECTS THAT NOT ALL IS RIGHT HERE, AT LEAST. BUT NO MATTER WHAT SHE THINKS SHE HAS GOTTEN INTO, THE TRUTH IS FAR, FAR WORSE --
-- AS, TO HER ETERNAL REGRET, SHE WILL SOON DISCOVER --!
There wasn't room for a title at the beginning, so call this one --
THE CAT CAME BACK!
-- and be on the lookout for more Deviltry -- in the All-new HELLCAT Limited Series by:
STEVE ENGLEHART & NORM BREYFOGLE
It's coming your way in July!
Don't Miss It!

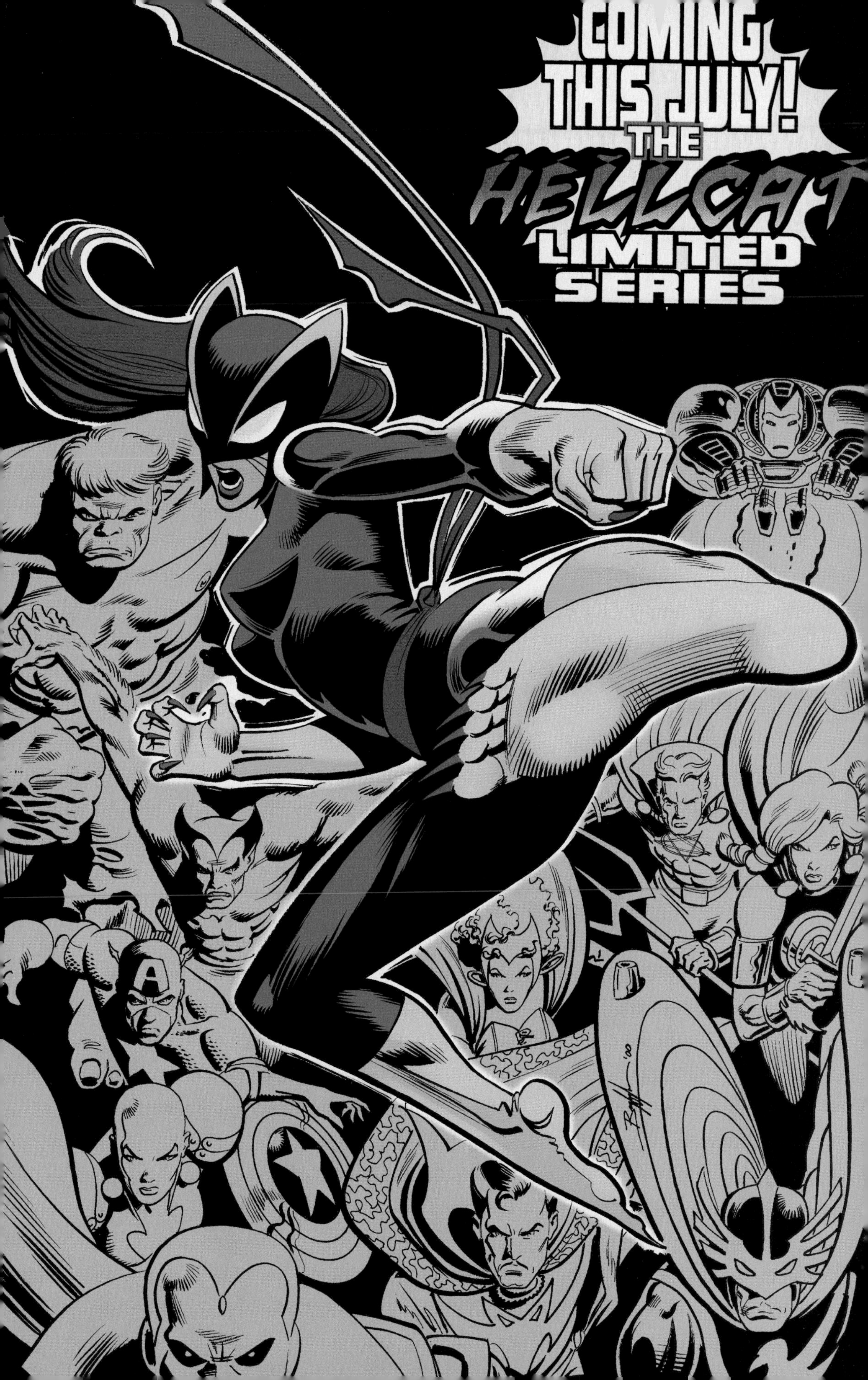
COMING THIS JULY!
THE
HELLCAT
LIMITED SERIES

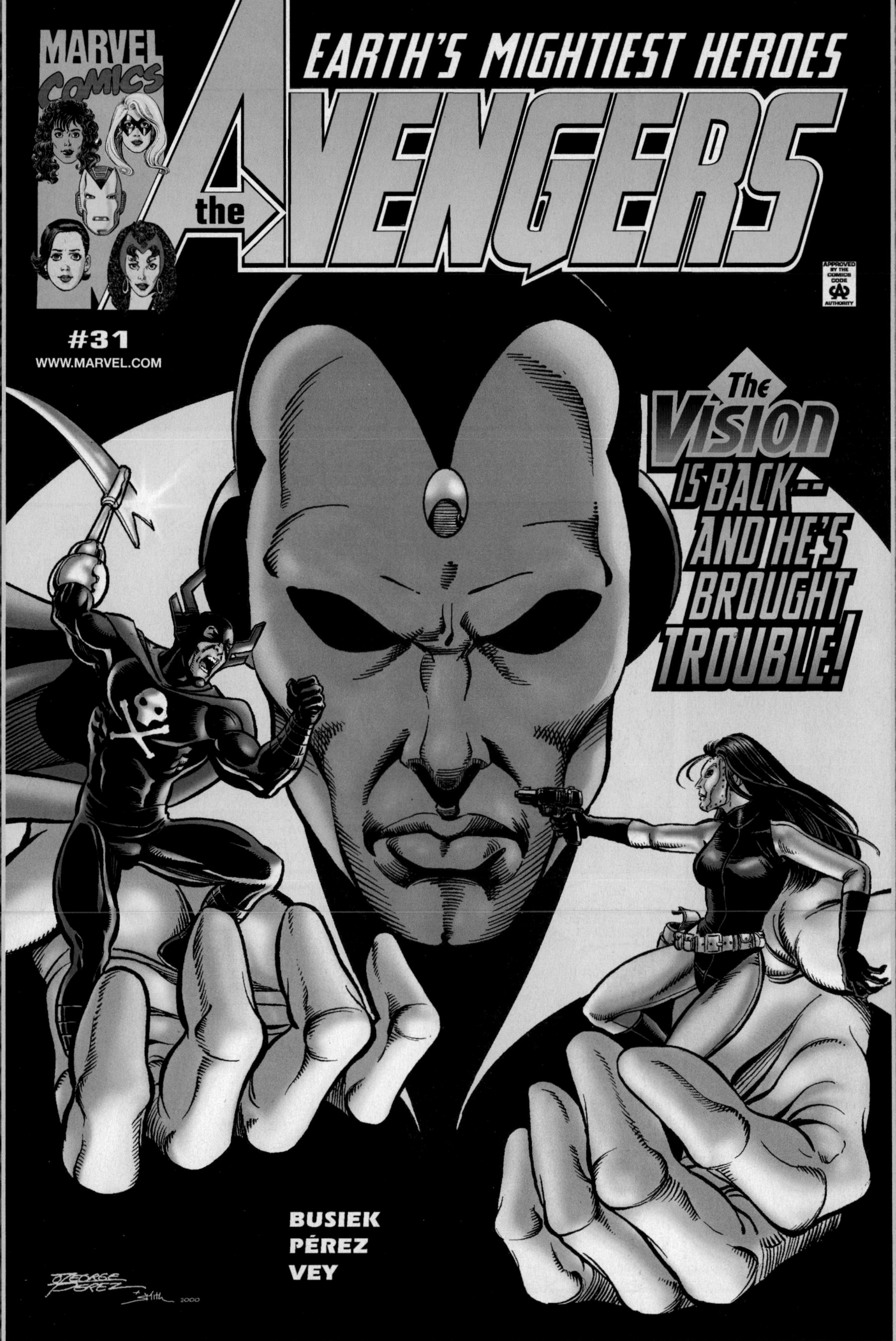
MARVEL COMICS
EARTH'S MIGHTIEST HEROES
the AVENGERS
APPROVED BY THE COMICS CODE AUTHORITY
#31
WWW.MARVEL.COM
The VISION IS BACK -- AND HE'S BROUGHT TROUBLE!
BUSIEK
PÉREZ
VEY
GEORGE PÉREZ + Smith 2000

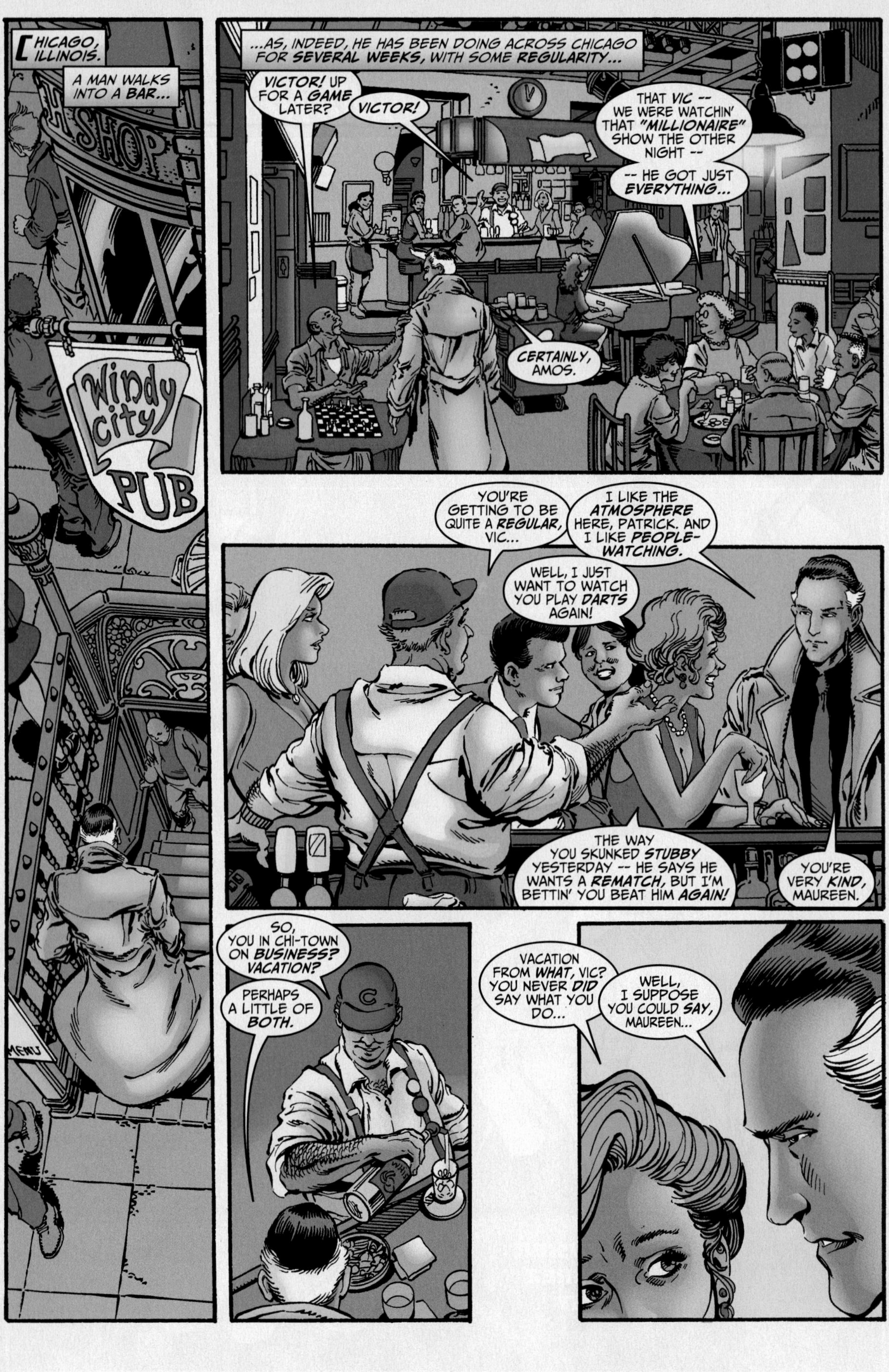
CHICAGO, ILLINOIS.
A MAN WALKS INTO A BAR...
SHOP
Windy City PUB
MENU
...AS, INDEED, HE HAS BEEN DOING ACROSS CHICAGO FOR SEVERAL WEEKS, WITH SOME REGULARITY...
VICTOR! UP FOR A GAME LATER?
VICTOR!
THAT VIC -- WE WERE WATCHIN' THAT "MILLIONAIRE" SHOW THE OTHER NIGHT --
-- HE GOT JUST EVERYTHING...
CERTAINLY, AMOS.
YOU'RE GETTING TO BE QUITE A REGULAR, VIC...
I LIKE THE ATMOSPHERE HERE, PATRICK. AND I LIKE PEOPLE-WATCHING.
WELL, I JUST WANT TO WATCH YOU PLAY DARTS AGAIN!
THE WAY YOU SKUNKED STUBBY YESTERDAY -- HE SAYS HE WANTS A REMATCH, BUT I'M BETTIN' YOU BEAT HIM AGAIN!
YOU'RE VERY KIND, MAUREEN.
SO, YOU IN CHI-TOWN ON BUSINESS? VACATION?
PERHAPS A LITTLE OF BOTH.
VACATION FROM WHAT, VIC? YOU NEVER DID SAY WHAT YOU DO...
WELL, I SUPPOSE YOU COULD SAY, MAUREEN...

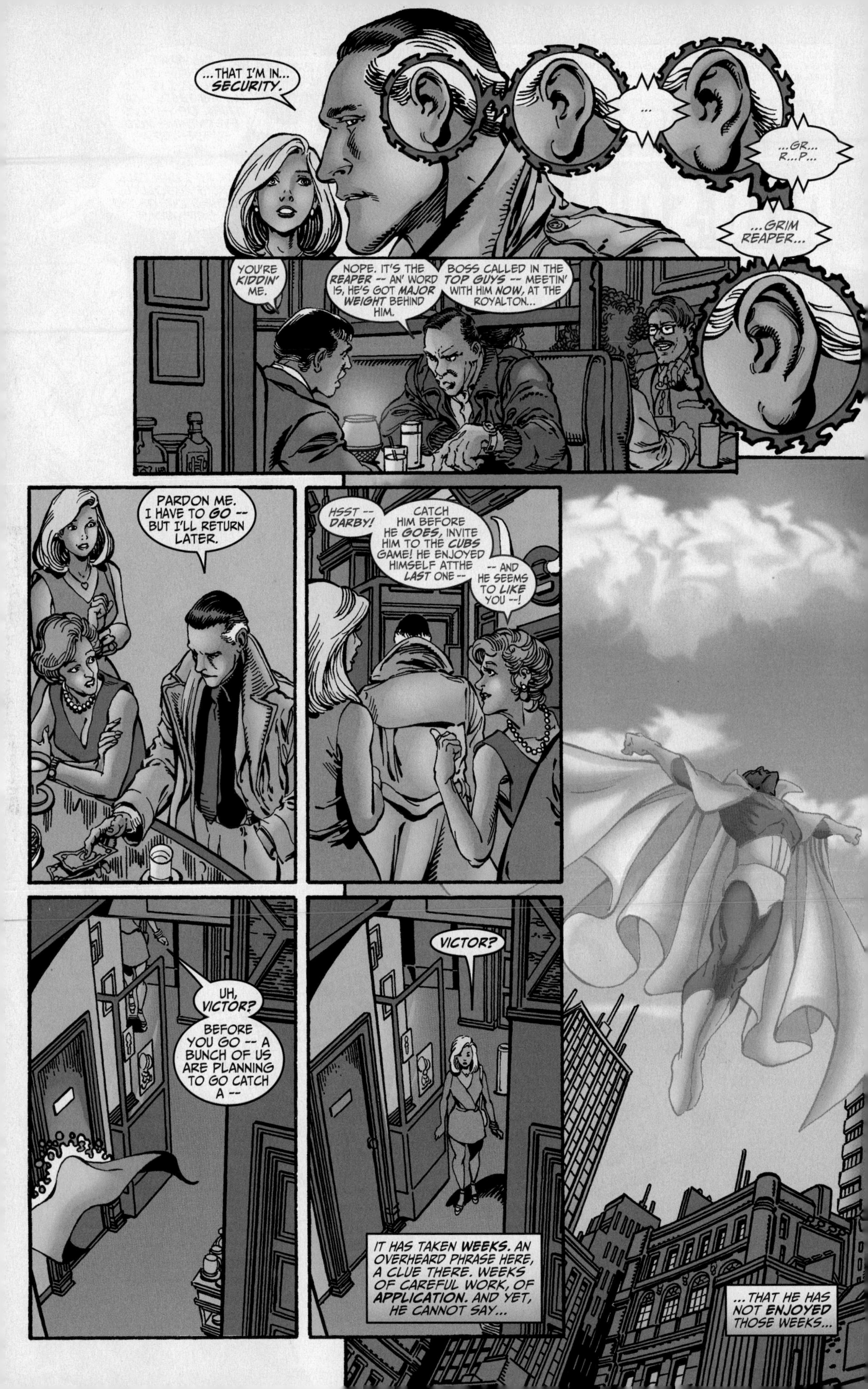
...THAT I'M IN... SECURITY.
...
...GR... R...P...
...GRIM REAPER...
YOU'RE KIDDIN' ME.
NOPE. IT'S THE REAPER -- AN' WORD IS, HE'S GOT MAJOR WEIGHT BEHIND HIM.
BOSS CALLED IN THE TOP GUYS -- MEETIN' WITH HIM NOW, AT THE ROYALTON...
PARDON ME. I HAVE TO GO -- BUT I'LL RETURN LATER.
HSST -- DARBY!
CATCH HIM BEFORE HE GOES, INVITE HIM TO THE CUBS GAME! HE ENJOYED HIMSELF ATTHE LAST ONE --
-- AND HE SEEMS TO LIKE YOU --!
UH, VICTOR?
BEFORE YOU GO -- A BUNCH OF US ARE PLANNING TO GO CATCH A --
VICTOR?
IT HAS TAKEN WEEKS. AN OVERHEARD PHRASE HERE, A CLUE THERE. WEEKS OF CAREFUL WORK, OF APPLICATION. AND YET, HE CANNOT SAY...
...THAT HE HAS NOT ENJOYED THOSE WEEKS...

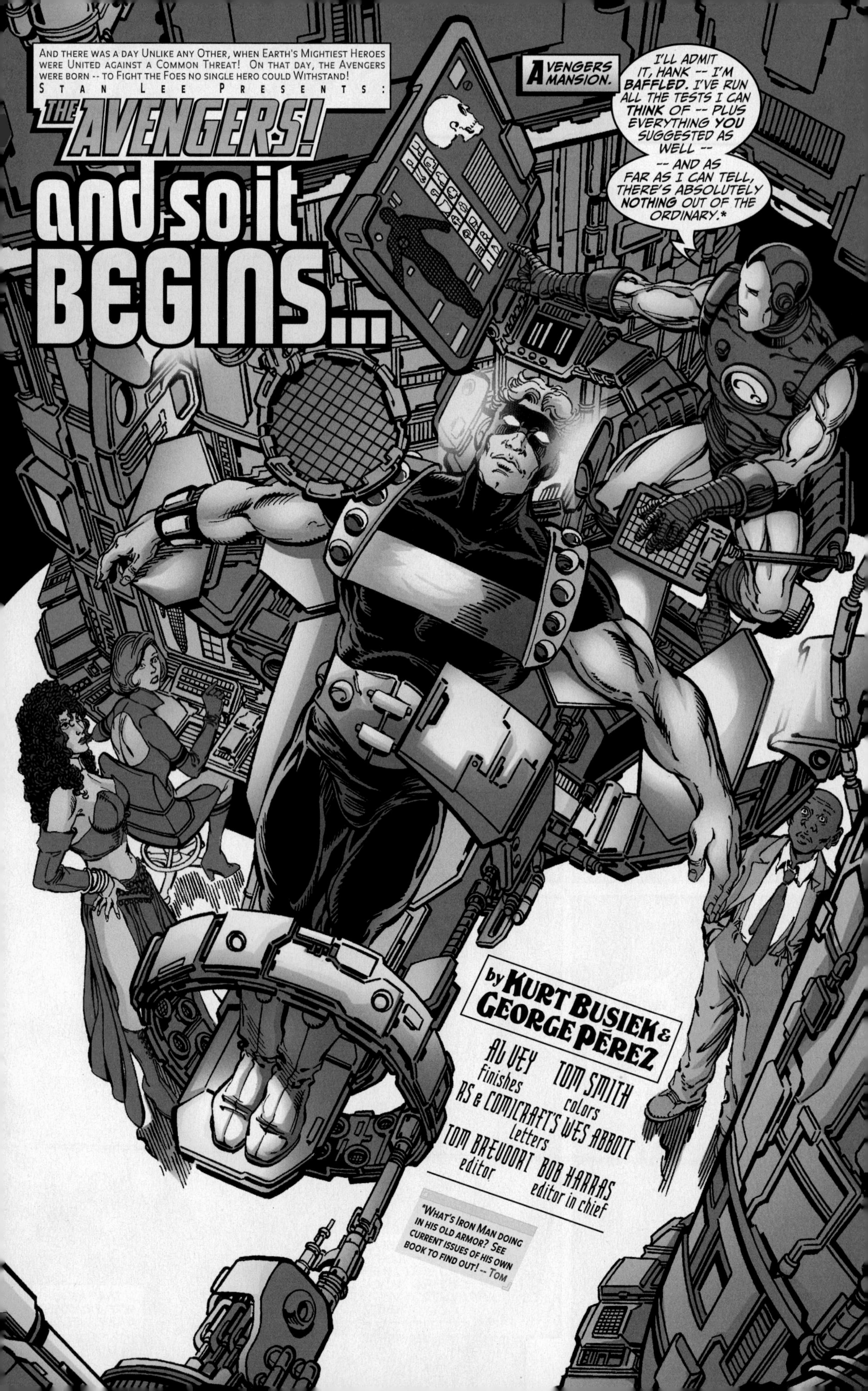

And there was a day Unlike any Other, when Earth's Mightiest Heroes were United against a Common Threat! On that day, the Avengers were born -- to Fight the Foes no single hero could Withstand!
Stan Lee Presents:
THE AVENGERS!
and so it BEGINS...
Avengers Mansion.
I'LL ADMIT IT, HANK -- I'M BAFFLED. I'VE RUN ALL THE TESTS I CAN THINK OF -- PLUS EVERYTHING YOU SUGGESTED AS WELL --
-- AND AS FAR AS I CAN TELL, THERE'S ABSOLUTELY NOTHING OUT OF THE ORDINARY.*
by KURT BUSIEK & GEORGE PÉREZ
AL VEY finishes
TOM SMITH colors
RS & COMICRAFT'S WES ABBOTT letters
TOM BREVOORT editor
BOB HARRAS editor in chief
*What's Iron Man doing in his old armor? See current issues of his own book to find out! -- Tom

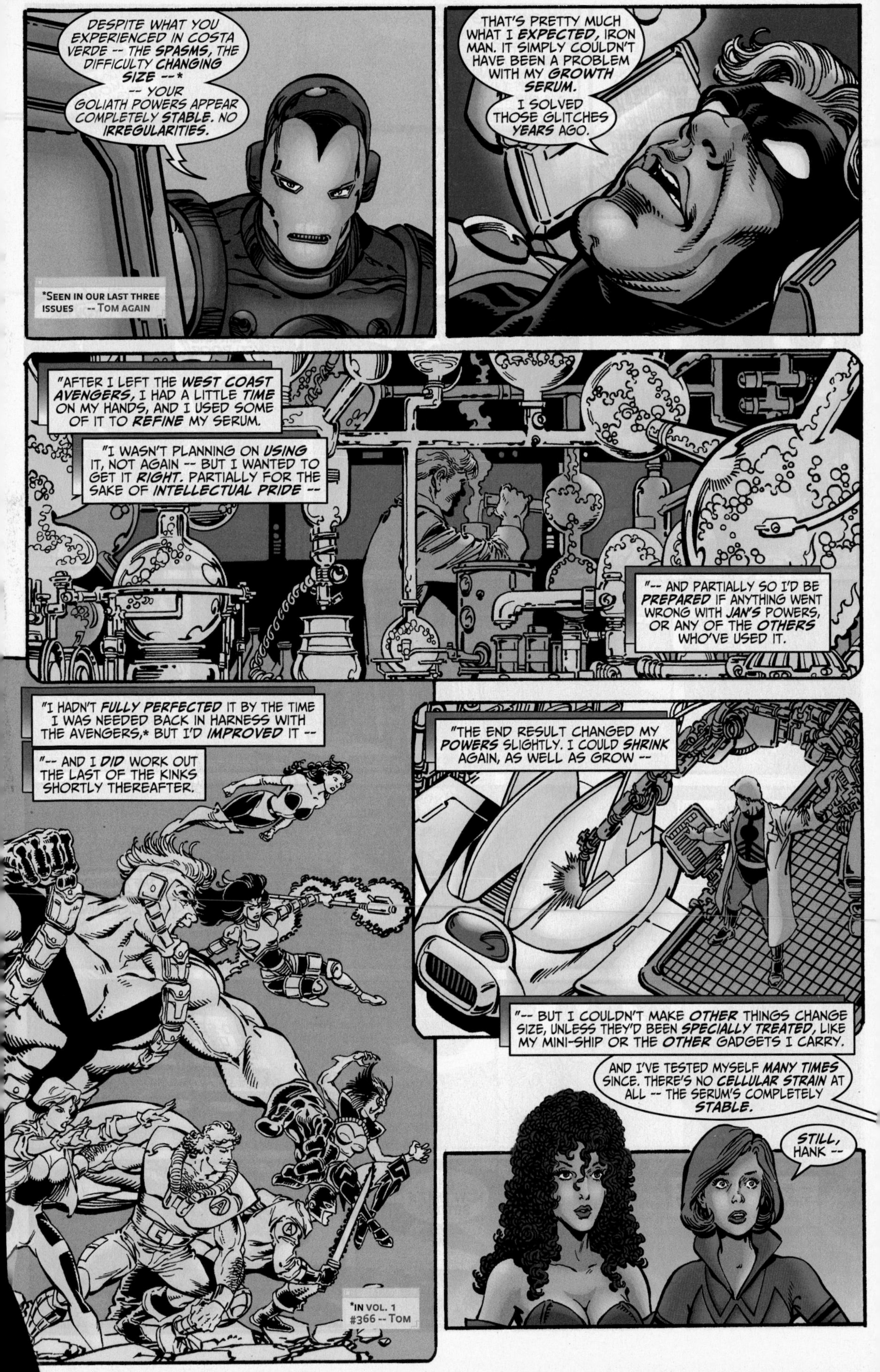
DESPITE WHAT YOU EXPERIENCED IN COSTA VERDE -- THE SPASMS, THE DIFFICULTY CHANGING SIZE --*
-- YOUR GOLIATH POWERS APPEAR COMPLETELY STABLE. NO IRREGULARITIES.
*SEEN IN OUR LAST THREE ISSUES -- TOM AGAIN
THAT'S PRETTY MUCH WHAT I EXPECTED, IRON MAN. IT SIMPLY COULDN'T HAVE BEEN A PROBLEM WITH MY GROWTH SERUM.
I SOLVED THOSE GLITCHES YEARS AGO.
"AFTER I LEFT THE WEST COAST AVENGERS, I HAD A LITTLE TIME ON MY HANDS, AND I USED SOME OF IT TO REFINE MY SERUM.
"I WASN'T PLANNING ON USING IT, NOT AGAIN -- BUT I WANTED TO GET IT RIGHT. PARTIALLY FOR THE SAKE OF INTELLECTUAL PRIDE --
"-- AND PARTIALLY SO I'D BE PREPARED IF ANYTHING WENT WRONG WITH JAN'S POWERS, OR ANY OF THE OTHERS WHO'VE USED IT.
"I HADN'T FULLY PERFECTED IT BY THE TIME I WAS NEEDED BACK IN HARNESS WITH THE AVENGERS,* BUT I'D IMPROVED IT --
"-- AND I DID WORK OUT THE LAST OF THE KINKS SHORTLY THEREAFTER.
*IN VOL. 1 #366 -- TOM
"THE END RESULT CHANGED MY POWERS SLIGHTLY. I COULD SHRINK AGAIN, AS WELL AS GROW --
"-- BUT I COULDN'T MAKE OTHER THINGS CHANGE SIZE, UNLESS THEY'D BEEN SPECIALLY TREATED, LIKE MY MINI-SHIP OR THE OTHER GADGETS I CARRY.
AND I'VE TESTED MYSELF MANY TIMES SINCE. THERE'S NO CELLULAR STRAIN AT ALL -- THE SERUM'S COMPLETELY STABLE.
STILL, HANK --

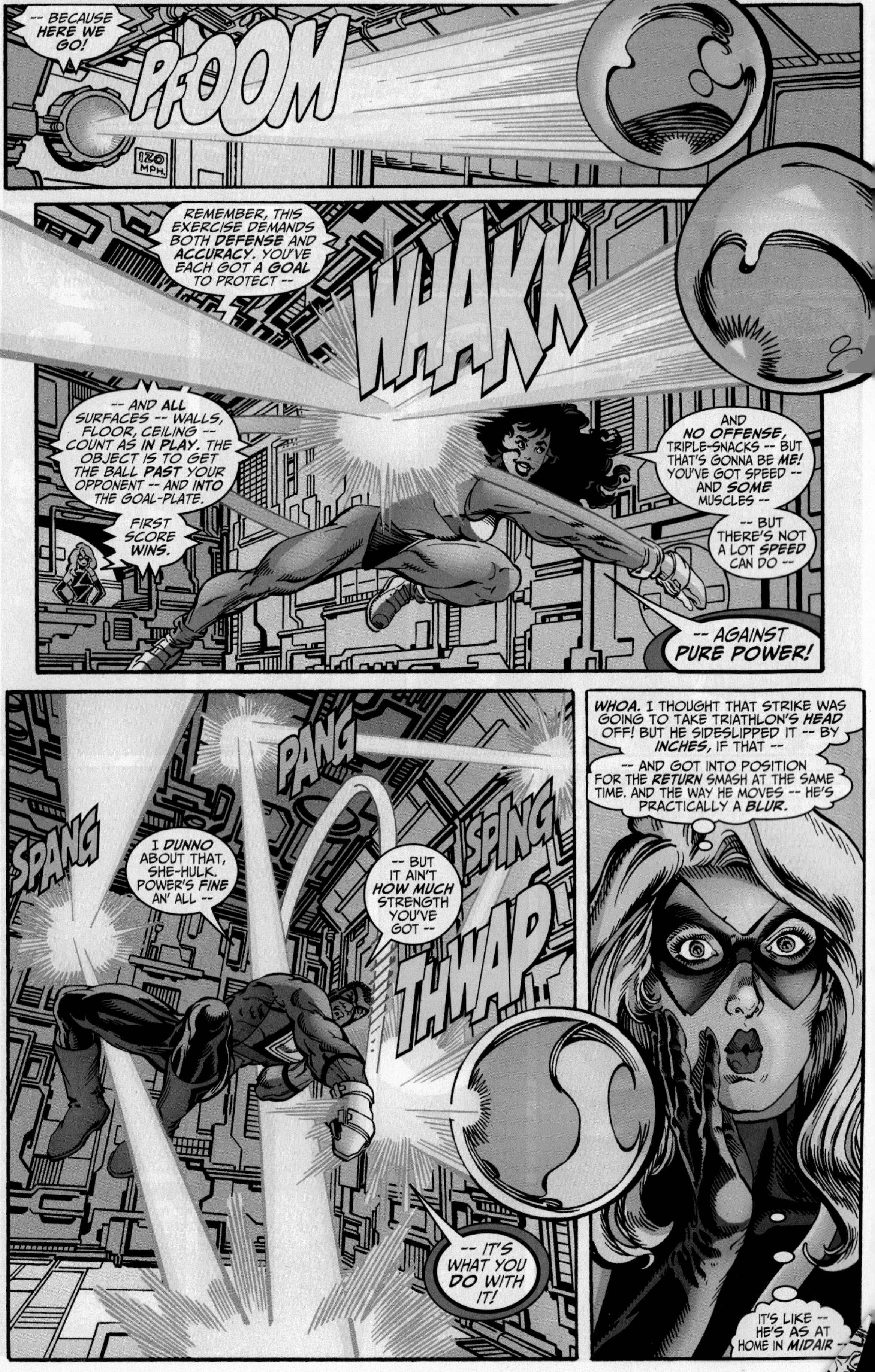
-- BECAUSE HERE WE GO!
PFOOM
120 MPH.
REMEMBER, THIS EXERCISE DEMANDS BOTH DEFENSE AND ACCURACY. YOU'VE EACH GOT A GOAL TO PROTECT --
WHAKK
-- AND ALL SURFACES -- WALLS, FLOOR, CEILING -- COUNT AS IN PLAY. THE OBJECT IS TO GET THE BALL PAST YOUR OPPONENT -- AND INTO THE GOAL-PLATE.
FIRST SCORE WINS.
AND NO OFFENSE, TRIPLE-SNACKS -- BUT THAT'S GONNA BE ME! YOU'VE GOT SPEED -- AND SOME MUSCLES --
-- BUT THERE'S NOT A LOT SPEED CAN DO --
-- AGAINST PURE POWER!
PANG
SPANG
I DUNNO ABOUT THAT, SHE-HULK. POWER'S FINE AN' ALL --
SPING
-- BUT IT AIN'T HOW MUCH STRENGTH YOU'VE GOT --
THWAP!
-- IT'S WHAT YOU DO WITH IT!
WHOA. I THOUGHT THAT STRIKE WAS GOING TO TAKE TRIATHLON'S HEAD OFF! BUT HE SIDESLIPPED IT -- BY INCHES, IF THAT --
-- AND GOT INTO POSITION FOR THE RETURN SMASH AT THE SAME TIME. AND THE WAY HE MOVES -- HE'S PRACTICALLY A BLUR.
IT'S LIKE -- HE'S AS AT HOME IN MIDAIR --

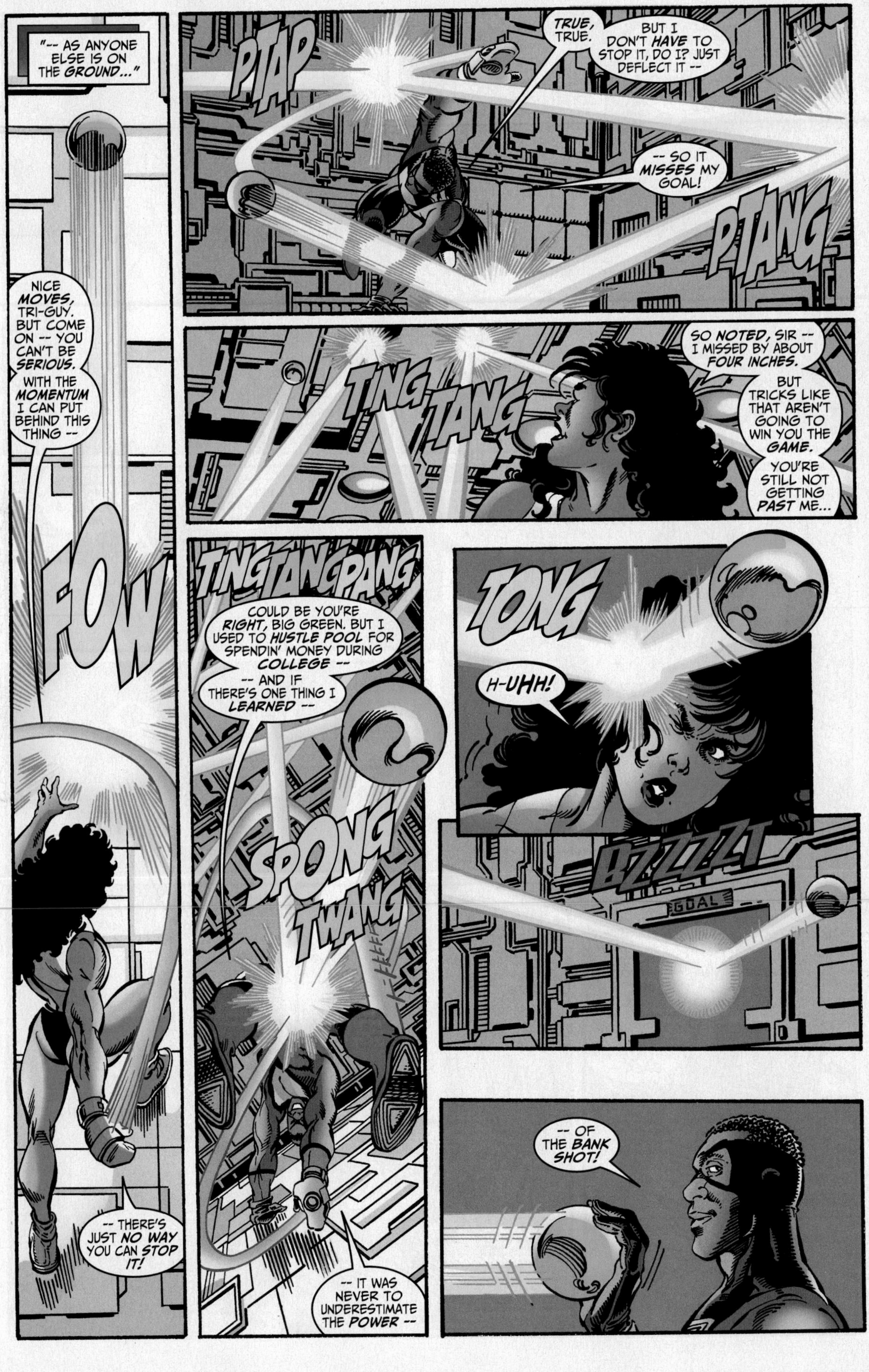

"-- AS ANYONE ELSE IS ON THE *GROUND*..."
NICE *MOVES*, TRI-GUY. BUT COME ON -- YOU CAN'T BE *SERIOUS*.
WITH THE *MOMENTUM* I CAN PUT BEHIND THIS THING --
FOW
-- THERE'S JUST *NO WAY* YOU CAN *STOP IT*!
PTAP
TRUE, TRUE.
BUT I DON'T *HAVE* TO STOP IT, DO I? JUST DEFLECT IT --
-- SO IT *MISSES* MY GOAL!
PTANG
TING TANG
SO *NOTED*, SIR -- I MISSED BY ABOUT *FOUR INCHES*.
BUT TRICKS LIKE THAT AREN'T GOING TO WIN YOU THE *GAME*.
YOU'RE STILL NOT GETTING *PAST* ME...
TINGTANGPANG
COULD BE YOU'RE *RIGHT*, BIG GREEN. BUT I USED TO *HUSTLE POOL* FOR SPENDIN' MONEY DURING *COLLEGE* --
-- AND IF THERE'S ONE THING I *LEARNED* --
SPONG
TWANG
-- IT WAS NEVER TO UNDERESTIMATE THE *POWER* --
TONG
H-UHH!
BZZZZZT
GOAL
-- OF THE *BANK SHOT*!

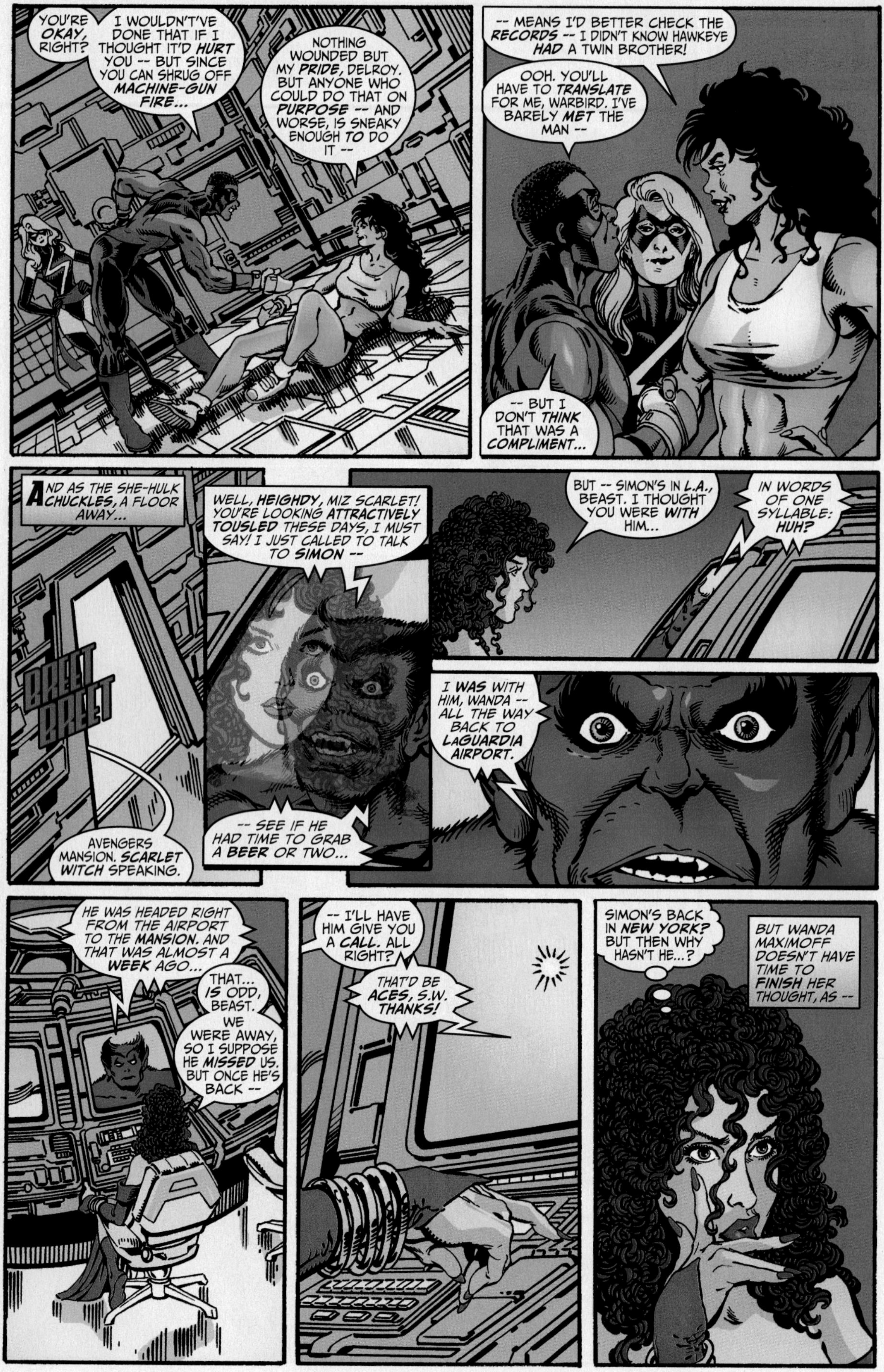
YOU'RE OKAY, RIGHT?
I WOULDN'T'VE DONE THAT IF I THOUGHT IT'D HURT YOU -- BUT SINCE YOU CAN SHRUG OFF MACHINE-GUN FIRE...
NOTHING WOUNDED BUT MY PRIDE, DELROY. BUT ANYONE WHO COULD DO THAT ON PURPOSE -- AND WORSE, IS SNEAKY ENOUGH TO DO IT --
-- MEANS I'D BETTER CHECK THE RECORDS -- I DIDN'T KNOW HAWKEYE HAD A TWIN BROTHER!
OOH. YOU'LL HAVE TO TRANSLATE FOR ME, WARBIRD. I'VE BARELY MET THE MAN --
-- BUT I DON'T THINK THAT WAS A COMPLIMENT...
AND AS THE SHE-HULK CHUCKLES, A FLOOR AWAY...
BREET BREET
AVENGERS MANSION. SCARLET WITCH SPEAKING.
WELL, HEIGHDY, MIZ SCARLET! YOU'RE LOOKING ATTRACTIVELY TOUSLED THESE DAYS, I MUST SAY! I JUST CALLED TO TALK TO SIMON --
-- SEE IF HE HAD TIME TO GRAB A BEER OR TWO...
BUT -- SIMON'S IN L.A., BEAST. I THOUGHT YOU WERE WITH HIM...
IN WORDS OF ONE SYLLABLE: HUH?
I WAS WITH HIM, WANDA -- ALL THE WAY BACK TO LAGUARDIA AIRPORT.
HE WAS HEADED RIGHT FROM THE AIRPORT TO THE MANSION. AND THAT WAS ALMOST A WEEK AGO...
THAT... IS ODD, BEAST. WE WERE AWAY, SO I SUPPOSE HE MISSED US. BUT ONCE HE'S BACK --
-- I'LL HAVE HIM GIVE YOU A CALL. ALL RIGHT?
THAT'D BE ACES, S.W. THANKS!
SIMON'S BACK IN NEW YORK? BUT THEN WHY HASN'T HE...?
BUT WANDA MAXIMOFF DOESN'T HAVE TIME TO FINISH HER THOUGHT, AS --

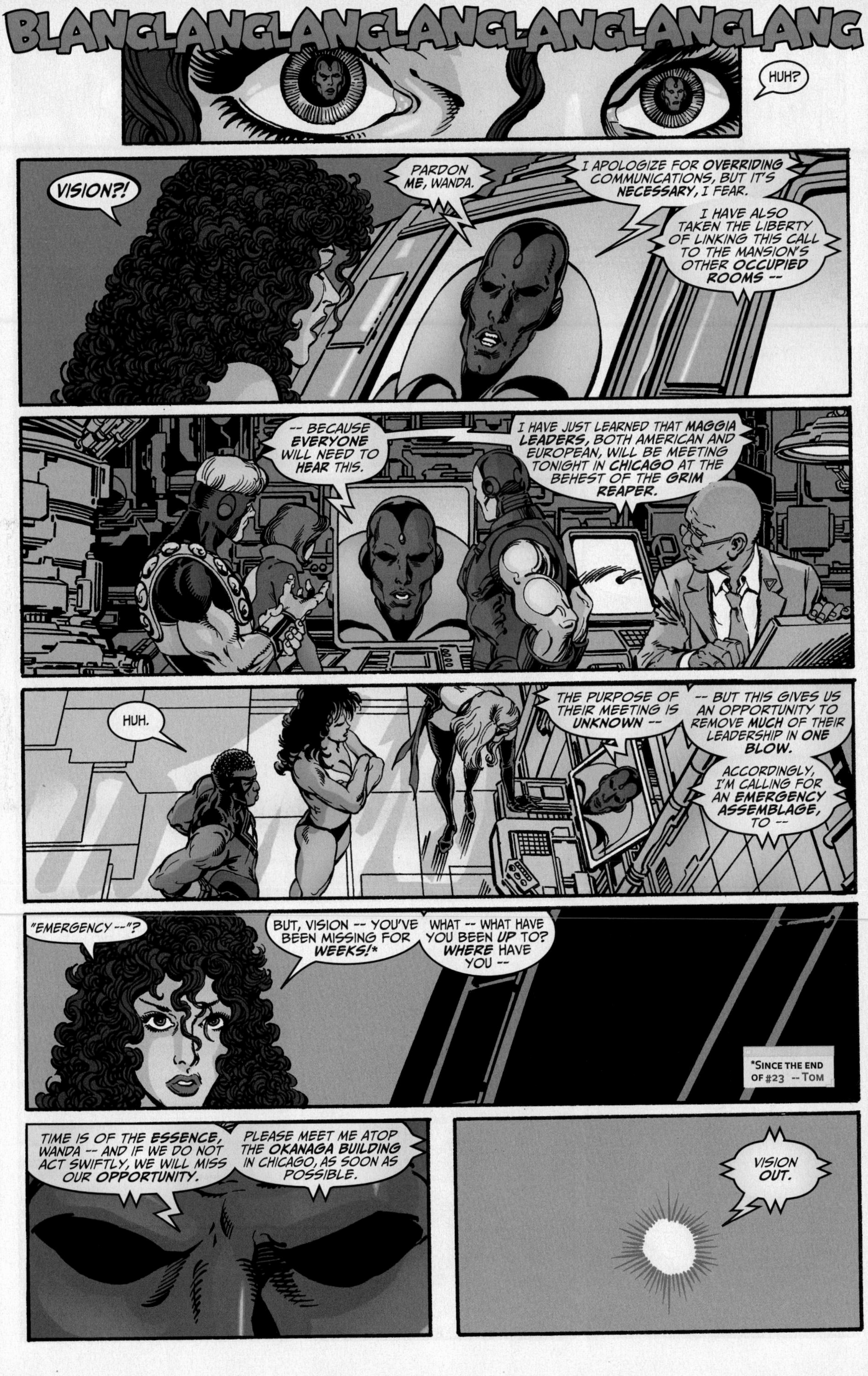
BLANGLANGLANGLANGLANGLANGLANG
HUH?
VISION?!
PARDON ME, WANDA.
I APOLOGIZE FOR OVERRIDING COMMUNICATIONS, BUT IT'S NECESSARY, I FEAR.
I HAVE ALSO TAKEN THE LIBERTY OF LINKING THIS CALL TO THE MANSION'S OTHER OCCUPIED ROOMS --
-- BECAUSE EVERYONE WILL NEED TO HEAR THIS.
I HAVE JUST LEARNED THAT MAGGIA LEADERS, BOTH AMERICAN AND EUROPEAN, WILL BE MEETING TONIGHT IN CHICAGO AT THE BEHEST OF THE GRIM REAPER.
HUH.
THE PURPOSE OF THEIR MEETING IS UNKNOWN --
-- BUT THIS GIVES US AN OPPORTUNITY TO REMOVE MUCH OF THEIR LEADERSHIP IN ONE BLOW.
ACCORDINGLY, I'M CALLING FOR AN EMERGENCY ASSEMBLAGE, TO --
"EMERGENCY --"?
BUT, VISION -- YOU'VE BEEN MISSING FOR WEEKS!*
WHAT -- WHAT HAVE YOU BEEN UP TO? WHERE HAVE YOU --
*SINCE THE END OF #23 -- TOM
TIME IS OF THE ESSENCE, WANDA -- AND IF WE DO NOT ACT SWIFTLY, WE WILL MISS OUR OPPORTUNITY.
PLEASE MEET ME ATOP THE OKANAGA BUILDING IN CHICAGO, AS SOON AS POSSIBLE.
VISION OUT.

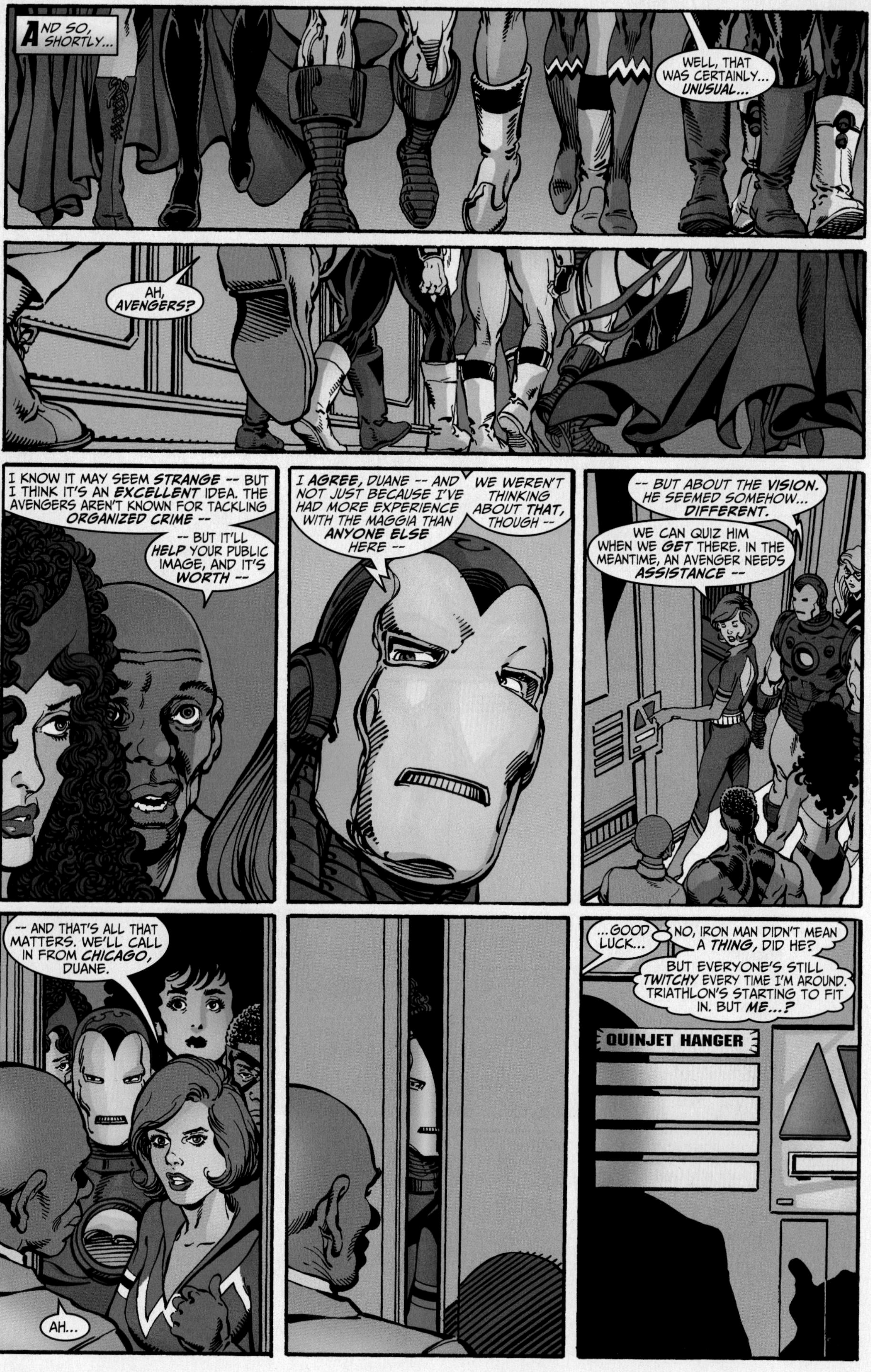
AND SO, SHORTLY...
WELL, THAT WAS CERTAINLY... UNUSUAL...
AH, AVENGERS?
I KNOW IT MAY SEEM STRANGE -- BUT I THINK IT'S AN EXCELLENT IDEA. THE AVENGERS AREN'T KNOWN FOR TACKLING ORGANIZED CRIME --
-- BUT IT'LL HELP YOUR PUBLIC IMAGE, AND IT'S WORTH --
I AGREE, DUANE -- AND NOT JUST BECAUSE I'VE HAD MORE EXPERIENCE WITH THE MAGGIA THAN ANYONE ELSE HERE --
WE WEREN'T THINKING ABOUT THAT, THOUGH --
-- BUT ABOUT THE VISION. HE SEEMED SOMEHOW... DIFFERENT.
WE CAN QUIZ HIM WHEN WE GET THERE. IN THE MEANTIME, AN AVENGER NEEDS ASSISTANCE --
-- AND THAT'S ALL THAT MATTERS. WE'LL CALL IN FROM CHICAGO, DUANE.
AH...
...GOOD LUCK...
NO, IRON MAN DIDN'T MEAN A THING, DID HE?
BUT EVERYONE'S STILL TWITCHY EVERY TIME I'M AROUND. TRIATHLON'S STARTING TO FIT IN. BUT ME...?
QUINJET HANGER

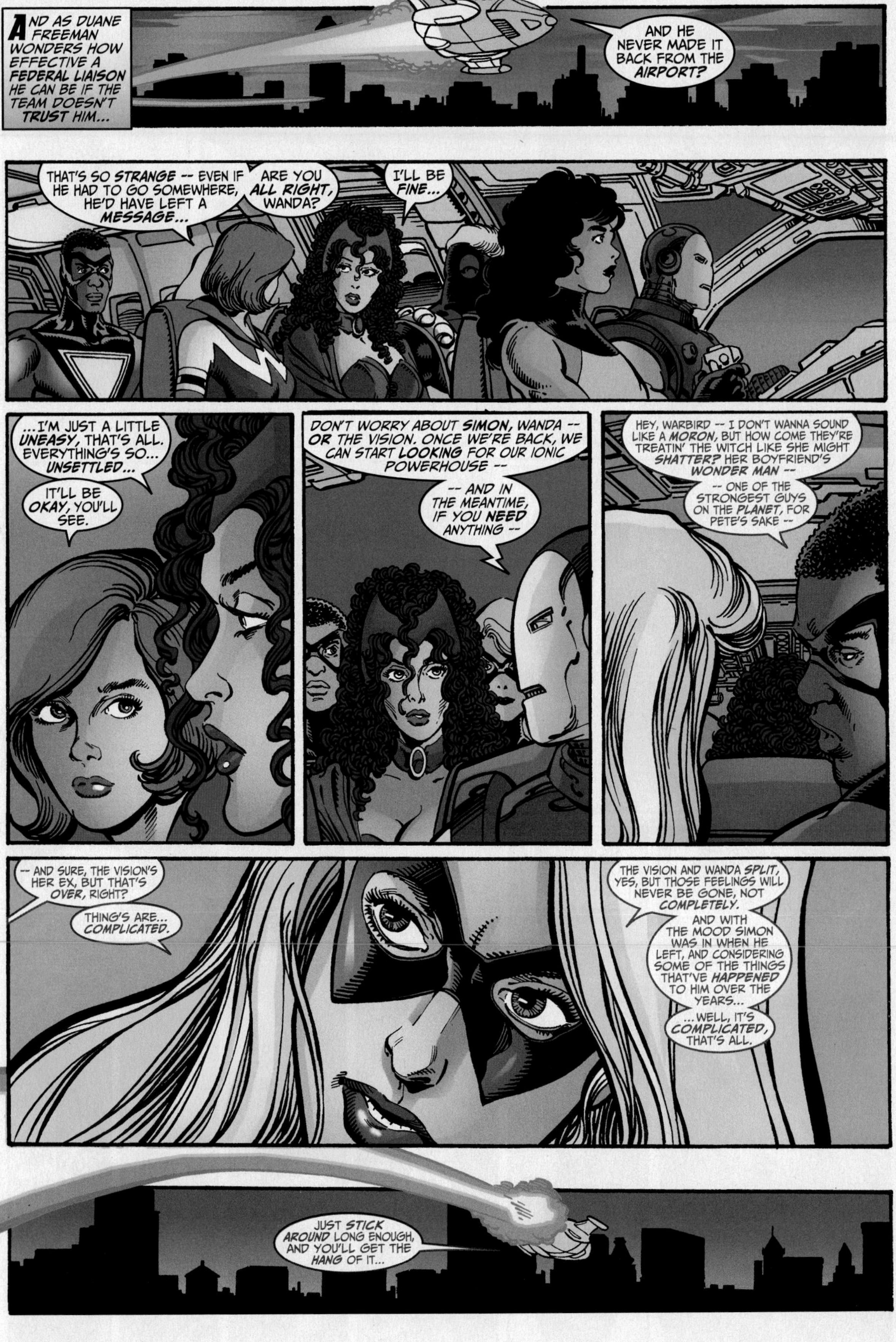
AND AS DUANE FREEMAN WONDERS HOW EFFECTIVE A FEDERAL LIAISON HE CAN BE IF THE TEAM DOESN'T TRUST HIM...
AND HE NEVER MADE IT BACK FROM THE AIRPORT?
THAT'S SO STRANGE -- EVEN IF HE HAD TO GO SOMEWHERE, HE'D HAVE LEFT A MESSAGE...
ARE YOU ALL RIGHT, WANDA?
I'LL BE FINE...
...I'M JUST A LITTLE UNEASY, THAT'S ALL. EVERYTHING'S SO... UNSETTLED...
IT'LL BE OKAY, YOU'LL SEE.
DON'T WORRY ABOUT SIMON, WANDA -- OR THE VISION. ONCE WE'RE BACK, WE CAN START LOOKING FOR OUR IONIC POWERHOUSE --
-- AND IN THE MEANTIME, IF YOU NEED ANYTHING --
HEY, WARBIRD -- I DON'T WANNA SOUND LIKE A MORON, BUT HOW COME THEY'RE TREATIN' THE WITCH LIKE SHE MIGHT SHATTER? HER BOYFRIEND'S WONDER MAN --
-- ONE OF THE STRONGEST GUYS ON THE PLANET, FOR PETE'S SAKE --
-- AND SURE, THE VISION'S HER EX, BUT THAT'S OVER, RIGHT?
THING'S ARE... COMPLICATED.
THE VISION AND WANDA SPLIT, YES, BUT THOSE FEELINGS WILL NEVER BE GONE, NOT COMPLETELY.
AND WITH THE MOOD SIMON WAS IN WHEN HE LEFT, AND CONSIDERING SOME OF THE THINGS THAT'VE HAPPENED TO HIM OVER THE YEARS...
...WELL, IT'S COMPLICATED, THAT'S ALL.
JUST STICK AROUND LONG ENOUGH, AND YOU'LL GET THE HANG OF IT...

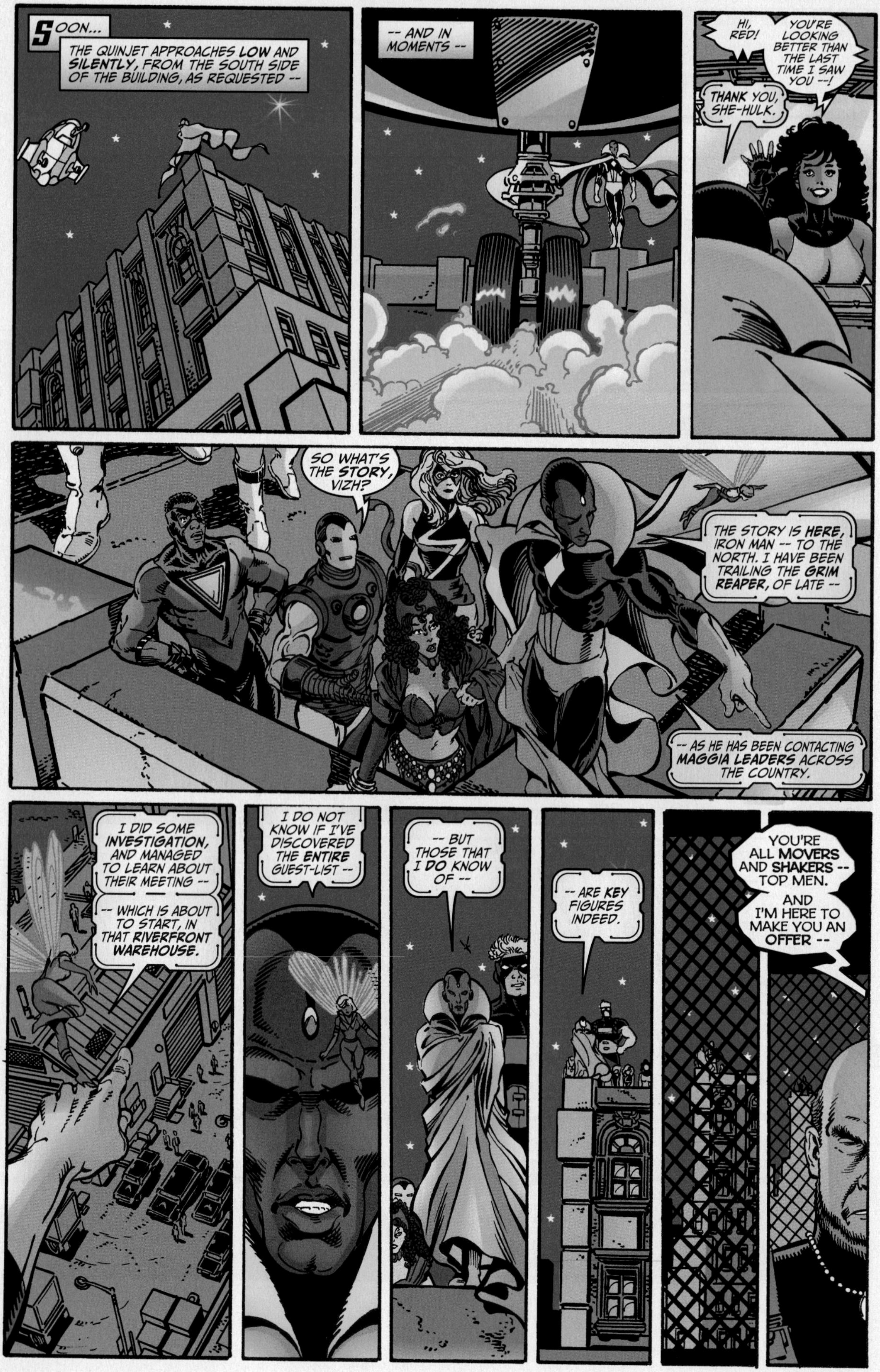
SOON...
THE QUINJET APPROACHES LOW AND SILENTLY, FROM THE SOUTH SIDE OF THE BUILDING, AS REQUESTED --
-- AND IN MOMENTS --
HI, RED!
YOU'RE LOOKING BETTER THAN THE LAST TIME I SAW YOU --!
THANK YOU, SHE-HULK.
SO WHAT'S THE STORY, VIZH?
THE STORY IS HERE, IRON MAN -- TO THE NORTH. I HAVE BEEN TRAILING THE GRIM REAPER, OF LATE --
-- AS HE HAS BEEN CONTACTING MAGGIA LEADERS ACROSS THE COUNTRY.
I DID SOME INVESTIGATION, AND MANAGED TO LEARN ABOUT THEIR MEETING --
-- WHICH IS ABOUT TO START, IN THAT RIVERFRONT WAREHOUSE.
I DO NOT KNOW IF I'VE DISCOVERED THE ENTIRE GUEST-LIST --
-- BUT THOSE THAT I DO KNOW OF --
-- ARE KEY FIGURES INDEED.
YOU'RE ALL MOVERS AND SHAKERS -- TOP MEN.
AND I'M HERE TO MAKE YOU AN OFFER --

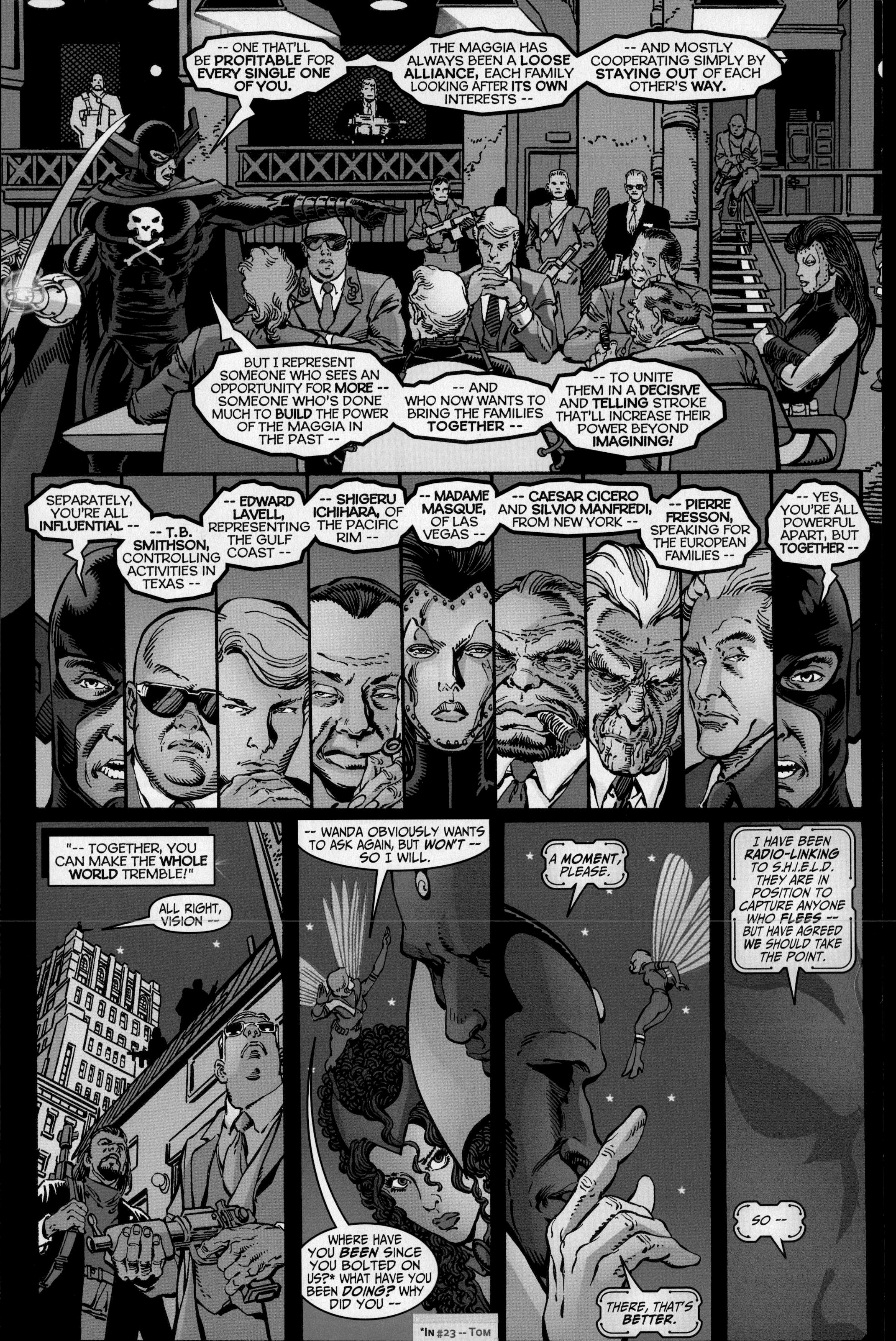
-- ONE THAT'LL BE PROFITABLE FOR EVERY SINGLE ONE OF YOU.
THE MAGGIA HAS ALWAYS BEEN A LOOSE ALLIANCE, EACH FAMILY LOOKING AFTER ITS OWN INTERESTS --
-- AND MOSTLY COOPERATING SIMPLY BY STAYING OUT OF EACH OTHER'S WAY.
BUT I REPRESENT SOMEONE WHO SEES AN OPPORTUNITY FOR MORE -- SOMEONE WHO'S DONE MUCH TO BUILD THE POWER OF THE MAGGIA IN THE PAST --
-- AND WHO NOW WANTS TO BRING THE FAMILIES TOGETHER --
-- TO UNITE THEM IN A DECISIVE AND TELLING STROKE THAT'LL INCREASE THEIR POWER BEYOND IMAGINING!
SEPARATELY, YOU'RE ALL INFLUENTIAL --
-- T.B. SMITHSON, CONTROLLING ACTIVITIES IN TEXAS --
-- EDWARD LAVELL, REPRESENTING THE GULF COAST --
-- SHIGERU ICHIHARA, OF THE PACIFIC RIM --
-- MADAME MASQUE, OF LAS VEGAS --
-- CAESAR CICERO AND SILVIO MANFREDI, FROM NEW YORK --
-- PIERRE FRESSON, SPEAKING FOR THE EUROPEAN FAMILIES --
-- YES, YOU'RE ALL POWERFUL APART, BUT TOGETHER --
"-- TOGETHER, YOU CAN MAKE THE WHOLE WORLD TREMBLE!"
ALL RIGHT, VISION --
-- WANDA OBVIOUSLY WANTS TO ASK AGAIN, BUT WON'T -- SO I WILL.
WHERE HAVE YOU BEEN SINCE YOU BOLTED ON US?* WHAT HAVE YOU BEEN DOING? WHY DID YOU --
A MOMENT, PLEASE.
THERE, THAT'S BETTER.
I HAVE BEEN RADIO-LINKING TO S.H.I.E.L.D. THEY ARE IN POSITION TO CAPTURE ANYONE WHO FLEES -- BUT HAVE AGREED WE SHOULD TAKE THE POINT.
SO --
*IN #23 -- TOM

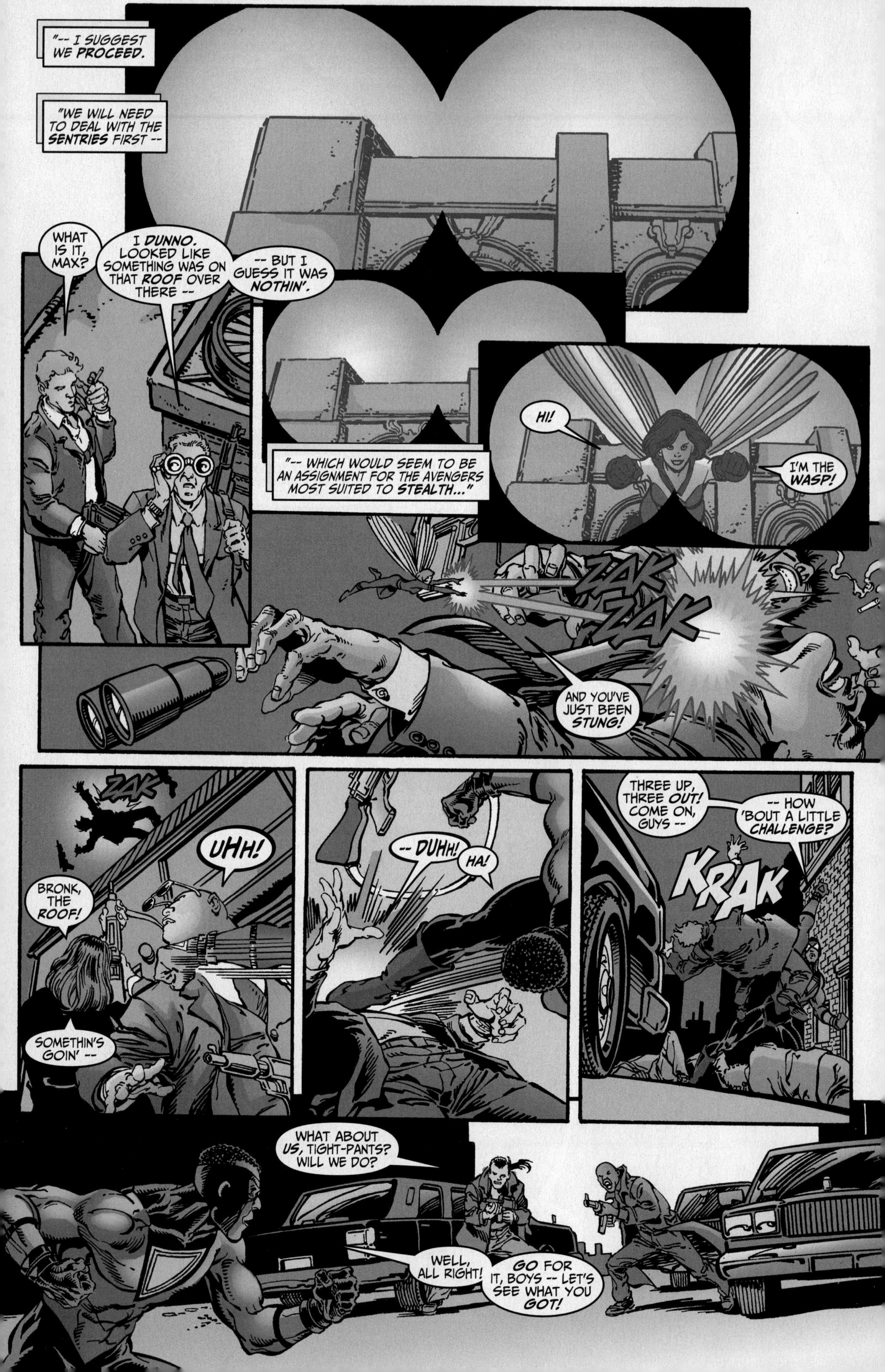
"-- I SUGGEST WE PROCEED.
"WE WILL NEED TO DEAL WITH THE SENTRIES FIRST --
WHAT IS IT, MAX?
I DUNNO. LOOKED LIKE SOMETHING WAS ON THAT ROOF OVER THERE --
-- BUT I GUESS IT WAS NOTHIN'.
"-- WHICH WOULD SEEM TO BE AN ASSIGNMENT FOR THE AVENGERS MOST SUITED TO STEALTH..."
HI!
I'M THE WASP!
ZAK ZAK
AND YOU'VE JUST BEEN STUNG!
ZAK
UHH!
BRONK, THE ROOF!
SOMETHIN'S GOIN' --
-- DUHH!
HA!
THREE UP, THREE OUT! COME ON, GUYS --
-- HOW 'BOUT A LITTLE CHALLENGE?
KRAK
WHAT ABOUT US, TIGHT-PANTS? WILL WE DO?
WELL, ALL RIGHT!
GO FOR IT, BOYS -- LET'S SEE WHAT YOU GOT!

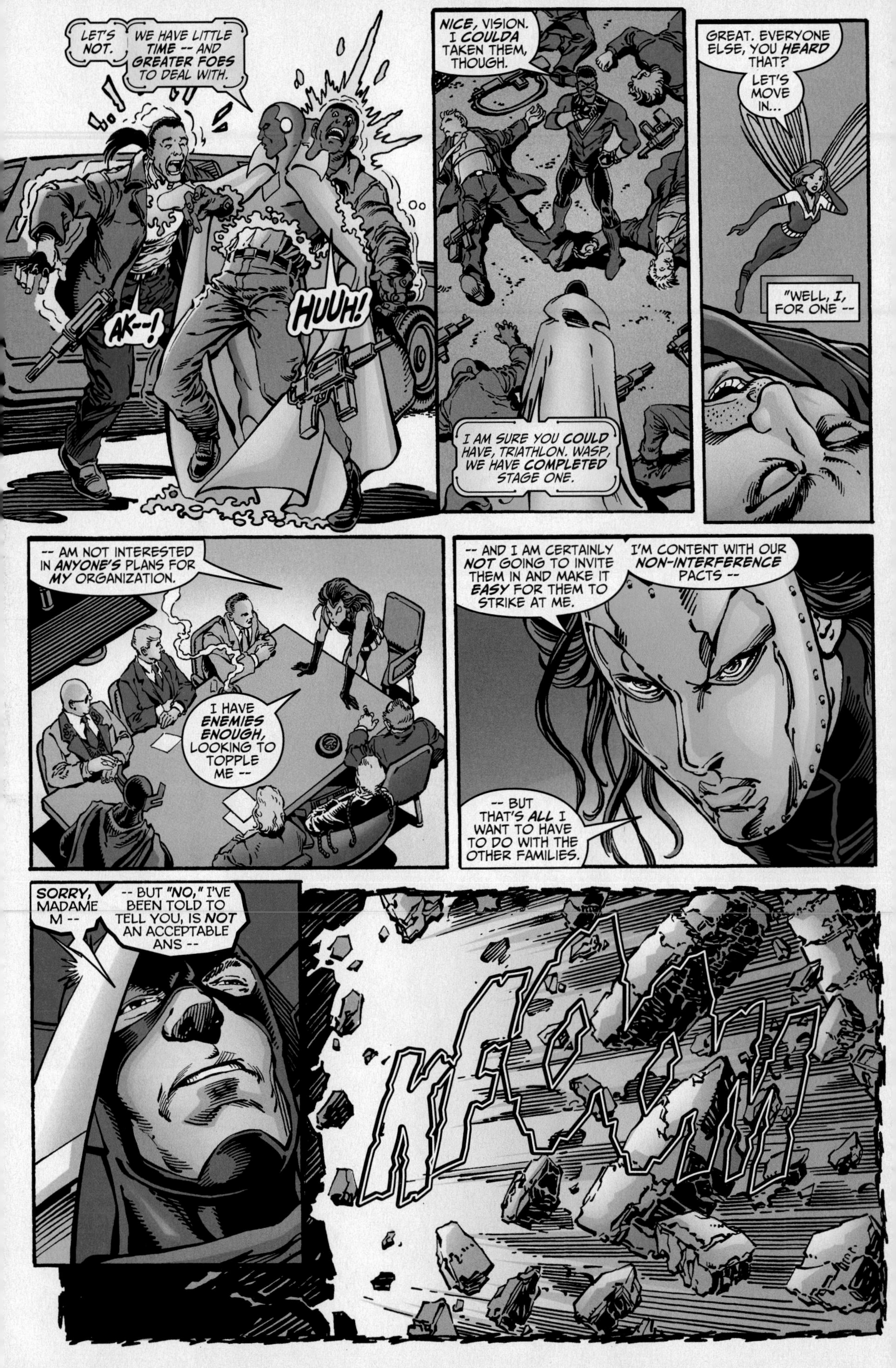
LET'S NOT.
WE HAVE LITTLE TIME -- AND GREATER FOES TO DEAL WITH.
AK--!
HUUH!
NICE, VISION. I COULDA TAKEN THEM, THOUGH.
I AM SURE YOU COULD HAVE, TRIATHLON. WASP, WE HAVE COMPLETED STAGE ONE.
GREAT. EVERYONE ELSE, YOU HEARD THAT?
LET'S MOVE IN...
"WELL, I, FOR ONE --
-- AM NOT INTERESTED IN ANYONE'S PLANS FOR MY ORGANIZATION.
I HAVE ENEMIES ENOUGH, LOOKING TO TOPPLE ME --
-- AND I AM CERTAINLY NOT GOING TO INVITE THEM IN AND MAKE IT EASY FOR THEM TO STRIKE AT ME.
I'M CONTENT WITH OUR NON-INTERFERENCE PACTS --
-- BUT THAT'S ALL I WANT TO HAVE TO DO WITH THE OTHER FAMILIES.
SORRY, MADAME M --
-- BUT "NO," I'VE BEEN TOLD TO TELL YOU, IS NOT AN ACCEPTABLE ANS --
KRAKOOM

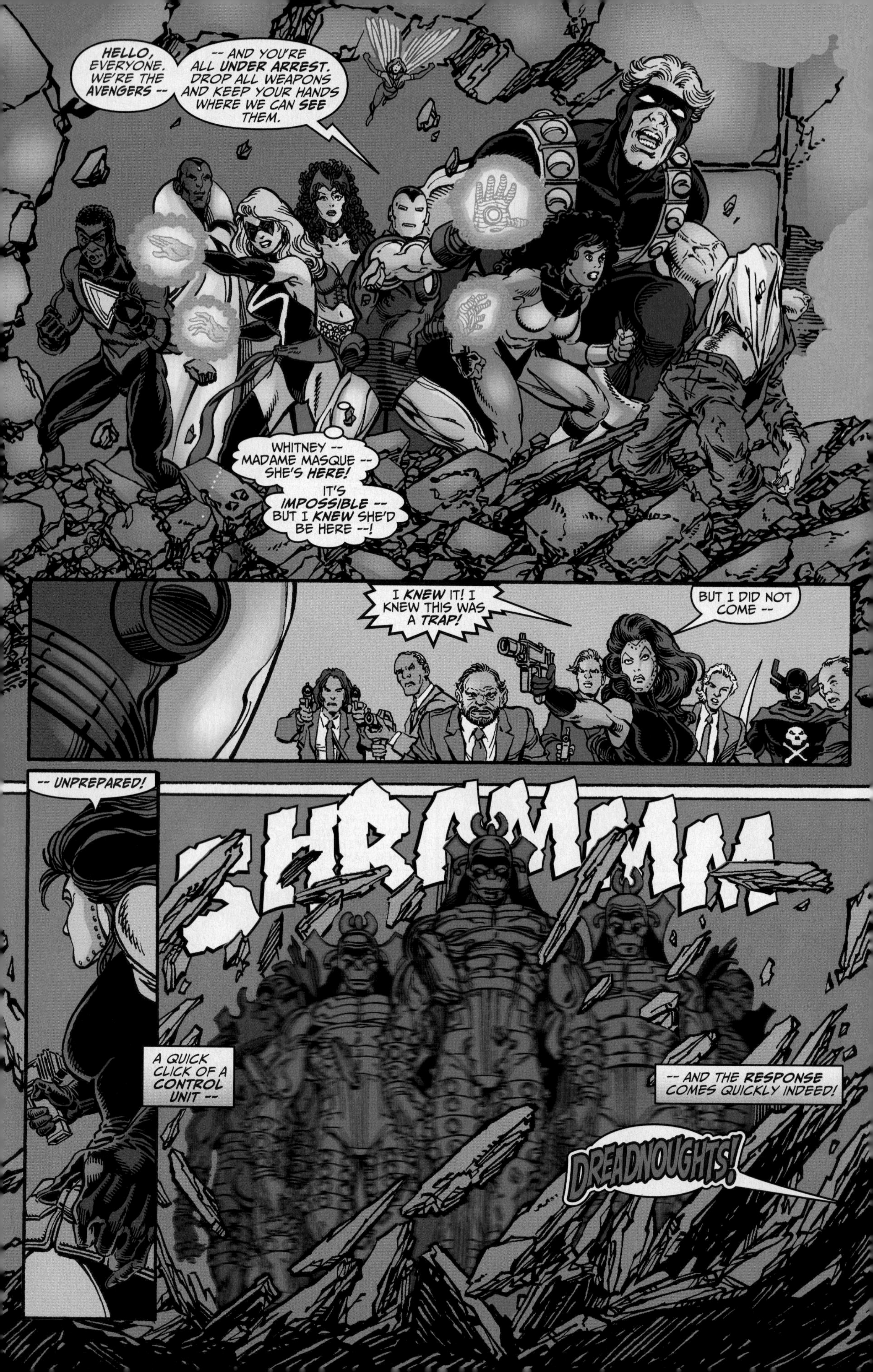
HELLO, EVERYONE. WE'RE THE AVENGERS --
-- AND YOU'RE ALL UNDER ARREST. DROP ALL WEAPONS AND KEEP YOUR HANDS WHERE WE CAN SEE THEM.
WHITNEY -- MADAME MASQUE -- SHE'S HERE!
IT'S IMPOSSIBLE -- BUT I KNEW SHE'D BE HERE --!
I KNEW IT! I KNEW THIS WAS A TRAP!
BUT I DID NOT COME --
-- UNPREPARED!
SHRMMM!
A QUICK CLICK OF A CONTROL UNIT --
-- AND THE RESPONSE COMES QUICKLY INDEED!
DREADNOUGHTS!

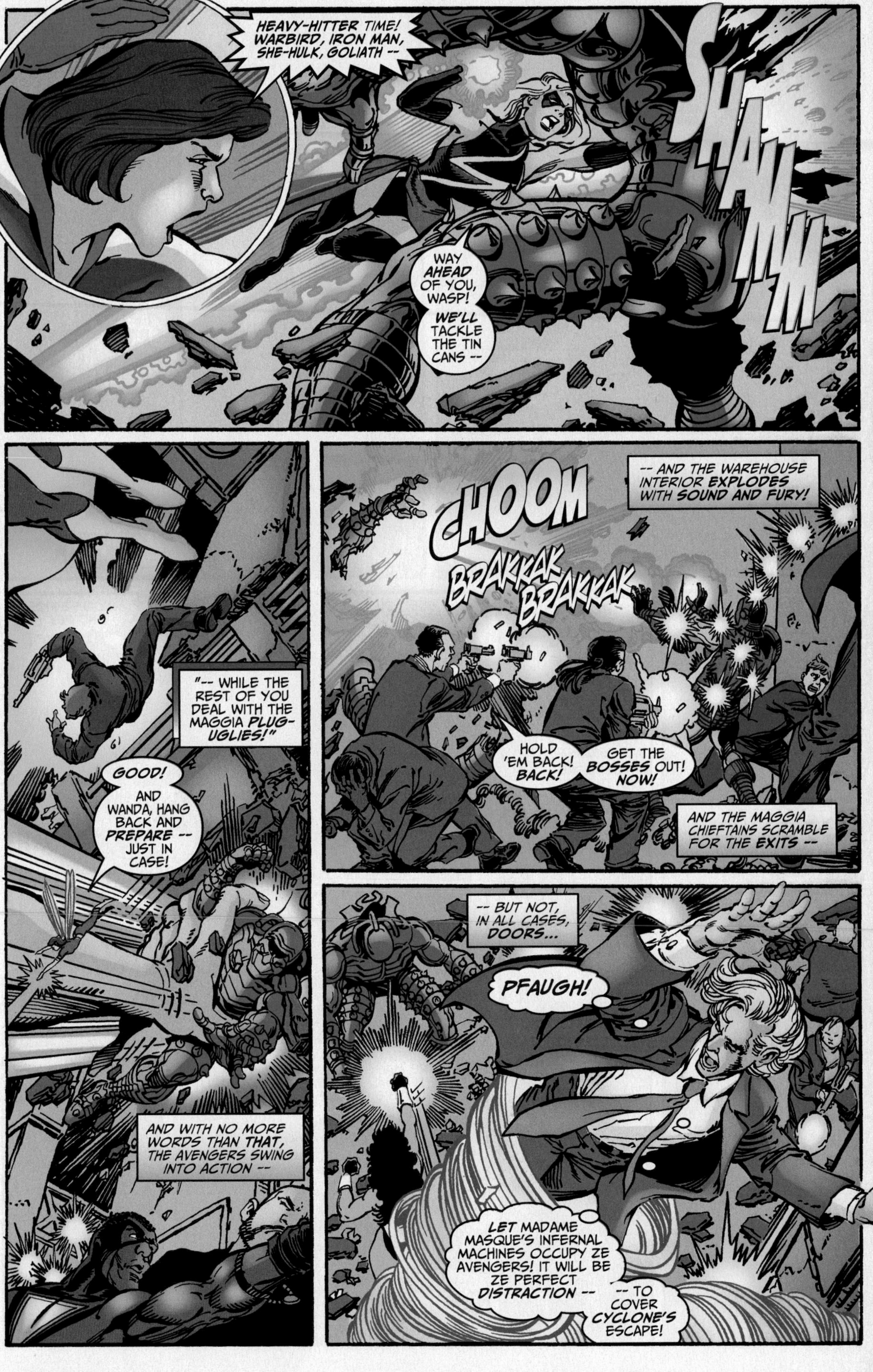
HEAVY-HITTER TIME! WARBIRD, IRON MAN, SHE-HULK, GOLIATH --
SHAMMM
WAY AHEAD OF YOU, WASP!
WE'LL TACKLE THE TIN CANS --
"-- WHILE THE REST OF YOU DEAL WITH THE MAGGIA PLUG-UGLIES!"
GOOD!
AND WANDA, HANG BACK AND PREPARE -- JUST IN CASE!
AND WITH NO MORE WORDS THAN THAT, THE AVENGERS SWING INTO ACTION --
-- AND THE WAREHOUSE INTERIOR EXPLODES WITH SOUND AND FURY!
CHOOM
BRAKKAK BRAKKAK
HOLD 'EM BACK! BACK!
GET THE BOSSES OUT! NOW!
AND THE MAGGIA CHIEFTAINS SCRAMBLE FOR THE EXITS --
-- BUT NOT, IN ALL CASES, DOORS...
PFAUGH!
LET MADAME MASQUE'S INFERNAL MACHINES OCCUPY ZE AVENGERS! IT WILL BE ZE PERFECT DISTRACTION --
-- TO COVER CYCLONE'S ESCAPE!

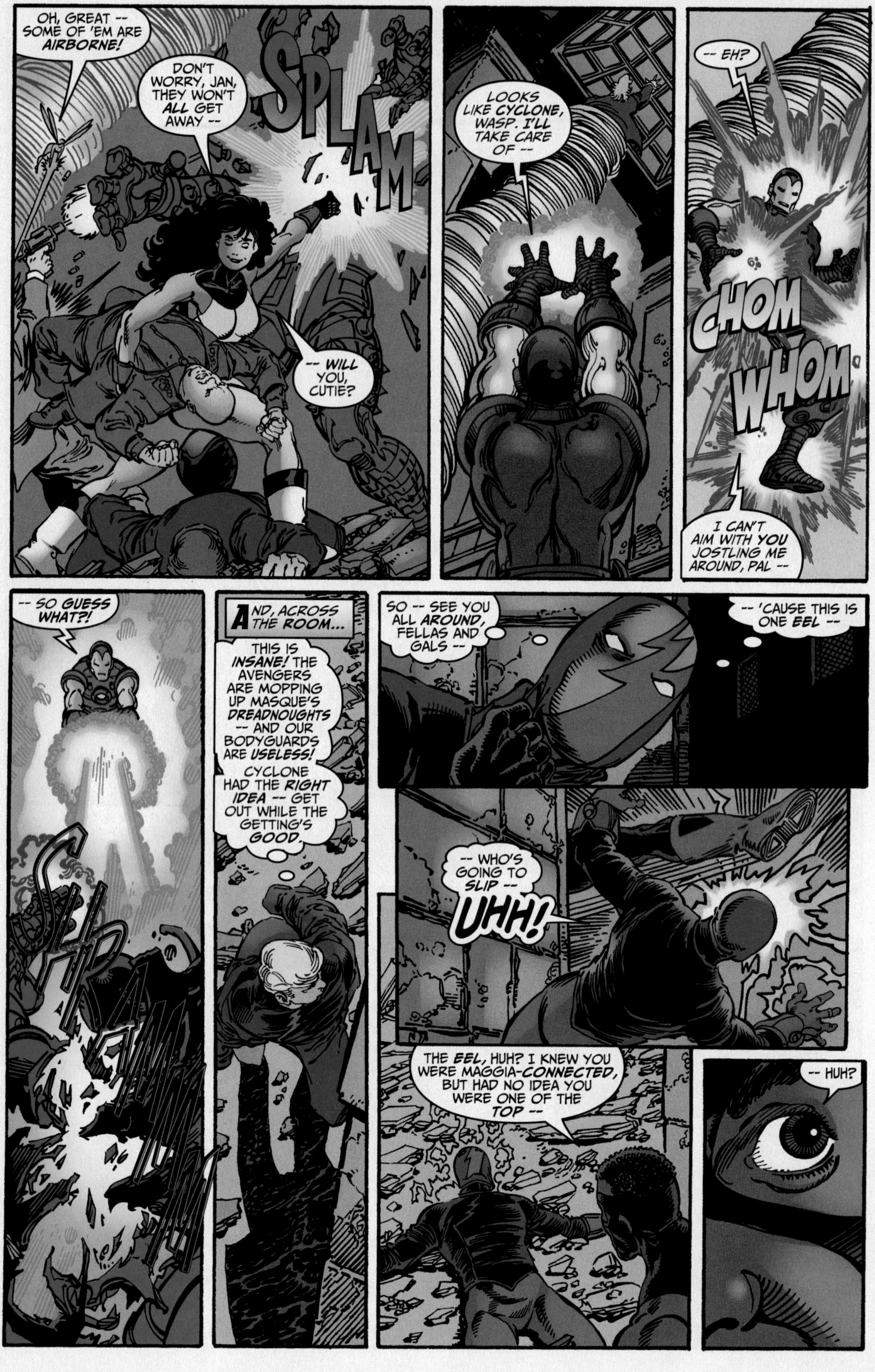
OH, GREAT -- SOME OF 'EM ARE AIRBORNE!
DON'T WORRY, JAN, THEY WON'T ALL GET AWAY --
SPLAM
-- WILL YOU, CUTIE?
LOOKS LIKE CYCLONE, WASP. I'LL TAKE CARE OF --
-- EH?
CHOM
WHOM
I CAN'T AIM WITH YOU JOSTLING ME AROUND, PAL --
-- SO GUESS WHAT?!
SHRAAAAM
AND, ACROSS THE ROOM...
THIS IS INSANE! THE AVENGERS ARE MOPPING UP MASQUE'S DREADNOUGHTS -- AND OUR BODYGUARDS ARE USELESS!
CYCLONE HAD THE RIGHT IDEA -- GET OUT WHILE THE GETTING'S GOOD.
SO -- SEE YOU ALL AROUND, FELLAS AND GALS --
-- 'CAUSE THIS IS ONE EEL --
-- WHO'S GOING TO SLIP --
UHH!
THE EEL, HUH? I KNEW YOU WERE MAGGIA-CONNECTED, BUT HAD NO IDEA YOU WERE ONE OF THE TOP --
-- HUH?

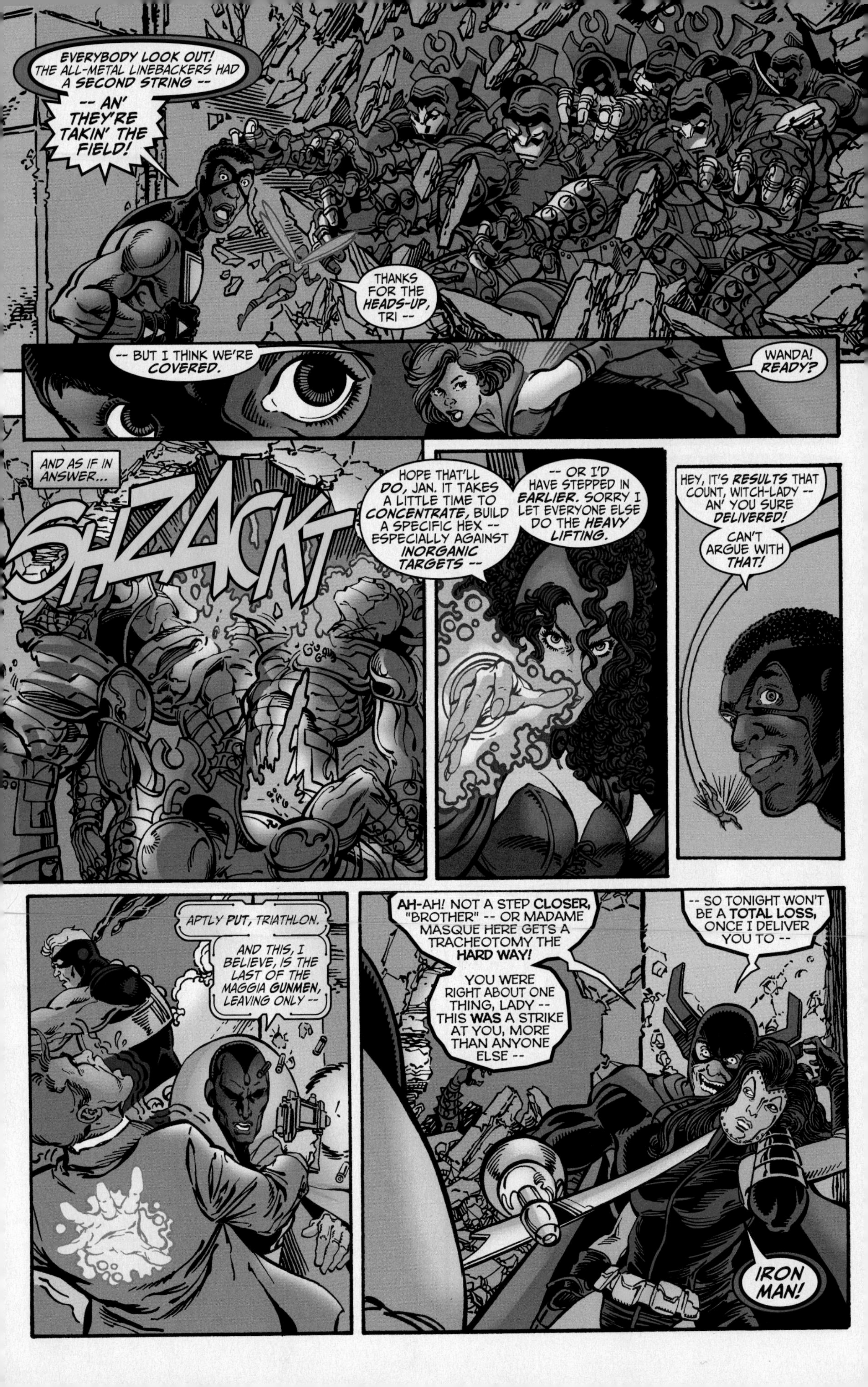
EVERYBODY LOOK OUT! THE ALL-METAL LINEBACKERS HAD A SECOND STRING --
-- AN' THEY'RE TAKIN' THE FIELD!
THANKS FOR THE HEADS-UP, TRI --
-- BUT I THINK WE'RE COVERED.
WANDA! READY?
AND AS IF IN ANSWER...
SHZACKT
HOPE THAT'LL DO, JAN. IT TAKES A LITTLE TIME TO CONCENTRATE, BUILD A SPECIFIC HEX -- ESPECIALLY AGAINST INORGANIC TARGETS --
-- OR I'D HAVE STEPPED IN EARLIER. SORRY I LET EVERYONE ELSE DO THE HEAVY LIFTING.
HEY, IT'S RESULTS THAT COUNT, WITCH-LADY -- AN' YOU SURE DELIVERED!
CAN'T ARGUE WITH THAT!
APTLY PUT, TRIATHLON.
AND THIS, I BELIEVE, IS THE LAST OF THE MAGGIA GUNMEN, LEAVING ONLY --
AH-AH! NOT A STEP CLOSER, "BROTHER" -- OR MADAME MASQUE HERE GETS A TRACHEOTOMY THE HARD WAY!
YOU WERE RIGHT ABOUT ONE THING, LADY -- THIS WAS A STRIKE AT YOU, MORE THAN ANYONE ELSE --
-- SO TONIGHT WON'T BE A TOTAL LOSS, ONCE I DELIVER YOU TO --
IRON MAN!

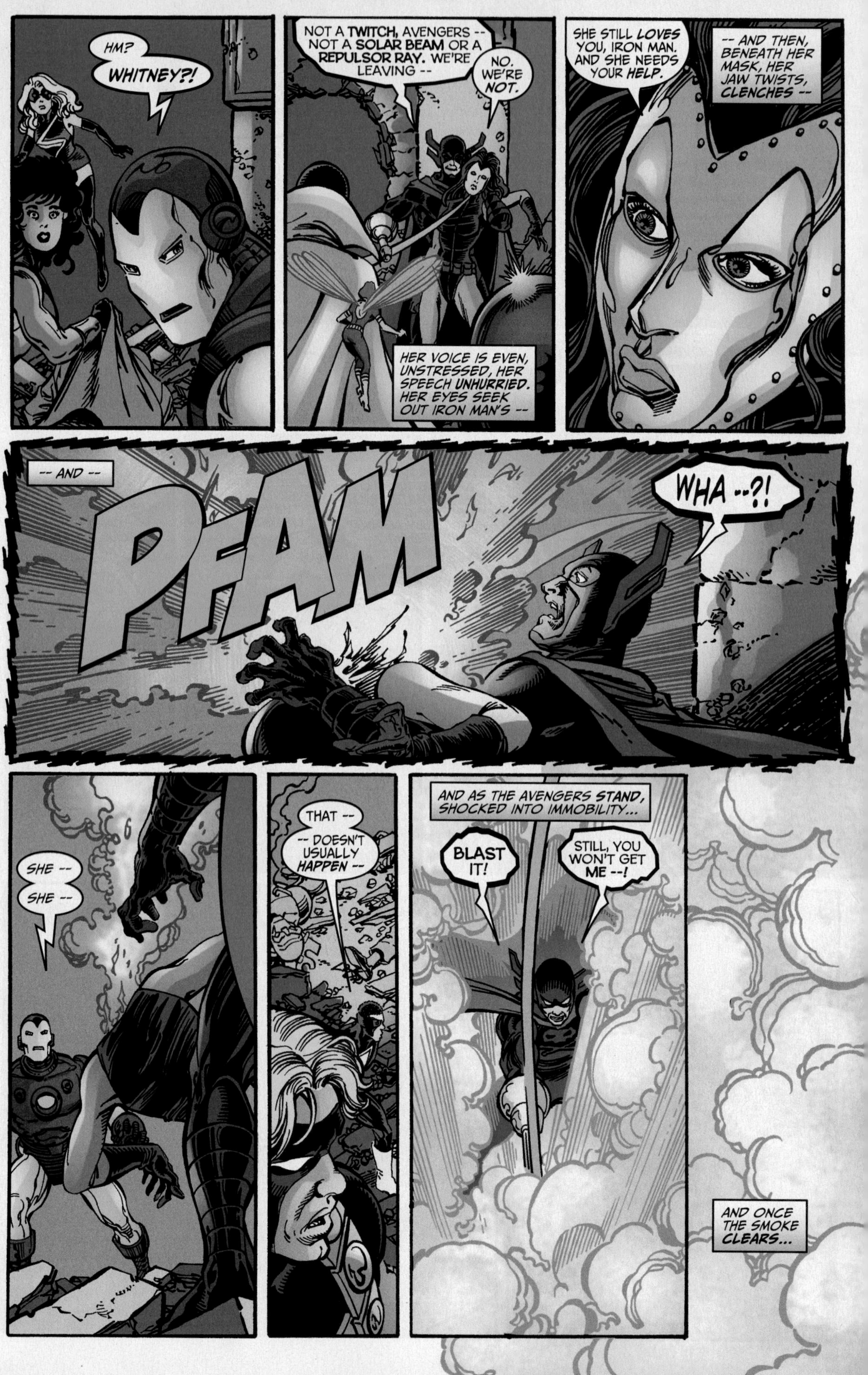
HM?
WHITNEY?!
NOT A TWITCH, AVENGERS -- NOT A SOLAR BEAM OR A REPULSOR RAY. WE'RE LEAVING --
NO. WE'RE NOT.
HER VOICE IS EVEN, UNSTRESSED, HER SPEECH UNHURRIED. HER EYES SEEK OUT IRON MAN'S --
SHE STILL LOVES YOU, IRON MAN. AND SHE NEEDS YOUR HELP.
-- AND THEN, BENEATH HER MASK, HER JAW TWISTS, CLENCHES --
-- AND --
PFAM
WHA --?!
SHE --
SHE --
THAT --
-- DOESN'T USUALLY HAPPEN --
AND AS THE AVENGERS STAND, SHOCKED INTO IMMOBILITY...
BLAST IT!
STILL, YOU WON'T GET ME --!
AND ONCE THE SMOKE CLEARS...

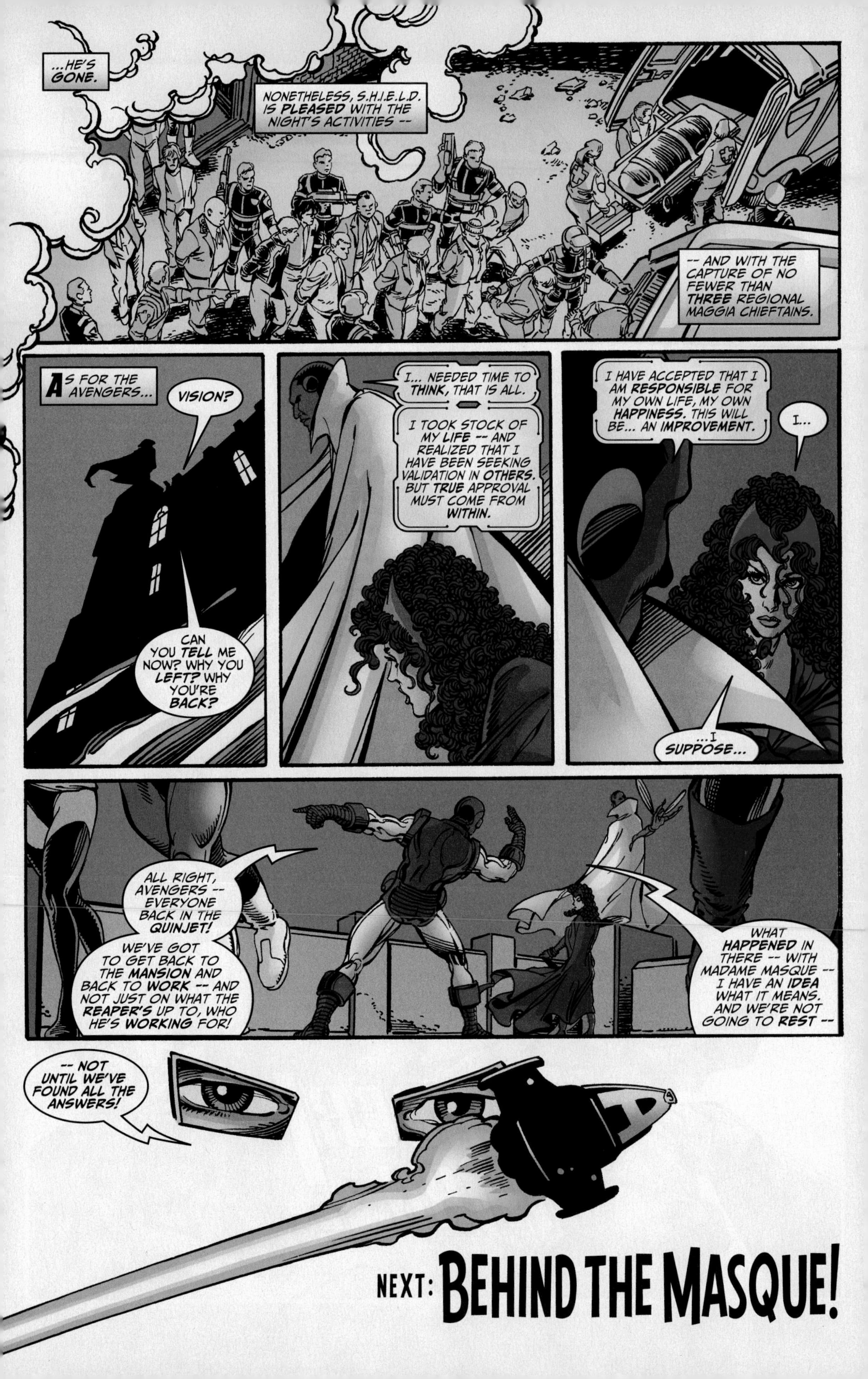
...HE'S GONE.
NONETHELESS, S.H.I.E.L.D. IS PLEASED WITH THE NIGHT'S ACTIVITIES --
-- AND WITH THE CAPTURE OF NO FEWER THAN THREE REGIONAL MAGGIA CHIEFTAINS.
AS FOR THE AVENGERS...
VISION?
CAN YOU TELL ME NOW? WHY YOU LEFT? WHY YOU'RE BACK?
I... NEEDED TIME TO THINK, THAT IS ALL.
I TOOK STOCK OF MY LIFE -- AND REALIZED THAT I HAVE BEEN SEEKING VALIDATION IN OTHERS. BUT TRUE APPROVAL MUST COME FROM WITHIN.
I HAVE ACCEPTED THAT I AM RESPONSIBLE FOR MY OWN LIFE, MY OWN HAPPINESS. THIS WILL BE... AN IMPROVEMENT.
I...
...I SUPPOSE...
ALL RIGHT, AVENGERS -- EVERYONE BACK IN THE QUINJET!
WE'VE GOT TO GET BACK TO THE MANSION AND BACK TO WORK -- AND NOT JUST ON WHAT THE REAPER'S UP TO, WHO HE'S WORKING FOR!
WHAT HAPPENED IN THERE -- WITH MADAME MASQUE -- I HAVE AN IDEA WHAT IT MEANS. AND WE'RE NOT GOING TO REST --
-- NOT UNTIL WE'VE FOUND ALL THE ANSWERS!
NEXT: BEHIND THE MASQUE!

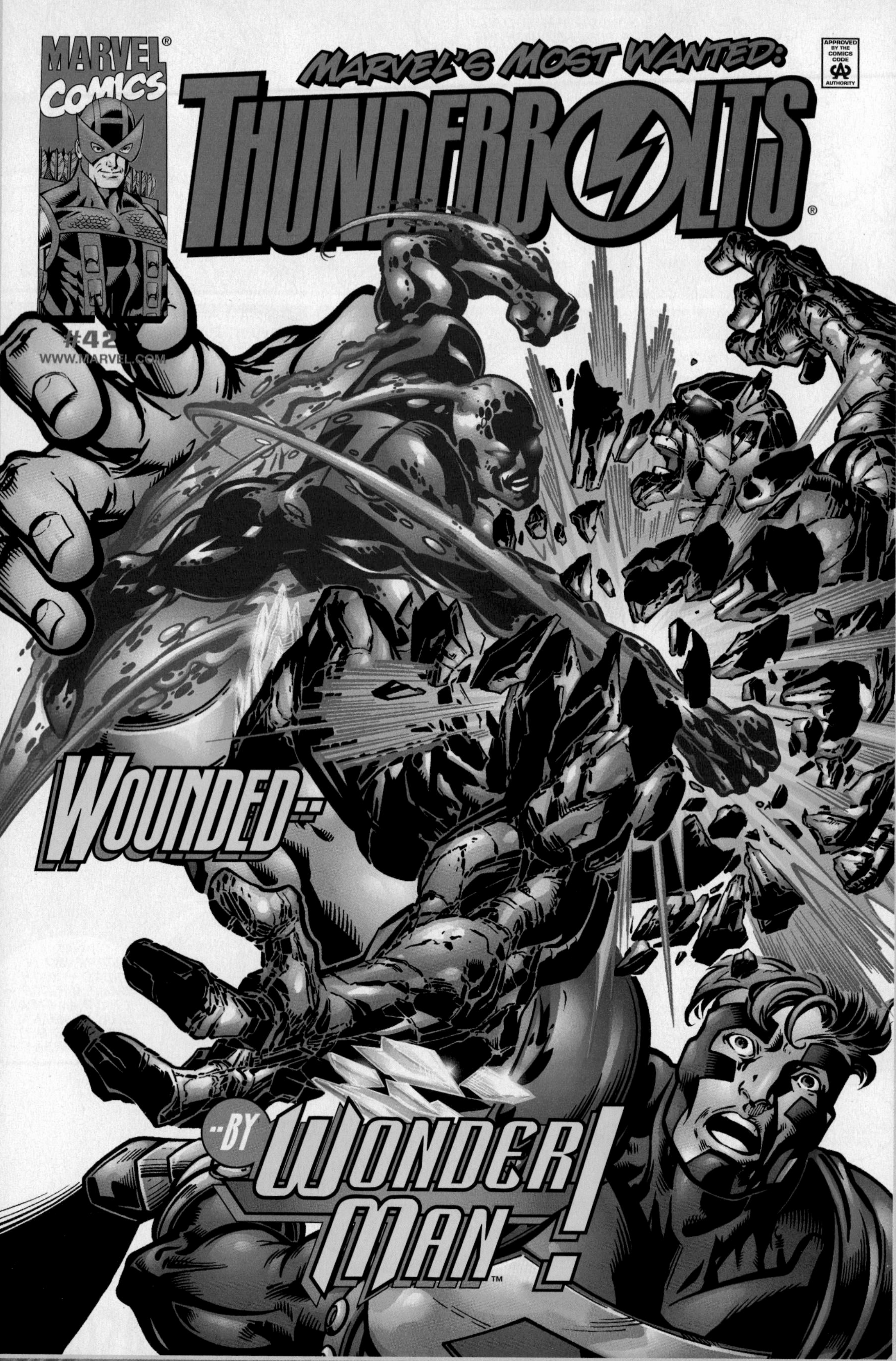
MARVEL® COMICS
MARVEL'S MOST WANTED:
THUNDERBOLTS®
APPROVED BY THE COMICS CODE AUTHORITY
#42
WWW.MARVEL.COM
WOUNDED--
--BY WONDER MAN!™

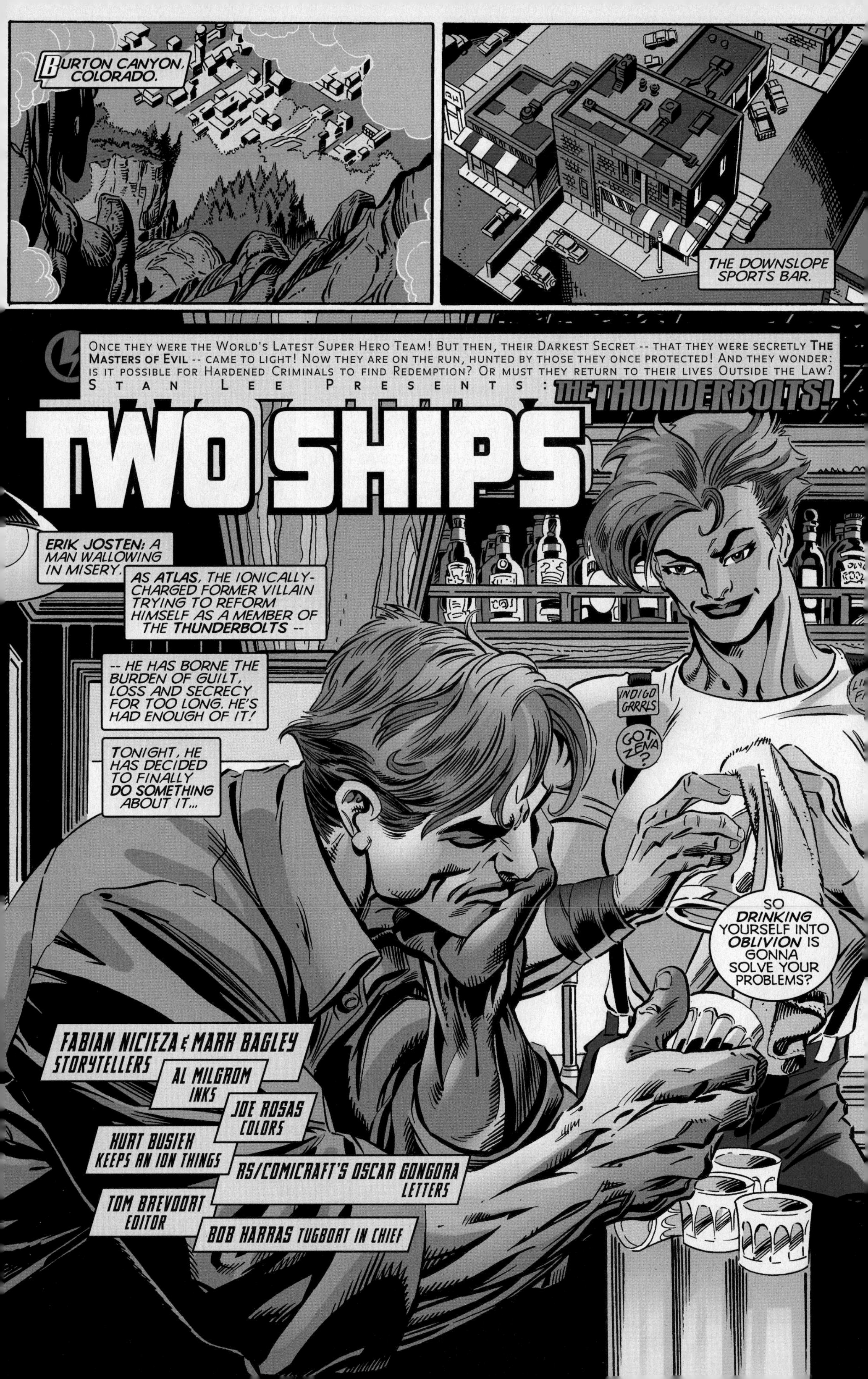
BURTON CANYON, COLORADO.
THE DOWNSLOPE SPORTS BAR.
ONCE THEY WERE THE WORLD'S LATEST SUPER HERO TEAM! BUT THEN, THEIR DARKEST SECRET -- THAT THEY WERE SECRETLY THE MASTERS OF EVIL -- CAME TO LIGHT! NOW THEY ARE ON THE RUN, HUNTED BY THOSE THEY ONCE PROTECTED! AND THEY WONDER: IS IT POSSIBLE FOR HARDENED CRIMINALS TO FIND REDEMPTION? OR MUST THEY RETURN TO THEIR LIVES OUTSIDE THE LAW?
STAN LEE PRESENTS: THE THUNDERBOLTS!
TWO SHIPS
ERIK JOSTEN: A MAN WALLOWING IN MISERY.
AS ATLAS, THE IONICALLY-CHARGED FORMER VILLAIN TRYING TO REFORM HIMSELF AS A MEMBER OF THE THUNDERBOLTS --
-- HE HAS BORNE THE BURDEN OF GUILT, LOSS AND SECRECY FOR TOO LONG. HE'S HAD ENOUGH OF IT!
TONIGHT, HE HAS DECIDED TO FINALLY DO SOMETHING ABOUT IT...
INDIGO GRRRLS
GOT ZENA?
SO DRINKING YOURSELF INTO OBLIVION IS GONNA SOLVE YOUR PROBLEMS?
FABIAN NICIEZA & MARK BAGLEY STORYTELLERS
AL MILGROM INKS
JOE ROSAS COLORS
KURT BUSIEK KEEPS AN ION THINGS
RS/COMICRAFT'S OSCAR GONGORA LETTERS
TOM BREVOORT EDITOR
BOB HARRAS TUGBOAT IN CHIEF

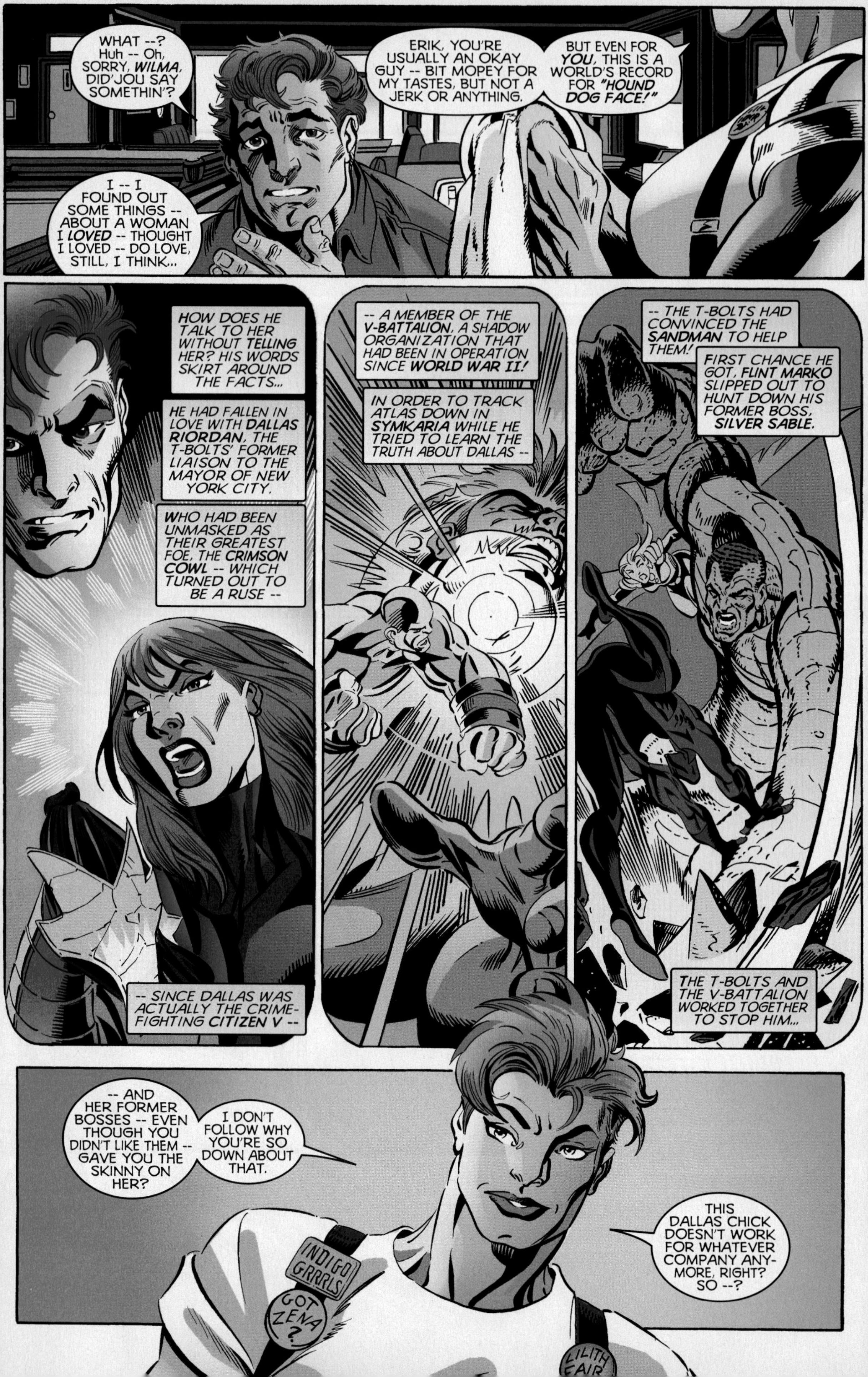
WHAT --? Huh -- Oh, SORRY, WILMA, DID'JOU SAY SOMETHIN'?
ERIK, YOU'RE USUALLY AN OKAY GUY -- BIT MOPEY FOR MY TASTES, BUT NOT A JERK OR ANYTHING.
BUT EVEN FOR YOU, THIS IS A WORLD'S RECORD FOR "HOUND DOG FACE!"
I -- I FOUND OUT SOME THINGS -- ABOUT A WOMAN I LOVED -- THOUGHT I LOVED -- DO LOVE, STILL, I THINK...
HOW DOES HE TALK TO HER WITHOUT TELLING HER? HIS WORDS SKIRT AROUND THE FACTS...
HE HAD FALLEN IN LOVE WITH DALLAS RIORDAN, THE T-BOLTS' FORMER LIAISON TO THE MAYOR OF NEW YORK CITY.
WHO HAD BEEN UNMASKED AS THEIR GREATEST FOE, THE CRIMSON COWL -- WHICH TURNED OUT TO BE A RUSE --
-- SINCE DALLAS WAS ACTUALLY THE CRIME-FIGHTING CITIZEN V --
-- A MEMBER OF THE V-BATTALION, A SHADOW ORGANIZATION THAT HAD BEEN IN OPERATION SINCE WORLD WAR II!
IN ORDER TO TRACK ATLAS DOWN IN SYMKARIA WHILE HE TRIED TO LEARN THE TRUTH ABOUT DALLAS --
-- THE T-BOLTS HAD CONVINCED THE SANDMAN TO HELP THEM!
FIRST CHANCE HE GOT, FLINT MARKO SLIPPED OUT TO HUNT DOWN HIS FORMER BOSS, SILVER SABLE.
THE T-BOLTS AND THE V-BATTALION WORKED TOGETHER TO STOP HIM...
-- AND HER FORMER BOSSES -- EVEN THOUGH YOU DIDN'T LIKE THEM -- GAVE YOU THE SKINNY ON HER?
I DON'T FOLLOW WHY YOU'RE SO DOWN ABOUT THAT.
THIS DALLAS CHICK DOESN'T WORK FOR WHATEVER COMPANY ANY-MORE, RIGHT? SO --?
INDIGO GRRRLS
GOT ZENA ?

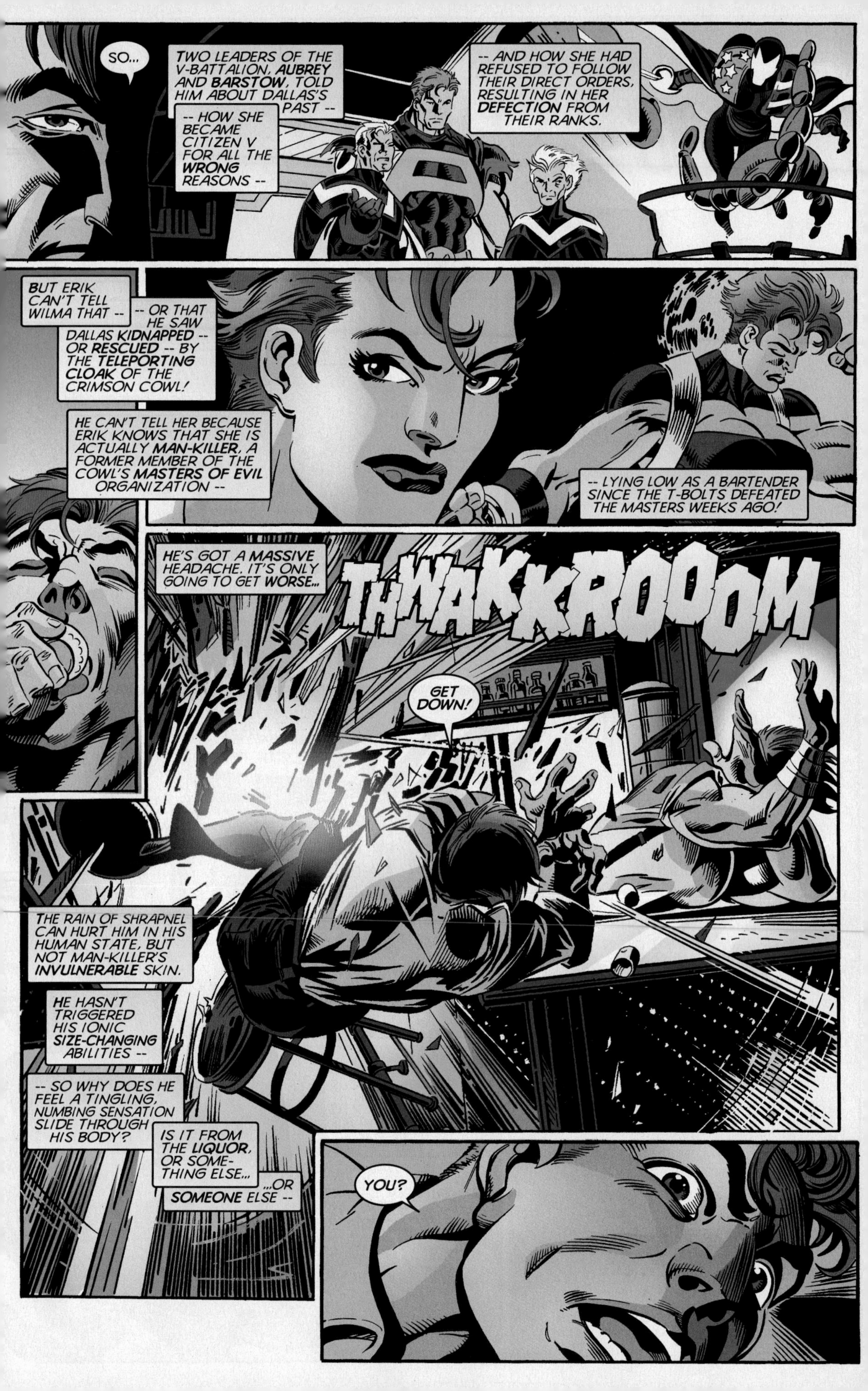
SO...
TWO LEADERS OF THE V-BATTALION, AUBREY AND BARSTOW, TOLD HIM ABOUT DALLAS'S PAST --
-- HOW SHE BECAME CITIZEN V FOR ALL THE WRONG REASONS --
-- AND HOW SHE HAD REFUSED TO FOLLOW THEIR DIRECT ORDERS, RESULTING IN HER DEFECTION FROM THEIR RANKS.
BUT ERIK CAN'T TELL WILMA THAT --
-- OR THAT HE SAW DALLAS KIDNAPPED -- OR RESCUED -- BY THE TELEPORTING CLOAK OF THE CRIMSON COWL!
HE CAN'T TELL HER BECAUSE ERIK KNOWS THAT SHE IS ACTUALLY MAN-KILLER, A FORMER MEMBER OF THE COWL'S MASTERS OF EVIL ORGANIZATION --
-- LYING LOW AS A BARTENDER SINCE THE T-BOLTS DEFEATED THE MASTERS WEEKS AGO!
HE'S GOT A MASSIVE HEADACHE. IT'S ONLY GOING TO GET WORSE...
THWAKKROOOOM
GET DOWN!
THE RAIN OF SHRAPNEL CAN HURT HIM IN HIS HUMAN STATE, BUT NOT MAN-KILLER'S INVULNERABLE SKIN.
HE HASN'T TRIGGERED HIS IONIC SIZE-CHANGING ABILITIES --
-- SO WHY DOES HE FEEL A TINGLING, NUMBING SENSATION SLIDE THROUGH HIS BODY?
IS IT FROM THE LIQUOR, OR SOMETHING ELSE...
...OR SOMEONE ELSE --
YOU?

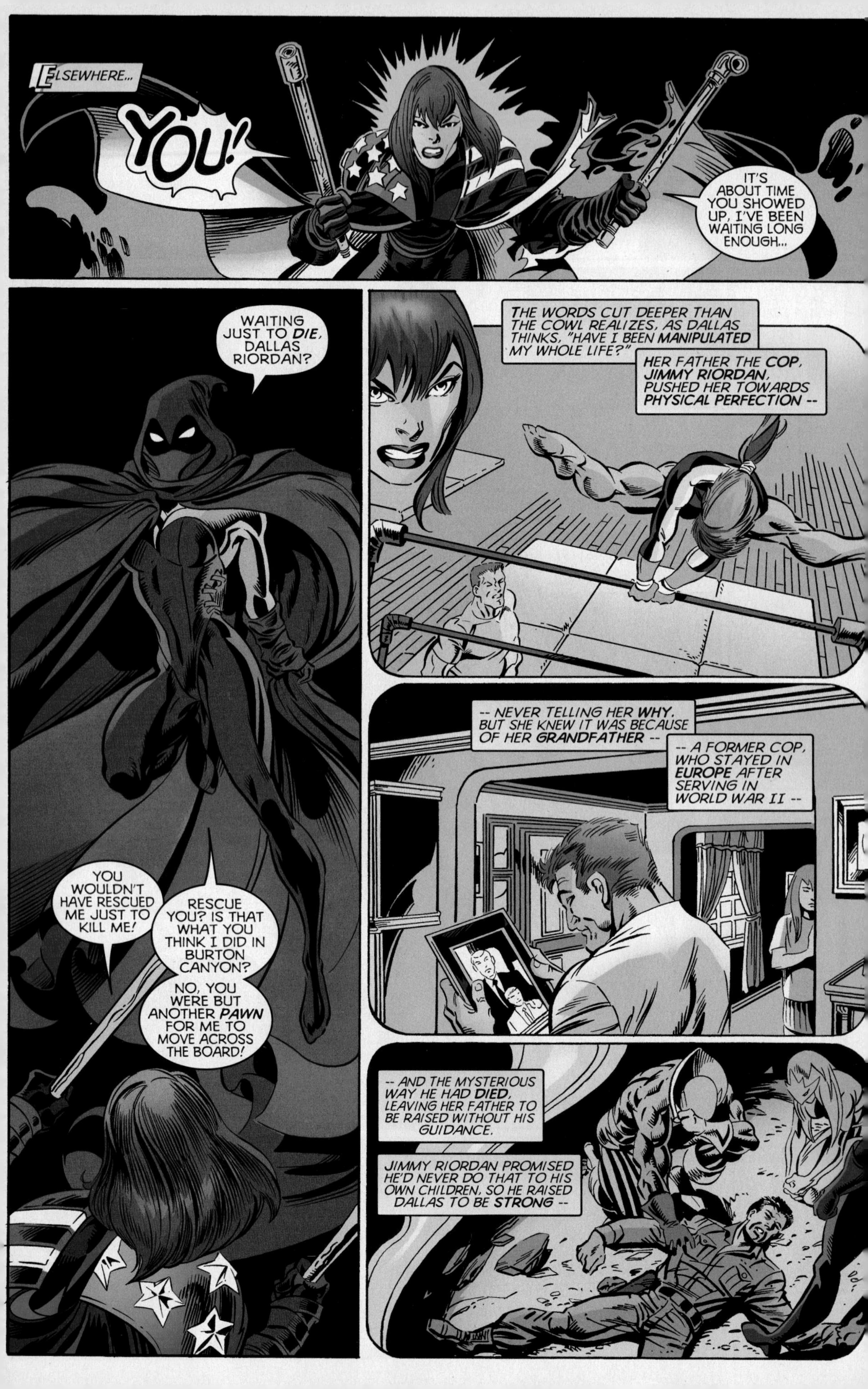
ELSEWHERE...
YOU!
IT'S ABOUT TIME YOU SHOWED UP, I'VE BEEN WAITING LONG ENOUGH...
WAITING JUST TO *DIE*, DALLAS RIORDAN?
YOU WOULDN'T HAVE RESCUED ME JUST TO KILL ME!
RESCUE YOU? IS THAT WHAT YOU THINK I DID IN BURTON CANYON?
NO, YOU WERE BUT ANOTHER *PAWN* FOR ME TO MOVE ACROSS THE BOARD!
THE WORDS CUT DEEPER THAN THE COWL REALIZES, AS DALLAS THINKS, "HAVE I BEEN *MANIPULATED* MY WHOLE LIFE?"
HER FATHER THE *COP*, *JIMMY RIORDAN*, PUSHED HER TOWARDS *PHYSICAL PERFECTION* --
-- NEVER TELLING HER *WHY*, BUT SHE KNEW IT WAS BECAUSE OF HER *GRANDFATHER* --
-- A FORMER COP, WHO STAYED IN *EUROPE* AFTER SERVING IN WORLD WAR II --
-- AND THE MYSTERIOUS WAY HE HAD *DIED*, LEAVING HER FATHER TO BE RAISED WITHOUT HIS GUIDANCE.
JIMMY RIORDAN PROMISED HE'D NEVER DO THAT TO HIS OWN CHILDREN, SO HE RAISED DALLAS TO BE *STRONG* --

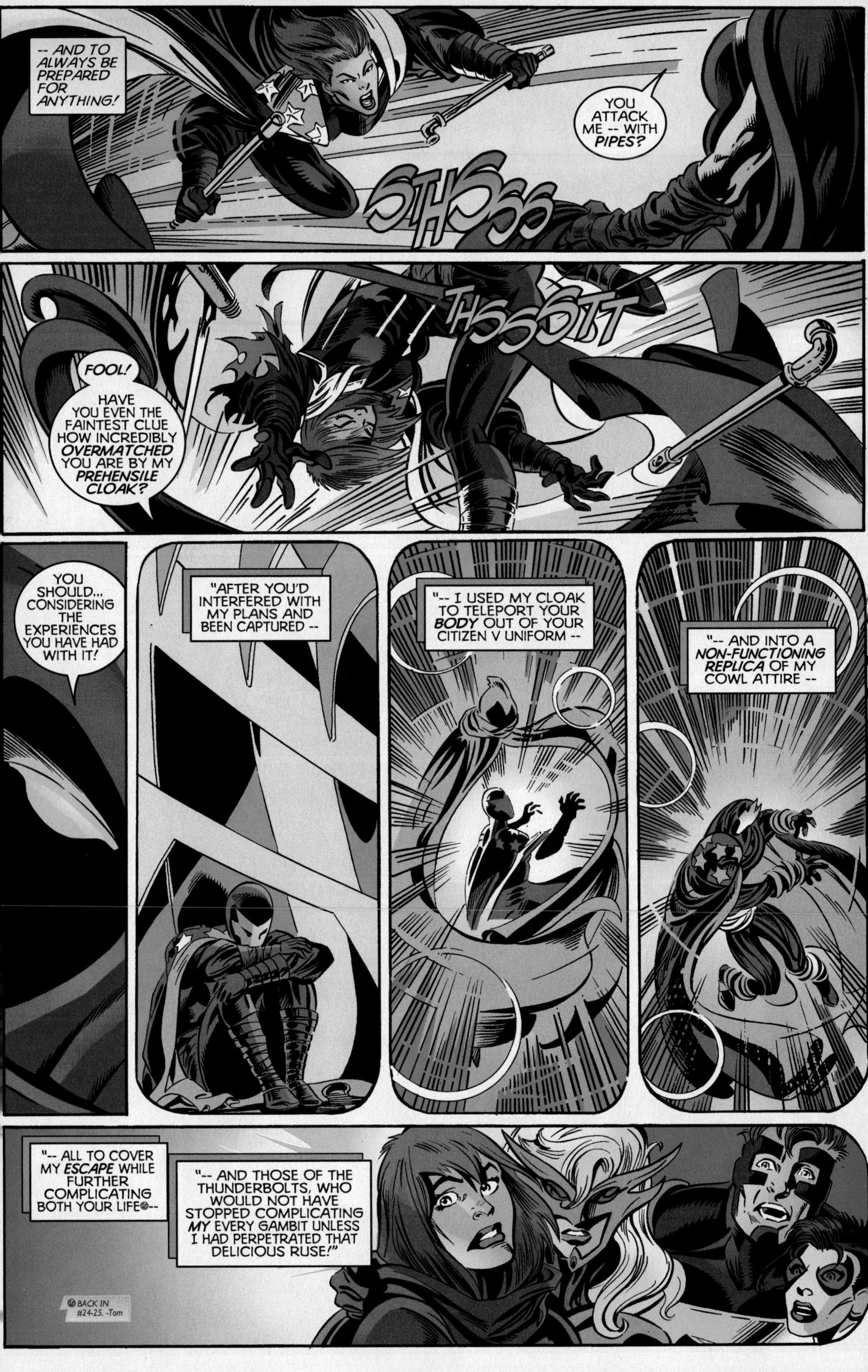
-- AND TO ALWAYS BE PREPARED FOR ANYTHING!
YOU ATTACK ME -- WITH PIPES?
SSSCHS
THSSSTT
FOOL!
HAVE YOU EVEN THE FAINTEST CLUE HOW INCREDIBLY OVERMATCHED YOU ARE BY MY PREHENSILE CLOAK?
YOU SHOULD... CONSIDERING THE EXPERIENCES YOU HAVE HAD WITH IT!
"AFTER YOU'D INTERFERED WITH MY PLANS AND BEEN CAPTURED --
"-- I USED MY CLOAK TO TELEPORT YOUR BODY OUT OF YOUR CITIZEN V UNIFORM --
"-- AND INTO A NON-FUNCTIONING REPLICA OF MY COWL ATTIRE --
"-- ALL TO COVER MY ESCAPE WHILE FURTHER COMPLICATING BOTH YOUR LIFE--
"-- AND THOSE OF THE THUNDERBOLTS, WHO WOULD NOT HAVE STOPPED COMPLICATING MY EVERY GAMBIT UNLESS I HAD PERPETRATED THAT DELICIOUS RUSE!"
BACK IN #24-25. -Tom

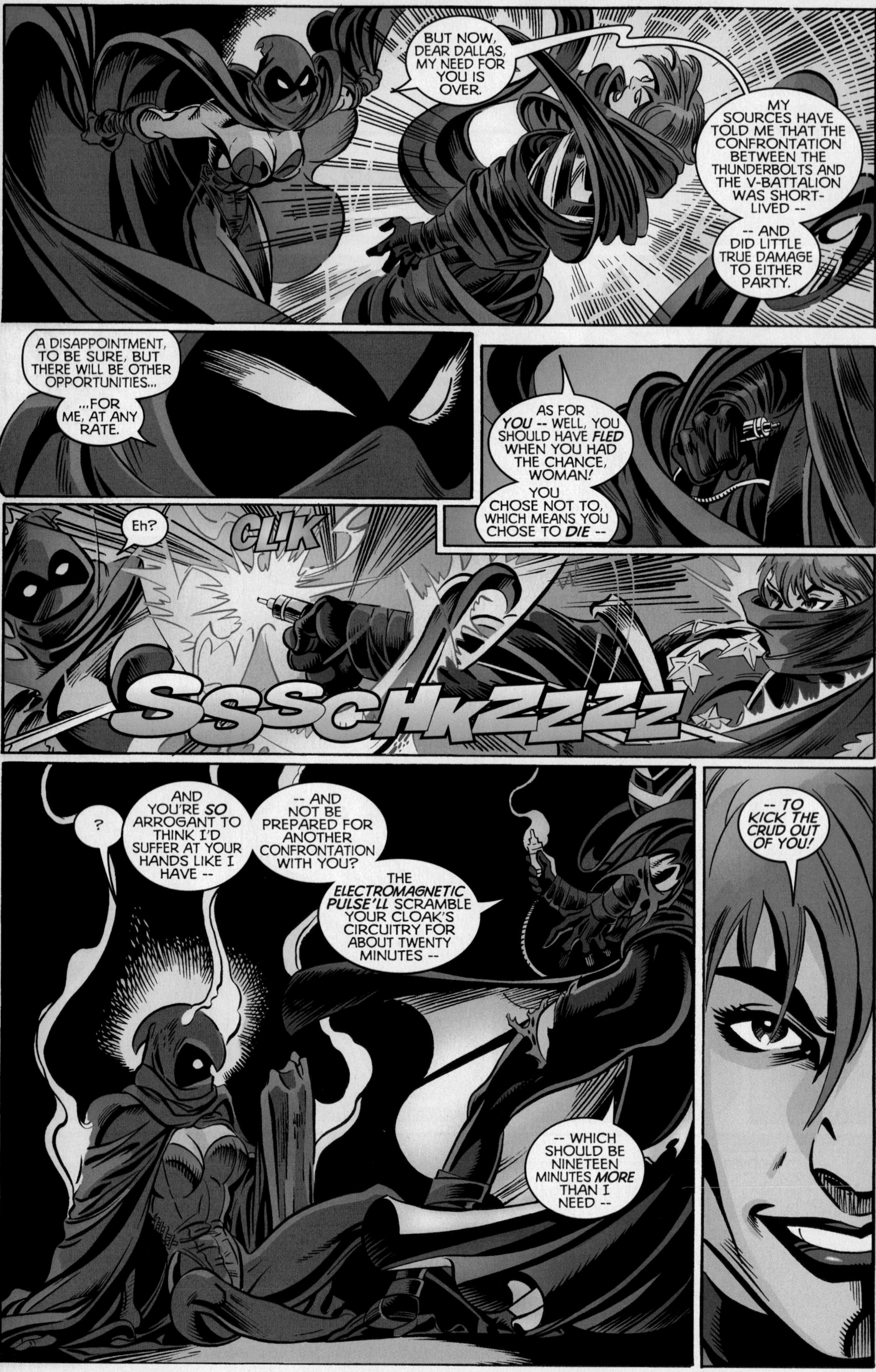
BUT NOW, DEAR DALLAS, MY NEED FOR YOU IS OVER.
MY SOURCES HAVE TOLD ME THAT THE CONFRONTATION BETWEEN THE THUNDERBOLTS AND THE V-BATTALION WAS SHORT-LIVED --
-- AND DID LITTLE TRUE DAMAGE TO EITHER PARTY.
A DISAPPOINTMENT, TO BE SURE, BUT THERE WILL BE OTHER OPPORTUNITIES...
...FOR ME, AT ANY RATE.
AS FOR *YOU* -- WELL, YOU SHOULD HAVE *FLED* WHEN YOU HAD THE CHANCE, WOMAN!
YOU CHOSE NOT TO, WHICH MEANS YOU CHOSE TO *DIE* --
Eh?
CLIK
SSSCHKZZZZ
?
AND YOU'RE *SO* ARROGANT TO THINK I'D SUFFER AT YOUR HANDS LIKE I HAVE --
-- AND NOT BE PREPARED FOR ANOTHER CONFRONTATION WITH YOU?
THE *ELECTROMAGNETIC PULSE'LL* SCRAMBLE YOUR CLOAK'S CIRCUITRY FOR ABOUT TWENTY MINUTES --
-- WHICH SHOULD BE NINETEEN MINUTES *MORE* THAN I NEED --
-- *TO KICK THE CRUD OUT OF YOU!*

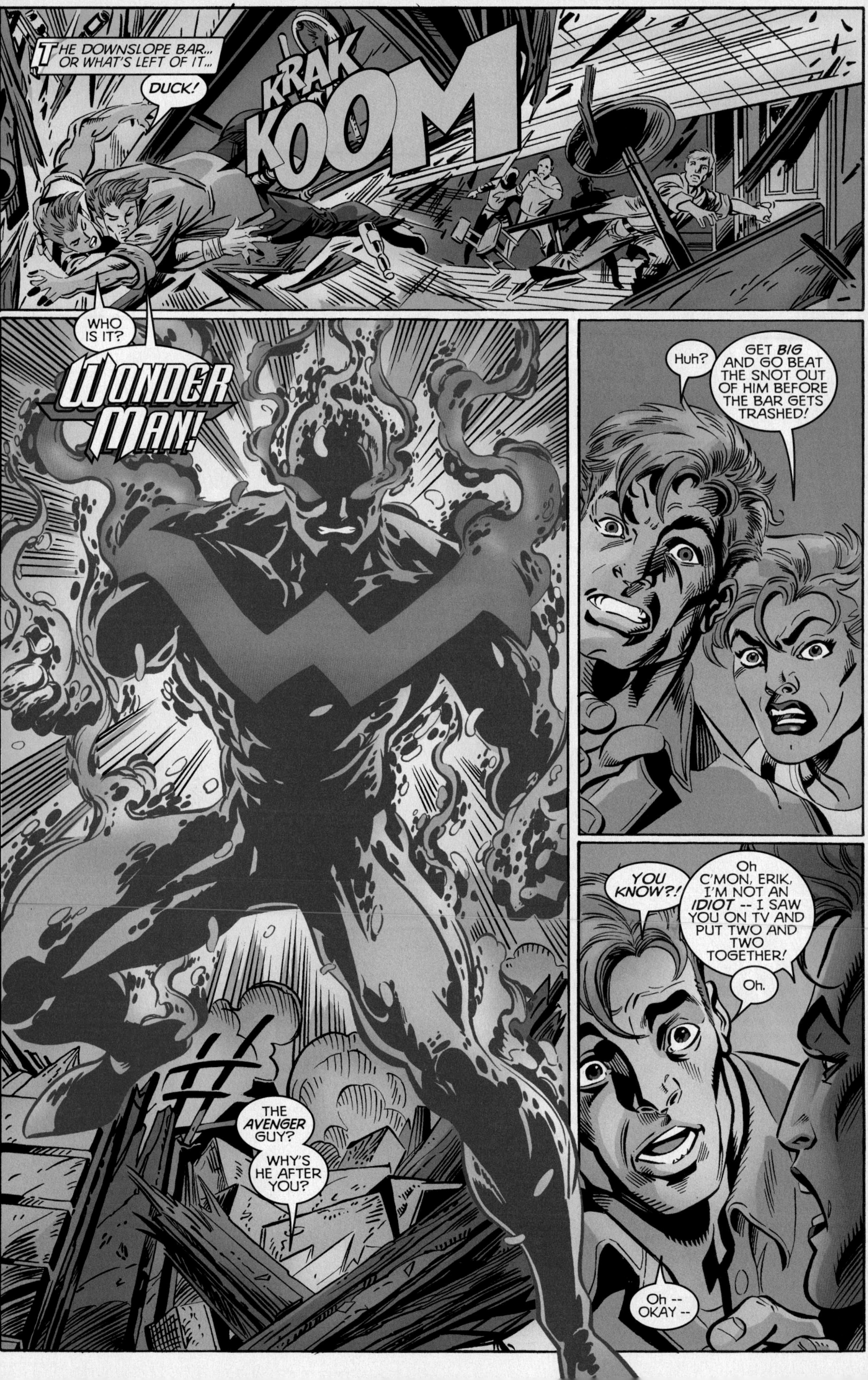
THE DOWNSLOPE BAR... OR WHAT'S LEFT OF IT...
DUCK!
KRAK KOOM
WHO IS IT?
WONDER MAN!
Huh?
GET BIG AND GO BEAT THE SNOT OUT OF HIM BEFORE THE BAR GETS TRASHED!
THE AVENGER GUY?
WHY'S HE AFTER YOU?
YOU KNOW?!
Oh C'MON, ERIK, I'M NOT AN IDIOT -- I SAW YOU ON TV AND PUT TWO AND TWO TOGETHER!
Oh.
Oh -- OKAY --

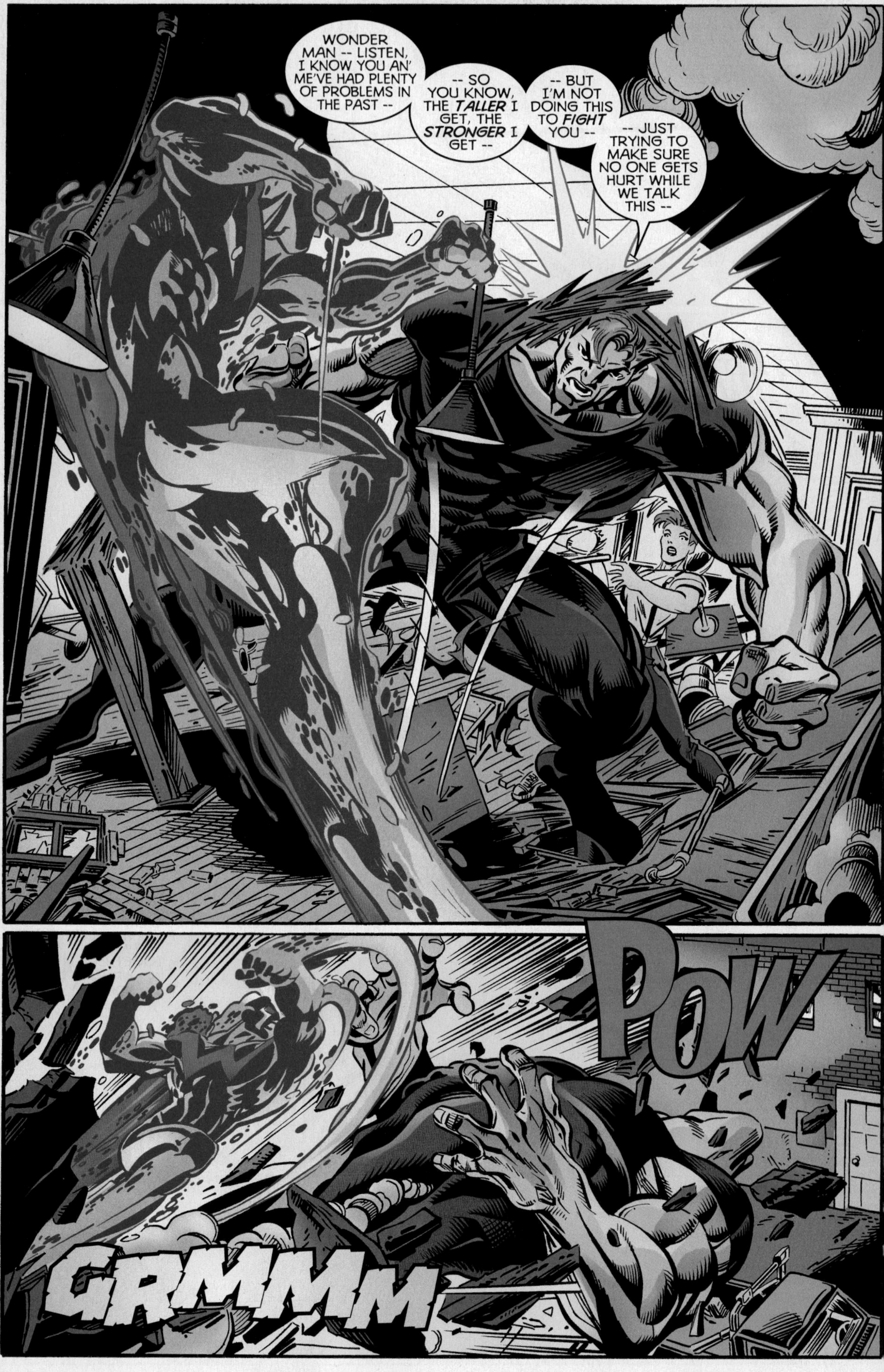
WONDER MAN -- LISTEN, I KNOW YOU AN' ME'VE HAD PLENTY OF PROBLEMS IN THE PAST --
-- SO YOU KNOW, THE *TALLER* I GET, THE *STRONGER* I GET --
-- BUT I'M NOT DOING THIS TO *FIGHT* YOU --
-- JUST TRYING TO MAKE SURE NO ONE GETS HURT WHILE WE TALK THIS --
POW
GRMMMM

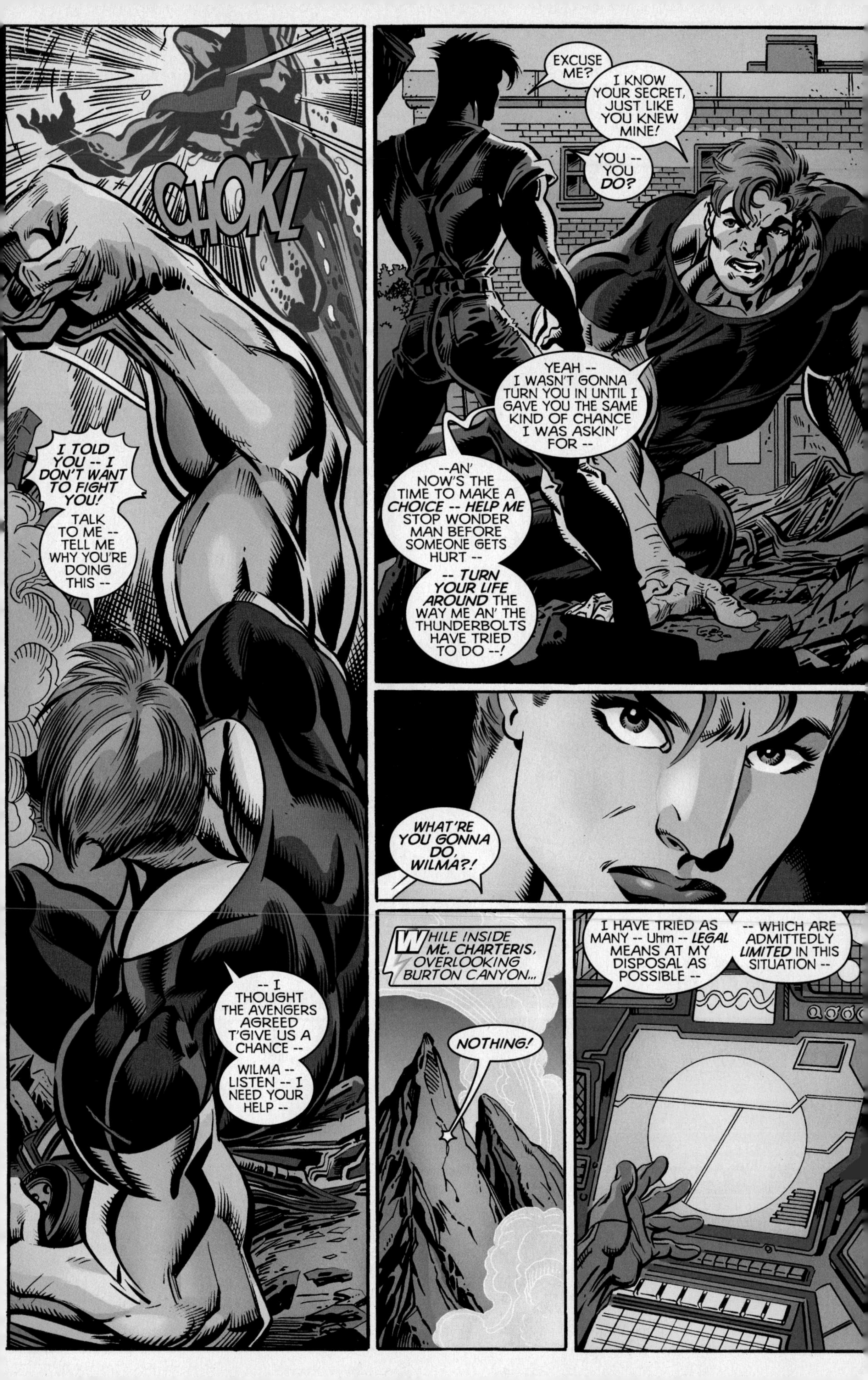
CHOK!
I TOLD YOU -- I DON'T WANT TO FIGHT YOU!
TALK TO ME -- TELL ME WHY YOU'RE DOING THIS --
-- I THOUGHT THE AVENGERS AGREED T'GIVE US A CHANCE --
WILMA -- LISTEN -- I NEED YOUR HELP --
EXCUSE ME?
I KNOW YOUR SECRET, JUST LIKE YOU KNEW MINE!
YOU -- YOU DO?
YEAH -- I WASN'T GONNA TURN YOU IN UNTIL I GAVE YOU THE SAME KIND OF CHANCE I WAS ASKIN' FOR --
--AN' NOW'S THE TIME TO MAKE A CHOICE -- HELP ME STOP WONDER MAN BEFORE SOMEONE GETS HURT --
-- TURN YOUR LIFE AROUND THE WAY ME AN' THE THUNDERBOLTS HAVE TRIED TO DO --!
WHAT'RE YOU GONNA DO, WILMA?!
WHILE INSIDE Mt. CHARTERIS, OVERLOOKING BURTON CANYON...
NOTHING!
I HAVE TRIED AS MANY -- Uhm -- LEGAL MEANS AT MY DISPOSAL AS POSSIBLE --
-- WHICH ARE ADMITTEDLY LIMITED IN THIS SITUATION --

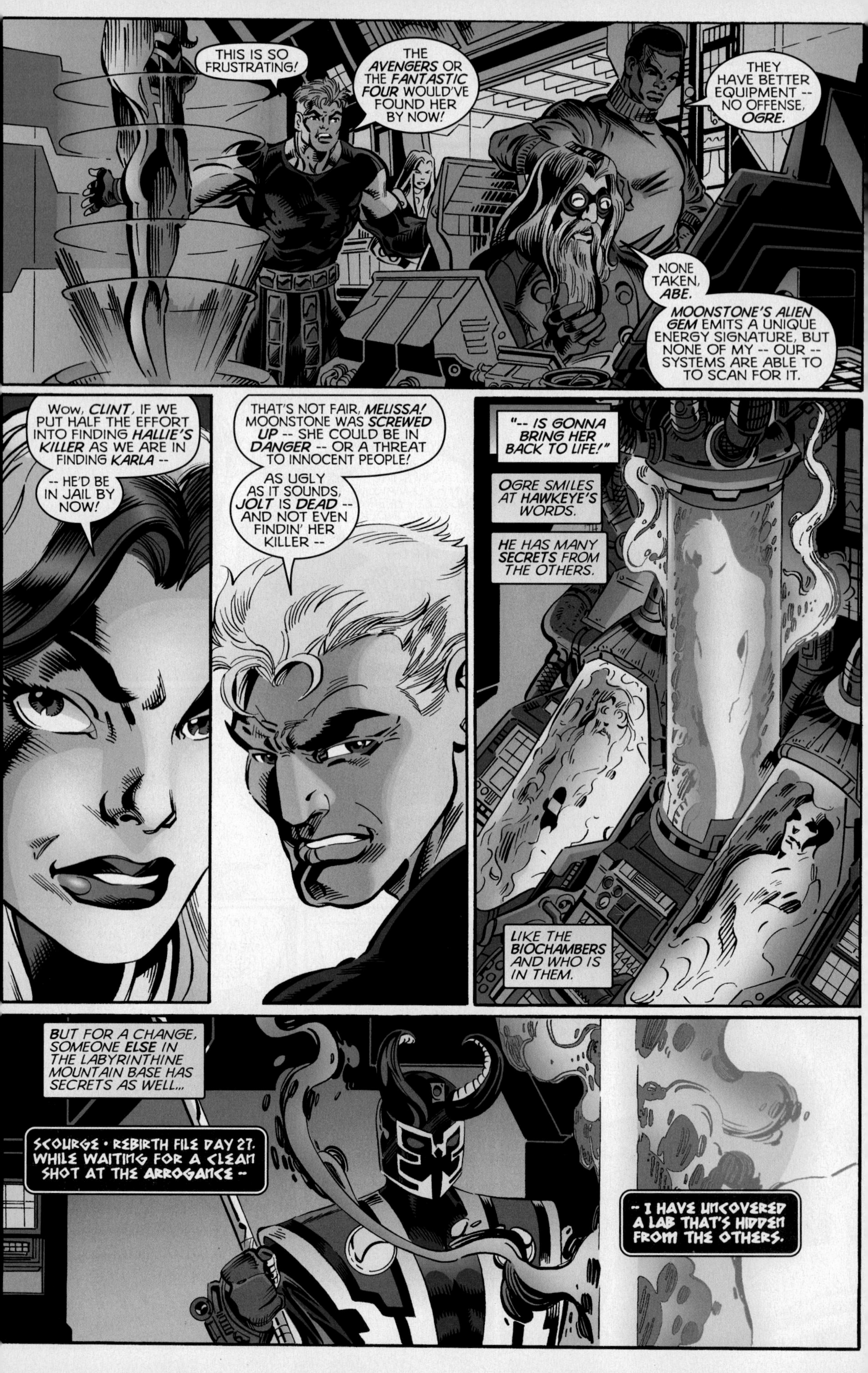
THIS IS SO FRUSTRATING!
THE AVENGERS OR THE FANTASTIC FOUR WOULD'VE FOUND HER BY NOW!
THEY HAVE BETTER EQUIPMENT -- NO OFFENSE, OGRE.
NONE TAKEN, ABE.
MOONSTONE'S ALIEN GEM EMITS A UNIQUE ENERGY SIGNATURE, BUT NONE OF MY -- OUR -- SYSTEMS ARE ABLE TO TO SCAN FOR IT.
WOW, CLINT, IF WE PUT HALF THE EFFORT INTO FINDING HALLIE'S KILLER AS WE ARE IN FINDING KARLA --
-- HE'D BE IN JAIL BY NOW!
THAT'S NOT FAIR, MELISSA! MOONSTONE WAS SCREWED UP -- SHE COULD BE IN DANGER -- OR A THREAT TO INNOCENT PEOPLE!
AS UGLY AS IT SOUNDS, JOLT IS DEAD -- AND NOT EVEN FINDIN' HER KILLER --
"-- IS GONNA BRING HER BACK TO LIFE!"
OGRE SMILES AT HAWKEYE'S WORDS.
HE HAS MANY SECRETS FROM THE OTHERS.
LIKE THE BIOCHAMBERS AND WHO IS IN THEM.
BUT FOR A CHANGE, SOMEONE ELSE IN THE LABYRINTHINE MOUNTAIN BASE HAS SECRETS AS WELL...
SCOURGE • REBIRTH FILE DAY 27. WHILE WAITING FOR A CLEAN SHOT AT THE ARROGANCE --
-- I HAVE UNCOVERED A LAB THAT'S HIDDEN FROM THE OTHERS.

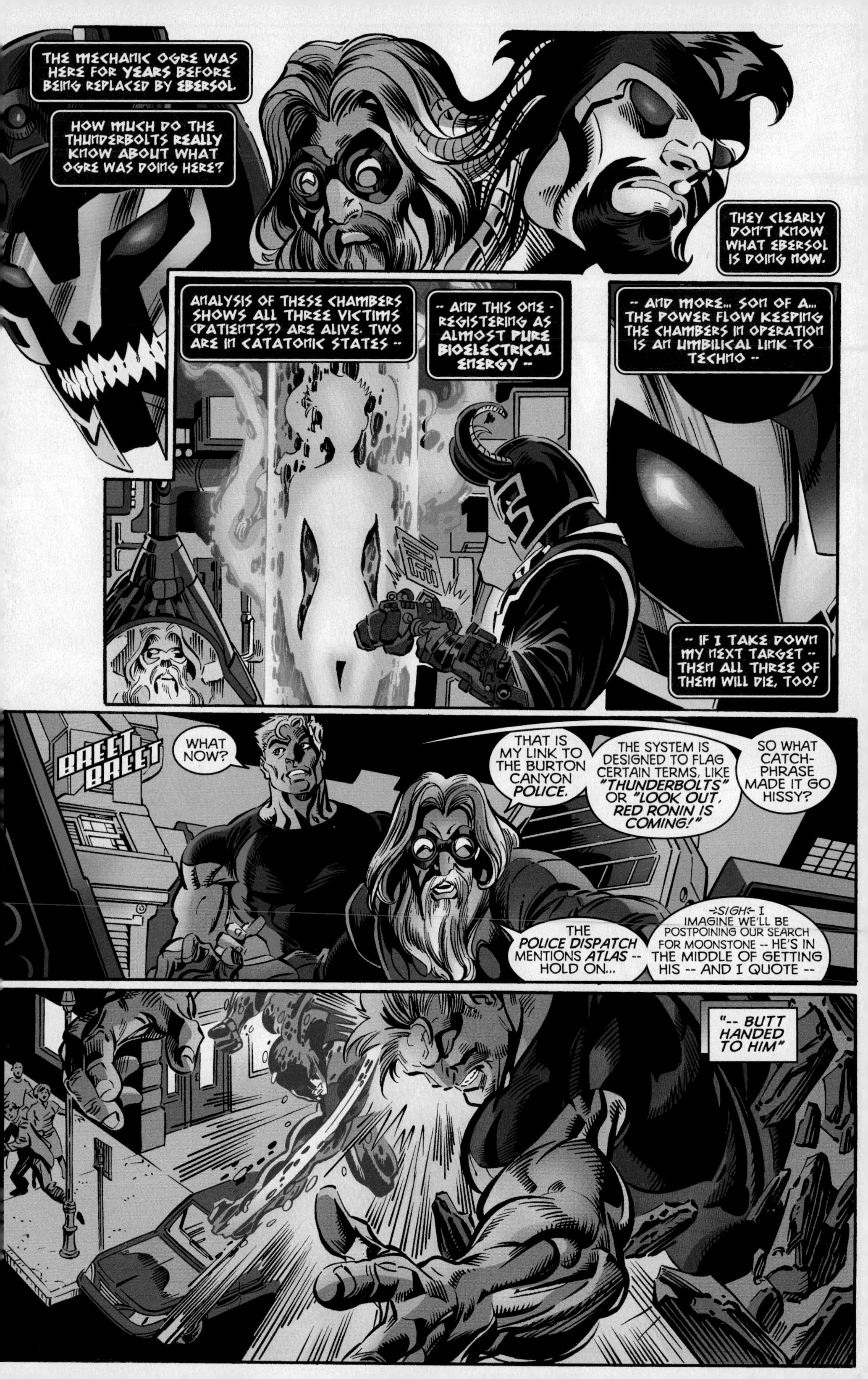
THE MECHANIC OGRE WAS HERE FOR YEARS BEFORE BEING REPLACED BY EBERSOL.
HOW MUCH DO THE THUNDERBOLTS REALLY KNOW ABOUT WHAT OGRE WAS DOING HERE?
THEY CLEARLY DON'T KNOW WHAT EBERSOL IS DOING NOW.
ANALYSIS OF THESE CHAMBERS SHOWS ALL THREE VICTIMS (PATIENTS?) ARE ALIVE. TWO ARE IN CATATONIC STATES --
-- AND THIS ONE -- REGISTERING AS ALMOST PURE BIOELECTRICAL ENERGY --
-- AND MORE... SON OF A... THE POWER FLOW KEEPING THE CHAMBERS IN OPERATION IS AN UMBILICAL LINK TO TECHNO --
-- IF I TAKE DOWN MY NEXT TARGET -- THEN ALL THREE OF THEM WILL DIE, TOO!
BREET BREET
WHAT NOW?
THAT IS MY LINK TO THE BURTON CANYON POLICE.
THE SYSTEM IS DESIGNED TO FLAG CERTAIN TERMS, LIKE "THUNDERBOLTS" OR "LOOK OUT, RED RONIN IS COMING!"
SO WHAT CATCH-PHRASE MADE IT GO HISSY?
THE POLICE DISPATCH MENTIONS ATLAS -- HOLD ON...
<SIGH> I IMAGINE WE'LL BE POSTPOINING OUR SEARCH FOR MOONSTONE -- HE'S IN THE MIDDLE OF GETTING HIS -- AND I QUOTE --
"-- BUTT HANDED TO HIM"

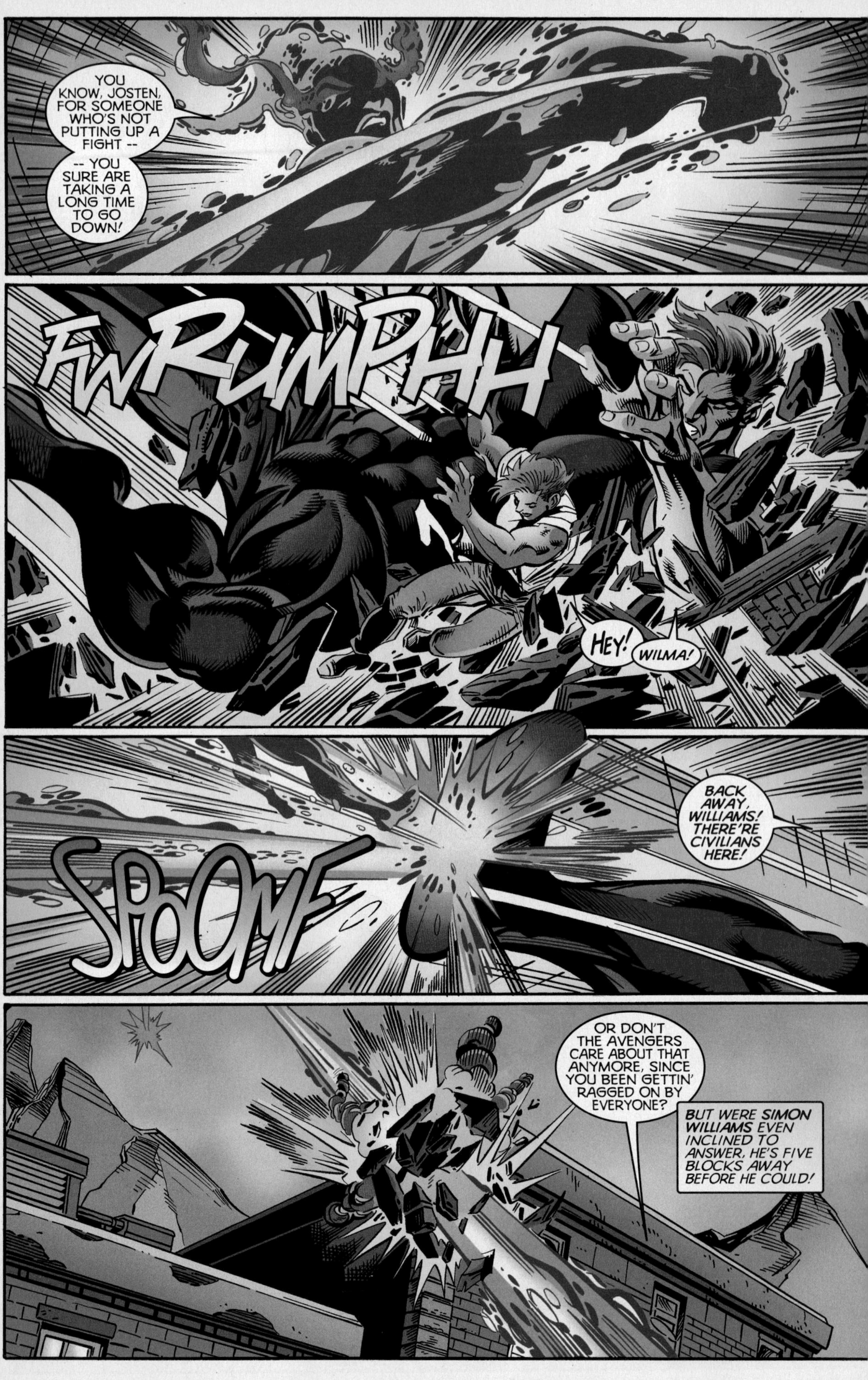
YOU KNOW, JOSTEN, FOR SOMEONE WHO'S NOT PUTTING UP A FIGHT --
-- YOU SURE ARE TAKING A LONG TIME TO GO DOWN!
FWRUMPHH
HEY!
WILMA!
BACK AWAY, WILLIAMS! THERE'RE CIVILIANS HERE!
SPOOMF
OR DON'T THE AVENGERS CARE ABOUT THAT ANYMORE, SINCE YOU BEEN GETTIN' RAGGED ON BY EVERYONE?
BUT WERE SIMON WILLIAMS EVEN INCLINED TO ANSWER, HE'S FIVE BLOCKS AWAY BEFORE HE COULD!

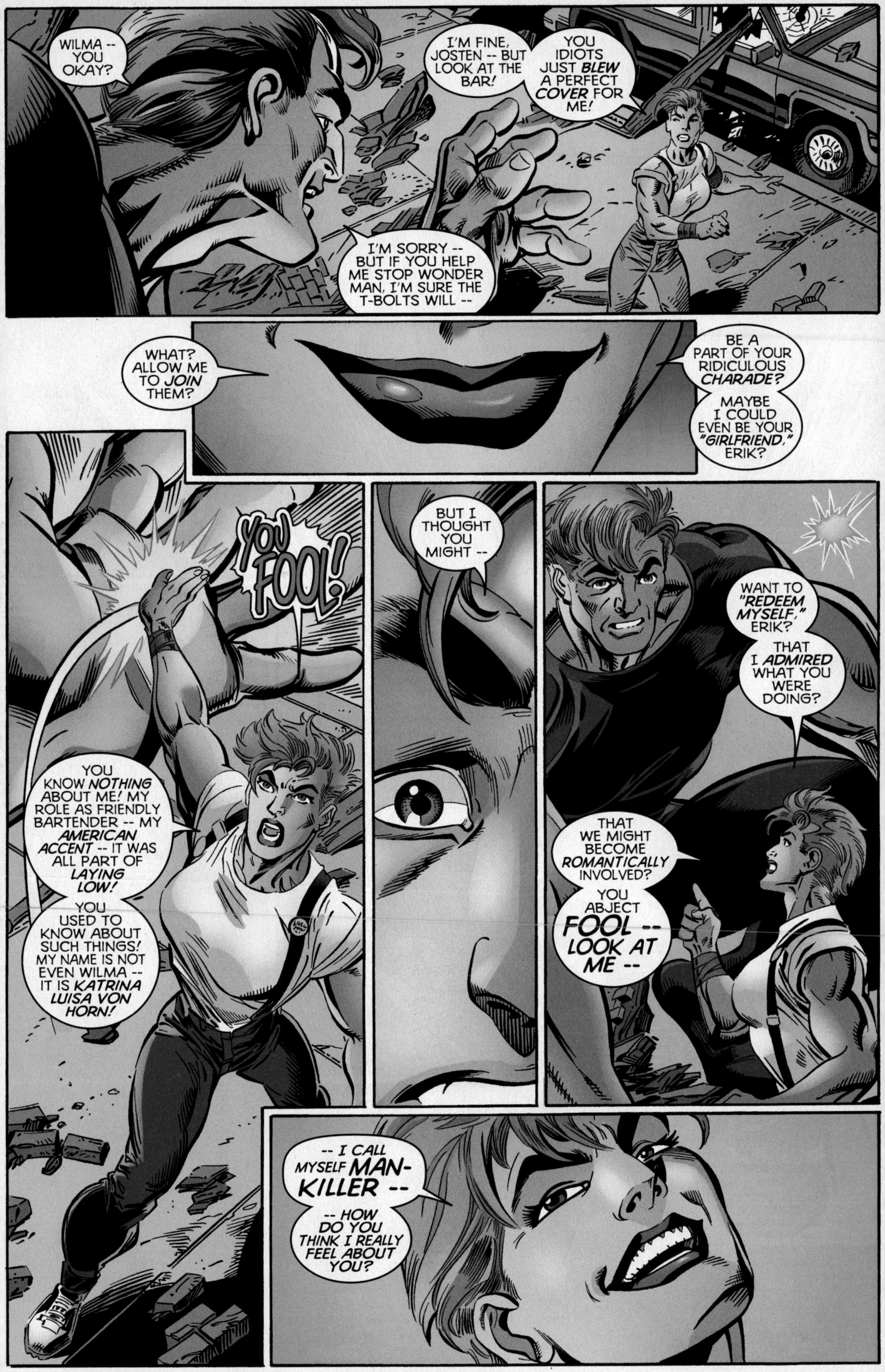
WILMA -- YOU OKAY?
I'M FINE, JOSTEN -- BUT LOOK AT THE BAR!
YOU IDIOTS JUST BLEW A PERFECT COVER FOR ME!
I'M SORRY -- BUT IF YOU HELP ME STOP WONDER MAN, I'M SURE THE T-BOLTS WILL --
WHAT? ALLOW ME TO JOIN THEM?
BE A PART OF YOUR RIDICULOUS CHARADE?
MAYBE I COULD EVEN BE YOUR "GIRLFRIEND," ERIK?
YOU FOOL!
YOU KNOW NOTHING ABOUT ME! MY ROLE AS FRIENDLY BARTENDER -- MY AMERICAN ACCENT -- IT WAS ALL PART OF LAYING LOW!
YOU USED TO KNOW ABOUT SUCH THINGS! MY NAME IS NOT EVEN WILMA -- IT IS KATRINA LUISA VON HORN!
BUT I THOUGHT YOU MIGHT --
WANT TO "REDEEM MYSELF," ERIK?
THAT I ADMIRED WHAT YOU WERE DOING?
THAT WE MIGHT BECOME ROMANTICALLY INVOLVED?
YOU ABJECT FOOL -- LOOK AT ME --
-- I CALL MYSELF MAN-KILLER --
-- HOW DO YOU THINK I REALLY FEEL ABOUT YOU?

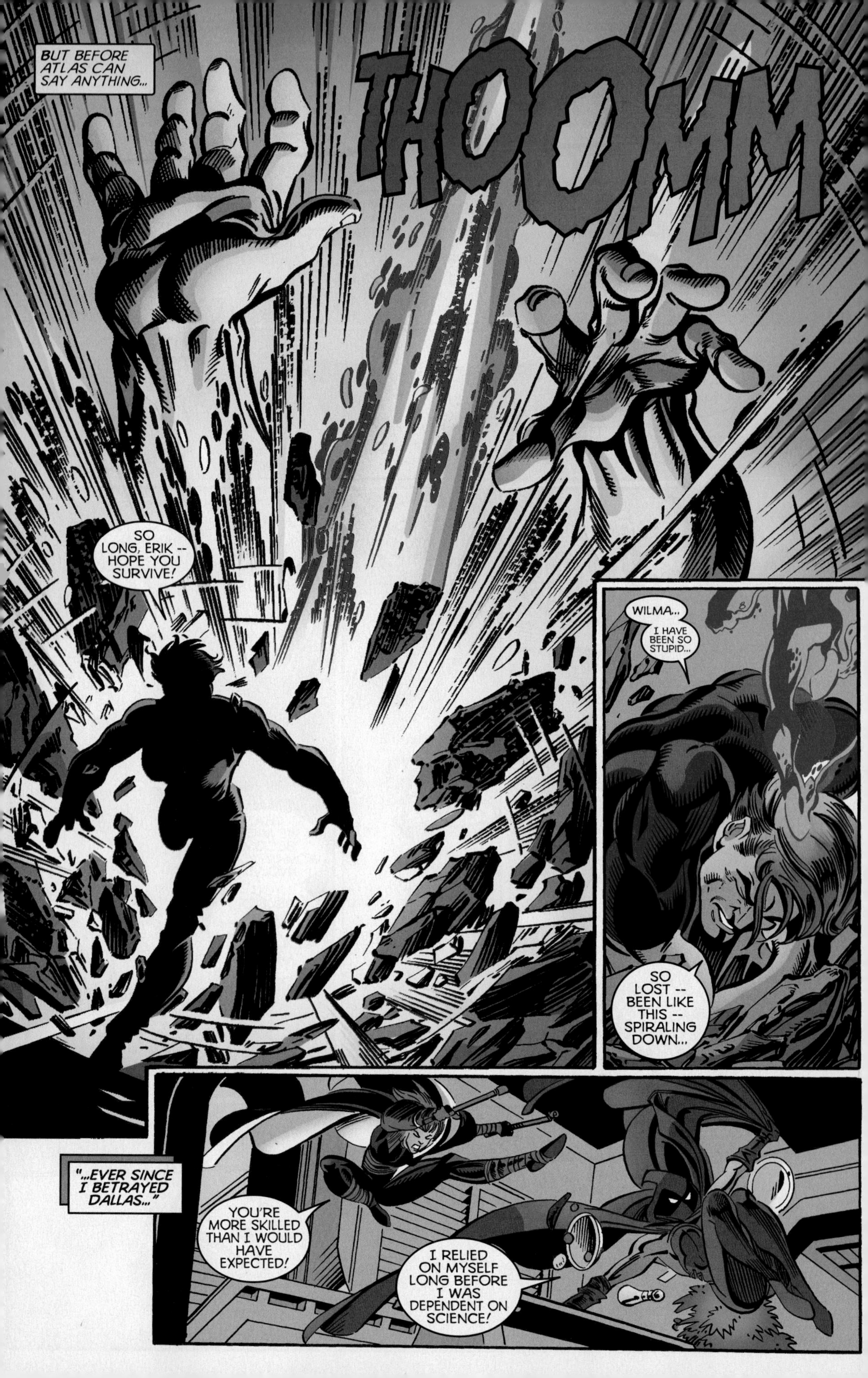
BUT BEFORE ATLAS CAN SAY ANYTHING...
THOOMM
SO LONG, ERIK -- HOPE YOU SURVIVE!
WILMA...
I HAVE BEEN SO STUPID...
SO LOST -- BEEN LIKE THIS -- SPIRALING DOWN...
"...EVER SINCE I BETRAYED DALLAS..."
YOU'RE MORE SKILLED THAN I WOULD HAVE EXPECTED!
I RELIED ON MYSELF LONG BEFORE I WAS DEPENDENT ON SCIENCE!

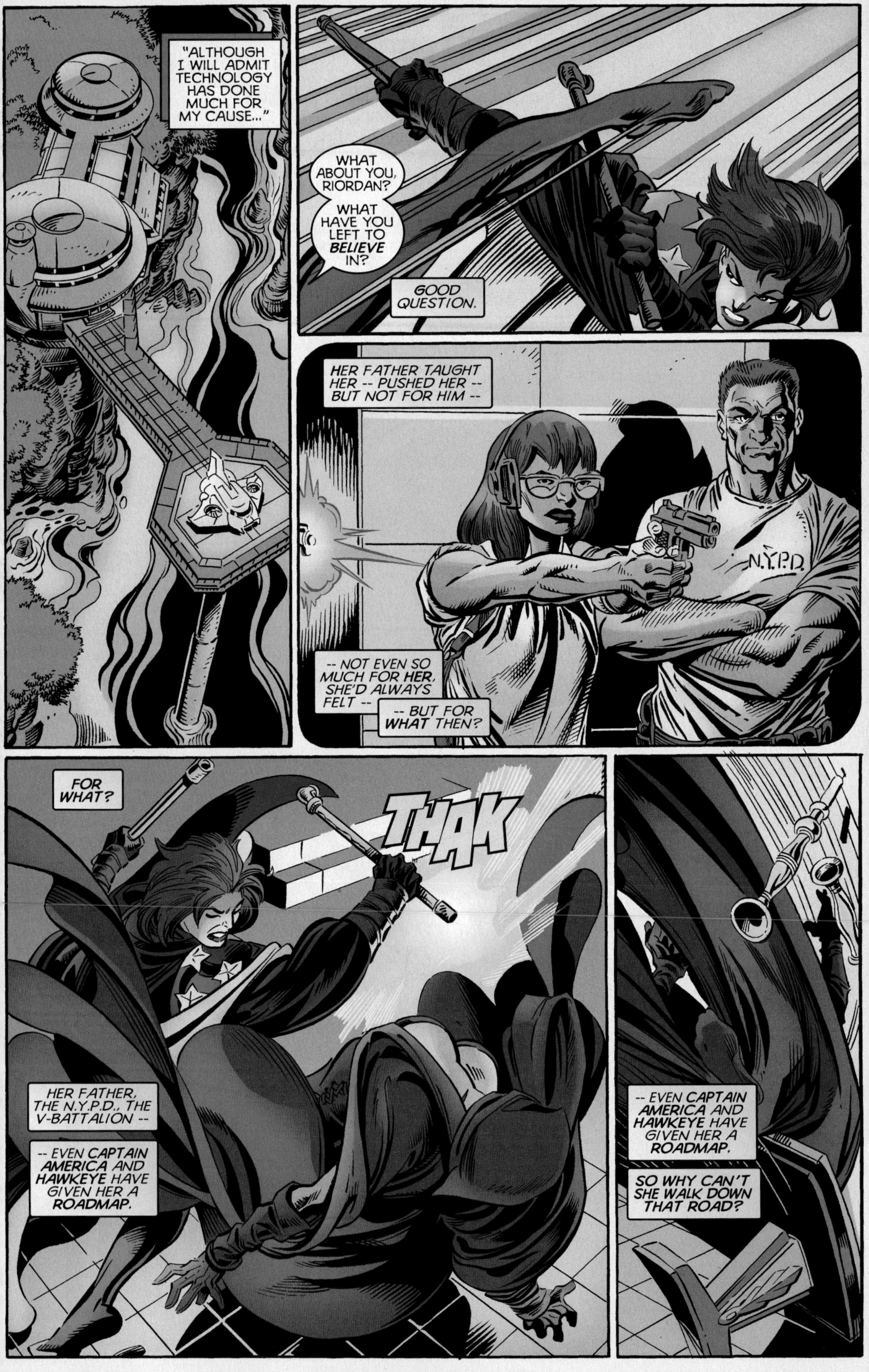
"ALTHOUGH I WILL ADMIT TECHNOLOGY HAS DONE MUCH FOR MY CAUSE..."
WHAT ABOUT YOU, RIORDAN?
WHAT HAVE YOU LEFT TO **BELIEVE** IN?
GOOD QUESTION.
HER FATHER TAUGHT HER -- PUSHED HER -- BUT NOT FOR HIM --
N.Y.P.D.
-- NOT EVEN SO MUCH FOR **HER**, SHE'D ALWAYS FELT --
-- BUT FOR **WHAT** THEN?
FOR **WHAT**?
THAK
HER FATHER, THE N.Y.P.D., THE V-BATTALION --
-- EVEN **CAPTAIN AMERICA** AND **HAWKEYE** HAVE GIVEN HER A **ROADMAP**.
-- EVEN **CAPTAIN AMERICA** AND **HAWKEYE** HAVE GIVEN HER A **ROADMAP**.
SO WHY CAN'T SHE WALK DOWN THAT ROAD?

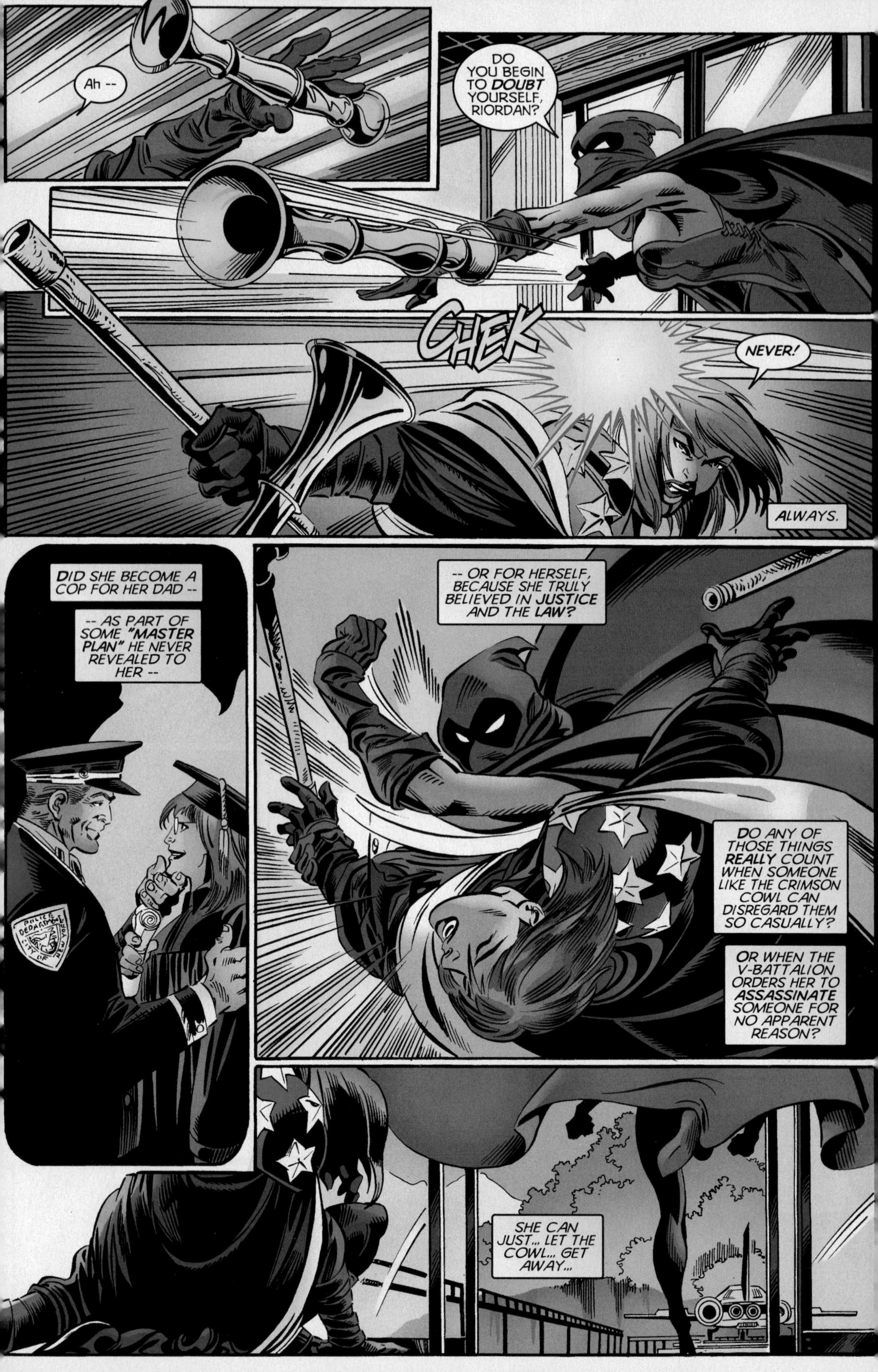
Ah --
DO YOU BEGIN TO **DOUBT** YOURSELF, RIORDAN?
CHEK
NEVER!
ALWAYS.
DID SHE BECOME A COP FOR HER DAD --
-- AS PART OF SOME **"MASTER PLAN"** HE NEVER REVEALED TO HER --
-- OR FOR HERSELF, BECAUSE SHE TRULY BELIEVED IN **JUSTICE** AND THE **LAW?**
DO ANY OF THOSE THINGS **REALLY** COUNT WHEN SOMEONE LIKE THE CRIMSON COWL CAN DISREGARD THEM SO CASUALLY?
OR WHEN THE V-BATTALION ORDERS HER TO **ASSASSINATE** SOMEONE FOR NO APPARENT REASON?
SHE CAN JUST... LET THE COWL... GET AWAY...

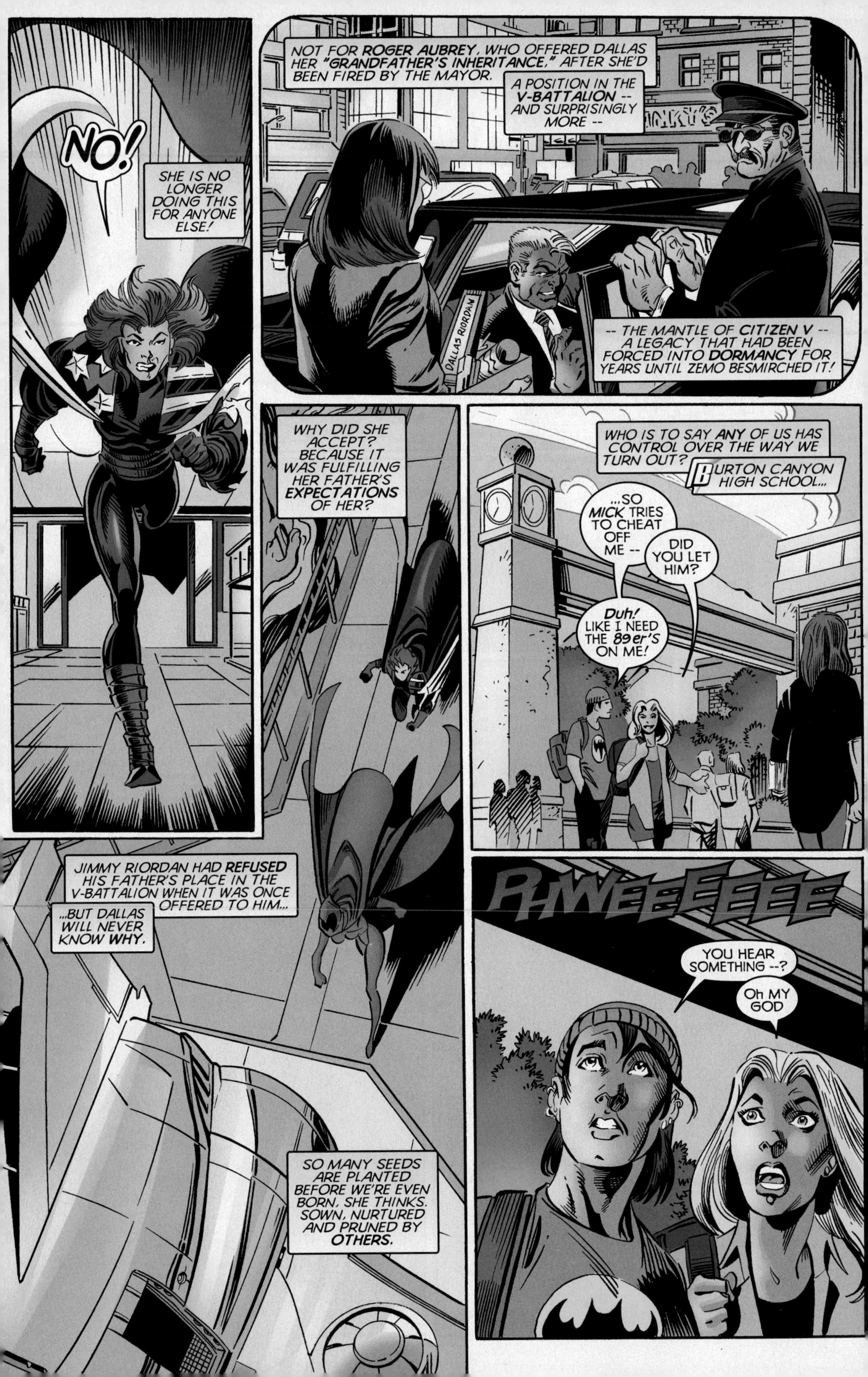
NO!
SHE IS NO LONGER DOING THIS FOR ANYONE ELSE!
NOT FOR ROGER AUBREY, WHO OFFERED DALLAS HER "GRANDFATHER'S INHERITANCE," AFTER SHE'D BEEN FIRED BY THE MAYOR.
A POSITION IN THE V-BATTALION -- AND SURPRISINGLY MORE --
DALLAS RIORDAN
-- THE MANTLE OF CITIZEN V -- A LEGACY THAT HAD BEEN FORCED INTO DORMANCY FOR YEARS UNTIL ZEMO BESMIRCHED IT!
WHY DID SHE ACCEPT? BECAUSE IT WAS FULFILLING HER FATHER'S EXPECTATIONS OF HER?
WHO IS TO SAY ANY OF US HAS CONTROL OVER THE WAY WE TURN OUT?
BURTON CANYON HIGH SCHOOL...
...SO MICK TRIES TO CHEAT OFF ME --
DID YOU LET HIM?
Duh! LIKE I NEED THE 89er'S ON ME!
JIMMY RIORDAN HAD REFUSED HIS FATHER'S PLACE IN THE V-BATTALION WHEN IT WAS ONCE OFFERED TO HIM...
...BUT DALLAS WILL NEVER KNOW WHY.
SO MANY SEEDS ARE PLANTED BEFORE WE'RE EVEN BORN, SHE THINKS. SOWN, NURTURED AND PRUNED BY OTHERS.
R-HWEEEEEEE
YOU HEAR SOMETHING --?
Oh MY GOD

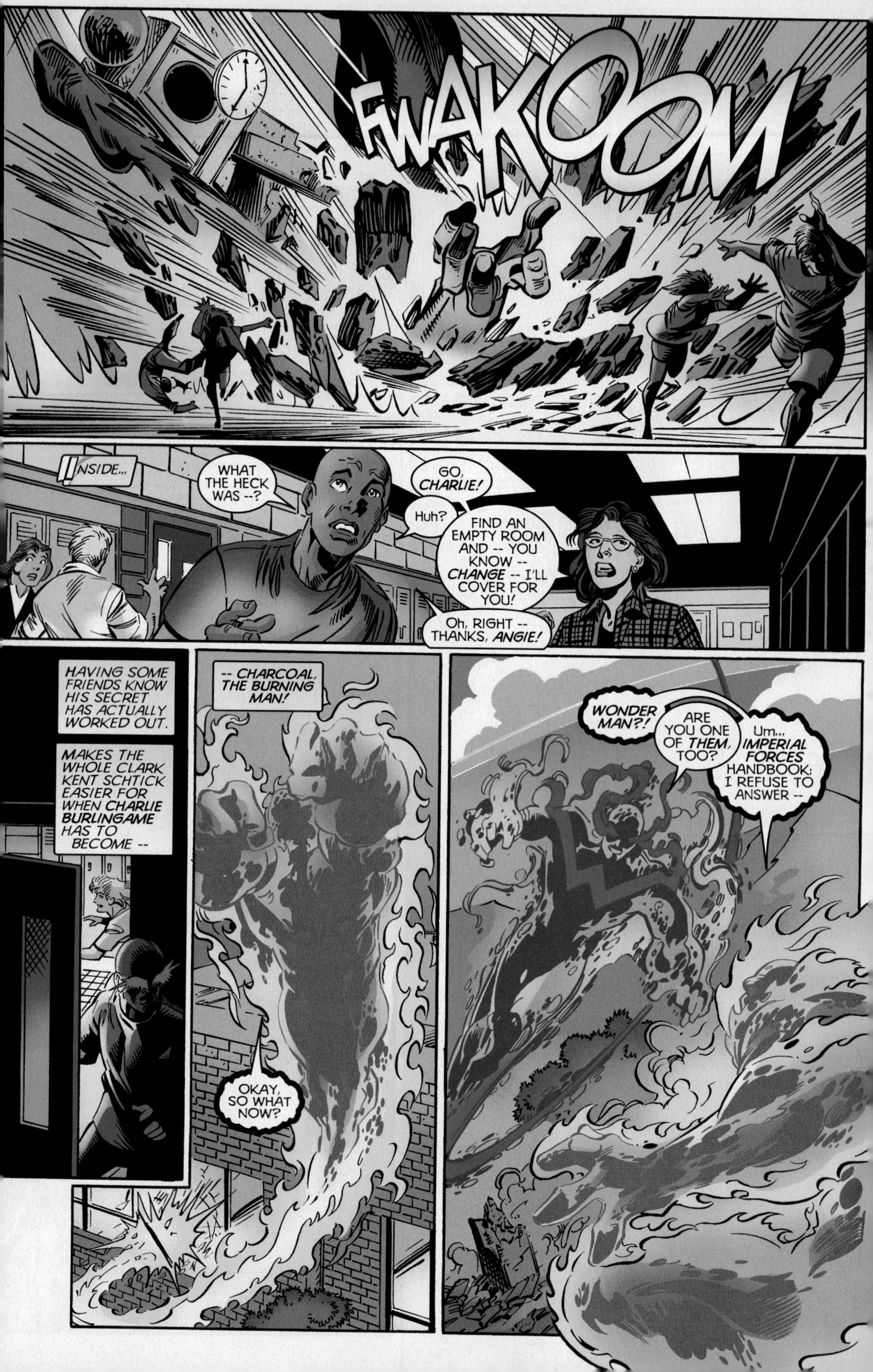
FWAKOOM
INSIDE...
WHAT THE HECK WAS --?
GO, CHARLIE!
Huh?
FIND AN EMPTY ROOM AND -- YOU KNOW -- CHANGE -- I'LL COVER FOR YOU!
Oh, RIGHT -- THANKS, ANGIE!
HAVING SOME FRIENDS KNOW HIS SECRET HAS ACTUALLY WORKED OUT.
MAKES THE WHOLE CLARK KENT SCHTICK EASIER FOR WHEN CHARLIE BURLINGAME HAS TO BECOME --
-- CHARCOAL, THE BURNING MAN!
OKAY, SO WHAT NOW?
WONDER MAN?!
ARE YOU ONE OF THEM, TOO?
Um... IMPERIAL FORCES HANDBOOK: I REFUSE TO ANSWER --

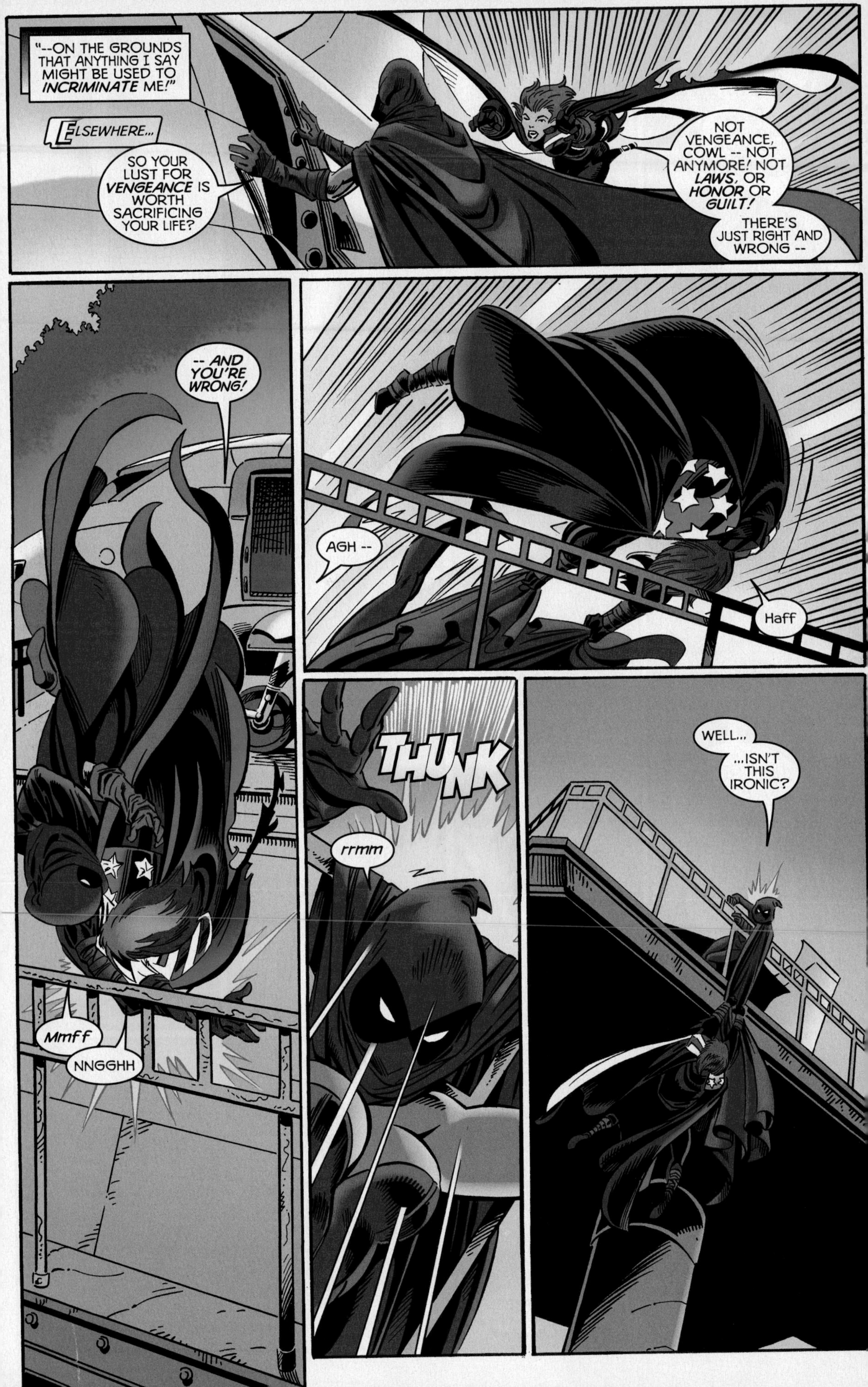
"--ON THE GROUNDS THAT ANYTHING I SAY MIGHT BE USED TO *INCRIMINATE* ME!"
ELSEWHERE...
SO YOUR LUST FOR *VENGEANCE* IS WORTH SACRIFICING YOUR LIFE?
NOT VENGEANCE, COWL -- NOT ANYMORE! NOT *LAWS*, OR *HONOR* OR *GUILT!*
THERE'S JUST RIGHT AND WRONG --
-- *AND YOU'RE WRONG!*
AGH --
Haff
Mmff
NNGGHH
THUNK
rrmm
WELL...
...ISN'T THIS IRONIC?

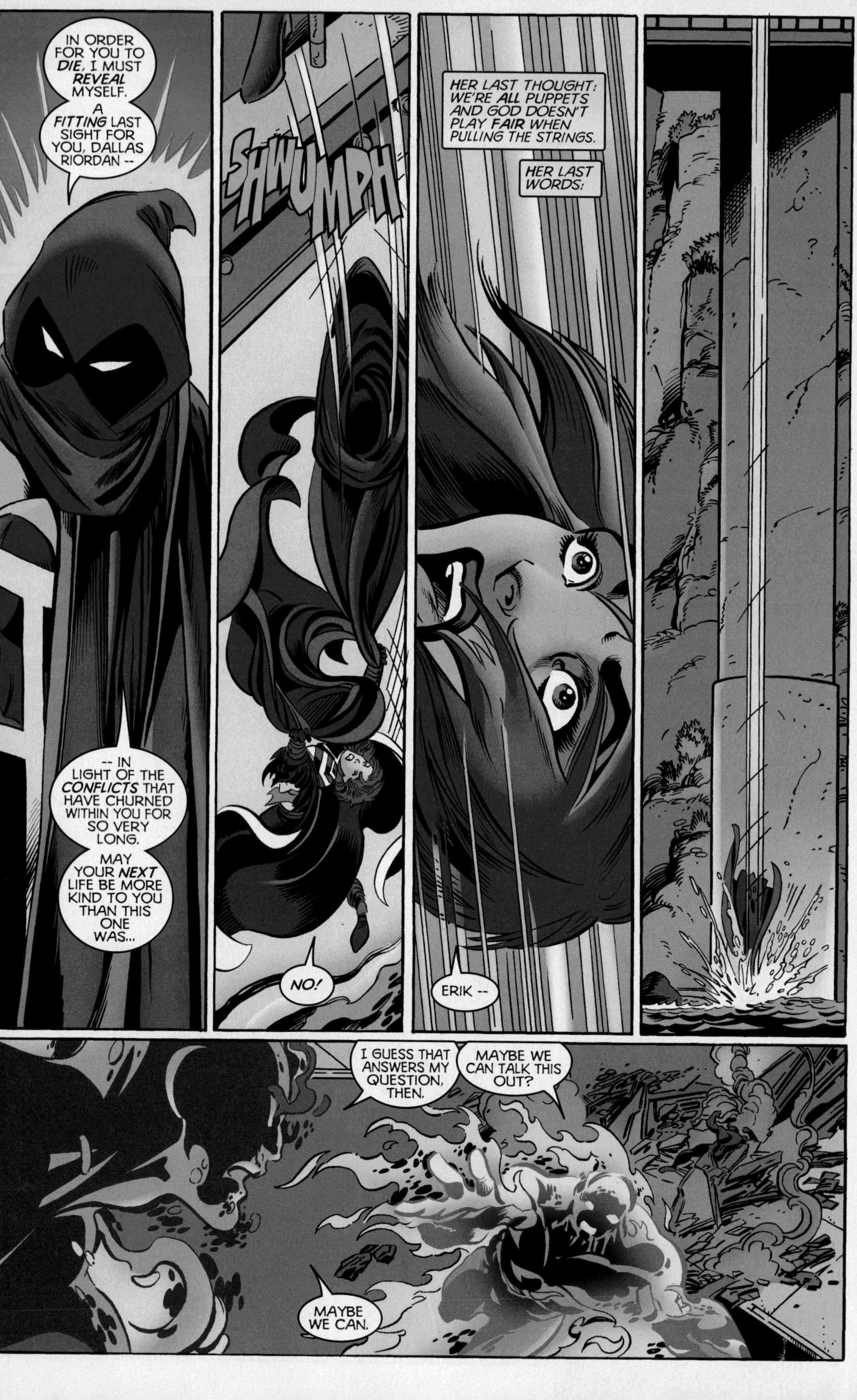
IN ORDER FOR YOU TO DIE, I MUST REVEAL MYSELF.
A FITTING LAST SIGHT FOR YOU, DALLAS RIORDAN --
-- IN LIGHT OF THE CONFLICTS THAT HAVE CHURNED WITHIN YOU FOR SO VERY LONG.
MAY YOUR NEXT LIFE BE MORE KIND TO YOU THAN THIS ONE WAS...
SHWUMPH
NO!
HER LAST THOUGHT: WE'RE ALL PUPPETS AND GOD DOESN'T PLAY FAIR WHEN PULLING THE STRINGS.
HER LAST WORDS:
ERIK --
I GUESS THAT ANSWERS MY QUESTION, THEN.
MAYBE WE CAN TALK THIS OUT?
MAYBE WE CAN.

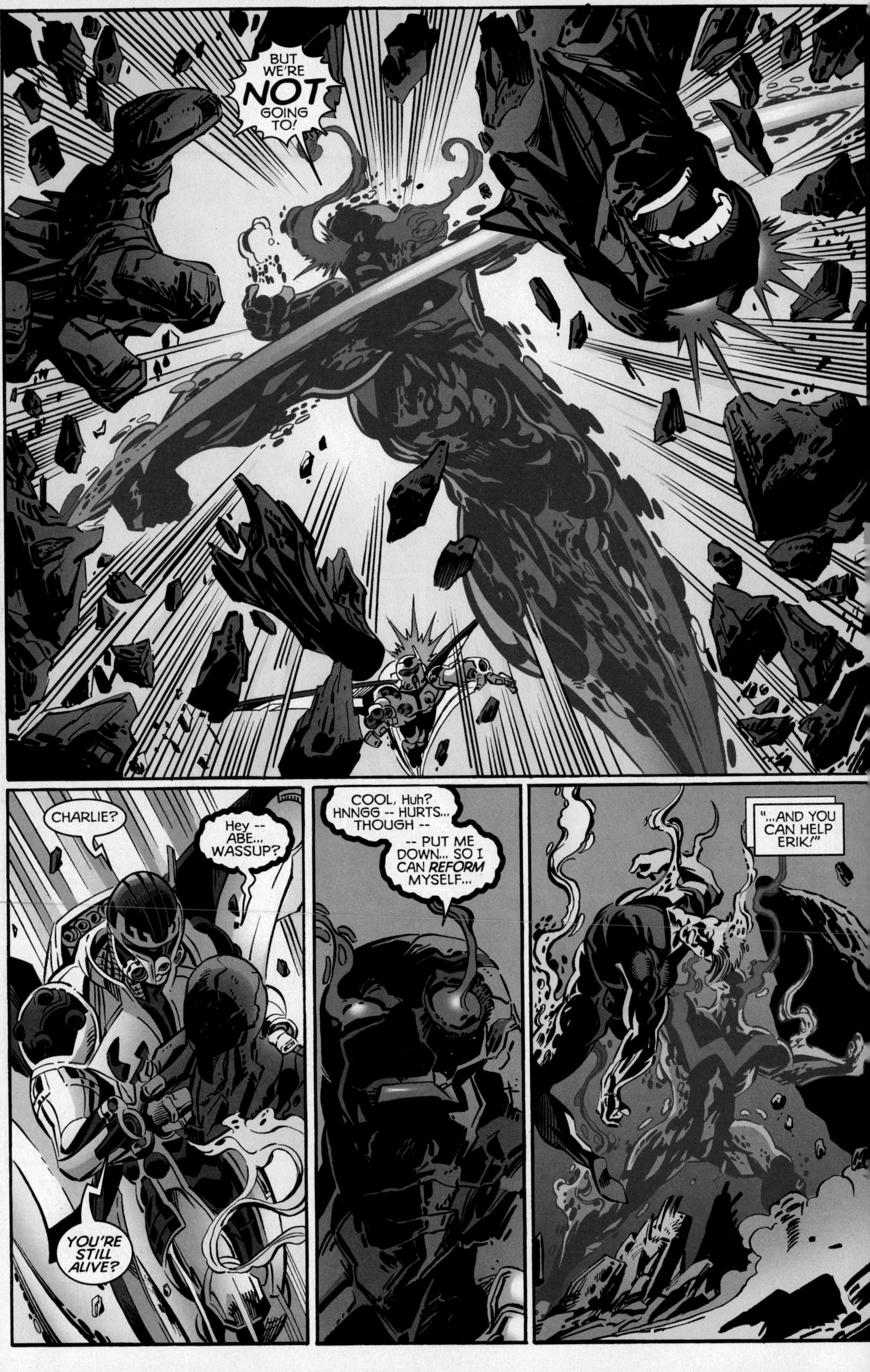

BUT WE'RE *NOT* GOING TO!
CHARLIE?
Hey -- ABE... WASSUP?
YOU'RE STILL ALIVE?
COOL, Huh? HNNGG -- HURTS... THOUGH --
-- PUT ME DOWN... SO I CAN *REFORM* MYSELF...
"...AND YOU CAN HELP ERIK!"

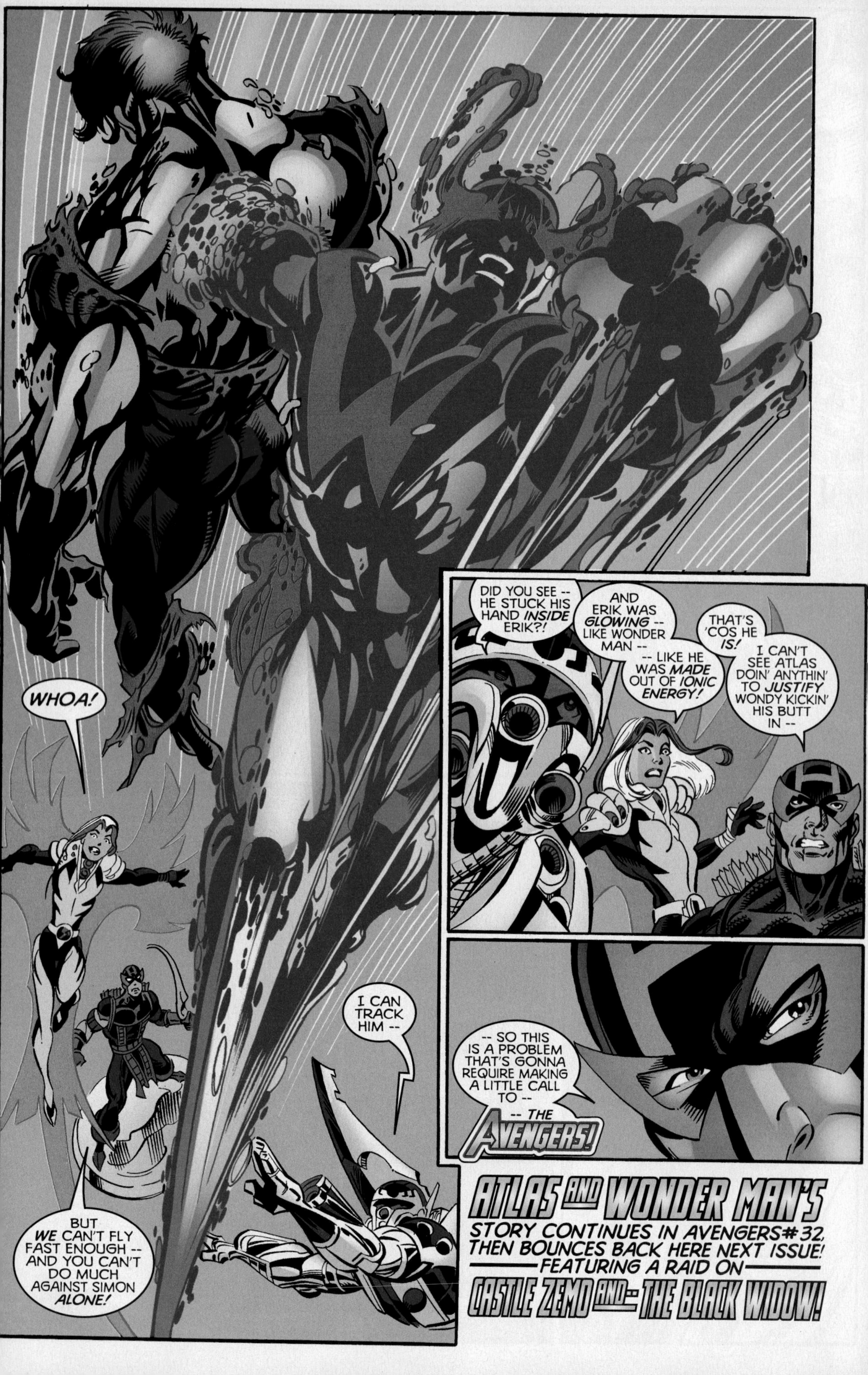
WHOA!
I CAN TRACK HIM --
BUT WE CAN'T FLY FAST ENOUGH -- AND YOU CAN'T DO MUCH AGAINST SIMON ALONE!
DID YOU SEE -- HE STUCK HIS HAND INSIDE ERIK?!
AND ERIK WAS GLOWING -- LIKE WONDER MAN --
-- LIKE HE WAS MADE OUT OF IONIC ENERGY!
THAT'S 'COS HE IS!
I CAN'T SEE ATLAS DOIN' ANYTHIN' TO JUSTIFY WONDY KICKIN' HIS BUTT IN --
-- SO THIS IS A PROBLEM THAT'S GONNA REQUIRE MAKING A LITTLE CALL TO --
-- THE AVENGERS!
ATLAS AND WONDER MAN'S STORY CONTINUES IN AVENGERS#32, THEN BOUNCES BACK HERE NEXT ISSUE! FEATURING A RAID ON CASTLE ZEMO AND-- THE BLACK WIDOW!

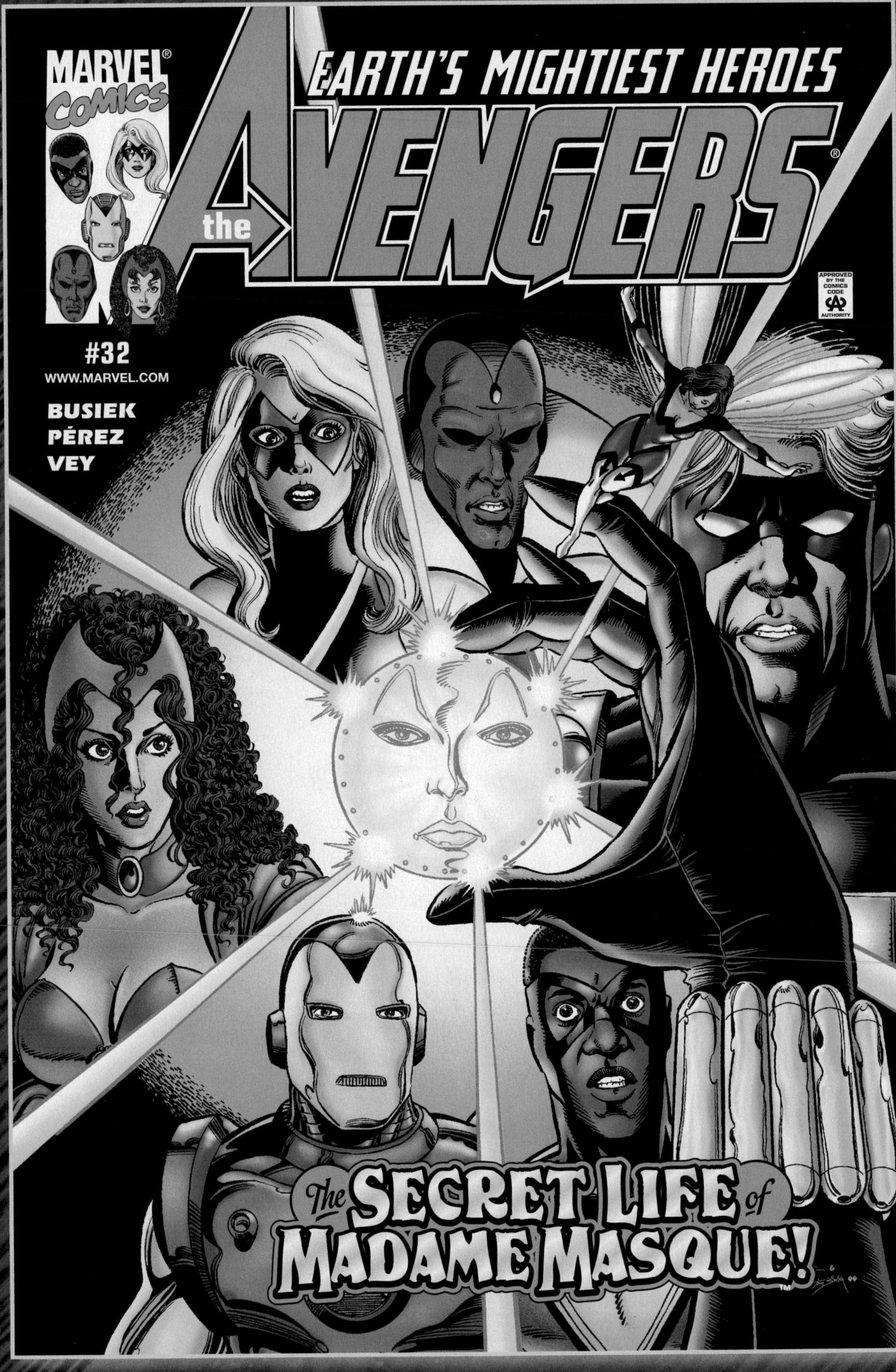
MARVEL® COMICS
EARTH'S MIGHTIEST HEROES
the AVENGERS®
APPROVED BY THE COMICS CODE AUTHORITY
#32
WWW.MARVEL.COM
BUSIEK
PÉREZ
VEY
The SECRET LIFE of MADAME MASQUE!™

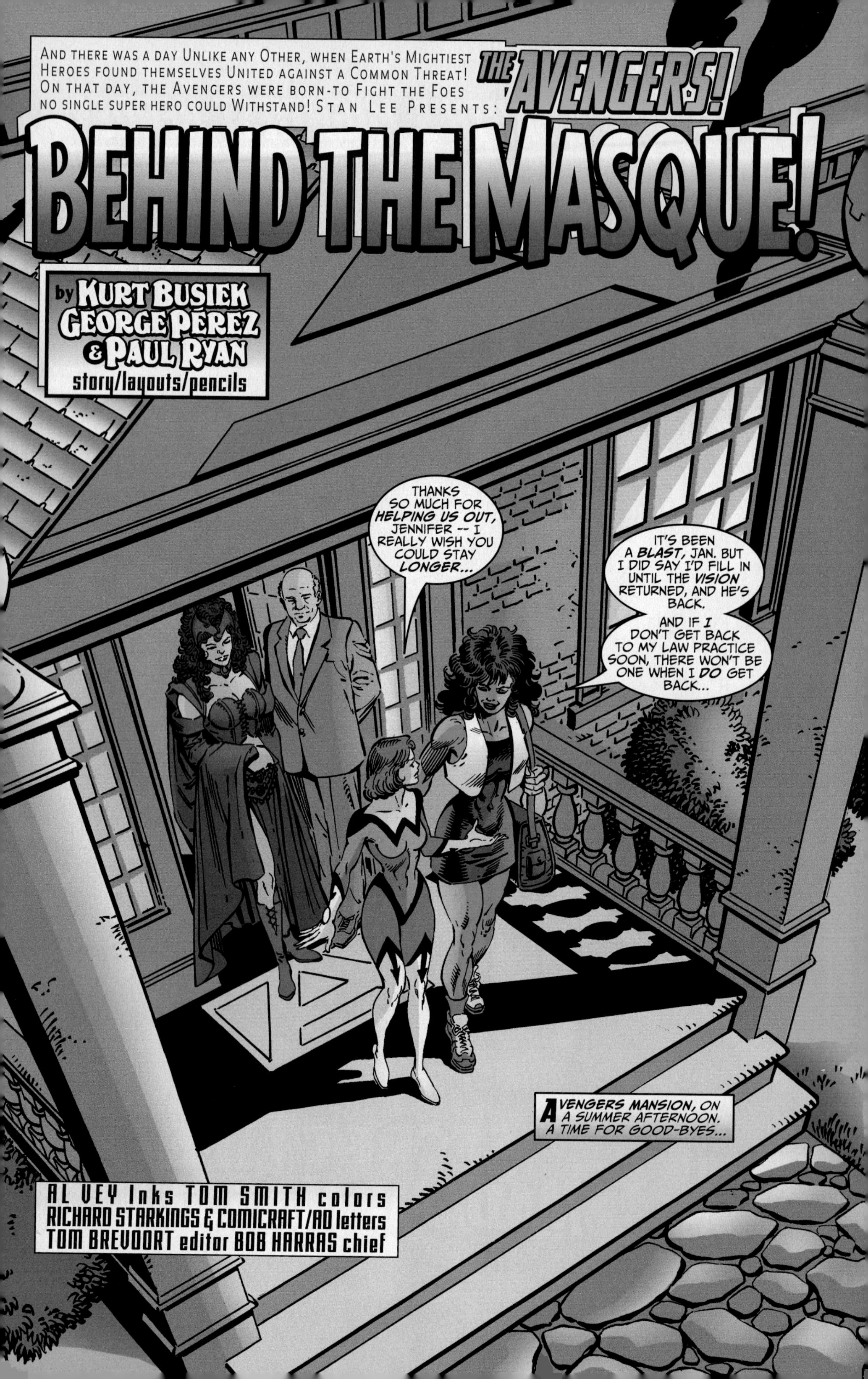
AND THERE WAS A DAY UNLIKE ANY OTHER, WHEN EARTH'S MIGHTIEST HEROES FOUND THEMSELVES UNITED AGAINST A COMMON THREAT! ON THAT DAY, THE AVENGERS WERE BORN-TO FIGHT THE FOES NO SINGLE SUPER HERO COULD WITHSTAND! STAN LEE PRESENTS:
THE AVENGERS!
BEHIND THE MASQUE!
by KURT BUSIEK GEORGE PÉREZ & PAUL RYAN story/layouts/pencils
THANKS SO MUCH FOR HELPING US OUT, JENNIFER -- I REALLY WISH YOU COULD STAY LONGER...
IT'S BEEN A BLAST, JAN. BUT I DID SAY I'D FILL IN UNTIL THE VISION RETURNED, AND HE'S BACK.
AND IF I DON'T GET BACK TO MY LAW PRACTICE SOON, THERE WON'T BE ONE WHEN I DO GET BACK...
AVENGERS MANSION, ON A SUMMER AFTERNOON. A TIME FOR GOOD-BYES...
AL VEY inks TOM SMITH colors RICHARD STARKINGS & COMICRAFT/AD letters TOM BREVOORT editor BOB HARRAS chief

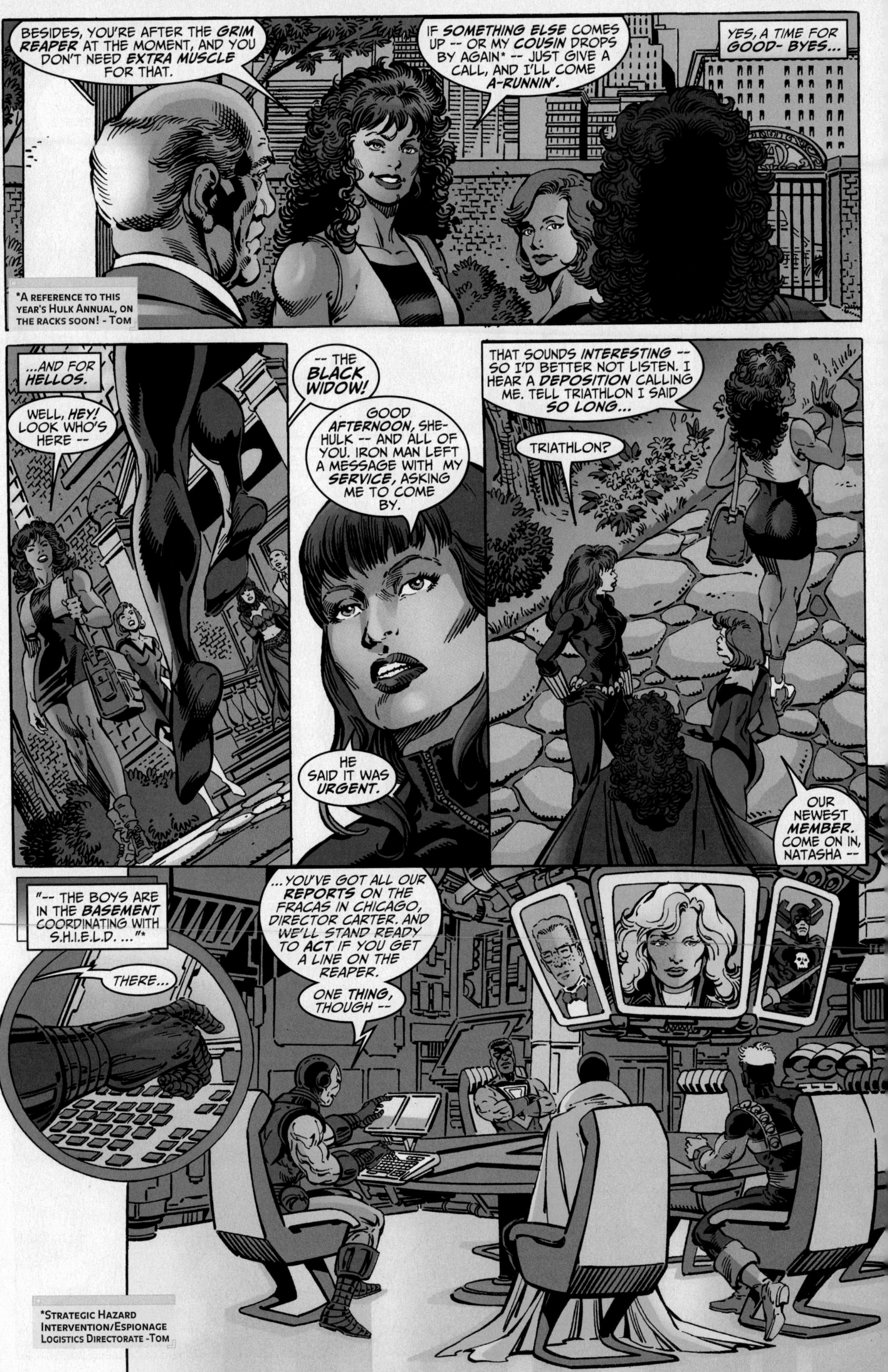
BESIDES, YOU'RE AFTER THE GRIM REAPER AT THE MOMENT, AND YOU DON'T NEED EXTRA MUSCLE FOR THAT.
IF SOMETHING ELSE COMES UP -- OR MY COUSIN DROPS BY AGAIN* -- JUST GIVE A CALL, AND I'LL COME A-RUNNIN'.
YES, A TIME FOR GOOD- BYES...
*A REFERENCE TO THIS YEAR'S HULK ANNUAL, ON THE RACKS SOON! - TOM
...AND FOR HELLOS.
WELL, HEY! LOOK WHO'S HERE --
-- THE BLACK WIDOW!
GOOD AFTERNOON, SHE-HULK -- AND ALL OF YOU. IRON MAN LEFT A MESSAGE WITH MY SERVICE, ASKING ME TO COME BY.
HE SAID IT WAS URGENT.
THAT SOUNDS INTERESTING -- SO I'D BETTER NOT LISTEN. I HEAR A DEPOSITION CALLING ME. TELL TRIATHLON I SAID SO LONG...
TRIATHLON?
OUR NEWEST MEMBER. COME ON IN, NATASHA --
"-- THE BOYS ARE IN THE BASEMENT COORDINATING WITH S.H.I.E.L.D. ..."*
THERE...
...YOU'VE GOT ALL OUR REPORTS ON THE FRACAS IN CHICAGO, DIRECTOR CARTER. AND WE'LL STAND READY TO ACT IF YOU GET A LINE ON THE REAPER.
ONE THING, THOUGH --
*STRATEGIC HAZARD INTERVENTION/ESPIONAGE LOGISTICS DIRECTORATE -TOM

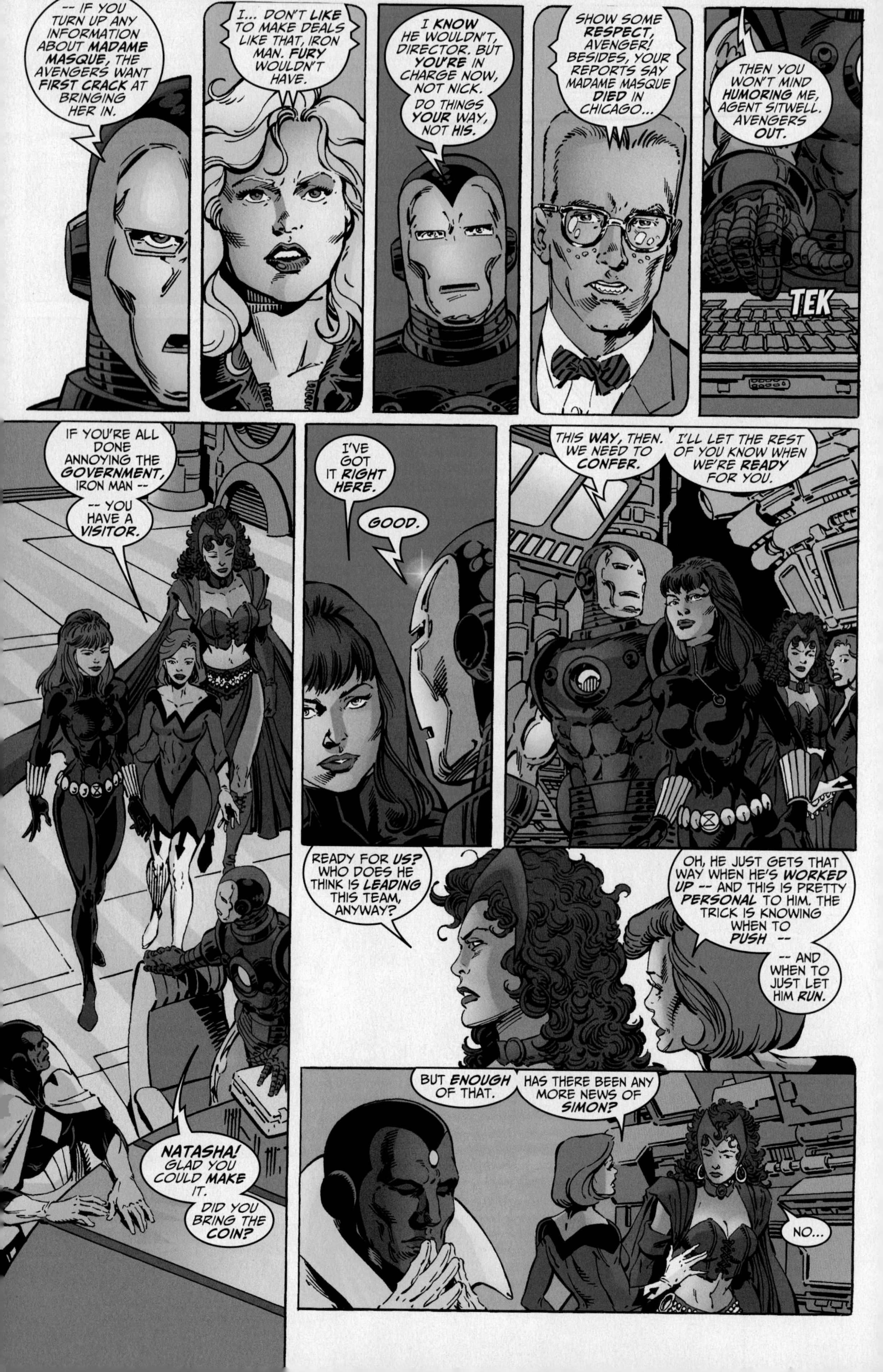
-- IF YOU TURN UP ANY INFORMATION ABOUT **MADAME MASQUE**, THE AVENGERS WANT **FIRST CRACK** AT BRINGING HER IN.
I... DON'T **LIKE** TO MAKE DEALS LIKE THAT, IRON MAN. **FURY** WOULDN'T HAVE.
I **KNOW** HE WOULDN'T, DIRECTOR. BUT **YOU'RE** IN CHARGE NOW, NOT NICK.
DO THINGS **YOUR** WAY, NOT **HIS**.
SHOW SOME **RESPECT**, AVENGER! BESIDES, YOUR REPORTS SAY MADAME MASQUE **DIED** IN CHICAGO...
THEN YOU WON'T MIND **HUMORING** ME, AGENT SITWELL. AVENGERS **OUT**.
TEK
IF YOU'RE ALL DONE ANNOYING THE **GOVERNMENT**, IRON MAN --
-- YOU HAVE A **VISITOR**.
I'VE GOT IT **RIGHT HERE**.
GOOD.
THIS **WAY**, THEN. WE NEED TO **CONFER**.
I'LL LET THE REST OF YOU KNOW WHEN WE'RE **READY** FOR YOU.
READY FOR **US?** WHO DOES HE THINK IS **LEADING** THIS TEAM, ANYWAY?
OH, HE JUST GETS THAT WAY WHEN HE'S **WORKED UP** -- AND THIS IS PRETTY **PERSONAL** TO HIM. THE TRICK IS KNOWING WHEN TO **PUSH** --
-- AND WHEN TO JUST LET HIM **RUN**.
NATASHA! GLAD YOU COULD **MAKE** IT.
DID YOU BRING THE **COIN?**
BUT **ENOUGH** OF THAT.
HAS THERE BEEN ANY MORE NEWS OF **SIMON?**
NO...

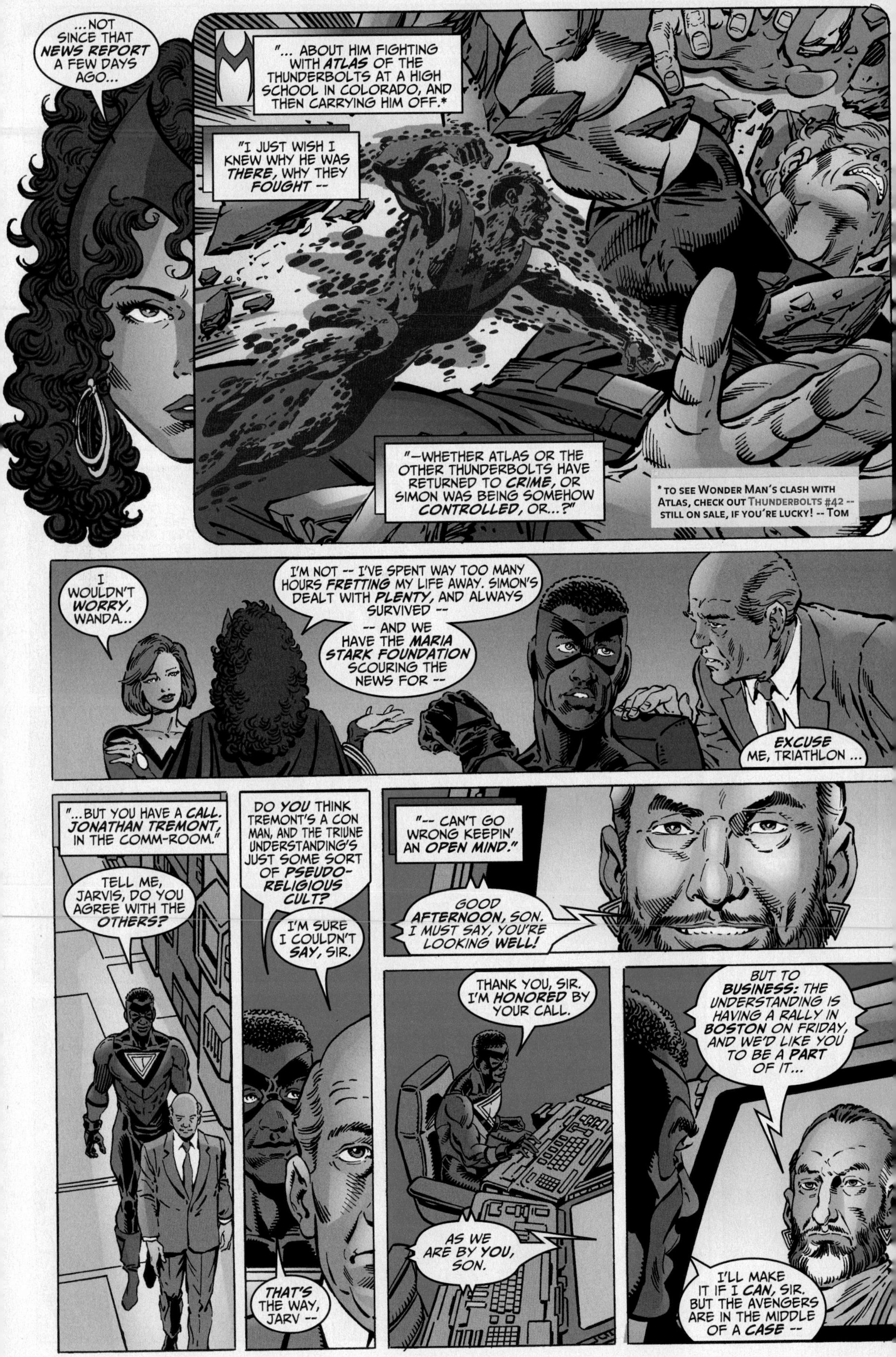
...NOT SINCE THAT NEWS REPORT A FEW DAYS AGO...
"... ABOUT HIM FIGHTING WITH ATLAS OF THE THUNDERBOLTS AT A HIGH SCHOOL IN COLORADO, AND THEN CARRYING HIM OFF.*
"I JUST WISH I KNEW WHY HE WAS THERE, WHY THEY FOUGHT --
"--WHETHER ATLAS OR THE OTHER THUNDERBOLTS HAVE RETURNED TO CRIME, OR SIMON WAS BEING SOMEHOW CONTROLLED, OR...?"
* TO SEE WONDER MAN'S CLASH WITH ATLAS, CHECK OUT THUNDERBOLTS #42 -- STILL ON SALE, IF YOU'RE LUCKY! -- TOM
I WOULDN'T WORRY, WANDA...
I'M NOT -- I'VE SPENT WAY TOO MANY HOURS FRETTING MY LIFE AWAY. SIMON'S DEALT WITH PLENTY, AND ALWAYS SURVIVED --
-- AND WE HAVE THE MARIA STARK FOUNDATION SCOURING THE NEWS FOR --
EXCUSE ME, TRIATHLON ...
"...BUT YOU HAVE A CALL. JONATHAN TREMONT, IN THE COMM-ROOM."
TELL ME, JARVIS, DO YOU AGREE WITH THE OTHERS?
DO YOU THINK TREMONT'S A CON MAN, AND THE TRIUNE UNDERSTANDING'S JUST SOME SORT OF PSEUDO-RELIGIOUS CULT?
I'M SURE I COULDN'T SAY, SIR.
THAT'S THE WAY, JARV --
"-- CAN'T GO WRONG KEEPIN' AN OPEN MIND."
GOOD AFTERNOON, SON. I MUST SAY, YOU'RE LOOKING WELL!
THANK YOU, SIR. I'M HONORED BY YOUR CALL.
AS WE ARE BY YOU, SON.
BUT TO BUSINESS: THE UNDERSTANDING IS HAVING A RALLY IN BOSTON ON FRIDAY, AND WE'D LIKE YOU TO BE A PART OF IT...
I'LL MAKE IT IF I CAN, SIR. BUT THE AVENGERS ARE IN THE MIDDLE OF A CASE --

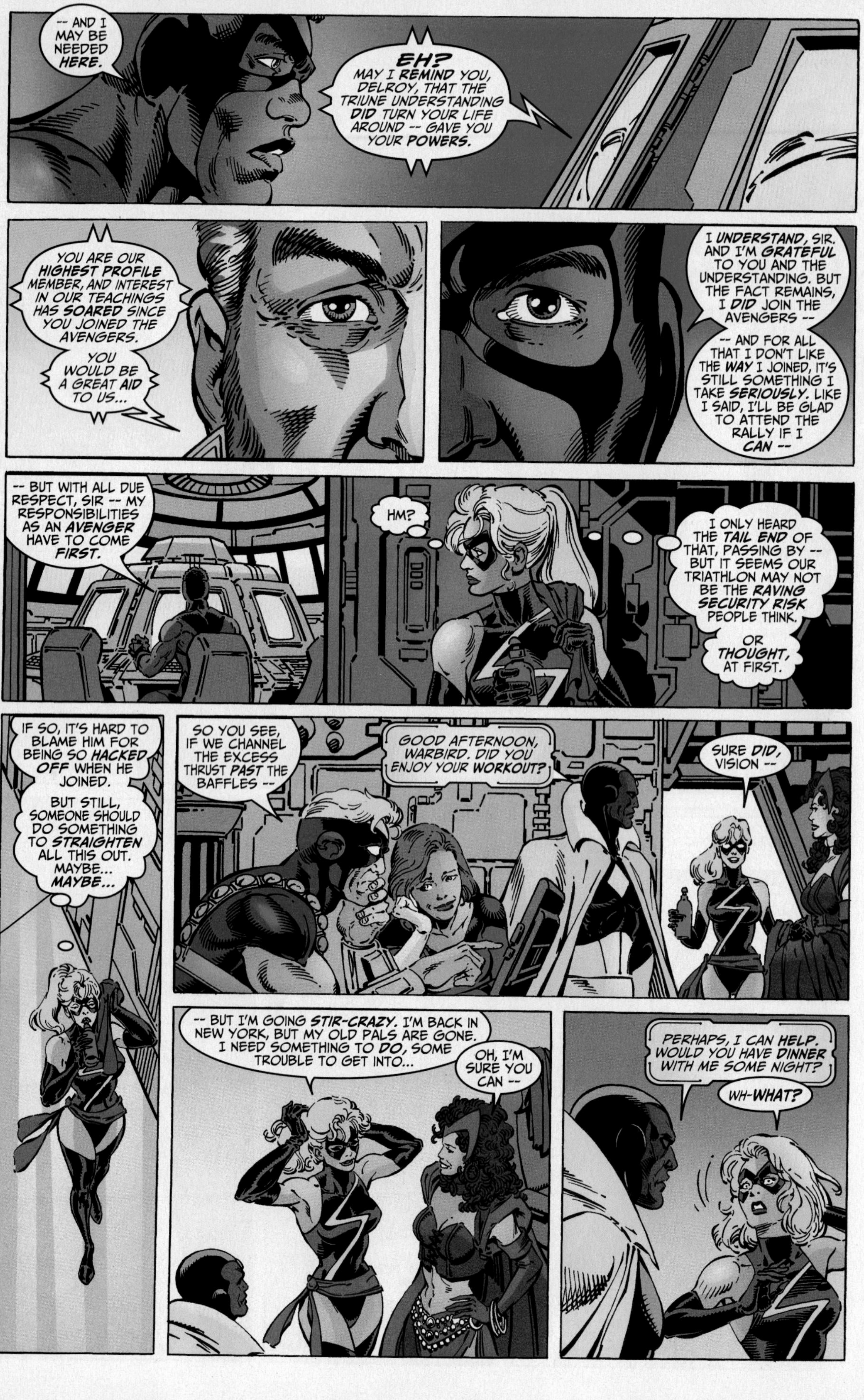
-- AND I MAY BE NEEDED HERE.
EH? MAY I REMIND YOU, DELROY, THAT THE TRIUNE UNDERSTANDING DID TURN YOUR LIFE AROUND -- GAVE YOU YOUR POWERS.
YOU ARE OUR HIGHEST PROFILE MEMBER, AND INTEREST IN OUR TEACHINGS HAS SOARED SINCE YOU JOINED THE AVENGERS.
YOU WOULD BE A GREAT AID TO US...
I UNDERSTAND, SIR. AND I'M GRATEFUL TO YOU AND THE UNDERSTANDING. BUT THE FACT REMAINS, I DID JOIN THE AVENGERS --
-- AND FOR ALL THAT I DON'T LIKE THE WAY I JOINED, IT'S STILL SOMETHING I TAKE SERIOUSLY. LIKE I SAID, I'LL BE GLAD TO ATTEND THE RALLY IF I CAN --
-- BUT WITH ALL DUE RESPECT, SIR -- MY RESPONSIBILITIES AS AN AVENGER HAVE TO COME FIRST.
HM?
I ONLY HEARD THE TAIL END OF THAT, PASSING BY -- BUT IT SEEMS OUR TRIATHLON MAY NOT BE THE RAVING SECURITY RISK PEOPLE THINK.
OR THOUGHT, AT FIRST.
IF SO, IT'S HARD TO BLAME HIM FOR BEING SO HACKED OFF WHEN HE JOINED.
BUT STILL, SOMEONE SHOULD DO SOMETHING TO STRAIGHTEN ALL THIS OUT. MAYBE... MAYBE...
SO YOU SEE, IF WE CHANNEL THE EXCESS THRUST PAST THE BAFFLES --
GOOD AFTERNOON, WARBIRD. DID YOU ENJOY YOUR WORKOUT?
SURE DID, VISION --
-- BUT I'M GOING STIR-CRAZY. I'M BACK IN NEW YORK, BUT MY OLD PALS ARE GONE. I NEED SOMETHING TO DO, SOME TROUBLE TO GET INTO...
OH, I'M SURE YOU CAN --
PERHAPS, I CAN HELP. WOULD YOU HAVE DINNER WITH ME SOME NIGHT?
WH-WHAT?

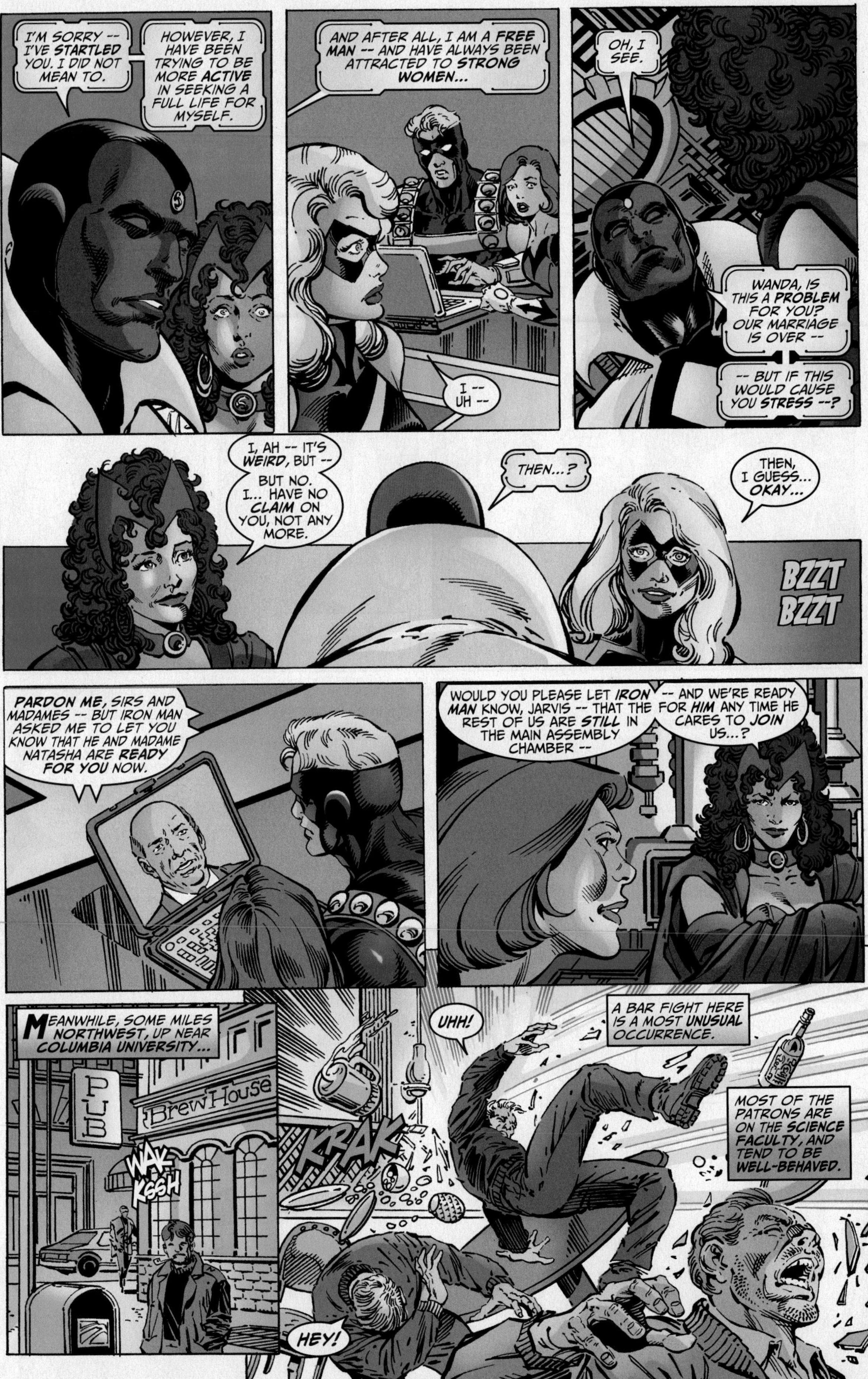
I'M SORRY -- I'VE STARTLED YOU. I DID NOT MEAN TO.
HOWEVER, I HAVE BEEN TRYING TO BE MORE ACTIVE IN SEEKING A FULL LIFE FOR MYSELF.
AND AFTER ALL, I AM A FREE MAN -- AND HAVE ALWAYS BEEN ATTRACTED TO STRONG WOMEN...
I -- UH --
OH, I SEE.
WANDA, IS THIS A PROBLEM FOR YOU? OUR MARRIAGE IS OVER --
-- BUT IF THIS WOULD CAUSE YOU STRESS --?
I, AH -- IT'S WEIRD, BUT --
BUT NO. I... HAVE NO CLAIM ON YOU, NOT ANY MORE.
THEN...?
THEN, I GUESS... OKAY...
BZZT BZZT
PARDON ME, SIRS AND MADAMES -- BUT IRON MAN ASKED ME TO LET YOU KNOW THAT HE AND MADAME NATASHA ARE READY FOR YOU NOW.
WOULD YOU PLEASE LET IRON MAN KNOW, JARVIS -- THAT THE REST OF US ARE STILL IN THE MAIN ASSEMBLY CHAMBER --
-- AND WE'RE READY FOR HIM ANY TIME HE CARES TO JOIN US...?
MEANWHILE, SOME MILES NORTHWEST, UP NEAR COLUMBIA UNIVERSITY...
PUB
BrewHouse
WAK KSSH
UHH!
A BAR FIGHT HERE IS A MOST UNUSUAL OCCURRENCE.
KRAK
MOST OF THE PATRONS ARE ON THE SCIENCE FACULTY, AND TEND TO BE WELL-BEHAVED.
HEY!

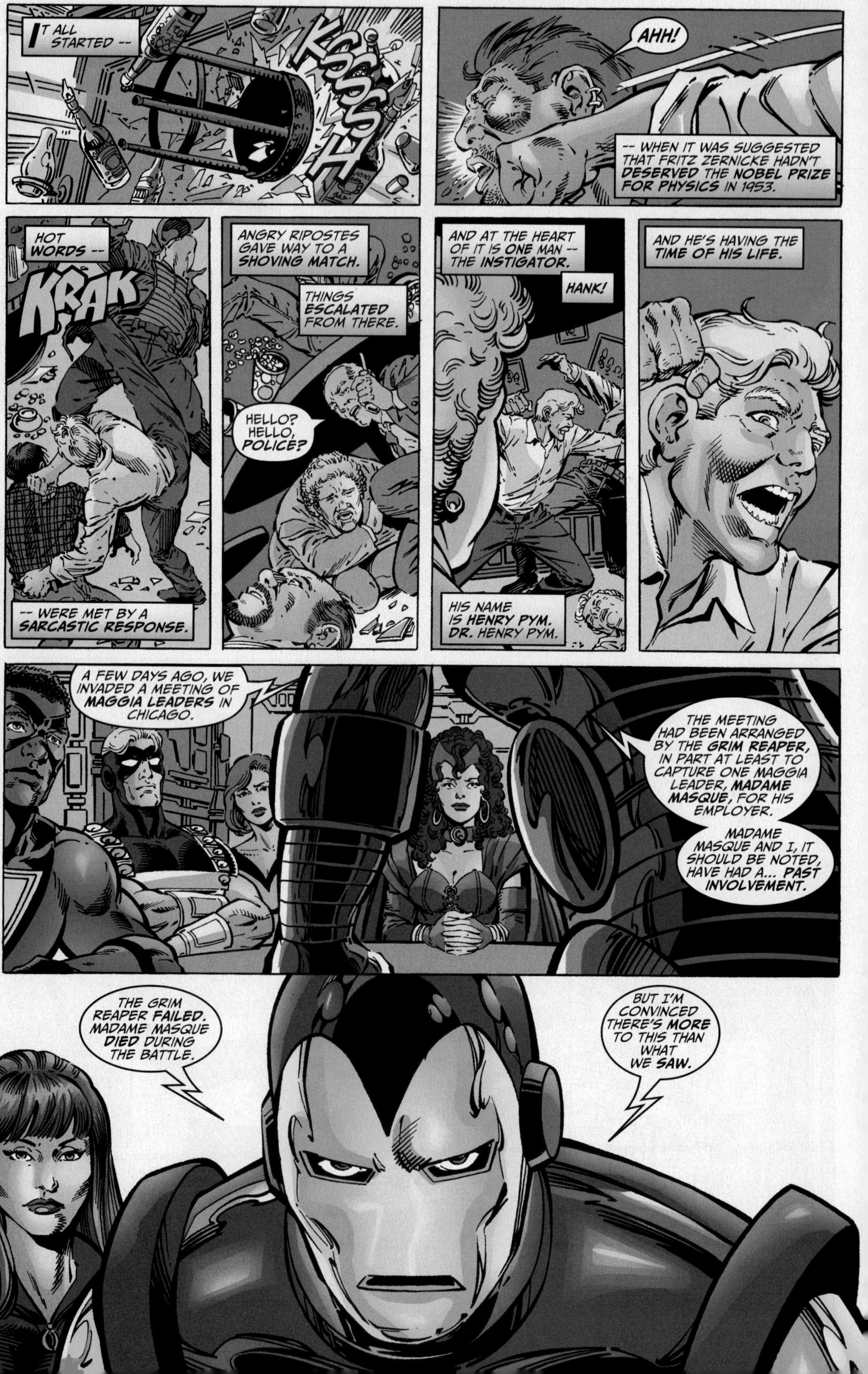
IT ALL STARTED --
KSSSH
AHH!
-- WHEN IT WAS SUGGESTED THAT FRITZ ZERNICKE HADN'T DESERVED THE NOBEL PRIZE FOR PHYSICS IN 1953.
HOT WORDS --
KRAK
-- WERE MET BY A SARCASTIC RESPONSE.
ANGRY RIPOSTES GAVE WAY TO A SHOVING MATCH.
THINGS ESCALATED FROM THERE.
HELLO? HELLO, POLICE?
AND AT THE HEART OF IT IS ONE MAN -- THE INSTIGATOR.
HANK!
HIS NAME IS HENRY PYM. DR. HENRY PYM.
AND HE'S HAVING THE TIME OF HIS LIFE.
A FEW DAYS AGO, WE INVADED A MEETING OF MAGGIA LEADERS IN CHICAGO.
THE MEETING HAD BEEN ARRANGED BY THE GRIM REAPER, IN PART AT LEAST TO CAPTURE ONE MAGGIA LEADER, MADAME MASQUE, FOR HIS EMPLOYER.
MADAME MASQUE AND I, IT SHOULD BE NOTED, HAVE HAD A... PAST INVOLVEMENT.
THE GRIM REAPER FAILED. MADAME MASQUE DIED DURING THE BATTLE.
BUT I'M CONVINCED THERE'S MORE TO THIS THAN WHAT WE SAW.

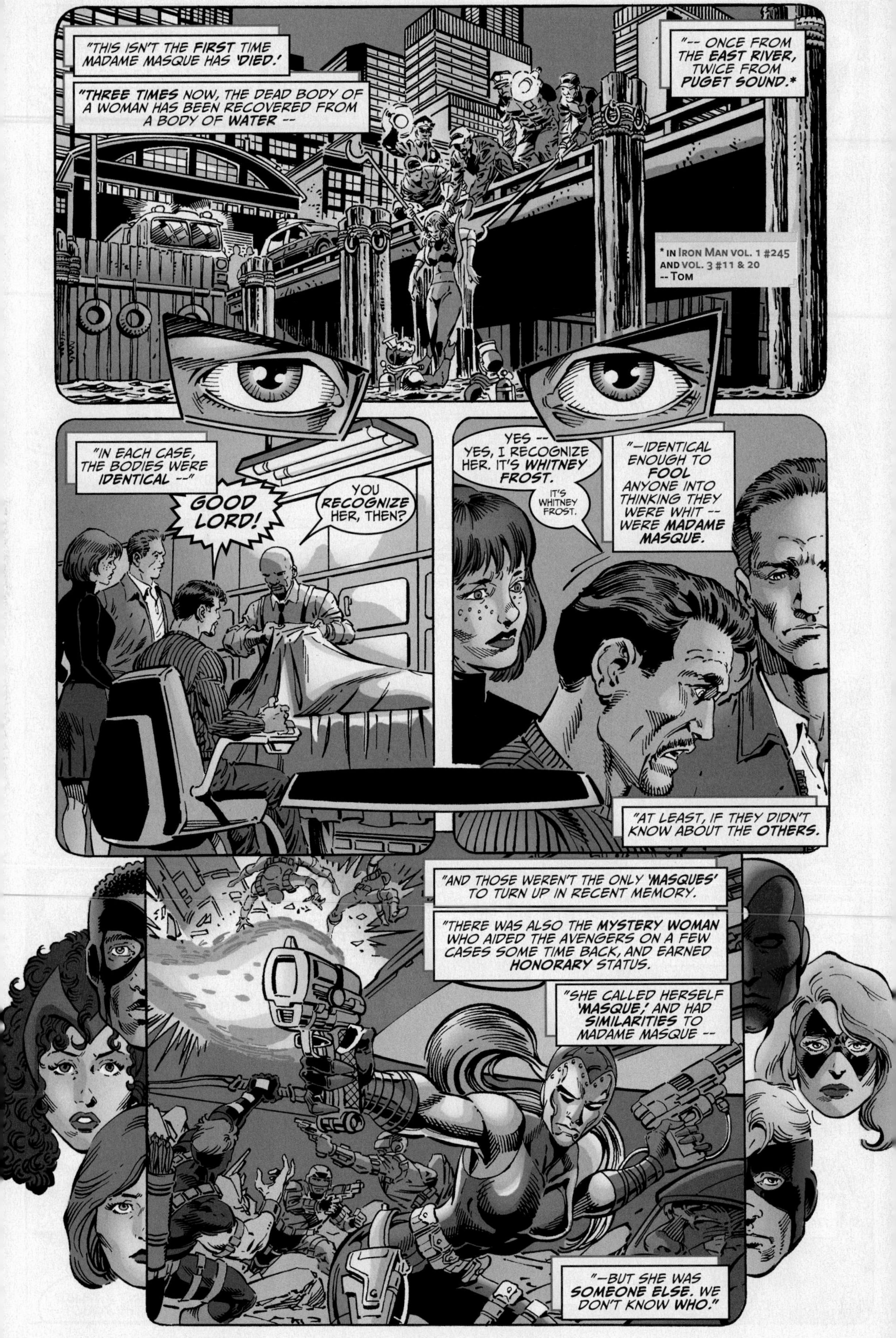
"THIS ISN'T THE FIRST TIME MADAME MASQUE HAS 'DIED.'
"THREE TIMES NOW, THE DEAD BODY OF A WOMAN HAS BEEN RECOVERED FROM A BODY OF WATER --
"-- ONCE FROM THE EAST RIVER, TWICE FROM PUGET SOUND.*
* IN IRON MAN VOL. 1 #245 AND VOL. 3 #11 & 20 --TOM
"IN EACH CASE, THE BODIES WERE IDENTICAL --"
GOOD LORD!
YOU RECOGNIZE HER, THEN?
YES -- YES, I RECOGNIZE HER. IT'S WHITNEY FROST.
IT'S WHITNEY FROST.
"—IDENTICAL ENOUGH TO FOOL ANYONE INTO THINKING THEY WERE WHIT -- WERE MADAME MASQUE.
"AT LEAST, IF THEY DIDN'T KNOW ABOUT THE OTHERS.
"AND THOSE WEREN'T THE ONLY 'MASQUES' TO TURN UP IN RECENT MEMORY.
"THERE WAS ALSO THE MYSTERY WOMAN WHO AIDED THE AVENGERS ON A FEW CASES SOME TIME BACK, AND EARNED HONORARY STATUS.
"SHE CALLED HERSELF 'MASQUE,' AND HAD SIMILARITIES TO MADAME MASQUE --
"—BUT SHE WAS SOMEONE ELSE. WE DON'T KNOW WHO."

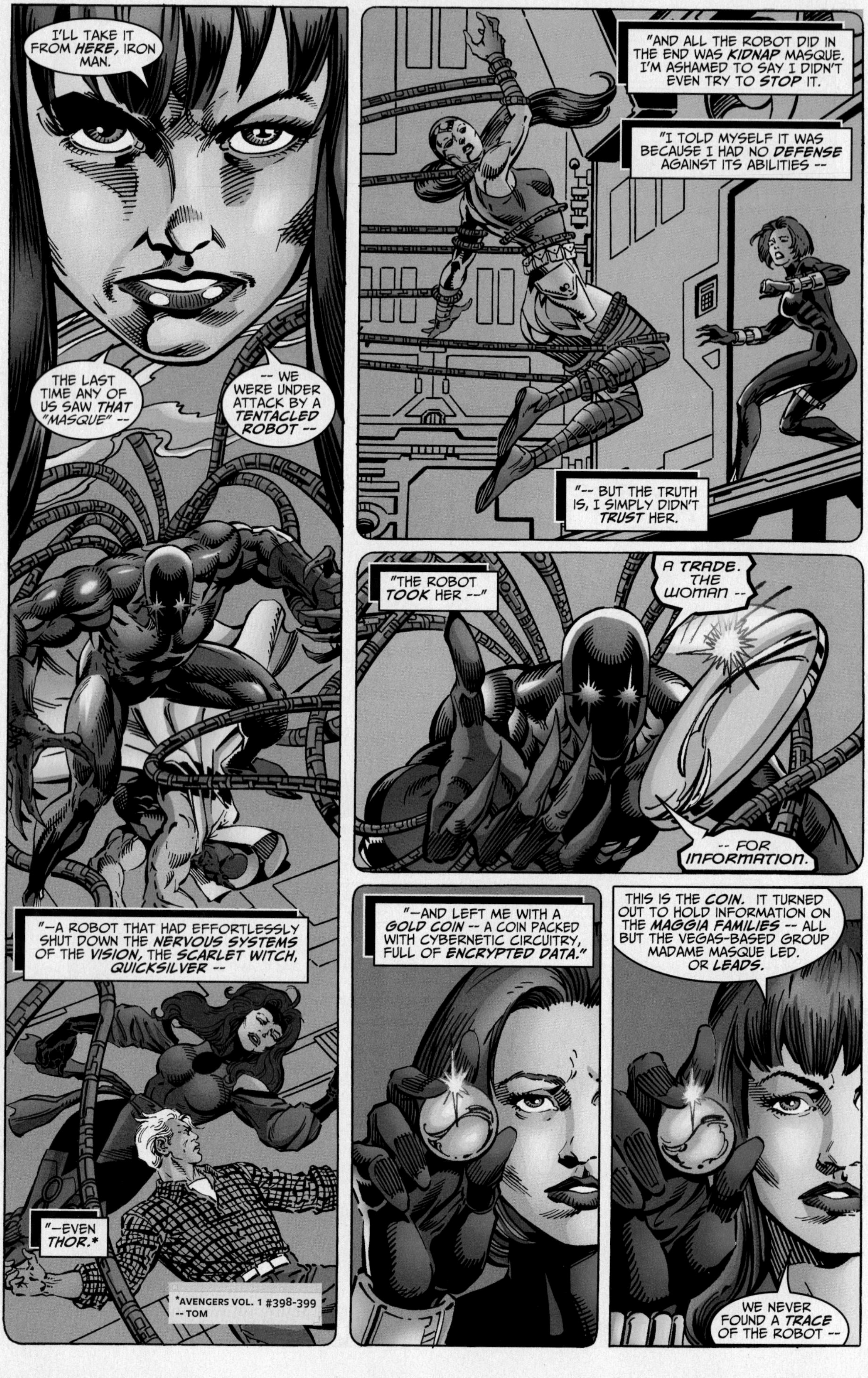
I'LL TAKE IT FROM HERE, IRON MAN.
THE LAST TIME ANY OF US SAW THAT "MASQUE" --
-- WE WERE UNDER ATTACK BY A TENTACLED ROBOT --
"—A ROBOT THAT HAD EFFORTLESSLY SHUT DOWN THE NERVOUS SYSTEMS OF THE VISION, THE SCARLET WITCH, QUICKSILVER --
"—EVEN THOR.*
*AVENGERS VOL. 1 #398-399 -- TOM
"AND ALL THE ROBOT DID IN THE END WAS KIDNAP MASQUE. I'M ASHAMED TO SAY I DIDN'T EVEN TRY TO STOP IT.
"I TOLD MYSELF IT WAS BECAUSE I HAD NO DEFENSE AGAINST ITS ABILITIES --
"-- BUT THE TRUTH IS, I SIMPLY DIDN'T TRUST HER.
"THE ROBOT TOOK HER --"
A TRADE. THE WOMAN --
-- FOR INFORMATION.
"—AND LEFT ME WITH A GOLD COIN -- A COIN PACKED WITH CYBERNETIC CIRCUITRY, FULL OF ENCRYPTED DATA."
THIS IS THE COIN. IT TURNED OUT TO HOLD INFORMATION ON THE MAGGIA FAMILIES -- ALL BUT THE VEGAS-BASED GROUP MADAME MASQUE LED. OR LEADS.
WE NEVER FOUND A TRACE OF THE ROBOT --

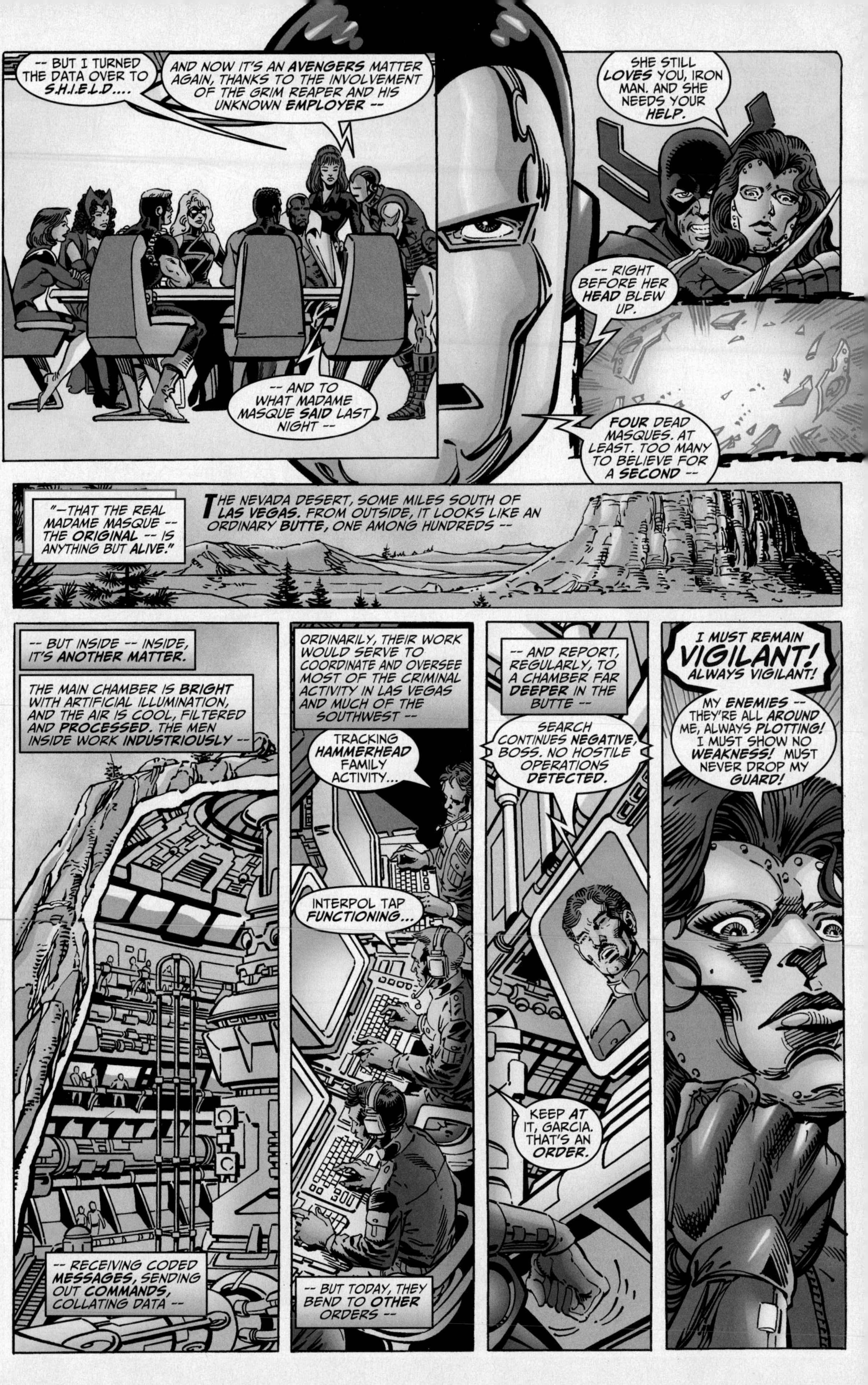
-- BUT I TURNED THE DATA OVER TO S.H.I.E.L.D....
AND NOW IT'S AN AVENGERS MATTER AGAIN, THANKS TO THE INVOLVEMENT OF THE GRIM REAPER AND HIS UNKNOWN EMPLOYER --
-- AND TO WHAT MADAME MASQUE SAID LAST NIGHT --
SHE STILL LOVES YOU, IRON MAN. AND SHE NEEDS YOUR HELP.
-- RIGHT BEFORE HER HEAD BLEW UP.
FOUR DEAD MASQUES. AT LEAST. TOO MANY TO BELIEVE FOR A SECOND --
"--THAT THE REAL MADAME MASQUE -- THE ORIGINAL -- IS ANYTHING BUT ALIVE."
THE NEVADA DESERT, SOME MILES SOUTH OF LAS VEGAS. FROM OUTSIDE, IT LOOKS LIKE AN ORDINARY BUTTE, ONE AMONG HUNDREDS --
-- BUT INSIDE -- INSIDE, IT'S ANOTHER MATTER.
THE MAIN CHAMBER IS BRIGHT WITH ARTIFICIAL ILLUMINATION, AND THE AIR IS COOL, FILTERED AND PROCESSED. THE MEN INSIDE WORK INDUSTRIOUSLY --
-- RECEIVING CODED MESSAGES, SENDING OUT COMMANDS, COLLATING DATA --
ORDINARILY, THEIR WORK WOULD SERVE TO COORDINATE AND OVERSEE MOST OF THE CRIMINAL ACTIVITY IN LAS VEGAS AND MUCH OF THE SOUTHWEST --
TRACKING HAMMERHEAD FAMILY ACTIVITY...
INTERPOL TAP FUNCTIONING...
-- BUT TODAY, THEY BEND TO OTHER ORDERS --
-- AND REPORT, REGULARLY, TO A CHAMBER FAR DEEPER IN THE BUTTE --
SEARCH CONTINUES NEGATIVE, BOSS. NO HOSTILE OPERATIONS DETECTED.
KEEP AT IT, GARCIA. THAT'S AN ORDER.
I MUST REMAIN VIGILANT! ALWAYS VIGILANT!
MY ENEMIES -- THEY'RE ALL AROUND ME, ALWAYS PLOTTING! I MUST SHOW NO WEAKNESS! MUST NEVER DROP MY GUARD!

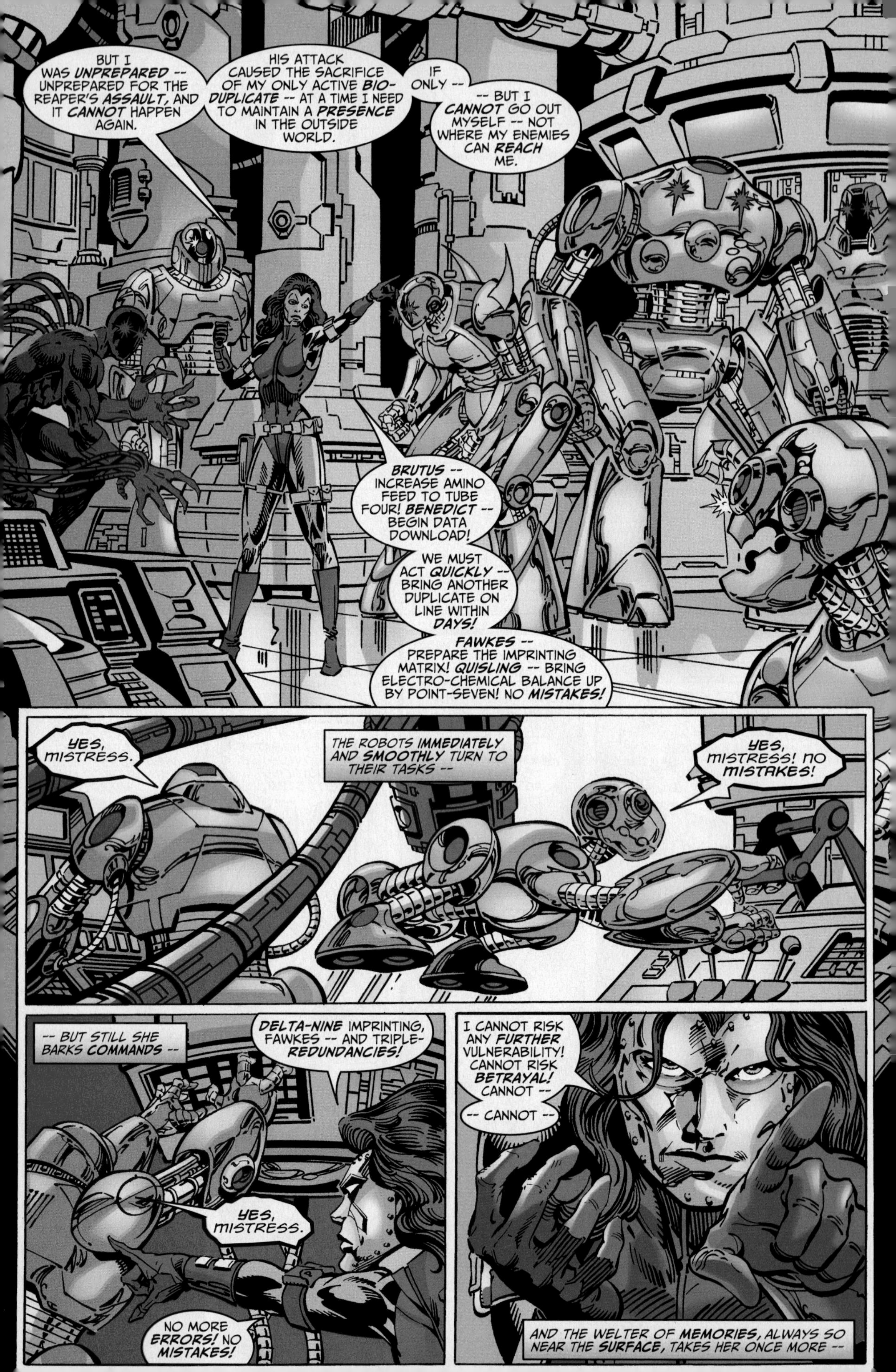
BUT I WAS UNPREPARED -- UNPREPARED FOR THE REAPER'S ASSAULT, AND IT CANNOT HAPPEN AGAIN.
HIS ATTACK CAUSED THE SACRIFICE OF MY ONLY ACTIVE BIO-DUPLICATE -- AT A TIME I NEED TO MAINTAIN A PRESENCE IN THE OUTSIDE WORLD.
IF ONLY --
-- BUT I CANNOT GO OUT MYSELF -- NOT WHERE MY ENEMIES CAN REACH ME.
BRUTUS -- INCREASE AMINO FEED TO TUBE FOUR! BENEDICT -- BEGIN DATA DOWNLOAD!
WE MUST ACT QUICKLY -- BRING ANOTHER DUPLICATE ON LINE WITHIN DAYS!
FAWKES -- PREPARE THE IMPRINTING MATRIX! QUISLING -- BRING ELECTRO-CHEMICAL BALANCE UP BY POINT-SEVEN! NO MISTAKES!
YES, MISTRESS.
THE ROBOTS IMMEDIATELY AND SMOOTHLY TURN TO THEIR TASKS --
YES, MISTRESS! NO MISTAKES!
-- BUT STILL SHE BARKS COMMANDS --
DELTA-NINE IMPRINTING, FAWKES -- AND TRIPLE-REDUNDANCIES!
YES, MISTRESS.
NO MORE ERRORS! NO MISTAKES!
I CANNOT RISK ANY FURTHER VULNERABILITY! CANNOT RISK BETRAYAL! CANNOT --
-- CANNOT --
AND THE WELTER OF MEMORIES, ALWAYS SO NEAR THE SURFACE, TAKES HER ONCE MORE --

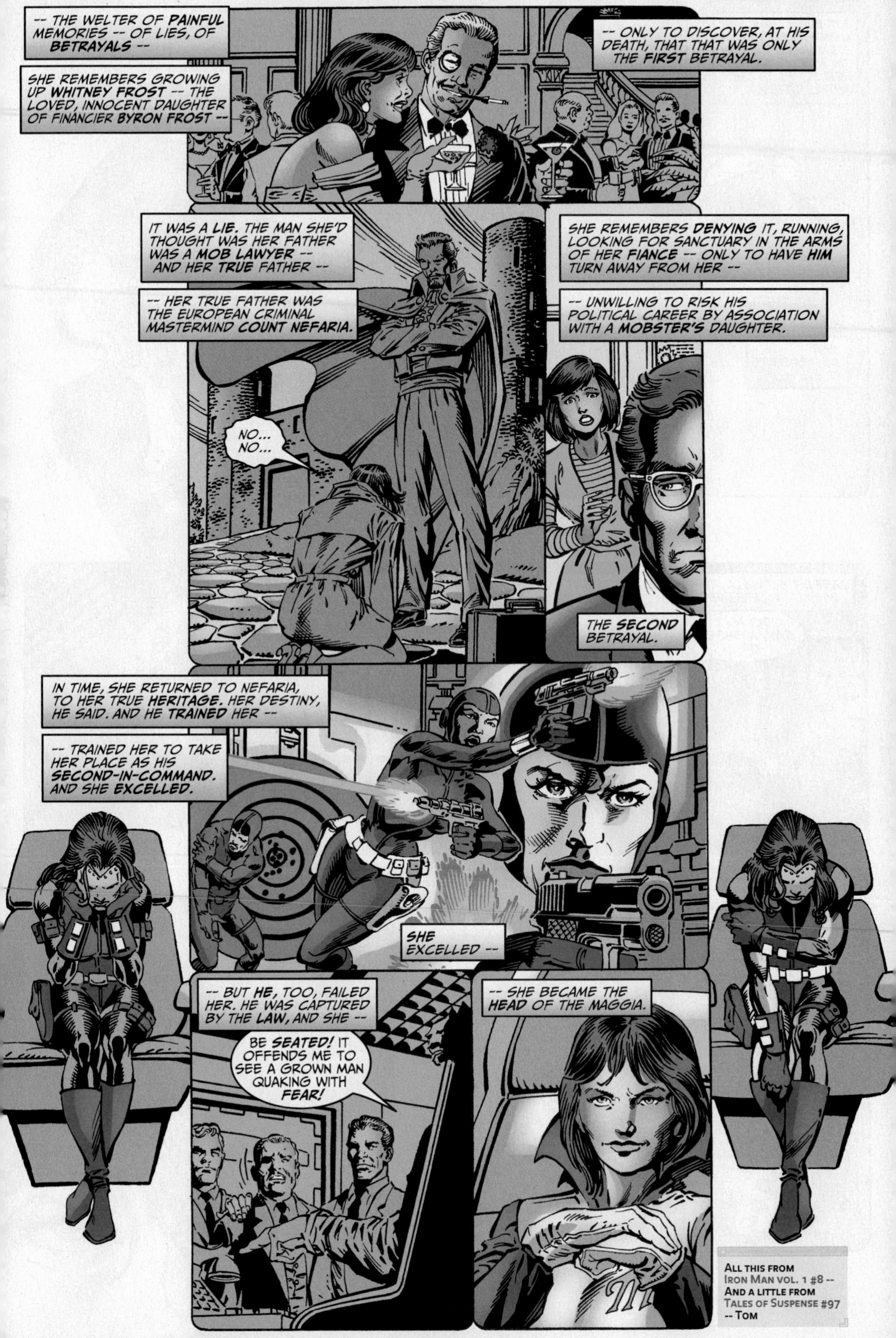
-- THE WELTER OF PAINFUL MEMORIES -- OF LIES, OF BETRAYALS --
SHE REMEMBERS GROWING UP WHITNEY FROST -- THE LOVED, INNOCENT DAUGHTER OF FINANCIER BYRON FROST --
-- ONLY TO DISCOVER, AT HIS DEATH, THAT THAT WAS ONLY THE FIRST BETRAYAL.
IT WAS A LIE. THE MAN SHE'D THOUGHT WAS HER FATHER WAS A MOB LAWYER -- AND HER TRUE FATHER --
-- HER TRUE FATHER WAS THE EUROPEAN CRIMINAL MASTERMIND COUNT NEFARIA.
NO... NO...
SHE REMEMBERS DENYING IT, RUNNING, LOOKING FOR SANCTUARY IN THE ARMS OF HER FIANCE -- ONLY TO HAVE HIM TURN AWAY FROM HER --
-- UNWILLING TO RISK HIS POLITICAL CAREER BY ASSOCIATION WITH A MOBSTER'S DAUGHTER.
THE SECOND BETRAYAL.
IN TIME, SHE RETURNED TO NEFARIA, TO HER TRUE HERITAGE. HER DESTINY, HE SAID. AND HE TRAINED HER --
-- TRAINED HER TO TAKE HER PLACE AS HIS SECOND-IN-COMMAND. AND SHE EXCELLED.
SHE EXCELLED --
-- BUT HE, TOO, FAILED HER. HE WAS CAPTURED BY THE LAW, AND SHE --
BE SEATED! IT OFFENDS ME TO SEE A GROWN MAN QUAKING WITH FEAR!
-- SHE BECAME THE HEAD OF THE MAGGIA.

ALL THIS FROM IRON MAN VOL. 1 #8 -- AND A LITTLE FROM TALES OF SUSPENSE #97 -- TOM

BUT EVEN THEN, HER **MEN** FAILED HER, EVENTUALLY TURNED ON HER, FORCING HER TO FLEE THE AUTHORITIES.

-- REMEMBERS **CRASHING** --

-- AND BEING **RESCUED** --

-- BY **MORDECAI MIDAS,** WHO HID HER RUINED FACE BEHIND A GOLDEN MASK FOR THE FIRST TIME, MADE HER INTO **MADAME MASQUE** --

OF COURSE, THAT WAS BEFORE **HE** TOO TURNED ON HER, TRIED TO KILL HER --

MEN!

ALL OF THEM -- FATHERS, LOVERS, **EMPLOYERS** -- THEY ALL BETRAYED HER! ALL FAILED HER!

SHE REMEMBERS IT ALL --

JASPER SITWELL, THE S.H.I.E.L.D. AGENT WHO'D **PROFESSED** TO LOVE HER --

DO AS I **SAY,** AVENGER! OR...!

IRON MAN -- TONY STARK -- WHO'D BEEN SO WARM, SO TENDER, SO SUPPORTIVE --

-- WHO SHE'D GIVEN HER **HEART** TO --

-- UNTIL HE **TORE** IT APART --

-- UNTIL SHE CAME TO HIM FOR **HELP,** TO SAVE HER FATHER'S LIFE, AND HE **REPAID** HER TRUST --

-- BY **MURDERING** HIM!

IT WAS **THEN** -- THEN THAT I CAME HERE --

-- BUILT THIS **REFUGE** --

THIS FACTUALLY-ACCURATE BUT EMOTIONALLY-COLORED ACCOUNT COURTESY OF IRON MAN VOL .1 #8, 17-19, 106, 109 AND 116 -- TOM

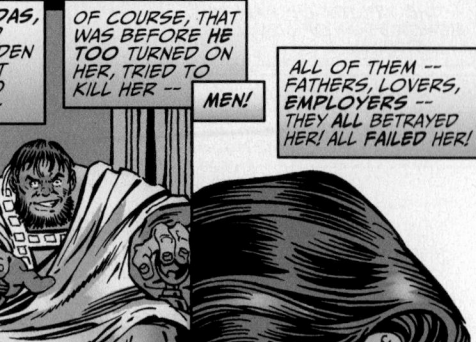

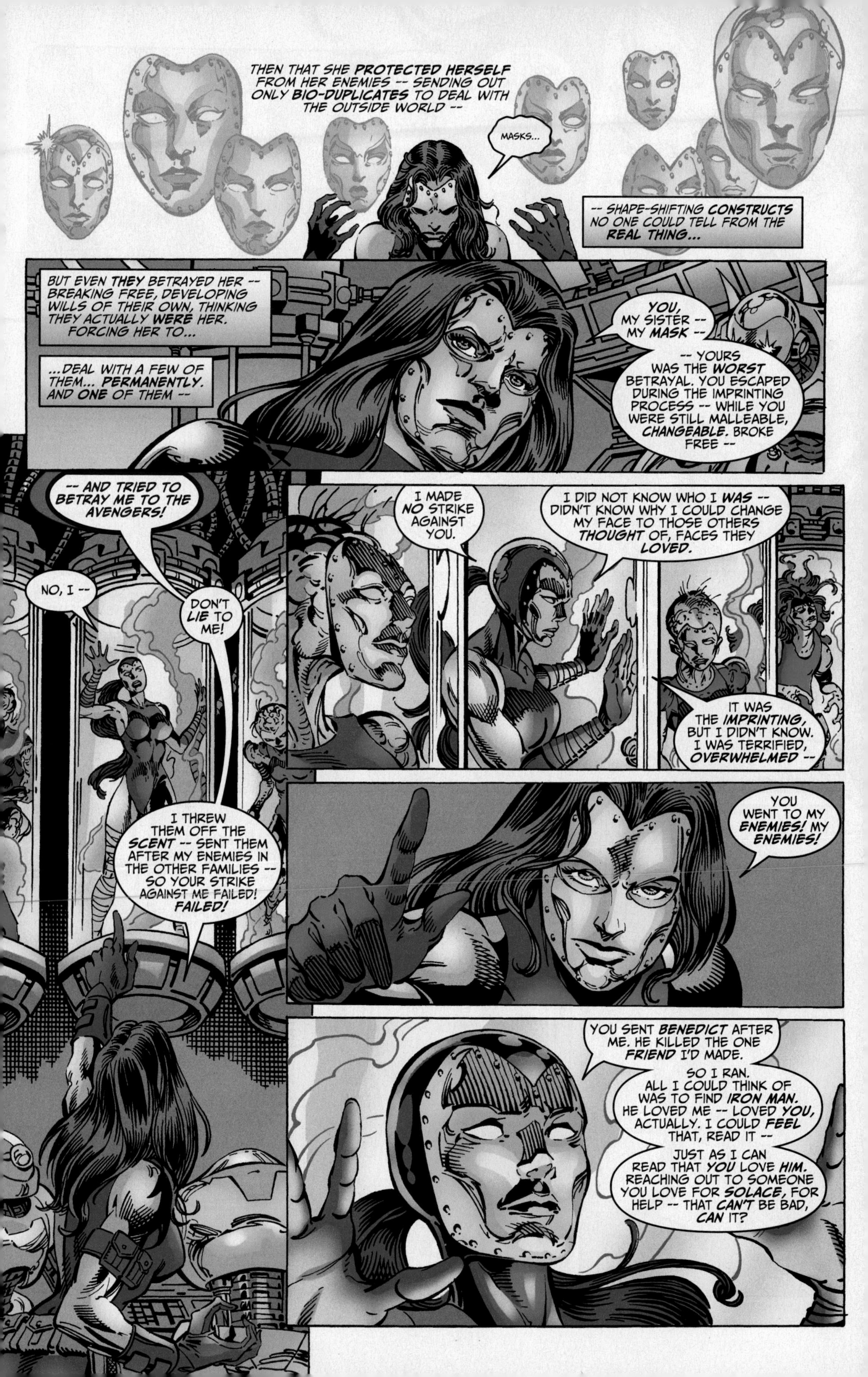
THEN THAT SHE PROTECTED HERSELF FROM HER ENEMIES -- SENDING OUT ONLY BIO-DUPLICATES TO DEAL WITH THE OUTSIDE WORLD --
MASKS...
-- SHAPE-SHIFTING CONSTRUCTS NO ONE COULD TELL FROM THE REAL THING...
BUT EVEN THEY BETRAYED HER -- BREAKING FREE, DEVELOPING WILLS OF THEIR OWN, THINKING THEY ACTUALLY WERE HER. FORCING HER TO...
...DEAL WITH A FEW OF THEM... PERMANENTLY. AND ONE OF THEM --
YOU, MY SISTER -- MY MASK --
-- YOURS WAS THE WORST BETRAYAL. YOU ESCAPED DURING THE IMPRINTING PROCESS -- WHILE YOU WERE STILL MALLEABLE, CHANGEABLE. BROKE FREE --
-- AND TRIED TO BETRAY ME TO THE AVENGERS!
NO, I --
DON'T LIE TO ME!
I THREW THEM OFF THE SCENT -- SENT THEM AFTER MY ENEMIES IN THE OTHER FAMILIES -- SO YOUR STRIKE AGAINST ME FAILED! FAILED!
I MADE NO STRIKE AGAINST YOU.
I DID NOT KNOW WHO I WAS -- DIDN'T KNOW WHY I COULD CHANGE MY FACE TO THOSE OTHERS THOUGHT OF, FACES THEY LOVED.
IT WAS THE IMPRINTING, BUT I DIDN'T KNOW. I WAS TERRIFIED, OVERWHELMED --
YOU WENT TO MY ENEMIES! MY ENEMIES!
YOU SENT BENEDICT AFTER ME. HE KILLED THE ONE FRIEND I'D MADE.
SO I RAN. ALL I COULD THINK OF WAS TO FIND IRON MAN. HE LOVED ME -- LOVED YOU, ACTUALLY. I COULD FEEL THAT, READ IT --
JUST AS I CAN READ THAT YOU LOVE HIM. REACHING OUT TO SOMEONE YOU LOVE FOR SOLACE, FOR HELP -- THAT CAN'T BE BAD, CAN IT?

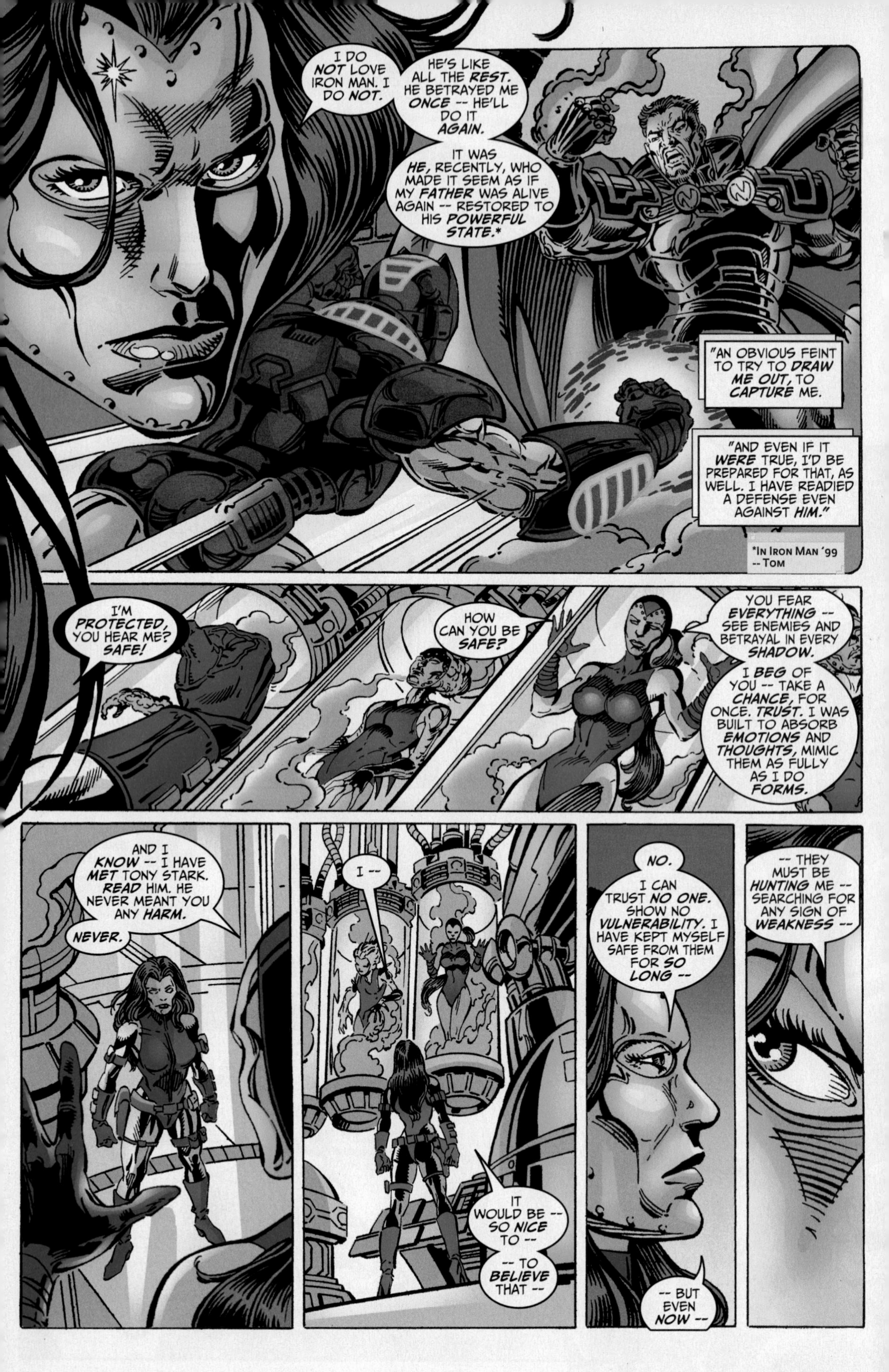
I DO NOT LOVE IRON MAN. I DO NOT.
HE'S LIKE ALL THE REST. HE BETRAYED ME ONCE -- HE'LL DO IT AGAIN.
IT WAS HE, RECENTLY, WHO MADE IT SEEM AS IF MY FATHER WAS ALIVE AGAIN -- RESTORED TO HIS POWERFUL STATE.*
"AN OBVIOUS FEINT TO TRY TO DRAW ME OUT, TO CAPTURE ME.
"AND EVEN IF IT WERE TRUE, I'D BE PREPARED FOR THAT, AS WELL. I HAVE READIED A DEFENSE EVEN AGAINST HIM."
*IN IRON MAN '99 -- TOM
I'M PROTECTED, YOU HEAR ME? SAFE!
HOW CAN YOU BE SAFE?
YOU FEAR EVERYTHING -- SEE ENEMIES AND BETRAYAL IN EVERY SHADOW.
I BEG OF YOU -- TAKE A CHANCE, FOR ONCE. TRUST. I WAS BUILT TO ABSORB EMOTIONS AND THOUGHTS, MIMIC THEM AS FULLY AS I DO FORMS.
AND I KNOW -- I HAVE MET TONY STARK. READ HIM. HE NEVER MEANT YOU ANY HARM.
NEVER.
I --
IT WOULD BE -- SO NICE TO --
-- TO BELIEVE THAT --
NO.
I CAN TRUST NO ONE. SHOW NO VULNERABILITY. I HAVE KEPT MYSELF SAFE FROM THEM FOR SO LONG --
-- BUT EVEN NOW --
-- THEY MUST BE HUNTING ME -- SEARCHING FOR ANY SIGN OF WEAKNESS --

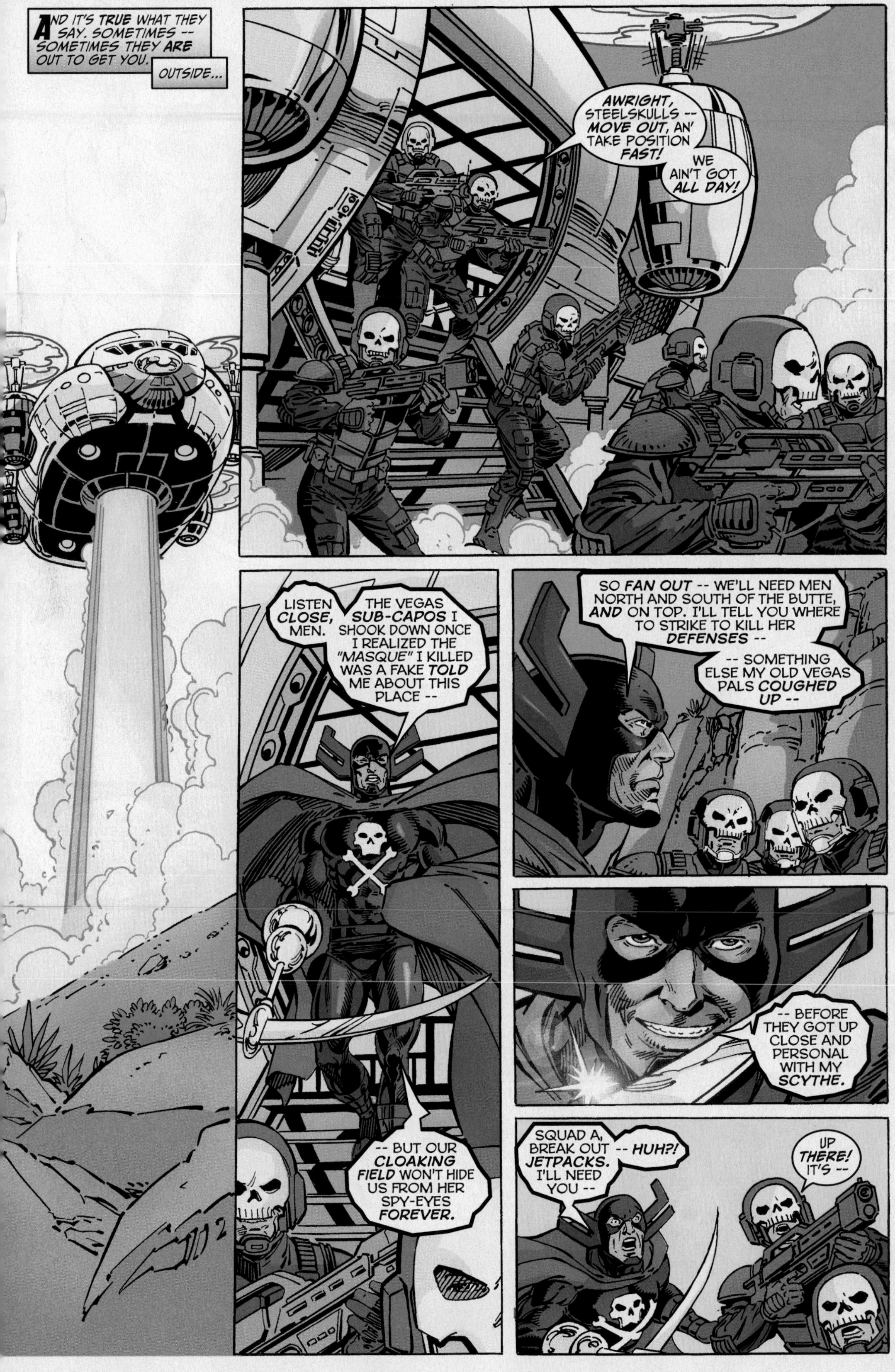
AND IT'S TRUE WHAT THEY SAY. SOMETIMES -- SOMETIMES THEY ARE OUT TO GET YOU.
OUTSIDE...
AWRIGHT, STEELSKULLS -- MOVE OUT, AN' TAKE POSITION FAST!
WE AIN'T GOT ALL DAY!
LISTEN CLOSE, MEN.
THE VEGAS SUB-CAPOS I SHOOK DOWN ONCE I REALIZED THE "MASQUE" I KILLED WAS A FAKE TOLD ME ABOUT THIS PLACE --
-- BUT OUR CLOAKING FIELD WON'T HIDE US FROM HER SPY-EYES FOREVER.
SO FAN OUT -- WE'LL NEED MEN NORTH AND SOUTH OF THE BUTTE, AND ON TOP. I'LL TELL YOU WHERE TO STRIKE TO KILL HER DEFENSES --
-- SOMETHING ELSE MY OLD VEGAS PALS COUGHED UP --
-- BEFORE THEY GOT UP CLOSE AND PERSONAL WITH MY SCYTHE.
SQUAD A, BREAK OUT JETPACKS. I'LL NEED YOU --
-- HUH?!
UP THERE! IT'S --

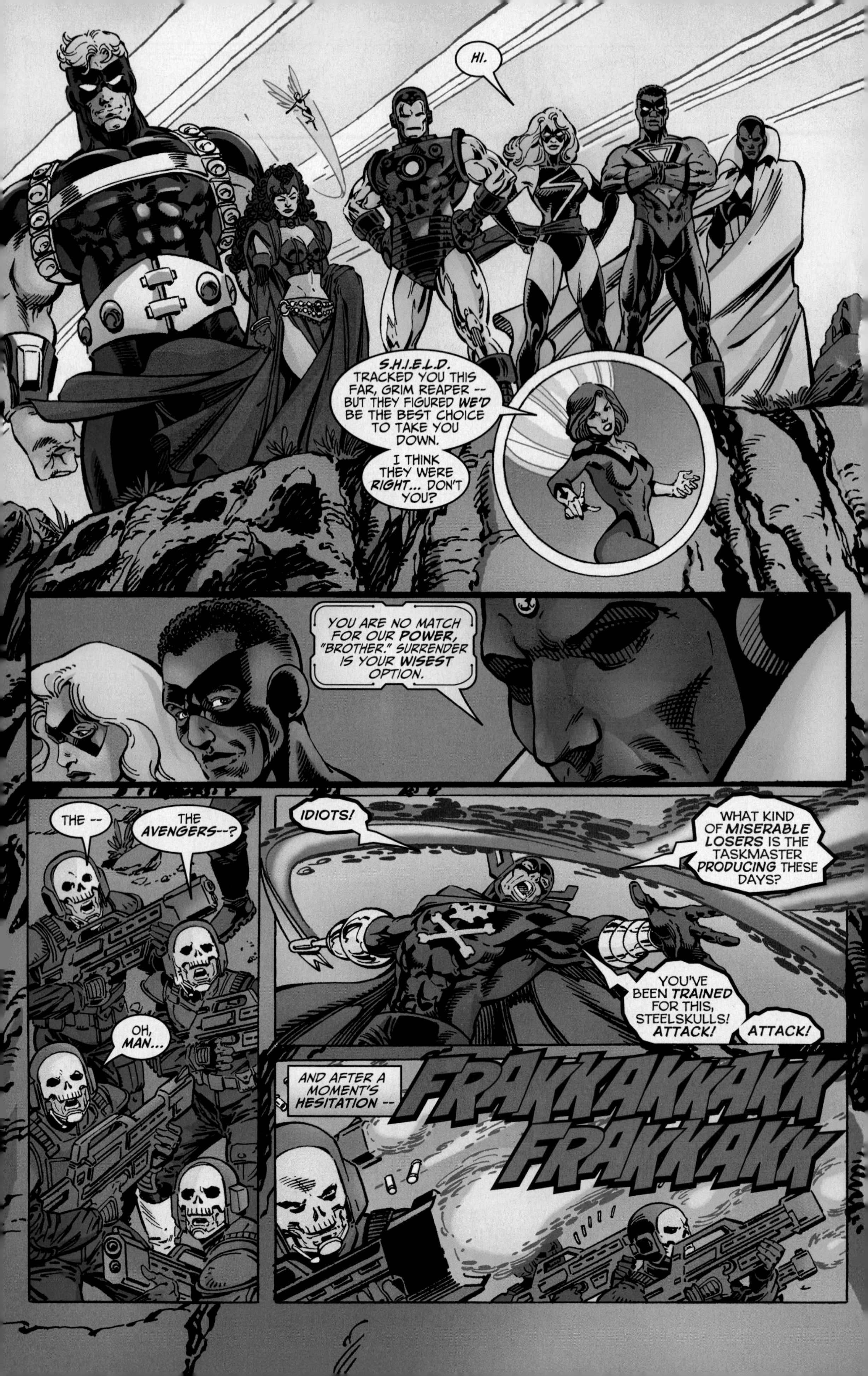
HI.
S.H.I.E.L.D. TRACKED YOU THIS FAR, GRIM REAPER -- BUT THEY FIGURED WE'D BE THE BEST CHOICE TO TAKE YOU DOWN.
I THINK THEY WERE RIGHT... DON'T YOU?
YOU ARE NO MATCH FOR OUR POWER, "BROTHER." SURRENDER IS YOUR WISEST OPTION.
THE --
THE AVENGERS--?
OH, MAN...
IDIOTS!
WHAT KIND OF MISERABLE LOSERS IS THE TASKMASTER PRODUCING THESE DAYS?
YOU'VE BEEN TRAINED FOR THIS, STEELSKULLS! ATTACK!
ATTACK!
AND AFTER A MOMENT'S HESITATION --
FRAKKAKKAKK
FRAKKAKK

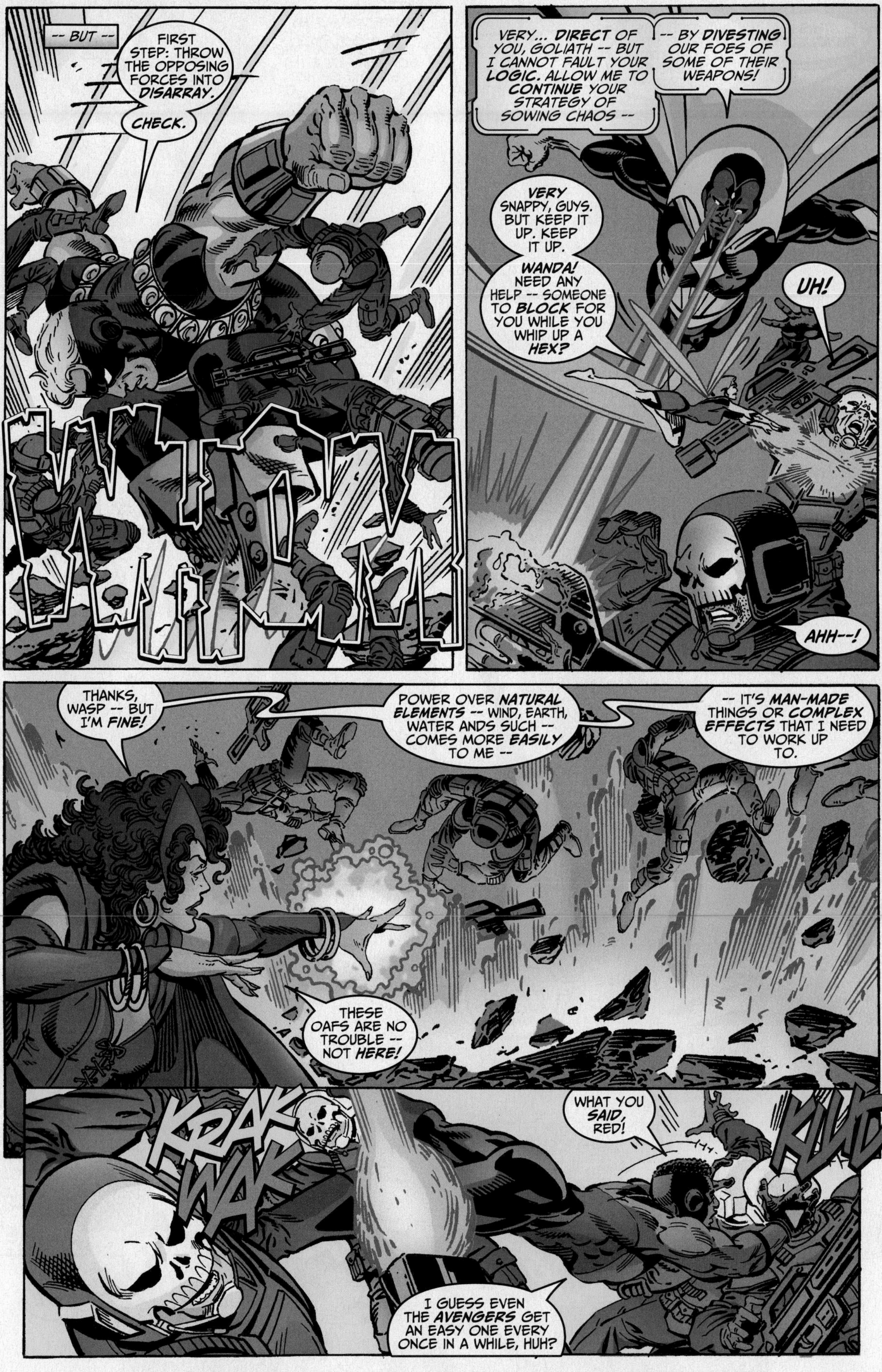
-- BUT --
FIRST STEP: THROW THE OPPOSING FORCES INTO DISARRAY.
CHECK.
VERY... DIRECT OF YOU, GOLIATH -- BUT I CANNOT FAULT YOUR LOGIC. ALLOW ME TO CONTINUE YOUR STRATEGY OF SOWING CHAOS --
-- BY DIVESTING OUR FOES OF SOME OF THEIR WEAPONS!
VERY SNAPPY, GUYS. BUT KEEP IT UP. KEEP IT UP.
WANDA! NEED ANY HELP -- SOMEONE TO BLOCK FOR YOU WHILE YOU WHIP UP A HEX?
UH!
AHH--!
THANKS, WASP -- BUT I'M FINE!
POWER OVER NATURAL ELEMENTS -- WIND, EARTH, WATER ANDS SUCH -- COMES MORE EASILY TO ME --
-- IT'S MAN-MADE THINGS OR COMPLEX EFFECTS THAT I NEED TO WORK UP TO.
THESE OAFS ARE NO TROUBLE -- NOT HERE!
KRAK
WAK
WHAT YOU SAID, RED!
KUD
I GUESS EVEN THE AVENGERS GET AN EASY ONE EVERY ONCE IN A WHILE, HUH?

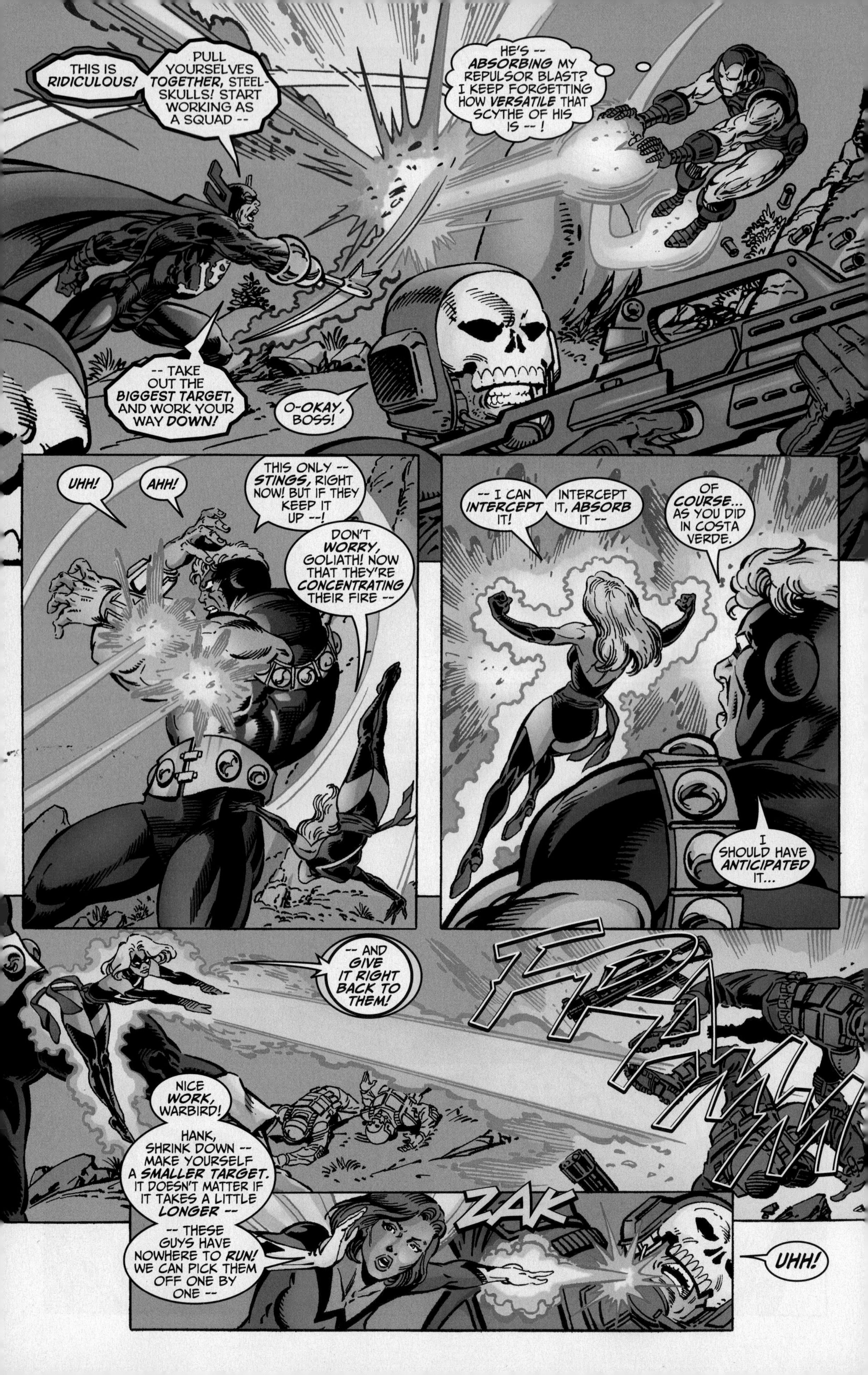
THIS IS RIDICULOUS!
PULL YOURSELVES TOGETHER, STEEL-SKULLS! START WORKING AS A SQUAD --
HE'S -- ABSORBING MY REPULSOR BLAST? I KEEP FORGETTING HOW VERSATILE THAT SCYTHE OF HIS IS -- !
-- TAKE OUT THE BIGGEST TARGET, AND WORK YOUR WAY DOWN!
O-OKAY, BOSS!
UHH!
AHH!
THIS ONLY -- STINGS, RIGHT NOW! BUT IF THEY KEEP IT UP --!
DON'T WORRY, GOLIATH! NOW THAT THEY'RE CONCENTRATING THEIR FIRE --
-- I CAN INTERCEPT IT!
INTERCEPT IT, ABSORB IT --
OF COURSE... AS YOU DID IN COSTA VERDE.
I SHOULD HAVE ANTICIPATED IT...
-- AND GIVE IT RIGHT BACK TO THEM!
TTRRAMMM
NICE WORK, WARBIRD!
HANK, SHRINK DOWN -- MAKE YOURSELF A SMALLER TARGET. IT DOESN'T MATTER IF IT TAKES A LITTLE LONGER --
-- THESE GUYS HAVE NOWHERE TO RUN! WE CAN PICK THEM OFF ONE BY ONE --
ZAK
UHH!

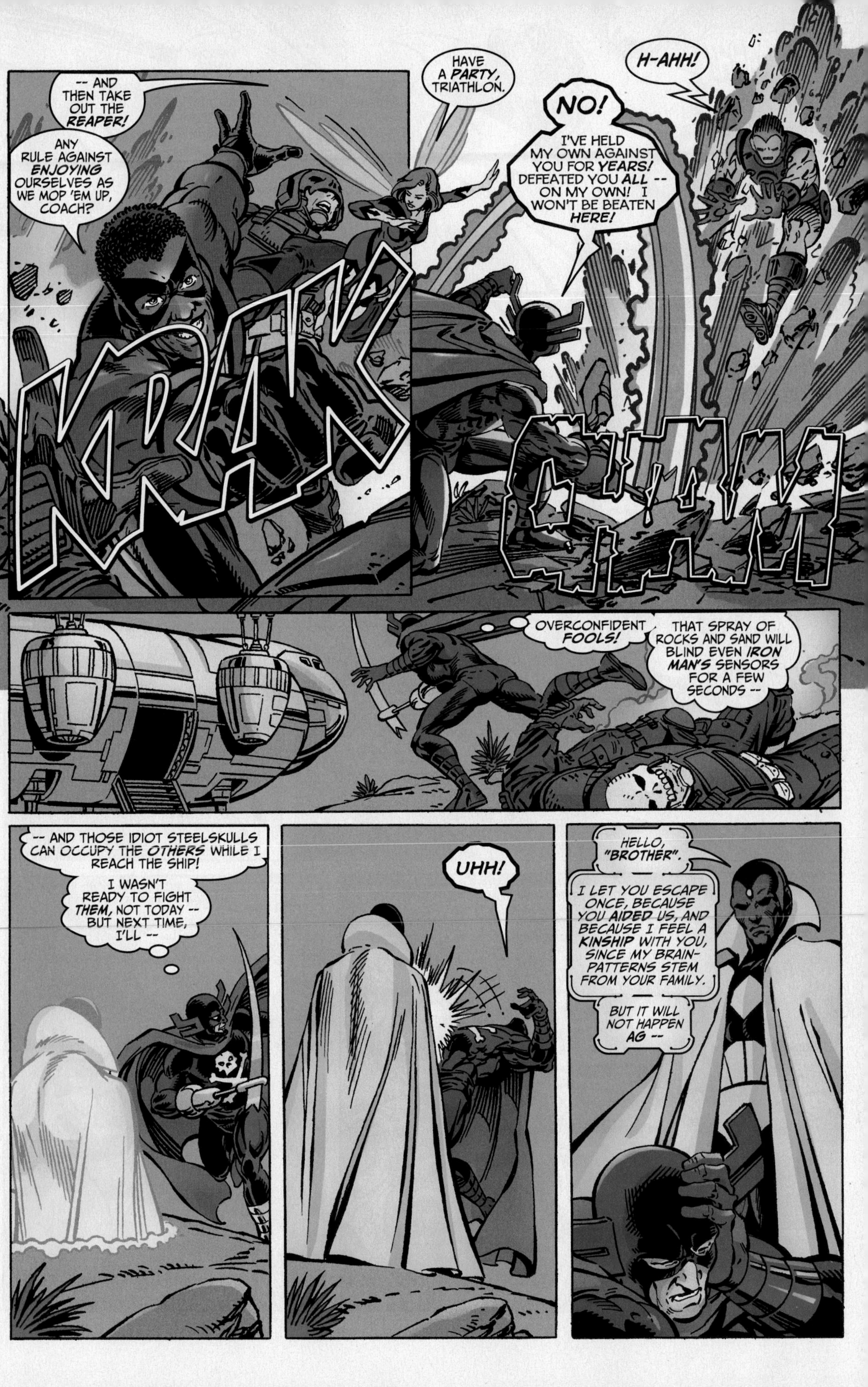
-- AND THEN TAKE OUT THE *REAPER!*
ANY RULE AGAINST *ENJOYING* OURSELVES AS WE MOP 'EM UP, COACH?
HAVE A *PARTY,* TRIATHLON.
KRAK
H-AHH!
NO!
I'VE HELD MY OWN AGAINST YOU FOR *YEARS!* DEFEATED YOU *ALL* -- ON MY OWN! I WON'T BE BEATEN *HERE!*
OVERCONFIDENT *FOOLS!*
THAT SPRAY OF ROCKS AND SAND WILL BLIND EVEN *IRON MAN'S* SENSORS FOR A FEW SECONDS --
-- AND THOSE IDIOT STEELSKULLS CAN OCCUPY THE *OTHERS* WHILE I REACH THE SHIP!
I WASN'T READY TO FIGHT *THEM,* NOT TODAY -- BUT NEXT TIME, I'LL --
UHH!
HELLO, "BROTHER".
I LET YOU ESCAPE ONCE, BECAUSE YOU *AIDED* US, AND BECAUSE I FEEL A *KINSHIP* WITH YOU, SINCE MY BRAIN-PATTERNS STEM FROM YOUR FAMILY.
BUT IT WILL NOT HAPPEN *AG* --

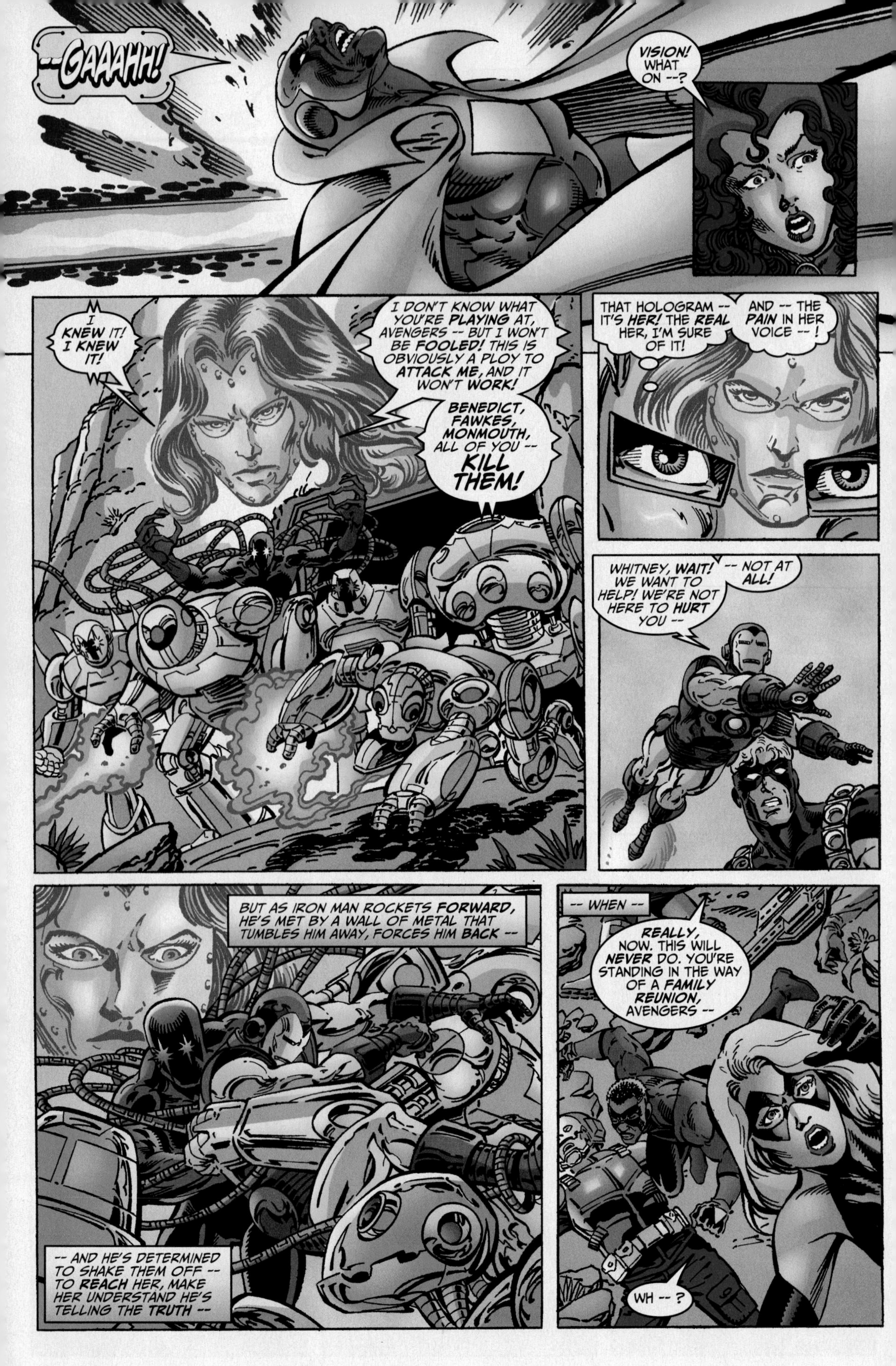
--GAAAHH!
VISION! WHAT ON --?
I KNEW IT! I KNEW IT!
I DON'T KNOW WHAT YOU'RE PLAYING AT, AVENGERS -- BUT I WON'T BE FOOLED! THIS IS OBVIOUSLY A PLOY TO ATTACK ME, AND IT WON'T WORK!
BENEDICT, FAWKES, MONMOUTH, ALL OF YOU -- KILL THEM!
THAT HOLOGRAM -- IT'S HER! THE REAL HER, I'M SURE OF IT!
AND -- THE PAIN IN HER VOICE -- !
WHITNEY, WAIT! WE WANT TO HELP! WE'RE NOT HERE TO HURT YOU --
-- NOT AT ALL!
BUT AS IRON MAN ROCKETS FORWARD, HE'S MET BY A WALL OF METAL THAT TUMBLES HIM AWAY, FORCES HIM BACK --
-- AND HE'S DETERMINED TO SHAKE THEM OFF -- TO REACH HER, MAKE HER UNDERSTAND HE'S TELLING THE TRUTH --
-- WHEN --
REALLY, NOW. THIS WILL NEVER DO. YOU'RE STANDING IN THE WAY OF A FAMILY REUNION, AVENGERS --
WH -- ?

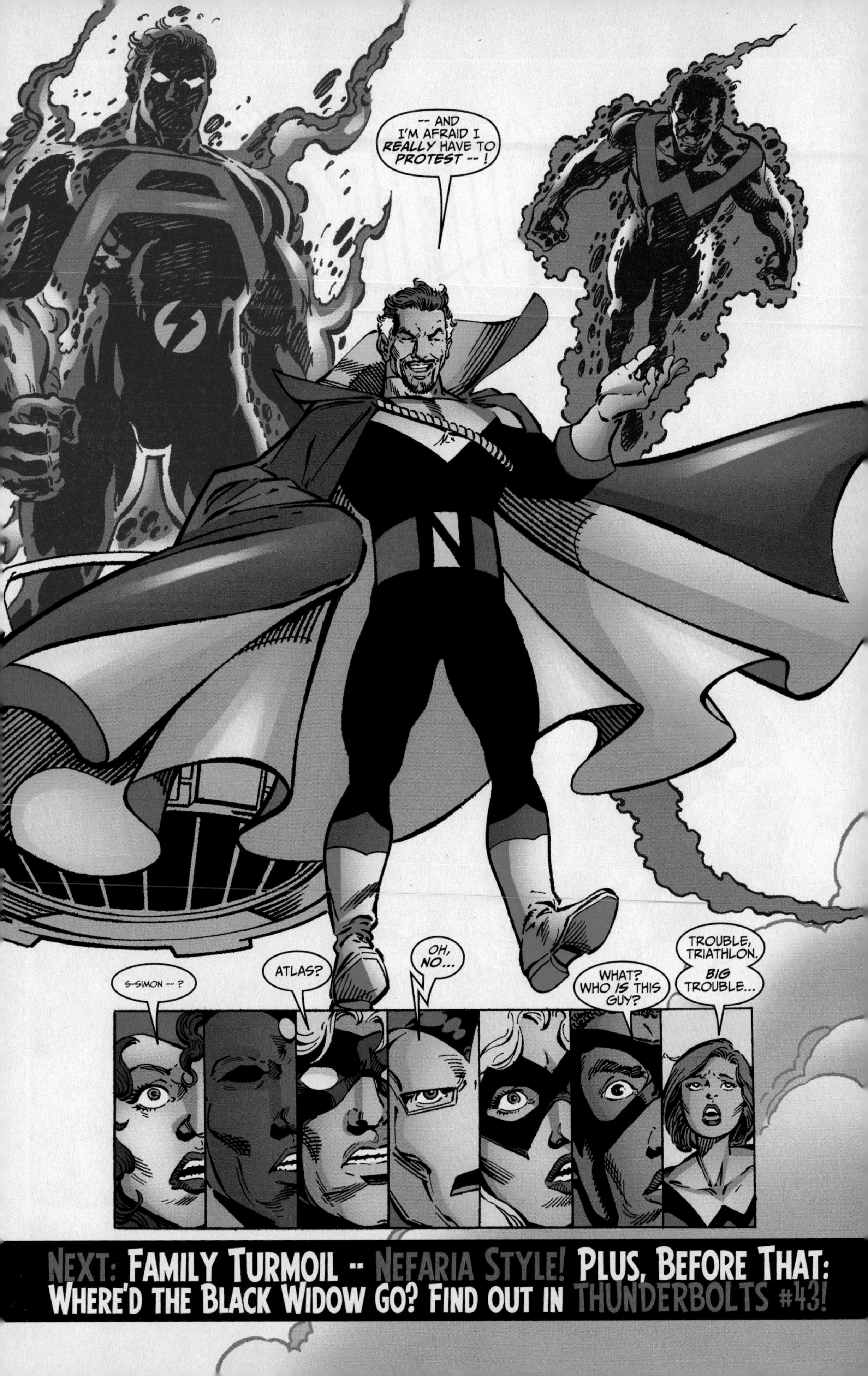
-- AND I'M AFRAID I REALLY HAVE TO PROTEST -- !
S-SIMON -- ?
ATLAS?
OH, NO...
WHAT? WHO IS THIS GUY?
TROUBLE, TRIATHLON. BIG TROUBLE...
NEXT: FAMILY TURMOIL -- NEFARIA STYLE! PLUS, BEFORE THAT: WHERE'D THE BLACK WIDOW GO? FIND OUT IN THUNDERBOLTS #43!

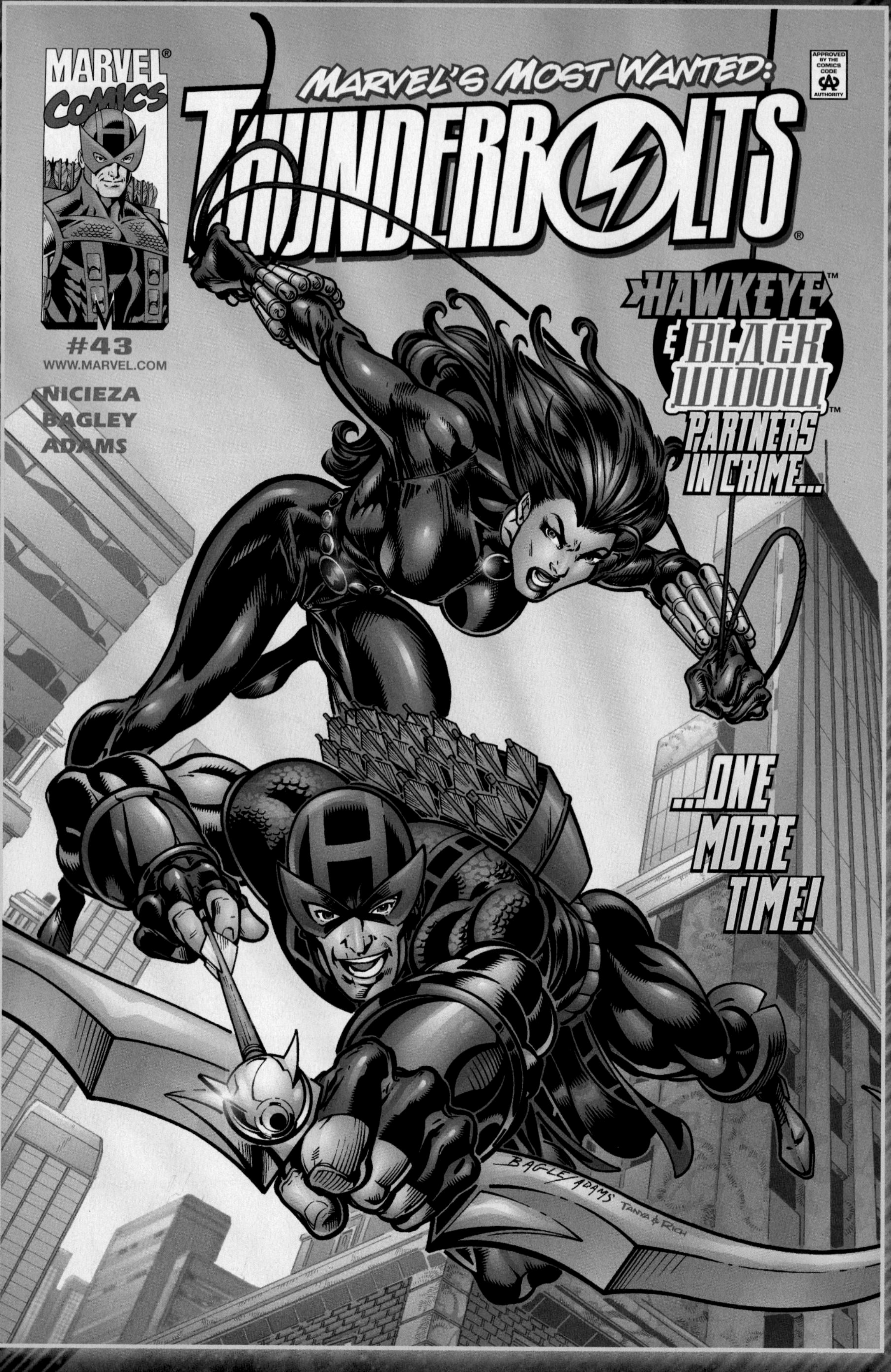
MARVEL COMICS
MARVEL'S MOST WANTED:
THUNDERBOLTS
APPROVED BY THE COMICS CODE AUTHORITY
#43
WWW.MARVEL.COM
NICIEZA
BAGLEY
ADAMS
HAWKEYE & BLACK WIDOW PARTNERS IN CRIME...
...ONE MORE TIME!
BAGLEY/ADAMS TANYA & RICH

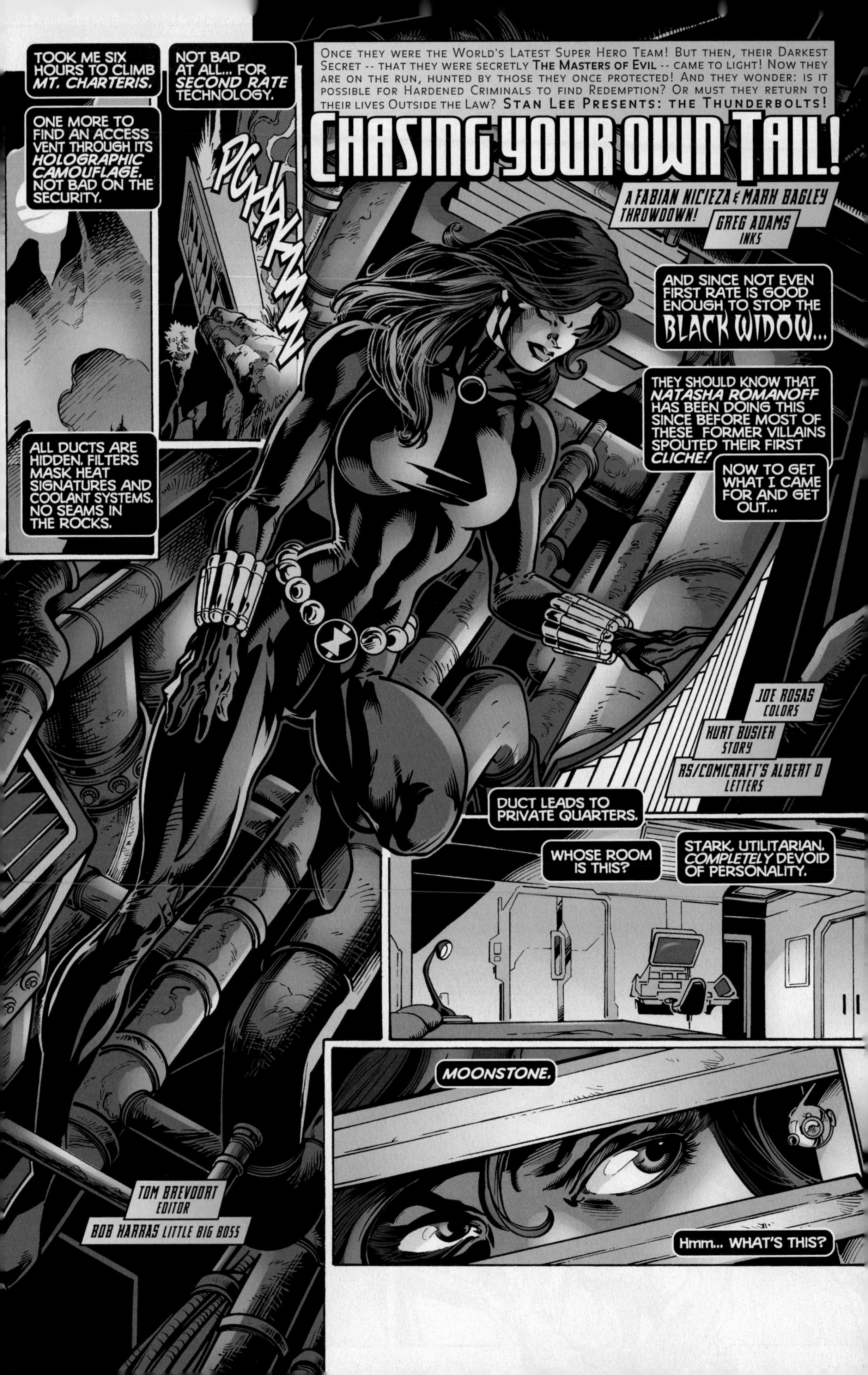

TOOK ME SIX HOURS TO CLIMB MT. CHARTERIS.
NOT BAD AT ALL... FOR SECOND RATE TECHNOLOGY.
ONCE THEY WERE THE WORLD'S LATEST SUPER HERO TEAM! BUT THEN, THEIR DARKEST SECRET -- THAT THEY WERE SECRETLY THE MASTERS OF EVIL -- CAME TO LIGHT! NOW THEY ARE ON THE RUN, HUNTED BY THOSE THEY ONCE PROTECTED! AND THEY WONDER: IS IT POSSIBLE FOR HARDENED CRIMINALS TO FIND REDEMPTION? OR MUST THEY RETURN TO THEIR LIVES OUTSIDE THE LAW? STAN LEE PRESENTS: THE THUNDERBOLTS!
CHASING YOUR OWN TAIL!
ONE MORE TO FIND AN ACCESS VENT THROUGH ITS HOLOGRAPHIC CAMOUFLAGE. NOT BAD ON THE SECURITY.
PCHAKAKMM
A FABIAN NICIEZA & MARK BAGLEY THROWDOWN!
GREG ADAMS INKS
AND SINCE NOT EVEN FIRST RATE IS GOOD ENOUGH TO STOP THE BLACK WIDOW...
THEY SHOULD KNOW THAT NATASHA ROMANOFF HAS BEEN DOING THIS SINCE BEFORE MOST OF THESE FORMER VILLAINS SPOUTED THEIR FIRST CLICHE!
NOW TO GET WHAT I CAME FOR AND GET OUT...
ALL DUCTS ARE HIDDEN. FILTERS MASK HEAT SIGNATURES AND COOLANT SYSTEMS. NO SEAMS IN THE ROCKS.
JOE ROSAS COLORS
KURT BUSIEK STORY
RS/COMICRAFT'S ALBERT D LETTERS
DUCT LEADS TO PRIVATE QUARTERS.
WHOSE ROOM IS THIS?
STARK. UTILITARIAN. COMPLETELY DEVOID OF PERSONALITY.
MOONSTONE.
TOM BREVOORT EDITOR
BOB HARRAS LITTLE BIG BOSS
Hmm... WHAT'S THIS?

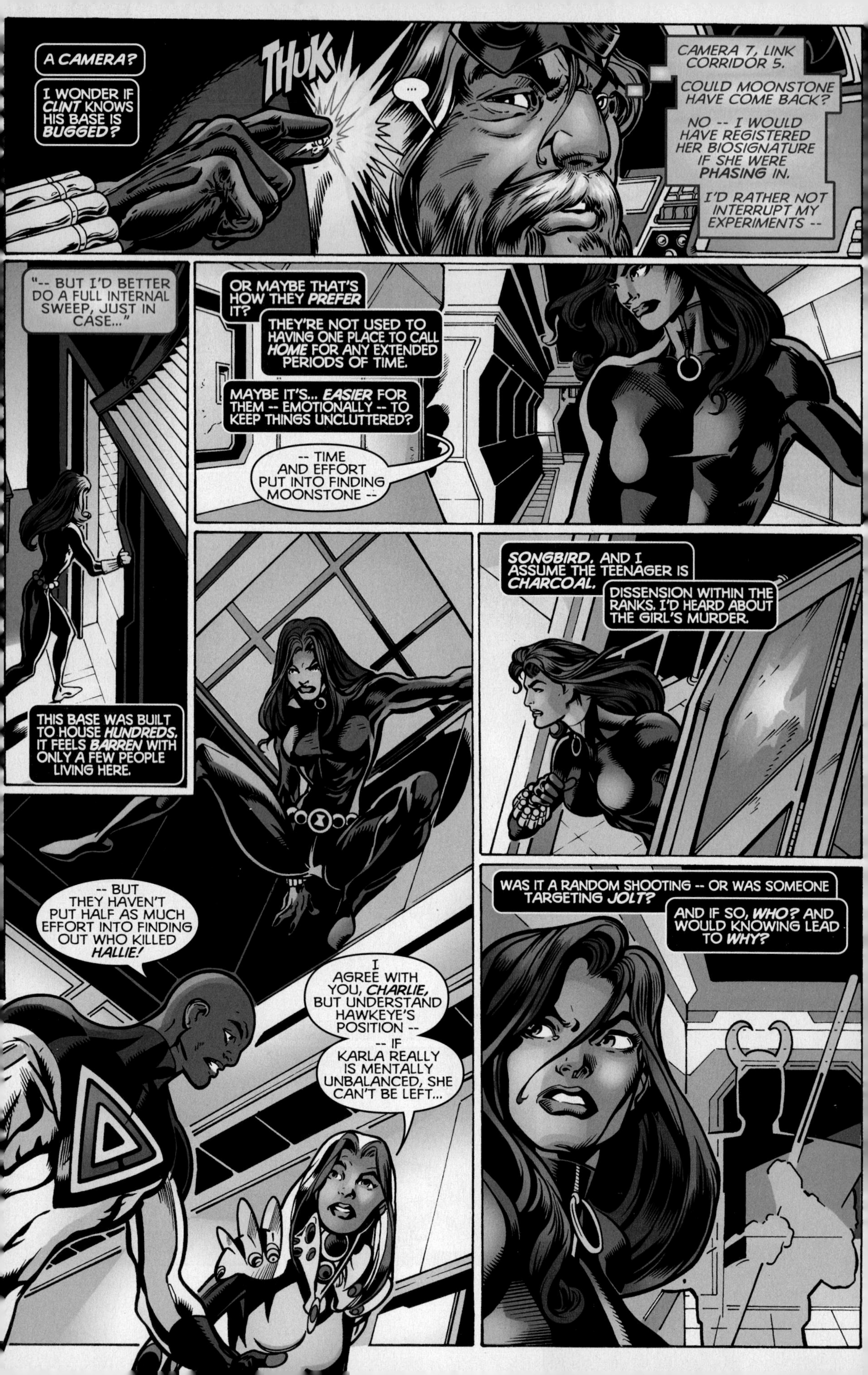
A CAMERA?
I WONDER IF CLINT KNOWS HIS BASE IS BUGGED?
THUK!
...
CAMERA 7, LINK CORRIDOR 5.
COULD MOONSTONE HAVE COME BACK?
NO -- I WOULD HAVE REGISTERED HER BIOSIGNATURE IF SHE WERE PHASING IN.
I'D RATHER NOT INTERRUPT MY EXPERIMENTS --
"-- BUT I'D BETTER DO A FULL INTERNAL SWEEP, JUST IN CASE..."
THIS BASE WAS BUILT TO HOUSE HUNDREDS. IT FEELS BARREN WITH ONLY A FEW PEOPLE LIVING HERE.
OR MAYBE THAT'S HOW THEY PREFER IT?
THEY'RE NOT USED TO HAVING ONE PLACE TO CALL HOME FOR ANY EXTENDED PERIODS OF TIME.
MAYBE IT'S... EASIER FOR THEM -- EMOTIONALLY -- TO KEEP THINGS UNCLUTTERED?
-- TIME AND EFFORT PUT INTO FINDING MOONSTONE --
SONGBIRD. AND I ASSUME THE TEENAGER IS CHARCOAL.
DISSENSION WITHIN THE RANKS. I'D HEARD ABOUT THE GIRL'S MURDER.
-- BUT THEY HAVEN'T PUT HALF AS MUCH EFFORT INTO FINDING OUT WHO KILLED HALLIE!
I AGREE WITH YOU, CHARLIE, BUT UNDERSTAND HAWKEYE'S POSITION --
-- IF KARLA REALLY IS MENTALLY UNBALANCED, SHE CAN'T BE LEFT...
WAS IT A RANDOM SHOOTING -- OR WAS SOMEONE TARGETING JOLT?
AND IF SO, WHO? AND WOULD KNOWING LEAD TO WHY?

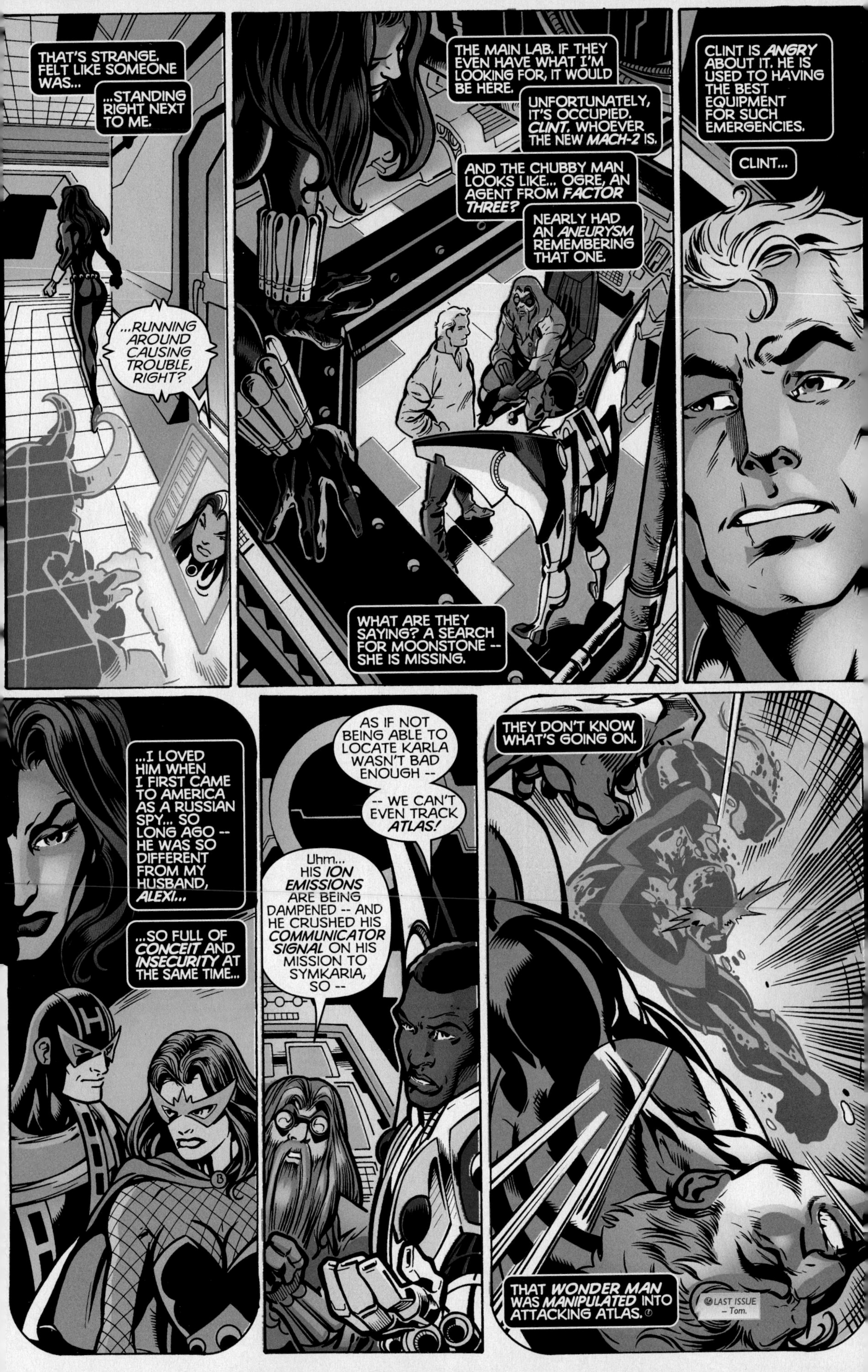

THAT'S STRANGE. FELT LIKE SOMEONE WAS...
...STANDING RIGHT NEXT TO ME.
...RUNNING AROUND CAUSING TROUBLE, RIGHT?
THE MAIN LAB. IF THEY EVEN HAVE WHAT I'M LOOKING FOR, IT WOULD BE HERE.
UNFORTUNATELY, IT'S OCCUPIED. *CLINT*. WHOEVER THE NEW *MACH-2* IS.
AND THE CHUBBY MAN LOOKS LIKE... OGRE, AN AGENT FROM *FACTOR THREE*?
NEARLY HAD AN *ANEURYSM* REMEMBERING THAT ONE.
WHAT ARE THEY SAYING? A SEARCH FOR MOONSTONE -- SHE IS MISSING.
CLINT IS *ANGRY* ABOUT IT. HE IS USED TO HAVING THE BEST EQUIPMENT FOR SUCH EMERGENCIES.
CLINT...
...I LOVED HIM WHEN I FIRST CAME TO AMERICA AS A RUSSIAN SPY... SO LONG AGO -- HE WAS SO DIFFERENT FROM MY HUSBAND, *ALEXI*...
...SO FULL OF *CONCEIT* AND *INSECURITY* AT THE SAME TIME...
AS IF NOT BEING ABLE TO LOCATE KARLA WASN'T BAD ENOUGH --
-- WE CAN'T EVEN TRACK *ATLAS!*
Uhm... HIS *ION EMISSIONS* ARE BEING DAMPENED -- AND HE CRUSHED HIS *COMMUNICATOR SIGNAL* ON HIS MISSION TO SYMKARIA, SO --
THEY DON'T KNOW WHAT'S GOING ON.
THAT *WONDER MAN* WAS *MANIPULATED* INTO ATTACKING ATLAS.
LAST ISSUE – Tom.

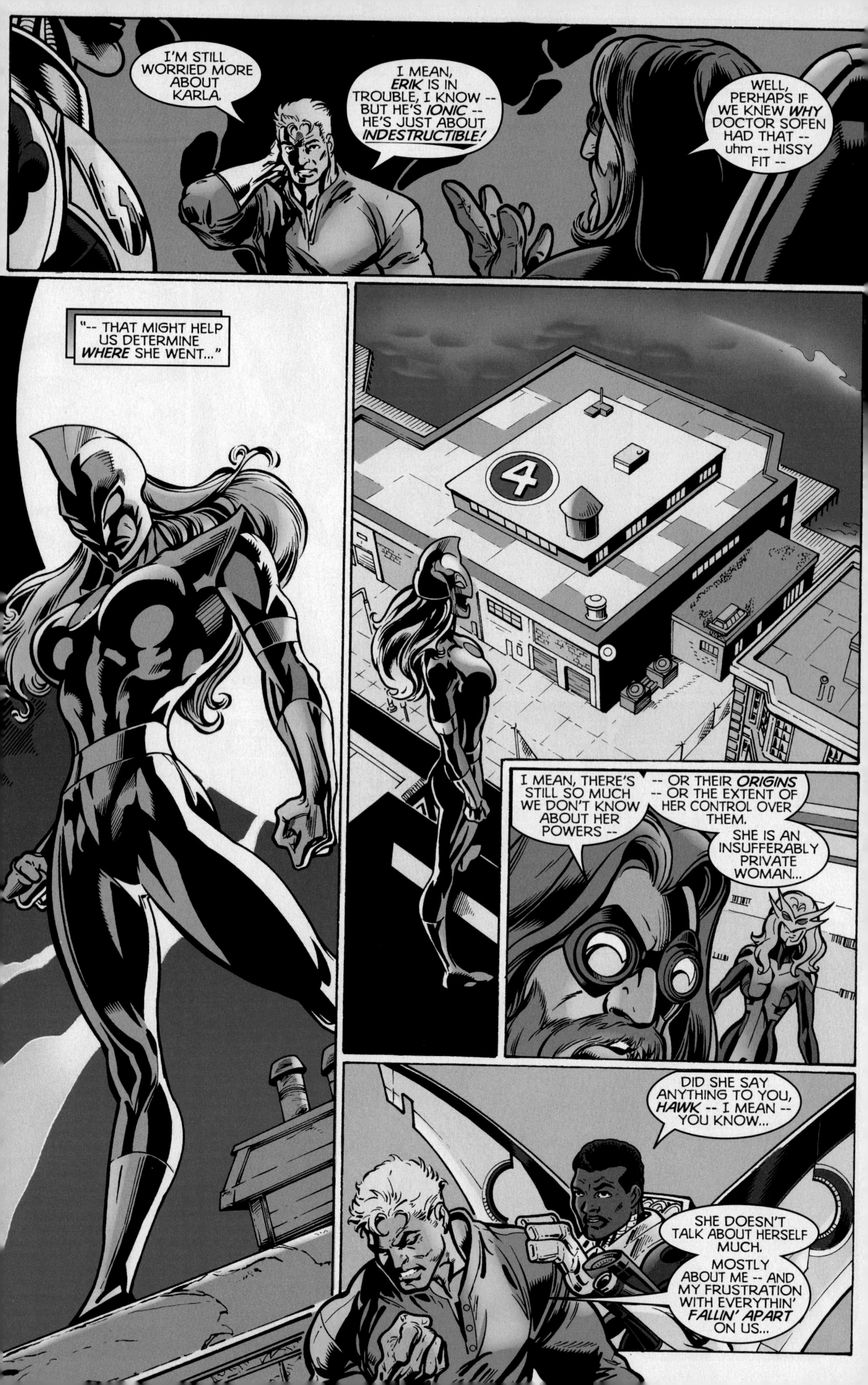
I'M STILL WORRIED MORE ABOUT KARLA.
I MEAN, ***ERIK*** IS IN TROUBLE, I KNOW -- BUT HE'S ***IONIC*** -- HE'S JUST ABOUT ***INDESTRUCTIBLE!***
WELL, PERHAPS IF WE KNEW ***WHY*** DOCTOR SOFEN HAD THAT -- uhm -- HISSY FIT --
"-- THAT MIGHT HELP US DETERMINE ***WHERE*** SHE WENT..."
I MEAN, THERE'S STILL SO MUCH WE DON'T KNOW ABOUT HER POWERS --
-- OR THEIR ***ORIGINS*** -- OR THE EXTENT OF HER CONTROL OVER THEM.
SHE IS AN INSUFFERABLY PRIVATE WOMAN...
DID SHE SAY ANYTHING TO YOU, ***HAWK*** -- I MEAN -- YOU KNOW...
SHE DOESN'T TALK ABOUT HERSELF MUCH.
MOSTLY ABOUT ME -- AND MY FRUSTRATION WITH EVERYTHIN' ***FALLIN' APART*** ON US...

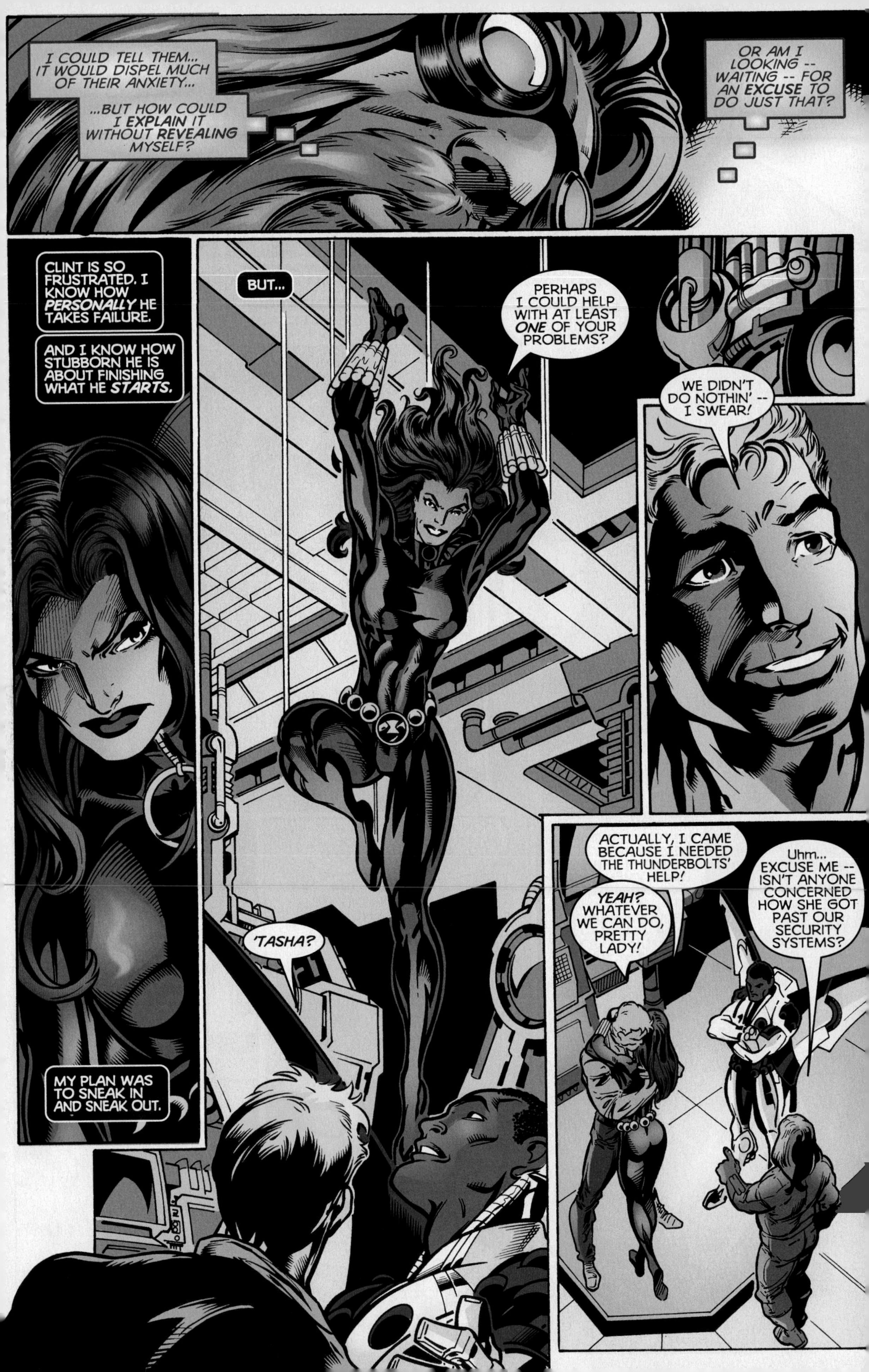
I COULD TELL THEM... IT WOULD DISPEL MUCH OF THEIR ANXIETY...
...BUT HOW COULD I EXPLAIN IT WITHOUT REVEALING MYSELF?
OR AM I LOOKING -- WAITING -- FOR AN EXCUSE TO DO JUST THAT?
CLINT IS SO FRUSTRATED. I KNOW HOW PERSONALLY HE TAKES FAILURE.
AND I KNOW HOW STUBBORN HE IS ABOUT FINISHING WHAT HE STARTS.
MY PLAN WAS TO SNEAK IN AND SNEAK OUT.
BUT...
PERHAPS I COULD HELP WITH AT LEAST ONE OF YOUR PROBLEMS?
'TASHA?
WE DIDN'T DO NOTHIN' -- I SWEAR!
ACTUALLY, I CAME BECAUSE I NEEDED THE THUNDERBOLTS' HELP!
YEAH? WHATEVER WE CAN DO, PRETTY LADY!
Uhm... EXCUSE ME -- ISN'T ANYONE CONCERNED HOW SHE GOT PAST OUR SECURITY SYSTEMS?

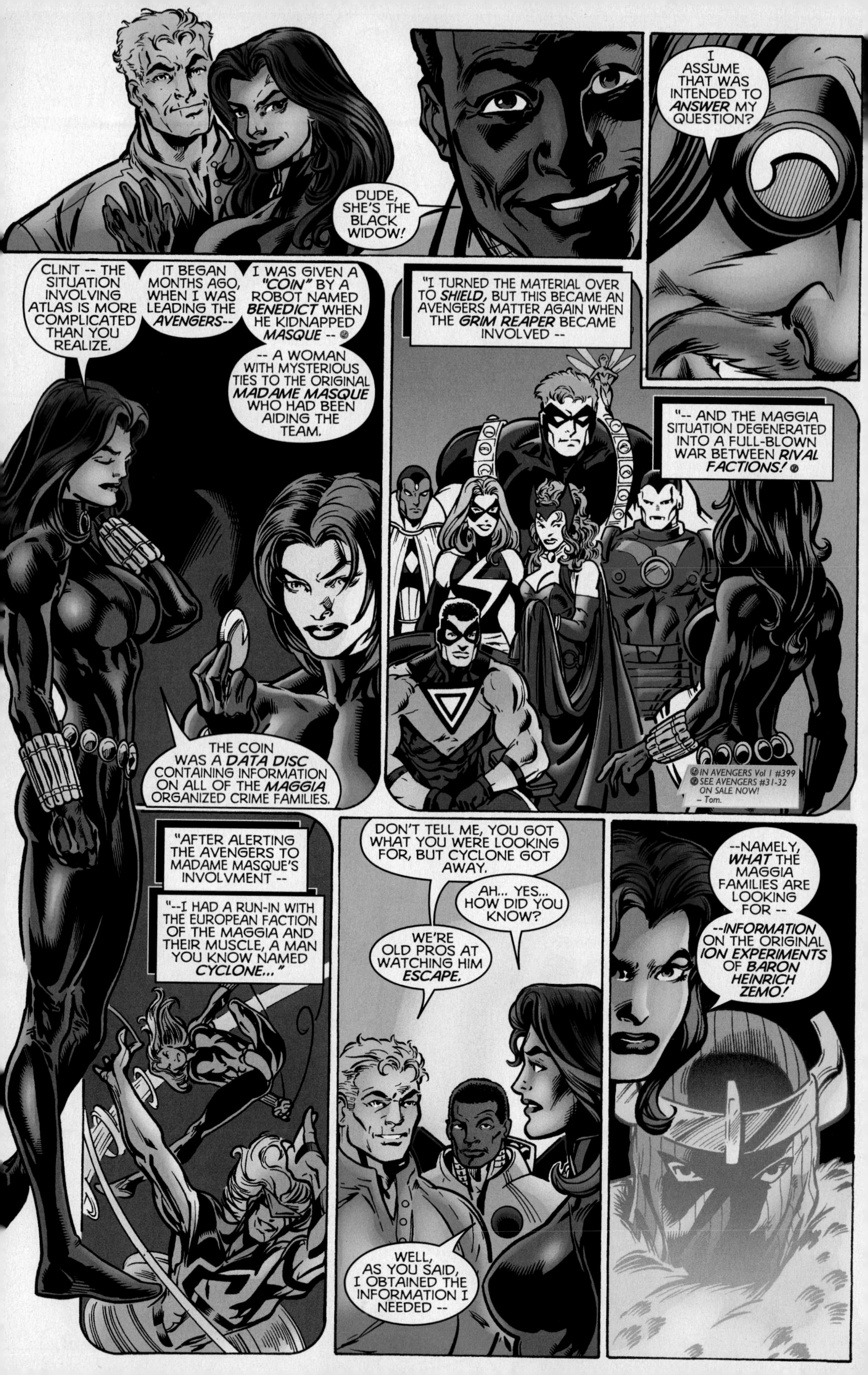

DUDE, SHE'S THE BLACK WIDOW!
I ASSUME THAT WAS INTENDED TO ANSWER MY QUESTION?
CLINT -- THE SITUATION INVOLVING ATLAS IS MORE COMPLICATED THAN YOU REALIZE.
IT BEGAN MONTHS AGO, WHEN I WAS LEADING THE AVENGERS--
I WAS GIVEN A "COIN" BY A ROBOT NAMED BENEDICT WHEN HE KIDNAPPED MASQUE --
-- A WOMAN WITH MYSTERIOUS TIES TO THE ORIGINAL MADAME MASQUE WHO HAD BEEN AIDING THE TEAM.
THE COIN WAS A DATA DISC CONTAINING INFORMATION ON ALL OF THE MAGGIA ORGANIZED CRIME FAMILIES.
"I TURNED THE MATERIAL OVER TO SHIELD, BUT THIS BECAME AN AVENGERS MATTER AGAIN WHEN THE GRIM REAPER BECAME INVOLVED --
"-- AND THE MAGGIA SITUATION DEGENERATED INTO A FULL-BLOWN WAR BETWEEN RIVAL FACTIONS!
IN AVENGERS Vol 1 #399
SEE AVENGERS #31-32 ON SALE NOW!
– Tom.
"AFTER ALERTING THE AVENGERS TO MADAME MASQUE'S INVOLVMENT --
"--I HAD A RUN-IN WITH THE EUROPEAN FACTION OF THE MAGGIA AND THEIR MUSCLE, A MAN YOU KNOW NAMED CYCLONE..."
DON'T TELL ME, YOU GOT WHAT YOU WERE LOOKING FOR, BUT CYCLONE GOT AWAY.
AH... YES... HOW DID YOU KNOW?
WE'RE OLD PROS AT WATCHING HIM ESCAPE.
WELL, AS YOU SAID, I OBTAINED THE INFORMATION I NEEDED --
--NAMELY, WHAT THE MAGGIA FAMILIES ARE LOOKING FOR --
--INFORMATION ON THE ORIGINAL ION EXPERIMENTS OF BARON HEINRICH ZEMO!

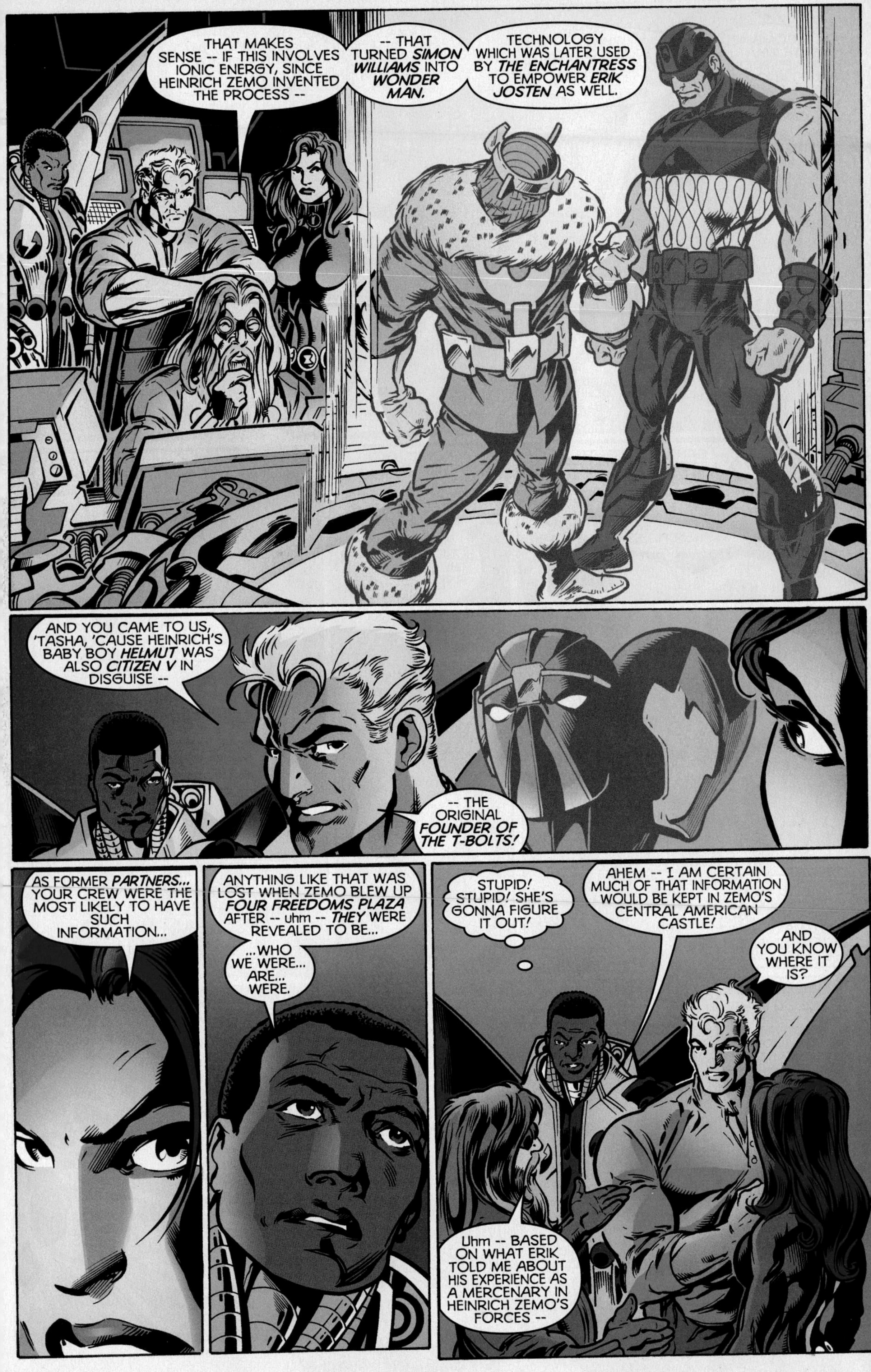
THAT MAKES SENSE -- IF THIS INVOLVES IONIC ENERGY, SINCE HEINRICH ZEMO INVENTED THE PROCESS --
-- THAT TURNED *SIMON WILLIAMS* INTO *WONDER MAN.*
TECHNOLOGY WHICH WAS LATER USED BY *THE ENCHANTRESS* TO EMPOWER *ERIK JOSTEN* AS WELL.
AND YOU CAME TO US, 'TASHA, 'CAUSE HEINRICH'S BABY BOY *HELMUT* WAS ALSO *CITIZEN V* IN DISGUISE --
-- THE ORIGINAL *FOUNDER OF THE T-BOLTS!*
AS FORMER *PARTNERS...* YOUR CREW WERE THE MOST LIKELY TO HAVE SUCH INFORMATION...
ANYTHING LIKE THAT WAS LOST WHEN ZEMO BLEW UP *FOUR FREEDOMS PLAZA* AFTER -- uhm -- *THEY* WERE REVEALED TO BE...
...WHO WE WERE... ARE... WERE.
STUPID! STUPID! SHE'S GONNA FIGURE IT OUT!
AHEM -- I AM CERTAIN MUCH OF THAT INFORMATION WOULD BE KEPT IN ZEMO'S CENTRAL AMERICAN CASTLE!
AND YOU KNOW WHERE IT IS?
Uhm -- BASED ON WHAT ERIK TOLD ME ABOUT HIS EXPERIENCE AS A MERCENARY IN HEINRICH ZEMO'S FORCES --

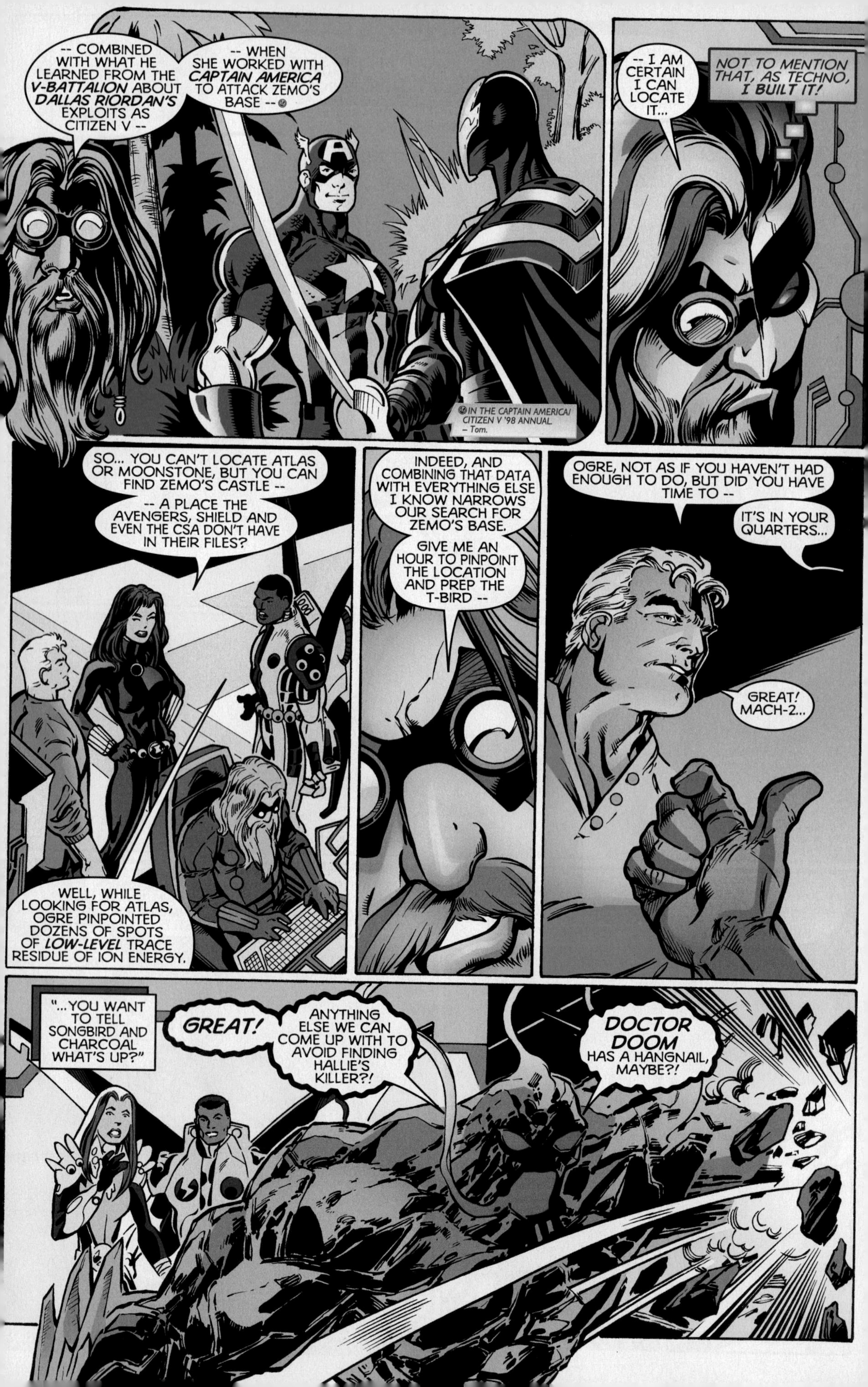
-- COMBINED WITH WHAT HE LEARNED FROM THE *V-BATTALION* ABOUT *DALLAS RIORDAN'S* EXPLOITS AS CITIZEN V --
-- WHEN SHE WORKED WITH *CAPTAIN AMERICA* TO ATTACK ZEMO'S BASE --
IN THE CAPTAIN AMERICA/ CITIZEN V '98 ANNUAL. – Tom.
-- I AM CERTAIN I CAN LOCATE IT...
NOT TO MENTION THAT, AS TECHNO, I BUILT IT!
SO... YOU CAN'T LOCATE ATLAS OR MOONSTONE, BUT YOU CAN FIND ZEMO'S CASTLE --
-- A PLACE THE AVENGERS, SHIELD AND EVEN THE CSA DON'T HAVE IN THEIR FILES?
WELL, WHILE LOOKING FOR ATLAS, OGRE PINPOINTED DOZENS OF SPOTS OF *LOW-LEVEL* TRACE RESIDUE OF ION ENERGY.
INDEED, AND COMBINING THAT DATA WITH EVERYTHING ELSE I KNOW NARROWS OUR SEARCH FOR ZEMO'S BASE.
GIVE ME AN HOUR TO PINPOINT THE LOCATION AND PREP THE T-BIRD --
OGRE, NOT AS IF YOU HAVEN'T HAD ENOUGH TO DO, BUT DID YOU HAVE TIME TO --
IT'S IN YOUR QUARTERS...
GREAT! MACH-2...
"...YOU WANT TO TELL SONGBIRD AND CHARCOAL WHAT'S UP?"
GREAT!
ANYTHING ELSE WE CAN COME UP WITH TO AVOID FINDING HALLIE'S KILLER?!
DOCTOR DOOM HAS A HANGNAIL, MAYBE?!

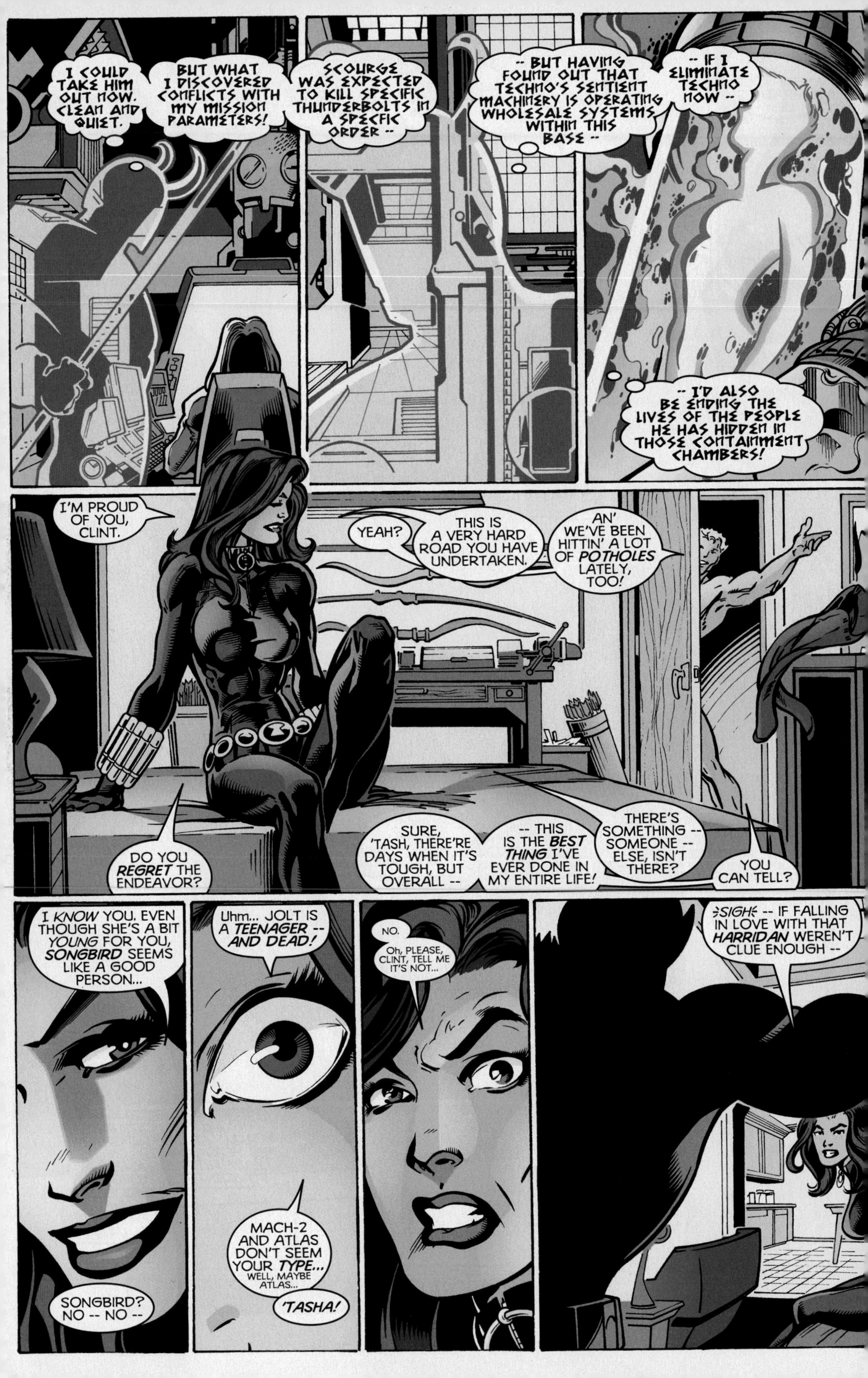
I COULD TAKE HIM OUT NOW. CLEAN AND QUIET.
BUT WHAT I DISCOVERED CONFLICTS WITH MY MISSION PARAMETERS!
SCOURGE WAS EXPECTED TO KILL SPECIFIC THUNDERBOLTS IN A SPECIFIC ORDER --
-- BUT HAVING FOUND OUT THAT TECHNO'S SENTIENT MACHINERY IS OPERATING WHOLESALE SYSTEMS WITHIN THIS BASE --
-- IF I ELIMINATE TECHNO NOW --
-- I'D ALSO BE ENDING THE LIVES OF THE PEOPLE HE HAS HIDDEN IN THOSE CONTAINMENT CHAMBERS!
I'M PROUD OF YOU, CLINT.
YEAH?
THIS IS A VERY HARD ROAD YOU HAVE UNDERTAKEN.
AN' WE'VE BEEN HITTIN' A LOT OF POTHOLES LATELY, TOO!
DO YOU REGRET THE ENDEAVOR?
SURE, 'TASH, THERE'RE DAYS WHEN IT'S TOUGH, BUT OVERALL --
-- THIS IS THE BEST THING I'VE EVER DONE IN MY ENTIRE LIFE!
THERE'S SOMETHING -- SOMEONE -- ELSE, ISN'T THERE?
YOU CAN TELL?
I KNOW YOU. EVEN THOUGH SHE'S A BIT YOUNG FOR YOU, SONGBIRD SEEMS LIKE A GOOD PERSON...
SONGBIRD? NO -- NO --
Uhm... JOLT IS A TEENAGER -- AND DEAD!
MACH-2 AND ATLAS DON'T SEEM YOUR TYPE... WELL, MAYBE ATLAS...
'TASHA!
NO.
Oh, PLEASE, CLINT, TELL ME IT'S NOT...
SIGH -- IF FALLING IN LOVE WITH THAT HARRIDAN WEREN'T CLUE ENOUGH --

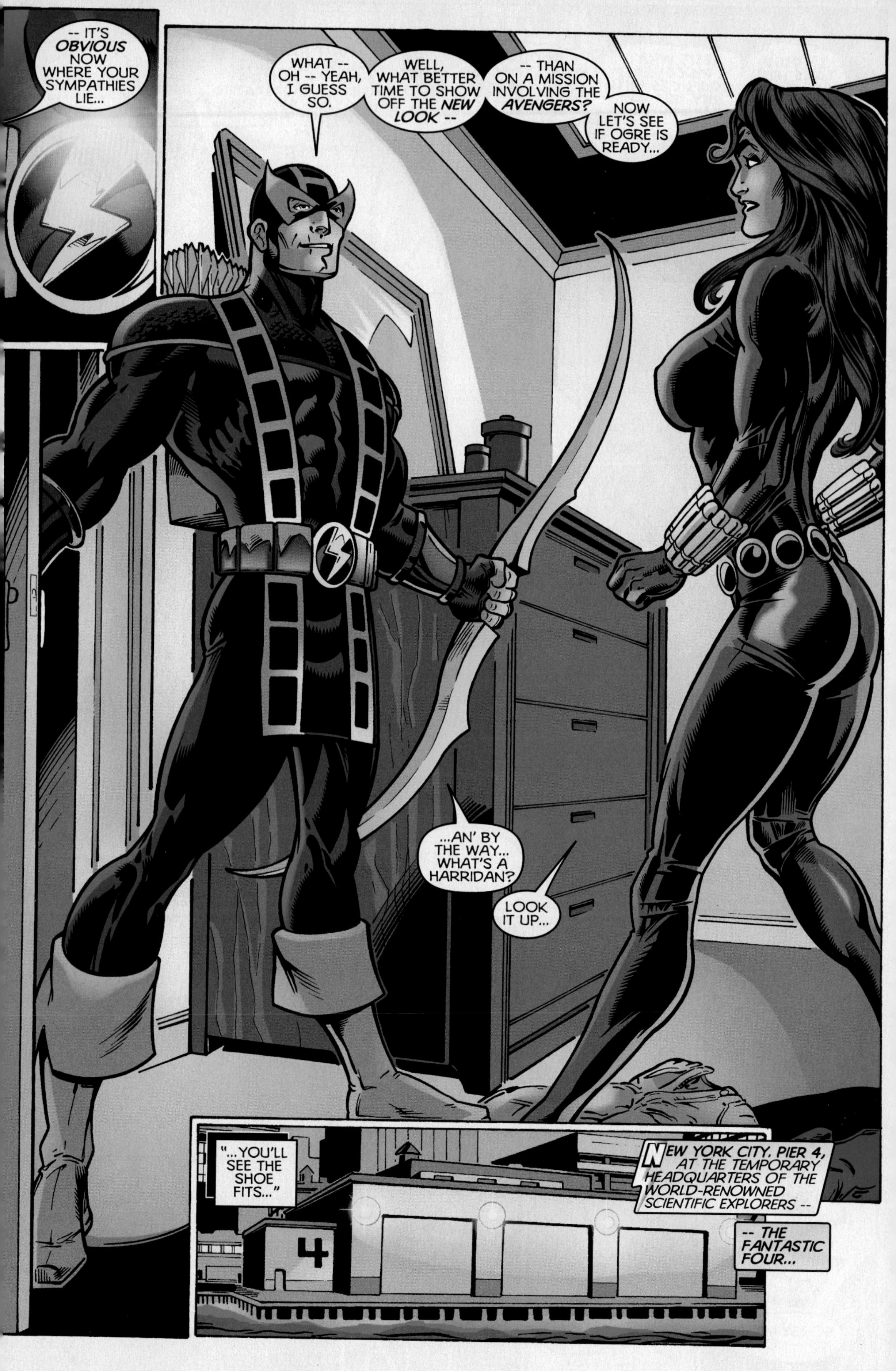

-- IT'S OBVIOUS NOW WHERE YOUR SYMPATHIES LIE...
WHAT -- OH -- YEAH, I GUESS SO.
WELL, WHAT BETTER TIME TO SHOW OFF THE NEW LOOK --
-- THAN ON A MISSION INVOLVING THE AVENGERS?
NOW LET'S SEE IF OGRE IS READY...
...AN' BY THE WAY... WHAT'S A HARRIDAN?
LOOK IT UP...
NEW YORK CITY, PIER 4, AT THE TEMPORARY HEADQUARTERS OF THE WORLD-RENOWNED SCIENTIFIC EXPLORERS --
-- THE FANTASTIC FOUR...
"...YOU'LL SEE THE SHOE FITS..."
4

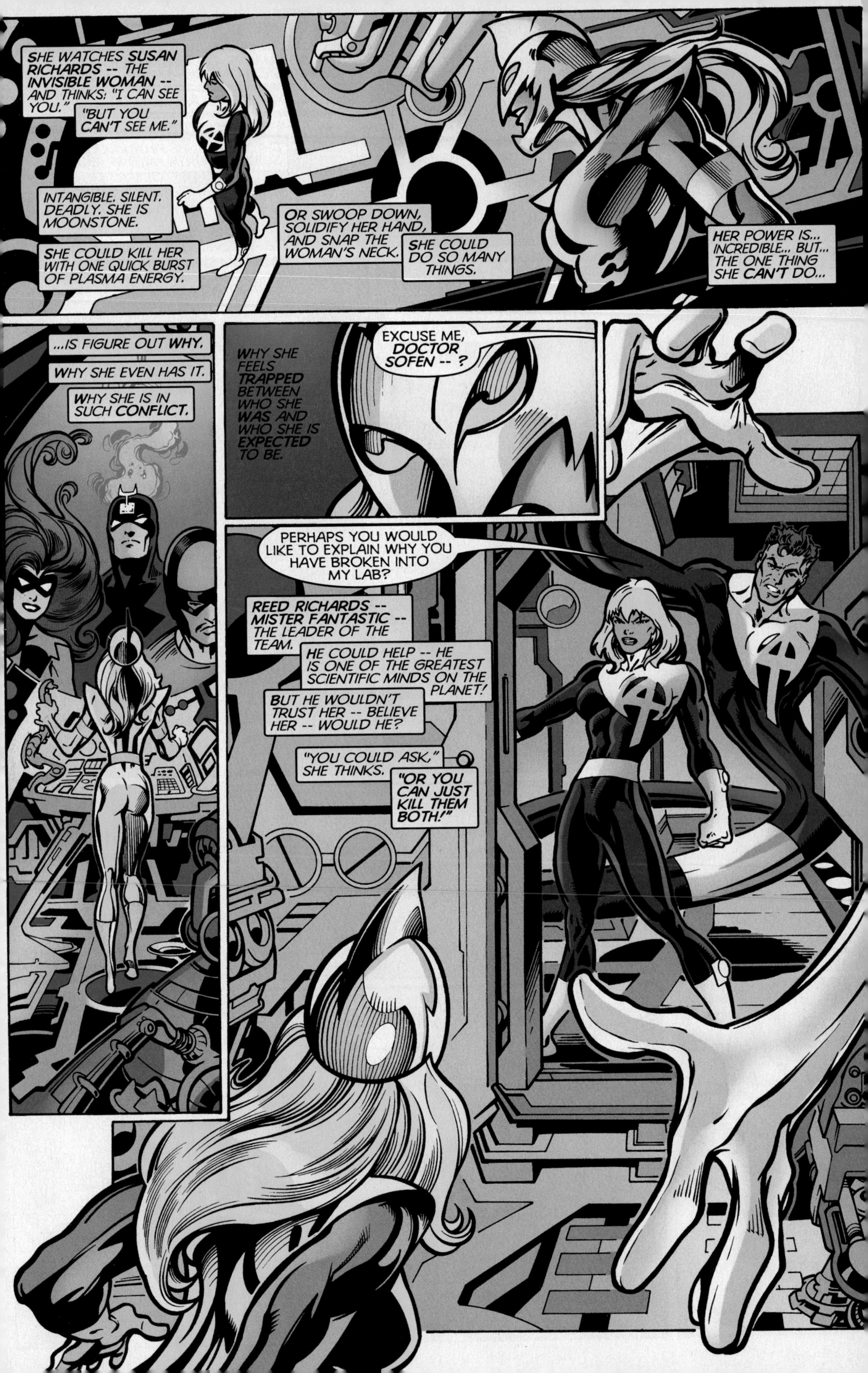

SHE WATCHES SUSAN RICHARDS -- THE INVISIBLE WOMAN -- AND THINKS: "I CAN SEE YOU."
"BUT YOU CAN'T SEE ME."
INTANGIBLE. SILENT. DEADLY. SHE IS MOONSTONE.
SHE COULD KILL HER WITH ONE QUICK BURST OF PLASMA ENERGY.
OR SWOOP DOWN, SOLIDIFY HER HAND, AND SNAP THE WOMAN'S NECK.
SHE COULD DO SO MANY THINGS.
HER POWER IS... INCREDIBLE... BUT... THE ONE THING SHE CAN'T DO...
...IS FIGURE OUT WHY.
WHY SHE EVEN HAS IT.
WHY SHE IS IN SUCH CONFLICT.
WHY SHE FEELS TRAPPED BETWEEN WHO SHE WAS AND WHO SHE IS EXPECTED TO BE.
EXCUSE ME, DOCTOR SOFEN -- ?
PERHAPS YOU WOULD LIKE TO EXPLAIN WHY YOU HAVE BROKEN INTO MY LAB?
REED RICHARDS -- MISTER FANTASTIC -- THE LEADER OF THE TEAM.
HE COULD HELP -- HE IS ONE OF THE GREATEST SCIENTIFIC MINDS ON THE PLANET!
BUT HE WOULDN'T TRUST HER -- BELIEVE HER -- WOULD HE?
"YOU COULD ASK," SHE THINKS.
"OR YOU CAN JUST KILL THEM BOTH!"

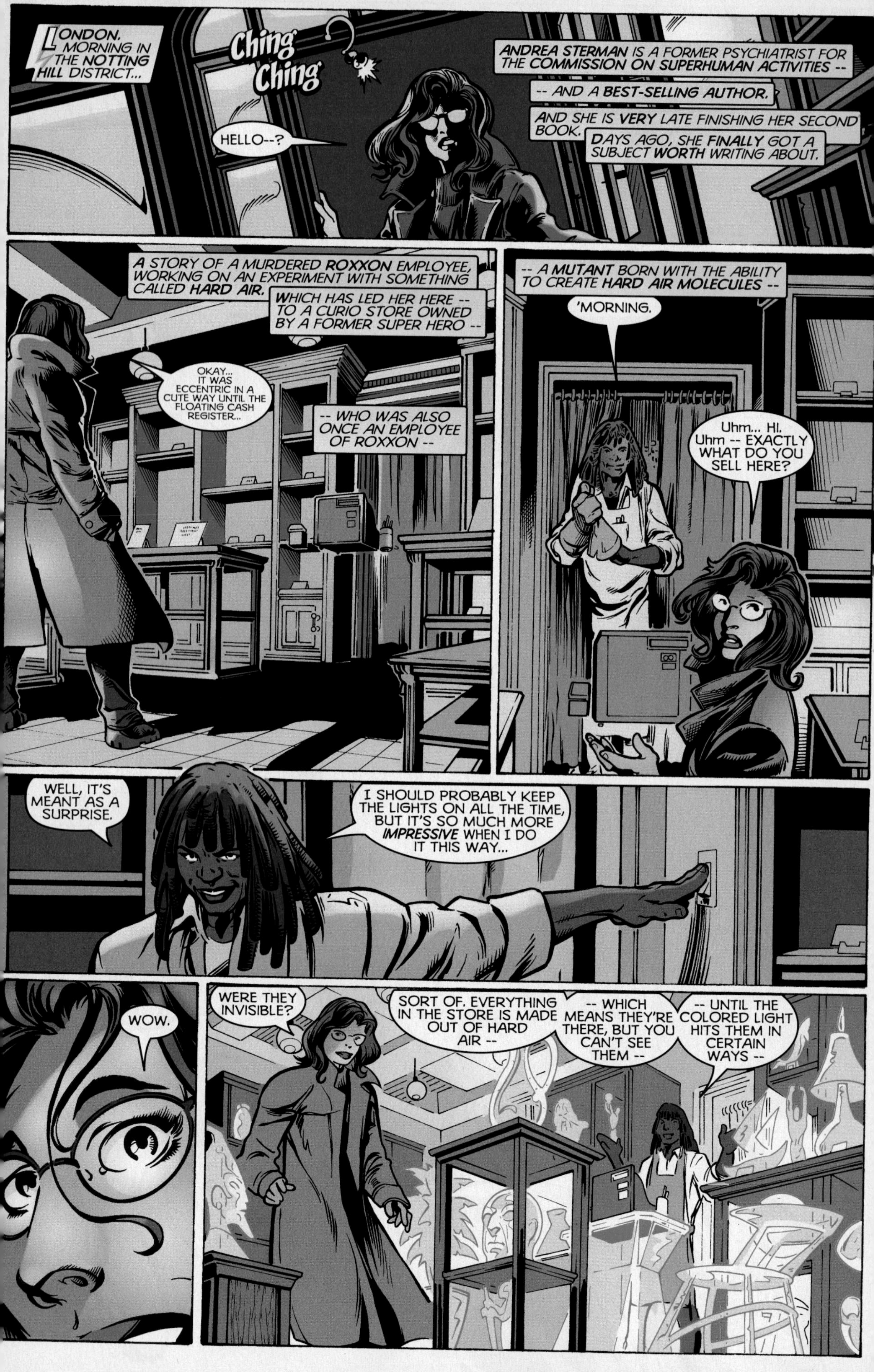
LONDON. MORNING IN THE NOTTING HILL DISTRICT...
Ching Ching
ANDREA STERMAN IS A FORMER PSYCHIATRIST FOR THE COMMISSION ON SUPERHUMAN ACTIVITIES --
-- AND A BEST-SELLING AUTHOR.
AND SHE IS VERY LATE FINISHING HER SECOND BOOK.
DAYS AGO, SHE FINALLY GOT A SUBJECT WORTH WRITING ABOUT.
HELLO--?
A STORY OF A MURDERED ROXXON EMPLOYEE, WORKING ON AN EXPERIMENT WITH SOMETHING CALLED HARD AIR.
WHICH HAS LED HER HERE -- TO A CURIO STORE OWNED BY A FORMER SUPER HERO --
OKAY... IT WAS ECCENTRIC IN A CUTE WAY UNTIL THE FLOATING CASH REGISTER...
-- WHO WAS ALSO ONCE AN EMPLOYEE OF ROXXON --
-- A MUTANT BORN WITH THE ABILITY TO CREATE HARD AIR MOLECULES --
'MORNING.
Uhm... HI. Uhm -- EXACTLY WHAT DO YOU SELL HERE?
WELL, IT'S MEANT AS A SURPRISE.
I SHOULD PROBABLY KEEP THE LIGHTS ON ALL THE TIME, BUT IT'S SO MUCH MORE IMPRESSIVE WHEN I DO IT THIS WAY...
WOW.
WERE THEY INVISIBLE?
SORT OF. EVERYTHING IN THE STORE IS MADE OUT OF HARD AIR --
-- WHICH MEANS THEY'RE THERE, BUT YOU CAN'T SEE THEM --
-- UNTIL THE COLORED LIGHT HITS THEM IN CERTAIN WAYS --

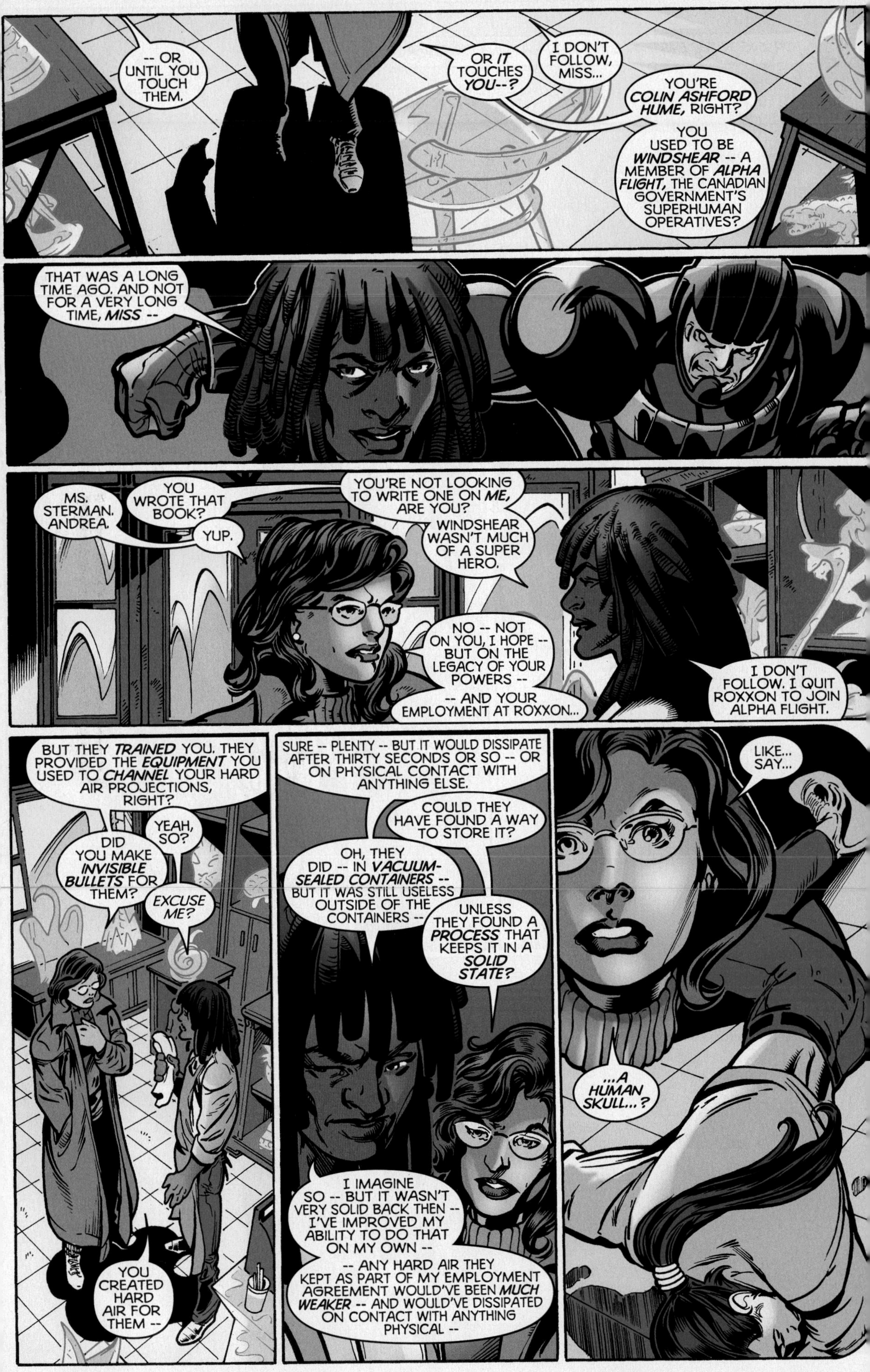
-- OR UNTIL YOU TOUCH THEM.
OR *IT* TOUCHES *YOU*--?
I DON'T FOLLOW, MISS...
YOU'RE *COLIN ASHFORD HUME,* RIGHT?
YOU USED TO BE *WINDSHEAR* -- A MEMBER OF *ALPHA FLIGHT,* THE CANADIAN GOVERNMENT'S SUPERHUMAN OPERATIVES?
THAT WAS A LONG TIME AGO. AND NOT FOR A VERY LONG TIME, *MISS* --
MS. STERMAN. ANDREA.
YOU WROTE THAT BOOK?
YUP.
YOU'RE NOT LOOKING TO WRITE ONE ON *ME,* ARE YOU?
WINDSHEAR WASN'T MUCH OF A SUPER HERO.
NO -- NOT ON YOU, I HOPE -- BUT ON THE LEGACY OF YOUR POWERS --
-- AND YOUR EMPLOYMENT AT ROXXON...
I DON'T FOLLOW. I QUIT ROXXON TO JOIN ALPHA FLIGHT.
BUT THEY *TRAINED* YOU. THEY PROVIDED THE *EQUIPMENT* YOU USED TO *CHANNEL* YOUR HARD AIR PROJECTIONS, RIGHT?
YEAH, SO?
DID YOU MAKE *INVISIBLE BULLETS* FOR THEM?
EXCUSE ME?
YOU CREATED HARD AIR FOR THEM --
SURE -- PLENTY -- BUT IT WOULD DISSIPATE AFTER THIRTY SECONDS OR SO -- OR ON PHYSICAL CONTACT WITH ANYTHING ELSE.
COULD THEY HAVE FOUND A WAY TO STORE IT?
OH, THEY DID -- IN *VACUUM-SEALED CONTAINERS* -- BUT IT WAS STILL USELESS OUTSIDE OF THE CONTAINERS --
UNLESS THEY FOUND A *PROCESS* THAT KEEPS IT IN A *SOLID STATE?*
I IMAGINE SO -- BUT IT WASN'T VERY SOLID BACK THEN -- I'VE IMPROVED MY ABILITY TO DO THAT ON MY OWN --
-- ANY HARD AIR THEY KEPT AS PART OF MY EMPLOYMENT AGREEMENT WOULD'VE BEEN *MUCH WEAKER* -- AND WOULD'VE DISSIPATED ON CONTACT WITH ANYTHING PHYSICAL --
LIKE... SAY...
...A *HUMAN SKULL*...?

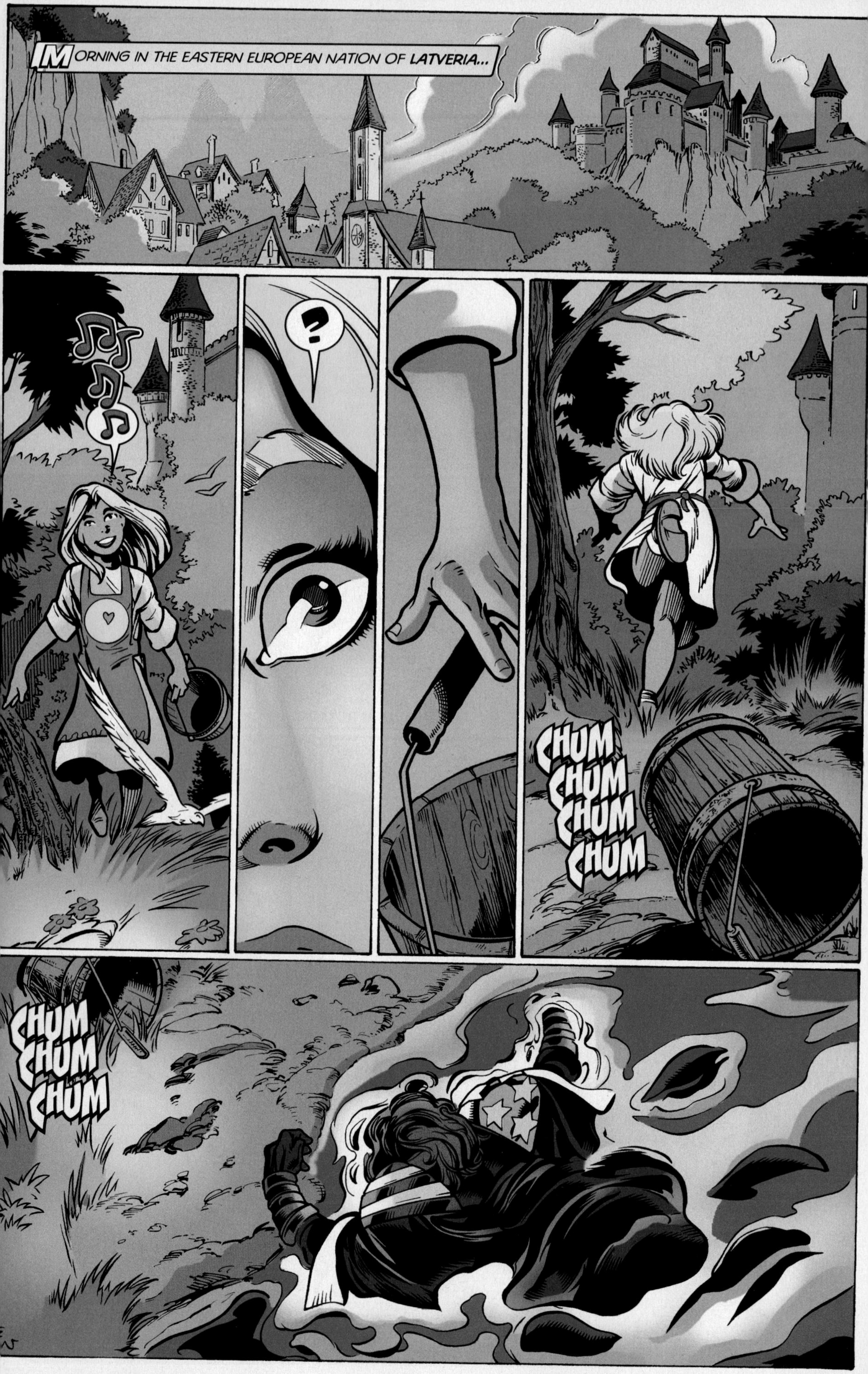
MORNING IN THE EASTERN EUROPEAN NATION OF LATVERIA...
?
CHUM CHUM CHUM CHUM
CHUM CHUM CHUM

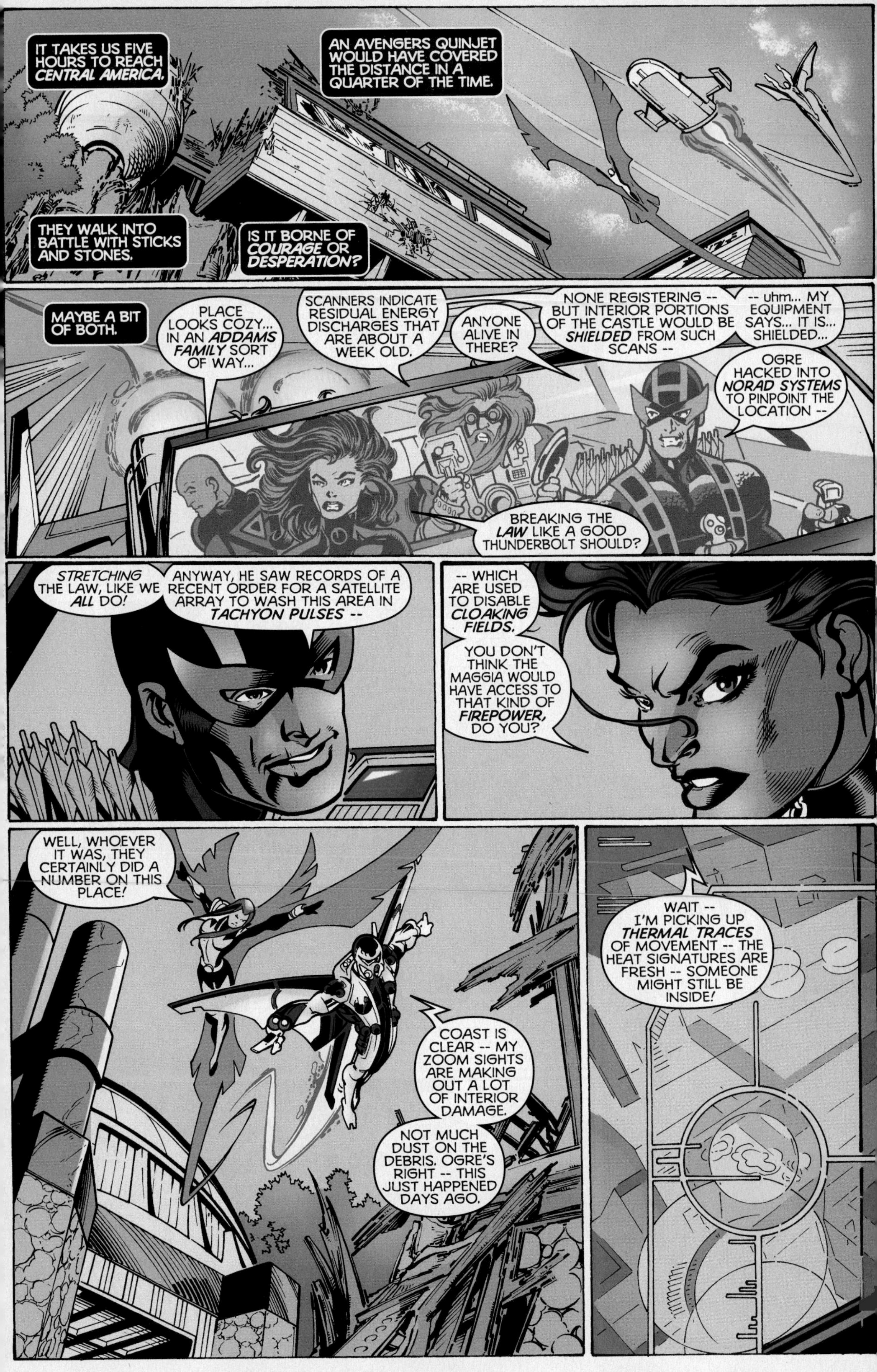
IT TAKES US FIVE HOURS TO REACH *CENTRAL AMERICA.*
AN AVENGERS QUINJET WOULD HAVE COVERED THE DISTANCE IN A QUARTER OF THE TIME.
THEY WALK INTO BATTLE WITH STICKS AND STONES.
IS IT BORNE OF *COURAGE* OR *DESPERATION?*
MAYBE A BIT OF BOTH.
PLACE LOOKS COZY... IN AN *ADDAMS FAMILY* SORT OF WAY...
SCANNERS INDICATE RESIDUAL ENERGY DISCHARGES THAT ARE ABOUT A WEEK OLD.
ANYONE ALIVE IN THERE?
NONE REGISTERING -- BUT INTERIOR PORTIONS OF THE CASTLE WOULD BE *SHIELDED* FROM SUCH SCANS --
-- uhm... MY EQUIPMENT SAYS... IT IS... SHIELDED...
OGRE HACKED INTO *NORAD SYSTEMS* TO PINPOINT THE LOCATION --
BREAKING THE *LAW* LIKE A GOOD THUNDERBOLT SHOULD?
STRETCHING THE LAW, LIKE WE *ALL* DO!
ANYWAY, HE SAW RECORDS OF A RECENT ORDER FOR A SATELLITE ARRAY TO WASH THIS AREA IN *TACHYON PULSES* --
-- WHICH ARE USED TO DISABLE *CLOAKING FIELDS.*
YOU DON'T THINK THE MAGGIA WOULD HAVE ACCESS TO THAT KIND OF *FIREPOWER,* DO YOU?
WELL, WHOEVER IT WAS, THEY CERTAINLY DID A NUMBER ON THIS PLACE!
COAST IS CLEAR -- MY ZOOM SIGHTS ARE MAKING OUT A LOT OF INTERIOR DAMAGE.
NOT MUCH DUST ON THE DEBRIS. OGRE'S RIGHT -- THIS JUST HAPPENED DAYS AGO.
WAIT -- I'M PICKING UP *THERMAL TRACES* OF MOVEMENT -- THE HEAT SIGNATURES ARE FRESH -- SOMEONE MIGHT STILL BE INSIDE!

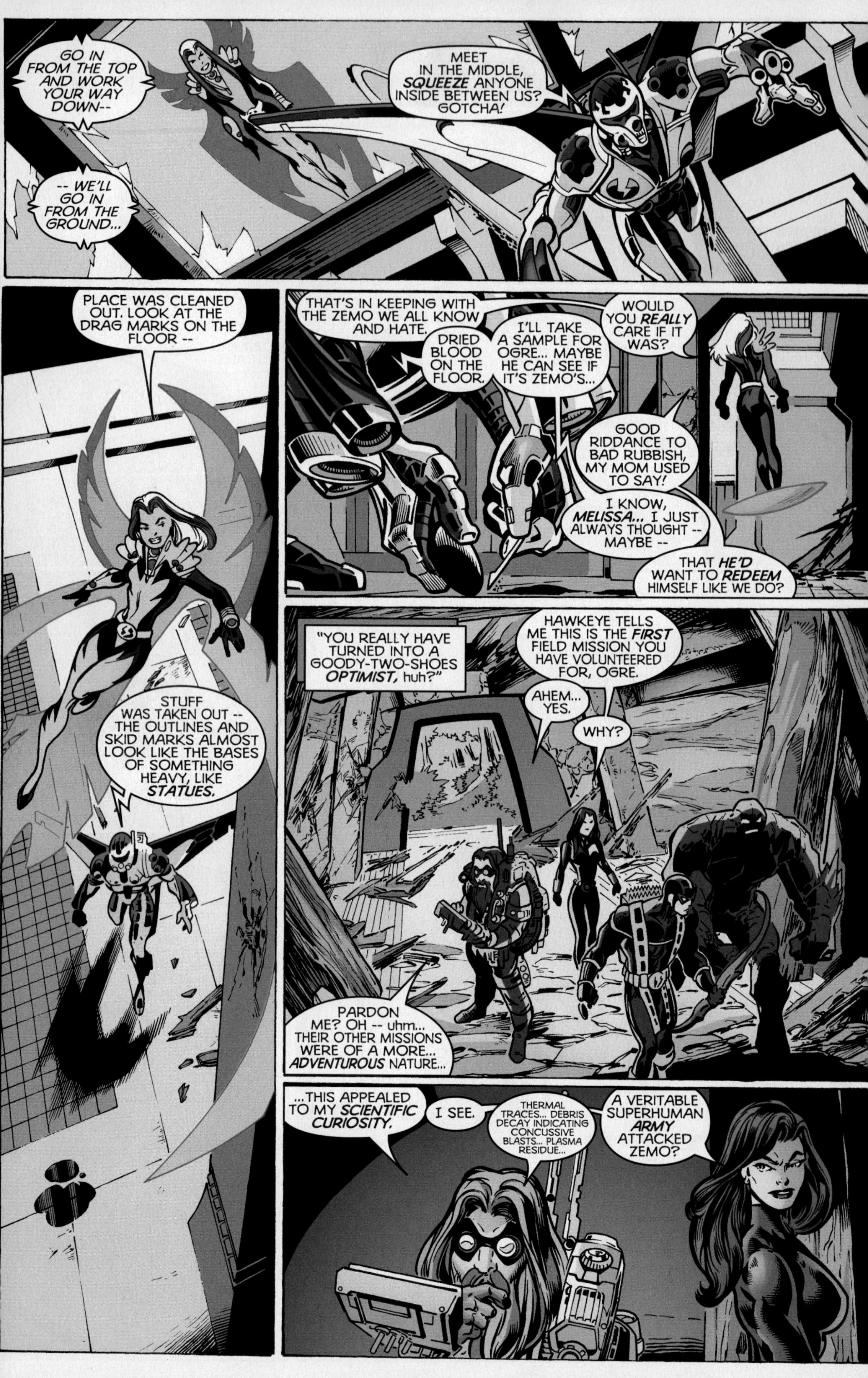
GO IN FROM THE TOP AND WORK YOUR WAY DOWN--
MEET IN THE MIDDLE, SQUEEZE ANYONE INSIDE BETWEEN US? GOTCHA!
-- WE'LL GO IN FROM THE GROUND...
PLACE WAS CLEANED OUT. LOOK AT THE DRAG MARKS ON THE FLOOR --
STUFF WAS TAKEN OUT -- THE OUTLINES AND SKID MARKS ALMOST LOOK LIKE THE BASES OF SOMETHING HEAVY, LIKE STATUES.
THAT'S IN KEEPING WITH THE ZEMO WE ALL KNOW AND HATE.
DRIED BLOOD ON THE FLOOR.
I'LL TAKE A SAMPLE FOR OGRE... MAYBE HE CAN SEE IF IT'S ZEMO'S...
WOULD YOU REALLY CARE IF IT WAS?
GOOD RIDDANCE TO BAD RUBBISH, MY MOM USED TO SAY!
I KNOW, MELISSA... I JUST ALWAYS THOUGHT -- MAYBE --
THAT HE'D WANT TO REDEEM HIMSELF LIKE WE DO?
"YOU REALLY HAVE TURNED INTO A GOODY-TWO-SHOES OPTIMIST, huh?"
HAWKEYE TELLS ME THIS IS THE FIRST FIELD MISSION YOU HAVE VOLUNTEERED FOR, OGRE.
AHEM... YES.
WHY?
PARDON ME? OH -- uhm... THEIR OTHER MISSIONS WERE OF A MORE... ADVENTUROUS NATURE...
...THIS APPEALED TO MY SCIENTIFIC CURIOSITY.
I SEE.
THERMAL TRACES... DEBRIS DECAY INDICATING CONCUSSIVE BLASTS... PLASMA RESIDUE...
A VERITABLE SUPERHUMAN ARMY ATTACKED ZEMO?

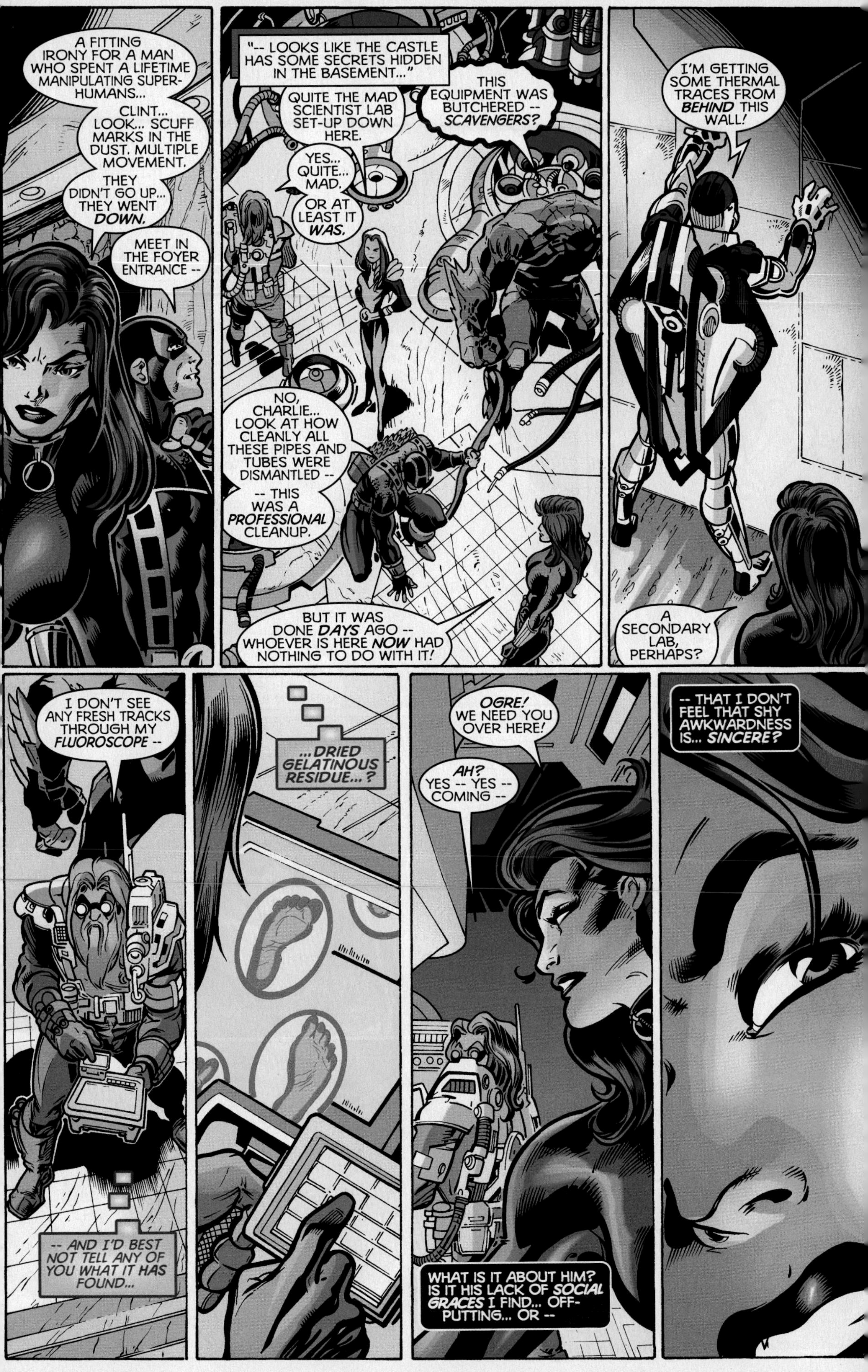
A FITTING IRONY FOR A MAN WHO SPENT A LIFETIME MANIPULATING SUPER-HUMANS...
CLINT... LOOK... SCUFF MARKS IN THE DUST. MULTIPLE MOVEMENT.
THEY DIDN'T GO UP... THEY WENT *DOWN.*
MEET IN THE FOYER ENTRANCE --
"-- LOOKS LIKE THE CASTLE HAS SOME SECRETS HIDDEN IN THE BASEMENT..."
QUITE THE MAD SCIENTIST LAB SET-UP DOWN HERE.
YES... QUITE... MAD.
OR AT LEAST IT *WAS.*
THIS EQUIPMENT WAS BUTCHERED -- *SCAVENGERS?*
NO, CHARLIE... LOOK AT HOW CLEANLY ALL THESE PIPES AND TUBES WERE DISMANTLED --
-- THIS WAS A *PROFESSIONAL* CLEANUP.
BUT IT WAS DONE *DAYS* AGO -- WHOEVER IS HERE *NOW* HAD NOTHING TO DO WITH IT!
I'M GETTING SOME THERMAL TRACES FROM *BEHIND* THIS WALL!
A SECONDARY LAB, PERHAPS?
I DON'T SEE ANY FRESH TRACKS THROUGH MY *FLUOROSCOPE* --
-- AND I'D BEST NOT TELL ANY OF YOU WHAT IT *HAS* FOUND...
...DRIED GELATINOUS RESIDUE...?
OGRE! WE NEED YOU OVER HERE!
AH? YES -- YES -- COMING --
WHAT IS IT ABOUT HIM? IS IT HIS LACK OF *SOCIAL GRACES* I FIND... OFF-PUTTING... OR --
-- THAT I DON'T FEEL THAT SHY AWKWARDNESS IS... *SINCERE?*

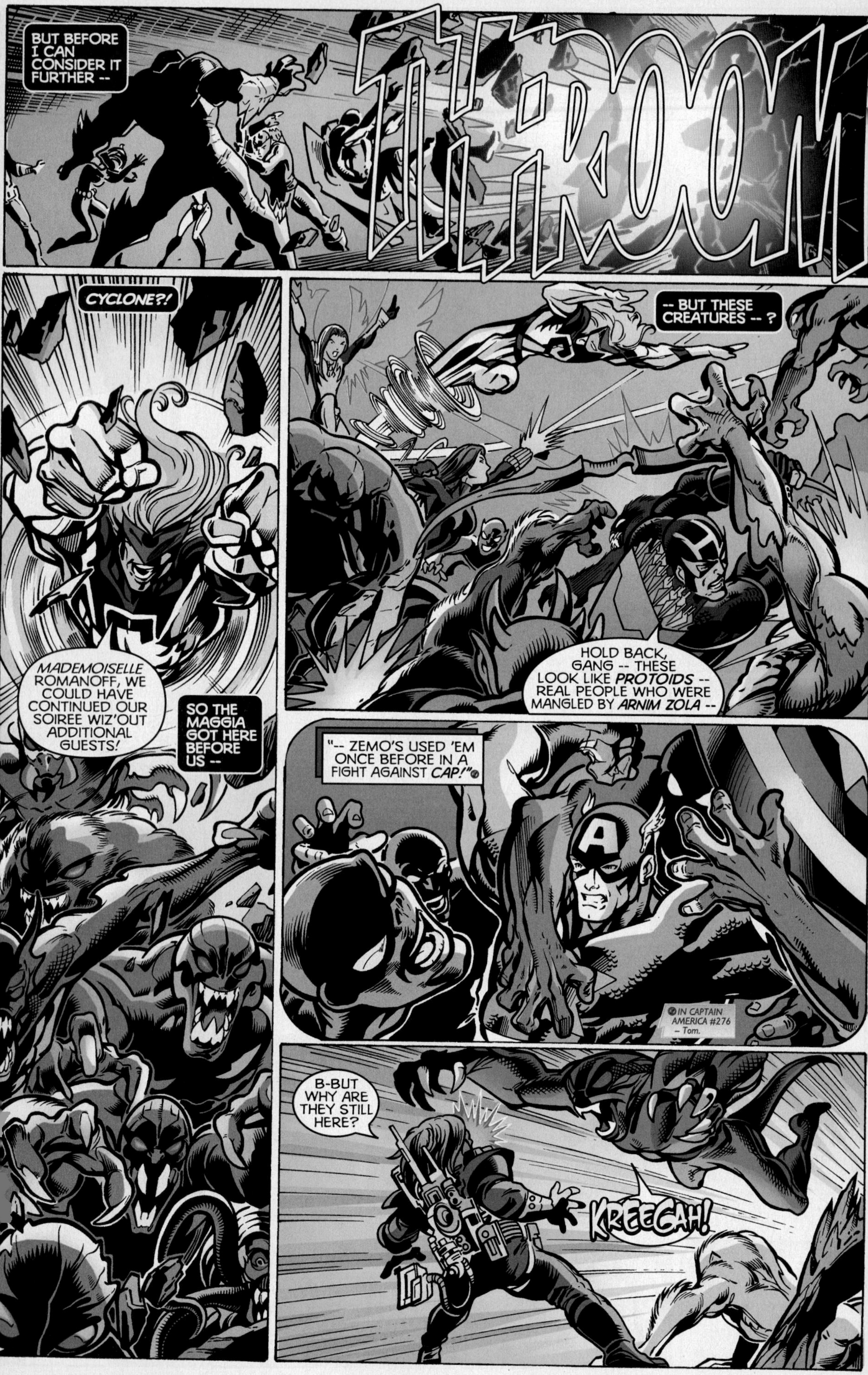
BUT BEFORE I CAN CONSIDER IT FURTHER --
THROOOM
CYCLONE?!
MADEMOISELLE ROMANOFF, WE COULD HAVE CONTINUED OUR SOIREE WIZ'OUT ADDITIONAL GUESTS!
SO THE MAGGIA GOT HERE BEFORE US --
-- BUT THESE CREATURES -- ?
HOLD BACK, GANG -- THESE LOOK LIKE PROTOIDS -- REAL PEOPLE WHO WERE MANGLED BY ARNIM ZOLA --
"-- ZEMO'S USED 'EM ONCE BEFORE IN A FIGHT AGAINST CAP!"
IN CAPTAIN AMERICA #276 – Tom.
B-BUT WHY ARE THEY STILL HERE?
KREEGAH!

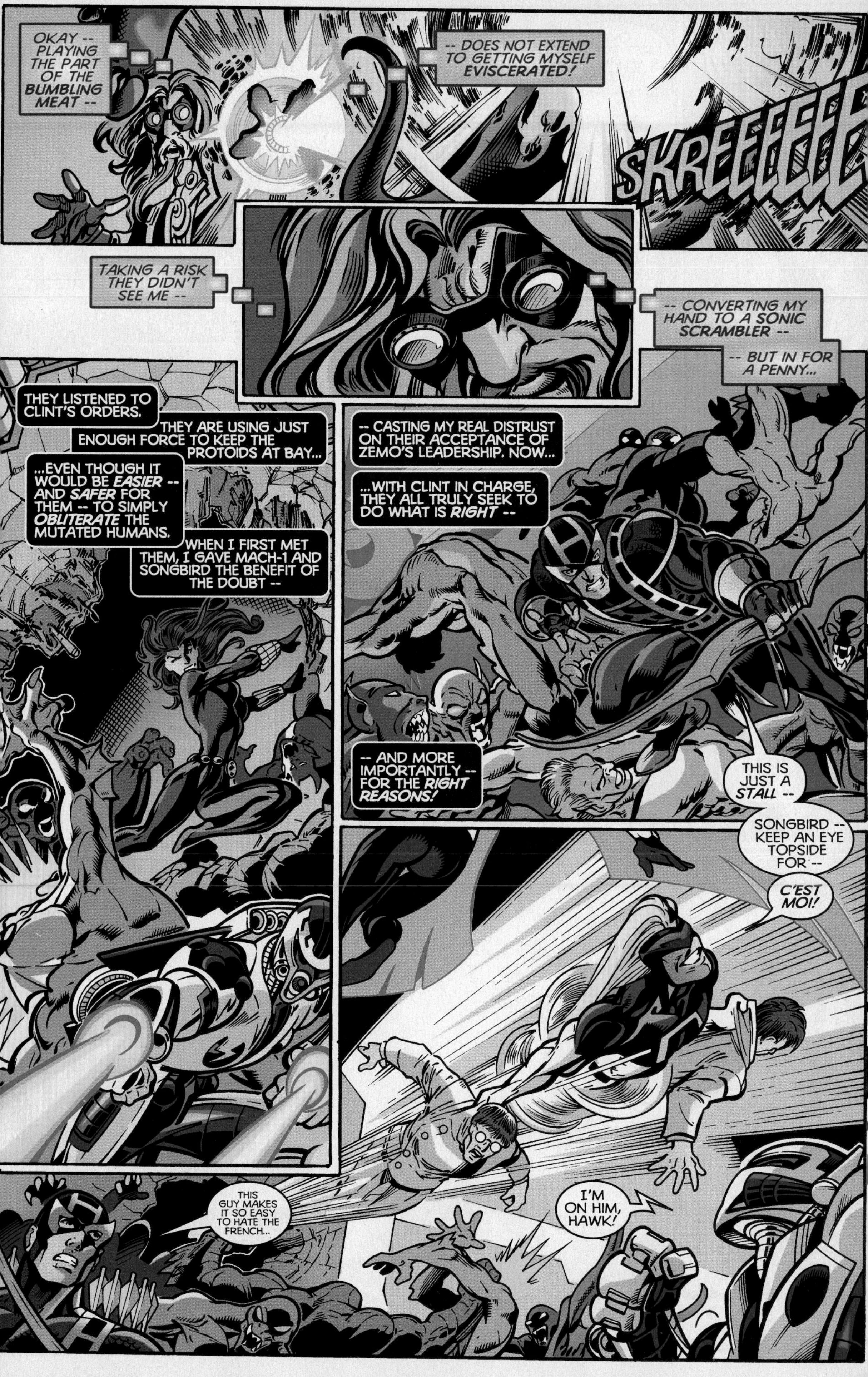
OKAY -- PLAYING THE PART OF THE BUMBLING MEAT --
-- DOES NOT EXTEND TO GETTING MYSELF EVISCERATED!
SKREEEEEE
TAKING A RISK THEY DIDN'T SEE ME --
-- CONVERTING MY HAND TO A SONIC SCRAMBLER --
-- BUT IN FOR A PENNY...
THEY LISTENED TO CLINT'S ORDERS.
THEY ARE USING JUST ENOUGH FORCE TO KEEP THE PROTOIDS AT BAY...
...EVEN THOUGH IT WOULD BE EASIER -- AND SAFER FOR THEM -- TO SIMPLY OBLITERATE THE MUTATED HUMANS.
WHEN I FIRST MET THEM, I GAVE MACH-1 AND SONGBIRD THE BENEFIT OF THE DOUBT --
-- CASTING MY REAL DISTRUST ON THEIR ACCEPTANCE OF ZEMO'S LEADERSHIP. NOW...
...WITH CLINT IN CHARGE, THEY ALL TRULY SEEK TO DO WHAT IS RIGHT --
-- AND MORE IMPORTANTLY -- FOR THE RIGHT REASONS!
THIS IS JUST A STALL --
SONGBIRD -- KEEP AN EYE TOPSIDE FOR --
C'EST MOI!
THIS GUY MAKES IT SO EASY TO HATE THE FRENCH...
I'M ON HIM, HAWK!

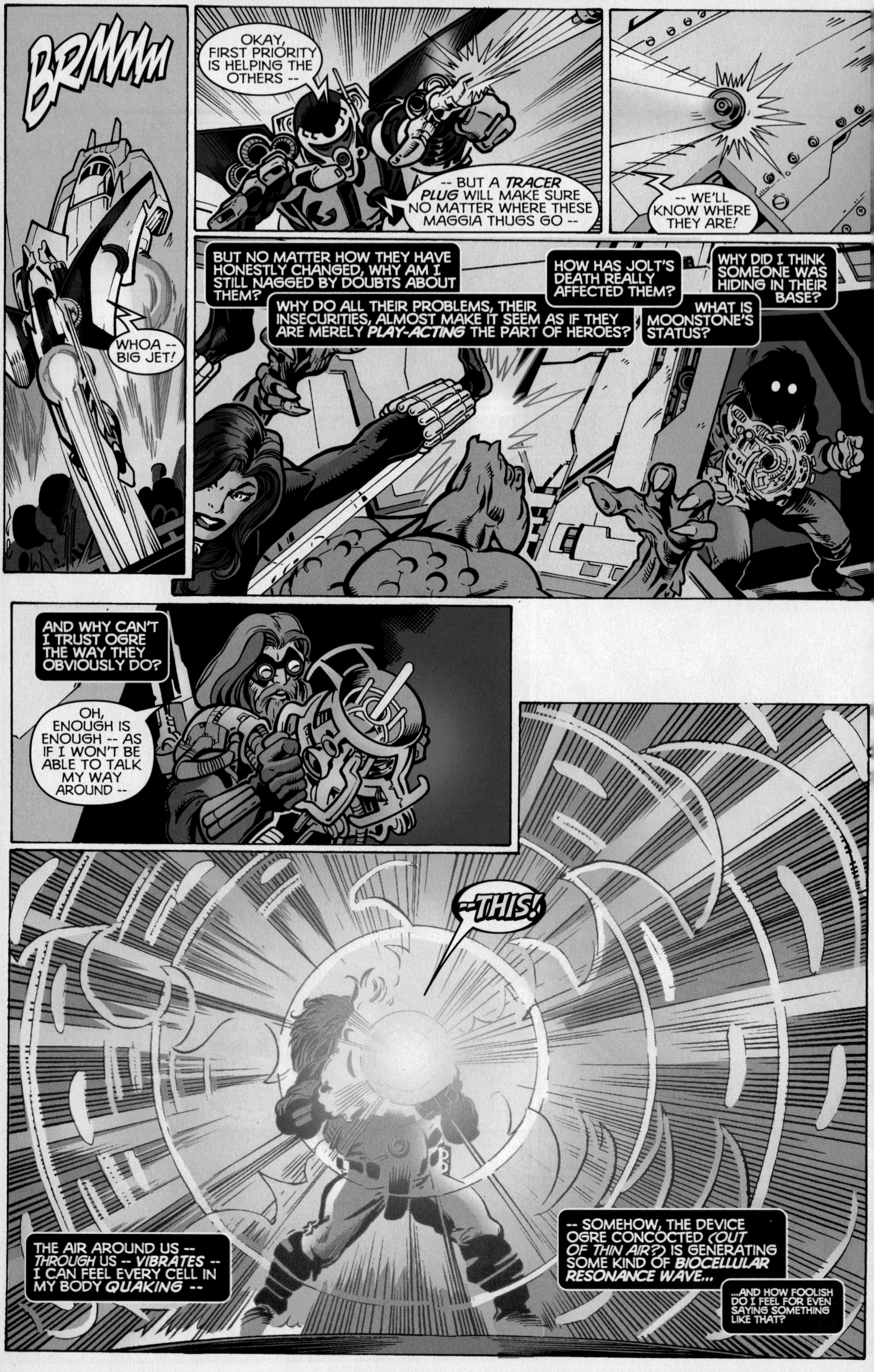
BRMMM
WHOA -- BIG JET!
OKAY, FIRST PRIORITY IS HELPING THE OTHERS --
-- BUT A TRACER PLUG WILL MAKE SURE NO MATTER WHERE THESE MAGGIA THUGS GO --
-- WE'LL KNOW WHERE THEY ARE!
BUT NO MATTER HOW THEY HAVE HONESTLY CHANGED, WHY AM I STILL NAGGED BY DOUBTS ABOUT THEM?
WHY DO ALL THEIR PROBLEMS, THEIR INSECURITIES, ALMOST MAKE IT SEEM AS IF THEY ARE MERELY PLAY-ACTING THE PART OF HEROES?
HOW HAS JOLT'S DEATH REALLY AFFECTED THEM?
WHY DID I THINK SOMEONE WAS HIDING IN THEIR BASE?
WHAT IS MOONSTONE'S STATUS?
AND WHY CAN'T I TRUST OGRE THE WAY THEY OBVIOUSLY DO?
OH, ENOUGH IS ENOUGH -- AS IF I WON'T BE ABLE TO TALK MY WAY AROUND --
--THIS!
THE AIR AROUND US -- THROUGH US -- VIBRATES -- I CAN FEEL EVERY CELL IN MY BODY QUAKING --
-- SOMEHOW, THE DEVICE OGRE CONCOCTED (OUT OF THIN AIR?) IS GENERATING SOME KIND OF BIOCELLULAR RESONANCE WAVE...
...AND HOW FOOLISH DO I FEEL FOR EVEN SAYING SOMETHING LIKE THAT?

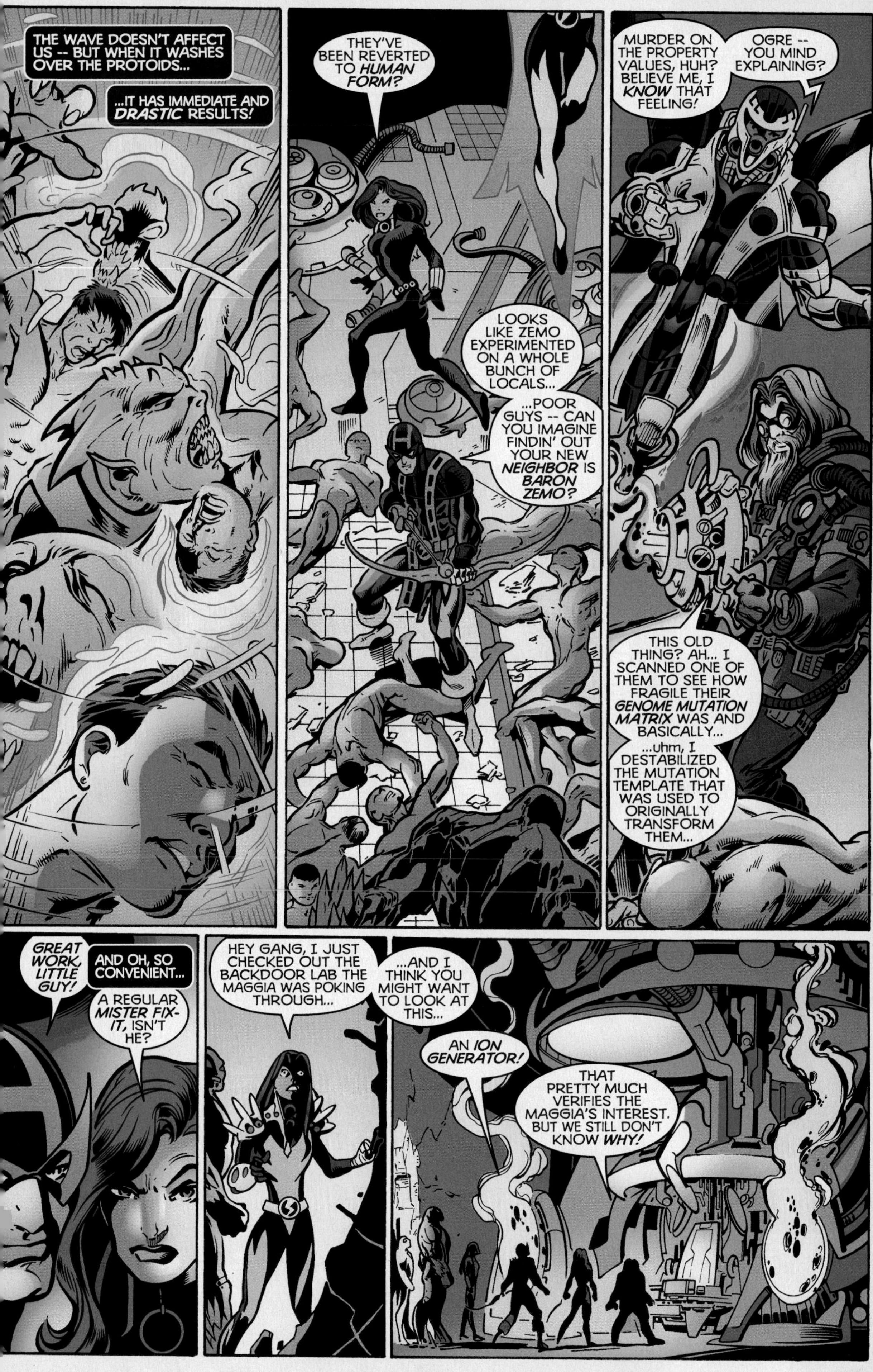
THE WAVE DOESN'T AFFECT US -- BUT WHEN IT WASHES OVER THE PROTOIDS...
...IT HAS IMMEDIATE AND *DRASTIC* RESULTS!
THEY'VE BEEN REVERTED TO *HUMAN FORM?*
LOOKS LIKE ZEMO EXPERIMENTED ON A WHOLE BUNCH OF LOCALS...
...POOR GUYS -- CAN YOU IMAGINE FINDIN' OUT YOUR NEW *NEIGHBOR* IS *BARON ZEMO?*
MURDER ON THE PROPERTY VALUES, HUH? BELIEVE ME, I *KNOW* THAT FEELING!
OGRE -- YOU MIND EXPLAINING?
THIS OLD THING? AH... I SCANNED ONE OF THEM TO SEE HOW FRAGILE THEIR *GENOME MUTATION MATRIX* WAS AND BASICALLY...
...uhm, I DESTABILIZED THE MUTATION TEMPLATE THAT WAS USED TO ORIGINALLY TRANSFORM THEM...
GREAT WORK, LITTLE GUY!
AND OH, SO CONVENIENT...
A REGULAR *MISTER FIX-IT,* ISN'T HE?
HEY GANG, I JUST CHECKED OUT THE BACKDOOR LAB THE MAGGIA WAS POKING THROUGH...
...AND I THINK YOU MIGHT WANT TO LOOK AT THIS...
AN ION GENERATOR!
THAT PRETTY MUCH VERIFIES THE MAGGIA'S INTEREST. BUT WE STILL DON'T KNOW *WHY!*

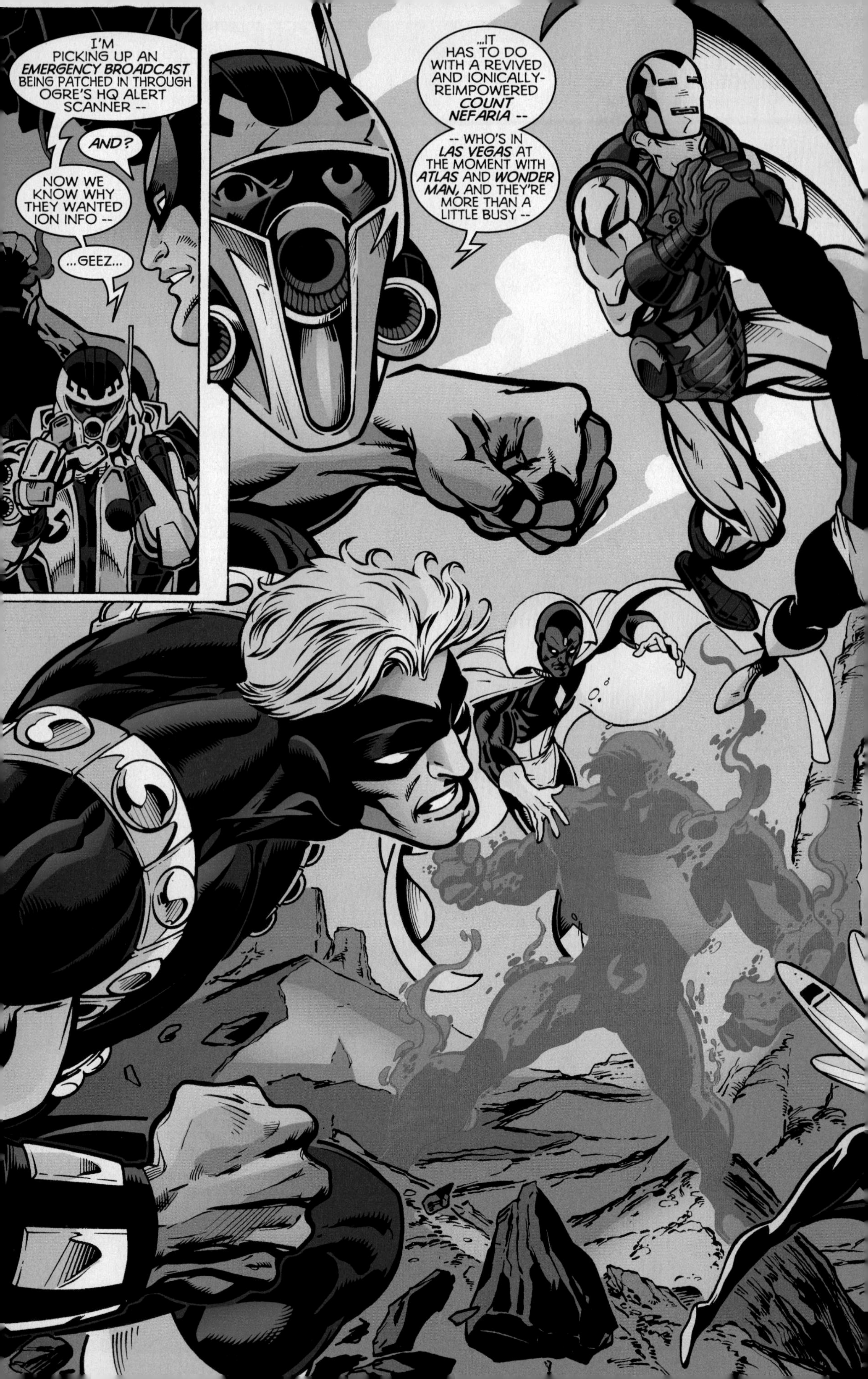
I'M PICKING UP AN EMERGENCY BROADCAST BEING PATCHED IN THROUGH OGRE'S HQ ALERT SCANNER --
AND?
NOW WE KNOW WHY THEY WANTED ION INFO --
...GEEZ...
...IT HAS TO DO WITH A REVIVED AND IONICALLY-REIMPOWERED COUNT NEFARIA --
-- WHO'S IN LAS VEGAS AT THE MOMENT WITH ATLAS AND WONDER MAN, AND THEY'RE MORE THAN A LITTLE BUSY --

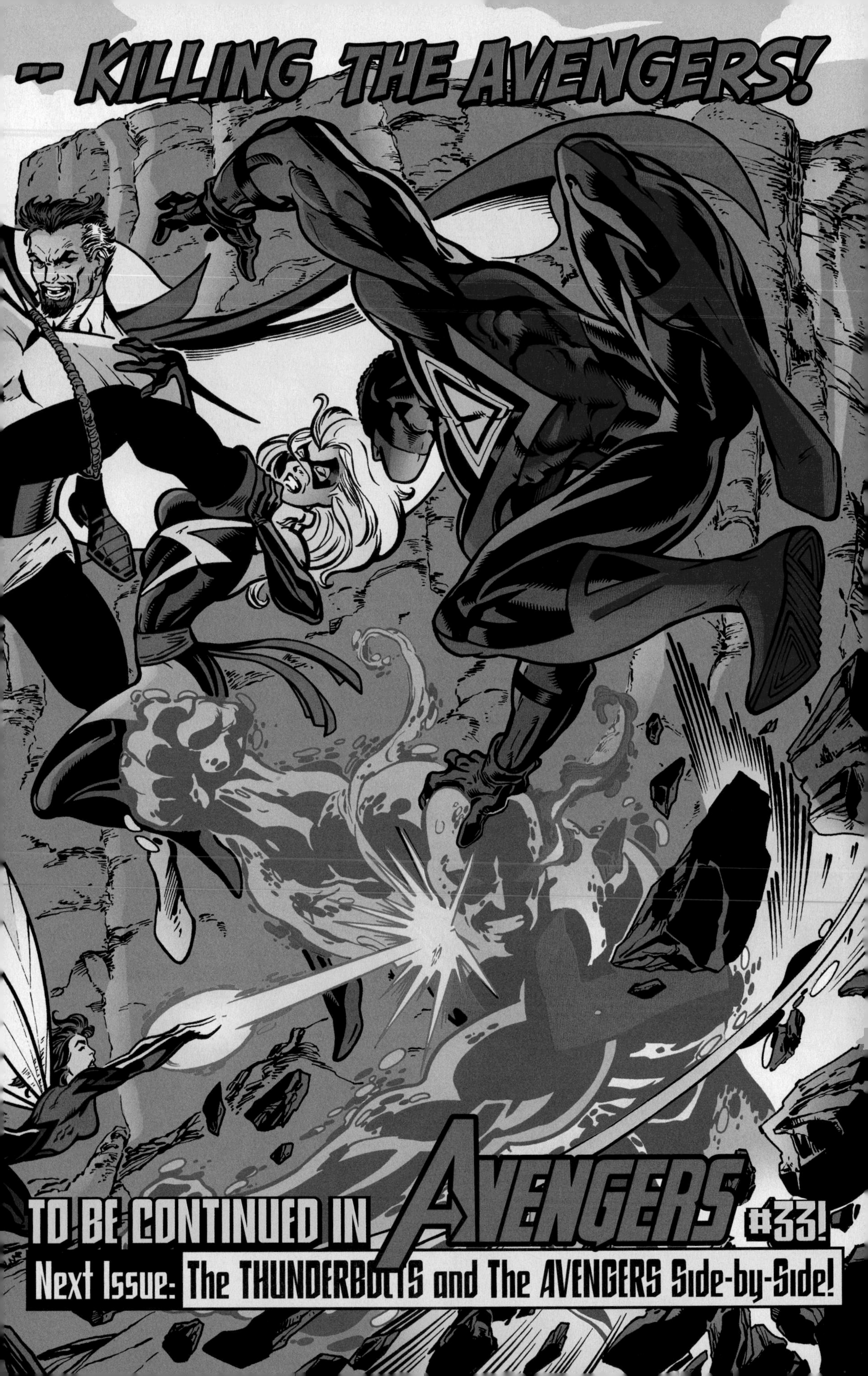
-- KILLING THE AVENGERS!
TO BE CONTINUED IN AVENGERS #33!
Next Issue: The THUNDERBOLTS and The AVENGERS Side-by-Side!

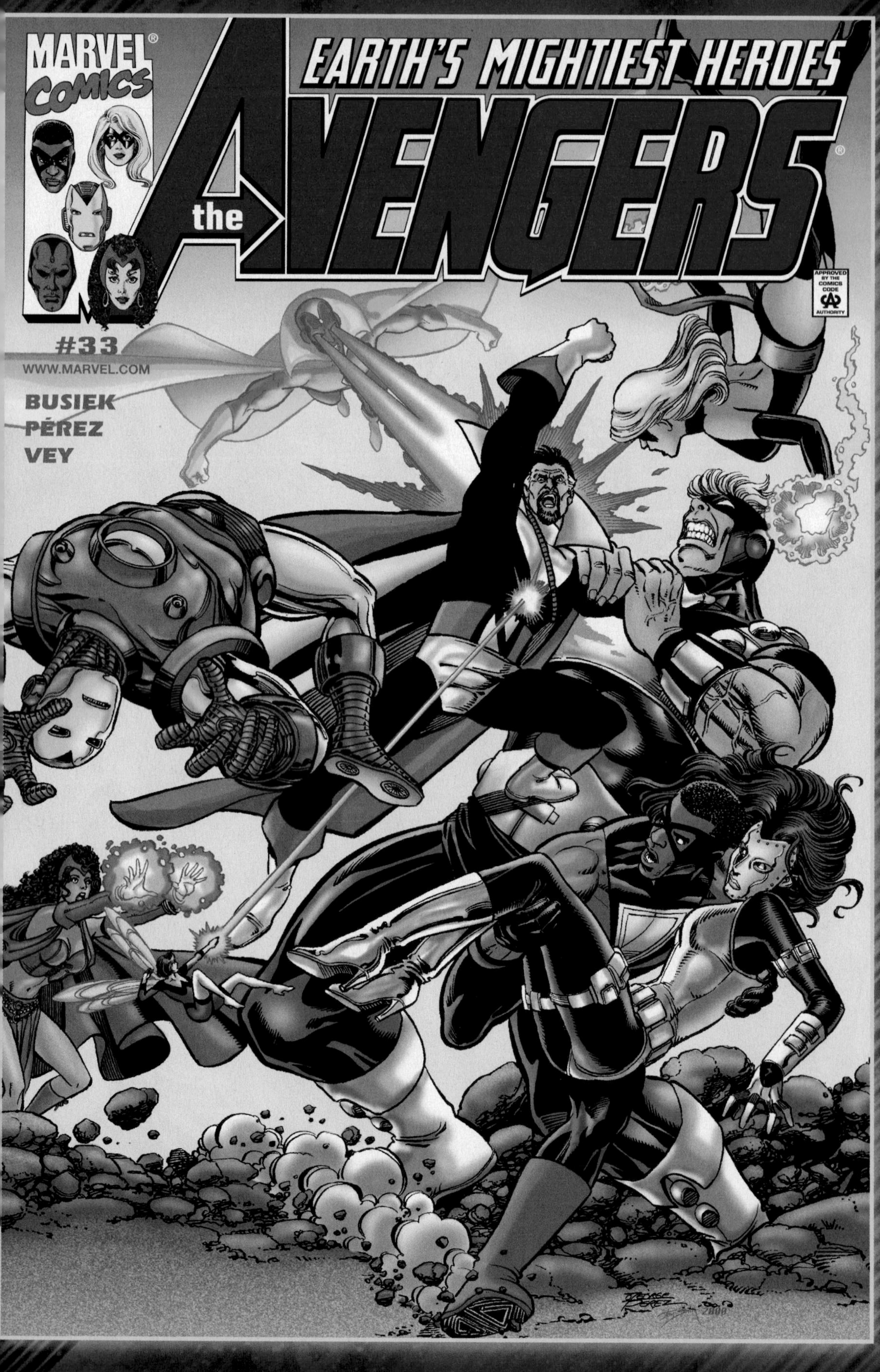
MARVEL®
COMICS
EARTH'S MIGHTIEST HEROES
the
AVENGERS®
APPROVED BY THE COMICS CODE AUTHORITY
#33
WWW.MARVEL.COM
BUSIEK
PÉREZ
VEY

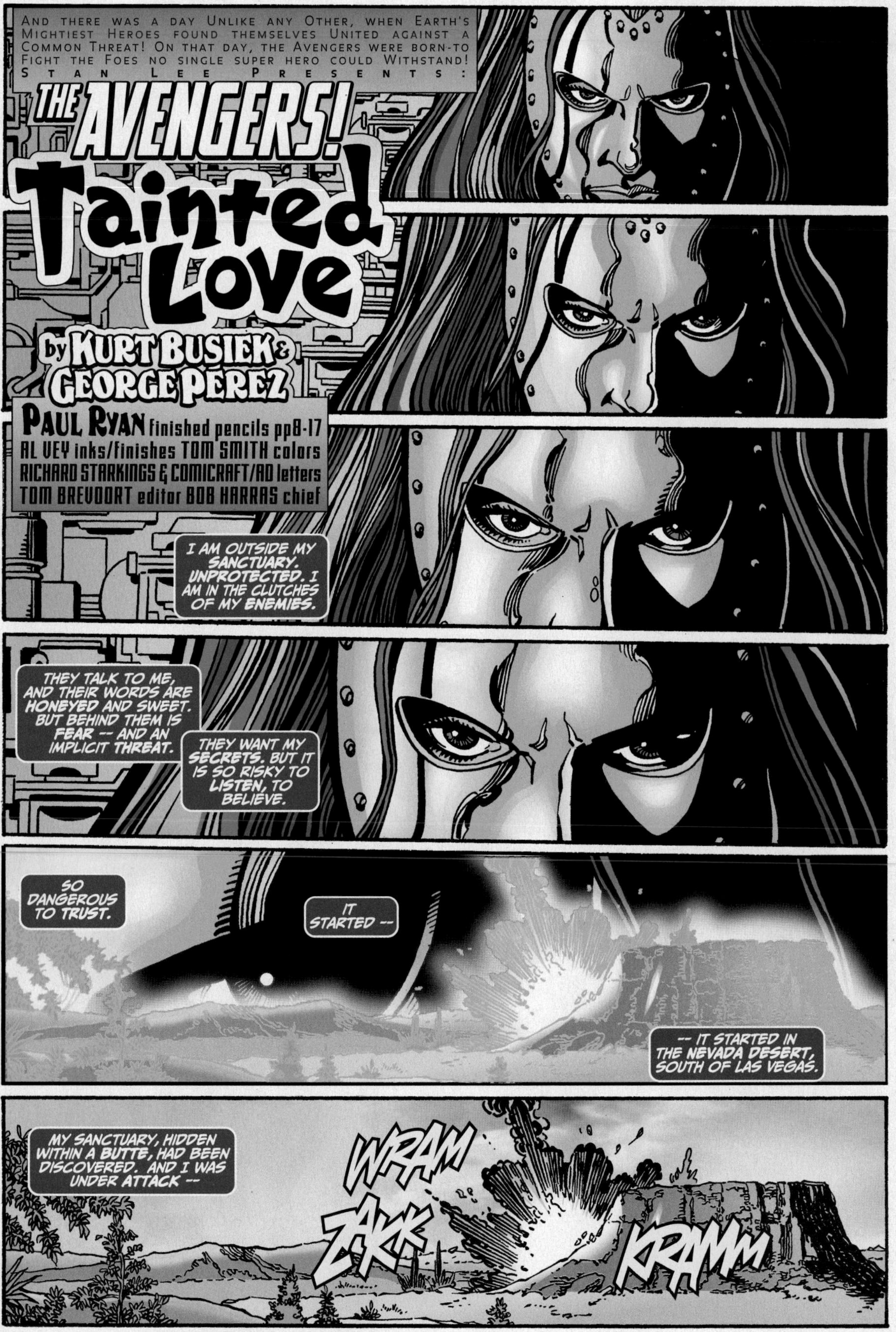
AND THERE WAS A DAY UNLIKE ANY OTHER, WHEN EARTH'S MIGHTIEST HEROES FOUND THEMSELVES UNITED AGAINST A COMMON THREAT! ON THAT DAY, THE AVENGERS WERE BORN-TO FIGHT THE FOES NO SINGLE SUPER HERO COULD WITHSTAND!
STAN LEE PRESENTS:
THE AVENGERS!
Tainted Love
by KURT BUSIEK & GEORGE PEREZ
PAUL RYAN finished pencils pp8-17
AL VEY inks/finishes TOM SMITH colors
RICHARD STARKINGS & COMICRAFT/AD letters
TOM BREVOORT editor BOB HARRAS chief
I AM OUTSIDE MY SANCTUARY. UNPROTECTED. I AM IN THE CLUTCHES OF MY ENEMIES.
THEY TALK TO ME, AND THEIR WORDS ARE HONEYED AND SWEET. BUT BEHIND THEM IS FEAR -- AND AN IMPLICIT THREAT.
THEY WANT MY SECRETS. BUT IT IS SO RISKY TO LISTEN, TO BELIEVE.
SO DANGEROUS TO TRUST.
IT STARTED --
-- IT STARTED IN THE NEVADA DESERT, SOUTH OF LAS VEGAS.
MY SANCTUARY, HIDDEN WITHIN A BUTTE, HAD BEEN DISCOVERED. AND I WAS UNDER ATTACK --
WRAM
ZAKK
KRAMM

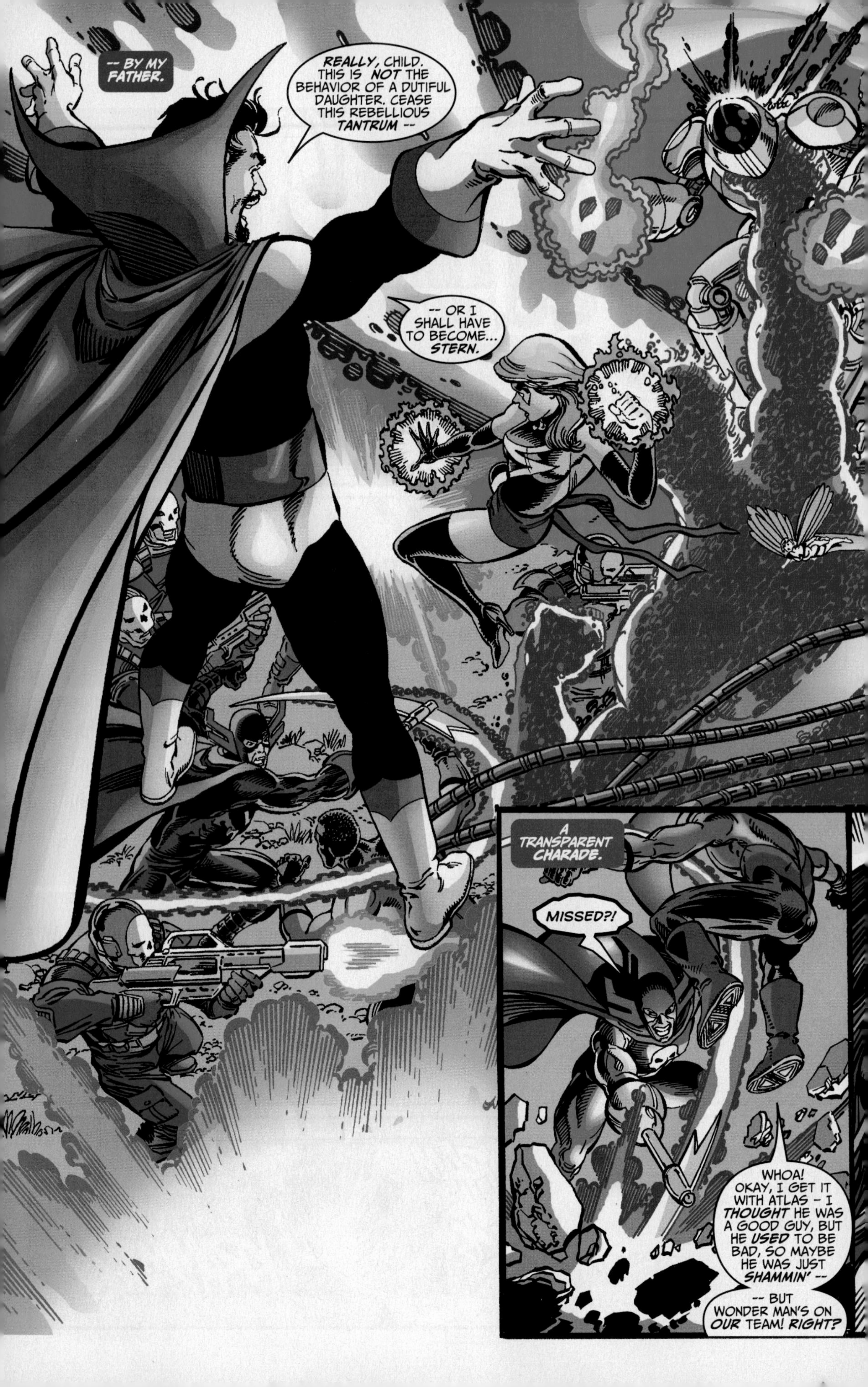
-- BY MY FATHER.
REALLY, CHILD. THIS IS NOT THE BEHAVIOR OF A DUTIFUL DAUGHTER. CEASE THIS REBELLIOUS TANTRUM --
-- OR I SHALL HAVE TO BECOME... STERN.
A TRANSPARENT CHARADE.
MISSED?!
WHOA! OKAY, I GET IT WITH ATLAS – I THOUGHT HE WAS A GOOD GUY, BUT HE USED TO BE BAD, SO MAYBE HE WAS JUST SHAMMIN' --
-- BUT WONDER MAN'S ON OUR TEAM! RIGHT?

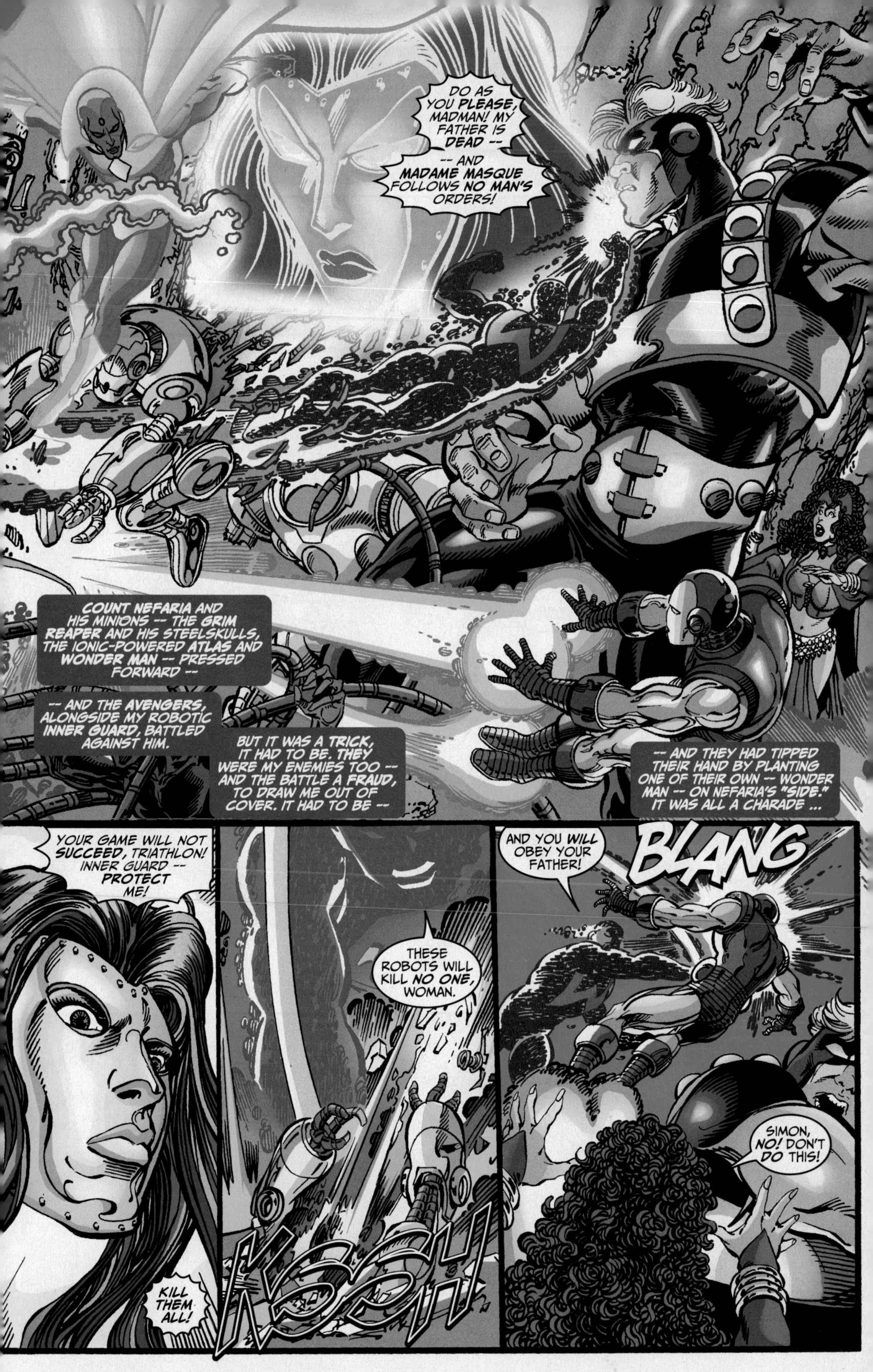
DO AS YOU PLEASE, MADMAN! MY FATHER IS DEAD --
-- AND MADAME MASQUE FOLLOWS NO MAN'S ORDERS!
COUNT NEFARIA AND HIS MINIONS -- THE GRIM REAPER AND HIS STEELSKULLS, THE IONIC-POWERED ATLAS AND WONDER MAN -- PRESSED FORWARD --
-- AND THE AVENGERS, ALONGSIDE MY ROBOTIC INNER GUARD, BATTLED AGAINST HIM.
BUT IT WAS A TRICK, IT HAD TO BE. THEY WERE MY ENEMIES TOO -- AND THE BATTLE A FRAUD, TO DRAW ME OUT OF COVER. IT HAD TO BE --
-- AND THEY HAD TIPPED THEIR HAND BY PLANTING ONE OF THEIR OWN -- WONDER MAN -- ON NEFARIA'S "SIDE." IT WAS ALL A CHARADE ...
YOUR GAME WILL NOT SUCCEED, TRIATHLON! INNER GUARD -- PROTECT ME!
KILL THEM ALL!
THESE ROBOTS WILL KILL NO ONE, WOMAN.
KSSSH
AND YOU WILL OBEY YOUR FATHER!
BLANG
SIMON, NO! DON'T DO THIS!

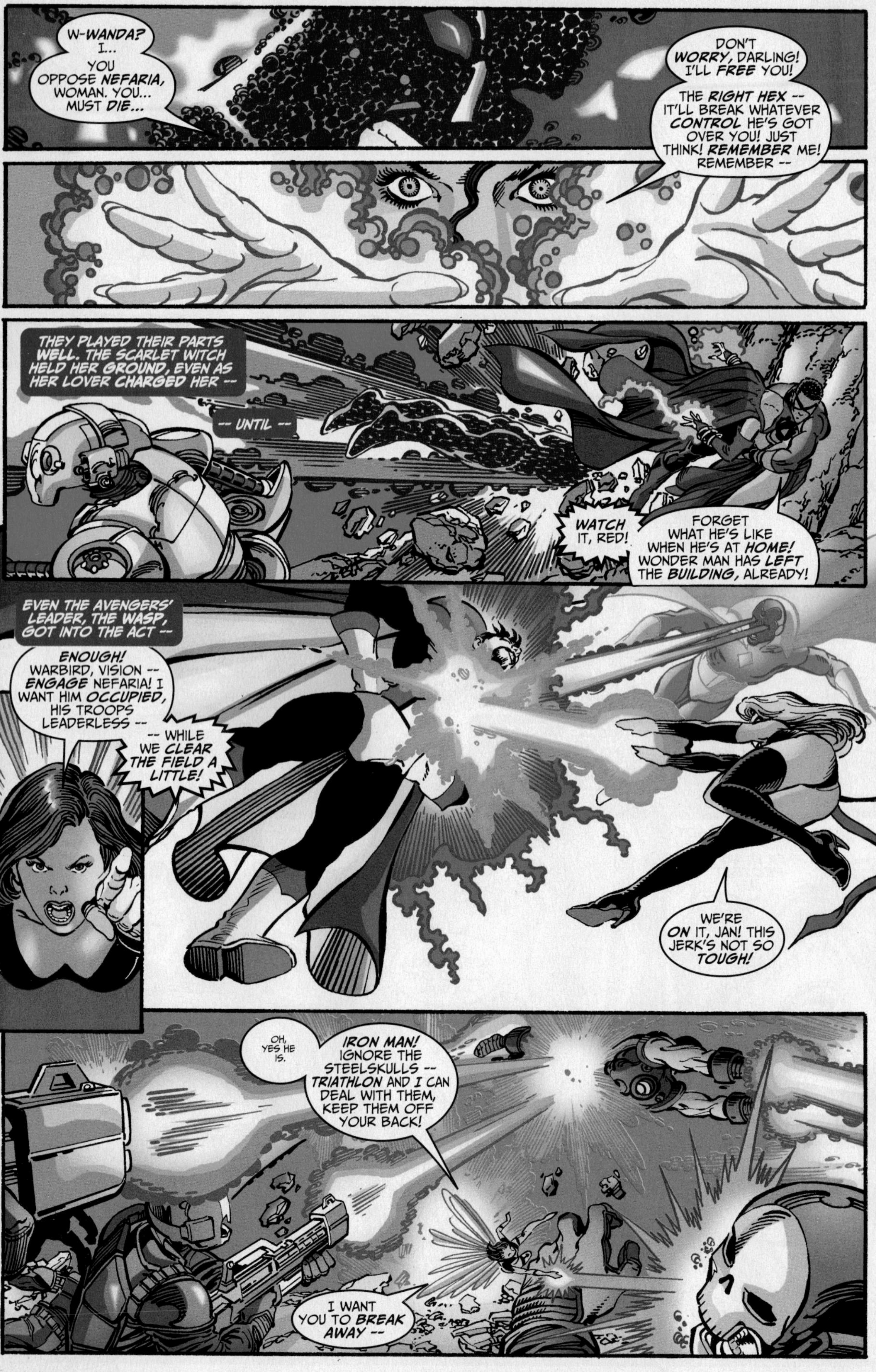
W-WANDA? I... YOU OPPOSE NEFARIA, WOMAN. YOU... MUST DIE...
DON'T WORRY, DARLING! I'LL FREE YOU!
THE RIGHT HEX -- IT'LL BREAK WHATEVER CONTROL HE'S GOT OVER YOU! JUST THINK! REMEMBER ME! REMEMBER --
THEY PLAYED THEIR PARTS WELL. THE SCARLET WITCH HELD HER GROUND, EVEN AS HER LOVER CHARGED HER --
-- UNTIL --
WATCH IT, RED!
FORGET WHAT HE'S LIKE WHEN HE'S AT HOME! WONDER MAN HAS LEFT THE BUILDING, ALREADY!
EVEN THE AVENGERS' LEADER, THE WASP, GOT INTO THE ACT --
ENOUGH! WARBIRD, VISION -- ENGAGE NEFARIA! I WANT HIM OCCUPIED, HIS TROOPS LEADERLESS --
-- WHILE WE CLEAR THE FIELD A LITTLE!
WE'RE ON IT, JAN! THIS JERK'S NOT SO TOUGH!
OH, YES HE IS.
IRON MAN! IGNORE THE STEELSKULLS -- TRIATHLON AND I CAN DEAL WITH THEM, KEEP THEM OFF YOUR BACK!
I WANT YOU TO BREAK AWAY --

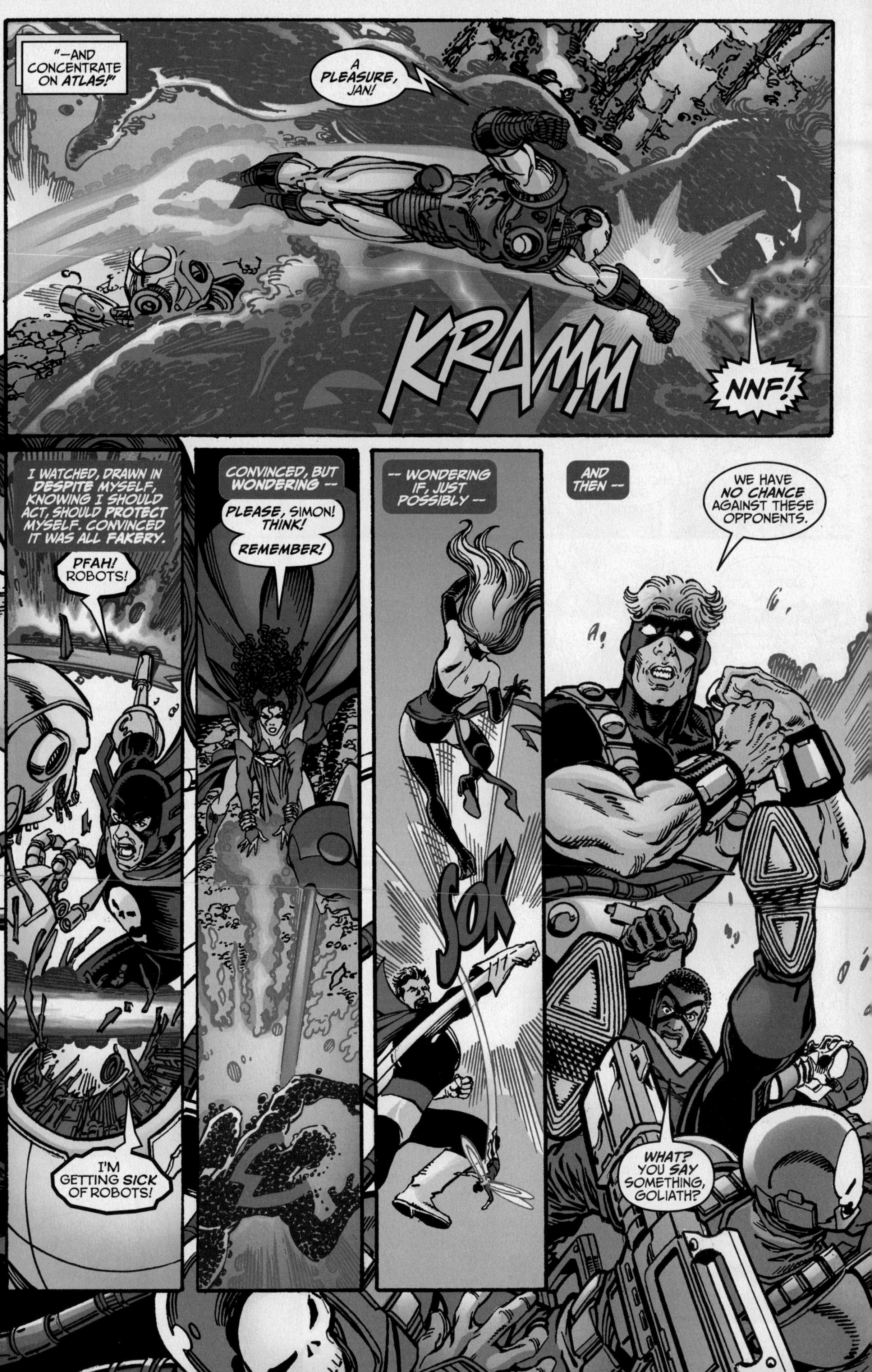
"—AND CONCENTRATE ON ATLAS!"
A PLEASURE, JAN!
KRAMM
NNF!
I WATCHED, DRAWN IN DESPITE MYSELF, KNOWING I SHOULD ACT, SHOULD PROTECT MYSELF. CONVINCED IT WAS ALL FAKERY.
PFAH! ROBOTS!
I'M GETTING SICK OF ROBOTS!
CONVINCED, BUT WONDERING --
PLEASE, SIMON! THINK!
REMEMBER!
-- WONDERING IF, JUST POSSIBLY --
SOK
AND THEN --
WE HAVE NO CHANCE AGAINST THESE OPPONENTS.
WHAT? YOU SAY SOMETHING, GOLIATH?

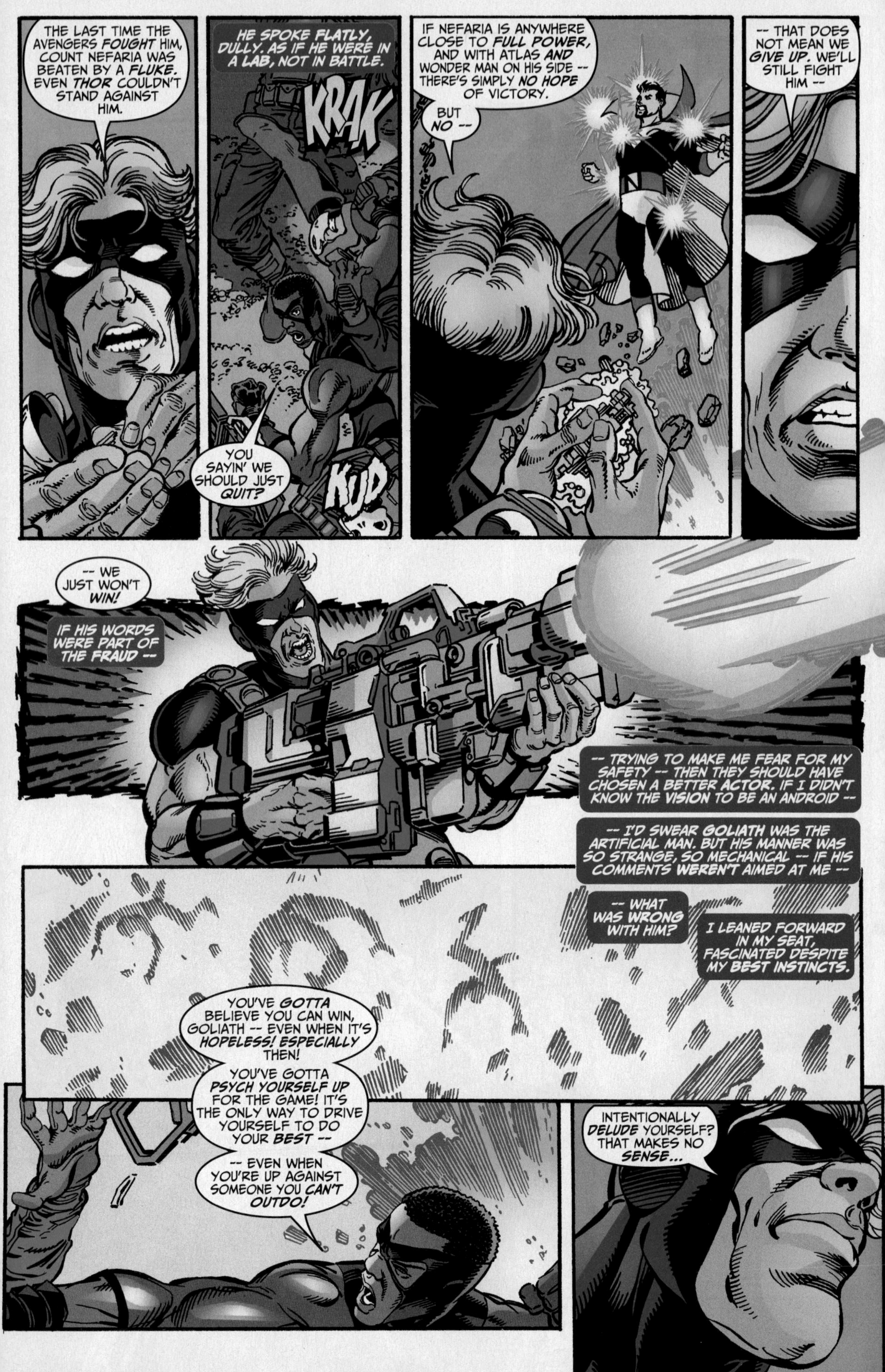
THE LAST TIME THE AVENGERS *FOUGHT* HIM, COUNT NEFARIA WAS BEATEN BY A *FLUKE*. EVEN *THOR* COULDN'T STAND AGAINST HIM.
HE SPOKE FLATLY, DULLY, AS IF HE WERE IN A LAB, NOT IN BATTLE.
KRAK
YOU SAYIN' WE SHOULD JUST *QUIT?*
KUD
IF NEFARIA IS ANYWHERE CLOSE TO *FULL POWER*, AND WITH ATLAS *AND* WONDER MAN ON HIS SIDE -- THERE'S SIMPLY *NO HOPE* OF VICTORY.
BUT *NO* --
-- THAT DOES NOT MEAN WE *GIVE UP*. WE'LL STILL FIGHT HIM --
-- WE JUST WON'T *WIN!*
IF HIS WORDS WERE PART OF THE FRAUD --
-- TRYING TO MAKE ME FEAR FOR MY SAFETY -- THEN THEY SHOULD HAVE CHOSEN A BETTER ACTOR. IF I DIDN'T KNOW THE VISION TO BE AN ANDROID --
-- I'D SWEAR GOLIATH WAS THE ARTIFICIAL MAN. BUT HIS MANNER WAS SO STRANGE, SO MECHANICAL -- IF HIS COMMENTS WEREN'T AIMED AT ME --
-- WHAT WAS WRONG WITH HIM?
I LEANED FORWARD IN MY SEAT, FASCINATED DESPITE MY BEST INSTINCTS.
YOU'VE *GOTTA* BELIEVE YOU CAN WIN, GOLIATH -- EVEN WHEN IT'S *HOPELESS! ESPECIALLY* THEN!
YOU'VE GOTTA *PSYCH YOURSELF UP* FOR THE GAME! IT'S THE ONLY WAY TO DRIVE YOURSELF TO DO YOUR *BEST* --
-- EVEN WHEN YOU'RE UP AGAINST SOMEONE YOU *CAN'T OUTDO!*
INTENTIONALLY *DELUDE* YOURSELF? THAT MAKES NO *SENSE*...

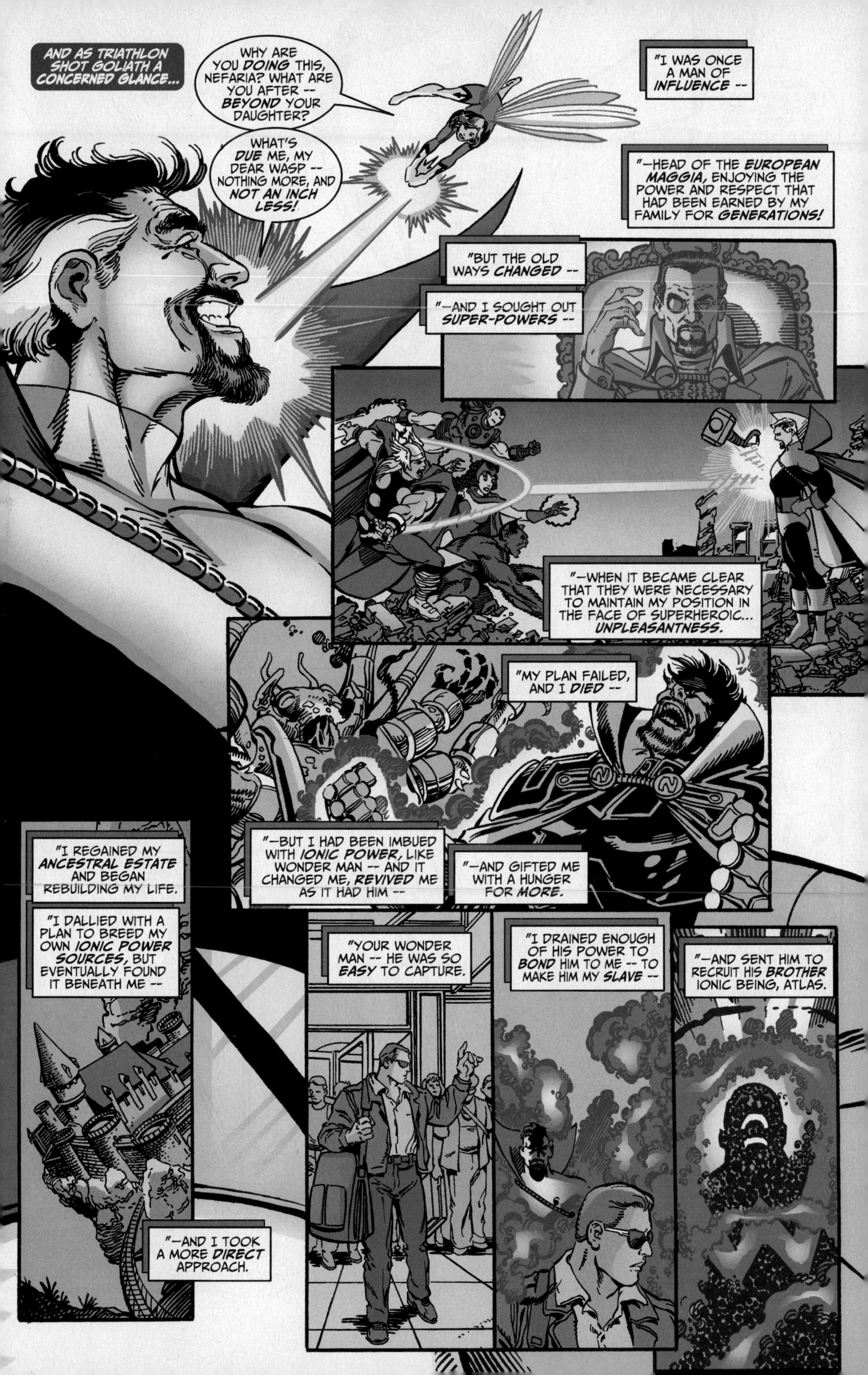
AND AS TRIATHLON SHOT GOLIATH A CONCERNED GLANCE...
WHY ARE YOU DOING THIS, NEFARIA? WHAT ARE YOU AFTER -- BEYOND YOUR DAUGHTER?
WHAT'S DUE ME, MY DEAR WASP -- NOTHING MORE, AND NOT AN INCH LESS!
"I WAS ONCE A MAN OF INFLUENCE --
"—HEAD OF THE EUROPEAN MAGGIA, ENJOYING THE POWER AND RESPECT THAT HAD BEEN EARNED BY MY FAMILY FOR GENERATIONS!
"BUT THE OLD WAYS CHANGED --
"—AND I SOUGHT OUT SUPER-POWERS --
"—WHEN IT BECAME CLEAR THAT THEY WERE NECESSARY TO MAINTAIN MY POSITION IN THE FACE OF SUPERHEROIC... UNPLEASANTNESS.
"MY PLAN FAILED, AND I DIED --
"—BUT I HAD BEEN IMBUED WITH IONIC POWER, LIKE WONDER MAN -- AND IT CHANGED ME, REVIVED ME AS IT HAD HIM --
"—AND GIFTED ME WITH A HUNGER FOR MORE.
"I REGAINED MY ANCESTRAL ESTATE AND BEGAN REBUILDING MY LIFE.
"I DALLIED WITH A PLAN TO BREED MY OWN IONIC POWER SOURCES, BUT EVENTUALLY FOUND IT BENEATH ME --
"—AND I TOOK A MORE DIRECT APPROACH.
"YOUR WONDER MAN -- HE WAS SO EASY TO CAPTURE.
"I DRAINED ENOUGH OF HIS POWER TO BOND HIM TO ME -- TO MAKE HIM MY SLAVE --
"—AND SENT HIM TO RECRUIT HIS BROTHER IONIC BEING, ATLAS.

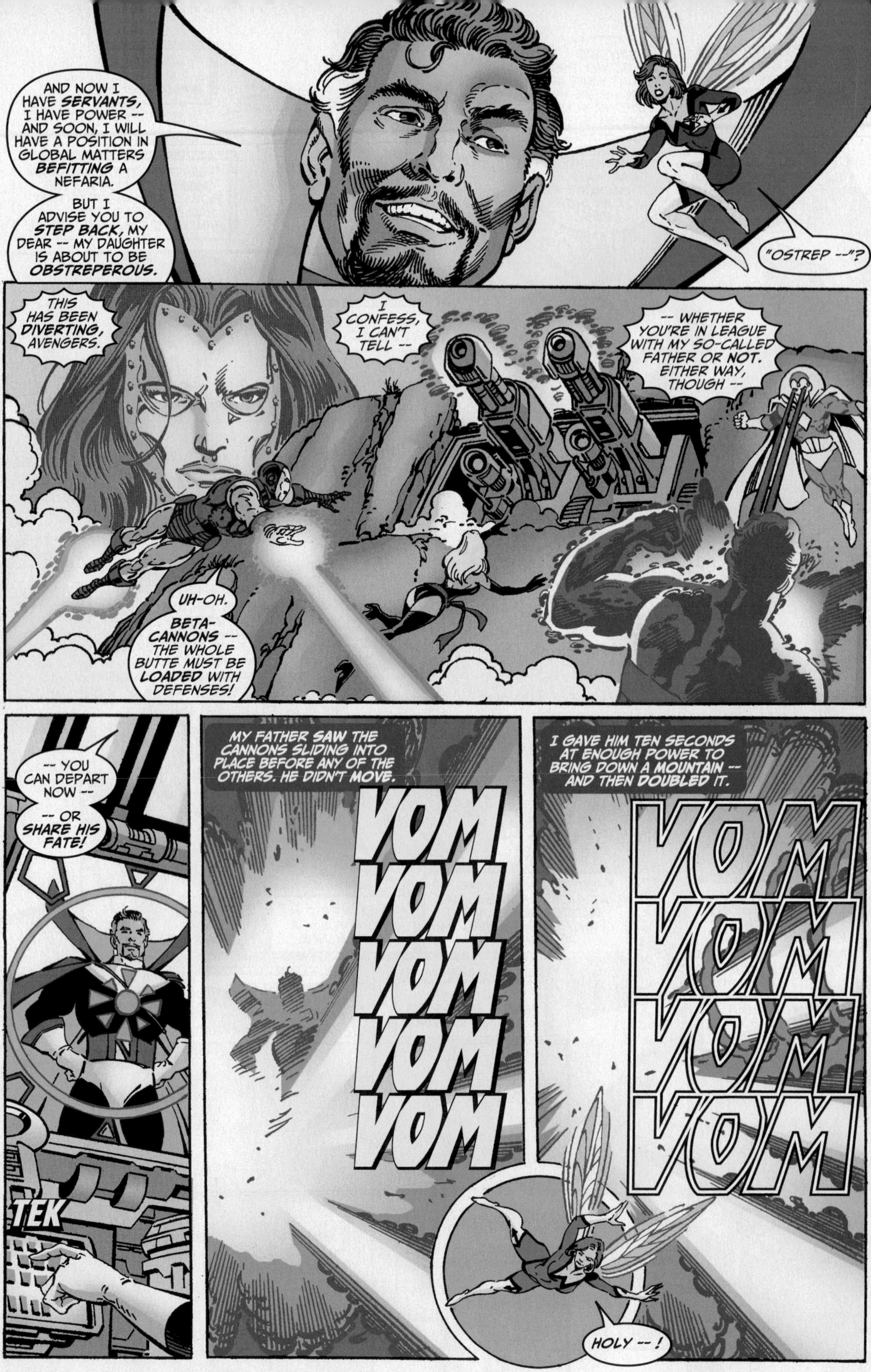

AND NOW I HAVE **SERVANTS**, I HAVE POWER -- AND SOON, I WILL HAVE A POSITION IN GLOBAL MATTERS **BEFITTING** A NEFARIA.
BUT I ADVISE YOU TO **STEP BACK**, MY DEAR -- MY DAUGHTER IS ABOUT TO BE **OBSTREPEROUS**.
"OSTREP --"?
THIS HAS BEEN **DIVERTING**, AVENGERS.
I CONFESS, I CAN'T TELL --
-- WHETHER YOU'RE IN LEAGUE WITH MY SO-CALLED FATHER OR **NOT**. EITHER WAY, THOUGH --
UH-OH.
BETA-CANNONS -- THE WHOLE BUTTE MUST BE **LOADED** WITH DEFENSES!
-- YOU CAN DEPART NOW --
-- OR **SHARE HIS FATE!**
TEK
MY FATHER **SAW** THE CANNONS SLIDING INTO PLACE BEFORE ANY OF THE OTHERS. HE DIDN'T **MOVE**.
VOM VOM VOM VOM VOM
I GAVE HIM TEN SECONDS AT ENOUGH POWER TO BRING DOWN A **MOUNTAIN** -- AND THEN **DOUBLED** IT.
VOM VOM VOM VOM
HOLY -- !

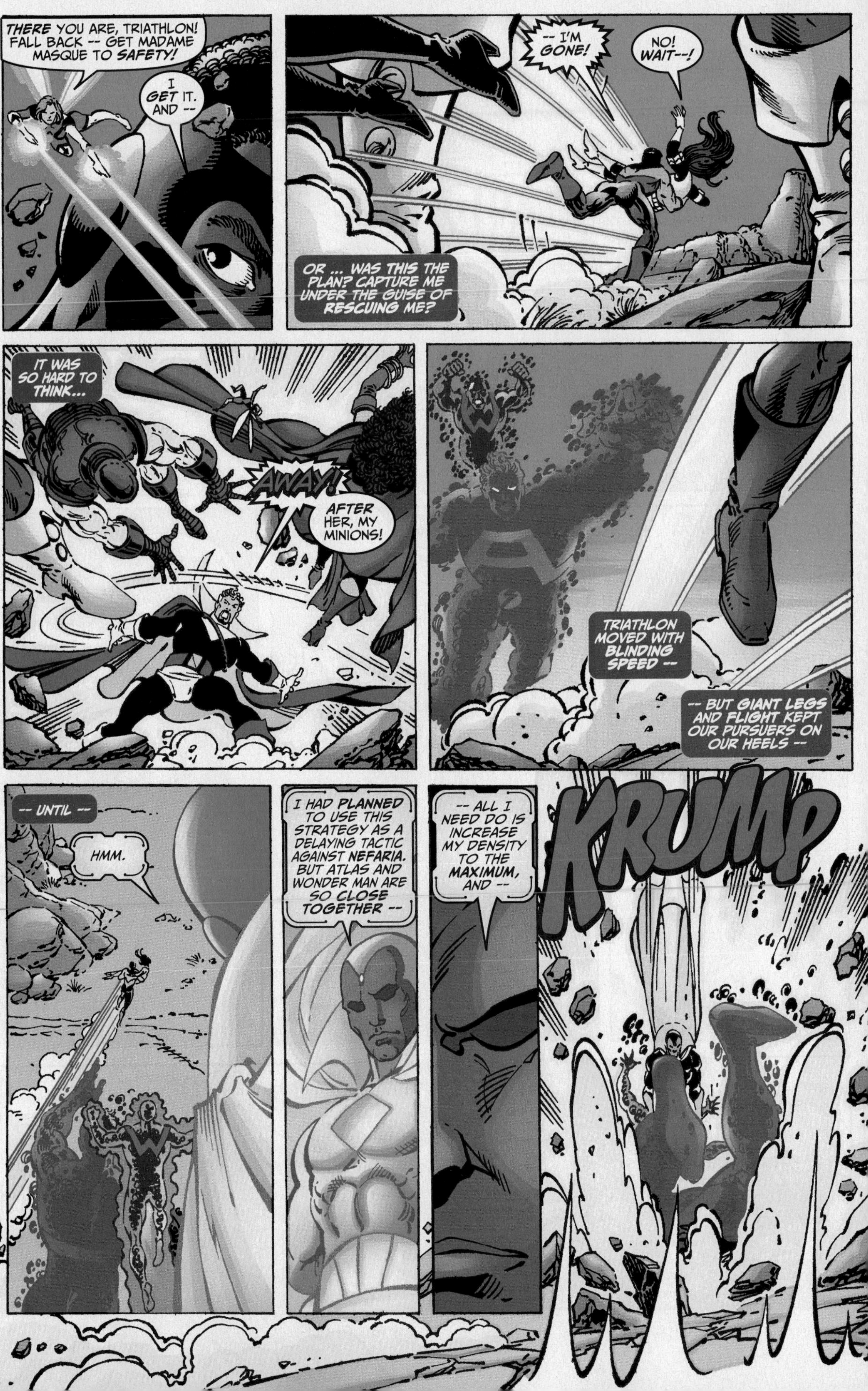
THERE YOU ARE, TRIATHLON! FALL BACK -- GET MADAME MASQUE TO SAFETY!
I GET IT. AND --
-- I'M GONE!
NO! WAIT--!
OR ... WAS THIS THE PLAN? CAPTURE ME UNDER THE GUISE OF RESCUING ME?
IT WAS SO HARD TO THINK...
AWAY!
AFTER HER, MY MINIONS!
TRIATHLON MOVED WITH BLINDING SPEED --
-- BUT GIANT LEGS AND FLIGHT KEPT OUR PURSUERS ON OUR HEELS --
-- UNTIL --
HMM.
I HAD PLANNED TO USE THIS STRATEGY AS A DELAYING TACTIC AGAINST NEFARIA. BUT ATLAS AND WONDER MAN ARE SO CLOSE TOGETHER --
-- ALL I NEED DO IS INCREASE MY DENSITY TO THE MAXIMUM, AND --
KRUMP

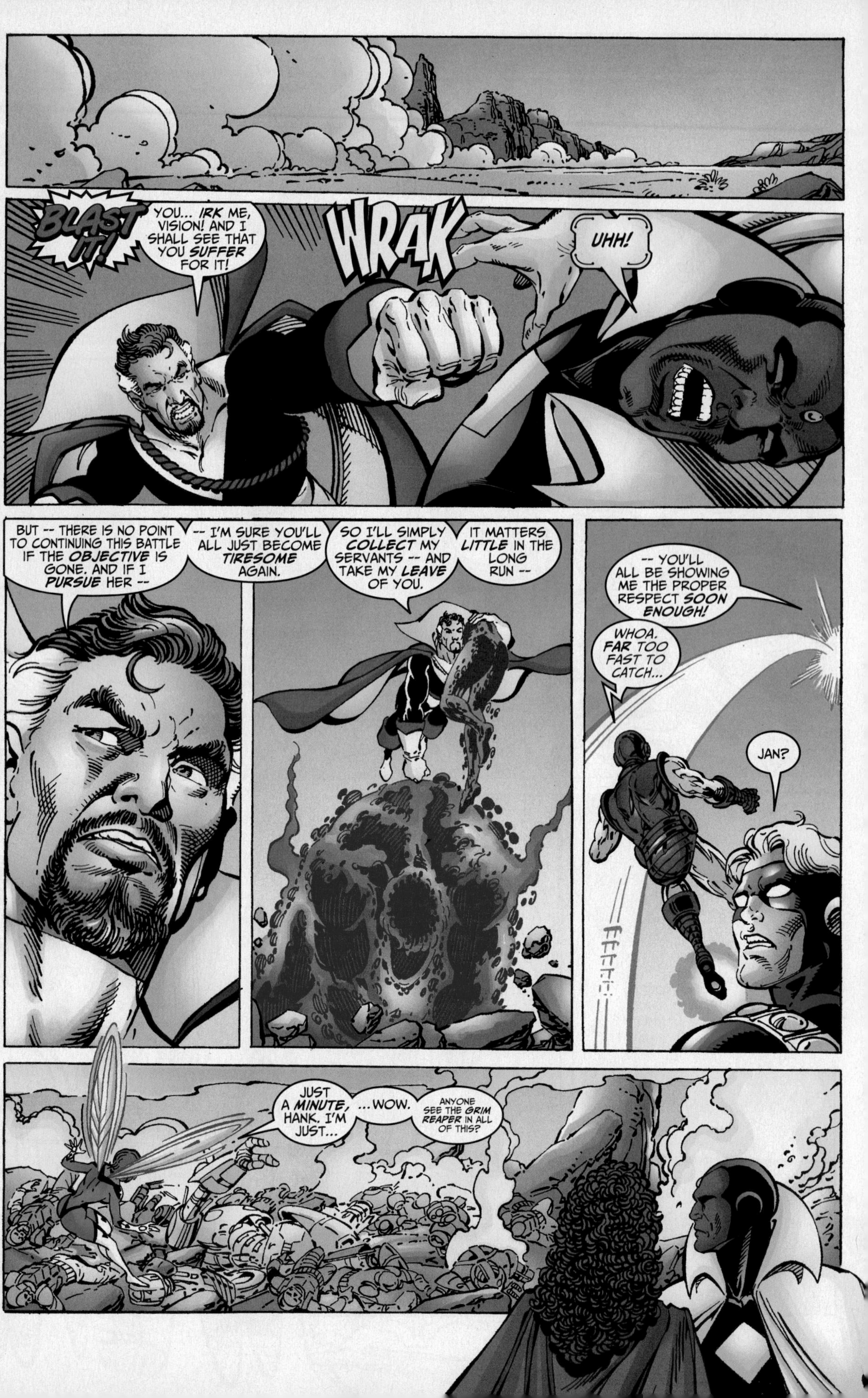
BLAST IT!
YOU... IRK ME, VISION! AND I SHALL SEE THAT YOU SUFFER FOR IT!
WRAK
UHH!
BUT -- THERE IS NO POINT TO CONTINUING THIS BATTLE IF THE OBJECTIVE IS GONE. AND IF I PURSUE HER --
-- I'M SURE YOU'LL ALL JUST BECOME TIRESOME AGAIN.
SO I'LL SIMPLY COLLECT MY SERVANTS -- AND TAKE MY LEAVE OF YOU.
IT MATTERS LITTLE IN THE LONG RUN --
-- YOU'LL ALL BE SHOWING ME THE PROPER RESPECT SOON ENOUGH!
WHOA. FAR TOO FAST TO CATCH...
JAN?
FFFTTT!
JUST A MINUTE, HANK. I'M JUST...
...WOW.
ANYONE SEE THE GRIM REAPER IN ALL OF THIS?

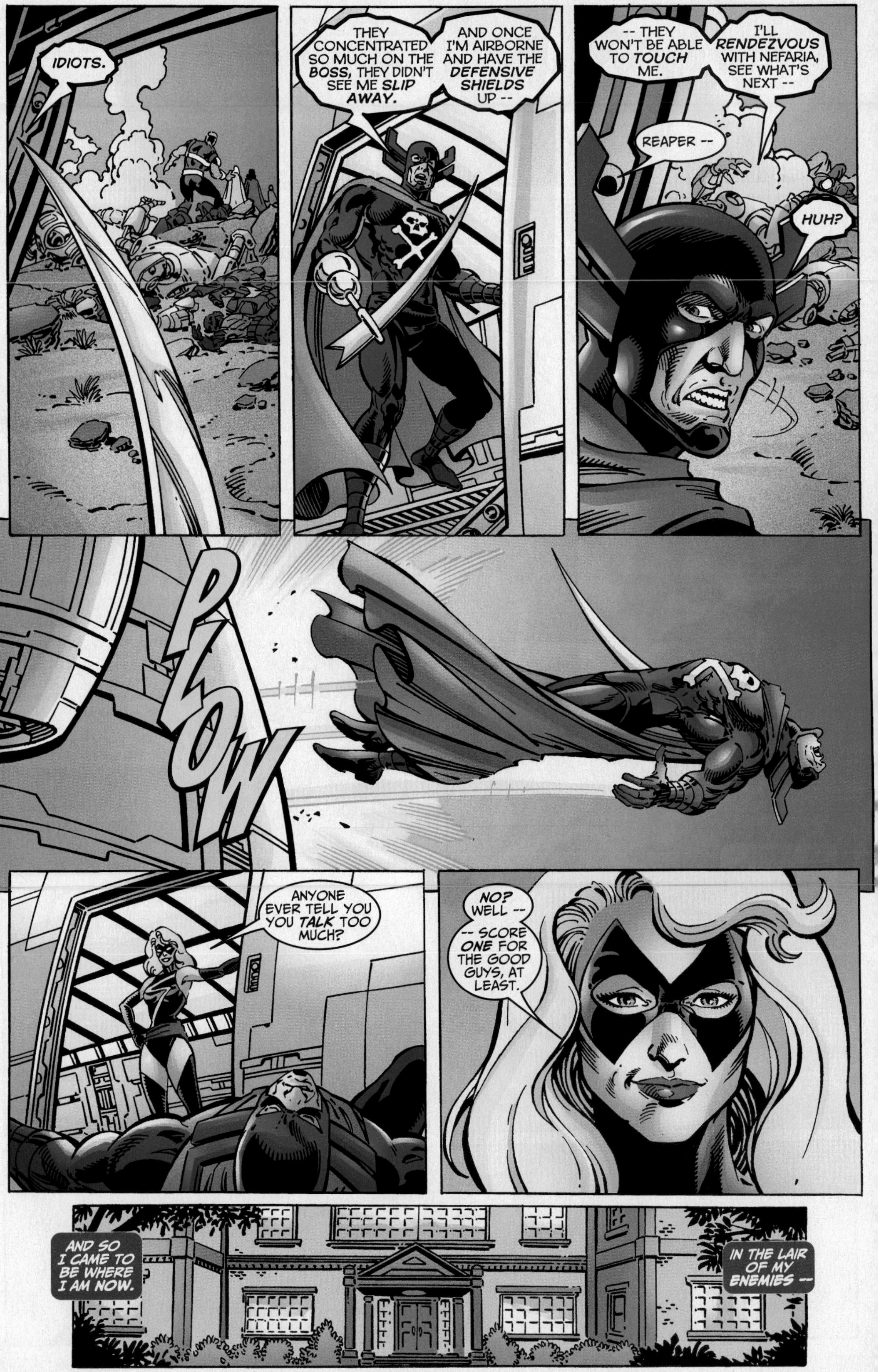
IDIOTS.
THEY CONCENTRATED SO MUCH ON THE BOSS, THEY DIDN'T SEE ME SLIP AWAY.
AND ONCE I'M AIRBORNE AND HAVE THE DEFENSIVE SHIELDS UP --
-- THEY WON'T BE ABLE TO TOUCH ME.
I'LL RENDEZVOUS WITH NEFARIA, SEE WHAT'S NEXT --
REAPER --
HUH?
PLOW
ANYONE EVER TELL YOU YOU TALK TOO MUCH?
NO? WELL --
-- SCORE ONE FOR THE GOOD GUYS, AT LEAST.
AND SO I CAME TO BE WHERE I AM NOW.
IN THE LAIR OF MY ENEMIES --

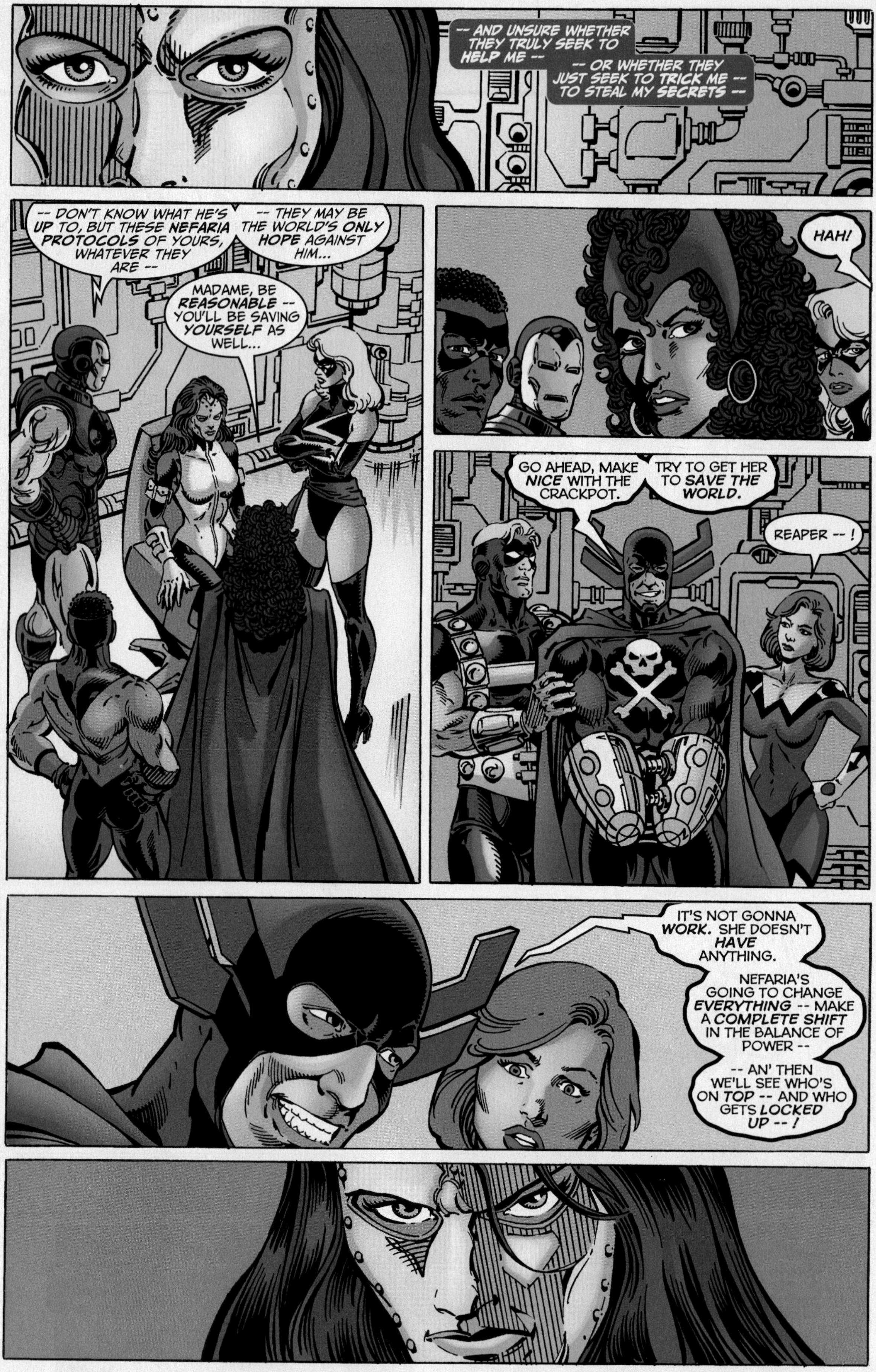
-- AND UNSURE WHETHER THEY TRULY SEEK TO HELP ME --
-- OR WHETHER THEY JUST SEEK TO TRICK ME -- TO STEAL MY SECRETS --
-- DON'T KNOW WHAT HE'S UP TO, BUT THESE NEFARIA PROTOCOLS OF YOURS, WHATEVER THEY ARE --
-- THEY MAY BE THE WORLD'S ONLY HOPE AGAINST HIM...
MADAME, BE REASONABLE -- YOU'LL BE SAVING YOURSELF AS WELL...
HAH!
GO AHEAD, MAKE NICE WITH THE CRACKPOT.
TRY TO GET HER TO SAVE THE WORLD.
REAPER -- !
IT'S NOT GONNA WORK. SHE DOESN'T HAVE ANYTHING.
NEFARIA'S GOING TO CHANGE EVERYTHING -- MAKE A COMPLETE SHIFT IN THE BALANCE OF POWER --
-- AN' THEN WE'LL SEE WHO'S ON TOP -- AND WHO GETS LOCKED UP -- !

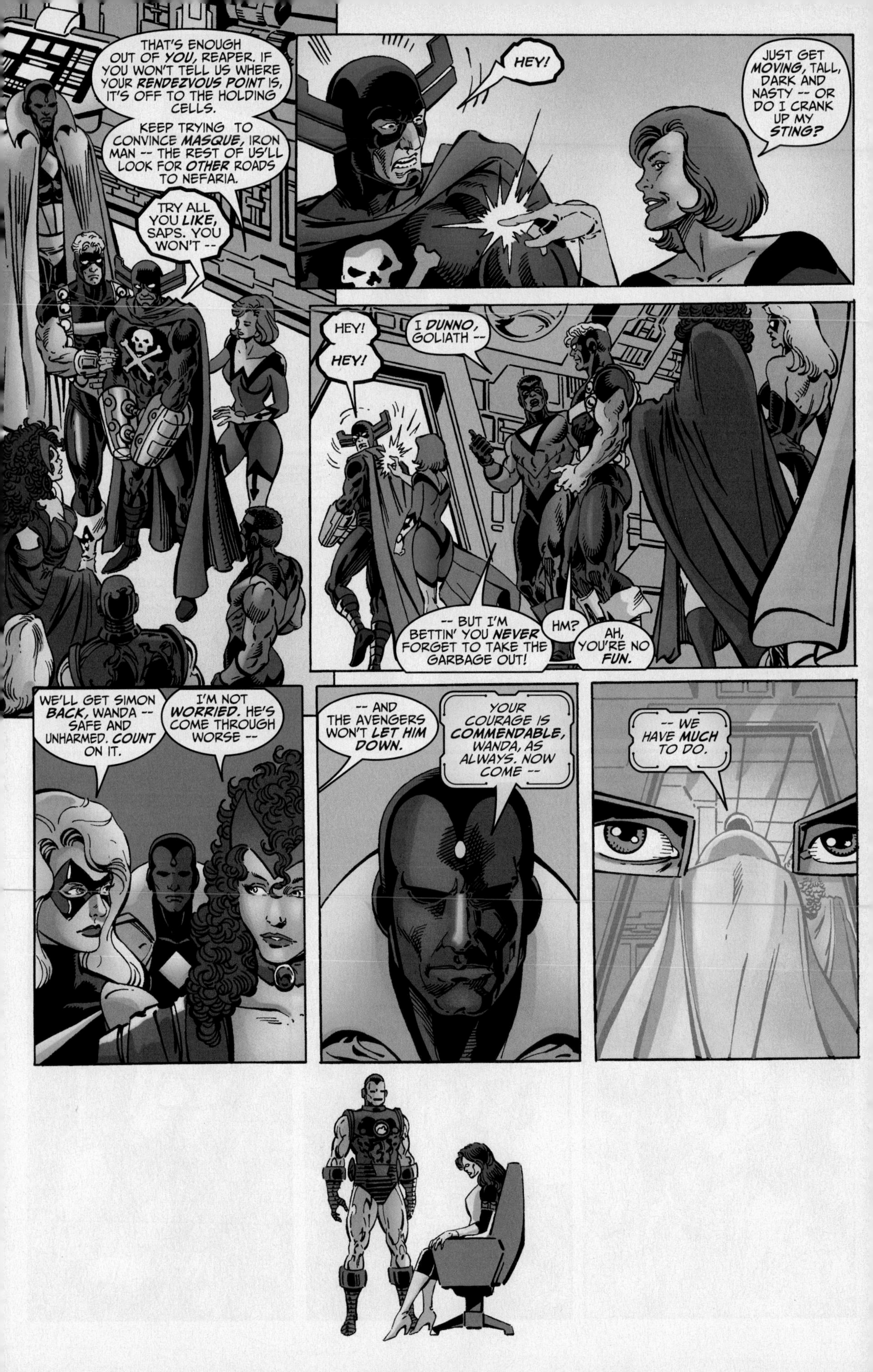
THAT'S ENOUGH OUT OF YOU, REAPER. IF YOU WON'T TELL US WHERE YOUR RENDEZVOUS POINT IS, IT'S OFF TO THE HOLDING CELLS.
KEEP TRYING TO CONVINCE MASQUE, IRON MAN -- THE REST OF US'LL LOOK FOR OTHER ROADS TO NEFARIA.
TRY ALL YOU LIKE, SAPS. YOU WON'T --
HEY!
JUST GET MOVING, TALL, DARK AND NASTY -- OR DO I CRANK UP MY STING?
HEY!
HEY!
I DUNNO, GOLIATH --
-- BUT I'M BETTIN' YOU NEVER FORGET TO TAKE THE GARBAGE OUT!
HM?
AH, YOU'RE NO FUN.
WE'LL GET SIMON BACK, WANDA -- SAFE AND UNHARMED. COUNT ON IT.
I'M NOT WORRIED. HE'S COME THROUGH WORSE --
-- AND THE AVENGERS WON'T LET HIM DOWN.
YOUR COURAGE IS COMMENDABLE, WANDA, AS ALWAYS. NOW COME --
-- WE HAVE MUCH TO DO.

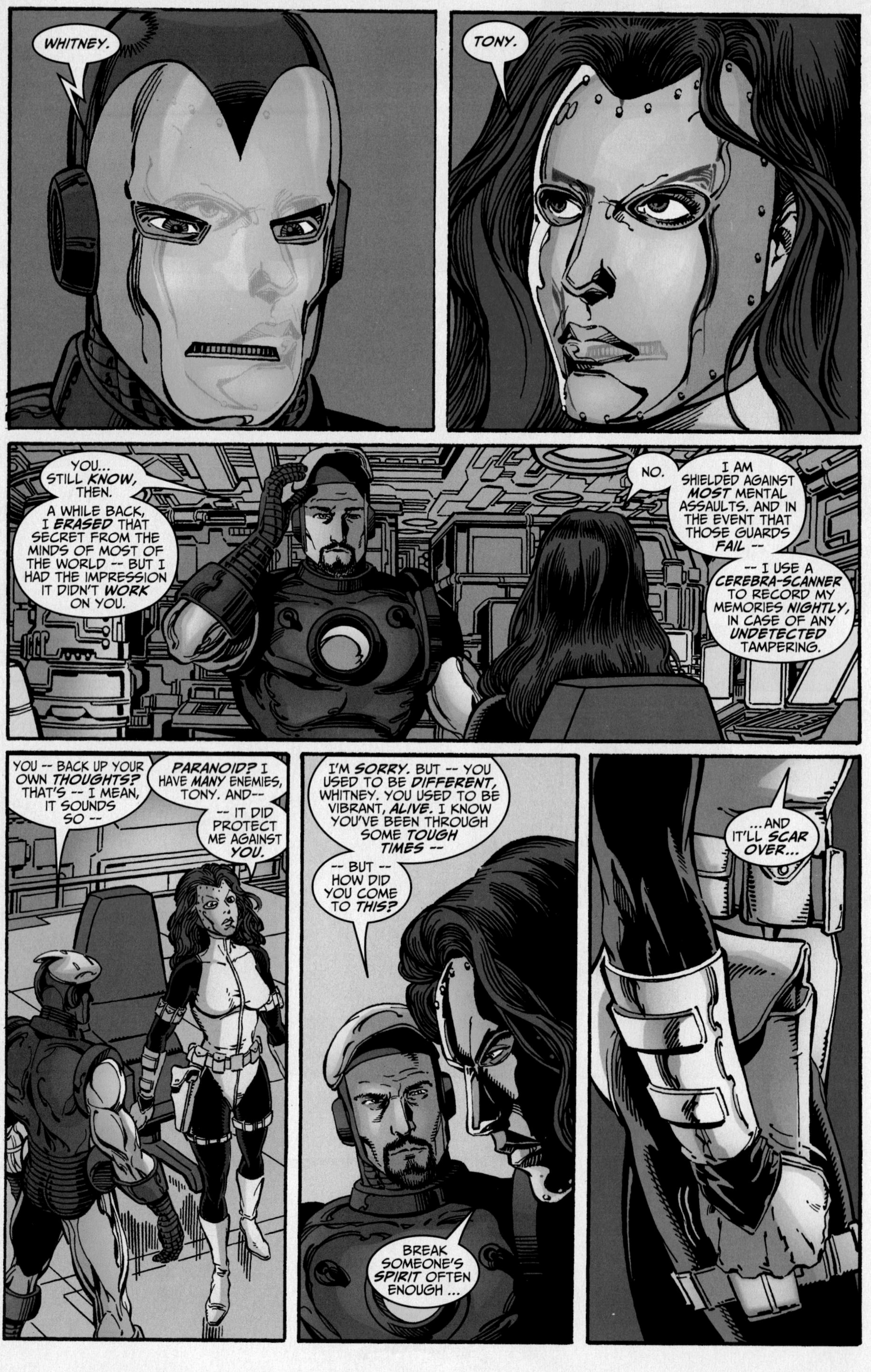
WHITNEY.
TONY.
YOU... STILL KNOW, THEN.
A WHILE BACK, I ERASED THAT SECRET FROM THE MINDS OF MOST OF THE WORLD -- BUT I HAD THE IMPRESSION IT DIDN'T WORK ON YOU.
NO.
I AM SHIELDED AGAINST MOST MENTAL ASSAULTS. AND IN THE EVENT THAT THOSE GUARDS FAIL --
-- I USE A CEREBRA-SCANNER TO RECORD MY MEMORIES NIGHTLY, IN CASE OF ANY UNDETECTED TAMPERING.
YOU -- BACK UP YOUR OWN THOUGHTS? THAT'S -- I MEAN, IT SOUNDS SO --
PARANOID? I HAVE MANY ENEMIES, TONY. AND--
-- IT DID PROTECT ME AGAINST YOU.
I'M SORRY. BUT -- YOU USED TO BE DIFFERENT, WHITNEY. YOU USED TO BE VIBRANT, ALIVE. I KNOW YOU'VE BEEN THROUGH SOME TOUGH TIMES --
-- BUT -- HOW DID YOU COME TO THIS?
BREAK SOMEONE'S SPIRIT OFTEN ENOUGH ...
...AND IT'LL SCAR OVER...

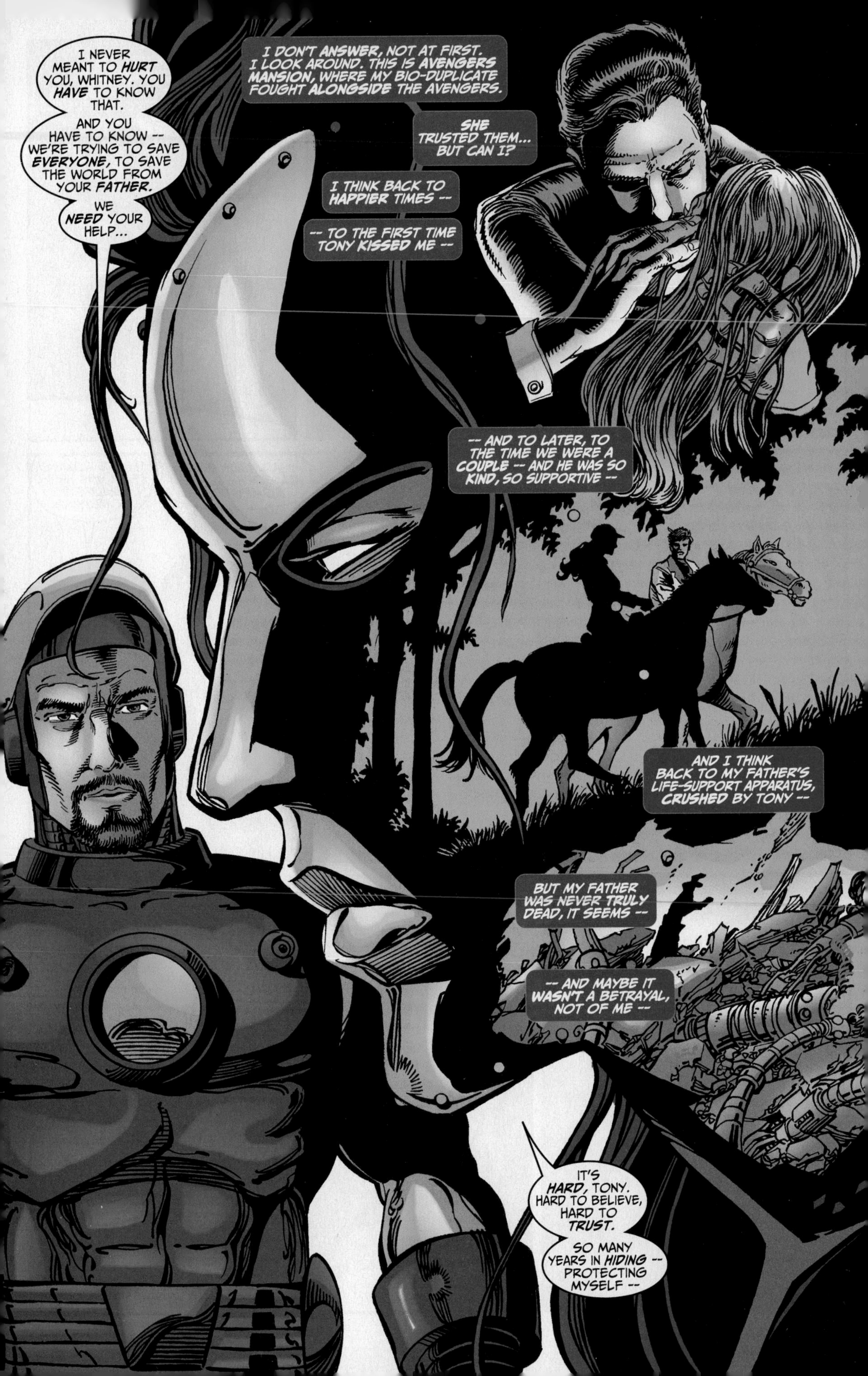
I NEVER MEANT TO HURT YOU, WHITNEY. YOU HAVE TO KNOW THAT.
AND YOU HAVE TO KNOW -- WE'RE TRYING TO SAVE EVERYONE, TO SAVE THE WORLD FROM YOUR FATHER.
WE NEED YOUR HELP...
I DON'T ANSWER, NOT AT FIRST. I LOOK AROUND. THIS IS AVENGERS MANSION, WHERE MY BIO-DUPLICATE FOUGHT ALONGSIDE THE AVENGERS.
SHE TRUSTED THEM... BUT CAN I?
I THINK BACK TO HAPPIER TIMES --
-- TO THE FIRST TIME TONY KISSED ME --
-- AND TO LATER, TO THE TIME WE WERE A COUPLE -- AND HE WAS SO KIND, SO SUPPORTIVE --
AND I THINK BACK TO MY FATHER'S LIFE-SUPPORT APPARATUS, CRUSHED BY TONY --
BUT MY FATHER WAS NEVER TRULY DEAD, IT SEEMS --
-- AND MAYBE IT WASN'T A BETRAYAL, NOT OF ME --
IT'S HARD, TONY. HARD TO BELIEVE, HARD TO TRUST.
SO MANY YEARS IN HIDING -- PROTECTING MYSELF --

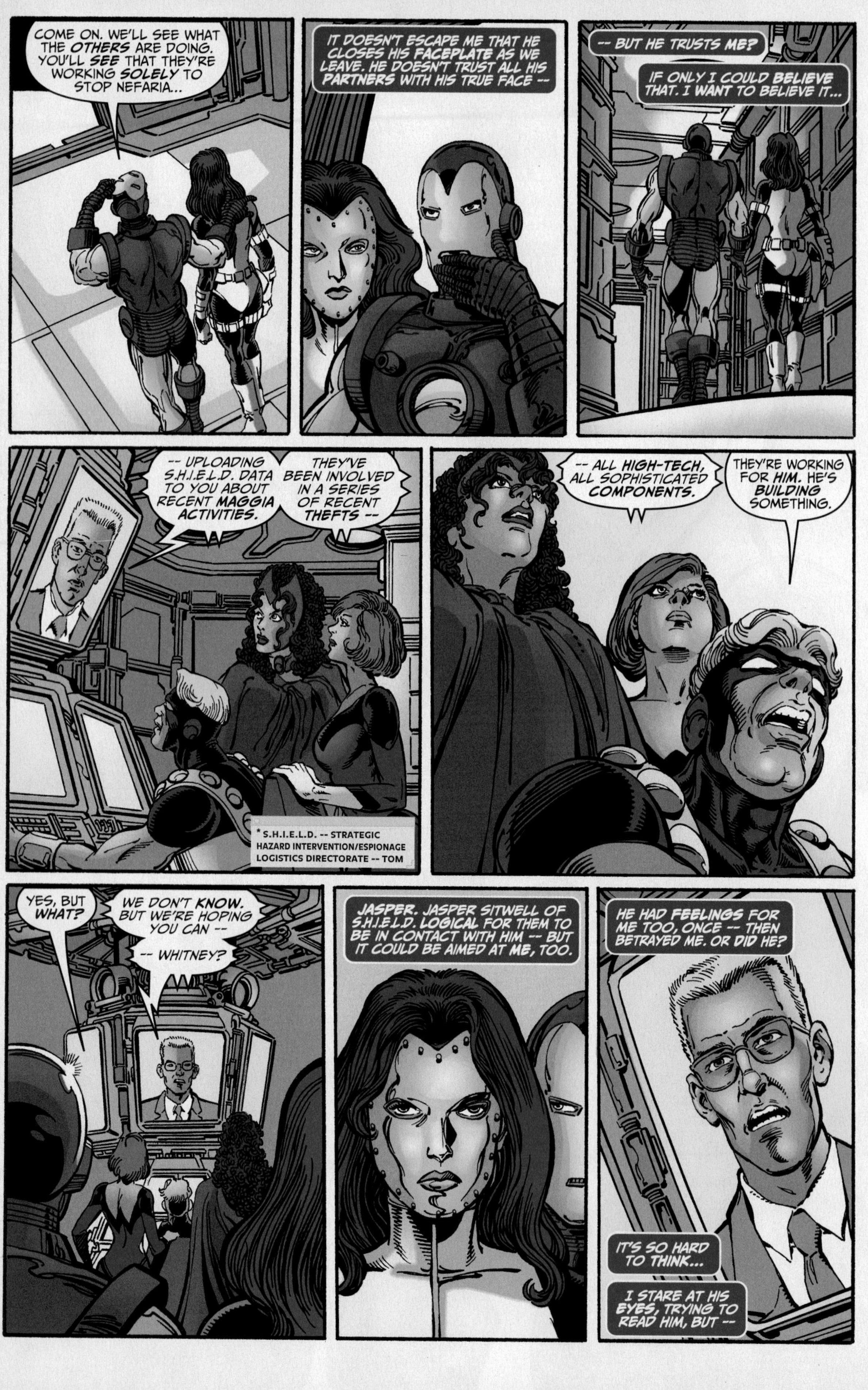
COME ON. WE'LL SEE WHAT THE *OTHERS* ARE DOING. YOU'LL *SEE* THAT THEY'RE WORKING *SOLELY* TO STOP NEFARIA...
IT DOESN'T ESCAPE ME THAT HE CLOSES HIS *FACEPLATE* AS WE LEAVE. HE DOESN'T TRUST ALL HIS *PARTNERS* WITH HIS TRUE FACE --
-- BUT HE TRUSTS *ME*?
IF ONLY I COULD *BELIEVE* THAT. I *WANT* TO BELIEVE IT...
-- UPLOADING S.H.I.E.L.D. DATA TO YOU ABOUT RECENT *MAGGIA* *ACTIVITIES*.
THEY'VE BEEN INVOLVED IN A SERIES OF RECENT *THEFTS* --
* S.H.I.E.L.D. -- STRATEGIC HAZARD INTERVENTION/ESPIONAGE LOGISTICS DIRECTORATE -- TOM
-- ALL *HIGH-TECH*, ALL SOPHISTICATED *COMPONENTS*.
THEY'RE WORKING FOR *HIM*. HE'S *BUILDING* SOMETHING.
YES, BUT *WHAT*?
WE DON'T *KNOW*. BUT WE'RE HOPING YOU CAN --
-- WHITNEY?
JASPER. JASPER SITWELL OF S.H.I.E.L.D. *LOGICAL* FOR THEM TO BE IN CONTACT WITH HIM -- BUT IT COULD BE AIMED AT *ME*, TOO.
HE HAD *FEELINGS* FOR ME TOO, ONCE -- THEN BETRAYED ME. OR *DID* HE?
IT'S SO HARD TO THINK...
I STARE AT HIS *EYES*, TRYING TO READ HIM, BUT --

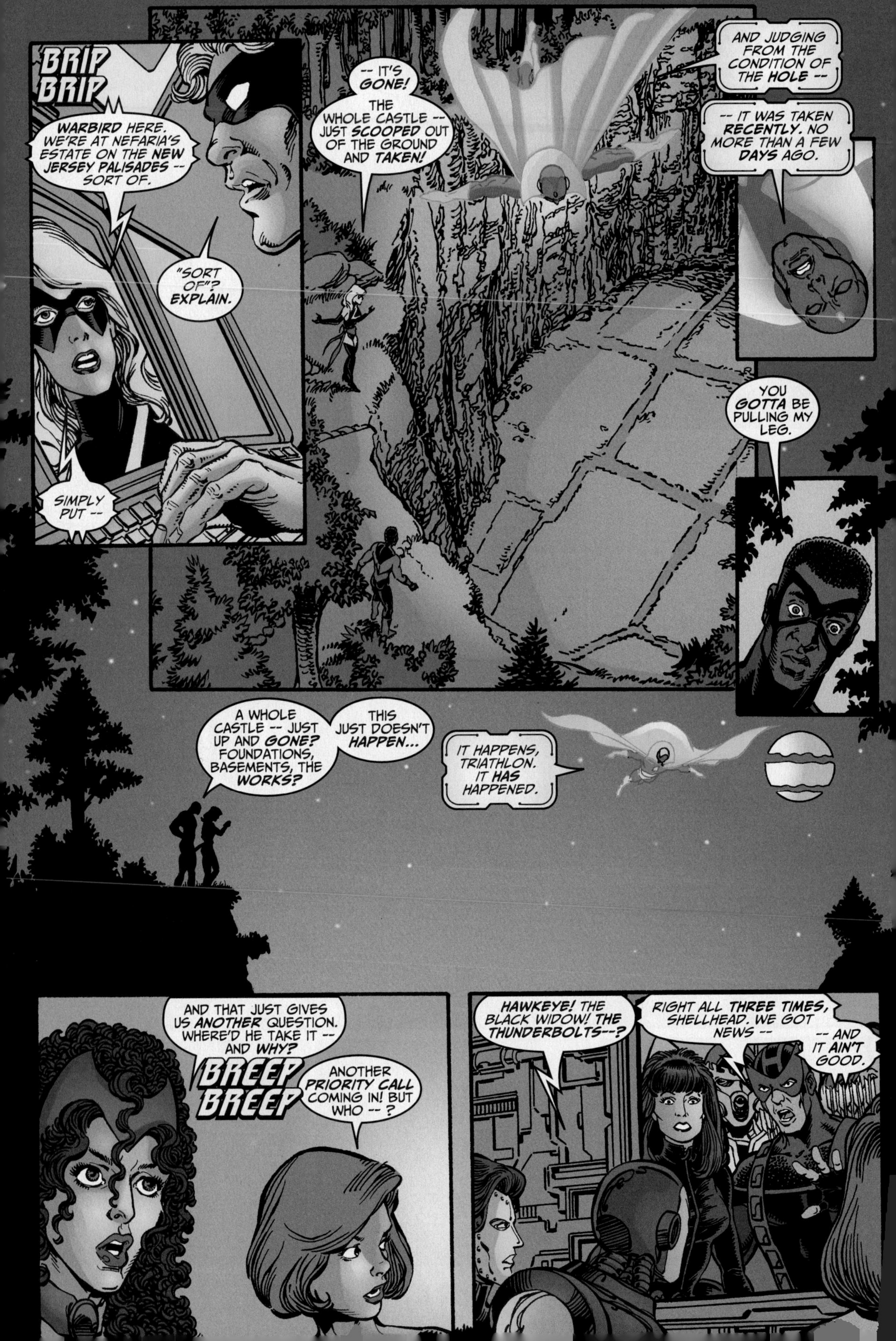
BRIP BRIP
WARBIRD HERE. WE'RE AT NEFARIA'S ESTATE ON THE NEW JERSEY PALISADES -- SORT OF.
"SORT OF"? EXPLAIN.
SIMPLY PUT --
-- IT'S GONE!
THE WHOLE CASTLE -- JUST SCOOPED OUT OF THE GROUND AND TAKEN!
AND JUDGING FROM THE CONDITION OF THE HOLE --
-- IT WAS TAKEN RECENTLY. NO MORE THAN A FEW DAYS AGO.
YOU GOTTA BE PULLING MY LEG.
A WHOLE CASTLE -- JUST UP AND GONE? FOUNDATIONS, BASEMENTS, THE WORKS?
THIS JUST DOESN'T HAPPEN...
IT HAPPENS, TRIATHLON. IT HAS HAPPENED.
AND THAT JUST GIVES US ANOTHER QUESTION. WHERE'D HE TAKE IT -- AND WHY?
BREEP BREEP
ANOTHER PRIORITY CALL COMING IN! BUT WHO -- ?
HAWKEYE! THE BLACK WIDOW! THE THUNDERBOLTS--?
RIGHT ALL THREE TIMES, SHELLHEAD. WE GOT NEWS --
-- AND IT AIN'T GOOD.

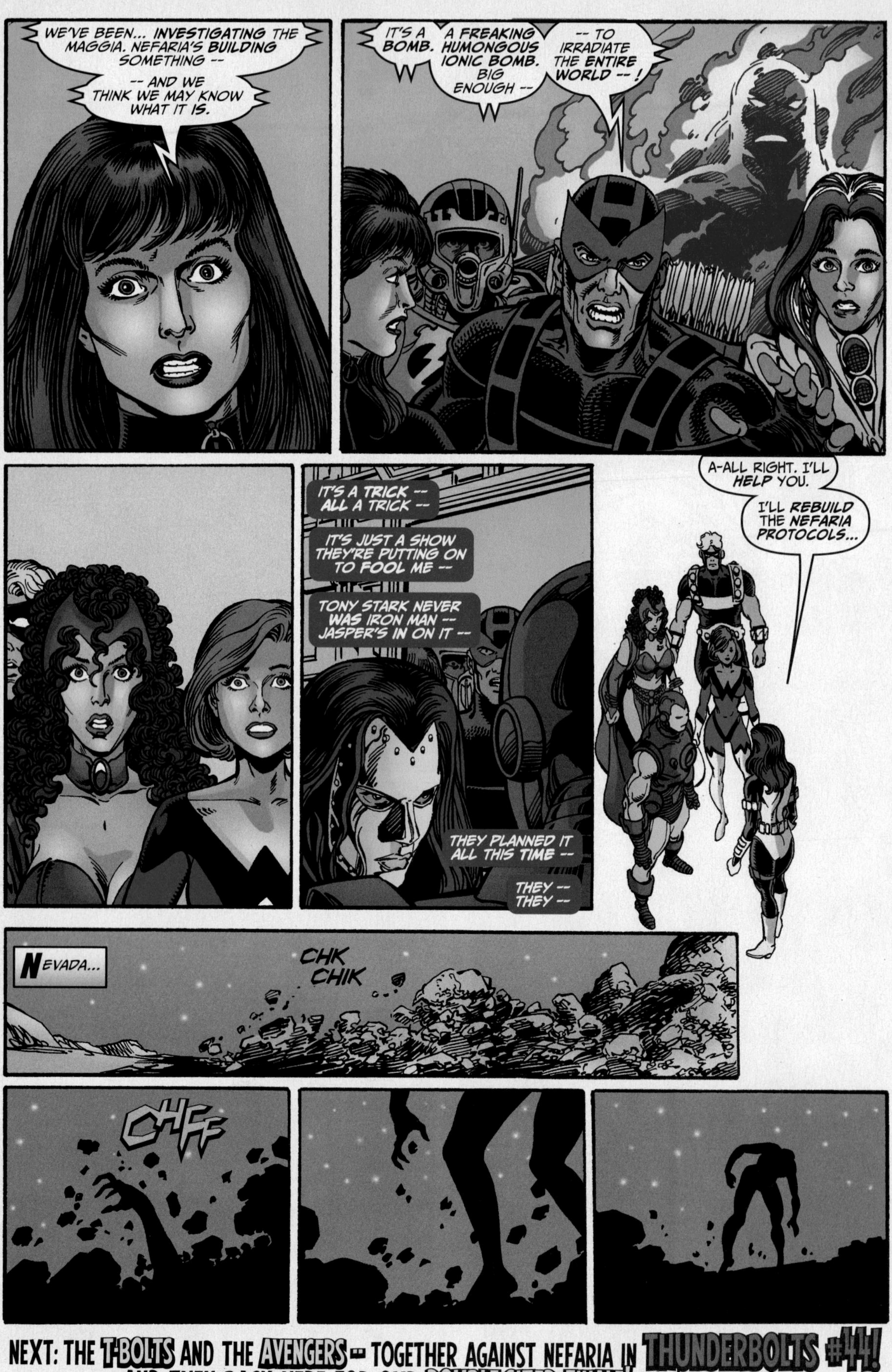
WE'VE BEEN... INVESTIGATING THE MAGGIA. NEFARIA'S BUILDING SOMETHING --
-- AND WE THINK WE MAY KNOW WHAT IT IS.
IT'S A BOMB.
A FREAKING HUMONGOUS IONIC BOMB. BIG ENOUGH --
-- TO IRRADIATE THE ENTIRE WORLD -- !
IT'S A TRICK -- ALL A TRICK --
IT'S JUST A SHOW THEY'RE PUTTING ON TO FOOL ME --
TONY STARK NEVER WAS IRON MAN -- JASPER'S IN ON IT --
THEY PLANNED IT ALL THIS TIME --
THEY -- THEY --
A-ALL RIGHT. I'LL HELP YOU.
I'LL REBUILD THE NEFARIA PROTOCOLS...
NEVADA...
CHK CHIK
CHFF

NEXT: THE T-BOLTS AND THE AVENGERS -- TOGETHER AGAINST NEFARIA IN THUNDERBOLTS #44!
AND THEN BACK HERE FOR OUR DOUBLE-SIZED FINALE! DON'T MISS IT!

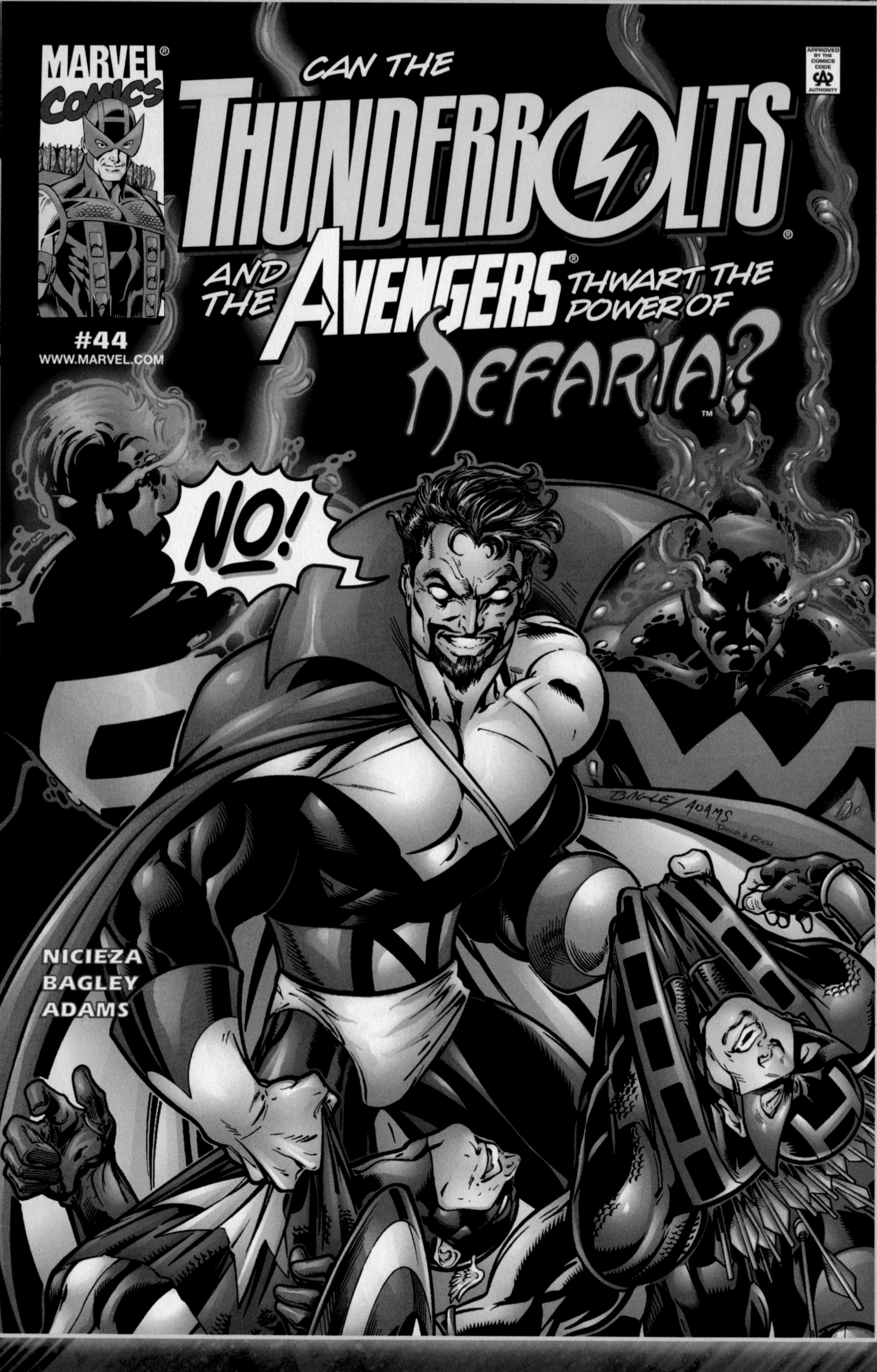
MARVEL® COMICS
CAN THE
THUNDERBOLTS®
AND THE AVENGERS® THWART THE POWER OF
NEFARIA?™
#44
WWW.MARVEL.COM
APPROVED BY THE COMICS CODE AUTHORITY
NO!
BAGLEY/ADAMS
NICIEZA
BAGLEY
ADAMS

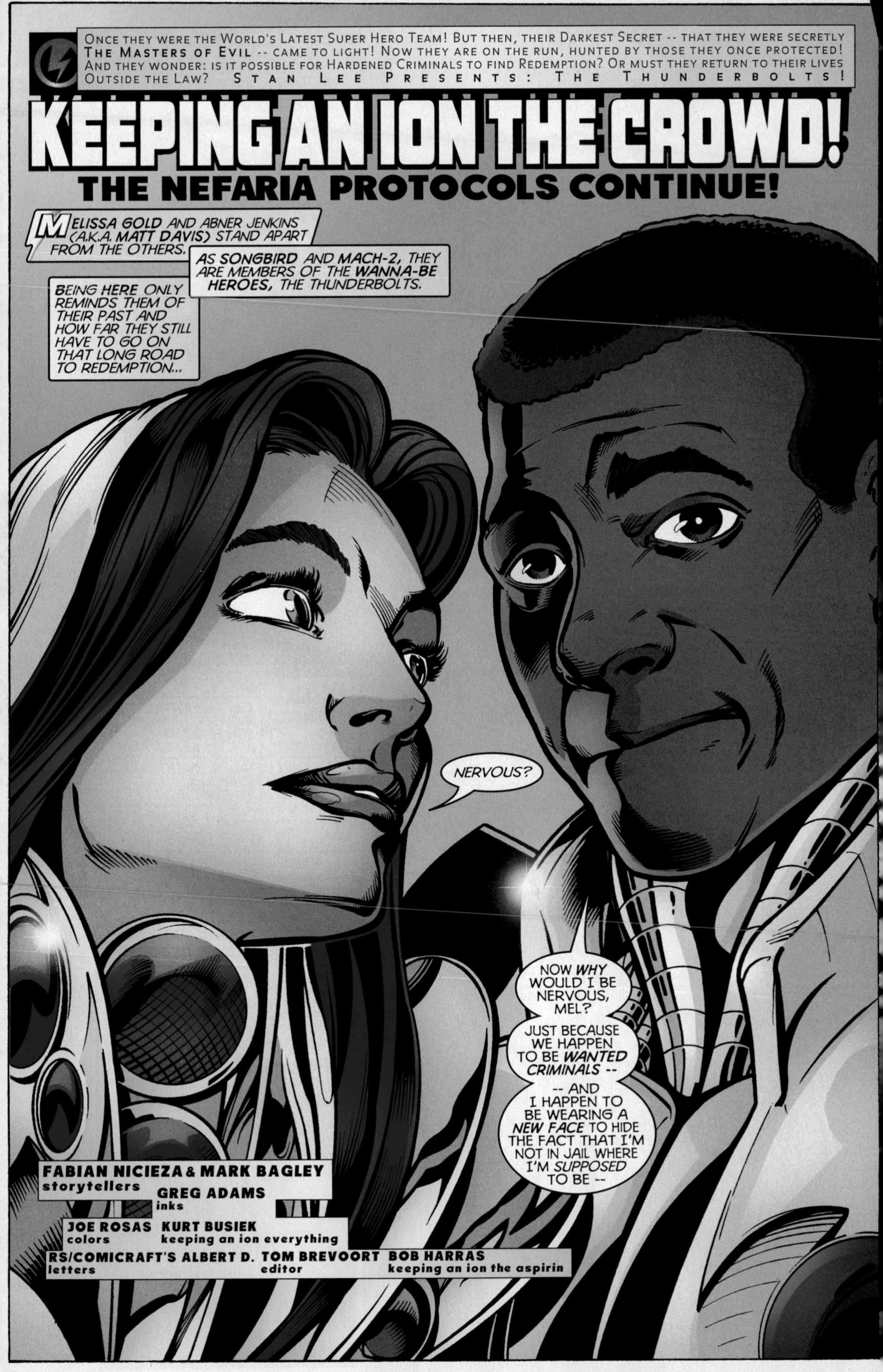

Once they were the World's Latest Super Hero Team! But then, their Darkest Secret -- that they were secretly The Masters of Evil -- came to light! Now they are on the run, hunted by those they once protected! And they wonder: is it possible for Hardened Criminals to find Redemption? Or must they return to their lives Outside the Law? Stan Lee Presents: The Thunderbolts!
KEEPING AN ION THE CROWD!
THE NEFARIA PROTOCOLS CONTINUE!
MELISSA GOLD AND ABNER JENKINS (A.K.A. MATT DAVIS) STAND APART FROM THE OTHERS.
AS SONGBIRD AND MACH-2, THEY ARE MEMBERS OF THE WANNA-BE HEROES, THE THUNDERBOLTS.
BEING HERE ONLY REMINDS THEM OF THEIR PAST AND HOW FAR THEY STILL HAVE TO GO ON THAT LONG ROAD TO REDEMPTION...
NERVOUS?
NOW WHY WOULD I BE NERVOUS, MEL?
JUST BECAUSE WE HAPPEN TO BE WANTED CRIMINALS --
-- AND I HAPPEN TO BE WEARING A NEW FACE TO HIDE THE FACT THAT I'M NOT IN JAIL WHERE I'M SUPPOSED TO BE --
FABIAN NICIEZA & MARK BAGLEY storytellers
GREG ADAMS inks
JOE ROSAS colors
KURT BUSIEK keeping an ion everything
RS/COMICRAFT'S ALBERT D. letters
TOM BREVOORT editor
BOB HARRAS keeping an ion the aspirin

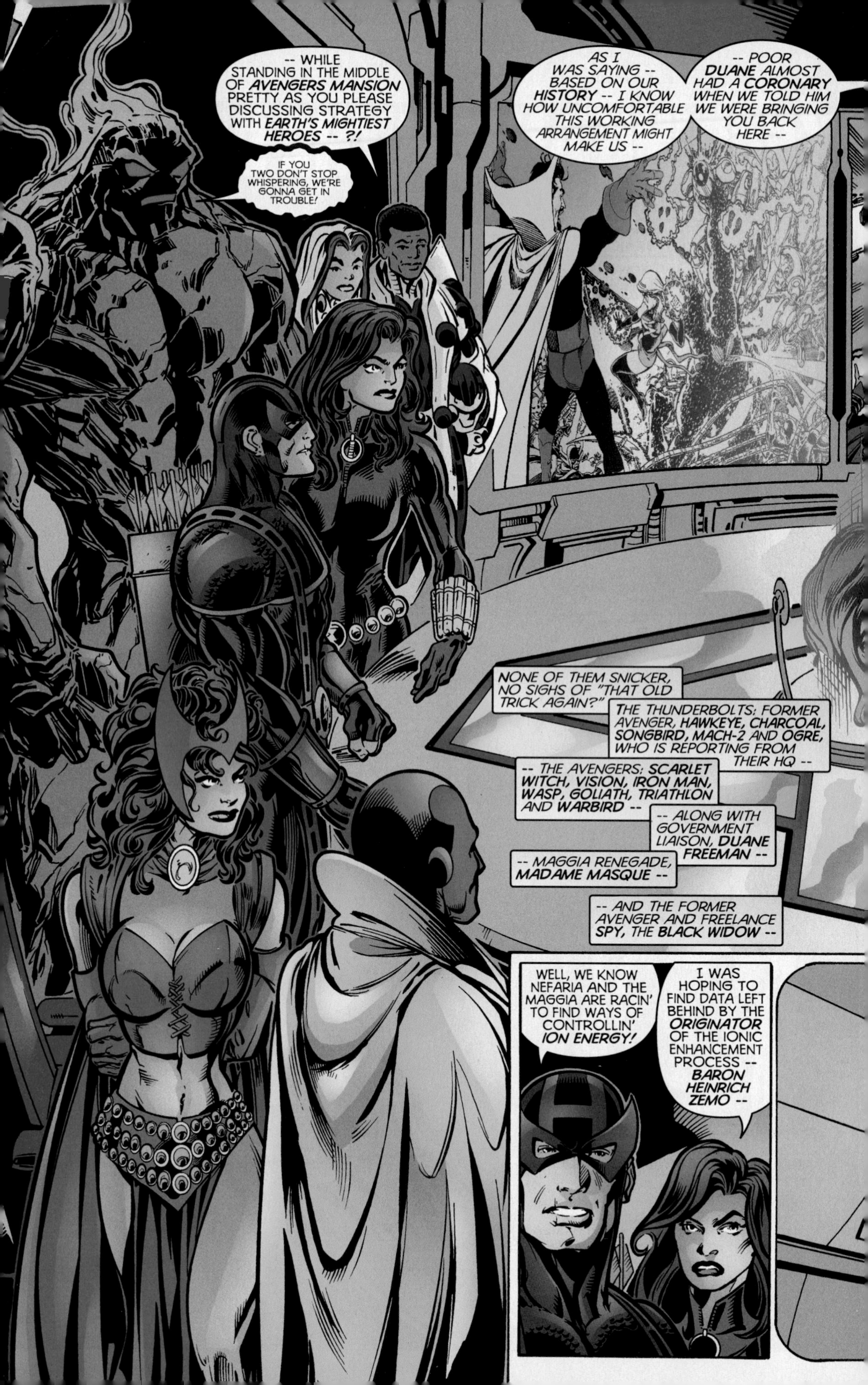
-- WHILE STANDING IN THE MIDDLE OF AVENGERS MANSION PRETTY AS YOU PLEASE DISCUSSING STRATEGY WITH EARTH'S MIGHTIEST HEROES -- ?!
IF YOU TWO DON'T STOP WHISPERING, WE'RE GONNA GET IN TROUBLE!
AS I WAS SAYING -- BASED ON OUR HISTORY -- I KNOW HOW UNCOMFORTABLE THIS WORKING ARRANGEMENT MIGHT MAKE US --
-- POOR DUANE ALMOST HAD A CORONARY WHEN WE TOLD HIM WE WERE BRINGING YOU BACK HERE --
NONE OF THEM SNICKER, NO SIGHS OF "THAT OLD TRICK AGAIN?"
THE THUNDERBOLTS: FORMER AVENGER, HAWKEYE, CHARCOAL, SONGBIRD, MACH-2 AND OGRE, WHO IS REPORTING FROM THEIR HQ --
-- THE AVENGERS: SCARLET WITCH, VISION, IRON MAN, WASP, GOLIATH, TRIATHLON AND WARBIRD --
-- ALONG WITH GOVERNMENT LIAISON, DUANE FREEMAN --
-- MAGGIA RENEGADE, MADAME MASQUE --
-- AND THE FORMER AVENGER AND FREELANCE SPY, THE BLACK WIDOW --
WELL, WE KNOW NEFARIA AND THE MAGGIA ARE RACIN' TO FIND WAYS OF CONTROLLIN' ION ENERGY!
I WAS HOPING TO FIND DATA LEFT BEHIND BY THE ORIGINATOR OF THE IONIC ENHANCEMENT PROCESS -- BARON HEINRICH ZEMO --

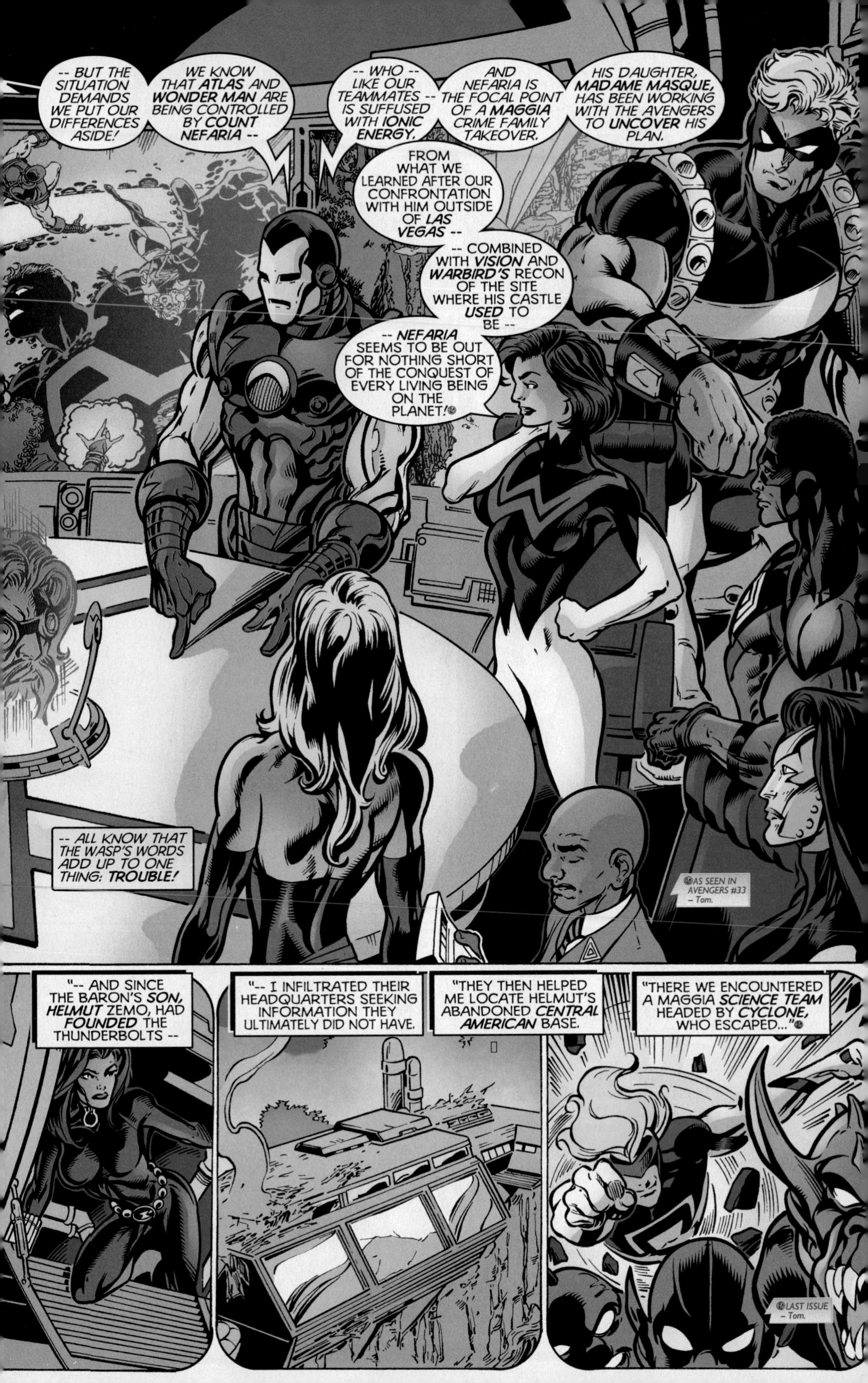
-- BUT THE SITUATION DEMANDS WE PUT OUR DIFFERENCES ASIDE!
WE KNOW THAT ATLAS AND WONDER MAN ARE BEING CONTROLLED BY COUNT NEFARIA --
-- WHO -- LIKE OUR TEAMMATES -- IS SUFFUSED WITH IONIC ENERGY.
AND NEFARIA IS THE FOCAL POINT OF A MAGGIA CRIME FAMILY TAKEOVER.
HIS DAUGHTER, MADAME MASQUE, HAS BEEN WORKING WITH THE AVENGERS TO UNCOVER HIS PLAN.
FROM WHAT WE LEARNED AFTER OUR CONFRONTATION WITH HIM OUTSIDE OF LAS VEGAS --
-- COMBINED WITH VISION AND WARBIRD'S RECON OF THE SITE WHERE HIS CASTLE USED TO BE --
-- NEFARIA SEEMS TO BE OUT FOR NOTHING SHORT OF THE CONQUEST OF EVERY LIVING BEING ON THE PLANET!
-- ALL KNOW THAT THE WASP'S WORDS ADD UP TO ONE THING: TROUBLE!
AS SEEN IN AVENGERS #33 – Tom.
"-- AND SINCE THE BARON'S SON, HELMUT ZEMO, HAD FOUNDED THE THUNDERBOLTS --
"-- I INFILTRATED THEIR HEADQUARTERS SEEKING INFORMATION THEY ULTIMATELY DID NOT HAVE.
"THEY THEN HELPED ME LOCATE HELMUT'S ABANDONED CENTRAL AMERICAN BASE.
"THERE WE ENCOUNTERED A MAGGIA SCIENCE TEAM HEADED BY CYCLONE, WHO ESCAPED..."
LAST ISSUE – Tom.

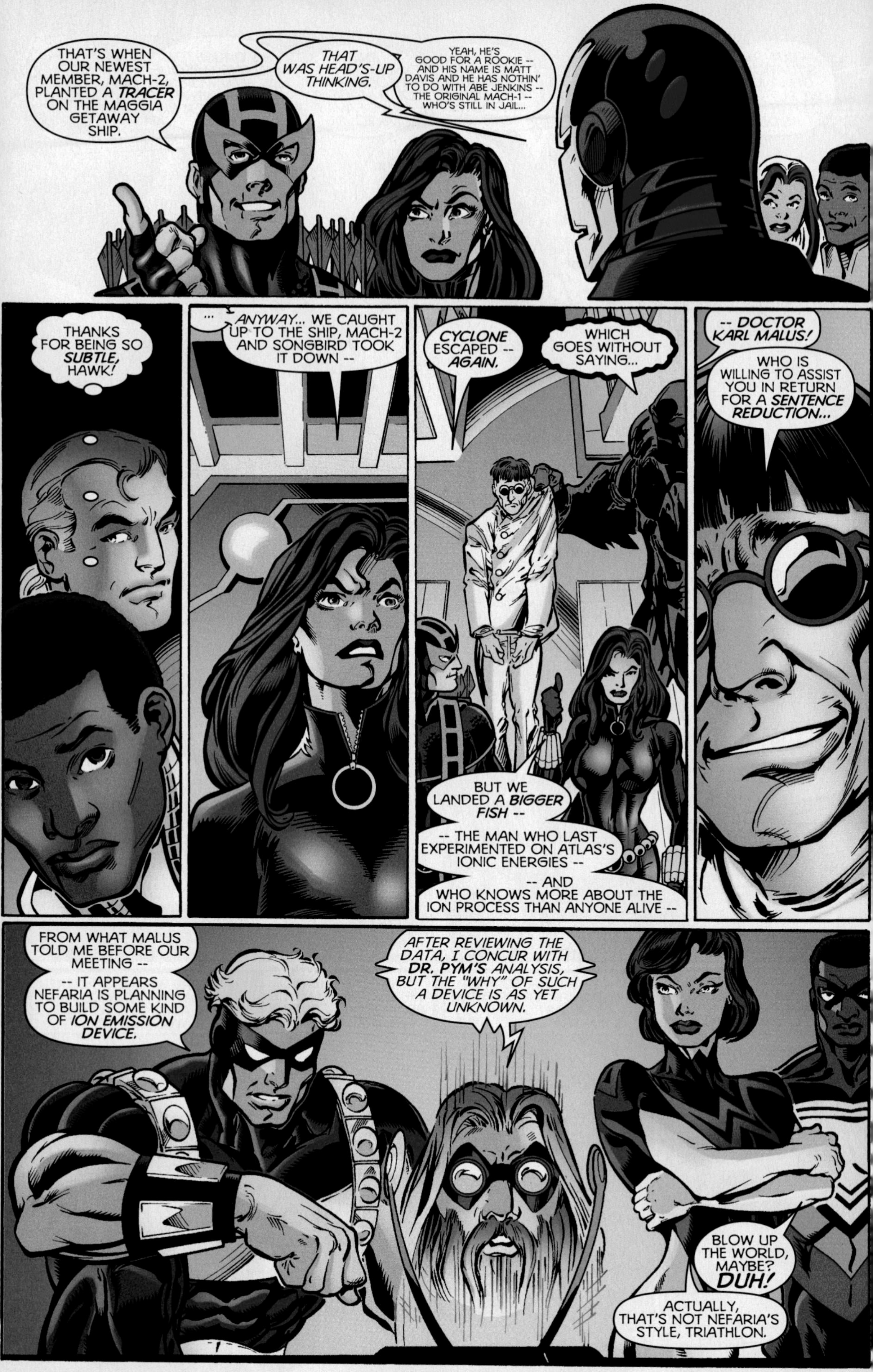
THAT'S WHEN OUR NEWEST MEMBER, MACH-2, PLANTED A *TRACER* ON THE MAGGIA GETAWAY SHIP.
THAT WAS HEAD'S-UP THINKING.
YEAH, HE'S GOOD FOR A ROOKIE -- AND HIS NAME IS MATT DAVIS AND HE HAS NOTHIN' TO DO WITH ABE JENKINS -- THE ORIGINAL MACH-1 -- WHO'S STILL IN JAIL...
THANKS FOR BEING SO *SUBTLE,* HAWK!
... *ANYWAY*... WE CAUGHT UP TO THE SHIP, MACH-2 AND SONGBIRD TOOK IT DOWN --
CYCLONE ESCAPED -- *AGAIN.*
WHICH GOES WITHOUT SAYING...
BUT WE LANDED A *BIGGER FISH* --
-- THE MAN WHO LAST EXPERIMENTED ON ATLAS'S IONIC ENERGIES --
-- AND WHO KNOWS MORE ABOUT THE ION PROCESS THAN ANYONE ALIVE --
-- *DOCTOR KARL MALUS!*
WHO IS WILLING TO ASSIST YOU IN RETURN FOR A *SENTENCE REDUCTION...*
FROM WHAT MALUS TOLD ME BEFORE OUR MEETING --
-- IT APPEARS NEFARIA IS PLANNING TO BUILD SOME KIND OF *ION EMISSION DEVICE.*
AFTER REVIEWING THE DATA, I CONCUR WITH **DR. PYM'S** *ANALYSIS, BUT THE "WHY" OF SUCH A DEVICE IS AS YET UNKNOWN.*
BLOW UP THE WORLD, MAYBE? ***DUH!***
ACTUALLY, THAT'S NOT NEFARIA'S STYLE, TRIATHLON.

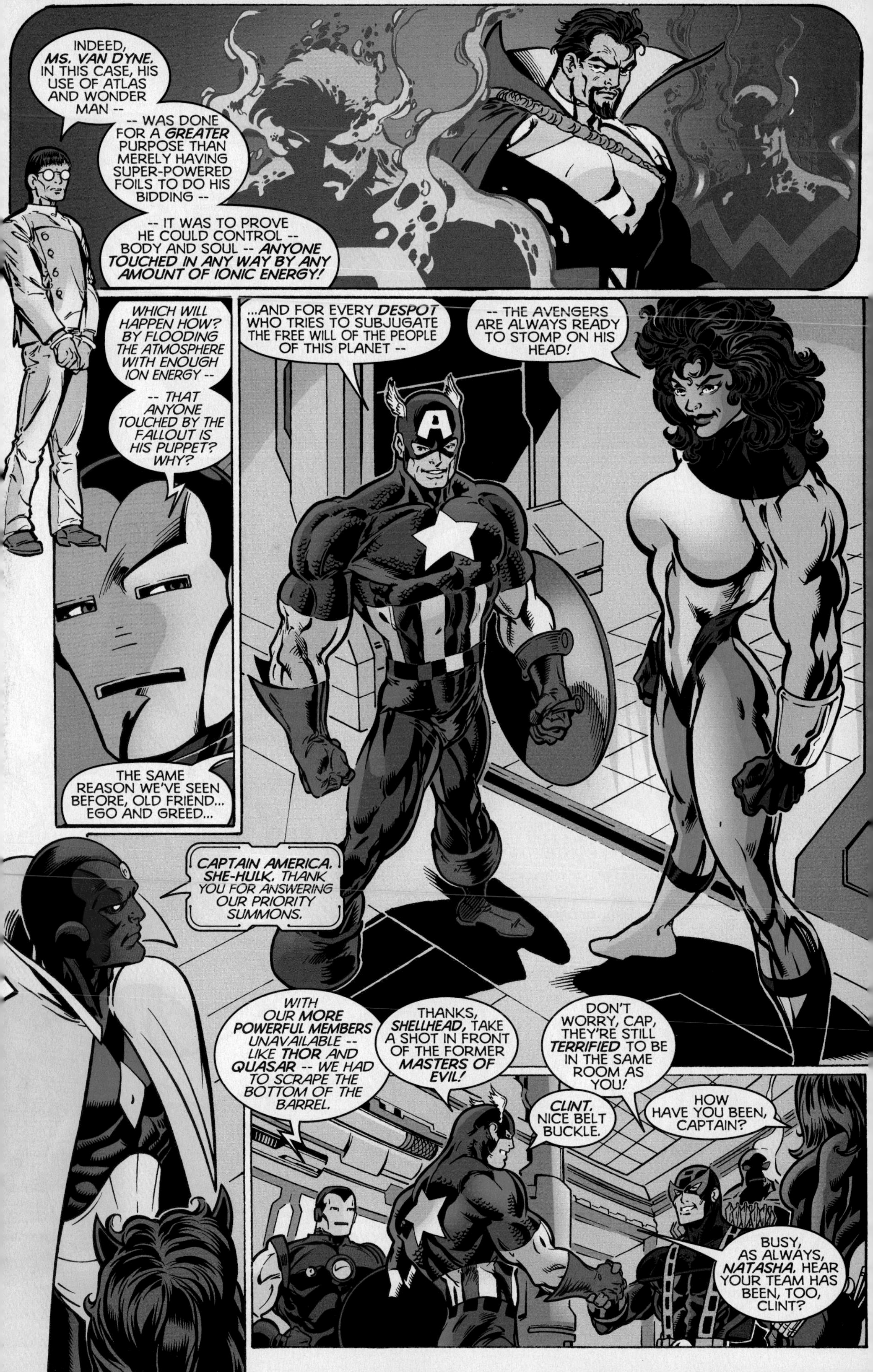

INDEED, **MS. VAN DYNE.** IN THIS CASE, HIS USE OF ATLAS AND WONDER MAN --
-- WAS DONE FOR A ***GREATER*** PURPOSE THAN MERELY HAVING SUPER-POWERED FOILS TO DO HIS BIDDING --
-- IT WAS TO PROVE HE COULD CONTROL -- BODY AND SOUL -- ***ANYONE TOUCHED IN ANY WAY BY ANY AMOUNT OF IONIC ENERGY!***
WHICH WILL HAPPEN HOW? BY FLOODING THE ATMOSPHERE WITH ENOUGH ION ENERGY --
-- THAT ANYONE TOUCHED BY THE FALLOUT IS HIS PUPPET? WHY?
THE SAME REASON WE'VE SEEN BEFORE, OLD FRIEND... EGO AND GREED...
...AND FOR EVERY ***DESPOT*** WHO TRIES TO SUBJUGATE THE FREE WILL OF THE PEOPLE OF THIS PLANET --
-- THE AVENGERS ARE ALWAYS READY TO STOMP ON HIS HEAD!
CAPTAIN AMERICA. SHE-HULK. *THANK YOU FOR ANSWERING OUR PRIORITY SUMMONS.*
WITH OUR **MORE POWERFUL MEMBERS** UNAVAILABLE -- LIKE **THOR** AND **QUASAR** -- WE HAD TO SCRAPE THE BOTTOM OF THE BARREL.
THANKS, ***SHELLHEAD,*** TAKE A SHOT IN FRONT OF THE FORMER ***MASTERS OF EVIL!***
DON'T WORRY, CAP, THEY'RE STILL ***TERRIFIED*** TO BE IN THE SAME ROOM AS YOU!
CLINT. NICE BELT BUCKLE.
HOW HAVE YOU BEEN, CAPTAIN?
BUSY, AS ALWAYS, ***NATASHA.*** HEAR YOUR TEAM HAS BEEN, TOO, CLINT?

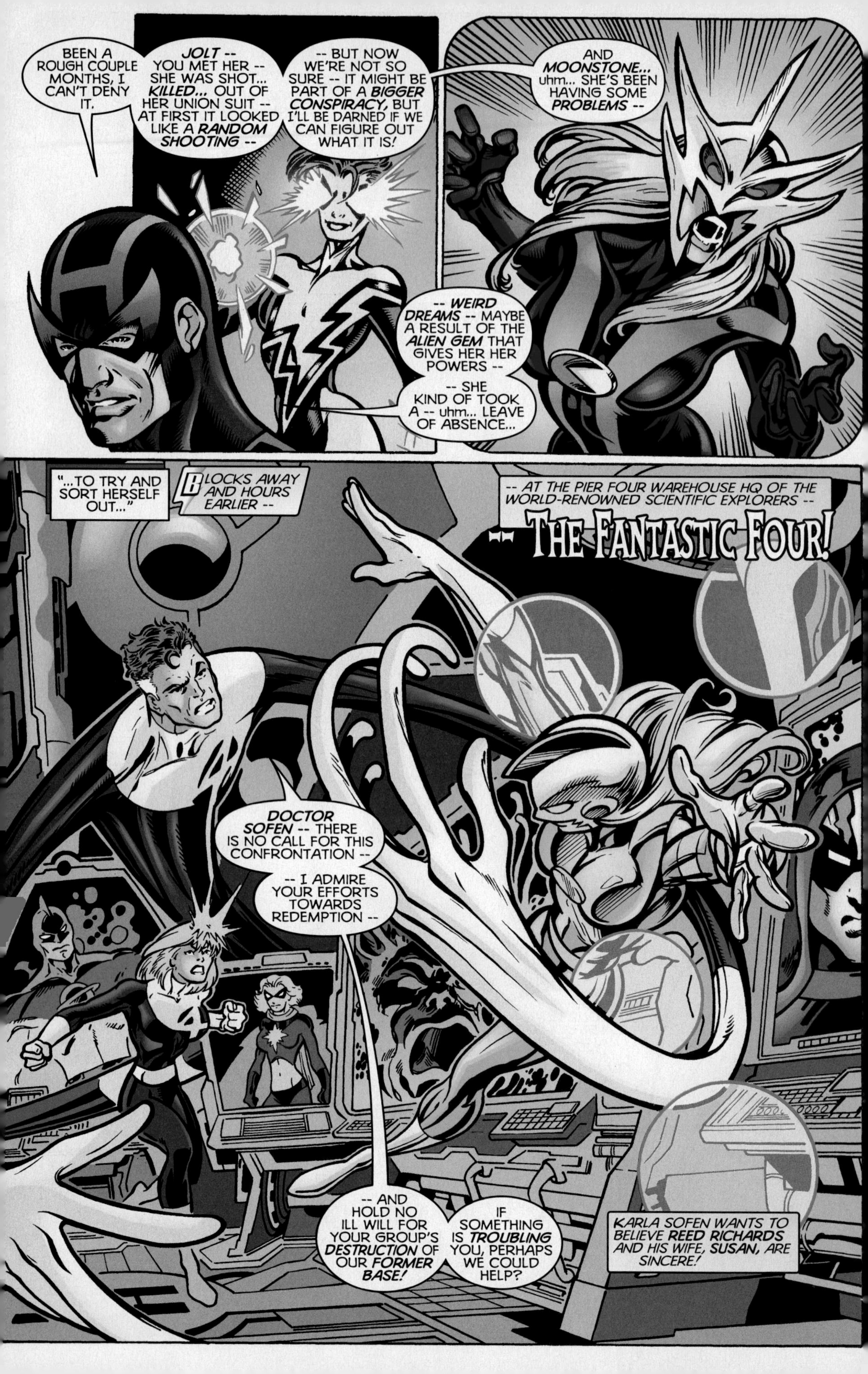
BEEN A ROUGH COUPLE MONTHS, I CAN'T DENY IT.
JOLT -- YOU MET HER -- SHE WAS SHOT... KILLED... OUT OF HER UNION SUIT -- AT FIRST IT LOOKED LIKE A RANDOM SHOOTING --
-- BUT NOW WE'RE NOT SO SURE -- IT MIGHT BE PART OF A BIGGER CONSPIRACY, BUT I'LL BE DARNED IF WE CAN FIGURE OUT WHAT IT IS!
AND MOONSTONE... uhm... SHE'S BEEN HAVING SOME PROBLEMS --
-- WEIRD DREAMS -- MAYBE A RESULT OF THE ALIEN GEM THAT GIVES HER HER POWERS --
-- SHE KIND OF TOOK A -- uhm... LEAVE OF ABSENCE...
"...TO TRY AND SORT HERSELF OUT..."
BLOCKS AWAY AND HOURS EARLIER --
-- AT THE PIER FOUR WAREHOUSE HQ OF THE WORLD-RENOWNED SCIENTIFIC EXPLORERS --
-- THE FANTASTIC FOUR!
DOCTOR SOFEN -- THERE IS NO CALL FOR THIS CONFRONTATION --
-- I ADMIRE YOUR EFFORTS TOWARDS REDEMPTION --
-- AND HOLD NO ILL WILL FOR YOUR GROUP'S DESTRUCTION OF OUR FORMER BASE!
IF SOMETHING IS TROUBLING YOU, PERHAPS WE COULD HELP?
KARLA SOFEN WANTS TO BELIEVE REED RICHARDS AND HIS WIFE, SUSAN, ARE SINCERE!

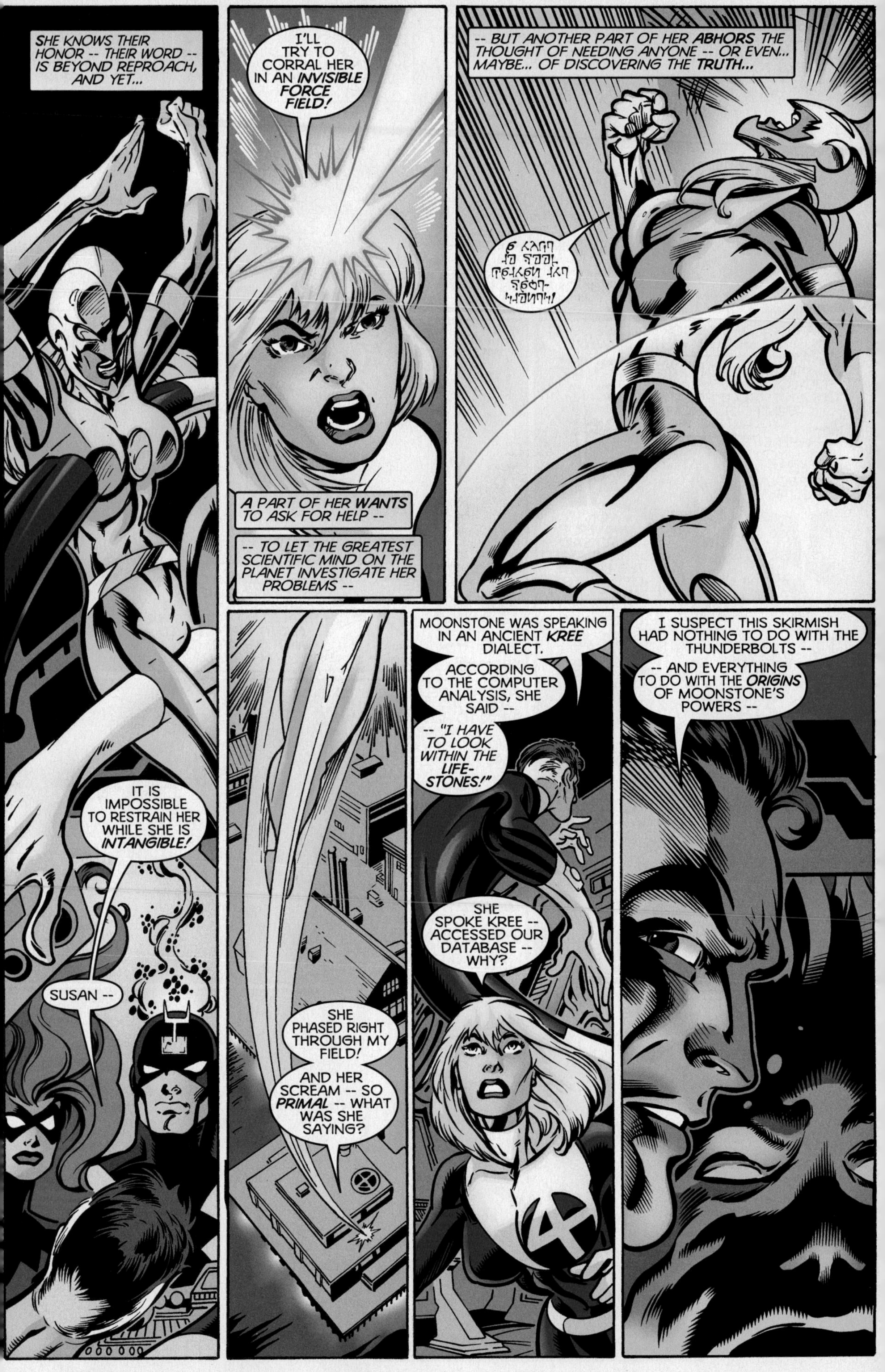
SHE KNOWS THEIR HONOR -- THEIR WORD -- IS BEYOND REPROACH, AND YET...
I'LL TRY TO CORRAL HER IN AN INVISIBLE FORCE FIELD!
A PART OF HER WANTS TO ASK FOR HELP --
-- TO LET THE GREATEST SCIENTIFIC MIND ON THE PLANET INVESTIGATE HER PROBLEMS --
-- BUT ANOTHER PART OF HER ABHORS THE THOUGHT OF NEEDING ANYONE -- OR EVEN... MAYBE... OF DISCOVERING THE TRUTH...
IT IS IMPOSSIBLE TO RESTRAIN HER WHILE SHE IS INTANGIBLE!
SUSAN --
SHE PHASED RIGHT THROUGH MY FIELD!
AND HER SCREAM -- SO PRIMAL -- WHAT WAS SHE SAYING?
MOONSTONE WAS SPEAKING IN AN ANCIENT KREE DIALECT.
ACCORDING TO THE COMPUTER ANALYSIS, SHE SAID --
-- "I HAVE TO LOOK WITHIN THE LIFE-STONES!"
SHE SPOKE KREE -- ACCESSED OUR DATABASE -- WHY?
I SUSPECT THIS SKIRMISH HAD NOTHING TO DO WITH THE THUNDERBOLTS --
-- AND EVERYTHING TO DO WITH THE ORIGINS OF MOONSTONE'S POWERS --

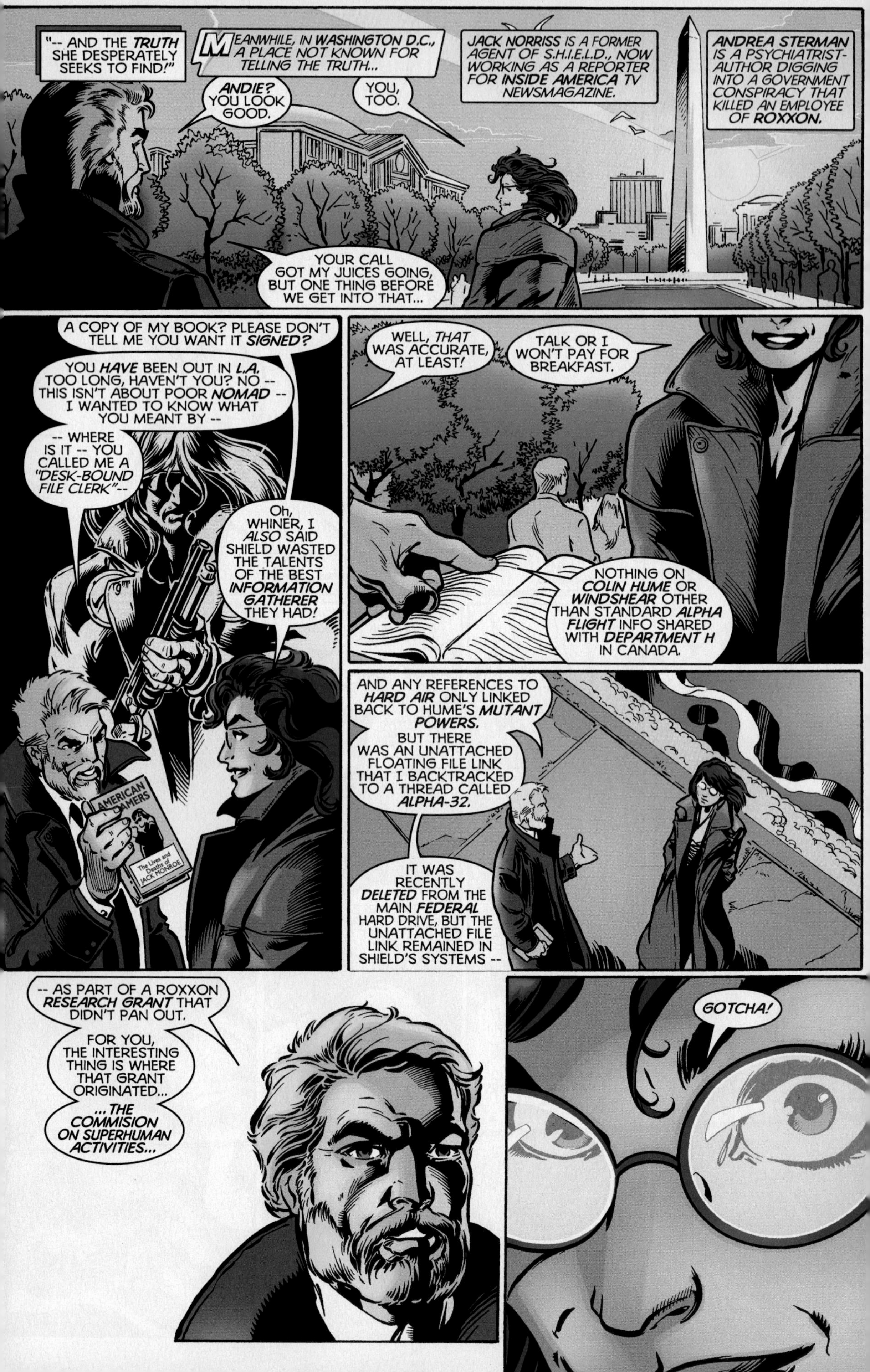

"-- AND THE TRUTH SHE DESPERATELY SEEKS TO FIND!"
MEANWHILE, IN WASHINGTON D.C., A PLACE NOT KNOWN FOR TELLING THE TRUTH...
JACK NORRISS IS A FORMER AGENT OF S.H.I.E.L.D., NOW WORKING AS A REPORTER FOR INSIDE AMERICA TV NEWSMAGAZINE.
ANDREA STERMAN IS A PSYCHIATRIST-AUTHOR DIGGING INTO A GOVERNMENT CONSPIRACY THAT KILLED AN EMPLOYEE OF ROXXON.
ANDIE? YOU LOOK GOOD.
YOU, TOO.
YOUR CALL GOT MY JUICES GOING, BUT ONE THING BEFORE WE GET INTO THAT...
A COPY OF MY BOOK? PLEASE DON'T TELL ME YOU WANT IT SIGNED?
YOU HAVE BEEN OUT IN L.A. TOO LONG, HAVEN'T YOU? NO -- THIS ISN'T ABOUT POOR NOMAD -- I WANTED TO KNOW WHAT YOU MEANT BY --
-- WHERE IS IT -- YOU CALLED ME A "DESK-BOUND FILE CLERK"--
Oh, WHINER, I ALSO SAID SHIELD WASTED THE TALENTS OF THE BEST INFORMATION GATHERER THEY HAD!
AMERICAN DAMERS
The Lives and Deaths of JACK MONROE
WELL, THAT WAS ACCURATE, AT LEAST!
TALK OR I WON'T PAY FOR BREAKFAST.
NOTHING ON COLIN HUME OR WINDSHEAR OTHER THAN STANDARD ALPHA FLIGHT INFO SHARED WITH DEPARTMENT H IN CANADA.
AND ANY REFERENCES TO HARD AIR ONLY LINKED BACK TO HUME'S MUTANT POWERS.
BUT THERE WAS AN UNATTACHED FLOATING FILE LINK THAT I BACKTRACKED TO A THREAD CALLED ALPHA-32.
IT WAS RECENTLY DELETED FROM THE MAIN FEDERAL HARD DRIVE, BUT THE UNATTACHED FILE LINK REMAINED IN SHIELD'S SYSTEMS --
-- AS PART OF A ROXXON RESEARCH GRANT THAT DIDN'T PAN OUT.
FOR YOU, THE INTERESTING THING IS WHERE THAT GRANT ORIGINATED...
...THE COMMISION ON SUPERHUMAN ACTIVITIES...
GOTCHA!

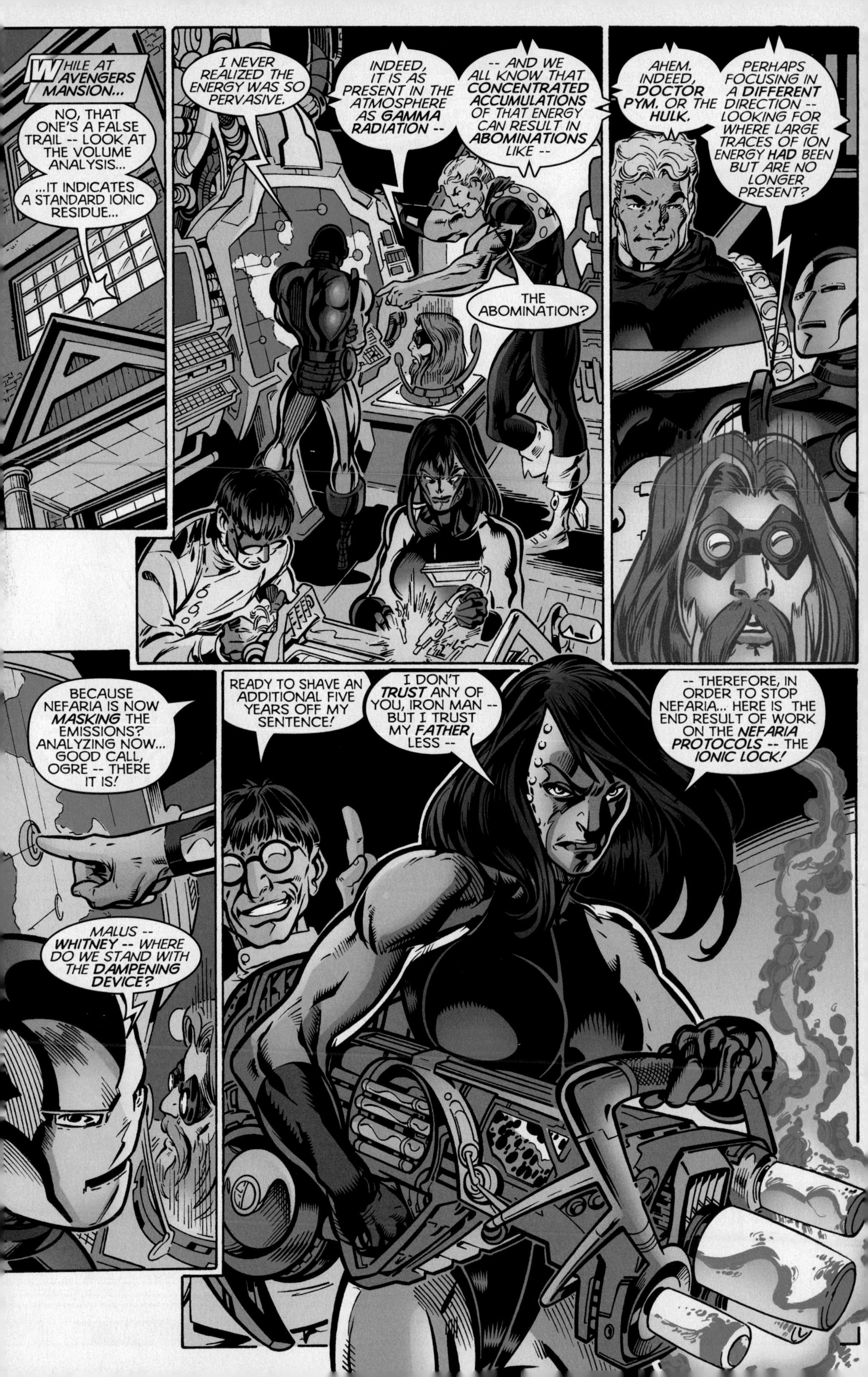
WHILE AT AVENGERS MANSION...
NO, THAT ONE'S A FALSE TRAIL -- LOOK AT THE VOLUME ANALYSIS...
...IT INDICATES A STANDARD IONIC RESIDUE...
I NEVER REALIZED THE ENERGY WAS SO PERVASIVE.
INDEED, IT IS AS PRESENT IN THE ATMOSPHERE AS GAMMA RADIATION --
-- AND WE ALL KNOW THAT CONCENTRATED ACCUMULATIONS OF THAT ENERGY CAN RESULT IN ABOMINATIONS LIKE --
THE ABOMINATION?
AHEM. INDEED, DOCTOR PYM. OR THE HULK.
PERHAPS FOCUSING IN A DIFFERENT DIRECTION -- LOOKING FOR WHERE LARGE TRACES OF ION ENERGY HAD BEEN BUT ARE NO LONGER PRESENT?
BECAUSE NEFARIA IS NOW MASKING THE EMISSIONS? ANALYZING NOW... GOOD CALL, OGRE -- THERE IT IS!
MALUS -- WHITNEY -- WHERE DO WE STAND WITH THE DAMPENING DEVICE?
READY TO SHAVE AN ADDITIONAL FIVE YEARS OFF MY SENTENCE!
I DON'T TRUST ANY OF YOU, IRON MAN -- BUT I TRUST MY FATHER LESS --
-- THEREFORE, IN ORDER TO STOP NEFARIA... HERE IS THE END RESULT OF WORK ON THE NEFARIA PROTOCOLS -- THE IONIC LOCK!

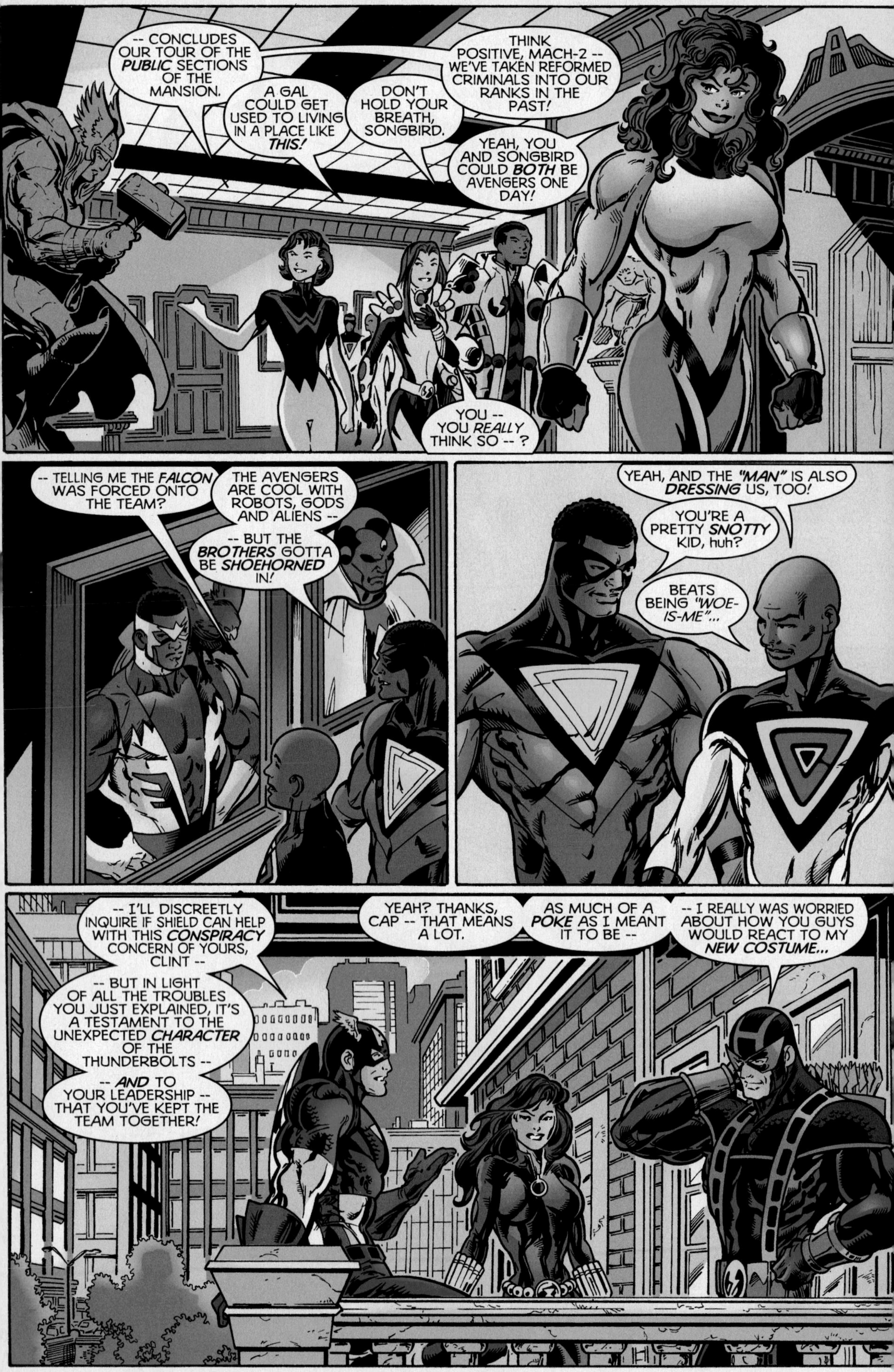
-- CONCLUDES OUR TOUR OF THE *PUBLIC* SECTIONS OF THE MANSION.
A GAL COULD GET USED TO LIVING IN A PLACE LIKE *THIS!*
DON'T HOLD YOUR BREATH, SONGBIRD.
THINK POSITIVE, MACH-2 -- WE'VE TAKEN REFORMED CRIMINALS INTO OUR RANKS IN THE PAST!
YEAH, YOU AND SONGBIRD COULD *BOTH* BE AVENGERS ONE DAY!
YOU -- YOU *REALLY* THINK SO -- ?
-- TELLING ME THE *FALCON* WAS FORCED ONTO THE TEAM?
THE AVENGERS ARE COOL WITH ROBOTS, GODS AND ALIENS --
-- BUT THE *BROTHERS* GOTTA BE *SHOEHORNED* IN!
YEAH, AND THE *"MAN"* IS ALSO *DRESSING* US, TOO!
YOU'RE A PRETTY *SNOTTY* KID, huh?
BEATS BEING *"WOE-IS-ME"*...
-- I'LL DISCREETLY INQUIRE IF SHIELD CAN HELP WITH THIS *CONSPIRACY* CONCERN OF YOURS, CLINT --
-- BUT IN LIGHT OF ALL THE TROUBLES YOU JUST EXPLAINED, IT'S A TESTAMENT TO THE UNEXPECTED *CHARACTER* OF THE THUNDERBOLTS --
-- *AND* TO YOUR LEADERSHIP -- THAT YOU'VE KEPT THE TEAM TOGETHER!
YEAH? THANKS, CAP -- THAT MEANS A LOT.
AS MUCH OF A *POKE* AS I MEANT IT TO BE --
-- I REALLY WAS WORRIED ABOUT HOW YOU GUYS WOULD REACT TO MY *NEW COSTUME...*

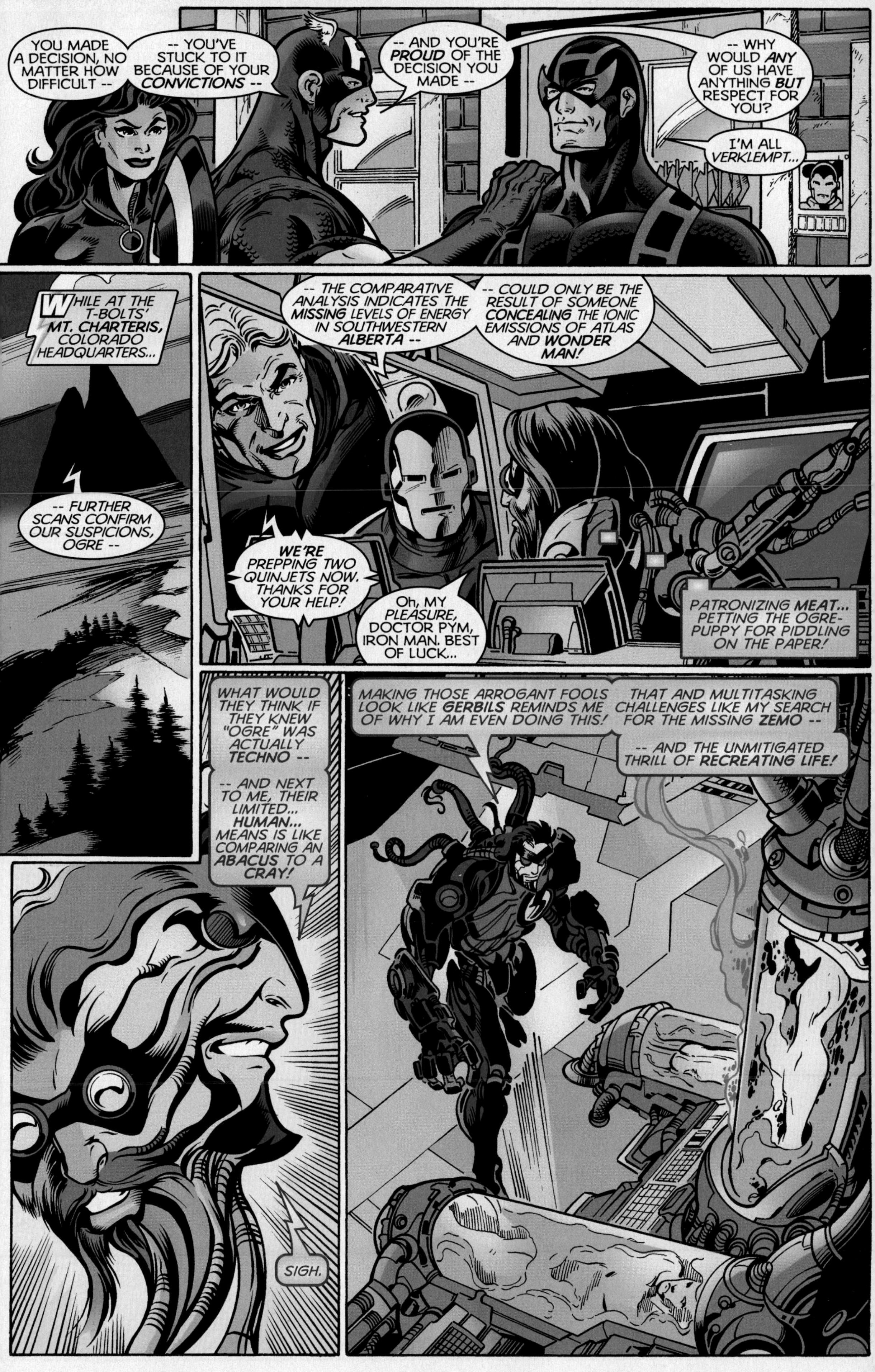
YOU MADE A DECISION, NO MATTER HOW DIFFICULT --
-- YOU'VE STUCK TO IT BECAUSE OF YOUR CONVICTIONS --
-- AND YOU'RE PROUD OF THE DECISION YOU MADE --
-- WHY WOULD ANY OF US HAVE ANYTHING BUT RESPECT FOR YOU?
I'M ALL VERKLEMPT...
WHILE AT THE T-BOLTS' MT. CHARTERIS, COLORADO HEADQUARTERS...
-- THE COMPARATIVE ANALYSIS INDICATES THE MISSING LEVELS OF ENERGY IN SOUTHWESTERN ALBERTA --
-- COULD ONLY BE THE RESULT OF SOMEONE CONCEALING THE IONIC EMISSIONS OF ATLAS AND WONDER MAN!
-- FURTHER SCANS CONFIRM OUR SUSPICIONS, OGRE --
WE'RE PREPPING TWO QUINJETS NOW. THANKS FOR YOUR HELP!
Oh, MY PLEASURE, DOCTOR PYM, IRON MAN. BEST OF LUCK...
PATRONIZING MEAT... PETTING THE OGRE-PUPPY FOR PIDDLING ON THE PAPER!
WHAT WOULD THEY THINK IF THEY KNEW "OGRE" WAS ACTUALLY TECHNO --
-- AND NEXT TO ME, THEIR LIMITED... HUMAN... MEANS IS LIKE COMPARING AN ABACUS TO A CRAY!
SIGH.
MAKING THOSE ARROGANT FOOLS LOOK LIKE GERBILS REMINDS ME OF WHY I AM EVEN DOING THIS!
THAT AND MULTITASKING CHALLENGES LIKE MY SEARCH FOR THE MISSING ZEMO --
-- AND THE UNMITIGATED THRILL OF RECREATING LIFE!

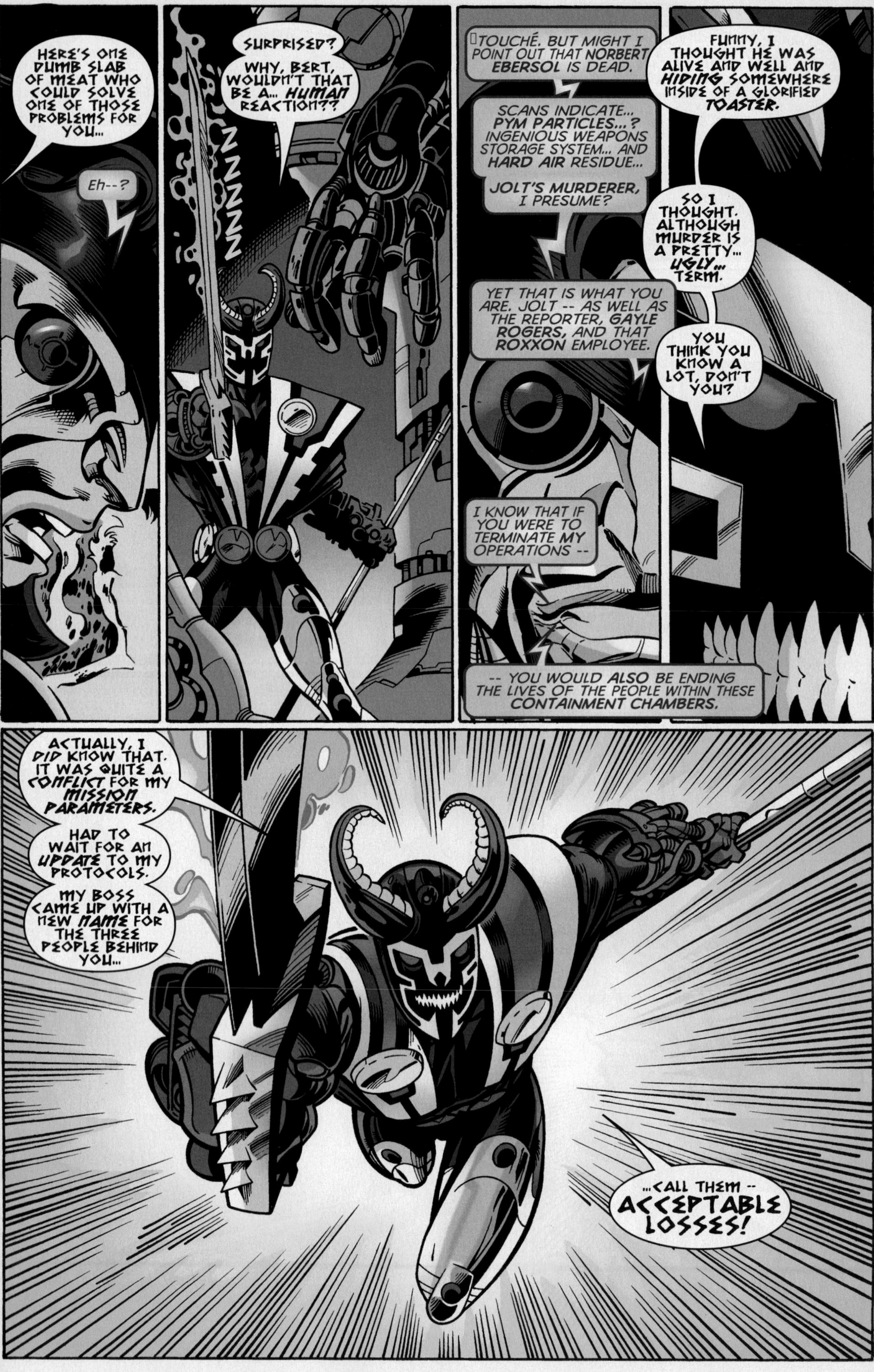

HERE'S ONE DUMB SLAB OF MEAT WHO COULD SOLVE ONE OF THOSE PROBLEMS FOR YOU...
Eh--?
SURPRISED?
WHY, BERT, WOULDN'T THAT BE A... HUMAN REACTION??
ZZZZZZ
TOUCHÉ. BUT MIGHT I POINT OUT THAT NORBERT EBERSOL IS DEAD.
SCANS INDICATE... PYM PARTICLES...? INGENIOUS WEAPONS STORAGE SYSTEM... AND HARD AIR RESIDUE...
JOLT'S MURDERER, I PRESUME?
FUNNY, I THOUGHT HE WAS ALIVE AND WELL AND HIDING SOMEWHERE INSIDE OF A GLORIFIED TOASTER.
SO I THOUGHT. ALTHOUGH MURDER IS A PRETTY... UGLY... TERM.
YET THAT IS WHAT YOU ARE. JOLT -- AS WELL AS THE REPORTER, GAYLE ROGERS, AND THAT ROXXON EMPLOYEE.
YOU THINK YOU KNOW A LOT, DON'T YOU?
I KNOW THAT IF YOU WERE TO TERMINATE MY OPERATIONS --
-- YOU WOULD ALSO BE ENDING THE LIVES OF THE PEOPLE WITHIN THESE CONTAINMENT CHAMBERS.
ACTUALLY, I DID KNOW THAT. IT WAS QUITE A CONFLICT FOR MY MISSION PARAMETERS.
HAD TO WAIT FOR AN UPDATE TO MY PROTOCOLS.
MY BOSS CAME UP WITH A NEW NAME FOR THE THREE PEOPLE BEHIND YOU...
...CALL THEM -- ACCEPTABLE LOSSES!

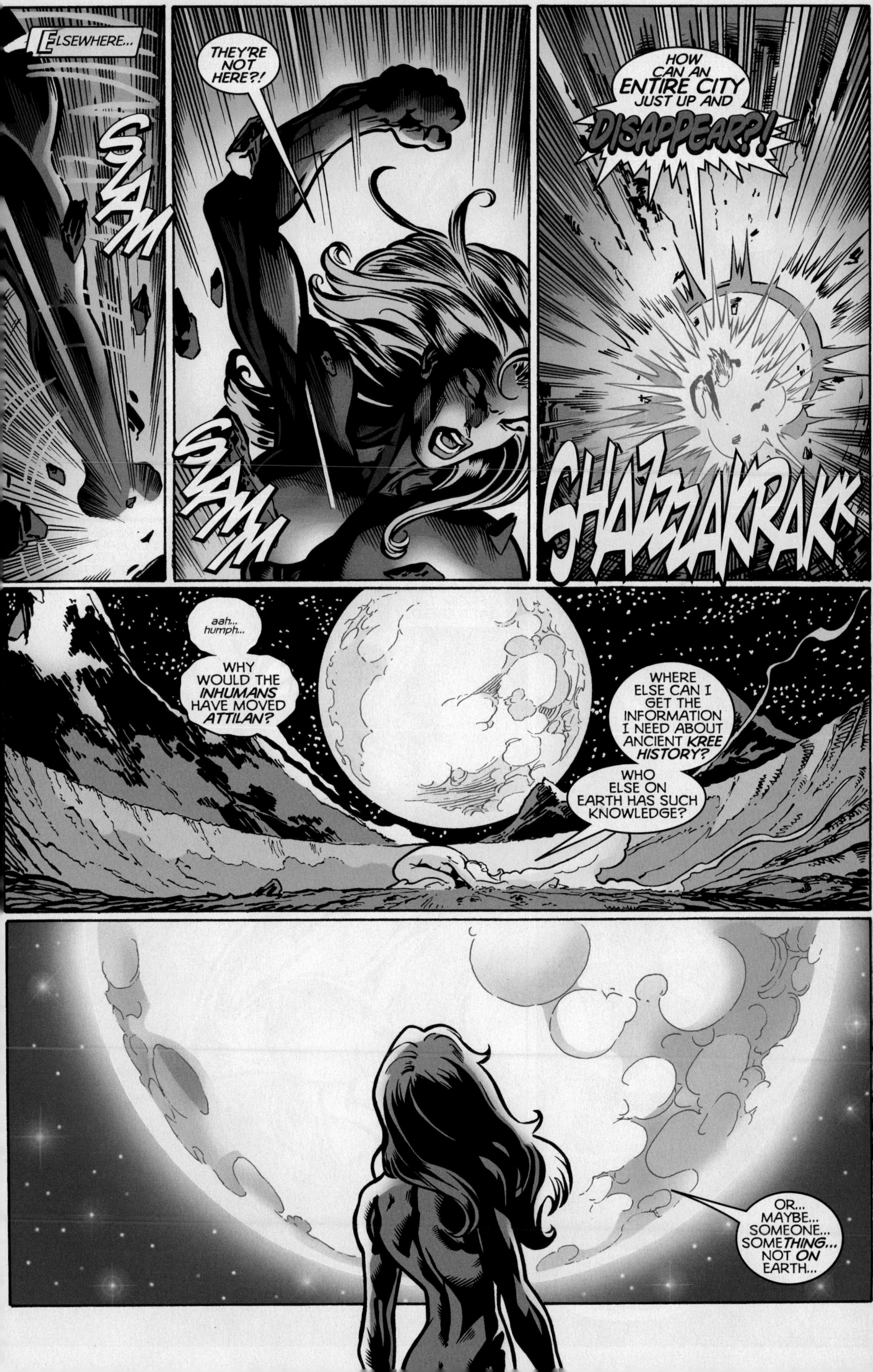
ELSEWHERE...
SLAM
THEY'RE NOT HERE?!
SLAMM
HOW CAN AN ENTIRE CITY JUST UP AND DISAPPEAR?!
SHAZZZAKRAKK
aah... humph...
WHY WOULD THE INHUMANS HAVE MOVED ATTILAN?
WHERE ELSE CAN I GET THE INFORMATION I NEED ABOUT ANCIENT KREE HISTORY?
WHO ELSE ON EARTH HAS SUCH KNOWLEDGE?
OR... MAYBE... SOMEONE... SOMETHING... NOT ON EARTH...

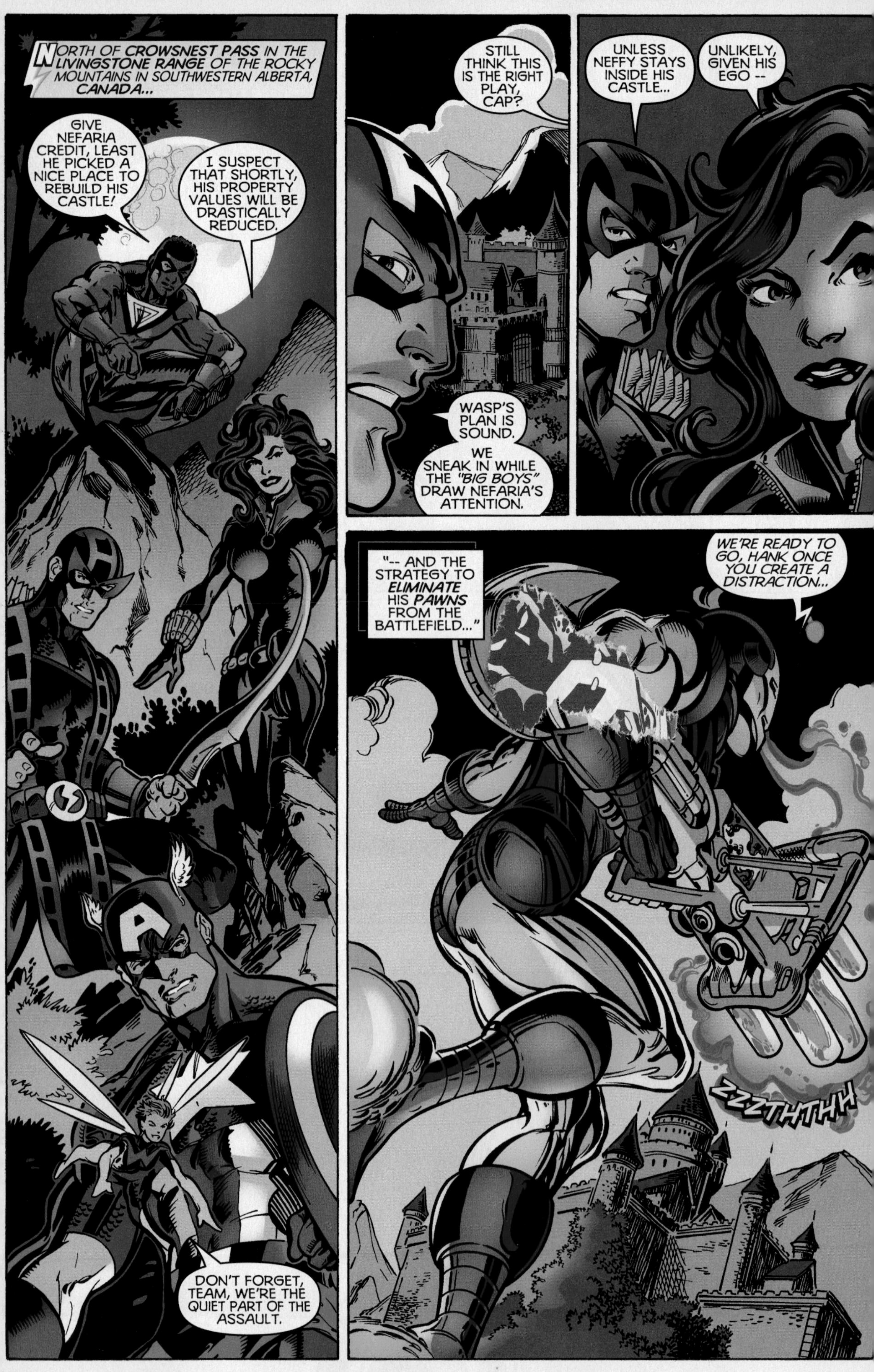
NORTH OF CROWSNEST PASS IN THE LIVINGSTONE RANGE OF THE ROCKY MOUNTAINS IN SOUTHWESTERN ALBERTA, CANADA...
GIVE NEFARIA CREDIT, LEAST HE PICKED A NICE PLACE TO REBUILD HIS CASTLE!
I SUSPECT THAT SHORTLY, HIS PROPERTY VALUES WILL BE DRASTICALLY REDUCED.
DON'T FORGET, TEAM, WE'RE THE QUIET PART OF THE ASSAULT.
STILL THINK THIS IS THE RIGHT PLAY, CAP?
WASP'S PLAN IS SOUND.
WE SNEAK IN WHILE THE "BIG BOYS" DRAW NEFARIA'S ATTENTION.
UNLESS NEFFY STAYS INSIDE HIS CASTLE...
UNLIKELY, GIVEN HIS EGO --
"-- AND THE STRATEGY TO ELIMINATE HIS PAWNS FROM THE BATTLEFIELD..."
WE'RE READY TO GO, HANK ONCE YOU CREATE A DISTRACTION...
ZZZTHTHH

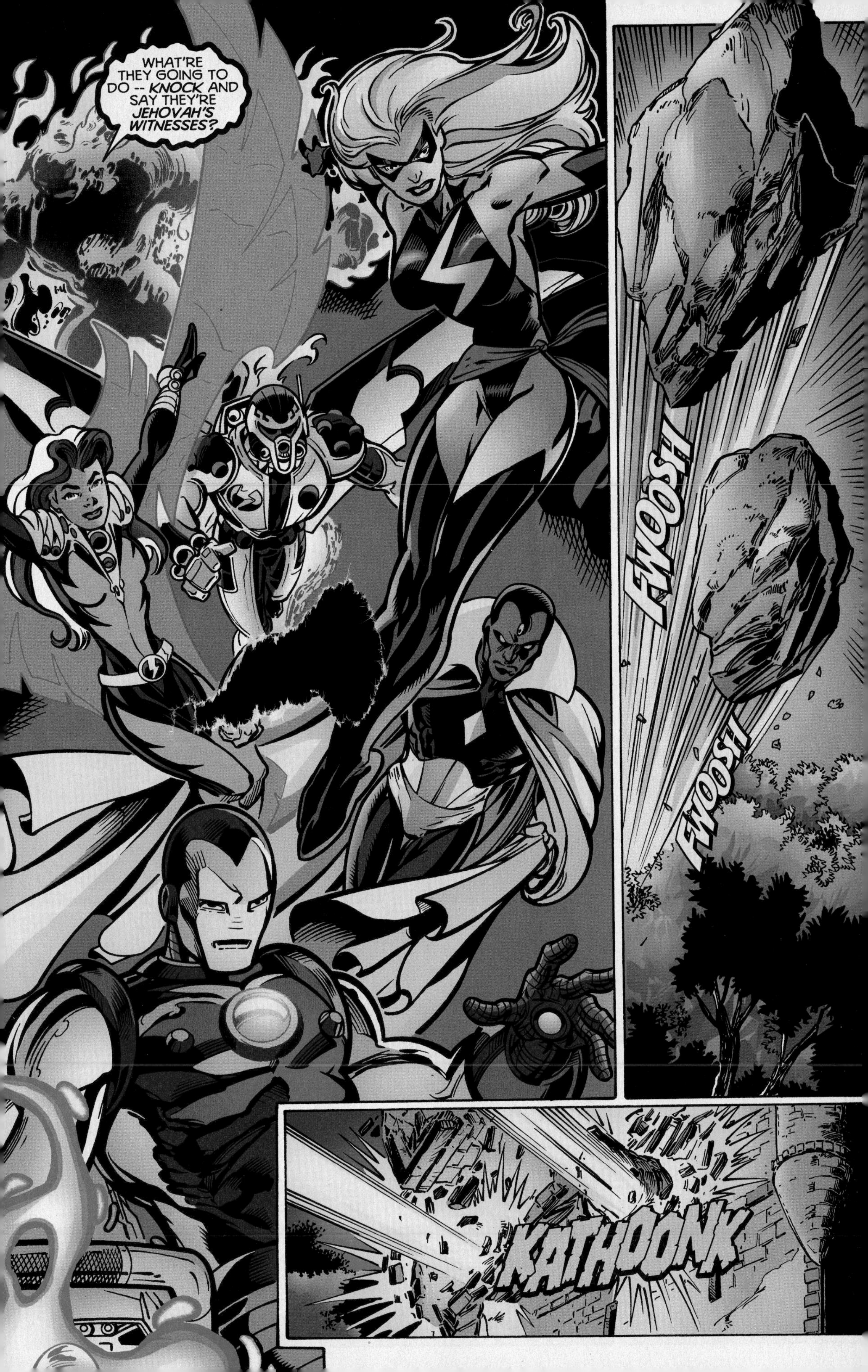
WHAT'RE THEY GOING TO DO -- KNOCK AND SAY THEY'RE JEHOVAH'S WITNESSES?
FWOOSH
FWOOSH
KATHOONK

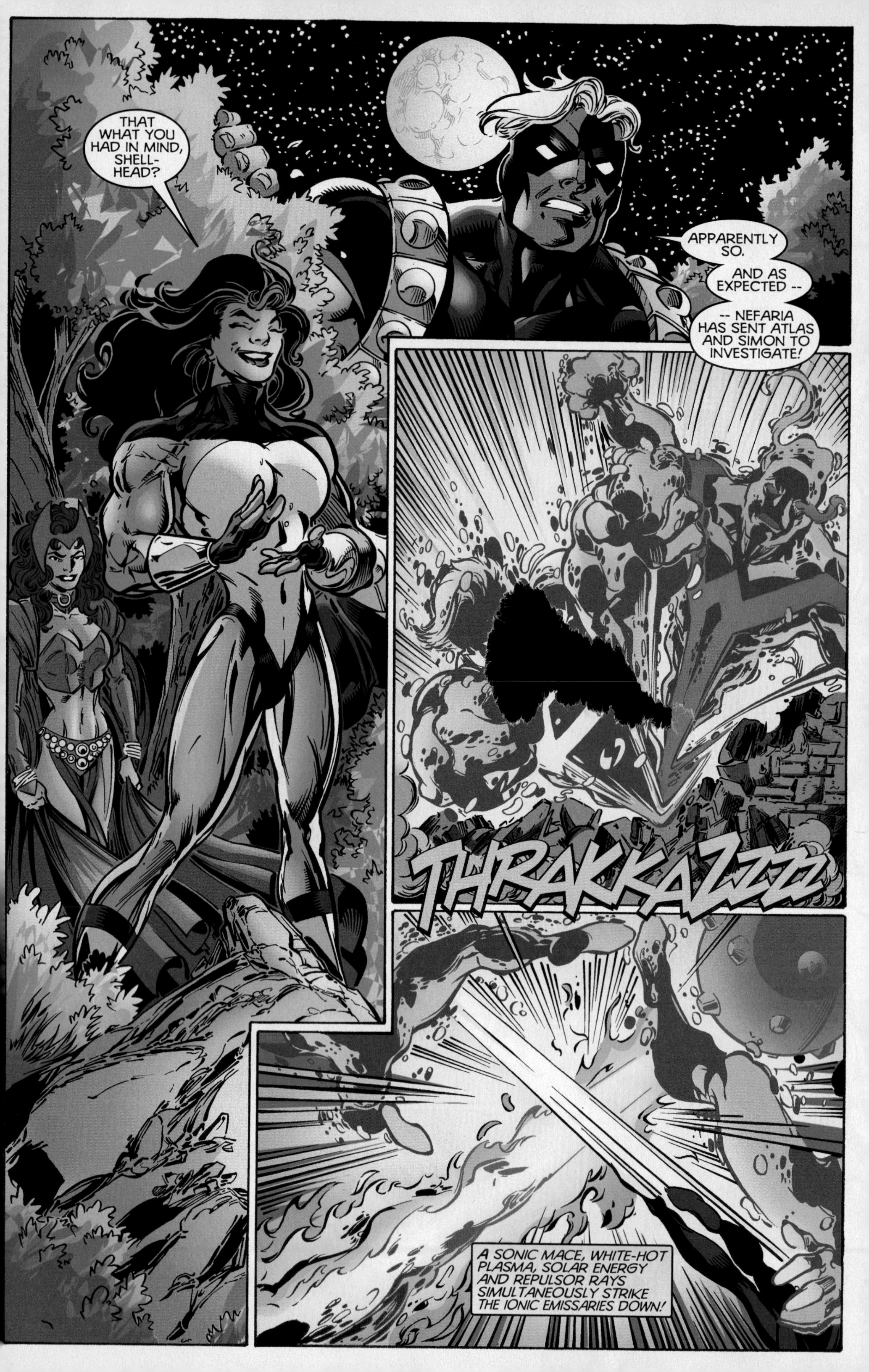
THAT WHAT YOU HAD IN MIND, SHELL-HEAD?
APPARENTLY SO.
AND AS EXPECTED --
-- NEFARIA HAS SENT ATLAS AND SIMON TO INVESTIGATE!
THRAKKAZZZZ
A SONIC MACE, WHITE-HOT PLASMA, SOLAR ENERGY AND REPULSOR RAYS SIMULTANEOUSLY STRIKE THE IONIC EMISSARIES DOWN!

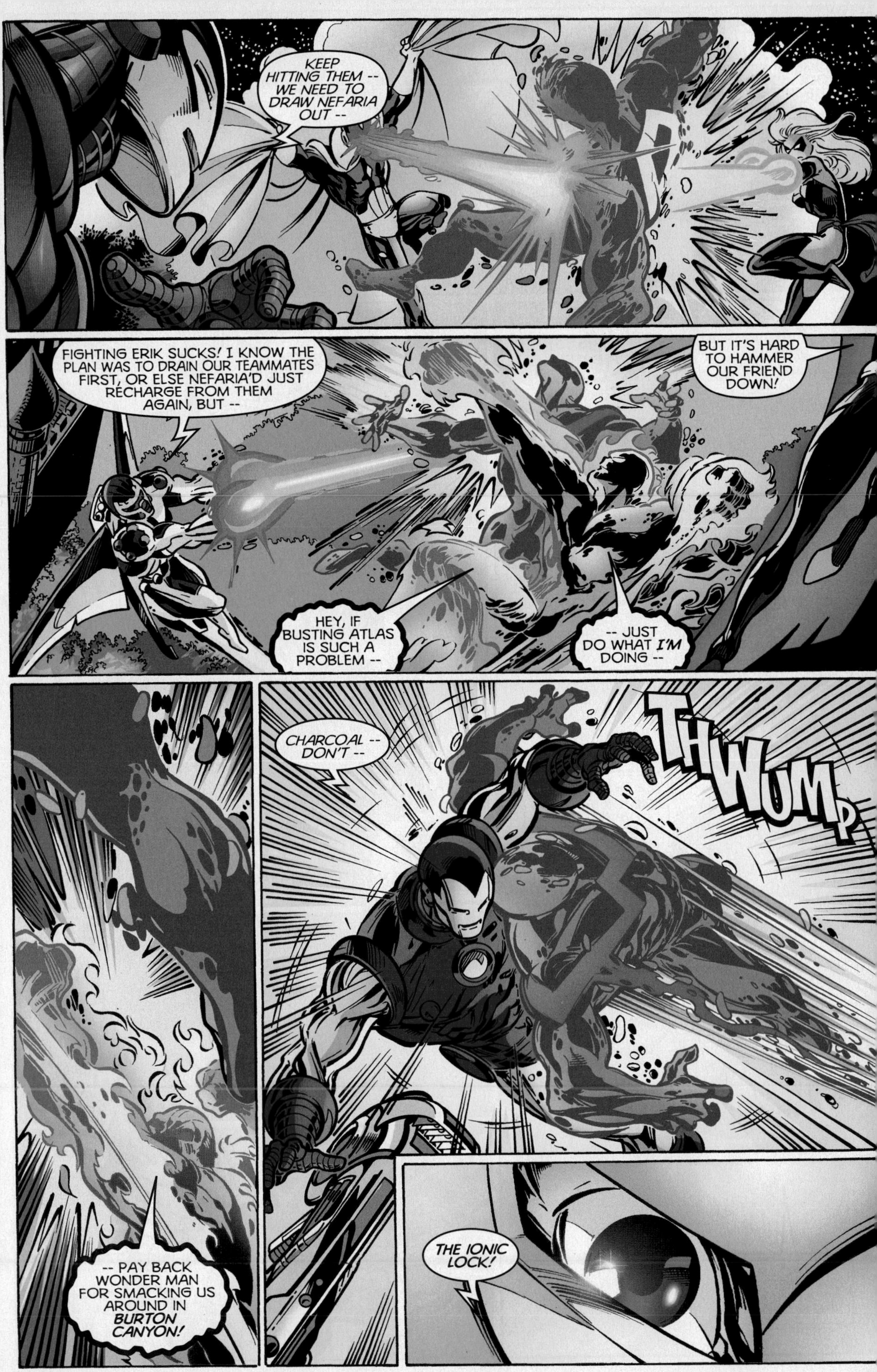
KEEP HITTING THEM -- WE NEED TO DRAW NEFARIA OUT --
FIGHTING ERIK SUCKS! I KNOW THE PLAN WAS TO DRAIN OUR TEAMMATES FIRST, OR ELSE NEFARIA'D JUST RECHARGE FROM THEM AGAIN, BUT --
BUT IT'S HARD TO HAMMER OUR FRIEND DOWN!
HEY, IF BUSTING ATLAS IS SUCH A PROBLEM --
-- JUST DO WHAT I'M DOING --
-- PAY BACK WONDER MAN FOR SMACKING US AROUND IN BURTON CANYON!
CHARCOAL -- DON'T --
THWUMP
THE IONIC LOCK!

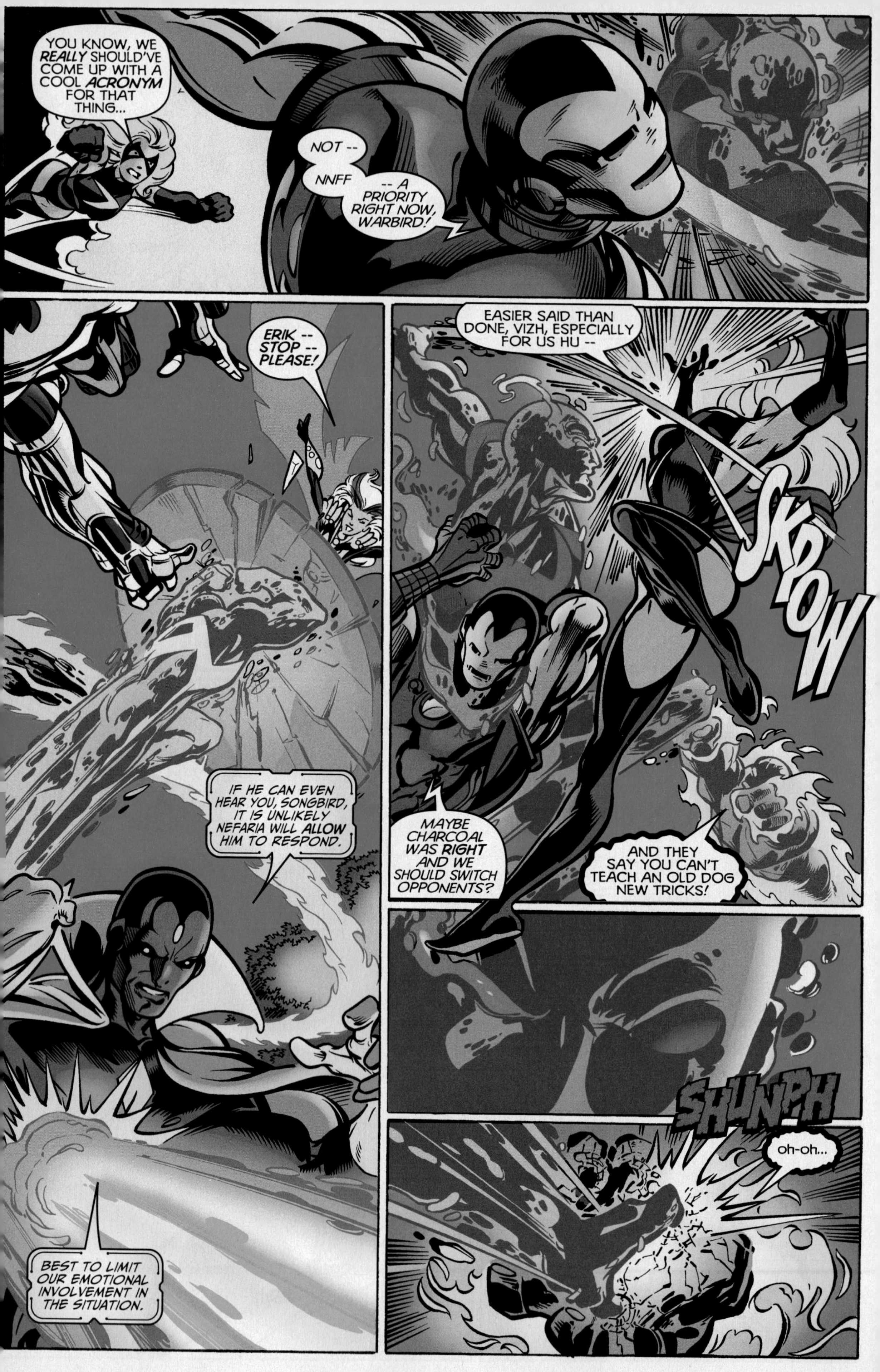
YOU KNOW, WE REALLY SHOULD'VE COME UP WITH A COOL ACRONYM FOR THAT THING...
NOT --
NNFF
-- A PRIORITY RIGHT NOW, WARBIRD!
ERIK -- STOP -- PLEASE!
IF HE CAN EVEN HEAR YOU, SONGBIRD, IT IS UNLIKELY NEFARIA WILL ALLOW HIM TO RESPOND.
BEST TO LIMIT OUR EMOTIONAL INVOLVEMENT IN THE SITUATION.
EASIER SAID THAN DONE, VIZH, ESPECIALLY FOR US HU --
SKROW
MAYBE CHARCOAL WAS RIGHT AND WE SHOULD SWITCH OPPONENTS?
AND THEY SAY YOU CAN'T TEACH AN OLD DOG NEW TRICKS!
SHUNPH
oh-oh...

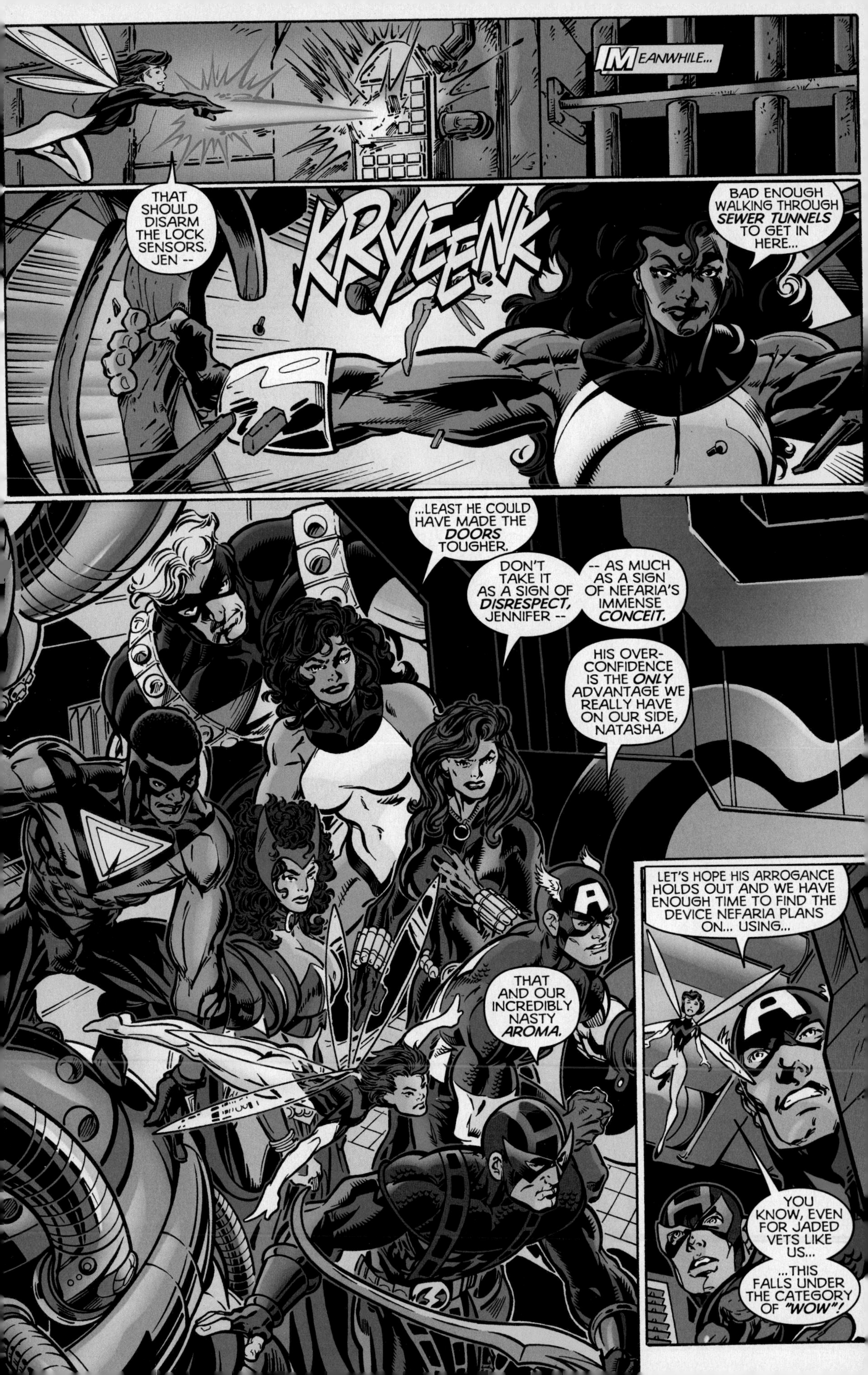
MEANWHILE...
THAT SHOULD DISARM THE LOCK SENSORS. JEN --
KRYEENK
BAD ENOUGH WALKING THROUGH SEWER TUNNELS TO GET IN HERE...
...LEAST HE COULD HAVE MADE THE DOORS TOUGHER.
DON'T TAKE IT AS A SIGN OF DISRESPECT, JENNIFER --
-- AS MUCH AS A SIGN OF NEFARIA'S IMMENSE CONCEIT.
HIS OVER-CONFIDENCE IS THE ONLY ADVANTAGE WE REALLY HAVE ON OUR SIDE, NATASHA.
THAT AND OUR INCREDIBLY NASTY AROMA.
LET'S HOPE HIS ARROGANCE HOLDS OUT AND WE HAVE ENOUGH TIME TO FIND THE DEVICE NEFARIA PLANS ON... USING...
YOU KNOW, EVEN FOR JADED VETS LIKE US...
...THIS FALLS UNDER THE CATEGORY OF "WOW"!

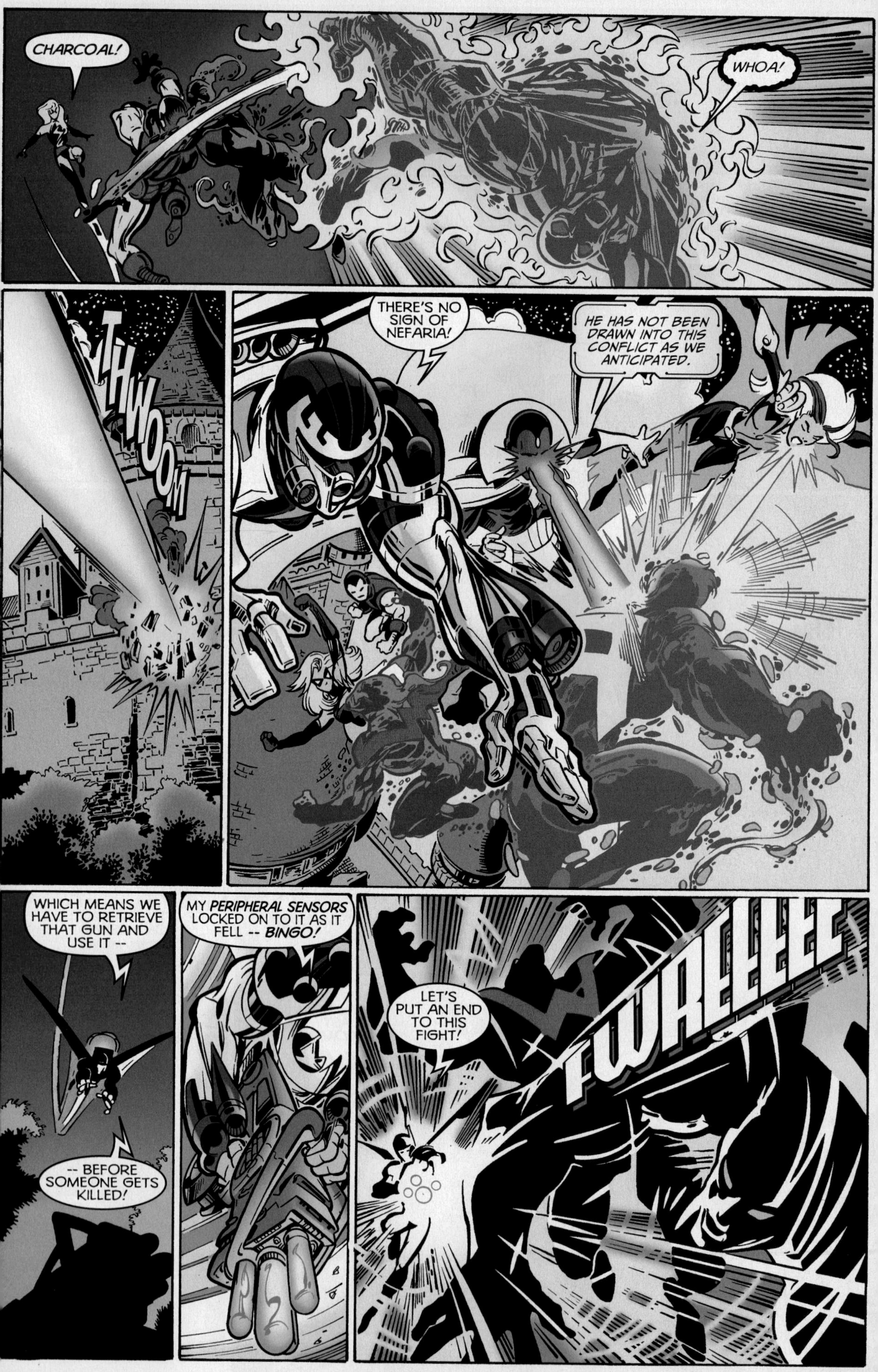
CHARCOAL!
WHOA!
THWOOM
THERE'S NO SIGN OF NEFARIA!
HE HAS NOT BEEN DRAWN INTO THIS CONFLICT AS WE ANTICIPATED.
WHICH MEANS WE HAVE TO RETRIEVE THAT GUN AND USE IT --
-- BEFORE SOMEONE GETS KILLED!
MY PERIPHERAL SENSORS LOCKED ON TO IT AS IT FELL -- BINGO!
LET'S PUT AN END TO THIS FIGHT!
FWREEEE

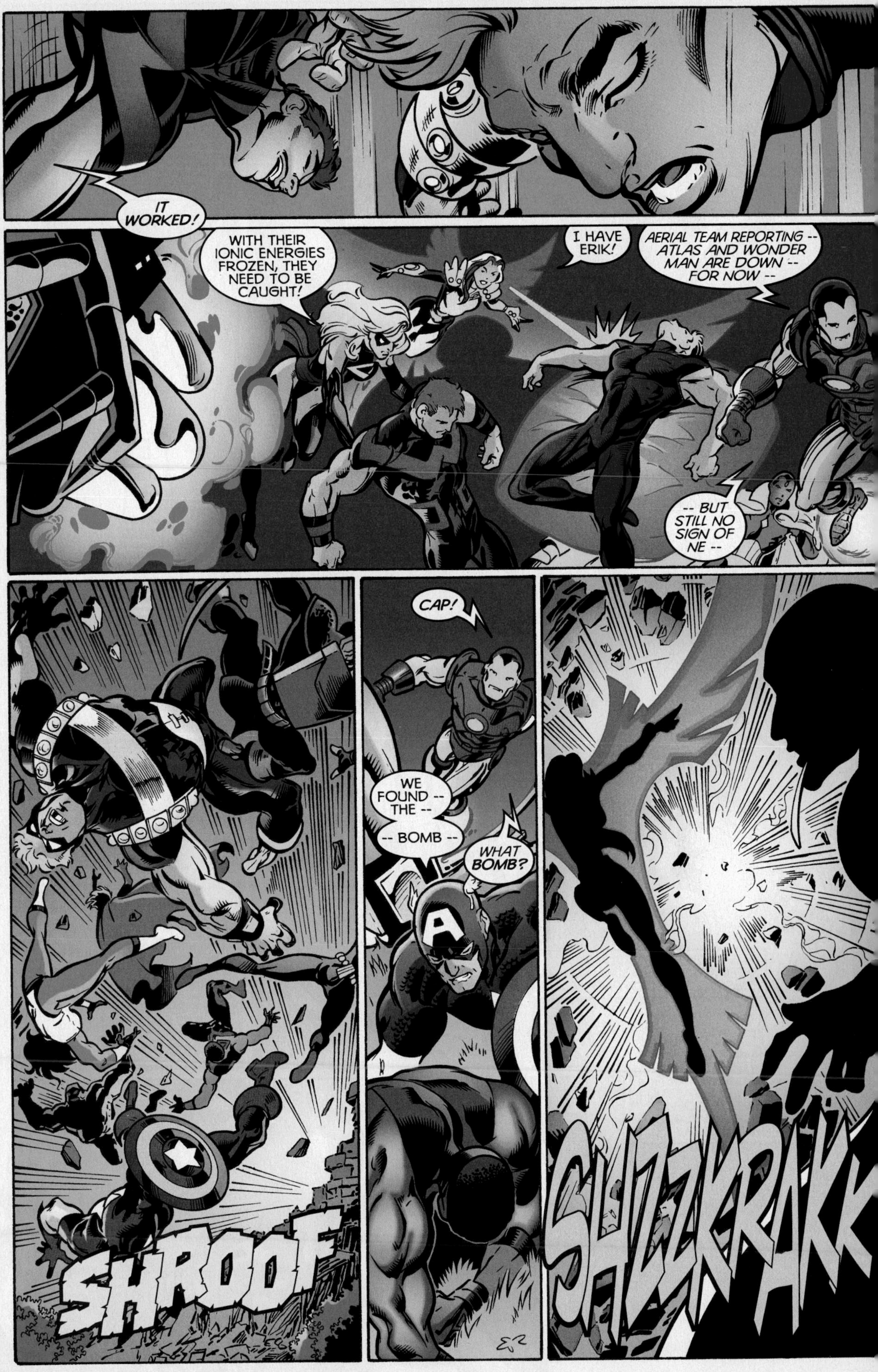

IT WORKED!
WITH THEIR IONIC ENERGIES FROZEN, THEY NEED TO BE CAUGHT!
I HAVE ERIK!
AERIAL TEAM REPORTING -- ATLAS AND WONDER MAN ARE DOWN -- FOR NOW --
-- BUT STILL NO SIGN OF NE --
SHROOF
CAP!
WE FOUND -- THE --
-- BOMB --
WHAT BOMB?
SHZZKRAKK

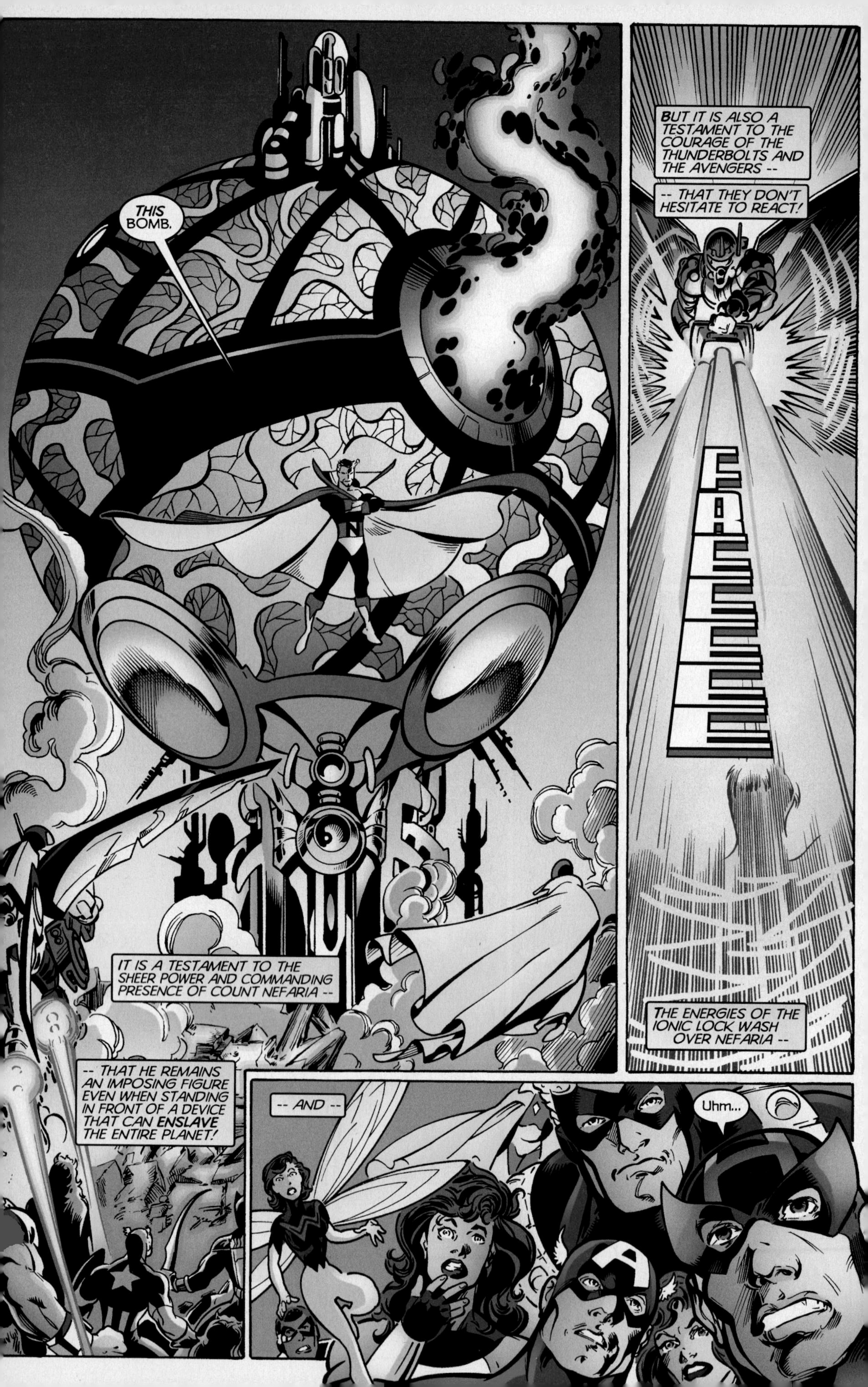
THIS BOMB.
IT IS A TESTAMENT TO THE SHEER POWER AND COMMANDING PRESENCE OF COUNT NEFARIA --
-- THAT HE REMAINS AN IMPOSING FIGURE EVEN WHEN STANDING IN FRONT OF A DEVICE THAT CAN ENSLAVE THE ENTIRE PLANET!
BUT IT IS ALSO A TESTAMENT TO THE COURAGE OF THE THUNDERBOLTS AND THE AVENGERS --
-- THAT THEY DON'T HESITATE TO REACT!
FREEEEE
THE ENERGIES OF THE IONIC LOCK WASH OVER NEFARIA --
-- AND --
Uhm...

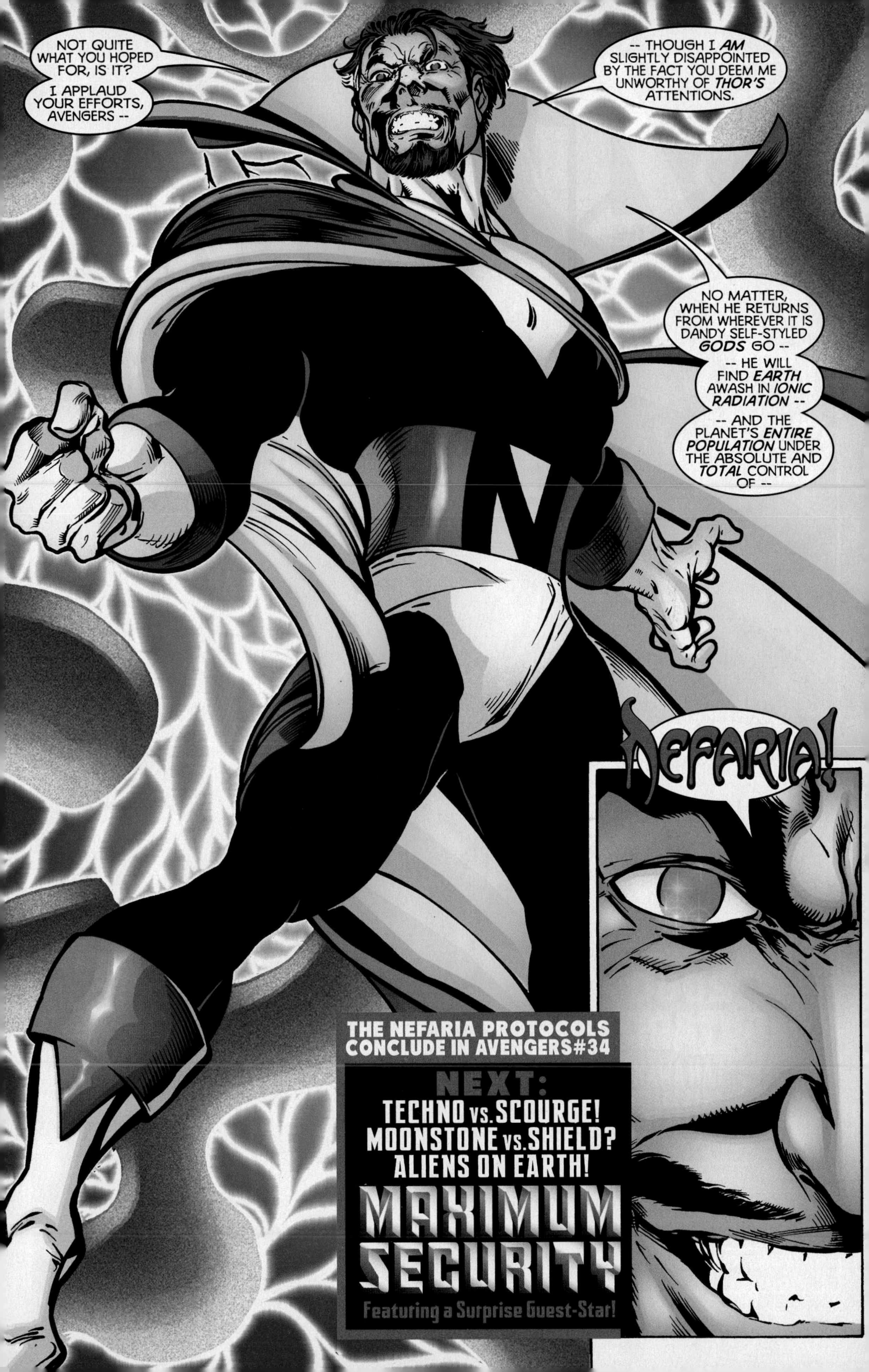
NOT QUITE WHAT YOU HOPED FOR, IS IT?
I APPLAUD YOUR EFFORTS, AVENGERS --
-- THOUGH I AM SLIGHTLY DISAPPOINTED BY THE FACT YOU DEEM ME UNWORTHY OF THOR'S ATTENTIONS.
NO MATTER, WHEN HE RETURNS FROM WHEREVER IT IS DANDY SELF-STYLED GODS GO --
-- HE WILL FIND EARTH AWASH IN IONIC RADIATION --
-- AND THE PLANET'S ENTIRE POPULATION UNDER THE ABSOLUTE AND TOTAL CONTROL OF --
NEFARIA!
THE NEFARIA PROTOCOLS CONCLUDE IN AVENGERS#34
NEXT:
TECHNO vs. SCOURGE!
MOONSTONE vs. SHIELD?
ALIENS ON EARTH!
MAXIMUM SECURITY
Featuring a Surprise Guest-Star!

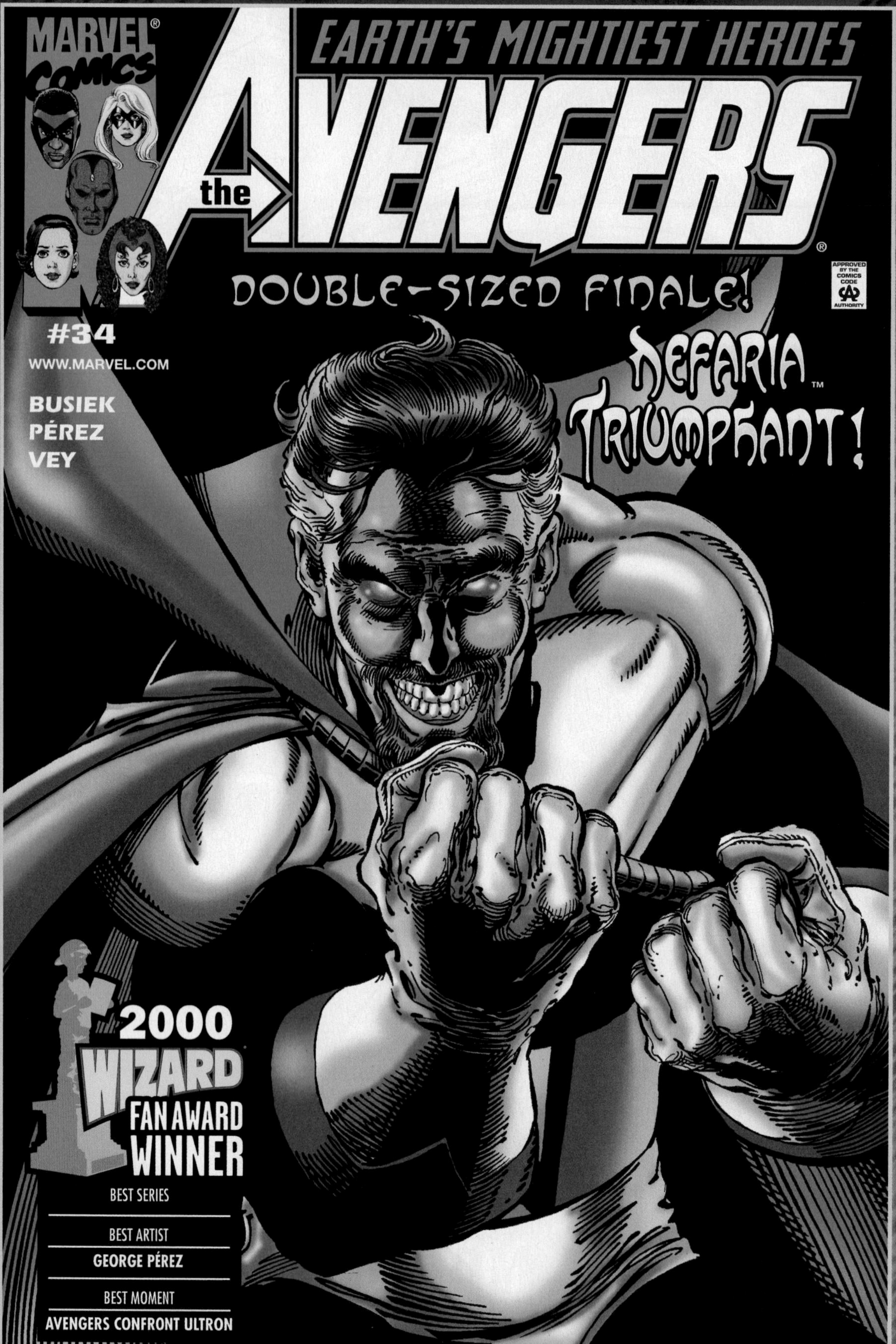
MARVEL®
COMICS
EARTH'S MIGHTIEST HEROES
the AVENGERS®
APPROVED BY THE COMICS CODE AUTHORITY
DOUBLE-SIZED FINALE!
#34
WWW.MARVEL.COM
BUSIEK
PÉREZ
VEY
NEFARIA™ TRIUMPHANT!
2000
WIZARD
FAN AWARD
WINNER
BEST SERIES
BEST ARTIST
GEORGE PÉREZ
BEST MOMENT
AVENGERS CONFRONT ULTRON

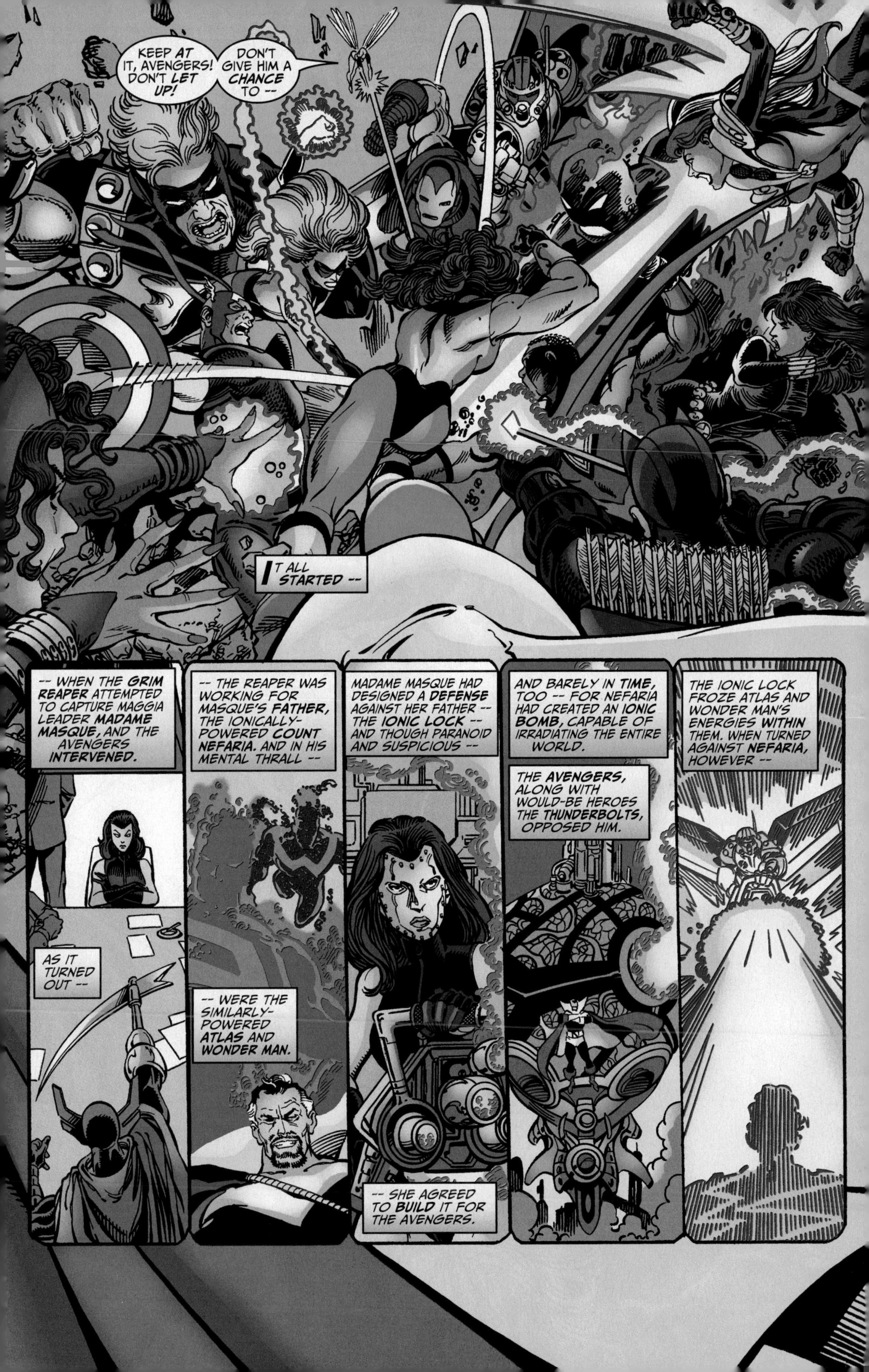

KEEP AT IT, AVENGERS! DON'T LET UP!
DON'T GIVE HIM A CHANCE TO --
IT ALL STARTED --
-- WHEN THE GRIM REAPER ATTEMPTED TO CAPTURE MAGGIA LEADER MADAME MASQUE, AND THE AVENGERS INTERVENED.
AS IT TURNED OUT --
-- THE REAPER WAS WORKING FOR MASQUE'S FATHER, THE IONICALLY-POWERED COUNT NEFARIA. AND IN HIS MENTAL THRALL --
-- WERE THE SIMILARLY-POWERED ATLAS AND WONDER MAN.
MADAME MASQUE HAD DESIGNED A DEFENSE AGAINST HER FATHER -- THE IONIC LOCK -- AND THOUGH PARANOID AND SUSPICIOUS --
-- SHE AGREED TO BUILD IT FOR THE AVENGERS.
AND BARELY IN TIME, TOO -- FOR NEFARIA HAD CREATED AN IONIC BOMB, CAPABLE OF IRRADIATING THE ENTIRE WORLD.
THE AVENGERS, ALONG WITH WOULD-BE HEROES THE THUNDERBOLTS, OPPOSED HIM.
THE IONIC LOCK FROZE ATLAS AND WONDER MAN'S ENERGIES WITHIN THEM. WHEN TURNED AGAINST NEFARIA, HOWEVER --

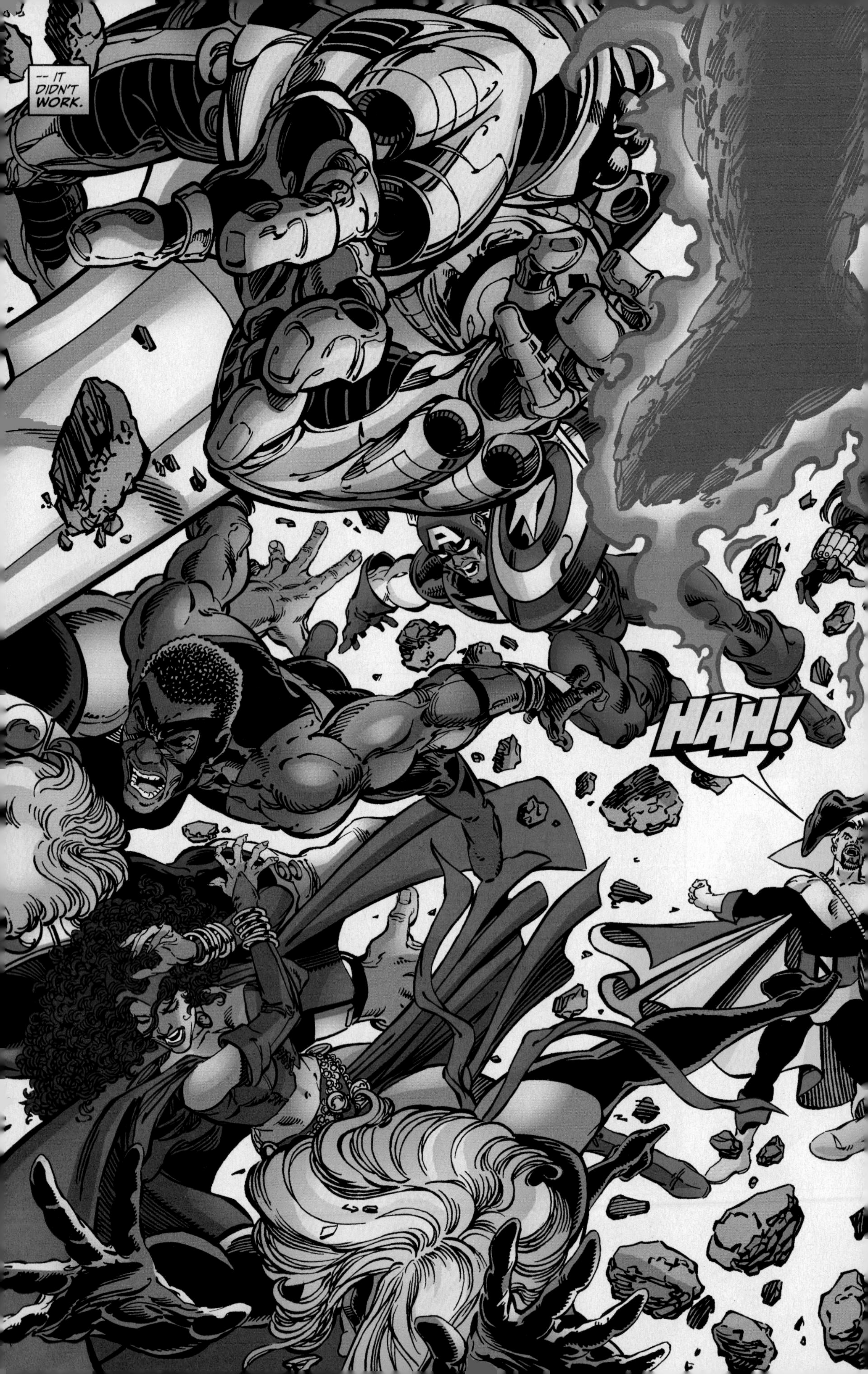
-- IT DIDN'T WORK.
HAH!

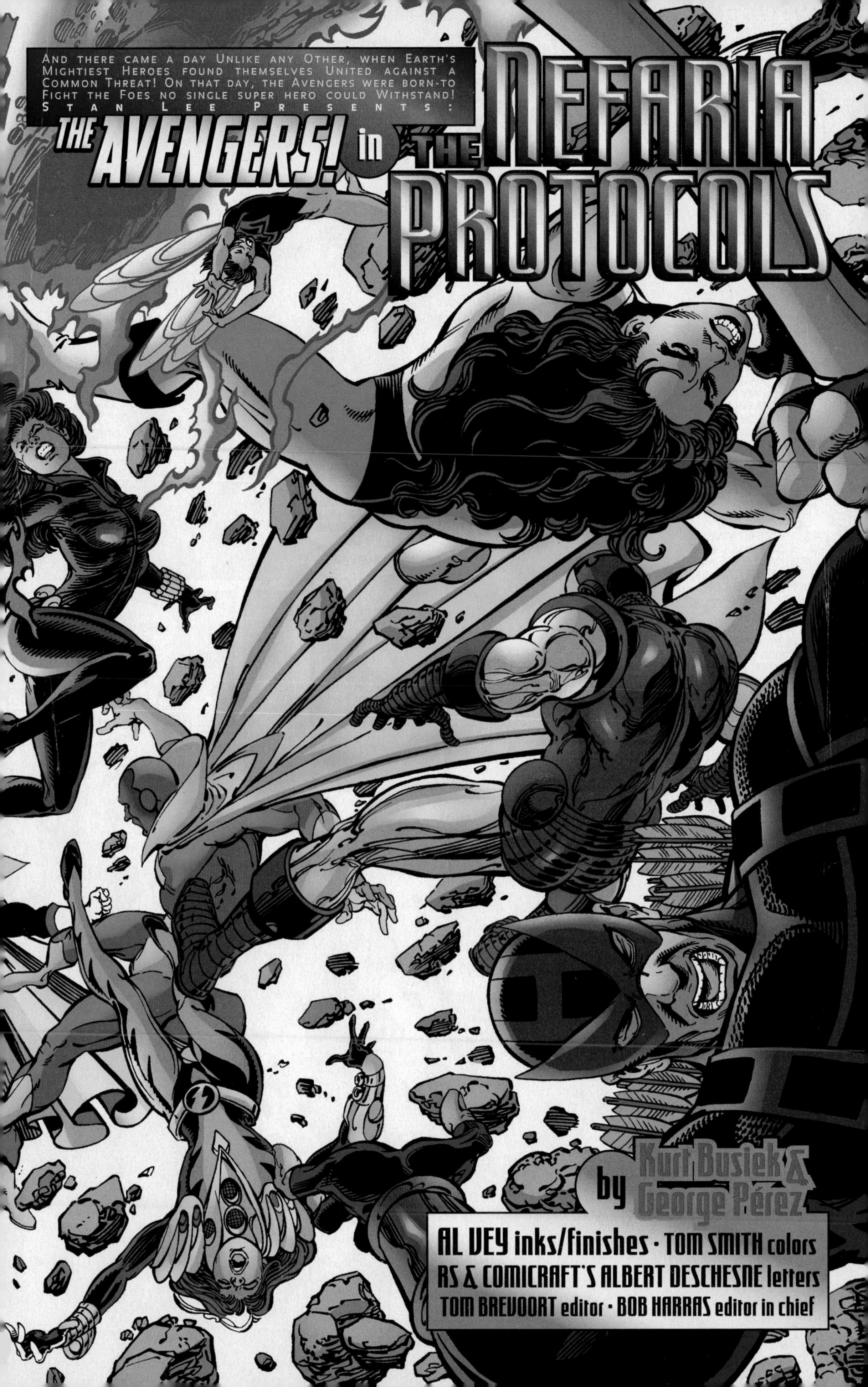
And there came a day Unlike any Other, when Earth's Mightiest Heroes found themselves United against a Common Threat! On that day, the Avengers were born-to Fight the Foes no single super hero could Withstand!
Stan Lee Presents:
The Avengers! in The Nefaria Protocols
by Kurt Busiek & George Pérez
Al Vey inks/finishes • Tom Smith colors
RS & Comicraft's Albert Deschesne letters
Tom Brevoort editor • Bob Harras editor in chief

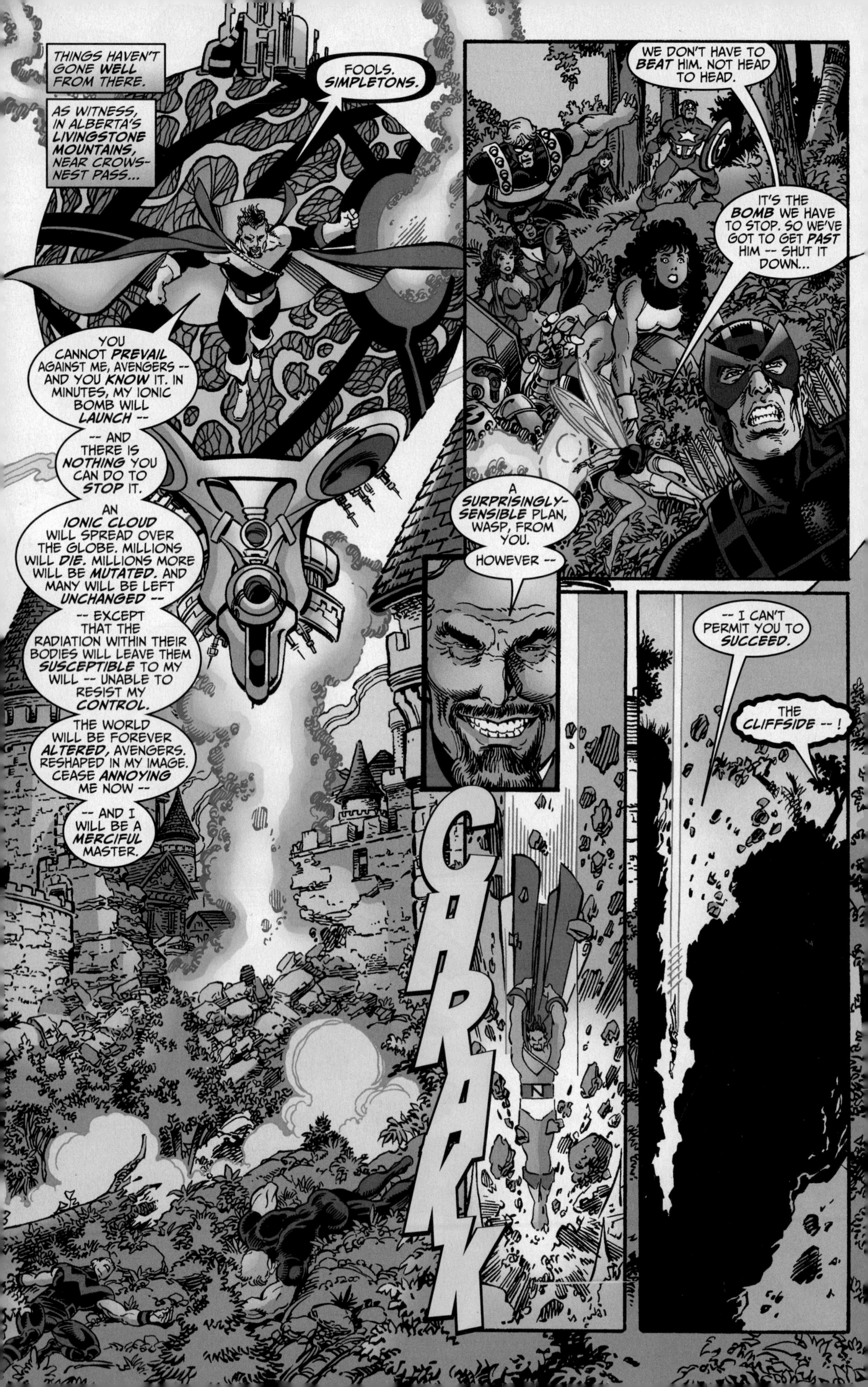
THINGS HAVEN'T GONE WELL FROM THERE.
AS WITNESS, IN ALBERTA'S LIVINGSTONE MOUNTAINS, NEAR CROWS-NEST PASS...
FOOLS. SIMPLETONS.
YOU CANNOT PREVAIL AGAINST ME, AVENGERS -- AND YOU KNOW IT. IN MINUTES, MY IONIC BOMB WILL LAUNCH --
-- AND THERE IS NOTHING YOU CAN DO TO STOP IT.
AN IONIC CLOUD WILL SPREAD OVER THE GLOBE. MILLIONS WILL DIE. MILLIONS MORE WILL BE MUTATED. AND MANY WILL BE LEFT UNCHANGED --
-- EXCEPT THAT THE RADIATION WITHIN THEIR BODIES WILL LEAVE THEM SUSCEPTIBLE TO MY WILL -- UNABLE TO RESIST MY CONTROL.
THE WORLD WILL BE FOREVER ALTERED, AVENGERS. RESHAPED IN MY IMAGE. CEASE ANNOYING ME NOW --
-- AND I WILL BE A MERCIFUL MASTER.
WE DON'T HAVE TO BEAT HIM. NOT HEAD TO HEAD.
IT'S THE BOMB WE HAVE TO STOP. SO WE'VE GOT TO GET PAST HIM -- SHUT IT DOWN...
A SURPRISINGLY-SENSIBLE PLAN, WASP, FROM YOU.
HOWEVER --
-- I CAN'T PERMIT YOU TO SUCCEED.
CHRAKK
THE CLIFFSIDE -- !

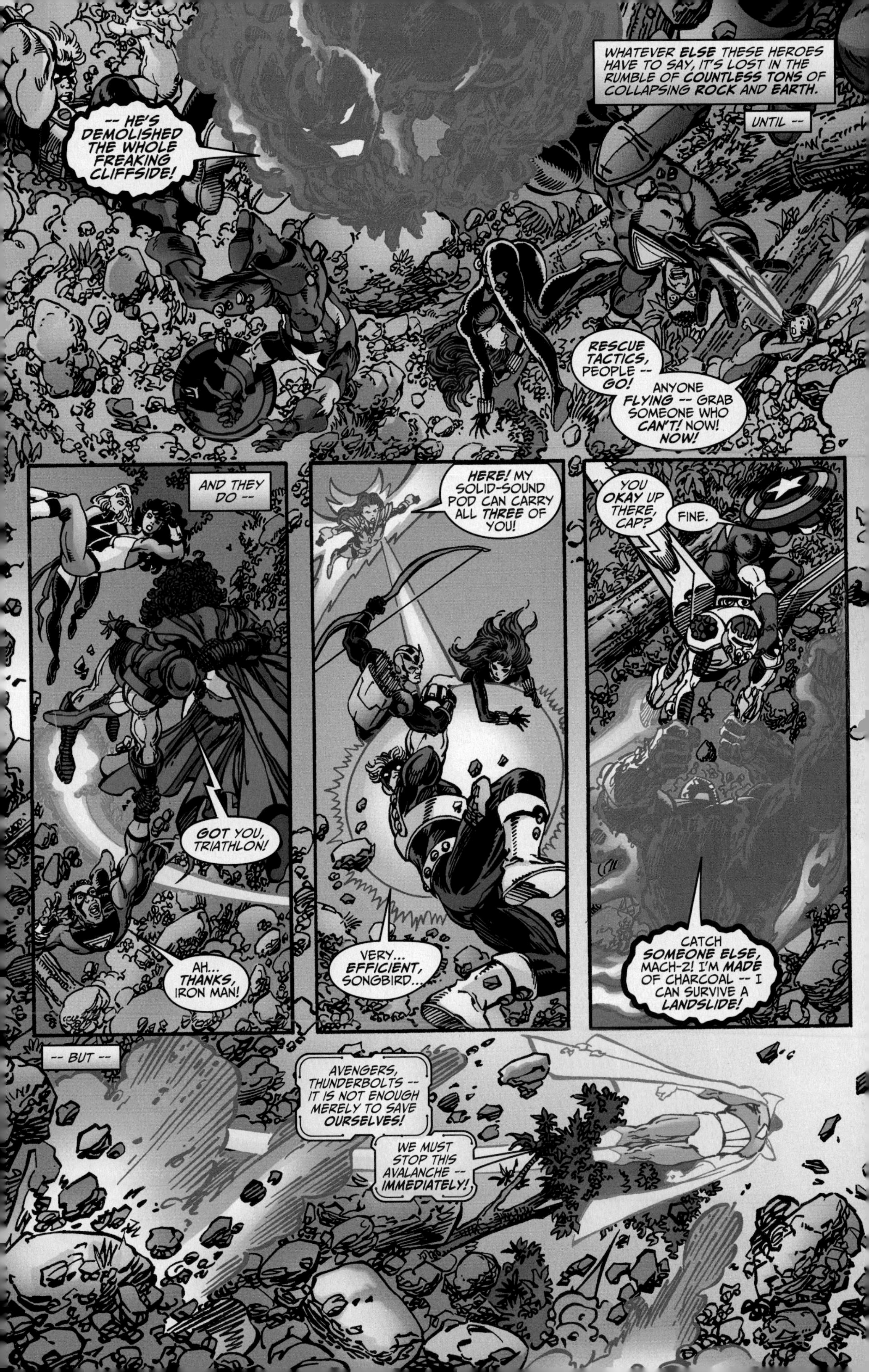

WHATEVER ELSE THESE HEROES HAVE TO SAY, IT'S LOST IN THE RUMBLE OF COUNTLESS TONS OF COLLAPSING ROCK AND EARTH.
-- HE'S DEMOLISHED THE WHOLE FREAKING CLIFFSIDE!
UNTIL --
RESCUE TACTICS, PEOPLE -- GO!
ANYONE FLYING -- GRAB SOMEONE WHO CAN'T! NOW! NOW!
AND THEY DO --
GOT YOU, TRIATHLON!
AH... THANKS, IRON MAN!
HERE! MY SOLID-SOUND POD CAN CARRY ALL THREE OF YOU!
VERY... EFFICIENT, SONGBIRD...
YOU OKAY UP THERE, CAP?
FINE.
CATCH SOMEONE ELSE, MACH-2! I'M MADE OF CHARCOAL -- I CAN SURVIVE A LANDSLIDE!
-- BUT --
AVENGERS, THUNDERBOLTS -- IT IS NOT ENOUGH MERELY TO SAVE OURSELVES!
WE MUST STOP THIS AVALANCHE -- IMMEDIATELY!

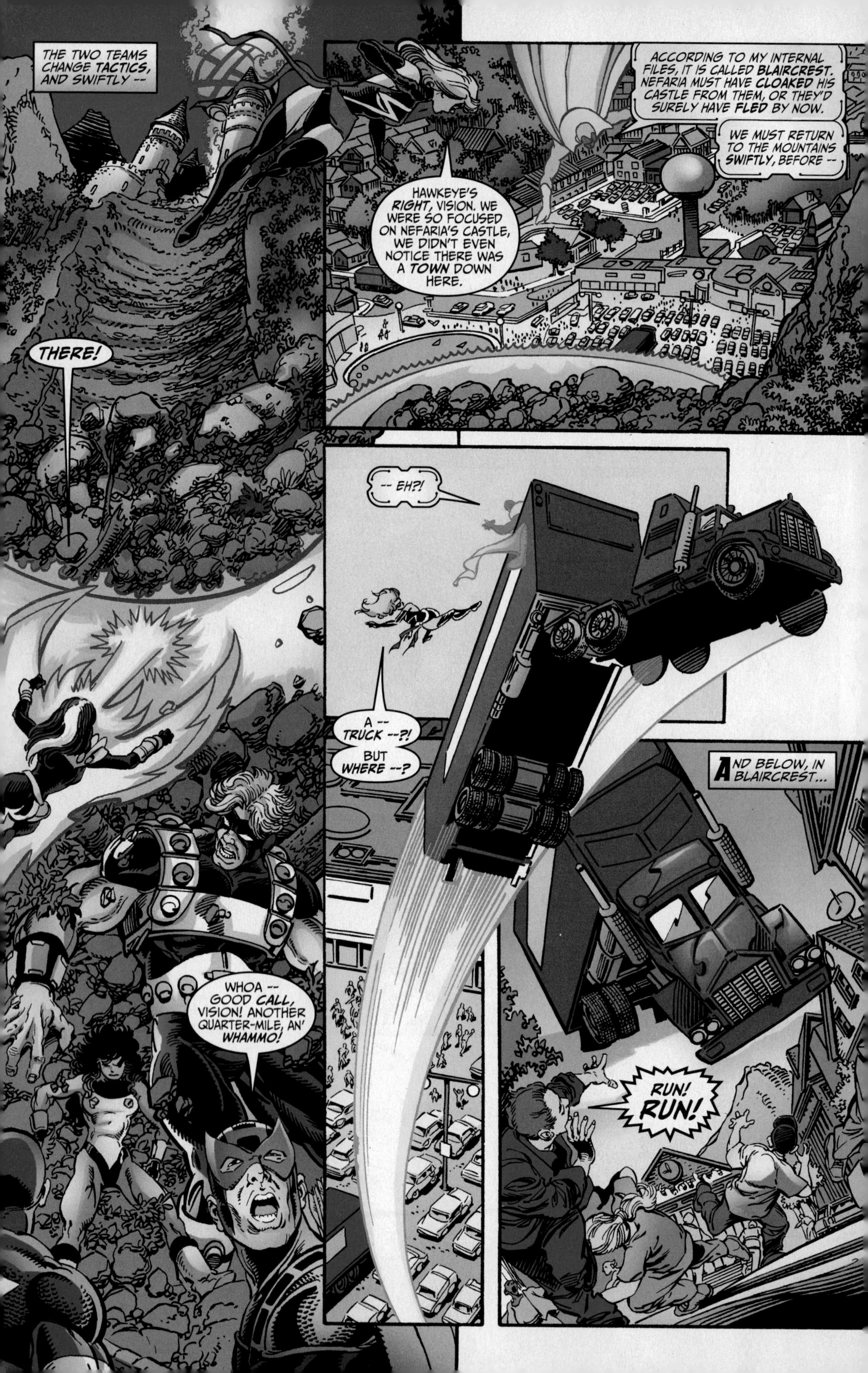
THE TWO TEAMS CHANGE TACTICS, AND SWIFTLY --
HAWKEYE'S RIGHT, VISION. WE WERE SO FOCUSED ON NEFARIA'S CASTLE, WE DIDN'T EVEN NOTICE THERE WAS A TOWN DOWN HERE.
ACCORDING TO MY INTERNAL FILES, IT IS CALLED BLAIRCREST. NEFARIA MUST HAVE CLOAKED HIS CASTLE FROM THEM, OR THEY'D SURELY HAVE FLED BY NOW.
WE MUST RETURN TO THE MOUNTAINS SWIFTLY, BEFORE --
THERE!
-- EH?!
A -- TRUCK --?! BUT WHERE --?
WHOA -- GOOD CALL, VISION! ANOTHER QUARTER-MILE, AN' WHAMMO!
AND BELOW, IN BLAIRCREST...
RUN! RUN!

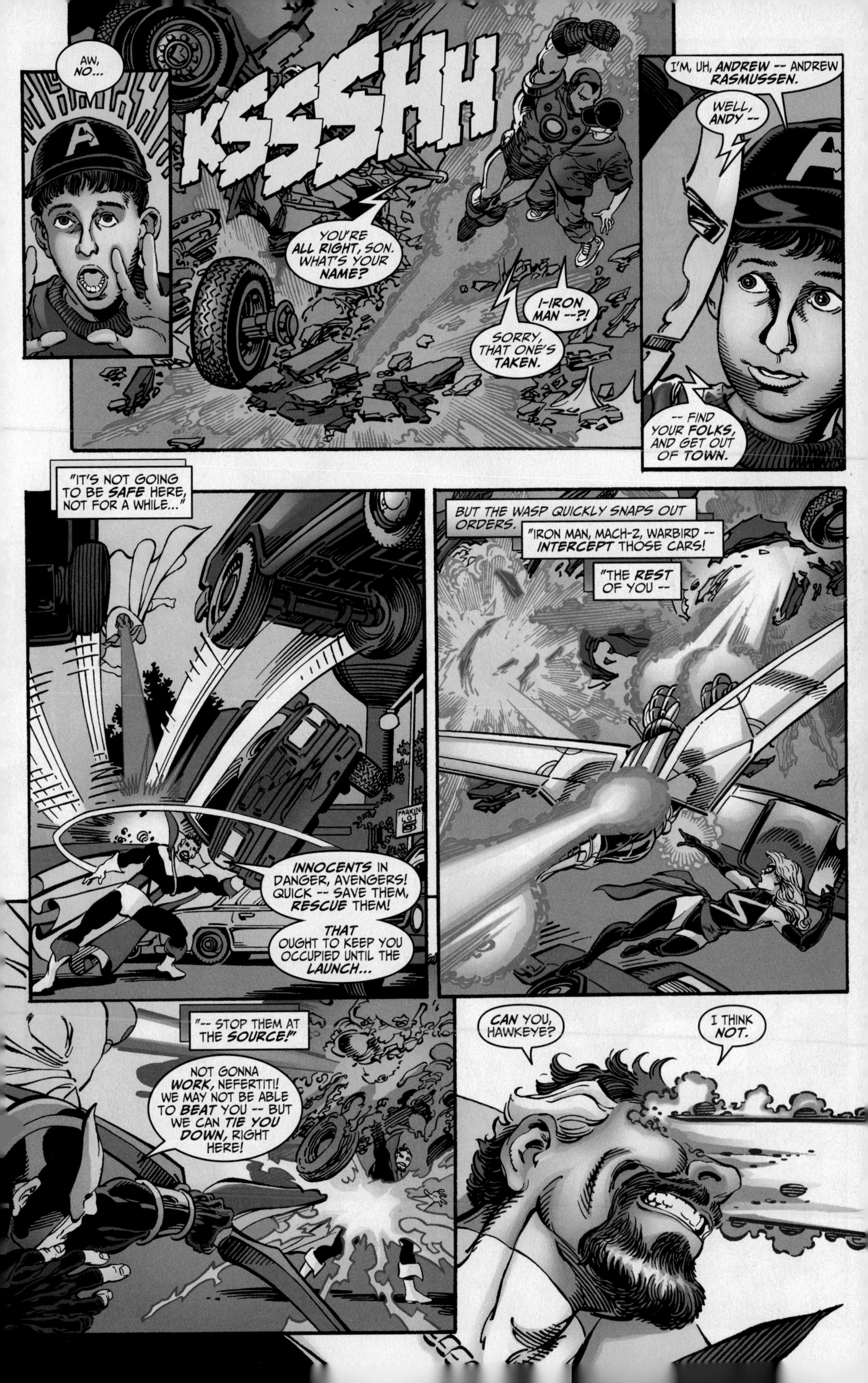
AW, NO...
KSSSHH
YOU'RE ALL RIGHT, SON. WHAT'S YOUR NAME?
I-IRON MAN --?!
SORRY, THAT ONE'S TAKEN.
I'M, UH, ANDREW -- ANDREW RASMUSSEN.
WELL, ANDY --
-- FIND YOUR FOLKS, AND GET OUT OF TOWN.
"IT'S NOT GOING TO BE SAFE HERE, NOT FOR A WHILE..."
INNOCENTS IN DANGER, AVENGERS! QUICK -- SAVE THEM, RESCUE THEM!
THAT OUGHT TO KEEP YOU OCCUPIED UNTIL THE LAUNCH...
BUT THE WASP QUICKLY SNAPS OUT ORDERS.
"IRON MAN, MACH-2, WARBIRD -- INTERCEPT THOSE CARS!
"THE REST OF YOU --
"-- STOP THEM AT THE SOURCE!"
NOT GONNA WORK, NEFERTITI! WE MAY NOT BE ABLE TO BEAT YOU -- BUT WE CAN TIE YOU DOWN, RIGHT HERE!
CAN YOU, HAWKEYE?
I THINK NOT.

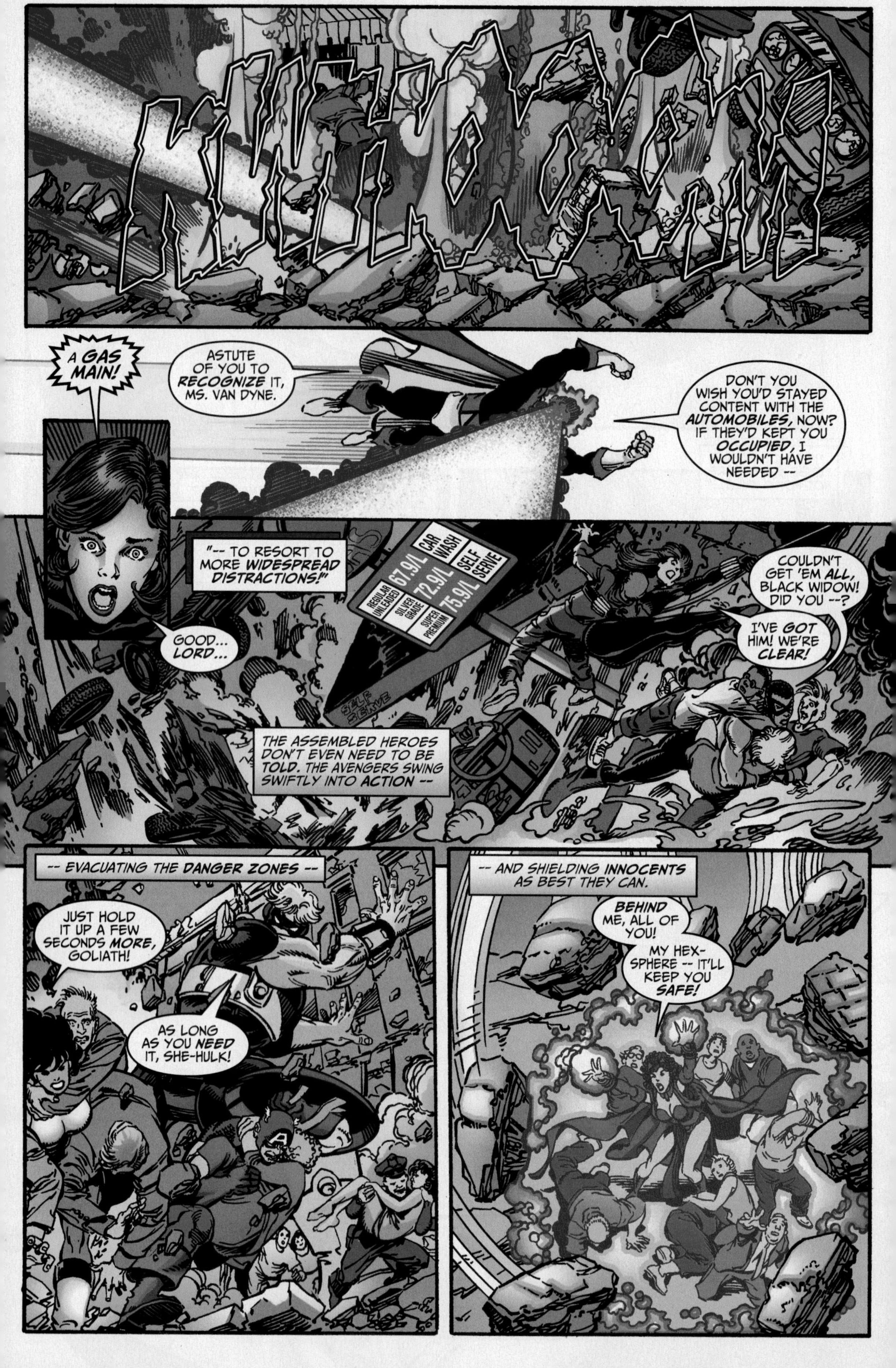
KRRRROOOOMMB
A GAS MAIN!
ASTUTE OF YOU TO RECOGNIZE IT, MS. VAN DYNE.
DON'T YOU WISH YOU'D STAYED CONTENT WITH THE AUTOMOBILES, NOW? IF THEY'D KEPT YOU OCCUPIED, I WOULDN'T HAVE NEEDED --
"-- TO RESORT TO MORE WIDESPREAD DISTRACTIONS!"
GOOD... LORD...
CAR WASH
SELF SERVE
REGULAR UNLEADED 67.9/L
SILVER GRADE 72.9/L
SUPER PREMIUM 75.9/L
COULDN'T GET 'EM ALL, BLACK WIDOW! DID YOU --?
I'VE GOT HIM! WE'RE CLEAR!
THE ASSEMBLED HEROES DON'T EVEN NEED TO BE TOLD. THE AVENGERS SWING SWIFTLY INTO ACTION --
-- EVACUATING THE DANGER ZONES --
JUST HOLD IT UP A FEW SECONDS MORE, GOLIATH!
AS LONG AS YOU NEED IT, SHE-HULK!
-- AND SHIELDING INNOCENTS AS BEST THEY CAN.
BEHIND ME, ALL OF YOU!
MY HEX-SPHERE -- IT'LL KEEP YOU SAFE!

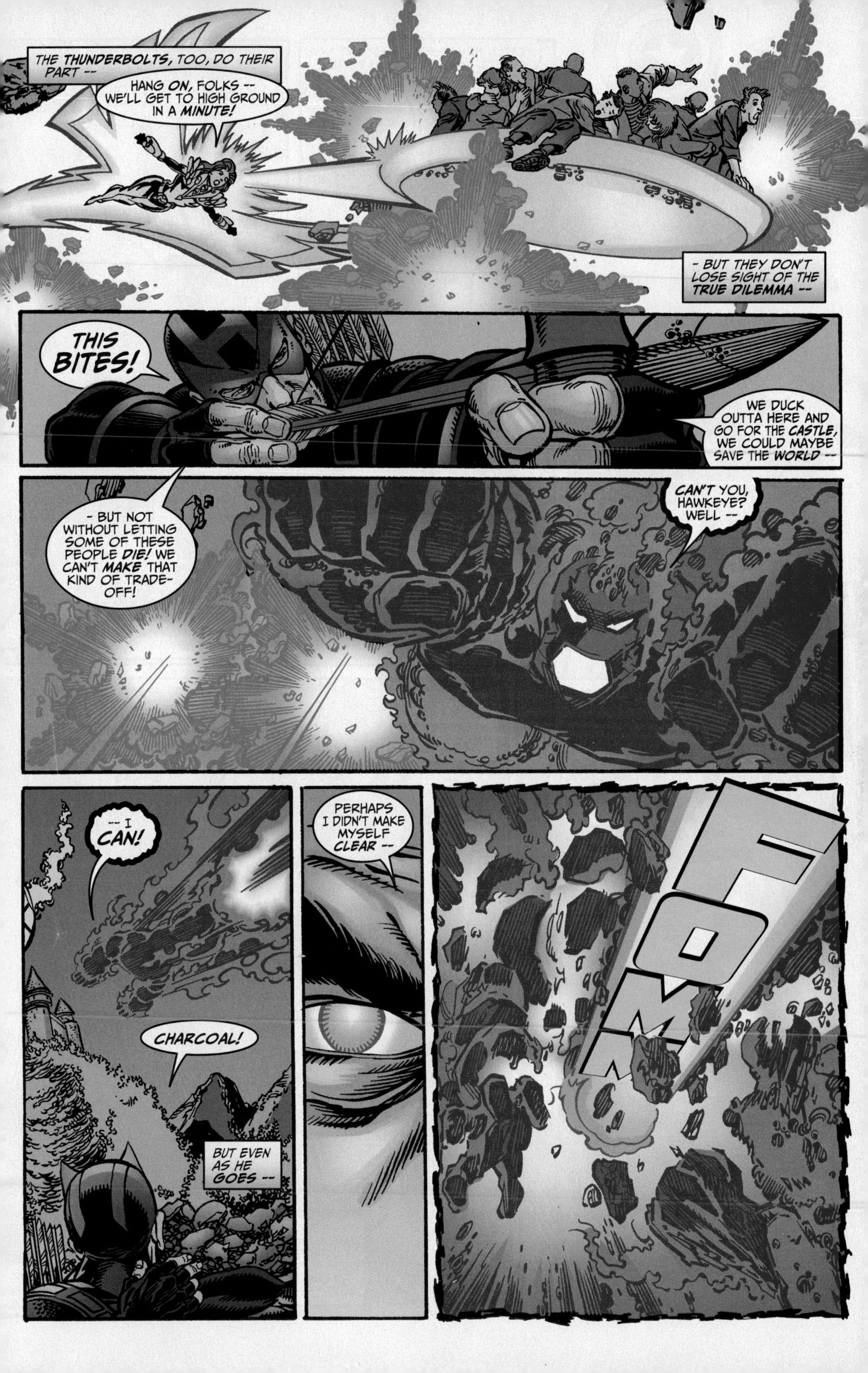
THE THUNDERBOLTS, TOO, DO THEIR PART --
HANG ON, FOLKS -- WE'LL GET TO HIGH GROUND IN A MINUTE!
- BUT THEY DON'T LOSE SIGHT OF THE TRUE DILEMMA --
THIS BITES!
WE DUCK OUTTA HERE AND GO FOR THE CASTLE, WE COULD MAYBE SAVE THE WORLD --
- BUT NOT WITHOUT LETTING SOME OF THESE PEOPLE DIE! WE CAN'T MAKE THAT KIND OF TRADE-OFF!
CAN'T YOU, HAWKEYE? WELL --
-- I CAN!
CHARCOAL!
BUT EVEN AS HE GOES --
PERHAPS I DIDN'T MAKE MYSELF CLEAR --
FOOMM

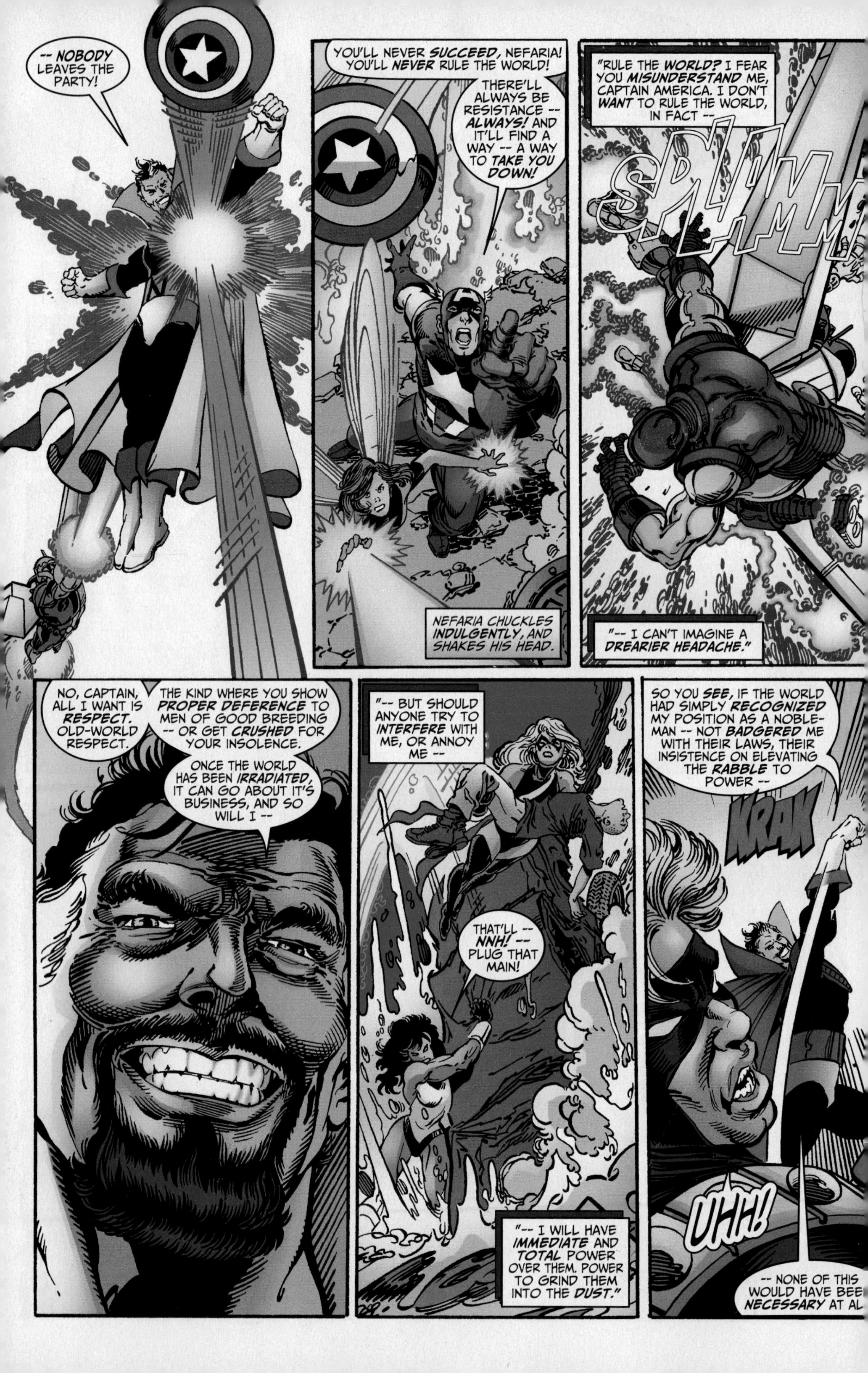

-- NOBODY LEAVES THE PARTY!
YOU'LL NEVER SUCCEED, NEFARIA! YOU'LL NEVER RULE THE WORLD!
THERE'LL ALWAYS BE RESISTANCE -- ALWAYS! AND IT'LL FIND A WAY -- A WAY TO TAKE YOU DOWN!
NEFARIA CHUCKLES INDULGENTLY, AND SHAKES HIS HEAD.
"RULE THE WORLD? I FEAR YOU MISUNDERSTAND ME, CAPTAIN AMERICA. I DON'T WANT TO RULE THE WORLD, IN FACT --
SPLAMM
"-- I CAN'T IMAGINE A DREARIER HEADACHE."
NO, CAPTAIN, ALL I WANT IS RESPECT. OLD-WORLD RESPECT.
THE KIND WHERE YOU SHOW PROPER DEFERENCE TO MEN OF GOOD BREEDING -- OR GET CRUSHED FOR YOUR INSOLENCE.
ONCE THE WORLD HAS BEEN IRRADIATED, IT CAN GO ABOUT IT'S BUSINESS, AND SO WILL I --
"-- BUT SHOULD ANYONE TRY TO INTERFERE WITH ME, OR ANNOY ME --
THAT'LL -- NNH! -- PLUG THAT MAIN!
"-- I WILL HAVE IMMEDIATE AND TOTAL POWER OVER THEM. POWER TO GRIND THEM INTO THE DUST."
SO YOU SEE, IF THE WORLD HAD SIMPLY RECOGNIZED MY POSITION AS A NOBLEMAN -- NOT BADGERED ME WITH THEIR LAWS, THEIR INSISTENCE ON ELEVATING THE RABBLE TO POWER --
KRAK
UHH!
-- NONE OF THIS WOULD HAVE BEE NECESSARY AT AL

I -- I DON'T *BELIEVE* THIS!

YOU'D MURDER *MILLIONS* -- MUTATE EVEN MORE -- JUST SO PEOPLE WILL BE *POLITE* TO YOU?!

IT'S A *SADLY* ILL-MANNERED WORLD, WASP.

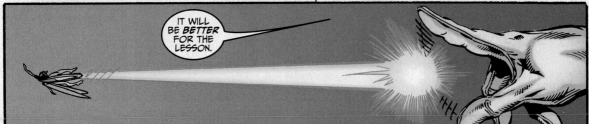

IT WILL BE *BETTER* FOR THE LESSON.

BUT THEN, AS NEFARIA TURNS BACK TO THE *OTHERS...*

NNGH!

WHAT IN SEVEN *HELLS?!*

CHAOS-MAGIC, NEFARIA! MY *HEX-POWER!* MY BIRTHRIGHT -- AS THE *SCARLET WITCH!*

I'LL *SUFFUSE* YOU WITH IT -- TAKE OVER *YOUR* POWER -- SHUT YOU *DOWN!*

YOU... CAN *TRY,* MS. MAXIMOFF!

OH, *MAN.* DOES *NOTHING* STOP THIS GUY?

I DUNNO, JEN...

TRIATHLON! SHE-HULK! I'VE GOT A *PLAN!*

BUT WE HAVE TO BE *FAST* -- WANDA'S NOT GOING TO BE ABLE TO *HOLD* HIM MUCH LONGER --

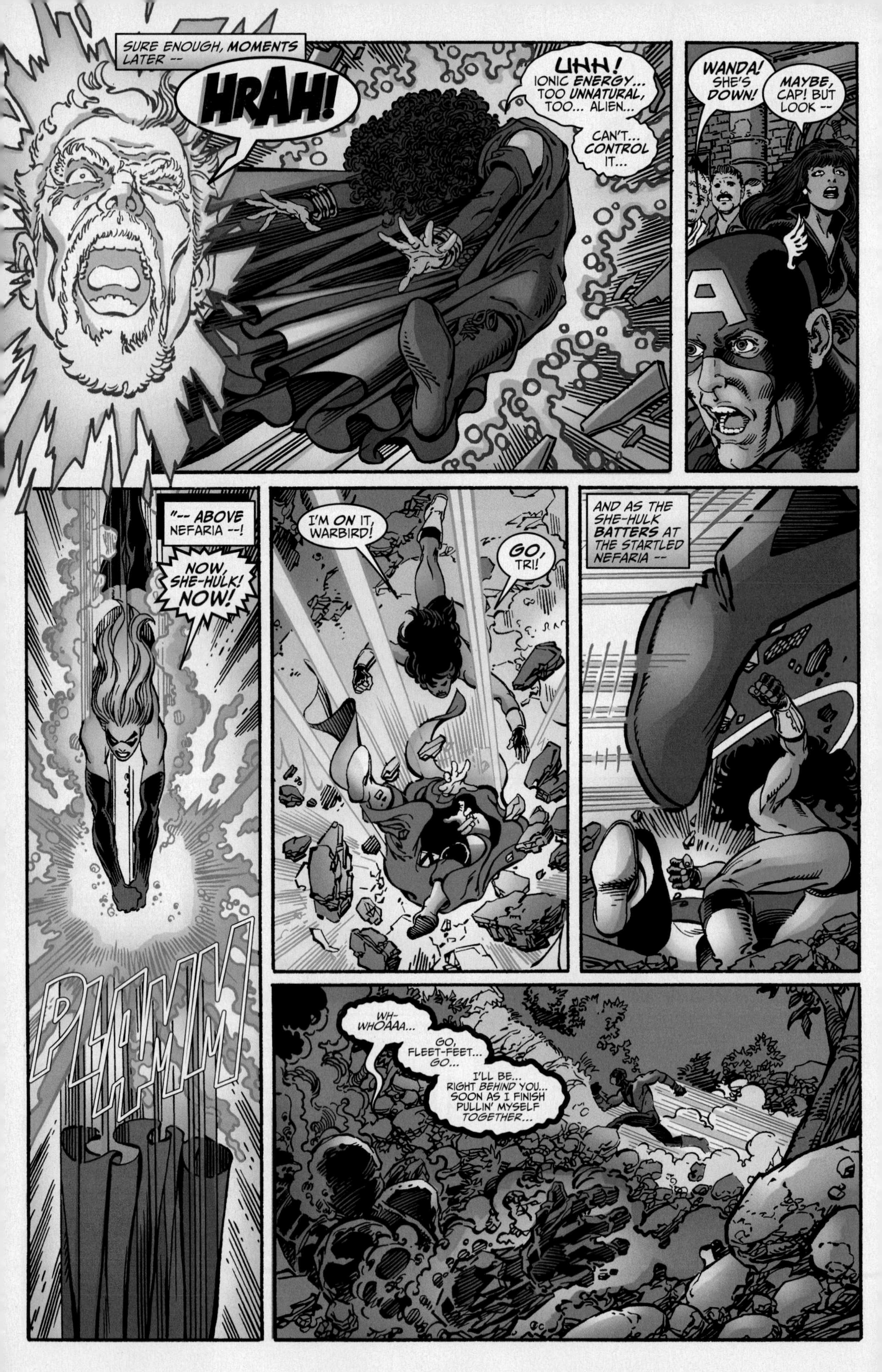
SURE ENOUGH, MOMENTS LATER --
HRAH!
UHH! IONIC ENERGY... TOO UNNATURAL, TOO... ALIEN...
CAN'T... CONTROL IT...
WANDA! SHE'S DOWN!
MAYBE, CAP! BUT LOOK --
"-- ABOVE NEFARIA --!
NOW, SHE-HULK! NOW!
I'M ON IT, WARBIRD!
GO, TRI!
AND AS THE SHE-HULK BATTERS AT THE STARTLED NEFARIA --
WH-WHOAAA...
GO, FLEET-FEET... GO...
I'LL BE... RIGHT BEHIND YOU... SOON AS I FINISH PULLIN' MYSELF TOGETHER...

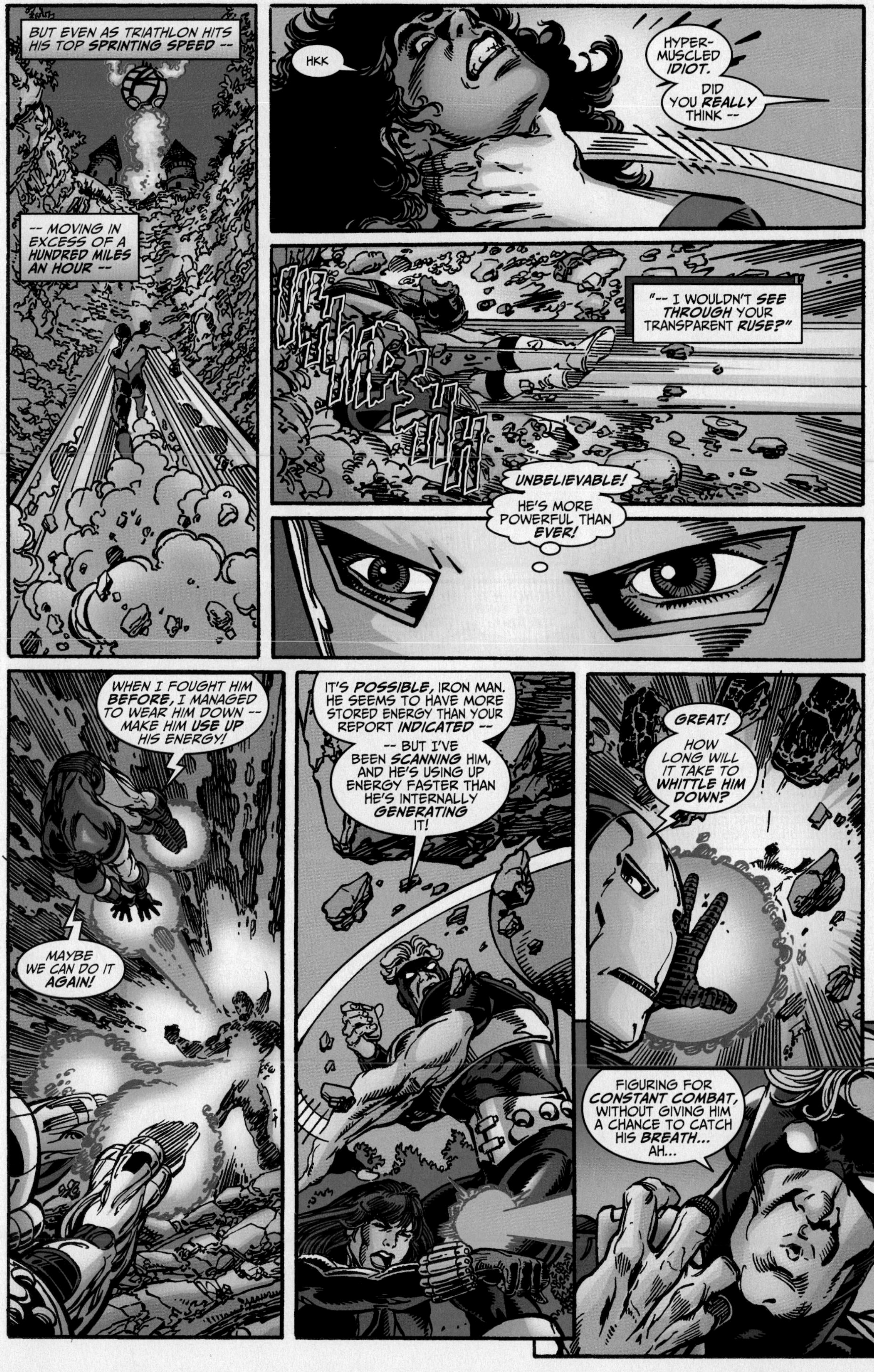

BUT EVEN AS TRIATHLON HITS HIS TOP SPRINTING SPEED --
-- MOVING IN EXCESS OF A HUNDRED MILES AN HOUR --
HKK
HYPER-MUSCLED IDIOT.
DID YOU REALLY THINK --
"-- I WOULDN'T SEE THROUGH YOUR TRANSPARENT RUSE?"
WHMPTH
UNBELIEVABLE!
HE'S MORE POWERFUL THAN EVER!
WHEN I FOUGHT HIM BEFORE, I MANAGED TO WEAR HIM DOWN -- MAKE HIM USE UP HIS ENERGY!
MAYBE WE CAN DO IT AGAIN!
IT'S POSSIBLE, IRON MAN. HE SEEMS TO HAVE MORE STORED ENERGY THAN YOUR REPORT INDICATED --
-- BUT I'VE BEEN SCANNING HIM, AND HE'S USING UP ENERGY FASTER THAN HE'S INTERNALLY GENERATING IT!
GREAT!
HOW LONG WILL IT TAKE TO WHITTLE HIM DOWN?
FIGURING FOR CONSTANT COMBAT, WITHOUT GIVING HIM A CHANCE TO CATCH HIS BREATH... AH...

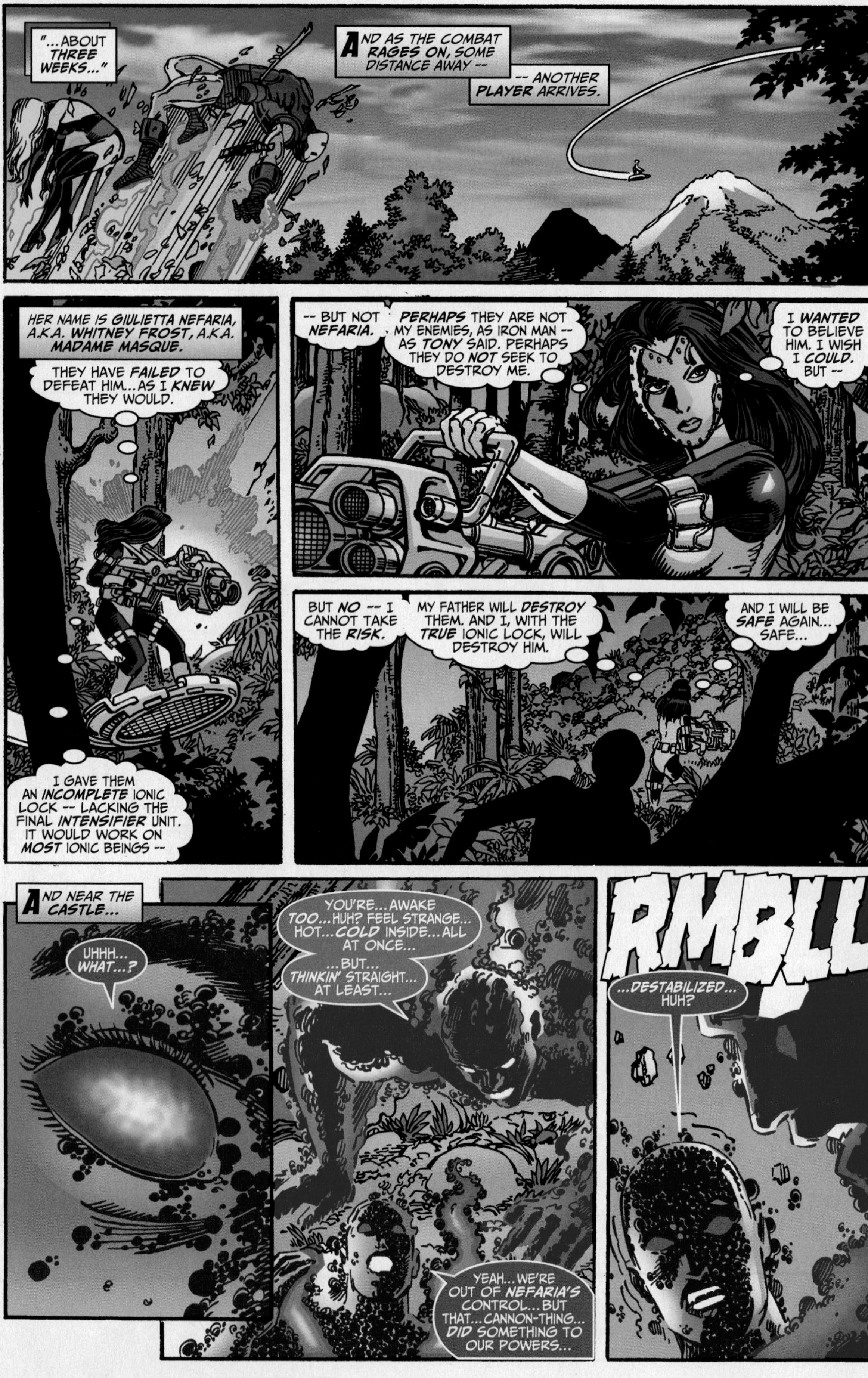
"...ABOUT THREE WEEKS..."
AND AS THE COMBAT RAGES ON, SOME DISTANCE AWAY --
-- ANOTHER PLAYER ARRIVES.
HER NAME IS GIULIETTA NEFARIA, A.K.A. WHITNEY FROST, A.K.A. MADAME MASQUE.
THEY HAVE FAILED TO DEFEAT HIM...AS I KNEW THEY WOULD.
I GAVE THEM AN INCOMPLETE IONIC LOCK -- LACKING THE FINAL INTENSIFIER UNIT. IT WOULD WORK ON MOST IONIC BEINGS --
-- BUT NOT NEFARIA.
PERHAPS THEY ARE NOT MY ENEMIES, AS IRON MAN -- AS TONY SAID. PERHAPS THEY DO NOT SEEK TO DESTROY ME.
I WANTED TO BELIEVE HIM. I WISH I COULD. BUT --
BUT NO -- I CANNOT TAKE THE RISK.
MY FATHER WILL DESTROY THEM. AND I, WITH THE TRUE IONIC LOCK, WILL DESTROY HIM.
AND I WILL BE SAFE AGAIN... SAFE...
AND NEAR THE CASTLE...
UHHH... WHAT...?
YOU'RE... AWAKE TOO...HUH? FEEL STRANGE... HOT...COLD INSIDE...ALL AT ONCE...
...BUT... THINKIN' STRAIGHT... AT LEAST...
YEAH...WE'RE OUT OF NEFARIA'S CONTROL...BUT THAT...CANNON-THING... DID SOMETHING TO OUR POWERS...
RMBLL
...DESTABILIZED... HUH?

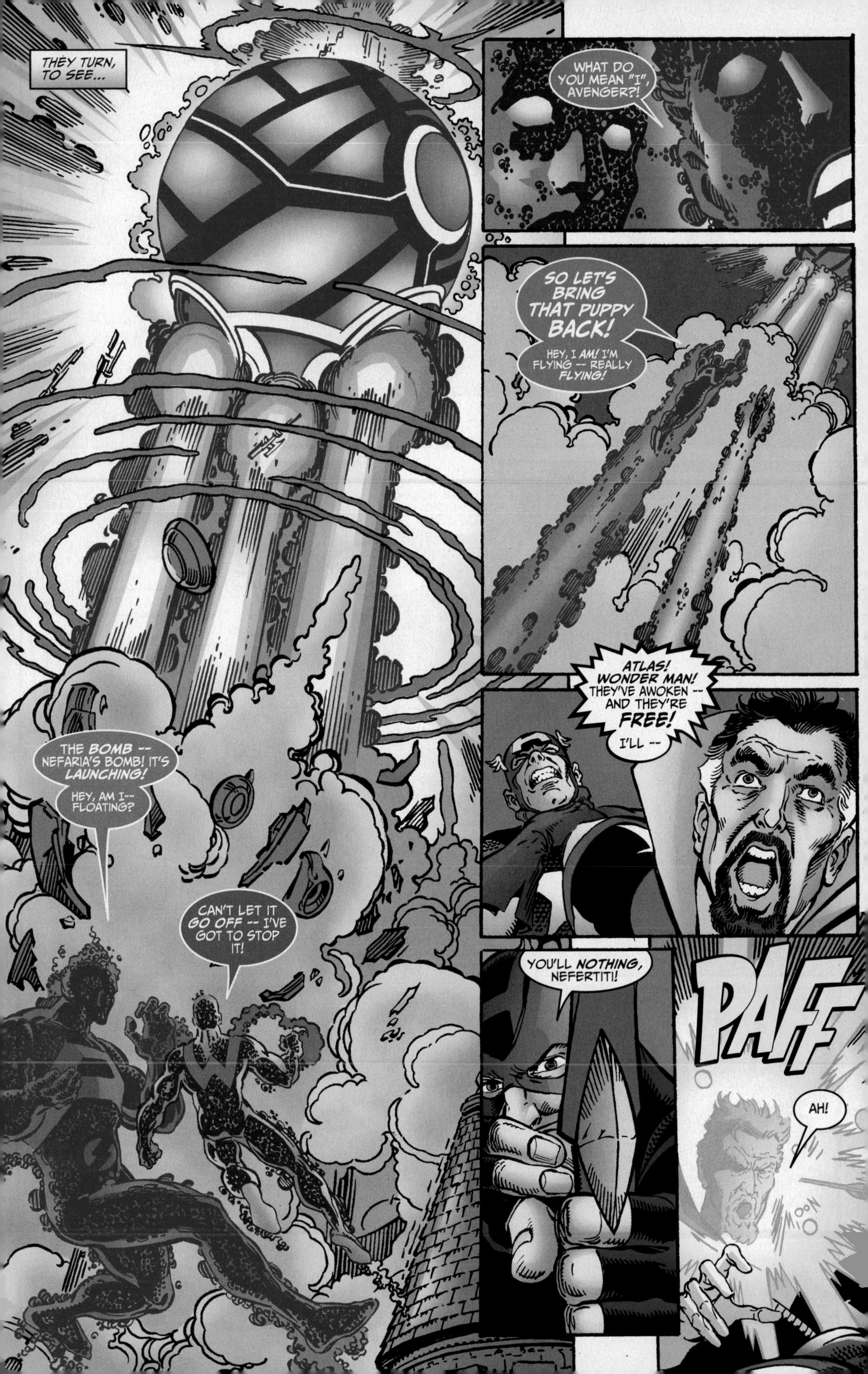
THEY TURN, TO SEE...
WHAT DO YOU MEAN "I", AVENGER?!
SO LET'S BRING THAT PUPPY BACK!
HEY, I AM! I'M FLYING -- REALLY FLYING!
THE BOMB -- NEFARIA'S BOMB! IT'S LAUNCHING!
HEY, AM I-- FLOATING?
CAN'T LET IT GO OFF -- I'VE GOT TO STOP IT!
ATLAS! WONDER MAN! THEY'VE AWOKEN -- AND THEY'RE FREE!
I'LL --
YOU'LL NOTHING, NEFERTITI!
PAFF
AH!

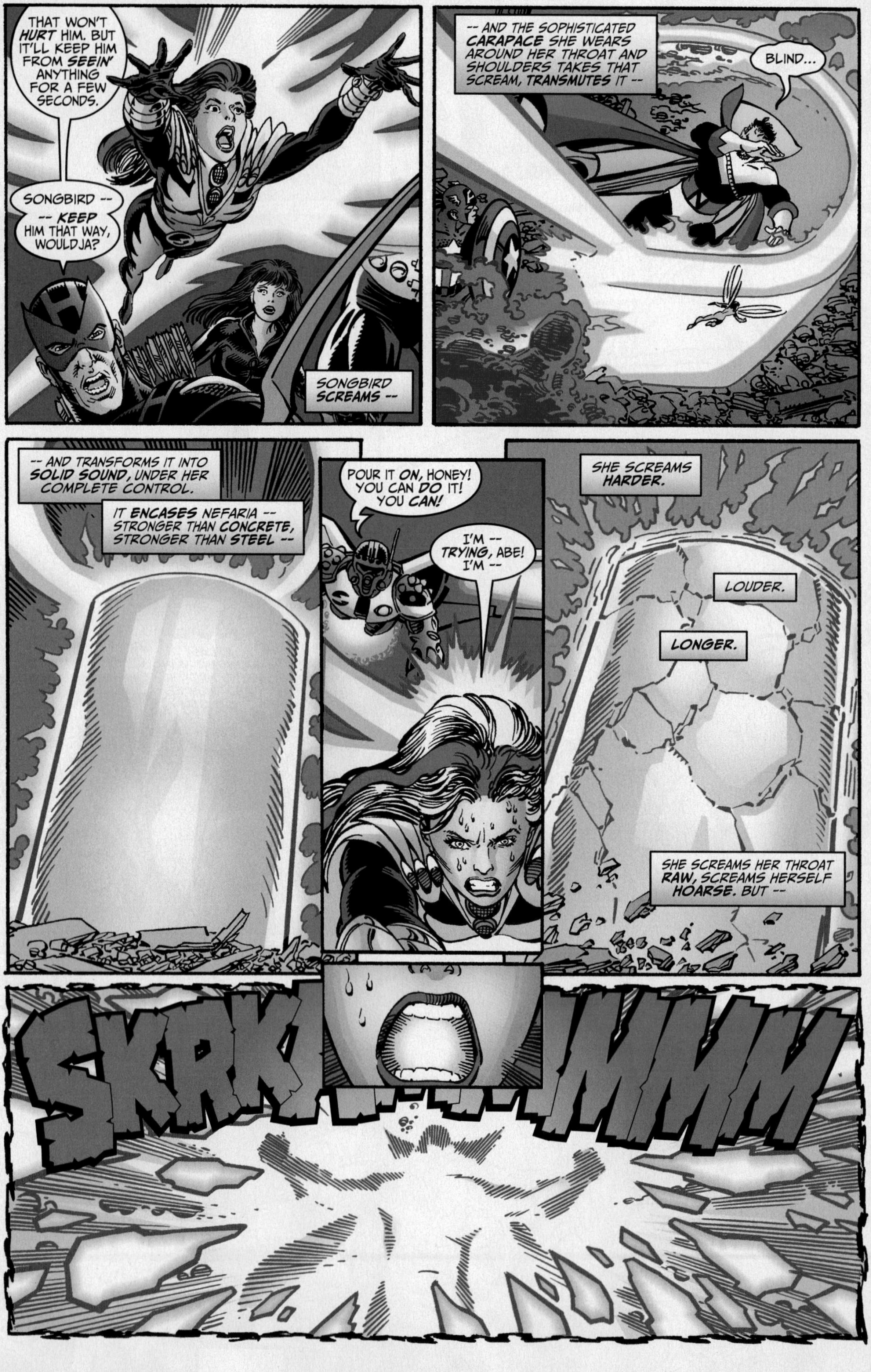

THAT WON'T HURT HIM. BUT IT'LL KEEP HIM FROM SEEIN' ANYTHING FOR A FEW SECONDS.
SONGBIRD --
-- KEEP HIM THAT WAY, WOULDJA?
SONGBIRD SCREAMS --
-- AND THE SOPHISTICATED CARAPACE SHE WEARS AROUND HER THROAT AND SHOULDERS TAKES THAT SCREAM, TRANSMUTES IT --
BLIND...
-- AND TRANSFORMS IT INTO SOLID SOUND, UNDER HER COMPLETE CONTROL.
IT ENCASES NEFARIA -- STRONGER THAN CONCRETE, STRONGER THAN STEEL --
POUR IT ON, HONEY! YOU CAN DO IT! YOU CAN!
I'M -- TRYING, ABE! I'M --
SHE SCREAMS HARDER.
LOUDER.
LONGER.
SHE SCREAMS HER THROAT RAW, SCREAMS HERSELF HOARSE. BUT --
SKRK
MMM

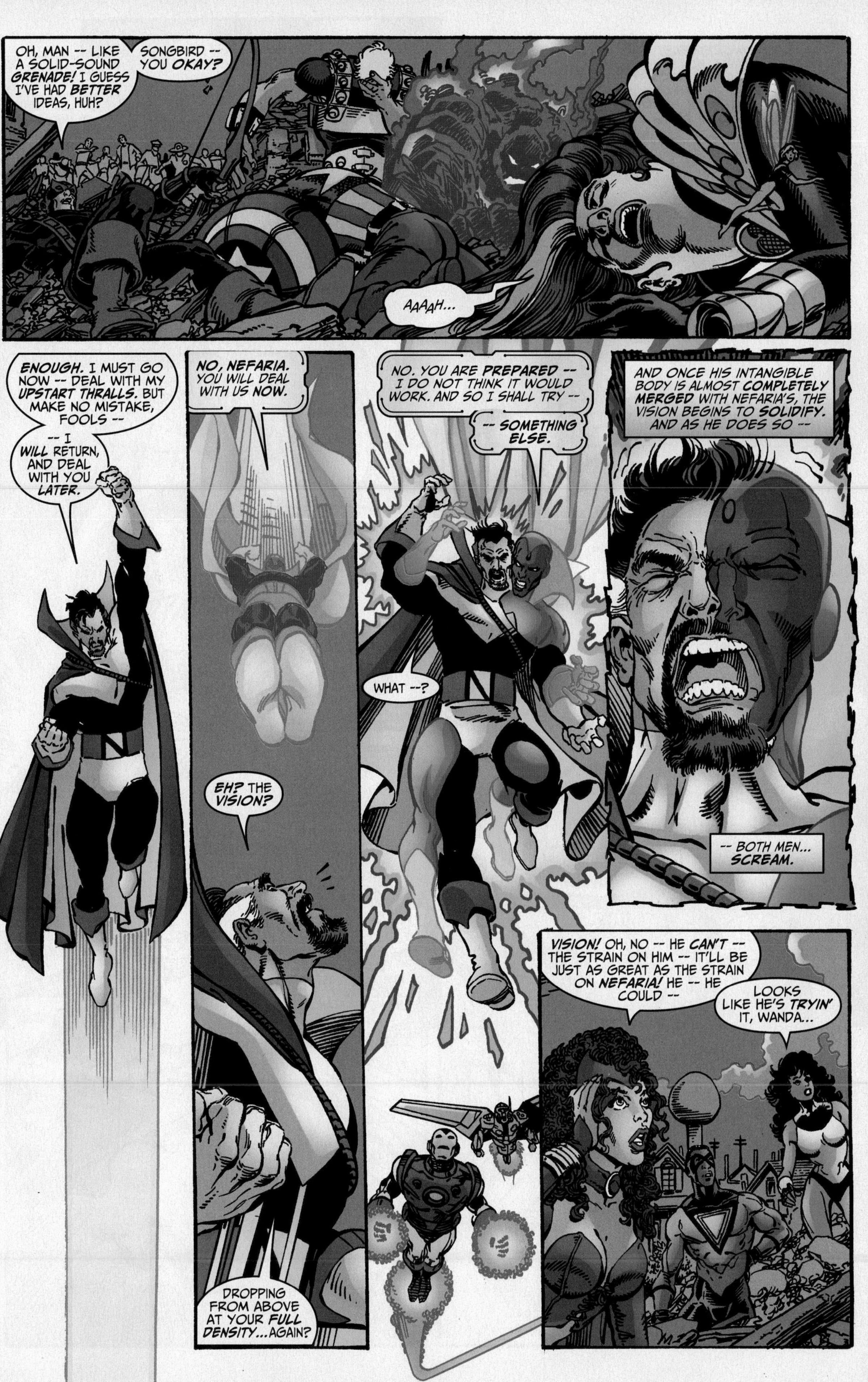
OH, MAN -- LIKE A SOLID-SOUND GRENADE! I GUESS I'VE HAD BETTER IDEAS, HUH?
SONGBIRD -- YOU OKAY?
AAAAH...
ENOUGH. I MUST GO NOW -- DEAL WITH MY UPSTART THRALLS. BUT MAKE NO MISTAKE, FOOLS --
-- I WILL RETURN, AND DEAL WITH YOU LATER.
NO, NEFARIA. YOU WILL DEAL WITH US NOW.
EH? THE VISION?
DROPPING FROM ABOVE AT YOUR FULL DENSITY... AGAIN?
NO. YOU ARE PREPARED -- I DO NOT THINK IT WOULD WORK. AND SO I SHALL TRY --
-- SOMETHING ELSE.
WHAT --?
AND ONCE HIS INTANGIBLE BODY IS ALMOST COMPLETELY MERGED WITH NEFARIA'S, THE VISION BEGINS TO SOLIDIFY. AND AS HE DOES SO --
-- BOTH MEN... SCREAM.
VISION! OH, NO -- HE CAN'T -- THE STRAIN ON HIM -- IT'LL BE JUST AS GREAT AS THE STRAIN ON NEFARIA! HE -- HE COULD --
LOOKS LIKE HE'S TRYIN' IT, WANDA...

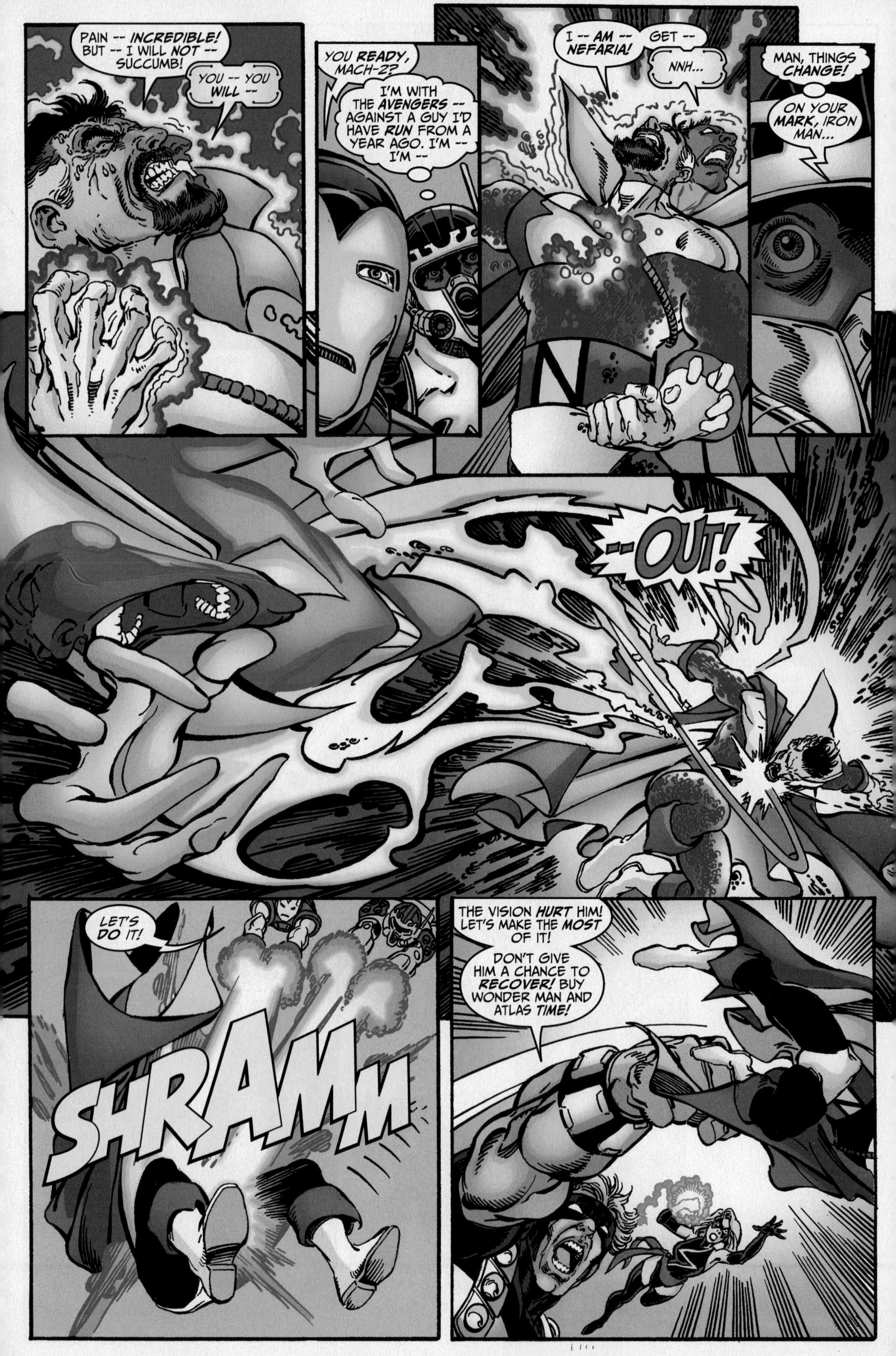
PAIN -- INCREDIBLE! BUT -- I WILL NOT -- SUCCUMB!
YOU -- YOU WILL --
YOU READY, MACH-2?
I'M WITH THE AVENGERS -- AGAINST A GUY I'D HAVE RUN FROM A YEAR AGO. I'M -- I'M --
I -- AM -- NEFARIA!
GET --
NNH...
MAN, THINGS CHANGE!
ON YOUR MARK, IRON MAN...
--OUT!
LET'S DO IT!
SHRAMM
THE VISION HURT HIM! LET'S MAKE THE MOST OF IT!
DON'T GIVE HIM A CHANCE TO RECOVER! BUY WONDER MAN AND ATLAS TIME!

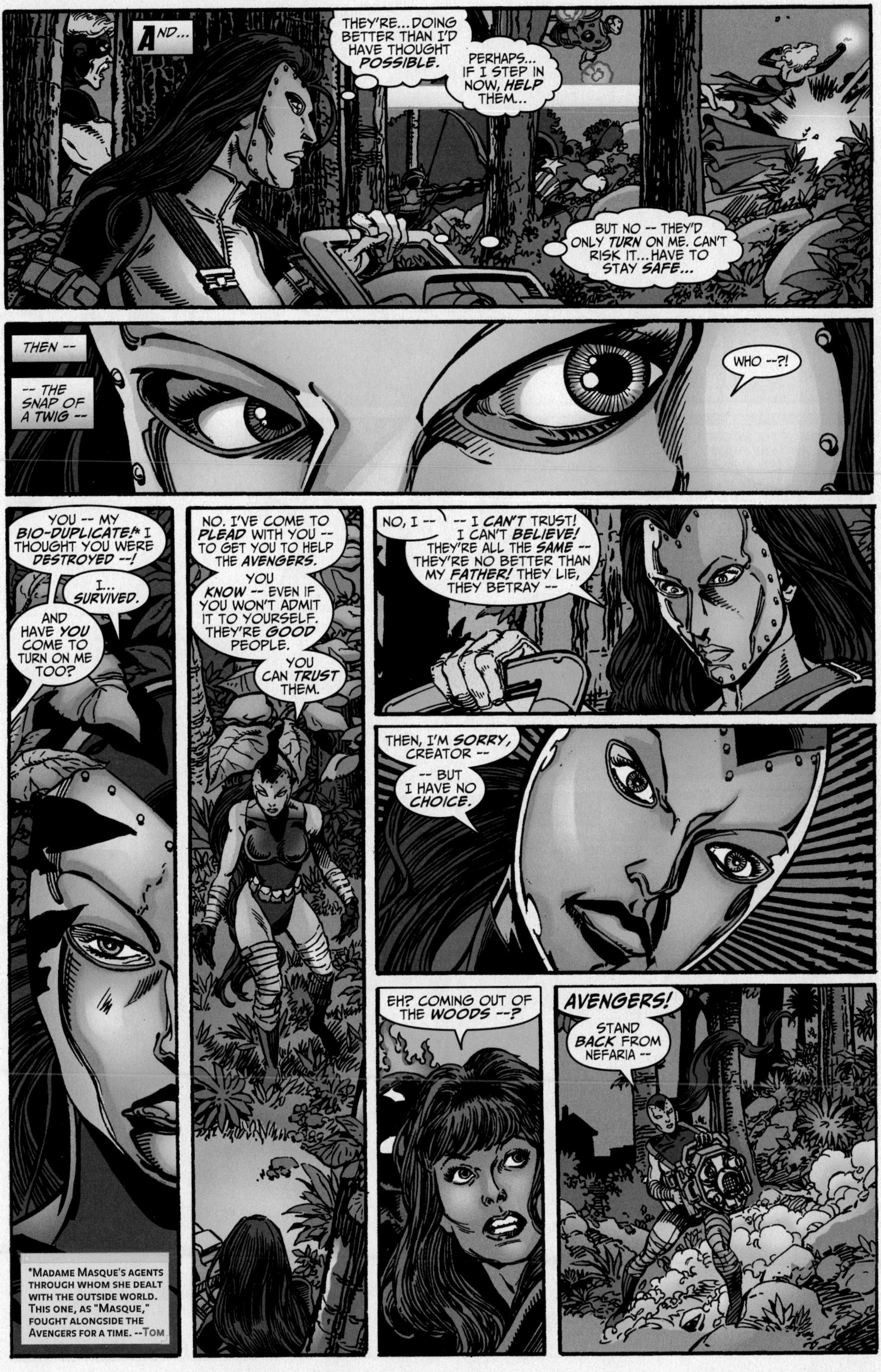
AND...
THEY'RE...DOING BETTER THAN I'D HAVE THOUGHT POSSIBLE.
PERHAPS... IF I STEP IN NOW, HELP THEM...
BUT NO -- THEY'D ONLY TURN ON ME. CAN'T RISK IT...HAVE TO STAY SAFE...
THEN --
-- THE SNAP OF A TWIG --
WHO --?!
YOU -- MY BIO-DUPLICATE!* I THOUGHT YOU WERE DESTROYED --!
I... SURVIVED.
AND HAVE YOU COME TO TURN ON ME TOO?
NO. I'VE COME TO PLEAD WITH YOU -- TO GET YOU TO HELP THE AVENGERS.
YOU KNOW -- EVEN IF YOU WON'T ADMIT IT TO YOURSELF. THEY'RE GOOD PEOPLE.
YOU CAN TRUST THEM.
NO, I --
-- I CAN'T TRUST! I CAN'T BELIEVE! THEY'RE ALL THE SAME -- THEY'RE NO BETTER THAN MY FATHER! THEY LIE, THEY BETRAY --
THEN, I'M SORRY, CREATOR --
-- BUT I HAVE NO CHOICE.
EH? COMING OUT OF THE WOODS --?
AVENGERS!
STAND BACK FROM NEFARIA --
*MADAME MASQUE'S AGENTS THROUGH WHOM SHE DEALT WITH THE OUTSIDE WORLD. THIS ONE, AS "MASQUE," FOUGHT ALONGSIDE THE AVENGERS FOR A TIME. --TOM

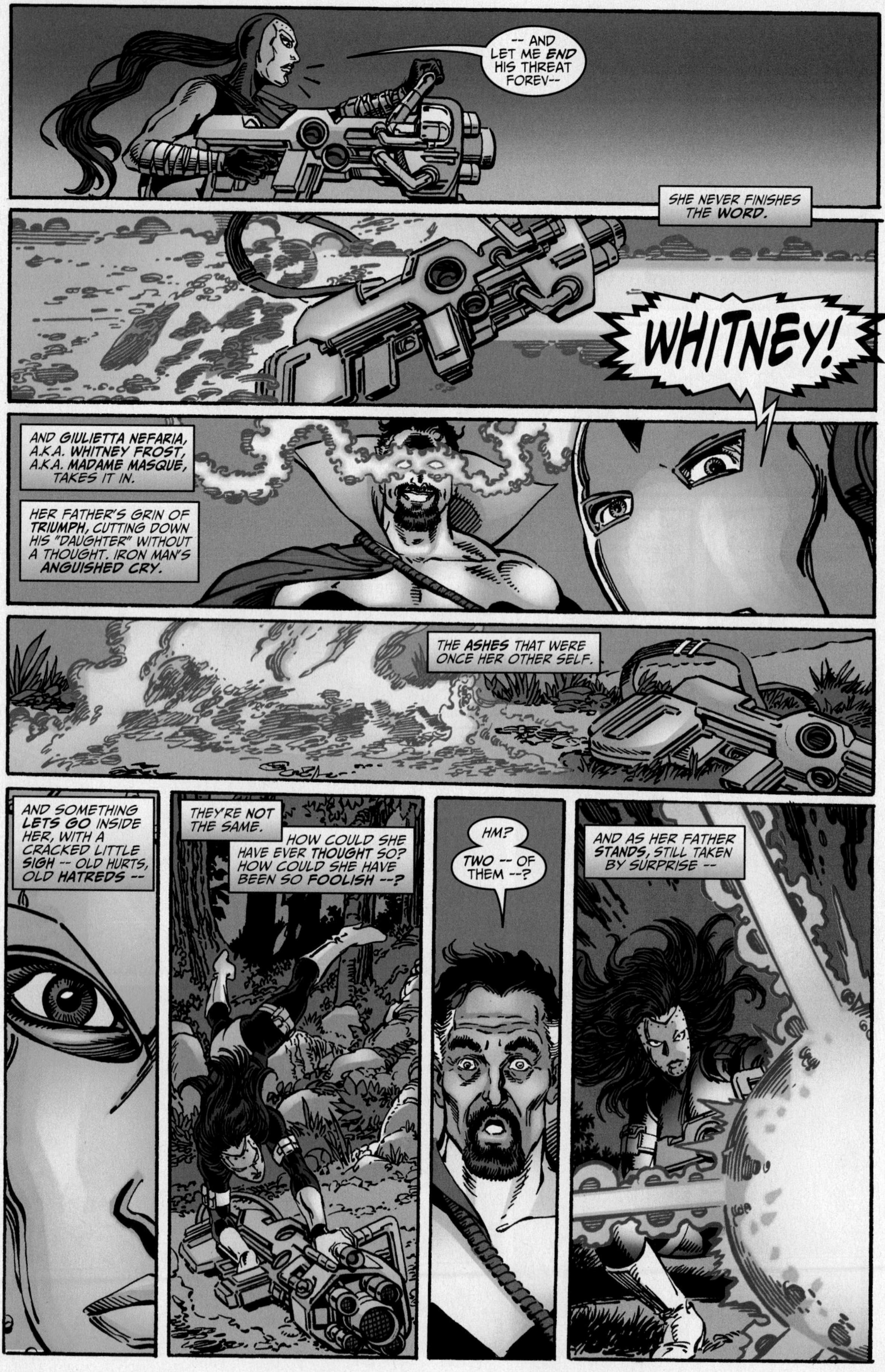
-- AND LET ME END HIS THREAT FOREV--
SHE NEVER FINISHES THE WORD.
WHITNEY!
AND GIULIETTA NEFARIA, A.K.A. WHITNEY FROST, A.K.A. MADAME MASQUE, TAKES IT IN.
HER FATHER'S GRIN OF TRIUMPH, CUTTING DOWN HIS "DAUGHTER" WITHOUT A THOUGHT. IRON MAN'S ANGUISHED CRY.
THE ASHES THAT WERE ONCE HER OTHER SELF.
AND SOMETHING LETS GO INSIDE HER, WITH A CRACKED LITTLE SIGH -- OLD HURTS, OLD HATREDS --
THEY'RE NOT THE SAME.
HOW COULD SHE HAVE EVER THOUGHT SO? HOW COULD SHE HAVE BEEN SO FOOLISH --?
HM?
TWO -- OF THEM --?
AND AS HER FATHER STANDS, STILL TAKEN BY SURPRISE --

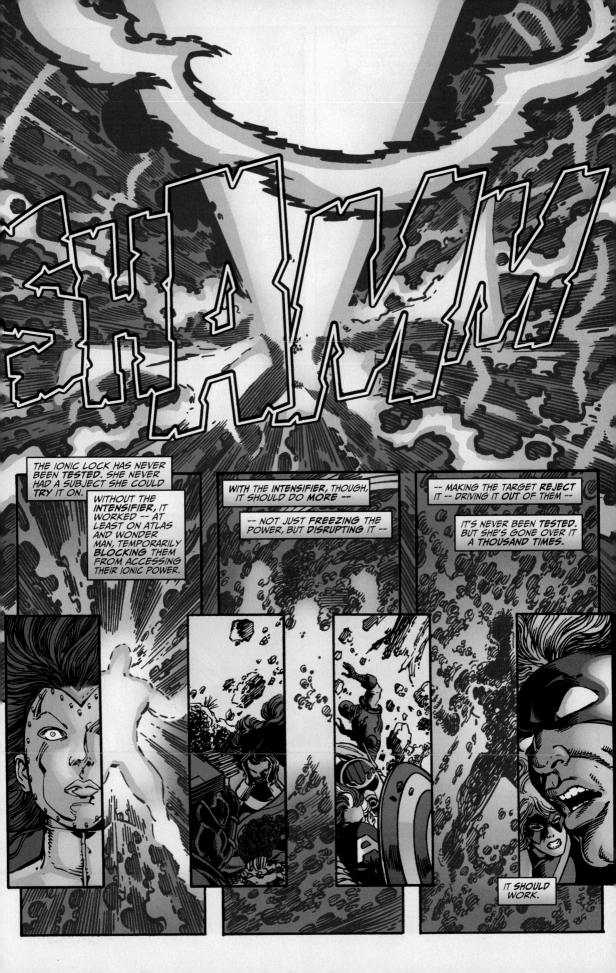

SHAKKM

THE IONIC LOCK HAS NEVER BEEN **TESTED.** SHE NEVER HAD A SUBJECT SHE COULD TRY IT ON.

WITHOUT THE **INTENSIFIER,** IT WORKED -- AT LEAST ON ATLAS AND WONDER MAN, TEMPORARILY **BLOCKING** THEM FROM ACCESSING THEIR IONIC POWER.

WITH THE **INTENSIFIER,** THOUGH, IT SHOULD DO **MORE** --

-- NOT JUST **FREEZING** THE POWER, BUT **DISRUPTING** IT --

-- MAKING THE TARGET **REJECT** IT -- DRIVING IT **OUT** OF THEM --

IT'S NEVER BEEN **TESTED.** BUT SHE'S GONE OVER IT A **THOUSAND TIMES.**

IT **SHOULD** WORK.

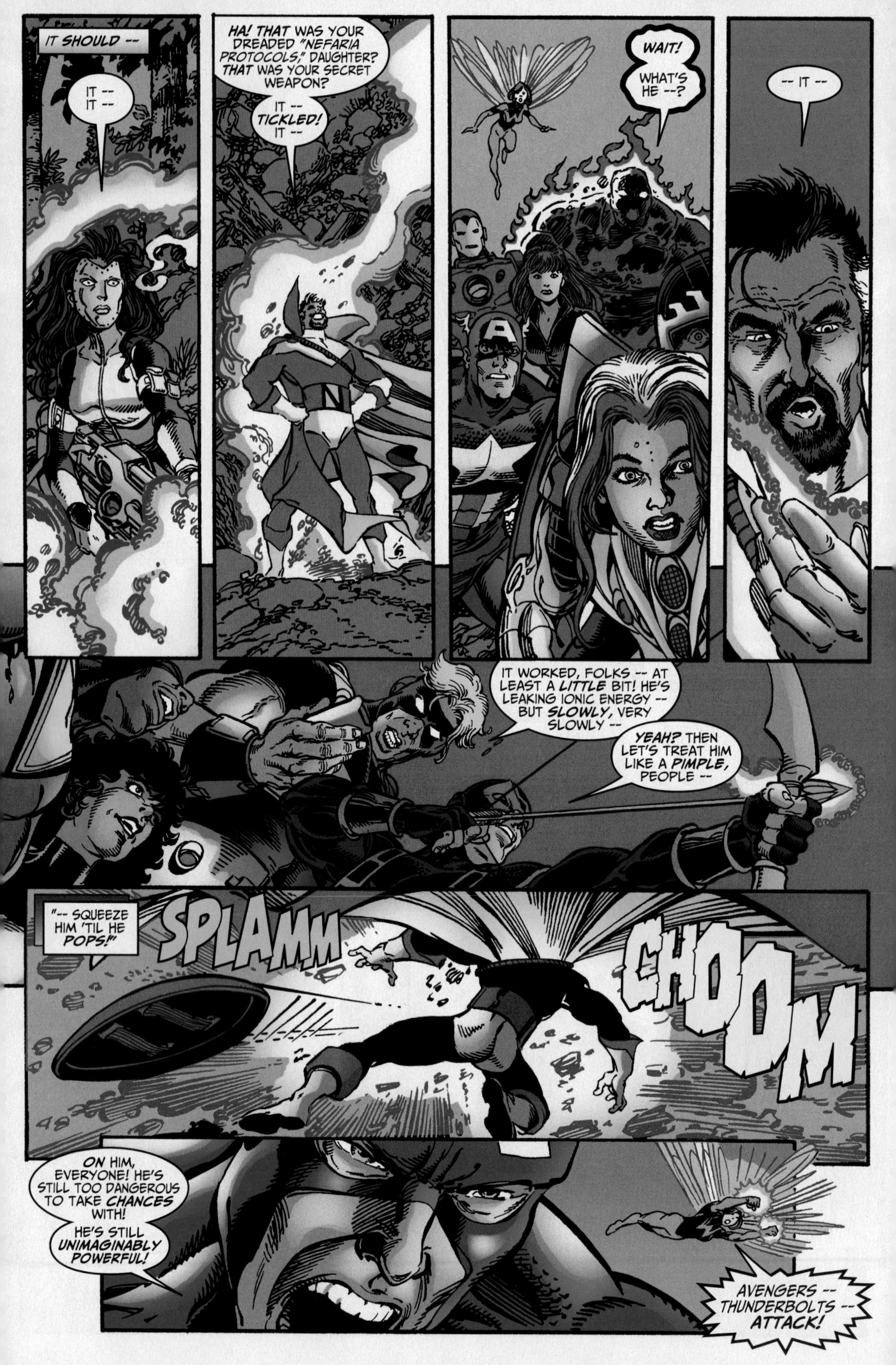
IT SHOULD --
IT -- IT --
HA! THAT WAS YOUR DREADED "NEFARIA PROTOCOLS," DAUGHTER? THAT WAS YOUR SECRET WEAPON?
IT -- TICKLED! IT --
WAIT!
WHAT'S HE --?
-- IT --
IT WORKED, FOLKS -- AT LEAST A LITTLE BIT! HE'S LEAKING IONIC ENERGY -- BUT SLOWLY, VERY SLOWLY --
YEAH? THEN LET'S TREAT HIM LIKE A PIMPLE, PEOPLE --
"-- SQUEEZE HIM 'TIL HE POPS!"
SPLAMM
CHOOOM
ON HIM, EVERYONE! HE'S STILL TOO DANGEROUS TO TAKE CHANCES WITH!
HE'S STILL UNIMAGINABLY POWERFUL!
AVENGERS -- THUNDERBOLTS -- ATTACK!

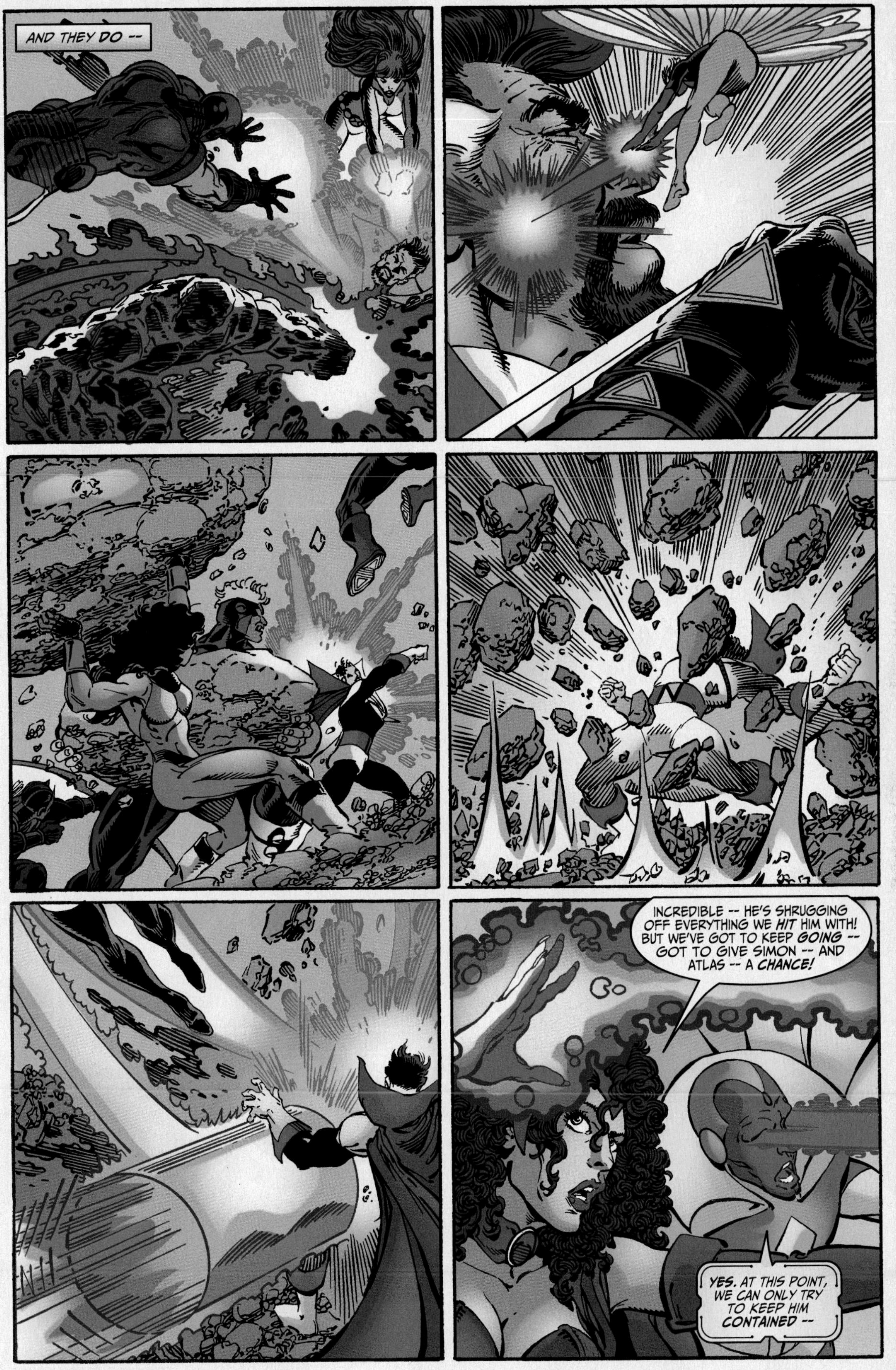
AND THEY DO --
INCREDIBLE -- HE'S SHRUGGING OFF EVERYTHING WE HIT HIM WITH! BUT WE'VE GOT TO KEEP GOING -- GOT TO GIVE SIMON -- AND ATLAS -- A CHANCE!
YES. AT THIS POINT, WE CAN ONLY TRY TO KEEP HIM CONTAINED --

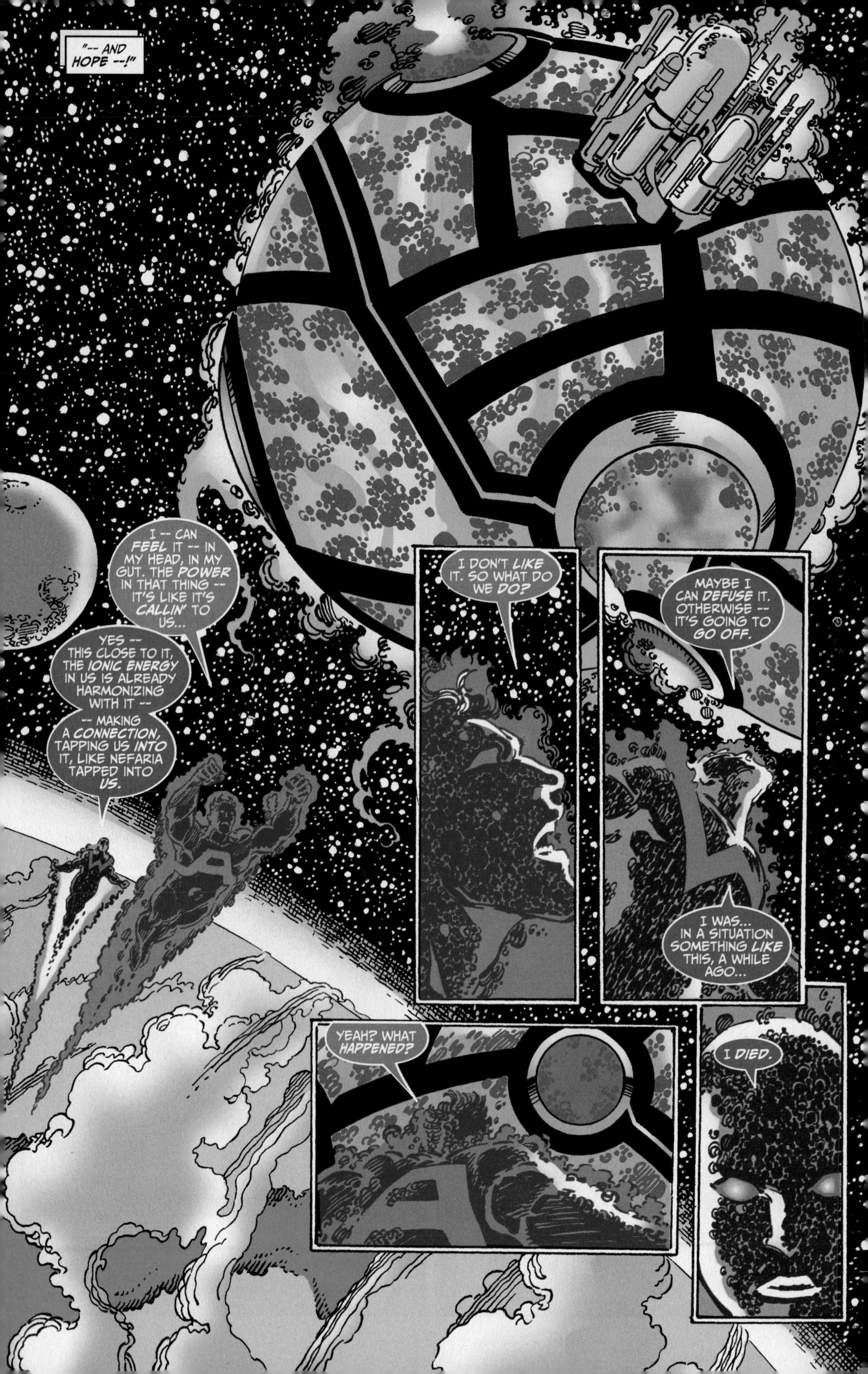
"-- AND HOPE --!"
I -- CAN FEEL IT -- IN MY HEAD, IN MY GUT. THE POWER IN THAT THING -- IT'S LIKE IT'S CALLIN' TO US...
YES -- THIS CLOSE TO IT, THE IONIC ENERGY IN US IS ALREADY HARMONIZING WITH IT --
-- MAKING A CONNECTION, TAPPING US INTO IT, LIKE NEFARIA TAPPED INTO US.
I DON'T LIKE IT. SO WHAT DO WE DO?
MAYBE I CAN DEFUSE IT. OTHERWISE -- IT'S GOING TO GO OFF.
I WAS... IN A SITUATION SOMETHING LIKE THIS, A WHILE AGO...
YEAH? WHAT HAPPENED?
I DIED.

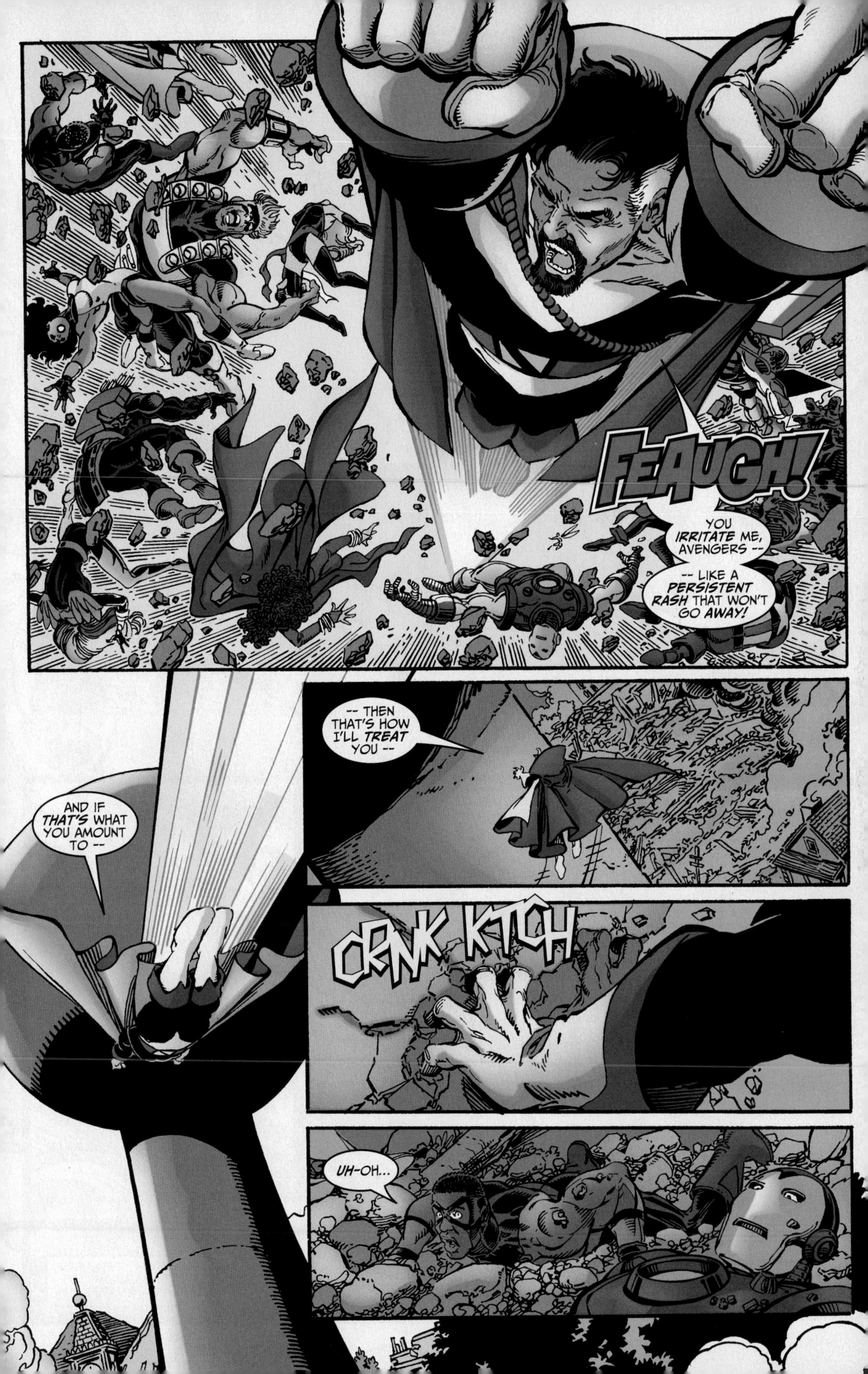
FEAUGH!
YOU IRRITATE ME, AVENGERS --
-- LIKE A PERSISTENT RASH THAT WON'T GO AWAY!
AND IF THAT'S WHAT YOU AMOUNT TO --
-- THEN THAT'S HOW I'LL TREAT YOU --
CRNK KTCH
UH-OH...

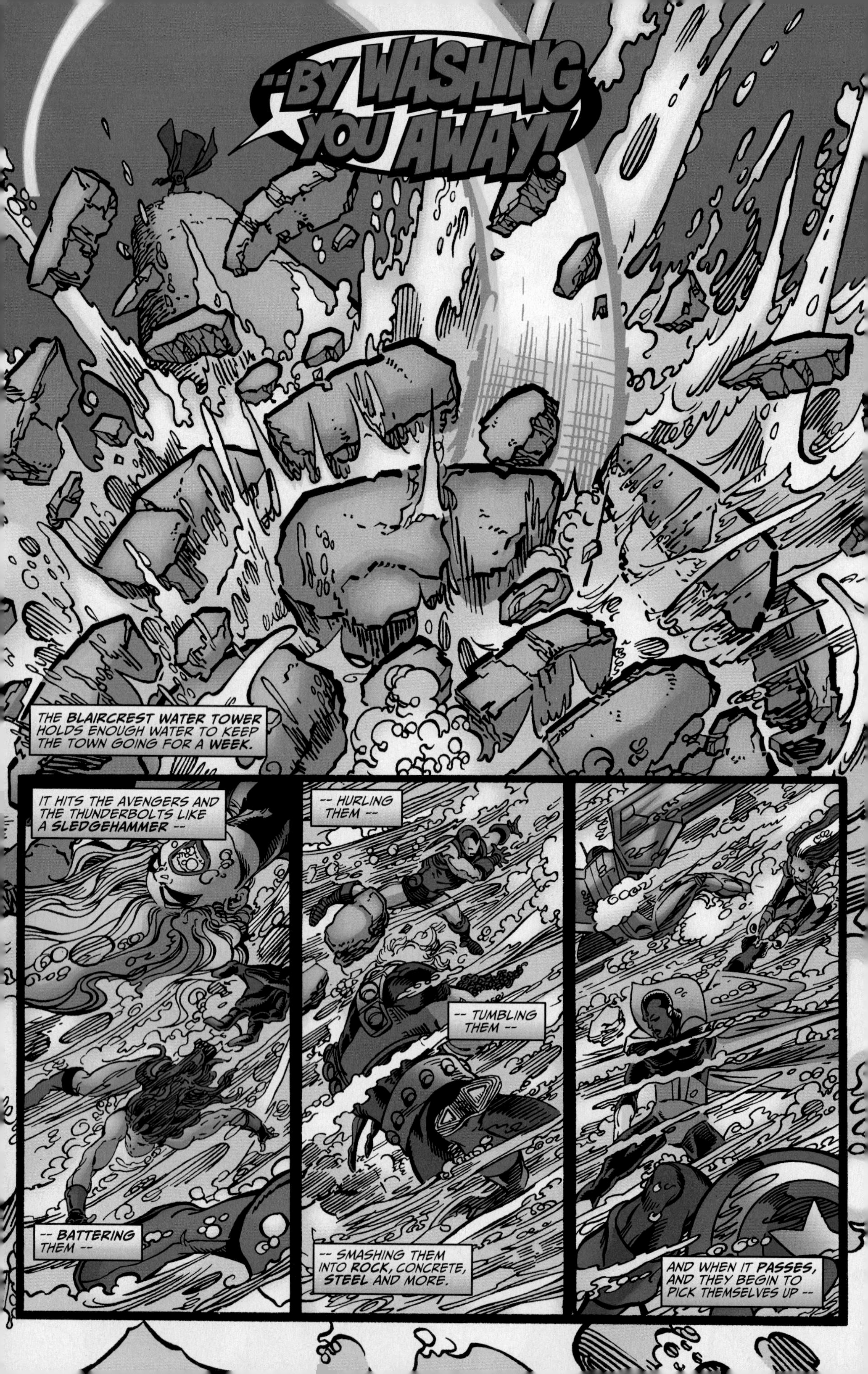
--BY WASHING YOU AWAY!
THE BLAIRCREST WATER TOWER HOLDS ENOUGH WATER TO KEEP THE TOWN GOING FOR A WEEK.
IT HITS THE AVENGERS AND THE THUNDERBOLTS LIKE A SLEDGEHAMMER --
-- BATTERING THEM --
-- HURLING THEM --
-- TUMBLING THEM --
-- SMASHING THEM INTO ROCK, CONCRETE, STEEL AND MORE.
AND WHEN IT PASSES, AND THEY BEGIN TO PICK THEMSELVES UP --

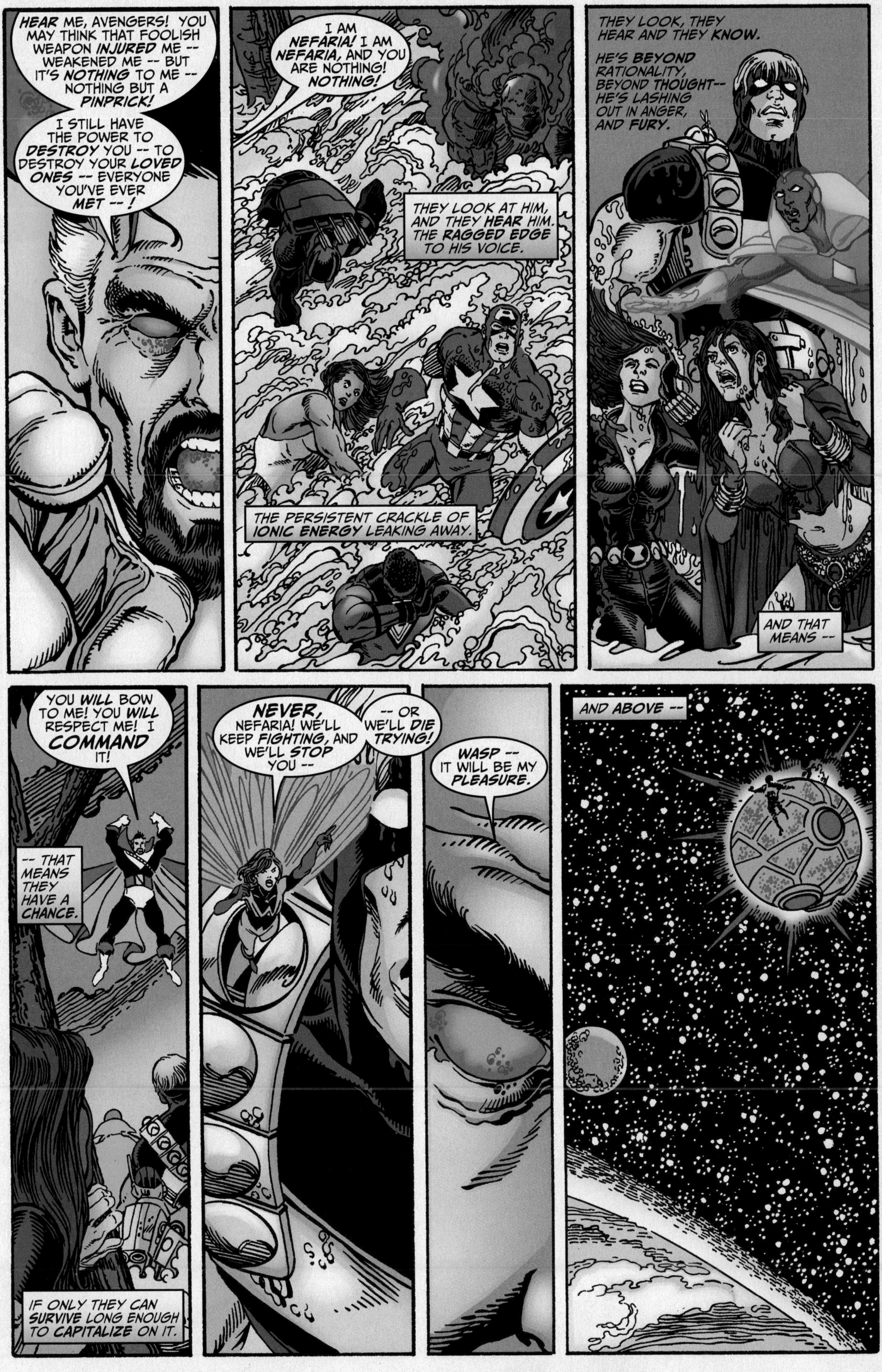
HEAR ME, AVENGERS! YOU MAY THINK THAT FOOLISH WEAPON INJURED ME -- WEAKENED ME -- BUT IT'S NOTHING TO ME -- NOTHING BUT A PINPRICK!
I STILL HAVE THE POWER TO DESTROY YOU -- TO DESTROY YOUR LOVED ONES -- EVERYONE YOU'VE EVER MET -- !
I AM NEFARIA! I AM NEFARIA, AND YOU ARE NOTHING! NOTHING!
THEY LOOK AT HIM, AND THEY HEAR HIM. THE RAGGED EDGE TO HIS VOICE.
THE PERSISTENT CRACKLE OF IONIC ENERGY LEAKING AWAY.
THEY LOOK, THEY HEAR AND THEY KNOW.
HE'S BEYOND RATIONALITY, BEYOND THOUGHT-- HE'S LASHING OUT IN ANGER, AND FURY.
AND THAT MEANS --
YOU WILL BOW TO ME! YOU WILL RESPECT ME! I COMMAND IT!
-- THAT MEANS THEY HAVE A CHANCE.
IF ONLY THEY CAN SURVIVE LONG ENOUGH TO CAPITALIZE ON IT.
NEVER, NEFARIA! WE'LL KEEP FIGHTING, AND WE'LL STOP YOU --
-- OR WE'LL DIE TRYING!
WASP -- IT WILL BE MY PLEASURE.
AND ABOVE --

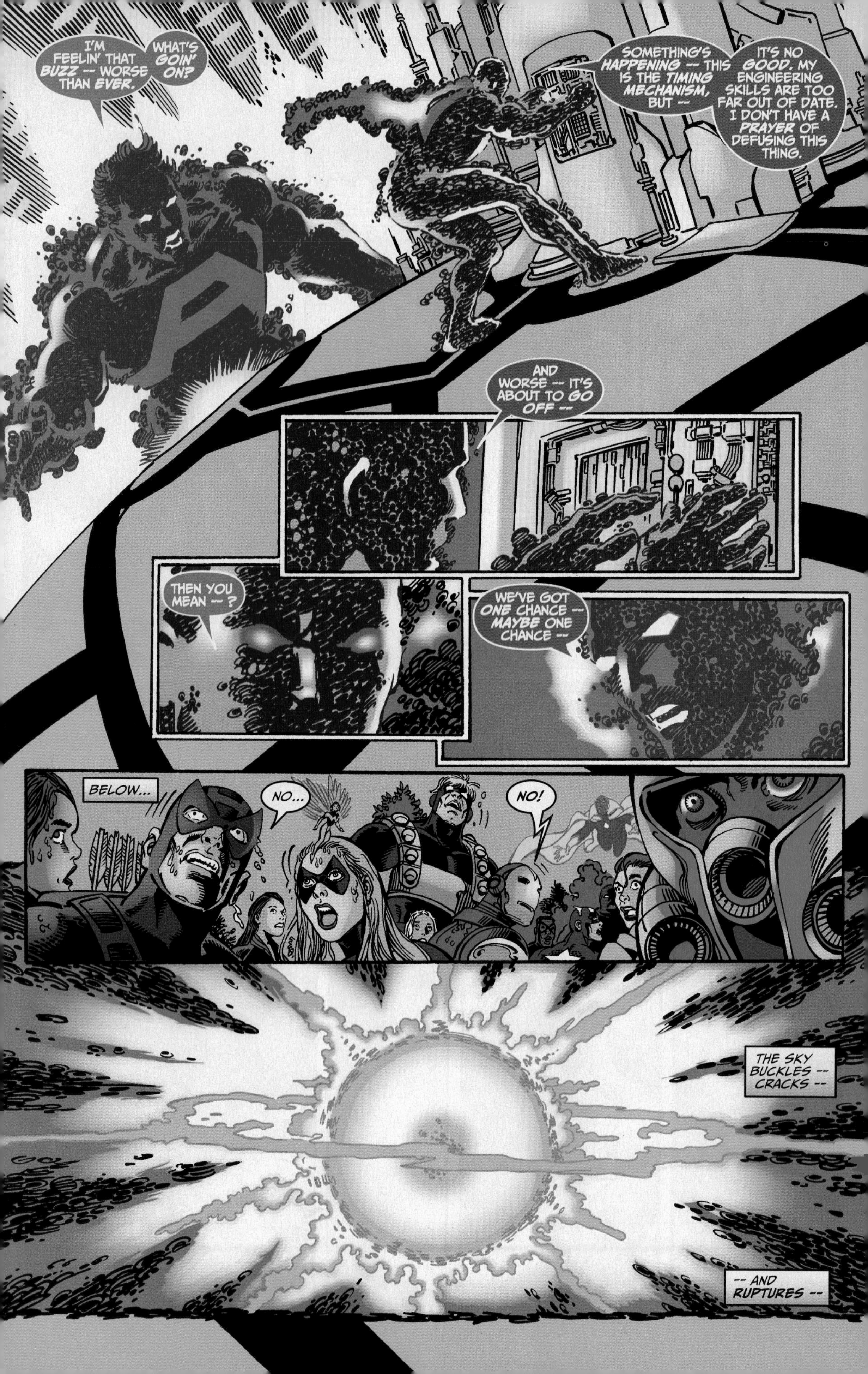
I'M FEELIN' THAT *BUZZ* -- WORSE THAN *EVER*.
WHAT'S *GOIN'* ON?
SOMETHING'S *HAPPENING* -- THIS IS THE *TIMING MECHANISM*, BUT --
IT'S NO *GOOD*. MY ENGINEERING SKILLS ARE TOO FAR OUT OF DATE. I DON'T HAVE A *PRAYER* OF DEFUSING THIS THING.
AND WORSE -- IT'S ABOUT TO *GO OFF* --
THEN YOU MEAN -- ?
WE'VE GOT *ONE CHANCE* -- *MAYBE* ONE CHANCE --
BELOW...
NO...
NO!
THE SKY BUCKLES -- CRACKS --
-- AND RUPTURES --

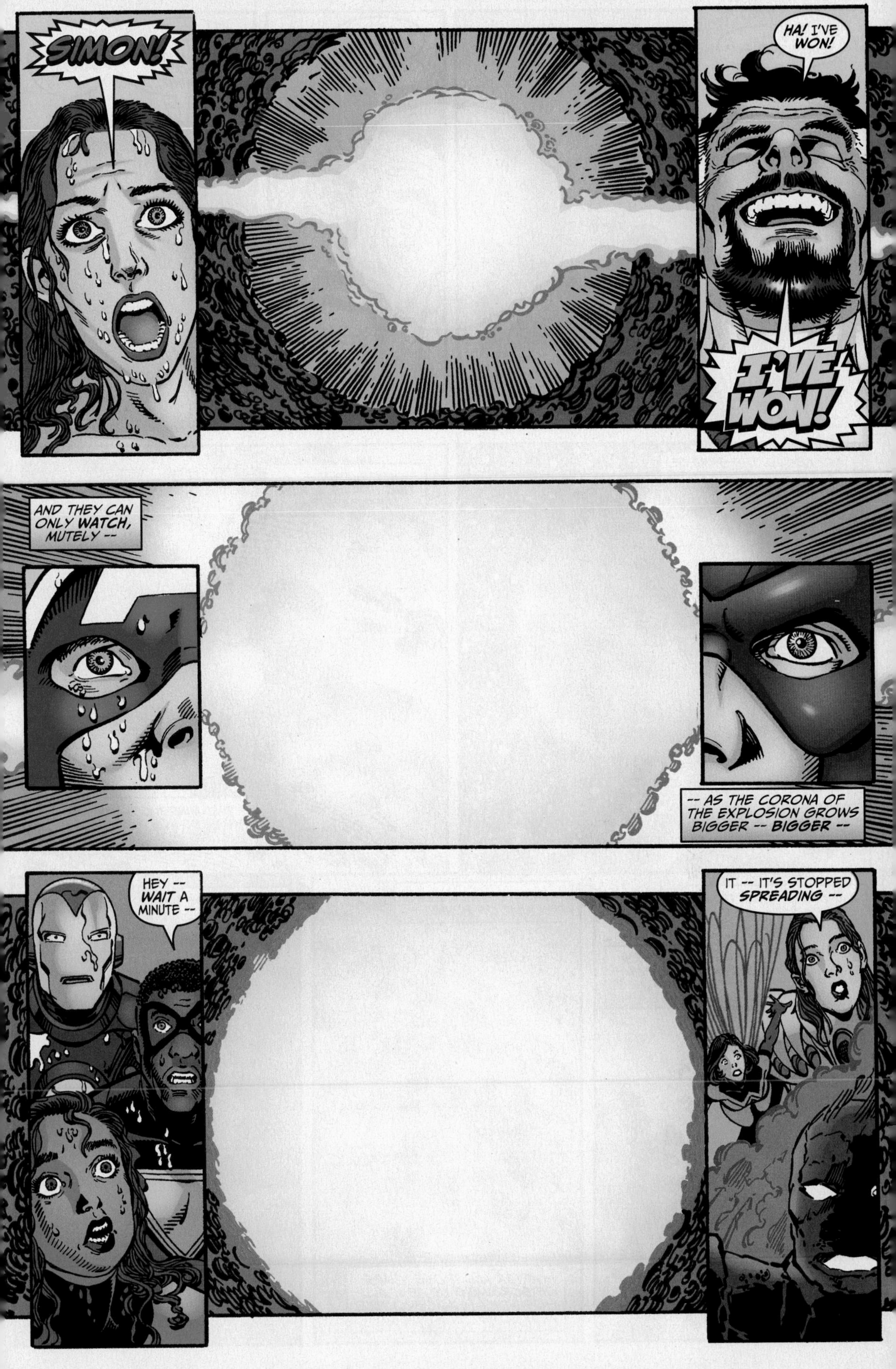
SIMON!
HA! I'VE WON!
I'VE WON!
AND THEY CAN ONLY WATCH, MUTELY --
-- AS THE CORONA OF THE EXPLOSION GROWS BIGGER -- BIGGER --
HEY -- WAIT A MINUTE --
IT -- IT'S STOPPED SPREADING --

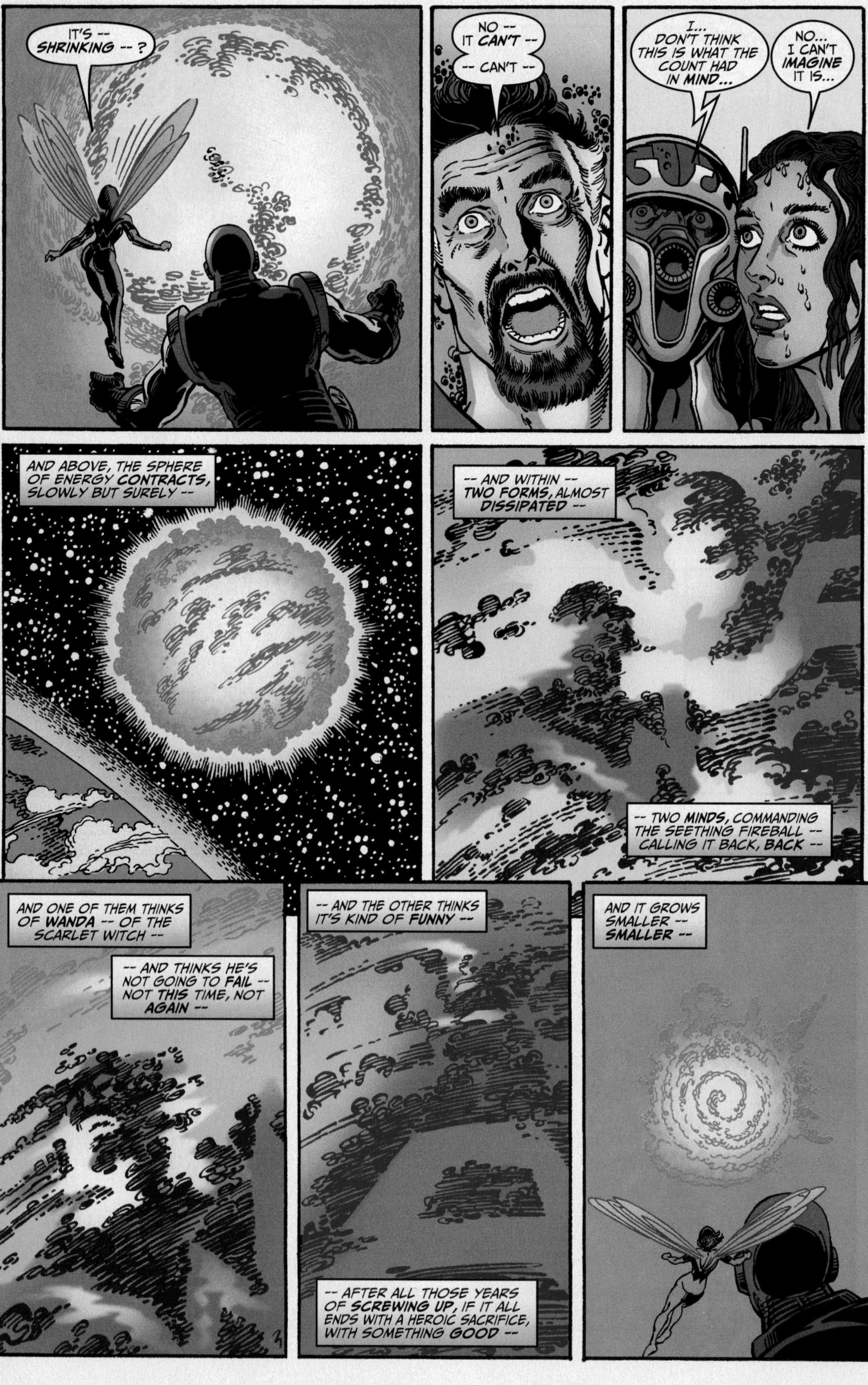
IT'S -- SHRINKING -- ?
NO -- IT CAN'T --
-- CAN'T --
I... DON'T THINK THIS IS WHAT THE COUNT HAD IN MIND...
NO... I CAN'T IMAGINE IT IS...
AND ABOVE, THE SPHERE OF ENERGY CONTRACTS, SLOWLY BUT SURELY --
-- AND WITHIN TWO FORMS, ALMOST DISSIPATED --
-- TWO MINDS, COMMANDING THE SEETHING FIREBALL -- CALLING IT BACK, BACK --
AND ONE OF THEM THINKS OF WANDA -- OF THE SCARLET WITCH --
-- AND THINKS HE'S NOT GOING TO FAIL -- NOT THIS TIME, NOT AGAIN --
-- AND THE OTHER THINKS IT'S KIND OF FUNNY --
-- AFTER ALL THOSE YEARS OF SCREWING UP, IF IT ALL ENDS WITH A HEROIC SACRIFICE, WITH SOMETHING GOOD --
AND IT GROWS SMALLER -- SMALLER --

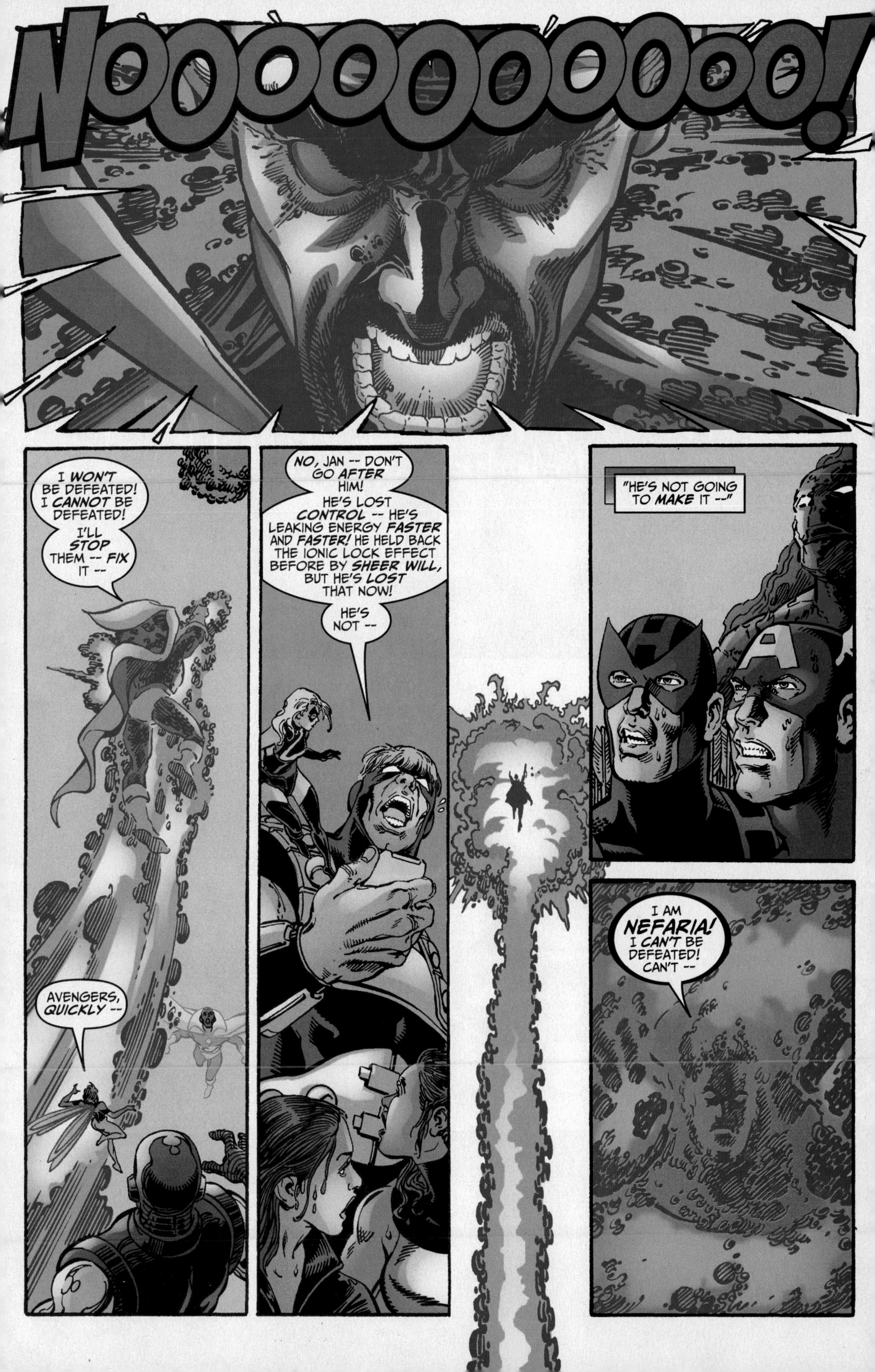
NOOOOOOOOOOO!
I WON'T BE DEFEATED! I CANNOT BE DEFEATED!
I'LL STOP THEM -- FIX IT --
AVENGERS, QUICKLY --
NO, JAN -- DON'T GO AFTER HIM!
HE'S LOST CONTROL -- HE'S LEAKING ENERGY FASTER AND FASTER! HE HELD BACK THE IONIC LOCK EFFECT BEFORE BY SHEER WILL, BUT HE'S LOST THAT NOW!
HE'S NOT --
"HE'S NOT GOING TO MAKE IT --"
I AM NEFARIA! I CAN'T BE DEFEATED! CAN'T --

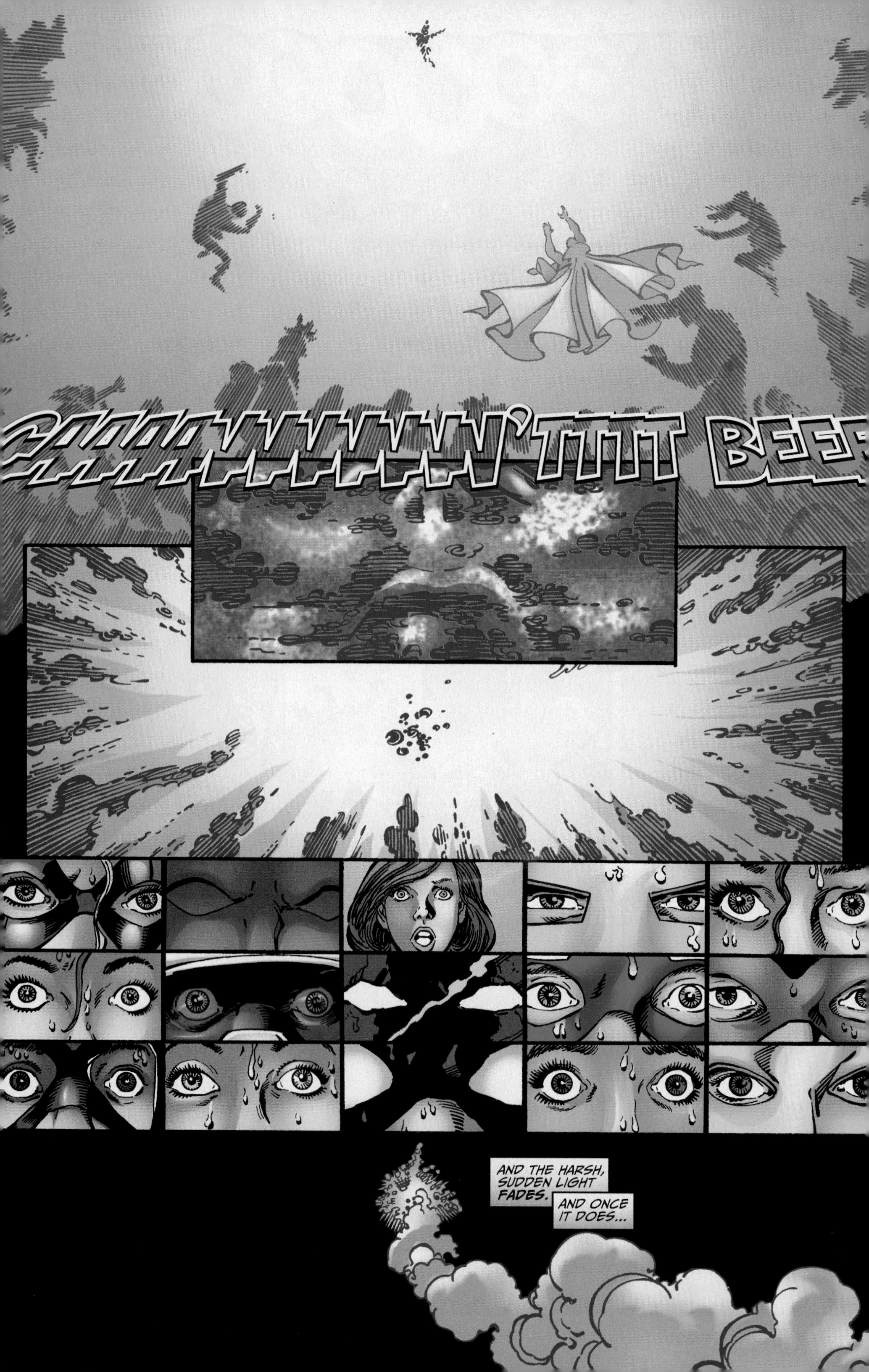
AND THE HARSH, SUDDEN LIGHT FADES.
AND ONCE IT DOES...

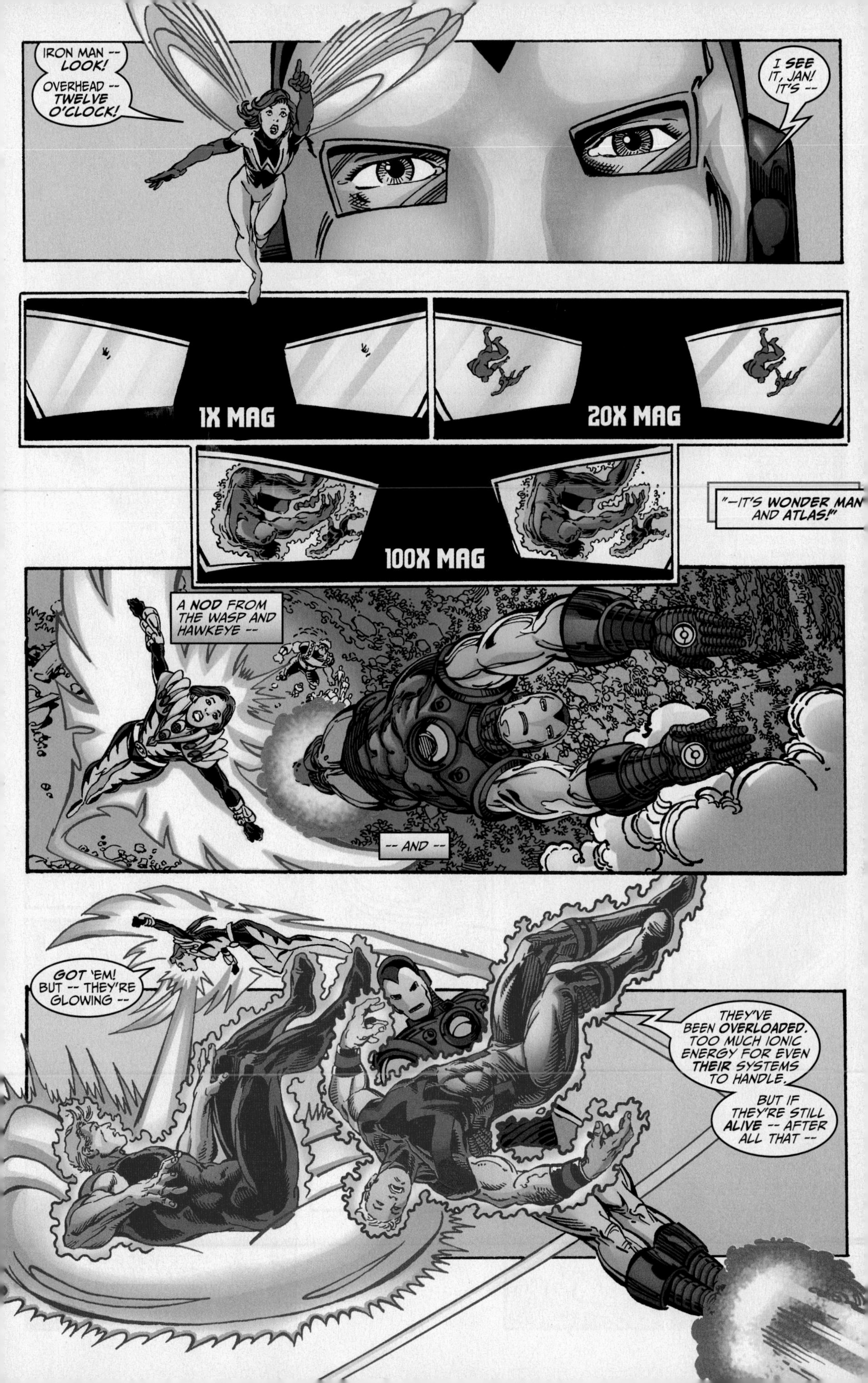
IRON MAN -- LOOK!
OVERHEAD -- TWELVE O'CLOCK!
I SEE IT, JAN! IT'S --
1X MAG
20X MAG
100X MAG
"--IT'S WONDER MAN AND ATLAS!"
A NOD FROM THE WASP AND HAWKEYE --
-- AND --
GOT 'EM! BUT -- THEY'RE GLOWING --
THEY'VE BEEN OVERLOADED. TOO MUCH IONIC ENERGY FOR EVEN THEIR SYSTEMS TO HANDLE.
BUT IF THEY'RE STILL ALIVE -- AFTER ALL THAT --

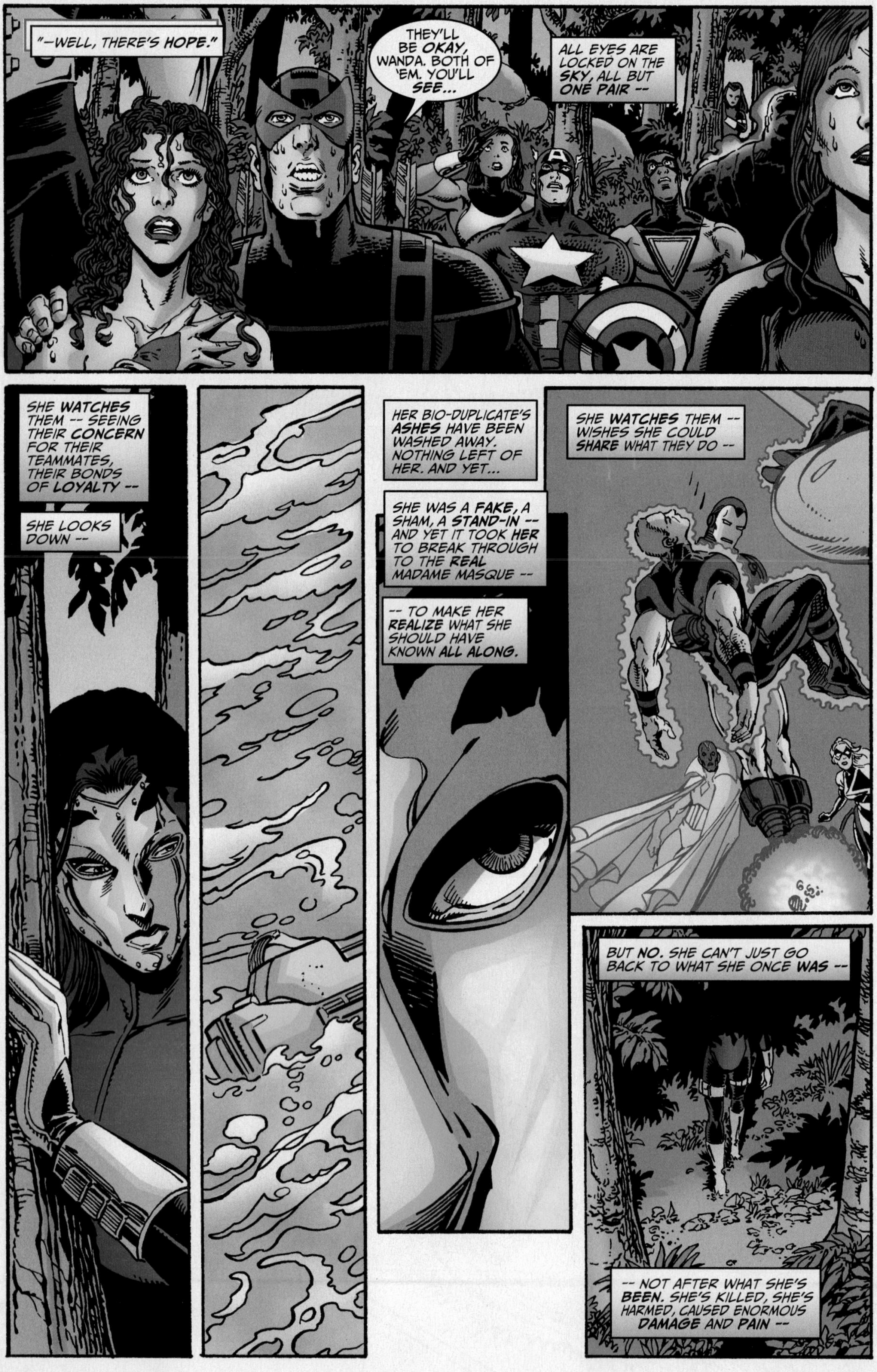
"—WELL, THERE'S HOPE."
THEY'LL BE OKAY, WANDA. BOTH OF 'EM. YOU'LL SEE...
ALL EYES ARE LOCKED ON THE SKY, ALL BUT ONE PAIR --
SHE WATCHES THEM -- SEEING THEIR CONCERN FOR THEIR TEAMMATES, THEIR BONDS OF LOYALTY --
SHE LOOKS DOWN --
HER BIO-DUPLICATE'S ASHES HAVE BEEN WASHED AWAY. NOTHING LEFT OF HER. AND YET...
SHE WAS A FAKE, A SHAM, A STAND-IN -- AND YET IT TOOK HER TO BREAK THROUGH TO THE REAL MADAME MASQUE --
-- TO MAKE HER REALIZE WHAT SHE SHOULD HAVE KNOWN ALL ALONG.
SHE WATCHES THEM -- WISHES SHE COULD SHARE WHAT THEY DO --
BUT NO. SHE CAN'T JUST GO BACK TO WHAT SHE ONCE WAS --
-- NOT AFTER WHAT SHE'S BEEN. SHE'S KILLED, SHE'S HARMED, CAUSED ENORMOUS DAMAGE AND PAIN --

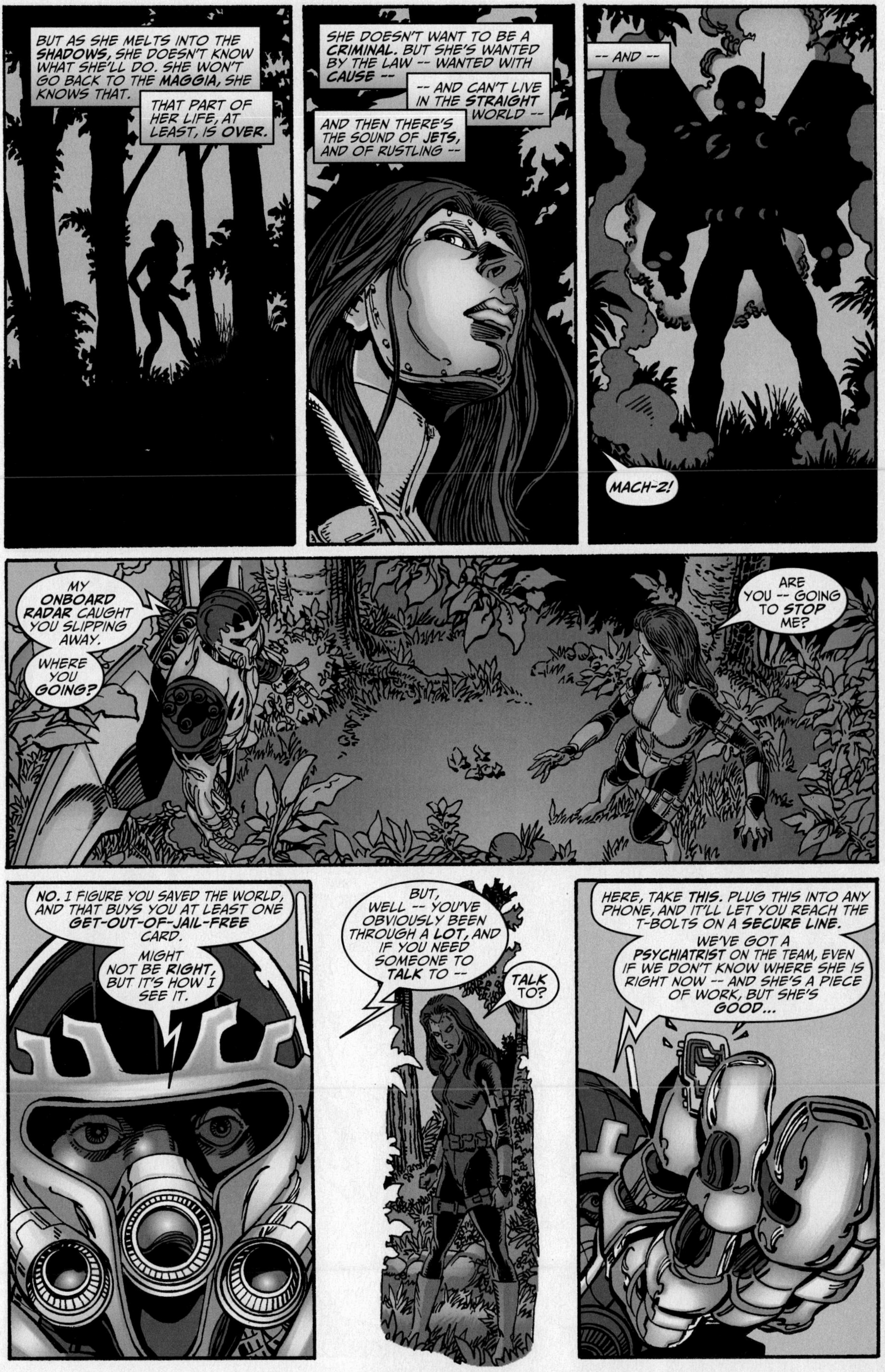

BUT AS SHE MELTS INTO THE SHADOWS, SHE DOESN'T KNOW WHAT SHE'LL DO. SHE WON'T GO BACK TO THE MAGGIA, SHE KNOWS THAT.
THAT PART OF HER LIFE, AT LEAST, IS OVER.
SHE DOESN'T WANT TO BE A CRIMINAL. BUT SHE'S WANTED BY THE LAW -- WANTED WITH CAUSE --
-- AND CAN'T LIVE IN THE STRAIGHT WORLD --
AND THEN THERE'S THE SOUND OF JETS, AND OF RUSTLING --
-- AND --
MACH-2!
MY ONBOARD RADAR CAUGHT YOU SLIPPING AWAY.
WHERE YOU GOING?
ARE YOU -- GOING TO STOP ME?
NO. I FIGURE YOU SAVED THE WORLD, AND THAT BUYS YOU AT LEAST ONE GET-OUT-OF-JAIL-FREE CARD.
MIGHT NOT BE RIGHT, BUT IT'S HOW I SEE IT.
BUT, WELL -- YOU'VE OBVIOUSLY BEEN THROUGH A LOT, AND IF YOU NEED SOMEONE TO TALK TO --
TALK TO?
HERE, TAKE THIS. PLUG THIS INTO ANY PHONE, AND IT'LL LET YOU REACH THE T-BOLTS ON A SECURE LINE.
WE'VE GOT A PSYCHIATRIST ON THE TEAM, EVEN IF WE DON'T KNOW WHERE SHE IS RIGHT NOW -- AND SHE'S A PIECE OF WORK, BUT SHE'S GOOD...

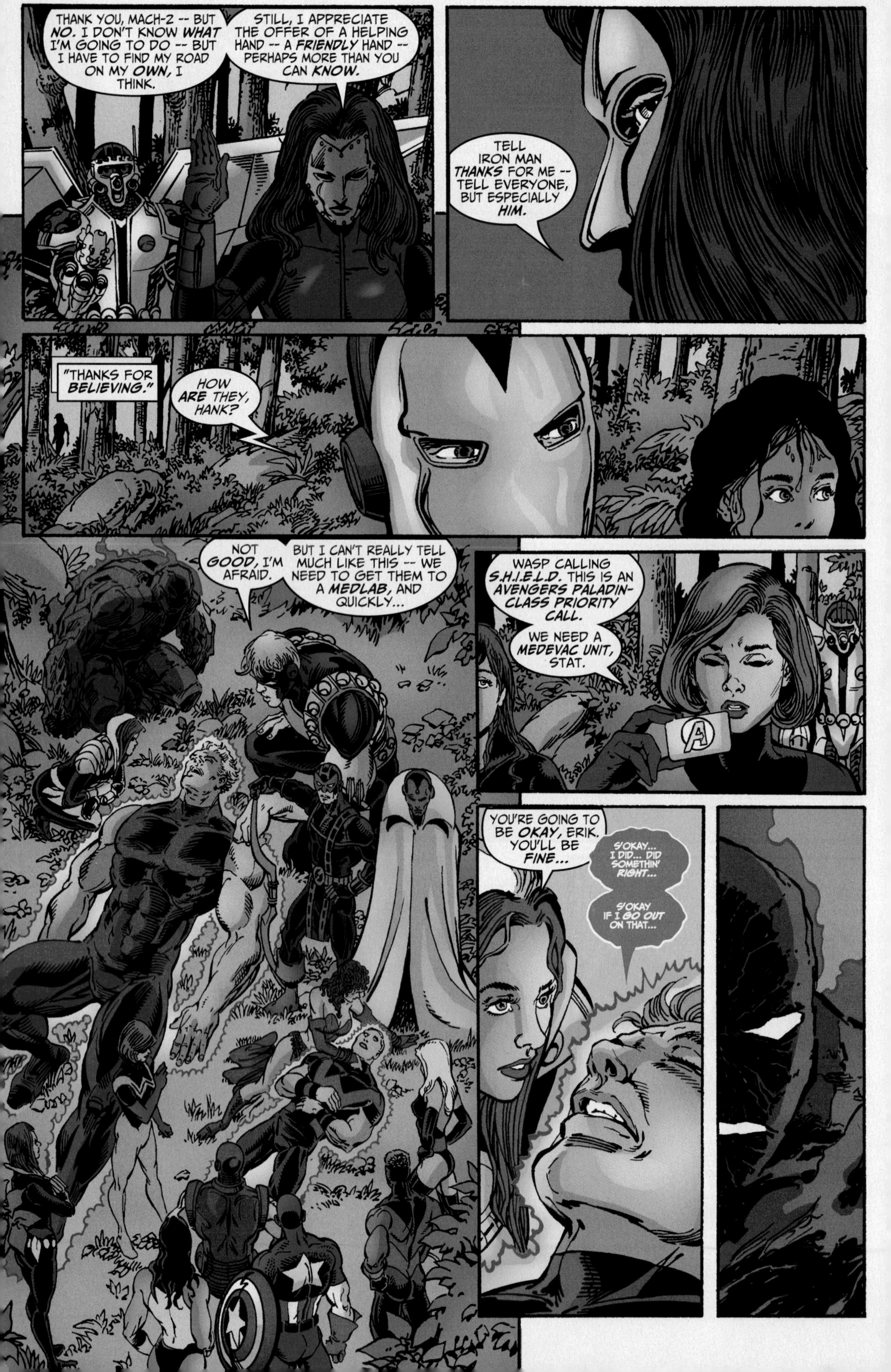
THANK YOU, MACH-2 -- BUT NO. I DON'T KNOW WHAT I'M GOING TO DO -- BUT I HAVE TO FIND MY ROAD ON MY OWN, I THINK.
STILL, I APPRECIATE THE OFFER OF A HELPING HAND -- A FRIENDLY HAND -- PERHAPS MORE THAN YOU CAN KNOW.
TELL IRON MAN THANKS FOR ME -- TELL EVERYONE, BUT ESPECIALLY HIM.
"THANKS FOR BELIEVING."
HOW ARE THEY, HANK?
NOT GOOD, I'M AFRAID.
BUT I CAN'T REALLY TELL MUCH LIKE THIS -- WE NEED TO GET THEM TO A MEDLAB, AND QUICKLY...
WASP CALLING S.H.I.E.L.D. THIS IS AN AVENGERS PALADIN-CLASS PRIORITY CALL.
WE NEED A MEDEVAC UNIT, STAT.
YOU'RE GOING TO BE OKAY, ERIK. YOU'LL BE FINE...
S'OKAY... I DID... DID SOMETHIN' RIGHT...
S'OKAY IF I GO OUT ON THAT...

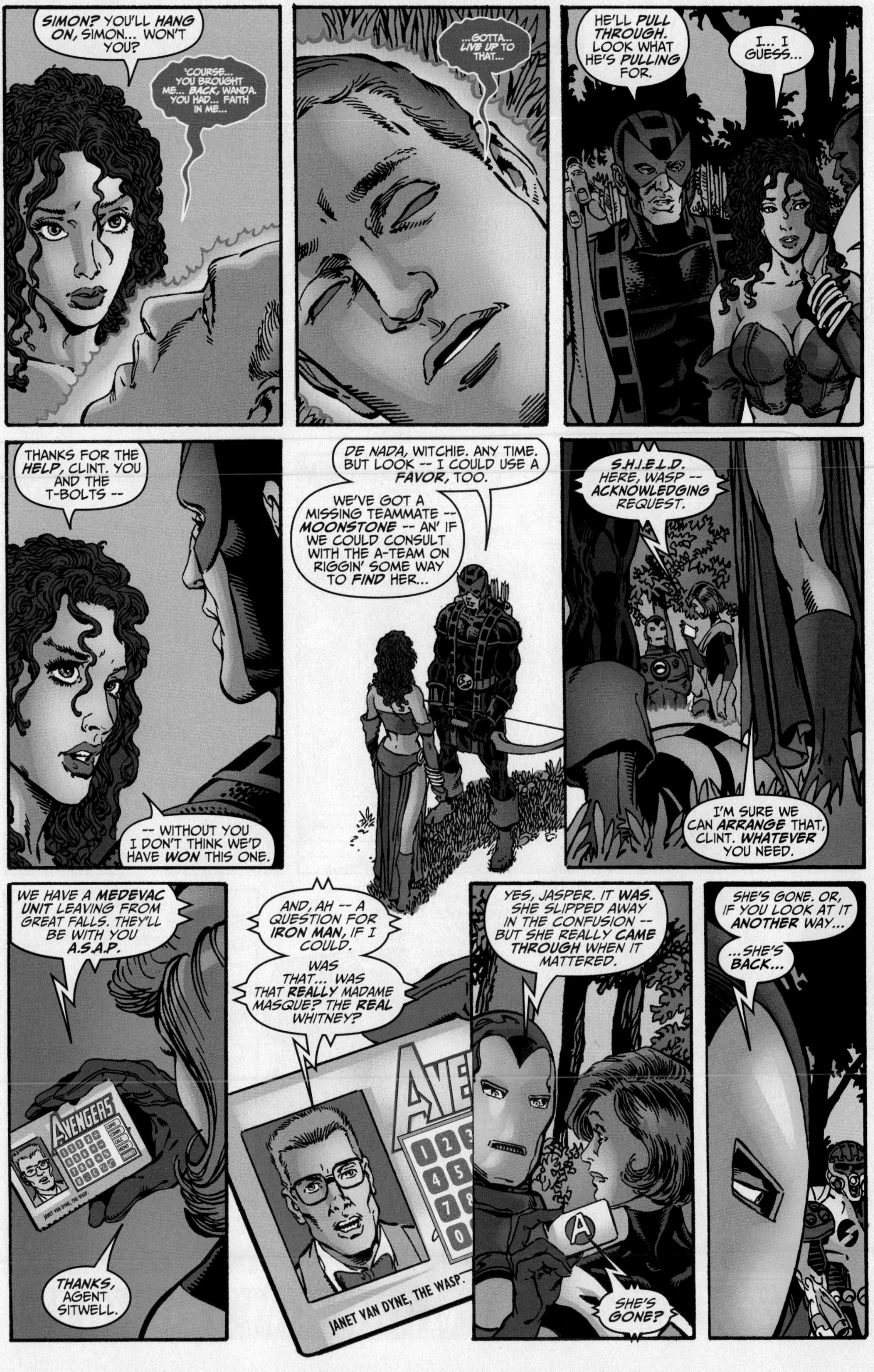
SIMON? YOU'LL HANG ON, SIMON... WON'T YOU?
'COURSE... YOU BROUGHT ME... BACK, WANDA. YOU HAD... FAITH IN ME...
...GOTTA... LIVE UP TO THAT...
HE'LL PULL THROUGH. LOOK WHAT HE'S PULLING FOR.
I... I GUESS...
THANKS FOR THE HELP, CLINT. YOU AND THE T-BOLTS --
-- WITHOUT YOU I DON'T THINK WE'D HAVE WON THIS ONE.
DE NADA, WITCHIE. ANY TIME. BUT LOOK -- I COULD USE A FAVOR, TOO.
WE'VE GOT A MISSING TEAMMATE -- MOONSTONE -- AN' IF WE COULD CONSULT WITH THE A-TEAM ON RIGGIN' SOME WAY TO FIND HER...
S.H.I.E.L.D. HERE, WASP -- ACKNOWLEDGING REQUEST.
I'M SURE WE CAN ARRANGE THAT, CLINT. WHATEVER YOU NEED.
WE HAVE A MEDEVAC UNIT LEAVING FROM GREAT FALLS. THEY'LL BE WITH YOU A.S.A.P.
THANKS, AGENT SITWELL.
AND, AH -- A QUESTION FOR IRON MAN, IF I COULD.
WAS THAT... WAS THAT REALLY MADAME MASQUE? THE REAL WHITNEY?
JANET VAN DYNE, THE WASP.
YES, JASPER. IT WAS. SHE SLIPPED AWAY IN THE CONFUSION -- BUT SHE REALLY CAME THROUGH WHEN IT MATTERED.
SHE'S GONE?
SHE'S GONE. OR, IF YOU LOOK AT IT ANOTHER WAY...
...SHE'S BACK...

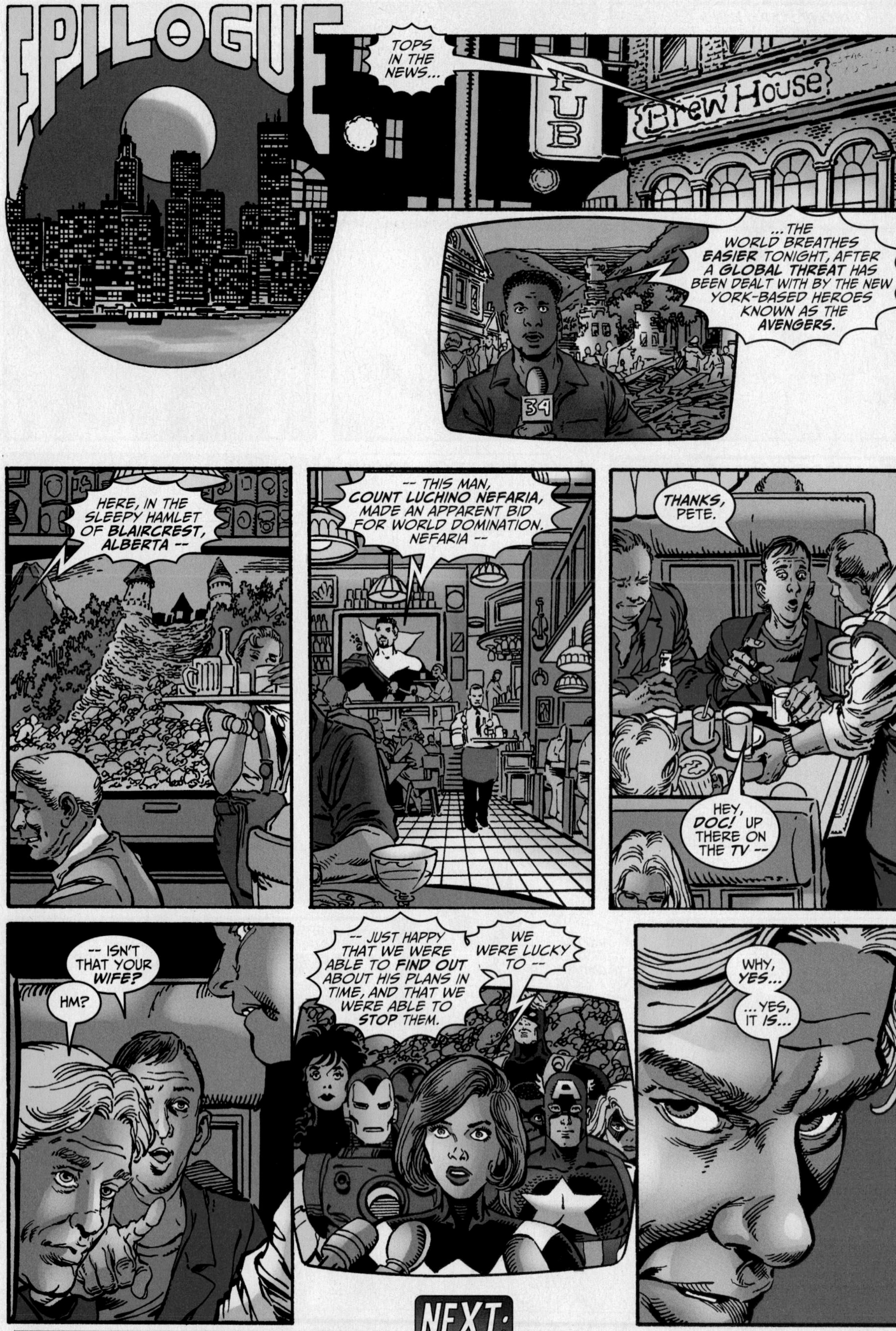
EPILOGUE
TOPS IN THE NEWS...
PUB
Brew House
...THE WORLD BREATHES EASIER TONIGHT, AFTER A GLOBAL THREAT HAS BEEN DEALT WITH BY THE NEW YORK-BASED HEROES KNOWN AS THE AVENGERS.
34
HERE, IN THE SLEEPY HAMLET OF BLAIRCREST, ALBERTA --
-- THIS MAN, COUNT LUCHINO NEFARIA, MADE AN APPARENT BID FOR WORLD DOMINATION. NEFARIA --
THANKS, PETE.
HEY, DOC! UP THERE ON THE TV --
-- ISN'T THAT YOUR WIFE?
HM?
-- JUST HAPPY THAT WE WERE ABLE TO FIND OUT ABOUT HIS PLANS IN TIME, AND THAT WE WERE ABLE TO STOP THEM.
WE WERE LUCKY TO --
WHY, YES...
...YES, IT IS...

TO KURT, AL, TOM S., TOM B. AND EVERYONE WHO WORKED ON THIS SERIES THESE PAST 3 YEARS -- **THANKS FOR A HELLUVA RIDE!** George Perez

NEXT: MAXIMUM SECURITY

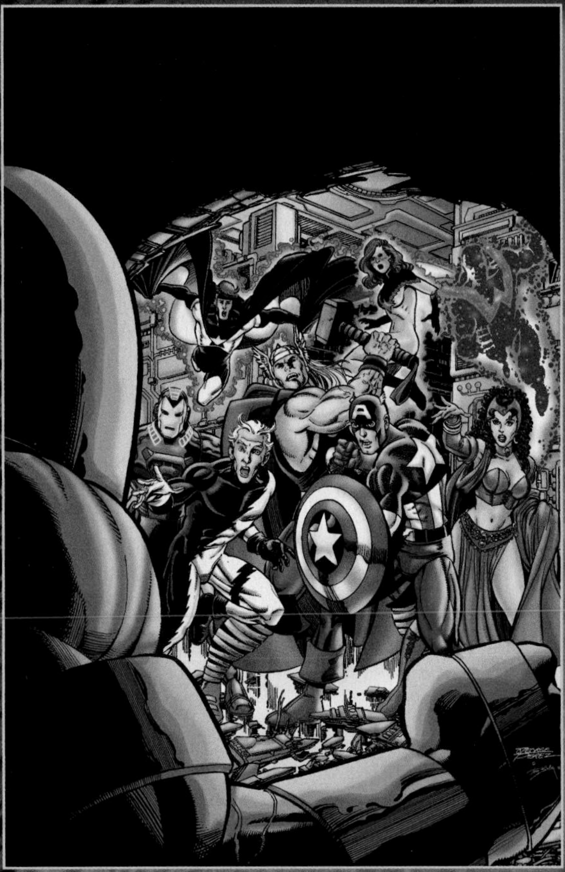

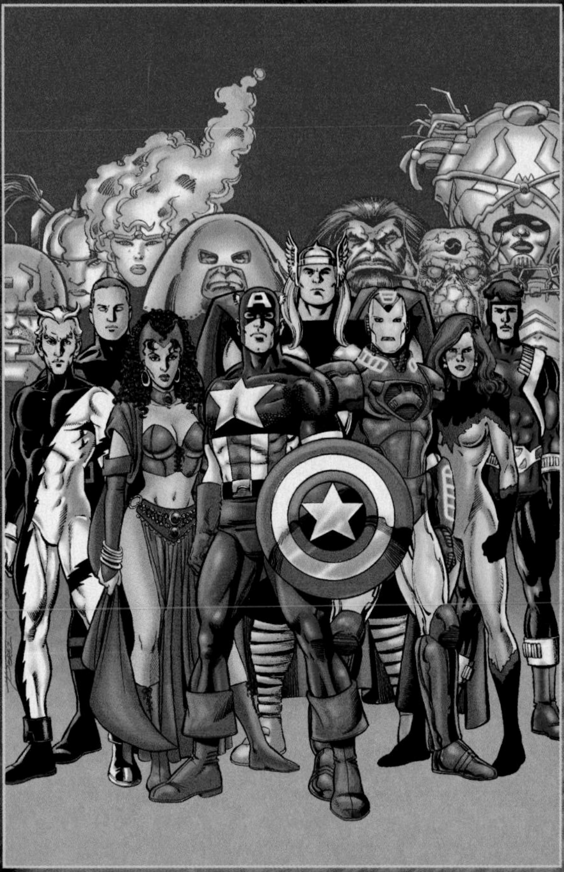

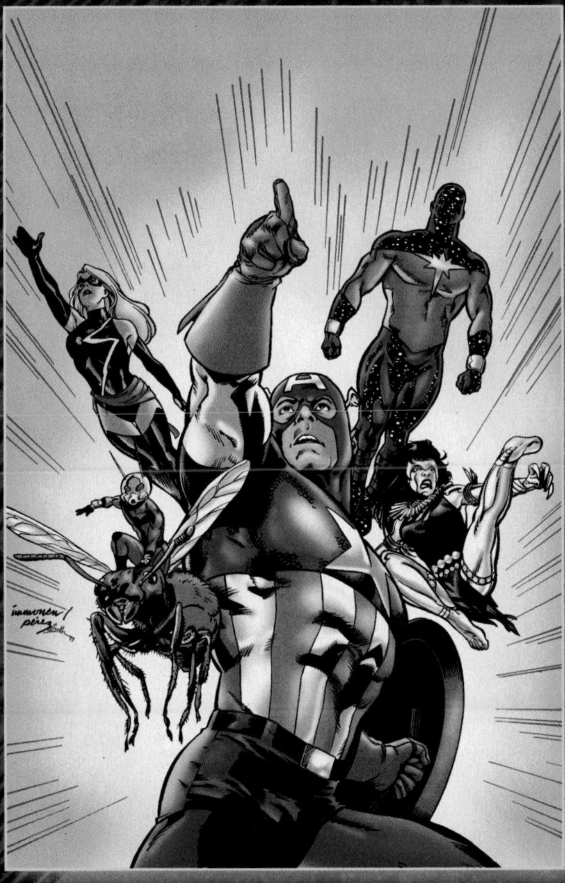

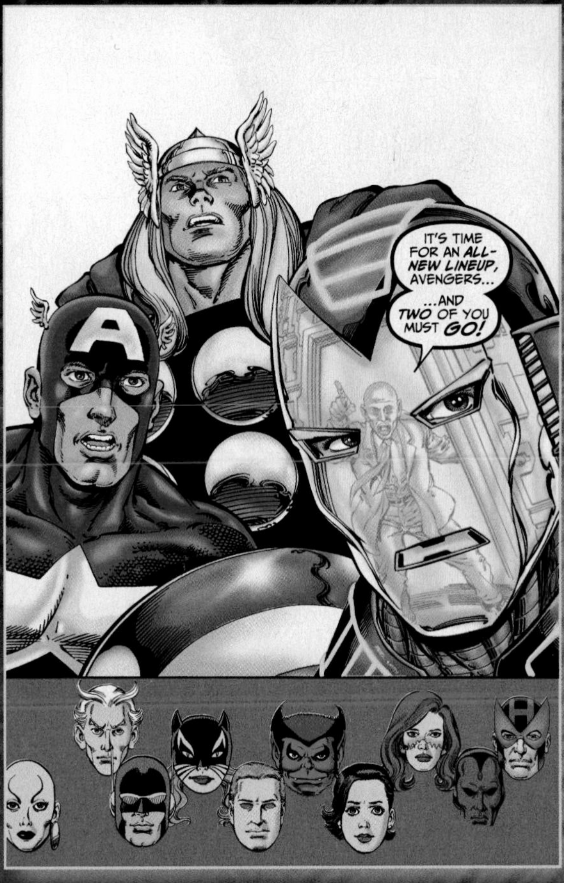
IT'S TIME FOR AN ALL-NEW LINEUP, AVENGERS... ...AND TWO OF YOU MUST GO!

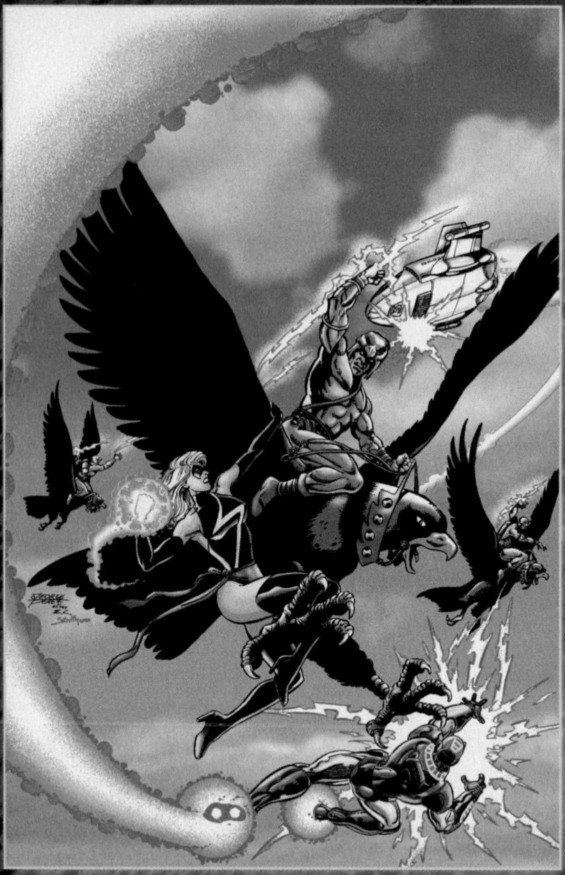
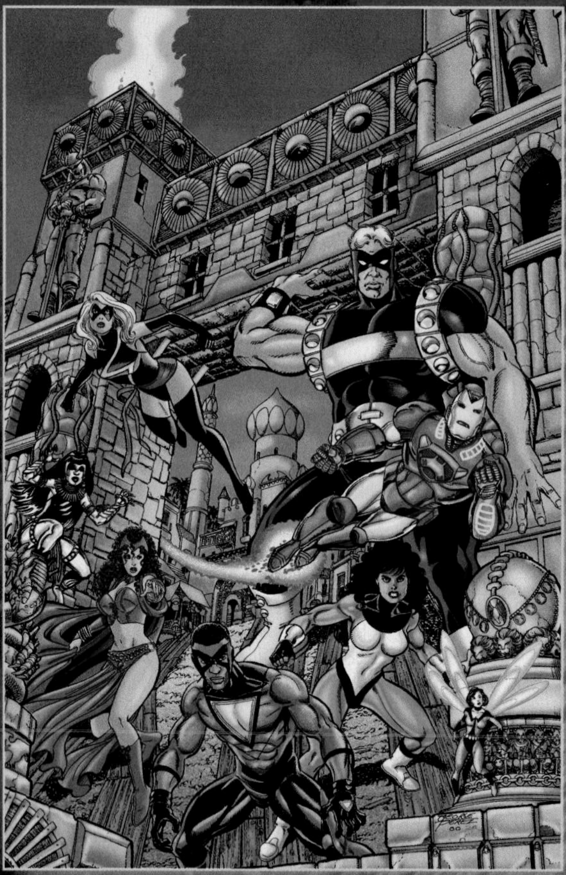
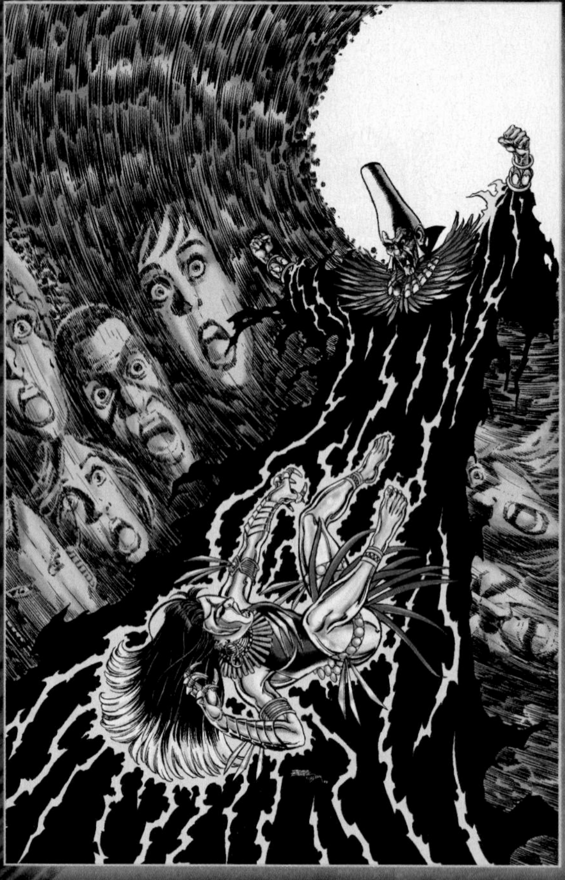
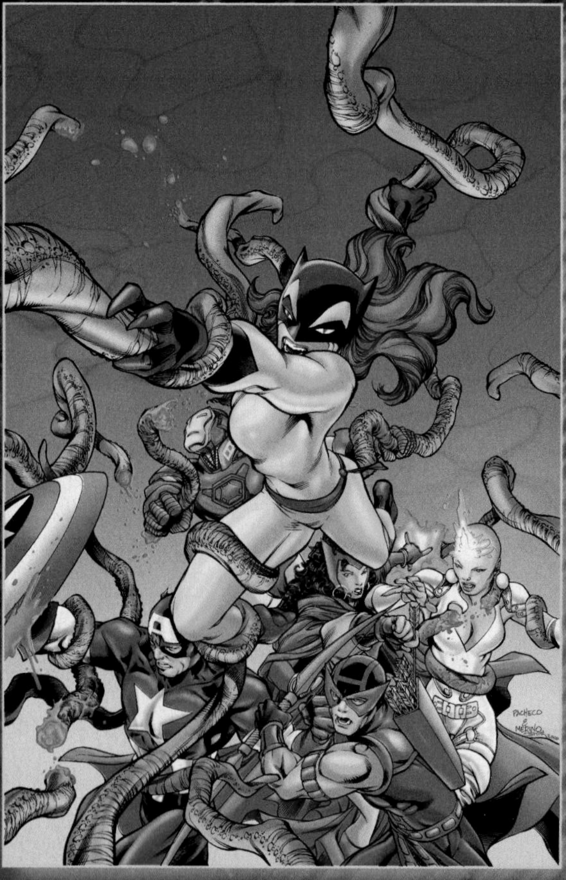

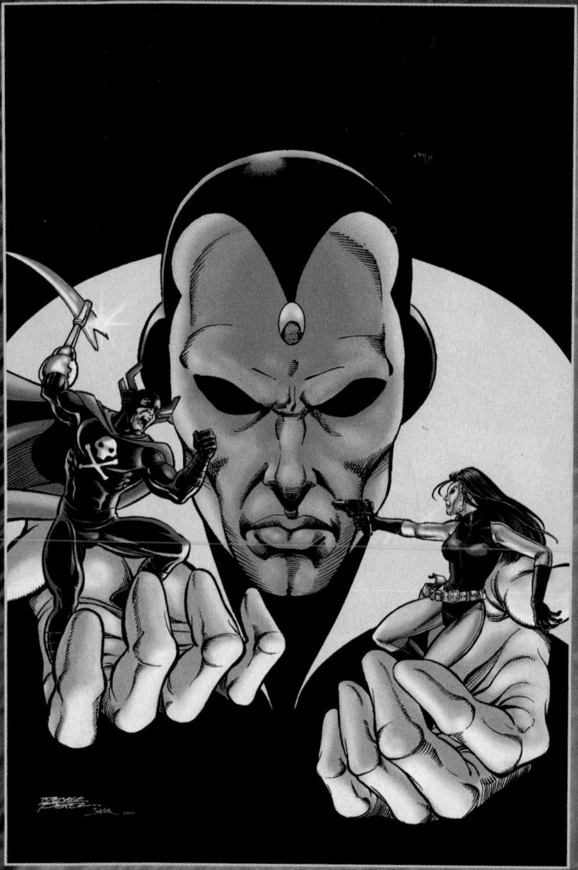

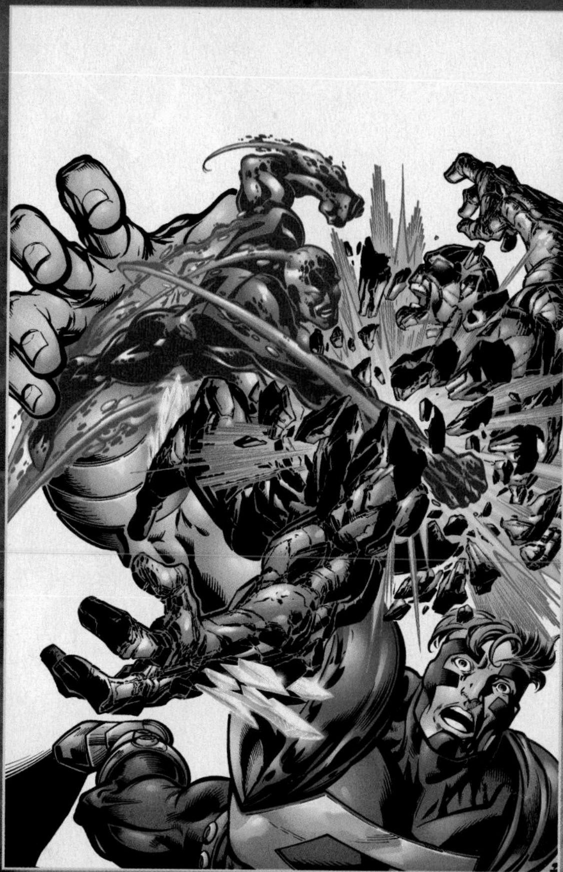

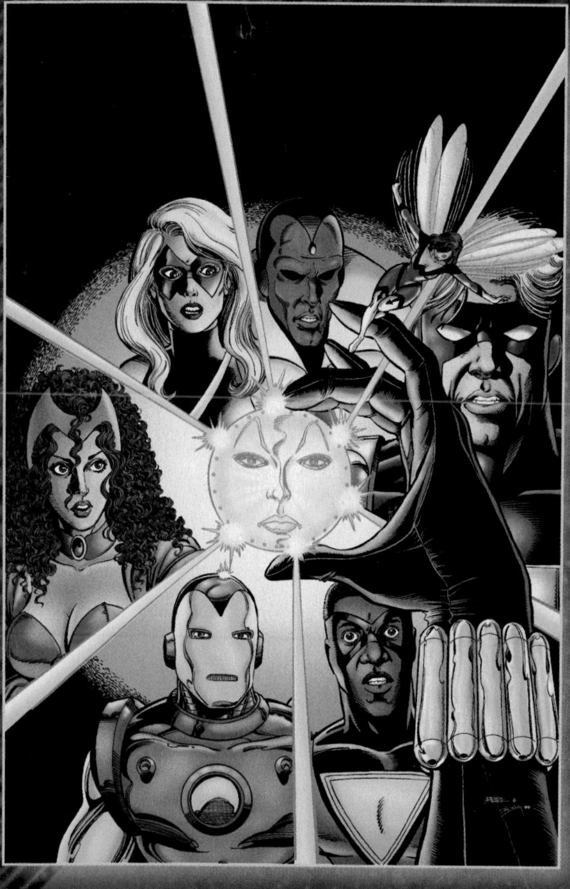

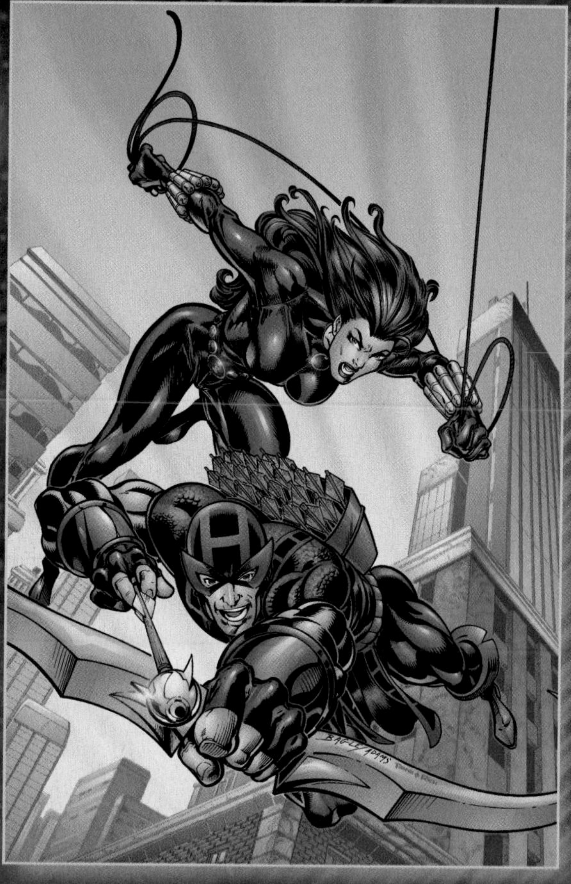

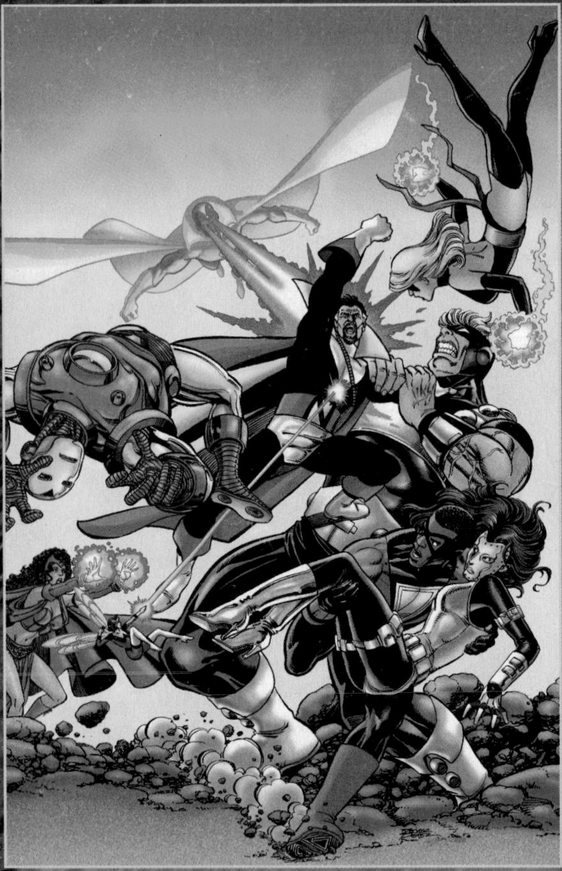
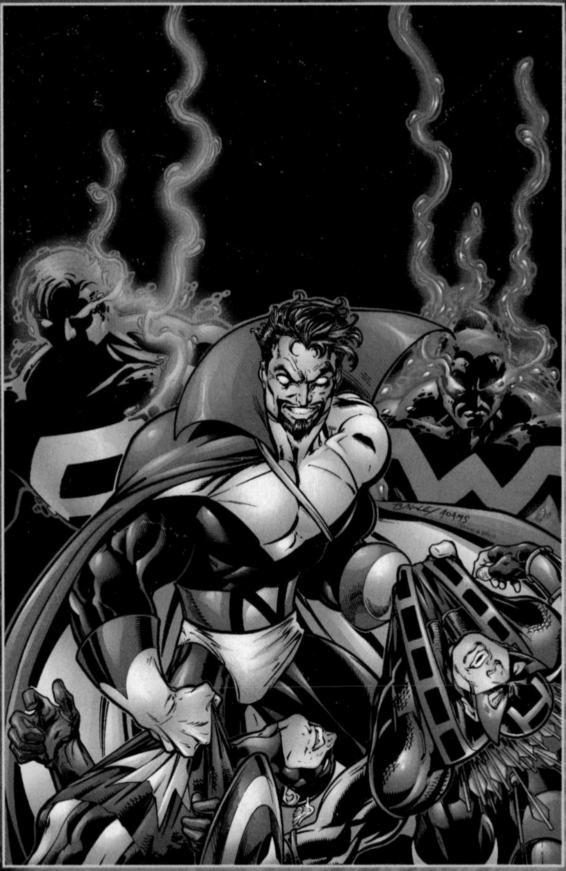
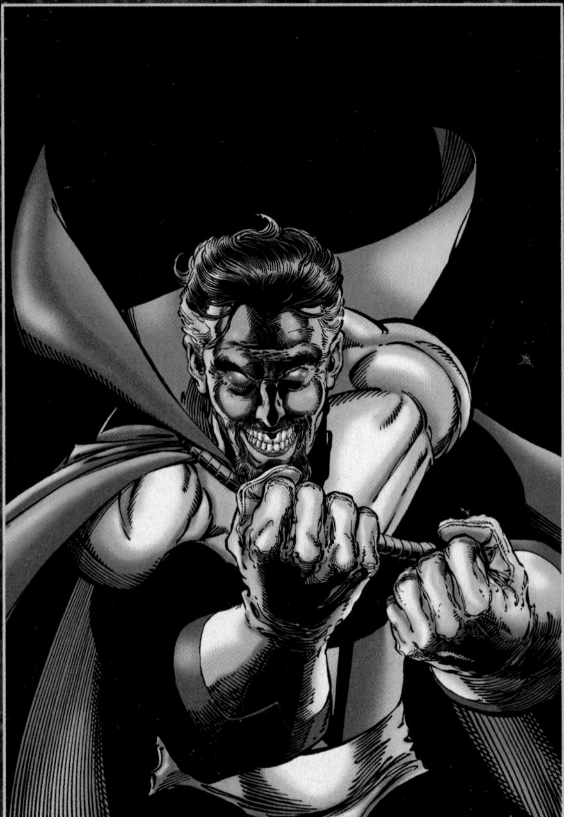

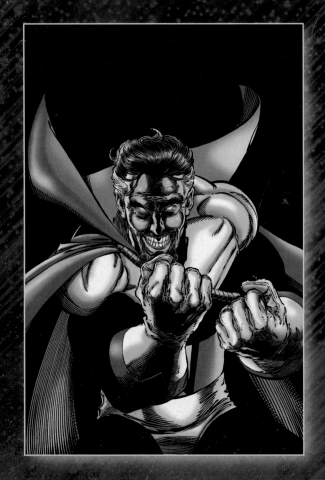